ISBN 978-1-332-31064-7
PIBN 10312351

William Winslow Eaton MD

GENEALOGICAL

AND

PERSONAL MEMOIRS

Relating to the Families of Boston and Eastern Massachusetts.

PREPARED UNDER THE EDITORIAL SUPERVISION OF

WILLIAM RICHARD CUTTER, A. M.

Historian of the New England Historic Genealogical Society; Librarian of Woburn Public Library; Author of "The Cutter Family," "History of Arlington," "Bibliography of Woburn," etc., etc.

VOLUME IV.

ILLUSTRATED.

NEW YORK

LEWIS HISTORICAL PUBLISHING COMPANY

. . . . 1908 . . . .

Boston and Eastern Massachusetts.

TEWKSBURY "Henrie Tuxburie tooke ye oath of fidelity to this govern't this 17 day of May 1669." Thus it is written in the ancient records of "Old Newbury," and the record has reference to Henry Tewksbury (1), of English birth and parentage and whose descendant is traced to an ancient family of the surname Tewksbury, or Tukesbery, or Tewxbury, or Tuxbury, in the borough of Tewk. But this Henry Tewksbury, immigrant, weaver, is believed to have come to America several years at least before he sat down at Newbury and took the oath of fidelity there in 1669, for he was in Boston and married there in 1659. In 1669 he sold his lands and removed to Amesbury, took the oath of allegiance there in 1677, was made freeman in 1690, and was tithingman in 1693. He married, November 10, 1659, in Boston, Martha Copp, widow of William Harvey, and was still living in 1697. His children: 1. Elizabeth, born August 22, 1660. 2. Hannah, September 1, 1662. 3. Henry, December 25, 1664. 4. Naomi, January 18, 1666-67. 5. Ruth, March 10, 1668-69. 6. Mary, January 13, 1670-71. 7. Martha, March 3, 1672-73. 8. John, July 11, 1674.

(II) Henry Tewksbury, son of the immigrant, was born in Newbury, December 25, 1664, lived in Amesbury, married Hannah ———; children: 1. Henry, born December 0, 1694. 2. Jonathan, February 27, 1695-96. 3. Hannah, August 26, 1697. 4. Naomi, August 6, 1702. 5. Jane, March 18, 1704. 6. John, March 26, 1707. 7. Abner, January 13, 1709. 8. James, November 15, 1712.

(III) John Tewksbury, of Pullen Point, son of Henry and Hannah Tewksbury, was born in Newbury, March 26, 1707, died in Chelsea in 1752. He was progenitor of a remarkable family in the history of the region in which the later years of his life were spent and he himself also was a remarkable man, although he did not live to take part in the events which distinguished the lives of his sons. The name of his wife does not appear, nor have we record of his children except sons, Andrew, John and James, whose descendants now number more than one hundred persons in the town of Winthrop alone, and of these more than fifty bear the name of Tewksbury.

The brothers Andrew, John and James, and John, Jr., the young son of John, were all privates in Captain Samuel Sprague's company of Chelsea men "that kept guard at Pullen Point in Chelsea" from April 19, 1775, until discharged by their commanding officer. In many other ways they were identified with the best interests of the town in later years, and each was progenitor of a good family.

(IV) John Tewksbury, son of John Tewksbury, of Pullen Point, was born probably in 1735, and died in Chelsea, March 11, 1816, aged eighty-one years. He was living at Shirley Point with his father in 1750; was baptized and owned the covenant in 1766; served as one of the committee on the Bellingham will in 1770, stood guard at the Point for thirty days in 1775. On September 21, 1758, he married Anna Bill. His posterity living at the present time (1908) in Winthrop, says Judge Chamberlain, number eighty-six persons, bearing the surnames Tewksbury, Floyd, Paine, Richardson, Strout, Smith, Patch, Lindsey, Durham, Gilmore, Griffin, Cobb and Westlake.

(IV) James Tewksbury, son of John Tewksbury, of Pullen Point, was born in 1744, baptized and joined the church in 1769, married in 1770, stood guard with his brother at Pullen Point in 1775, and died November 7, 1800, aged fifty-six years. He married, August 16, 1770, Mary, daughter of John and Susanna Sargeant. His Winthrop descendants number thirty-one persons and are represented in the family names, Tewksbury, Ingalls, Richardson, Eldridge, Tucker, Durham, Greeley, Sanford, Shattuck, Griffin, Whittemore and Cobb.

(IV) Andrew Tewksbury, son of John Tewksbury, of Pullen Point, was born in 1739 and died in 1814, aged seventy-five years. He was at Point Shirley with his father in 1750, was admitted to church communion in 1658, stood guard for thirty days with Captain Sprague's company of Chelsea men in July, 1775, and by principal occupation was a farmer. He married, February 18, 1762, Susanna Hasey, born 1741, died 1832, daughter of John and Mary (Chamberlain) Hasey. John Hasey was born in 1710 and died in 1753; married first, in 1730, Abigail Dexter, died in 1731-32; second, 1734-35, Abigail Chamberlain. John Hasey was son of William Hasey, who was born 1679, died 1753; married first, Elizabeth ———, second, 1709, Sarah Tuttle, third, Abigail Hathorn. William Hasey was a son of William Hasey, who was born 1652, married, before 1675, Judith Jacob. William Hasey was a son of Lieutenant William Hasey, who married first, Sarah ———, second, Judith Poole. He bought the Cole farm at Rumney Marsh in 1653-54, was made freeman, 1665, cornet of the Three County Troop, 1665, and commander in 1675. Andrew Tewksbury's wife, Susanna, taught a school at Pullen Point in 1765, and from a report of the children in attendance the school kept in John Tewksbury's house in 1779 we find the names of the children of Andrew and Hannah at that time, and who were taught "Reading & Writeing." They were Andrew, Jr., Susanna, Hannah, Elizabeth and Carter. They had other children, William, Esther and Lois, and perhaps others. Judge Chamberlain in his recent "History of Chelsea," says that in 1908 there were thirty-one descendants of Andrew Tewksbury living in Winthrop, represented in the family names of Tewksbury, Floyd, Magee, Wyman, Haggerston, Hall, Gilmore and Brown.

(V) Andrew Tewksbury Jr., son of Andrew and Susanna (Hasey) Tewksbury, was born in Chelsea, October 18, 1763, although the date of his baptism is mentioned in one record as 1762. He married, April 26, 1787, Polly Williams, who was born in Chelsea, October 15, 1766, and by whom he had eleven children, all born at Point Shirley: 1. Sally, born March 2, 1788. 2. Andrew, Jr., October 17, 1789. 3. Polly, August 10, 1791. 4. Lydia, July 12, 1793. 5. Elizabeth, July 29, 1795. 6. John W., September 9, 1797. 7. Lucinda, April 7, 1800. 8. Harriet, February 13, 1802. 9. Adeline, January 30, 1804. 10. Samuel, December 6, 1806. 11. Gerry, June 16, 1810. Of these children Andrew, Jr., died at the age of about forty years; all the others lived to between seventy-eight and eighty-five years, and one lived to more than ninety years.

(VI) John W. Tewksbury, son of Andrew Jr. and Polly (Williams) Tewksbury, was born in Chelsea, September 9, 1797, and for many years was one of the most energetic and progressive business men of the town. After the death of his wife's father, Samuel Sturgis, in company with Samuel Leeds, of South Boston, he became joint owner of the Point Shirley Salt Works, which Mr. Sturgis had founded soon after 1812, and as partners they operated the works about five years. Then Mr. Tewksbury became sole proprietor and carried on the business until 1845, when he sold the plant and a portion of the land to the Revere Copper Company. In 1852 he disposed of the remaining part of his lands in that vicinity and purchased a desirable farm farther up the neck. This purchase included what in later years has been known as Cottage Hill and there he lived the quiet and contented life of a farmer and gardener until about 1860, when he gave the management of the estate into the hands of his son and retired from active pursuits. Mr. Tewksbury died in 1884, having attained the ripe old age of eighty-seven years. He lived to witness the growth of his town from a sparsely settled region into a healthful and progressive municipality, and indeed he himself was an important factor in that growth and development and for many years was counted among the foremost men of the town. He was something of a public man in politics, a firm Republican, and was one of the first selectmen of the new town of Winthrop. In 1822, Mr. Tewksbury married Abigail Sturgis, daughter of Samuel Sturgis, of Boston, and for many years one of the most enterprising business men of Chelsea. In Boston Mr. Sturgis was a merchant and otherwise was engaged in various large enterprises. At one time and for several years he was owner and proprietor of the "Golden Key," which later became "Oak Hall," as now known. In 1812 he went to Chelsea and made extensive land purchases, acquiring about two-thirds of Point Shirley, including Great Head, where he established the once famous Point Shirley Salt Works, which in some respects was one of the greatest business enterprises in New England, and which he operated with good success for many years. His father was Captain William Sturgis, of Cape Cod, master mariner, whose life and experiences are ample for a volume of history. He came of that old Barnstable Sturgis (or Sturges) family of which John Sturges was the founder and immigrant ancestor.

(VII) Charles S. Tewksbury, son of John W. and Abigail (Sturgis) Tewksbury, was born on his father's home farm in Chelsea, May 14, 1824, died in that town July 12, 1875. He appears to have inherited many of the excellent business qualities of his father, and from early young manhood was closely associated with him in various enterprises of an important character In 1860, when his father retired from active pursuits, Charles S. took a lease of the farm on "the neck," brought it to a condition of high fertility and for the next fifteen years gathered from its acres an annual crop of market products that yielded a gratifying revenue to the proprietor. In the meantime the natural beauties of the locality had begun to attract the attention of the annual colony of summer visitors, and quick to see the advantages of such an acquisition, with the co-operation of his son, Ensign Kimball, Mr. Tewksbury caused his farm lands to be subdivided and laid out into lots for summer cottages, with all the desirable appointments of streets and avenues; and now, after the lapse of hardly more than a score of years the old farm site has become the very center of the most attractive part of Winthrop Beach. But still, with all these changes of years Mr. Tewksbury with thoughtful consideration has preserved many reminders of the old town by naming the principal thoroughfares of his subdivided tract of land in allusion to the old sites and families which once were familiar to former residents in the locality; and now in visiting the town one finds Cottage Hill, Beacon, Tewksbury, Perkins, Underhill, Sturgis, Irwin and other streets, Hathorne and Shirley avenues to recall past memories and noted characters in the old life of the locality. Mr. Tewksbury died July 12, 1895. He was an excellent business man, and withal a good man in every respect. He did much for the permanent welfare of his native town, and its people always respected him according to his worth. He married first, Armenia Parker, who was born in Ludlow, Vermont, and died in Winthrop, having borne her husband five children, all of whom except one died young: Albert, Ensign Kimball (who alone survives), John William, Joshua B. and Almena. For his second wife Mr. Tewksbury married Nancy Moore, who was born in Chelsea, Vermont, and died while visiting in Boston in April, 1898, having survived her husband nearly three years. No children were born of this marriage.

(VIII) Ensign Kimball Tewksbury, son and only surviving child of Charles S. and Armenia (Parker) Tewksbury, was born in the then town of Chelsea, near where now stands his own pleasant house, March 27, 1852. His life has been spent in the town, there he was educated in the public schools, and he received an excellent business training by having early associated himself with the several enterprises in which his father was interested and in which he too had an interest. For himself, however, he learned the trade of carpenter and joiner and having become a practical workman he soon became a building contractor. In this vocation he always found much work to be done, especially in connection with the land operations in which both his father and himself were so extensively interested for many years. During the last twenty-five or thirty years Mr. Tewksbury has built more than three hundred dwelling houses, besides many business structures and other buildings. And besides his connection with his father's real estate operations he has carried on improvement enterprises on his own account; also in company with Mr. Nickerson, with whom he is now engaged in building and real estate undertakings, all of which have contributed materially to the welfare of the town and its people. Thus it will be seen that Mr. Tewksbury has been a pretty busy man during the last more than quarter of a century, but it cannot be said that he has been selfish of his time for purely personal ends, for he always has been found in some way identified with every measure proposed for the public welfare, a leader in some of them and always ready to do his full share in whatever promises for the interests of the town. He is a public-spirited, liberal and progressive citizen, full worthy of success which has been the reward of his honest endeavors.

On November 29, 1873, Ensign Kimball Tewksbury married Mary F. Bugbee, who was born in Chelsea, Vermont, October 1, 1850, daughter of Erastus and Mary (Moore) Bugbee, both natives of Vermont and descendants of highly respectable old New England colonial families. Mrs. Tewksbury is a woman of education and social position and her congenial companionship and sound counsel have been material factors in her husband's success. They have two children: 1. Charles F., a successful farmer in Halifax, Massachusetts; he married Laura Estelle Wison, who was born in Kansas. 2. Ella, wife of Henry Ridgeway, an employee of the New England Telegraph and Telephone Company, Boston.

FENNO The name of Rebecca Ffenner is found in the list of passengers on board the ship "Truelove," bound from England to New England, 1635. This is the earliest mention of the Fenno surname in America, and it may be assumed that she was the same Rebecca Fenno who had a grant of sixty-eight acres of land from the town of Dorchester, situated in Unity, which two years later was incorporated as Milton, Massachusetts, where the name Fenno is still well known. Rebecca Fenno was admitted to the church in Milton, August 12, 1683.

(I) John Fenno, believed to be a son of Rebecca Fenno, was granted twenty acres of land in Equity (Milton) in 1660, and soon afterward built a house there, as testified by the Dorchester records, 1661: "We have layed out and staked the way two rodd and halfe broad from the meetinghouse at unquetie from John Gills land and Robert Redmans land to John Fennos house leading to the way to Blue Hills." The locality of his house long bore the name of Fenno Hill, recently changed by the Metropolitan park commission to Kitchamakin Hill. The farm now known as the Fenno farm, says a recent narrative, was granted by the town of Dorchester, December, 1657, to Lieutenant Roger Clapp, "where he shall find a convenient place" beyond the Blue Hills. Major Humphrey Atherton, Ensign Foster and William Sumner were empowered to lay it out. A plan was made in 1662 by Joshua Fisher, another in 1689, and on Butcher's map it is designated as Captain Clapp's farm. At the death of Captain Clapp, the next year, the farm descended to his sons Samuel and Hopestill. In 1692 an action to recover the farm was brought by Richard Thayer against the Clapp executors, the result being averse to plaintiffs, and the Clapp heirs, for a consideration of one hundred pounds, conveyed it, June 21, 1694, to John Fenno, who retained possession until his death, 1708. He willed the farm to his sons John, Benjamin and Ephraim; his son Joseph had gone with the expedition to Canada, and the father provided by will that if he returned his brothers should jointly pay him ninety pounds. In his will, dated August, 1702, he describes his property as in "Lancashire in ye Realme of England." He was a soldier in King Philip's war. He died in Milton, April 7, 1708, aged seventy-nine years. He married Rebecca Tucker, died June 12, 1690, aged seventy-nine. Children, born in Milton: 1. Rebecca, born September 23, 1662, died in Braintree, July, 1741; married, April 27, 1688, Dependence French. 2. John, see forward. 3. Elizabeth, died September 21, 1669. 4. Joseph, born September 1, 1670, probably killed in French and Indian war, as his father writes in his will, "my son Joseph formerly went to Canada in an expedition against the then common enemy, since which time I have never heard from him." 5. Mary, born July 31, 1677, married, February 18, 1709, James Badcock, of Milton; removed to Connecticut. 6. Elizabeth, born March 31, 1680, died 1746; married, October 3, 1706, John Waldo, of Windham, Connecticut. 7. Ephraim, born June 30, 1682.

(II) John Fenno, second child and eldest son of John Fenno (1), was born in Milton, August 29, 1665. He was a farmer, and lived in that part of Stoughton now Canton, where he died April 23, 1741. The house he built in 1694 is standing—a big-chimneyed red house with numerous outbuildings, on Farm street, south side of Porkipog pond. The land, five hundred acres, was bought by his father in 1694. John Fenno seems to be the only one of the brothers who settled in Canton. In 1695 he was chosen on committee on bounds by Dorchester, and was surveyor of highways in 1704 and 1709. In 1716 his house is represented on a plan as having two stories—a rarity in those days—and indicates that he was possessed of more than average property. At the organization of the precinct he was chosen assessor, and it also appears to have been his duty to keep the boys in order in the meeting house. June 25, 1690, he married Rachel Newcomb, of Braintree, who died October 16, 1750. Children: 1. Bethia, born October 12, 1692, died April 29, 1780; married, December 15, 1713, Charles Wentworth. 2. Joseph, born February 21, 1695, died in Canton, June 26, 1764; married, December 8, 1726, Sarah White, of Milton, who died September 29, 1760. 3. Rebecca, born September 8, 1697, died in Canton, March 13, 1783; married, January 2, 1727, John Pierce, of Watertown. 4. Isaac, born November 14, 1699, died July 2, 1771; married (first), January 9, 1728, Hannah Puffer; (second), April 10, 1732, Mary Niles. 5. John, see forward. 6. Ruth, born May 30, 1705, died March 28, 1768; married, October 10, 1728, Eliphalet Leonard, of Easton; he died February 4, 1786. 7. Elizabeth, born May 7, 1707, died October 17, 1783; married, June 9, 1727, Stephen Billings; he died June 10, 1767. 8. Seth, born October 28, 1709, died October 31, 1740. 9. Freelove, born February 1, 1714, married, April 18, 1733, John Brett, of Bridgewater.

(III) John Fenno, son of John and Rachel (Newcomb) Fenno, born in Milton, February 7, 1703, was a farmer, and lived in Canton, where he died, December 15, 1759. "In 1732 he confessed and bewailed the sin of fighting." He married, December 15, 1726, Hannah, born February 25, 1707, died October 23, 1768, daughter of Joseph and Rahanna (Babcock) Billings. Children: 1. Mary, born September 11, 1727, married, January 19,

1748, John French. 2. John, born February 11, 1730, died about 1763; married, December 14, 1752, Jerusha Wentworth. 3. Ruhanna, born December 6, 1732, married (first), November 7, 1751, Jonas Hartwell; (second), ——— Snell. 4. Joseph, born May 15, 1735, drowned June 19, 1767, while getting a vessel up Newport river; was in Crown Point expedition, 1755; married, July 16, 1761, Jerusha Robinson, of Dorchester. 5. William; see forward. 6. Rachel, born November 18, 1740, married, January 18, 1759, Ezra Winslow, of Stoughton. 7. Abigail, born April 1, 1743, married, May 12, 1760, John Howard Winslow, of Stoughton. 8. Freelove, married October 1, 1767, Caleb Kingman, of Bridgewater.

(IV) William Fenno, son of John and Hannah (Billings) Fenno, born in Canton, November 9, 1737, died there 1774. His widow was appointed administratrix July 22, 1774. He married, 1761, Sarah Endicott, born in Canton, August 10, 1741, daughter of James, and granddaughter of Gilbert Endicott, who settled near Dorchester early in the seventeenth century. Children, born in Canton: 1. Sarah, born February 27, 1762, married John Payson. 2. Hannah, born September 11, 1763, married Oliver Downs, December 25, 1787. 3. John, see forward. 4. William, born December 21, 1767, was a housewright in Boston, and died there July 24, 1813; married Sybil Hayward, born November 25, 1769. 5. Joseph, born November 21, 1769.

(V) Deacon John Fenno, son of William and Sarah (Endicott) Fenno, born in Canton, January 1, 1766, died in Boston, July 26, 1835. He kept a grocery store on Hanover street, Boston, and was a deacon of the New North Church, in the time of Rev. Francis Parkman. He was the first of the Fenno family to settle in Chelsea, where he bought a large tract of land. He married, 1793, Olive Pratt, born April 10, 1770, died in Chelsea, November 24, 1856, daughter of Nehemiah and Ruth (Torrey) Pratt, of South Weymouth, Massachusetts. Their wedding was the first in East Boston. Children: 1. John, born April 8, 1794, died August 24, 1859; married (first), Charlotte Fracker, July 9, 1820; (second), Lucy Elizabeth Heard, April 14, 1839. 2. Joseph, see forward. 3. Sarah, born October 24, 1797, died December 4, 1875; married Lewis Jenkins Bailey, April 12, 1819. 4. William, born March 1, 1800, died December 9, 1866; married Margaret Norwood Bailey, January 27, 1839. 5. Harriet Ardelia, born October 20, 1803, died June 6, 1836, married Henry Cutting, January 27, 1829. 6. Henry William, born November 25, 1805, died July 14, 1862; married Rebecca Hill Daricott, November 20, 1828. 7. Olive Augusta, born September 5, 1807, died September 3, 1878; married Rev. Horatio Alger, March 31, 1831. 8. Ann Catherine, died September 17, 1813, aged two years.

(VI) Joseph Fenno, son of Deacon John and Olive (Pratt) Fenno, born September 20, 1795, died May 20, 1863. In 1838 he erected a building in Chelsea, that part now Revere, corner of Beach street and Broadway, and has been since known as Fenno's Corner. There he conducted a mercantile business to the time of his death; was continued by his son, Joseph Henry, and by his son, Warren Fenno, and on the death of the latter, in 1905, the business was closed to settle the estate. Joseph Fenno married (first), June 30, 1822, Eliza Dupee Lillie, born February 25, 1802, died August 19, 1833; child: Joseph Henry. He married (second), August 24, 1836, Amelia Caroline Colby, born April 13, 1813, died January 10, 1840; child: Caroline Amelia, born December 17, 1837, married, June 16, 1859, Russell Tewkesbury; children: i. Ada Maria, born May 27, 1861, died December 21, 1889; ii. Russell Sturgis, born May 5, 1868. He married (third), January 3, 1841, Lydia Maria Pierce, born January 12, 1821, died June 27, 1886; children: 1. Thomas Lillie, born October 1, 1841, died January 29, 1891; married October 24, 1867, Adelaide Eliza Tucker, born April 12, 1844, daughter of John and Ann Sarah (Davenport) Tucker; he was born December 14, 1818, died June, 1899, she died December 1, 1861. Children, two eldest born in North Chelsea: i. Walter Davenport, born September 8, 1868, died August 25, 1869; ii. Harvey Chester, born August 25, 1870, died February 22, 1897; iii. Stanley Warner, born in Revere, February 2, 1877, graduate of Harvard, class 1904, since has been science teacher in Revere high school; closely identified with Unitarian church, treasurer and collector; married Bertha Pierce Whittaker, June 26, 1906. 2. Edward Augustus, see forward. 3. Charles Francis, see forward. 4. Sarah Pierce, born February 22, 1847, died February 5, 1882; married Fred E. Proctor, October 17, 1877; children: Ralph Fenno, Lucia Maria. 5. Maria Augusta, born February 8, 1849, died March 9, same year. 6. Walter Pierce, born May 20, 1850, died January 12, 1860. 7. Fred Austin, born February 5, 1853, married Mary

Ella Childs, October 21, 1886. 8. Morton, born July 6, 1855, died January 8, 1882. 9. Herbert, born August 18, 1858, married (first) Emma J. Sawtelle, of Holyoke; child: Emma J., married (second) Mary Lane, of Deerfield. 10. Parker, born May 10, 1862, died March 15, 1896, unmarried.

(VII) Edward Augustus Fenno, son of Joseph and Lydia Maria (Pierce) Fenno, born Chelsea, August 26, 1842, died at Holyoke, April 16, 1886. He was educated in his native town. He early went to Holyoke, and was there engaged successfully in the grocery business until his death. He married, in Chelsea, October 16, 1866, Sarah Yendell Derby, born Chelsea, February 21, 1843, daughter of Minot and Dorcas (Holliday) Derby. Children: 1. Minot Derby, see forward. 2. Jennie Clark, born in North Chelsea, September 20, 1874, died February 23, 1900, in Revere, unmarried. 3. Albert Edward, born in Revere, October 7, 1876, married Georgianna O. Miller.

(VII) Charles Francis Fenno, son of Joseph and Lydia Maria (Pierce) Fenno, was born July 30, 1844, died November 24, 1903. He was educated in Revere schools; worked in grocery store for his father and his stepbrother Joseph Henry up to the time of his marriage; after marriage learned trade of paper hanging and worked at that until 1883, when he was elected tax collector, in which capacity he served twenty-two years or until his death; he also served as constable, truant officer, member of police department fifteen years or more. He was a Republican, Unitarian in religion, and member of New England Order of Protection. He was upright, honest and conscientious, and was highly respected and greatly beloved by the poor whom he helped to the extent of his ability. He married, July 19, 1865, Emma Catherine, born April 20, 1846, daughter of John Tucker and wife, Ann Sarah (Davenport) Tucker; John Tucker was born in Milton, December 14, 1818, died June 12, 1898; his wife was born August 28, 1822, died December 1, 1861, daughter of James and Abigail (Lord) Davenport, of Dorchester, the former of whom was son of James Davenport. Children: 1. Alice Russell, born December 2, 1868, married, October 3, 1889, Vincent Farnsworth. 2. Charles Percy, born April 13, 1870, married Mary Louise Richardson, October 3, 1894.

(VIII) Minot Derby Fenno, eldest child of Edward Augustus and Sarah Yendell (Derby) Fenno, was born in North Chelsea, November 8, 1868. He received his early education in the schools of his native town, and finished his education in Holyoke, whither his parents had removed. On coming to young manhood he engaged in the grocery business with his father, with whom he was associated until the death of the parent. Minot D. Fenno then returned to Revere, and became actively identified with public affairs. In 1887 he became state auditor for the State Bath House at Revere, and was later town auditor, occupying that office until 1904, when he resigned to become tax collector of Revere, which office he still holds. Mr. Fenno married, in Revere, March 4, 1906, Clara I. Higgins. No children.

KENT In England the surname Kent is placed with the more numerous patronymics, and in its origin dates to the time of the Conquest; and besides being a name of remarkable antiquity as shown by the researches of students it also appears to have been borne by many persons of distinction, some of them famed because of valorous deeds in war, others by reason of incumbency of high official station in the service of the crown, and still others who were eminent scholars, jurists, theologians, and men schooled in diplomacy and statecraft. And as they wrought so well they of this house were honored by an appreciative sovereign with vast estates in land, amounting almost to principalities, and with enviable titles, barons, dukes and earls, with arms and other tokens of royal favor. Of arms there are not a few, and the bearings generally display the eagle on both the escutcheon and the crest.

So too may it be written of the Kents of America, now a numerous family, but not less noted in achievement than the ancient house in the mother country; and we have only to turn the pages of our national history for the honorable roll of statesmen, divines, heroes of wars, scholars, authors, and men of all professions who have sprung from the parent stock crossed the Atlantic and sat down in the New England plantations during the first half of the seventeenth century.

(I) John Kent, of Dedham, immigrant ancestor and founder of the New England family of his surname treated in this place, was not a son of Richard Kent Sr., of Newbury, as has been asserted by some chroniclers of the family history. He was admitted to the church in Dedham in 1652, was made freeman 1654, and he was taxed there from 1653 until

Charles F. Fenn.

November, 1664. He joined with others in a petition to the general court in 1662, was fence viewer in 1664-5, and removed from Dedham to Charlestown, where he and his wife Hannah were received into church membership in 1673. Their first child was born in Charlestown in 1667, and he was tithingman there in 1679. He died after 1707. He married, at Dedham, May 21, 1662, Hannah Griswold, born in Cambridge, March 4, 1644-5, died at Charlestown, January 9, 1690-1, daughter of Francis and Mary Griswold (or Grissell) of Charlestown. December 5, 1636, "there is granted unto Francis Greshold, the Drummer, two acres of land lying at the end of Barnabe Lambson's pole toward Charlestowne, in regard of his service amongst the soldiers upon all occasions, as long as he stayeth." Children of John and Hannah (Griswold) Kent: 1. Hannah, born July 2, 1667; married Joseph Cahoon. 2. Maria, born February 3, 1669. 3. John Jr., born 1670; married, first, December 22, 1692, Sarah Smith; second, Elizabeth ———; he removed to Scituate in 1698, to Mansfield, Connecticut, in 1709, and died there in 1753; representative in 1724. 4. Joshua, born June 15, 1672, died June 20, 1672. 5. Joshua, born July 4, 1674; married, November 4, 1697, Agnes Okeman; lived in Boston. 6. Joseph, born October 13, 1675. 7. Samuel, born March 23, 1678, died March 16, 1702-3. 8. Ebenezer, born August 18, 1680, died at Hingham, February 16, 1752; married, December 8, 1703, Hannah Gannett. 9. Lydia, born July 16, 1683; married, 1714, Ebenezer Simmons, of Scituate. 10. Mary, born May 12, 1686; married, 1710, Joseph Barber, of Hingham. 11. Susannah, born August 13, 1689.

(II) Ebenezer Kent, son of John and Hannah (Griswold) Kent, born in Charlestown, August 18, 1680, removed to Hingham between 1700 and 1703, and built the first dwelling house on the west side of Cohasset river, where he had a farm. He was a member of the Second church (Cohasset), constable in 1727 and 1736, owned lands in several towns, and died well possessed, February 16, 1752. He married Hannah, daughter of Joseph Gannett, born in Scituate, 1684, died in Hingham, March 27, 1767. Children: 1. Abigail, born October 12, 1706, died March 12, 1709. 2. Hannah, born 1707; married January 16, 1727-8, Israel Whitcomb. 3. Mercy, born July 31, 1709; married Stephen Stoddard. 4. Elizabeth, born September 6, 1710; married (1) May 7, 1735, Eliakim Mayo, (2) ——— Pitcher. 5. Isaac, born September 27, 1712. 6. Mary, born 1715; married, August 31, 1743, Joseph Blake. 7. Ebenezer Jr., born April 18, 1717, settled in Leicester, Massachusetts. 8. Seth, born April 3, 1721. 9. Abigail, born March 29, 1723; married, October 22, 1744, Joseph Souther. 10. Lydia, born April 24, 1725; married, December 22, 1743, Noah Ripley, settled at Barre, Massachusetts. 11. Abel, born August 7, 1730.

(III) Isaac Kent, son of Ebenezer and Hannah (Gannett) Kent, was born September 27, 1712, in Conihasset, near Hingham. He married first, October 25, 1739, Rachel, daughter of Andrew and Rachel (Bates) Beal, born in Hingham, August 25, 1719. They removed to Mendon, Massachusetts, (now Milford), and were received into the church there April 11, 1746, by letter from the Second church of Hingham. Their home in Milford was in the southeastern part of the Bear Hill district. He was selectman from 1750 to 1760. He is said to have removed to Bellingham, but in 1770 was dismissed to the church in Annapolis Granville. Rachel Kent died May 15, 1805, aged eighty-six. Children: 1. Rachel, born July 28, 1740, in Hingham, died 1746. 2. Isaac, born June 9, 1742. 3. Susanna, born July 30, 1744, died May 2, 1751. 4. Elizabeth, born August 15, 1746, died March 13, 1749. 5. Rebecca, born August 11, 1748-9, died June 9, 1791. 6. Anna, born July 25, 1750, died June 9, 1791. 7. Abigail, born March 1, 1752. 8. Arach, twin, October 4, 1754. 9. Zarah, twin, October 4, 1754. 10. John, January 31, 1757. 11. Caleb, twin, April 15, 1759. 12. Joshua, twin, April 15, 1759. 13. Hannah, September 12, 1764, died April 4, 1796.

(IV) Isaac Kent, son of Isaac and Rachel (Beal) Kent, was born in Mendon, June 9, 1742. He married first, May 17, 1770, (by Rev. Mr. Willard) Sarah Wheelock, died November 13, 1779, aged twenty-eight years; he married second, August 17, 1780, Sarah Way, died August 20, 1790; he married third, April 21, 1791, Sarah Holbrook, of Grafton, died February 27, 1813, aged fifty-nine years, he married fourth, October 26, 1814, at Wethersfield, Vermont, Rhoda Kenny, widow. He died January 1, 1835, aged ninety-three. He and his brother John petitioned for the incorporation of a religious society in Alstead. Isaac is said to have had a brother Benjamin who settled in New York. Isaac lived in Warwick, Massachusetts, until 1776, when he removed to Alstead. Several of his family, including his brother Zarah, were loyalists in the revolution and removed to Nova Scotia, probably refugees. Isaac Kent was a soldier in the revolution, private in Captain Reuben Butterfield's company, Twentieth regiment, 1776 (Colonel Thatcher). He enlisted in the continental army July 5, 1777, and served until January 1, 1778, in Captain Joshua Parker's company, Colonel Robinson's regiment. He may also have been in Captain Moses Barnes' company, Lieutenant Colonel Samuel Pierce's regiment, 1779. At the time of his death Rev. Mr. Gerould said, "He was a valuable member of society, always punctual to all engagements, and peculiarly so in his attendance on public worship." Children of Isaac and Sarah (Wheelock) Kent: 1. Israel, born May 28, 1773, died December 29, 1831. 2. Amariah, born March 4, 1775, died June 16, 1825. 3. Anna, born January 16, died February 6, 1777. 4. Rebecca, born January 13, 1778, died November 10, 1783. 5. Benjamin, born November 13, 1779. Children of Isaac and Sarah (Holbrook) Kent: 6. Sally, born August 17, 1792, died October 12, 1858. 7. Asa, born February 28, 1794; remained on the homestead; died 1882, aged eighty-eight. 8. Arad, born October 10, 1795, died August 4, 1831, in Marion, Ohio. 9. Stephen, born May 27, 1797, died August 10, 1834, leaving a son, a lawyer in Ohio.

(V) Benjamin Kent, son of Isaac and Sarah (Wheelock) Kent, was born in Alstead, New Hampshire, November 13, 1779, and although a man of large stature and great physical strength he died in the very prime of life. He first learned the trade of shoemaking, followed that occupation with his father for some time, and later became a blacksmith and farmer. He died leaving a wife Sarah, and son Abel W. Kent.

(VI) Abel Willard Kent, only child of Benjamin and Sarah Kent, born in Alstead, about 1800, was brought up there by Frank Phelps, in allusion to whom he named his elder son. He was educated in the district school in Alstead, later became a shoemaker, and also was a teamster and farmer. When about thirty-three years old he went west and found a suitable location for a new home for his young family in Casapolis, Michigan, but before his wife and children reached there he was stricken with fever and died. In religious preference Mr. Kent was a Congregationalist, a Whig in politics, and while living in Alstead was a member of the state militia. He married Lucinda Gould, of Marlborough, Massachusetts, daughter of Benjamin and Abigail (Clark) Gould, the former a soldier of the war of 1812, a blacksmith by trade, and who settled near Alstead. Children of Abel Willard and Lucinda (Gould) Kent: 1. Rebecca, now dead; married George Loveland. 2. Adeline, married William K. Ritchie, and had Marion, Sarah and Addie Ritchie. 3. Frank Phelps. 4. Pliny Payson.

(VII) Frank Phelps Kent, son of Abel Willard and Lucinda (Gould) Kent, was born in Alstead, New Hampshire, September 8, 1835, and was less than three years old when he went with his mother to Michigan. His father had died before the family arrived there, and soon afterward they returned to Alstead and two years later went to Nashua, where Frank P. was sent to school. After a few years in that town the family removed to Pelham, New Hampshire, and there he attended winter terms of school and worked out during the warm months of each year until he was about seventeen years old. He then went back to Nashua and found steady work in a grocery store and later in a meat market, and at twenty-one, having gained a good understanding of business, he came to Boston and for the next two years was clerk for James Eggerton, whose place of business was in Quincy market. About 1859 Mr. Kent began business on his own account, having saved money enough to purchase a restaurant in Hanover street, Boston. This he continued with good success for one year, then sold out at a fair profit to himself and started a similar business in Milton, New Hampshire, carried it on about three and a half years, then sold out and went to Wilton, New Hampshire. In the latter town he engaged in the same business and increased his enterprises by adding a well appointed meat market and also a livery and sales stable. In Wilton, Mr. Kent was counted among the substantial and enterprising business men of the town and made many warm friends there. In 1886 he sold his store, but retained his other interests until his stables were destroyed by fire, after which he sold out his restaurant and removed to West Medford, Massachusetts, and purchased the general grocery and meat business formerly carried on by Burroughs Bros. For the next six years he continued the business in its old location near the railroad station, then moved his stock to the Usher building, remained there ten years, and in 1902 erected the building now occupied by his largely increased stock of general groceries and provisions. Besides this, he has erected commodious stable buildings, owns other valuable property in West Medford and also in Wilton, New Hampshire. From what has been stated here it must be seen that Mr. Kent is a capable and successful business man, and whatever has been accomplished by him is entirely the result of his own personal effort and industry. He is interested in public affairs as a citizen and considerable taxpayer, yet takes no active part in them, preferring to devote his leisure hours to the pleasant associations of his comfortable home. He is a member of the congregation of the Unitarian church, and of Mount Vernon Lodge, I. O. O. F., and in politics is a Democrat. On August 15, 1863, Mr. Kent married Mary Elizabeth Blanchard, born in Concord, Massachusetts February 16, 1843, daughter of Bradley and Mary (Bowers) Blanchard, of Milford. Children: 1. Minnie Bowers, born in Milford, November 20, 1864, died July 13, 1873. 2. Edward Frank, born October 23, 1868. 3. Jessie Blanchard, born in Wilton, September 24, 1870; married September 28, 1892, John H. Chute, of Annapolis, N. S., and had Edward Kent Chute, born August 24, 1894, died August 26, 1894. 4. Bessie Lovejoy, born in Wilton February 15, 1872. 5. Kittie, born in Wilton, June 10, 1875; married, March 4, 1903, Albert H. Fisher, of Waltham, Massachusetts.

(VIII) Edward Frank Kent, son of Frank Phelps and Mary E. (Blanchard) Kent, was born in Wilton, New Hampshire, October 23, 1868. He graduated from Wilton high school, class of '84, and in the fall of 1885 began a special course of study in physiology and botany at Ashburnham Academy, with the purpose of laying the foundation of a thorough education in surgery, which profession he determined upon for his vocation in life. But this he was compelled to give up at the end of a year, and thereupon took a thorough course in Comer's Business College, Boston. He then returned to Wilton and acquired a partnership interest in the grocery and provision business carried on by his father; and from that to the present time the relation has continued under the style of F. P. Kent, a name and house well known in trade circles in eastern Massachusetts and New Hampshire. The several changes in location and the general character of the business conducted by this firm are sufficiently stated in earlier paragraphs, but it is proper to mention in this connection that a full measure of the success which has rewarded the endeavors of the firm of F. P. Kent has been due to the business capacity, enterprise and known integrity of the junior partner. In politics Mr. Kent is Republican, taking an active interest in local affairs, but has no strong ambition for public office. He is a Mason of high degree, member of Mount Vernon Lodge, F. and A. M., Mystic Chapter, R. A. M., Medford Council, R. and S M., all of Medford; Boston Commandery, K. T.; Lafayette Lodge of Perfection (14) Giles F. Yates Chapter (16) Princes of Jerusalem; Mt. Olivet Chapter (18) Rose Croix; and Massachusetts Consistory (32) A. A. S. R.; Aleppo Temple, A. A. O. N. M. S.; past patron of Middlesex Chapter, No. 64, O. E. S. of West Medford; member of Mount Vernon Lodge, No. 184, I. O. O. F., of West Medford, and has served as its sentinel and permanent secretary. He also is a member of the Neighborhood Club of West Medford, and at the time of its dissolution was a member of the Medford Club. On January 14, 1897, Mr. Kent married Harriet Havilah Gates, of Annapolis, N. S., daughter of Edwin and Horatia Nelson (Ryerson) Gates. Children: 1. Marjorie, born July 26, 1898, died same day. 2. Katherine Havilah, born November 4, 1902.

STONE Caleb Stone, son of James Stone, was born about 1750. He was of Boston when he married, February 1, 1780, Anna Williams, of Lynn. His wife died August 25, 1833, aged seventy-eight years. He died at Lynn, January 29, 1818. Children, born at Lynn: 1. John, February 8, 1781. 2. Thomas, January 5, 1782. 3. James, June 3, 1784; mentioned below. 4. Jonathan, August 18, 1786. 5. Anna, October 2, 1788. 6. Benjamin, April 6, 1791. 7. Joshua, March 30, 1792. 8. Caleb, February 12, 1794; married, June 11, 1818, Isna J. Wilkins. 9. Williams, April 26, 1796. 10. Polly, March 8, 1799. 11. Henry, April 28, 1802; died September 22, 1817. 12. George, born September 17, 1805. 13. Nancy, October 16, 1807.

(II) James Stone, son of Caleb Stone, was born in Lynn, June 3, 1784. He was commonly known as "Sir Stone." He was educated in the public schools of Lynn and learned the trade of shoemaker there. He was one of the pioneers in shoe manufacturing, which he followed all his life. He died at Lynn about sixty-five years of age. He married Eunice Thayer, of Dedham, Massachusetts, born at Dedham, died at Lynn, aged ninety-five years. Children: James, mentioned below; Abraham; William; Katherine; Lydia; Ann, died young; Lydia Ann. (See Thayer).

(III) James Stone, son of James Stone, was born in Lynn, 1811. He received his education in the district schools of his native place, and learned his father's business of shoemaking. He was appointed constable in Lynn when it was a town; later deputy city marshal; and was city marshal for a time, superintendent of streets, and continued throughout his active life in positions of honor and responsibility in the city. He was chief of the fire department for a number of years. In politics he was a Republican, but he held the confidence and esteem of all his townsmen, regardless of party affiliations. He was at one time a member of Bay State Lodge of Odd Fellows. He was an active and prominent member of the First Methodist Episcopal Church of Lynn, and for many years its sexton. He married, in 1832, Sally Breed, born at Lynn, 1811, daughter of Joseph and Mary (Sweetser) Breed (see Breed family). Both James Stone and his wife Sally died in Lynn, in July, 1898, lacking a month of sixty-six years of married life together. Children, born in Lynn. 1. Lydia Ann, resides in Lynn. 2. William, mentioned below. 3. James Wilbur, died aged five years. 4. Sarah Maria, died young. 5. James Edward, died at Lynn, about 1892, married Lucy Ellen Buxton. 6. Sarah Abbie, resides in Lynn. 7. Ella F., resides in Lynn.

(IV) William Stone, son of James Stone, was born at Lynn, January 21, 1836, and was educated there in the public schools. He worked for a time as a finisher in the shoe factory of Samuel Bubier. He was then appointed a special police officer and served several years, gaining useful experience and displaying unusual fitness for the duties of his office. He was later deputy under Marshal C. H. Kent, of Lynn, for two years. In 1879 he was deputy under Marshal Charles C. Frye for two years, then city marshal two years, 1879-80. Two years later he was appointed clerk of the Lynn police department. In 1886 he was elected superintendent of Pine Grove cemetery of Lynn, and served as such for the twenty-one years following to the time of his death in 1907. He was a faithful and efficient police officer, doing his duty conscientiously in every position he was called to fill and commanding the confidence of his townsmen. He was a member of the following lodges: Bay State Lodge, of Odd Fellows, of which he was for many years a trustee; charter member of Abraham Lincoln Lodge, Knights of Pythias; charter member of Sagamore Tribe, Improved Order of Red Men. He was also a member of the Lynn Historical Society and one of the council. He was a prime mover in the reorganization of the Houghton Horticultural Society, and afterward its president, and also president of the American Association of Cemetery Superintendents. He was the founder of Master King's school for boys, and later its president. He was an attendant of the First Methodist church. He married in Lynn, May 23, 1861, Eliza Ellen Tufts, born in Lynn, daughter of Robert D. and Eliza B. (Needham) Tufts. Her father was a native of Lynn, her mother of Danvers. Children, born in Lynn: 1. Fredilyn A., March 2, 1862; resides at home with her parents. 2. Wilbur F., November 10, 1866; married Cora L. Willis, of Lynn.

THAYER Richard Thayer, immigrant ancestor of this branch of the American family, (see other Thayer narrative), settled in Boston. He was born and baptized in Thornbury, Gloucestershire, England, April, 1601, and came to New England in 1641, bringing with him, according to a deposition of his son Richard, eight children. He had a brother Thomas who came to New England also. Richard's son Richard settled in Braintree. Richard (1) was a shoemaker by trade. He married, in Thornbury, England, April 5, 1624, Dorothy Mortimore; second, Jane, widow of John Parker, and in 1658 joined with her in a deed to her Parker children. He died before 1668. (See Suffolk Deeds, v, 446). Children: 1. Richard, baptized February 10, 1624-5. 2. Cornelius, mentioned below. 3. Deborah, baptized February, 1629-30; married April 11, 1653, Thomas Faxon. 4. Jael, married March 17, 1654, John Harbour Jr. 5. Sarah, married July 20, 1651, Samuel Davis. 6. Hannah, married May 28, 1664, Samuel Hayden. 7. Zachariah, died July 29, 1693; estate was administered by brother Richard. 8. Abigail, died August 6, 1717, aged sixty-six years. 9. Nathaniel, born about 1650; married Deborah ———; settled in Boston.

(II) Cornelius Thayer, son of Richard Thayer, was married to Abigail Copeland and settled in Braintree, Massachusetts. His wife died January 1, 1731. Children: 1. Cornelius, born 1695. 2. Moses, born 1698. 3. Gideon, born March 1, 1700. 4. David, born 1702. 5. Ezekiel, born 1704. 6. Eliakim, born 1706; mentioned below. 7. Hezekiah, born 1708. 8. Jeremiah, born 1710; died November 9, 1711. 9. Abigail, born January 11, 1712. 10. Jeremiah, born August 20, 1716.

(III) Eliakim Thayer, son of Cornelius Thayer, born 1706, settled in Dorchester, Massachusetts. He married, August 12, 1729, Deborah Hersey, of Milton, Massachusetts. Children: 1. Eliakim, born October 25, 1731. 2. Jesse, born April 28, 1733; mentioned below. 3. Cornelius, born February 10, 1738. 4. Gideon, 1740. 5. Solomon, September 23, 1744. 6. Benjamin, 1746. 7. Betsey, April 10. 1749. 8. Abigail, October 16, 1751.

(IV) Jesse Thayer, son of Eliakim Thayer, born in Dorchester, April 28, 1733, settled in Marblehead. He married May 28, 1763, Deborah Niles. Children: 1. Samuel, born 1764. 2. Jesse. 3. Nathaniel. 4. Isaac. 5. Catherine. 6. Lydia. 7. Hannah. 8. Eunice, married James Stone (See Stone).

BISHOP This surname is of ancient English origin. Just how the title of a sacred office of the Catholic church came to be used for a surname is lost in the obscurity of ancient history. It is suggested that it must have been a personal name or a nickname of some progenitor, as Major and Deacon are sometimes given. Other names, like Pope, are of the same class, however. Bishop was a common name in England many centuries ago. No less than eleven immigrants of this surname came to Massachusetts before 1650 with their families. Various branches of the English Bishops bear coats-of-arms and have had titles and dignities of various kind.

(I) John Bishop, immigrant ancestor, born in England, about 1600, was one of the twenty-five immigrants who came with Rev. Henry Whitfield's company from England and founded Guilford, Connecticut. His name was signed second to the Plantation Covenant made on shipboard June 1, 1639. Robert Kitchell signed first. The order of the name indicates the respective social and other standing of the company, judging from analogy in similar cases. He was fifth on the list of trustees of the Indian purchases, and one of the four magistrates appointed to administer justice and preserve peace in the community. He brought his family of several children with him, and is said to be brother of James Bishop of New Haven, a contemporary. His wife was Anne. He died February, 1661, and she died April, 1676. His estate was the largest in the colony with the exception of Mr. Whitfield's. The site of John Bishop's homestead was suitably marked at the celebration of the two hundred and fiftieth anniversary of the settlement of Guilford, Connecticut, held September 8, 9, 10, 1889. Children, probably all born in England: 1. John, mentioned below. 2. Stephen, married May 4, 1654, Tabitha Wilkinson, of Bermuda, who died December 21, 1692; he died at Guilford, June, 1690. 3. Bethia, married James Steele. 5. Daughter, married ——— Hubbard.

(II) John Bishop, son of John Bishop (1), was born about 1625 in England. He married, at Guilford, Connecticut, December 13, 1650, Susannah, daughter of Henry Goldham, of Guilford. She died November 1, 1703, and he died October 1, 1683. Children, born at Guilford: 1. Mary, September 20, 1652; married John Hodgkin. 2. John, 1655; mentioned below. 3. Susannah, 1657; married Moses Blatchley. 4. Elizabeth, 1660; married John Scranton. 5. Daniel, 1663; married Hannah Bradley. 6. Nathaniel, 1666; married Mercy Hughes. 7. Samuel, October 23, 1670; married Abigail Witmoor. 8. Sarah, January 22, 1674. 9. Abigail, January 25, 1681; married Samuel Lee.

(III) John Bishop, son of John Bishop (2), was born in Guilford, 1655. He married first, July 3, 1689, Elizabeth Hitchcock, died March 14, 1712; second, November 18, 1713, Mary Johnson, of New Haven. He died at Guilford, November 25, 1731. Children of first wife, born at Guilford: 1. Elizabeth, October 14, 1690; married Samuel Scranton. 2. John, August 12, 1692; married Abigail Spinning. 3. Ann, February 15, 1695; married David Field. 4. David, June 6, 1697; mentioned below. 5. Jonathan, November 8, 1699; married Hannah Chittenden. 6. Mary, December, 1700; married Caleb Jones. 7. Deborah, February 19, 1702. 8. Nathaniel, May 6, 1704; married Margaret Blinn. 9. Timothy, 1708; married Hannah Blinn. Children of second wife, born at Guilford: 10. William, October 18, 1714; married Patience ———. 11. Enos, May 26, 1717; married Abigail Burgis. 12. Esther, February 24, 1719. 13. Mercy, May 17, 1722; married Abraham Dowd.

(IV) David Bishop, son of John Bishop (3), was born in Guilford, June 6, 1697. He married Deborah (or Dorothy) Stanley, widow of Thomas Stanley. She died February 11, 1775. He died in Guilford, August 20, 1773. Children: 1. Deborah, born January 17, 1725; married January 10, 1743, Jehiel Evarts. 2. Huldah, born August 5, 1726; died September 15, 1735. 3. David, born September 20, 1728; mentioned below. 4. Chloe, born July 15, 1730;

married Handy Bushnell. 5. Sarah, born August 18, 1736; married February 3, 1762, Miles Hall.

(V) David Bishop, son of David Bishop (4), was born in Guilford, September 20, 1728. He married, April 17, 1755, Audrea Fowler, born September 12, 1724, died January 24, 1815, daughter of Benjamin and Audrea (Morgan) Fowler, of Guilford. Her mother was daughter of Captain John Morgan, of Preston, Connecticut. Bishop died June 25, 1792. Children, born at Guilford: 1. Audrea, February 28, 1856; did March 28, 1757. 2. David, July 29, 1757; mentioned below. 3. Huldah, March 4, 1759; married Eber Lee. 4. Margaret, November 10, 1760; died September 21, 1764. 5. Jonathan, October 19, 1762; married Huldah Chapman. 6. Jared, October 22, 1764; took place of his brother David in coast guard in revolution; married Mary Munson.

(VI) David Bishop, son of David Bishop (5), was born at Guilford, July 29, 1757. He was a soldier in the revolution, serving as a private seven months twenty-three days in 1781 in the coast guard at Guilford, in Captain Peter Vaill's company. His brother Jared took his place as substitute. He was deacon of the church at Guilford elected April 28, 1802. During the revolution his barn was burned a few days before the date of report, "last Friday night" before January 27, 1783, and an indignant protest against the outrage was sent to the general assembly signed by the selectmen and justices of the peace. He married, September 9, 1776, Deborah Fowler, born January 1, 1759, died August 16, 1825, daughter of Noah and Deborah (Pendleton) Fowler. Her father was of Guilford; her mother, who died August —, 1828, aged ninety years, was a native of Stonington. David Bishop died April 19, 1833, at Paris, New York, whither he removed about 1807 with his family and parents. Children, born at Guilford: 1. David, May 9, 1778; died May 17, 1778. 2. Deborah, April 28, 1779; married Joel Collins. 3. David, January 4, 1781; died August 20, 1782. 4. Amos, April 21, 1783; mentioned below. 5. Joel, June 14, 1785; died at about twenty-one years of age. He was drowned at sea during a storm, having been washed overboard as the ship was coming into the port of New York. 6. Clarissa, July 23, 1787; married Heaton Atwater. 7. Parnel, September 29, 1789; married John Townsend. 8. Dr. Leveret, July 19, 1791; married, first, Widow Lura (Bacon) Owen, second ———. 9. Bushnell, April 11, 1795; married first, Amanda Strong of Paris Hill, New York; second, Widow Eunice West DeLand. 10. Audrea, 1797; married Levi Linsley of Stony Creek, Connecticut. 11. Maria, 1799; married Otis Manchester, a successful merchant tailor of Utica, New York, and later of New York City.

(VII) Amos Bishop, son of David Bishop (6), was born in Guilford, April 21, 1783; died in Paris, New York, May 11, 1866. He was a successful farmer. He bought primeval forest land at Volney, New York, which he cleared up and where he built a log house. Later he exchanged his farm for one at Paris, New York, upon which he lived until his death. He married first, April 19, 1810, Fanny Prentiss, born June 8, 1791, the first white child born in Paris, Oneida county, New York. She died in Paris, New York, August 14, 1815. He married second, April 7, 1824, Amanda Russell, born February 1, 1795, daughter of Samuel Smithson Russell and Eunice (Camp) Russell. Children of first wife: 1. Daughter, born at Volney, New York, January 19, 1811, died in infancy. 2. Ann Maria, born in Volney, New York, April 15, 1812, died Paris, New York, February 8, 1819. 3. Joel Prentiss, born March 10, 1814; mentioned below. Children of second wife, born at Paris: 4. Amos, February 9, 1825; died March 17, 1825. 5. Amanda, February 9, 1825 (twin); died March 21, 1825. 6. Samuel Russell, April 3, 1826; died at New Hartford, New York, March, 1896. 7. David Fowler, September 24, 1828. He was a physician and surgeon of Lockport, New York, later president of American District Steam Company of that place, which position he held until his death, April 25, 1885; he married, September 21, 1859, Leah Eliza Howes. 8. Robert Smithson, November 22, 1831. He was a physician and surgeon at Medina, New York, and later succeeded his brother as president of the American District Steam Company, Lockport, which position he held until his death, at Lockport, December 31, 1896. He married, first, April 18, 1854, Mary Louisa Hutchins, died September 2, 1889; second, June 2, 1895, Mary Katharine Fitch. 9. Leverett Bushnell, born February 5, 1837, died at twenty years of age, unmarried. 10. Amanda, December 17, 1838, died May 28, 1843.

(VIII) Joel Prentiss Bishop, LL.D., son of Amos Bishop (7), was born March 10, 1814, in Volney, Oswego county, New York, in the small log house that his father built in the wilderness, remote from all other habitations

Joel P. Bishop

but one. He was an infant when his mother died, and his father in order to get better medical attendance for her in her mortal sickness removed the family to Paris, where he continued to live after her death, exchanging his farm at Volney for one at Paris, where he had formerly lived. Here, in close communion with nature, young Joel spent his childhood and early youth, assisting his father on the farm while attending a remote district school and afterwards the academy. He attended both the Whitestown Seminary and the Oneida Institute at Whitestown, Oneida county, New York, and Stockbridge Academy, Stockbridge, Madison county, New York, and was a member of the alumni association of the seminary. He proved to be an unusually brilliant student and his ambition was stimulated by the unqualified commendation of his instructors. To quote his own words: "My aspirations grew, and at about the age of sixteen an arrangement was made with my father to permit me to leave the farm and get an education by my own exertions. I found poverty to be no obstruction. While yet sixteen I taught a public school, and by such and other means I readily obtained the money for clothing, tuition and books. I could always earn my board without hindrance to my studies. But health soon failed, and then began the struggle. I did everything to baffle disease; relinquished study, returned to it under circumstances thought to be more favorable, broke down again, varied the experiment and so on, for how many times I do not remember. When twenty-one I became fully satisfied that the struggle was useless, and gave it up. I did not, like Blackstone, write a 'Farewell to the Muse', but a 'Farewell to Science.' It was dated July 19, 1835, and published in the *Literary Emporium* of New Haven, Connecticut, near which place I then was, in the number for October 3, 1835."

After his pathetic "Farewell to Science," but with courage still good, he sought a business opening suited to his state of health. His interest in the anti-slavery movement at that time brought to him an opportunity, and he became general business manager, publishing agent and assistant treasurer of the New York Anti-slavery Society and assistant editor of the *Friend of Man,* an anti-slavery publication of Utica, New York. He afterwards declined the offer of the editorship of the paper, fearing that with his other interests and duties it might prove too great a tax on his strength. Hoping to benefit from a change of occupation and place of residence, he entered the law office of Henry B. Stanton and Henry A. Bolles as a student in the fall of 1842, not expecting that his health would permit him actually to practice law, but was happily disappointed. He was admitted to the bar April 9, 1844, in Suffolk county, after studying for a year and four months, supporting himself in the meantime by editing the *Social Monitor and Orphan's Advocate.* Notwithstanding the fact that he qualified himself as an attorney in half the usual time, the judge who passed upon his qualifications took particular pains to see his preceptors afterward and to commend them for the unusually thorough preparation the student had received in their office. Before opening an office he declined several flattering offers of partnership and began to practice on his own account. Showing an unusual penetration and skill in solving and conducting perplexing and difficult cases, he soon established a reputation at the bar and had no lack of clients, no period of waiting for business at the start. Indeed, his legal business began six weeks after he was enrolled as a law student, when under what proved to be fortunate circumstances for him he was required to draw without other help than a little previous explanation, a special declaration in an important case. This went through the courts and stood all the tests, and afterwards he was entrusted with the management of the business of the firm in the lower courts, consulting with clients and trying their cases. And he also tried and won his first jury case in the higher court while yet a student. His first commission as justice of the peace was issued by Governor Briggs, dated July 1, 1846.

Some years of practice found him with his business divided between large and small cases, much of it being of the latter description. Preferring the former, he determined to avoid the latter and to use his leisure in writing a law book. He published his "Marriage and Divorce" just ten years after he entered a law office as a student. The book was received with instant and unusual favor by the profession, and it brought to him a constant succession of requests and advice to write other books. But he felt that it was not possible for one both to practice law and have the time necessary to make the research that an honest and thorough treatment of legal subjects demanded. So, after due consideration and with the approval of the only one whom he thought entitled to object,—his wife,—he decided upon making what he always considered as the greatest sacrifice of life; relinquished his lucrative practice and devoted himself exclusively to the drudgery of legal authorship. He believed, however, that he could be of genuine service to his profession by expounding some important subjects not adequately treated by other authors. No better evidence that he proved eminently successful in his effort and life work could be desired than the universal commendation and praise with which his works on legal subjects have been received by the bench and bar. And the standing of his works in legal literature has gained in strength with the passage of time. Justice Woods, of the United States supreme court, once said of the works of Mr. Bishop: "The volumes leave nothing to be desired in the exposition of the subject of which they treat. I cannot too highly commend their arrangement and the lucid style and the clear discrimination and good sense with which they are written. The industry and learning of which they are proofs are indeed marvelous." Equally strong and sweeping is the word of Hon. W. C. Robinson of Yale University: "Whether they are students, lawyers, judges, or teachers, to these Bishop's books have no superior in any branch of legal literature."

As might be expected the knowledge and appreciation of his labors as a writer of jurisprudence are not by any means confined within the boundaries of the American continent. He received the honorary degree of *Doctor Juris Utriusque* conferred upon him by the University of Berne, Switzerland, on the occasion of celebrating the fiftieth anniversary of the founding of the university. It was in express recognition of the "great services" rendered by his legal works to his country "and to the science of law." The degree was announced in the presence of the representatives of the principal universities of Europe and the specially invited American minister to Switzerland, and to complete the character of the event as an international courtesy, as well as a personal tribute to the author, the diploma was transmitted through the Department of State at Washington.

Following is a list of the more important works of Dr. Bishop: "Marriage and Divorce" (six editions, 1852-81); "Marriage, Divorce and Separation" (1891; two vols.); "Criminal Law" (two volumes, seven editions, 1856-82); "New Criminal Law" (two volumes, 1892); "Criminal Procedure" (two volumes, three editions, 1866-80): "New Criminal Procedure" (vol. I, 1895; vol. 2, 1896); "First Book of the Law" (1868); "The Law of Married Women" (vol. 1. 1871; vol. 2, 1875); "Statutory Crimes" (vol. 1, 1873, three editions, 1873-1901); "Law of Contracts" (vol. 1, 1878, enlarged edition 1887); "The Written Laws" (1882); "Directions and Forms" (1885); "Non-Contract Law" (1889); "Law in General and as a Profession" (1901). Among his monographs on quasi-legal subjects, published as pamphlets, are: "Thoughts for the Times" (1863); "Secession and Slavery" (1864); "The Law of *Nolle Prosequi* in Criminal Causes" (1876); "Strikes and their Related Question" (1886); "Common Law and Codification" (1888). He was an occasional contributor to the various law journals. It should be noted that when Dr. Bishop made a new edition of any of his works he rewrote it completely, making a new work based on the old, and not merely a reprint. Therefore, he kept his books up to date.

Although not insensible of his own attainments, Dr. Bishop always seemed to take pride and pleasure in showing indifference to the glitter of notoriety. Unlike the majority of lawyers, he always shunned politics and public office. He was a member of the board of trustees of the Social Law Library from 1854 to 1871, a period of seventeen years. Not long before he devoted himself to legal authorship exclusively, he was tendered the appointment of chief justice of the Hawaiian Islands by King Kamehameha III, but after giving the offer serious consideration, he finally declined it. He applied himself so assiduously to his self-imposed task of writing and research that he became perforce very much of a recluse and was seldom seen in public. He refused to accept any cases and only on rare occasions could he be induced to give an expert opinion in an important case, where the question itself was of interest and importance to legal science, rather than to the parties concerned. Among the few instances may be mentioned the Lauderdale Peerage Cases, involving the descent of an earldom and large estates in Scotland and depending upon the validity of a marriage celebrated in New York in 1772. In the famous Louisiana *Nolle Prosequi* cases he gave an opinion as to the right and power of the district attorney to enter a nolle prosequi after verdict and before sentence.

Dr. Bishop was an indefatigable worker and seldom took a rest or vacation. It was his custom to rise early, at six or before, employing the time before breakfast in reading or in the execution of any errands requiring his attention. Breakfasting at seven, by half past he was usually ready to begin the day's labors, which he generally continued until five in the afternoon, reserving only half an hour for luncheon at mid-day. Commonly he did no work in the evening, but retired early at from eight to half past. If, however, he were being pushed for copy by the printers, he would sometimes work an hour or more before breakfast and put in two or three extra hours after the evening meal, which was generally taken at half-past five or six. The reason that he did not mix more with the world at large was because he was afraid the extra energy it would require would detract in some degree from his remarkable power to sustain protracted mental concentration in his chosen field of labor, and thereby lessen the amount and quality of work he could accomplish. This explains his great reluctance to accept an invitation to deliver a public address. In fact the last invitation of this nature which he accepted was in 1887 when, December 7, he delivered the annual address of the South Carolina Bar Association in Columbia before a distinguished assembly of judges and lawyers in the Hall of the House of Representatives.

Physically Dr. Bishop was of medium height and inclined to stoutness, weighing nearly two hundred pounds, and of light complexion. He was naturally of a poetic temperament and in his younger days was considerably addicted to writing of verse, a weakness that he never fully overcame. He was possessed of great depth of feeling and a present, no matter how trivial, given him by a friend, would always be preserved as though it were something sacred. The certificates of merit which he obtained at school in early childhood were wrapped in paper with painstaking care and always preserved under lock and key. He was openhearted, kind and trustful to a degree that sometimes led to his being imposed upon by those with whom he had business transactions. He greatly enjoyed a good story, and could always relate one interestingly. It should be noted too that his laugh was very characteristic, aptly described as infectious. It was an excellent index of his simple, humor-loving, frank and joyous disposition when his mind was free from his engrossing labors. In his younger years he took an active interest in church work and at one time taught a Sunday school class at the Massachusetts state prison. He died in Cambridge, Massachusetts, November 4, 1901.

Mr. Bishop married, June 5, 1845, Mary Alice Perkins, born October 5, 1828, in Beverly, Massachusetts, died in Cambridge, January 9, 1901, daughter of George and Mary Ann (Larcom) Perkins of Amesbury. George Perkins was a merchant. His wife was daughter of Jonathan Larcom and wife Anna (Ives) Ober, who was a widow. Jonathan was brother of Captain Benjamin Larcom, the father of Lucy Larcom, the authoress. Children of Joel Prentiss and Mary Alice (Perkins) Bishop: 1. Herbert Lyon, born in Boston, July 27, 1849; died unmarried, at Eagle Creek, Minnesota, January 4, 1867. 2. Fannie Prentiss, born in Boston, March 28, 1860; died in Sharon, Massachusetts, December 7, 1894, unmarried. 3. Charles Sumner, born in Cambridge, Massachusetts, December 22, 1869; studied law under his father's instruction and is now engaged in the real estate business in Cambridge, residing at (the homestead) 1679 Massachusetts avenue, Cambridge; married May 4, 1904, De Lana Evelyn Storey, born March 29, 1880, at Montville, Connecticut, daughter of William Thomas and Mary Tracy (Fielding) Storey; children: i. Audrea Bishop, born February 11, 1905; ii. Richard Storey, born May 16, 1906; iii. Charles Prentiss, born February 20, 1908.

COLLINS Benjamin Collins resided in Salisbury, and was a householder there in 1677. He may have been brother to Robert, who settled in Ipswich, and was perhaps son of Henry the immigrant. He died December 10, 1683, and the inventory of his estate was filed January 3, 1684. He married, November 5, 1668, Martha, daughter of John Eaton; she married second, November 4, 1686, Philip Flanders. Children: 1. Mary, born January 8, 1669. 2. John, born 1673; mentioned below. 3. Samuel, born January 18, 1676; married March 16, 1698-9 Sarah White. 4. Anna, born April 1, 1679. 5. Benjamin, May 29, 1681. 6. Ephraim, September 30, 1683.

(II) John Collins, son of Benjamin Collins, was born in Salisbury, 1673, and was a Quaker. He resided in Salisbury. He married Elizabeth ——, who was also a Quaker. Children: 1. Jonathan, born October 11, 1695. 2. Daughter, born October, died November, 1697. 3. Benjamin, mentioned below. Probably others.

(III) Benjamin Collins, son of John Collins, born 1708, settled in Hawke, now Danville, New Hampshire. He is the ancestor of all of the name in Weare, New Hampshire, and vicinity. He married Mary Jones.

(IV) Thomas Collins, doubtless a direct descendant of Benjamin Collins (3), was born at Merrimac, New Hampshire, October 10, 1801. The public records necessary to trace the intervening generations are lacking. He died at Woburn, Massachusetts, April 5, 1874, aged according to the state record, seventy-two years and five months twenty-five days. He attended the public schools of Merrimac and vicinity, and when a young man came to Medford, Massachusetts, finding employment there on the farm of Ebenezer Parker, whose daughter he afterward married. He was industrious and capable in his work. He had the management of the farm after a time, and made it profitable. At length Mr. Parker sold his Medford farm after the marriage of his daughter, and Mr. and Mrs. Collins went with him to Winchester, then part of Woburn, buying a large farm near the depot center. Mr. Collins managed the place. He bought a farm on his own account and on the death of his wife and her parents inherited half of the Parker farm at Winchester. He sold out a few years later, but remained in Winchester several years and then leased a farm in Woburn. His last years were spent in that town and he died there April 5, 1874. He was well known and universally respected in each of the towns where he had made his home. He and his first wife were active and faithful members of the Congregational church in Winchester. He was a Whig in his younger days, afterward a Republican in politics. He married, December 20, 1830, Mary Ann Parker, born December 23, 1812, died September 20, 1861, daughter of Ebenezer and Margaret Parker, of Medford and Woburn. Their children, born at Winchester: 1. George Franklin, October 24, 1831; died March 18, 1885; married, 1855, Ann Maria Houghton, of Calais, Maine; child, Frank H., born October 23, 1856, died November 19, 1874. 2. Margaret Ann, born November 21, 1835; died January 22, 1839. 3. Parker Thompson, born September 11, 1838; died October 21, 1884. 4. Jerome Erastus, born December 11, 1839; mentioned below. 5. Charles Edward, born October 1, 1841; died May 3, 1866. 6. Martha Ann, born February 26, 1848; married May 1, 1871, Henry Ward, of Marlborough, New Hampshire; children: i. George, and two others.

(V) Jerome Erastus Collins, son of Thomas Collins (4), born at Woburn, December 11, 1839, on the homestead near the center of what is now Winchester, died at West Medford, September 12, 1901. He received his education in the public schools of his native town and at Warren Academy. In the meantime he worked with his father on the farm. He was the only son who remained at home on the farm until he came of age. He began to learn the trade of shirt-cutting in Boston, when he was twenty-one years old, in the employ of the Hub shirt factory, 221 Washington street. He was with this concern five years, and then in the same line of business in New York city for three years. He returned to Boston to work as cutter in the shirt factory of Hawley, Folsom & Martin, 13 Otis street, and was with that house eleven years. After two more years in the same business with another Boston firm he decided to give up his trade, his health having suffered from the close confinement in the factory, and he opened a meat and provision store in the Usher Block at West Medford. But after five years of successful business he sold out, and about 1893 returned to his trade as cutter in the Goodhue shirt factory at Derby Line, Vermont, continuing with this concern until he had to give up work eight years later, on account of illness. He returned to West Medford in July, 1901, and died of Bright's disease, September 12 following. Mr. Collins was well known and highly esteemed in West Medford, where he made his home for about twenty-five years. He purchased his first residence there in 1874 at 44 Allston street, of Charles Davis. After selling that house he bought of Oscar Patch, in 1896, the property at 50 Allston street, where he was living at the time of his death. He was devoted to his home and family, and attracted many friends. He was upright, earnest and honorable in all the relations of life, of strict integrity and sterling character, firm in supporting what he thought right and in opposing what he believed wrong. He attended the First Congregational Church of West Medford. He was a Republican in politics. He was a member of the Paul Revere Colony of Pilgrim Fathers, and later of the Craddock Colony, and held the office of governor in that order. He married, October 5, 1865, Regina Louise Van Kampen, born at Boston, April 17, 1845, daughter of Antony and Celia (Andrews) Van Kampen, of Boston. Her father was a stone cutter. Children: 1. Mary Louise, born June 28, 1884; died October 9, 1884. 2. Maud Florence McInnis, of Boston, adopted April 9, 1878, born October 17, 1873.

(For early generations see William Osborne 1)

OSBORNE (III) Samuel Osborne, son of William and Hannah (Burton) Osborne, was born in Salem, April 27, 1675, married first, Eleanor Southwick, born 1674, died October 26, 1702, daughter of Daniel and granddaughter of Lawrence Southwick; married second, June 3, 1705, Sarah, daughter of Abraham Clark, of Oyster river, Piscataqua. He had eight children, four by each marriage, and all born in Salem: 1. Samuel, February 4, 1697. 2. Elizabeth, January 14, 1699. 3. Hannah, November 14, 1700. 4. Joseph, October 26, 1702. 5. Thomas, April 1, 1706. 6. Sarah, November 4, 1707. 7. Mary, July 27, 1709. 8. Isaac, February 13, 1711.

(IV) Joseph Osborne, son of Samuel and Eleanor (Southwick) Osborne, was born in Salem, or Danvers, October 26, 1702, and died after November 17, 1780. He married first, Rachel Foster, who died before 1734; married second, Sarah Gardner. He had nine children, all born in Danvers: 1. Joseph, August 26, 1726. 2. Rachel, baptized 1734. 3. Ginger, baptized 1734. 4. Eunice, baptized 1736. 5. Israel, baptized May 27, 1739. 6. Mehitable, November 15, 1741, married first, Ezra Porter, second, Sylvester Procter. 7. Aaron, born November 15, 1742, died February 8, 1803; married, 1774, Lydia Procter. 8. Abel, baptized August 18, 1745, died young. 9. Abel, baptized November 9, 1746, married Lydia Foster.

(V) Joseph Osborne, son of Joseph and Rachel (Foster) Osborne, was born in Danvers, August 26, 1726, died January 30, 1791. He married, January 6, 1756, Mary Procter, born December 3, 1733, died July 9, 1804. They had eight children, all born in Danvers: 1. Joseph, January 5, 1757, died August 29, 1829; married first, Mary Shillaber, second, Judith Francis. 2. Sylvester, November 10, 1758, died October 2, 1845; married first, Susanna Southwick; second, Elizabeth Pool; third, Mrs. L. W. Saunders. 3. Rachel, January 31, 1761, died December 27, 1813; married Jonathan Howard, died March 22, 1826. 4. Jonathan, August 30, 1763. 5. John, November 22, 1765, died November 3, 1845; married Lydia Southwick. 6. Daniel, September 10, 1768, died February 11, 1826; married Mehitable Procter. 7. Amos, April 2, 1773, died June 21, 1836; married Nancy Fowler. 8. Mary, August 14, 1779, died June 1, 1850.

(VI) Jonathan Osborne, son of Joseph and Mary (Procter) Osborne, was born in Danvers, August 30, 1763, died July 29, 1833; married, 1784, Sukey (Susanna) Smith and had eight children, all born in Danvers: 1. Sukey (Susanna), September 2, 1785. 2. George, February 14, 1787, died young. 3. Richard, February 8, 1788. 4. George, September 25, 1792. 5. Silas, July 26, 1794. 6. Rachel, April 26, 1797. 7. Jonathan, May 16, 1806. 8. Hannah, February 5, 1810.

(VII) Richard Osborne, son of Jonathan and Sukey (Smith) Osborne, was born in Danvers, now Peabody, Massachusetts, February 8, 1788, and married, at Salem, New Hampshire, December 31, 1815, Alice Wheeler. The Danvers vital records show the dates of birth of three of their children, although they probably had others. Those whose names appear were Dennison, born about 1816. William Sumner, born January 4, 1819, probably died young, for mention is made of William Sumner, born July, 1820. The third child was Almira, born August 30, 1821.

(VIII) William Sumner Osborne, son of Richard and Alice (Wheeler) Osborne, was born in South Danvers, now Peabody. He married first, November 27, 1843, Caroline M. Grove, who was born in Weare, New Hampshire, and died in Peabody, August 25, 1845, aged twenty years ten months. He married second, April 30, 1848, Catherine Ann Stevenson. He married third, Maria N. Miller. Children: 1. Caroline Gove, born November 23, 1852, married, November 11, 1874, Charles Kendall Clark; two children: Sarah L. and Richard Osborne; the latter married Mary A. Sleeper. 2. Richard Abbott.

(IX) Richard Abbott Osborne, son of William Sumner and Catherine Ann (Stevenson) Osborne, was born in Peabody, July 1, 1854, and for many years has been teller of the National Shawmut Bank, of Boston. He married, October 5, 1881, Ellinor Laithe Higbee, who was born September 24, 1853, daughter of Charles and Sarah Maria (Brown) Higbee. Mr. and Mrs. Osborne have one child, Katharine Osborn, born Salem. (See Higbee).

HIGBEE

Charles Higbee (1), first appears in New Hampshire history as a resident in Claremont and was more than twenty-one years old in 1776, twelve years after that town was granted by Governor Wentworth to its original proprietors. Stephen Higbee also is mentioned in the records as being more than twenty-one years in 1776, when the selectmen were designating the town's available men for military service in the war then just begun. Stephen was one of the committee of safety for Claremont in 1776, and appears to have been a man of considerable influence in the town; wherefore it is probable that he then was a man of mature age and presumably the head of the family of which Charles was a member.

The Claremont Higbees are first mentioned in connection with events of the revolution, and there is nothing to show whence they came or where, but it certainly was later than 1764 and probably not before 1770. There is a tradition that the immigrant Higbees were three brothers who came to this country about the middle of the seventeenth century and settled one in Connecticut, another in New York and the third at Portsmouth, New Hampshire, but the Portsmouth records give no account of such settlement in that vicinity, and it is more probable that the New Hampshire Higbees are descended either from John or William Higbee, or of Edward, the son of John. A remarkable similarity of baptismal names in the families indicates something more than possible relationship, but there appears no present means by which to determine the precise connection.

Charles Higbee was a private in Captain John Marey's company of Colonel James Reed's regiment of New Hampshire troops, and was in service nineteen days from July 12, 1775; also private in Captain Samuel Wetherbee's company of Colonel Isaac Wyman's regiment which formed a part of the northern army in 1776, and was in service at Mt. Independence; also private in Captain Oliver Ashley's company of Colonel Benjamin Bellow's regiment at Ticonderoga in May, 1777. Levi Higbee, who is presumed to have been a younger brother of Charles, was at Ticonderoga, and also was with General Stark's army at the battle of Bennington in August, 1777. Charles Higbee was a merchant in Claremont as early as 1784 and for many years afterward, and in 1805 he was surveyor of highways. He appears to have carried on business quite extensively and in various directions, as is shown by some of his old account books and papers now in possession of his great-granddaughter, Mrs. Richard Abbott Osborne, of Salem. The name of his wife and the names and dates of birth of his children are not known, except of his son Lemuel.

(II) Lemuel Higbee was born in Claremont, August 21, 1784, and died in Salem, Massachusetts, January 15, 1843. He was one of the old Salem master mariners, a deep sea sailor, a man of great mental and physical energy, strong in his adherence to Jacksonian democracy and equally firm in his faith in the Congregational church. He married Betsey Francis, about 1812. She died January 4, 1875, having born her husband nine children: 1. Eliza, May 23, 1813, died February 5, 1830. 2. Lemuel, Jr., December 15, 1814. 3. Charles, November 13, 1816. 4. Abigail B., January 13, 1819. 5. Thomas F., November 23, 1822. 6. Susanna Francis, January 19, 1825. 7. Benjamin L., October 12, 1827. 8. Stephen Dexter, February 19, 1830. 9. Elizabeth Philinda, February 3, 1832.

(III) Charles Higbee, son of Lemuel and Betsey (Francis) Higbee, was born in Salem, November 13, 1816, and began his business career as a mechanic, having learned the trade of a carriage wheelwright in Danvers and worked for some time as a journeyman. Even from his early young manhood Mr. Higbee had aspired to an active business life and was quick to see that little real success could be achieved by following his trade, but he kept industriously at work until the right opportunity presented itself and then embarked in the leather business, in a rather small way at first and gradually increasing his operations until he became one of the proprietors of the largest leather concern of New England in its time. The firm of Blake, Higbee & Company, which he was chiefly instrumental in organizing, had large factories in Salem and Woburn, with principal offices and saleshouse in Boston. He proved himself to be an energetic, capable and straightforward business man and by honest endeavor won the gratifying success which followed his efforts. He had neither time nor inclination for the welfare of politics, but, never on that account was lacking in interest or public spirit in whatever measures were proposed for the welfare of his home city, its institutions and its people. He was very much a domestic man, devoted to family, loyal to friends, considerate of the happiness of others and generous in dispensing benevolences, but always giving in a manner which would not draw attention to the donor. Mr. Higbee married for his first wife ——— Hutchinson, who died childless. He married second, Sarah Maria Brown, who was born in Danvers, died November 1, 1883, daughter of George and Sally (Twiss) Brown. Four children were born of this marriage: Charles Henry, who married Ruth Miller and had Molly and Ruth. Annie, born November 17, 1848, died in infancy. Ellinor Laithe, born September 24, 1853. Eliza, who died at the age of four years.

(IV) Ellinor Laithe Higbee, daughter of Charles and Sarah Maria (Brown) Higbee, was born in Salem, September 24, 1853, and married, October 5, 1881, Richard Abbott Osborne, who was born in Peabody, Massachusetts, July 1, 1854, son of William Sumner and Catherine Ann (Stevenson) Osborne (see Osborne family). Mr. and Mrs. Osborne have one daughter, Katharine Osborne, born in Salem.

TAYLOR William Taylor was of Concord, Massachusetts, about 1640, and it is supposed that he was a younger brother of James Taylor, and came with him to America, settling in the plantation at Concord. William was a husbandman and owned a farm of more than one hundred acres on the East Bedford road. He died in Concord, December 6, 1696, and his wife, Mary Miriam, died December 10, 1699. Children, all born in Concord: 1. Mary, February 19, 1649-50. 2. John, October 19, 1653. 3. Samuel, July 3, 1655, died July 16, 1655. 4. Abraham, November 14, 1656. 5. Isaac, March 5, 1659. 6. Jacob, May 8, 1662. 7. Joseph, born April 7, 1665.

(II) Abraham Taylor, son of William and Mary (Miriam) Taylor, was born in Concord, November 14, 1656, and was a husbandman there all through his life. He married, December 16, 1681, Mary Whittaker, died February 16, 1756, aged ninety-three years eleven months. Children, all born in Concord: 1. Abraham, January 11, 1682-3. 2. Ebenezer, April 30, 1688. 3. Elizabeth, August 17, 1690. 4. Mary, March 15, 1691-2. 5. Jonathan, August 10, 1894. 6. Sarah, October 13, 1696. 7. David, January 31, 1698. 8. Benjamin, April 18, 1699. 9. Nathaniel, February 9, 1701-2. 10. Daniel, March 22, 1703-4. 11. Timothy, March 5, 1705, died March 28. 12. Samuel, October 1, 1708.

(III) Abraham Taylor, son of Abraham and Mary (Whittaker) Taylor, was born in Concord, January 11, 1682-3. His wife's name was Mary, and their children, so far as records show, were: Abraham, Samuel, Timothy, born 1718, Alice, Amos.

(IV) Amos Taylor, son of Abraham and Mary Taylor, baptized September 10, 1725, in Dunstable, Massachusetts, died probably in New Hampshire. In speaking of him the author of the "History of New Ipswich," New Hampshire, mentioned him as a brother of Reuben and Thaddeus Taylor, who were sons of Samuel Taylor, and the latter a son of Abraham Taylor and grandson of William Taylor the immigrant of Concord, Massachusetts. This statement, however, is an error, for Reuben and Thaddeus were cousins of Amos. He went from Dunstable to New Ipswich as early as 1757, settled on a farm next to that of Reuben Taylor, and was a member of the first church in the town, organized 1760. "It is believed," says the work referred to, " that he either returned to Dunstable before the incorporation of the town, or settled in one of the adjoining towns." He married, May 21, 1747, in Dunstable, Bridget Martin, and had two sons born in Dunstable—Amos, September 7, 1748, and Edmund. Doubtless they had other children of whom we have no account.

(V) Edmund Taylor, son of Amos and Bridget (Martin) Taylor, was born in Dunstable, Massachusetts, May 4, 1750, and from the summer of 1777 to the close of the war was actively identified with military events of the revolution. In July, 1777, he enlisted as private in Captain Samuel Fairfield's company of Colonel May's regiment, and with that command was attached to the northern army. He served there eighteen days and was paid for one hundred miles travel. After the close of the war he removed to Cavendish, Vermont, opened a farm in that town and lived there for several years, where he had sons Levi and Wilder, the latter settling in Bangor, Maine.

(VI) Levi Taylor, son of Edmund, the revolutionary soldier and Vermont pioneer, was born in Cavendish, Vermont, and died in Sherburne, Vermont, where the later years of his life were spent. He was a thrifty and successful farmer, and by his own enterprise gained a fair property for his time, but all of this was swept away by having been compelled to pay the principal of a surety bond which in the goodness of his heart he had executed in behalf of a friend while living in Weathersfield. After this misfortune he removed with his family to Sherburne, Vermont, purchased a farm there and succeeded once more to accumulating a comfortable property. He lived to good old age and came to accidental death by falling off the heavily snow laden roof of one of his outbuildings, in which he was at work at the time. He married Hannah, daughter of Ebenezer Farnsworth, a patriot and soldier of the revolution who followed the fortunes of the Continental army and fought at Trenton, Yorktown, Germantown and wintered at Valley Forge. Hannah Farnsworth Taylor died at the age of fifty years, having borne her husband seven children: 1. Lemira, married Luther Harrington (see Harrington family). 2. Mary Ann, married Theophilus Flagg Clark, a Vermont farmer; both now dead; children: Francis G., Charles, Ellen and Ann Clark. 3. James Harvey. 4. Hester Ann, married Frank Gates; lived on a farm in Vermont. 5. Charles Wesley, married Harriet Winslow, and lived in Windsor, Vermont, leaving children Frank, Charles, Edward and William Taylor. 6. Jane, died at the age of nineteen years. 7. Gilford D., married first, ——— Blake, and had one son, William S.; married second, Fanny Adams, and had two sons, Fred E., and Harry F. Taylor.

(VII) James Harvey Taylor, son of Levi and Hannah (Farnsworth) Taylor, born December 30, 1811, died June 29, 1887. He was a farmer, an earnest, honest and thrifty husbandman and a man highly respected by his fellow townsmen. Soon after marriage he went to the old homestead farm in Cavendish, Vermont, which had been first settled by his grandfather Edmund Taylor, the revolutionary soldier, more than half a century before, and there he lived to the end of his days. He married Emily Paige, born June 1, 1817, died 1893. She is remembered as a very estimable woman, a devout member of the Wesleyan Methodist church, and a descendant of an old New England colonial family. James Harvey and Emily (Paige) Taylor had eight children: 1. Edwin, died young. 2. Caroline, died young. 3. Jane Gray, married J. G. Upham, now deceased. She is living in Ludlow, Vermont. 4. George D., enlisted as private in a Vermont company for service during the civil war; was promoted for meritorious conduct to the rank of lieutenant, and died of fever contracted in the service. 5. Child, died in infancy. 6. Elwin P., married and settled in Weathersfield, Vermont. 7. Eugene S., now of Boston. 8. Mary E., married John E. Wetherbee.

(VIII) Eugene S. Taylor, son of James Harvey and Emily (Paige) Taylor, was born in Sherburne, Vermont, September 15, 1850, and spent his young life on his father's farm. As a boy he was sent to the district school during the winter seasons and in the summer months he helped with the work of the farm. Upon reaching his majority he determined to enter the profession of dentistry, and to that end pursued a course at the dental department of the University of Iowa, Iowa City, graduating from that institution with the degree of D. D. S. in 1876. For the next four years he practiced in Jones county, Iowa, then came back east and practiced in New Hampshire until 1885, and then established himself in Boston, where for more than twenty years he has been a prominent figure in professional circles and has become recognized as one of the leading practitioners of dental surgery in that city. A practitioner of long experience and excellent reputation, Dr. Taylor enjoys a lucrative practice, a large clientele and wide acquaintance in Boston and its vicinity. He is also a member of many societies and associations of a professional character, both general and local, while in Freemasonry he holds an enviable prominence, holding membership in the several subordinate as well as the more advanced bodies of the craft, and has served in various official capacities in nearly all of them. He is a Master, Royal Arch, Templar and Scottish Rite Mason, and also has traversed the hot desert sands to Aleppo Temple, A. A. O. N. M. S. In Odd Fellowship he has passed the chairs of the lodge and holds membership in the encampment and the grand lodge of the state. In political preference Dr. Taylor is a firm and unyielding Democrat, and in religious holdings is not bound by any creed nor allied to any sect, but he believes in doing right because it is right to do so, in being just, charitable and honest because thereby one always feels happier and can add to the comfort of those about him. His mind is naturally studious and inclined to be philosophical, and he is a careful reader of events and close analyst of men and measures and of the underlying motives which impel their action. Dr. Taylor married first, 1872, Isadora Albee, born in Rockingham, Vermont, 1851, died 1878. He married second, 1892, Mrs. Fanny M. (Curtis) Johnson, a descendant of William Curtis, of Scituate, Massachusetts.

BEEDE The earliest representatives of this family in this country came from the Isle of Jersey in the English channel, and their language indicated the old Norman French which is still spoken by the peasantry of that island. The chief seat of the family for more than a century has been in Sandwich, New Hampshire, whence come the Beedes of Lynn, Massachusetts.

(I) Eli Beede, the immigrant ancestor of the family, was a Frenchman, born 1699; came to America as a lad of fourteen years, working his passage. He was the only son of a widow residing on the Isle of Jersey. Remaining a few months in Boston, he then went to Hampton, New Hampshire, where he served a regular apprenticeship with a farmer. In 1720 he removed to the eastern part of Kingston, later incorporated under the name of East Kingston. He was a man of considerable local distinction, became an extensive land owner, and was called "doctor" on account of his skill in the treatment of sick horses and cattle, and "wizard" because of his power of teaching and training wild and vicious horses. After his settlement in Kingston he became a member of Rev. Mr. Seacombe's church. Eli Beede's will was made 1786, probated June 17, 1789. An inventory of his estate shows him to have been a very successful man owning stock farms in East Kingston, Poplin, Deerfield and Salisbury. He married Mehitable Sleeper, the first white female child born in Kingston, and they were the parents of: 1. Hezekiah, died March 12, 1772, married first, Hepzibah Smith; second, Judith Gove. 2. Daniel, see forward. 3. Thomas, died March 6, 1806; married Elizabeth Uraan. 4. Jonathan, born September 18, 1734, died June 14, 1825; married first, Anna Sleeper; second, Susanna Hoag. 5. Elizabeth, married John Huntoon. 6. Johanna, died prior to June 17, 1789; married Samuel Davis.

(II) Daniel Beede, second son and child of Eli and Mehitable (Sleeper) Beede, was born in East Kingston, New Hampshire, July 21, 1729, and died April 7, 1800. His education was a limited one, as the people of those times had little money to spare for that purpose. The Bible was the only book his father permitted to be read in the home, and extracts from this book, printed for that purpose, were almost all of the literature in use in the schools of the day. Under such circumstances it was a matter of great difficulty to acquire an education, but by the assistance of Rev. Mr. Seacombe and the use of a few books, among them a spelling book, loaned him, he obtained a stock of valuable information. Mr. Seacombe also instructed him in the higher mathematics, more particularly in trigonometry and surveying, and he afterward became a practical surveyor and surveyed the town of Sandwich, New Hampshire, for the proprietors who, as an inducement for him to settle in the town, gave him and each of his sons a grant of land of five hundred acres each. He resided for a time in Brentwood, New Hampshire, removed to Poplin, thence to Gilmanton, and finally settled in Sandwich, November, 1770. It was then a new town, which had been incorporated only a few years; there he acquired a valuable farm with good buildings, and spent the remainder of his days. He was for many years the representative of that town in the legislature, and justice of the peace. He was a selectman in Brentwood in 1754-60-61-62-63, held town office in Poplin in 1764-66, in 1788 was a member of the New Hampshire convention which ratified the constitution of the United States, in 1791 a member of the convention which revised and amended the constitution of his native state, and June 15, 1795, was appointed a judge of the court of common pleas for the county of Strafford, in which he lived. In the winter of 1799, at the close of the court over which he had presided, he invited the judges and lawyers to spend the evening with him at his lodgings, and when they had assembled, he announced that before the next term of court he would reach the legal age for retirement, and that he had invited them to meet him for the purpose of declaring his intention to resign and take his leave of them before he returned to private life. The gentlemen present expressed their approbation of his conduct while on the bench and their sorrow that the provisions of the constitution required his resignation. At the time of great excitement in Brentwood and its vicinity upon the subject of religion, Judge Beede adopted the tenets and principles of the Quakers, finding them preferable to all others with which he had become acquainted; he attended the Quaker meetings frequently and was attached to them, but he never became a member of that or any other church, deeming it better and wiser to be free from all the restraints of church government. He was liberal and charitable in his opinions, and his view was that there were good and bad men to be found in all sects; that genuine religion consisted of good works, not faith; in charity and acts of kindness, not professions; and that an honest infidel was better than a zealous, bigoted, immoral believer. He was a man of sound judgment, great prudence and strict integrity; and was superior to the narrow views of piety and the sordid spirit of selfishness. He was distinguished for his hospitality and kindness to strangers and travelers. At his house they always received a cordial welcome. Instead of thinking they were under obligation to him, he appeared gratified with having opportunity and means of accommodating them. In public as well as private life his great object, and one he pursued successfully, was to be useful to others; and in return he enjoyed the consolation arising from the respect, esteem and confidence of all who knew him. As those who differed from him in opinion never questioned the purity of his motives, they submitted to his decision. Indeed the mildness of his temper and the gentleness of his manner tended not less than the decision of his character to disarm opposition.

Judge Beede married first, January 22, 1749, Patience Prescott, daughter of Joshua Prescott. She was born in Kingston in 1724. He married second, February 27, 1795, Dorothy, widow of Captain Nathaniel Eldridge. Judge Daniel and Patience (Prescott) Beede had children: 1. Nathan, see forward. 2. Daniel Jr., born May 29, 1752. 3. Aaron, born September 22, 1754, died October 10, 1788. 4. Elijah, born May 16, 1757, was drowned in Squam Lake. 5. Joshua, born May 13, 1760. 6. Sarah, born February 19, 1762, married, October 27, 1785, Joseph Varney. 7. Mary, born March 26, 1764, married, October 27, 1785, Richard Varney. 8. Cyrus, born March 9, 1766. 9. Martha, born March 9, 1770, married, March 4, 1790, Stephen Hoag. 10. Phoebe, born December 6, 1771, married, November 28, 1793, John Purrington. 11. Lydia, born September 28, 1773, married, November 27, 1803, Samuel Tibbetts. 12. Patience, born September 2, 1777, married, July 3, 1802, Barzilla Hines. The first child Nathan was born in Kingston, the next seven children were born in Poplin, (now Fremont) New Hampshire, and the others in Sandwich in the same state.

(III) Nathan Beede, eldest child of Judge Daniel and Patience (Prescott) Beede, was born June 4, 1750, and died August 20, 1841. He was one of the company that settled in Sandwich, New Hampshire, and felled the first tree, being at that time a youth of eighteen years. He married, July 15, 1770, Dolly Scribner, who was born in Brentwood, November 4, 1750, and died in Sandwich, May 18, 1842. They had children: 1. Daniel, born June 15, 1771, died December 6, 1833; married, December 11, 1792, Lydia Hoag. 2. Betsy, born May 10, 1773, died October 16, 1788. 3. Elijah, see forward. 4. Elisha W., born March 31, 1777, died March 2, 1856; married, March 24, 1803, Sally Stephens. 5. Grace, born August 21, 1779, died December 31, 1802. 6. William Penn, born November 22, 1781, died February 3, 1817. 7. Nathan, born March 29, 1785, married Anna Hoar. 8. Dolly, born January 16, 1787, died July, 1874; married, May 27, 1810, David Vittum. 9. Betsey, born March 9, 1789, died September 15, 1790. 10. Hugh J., born January 20, 1791, died October 5, 1795. 11. Patience, born December 31, 1793, died July 20, 1847; married James Moulton.

(IV) Elijah Beede, second son and third child of Nathan and Dolly (Scribner) Beede, was born March 29, 1775, died December 12, 1855, and was a minister of the Quaker denomination in Sandwich. He married, September 2, 1802, Anna Felch, born May 24, 1785, died November 7, 1848. They had children: 1. Parker, born November 15, 1803, died February 10, 1890; married, February 16, 1836, Achsah Bradbury, born January 20, 1807, died February 8, 1872. Their children were: George, Ellen and Abby. 2. Grace, born February 4, 1805, died December 28, 1880; married Ira Huckins and had children: Charles, Jennie and Gilbert. 3. David, born May 2, 1806, died August 11, 1808. 4. Asa, born November 9, 1807, died August 15, 1808. 5. Jane R., born March 16, 1809, died April 17, 1851; married, December 12, 1831, Joseph Gilman and had children: Mary Jane, Lydia B., Andrew, Albert and George Edwin. 6. Lydia, born September 17, 1810, died February 21, 1819. 7. David, born April 14, 1812, died the same day. 8. Solomon, see forward. 9. Valentine, born March 11, 1815, died February 23, 1873; married, June 28, 1840, Charlotte Pierce and had children: Anna Maria, Henry, Ellen, Abbie, Charles, Caroline, Frank and Edward. 10. Phoebe Purrington, born January 31, 1817, died January 15, 1890; married, January 31, 1838, Daniel Davis Clark and had children: Anna Maria, Daniel E., George William and Alberta M. 11. Martha, born March 30, 1819, died April 16 of the same year. 12. Lydia, born June 28, 1820, died June 30 of the same year. 13. Anna Maria, born May 24, 1821, died November 25, 1886-87; married, January 27, 1843, Langdon Goddard Clark and had children: George Langdon, Anna Phoebe, Sarah Jane, Millard Frank, Selwyn Beede, Charles Sumner, Amy Maretta, Lulie May, Arthur Moses. 14. Moses H., born January 19, 1823, died February 3, 1869; married Mehitable Lee and had children: Althea Maria, Warren Herbert, Alfred Wesley and Andrew Freemont. 15. William Penn, born November 2, 1825, died April 16, 1891; married, November 23, 1848, Susan M. Burnell and had children: Emily F., Daniel William, Clara M., Frederick A. and M. Addie, of whom the two last named were twins. 16. George, born June 11, 1828, died 1829.

Charles O. Beede

(V) Solomon Beede, fifth son and eighth child of Elijah and Anna (Felch) Beede, was born in Sandwich, New Hampshire, August 10, 1813, and died in Lynn, Massachusetts, April 10, 1843. He was never very strong physically, and his death at the age of less than thirty years was the result of consumption. He married, December 20, 1836, Lucy Moulton French, born September 16, 1815, died August 24, 1858. Their children were: 1. George Freeman, born July 29, 1838, died December 31, 1870; married, November 20, 1864, Charlotte W. Freeman, born June 21, 1839, died November 2, 1900. Their children were: Charles Warren, born March 17, 1867, died September 9, 1868; Grace Freeman, born February 13, 1870, died July 19, 1872. 2. Charles Otis, see forward.

(VI) Charles Otis Beede, second and youngest son and child of Solomon and Lucy M. (French) Beede, was born in Lynn, Massachusetts, December 29, 1840, died August 27, 1898. He attended the public schools at Lynn, and later went to Sandwich, New Hampshire, where he completed his education at the New Hampton Institute. He then returned to his native town where he found employment in one of the large shoe manufacturing establishments, and where he remained until he had obtained a thorough practical knowledge of all branches of this industry. He, in 1865, with a small capital, started in business for himself, working personally when there was necessity for him to do so, devoting to it all of his time and energy, and frequently spending the evening hours in looking after the business details. He succeeded in building up a large and profitable trade, but the cares and responsibilities of business to which he so persistently devoted himself, at length made inroads upon his health and in 1872 he was obliged to retire for a time and sought rest and recuperation in New Hampshire. At the expiration of one year he returned to Lynn and again became a prominent factor in the industrial life of the city, devoting his attention particularly to the manufacture of boot and shoe supplies, and becoming proprietor of one of the largest establishments of the kind in the country; he disposed of this business shortly before the great fire of 1898. In addition to this he conducted a retail store for the sale of rubber goods, which business he carried on successfully for a number of years, but after the Lynn fire he disposed of it to Mr. O. R. Howe, who had long been associated with him as a bookkeeper. Shortly afterward he engaged in the real estate business which he continued until his death. Mr. Beede was one of the best representatives of the purely self-made and successful business men of whom Lynn can boast, and whatever measure of success he achieved was the result of his own personal effort and industry. One considerable factor that tended to this result was the regard and consideration he had always shown his employes, giving them an annual holiday at his own expense, sharing in their pleasures, listening and giving heed to their requests, making them his friends at all times, and permitting them in return to regard him as their true benefactor and friend. He took a commendable interest in the municipal government of Lynn, served as a member of the board of aldermen in 1881-82, and was otherwise identified with important measures proposed for the promotion of the welfare of the city. At the time of his death he was completing the third year of his service as a member of the water board. He was a member of the Massachusetts Legislature in 1897 and 1898. The first year he won, over a number of candidates, and such satisfaction did his service give that the following year there was no opposition. In this position his sound judgment and discriminating mind enabled him to support every measure which he believed for the interests of the city. At the time of his death he was a candidate for senator in the First Essex district. Among other positions of trust he held were those of director in the Manufacturers' National Bank, trustee in the Lynn Five Cents Savings Bank, and member of the Lynn Safe Deposit and Trust Company. He was an active member of Mount Carmel Lodge, Free and Accepted Masons; Sutton Chapter, Royal Arch Masons; Mount Olivet Commandery, Knights Templar; and a charter member of the Oxford Club.

He and his wife were members of the First Methodist Episcopal Church of Lynn for nearly thirty years, during all of which time Mr. Beede served on the board of trustees, and for several years previous to his death was in point of service the senior member of this board. He was apparently in good health until the day before his death, which followed an illness of but a few hours, being caused by an attack of heart disease. He was a great-hearted man and a model humanitarian, his charities being judicious and numerous, his sympathies genuine, sincere and tender. His life was a credit to the church, an honor to the city and a precious legacy to the family.

Mr. Beede married, December 22, 1864, Irene S. Rich, born December 24, 1839. The children of this union were: 1. Elizabeth L., born September 4, 1865. 2. George W., born October 26, 1868, resides in Wakefield, Massachusetts; married, March 17, 1892, Nellie M. Black, born January 18, 1868, and has children: Merton, born March 6, 1893, died July 11, 1906; Irene Estelle, born April 2, 1899. 3. Arthur Crosby, born June 22, 1874, died November 17, 1875.

WHITTEMORE The surname Whittemore is of Anglo-Saxon origin, from Whytemore, (a white lake or meadow). The first John, Lord of Whytemore, took the name from the place where the family originally dwelt. His home was on the northeast side of the parish of Bobbington, in the meadow of Claverly, in Shropshire, England. The place now bears the name of Whittemore. It is recorded by two historians that Whittemore Hall, at Whittemore, was the home of the progenitors of the American family.

The genealogy of the Whittemore family has been traced back in England to the twelfth century. Mr. Eli Jones Whittemore, of Worcester, has the result of researches of D. J. Whittemore, chief engineer of the Chicago, Milwaukee & St. Paul railroad, which were carried on for a number of years in England at considerable expense and infinite pains to secure accuracy. A vast amount of information which he collected should be edited. A brief abstract only can be used here. It will serve to correct some of the errors in the Whittemore and Whitmore genealogists. The name is commonly spelled Whitmore in England, while some of the descendants of the original stock spell their name Wetmore.

(I) The Whitmores of Staffordshire, England, were originally termed de Boterel. The name of the father of William de Boterel (1100-1135) and his brother, Peter de Boterel, is unknown. William had a son William (1158-1163).

(II) Peter de Boterel, of Staffordshire, had a son Radulph or Ralph.

(III) Ralph de Boterel (1152-1171) married twice. His son William by the first wife married Avisa de Whitmore in 1179. William (IV) (1174) had a son Reginald (V) (1238), who had a son Robert (VI) (1260). This is not the American line. That descends from the second wife, by her son Ralph de Boterel, and not by Rad Fitz Wetmore (1220-40), an illegitimate son. Rad had a son Will de Burgvyllon (1242-54).

(IV) Ralph de Boterel had a son Sir John.

(V) Sir John de Whitmore married Agnes (1252-76) and had at least three sons; John, Lord of Whitmore, founder of what the genealogists call the Caunton line; William, married Alice Fenners, had a son Philip (VII), founded what is called the Claverly branch; Ralph (VI). This John was the first to bear the name Whitmore, as mentioned above.

(VI) John Whitmore, son of Sir John Whitmore, married Margerie (1270-1301).

(VII) Richard of Whitmore married Susannah Draycote, daughter of Sir Philip Draycote, of Painesley, knight, and had: 1. Jane, married John Blunt. 2. Mary, married John Gifford. 3. Beatrix, married John Chetwind. 4. Christina, married Richard Fleetwood. 5. Philip, mentioned below.

(VIII) Philip Whitmore married Thomasine, daughter of Richard Oliver(?) and had a son Richard.

(IX) Richard Whitmore, son of Philip Whitmore (8), married first a daughter of Sir Ralph Bagot; second, a daughter of Richard Devereaux; third, a daughter of Simon Harcourt, probably of Ellenhall, Staffordshire, and by her had a son Nicholas.

(X) Nicholas Whitmore, son of Richard Whitmore (9), married Annie Aston, daughter of Thomas of Tixhall, Staffordshire, and had Mary, married William Lusone; and Anthony, mentioned below.

(XI) Anthony Whitmore, son of Nicholas Whitmore (10), married Christina Vaux, daughter and heir of Nicholas Vaux, and had Joan and William.

(XII) William Whitmore, son of Anthony Whitmore (11), had a son John.

(XIII) John Whitmore, of Caunton, second son of William Whitmore (12), in the reign of Henry VI, married Alice Blyton, daughter and heir of Robert Blyton, of Caunton, county Notts. He married second, Catherine Compton, daughter and heir of Robert Compton, of Hawton (Visitation of York, 1563), and had William, and Robert, who was the heir.

(XIV) Robert Whitmore, son of John Whitmore, of Caunton (13), married Catherine Claye, daughter of George Claye, of Finningly, county Notts. (Visitation of Yorkshire), and had a son William, the heir, who married a daughter of John Ridley. William of Rotterham died in 1568. Robert Whitmore married second, Alice Atwoode, of Harlington, Bedfordshire. He died at Caunton in 1540. By this marriage were children: 1. Richard, died without issue in 1559. 2. John, living in 1545. 3. Charles, died 1568. 4. Thomas, living in 1559, probably died about 1603. 5. Edmund, living in 1559. 6. Rowland, living in 1591. 7. James. 8. Randall; and three daughters. Thomas Whitmore Sr., of Hitchin, was the son of Edmund or Rowland, sons of Robert. Hitchin is the parish where the immigrant, Thomas Whitmore, was born, but he was the son of another Thomas Whitmore, as will be seen later.

(XV) Charles Whitmore, son of Robert Whitmore (14), died in 1568. He lived in Tuxforth, county Notts. Children: 1. William, died in 1582 in county Notts. 2. John, supposed to have lived in Staffordshire and died 1571. 3. Robert, died 1608. 4. Richard, died 1578. 5. James, died 1614. 6. Thomas the elder, died 1649. 7. Roger of Hitchin. 8. Christopher, of county Beds, died 1640. Four daughters and a posthumous child supposed to have been George. Three of the sons spelled the name Whittamore, three Watmore, and one Whitmore, the prevailing English spelling.

(XVI) Thomas Whitmore, son of Charles Whitmore (15), lived in Hitchin, Hertfordshire. He married Mary ———. His two sons emigrated to New England. Thomas went to Malden and John to Stamford, Connecticut. Thomas is the ancestor of most of the American Whittemores, John had a daughter Elizabeth and son John, who was of age in 1649, and lived at Stamford and Middletown, Connecticut.

(XVI) Roger Whitmore, son of Charles Whitmore (15), and brother of Thomas of Hitchin, was the father of Nicholas Whitmore. Nicholas had two sons also who went to New England. Francis Whitmore to Boston and Thomas to Middletown, Connecticut. From these are descended the American Whitmores. Their father was a first cousin to the Malden emigrant, Thomas Whittemore mentioned below.

(I) Thomas Whittemore, the immigrant ancestor, son of Thomas Whitmore (16), of the English lineage, came to New England about the year 1643 from the town of Hitchin, Hertfordshire, England. He was an early settler of Charlestown, Massachusetts, and his home was in the southeast part of what became Malden, now Everett, about three miles from Boston. In 1645 he purchased of Rev. John Cotton of Boston, "meadow for two cow's grass," a piece of land adjoining his own farm. His farm was bounded on the east by Chelsea, and south by the Mystic river. It is remarkable that the homestead remained in the family until May 1, 1845, when it was sold by the late William Whittemore to Nathaniel Sands, of New York City. The site of the dwelling house erected by Thomas Whittemore is still to be identified by the old cellar hole, on which in 1806 a house was built by Joseph Whittemore. In 1866 this house was burned. The site is a fine one, commanding a beautiful view of the surrounding country.

Thomas Whittemore was baptized January 6, 1593, son of Thomas and Mary Whittemore, of Hitchin, Hertfordshire, England. He died in Malden, May 25, 1661. He married first, Sarah ———, who died October 31, 1616. He married second, Sarah Deardes, April 14, 1623, in England. She was buried November 17, 1628. He married third, Hannah ———, who according to her own deposition was born in 1612. She married second, June 3, 1663, at Chelmsford, Benjamin Butterfield. His will was proved June 25, 1661. Child of first wife: 1. Sarah, baptized April 14, 1616. Children of second wife: 2. Mary, baptized May 12, 1624. 3. Thomas, baptized October 6, 1626, lived in England. Children of third wife: 4. Daniel, baptized July 31, 1633, mentioned below. 5. John, baptized April 27, 1635, buried April 29, 1635. 6. Nathaniel, baptized May 1, 1636, married Mary Knower and left no male descendants. 7. John, baptized February 11, 1638-39, at Hitchin, England, as were all the preceding; settled in Cambridge, Massachusetts, and has many descendants. 8. Elizabeth, born in New England in 1641. 9. Benjamin, baptized 1643, married Elizabeth Bucknam; died July 16, 1726. 10. Thomas (one of the few cases where there are two sons of the same name living at the same time, the elder Thomas never came to this country), baptized 1645, married, November 9, 1666, Elizabeth Pierce, of Woburn. 11. Samuel, baptized 1647, married Hannah ———; removed to Dover, New Hampshire, thence to Somerville, Massachusetts, and died September 15, 1726. 12. Pelletiah, baptized 1653. 13. Abraham, baptized 1656, was in King Philip's war; died January 14, 1690-91.

(II) Daniel Whittemore, son of Thomas Whittemore (1), was born at Hitchin, Hertfordshire, England, and baptized there July

31, 1633. He married, March 7, 1662, Mary Mellins, daughter of Richard Mellins, of Charlestown. Her father removed to Weymouth, where he was admitted a freeman September 7, 1639. Daniel Whittemore inherited the homestead from his father and settled on it; he bequeathed the homestead to his sons Daniel and John. The will was nuncupative and was not proved until nearly two years after his death. His widow Mary was the administratrix. Children: 1. Daniel, born April 27, 1663, resided in Charlestown and Malden; died September 21, 1756; left the homestead to his son Daniel. 2. John, February 12, 1664-65, mentioned below. 3. Thomas, March 5, 1667. 4. Mary, February 15, 1668-69. 5. Nathaniel, February 7, 1670. 6. Peletiah, 1680, married, October 25, 1709, Elizabeth Eustis; died October 21, 1725. 7. James, married first, 1703, Hannah Paul; second, Mary Grover.

(III) John Whittemore, son of Daniel Whittemore (2), was born February 12, 1664-65, died in 1730. He married Ruth Bassett, sister of Lydia Bassett, who married his brother, Daniel Whittemore. They were daughters of Joseph Bassett, and granddaughters of William Bassett, the immigrant, who came over in the ship "Fortune," in 1621, lived in Duxbury in 1637, was deputy to the general court several years, and joined Governor Bradford and others in the purchase of Dartmouth, Massachusetts, and removed to Bridgewater where he died in 1667. Ruth Whittemore was appointed April 3, 1730, administratrix of her husband's estate, which was inventoried at five hundred and three pounds. Children: 1. John, born September 12, 1694, settled in Leicester; married Rebecca Richardson; died 1771. 2. Jeremiah, born 1696, settled in Concord; married first, March 15, 1722, Patience Reed; second, June 5, 1746, Abigail Wooley; died March 31, 1783. 3. Joseph, born 1698, probably removed to Mansfield, Connecticut. 4. Benjamin, born 1700, mentioned below. 5. Elias, born 1702, married, November 13, 1728, Rhoda Holt, of Andover; died at Concord, December 29, 1793. 6. Patience, born 1704, married Timothy Lamson. 7. David, born April 16, 1706, married first, Alice Kendall, of Boston; second, Sarah ———; died September, 1782, at Litchfield, New Hampshire. 8. Deborah, born March 1, 1708, married, February 2, 1738, Moses Gleason. 9. Peletiah, born October 30, 1710, married, July 30, 1738, Deborah Kendall, of Dunstable, who died August 2, 1799.

(IV) Benjamin Whittemore, son of John Whittemore (3), was born in 1700. He resided in Rumney Marsh (Chelsea), and was constable there for several years. He married, December 10, 1723, Sarah Kendall, of Chelsea. Children: 1. Benjamin, born October 9, 1724, mentioned below. 2. Esther, October 5, 1729. 3. Phebe, February 6, 1731. 4. Rebecca, June 16, 1734. 5. Abraham, March 7, 1736. 6. Amos, February 26, 1738.

(V) Benjamin Whittemore, son of Benjamin Whittemore (4), was born October 9, 1724, and died at Greenfield, New Hampshire, January 10, 1798. He probably moved from Chelsea to Nottingham West, now Hudson, about 1748, where the last five of his children were born. He was in the revolution, in Captain Samuel Greeley's company from Hudson. He was in Nottingham West in 1777, and removed to Greenfield late in life, and lived with his eldest son, Major Amos Whittemore, at the time of his death. He married, April 28, 1746, Hannah Collins, of Chelsea. Children: 1. Amos, born February 9, 1747, mentioned below. 2. Infant, died young. 3. Peter. 4. Benjamin, March 6, 1752, at Nottingham West. 5. Sarah, June 8, 1754. 6. Hannah, April 9, 1756. 7. Phebe, August 18, 1763. 8. Esther, May 18, 1766.

(VI) Major Amos Whittemore, son of Benjamin Whittemore (5), was born in Chelsea, February 9, 1747, and died August 18, 1827. He went when a child with his father to Hudson, where he lived until after he was married. In 1769 he was living in Monson, afterward incorporated into the towns of Hollis and Amherst. He removed in 1771 to what was then a part of the Lyndeborough Gore, which became a part of Greenfield in 1790. He was one of the first settlers there and bought the farm where he lived the remainder of his life, now or lately owned by his grandson, A. Marshall Whittemore. He was a major in the revolution, and answered the Lexington alarm, April 19, 1775, returning with Lieutenant Barron. He was at Ticonderoga in 1776, and enlisted in the Continental army and went to New York, September 26, 1776. He was at Bennington under General Stark in 1777. In 1807 he returned to Greenfield and afterwards held various town offices. He married Molly Taylor, of Milford, who died November 27, 1837. Children: 1. Collins, born June 7, 1767, at Hudson, married Mehitable Fuller. 2. Asa, born 1769, married Hannah Burnham, of Greenfield, and resided in Hancock. 3. Amos, married Polly Savage.

4. Benjamin, married Deborah Perry and resided at Bennington; had sons Charles P. and Timothy of Boston; Emily F.; Francis M. and other children. 5. Polly, married Paul Cragin, of Greenfield. 6. Betsey, married Dr. Moses Marsh. 7. Jacob, resided at Antrim, New Hampshire. 8. William, resided at Greenfield. 9. Abram, mentioned below.

(VII) Abram Whittemore, son of Major Amos Whittemore (6), was born November 26, 1786, and died September 4, 1860. He married Martha Marshall, born October 17, 1790, died March 31, 1860. Children: 1. Amos M., born January 25, 1815, married Jane Bates. 2. Joseph R., May 16, 1817, was living in Kansas City in 1890. 3. John Mark, July 27, 1819, mentioned below. 4. Paul C., May 3, 1821, married twice and left descendants. 5. Abram, February 8, 1823, went west. 6. Martha A., October 28, 1825, married Willard Hardy, died 1890. 7. Mary M., September 28, 1827, married Andrew J. Mitchell, of New Hampshire.

(VIII) John Mark Whittemore, son of Abram Whittemore (7), was born in Greenfield, New Hampshire, July 27, 1819, and died November 18, 1901. He received a liberal education when a young man and went to Boston and engaged in the publishing business, and later as a manufacturer of stationery. He married Mary C. Loud, of Boston. (See Loud family herewith). Children: 1. Mary C., born 1844, married Benjamin F. Guild and had Mary and Helen Guild. 2. John Marshall, born January 6, 1846, mentioned below. 3. George C., born 1857; never married.

(IX) John Marshall Whittemore, son of John Mark Whittemore (8), was born January 6, 1846, and died April 20, 1893. He was a graduate of Harvard University, class of 1866. He went into business with his father, manufacturing stationery, and remained with him a number of years. From 1884 to 1885 he was secretary of Harvard College. He was a member and vestryman of St. John's Church (Episcopal) of Cambridge. He married Louisa Adams Kelsey, born February 15, 1848, died December 30, 1885, daughter of James Harvey and Caroline Louise (Adams) Kelsey. (See Kelsey family herewith). Children: 1. Rev. Francis Lee, born May 6, 1871, mentioned below. 2. James Kelsey, April 13, 1875, married Elizabeth DeBlois Lane, of Weston; professor of mathematics at Harvard. 3. Wyman, April 6, 1879, physician.

(X) Rev. Francis Lee Whittemore, son of John Marshall Whittemore (9), was born in Cambridge, Massachusetts, May 6, 1871. He was educated in private schools and at Harvard University, graduating with the class of 1892. He then attended the Episcopal Theological School at Cambridge, graduating in 1895. At this time he was ordained deacon, and in 1897 priest, in the meantime continuing his studies in England and Germany. In 1897 he was appointed assistant of Grace Church at New Bedford, Massachusetts, and later vicar at Providence, Rhode Island, in the Church of the Savior. In 1904 he became rector of St. Paul's Episcopal Church at Dedham, Massachusetts, where he is now situated.

LOUD

The early history of the Loud family in this country is particularly difficult, on account of missing records or lack of records. Savage mentions only Solomon Loud who was a soldier from the East (meaning Maine probably) at Northampton, Massachusetts, in King Philip's war under Captain Turner. The name is the same as that of the ancestor of the family a hundred years later and it is impossible to doubt that both were of the same family. We know that Francis Loud, the ancestor from whom most of the family in this country are descended, was in the Sagadahoc Valley, Maine, in 1675, and we may assume that Solomon was a brother or a near relative. No others of the name can be found at that time. Francis Loud Jr. married a sister or niece of Thomas Prince, the annalist. We are told by one genealogist that Honor Prince was of the fifth generation from Elder Brewster of the "Mayflower." The Loud family settled in Weymouth, Massachusetts, where it has been well represented to the present time.

(I) Solomon Loud, ancestor of the family of this sketch, seems to have come to Boston from Maine. We find the marriage of Solomon Loud and Sarah Heard, of Dover, solemnized January 19, 1789, at Dover, New Hampshire, by the minister of the parish, Rev. Jeremy Belknap. Solomon Loud was a cabinet-maker by trade. He followed his trade in Boston in partnership with Nathaniel Bryant. Together they bought Lot 38 of a section of land owned by John M. Germain and Benjamin Longley. In September, 1811, he bought the interests of his partner in this land. He died in 1833, leaving a widow Abigail who administered his estate. His daughter, Mary C. Loud, married John Mark Whittemore. (See Whittemore family herewith).

KELSEY The surname Kelso and Kelsey seem to have the same origin, though Kelso is the common spelling of the Scotch families and Kelsey of the English. Other spellings such as Calsey, Kelse, Kelsea, Kelsa, Kelsy are also found in both families in America and in the old country. There is a parish of North and South Kelsey in Lincolnshire, England. A Kelsey family had its seat at Chelmsford and Thorp, county Essex, in 1634, and had a coat-of-arms.

The founder of the Scotch family of Kelso lived at Kelso-land, county Ayr, Scotland, Hugo de Kelso, by name, as early as 1296. John Kelso, a descendant, alienated the property in 1676 and his second son William acquired lands in Dankerth, Ayrshire, near the family estate. Arms: Sable a fesse engrailed between three garbs or. Crest: A garb or. Motto: Otium cum dignitate. Another seat of the Kelso family is in Roxburghshire. One of the Scotch Kelso family was the Presbyterian minister of Enniskillen, Ireland, at the time of the revolution of 1688 when William took the throne of the United Kingdom from James. Enniskillen was an unwalled village of eighty houses, situated on an island in the river which joins the two sheets of water known as Lough Erne. The Rev. Robert Kelso urged resistance to the Roman Catholic soldiers who were to be placed there for a garrison and labored both in public and private to animate "his hearers to take up arms and stand upon their own defence; showing example himself by wearing arms, and marching in the head of them when together." They had at first but eighty men poorly armed, but were soon augmented by friends of the same race and religion who fled from the murderous attacks of the Irish Roman Catholics in the south and west. From that time to the end of the war the men of Enniskillen waged a vigorous and successful campaign. The family in Ireland settled in Antrim in Ulster Province and was doubtless descended from the redoubtable minister.

Among the early settlers of Londonderry, New Hampshire, was a branch of this Scotch-Irish family of Kelso. From Londonderry they removed to New Boston and the history of Nottingham, New Hampshire, claims relationship with them, but the evidence of the Connecticut origin of the Nottingham family is too strong.

(I) William Kelsey, immigrant ancestor, was born doubtless in England, but may have been of the Scotch family of Kelso, as the name was frequently spelled in early records. He settled in Cambridge, Massachusetts, as early as 1632 and was a proprietor in 1633. He was admitted a freeman March 4, 1634-35. He sold a meadow there April 19, 1636. He removed to Hartford where he lived until 1663 and then settled in the adjacent town of Killingworth, Connecticut. He was deputy to the general court in 1671. Children: 1. Abigail, born April, 1645. 2. Stephen, November 7, 1647, mentioned below. 3. Daniel, born 1650. 4. Mark, married, March 8, 1658-59, Rebecca Hoskins; second, December 26, 1683, Abigail Atwood; resided in Wethersfield and Windsor, Connecticut; children: i. Rebecca, born January 2, 1659; ii. Thomas, October 16, 1663; iii. John, died June 18, 1685. 5. Lieutenant John, resided in Hartford; was admitted freeman 1658; removed to Killingworth; married Phebe Disbrow, daughter of Nicholas; children: John, Joseph, Josiah and three daughters.

(II) Stephen Kelsey, son of William Kelsey (1), was born November 7, 1647, and died November 30, 1710, married, November 15, 1672, Hannah Ingersoll, daughter of John. Children: 1. Hannah, born 1675. 2. Stephen, September 20, 1677, married, January 11, 1699, Dorothy Brownson. 3. John, January 20, 1680, mentioned below. 4. Daniel, September 14, 1682. 5. William, February 19, 1685. 6. James, August 21, 1687. 7. Charles, June 15, 1692.

(III) John Kelsey, son of Stephen Kelsey (2), was born in Wethersfield, Connecticut, January 20, 1680. He married, November 23, 1704, Mary Buck, daughter of Ezekiel. He resided in the west Beckley quarter and petitioned in 1712 with others for a new parish. Children, born at Wethersfield: 1. Mary, born September 14, 1705. 2. John, November 22, 1706. 3. Hannah, January 6, 1708. 4. James, November 16, 1709, mentioned below. 5. Charles, September 16, 1711, married, March 4, 1742, Mabel Andrews. 6. Ezekiel, January 26, 1713, married Sarah Allen. 7. Rachel, August 21, 1714. 8. Comfort, February 27, 1715-16. 9. Enoch, August 27, 1717, married, August 30, 1744, Mary Bidwell. 10. Esther, May 22, 1725. 11. Ruth, December 6, 1727.

(IV) James Kelsey, son of John Kelsey (3), was born in Wethersfield, Connecticut, November 16, 1709. He married, November 10, 1737, Eunice Andrews. Children: 1. Joseph, born August 28, 1738, at Wethersfield.

2. James, born at Wethersfield probably. 3. Zachariah, (perhaps nephew instead of son) was in Captain Pride's company, Colonel Erastus Wolcott's regiment at Boston in 1775-76; he was of Connecticut at that time; in 1780 he was aged twenty-three years when he was in a New Hampshire regiment and was allowed seven pounds, eleven shillings, for losses at the battle of Ticonderoga. Besides Zachariah many of the family were in the revolution in Massachusetts and New Hampshire regiments, as well as Connecticut. Many of the family went from Killingworth, Connecticut, to Newport, New Hampshire. Moses and Hugh Kelsey settled in Moultonborough; Robert and Hugh at Center Harbor. A James Kelsey lived at Bristol and Topsham, and served in the revolution in 1777 and 1780. Seymour and Hugh were in western Massachusetts regiments as well as in New Hampshire. The western Massachusetts families seem to be from the Connecticut family.

(V) James Kelsey, son of James Kelsey (4), was born in Wethersfield, or vicinity about 1740. He and Zachariah Kelsey appear to have come from Connecticut during or before the revolution and settled in Northfield or Nottingham, where James Albert Kelsey had his residence lately, and built the main part of the house on this farm, a half mile west of the Lee line in the Kelsey district on the road from Deerfield Parade to Levi Hall's house. He died April 23, 1795. He married Elizabeth Harvey, sister of John Harvey, of Nottingham, New Hampshire. He was probably the same James that served from New London, Connecticut, as a corporal in Captain Martin Kirkland's company, Colonel Walcott's regiment. Children, recorded at Nottingham: 1. Margaret, born November 3, 1762, married Miles Reynolds and resided in Lee; children: Betsey, Lois, John and Olive Reynolds. 2. William, born October 1, 1764, married Hannah Harvey and had the homestead; children: i. Daniel, born June 2, 1805; ii. Elizabeth, October 16, 1806; iii. William; iv. John H.; v. James, April 5, 1814; vi. James Albert, April 5, 1818, married Abbie A. Sears. 3. James Jr., born May 6, 1766; children: Sally, Rendal, Harvey, James, John, Robert, Moses, Sally, Hiram, Hugh. 4. Jane, born March 10, 1768, married Jonathan Thompson, of Lee; children: James, Susan, Noah, Hugh and Mary Thompson. 5. Moses, born February 17, 1770, died unmarried. 6. John, born October 5, 1771, mentioned below. 7. Hugh, born September 19, 1773, married Ann Harvey; son Hugh inherited his farm.

(VI) John Kelsey, son of James Kelsey (5), was born in Nottingham, New Hampshire, October 5, 1771. Married Mary Roberts, of Waterborough, Maine. He lived on what is known as the John Kelsey place. Children, born at Nottingham: James H., mentioned below; Susan, Eliza, John, Mary, Ichabod, Hiram.

(VII) James Harvey Kelsey, son of John Kelsey (6), was born in Nottingham. He married Caroline Louise Adams, daughter of William Parker Adams, of Portsmouth, New Hampshire. He was a well-to-do merchant in Boston. Children: 1. Louisa Adams, born February 15, 1848, died December 30, 1885; she married John Marshall Whittemore. 2. Kate, born November 15, 1852, married Nicholas Baron von Zedlitz-Neukirch of Kauffung, Silesia.

WEBER

The late Nicholas Weber, for many years a prominent leather manufacturer of Lynn, Massachusetts, and a successful business man in that city for almost a quarter of a century, was of French birth, although in common with nearly all others who bear the surnames Webber or Weber he doubtless was descended from Holland Dutch ancestors. The American Webbers and Webers generally claim descent from Wolfert Webber, of Amsterdam, Holland, where he was born, and of New Amsterdam (New York City), where he came about 1633 with Van Twiller, the Dutch governor of New Netherlands, and where he became owner of a large tract of land which now and for many years has been a part of the vast property owned by the corporation of Trinity Church.

Nicholas Weber was born in Alsace Lorraine, France, now Germany, September 29, 1836, son of Nicholas and Anne (Weber) Weber, the former of whom was born in Luxembourg, and the latter in Lorraine. He learned the trade of leather dressing in his native country, and was there when the Prussian war broke out. He took an active part in the war, shared the privations that came to a people at such a time, and saw his native province pass from the control of France to that of Germany. In 1873, with his wife and three children, he came to the United States, settling first in Quebec, from whence he removed to Boston, later to Cambridge, where he remained one year, and finally to Lynn, where he obtained a position as foreman for A. B. Martin. His trade, which he had learned at home, and subsequent twelve years experience with Levin Foreres, in Paris, France, stood him in good stead in his new position, and he soon took the front rank in his vocation. After serving faithfully for Mr. Martin, he went into business for himself and engaged in the manufacture of gloves and white sheep stock, and for a dozen or more years turned out that quality of stock for Lucius Beebe & Son. His large factory was located at the corner of Western avenue and Federal street, and he gave employment to nearly two hundred hands. In January, 1892, he organized the Weber Leather Company, of which he was president till the time of his death, taking his oldest son, Nicholas M., in company with him. He invented a staking machine, which is used in all the factories in this country and in several other countries where leather is made. By close attention to business he built up a trade that is not confined to the United States, the company having agents in France, Germany, Austria and other countries. Mr. Weber is remembered as a skillful workman, a capable and straightforward business man, and one who enjoyed the respect of all persons with whom he was acquainted either socially or in a business way. He was a member of the National Morocco Manufacturers' Association, Lynn Manufacturers' Association, of which he was at one time a member of the executive committee, St. Jean de Baptiste Benevolent Society, and a charter member of Lynn Lodge of Elks.

Nicholas Weber married, November 23, 1867, Marie B., daughter of Matthias and Barbara (Peiffer) Kline, of Lorraine. The father of Matthias Kline was a soldier under Napoleon I. Mr. and Mrs. Weber had nine children: 1. Nicholas M., born St. Denis, France, October 28, 1868, married, June 2, 1897, Mary A. Quill, daughter of John and Mary (Dorgan) Quill, of Ipswich; children: i. Ruth Marie, born April 24, 1898; ii. Madeline, May 2, 1899, died May 17, 1905; iii. Dorothy Mildreth, August 10, 1900; iv. Mabel Marie, June 10, 1902, died December 12, 1902. 2. Charles P., born January 29, 1871, in Paris, at the time of the siege of that city, married Agnes Fitzpatrick, of Lynn; children: i. Claire Agnes, died in infancy; ii. Nicholas, died in infancy; iii. Alfred Joseph, born July 17, 1900; iv. Nicholas Charles, March 1, 1901. 3. Eugene, born in Paris, April 30, 1872, died in Lynn, aged five years. 4. John L., born in Lynn, February 11, 1877, see forward. 5. Albert Arthur, born March 26, 1879, married, September 14, 1904, Mary E. Donahue, of Salem; children: i. Genevieve Marie, born September 27, 1905; ii. Albert Nicholas, June 23, 1906; iii. William Francis, September 4, 1908. 6. Marie, born July 26, 1880. 7. William Simon, born February 18, 1884. 8. Alice Madeline, born August 27, 1885, a graduate of St. Ann's Academy, Marlboro, Massachusetts, class of 1904. 9. Joseph George, born April 23, 1889, a graduate of Mt. St. Louis Institute, Montreal. Nicholas Weber, father of these children, died December 12, 1900, aged fifty-four years. All of Mr. Weber's children are stockholders in the Weber Leather Company and the following hold offices: Nicholas M., president and treasurer; John L., vice-president; Albert A., secretary; Charles P., foreman of the factory.

John L. Weber, son of Nicholas and Marie B. (Kline) Weber, was born in Lynn, Massachusetts, February 11, 1877. He received his education in public schools in that city, and also in Mount St. Louis Institute, Montreal. Returning home he began work in his father's factory, and in 1898 acquired an interest in the Weber Leather Company, of which he is still a member. Although his business interests are largely in Lynn, Mr. Weber lives in the adjoining village of Cliftondale, town of Saugus, where he is prominently identified with local institutions. Since 1900 he has been a member of the Saugus Fire Department, was a member of its board of engineers in 1904, and in 1906 was appointed chief engineer of the department. He is a member of Malden Lodge, No. 965, Benevolent and Protective Order of Elks, and of Valladolid Council, No. 70, Knights of Columbus.

Mr. Weber married, June 19, 1898, Mary E. Guy, of Lynn, daughter of John W. Guy. Children: 1. Lauretta Marie, born April 11, 1899. 2. John Louis, August 15, 1900. 3. Marion, October 12, 1901. 4. Leo Francis, July 19, 1903. 5. Alice Madeline, April 2, 1906.

HOOD The family name Hood has been known in the history of Lynn, Massachusetts, for more than two and a half centuries, and as evidence of the highly respectable character of him who first bore that surname in the region it may be said that in 1692 the town voted Richard Hood, senior, should have a seat in the pulpit in the meeting house. On May 23 same year, Sarah Hood, daughter of Richard Sr. and wife of William Bassett, was placed on trial in Salem on a charge of witchcraft, and after the hollow mockery of trial was finished she was committed to the common jail in Boston and confined there until December 3 following. In the jail with her she was allowed the company of her child, then less than three years old, and her next child was christened Deliverance, in allusion to her release from imprisonment.

(I) Richard Hood, immigrant ancestor of the branch of the family here considered, came to New England from Lynn Regis, Yorkshire or Norfolk, England, in 1640, and was an early settler in Lynn, a town which had been founded ten years before by people who came largely from the town of that name in England. He was a member of the Society of Friends, and a man of good report in the town; the appointment mentioned to a seat in the pulpit with the minister was a mark of distinction and an evidence of the respect in which he was held by the townsfolk. The home of Richard Hood was in that part of Lynn which was and is called Nahant, where previous to 1800 the only dwellers were the Breeds and Hoods and later the Johnsons, and they all were counted among the most substantial and respectable inhabitants of the town. Richard Hood died September 12, 1695. The name of his wife was Agnes, and Savage's "Genealogical Dictionary" mentions their children as follows: 1. Richard, born November 18, 1655. 2. Sarah, August 2, 1657, married William Bassett. 3. Rebecca, February 7, 1663, married Hugh Alley. 4. John, May 7, 1664. 5. Hannah, October 21, 1665. 6. Samuel, May 12, 1667. 7. Ann, February 13, 1672. 8. Joseph, July 8, 1674. 9. Benjamin, January 3, 1678; made freeman 1691; died September 12, 1695.

(II) Richard Hood Jr., born November 18, 1655, son of Richard Hood (1), had sons Samuel, born October 18, 1690; Richard, March 30, 1692; Zebulon, 1693, died December, 1693; Zebulon, 1694, died July 12, 1695. It is quite probable that Richard Jr. had other children whose names do not appear in the published records.

(III) Richard Hood, born March 30, 1692, died October 4, 1762, was son of Richard Hood Jr. He married, May 20, 1718, Theodate, daughter of Samuel Collins, gunsmith, of Lynn. Richard Hood was appointed a constable for collection of taxes in Lynn, Massachusetts, by the English crown in 1732. Children: 1. Theodate, born October 27, 1719. 2. Jedediah, September 25, 1721. 3. Content, December 20, 1722. 4. Rebecca, April 3, 1725. 5. Hannah, December 9, 1727. 6. Patience, September 9, 1730. 7. Abner, September 26, 1733: 8. Abigail, September 14, 1736.

(IV) Abner Hood, son of Richard and Theodate (Collins) Hood, born at Nahant, a part of Lynn, September 26, 1733, died there March 11, 1818. He married, June 11, 1783, Kezia Breed, born August 25, 1750, died November 4, 1825, daughter of Benjamin and Ruth (Allen) Breed, granddaughter of Samuel and Anna (Hood) Breed, great-granddaughter of Allen and Anna (Breed) Breed, and great-great-granddaughter of Allen Bread, immigrant ancestor of the Breed families in this country, and of whom and his descendants mention will be found in these annals. Abner and Kezia (Breed) Hood had (vital records) six children: 1. Abner, born April 1, 1784, see forward. 2. Richard, March 13, 1786. 3. Theodate, May 23, 1787. 4-5. Ebenezer and Benjamin (twins), born April 7, 1790: for history of Benjamin see forward. 6. Content, born December 21, 1792. Three of the sons of Abner Hood were the first men to contribute money to build one of the first public libraries in the country in 1819.

(V) Abner Hood, eldest child of Abner and Kezia (Breed) Hood, was born in Lynn, April 1, 1784. He married, September 28, 1805, Polly (Mary) Richardson; children: 1. George, born November 10, 1806; see forward. 2. Martha Ann, January 21, 1809. 3. Abner, July 29, 1812. 4. Charles Green, December 23, 1814. 5. James Magee, November 2, 1820.

(V) Benjamin Hood, son of Abner and Kezia (Breed) Hood, was born in Nahant, Massachusetts, April 7, 1790. He received his early education at the old homestead, being taught by a tutor in a room which had been set apart from the rest of the house and called at that time the school room, but later went through a course of studies at the Andover Academy. He later returned to his home and during his life was never engaged in any practical business, but remained at home to assist in the care of the property and led the life of a farmer. During the summer months Mr. Hood opened the old home for summer boarders, and it became a favorite resort for pleasure and comfort; it was there that Longfellow wrote a part of his poem "Hiawatha." Mr. Hood was of the old Whig party, but never served in any town office, having confined his interest entirely to the care of the old homestead, which was owned by the family for nearly two hundred years, and was sold in 1865. He was of Quaker faith, but was read out of the church when he purchased a piano for the pleasure of his children, such an act being contrary to the laws of the church. He married Hannah Philips, born in Swampscott, 1800, daughter of John and Judith (Dow) Philips, of Swampscott; children: 1. Louise P., born March 14, 1821, died 1876; married Albert Wyer, no children. 2. Ann Maria, January 9, 1824, died 1875; married, 1846, Dexter Stetson, see forward. 3. Anna Amelia, January 27, 1832, died 1900. 4. Julia Pond, July 1, 1834, resides on Nahant street, Lynn. Benjamin Hood (father) died at the old homestead at Nahant, 1857; his wife died in 1859, aged fifty-nine years.

Dexter Stetson, born in Freeport, Maine, 1815, died in Lynn, Massachusetts, 1899, was a son of Charles and Abigail (Dennison) Stetson. After learning the trade of carpenter at Durham, Maine, Dexter Stetson went at an early age to Nahant, Massachusetts, where he built many of the finest summer cottages. He was a respected and public-spirited citizen, and served his town in many capacities, being one of the first selectmen of Nahant, but his ambition led him to a larger field of action, and he went to New Orleans, Louisiana, as a contractor and builder for the United States government, and there built large storehouses, but was later transferred to the Atlantic coast and built light houses from Florida to North Carolina, erecting some of the finest light houses on the coast. He served the government faithfully for thirty years, and after his retirement constantly received complimentary letters from many parts of the country for his elegant workmanship. He married Ann Maria Hood, mentioned above, and is survived by his only daughter, Helen L. Stetson, who was born at Nahant and now resides on Nahant street, Lynn.

(VI) George Hood, son of Abner and Mary (Richardson) Hood, was born in Lynn, November 10, 1806, and received his early education in the public schools at Nahant, in which locality his youth was spent. After leaving school he learned the trade of shoemaking, followed that occupation for a few years, but soon after attaining his majority went west with John C. Abbott and in company with him located in St. Louis and established a shoe business in that city. This was in 1829, and although the country was comparatively new to the line of trade they established, it proved a successful venture and was soon followed by a branch store in Natchez, Mississippi, which Mr. Hood started for his firm and gave to it his personal attention until 1835, when he returned to Lynn. However, he retained his interest in the business in St. Louis and Natchez until 1841. Having returned to the east Mr. Hood established a commission shoe and leather house in Boston and continued at its head until his death, although in many ways his attention was directed in other channels of business and at the same time he became an active figure in local and general politics. In this field his fortunes were cast with the Democratic party, the minority party always in Essex county politics and generally in the state; yet frequently he was called to stand as the nominee of his party in the hope that his known personal influence, high character and popularity might turn the scale of doubtful contest. He filled various offices of local importance, served several times in the lower house of the general court and in 1843 was elected to the senate. In 1846 he was nominated by the Democratic state convention for the lieutenant-governorship, but was defeated at the polls by the natural opposition majority in the state, and in 1852 he stood as the Democratic candidate for a seat in the lower house of the federal congress, but the Republican majority in the district was too great to overcome. In 1853 he was chosen a delegate to the convention for revising the constitution of the commonwealth. The crowning achievement of Mr. Hood's political career was the great good he was so largely instrumental in accomplishing in connection with the movement to incorporate the city of Lynn and supercede the old with a new form of government. The charter proposed in 1849 contained provisions which were unsatisfactory to many of the people, and he led the forces which opposed and defeated its adoption. In the spring of the year 1850 another charter was granted, and was accepted by vote of the people. Although he had opposed the second charter and was not at all in sympathy with the movement to establish the so-called high form of municipal government, Mr. Hood was nominated and elected the first mayor of Lynn; and so satisfactory was his administration of the city government during that year, that in March, 1851, he was re-elected by a largely increased majority and served two years in office.

But not politics alone occupied Mr. Hood's attention during the period of his activity in that field, for he continued his mercantile business in Boston, and in 1853 was one of the principal organizers of the Shoe and Leather Fire Insurance Company of Boston, and its

Dexter Stetson.

Lewis Historical Pub, Co.

George Hood

president from 1853 to 1858, when he resigned. Besides these and other personal concerns, he always manifested a wholesome interest in the social and industrial welfare of his native town and its institutions. He was in all respects a model citizen, universally esteemed for his high moral character, his unselfish liberality and public spirit, and for his real worth as a man.

Mr. Hood died at his home in Lynn, June 29, 1859, being then a little less than fifty-three years old. He married, September 11, 1833, Hermione Breed, born in Lynn, March 18, 1812, died January 20, 1887, daughter of Major Aaron Breed and his second wife, Mary Kemp, granddaughter of Amos Breed and Ruth Newhall, great-granddaughter of Jabez and Desire Breed, great-great-granddaughter of Samuel Breed and Anna Hood, and great-great-great-granddaughter of Allen Breed (or Bread) who was the son of Allen Bread, the immigrant ancestor of the family of that surname in America. Children of George and Hermione (Breed) Hood: 1. Harriet M. 2. George Abbott, September 7, 1835. 3. Adelaide M. 4. Edwin E. 5. Edwin. 6. Julius S. 7. Henrietta A., married A. Bigelow, of Nova Scotia. 8. Henry, born May 28, 1844, died May 29, 1844. 9. Caroline P. 10. Aubrey, born July 18, 1846. 11. Ada H., married Louis H. Bonelli; (see Bonelli). 12. Edward K. 13. Mary.

BONELLI Among the successful and representative business men of Boston may be mentioned Louis Henry Bonelli, a native of St. Thomas, West Indies, second son of Andre and Annette (Bessupp) Bonelli. Andre Bonelli (father), a native of Italy, went to the West Indies about the age of eighteen, and shortly afterward opened a hotel, which became one of the leading hostelries of the place, and continued in that line of business throughout the active years of his life, his death occurring there in 1876. He married, in 1842, Annette Bessupp, of Holland; children: Andrew, Louis Henry, Annette, Charles A., Eugene, all born in the West Indies.

Louis Henry Bonelli acquired his education in Hamburg College, Germany, which he attended five years, after which he returned to his native land, and one year later removed to Boston, Massachusetts, about 1871. He at once established a cigar business which he conducted successfully for two years, and then turned his attention to the real estate business, continuing in the same up to the present time (1908), with office at 60 State street, Boston, with his sons Walter, George and Edward. He is a member of the Unitarian church, a Republican in politics, and a member of the Masonic fraternity. He married Ada H. Hood; (see Hood); their children: 1. Walter Hood, born in Lynn, Massachusetts, February 10, 1875, acquired his early education in the schools of his native place, went to Boston, 1887, graduated from Phillips grammar school, then pursued a course in Boston Latin school, after which he entered Harvard College, remaining two years. He entered the employ of the Prudential Life Insurance Company, New York, remaining two years, and then received and accepted the appointment of head clerk in Charlestown navy yard. At the present time he is interested in the real estate business with his father at 60 State street, Boston. 2. Anna Hermione, born in Lynn, September 3, 1876, resides at home, unmarried. 3. Louis Henry Jr., born in Newport, September 2, 1878, graduate from Boston Latin school, 1897, and Harvard College, 1901. He was appointed, through Harvard College, as supervisor of schools in the Philippine Islands by the government at Washington, 1901, going there in July of that year and remaining three years. In 1904 he returned to Boston, having traveled around the world. He became interested in the real estate business and has since been engaged in the same with his father and brothers—Walter, George and Edward—under the firm name of Hood Land Company. He is a member of the Real Estate Exchange, also the City Club. He attends the Unitarian church, and is a Republican in politics. He is unmarried. 4. George Hood, born Cambridge, Massachusetts, October 15, 1880, a graduate of Rice grammar school, after which he pursued a course in Boston Latin school. He is engaged in the real estate business in Boston, with his father and brothers. He served as librarian of the Second Unitarian Church of Boston three years, which church he attends, and his political affiliations are with the Republican party. He is unmarried. 5. Edward Hood, born in Lynn, Massachusetts, November 15, 1882, graduate of Boston Latin school, 1902, and Harvard College, 1906; was member of the Ivy Club and Harvard Crew at Harvard. He is engaged in the real estate business with his father, at 60 State street, Boston. He is a member of the Real Estate Exchange, the City Club, Boston, attends the Unitarian church, and is a Republican in politics. He married, at Trinity Church, Boston, November 27, 1907, Emma A. White, a native of Augusta, Maine, but whose home has been in Boston. 6. Mabel Hermione, born Boston, Massachusetts, February 24, 1889; educated in the schools of Boston, graduated from Girls' Latin school, June, 1907. She resides at home.

PROCTER So far as American references disclose, the first representatives of the Procter surname in New England were George Procter of Dorchester, Robert Procter of Concord, and John Procter, of Ipswich and Salem, from whom have descended nearly all who now bear that name in the region mentioned; and many among them, in every generation from the time of the ancestors, have been found men of character, worth and prominence in the activities of life. This narrative, however, has to deal particularly with John Procter of Ipswich and Salem and his descendants.

According to authenticated records, John Procter was born in England in 1588, married there, and emigrated to New England in 1635, with wife Martha, age twenty-eight, and their two children—John, age three, and Mary, age one, in the ship "Susan and Ellen," and settled first in the plantation at Ipswich. After a few years he removed with his family to Salem and lived there to the end of his days. His wife Martha died June 13, 1659, and he afterward took a second wife of the same baptismal name and who survived him. He died some time between August 28 and November 28, 1672, and in his will mentions his sons John, Joseph and Benjamin, and daughters Martha White, Abigail Varney, Sarah Dodge and Hannah Weeden. His estate inventoried 1,228 pounds, which indicated that he was a man of substance, and well settled tradition, borne out by frequent mention of his name in connection with affairs relating to the government of the town, also indicates that he was a man of consequence among the planters.

(II) John Procter, son of John Procter the immigrant and Martha his wife, was born in England in 1632, and was three years old when his parents came to New England and settled at Ipswich. He lived many years in that town, and removed thence to Salem, where in 1692 both he and his wife were accused with the heresy of witchcraft and the judgment of death was pronounced against them. John Procter suffered the death penalty, but his wife was set free because of her pregnancy at that time. This, however, was his second wife. He married, first, December, 1662, Elizabeth, daughter of John Thorndike. She died August 3, 1672, and April 1, 1674, he married Elizabeth Basset. By both marriages he had twelve children, and at his death he left lands in Ipswich and Salem of the value of 208 pounds. Children: 1. Benjamin, born in Ipswich probably about 1664, died 1720. 2. Martha, born June 4, 1666. 3. Mary, born October 20, 1667, died February 15, 1668. 4. John, born October 28, 1668. 5. Mary, January 30, 1670. 6. Thorndike, July 15, 1672. 7. William, February 6, 1675. 8. Sarah, January 28, 1677. 9. Samuel, January 1, 1686. 10. Elisha, born April 28, 1687, died November 11, 1688. 11. Abigail, born January 27, 1689.

Some accounts of the Procter family make no mention of Benjamin, who is here given as the eldest of John Procter's children, nor of his daughter Elizabeth, who in 1681 became the wife of Thomas Very, and therefore must have been the eldest of his children. In the "Essex Institute Historical Collections" an account is given of the children of John Procter, "late of Ipswich," and there both Elizabeth and Benjamin are mentioned as "the eldest of these children." Benjamin Procter is mentioned in the division of his father's estate and from the best information to be obtained it is believed that he must have been born about 1664.

(III) Benjamin Procter, son of John Procter "the sufferer," married, December 8, 1694, ——— Whitridge; children: Mary Priscilla, Sarah and John Procter.

(IV) John Procter, son of Benjamin and ——— (Whitridge) Procter, born in Salem, 1704, died September 3, 1773. He married, December 14, 1727, Lydia Waters, the mother of all of his children, and who "departed this life" October 14, 1750. That he married a second wife is shown by his will made February 6, 1772, proved October 4, 1773, in which is mentioned a wife Eunice, and makes provision for her, but says that "in case she doth marry again she shall have no liberty to live in my house nor to any of above articles of living." John and Lydia (Waters) Procter had ten children, all of whom except Daniel, the youngest (who is mentioned in "Bridgman's Memorials" as one of them), were baptized by Rev. Benjamin Prescott, minister of the middle precinct of Salem: 1. John, born September 14, 1728; married twice, died August 27, 1771. 2. Lydia, baptized May 10, 1730; married a Flint. 3. Benjamin, baptized April 30, 1732. 4. Mary, baptized December 9, 1733; married an Osborn. 5. Sarah, baptized August 20, 1736; married a Gould. 6. Sylvester, baptized October 29, 1738, died March 21, 1790. 7. Prudence, baptized November 23, 1740; married James Buffington. 8. Joseph, born August 23, 1743; married Elizabeth Epes. 9. Daniel, of whom little is known other than has been mentioned.

(V) Joseph Procter, youngest but one of the children of John and Lydia (Waters) Procter, born in Danvers, August 23, 1743, baptized September 4 same year, died January 20, 1805. Of his early life and occupation little is now known, but from subsequent events it may properly be assumed that the foundation of his career as a man of business, a husband, a father, and a true Christian, were deeply and broadly laid, under judicious culture, and that, aided by his naturally strong common sense, his integrity of character and honesty of principle and purpose, produced in his life the most substantial results and left their impress in the hearts of his children and descendants in all subsequent generations. He moved to Gloucester about 1766 and purchased lands fronting on what became known as Canal street. That part of the town at one time was known as the "Cut," so called in allusion to its proximity to the small watercourse known by the same name, where the canal was afterward constructed. From that point his lands extended northerly nearly to Washington street, including what afterward became Mansfield street, which formed the old bed of the mill pond from which he obtained power for operating his mill machinery. In this locality he erected his mill, several dwelling houses, barns and other buildings, and also store houses for fish, grain and merchandise.

Mr. Procter first erected suitable buildings, built in 1768 the house on Canal street, then brought his bride from Danvers and established himself as a miller and potter, and engaged extensively in the manufacture of earthenware, which at that time was in general use for all domestic purposes. His mill was considered a triumph of mechanical engineering, and by its peculiar construction was made to accomplish a very great amount of work with a comparatively small expenditure of power. He also had a cooperage for making hogsheads, barrels and other utensils, and a forge for light iron work and repairing. He established and carried on a fishing business, sending his vessels to the Grand Banks, and also built several vessels for fishing and other purposes, employing some of them in the foreign trade, but particularly for shipping fish and earthenware to southern ports and the West Indies; and on the return voyage the vessels brought back cargoes of foreign produce, cocoa, and corn for his mill, and frequently goodly sums of money.

For five successive years Mr. Procter filled the office of selectman of Gloucester, and in later years several of his descendants served in the same capacity. At a meeting of the officers of the Sixth Regiment of militia, held at Gloucester, January 27, 1775, he was chosen first lieutenant of the sixth company, commanded by Captain Jacob Allen; Samuel Gorham was second lieutenant, and Eben Parsons ensign. During the revolutionary war he was agent for the owners of the privateer "General Stark," by the operations of which several rich prizes were taken and sent into American ports; and there is a tradition in the family that Joseph Procter was the first man in Gloucester to reduce granite blocks by the use of steel wedges. The sickness which resulted in Mr. Procter's death was due to fatigue and exposure consequent to getting afloat one of his vessels which had been driven on Coffin's beach in a heavy storm. He died January 29, 1805, aged sixty-two years.

On March 3, 1768, Joseph Procter married Elizabeth Epes, born in Danvers, April 24, 1743, died July 29, 1817, daughter of Captain Daniel and Hannah (Prescott) Epes, and granddaughter of Colonel Daniel Epes of Salem, and Hannah his wife. Hannah Prescott, born 1719, died 1775, married, 1737, Captain Daniel Epes, was daughter of Rev. Benjamin Prescott, born Concord, 1686, died Danvers 1777, and his wife Elizabeth Higginson, born 1696, died 1722-23; and Rev. Benjamin Prescott was a son of Captain Jonathan Prescott of Concord, by his first wife, Elizabeth Hoar. Elizabeth Higginson, wife of Rev. Benjamin Prescott, was daughter of John Higginson, and his wife Hannah Gardner (daughter of Samuel Gardner Jr., granddaughter of Lieutenant Colonel John Higginson, of Guilford, Connecticut, and Salem, and Sarah, daughter of Thomas Savage of Boston and his wife Mary Symmes), great-granddaughter of Rev. John Higginson, 1616-1708, of Clay Brook and Salem, and his wife Sarah Whitford (daughter of Rev. Henry Whitford) and great-granddaughter of Rev. Francis Higginson, born 1587, died Salem

1630. Samuel Gardner Jr., father of Hannah Gardner, who married John Higginson, was a son of Samuel Gardner and his wife Mary White, and grandson of Thomas Gardner. (See Gardner).

In this connection it is interesting to note that Mary Symmes, who married Thomas Savage, his second wife (his first wife was Faith Hutchinson, by whom he had seven children), was a daughter of Rev. Zachariah Simmes, son of Rev. William Simmes, and was born in Canterbury, England, April 5, 1599, rector of Dunstable in 1625, and the second minister of Charlestown, Massachusetts. He arrived in New England, September 18, 1634, with Rev. John Lothrop and William Hutchinson and his famous wife, Ann. With Rev. Zachariah also came to New England his wife Sarah and several children. He lived with her fifty years, and according to Mather they had thirteen children, five of whom were sons. Savage says that Rev. Zachariah died January 28, 1672, and that his widow died in 1676.

It may also be mentioned that John Higginson, who married Sarah Gardner, was born August 20, 1675, and was a Salem merchant. He married, September 11, 1695, and died April 26, 1718, having survived his wife, who died June 20, 1713. John Higginson, father of John last mentioned, was born at Guilford, Connecticut, in 1646, and afterward settled permanently at Salem, where he was a merchant. He married Sarah Savage, of Boston, October 9, 1672, and died March 23, 1719. His father, Rev. John Higginson, was born at Clay Brook, England, August 6, 1616, and kept a grammar school at Hartford, Connecticut. He married Sarah Whitfield of Guilford and assisted her father in his work in the ministry of that town. He left Guilford in 1659 and, stopping over for a brief season at Salem, was persuaded to settle as minister over the church there which his father had planted more than thirty years before. He was ordained there in 1660 and continued the work of the ministry at Salem until his death, December 9, 1708, aged ninety-two years. His wife Sarah died July 8, 1675. Rev. Francis Higginson was son of Rev. John Higginson, of England, where Francis was born in 1587. He was settled in the ministry at Clay Brook in Leicester, but having become a Puritan was invited to settle in New England. He arrived at Salem June 29, 1629, and in August of the same year gathered and planted the first church in the colony of Massachusetts Bay.

Thus it was that by his marriage with Elizabeth Epes, Joseph Procter and his descendants after him in all generations became connected with some of the best Puritan stock of New England, and who in the early times of the colony were largely engaged in the work of the ministry. Children of Joseph and Sarah (Epes) Procter: 1. Daniel Epes, born December 18, 1768, died March 9, 1851. 2. Elizabeth, born November 10, 1770, died April 15, 1845. 3. Joseph, born June 27, 1772, died October 21, 1842. 4. Hannah, born April 9, 1774, died 1841. 5. Lydia, born May 26, 1776, died July 1, 1843. 6. John, born March 24, 1778, died November 10, 1852. 7. Polly, born September 8, 1780, died February 20, 1807. 8. Denmark, born November 26, 1782, died in infancy. 9. Greenwich, born November 26, 1782, died November 19, 1854.

(VI) Daniel Epes Procter, eldest child of Joseph and Elizabeth (Epes) Procter, born in Gloucester, December 18, 1768, died in that town March 9, 1851. He married, October 4, 1792, Lydia Gould; children: 1. Epes, born July 31, 1793, died March 4, 1795. 2. Lydia, born May 14, 1795, died November 19, 1873. 3. Joseph, born November 22, 1796, died March 25, 1881. 4. Sarah, born October 26, 1797, died October 19, 1798. 5. Sarah, born May 22, 1799, died May 31, 1801. 6. Eliza, born March 9, 1801, died January 5, 1847. 7. Mary, born August 7, 1802, died February 24, 1867. 8. Francis Epes, born July 30, 1804, died August 19, 1846. 9. Hannah, born September 23, 1806, died September 21, 1842. 10. Nancy, born October 7, 1808, died January 17, 1889. 11. Sarah, born December 23, 1810, died May 5, 1882.

(VII) Francis Epes Procter, eighth child and third son of Daniel Epes and Lydia (Gould) Procter, born in Gloucester, July 30, 1804, died there August 19, 1846. Like his father he was a seafaring man, trading at foreign ports and also along the American coast. His advice to his sons was that they should not follow the sea, and generally they gave heed to the paternal admonition. He married, November 25, 1829, Ann Allen, daughter of Thomas Allen, of Gloucester, whose old home farm in that town has remained in the family for more than two hundred years. Children of Francis Epes and Ann (Allen) Procter: 1. Frances Ann, born February, 1831, died February 9, 1832. 2. Francis, born March 16, 1833, senior member of firm of Procter Brothers, publishers and booksellers. 3. George H., born July 4, 1835, junior mem-

Francis Procter

ber of firm of Procter Brothers. 4. William Allen, born ———, 1838, died February 2, 1849.

(VIII) Francis Procter, elder of the two surviving children of Francis Epes and Ann (Allen) Procter, was born in what then was the town of Gloucester, March 16, 1833, and for more than three score years has been closely identified with the business history of that town and subsequent city. As a boy he attended the common school, but his best education was acquired more by association and contact with men than by study in the schoolroom. When he was thirteen years old his father died, but even before that time the young boy had learned to depend on himself and was earning money for his own support. As a boy he had seen others peddling city papers, and believed that he could do as well as they, and with that end in view he wrote to the publisher of a Boston paper asking that a number of copies be sent him with which to begin business; but was surprised to learn that a cash remittance must accompany his order. He therefore borrowed a dollar from his mother, and with that as a starting capital purchased thirty-three copies of *The Flag of Our Union,* and sold them all in Gloucester in a single day, realizing a profit of thirty-three cents for his work. This was the beginning of Mr. Procter's business career, and upon the foundation then laid the present extensive business carried on by the firm, of which he is senior member, has been built up and established. His early earnings were put back into the business as capital, and in the course of a short time he was able to open a store on Main street, where newspapers, periodicals and books were kept for sale, and at one time his stock included confectionery, fruits and nuts, but this branch of the business proved unprofitable, and was soon discontinued. Later on his brother, George H. Procter, was taken into the store, and in 1857 the firm of Procter Brothers was established, and has since been well known in trade and newspaper circles in New England and the Canadian provinces.

In 1853, on account of certain annoyance at the hands of publishers, Mr. Procter determined to become himself a publisher, and in July of that year issued the first number of *Procter's Able Sheet.* At first it was published monthly, and from the outset proved a successful journalistic venture, showing, as the headline indicated, that the Procters were "able" to publish a "sheet" of their own. Subsequently the name was changed to *Gloucester Advertiser,* and the paper was issued semi-monthly. In 1856 the firm started publication of the *Cape Ann Advertiser,* a weekly paper, and continued it until July 1, 1891, when it was merged with the *Times.* The *Gloucester Daily Times* appeared June 16, 1888, and has since been continued as an independent Republican newspaper—not the avowed organ of any political party, but rather as an independent paper, representing the best interests and institutions of Gloucester and Cape Ann, and one which has gained a wide circulation in Essex county, eastern Massachusetts, Nova Scotia and the provinces. In the division of work and responsibility in connection with its publication the senior member of the firm has given particular attention to the business and general management, while the junior partner has capably filled the equally important position of managing editor. Since 1850 the place of business of the founders of these newspaper enterprises has been at the corner of Main and Centre streets, Gloucester. The building (which was the family homestead) and plant was destroyed by fire in the disastrous conflagration of 1864, and was at once replaced with the present building, in which the "old corner bookstore" is still maintained, with the editorial and composing rooms on the second and third floors and press room in the rear, on Centre street.

While the business and general management of the papers published by the firm has always occupied a large share of Mr. Procter's attention as editor and publisher, he nevertheless has for many years been regarded as a public man in Gloucester, and has been identified in some prominent manner with nearly every measure which has been proposed for the promotion of public interests in the city during the last fifty years. Politically he is a Republican, and was chosen as delegate to the first Free Soil convention held at Worcester, before the Republican party was brought into existence. In 1861 he was auditor of town accounts. In 1872 he was elected a delegate to the Liberal Republican convention that nominated Mr. Greeley for the presidency, and also was a member of the conference that nominated Charles Sumner for the governorship of Massachusetts. He was elected alderman of ward four of Gloucester in 1876, when perhaps no other Republican candidate could have been elected in that always Democratic stronghold. He has been largely interested in Press associations, is a charter member of the Massachusetts Press Association, founded in 1869, served as secretary two years, vice-president five years, president three years, was a delegate to the first National Editorial Association, which met at Cincinnati in 1880, and chosen member of the executive committee, and in connection has travelled on excursion from Prince Edwards Island to the City of Mexico. He also spent two winters (1879-1880) in Bermuda for the benefit of his health.

Mr. Procter became a Mason when he was a young man, and for two years was secretary of Tyrian Lodge. From 1883 to 1889 he was chairman of the Independent Christian Society (the oldest Universalist society in America). For many years he has been a director of the Gloucester Board of Trade and of the Gloucester Co-operative Bank. He is one of the original park commissioners of Gloucester, appointed by Mayor Asa G. Andrews, the first meeting of which body was held November 27, 1894, and he has been secretary of the board since it was organized. He also has been interested in various land improvement enterprises on Cape Ann, the laying out of Bellevue Heights, Wolf Hill and Willoughby Park; Procter street in Gloucester, where he built his home in 1859, is named in allusion to him. Mr. Procter served as general secretary of the 250th anniversary, which was celebrated in 1892 with great success.

On March 15, 1856, Francis Procter married Mary Melissa Rice, born March 14, 1838, daughter of Solomon and Mary Rice, of Marlboro, Massachusetts. Mrs. Procter passed away July 2, 1907, in her sixty-ninth year. Children: 1. Frank Rice, born Gloucester, January 1, 1857; married December 18, 1877, Carrie L., daughter of William C. and Susan (Leach) Rust, of Manchester-by-the-Sea; children, born in Gloucester: Ethel, born April 11, 1879, died November 14, 1903; Edna, born July 5, 1881; Vera, born December 25, 1887, died August 30, 1888; Narda, born July 16, 1892. 2. George Perkins, born Gloucester, October 17, 1859, died October 18, 1860. 3. William Allen, born in Gloucester, October 28, 1860; married July 5, 1883, Geneva W., daughter of Cephas and Tabitha Smith, of Rockport; children: Marian, born Gloucester, January 18, 1887; Carleton S., born Gloucester, November 6, 1891. 4. Mary Melissa, born Gloucester, July 23, 1873; married October 24, 1900, George V. Fisher, son of George and Sarah (Marchant) Fisher.

(VIII) George Henry Procter, managing editor of the Gloucester *Daily Times*, and for more than half a century the active editorial head of the several newspapers published by the firm of Procter Brothers, and the subsequently incorporated company of the same name, was born in Gloucester July 4, 1835, youngest surviving child of Francis Epes Procter. When a boy in school he worked evenings in his brother's news store, and carried newspapers in the town, traveling on foot from "the cut" to Eastern Point on Rocky Neck. When a little older he was apprenticed to learn the trade of tinsmithing, with a reservation of a fourth of his time for the purpose of attending school, but later on he gave up the trade and took charge of the outside work of his brother's business. In 1854 he became partner with his brother under the firm name of Procter Brothers. He was editor of *Procter's Able Sheet,* of which mention is made in a preceding paragraph, and he has been editor of each of the papers, monthly, semimonthly, weekly and daily, which have been published by the firm in all later years. Mr. Procter is counted among the oldest newspaper editors in active service in New England, having filled the editorial chair for somthing more than half a century. In journalistic circles he is well known, and as a writer on all general subjects his editorials have attracted attention by reason of their logic and strength, and his evident capacity of fervent analysis displayed in them. A Republican himself, his papers have been conducted on an independent basis so far as party politics is concerned, but he never has been known to occupy a neutral position on any important question of national or state politics. His papers always have been kept clean, free from sensationalism, but he has given the news of the day and commented on it in a way calculated to awaken public interest rather than to arouse passion or prejudice. In the early part of his career as a newspaper man Mr. Procter was for a time in seriously impaired health, and in 1858, on the advice of his physician, spent a part of that and the following year in Surinam, South America, and while there he wrote several articles on subjects of importance to Gloucester commercial interests. He has not taken a conspicuous part in Gloucester politics, having little inclination in that direction, although he did serve two years in the common council. On nearly all public occasions he has taken an active part and was a member of the literary committee on the celebration of the 250th anniversary of the incorporation of the town of

George H. Procter.

Gloucester; also on Gloucester Day in 1907, and frequently has served on Fourth of July celebration committees. For several years he served as historian of the Massachusetts Press Association. Mr. Procter has been a Master Mason since 1856. In religious preference he has been a Universalist, the greater portion of his life, but is now investigating Christian Science. He married, December 23, 1856, Sarah Steele, born August 3, 1838, daughter of James and Sarah D. Steele. Children: 1. Annie S., born in Gloucester, November 22, 1857; married Bryant G. Smith; children, all born in Boston: Infant, born September 10, 1878, died same day; Kenneth Procter Smith, born September 5, 1879; Mary Bates Smith, born December 30, 1884; Conrad Alaric Smith, born June 20, 1887; Sarah Procter Smith, born October 11, 1889; Gladys Louise Smith, born June 1, 1893. 2. George Henry, Jr., born April 5, 1860; married October 12, 1889, Emily D. Jones; one child. 3. Eddie, born August 30, 1862, died September 9, 1862. 4. Frances Mens, born February 23, 1866; married January 14, 1889, John J. Stanwood; children: Barnard Lewis Stanwood, born July 17, 1890; Marjorie Procter Stanwood, born February 19, 1892; Philip Stanwood, born July 22, 1893. 4. Mabel Bigelow, born August 20, 1868; married July 29, 1889, Gardner W. Tarr; one child: Donald Procter Tarr, born October 31, 1890. 5. John Murray, born November 10, 1870, died February 9, 1871. 6. James Lester, born April 25, 1876; married September 3, 1900, Elizabeth Clark Burt; one child: Alonzo, born June 24, 1901.

(For ancestry see preceding sketch.)

PROCTER

(VI) Joseph Procter, third child and second son of Joseph and Elizabeth (Epes) Procter, born in Gloucester, June 27, 1772, died there October 21, 1842. He appears to have been a substantial man in the town, and followed the excellent example of his father in his business life, as well as in town affairs, the records showing that he was selectman of Gloucester 1808-9. It is believed that he engaged extensively in the fishing business, and also that he had an interest if not the sole proprietorship in the old rope walk on the shore not far from his residence. He married, February 7, 1801, Elizabeth Piper, born January 17, 1777, died June 24, 1863. Children: 1. Joseph Johnston, born July 2, 1802, died September 2, 1846. 2. Mary, born September 20, 1804, died July 2, 1888. 3. John Piper, born February 23, 1807, died September 1, 1891. 4. Addison, born August 27, 1809, died October 29, 1883. 5. Infant son, born and died January 11, 1811. 6. Elizabeth, born February 5, 1813, died January 5, 1817. 7. Martha, born December 17, 1815. 8. Elizabeth, born October 20, 1823, died November 18, 1848.

(VII) Joseph Johnston Procter, eldest child of Joseph Procter, was born in Gloucester, at his father's house down in the "Cut," July 2, 1802, and died September 2, 1848, at the age of forty-six years. As early as the year 1829 he established himself in the fishing business on the site now occupied by his grandson, Joseph Osborne Procter, and conducted it for many years, until about the time of his death in the prime of his manhood, just when he had succeeded in laying the foundation of a substantial fortune; but his untimely taking off placed the burden of responsibility on his eldest son, Joseph Osborne Procter, who assumed charge of the business just before he had attained his majority. On June 17, 1826, Joseph J. Proctor married Eliza Ann Gilbert, born July 18, 1805, died March 24, 1887. Their children: 1. Eliza Ann, born November 22, 1827; married November 25, 1852. 2. Joseph Osborne, born May 4, 1829, died September 5, 1904. 3. David Ranney, born October 1, 1830; married February 24, 1851. 4. Ellen Maria, born August 10, 1832; married November 17, 1850. 5. Sarah Augusta, born July 14, 1834; married October 6, 1854. 6. Martha Jane, born April 8, 1836, died August 25, 1853. 7. Addison Gilbert, born July 29, 1838; married July 10, 1860. 8. Lucy Elizabeth, born January 11, 1840; married January 5, 1859. 9. Mary Adelia, born August 25, 1842; married November 17, 1861. 10. William Otis, born October 12, 1844; married June 16, 1864. 11. Howard, born June 6, 1847, died September 16, 1848.

(VIII) Joseph Osborne Procter, second son and child of Joseph Johnston Procter and Eliza Ann Gilbert, his wife, was born in Gloucester, Massachusetts, May 4, 1829, and died suddenly in that city, September 5, 1904. With his daughters Ella and Adeline he had attended a house party at Long Beach, and while there suffered an attack of acute indigestion. He rallied, however, and was being taken to his summer home when he was stricken with apoplexy and died almost immediately.

For many years Mr. Procter was prominent among the men engaged in the vast Gloucester fisheries, and in many respects was one of the most representative business men of the city. Having succeeded his father in business upon the death of the latter in 1848, he continued it until January, 1878, and then passed it over to his son. He often had as many as fifteen vessels engaged in the fishing business and employed about one hundred and fifty men. In 1852 Mr. Procter was elected a director of the Gloucester Mutual Fishing Insurance Company, and for the next twenty years exercised a dominant influence in the management of that company, having been its president and treasurer during the last fifteen years of that period. For fourteen years he was a director of the Holyoke Mutual Fire Innsurance Company of Salem, and for two years its treasurer. From 1858 to 1862 he was a director of the old Bank of Cape Ann, and in 1864 was one of the organizers of the First National Bank of Gloucester, a member of its first board of directors, serving in that capacity until 1896, and being president of the bank during the last sixteen years of that time. He was a charter member of the Gloucester Water Supply Company and its president from the time of organization. He also was vice-president of the Gloucester Electric Company, a director of the Gloucester Net and Twine Company, and the first president of the Gloucester Board of Trade, serving in that capacity from 1866 to 1890. In religion Mr. Procter was strictly orthodox; and having united with what is now Trinity Congregational Church in 1858, he was for several years a member of its standing committee, three years treasurer, twenty-eight years clerk, and for more than thirty years superintendent of the Sunday school, librarian, teacher or secretary. He took an active part in the promotion of the Gloucester Young Men's Christion Association, was always liberal in its support, and was honored by being selected to turn the first shovelful of earth for the new building on Middle street. He was named one of the trustees of the Sawyer Free Library by the late Samuel E. Sawyer, and for forty years was one of its directors. He also served as a director of the Gloucester Seamen's and Fishermen's Widows' Aid Society, a director and corporate member of the Gloucester Fishermen's Institute, and for a time was president of the latter institution, and he also was a director of the Gloucester Salt Company. In politics Mr. Procter was originally a Whig and later a firm Republican; and he was a member of the convention at Worcester which gave birth to the Republican party in Massachusetts. Frequently he was a delegate to state and county conventions, a member and chairman of the Gloucester board of selectmen in 1868 and 1869, county commissioner from 1874 to 1880, being chairman of the board during the last three years. He was appointed by Mayor Andrews a member of the park commission on the organization of that body in 1896 and continued as a member until 1902.

At the Procter family gathering held March 3, 1868, in commemoration of the one hundredth anniversary of the wedding day of its progenitors, Mr. Procter took an active part as chairman of the preliminary meetings and also furnished the genealogy of the family, which was published in pamphlet. He was the first civilian elected an honorary member of Colonel Allen Post No. 25, Grand Army of the Republic, and did much work to aid the post in its charitable and benevolent work.

Few men in Gloucester have done more for their native city than Joseph Osborne Procter. Possessed of a high order of executive ability and business talent, together with an energetic will, with untiring industry and perseverance, he had the faculty of doing an immense amount of clerical labor with little apparent effort. Left at an early age by the death of his father in charge of a large business, he assumed burdens which developed his latent energies and helped in the formation of a character which shone to advantage all along his pathway in life as an energetic public spirited citizen who gained the respect of his fellow men and whose presence has been greatly missed in the community in which he lived so long and so well.

Mr. Procter married first, November 28, 1849, Lydia Ann Gaffney, born November 28, 1828, died December 3, 1852, by whom he had one child, Ella Lucinda, born September 13, 1850. He married second, October 14, 1853, Martha Ann Morse, born December 3, 1825, died February 15, 1860, who bore him two children: Joseph Osborne, born July 26, 1854, and Martha Ann, born February 1, 1860, died August 12, 1860. He married third, September 11, 1860, Lucy Anna Evans, born November 7, 1828, died April 24, 1904, by whom he had two children: Annie Burroughs, born December 17, 1862, died December 19, 1862; Adeline Winthrop, born December 2, 1871.

(IX) Joseph Osborne Procter, son of Joseph O. and Martha Ann (Morse) Procter, was born in Gloucester, July 26, 1854, and received his education in the public and high schools of that city. When not in the schoolroom his time was generally occupied with some kind of work in connection with his father's business affairs, and when he reached the age of twenty-two years he succeeded his father and became sole owner and manager of the Gloucester Mackerel Company, an important element of the Gloucester fisheries in general, and which under his proprietorship has become one of the most extensive enterprises of its kind on the Atlantic coast, while to-day Mr. Procter himself is the largest handler of salt mackerel in the entire country. In respect to his capacity to build up and successfully direct a large business undertaking Mr. Procter is much like his father, but otherwise is differently constituted, in that his business methods and domestic habits are more conservative; and while he is not in any respect wanting in what is usually called progressive public spirit, he much prefers the comfort and congenial associations of home rather than the distractions of politics or monetary investments in enterprises which demand constant personal attention, frequently at the sacrifice of the rightful claims of home and family upon his time. He is a thorough Republican, but never has allowed himself to become actively identified with the political life of his home city beyond the natural requirements of good citizenship. With his family he enjoys both domestic and foreign travel, an indulgence which to all of them has been found a source of educational improvement as well as of pleasure.

On December 5, 1876, Mr. Procter married Florence Cunningham, daughter of Sylvester and Mary P. (Tarr) Cunningham; Mary P. Tarr was a daughter of William and Sarah (Knutsford) Tarr, and granddaughter of Nehemiah and ——— (Parsons) Cunningham. Mr. and Mrs. Procter have five children; all born in Gloucester: 1. Mabel D., born June 12, 1878; married James C. Tate, of Kansas City, Missouri; children: Florence Procter Tate and Frances Marshall Tate. 2. Joseph Osborne, born September 17, 1880; graduated from Harvard College, A. B., 1901; Harvard Law School, LL. B., *cum laude*, 1904; now in practice in Boston. 3. Helen Mansfield, born July 2, 1885. 4. Richard Cunningham, born March 3, 1891. 5. Dorothy Knutsford, born September 29, 1893.

IVERS The Ivers family came to New England about 1720 with the pioneer Scotch settlers from the north of Ireland. It is likely that the family is English in origin, but like all the Protestants from Ulster Province, Ireland, came to be called Scotch-Irish. Doubtless several generations had intermarried with the Scotch families in Ireland.

(I) We find two settlers in Boston. William Ivers married in Boston, April 28, 1724, Jane Barber. The Presbyterian minister officiated. His son William married (intention dated December 28, 1750) Sarah Flagg, of Boston. Gregory Ivers married within about a month of his brother William, Elizabeth Green, March 23, 1724, and their son Gregory married, February 19, 1755, Elizabeth Ivers, probably a sister of Gregory, and William Ivers, married August 17, 1737, at Boston, Elizabeth Green. All were Presbyterians. The name is found nowhere else in this country before the revolution. Owing to the defective condition of the Boston records it is impossible to give complete information of the early generations. The family of James is the most complete.

(II) James Ivers, son of William Ivers (1), born in Boston, about 1730; married, August 18, 1753, at Boston, Hannah Trecothick. He was a wealthy merchant, owning land on Chardon street, Ivers street, Vine street, where he resided; Green's Wharf; store on Broad street; brick store in Merchant's Row; a sugar house and a distillery. He died August 5, 1812. His estate was finally divided September 15, 1823. The widow's brother Barlow Trecothick is mentioned. Children, born in Boston: 1. James, born July 7, 1754; married January 14, 1779, Elizabeth Hughes. 2. Hannah, born March 20, 1756; married Jonathan Loring Austin. 3. Jane, born March 17, 1758; married Benjamin Austin. 4. Daughter married James T. Austin (?). Jane Ivers, widow of William Ivers (1), died at Boston, 1789. Her will, dated April 29, 1776, proved April 13, 1789, Captain Job Prince executor; bequeathed to son James, mentioned above, and to Thomas, mentioned below, and his children.

(II) Thomas Ivers, son of William Ivers (1), died 1781, just before his "aged mother" Jane. His will, dated April, 1781, bequeaths to his mother, his wife Mary, and daughters Elizabeth and Ann Ivers. His executors were his wife and Rev. Samuel Parker. He married, September 19, 1776, Mary Cutler at Boston.

(III) Samuel Ivers, grandson of Gregory (1), and doubtless son of William Ivers (2); married at Boston, April 11, 1784, Mary Brazier; second, August 9, 1807, Mary Nanning (Manning?). No record of his estate or death has been found.

(IV) Samuel Ivers, doubtless son of Samuel (3), born in Boston, about 1795, died 1869. He received his early education in the public schools of Boston. He came to Dedham when a young man, and lived a number of years, removing later to Cambridge and finally to Somerville, Massachusetts, where he died. He was a carpenter and cabinet-maker by trade, and became a contractor and builder. In his later years he was engaged in the retail furniture business. He married Caroline Fuller. Children: 1. George, married Eunice White, of Kennebunkport, Maine; four children, all deceased. 2. William H., born April 30, 1822; mentioned below. 3. Caroline, married James Hunniwell (Honeywell?); still living at Cambridge; children: i. James; ii. Frank Hunniwell. 4. Samuel, died 1905; married first, Jane Goby; second, Elizabeth Perkins; daughter Ella living at New Bedford. 5. Francis, married first, Sarah Porter; one child, Carrie; second, Grace Haywood; one son, Francis Haywood, married Levina Sidney Norton, of Nashua, N. H.; children: i. Leonie; ii. Grace. 6. Warren, married Jennie Lovejoy.

(V) William H. Ivers, son of Samuel Ivers (4), was born in Dedham, April 30, 1822. He was reared in Dedham and educated in the public schools of that town. When thirteen years old he found employment in Boston as clerk in a retail grocery store, and was thus employed for five years. He then returned to Dedham and worked at cabinet-making for his father. Later he engaged in the business of cabinetmaking on his own account in Dedham. He went to Cambridge with his father, and thence to Roxbury, where he worked at his trade, cabinetmaker, manufacturing and finishing chairs. In 1846 he went to work in the Chickering piano factory, and for the next twenty-five years was employed by the Chickerings in various positions of responsibility. In 1871 and 1872 he was with the Hallett & Davis Piano Company. He resigned his position to begin the manufacture of pianos on his own account, in 1871, at Dedham, with a limited capital and upon a very modest scale. His pianos found a ready sale on account of his superior workmanship and good taste, and his little business developed rapidly. He interested some capitalists and formed the now famous firm of Ivers & Pond Company. From year to year the business increased until it became one of the largest in New England. The pianos and organs manufactured by Mr. Ivers's house have the highest standing for every quality that counts in a musical instrument. In the perfection of their pianos this company has kept in the foremost ranks. Owing to his age, Mr. Ivers sold out his interests and retired from the company in 1897. The business continues under the old name, and is still flourishing. The factory is at Cambridgeport, and the main offices are at Boylston street, Boston. Mr. Ivers resided in Dedham for more than fifty years in his home which he bought in 1855. It was called the old Howe homestead before he owned it. He was a member of the Unitarian Church of Dedham; a member of the Masonic fraternity, and politically was a Republican. He married April 22, 1845, Lucy Jane Allen, born in Roxbury, September 30, 1825, daughter of John White and Camelia (Knight) Allen. Her father was born in 1796, and died in 1844; his children: Mary Allen, Frances Allen, Caroline Allen, Lucy Allen, Hannah Allen, John Allen, Alice Allen. Children of William and H. Ivers: 1. William H. Jr.; married Nancy Jane Wilkinson (nee Hayes); child: Jeanne. 2. Charles Francis, married first, Martha Dunham Chapman; second, Lavinia Vynal; children of first wife: Helen Louise, Hester Adelaide. 3. Lucy Adelaide; married William E. Pedrick; daughter Mary Alice. 4. Jane Amelia; married George Ingalls; daughter, Lucy Eleanor. William H. Ivers died February 9, 1908.

STONE Within the first quarter of a century following the landing of the Pilgrims at Plymouth in New England there were no less than ten persons of the name John Stone settled in the plantations of the region, and by reason of frequent removals on the part of some of them from one place to another much confusion of names and heads of families has long been a source of annoyance to chroniclers of Stone genealogy.

(I) In speaking of John Stone, the immigrant ancestor of the particular family under consideration here, so good an authority as Savage says that he was of Salem, Massachusetts, in 1636, and "kept the ferry across Bass river at the earliest day," meaning that he was the first keeper of a ferry at that place; that he had a grant of land on the Beverly side in 1637, and was one of the founders of the church in Beverly, June 23, 1667; that he was called John Stone, senior, from which it is supposed that he had a son of the same name, and perhaps other children. The same author also suggests that John Stone may have been a passenger in the "Elizabeth" from London in 1635, when, according to the ship's list of passengers, he was forty years old. There is no doubt of the general correctness of the statements made concerning John Stone, which are narrated in the preceding paragraph, but insomuch as the name of the old pioneer ferryman disappears from the Salem and Beverly records within a few years after he settled there and does not again appear until he is mentioned in connection with founding the Beverly church in 1667, it is well to quote what is written of this John Stone in one of the more recent Stone genealogies:

John Stone came to Salem, Massachusetts, in April, 1635, from Hawkhurst, Kent county, England, in the "Elizabeth," remained there for some time plying a ferry between Salem and Beverly, and finally removed to Guilford, Connecticut. This appears to account for the absence of his name from the Salem and Beverly records after the term of his ferry lease had expired, but it has been questioned whether the John Stone who helped establish the Beverly church was John the immigrant, or John his son, although in the list of original members the name is plainly written John Stone, sen.

The name of John Stone in early Salem and Beverly history figures most prominently in connection with the establishment of the first ferry across Bass river, which was done in pursuance of an agreement with the town of Salem, entered into on December 26, 1636. "It is agreed that John Stone shall keepe a ferry, to begin this day, betwixt his home on the neck vpon the north point and Cape Ann side, and shall giue diligent attendance therevpon dureing the space of three years, vnless he shall giue just occation to the contrary, and in consideracon thereof, he is to haue two pence from a stranger and one penny from an inhabitant. Moreover, the said John Stone doth promise to provide a convenient boat for the said purpose, betwixt this and the first month next coming after the date hereof." In 1639 the ferry lease was given to William Dexey, to continue for three years.

The name of the wife of John Stone, the elder, does not appear, but he had a son John, who died in 1691, leaving a widow Abigail. He had also a daughter Abigail and perhaps other children whose names do not appear.

(II) John Stone, son of John Stone, senior, married Abigail ———, and had a son Samuel.

(III) Samuel Stone, son of John and Abigail Stone, born Beverly, about 1658, died November 23, 1717, aged about fifty-nine years. He married, March 11, 1683-84, Elizabeth Herrick, and had, according to the published records of Beverly, six children: 1. Zachariah, born May 22, 1685. 2. Samuel, born April 15, 1687, drowned in Squam river in 1743. 3. John, born May 3, 1689. 4. Robert, born April 28, 1692. 5. Abigail, born November 17, 1695. 6. Elizabeth, born August 1, 1698.

(IV) Robert Stone, son of Samuel and Elizabeth (Herrick) Stone, born Beverly, April 28, 1692, married, January 23, 1723, Elizabeth Elliot. She was a granddaughter of Andrew Elliot, the first town clerk of Beverly and who died March 1, 1703-04, aged seventy-six years. Robert and Elizabeth (Elliot) Stone had (according to the published vital records of Beverly) three children: 1. Robert, born September 27, 1725, drowned in Squam river, December 7, 1743. 2. John, born September 8, 1728, see forward. 3. Zacharias, born October 2, 1731.

(V) John Stone, son of Robert and Elizabeth (Elliot) Stone, born Beverly, September 8, 1728, married, February 18, 1752, Hannah Rea. She was born in Beverly, September 13, 1732, and was a daughter of John and Hannah (Brown) Rea. The names and number of their children are not known, but they had a son John Stone.

(VI) John Stone, son of John and Hannah (Rea) Stone, born Beverly, April 1, 1755, died there January 22, 1832. He was a soldier of the revolution, having enlisted twice during the war, and on one occasion served under Washington's command at Harlem Heights in the province of New York. He married, June 28, 1755, Hannah Obear (Ober), who died October 24, 1846, aged eighty-nine years, six months, daughter of Captain James and Lydia (Cleaves) Ober. Children of John and Hannah (Ober) Stone: 1. Molly, born March 28, 1776, married ——— Edwards. 2. John, born January 1, 1778, died at sea, November 16, 1801. 3. Nancy, married Dr. Jones, of Wenham. 4. Hannah, born February 28, 1783, married (first) Captain Groves; (second) Edward Stone. 5. Robert, born March 15, 1785, died March 23, 1846. 6. Ezra. 7. James, born December 4, 1789, see forward. 8. Lydia, born March 11, 1793. 9. Anna, born June 20, 1795. 10. Louisa, born July 14, 1797. 11. Henry, born September 20, 1800.

(VII) James Stone, son of John and Hannah (Ober) Stone, born Beverly, December 4, 1789, died there September 26, 1881, having lived to attain the age of more than ninety years, after a life of hard, earnest and successful work. He early took to the sea, first as a fisherman and from that modest place gradually advanced through his own efforts and enterprise to the ownership of the largest fleet of deep sea fishing vessels that ever put out of the port of Beverly. He was not only a successful man, but he was a thoroughly good man, straightforward in his dealings with others, honest, liberal with his employees, of whom during his long business career there were perhaps thousands, and he often made liberal charitable contributions for the relief of the families of unfortunate fishermen. He always felt a deep interest in the welfare of his native town of Beverly, and served in various offices of local importance. For several years he was a member of the school committee, and for many years was a member of the Unitarian church. Originally he was an old line Whig, and afterward a Republican in politics. On November 13, 1817, James Stone married Lydia Foster, of Beverly, born March 25, 1788, died November 16, 1878. She was a daughter of Ezra T. and Sarah (Stickney) Foster. Sarah (Stickney) Foster was born March 31, 1754, the youngest but one of fourteen children of Deacon William Stickney, of Billerica, Massachusetts, who was born in Bradford, Massachusetts, October 14, 1704-05, and died August 27, 1781. He was brought up in the family of his grandfather, David Hazeltine, of Bradford, his own father having died when William was about two years old, and returned to live with his mother after her marriage with Samuel Hunt, of Billerica.

William Stickney was a prominent man in his day, and when about eighteen years old (July, 1722) was a servant to Joshua Abbot and served under Sergeant Jonathan Butterfield during the early Indian wars. He was deacon of the Church of Christ in Billerica as early as 1751 and performed various important offices in the church, having been its clerk from 1760 to 1763, moderator in 1762, and frequently a delegate from his church to ecclesiastical conventions. He was town clerk of Billerica twelve years, selectman as early as 1747, representative to the general court, and justice of the peace and quorum as early as 1765. He represented Billerica in the first provincial congress at Salem in 1774, at Cambridge and Watertown in 1775, and in 1776 was one of a committee in Billerica in behalf of the general court to purchase soldiers clothing for the army. He married twice. His first wife, whom he married in June, 1729, was Ann Whiting, who died March 26, 1749, and he married (second), November 23, 1749, Hannah Abbott, widow of Jeremiah Abbott and whose maiden name was Hannah Ballard. She died February 17, 1789.

Deacon William Stickney, father of William Stickney, was the second of three sons of William and Anna (Hazeltine) Stickney, who married in Bradford, Massachusetts, September 14, 1701. He was born in Bradford, January 27, 1674, and died there February 21, 1706, aged thirty-two years. He was a son of Lieutenant Samuel Stickney, who was born in England in 1633, came with his father to this country in 1638, settling first at Boston and afterward at Rowley, Massachusetts. He was selectman of Bradford eight years, constable in 1676, took the oath of fidelity in 1678, the freeman's oath in 1682, and represented Bradford in the general court in 1689-90. He is mentioned as lieutenant in the Bradford records in 1691, grand juror in 1697 and tythingman in 1704. He married (first), in Rowley, February 18, 1653-54, Julia Swan, and married (second), April 6, 1674, Mrs. Prudence Gage, whose family name was Leaver.

Lieutenant Samuel Stickney was the eldest son and child of William Stickney, who was baptized in St. Mary's church, Frampton, Lincolnshire, England, September 6, 1592, and came from Hull, Yorkshire, to America in 1637, with his wife Elizabeth and three children—Samuel, Amos and Mary—and was one of the original settlers of Rowley. He was the immigrant ancestor of the Stickney family of the line here briefly mentioned, and was himself a son of William Stickney, of Frampton, baptized 1558, married, June 16, 1585, Margaret Pierson, and grandson of Robert Stickney, of Frampton, who was buried October 18, 1582. Frampton is a parish in the wapentake of Kirton, Lincolnshire, England, and the church there is dedicated to St. Mary. Its parish register contains many records of baptisms, marriages and burials of Stickneys from 1588 to 1609.

Lydia Foster who married James Stone was born in Beverly, March 25, 1788, and died there November 16, 1878. Her father, Ezra Trask Foster, born in Beverly, January 29, 1752, married, October 3, 1784, Sarah Stickney, of whom mention is made in a preceding paragraph. Ezra Trask and Sarah (Stickney) Foster had six children, of whom Lydia was fifth in order of birth.

Ezra Trask Foster was a son of Deacon Joseph Foster, who was born in Ipswich, Massachusetts, February 14, 1714, and died February 27, 1767. He was town clerk, selectman and overseer of the poor, and in 1761 received from the town three pounds for disbursements for the French neutrals. He married, November 12, 1735, Hannah Trask, who died August 11, 1778, having borne her husband twelve children, of whom Ezra Trask Foster was eighth in order of birth.

Deacon Joseph Foster was a son of Joseph Foster, who was born in Ipswich, Massachusetts, September 14, 1680, and died February 22, 1755. He was a cordwainer, attended the South meeting-house in Ipswich and owned one-half of a pew in the gallery. He married (first), January 23, 1704, Elizabeth Goodwin; married (second), August 13, 1712, Mary Cressy, of Salem; married (third), November 30, 1714, widow Mary Brown, whose family name was Linforth. He had in all eleven children, of whom Joseph was third in order of seniority.

Joseph Foster was a son of Deacon Jacob Foster, who was born in England, 1635, died in Ipswich, Massachusetts, July 7, 1710. He was a deacon of the First Church in Ipswich. He married (first), January 12, 1658, Martha Kinsman, who died October 15, 1666, daughter of Robert Kinsman, of Ipswich. He married (second), February 26, 1667, Abigail Lord, who died June 4, 1729. Of his fourteen children Joseph was twelfth in order of birth.

Deacon Jacob Foster was a son of Reginald Foster, who was born in England about 1595, and died in Ipswich, Massachusetts, in 1681. He came from England in 1638 and had a grant of land in Ipswich, April 6, 1641. He brought with him his seven children by his first wife. He married three times, the name of his first wife being unknown. His second wife, Judith ———, died in October, 1664, and he married for his third wife, September 19, 1665, Sarah Martin, widow of John Martin and whose family name was White. She died February 22, 1683. Reginald Foster, of Little Badow, county of Essex, England, belonged to the Fosters of Bamborough and Etherstone Castle, county of Northumberland, England, (see Foster family elsewhere in this work).

James and Lydia (Foster) Stone had four children, all born in Beverly: 1. James W., born September 12, 1821, died August 10, 1901; married Lila E. Long, a southern woman, who was born January 11, 1827, and died August 8, 1905. Their children: Carrie L., born September 12, 1853, married Francis M. Nash and lives in New York City; Lila F., born August 25, 1859, lives in New York City. 2. John, born November 5, 1823, died September 7, 1867; never married. 3. Ezra F., born September 17, 1825, died March 28, 1885; never married. 4. Lydia, born October 23, 1828, lives in Beverly. She is a woman of high educational and social attainments and has taken an earnest interest in benevolent and church work in Beverly for many years.

ARRINGTON For the origin of the name in England, see sketch of the Harrington family in this work. The surnames Arrington, Harrington and Errington are identical in derivation.

(I) Captain James Arrington, doubtless the immigrant, is said to have come from Virginia to Salem. He settled in Salem and married there August 2, 1768, Mary Pickering, sister of Colonel Timothy Pickering. (See Pickering). He married second, September 11, 1783, Mary Abbott. (See Salem records). Children of the first wife: 1. James, born about 1770; mentioned below. 2. Joseph, married, November 27, 1796, Katherine Richards. Perhaps daughters.

(II) Captain James Arrington, son of Captain James Arrington, was born in Salem about 1770, and educated in the public schools. He was a master mariner. He lost his life during a storm at sea, being washed overboard. He was a member of the First Unitarian Church. In politics he was a staunch Whig. He married, March 10, 1797, Deborah (Richards) Scott, widow of George Scott. He died in 1810 and his widow Deborah was appointed guardian of the children July 10, 1810; administratrix July 17, 1810. Children, born in Salem: 1. James, mentioned below. 2. George, born 1804, married Jane Monies; children: i. Mary Jane, died young; ii. Elizabeth, died young; iii. George, died unmarried;

iv. Deborah R.; v. Eliza, married Charles Williams; resides at Salem and has a son George S. Williams. 3. Benjamin, born 1807, followed the sea; died unmarried. 4. Polly, died young. 5. Lydia, born October, 1809, died unmarried.

(III) Captain James Arrington, son of Captain James Arrington, born at Salem, Massachusetts, February 21, 1801, died there July 19, 1866. He was educated in the public school, and at an early age began to follow the sea. He became a prominent ship-master at Salem. In politics he was a Whig, and in religion a Universalist. He was a member of East India Marine Society. Among the vessels he commanded were the "Three Brothers" and "Mary Ann." He married, July 23, 1829, at Salem, Elizabeth R. Arrington, a cousin, born September 10, 1810, died January 30, 1840, daughter of Joseph and Catherine (Richards) Arrington. He married (second) Mary Ann Tufts, daughter of Aaron and Sally (Ward) Tufts. (See Tufts and Ward). Mary Ann Tufts married (first) Benjamin McAllister Richards, a seaman, son of Benjamin and Mary (Fowle) Richards. She had one daughter, Mary A. Richards, born October 1, 1837, married Henry M. Robinson, of Salem, and had two children who died young. The Pickering Genealogy gives among the families from which James Arrington descends (largely through the line of his mother): Arrington, Pickering, Flint, Hobby, Symonds, Browning, Foster, Stuart and Richards. His great-great-grandmother, Jane Hobby, married Benjamin Pickering, grandson of John Pickering (1), the immigrant. He was cousin of Hon. Timothy Pickering, of Washington's cabinet, one of the most prominent men of revolutionary days in Massachusetts. Captain Arrington was one of the best known and most prominent master mariners of Salem, one of the best navigators. He accumulated a comfortable fortune. He was a Whig in politics, and a Unitarian in religion. Children of first wife: 1. Mary, born October 11, 1830, married Edward Pierce; she lives in Brockton. 2. James, born September 10, 1832, married (first) Melinda Bickford; (second) Mary Kimball. 3. Benjamin, born February 21, 1835, died young. 4. Benjamin F., born June 13, 1836, died April 9, 1871; married Lydia Manning, who died December 30, 1870. Children of second wife: 5. Samuel W., born February 10, 1846, died February 9, 1877; married Sarah Jane Morse, who lives in Salem; children: i. Sarah Jane, born July 2, 1868, unmarried; ii. Samuel W., born December 26, 1869, unmarried; iii. James, born January 9, 1872, died young; iv. Mary, born September 2, 1873; v. James, born October 16, 1875, unmarried. 6. Deborah Richards, born May 26, 1847, married Charles H. Allen; no children; they reside in Providence, Rhode Island. 7. Lydia Ward, born March 12, 1849, married William H. Varney, born at Boscawen, New Hampshire, died November 28, 1888; they had no children; widow lives with Philip Payne Pinel Arrington. 8. Zachariah Taylor, born October 1, 1850, married Fannie Stingle, of Digby, Nova Scotia; they live at Lynn; have no children. 9. Philip Payne Pinel, born April 6, 1852, mentioned below. 10. Sally Ward, born March 2, 1854, died July 11, 1905; married George A. Newhall; he lives at Salem; children: i. George E. Newhall, died young; ii. Beatrice Newhall, born July 12, 1889. 11. Helen Marr, born April 1, 1857, died in infancy. 12. Helen Marr, born January 29, 1859, married (first) Frederick Frothingham; (second) Charles Alley, of Lynn; child of first marriage, Frederick Herbert Frothingham, born June 12, 1882; child of second marriage, Ruth Evelyn Alley, born July 28, 1900; they live in Lynn.

(IV) Philip Payne Pinel Arrington, son of Captain James Arrington (3), was born in Salem, April 6, 1852. He was educated in the public schools there. He has never been in active business, having been occupied in the care of his real estate and other investments. He has lived in the old Arrington home at 6 Andover street, and has always been greatly interested and useful in church work. He is a prominent member and deacon of the First Unitarian Church of Salem, the original church organized in Salem in 1629. In politics Mr. Arrington is non-partisan. He is opposed to machine politics of all kinds and votes for the men whom he prefers regardless of the party nominating them. He is a member of no lodge or secret society. He has never married.

(For ancestry see Peter Tufts 1.)

TUFTS (IV) Peter Tufts, son of Peter Tufts, born April 24, 1728, died May 4, 1791, aged sixty-three years. He resided in Charlestown and was taxed there from 1756 to 1770. In his will, dated March 1, and proved May 3, 1791, he mentions his wife and ten children. He married, April 19, 1750, Ann Adams, who died February 7, 1813, aged eighty-four years. Her grave is marked by a headstone. Children, born at Charlestown: 1. Peter, born May 20,

1751, died March 19, 1752. 2. Peter, born January 9, 1753, mentioned below. 3. John, born November 24, 1754. 4. Ann, born January 25, 1757, married Abel Richardson. 5. Elizabeth, born October 23, 1758, married Daniel Swan. 6. Joseph, born July 12, 1760. 7. Lydia, born June 10, 1762, married Rev. Robert Gray. 8. Asa, born July 2, 1764. 9. Thomas, born May 18, 1766. 10. Lucy, born November 12, 1767, married Jacob Osgood. 11. Rebecca, born September 20, 1769, married Nathan Adams. 12. Sarah, married Joseph Adams.

(V) Peter Tufts, son of Peter Tufts, was born in Charlestown, January 9, 1753. He was in the revolution in Captain Benjamin Blaney's company, Colonel Eleazer Brooks' regiment, in 1778, and was in camp seventy-one days. He married, at Cambridge, July 22, 1773, Hannah Adams, who died in 1816, aged sixty. Children, born in Charlestown: 1. Peter, born December 10, 1774. 2. Hannah. 3. Anna, born December 21, 1777, married Isaac Tufts. 4. Thomas. 5. Rebecca. 6. Sally. 7. Aaron, born about 1787, married October 24, 1813, Sarah Ward (See sketch of Ward family herewith). 8. Eliza. 9. Lucretia. 10. Ivory. 11. William.

(For preceding generations see Miles Ward 1.)

WARD

(IV) John Ward, son of Miles Ward (3), was born in Salem, July 7, 1707. He married, September 17, 1734, Hannah Higginson, born November 8, 1712, daughter of Nathaniel and Hannah (Gerrish) Higginson. He married (second), September 14, 1758, Martha Batter, born September 21, 1712, died October 12, 1787, daughter of Edmund and Martha (Pickman) Batter. Children, born in Salem: 1. Hannah, born December 21, 1735, married Samuel Webb. 2. Mary, born August 9, 1737, died May 27, 1740. 3. John, born January 10, 1738, married (first), June 4, 1761, Bethia Archer; (second), October 24, 1784, Molly (Lufkin) Emmerton, widow. 4. Nathaniel, born January 29, 1739. 5. Andrew, born October 6, 1742, mentioned below.

(V) Andrew Ward, son of John Ward, born in Salem, October 6, 1742, died January, 1816. The Pickering Genealogy gives a list of the families from which he is descended as: Ward, Flint, Massey, Wells, Warner, Higginson, Whitfield, Sheafe, Savage, Symmes, Gerrish, Lowell, Ruch and Spooner. He was a soldier in the revolution in the company of Captain Benjamin Ward, Jr., from January 22, 1776, to November 18 following, on coast defense duty at Salem; also in Captain Miles Greenwood's company, Colonel Jacob Gerrish's regiment in 1777-78. He married, May 21, 1773, Sarah Henfield, who died December, 1817, aged sixty-seven years, daughter of Edmund Henfield. Edmund Henfield, born at Salem, was the son of Joseph and Lydia (Baston) Henfield; died in 1794; married Lydia Hardy, born in Salem, 1723, died there March, 1794, daughter of Joseph and Sarah (Pickering) Hardy. Joseph Hardy was a ship-builder on Hardy street, Salem; resided also at Haverhill and Boston; son of Joseph and Mary (Grafton) Hardy; left no descendants in the male line. Lieutenant John Pickering, father of Sarah (Pickering) Hardy, was son of the immigrant John Pickering (See sketch of the Pickering family); was born at Salem in 1637 and resided there on his farm; was selectman, constable in 1664, on committee to determine the Lynn line in 1664, collector of subscriptions for Harvard College, signed the protest against various imposts in 1668, ensign of the military company in King Philip's war and took part in the battle of Bloody Brook.

Children of Edmund and Lydia (Hardy) Henfield: 1. Joseph Henfield, died March 1, 1809, aged sixty-six years. 2. Lydia Henfield, baptized May 13, 1744, married George Chapman, July 2, 1764. 3. Edmund Henfield, born at Salem, drowned; married Mary Bendle. 4. Sarah Henfield, married Andrew Ward; mentioned above. 5. Mary Henfield, married Joshua Goodall, baptized June 17, 1753. 6. John Henfield. 7. Martha Henfield, married David Neal. 8. Jonathan Henfield, married ——— Dowst. 9. Ruth Henfield, married John Chapman. Children of Andrew and Sarah (Henfield) Ward: 1. Andrew, married, November 18, 1798, Betsey Bowman. 2. Nathaniel, drowned March 31, 1824, aged forty-nine, light-house keeper at Baker Island; married Mary Cutler. 3. John, died October 18, 1821, aged forty years; married Lucy How. 4. Samuel, prominent citizen, representative to the general court. 5. Sarah, married, October 24, 1813, Aaron Tufts (See sketch of the Tufts family herewith). 6. Lydia, married (first) ——— Scagel; (second) Moses Smith.

(For preceding generations see John Pickering 1.)

PICKERING

(IV) William Pickering, son of Benjamin Pickering (3), was born at Salem. He was a cordwainer by trade. His will was dated February 16, 1765, and proved March 18 following, bequeathing to two sons, John and William, his shoemaking tools, etc.; to two daughters, Hannah Foster and Abigail Scollay; and to his wife Eunice who had the whole estate during life. He married Eunice (Pickering) Neale, widow of Joseph Neale, daughter of John Pickering (3) mentioned below. Children of William and Eunice Pickering: 1. Rev. John, baptized January 2, 1738-39, died October 27, 1823; married Hannah Ingersoll, daughter of Nathaniel Ingersoll. 2. William, born at Salem, died at Warwick, Massachusetts; removed to Richmond, New Hampshire, and later to Warwick; married Philadelphia Kempton, born at Richmond, daughter of Stephen and Catherine (Boyce) Kempton. 3. Hannah, baptized February 8, 1740-41, died October, 1801, aged sixty; married Joseph Foster; second, Joseph Lakeman; third, David Masury, of Salem. 4. Abigail, baptized June 12, 1743, died March 28, 1808, married James Scollay; second, William Baldwin. 5. Mary, baptized at Salem, June 12, 1743, probably died at Salem; married James Arrington. (See sketch of Arrington family. Colonel Timothy Pickering's sister did not marry an Arrington).

(III) John Pickering, son of John Pickering (2), and grandson of John Pickering, immigrant, was a farmer in Salem; admitted to the church in his native town, December 16, 1688. He inherited the homestead and became a prominent citizen of Salem; was selectman from 1710 to 1716 inclusive and deputy to the general court 1714-16-17. He was prosperous and left a goodly estate. His death was caused by cancer of the face. He was buried in the private yard of the Pickering family where his grave is marked by a stone. He died June 19, 1722, the inscription on the stone being wrong. He married Sarah Burrill, of the "royal family of Salem", as the Burrills were nicknamed on account of the prominence of the family.

George Burrill, immigrant, was her grandfather; he came to Lynn before 1637 soon after the first settlement and lived on the west side of Tower Hill where he owned two hundred acres or more; married, in Boston, 1626, Mary Cooper; children: i. Francis Burrill, born 1626, died 1704; ii. John Burrill, mentioned below; iii. George Burrill, died 1698.

Captain John Burrill, father of Sarah Burrill, and son of George Burrill, was a prominent citizen of Lynn; selectman, deputy to the general court; lived on Tower Hill also; married Lois Ivory, born 1631, died June 24, 1703, daughter of Thomas Ivory; will dated August 14, 1703; children: i. John Burrill, born December 15, 1658; ii. Sarah Burrill, born August 6, 1661, married John Pickering, mentioned above; iii. Thomas, born March 7, 1663-64; iv. Anna Burrill, born November 15, 1666-67; v. Theophilus Burrill. vi. Lois Burrill, born March 27, 1671-72; vii. Samuel Burrill, born 1674; viii. Mary Burrill, born April 18, 1676-77, died December 26, 1694; ix. Ebenezer, born September 13, 1679, married Martha Farrington; x. Ruth Burrill, born July 17, 1682, married Benjamin Potter.

Children of John and Sarah (Burrill) Pickering: 1. John, baptized February 6, 1688. 2 Lydia, drowned October 14, 1704. 3. Rev. Theophilus, baptized September 29, 1700, graduate of Harvard, 1719, settled at Chebacco. 4. Deacon Timothy, had father's homestead, baptized February 14, 1702-03; was father of Colonel Timothy Pickering of Washington's cabinet, one of the most famous men of the revolution and subsequent days. 5. Lois, baptized September 22, 1683, married Timothy Orne, baptized 1683, son of Joseph Orne, and grandson of John Horne or Orne, of Salem, a celebrated family. 6. Sarah, married Joseph Hardy, of Salem. 7. Eunice, mentioned below.

(IV) Eunice Pickering, daughter of John Pickering (3), was baptized in Salem, November 17, 1705. She married first, Joseph Neale, fisherman; second, William Pickering, mentioned above. She bequeathed to her children. Children of first husband: i. Emma Neale, baptized May 28, 172—, married Benjamin Bacon; ii. Mary Neale, baptized April 5, 1730, married John Foster and second, John Cleveland. Children of second husband—see William Pickering (4) above.

ALLEY

Hugh Alley Sr. was one of the earliest and most prominent settlers at Nahant and the only one who kept his home there in opposition to the decree of Lynn that it should be "sown down to English grass, and that no house should be left standing", as a final settlement of the fierce controversy raging as to the proprietorship of the land at Nahant.

(I) The first that is known of Hugh Alley is in 1635, when at the age of twenty-seven years he embarked, a "no subsidy" man, from Stepney parish in England, in the ship "Abigail" bound for New England. In company with him were Henry and Ann Collins with three children—Henry, John and Margery. He must have settled at Nahant as early as

1647 or 1648, as six of his children were born there. By the depositions of various individuals who testified in the contest over the Nahant lands, is shown that one Thomas Graves was the first inhabitant of Nahant, and Hugh Alley the second, and that his house and barn were standing in 1673 or 1674. His homestead was a most desirable dwelling place, with the bounty of land and sea at its very doors. He served in the Pequot war, as by deposition of Benjamin Collins and others, "the land now in controversie, called the Hope Well, was given to Hugh Alley for his services in the Pequot war". It would seem that they were a sturdy fighting family, for his son Solomon was killed afterward in King Philip's war. Hugh Alley died January 25, 1674. He married, 1641, Mary Graves, who came from England with her sister Joanna Graves in the ship "Hopewell", which arrived in Salem in September, 1635; these two were children of Thomas Graves, as they went to Nahant where Graves was settled. Children of Hugh and Mary Alley: 1. Mary, born January 6, 1641-2; married June 6, 1667, John Linsey. 2. John, November 30, 1646; married August 15, 1670, Joanna Furnill. 3. Martha, July 31, 1649; married, 1671, James Mills. 4. Sarah, April 15, 1651; married "beginning of August", 1668, Eleazer Linsey, a brother of John Linsey, who married Mary, see above. 5. Hugh, born May 15, 1653 (see post). 6. Solomon, born August 2, 1656; located in Deerfield, Massachusetts; one of Captain Lothrop's company, "the flower of Essex", and was killed at Bloody Brook, September 18, 1675. 7. Hannah, born June 1, 1661, died August 30, 1674. 8. Jacob, born September 5, 1663, died January 25, 1674.

(II) Hugh Alley, second son and fifth child of Hugh Alley, was born in Lynn, October 13, 1653. He was a weaver by trade, and spent his life in his native town, Lynn. He married, December 9, 1681, Rebecca Hood, who survived him and was his widow in 1722. He divided his estate between his wife Rebecca and his children in 1712. Children, born in Lynn: 1. Solomon, born October 11, 1682; killed in the Pequot war. 2. Jacob, January 28, 1683; perhaps died before 1712. 3. Eleazer, November 1, 1686; perhaps died before 1712. 4. Hannah, August 16, 1689; unmarried in 1712. 5. Richard, July 31, 1691; living in 1712. 6. Joseph, June 22, 1693; died in autumn 1767; lived in Lynn, a shipwright by trade; married first, Hepzibah Newhall, January 14, 1724-5; second, Anna Johnson, December 10, 1755. 7. Benjamin, February 24, 1695 (see post). 8. Samuel, died between March 3 and November 2, 1767; married December 12, 1728, Abigail Basset; housewright by trade, also fisherman several years.

(III) Benjamin Alley, sixth son and seventh child of Hugh and Rebecca (Hood) Alley, was born in Lynn, February 24, 1695. He was a farmer and fisherman, and lived in Lynn. He married first, Elizabeth Newhall, of Lynn (published September 26, 1717). She was living in 1741. He married second, Hannah Hart, of Lynn (published March 20, 1742-3). He made his will May 19, 1756, and it was proved June 21, 1756. His wife Hannah survived him. Children, born in Lynn: 1. Jacob, September 19, 1719 (see post). 2. Solomon, born January 2, 1721; married Rebecca ———, both living in 1771; he was a fisherman and lived in Lynn. 3. Eleazer, April 16, 1723; lived in Lynn; shipwright, 1749; married Tabitha Ingalls, of Lynn (published September 20, 1747); was living in 1756. 4. Richard, October 9, 1726; perhaps died young. 5. Hannah, July 28, 1728, died before 1756; married March 22, 1749-50, John Ingalls of Lynn. 6. Benjamin, April 9, 1731; of Boston; shipwright, 1749; living in 1756. 7. John, March 25, 1738; died in Lynn, March 10, 1807; married, before 1762, Sarah Hood, of Lynn; she was living in 1799; he was first a cordwainer, afterward a yeoman. 8. Abner, twin, February 18, 1741; married May 25, 1762, Sarah Webber; he was called cordwainer, but went to sea in 1778 and believed to have been lost. 9. Elizabeth, twin with Abner, married November 1, 1757, John Richards.

(IV) Jacob Alley, eldest child of Benjamin and Elizabeth (Newhall) Alley, was born in Lynn, Massachusetts, September 19, 1719. He was yeoman and cordwainer, and lived in Lynn, succeeding his father on the homestead, on corner of Sea and Market streets, present site of Boston and Revere Beach Railroad, Lynn. He married Huldah Newhall, of Lynn, June 26, 1753, but there is a question if he did not marry, for first wife, Mary Provender, of Lynn, February 21, 1738-9. He was still living in 1773. Administration upon his estate was granted April 28, 1777. His wife Huldah Newhall survived him, and died April 22, 1808. His children: 1. Jacob, living in Sherburne, Nantucket county, 1780; Quaker; shipwright; eldest son born 1777. 2. Timothy, born October 10, 1760 (see post). 3. Jerusha, born about 1764; married William Richards, of Lynn (published June 5, 1785). 4. Benjamin, born about 1765; cordwainer, lived in Lynn;

married February 1, 1785, Sarah Graves, of Lynn; died July 5, 1842, aged seventy-seven. 5. Solomon, born about 1768, died January 19, 1829, aged sixty years; was a blacksmith, lived in Lynn; married first, Bethia Hayward (or Howard) of Danvers (published March 18, 1792), who died December 1, 1794, aged twenty-six years; married second, June 10, 1796, Rachel Berry, of Lynn, who was living in 1828.

(V) Timothy Alley, second son and child of Jacob and Huldah (Newhall) Alley, born October 10, 1760, died December 16, 1850, aged ninety years. He lived in Lynn, and was a cordwainer. He married, April 8, 1787, Abigail Witt, of Lynn, born October 9, 1763, died 1834, on her seventy-first birthday. Children, born in Lynn: 1. Nabby, July 31, 1788, died May 1, 1838; married John D. Pecker, of Salisbury, born September 2, 1784, died January 16, 1865. 2. Sally, February 26, 1790, married Aaron Newhall. 3. Lydia, December 28, 1791, died July 24, 1792. 4. Timothy (3), April 30, 1793, see forward. 5. John, March 28, 1795, died November 29, 1865; married Sarah Homan, of Marblehead, died June 12, 1864. 6. Lydia, May 18, 1800, died October 10, 1884; married Benjamin Clifford, born 1795, died April 20, 1842. 7. Jacob Randolph, March 12, 1802, died December 17, 1872; married Tabitha Doliver, born 1801, died August 19, 1855. 8. Reuben, born November 15, 1805; married Hannah Moulton. 9. James, April 6, 1808, died March 25, 1899; married Abigail, daughter of Major Witt.

(VI) Timothy Alley, eldest son and fourth child of Timothy and Abigail (Witt) Alley, born April 30, 1793, died December 16, 1850. Married first, June 4, 1820, Elizabeth S. Follet, died July 8, 1843, daughter of Thomas and Mary Elizabeth Follet, of Marblehead, and who had five children. He married second, January 4, 1844, Widow Sarah Allen Wiggins, daughter of John Woodbury, of Lynn. No children were born of this marriage, but a child was adopted—Sarah Ellen Varney, born February 18, 1843, whose name was changed May 10, 1848. She was wife of N. Everett Silsbee, of Lynn, and is deceased. Children of Timothy and Elizabeth S. (Follet) Alley: 1. Timothy Norval, born February 28, 1823, see forward. 2. Anathasia Maria, born November 28, 1824, died October 16, 1829. 3. Edgar, born November 11, 1831, died November 14, 1831. 4. Edgar, born May 6, 1834, died May 7, 1834. 5. Mary Elizabeth, born April 12, 1839, died December 7, 1868.

(VII) Timothy Norval Alley, eldest child of Timothy and Elizabeth S. (Follet) Alley, was born in Lynn, February 28, 1823, and died May 24, 1887. He was educated at the academy in Lynn, and always lived there, and during his active life was engaged in the pressed leather business. First had a shop at corner of Union and Mailey streets, later next to the old Goodwin factory on Mt. Vernon street, later retired from business. Politically he was a staunch Democrat. His family attended services at the Universalist church in Lynn. He married, January 1, 1852, Harriet Augusta Burrill, born April 9, 1828, died November 26, 1878, daughter of Nathaniel Fuller Burrill, of Lynn. Children: 1. Alden Burrill, born November 6, 1852, died June 3, 1901; married Mary T. Noyes; no children. 2. Lizzie, born May 29, 1855, died in infancy. 3. Charles A., born in Lynn, October 16, 1856; in real estate business in Lynn. 4. Eva Maria, born April 1, 1859, died June 7, 1884; unmarried. 5. Reuben, born March 6, 1863, died April 23, 1865. 6. Addie Horton, born March 24, 1866; unmarried; lives in Lynn.

(VIII) Charles Albert Alley, second son of Timothy Norval and Harriet Augusta (Burrill) Alley, was born in Lynn, Massachusetts, October 16, 1856. He was educated in the common schools of Lynn, also at Johnson's private school, and on completing his studies engaged in cutting shoes for his uncle, Albert B. Ingalls, remaining in his employ between twelve and fifteen years, cutting, packing and finishing shoes. Later he worked at shoe making for different concerns in Lynn for a period of almost a quarter of a century, after which he and his cousin, C. R. Smith, engaged in the manufacture of shoes, continuing until the fire of 1889, when he engaged in the real estate business on his own account, building and developing property, especially the old Burrill farm in Lynn. Mr. Alley is past master of Mt. Carmel Lodge, F and A. M., past high priest Sutton Royal Arch Chapter, and past eminent commander Olivet Commandery, No. 36, K. T.; at present he is secretary of the board of trustees of the Masonic Fraternity of Lynn, member of Bay State Lodge, I. O. O. F.

Mr. Alley married, January 21, 1890, Helen Marr Arrington, born Salem, Massachusetts, January 29, 1859, daughter of James and Mary A. (Tufts) Arrington, natives of Salem. (See Arrington). They have one child, Ruth Evelyn, born Lynn, July 28, 1900. Mrs. Alley had by a former marriage a son, Fred Herbert Frothingham, born Lynn, June 12, 1881, at

Gustavus Attwill

present a salesman for Blodgett, Ordway & Webber at 100 Essex street, Boston, Massachusetts.

ATTWILL Extract from English records: Atwell Family. Lion rampant on one leg. Arms: Argent a pile sable surmounted by four chevrons countershaped. The crest of this family was given to John Atwell, of Manhead, in Devon, by William Camden Clarenceaux, 1614. Four generations given, Fred, John, William, Peter, 1620. Thomas, of Walkhampton, four generations, John Roger, Richard, Tristram, Grace. Richard aged fifty, 1620. Arms: Argent on a chevron sable. Three roses of the field. William Gilbert, View of Devonshire in 1630, by Thomas Westcote, John Atwell, of Kempton and Manhead, historian, born 1567. Attwill of Devonshire: Argent three leopards heads azure. Atwyl: Sable a pile H; a chevron counterchanged same with some others, pat. 1614. Atwill or Atwell: A pile gules, depressed by chevron azure, all within a border ingrailed argent; Devonshire.

(I) John Atwell settled in Casco, Maine, between the years 1630 and 1640, coming from Devonshire in England with John Maine, whose fifth daughter he married. In Maine Historic-Genealogical Records, vol. 2, p. 224, we find Maine's Point named after John Maine, father-in-law of John Atwell. He came to Lynn between the years 1650 and 1675 (See Lewis's History of Lynn, p. 96). John Atwell and his wife had children: John, Joseph, Richard and Sarah.

(II) John Atwell, eldest son of John and Elizabeth (Maine) Atwell, married Margaret Max, of Wenham, who bore him three children: Joseph, Nathan and John. Up to this time the name was spelled Atwell, since then Attwill.

(III) Nathan Attwill, second son of John and Margaret (Max) Atwell, lived in a certain dwelling in Lynn with barn and land situated near the old "Tunnel" meeting house; land bounded on every side by town common. This dwelling, built 1789, is still standing on Whiting street, Lynn. He married, November 27, 1727, Anna Ramsdell; children: William, Nathan and John. Nathan Attwill died previous to May 24, 1784, and his wife died about that date.

(IV) William Attwill, eldest son of Nathan and Anna (Ramsdell) Attwill, was born in Lynn, 1730, died November 5, 1806. He resided in the old Attwill house on site of Lynn common, built 1789 and moved about 1836; see above. He was a farmer, and lived and died in Lynn. He enlisted as private at Malden, Massachusetts, December 22, 1775, and at Winter Hill, January 22, 1778. He married, April 12, 1753, Lydia Hicks, born October 31, 1732, died January 8, 1812. Children: 1. Lydia, married William Tarbox. 2. Zachariah, born October 9, 1775, died November 6, 1836. 3. Anna. 4. Mary. 5. Hannah Hicks, married James Alley. 6. Thomas, served in Jacob Gerrish's regiment. 7. William. 8. Sally, married Aaron Breed. 9. John Daggett, see forward. 10. Betsey.

(V) John Daggett Attwill, youngest son of William and Lydia (Hicks) Attwill, was born in Lynn, May 7, 1771, died April 12, 1842. He was a shoe manufacturer in Lynn. He later went to New Orleans and opened a commission house with his son, John Daggett Jr., who died there at the age of thirty-three years. He continued in business there a number of years successfully, but in his last years returned to Lynn, where his death occurred. He is buried in what is known as the West End Burying Ground or Union Street Graveyard. He was a major in Lynn militia and was known by the name of Major Attwill. He married first, in Lynn, November 15, 1794, Martha Ingalls, born March 2, 1775. He married second, April 12, 1842, Hannah Palfrey. Children: 1. Martha, born March 20, 1797. 2. Nelson, September 1, 1798. 3. John Daggett, May 1, 1800. 4. Mary, April 25, 1802. 5. Betsy, February 4, 1804. 6. Alfred, January 9, 1806. 7. Gustavus, May 22, 1808, see forward. 8. Edwin, August 7, 1810. 9. Richard I., July 17, 1812, see forward. 10. William A., March 22, 1814. 11. Joseph W., July 3, 1817. 12. Benjamin, twin of Joseph W., July 3, 1817. 13. Jacob, March 26, 1816, died in infancy.

(VI) Gustavus Attwill, fourth son and seventh child of John Daggett and Martha (Ingalls) Attwill, was born in Lynn, May 22, 1808, died in Lynn, August 18, 1873. He was educated in schools of Lynn, and learned shoemaking. He took up shoe manufacturing and continued in same during his active career, for a number of years having his place of business on Broad street. He accumulated considerable property, and lived several years in a house which he built at the head of Union on Chestnut street, later residing on Newhall street. He was well known and respected. He took an active interest in city affairs; was member of old Whig party; became a Republican when that party was formed; member of general court and in the only constitutional convention ever held to amend the constitution; served in common council in Lynn, and president of same a number of years. He was major in the old Lynn militia, member of Universalist church and trustee a great number of years. He married, in Lynn, first, March 24, 1836, Almira Mudge, of Lynn (see history of Mudge family). Children: Charles Anderson, Frances Maria, Josephine, married George H. Rich, one child, Maria E. Rich; John D., Almira. Mr. Attwill married second, Maria A. Burrill, of Lynn, born October 20, 1823, died August 27, 1905; children: Alfred Mudge, see forward; Gustavus, see forward.

(VI) Richard Ingalls Attwill, ninth child and sixth son of John D. Attwill, was born July 17, 1812, in Lynn, died in Boston, December 8, 1902. He was for many years a well known newspaper man in Lynn and Boston. He began his career in 1845 as editor of the *Lynn Freeman*, a weekly paper published in Lynn. He later became connected with the *Boston Transcript*, reporting the proceedings of the legislature, and remaining for many years. He then went to Alton, Illinois, and was in the office of Editor Lovejoy at the time that a mob took possession of the office of his newspaper, killing Mr. Lovejoy and burning the building. He then returned to Boston and acted as reporter for the leading newspapers for some years, when he received an appointment in the United States internal revenue office, where he remained until his retirement from active pursuits.

(VII) Alfred Mudge Attwill, son of Gustavus and Maria A. (Burrill) Attwill, was born in Lynn, January 15, 1857. He was educated in public schools, and then worked for a time in shoe factory of Mr. B. F. Spinney, of Lynn. He next entered office of Great Western Insurance Company of Boston in 1874, remaining twenty years until 1894, when he engaged with Nathan Matthews, of Boston, as private secretary, remaining until 1904, during which time he acquired a thorough knowledge of real estate, and in 1904 opened an office of his own and has continued successfully in same since with offices in Lynn and Boston. He is a Republican in politics, and attends the Universalist church. In 1901 he built a house in Kensington Square, Lynn, where he resides. He is unmarried. Mr. Attwill has for many years taken a deep interest in the genealogy of his family and the record found here has been compiled from his manuscript. In memory of his father, Gustavus Attwill, and his uncle, Richard Ingalls Attwill, he has placed an engraving of each in this work.

(VII) Gustavus Attwill, son of Gustavus and Maria A. (Burrill) Attwill, was born March 25, 1865. He received his education in the public schools, and in 1881 entered the employ of the Shoe and Leather Fire Insurance Company of Boston and continued with them until the company went out of business, when he entered W. H. Brewster's Insurance Agency, where he still remains. He married Flora May, daughter of Henry L. Chase, of Lynn, who was a schoolmaster for many years in ward 4 of Lynn. Children: Orrissa M., born October 19, 1894, and Gustavus L., October 8, 1900.

FIELD The English surname Field, which has many thousands of representatives in both Great Britain and America, is one of the most ancient patronymics and can be traced in its origin to an era far antedating the Norman conquest, to the time when it was written De la Feld and De la Felde, and was applied to certain persons and families whose places of abode were in or near some field. Burke's "Landed Gentry of Great Britain and Ireland" gives the family an original place in Alsace, in the vicinity of the Vosges mountains, and speaks of its having been seated there at the Chateau de la Feld, near Colmar, from "the darkest period of the middle ages"; and "that the counts de la Feld were the once powerful proprietors of the desmenes and castles near Colmar, of which the latter still bears their name. These lords had large possessions in Alsace and Lorraine, and are frequently mentioned in the wars of those countries. The Croix d'Or of La Feld, their ancient badge, is still the coat of armor of the Delafields.

Hubertus de la Feld was the first of his race that emigrated to England. He went over with the crowd of foreigners who attended the Conqueror hither, his name appearing enrolled in the county of Lancaster in 1069, the third year of the reign of William I (Field Gen.). Hubertus de la Feld received large grants of land from William as a reward of fealty and honorable military service. In the fourteenth century the English de la Fields discontinued their old French prefix and adopted the more ordinary surname of Field. Roger Del Field, of Sowerby, England, born about 1240, was descended from Sir Hubertus de la Feld, and was the head of the Field fam-

Richard J. Attwill.

ilies that settled in Lancaster and Kent counties. His son, Thomas Del Feld, born about 1278, had a son John, born 1300, who had son Thomas, born 1330, married Annabelle ——— and had son Thomas Del Field, born 1360, who by wife Isabel had son William Feld, born Bradford, England, married Katherine ———, and by her had son William Field, born Bradford, married and had son Richard who married Elizabeth ———; he was born probably in East Ardsley, England, and died December, 1542. His son John, born about 1525, in East Ardsley, England, married, 1560, Jane Amyas, daughter of John; she died August 30, 1609; he died May, 1587: resided in Ardislawe, England. Their son John, born about 1568, in Ardsley, England, married, and is supposed to have died young. His son Zachariah, born in East Ardsley, Yorkshire, England, see forward.

(I) Zachariah Field, son of John Field, the first American progenitor of the family, was born at East Ardsley, Yorkshire, England, 1596. He sailed from Bristol to New England in 1629, and settled first in Dorchester. In 1636 he with others settled in Hartford, Connecticut. His residence was on Sentinel Hill, near the present north end of Main street. He was one of the forty-two men furnished by Hartford to take part in the Pequod war. He owned large tracts of land in Hartford. In 1644 dissensions arose in the church, and he with sixty others, being the minority in the dispute, bought of the Nonotuck Indians a tract of land nine miles square on the east side of the Connecticut river above Northampton. Here he was engaged in the mercantile business and had a large trade with the Indians. He was one of the twenty-five persons who engaged to settle in what is now Hatfield, and was one of the committee to lay out the lands. They were to have their houses built and occupy them before Michaelmas, (September 19, 1661) but he did not probably go there until the following year. His home lot contained eight acres, and was the first log north of the Northampton road, and is or was lately owned by William Billings. He died there June 30, 1666. He married, about 1641, Mary ———, who died about 1670. Children: 1. Mary, born about 1643, married, October 6, 1663, Joshua Carter, Jr., of Northampton, who was killed by Indians at Bloody Brook, September 18, 1675, while removing some of his effects to Northampton for safety. 2. Zachariah, born about 1645, married Sarah Webb. 3. John, born about 1648, married Mary Edwards. 4. Samuel, born about 1651, mentioned below. 5. Joseph, born about 1658, married first, Joanna Wyatt; second, Mary Belding.

(II) Sergeant Samuel Field, son of Zachariah Field (1), was born at Hartford, Connecticut, about 1651. He came with his father to Northampton in 1663. He removed to Hatfield, where he was slain by Indians in ambush while hoeing corn in Hatfield Meadows, June 24, 1697. He was a sergeant in the Turners Falls fight, May 19, 1676. He was a prominent and influential man in Hatfield, holding many town offices. He left no will and his estate was settled September 20, 1701. He married, August 9, 1676, Sarah Gilbert, born December 19, 1655, died February 4, 1712, daughter of Thomas and Catherine (Bliss) Gilbert, of Springfield. She married second, October 17, 1702, Ebenezer Chapin, of Springfield. Children: 1. Samuel, born September 27, 1678, married Mrs. Hannah E. Hoyt. 2. Thomas, born June 30, 1680, married Abigail Dickinson. 3. Sarah, born June 30, 1683, married, November 18, 1702, Samuel Warner, of Springfield. 4. Zachariah, born August 29, 1685. 5. Ebenezer, born March 17, 1688, mentioned below. 6. Mary, born July 23, 1690, married, June 26, 1712, Jonathan, son of David Hoyt; resided at Deerfield; with his father David, mother, brother Ebenezer and two sisters he was taken captive by the Indians in the battle of Deerfield, taken to Canada, and returned later. The father died of hunger near the lower Cohoes; his sister Abigail was killed on the way to Canada; Ebenezer remained among the Indians. 7. Josiah, born November 5, 1692, married Elizabeth ———. 8. Joshua, born April 9, 1695, married Elizabeth Cooley.

(III) Ebenezer Field, son of Sergeant Samuel Field (2), was born at Hatfield, Massachusetts, March 17, 1688. He married, 1714, Elizabeth, born 1695, daughter of William Arms; she married second, Azariah Wright. Ebenezer Field settled about 1710 in Deerfield, and in 1717 moved to Northfield, where he followed his trades of blacksmith and gunsmith. There is a tradition that being mistaken by the guard in the twilight for an Indian, while pitching peas into his barn, he was fired upon and wounded in the hip. There being no surgeon at Northfield, he was taken to Deerfield for treatment, and wearied by the journey, died before his wound could be dressed. He married Elizabeth, daughter of William and Joanna (Hawks) Arms, of Deerfield. She was born 1695; married second,

January 27, 1727, Azariah Wright, of Northfield; she died October, 1772. Ebenezer Field died September 12, 1723. Their children: 1. Ebenezer, born June 15, 1715, mentioned below. 2. Joanna, born April 6, 1717, married, 1737, Colonel Phineas Wright. 3. Moses, born February 19, 1719, married Ann Dickinson and Martha Root. 4. Aaron, born March 17, 1722, married Eunice Tracy. 5. Elizabeth, born January 3, 1723, married, February 14, 1745, Captain Ebenezer Wells.

(IV) Ebenezer Field, son of Ebenezer Field (3), was born in Deerfield, June 15, 1715. He married first, March 27, 1746, Sarah, daughter of Eleazer Mattoon, born 1722, died October 20, 1785; second, May 24, 1786, Mrs. Christian (Hubbard) Field, wife of Paul, born 1733, died November 6, 1795; he married third, Mrs. Abigail Chapin, of Orange, born 1728, died June 7, 1801. He was an innkeeper and tailor. He settled in Northfield, where he kept a tavern and conducted a tailoring business. He died at Northfield, August 12, 1801. His children: 1. Lydia, born September 12, 1742. 2. Ebenezer, born October 11, 1744, mentioned below. 3. Sarah, born November 4, 1747, married, April 29, 1784, David Allen, of East Windsor, Connecticut. 4. Abner, born May 27, 1750, married Mary Mattoon. 5. Lucy, born September 20, 1752, married Oliver Watrise. 6. Keziah, born February 3, 1755, died February 3, 1755. 7. Keziah, born October 24, 1756, married first, July 13, 1806, ——— Stiles, of Gill; second, July 3, 18—, James King, of Guildford, Vermont; she died in Boston.

(V) Ebenezer Field, son of Ebenezer Field (4), was born October 11, 1744, died 1811. He married, July 21, 1767, Eunice, born January 26, 1752, died July 6, 1826, daughter of Benoni and Martha (Sheldon) Wright. He was born in Northfield, Massachusetts, set off to Gill in 1805, resided at Weston some time, then returned to Gill, where he died. He was one of the company of minute-men, with the rank of corporal, on the Lexington alarm roll, Captain Reuben Read's company, Colonel Jonathan Warner's regiment, which marched April 20, in response to the alarm of April 19, 1775, from Weston to Roxbury; he was sergeant in Captain Granger's company, Colonel Ebenezer Learned's regiment, October 7, 1775, enlisted in Weston; was in Colonel Shepard's regiment, January 1, 1777, to December 31, 1779; also from January 1, to April 14, 1780; lieutenant; rolls dated at Providence, November 13, 1778, and May 5, 1779; reported furloughed May 4 for ten days by Colonel Shepard. By occupation Mr. Field was a farmer; he owned several hundred acres in what is now known as Gill, and was for years known as the richest man in that section. The farm was a fine one, and always under admirable cultivation; it was portioned off to various sons and daughters. His children: 1. Aurilla, baptized October 16, 1768, died November 13, 1768. 2. Rodolphus Wright, baptized October 22, 1769, married Hannah D. Hollister. 3. Bohan Prentice, baptized April 26, 1772, died young. 4. Ebenezer Sereno, baptized May 7, 1775, married Amelia Connable. 5. Aurilla, baptized March 11, 1778, married, 1793, Deacon Elihu Hollister. 6. Eunice, baptized April 3, 1780, married Zephaniah Pitts, of Gill. 7. Asaph Warren, baptized June 5, 1783, died unmarried. 8. Loren Sheldon, baptized April 9, 1786, married Mary Hubbard. 9. Gratin, baptized October 11, 1789, died unmarried. 10. Filena, baptized January 7, 1794, married (first) Leonard Jacobs; (second) John Warner. 11. Bohan Prentice (judge), born May 23, 1773, mentioned below.

(VI) Bohan Prentice Field, youngest child of Ebenezer Field (5), born May 23, 1773, was a native of Northfield, Massachusetts. He was a graduate of Dartmouth College, 1795; studied law in Portsmouth, New Hampshire, and later entered the office of Hon. Samuel Dana, of Amherst, New Hampshire, where he finished his studies preparatory to being admitted to the bar. In 1798 he settled in North Yarmouth, Maine, being the first lawyer to settle in that place. In 1799 he removed to Belfast, Maine, and became the pioneer of his profession in that town, then in Hancock county, and in 1800 contained but six hundred and seventy-four inhabitants, and in 1900 contained four thousand six hundred and fifteen. Mr. Field resided there forty-four years. On the organization of the county of Waldo in 1827, he was appointed by Governor Lincoln chief justice of the court of session for the county, which was a surprise to him, as they were political opponents. He continued to discharge the duties of the office for the term of ten years with industry and to the satisfaction of the county. He was a well-read lawyer, and his opinions were regarded as good authority and entitled to great weight. He rarely appeared as an advocate, but when he found it necessary or expedient to address a jury he did it with force and clearness, without any display of rhetoric, arguing for the cause and not for outside effect. He was valued in the community where he lived for his general intelligence, soundness of judgment and integrity of character. He died March 13, 1843. He married, October 23, 1807, Abigail, daughter of Benjamin and Mary (Mann) Davis, of Billerica, Massachusetts, born October 23, 1787, died November 3, 1863. Children: 1. Henry Cummings, born September 14, 1809, married Aseneth Harriman. 2. William Patten, born January 31, 1811, married Sarah Ingraham. 3. Abigail Eleanor, born March 2, 1812, died October 1, 1813. 4. Ebenezer Wright, born September 23, 1813, died October 7, 1813. 5. Charles Davis, born August 5, 1814, married Eliza Osgood. 6. Bohan Prentice, Jr., born September 11, 1815, mentioned below. 7. George Warner, born December 9, 1818, married Lucy H. Humphrey. 8. Benjamin Franklin, born October 10, 1820, married Caroline Williams Toby, and Annie Fuller Toby. 9. Edward Mann, born July 27, 1822, married Sarah Ross McRuer.

(VII) Bohan Prentice Field, sixth child of Judge Bohan Prentice Field (6), was a native of Belfast, Maine, born September 11, 1815, died October 1, 1897. He married, at Belfast, September 11, 1843, Lucy Haraden, born October, 1817, died July 20, 1892. He was a lawyer, read law in his father's office and with Hon. Jacob McGraw, of Bangor, Maine. He began practice in Searsmont, Waldo county, Maine, but later returned to Belfast and succeeded to his father's business. He was never known to have an enemy; a man endeared to the community, and well known and esteemed by his legal brethren in the state. In his manners he was bland, social and affectionate; in his morals pure and unaffected. He was a model in his office duties, and faithful to all his trusts. Through all party changes and administrations he held the office of register of probate for over forty years. He was one of the first to interest himself in insurance business in the state, and instructed his sons in law pertaining to that department, which they chose for their profession in life. He was deacon of the Congregational church, and was punctual at church, as he was in office; he gave the entire influence of his example to the observance of the Sabbath, and all the practical duties of religion. Children: 1. George Prentice, born October 17, 1844, mentioned below. 2. Abby Ellen, born December 8, 1849, married, January 10, 1872, Charles Spofford Pearl, born May 20, 1843; they have two children: Alice Field, born December 31, 1873, married W. H. Whitemore, of Portland, Maine, one child, Alice; Haraden Spofford, born June 27, 1879. 3. Charles Haraden, born November 25, 1855, married (first), May 16, 1877, Bertha Frances Chase; (second), June 2, 1886, Emma Moreland.

(VIII) George Prentice Field, eldest child of Bohan Prentice Field (7), was born at Searsmont, Maine, October 17, 1844. He was educated in the public schools of Belfast, Maine, and after graduating from the high school entered his father's office, in the insurance business. At the breaking out of the civil war he was appointed deputy provost marshal of the Fifth District of Maine, which position he held until the surrender of Richmond. He then after serving for two years as deputy collector of customs, resumed the insurance business, becoming first the assistant secretary of the National Fire Insurance Company of Bangor, Maine; then later secretary of the First National Fire Insurance Company of Worcester, Massachusetts. In 1873 he resigned that position to become special agent of the Royal Insurance Company of England, under its then New England managers, Foster & Scull. Here he became successively general agent, assistant manager, and later a member of the firm. The house dates back to 1858, when it began business as Foster & Cole, then in succession, Foster & Scull, Scull & Bradley, Scull & Field, and finally, as it is now, Field & Cowles. It is one of the oldest as it is the largest house in its line in Boston and New England, employing about seventy people in its office at 85 Water street, Boston, and maintaining a branch office at 65 Warren street, Roxbury. Every description of insurance is written with the exception of life lines. The firm is the representative in all New England of the Royal Insurance Company of Liverpool, England; and Boston agent for the Insurance Company of North America of Philadelphia, the Alliance of Philadelphia, and the National of Hartford, Connecticut. Mr. Field has long been prominent in insurance circles, aside from his business relations, and has served as president of the Boston Board of Underwriters of New England, as director and president of the Boston Protective Department, chairman of the board of trustees of the Insurance Library Association of Boston. He is also connected with various organizations—the Merchants' Association, the Board of Trade, of which he is vice-president; the Boston Firemen's Monument Association, of which he is treasurer; and the following clubs: the Algonquin, Boston Art, Country, Eastern Yacht, Essex County, Merchants' Exchange and City. He is vestryman of Emanuel Protestant Episcopal Church of Boston. Mr. Field married, at New Bedford, Massachusetts, June 12, 1868, Alma Claghorn Field (a cousin), born March, 1843, died August 5, 1908. Children: 1. Walter Ingram, born March 9, 1869, died February 7, 1894. 2. Edith Alma, born October 7, 1873, married, November 14, 1895, Horace Bertram Pearson; children: Robert Field, born 1900, and George Field, born 1902.

BREED The name of Breed has been a familiar one in Lynn from the earliest days of her history, Allen Breed having been a prominent settler there as early as 1630, while others bearing the name have been active in succeeding years in the development of the country and in furthering the best interests of the community. More especially active in recent years was the late Amos Franklin Breed, to whose far-seeing policy alone is due the excellent network of railways throughout the entire section, and a man who fulfilled in every way the highest ideals of citizenship.

(I) Allen Breed, mentioned above, was born in Westonning, England, in 1601, and settling in Lynn, Massachusetts, made his home in the western part of Summer street, the vicinity being called "Breed's End." He was the owner of two hundred acres of land, and actively and successfully engaged in its cultivation. As early as 1640 he was one of the grantees in the deed from the Indians of Southampton, Long Island, but either he did not remove to that place, or if he did, he soon returned to Massachusetts. He was made a freeman in 1681, and his death occurred in 1692. He married Elizabeth Knight, who was probably his second wife, and his children, who are presumed to be of his first union, were Allen and John.

(II) Allen, son of Allen Breed, was born in England in 1626, and was made a freeman in 1684. He married Mary ———, who died November 30, 1671, and their children were: Joseph, born February 12, 1658; Allen, August 3, 1660; John, January 18, 1663; Mary August 24, 1665; Elizabeth, November 1, 1667; and Samuel, September 25, 1669.

(III) Samuel, fourth son and youngest child of Allen and Mary Breed, probably spelled the name Bread. He married Anna, daughter of Richard Hood, February 5, 1691-2, and their children were: Samuel, born November 11, 1692; Amos, July 20, 1694; Jabez, January 26, 1696; Abigail, September 7, 1698; Nathan, January 3, 1703; Keziah, October 16, 1704; Anna, July 28, 1706; Ebenezer, May 1, 1710; Ruth, March 10, 1712, and Benjamin, July 4, 1715.

(IV) Ebenezer, son of Samuel and Anna (Hood) Breed, married Rebecca Phillips, of Boston, November 29, 1737, and their children were: Richard, born September 11, 1738; Amos, November 4, 1739; Ebenezer, May 1, 1741; Rebecca, December 29, 1742; Samuel, April 10, 1747; James, April 19, 1749; Elizabeth, March 19, 1751; William, February 20, 1753, and Simeon, September 13, 1755.

(V) Amos, son of Ebenezer and Rebecca Breed, married Ruth Estes, April 30, 1766, and their children were: Amos, born April 19, 1772; Hannah, February 16, 1781, and Rebecca, June 17, 1784.

(VI) Amos, only son of Amos and Ruth (Estes) Breed, married Frances Reed, of Salem, January 14, 1827. Their children were: Ruth Ann, born December 8, 1827, died January 26, 1831; Amos Franklin, born October 15, 1830, died May 22, 1900; Wilbur Fisk, born May 11, 1834, died January 8, 1837, and Wilbur Fisk, born December 5, 1836, married Susan Estelle Keith, April 6, 1864, who died April 27, 1907.

(VII) Amos Franklin, second child and eldest son of Amos and Frances (Reed) Breed, was born in Lynn, Massachusetts, October 15, 1830, and died in the same city, May 22, 1900. His education was acquired in the public schools, and he soon engaged in the shoe business, where he gave evidence of those remarkable traits of industry and integrity coupled with a natural aptitude for business and its practical and successful management and expansion. He retired from the manufacturing field directly after the great fire of 1889. His advice was early sought by financial institutions, and in 1884 he became president of the First National Bank, an office he filled until his decease. He was a director and vice-president of the Lynn Institution for Savings, director of the Boston, Revere Beach & Lynn Railroad Company, and a director of the Lynn Gas & Electric Company. He became best known, however, through his management of the Lynn & Boston Railroad Company, wherein his success was little short of miraculous. He assumed the manager's chair when the stock was considered almost

H. J. Breed

worthless, and inaugurated a policy which made it one of the best in the commonwealth, extended its tracks in all directions, improved the rolling stock, and eventually absorbed the Belt Line road. This was all accomplished quietly and was an established success by the time the investors realized his enterprise. Attracted by the phenomenal rise in the value of the stock of this road, the North Shore Traction Company was organized, absorbing the Lynn & Boston road and all its subsidiary branches, Mr. Breed becoming president of the new corporation and repeating his former successes. On July 30, 1899, the system of the North Shore Traction Company was bought by a company of Boston capitalists, and several of the roads were combined under the name of the Massachusetts Electric Companies, and again Mr. Breed was made president, a high and deserved compliment to his business acumen and executive ability. Mr. Breed was a most exemplary citizen, a man of inborn courtesy, with a bearing of confidence inspired by the courage to do and the will to act.

His active interest in politics and the Republican party dated from the time of his majority, and in 1864 he was elected to the common council. He was a member of the board of aldermen in 1865-6-7-8-70, and was elected to the state legislature in 1865-6, and again in 1876. In 1877-8 he was a member of the state senate, and in the latter year served as chairman of the committee on street railways. He was a presidential elector in 1872 and 1880, and a delegate to the Republican national convention in 1880 and 1896. He gave his time so freely, and his public spirit and general worth were so widely recognized, that he was continually sought to fill those positions which show the confidence of neighbors and friends. He was commissioner of the sinking fund of the city, and chairman of the commissioners of Pine Grove Cemetery, the latter an office he filled for nearly twenty years. Mr. Breed was naturally a charitable man, and gave freely to all measures for the relief of distress. He was married, December 7, 1854, to Mary A. Lindsey, of Lynn, and they were blessed with four children: Amos F. Jr., who died in infancy; Ruth Ann, born February 20, 1856, died August 31, 1872; Amos F. Jr., the second, born January 15, 1858, who still survives: Sylvester B., born January 18, 1867, died July 8, 1902; married, September 29, 1887, Mary B. Harrington, of Salem, and had one son, Amos Francis, born March 17, 1890.

The land upon which the old homestead now stands was purchased by the grandfather of Mr. Breed from his father-in-law, William Estes, January 4, 1774, and the house, which in those days was called a "mansion house," was probably erected soon after.

WILLARD The surname Willard was in use as a personal name from ancient times. Earlier than its use as a surname it was also a local or place name, in England. The ancient coat-of-arms used by many branches of this family: Argent, a chevron sable between three fish weels proper five ermine spots. Crest: A griffin's head erased or. Motto: Gaudet patientia duris.

(I) Richard Willard, to whom the line is traced, grandfather of the American immigrant, was a yeoman at Brenchley, England, where he died leaving a will dated September 18, 1558, proved October 24, 1558. Children: Robert, Alexander, George, Richard, Andrew, Symon, Thomas, William, Alice, Agnes.

(II) Richard Willard, son of Richard Willard (1), resided at Horsmonden, county Kent, England. He married first, Catherine ———, buried March 11, 1559; second, Margery, died December 12, 1608; third, January 17, 1610, Joan Morebread, buried February 25, 1617. His will mentioned children George, Mary, Elizabeth, Margery, Catherine, Richard; brother Thomas Willard; brother-in-law Thomas Humphrey; son Symon and sister-in-law Mary Davy. Children: 1. Richard, died young. 2. Thomas, baptized May 6, 1593, buried January 15, 1608. 3. Edward, baptized March 21, 1611-2, buried April 16, 1612. 4. John, baptized March 3, 1612-3; buried June 20, 1613. 6. George. 7. George. 8. Mary. 9. Elizabeth. 10. Margery, married Dolor Davis. 11. Catherine, baptized August 30, 1607. 12. Richard. 13. Simon, mentioned below.

(III) Major Simon Willard, son of Richard Willard (2), was the immigrant ancestor, born at Horsmonden, Kent, England, in 1604, baptized December 4, 1614. He was a soldier in Kent when a young man. He came to New England in 1634, in April, in the same ship with Dolor Davis, his brother-in-law. He was a merchant, and began to trade with the Indians as soon as he was fairly established at Cambridge. Davis, progenitor of many distinguished Massachusetts families, settled on the farm adjoining, on the Brighton side of the Charles river. Here Willard acquired a thousand acres, bounded by the farm of Davis,

Charles river and the Boston town line. He had many grants of land from time to time. He was one of the founders and first settlers of Concord, and was the first deputy to the general court, elected in December, 1636, serving every year after that until 1654, excepting 1643, 1647 and 1648, and was elected but declined to serve in 1654. He was a member of the council fifteen years, and for twenty-two years an assistant. He was given a patent by the general court in 1641 for trading with the Indians and collecting tribute from them. He was appointed magistrate, and during his life attended between seventy and eighty terms of the county court, his first term beginning November 28, 1654, his last April 4, 1676. For forty years he was active in military life. He rose to the rank of major, and commanded the provincial troops against the Indians. Both in military and civil life he became one of the most famous men of the province. He led the expedition against the Narragansetts in 1655, and was at Brookfield and Hadley in King Philip's war leading the Middlesex regiment. The town of Lancaster invited him by a personal letter dated February 7, 1658-9, to make his home in that town, promising lands and privileges. He decided to locate in Lancaster, and sold out his Concord estates to Captain Thomas Marshall, of Lynn, in 1659. His first home in Lancaster was near the opening of the present Center road, bounded on two sides by the Nashua river, and commanding a superb view of the valley and surrounding country. He lived there twelve years, and in 1670-1 removed to the large farm in the south part of Groton, where in 1671-2 he served as chairman of the committee to seat the meeting house. In 1673 he was chairman of the Groton selectmen. He had a fine farm at Still river, now Harvard, and doubtless moved to Groton in order to be nearer this property. He left Lancaster enjoying peace and good order, though King Philip's war was soon to devastate the country. In civil life Major Willard was a surveyor and was often called upon to fix town boundaries. He died of influenza, an epidemic of which occurred in 1676. He was one of the most conspicuous and honored men of his day and he died at the close of King Philip's war, after reaping his greatest triumphs April 24, 1676. He was a stalwart Puritan, conscientious and of sound understanding, of brave and enduring spirit. He had wealth as well as honor, bringing to this country an ample patrimony, giving large amounts of land to his children and leaving thirteen hundred acres besides other property at his death. Yet his widow petitioned the general court for reimbursement for losses occasioned by Indian wars, stating that the Major often said he had lost a thousand pounds in this way. The court answered this petition by a grant of a thousand acres to be divided among the six youngest children. He was buried April 27, 1676, and the inventory of his estate filed later by Mrs. Willard. He married first, Mary Sharpe, born 1614, at Horsmonden, daughter of Henry and Jane (Field) Sharpe; second, Elizabeth Dunster, sister of Henry Dunster, first president of Harvard College, and Willard's third wife was her sister Mary. His widow married Deacon Joseph Noyes, of Sudbury. His children were by first and third wives. Children: 1. Mary, married Joshua Edmunds. 2. Elizabeth, died young. 3. Elizabeth, married Robert Blood, of Concord, April 8, 1653, and she died August 29, 1690. 4. Dorothy, died young. 5. Josiah, married Hannah Hosmer. Children, born in Concord: 6. Samuel, born January 31, 1639-40, graduate of Harvard College, 1659; married Abigail, daughter of Rev. John Sherman, who married second, Eunice Tyng, daughter of Edward. 7. Sarah, born June 27, 1642; married Nathaniel Howard. 8. Abovehope, born October 30, 1646; died at Lancaster, December 23, 1663. 9. Simon, born November 23, 1649; married Martha Jacobs; second, Priscilla Buttolph; prominent man of Salem, Massachusetts. 10. Mary, born September 7, 1653; married Cyprian Stevens, ancestor of Worcester county Stevens families. 11. Henry, born June 4, 1655; mentioned below. 12. John, born February 12, 1656-7; married Mary Hayward. 13. Daniel, born December 29, 1658; married Hannah Cutler. Children, born at Lancaster: 14. Joseph, born January 4, 1660-1; resided in London, England. 15. Benjamin, born 1665; married Sarah Lakin. 16. Hannah, born October 6, 1666; married Captain Thomas Brintnall, May 23, 1693; lived at Sudbury. 17. Jonathan, born December 14, 1669; married Mary, daughter of Major Thomas and Patience Browne, of Sudbury.

A tablet inscribed as follows is fixed in the wall outside the crypt near St. Gabriel's Chapel, Canterbury Cathedral, England: "In Memoriam: Major Simon Willard, born 1604, died 1676, exactly one hundred years before the Declaration of Independence. A Kentish soldier, and an early pioneer in the settlement of the British colony of New England, America, 1634. He was made commander-in-chief of the British forces against the hostile Indian tribes. He was distinguished in the military, legislative and judicial service of the American commonwealth until his death, aged 72. Of Simon Willard's ancestry, one was Provost of Canterbury, 1218, and another was Baron of the Cinque Ports, 1377; and his descendants to the present day have held eminent positions in the United States. Erected by Sylvester D. Willard, London, 1902." The late Mrs. Francis Willard has also erected a brass tablet in the church of Horsmonden—the old home.

(IV) Henry Willard, son of Major Simon Willard (3), was born in Concord, June 4, 1655. He was a soldier in King Philip's war, 1675. He was a farmer, and left a considerable estate at Groton and Lancaster. He married first, Mary Lakin, of Groton. She died 1688, and he married, 1689, Dorcas Cutler. Willard died 1701, and his widow married second, Benjamin Bellows. Children, born at Groton: 1. Henry, April 11, 1675; married Sarah Nutting and Abigail Temple. 2. Simon, October 8, 1678; married Mary Whitcomb. 3. John, born September 3, 1682; married Anne Hill. Children, born at Lancaster. 4. Hezekiah, about 1712; married Anna Wilder, daughter of Thomas; Hezekiah was first selectman of Harvard, 1733-38. 5. Joseph, born about 1686; married Elizabeth Tarbell. Children, of wife Dorcas: 6. Samuel, born May 31, 1690; married Elizabeth Phelps, August 19, 1717, daughter of Edward and Ruth; had homestead of Major Simon, and it remained in the family of descendants to the present time; was deputy to general court, judge of county court; commanded colonial regiment at Louisburg; died November, 1752. 7. James, married Hannah Houghton. 8. Josiah, born 1693; mentioned below. 9. Jonathan, born 1695; married, August 17, 1719, Keziah White. Children of wife Mary: 10. Mary, born 1680; married Isaac Hunt. 11. Sarah, married Samuel Rogers. 12. Abigail, died unmarried. 13. Susanna, married March 19, 1723-4, John Moore. 14. Tabitha, died unmarried.

(V) Colonel Josiah Willard, son of Henry Willard (4), was born at Lancaster, 1693. He was one of the first settlers and principal officers of Lunenburg, Massachusetts; was prominent in military life, commanding a company in excursions against the Indian enemy on the frontiers, and afterwards was colonel and commander at Fort Dummer (now Brattleboro), Vermont. In both public and private life he had an excellent reputation, and did good service for his country. He died December 8, 1750, in his fifty-eighth year. A newspaper of that time says of him: "He was a grandson of the renowned Major Simon Willard, and was a gentleman of superior natural powers, of a pleasant happy and agreeable temper of mind; a faithful friend; one that paid singular regard to ministers of the Gospel; a kind husband and kinder parent. His death is a great loss to the public, considering his usefulness in many respects, particularly on the western frontiers where in late wars in his betrustments he has shown himself faithful, vigilant and careful. Of late he has had command of Fort Dummer, and always used his best endeavors for the protection of our exposed infant towns and his loss will be greatly regretted by them." He married, about 1715, Hannah, daughter of John and granddaughter of Thomas Wilder, who was among the earliest settlers in Lancaster. Children, born at Lunenburg: 1. Josiah, January 21, 1715-6; mentioned below. 2. Abigail, July 4, 1718; baptized at Lancaster, with Josiah and Susanna; married, August 2, 1737, Thomas Prentice. 3. Susanna, July 9, 1720; married John Arms. 4. Lois, December 16, 1722; married Valentine Butler. 5. Nathan, born May 28, 1726, commander at Fort Dummer; married Lucy Allen. 6. Prudence, September 30, 1727; married William Willard, magistrate, judge, prominent man at Brattleboro, Vermont. 7. Oliver, March 6, 1729-30; married Thankful Doolittle; captain, judge, grantee of various Vermont towns. 8. Sampson, June 27, 1732, drowned December 15, 1739, at Winchester. 9. Wilder, June 30, 1735; married Susanna Hubbard.

(VI) Colonel Josiah Willard, son of Colonel Josiah Willard (5), was born at Lunenburg, January 21, 1715-6, baptized there August 6, 1721. He was the principal grantee of the township of Earlington or Arlington (Winchester), New Hampshire, 1733; was surveyor of land at the Upper Ashuelot, 1736, and later. He was commissary and commander at Fort Dummer in the old French and Indian war, 1744-50. The enemy was driven off in May, 1746, "by the spirited behavior of Major Willard at the head of a small party of soldiers." He held a captain's commission in the forces raised for the defence of the Upper and Lower Ashuelot, 1747-9; was promoted lieutenant-colonel and succeeded his father in command of Fort Dummer, December 18,

1750. He was an active agent in procuring from the legislature of New Hampshire a charter for the town of Winchester in 1753. He was active in the campaign of 1755, and was at Fort Edward in September, when the battle of Lake George was fought by General Johnson and Baron Dieskau. He was lieutenant-colonel of the regiment of Colonel Joseph Blanchard, of Dunstable, and in active service in the Crown Point expedition under General Johnson in 1755. He took up his residence in Winchester, and represented the town in the state legislature 1768-73. He was active in securing a new county, and was given full authority to speak and act for the town. He was the colonel commanding the Sixth New Hampshire regiment of militia in 1775, but was loyal to the crown, and his regiment was divided, leaving him without a command. He was a grantee of Putney, Vermont, from New Hampshire, 1753, and from New York, 1766; also of Westminster, Vermont, and Westmoreland, New Hampshire, but never lived in those towns. He died November 19, 1786, at Winchester. "A man of great activity and benevolence, possessed of an equable disposition and conciliatory address. He was a Christian by precept and example, very useful and influential. His heart was always open to his friends in general and to the learned, especially the clergy, in particular." "The wise," says his epitaph, "will imitate his virtues and fools lament they did not when he shall rise immortal." He married, November 23, 1732, Hannah Hubbard, of Groton, who died August 15, 1791. They had twelve children, of whom: 1. Solomon, was a graduate of Harvard. 2. Jonathan, graduated from Harvard in 1776. 3. Josiah, mentioned below.

(VII) Major Josiah Willard, son of Colonel Josiah Willard (6), born 1737, died June 29, 1801, aged sixty-four. He was buried with his three wives at the burial ground at the lower end of Main street, Keene, New Hampshire. He was sergeant at Fort Dummer, 1753-4, under his father's command. He settled at Keene, and was a sadler by trade. He was selectman there 1764-5-6-7; first representative in state legislature, 1768-70; first recorder of deeds in Cheshire county, 1771-76. He was major in his father's regiment when it was reorganized, throwing him as well as his father out of a command, on account of their Tory principles. His name was at the head of the list of those refusing to sign the association test in 1776, but he was not very obnoxious, and no radical steps were taken against him during the revolution. He was five years senator, seven years representative, and thirteen years selectman. He married first, Thankful Taylor; second, Mary ———; third, April 15, 1785, Susanna, daughter of Colonel Isaac Wyman. His first wife died July 24, 1767, aged twenty-six; his second July 20, 1779, aged thirty-eight, and his third October 25, 1785. Children, born at Keene: 1. Lockhart, May 15, 1763; died 1818; prominent citizen; married Salome, daughter of General James Reed. 2. Grate or Grata, February 27, 1765. 3. Cynthia, born November 19, 1766. 4. Rebecca, May 24, 1772. 5. Hannah, January 14, 1774. 6. Josiah, March 28, 1776; died November 5, 1776. 7. Josiah, January 9, 1778; married Bial ———. 8. Henry, mentioned below.

(VIII) Henry Willard, son of Major Josiah Willard (7), born at Keene, July 20, 1779, died at Washington, New Hampshire, February 26, 1815. When a young man he went to Washington, New Hampshire, and engaged in business, conducting a general store. He was a member of the firm of Dorr & Willard from 1802 until 1805, and after that time carried on the business alone for the rest of his life. He resided at Washington Centre, near the spot where the house now or lately of Elizabeth Perkins now stands. He died of malignant spotted fever. In his will he made a provision for the perpetual care of the graves of himself and wife, who died of grief the same week. He married March 1, 1804, Lovey Adams, born at Lincoln, March 21, 1769, died March 1, 1815, daughter of Joseph and Mary (Eveleth) Adams, of Lincoln. Her father was born October 5, 1724, and died March 28, 1807. (See Adams family). Children: 1. Mary Ann, born May 12, 1805; died 1827, unmarried. 2. Catherine Hannah, born January 1, 1807; married G. A. Kettell, June 12, 1832; children: i. Mary I. Kettell, born April 21, 1833; ii. Catherine Hannah Kettell, November 4, 1836; iii. Henry Augustus Kettell, February 8, 1838; iv. Francis E. Kettell, October 16, 1841; v. Louise Cary Kettell, November 11, 1843; vi. George Adams Kettell, May 10, 1846; vii. Charles Willard Kettell, November 3, 1848; viii. Helen Lee Kettell, March 1, 1851. 3. Joseph Henry, September 27, 1808; died at Littleton, 1833. 4. Elisha Wheeler, mentioned below. 5. Martha Lawrence, born September 17, 1812; married, February 14, 1839, Commodore C. H. Jackson; children: i. Catherine Theresa Jackson;

ii. Mary Alsop Jackson, married Francis Goodwin; iii. Martha Lawrence Jackson; iv. Alice Fenwick Jackson. 6. Sarah, born 1814, died at Littleton, 1821.

(IX) Elisha Wheeler Willard, son of Henry Willard (8), born in Washington, New Hampshire, May 22, 1810, died at Newport, Rhode Island, December 14, 1904. His parents died when he was only five years old, and he and his brothers and sisters were brought up by relatives. Elisha resided with his uncle David Lawrence at Littleton, Massachusetts, until he was about fifteen years old, going to school and working on the farm. He afterward went to Charlestown, Massachusetts, and lived with his uncle Nathan Adams, working in his grocery store for a number of years. Later he was employed by a leather firm in Boston. In 1833 he went west and settled at Fox River, Kendall county, Illinois. He and a companion named Pickering, with whom he took up a grant of six hundred and forty acres of government land, built a log cabin and started a farm. He finally bought out Pickering's interest and remained on the farm seven years. He carried the produce of his farm, which consisted mostly of grain and live stock, sixty miles by wagon, to Chicago, the nearest market. About 1840 he removed to Chicago, where for a time he was in a land office. He entered into partnership with George Smith in the banking business. Mr. Smith made an extended visit to England, and Mr. Willard retained the management of the business, and conducted it safely through the panic of 1857, when many of his contemporaries were forced to the wall. In 1863 he retired from the firm and undertook the management of a branch of the Bank of Montreal, which later was discontinued. He served on the committee of safety in Chicago during the trying period preceding and during the civil war, and gave liberally to the cause. In the spring of 1865 he removed to Burlington, Massachusetts, where he bought a hundred acre farm and stayed for two years as a farmer, when he retired from active business. He sold the farm to Henry Cook and made his home in Ithaca, New York, and Boston. He toured England and the continent from 1870 to 1872, and returned again to Boston. About 1876 he removed to Newport, Rhode Island, and erected a house where he lived until his death. His daughter, Mary Adams Willard, makes her home there at the present time. Mr. Willard was a selfmade man in the highest sense. His education and success were won by hard work, with a fixed determination to win. He believed in being temperate in all things, and his ideals were of the purest and best. A great reader and deep thinker, he was well informed on all the topics of the day. One of his mottoes in life was "to be just before being generous," and he lived up to this motto. In politics Mr. Willard was a Republican, and during the civil war he was especially active in supporting the Republican administration with his wealth and influence to the extent of his ability.

He married, November 20, 1836, at Squaw Grove, DeKalb county, Illinois, Mary Eleanor Eastabrooks, born September 26, 1815, Owego, Tioga county, and died January 7, 1899, at Newport, Rhode Island, daughter of John and Eliza Eastabrooks. Children: 1. Julia, born at Fox River, Illinois, October 11, 1837; died at Squaw Grove, Illinois, October 6, 1841; buried at Mount Auburn Cemetery, Cambridge, Massachusetts. 2. Joseph Henry, born at Chicago, February 28, 1844; graduate of West Point, class 1868; entered engineering corps United States Army, and after forty years of faithful service retired February 28, 1908; married September 23, 1888, Ella Quinn, Vicksburg, Mississippi; children: i. Eleanore, born September 11, 1889, died January 17, 1901; ii. Roberta, born July 17, 1891; iii. Natalia, July 11, 1893; iv. Dorothy, September 28, 1896. 3. Mary Adams, born at Chicago, October 21, 1851; lives in house built by her father, at Newport, on Miantonomi avenue. 4. John Howard, mentioned below.

(X) John Howard Willard, son of Elisha Wheeler Willard (9), was born in Chicago, Illinois, May 2, 1855. His elementary educational training was under private tutorship and in the old Boston Latin School. He traveled with his parents in their trip abroad, returning in the autumn of 1872, and in autumn that year entered Phillips Academy at Exeter, New Hampshire, taking a three-year course, graduating in 1875. He then entered Harvard College. At the end of his sophomore year he left college and went to live with his parents at Newport, where he began the study of law in Francis B. Peckham's law office. He did not, however, continue in the active practice of his profession. In 1880 he purchased his present homestead in Lexington, where he has resided to the present time (1908). He is regarded as a good and representative citizen in the town. Mr. Willard is a Republican in politics. He has never sought public office. He and his family belong to the Hancock Congregational Church at Lexington. He is a member of the Belfry Club and of the Lexington Historical Society. He married, March 24, 1880, Ida Lillian (Haven) Hutchinson, of Burlington, born July 25, 1859, daughter of Timothy and Laura (Tibbetts) Haven, of Burlington. She was adopted when ten years old by her uncle, John W. Hutchinson. Children: 1. Constance Alton, born December 14, 1880, graduate of Radcliffe College, Cambridge; married, May 5, 1906, Robert Watkinson Huntington, Jr., of Hartford, Connecticut; child: Robert Watkinson Huntington (3d) born July 2, 1907. 2. Helene Adams, born January 23, 1882; died June 10, 1902; married, October 16, 1901, William Starling Burgess, of Boston, Massachusetts; no children. 3. Edith, born June 13, 1885, secretary of School of Design at Museum of Fine Arts, Boston.

(For early generations see John Adams 1).

ADAMS (III) Captain Daniel Adams, son of Joseph Adams (2), and grandson of John Adams (1), of the same family as President John Adams, who was descended from the father of John (1). Henry Adams of Braintree, was born at Menotomy, January 3, 1690. He married, April 23, 1715, Elizabeth Minot, of Lincoln, Massachusetts, who died November 12, 1764, aged sixty-seven, daughter of James and Rebecca (Wheeler) Minot. Her father was of Dorchester and Concord; her mother was born January 29, 1697, at Concord. He married, October 30, 1765, Mrs. Hannah Benney, of Weston, died June 11, 1776. Captain Adams and Ephraim Jones, both of Concord, cut a road from Townsend, Massachusetts, to the Ashuelot river in New Hampshire in 1737, without compensation. He resided in that part of Concord set off as Lincoln. He died February 9, 1780, aged ninety. Children: 1. Captain Daniel Jr., born October 15, 1720. 2. Elizabeth, October 1, 1722; married Humphrey Barrett. 3. Captain Joseph, October 5, 1724; mentioned below. 4. Rebecca, September 2, 1727; married Nathan Brown. 5. Mary, May 18, 1730; married Peter Hubbard. 6. James, March 20, 1732. 7. Lydia, September 1, 1735; married Abel Miles. 8. Martha, April 13, 1738; married Joseph Wellington.

(IV) Captain Joseph Adams, son of Captain Daniel Adams (3), was born in Lincoln, October 5, 1724. He married first, 1746, Mary Eveleth, of Stow; second, (intentions dated July 20, 1795), Mrs. Priscilla Martin, of Cambridge. In his will he names wife Priscilla, sons Joseph, Daniel and Nathan, and daughter Sally Eames, heirs of Polly Wheeler and Lovey Willard and sister Rebecca Brown. He died March 28, 1807, aged eighty-three. Children: 1. Mary, born April 29, 1747; died June 4, 1748. 2. Dr. Joseph, born January 30, 1749; married, November 23, 1774, Love Adams Lawrence, daughter of Rev. William and Love (Adams) Lawrence, and granddaughter of John and Love (Minot) Adams (3); was called "a gentleman of Lincoln," a Loyalist who left home during the revolution and spent most of his life in England; served as surgeon in the British Navy, his farm in Townsend was confiscated and sold March, 1780; he died in England, February 3, 1803; children: i. Lovey, born in Lincoln, April 30, 1775; died June 10, 1776; ii. Lovey, born in Liskard, Cornwall, England, June, 1778; died unmarried, 1870; iii. Mary, born 1790, married William Teckell, a solicitor of Liskard, died without issue August 14, 1876; iv. Susanna, born 1792; married Lieutenant Robert Ede, E. N., who died 1834; she died December 5, 1879; of their nine children three were: Emeline Susan, Joseph Adam Ede, and Caroline Ede, who married Joseph Rock, a London merchant, and had seven children. 3. Dr. Charles, born in Lincoln, November 8, 1750; also a Loyalist, removed to Halifax, Nova Scotia. 4. Nathan, born in Lincoln, November 11, 1752; died August 11, 1756. 5. Mary, born October 11, 1754, died August 17, 1756. 6. Sarah, born September 13, 1756; married, August 14, 1783, Robert Eames, of Sudbury. 7. Mary, born July 14, 1758; married, May 4, 1779, Elisha Wheeler, of Sudbury. 8. Nathan, born March 1, 1760; married May 16, 1796, Hannah Soley McCarty. 9. Pattie, born July 15, 1763; married, December 23, 1790, David Lawrence Jr., born 1762, died March 29, 1827, only child of Captain David and Hannah (Sawtelle) Lawrence. 10. Dr. Daniel, born April 14, 1766; married Sarah Goldwaite, daughter of Benjamin; was third postmaster of Keene, New Hampshire. 11. Lovey, born in Lincoln, March 21, 1769; married, March 1, 1804, Henry Willard, of Keene, New Hampshire, born July 20, 1779; died February, 1815. She died a week after her husband. (See Willard).

NORTON There were several early settlers bearing the surname Norton. George Norton, of Ipswich, Salem, and elsewhere, came from London early, took the freeman's oath in 1634, and died in 1659, leaving a widow who married Philip Fowler and had ten children, but no son. William Norton, born 1610, in England, came in the ship "Hopewell," in 1635, was admitted a freeman in 1635-6; brother of Rev. John Norton; left son John, ancestor of Professor Charles Eliot Norton, of Harvard; son Bonus, who settled in Hampton, and no others mentioned in will; daughter Elizabeth. Rev. John Norton, born at Stortford, Hertfordshire, May 6, 1606, a godly man and preacher in England, came with his family on the invitation of Governor Edward Winslow in the fall of 1635, preached at Plymouth, but settled in Ipswich; removed to Boston as pastor of the first church; died April 5, 1663; mentions brothers William and Thomas Norton; left no sons. Nicholas Norton settled in Weymouth, 1635-40, removed to Martha's Vineyard and had sons Joseph, born 1652, too young to be Joseph (1) mentioned below. George Norton, a carpenter, settled in Salem in 1629; admitted freeman May 14, 1634; removed to Gloucester, and to Wenham; no son Joseph in list of children attached to inventory of estate in 1659. Francis Norton, of London, was in Charlestown as early as 1630; had charge of the armory at Boston and had interests at Salem. There were several others from England before 1630.

(I) Joseph Norton, born about 1640, may have been nephew of some of the immigrants named above, though no actual proof of relationship has been found. He settled in Salisbury, Massachusetts, in the vicinity of which the Nortons named above settled. He took the oath of allegiance and fidelity in 1677; was a soldier against the Indians in 1697. He died November 10, 1721, at Salisbury. He married, March 10, 1662, Susanna Getchell, who died his widow, August 18, 1724. Children, born at Salisbury: 1. Son, born 1662; died young. 2. Samuel, born October 11, 1663; soldier in Wells, Maine, 1696. 3. Joseph, born August 14, 1665; mentioned below. 4. Priscilla, born December 16, 1667; married John, son of Robert Ring. 5. Solomon, born January 31, 1669-70; died May 2, 1721. 6. Benjamin, born March 24, 1671-2; died October, 1693. 7. Caleb, born June 25, 1675; married March 6, 1699-1700, Susanna Frame; was soldier in 1697-8; removed to Brunswick, Maine. 8. Flower (daughter), born November 21, 1677. 9. Joshua, born October 13, 1690; died January 22, 1692-3.

(II) Joseph Norton, son of Joseph Norton, was born in Salisbury, August 14, 1665. He married, November 16, 1699, Elizabeth Brown, and settled in Salisbury. He was a soldier against the Indians in 1697. Children, born in Salisbury: 1. Joshua, February 16, 1700-1; mentioned below. 2. Mary, February 28, 1702-3; died May 7, 1703. 3. Judith, March 3, 1703-4; baptized an adult, April 28, 1723.

(III) Joshua Norton, son of Joseph Norton, was born at Salisbury, February 18, 1700-1. He settled in Newbury, and was a periwig maker. He was one of the signers of the petition dated March 9, 1762, presented to the town of Newbury stating that a company had been formed to care for the fire engine, and asking that members be relieved from certain other minor public duties while serving as firemen. The road known as Elbow Lane is mentioned in the Newbury records as running between his house and that of Samuel Swazey, and this land had been in use, though not accepted as a public way, for fully thirty years. It is now within the limits of the city of Newburyport and extends from Market Square to Liberty street. In 1783 it probably extended through what is now Centre street to New Lane, now Middle street. He bought the estate of Benjamin Bishop in 1767. He married Lydia Bishop. Children: 1. Michael, mentioned below. 2. Bishop, died 1808; married Anna ———; a prominent citizen of Newburyport. 3. Constantine. 4. William. 5. Miriam. 6. George, of Newburyport.

(IV) Michael Norton, son of Joshua Norton, was born probably about 1770, and died at China, Maine. He settled before 1790 on what was known as Jones' Plantation, later incorporated as China, Maine, and took up a large tract of land about two miles out of the village. He was a farmer and well-to-do for his day. Late in life he gave his farm to his youngest child, who cared for his parents in their old age. He was a Baptist in religion and a Whig in politics. He married Bethia Williams, daughter of a lawyer of Augusta, Maine. Children 1. Benjamin, mentioned below. 2. Bethia, married ——— Keller, and had son Horace Keller. 3. Ezra, born 1809, died May 30, 1852; married, May 31, 1837, Sarah L. Hanson, a native of Lebanon, Maine. Children: i. Henry C., born January 15, 1840, died April 29, 1852; ii. Albert E., born March 5, 1842, died November 25, 1874, married Lizzie Bennet, May 1, 1874; iii. Myra J., born December 4, 1844, married Ralph J. Whitaker, March 5, 1868; children: Albert E., born

January 9, 1869; Carrie E., April 14, 1871; Lilla M., September 23, 1873; James R., June 22, 1875; Laura G., April 7, 1878; Leroy G., November 29, 1880; Edgar H., February 4, 1883; Sadie B., July 7, 1885.

(V) Benjamin Norton, son of Michael Norton, born at China, Maine, June 20, 1800, died there June 13, 1874. He attended the district school and worked on the farm until he became of age. At this time his father gave him seventy-five acres of land and he settled there as a farmer. About the time of his marriage he built his house. The principal product of his farm was butter and cheese. He was a Baptist in religion and a Democrat in politics. Energetic, industrious, enterprising, he succeeded in business; of kindly, modest, and charitable nature, he possessed many sterling qualities and an exemplary Christian character. He married, 1826, Alice Prebble, born at Whitefield, Maine, died at China, Maine. Children: 1. John Henry, born June 17, 1827; mentioned below. 2. Martha, born April 6, 1829; married Joshua Robbins, of Vassalboro, Maine; had Charles Robbins. 3. Elizabeth, born February 10, 1831; died February, 1900; married Addison P. Gould, of Bangor, Maine; children: Susan, married Frank Jay; Frederick; Abbie, married Daniel Leary. 4. Bertha Williams, born December 3, 1833; resides at West Medford. 5. Orin, born December 20, 1835; married, 1867, Omenia Sarah Brown, of Vassalboro, Maine; children: i. William Herbert, born March 29, 1868, married Lucy H. Bennett, of Newtonville, Maine; ii. Henry Clark, born October 24, 1870; iii. Daniel Newbert, born February 29, 1872; married, June 27, 1900, Mabel Leighton Swan, of Lowell, Massachusetts, and had Doris Mabel, born April 22, 1901, and Newbert Kendall, born January 25, 1903; iv. Carrie Rebecca, born October 30, 1874, married, February 26, 1896, George R. Stevens, of Waterville, Maine; v. John Moffett, born February 21, 1877, died February 27, 1901; vi. Lois Minnie, born December 6, 1879, married Albert T. Merrill, of Waterville; vii. Perley Orin, born November 3, 1882. 6. Hannah Clark, born December 10, 1837; died unmarried, 1875. 7. Daniel, born May 29, 1840; died unmarried, February 1, 1906. 8. Ann Maria, born April 3, 1844; married, October 17, 1866, John Farris, of China, Maine, born September 30, 1839, died August 8, 1901, son of Samuel and Sybil (Hanson) Farris; children: i. Fred A. Farris, born May 3, 1867, died May 30, 1889; ii. Alice M. Farris, born March 6, 1868, married, January 13, 1889, Leon Lewis, of China, and had Ethel M. Lewis, born March 26, 1889, now deceased, and Scott W. Lewis, born February 19, 1892; iii. Sybil E. Farris, born August 4, 1870, married, August 16, 1892, Fred Atkins; iv. George R. Farris, born November 7, 1875, married first, March 9, 1897, Emma Spaulding, second, November 27, 1907, Annie Atkins.

(VI) John Henry Norton, son of Benjamin Norton, born at China, Maine, June 17, 1827, died at West Medford, Massachusetts, December 5, 1904. He attended the Wood district school near his home and assisted in the work of the farm. He learned the trade of carpenter, and removed when a young man to Bangor, Maine, where he worked at his trade. He removed to Arlington, Massachusetts, and engaged in carpentering until 1849, then going to West Medford, where he settled. As soon as he had acquired a small capital he started in business for himself, and became a successful and prosperous contractor and builder, erecting many of the best buildings in Medford and the surrounding towns. Among the contracts were the Brooks school building, the Neighborhood Club House, the Newton Upper Falls school house, and over a hundred private residences. He encouraged the building up of the residential section of Medford by making easy terms of payment for young men. In 1871 he offered to build a house for public worship if the lumber and materials were provided. It was not thought advisable to accept this offer at the time, but he took an active part in the organization of the Congregational church and society of West Medford the next year. It is not too much to say that without his influence and help the church would not have been organized at that time. He made the largest contribution toward the building fund of the old church edifice, and was the largest individual contributor toward the payment of the mortgage debt. For many years he was the largest contributor toward the current expenses of the church and society, and gave a parsonage built expressly for the purpose, located near the new church. He was a charter member of the church and one of its first deacons, taught in the Sunday School, and for several years was chairman of the standing committee of the society. In politics he was a Republican, and although a citizen of Medford for over fifty years never accepted public office. He was interested, however, in everything that pertained to the public good. He could

John H Horton

be called truly a man "diligent in business, fervent in spirit, serving the Lord." He was unassuming in manner, and his voice was seldom heard in public, but his deeds spoke for him. Always industrious, his energy seemed untiring. He married, 1849, Martha R. Huffmaster, born July 6, 1819, died May 22, 1888, daughter of Thomas and Mary (Reed) Huffmaster, of Medford. Her father was a farmer, and was fatally injured in the tornado of August 22, 1851. Children: 1. Thomas Henry, born January 7, 1853; mentioned below. 2. Benjamin J., born January 1, 1854; mentioned below. 3. Frederick L., born January 22, 1855; died July 16, 1860. 4. Susan Alice, born May 4, 1858; died September 15, (?). 5. Carrie R., born June 12, 1859; died January 17, 1869. 6. William S., born March 18, 1863; died September 20, 1863.

(VII) Thomas Henry Norton, son of John Henry Norton, was born at Medford, Massachusetts, January 7, 1853. He attended the public schools until sixteen years of age, and learned the carpenter's trade of his father. He worked as journeyman carpenter for his father, and with his brother, B. J. Norton, took charge of the building of many of the important structures of the town. In 1893 he met with a serious injury sustained by falling some distance to the frozen ground, permanently disabling him and compelling him to give up his work. He then removed to Barnet, Vermont, and resided on the Strobridge homestead, which had belonged to his father-in-law, a farm of thirty-five acres. This he conducted until 1905, when his father died, and he returned to West Medford to take charge of the estate. He is at present a large property owner, including many apartment houses, and his time is fully occupied in looking after his property. He resides at 19 Brooks street, in a house that was built for him by his father in 1885. He attends the First Congregational Church, and is a member of the Brotherhood of Andrew and Philip of that society. He is also a member of the Medford Historical Society and of the Royal House Association. In politics he is a Republican. Mr. Norton is highly esteemed by his townsmen for his many good qualities of heart and mind. He married, December 22, 1881, Lilla Margaret Strobridge, born at Barnet, Vermont, July 2, 1854, daughter of Ebenezer Hinds and Margaret (Somers) Strobridge. Her father was a farmer and prominent in the militia. They have no children.

(VII) Benjamin John Norton, son of John Henry Norton, was born at West Medford, January 1, 1854. He was educated in the public schools and at the Brooks grammar school, supplemented by a course in the Bryant & Stratton Business College at Boston. He learned the trade of carpenter of his father and early became associated with him in the business, beginning by driving the wagon for him. About 1883 he entered the baking business in the Usher Block, on High street, and for four years carried on a successful business. He sold it and entered the employ of the West End street railway in Boston as a conductor, remaining six years. He then entered the employ of William Ricker & Company as salesman on their produce farm. Six years later he became associated with his father again in the building trade, and remained with him until his father's death in 1904. At present he is engaged, like his brother, in looking out for his extensive real estate interests, and resides at 42 Woburn street. He and his family attend the Unitarian Church, and he is a member of the Unitarian Club. In politics he is a Republican. He married, June 29, 1887, Anna Christianna Walkling, born March 24, 1869, daughter of Frederick and Christianna (Kahlhoefer) Walkling of Medford. Children: 1. Ethel May, born June 5, 1888. 2. Gertrude Anna, December 26, 1889. 3. John Benjamin, March 21, 1892. 4. Alice, November 26, 1895. 5. Louis Henry, June 15, 1897. 6. George Henry, August 13, 1899. 7. Ruth, September 24, 1901. 8. Henry Thomas, December 16, 1903. 9. Ralph Edwin, March 7, 1907.

IRWIN This ancient Scotch family attained distinction through the friendship of Robert Bruce for Sir William de Irwin, who was the elder son of William Irwin, of Bonshaw, and sealed his favor with the gift of the estate of Drom, or Drum, and thus the Irwins of Drum became an old feudal baronial house, upon one of whom was conferred the governorship of Aberdeen, and twice its masters refused the earldom of the same province. Sir William was armor-bearer to Bruce, and with the estate he was favored with a coat-of-arms. The three holly leaves were graven on the armorial when he was exalted to the earldom of Carrick.

Sir Alexander Irwin, son of Sir William, married a daughter of Sir Gilbert Hay, lord high constable of Scotland, and had a son Alexander of Drum, who was commander of the Lowland forces at Harlaw, 1411, where he fell fighting. His title and estate then succeeded to his brother John, who took the name Alexander, married his brother's widow, who was a daughter of Sir Robert Keith, great marshal of Scotland. Sir Alexander the successor was knighted by James I, whom his loyal subject afterward repaid as a commissioner to treat for his majesty's ransom.

From the Irwins of Drum descended the Irwins, Irvins and Irvings of Lenturk, Hilltown, Kingcausie, Fortrie, Enniskillen, Murthill, Cutts and other municipalities of Ireland. Burke has this to say of the Irwin family in Ireland: "The Irwins of Tauragoe have maintained a position of great respectability amongst the gentry of the county of Sligo since their settlement in Ireland, but from which branch of the Scottish Irwins or Irvines they descend has not been ascertained. The peculiar name of Crinus, borne by members of the family, is traditionally derived from Krynin Abethnae, second husband of the mother of Duncan, king of Scotland, to whom and his descendants that monarch granted the privilege of bearing the thistle as a crest. John Irwin, who married a daughter of Colonel Lewis Jones, of Ardna-glass, held a commission in the parliamentary army, in which his father-in-law also served, and accompanying Cromwell to Ireland, settled at Sligo".

The emigration from Scotland to Ireland began about the middle of the seventeenth century, and about three-quarters of a century later the descendants of many of those who had become seated in that place of temporary refuge followed the tide of European emigration to the shores of America; and they would have come earlier, but they had fled from the country of their ancestors because of religious persecution and were reluctant to fly in the face of evils they knew not of. They were Protestants, many of them Presbyterians, and because they were not of the church founded by the New England Puritans, they were unwilling to subject themselves to the discipline and punishment visited upon the Quakers and all others who were not of their faith. Many of these Irwins and Irvines were soldiers of the crown and came to take part in the wars with the French for supremacy in the western world.

James Irvine, born 1735, son of George Irvine, was a soldier in his majesty's service.

James Irvine, the Canadian statesman, was born in England, 1766, a son of Adam Irvine who emigrated from Scotland to Canada soon after Cromwell's time.

William Irvine, soldier and surgeon, was born in Enniskillen, Ireland, 1741, graduated from a Dublin university, and was surgeon on board a British ship of war, 1756-1763.

Paulus Aemelius Irving, born Bonshaw, Dumfries, Scotland, 1714, entered the army; became major of foot under Wolfe and was wounded on the Plains of Abraham; administered the government of Quebec, 1765, being commander in chief of the forces. His son, Sir Paulus Aemelius Irving, born Waterford, Ireland, 1751, became lieutenant of foot, 1764, captain, 1768; major, 1775; fought under the British standard at Lexington and Bunker Hill, Three Rivers, Crown Point, Ticonderoga, and under Burgoyne at Saratoga, where the army of the king met its first decisive defeat in the war for American independence.

About the year 1740 two brothers, descendants of Scotch ancestors, left the north of Ireland for this country and settled, one in the valley of the Hudson river, and the other in the province of Lord Baltimore in Maryland. And there was still another of the descendants of the Irwins of Drum, Aberdeen, who also came to this country as a soldier of the king, and whose own descendants have continued to live in the land, and honored it and their noble house with loyal citizenship.

(I) John Irwin was born in the north of Ireland before the middle of the eighteenth century, and while it is not certain that his parents were of Scotch birth, it is known that they came of Scotch ancestors and reasonably certain that the father was descended from Sir William de Irwin, armor-bearer to Robert Bruce, and founder of the house of Irwins of Drum. A few years before his death, while living in Nova Scotia, John Irwin wrote an account of his life, which as a matter of general and family interest is worthy to be placed in these annals.

"This is to certify that I enlisted in the year 1771, in the city of Dublin, Ireland, under the command of Lord Langanier, 9th regiment of foot, he being full colonel, it being commanded by Lieut. Col. Taylor, and I done duty for several years through Ireland, and I Embarked early in the year 1776 for America under the command of Lieut. Col. Hill, and landed at Quebec, Canada; from thence proceeded on a heavy campaign under the command of General Charlton and suffered greatly therein, having wintered in Canada.

"Next summer proceeded on second campaign under the command of General Burgoyne at Saratoga, and suffered there greatly by reason of several engagements—everything but death itself; became a prisoner to General Gates by capitulation and remained a prisoner for 4 years in a dreadful state of confinement, having a family with me all this time, which increased my suffering: being released came into New York and joined the 40th regiment of foot, under the command of Lieut. Col. Musgrave; being discharged in October, 1783, came to Nova Scotia and settled in the county of Shelburne, where I remained, having done military duty since I came to Shelburne until age rendered me incapable"

"signed John Irwin"

John Irwin married probably in England and doubtless his wife accompanied him to Canada in 1776. A brief mention of their children may be made as follows: 1. Samuel, the eldest, was born in Canada and was a farmer there throughout his life of eighty-four years. He married Cynthia Horton. 2. Margaret, born while her father was away from home on military duty. She married Philip Hemeion, a farmer in Shelburne county, where their lives were spent. He lived to be ninety years old, and she died at the ripe age of ninety-six years. They had a large family of twelve children, six sons and six daughters. 3. Hannah, the third child, never married. She was born in the states and lived to be ninety-four years old. 4. Margia, born in Shelburne and died there; she married James Muir, a native Nova Scotian, a famous ship builder in his time, a man of means and much influence. 5. Robert G., of whom mention is made in the next paragraph.

(II) Robert Grandby Irwin, youngest of the children of John Irwin, the soldier immigrant, was born in Shelburne, Nova Scotia, and was brought up on his father's farm, a part of which, fifty acres in extent, he fell heir to. He was a man of good education and made use of his talent by teaching school during the winter seasons for many years. He also was a man of considerable local prominence and exercised a healthful influence among his fellow townsmen. He died at the age of sixty-five years. His wife, Isabella (Firth) Irwin, was born in the north of Ireland and came with her parents to the British provinces in America when she was a child. Her father was John Firth. She was a very faithful helpmeet to her husband and made his a life of contentment to the end of his days: and she survived him many years and died in 1802, aged eighty-four years. They had four children: 1. Captain Samuel G., of whom mention is made in the succeeding paragraph. 2. Thomas, died young. 3. Eliza Ann, died young. 4. Robert G., born in Shelburne and died there, aged seventy-five years. He was a business man, thrifty, industrious and successful. His wife, whose name before marriage was Isabella Archer, was born in Nova Scotia and still alive at the age of seventy-five years, having borne her husband ten children: Frank, a physician, now dead; Robert, a prominent business man, and now (1908) a member of the Nova Scotia legislature; Bessie, unmarried, and lives with her mother; Archer, a physician, now in practice in the Sandwich Islands; Samuel, a manufacturer in Weston, Massachusetts; Anna, died when sixteen years old; Mary, whose husband is a mining engineer in Mexico; Harry, a lawyer in the Sandwich Islands; Frederick, a physician in the Sandwich Islands; Wesley.

(III) Captain Samuel Grandby Irwin, eldest child of Robert G. and Isabella (Firth) Irwin, was born in Shelburne, June 15, 1827, and for something like twenty years was one of the most famous master mariners on the northern Atlantic coast. He seemed to have been born for a seafaring life and from the time he left school until of mature age he followed the life of a seaman, from deckhand to skipper and part owner. When only a boy he shipped on board a coast trader, but from his first trip out he showed the qualities of the true sailorman and it was not long until he was capable of navigating a ship in any waters on the coast from Greenland to below the Delaware capes. At the age of twenty-seven he was master of the "Itasca", afterward sailed other coast traders and eventually became master of the "George J. Marsh" and owner of a three-fifths share in her. While master of the "George J. Marsh" Captain Irwin had the only serious misfortune of all the years of his life on the ocean. In the fall of 1866 he loaded at Greenland for Philadelphia with a cargo of 600 tons of mineral ore and cleared for the passage under favorable conditions considering the fact that the vessel was bottom-heavy on account of the great weight of ore in her hold; but as there was no possible way in which to distribute the cargo and ease off the weight below, he took a sailor's chance and put to sea. The "George J. Marsh" was a stanch boat and behaved well under good handling until the night of September 10, 1866, when she ran into an awful sea in the gulf of St. Lawrence, which sent her down after a mighty struggle of fifteen hours, with all hands at the pumps and her master at the wheel. Under ordinary conditions she would have rode out the gale, but being so very heavy below she could not rise with the swell and therefore her deck was awash all through the night; and when the pumps failed to keep her from filling and she began to sink, the captain, his wife, and crew of fourteen men took to the big lifeboat and pulled clear of the foundered ship before she went down. For the next ten hours the crew, already much exhausted with overwork, succeeded by a hard struggle in keeping the lifeboat afloat until all were picked up by a passing vessel and carried to port. After this unfortunate experience Captain Irwin quit the sea; not because of the shipwreck itself, for he was a born sailorman, every inch of him, but in a large measure his action was influenced by his wife, who spent that September night with him aboard the "George J. Marsh", when their lives were in great peril and when the sinking ship carried down with her a large share of her husband's hard-earned means.

In 1867, having recovered from the effects of a serious illness, Captain Irwin went to Winthrop, Massachusetts, purchased a comfortable house and a large tract of land near the center of the town and began a general real estate and insurance business. At the same time he was constantly looking about for other opportunities, and seeing the need of improved transportation facilities from Winthrop to Maverick Square, East Boston, he purchased at foreclosure sale in 1877 the company franchise and equipment of the horse railroad formerly operated between those points, organized a successor corporation under the name of Boston, Winthrop & Point Shirley railroad, and converted the old system into a narrow guage steam road, connecting with the Revere Beach & Lynn railroad at Orion Heights, and thus constructing the first steam road in the town of Winthrop. At the organization of the new company Captain Irwin was elected president, serving in that capacity for the next three years and operating the road with a fair degree of success, but owing to the difficulty in securing a fair rate for passenger traffic between Orion Heights and Boston it became virtually compulsory that his road be sold to the Boston & Maine Company. But notwithstanding the ultimate outcome of the venture to those most directly interested from a financial standpoint, the fact remains that Captain Irwin did more than any and all other persons in promoting the welfare of the town of Winthrop at the time when Boston was beginning to assume the character of a metropolitan city and men of means were casting about for desirable sites for suburban homes. Indeed he was the leading spirit of this enterprise from its inception, just as he was in later years the prime mover in various other improvements which have been for the prosperity of the town and its people. For many years Captain Irwin was known as a public-spirited, progressive and broad-minded citizen, devoting his energies, time and means to the accomplishment of ends which have advanced the general welfare as well as his own personal concerns, and selfishness was a quality not to be found in his nature. His fine business ability had been utilized by the town in many ways as he had at various times served as sinking fund commissioner, collector of taxes, assessor, selectman, chairman of the appropriation committee, and in addition to these offices had many times been placed upon important committees and delegations connected with private enterprises and philanthropic work of various kinds. During his career as a seaman and officer his experiences were varied and many, and he told some highly interesting stories of the countries he had visited, as well as stirring incidents of his career during that time. Captain Irwin was always genial and lovable, was held in the very highest esteem by both young and old of the town. In the later years of his life both he and Mrs. Irwin had been greatly interested in charitable and educational work.

Captain Irwin married first, in Gloucester, January 3, 1853, H. Almira Deming, born in Nova Scotia, 1830, died in Winthrop, May 6, 1886. He married second, May 11, 1887, in Georgetown, Delaware, Mary E. McGill, a native of Nova Scotia, a woman of superior educational attainments and who has devoted many years of her life to teaching, and more than fifteen years to educational work in the south. Her acquaintance in and about Winthrop and Boston is large, and with grace and becoming dignity she fills an enviable place in the social life of those localities; her own home is a seat of comfort and refined hospitality. She is a regular attendant at the services of the Methodist Episcopal church, of which her husband was a member for more than forty years. One child was born to Captain and Mrs. Irwin, Irene Blanche, who died at the age of three years. By recent adoption they took a daughter into their home, Ruby Ray, born October 16, 1904. Captain Irwin died at his home in Winthrop, September 8, 1908.

LAWRENCE Among the early settlers of Watertown were John and George Lawrence. John Lawrence, a carpenter, settled there early in 1636, and was admitted a freeman March 9, 1636-37. He married first, Elizabeth ———; second, Susanna ———; he had twelve children by his first wife and two by his second wife. In 1662 he probably removed to Groton, Massachusetts. John and George were probably nearly related, possibly father and son, and it is from the latter that the families of Watertown, Waltham and Weston by this name are descended.

(I) George Lawrence was born in 1637, died March 21, 1708-09; his will was dated 1707. He married first, Elizabeth Crispe, born January 8, 1636-37, daughter of Benjamin and Bridget Crispe, of Watertown; she died May 28, 1681. He married second, August 16, 1691, Elizabeth Holland. Children: 1. Elizabeth, born January 30, 1658, married, October 18, 1681, Thomas Whitney, born August 24, 1656, died September 20, 1719. 2. Judith, born May 12, 1660, married, about 1681, John Stearns. 3. Hannah, born March 24, 1661-62, married Obadiah Sawtel, of Groton. 4. John, born March 25, 1664, killed June 15, 1674, by being run over by a load of bricks. 5. Benjamin, born May 2, 1666, married Anna Adams Coolidge. 6. Daniel, twin of Benjamin, was living in Charlestown in 1708. 7. George, see forward. 8. Sarah, married Thomas Rider. 9. Mary, born December 4, 1671, married, April 5, 1689, John Earl, of Boston. 10. Martha, married, November 29, 1697, John Dix, born March 6, 1672-73. 11. Grace, born June 3, 1680, married ——— Edes, of Charlestown. 12. Joseph. 13. Rachel. born July 14, 1694. 14. Patience, twin of Rachel.

(II) George Lawrence Jr., son of George and Elizabeth (Crispe) Lawrence, born June 4, 1668, died March 5, 1735-36. He married Mary ———. Children: 1. Mary, born February 15, 1696-97. 2. George, see forward. 3. Elizabeth, born October 9, 1700. 4. John, see forward. 5. David, born July 16, 1706. 6. Sarah, born January 20, 1708-09, married, 1726, John Baldwin, of Woburn. 7. William, see forward. 8. Anna, born March 1, 1713-14.

(III) George Lawrence, son of George and Mary Lawrence, born June 3, 1698, died August 2, 1773. He married, May 1, 1724, Mary Stearns, born July 20, 1699, died January 21, 1740, daughter of Lieutenant Samuel and Mary (Hawkins) Stearns. He married second, May 13, 1742, Grace Brown, born 1719, died September 9, 1787. He was assessor of Waltham, 1738-39-40-46-48. Children: 1. Abigail, born February 14, 1724-25, died December 8, 1726. 2. Benjamin, born January 30, 1727-28, died abroad in the wars, 1754. 3. Elijah, born April 10, 1732, died April 14, 1805. 4. Joshua, born February 8, 173—, died November, 1735. 5. Jonathan, born and died in 1737. 6. Eunice, born September 19, 1738, died February 8, 1802; married, November 17, 1768, Isaac Stearns Jr., son of Deacon and Elizabeth (Childs) Stearns. 7. Mary, baptized April 17, 1743. 8. George, see forward. 9. Mary, baptized December 14, 1755, married, February 14, 1782, John Herrick, of Andover, Massachusetts.

(III) John Lawrence, son of George and Mary Lawrence, born February 20, 1703-04, died August 23, 1770. He was a resident of Waltham. He married, January 24, 1733-34, Mary Hammond, born February 4, 1714-15, daughter of Thomas and Mary (Harrington) Hammond. Children: 1. Anna, born January 30, 1734-35, married, April 1, 1756, Edward Harrington. 2. Sarah, born July 21, 1737, married, June 15, 1762, Josiah Whitney, born November 22, 1730, died December 3, 1800, son of Ensign David and Rebecca Whitney. 3. John, born November 30, 1740, married, April 16, 1765, Sarah Fiske, born September 19, 1745. 4. Abigail, born December 6, 1744, died October 21, 1803; married, June 7, 1763, Jonathan Fiske, born May 14, 1735, died March 30, 1787. 5. Phineas, see forward.

(III) William Lawrence, son of George and Mary Lawrence, was born May 20, 1711. He was a resident of Weston. He married, November 28, 1734, Mary Perry, born September 7, 1718, daughter of Samuel and Margaret (Train) Perry. Children: 1. Samuel, born August 7, 1735, married, 1758, Mary Clarke, of Medfield. 2. Mary, married, 1758, Isaac Gregory, born February 4, 1734-35, son of Isaac and Grace (Harrington) Gregory. 3. Abigail, born May 7, 1739, married, December 27, 1772, James Priest, born 1749-50, died May 21, 1790. 4. Mercy, twin of Abigail. 5. William, born June 1, 1741, married, October 13, 1763, Hannah Hammond. 6. Josiah, born July 16, 1744. 7. Josiah, born September 29, 1745. 8. Daniel, born September 29, 1747, married, April 22, 1772, Elizabeth Graves. 9. Jonathan, born February 1, 1750, married, 1773, Lucy Morse, of Sudbury.

(IV) George Lawrence, son of George and Grace (Brown) Lawrence, was a resident of Waltham. He married, 1771, Esther Warren, born March 14, 1754, daughter of Asa and Tabitha Warren. Children: 1. Benjamin, born January 31, 1772, died November 25, 1800. 2. George, born December 12, 1773, died February 3, 1796. 3. Jonas, born May 13, 1779. 4. Grace, born March 23, 1782, married, January 23, 1806, Leonard Green, baptized January 30, 1785, son of Samuel and Lydia Green. 5. Eunice, born May 3, 1784. 6. Sally, born July 22, 1786. 7. Elijah, born September 23, 1789. 8. Josiah, born April 18, 1791. 9. Hannah, born May 12, 1793. 10. Esther, born May 17, 1794, married, 1814, Leonard Green.

(IV) Deacon Phineas Lawrence, son of John and Mary (Hammond) Lawrence, was born February 19, 1749. He served as selectman from 1781 to 1786. He married, November 5, 1770, Elizabeth Stearns, born March 17, 1752, daughter of Deacon Isaac and Elizabeth (Childs) Stearns. Children: 1. Susanna, born June 18, 1771-72, married, September 26, 1793, Rev. Nathan Underwood, of Hardwich, a graduate of Harvard in 1788. 2. Elizabeth, born and died in 1773. 3. Phineas, born February 19, 1775, married, December 22, 1796, Polly Wellington, born April 16, 1776, daughter of William and Mary (Whitney) Wellington: children: i. Isaac W., baptized 1797; ii. Louisa, baptized September 23, 1798; iii. Marion, baptized April 6, 1800; iv. Adeline, baptized November 1, 1801; v. William H., baptized November 28, 1803; vi. Sybil, baptized September 8, 1805; vii. Sydney, baptized December 28, 1806. 4. Leonard, born May 6, 1777, died December, 1851; married Nancy ———; child, Frederick, baptized October 7, 1809. 5. Elizabeth, born September 2, 1779, married, December 12, 1797, Abraham Wellington. 6. Priscilla, born December 26, 1780, died July 24, 1803, unmarried. 7. Mary, born May 25, 1785, married, September 23, 1810, Chester Lyman, of Roxbury. 8. Nathan, born May 27, 1787. 9. Abigail, born June 18, 1789, married, April 12, 1810, Jonas Viles, Jr. 10. Jacob, see forward. 11. Lucretia, born January 19, 1797.

(V) Jacob Lawrence, son of Deacon Phineas and Elizabeth (Stearns) Lawrence, was born in Waltham, June 11, 1792, died December 28, 1881. He came to live in the house now occupied by his son Phineas at the time of his marriage in 1817, and resided there until his death. The homestead house was built by his father in 1809; an earlier homestead house was built in 1759, and is now the residence of Charles E. Lawrence, a nephew of Phineas Lawrence, both of the houses (adjoining) stand on the land originally granted to the early settler, George Lawrence. Jacob Lawrence was a farmer, following that vocation all his life. He married, May 15, 1817, Hannah Brown, born December 5, 1795, daughter of Jonas and Relief (Pierce) Brown (a full account of the Brown ancestry appears in the sketch of George R. Beal, elsewhere in this work). She died August 24, 1877. Children: 1. Edward, born February 28, 1818, married Nancy Stearns: child, Charles E. 2. John G., born January 8, 1820, died August 12, 1896, unmarried. 3. George B., born May 14, 1822, died August 10, 1900, unmarried. 4. Martha B., born May 22, 1824, died January 16, 1904. 5. Phineas, see forward. 6. Frances J., born July 17, 1830, died August 13, 1903. 7. Nathan N., born March 10, 1833, died December 21, 1884. 8. Mary E., born February 4, 1837, died March 7, 1843.

(VI) Phineas Lawrence, son of Jacob and Hannah (Brown) Lawrence, was born in Waltham, August 12, 1826. He was reared on the homestead, where he has passed the eighty-one years of his life. His early education was received in the district school. At an early age he took up farming, and has followed that vocation up to the present time. Both he and his father made a specialty of dairy farming; in 1826 his father established a milk route to Boston, Massachusetts, and this business was carried on successfully for half a century. In politics Mr. Lawrence has always been a Republican, and served on the board of aldermen of Waltham the first two years after its incorporation as a city. He is a member of the Unitarian church. He has been a contributor to the local journal, notable among his papers being, "Trepelo, Past and Present," a series of articles historically descriptive of the part of the city in which he resides, which have often been referred to and quoted as authority. He has also furnished numerous articles on agriculture and horticulture, on which latter subject he may be said to be an enthusiast.

CLAPP This surname had its origin in the proper or personal name of Osgod Clapa, a Danish noble in the court of King Canute (1017-36). The site of his country place was known afterward as Clapham, county Surrey. The spelling in the early records varies from Clapa to the present form, Clapp. The ancient seat of the family in England is at Salcombe, Devonshire, where

Jacob Lawrence

important estates were held for centuries by this family. Their coat-of-arms: First and fourth three battle-axes, second sable a griffin passant argent; third sable an eagle with two heafs displayed with a border engrailed argent. A common coat-of-arms in general use by the family in America as well as England: Vaire gules and argent a quarter azure charged with the sun or. Crest: A pike naiant proper. Motto: "Fais ce que Dois advienne que pourra." The American branches of this family are descended from six immigrants, brothers and cousins, who settled in Dorchester, Massachusetts, whence they and their descendants have scattered to all parts of the country.

(I) Nicholas Clapp, progenitor of the family given herein, lived at Venn Ottery, Devonshire, England. Three of his sons and one daughter, wife of his nephew Edward Clapp, came to America. His brother William lived at Salcombe Regis, England, and besides his son Edward another son Roger Clapp immigrated to America and settled at Dorchester. The family genealogy gives the name of Richard instead of Nicholas (1). Children: 1. Thomas, born 1597; mentioned below. 2. Ambrose, lived and died in England. 3. Richard, had Richard, Elizabeth, and Deborah; remained in England. 4. Prudence, came to New England; married her cousin Edward Clapp, and died at Dorchester, 1650. 5. Nicholas, born at Dorchester, England, came from Venn Ottery, Devonshire, about 1633; town officer, deacon; married Sarah, daughter of William Clapp, of Salcombe Regis, mentioned above; married second, Abigail, widow of Robert Sharp; he died 1679. 6. John, came to Dorchester; died July 24, 1655; mentions brothers and sisters in his will, brother-in-law and cousin Roger; widow married second, John Ellis, of Medfield; left land at South Boston to the town; sold in 1835 for a thousand dollars an acre, about thirteen acres.

(II) Thomas Clapp, the immigrant, son of Nicholas Clapp (1), was born in England in 1597. He arrived from Weymouth, England, July 24, 1633, and in 1634 was at Dorchester, where Nicholas and John had settled; was admitted a freeman at Dorchester 1636; removed to Weymouth, Massachusetts, as early as 1639 and lived on the farm owned later by Hon. Christopher Webb. He removed to Scituate in 1640 and was deacon of the church there in 1647; admitted freeman of Plymouth colony June 5, 1644; deputy to general court 1649; overseer of the poor 1667; a useful and eminent citizen. His farm was in the southwest part of the town near Stockbridge's mill pond, later owned by Calvin Jenkins. He died April 20, 1684, aged eighty-seven. His will, dated April 19, 1684, stated he was in his eighty-seventh year, bequeathing to wife Abigail, children: Thomas, of Dedham, Samuel, Increase and four daughters, mentioned below. Children: 1. Thomas, born March 15, 1639; mentioned below. 2. Increase, born May, 1640, probably. 3. Samuel. 4. Eleazer, removed to Barnstable; killed March 15, 1676, by Indians. 5. Elizabeth, married Captain Michael P. Pierce. 6. Prudence, unmarried. 7. John, born October 18, 1658; died 1671. 8. Abigail, born January 29, 1659-60.

(III) Thomas Clapp, son of Thomas Clapp (2), was born at Weymouth, Massachusetts, March 15, 1639, and settled at Dedham, living in that part incorporated in 1724 as Walpole. He was a housewright. His will was dated December 14, 1688, and proved January 29, 1691. He married, November 10, 1662, Mary Fisher, of Dedham. Children, born in Dedham: 1. Thomas, September 26, 1663; died January 28, 1704. 2. John, February 29, 1665-6; died March 12, 1665-6. 3. Joshua, 1667; mentioned below. 4. Mary, December 13, 1669. 5. Eleazer, November 4, 1671. 6. Abigail. 7. Hannah. 8. Samuel, August 21, 1682; died June 13, 1772.

(IV) Joshua Clapp, son of Thomas Clapp (3), born in Dedham, 1667, died 1728. He resided in Dedham in what was later the town of Walpole, (incorporated 1724). He was a farmer, inheriting part of his father's estate, including half the field near the river bounded north by land of his brother John, six acres adjoining land of James Fales, twelve acres at north of Neponset river, also two cow rights. He married Mary Boyden, daughter of Jonathan. She died May 18, 1718, and he married second, December 4, 1718, Silence Wright, widow of William, and daughter of John Bird, of Dorchester. She was born February 4, 1690. Children, born at Dedham, by first wife: 1. Joshua, 1707; mentioned below. 2. John, 1709, died February 21, 1775, aged sixty-six. 3. Abigail, married ——— Morse. 4. Esther, married ——— Morse. 5. Mary, married Eliezer Robins, of Stoughton. 6. Thankful, 1716. Children of second wife: 7. Silence, 1720. 8. Seth, 1722.

(V) Joshua Clapp, son of Joshua Clapp (4), born in Dedham, 1707, died May 6, 1802, aged ninety-five years. He was a man of high character and a distinguished citizen; captain of his company; justice of the peace and magistrate; deputy to general court; deacon of church at Walpole, formerly Dedham. About 1745 he marched to Boston with his company to defend it from the attack of the French fleet, then expected. He married, December 12, 1728, Abigail Bullard, of Walpole. She died August 12, 1782; and he married second, Deborah, widow of Deacon Hewins. She died November 18, 1797, aged ninety. Children, born at Walpole: 1. Joshua, September 7, 1729; mentioned below. 2. Ebenezer, November 27, 1733; married ——— Fales, of Walpole. 4. Eliphalet, March 6, 1736. 5. Abigail, September 5, 1738; married Benjamin Hartshorn and Jeremiah Smith. 6. Elhanah J., October 2, 1740; died October 13, 1805; married, July 16, 1767, Abigail Partridge. 7. Oliver, January 13, 1743, captain of Walpole company; married Susanna Gray; second, Susannah Clapp, widow of Thomas. 8. Esther, March 23, 1746; married Swift Payson, of Foxborough, son of Rev. Phillips Payson.

(VI) Joshua Clapp, son of Joshua Clapp (5), born in Walpole, September 7, 1729; married Margaret Guild. Children, born at Walpole: 1. Margaret, June 12, 1750; married Benjamin Pettee. 2. Joshua, March 11, 1753. 3. Aaron, February 5, 1755; resided at Walpole; married Lois Holmes; second, Abigail Whitman. 4. Oliver, February 22, 1757; married John Boyden. 5. Eliphaz, September 3, 1760; resided at Walpole; married ——— Boyden. 6. Asa, March 26, 1763; mentioned below. 7. Thomas, born May 19, 1766; married Nancy Boyden. 8. Oliver, September 6, 1768; married Patience Copp.

(VII) Asa Clapp, son of Joshua Clapp (6), born in Walpole, March 26, 1763; married, September 7, 1790, Esther Allen, of Walpole, born December 16, 1771, died May 29, 1839. Asa removed to Marlborough, New Hampshire, about 1798, and settled in the northeast part of the town, near Clapp's Pond. He died there March 31, 1840. Children: 1. Allen, born April 28, 1784, at Walpole; had the homestead; died February 6, 1837; married, February 10, 1819, Hannah Newcomb, of Roxbury, who died March 26, 1846; children: i. John Newcomb, born November 27, 1819, died January 4, 1834; ii. Esther, born September 1, 1822; married Matthew Brown; iii. Lura N., born July 8, 1825, married Edwin Piper; iv. Lydia B., born March 5, 1828, married, January 1, 1861, Elbridge Cummings; v. Sarah, born November 17, 1830; married ——— Fiske; vi. Allen Newcomb, born January 2, 1837, married Josie M. Mason. 2. Asa, born February 11, 1801, at Marlborough, mentioned below. 3. Franklin, born June 17, 1805; died March 13, 1854; married Roxanna Tenney who died April 29, 1853; lived on part of homestead at Marlborough; children: i. Sabrina, born May 31, 1830, married William Guild and William Dort; ii. Charles A., born September 27, 1831, married Eugenia M. Smith; iii. William M., born December 25, 1832; married Elizabeth McCollester and Sarah M. Bryson; iv. Elmer Augustus, born August 15, 1835, went to California, thence to Chile, South America, married a Spanish girl, Damiana Corasco, and had four children, son William lives in Valparaiso, Chile; v. Maria S., born July 21, 1839; married Solon W. Stone. 4. Daniel, born July 16, 1810; married Fannie Snell, of Roxbury; died July 31, 1846; resided in Roxbury.

(VIII) Asa Clapp, son of Asa Clapp (7), born at Marlborough, New Hampshire, February 11, 1801, died 1880. He married, May 5, 1825, Delina Bullard, born January 18, 1801, on the old Bullard homestead at Walpole, and died November 5, 1872. Children: 1. Harriet S., born July 10, 1827; married Charles Robinson; children: George and Harriet Robinson; reside at Walpole. 2. Frances Delina, born December 1, 1829, died May 17, 1850; married William Allen; reside at West Dedham, Massachusetts. 3. Asa Elbridge, born January 29, 1834; mentioned below. 4. George Allen, born May 7, 1838; died February 24, 1850.

(IX) Asa Elbridge Clapp, son of Asa Clapp (8), born in Roxbury, Massachusetts, January 29, 1834, died October 21, 1876. He was educated in the public schools of his native town. He learned the trade of cabinetmaker, and was for many years employed at his trade in the old Everett factory. He married, July 18, 1859, Mary Elizabeth Annis, born at Montville, Maine. (See Annis). Children: 1. Elmer E., born in Walpole, May 23, 1861, mentioned below. 2. Mary Frances, born in Norwood, August 23, 1868; married, October 30, 1905, Herbert W. Fishlock, son of Thomas and Elizabeth Fishlock, born March 13, 1864, in Wiltshire, came to America in December, 1883, and resided first in Boston, now in Roslindale.

(X) Elmer E. Clapp, son of Asa Elbridge Clapp (9), was born in Walpole, May 23, 1861. He received his education in the public schools of South Dedham. He learned the millinery business in the store of J. K. C.

Sleeper & Company, and later engaged in business in partnership with W. F. Tilton, under the firm name of Clapp & Tilton, succeeding his former employers in the same quarters, 12 Summer street, Boston, and is well known in the trade throughout the country. Mr. Clapp is a Unitarian in religion, and has served on the parish committee of the Unitarian church at Dedham. He is a member and past master of Orient Lodge of Free Masons, Norwood; of Hebron Chapter, Royal Arch Masons; of Cypress Commandery, Knights Templar, of Hyde Park. He resides at 30 Highland street, Dedham, where he has made his home. He married Annie F., daughter of Charles and Sarah E. (Vaughan) Hill. (See Hill). Children: 1. Richard E., born May 25, 1883. 2. Elizabeth, born September 7, 1885; married H. D. Bixby. 3. Esther E., born November 28, 1889. 4. Ruth E., born April 3, 1891, died February 8, 1892. 5. Charles E., born October 12, 1892. 6. John B., January 7, 1897.

HILL John Hill, immigrant ancestor of this branch of the Hill family in America, was first recorded as moving from Plymouth to Boston in 1630. He was made a freeman March 18, 1642; was taxed in Dover, New Hampshire, December 8, 1639. He seems to have been interested in land speculation in several places. He was one of the grantees of "Nashaway" in 1640. He died in 1647, probably in Boston. The only child of which there is a record was John, mentioned below.

(II) John Hill, son of John Hill (1), was born about 1624. He inherited land from his father in Dover and was taxed for it in 1650. He lived in that part of Dover called Oyster River, now Durham, New Hampshire. He was a grand juryman 1668-71; was taxed in 1684, after which he is not mentioned. He married, January 16, 1656, Elizabeth Strong. Children, as far as known from deeds and incidental mention: 1. Joseph, born 1657. 2. Samuel, born probably 1659; mentioned below. 3. John, born 1661; married perhaps Sarah Brackett. 4. Benjamin, born April 8, 1665. 5. Hannah, married William Frye.

(III) Samuel Hill, son of John Hill (2), was born probably in 1659. He made a deposition September 27, 1682, in which he says that he was about twenty-five years of age. He was then a constable. In 1685 he sold land to John Smart, which the deed declares he bought of his father, John Hill. He married first, in Kittery, Maine, Catherine Knight; second, October 28, 1680, Elizabeth, daughter of William and Mary Williams, of Oyster River, New Hampshire. He bought land in Eliot, Maine, in 1686. He also owned estates in Portsmouth, New Hampshire. His will was dated August 26, 1713, and proved March 28, 1723. Children: 1. John, born November 30, 1681. 2. Elizabeth, November 7, 1683; married, February 25, 1701-2, George Marshall, of Portsmouth. 3. Mary, April 6, 1685; married Benjamin Welch. 4. Hannah, September 29, 1687; married Samuel More. 5. Abigail, September 29, 1689; married, June 10, 1714, Ebenezer Bennett. 6. Samuel, December 13, 1696; married Mary Nelson. 7. Sarah, July 28, 1701; married, January 13, 1725-6, Joseph Fogg, of Scarborough, Maine. 8. Benjamin, July 2, 1703; mentioned below. 9. Joseph, July 28, 1706; married Abigail Libby.

(IV) Benjamin Hill, son of Samuel Hill (3), was born July 2, 1703. He married, January 12, 1726, Mary, daughter of Andrew and Catherine (Furbish) Neal. Children: 1. John, born December 12, 1727. 2. Eunice, November 6, 1730; married, November 13, 1751, John Shackley. 3. Mary, July 20, 1733; married, October 22, 1761, John Adams. 4. James, December 20, 1734; mentioned below. 5. Catharine, November 6, 1735; married, July 25, 1773, Peter Nowel, of York, Maine. 6. Elizabeth, May 15, 1738; married Samuel Hodge, of Dover. 7. Benjamin, December 24, 1739. 8. Abigail, March 26, 1741; died young. 9. Andrew, December 11, 1742; died young. 10. Andrew, April 3, 1744; married Judith Gerrish, of Newbury, Massachusetts. 11. Abigail, September, 1745; married, August 25, 1768, Ezra Moody, of Newbury. 12. Daniel, April 2, 1748; died November 6, 1749. 13. Anne, November 12, 1750.

(V) General James Hill, son of Benjamin Hill (4), born at Kittery, Maine, December 20, 1734, died August 22, 1811. He married, January 31, 1760, Sarah Coffin, born July 11, 1740, died February 3, 1774, daughter of Edward and Shuah (Bartlett) Coffin; second, June 20, 1774, Sarah Burleigh, died December 10, 1789; third, Martha Folsom, widow, died June 7, 1812, daughter of Jonathan Wiggin. He was a soldier in the French and Indian war, and marched from Newbury, Massachusetts, in the Crown Point expedition from April to December, 1755. He worked as a ship-carpenter on the ship "Achilles." He was captain of a company of militia on Pierces Island for the defence of Portsmouth Harbor, November 6, 1755; was appointed captain of a battalion in the Continental army June 13, 1776. He signed the Association List at Newmarket, July 12, 1776. As lieutenant-colonel he commanded the Fourth regiment of New Hampshire militia, June 27, 1771; was ensign in Captain John Langdon's independent company and marched to Saratoga, where they joined General Gates' army in the defeat of Burgoyne, October, 1777. Although he had been in many engagements in both the French and Indian and the revolutionary wars, he returned home without a wound. With Michael Shute, of Newfields, he was delegated from Newmarket to the provincial congress at Exeter, New Hampshire, April, 1775; he was in the New Hampshire assembly, 1779 to 1785, and a candidate for state senator in 1786, 1787 and 1792. He served on the court martial at the trial of the insurrectionary officers in Shay's Rebellion, September 27, 1786. He was a candidate for congress in 1796, and for the governor's council in 1797. Children, of first wife: 1. Daniel, born July 16, 1761; mentioned below. 2. Sarah, January 5, 1763. 3. Mary, June 2, 1764. 4. James, March 2, 1766. 5. Aphia, December 4, 1767; died June 21, 1770. 6. Eunice, May 28, 1770. 7. Elizabeth, February 22, 1772. 8. William, April 7, 1773. Children of second wife: 9. Hannah, March 27, 1775. 10. John Burleigh, June 3, 1776. 11. Joseph Hoit, June 16, 1778. 12. Benjamin, September 19, 1779. 13. Deborah, May 3, 1781. 14. Aphia, July 4, 1783. 15. Mehitable Burleigh, April 2, 1785. 16. Olive Bridge, January 1, 1787. 17. Amos Shepard, March 30, 1788.

(VI) Daniel Hill, son of General James Hill (5), was born July 16, 1761. He married, August 22, 1784, Elizabeth Burleigh, born June 10, 1766, died March 29, 1845. Children: 1. John Burleigh, born April 22, 1785; died February 27, 1786. 2. Olivia F., born January 21, 1787; died April 6, 1822. 3. Elizabeth, born January 11, 1789; died July 1, 1867. 4. Daniel Jr., born February 13, 1791; died June 8, 1815. 5. Mary B., born November 23, 1792; died June 22, 1867. 6. John B., born January 5, 1795; died June 12, 1841. 7. Nathaniel R., born October 29, 1796; mentioned below. 8. James, born February 10, 1799; died September, 1875. 9. Henry, born April 13, 1800; died February 26, 1803. 10. Mehitable, born December 25, 1802; died December 27, 1874. 11. Sarah Ann Coffin, born January 15, 1806; died February 5, 1874. 12. George Henry, born September 23, 1807.

(VII) Nathaniel Rogers Hill, son of Daniel Hill (6), born October 29, 1796, died July 3, 1878. He resided at Dover and Newmarket, New Hampshire, and married May 18, 1825, Esther Ela, born February 2, 1802, died April 10, 1889, daughter of Nathaniel Whittier and Esther (Emerson) Ela. Children: 1. Esther Emerson, born March 17, 1826; died March 28, 1900; married, April 18, 1848, Oliver Tibbets, of Rochester, New Hampshire. 2. Nathaniel Ela, born November 26, 1827; married, January 21, 1858, Caroline G. Tufts, of Dover, New Hampshire. 3. Daniel, born October 22, 1830; died December 13, 1833. 4. Elizabeth B., born January 25, 1834; died March 12, 1850. 5. Charles Ela, born September 22, 1838; mentioned below. 6. Mary Ednah, born December 15, 1843. 7. Susan Frances, born July 9, 1845; died September 6, 1847.

(VIII) Charles Ela Hill, son of Nathaniel R. Hill (7), was born September 22, 1838. He married, June 20, 1860, Sarah E. Vaughan, daughter of Richard and Eliza P. (Baxter) Vaughan. Children: 1. Elizabeth Vaughan, born April 16, 1861; died October 25, 1866. 2. Annie Florence, born January 5, 1863; married Elmer E. Clapp; (see Clapp). 3. Minnie Alice, born March 9, 1868; died August 3, 1869.

ANNIS

The surname Annis or Ennis is of Irish origin. The usual spelling in Ireland at the present time is Ennis; both spellings prevail in this country.

(I) Curmac Annis, or Ennis (alias Charles Annis), was the first of the name in New England. He was born in 1638, and came with other Protestants from Enniskillen, in the north of Ireland, to Massachusetts. He was a planter in Newbury, Massachusetts, as early as 1666. He married, May 15, 1666, Sarah Chase, who died before 1722. Children: 1. Joseph, born about 1666, weaver, lived with his father; married Dorothy ——, who died at Newbury in 1740; he died August 12, 1758, aged ninety-two; sons Aquila, Jonathan, Joseph, Christopher and Charles. 2. Abraham, born August 18, 1668, weaver, resided at Newbury until 1736, then at Haverhill, his farm of a hundred acres falling in New Hampshire when the line was fixed. (See "Essex Antiquarian," vol. iii, p. 185). 3. Aquila, born June 6, 1670; died April 17, 1672. 4. Isaac, born April 12, 1672; widow Rebecca married Shimuel Griffin. 5. Sarah, married, 1704, Orlando Bagley. 6. Priscilla, born November 8, 1677; married William Godfrey. 7. Hannah, born November 15, 1679; married Ephraim Wood. 8. Anne, born December 28, 1781, married George Worthen.

(II) Andrew Annis, of Boston, may have been related to Curmac Annis, mentioned above, very likely a grandson. His name was spelled Ennis, Enis, Enness, etc., in the Boston records. He married, May 25, 1713, Hannah Belcher. They were married by the Presbyterian minister of Boston. Children: 1. Charles, born September 8, 1722; married, July 15, 1756, Eliza Green, at Boston. And the following probably, none of their births being recorded: 2. Hannah, married Richard Williams, 1739. 3. Mary, married, September 19, 1742, William Roads. 4. Samuel, married Mary Humble, of Wells, Maine, July 6, 1743. (Spelled Annis). 5. Captain John, mentioned below. 6. Jonathan, married, December 12, 1754, Hannah White. And perhaps Lucy, Betsey and Rebecca.

(III) Captain John Annis, born July 20, 1732, married Mary Melony, and came to Maine from Boston, according to the history of Warren, Maine, settling at Broad Cove, Cushing, removing later to Warren. He served in the revolution in the volunteer navy, called privateers, and was shot in battle, receiving a wound that caused his death. His widow married ——— Blaisdel and resided many years on Blaisdel's Island, but died in Camden, Maine. Children: 1. Amy, born July 13, 1754. 2. Susannah, September 28, 1758; married Samuel Boggs 3d; resided at Warren; died November 15, 1838, aged eighty-two. 3. Mary, October 11, 1759; married Alexander Bird, in Camden. 4. Hannah, November 8, 1761; died September 15, 1840. 5. John, January 1, 1764; mentioned below. 6. Thomas, October 5, 1766. 7. Samuel, March 4, 1769; married Sarah Thorndike. 8. Martha, January 24, 1772; resided and died at Boston. 9. Sarah, January 4, 1774; married John Thorndike; resided at Camden; died December 12, 1767, burned to death by accident. 10. James Calder, November 16, 1778, lost at sea.

(IV) John Annis 2d, son of Captain John Annis (3), was born in Warren, Maine, January 1, 1764; married in Boston, (by Rev. Peter Thatcher) Sally Caverly, March 3, 1795. Child: John, mentioned below.

(V) John Annis, son of John Annis (4), born in Belmont, near Belfast, Maine, 1809, died 1851. He married Esther Rowell. They lived at Montville, Maine. Children: 1. Mary E., born at Montville, July 18, 1839; married Asa E. Clapp. (See Clapp).

RADDIN

The Raddin family is identical with the Reading family of England, the difference in spelling having arisen through the custom of spelling in this country. In Marblehead, the original home of the family in this country, we find births, deaths and marriages recorded in this family under the following styles of spelling: Reading, Redding, Redden, Reddin, Reddaine, Reddain, Reddan, Ridden, Riddon, Raddan, Raddin, Readdin, Readin, Reddan, Rodden, Ridden, Readdan, Redan and Raddain. Doubtless this list could be extended by research in other records. The derivation of the name is unquestionably from the town of Reading, Berkshire, England, also spelled Redding, etc., in early records. The town is said to have been named for a Saxon tribe, the Radingas, descendants of Raeda. The town is now shire town of Berkshire, and was an important place before the year 900, though the Domesday Book gives but twenty-eight houses there in 1066. Some of the town was destroyed in 1006 at the time of the invasion of Sweyn, King of Denmark. The ancient coat-of-arms of the Readings was: Argent three boars' heads couped sable. The following is in general use: Argent three boars' heads erased sable. Crest: A griffin sejeant holding in the dexter paw a garland of laurel all proper. A notable branch of the family in America is descended from Colonel John Reading, who came from England to New Jersey in 1684.

(I) Thaddeus Raddin, the immigrant ancestor of the Marblehead Readings or Raddins, was born in England. For the sake of uniformity we shall spell the name Raddin in this sketch, though no uniform style was followed in the early days. Savage (p. 501, vol. iv.) says he was in Marblehead in 1674. He was a commoner at that time. (See New Eng. Reg. viii, p. 288). (See also Essex Inst. Collections ii 279, 280). He was a prominent citizen and was appointed with the selectmen and several others to look into an Indian claim against Marblehead property. But he settled in Lynn first and his children's births are recorded there. Children, born at Lynn: 1. Hannah (twin), born August 12, 1660, died November 13, 1660. 2. Sarah (twin), born August 12, 1660. 3. Hannah, born November, 1662. 4. John, born February 3, 1664-65, mentioned below. 5. Abigail, born June 4, 1671. Perhaps others not recorded.

(II) John Raddin, son of Thaddeus Raddin, was born at Lynn, February 3, 1664-65. He resided at Lynn and Marblehead. He was living at Marblehead Neck at the time of the division in 1724. He married, at Marblehead, March 12, 1692-93, Joan Hawkins, who was a member of the Marblehead Church. (Vital records p. 361). Children, born at Marblehead: 1. Thaddeus, baptized May 13, 1694, married three times. 2. John, baptized April 14, 1695. 3. Mary, baptized January 31, 1696-97. 4. Thomas, baptized June 11, 1699, mentioned below. 5. Hannah, baptized May 18, 1701, married, at Lynn, January 19, 1719-20, Aaron Browne, of Marblehead. 6. Joseph, baptized July 15, 1705. (Page 423, Marblehead vital records). 7. Elizabeth, baptized March 27, 1709.

(III) Thomas Raddin, son of John Raddin, was born at Marblehead about 1690, baptized June 11, 1699. He married (intentions at Lynn, July 9, 1720) Jerusha Collins. Children, born at Marblehead: 1. Sarah, born about 1721, baptized December 8, 1723. 2. John, baptized December 8, 1723, married, September 24, 1744, Sarah Bowden. 3. Eleazer, baptized February 20, 1725-26. 4. Elizabeth, baptized October 20, 1728. 5. Mary, baptized March 7, 1735-36. 6. Benjamin Bullard, baptized July 19, 1741, mentioned below.

(IV) Benjamin Bullard Raddin, son of Thomas Raddin, was born in Marblehead, July 5, 1741, baptized there July 19, 1741. There are very few instances of middle names as early as 1741. The reason for giving this name Bullard does not appear. There were Bullards at Dedham and Sherborn, Massachusetts, and it seems most probable that Benjamin Bullard must have been nearly related to Thomas Raddin or his wife. Benjamin B. Raddin died at Saugus, March 25, 1825. He was a soldier in the revolution in Captain David Parker's company which marched from Saugus on the Lexington alarm, April 19, 1775; and he was also in Captain William Blackler's company, Colonel John Glover's regiment in 1775. (See vol. xii, p. 899, Mass. Soldiers and Sailors in Rev.) He married at Lynn, October 10, 1771, Anna Mansfield. Children, born in Lynn and recorded there, probably of the third parish, which became finally the town of Saugus: 1. Thomas, born June 30, 1772, married, December 19, 1793, Sally Sweetser. 2. Jerusha, born January 29, 1774. 3. John, born March 3, 1775. 4. Robert, born January 10, 1777, married, May 26, 1801, Betsey Danforth. 5. Benjamin, born October 17, 1778, married (intentions November 7, 1807), Mary King, of Danvers. 6. Joseph, born July 10, 1780, mentioned below. 7. Mary, born November 17, 1782.

(V) Joseph Raddin, son of Benjamin Bullard Raddin, was born in Lynn, in what is now the town of Saugus, July 10, 1780, and died at Saugus. Children, born at Lynn, now Saugus: 1. Joseph, born October 19, 1805, died at Saugus, July 22, 1831. 2. Polly, born January 12, 1807. 3. Charles, born May 1, 1809, mentioned below. 4. William, born February 22, 1810. 5. Hiram, born November 19, 1811. 6. Hiram, born February 24, 1816. 7. Milton, born February 9, 1817. 8. Hiram Augustus, born February 17, 1819, cigar maker; married, June 5, 1845, Sarah Mansfield, aged twenty-eight years, daughter of Richard Shea Mansfield.

(VI) Charles Raddin, son of Joseph Raddin, was born in Lynn, now Saugus, May 1, 1809. He was educated in the public schools of Saugus. He became one of the largest cigar and tobacco manufacturers and dealers in the state and acquired a considerable estate. Most of the men of this family were tobacconists and tobacco manufacturers. In religion he was a Methodist, being a charter member of the First Methodist Episcopal Church of Cliftondale, and also its first treasurer, having held this office many years. He married, at Saugus, April 25, 1833, Elizabeth Mansfield, born August 4, 1812, daughter of Richard Shea Mansfield, sister of Hiram Raddin's wife. Children, born at Saugus: 1. Charles W., born February 5, 1834, died October 11, 1896. 2. Lucy Ann, born November 30, 1836, died March 2, 1839. 3. Richard Lowell, born 1838, died February 23, 1839. 4. Fales L., born January 19, 1839, died December 29, 1873. 5. Joseph A., born February 15, 1842, mentioned below. 6. Caroline E., born November 2, 1844. 7. George Pickering, born 1847, died November 9, 1847, at Saugus. 8. Janette, born July 12, 1850. 9. Everett W., born July 1, 1855.

(VII) Joseph A. Raddin, son of Charles Raddin, was born at Saugus, February 15, 1842. He was reared on a farm and in early youth he began to learn the tobacco and snuff business of his father, whom he succeeded in business, continuing this till his death, August 18, 1887. He was a member of Franklin Lodge of Odd Fellows of Boston, and a charter member of Cliftondale Methodist Episcopal Church, of which he was for ten years the treasurer. He married, March 7, 1872, Charlotte E. Breed, born in Lynn, daughter of Ephraim and Jane (Sweetser) Breed. Mrs. Joseph A. Raddin died September 23, 1897.

G. Arthur Tapley.

Children, born at Clifondale: 1. Joseph Arthur, born March 13, 1873, mentioned below. 2. Jennie Breed, born May 19, 1874. 3. Willis Albert, born April 8, 1883. 4. Ellery Herbert, born November 16, 1885. 5. Carrie Elizabeth, born June 21, 1887. 6. Ella May, born August 18, 1889.

(VIII) Joseph Arthur Raddin, son of Joseph A. Raddin, was born at the village of Cliftondale, town of Saugus, Massachusetts, March 13, 1873. He was educated in the public schools of his native town and at the Burdett Business College of Boston. Since 1895 he has been engaged in the retail dry goods business, and dealer in men's and ladies' furnishings in Cliftondale. He is also the owner of the Indian Chief Poultry Farm of Saugus, established in 1888, and has a model farm. Mr. Raddin is a Republican in politics and in 1908 was elected a selectman of the town. He is a member of Cliftondale Lodge of Odd Fellows, No. 193, and of Old Essex Chapter, S. A. R. He has been a member of the Methodist Episcopal church from his youth; is treasurer of the board of trustees of the First Methodist Episcopal Church of Cliftondale, and is superintendent of the Sunday school which is the largest numerically in the Southern Essex district outside the city of Lynn. He married, September 6, 1899, Lavinia Brundage, born in Nova Scotia, August 1, 1876, daughter of George Brundage. They have no children.

(For preceding generations see Mansfield Tapley 1).

TAPLEY. (III) John Tapley, son of Mansfield and Mary (Wyeth) Tapley, born Charlestown, Massachusetts, April, 1774, died September 9, 1847. He married, November 3, 1795, Lydia Tufts, born May 24, 1778, died July 15, 1860. He was a blacksmith by trade, or perhaps a shipsmith, for it was he who superintended the construction of iron work for the American frigate "Constitution," of fame during the second war with the mother country. Lydia Tufts, wife of John Tapley, was a daughter of Samuel Tufts, who was born November 24, 1737, and married, May 11, 1769, Martha Adams, who died August 28, 1811, aged sixty-five years. Samuel Tufts was a son of Peter Tufts, who was born in Medford, Massachusetts, May 10, 1697, and married Lydia Buckman, who died October 31, 1776, aged seventy-two years. Peter Tufts was a son of John Tufts, who was born in Medford, married Mary Putnam and died March 28, 1728. John Tufts was a son of Peter Tufts, who was born in England, and was an inhabitant of Charlestown, on the Malden side, before 1638. With his brother William he kept the ferry in 1646-47. He married Mary Pierce, who died in January, 1702-03, aged seventy-five years.

(IV) John Mansfield Tapley, son of John and Lydia (Tufts) Tapley, born April 24, 1798, died May 10, 1843. He lived in that part of Charlestown known as Trainingfield square. He married, March 10, 1819, Mary Brown, of Marblehead.

(V) George A. Tapley, son of John M. and Mary (Brown) Tapley, was born in Charlestown, February 28, 1820. He married Parnell Munroe Thorp, born September 24, 1821, died December 15, 1896, daughter of Ira, born April 15, 1786, died May 4, 1868, and Catherine (Munroe) Thorp, born July 24, 1791, died June 6, 1869, granddaughter on the paternal side of Eliphalet and Hannah (Lewis) Thorp, of Dedham, who married December 17, 1762, and granddaughter on the maternal side of Philemon and Rhoda (Mead) Munroe, of Lexington, Massachusetts. Eliphalet Thorp was sergeant of militia, April 19, 1775, and with his company marched on the occasion of the Lexington alarm. He continued in the service until June 13, 1783, when he held a commission as captain of the fourth company of Lieutenant-Colonel John Brooks' regiment of Massachusetts militia. Philemon Munroe fought at Lexington, private in Captain Parker's company. He died in 1806. His first wife was Elizabeth (Waite) Munroe, of Malden, who died in 1784, and in 1786 he married Rhoda Mead. Mr. Tapley attended the Unitarian church.

(VI) G. Arthur Tapley, son of George A. and Parnell Munroe (Thorp) Tapley, was born in what formerly was North Chelsea, but now is Revere, Massachusetts, August 12, 1845, and received his early education in the public schools of his native town and at French's Commercial College, Boston. His chief business occupation for many years has been that of farming and market gardening, which he has carried on with gratifying success, for he always has been a practical husbandman, just as in other occupations he has been a practical, common sense business man. He is member of board of trustees and of board of auditors of County Savings Bank of Chelsea. For many years Mr. Tapley has been closely identified with the civil and political life of North Chelsea and Revere, serving in various official capacities, and for the last more than twenty-one years has filled the office of town treasurer of Revere, having been first elected in 1887. He holds membership in the New England Order of Protection, and also since June, 1900, has been a member of Old Suffolk Chapter of the Massachusetts Society of the Sons of the American Revolution. Mr. Tapley's eligibility to membership in this famous organization is established through two principal lines—Thorp and Munroe: his great-grandfather, Eliphalet Thorp, 1738-1812, of Dedham, Massachusetts, a minute-man; sergeant, Lexington, April 19, 1775; sergeant, Captain Guild's company, Colonel Heath's regiment, enlisted April 30, 1775; Lieutenant-Colonel Brooks' regiment, continental army, January 1, 1777, to December 31, 1779; commissioned captain September 16, 1780; captain, Sixth Company, Seventh Massachusetts Regiment, 1781; captain, Fourth Company, Seventh Massachusetts Regiment 1781; captain, Fourth Company, Seventh Massachusetts Regiment to June, 1783. His great-grandfather, Philemon Munroe, 1753-1806; private, Captain Blaney's company, Colonel Eleazer Brooks' regiment, January 12 to February 3, 1778, as guard at Cambridge; private, Captain Walton's company, Colonel Brooks' regiment, September 4-11, 1778.

On October 29, 1889, Mr. Tapley married Helen A. Pickering, born July 16, 1863, daughter of William and Helen Althea (Doyle) Pickering, of Salem, and by whom he has two children: William Thorp, born October 5, 1893, and Thelma Althea, born May 25, 1895.

(For ancestry see Joseph Pope 1).

POPE (III) Joseph Pope, eldest surviving son of Joseph and Bethesda (Folger) Pope, born in Salem, June 16, 1687, died 1755. He was a farmer and lived at "the village" That he was a man of substance is shown by his own upright life and the prominence afterward attained by his sons and daughters. He married, February 17, 1715-16, Mehitable Putnam, born July 20, 1695, daughter of John and Hannah Putnam; children: 1. Joseph, baptized September 1, 1717; when grown to manhood settled in Pomfret, Connecticut; married, October 7, 1743, Hannah Shaw, of Salem; their son, Joseph Pope Jr., born in Pomfret, September 28, 1746, graduated from Harvard College 1770, ordained minister of Congregational church 1773, preached many years in Spencer, Massachusetts, and died March 8, 1826. 2. Mehitable, baptized May 3, 1719; married April 18, 1741, Joseph Gardner, son of Abel Gardner and Sarah Porter, and had Joseph, Mehitable, Nathaniel and Eunice Gardner. 3. Hannah, baptized September 23, 1721, died 1764; married June 30, 1739, Israel Putnam, born January 7, 1717-8; removed to Pomfret, Connecticut, 1739, and there Mr. Putnam engaged in farming and acquired both wealth and influence. He was Major General Israel Putnam of the Continental army during the revolutionary war, one of the famous characters of his time, and active both in military and civil life. He died May 19, 1790. 4. Nathaniel, baptized May 17, 1724, died November, 1800 (see post). 5. Eunice, baptized April 30, 1727, died January, 1821, aged ninety-four years; married October, 1745, Colonel John Baker, of Ipswich. "She was a remarkable woman, and retained her faculties to the last. She was a connection of the late General Putnam, and was full of the same ardor that possessed him". 6. Mary, baptized May 31, 1730; married November 28, 1748, Samuel Williams, of Pomfret, Connecticut. 7. Ebenezer, baptized June 9, 1734, died November 4, 1802; married October, 1754, Sarah Pope, died October 12, 1832, daughter of John and Mary (Eaton) Pope; their children: Lucretia, John, Eben, Lucy, Oliver, Mary, Elizabeth, Jane and Abraham Gould Pope. 8. Eleazer, baptized November 14, 1736; married July 7, 1757, Nanny Putnam; children: Eleazer, Rebecca, Molly, Joseph, Mehitable, Nanna, Allen, Huldah, Perley Putnam, Betsey, Jasper and William Pope. 9. Elizabeth, baptized October 14, 1739; no further record.

(IV) Nathaniel Pope, second son of Joseph and Mehitable (Putnam) Pope, born in Salem, had his home and farm at "the village". Like his brothers and others of his father's family he was a man of high character, although he led a comparatively quiet life. He married first, Mary, daughter of Jasper Swinnerton, born 1728, died December 20, 1773, having borne her husband eleven children. He married second, December 23, 1784, Sarah Clark, daughter of Rev. Peter and Deborah (Hobart) Clark, of Danvers, Massachusetts, born December 18, 1738, died February 12, 1802, having survived her husband about two years. He died in November, 1800, and his estate was administered by his sons Elijah and Amos. Children of Nathaniel and Mary (Swinnerton) Pope: 1. Mary, born December 12, 1748; married June 4, 1777, Aaron Gilbert. 2. Eunice, born February 19, 1751; married September 6, 1773, James Putnam. 3. Nathaniel, born March 22, 1753, died unmarried, February 10, 1778. 4. Rebecca, born April 16, 1755; married January 27, 1784, Jonathan Proctor. 5. Hannah, born August 21, 1757, died aged twenty-one years. 6. Jasper, born October 10, 1759; died aged nineteen years. 7. Ruth, born November 7, 1761, died aged two years. 8. Zephaniah, born May 6, 1764, died unmarried, aged thirty-two years. 9. Elijah, born January 28, 1766, (see post). 10. Mehitable, born April 3, 1768, died June 2, 1837; married Caleb Oakes, of Danvers, and was mother of William Oakes, of Ipswich, the botanist, who was born July 1, 1799, died July 31, 1848, graduated from Harvard College in 1820. 11. Amos, born in Danvers, February 20, 1772, died there January 26, 1837; married January 16, 1806, Sarah Goodale, born April 19, 1773, died September 7, 1832; children: Zephaniah, born December 15, 1807, and Eunice, born May 30, 1810, died October 20, 1834.

(V) Elijah Pope, fourth son and ninth child of Nathaniel and Mary (Swinnerton) Pope, born January 28, 1766, died in Danvers, February 16, 1846. He married, June 20, 1791, Hannah Putnam, who died in Danvers, September 10, 1844. Children: 1. Nathaniel, born August 2, 1792 (see post). 2. Hannah, born September 29, 1794; married Francis Fletcher, of Dunstable, Massachusetts; daughters, Rachel, Hannah and Mary Fletcher. 3. Betsey, born February 18, 1797; married Samuel Putnam; removed to Brooklyn, New York. 4. Mary, born April 19, 1799, died single, June 25, 1823. 5. Jasper, born July 14, 1802; married first, December 13, 1830, Harriet Felton, born September 19, 1803, died November 24, 1843; second, February 9, 1846, Sarah Felton, born January 4, 1807. One son by second wife, Jasper Elijah Felton, born February 12, 1847. 6. Phebe, born November 8, 1807, died August 25, 1830. 7. Elijah, born July 13, 1809; married, 1831, Eunice Prince, born May 19, 1811; children: Francis Elijah, Nathaniel A., Samuel Putnam, Mary Elizabeth and James Arthur Pope.

(VI) Nathaniel Pope, eldest son and child of Elijah and Hannah (Putnam) Pope, was born in Danvers, Massachusetts, and was a successful and substantial farmer of that town, where his life was spent. He occupied a position of influence among the townsmen, filled various important offices, being selectman many years, member of the school committee, and a prominent member of The First Religious Society of the first parish, sometimes called Dr. Braman's church. He married first, August 8, 1814, Abi, daughter of John Preston; she was born February 13, 1791, and died March 1, 1841, and was the mother of all of his children. He married second, March 9, 1848, Charlotte Flint, born May 12, 1801, daughter of Elijah Flint and Elizabeth Putnam. Children of Nathaniel Pope: 1. Elizabeth Putnam, born February 12, 1816; married Andrew M. Putnam, of Danvers. 2. Harriet Adeline, born September 8, 1817; married Henry F. Putnam, of Danvers. 3. Mary Putnam, born July 26, 1819; married Calvin Putnam, of Danvers. 4. Aseneth Preston, born September 19, 1821; married Nathan Tapley, of Danvers. 5. Ira Preston, born September 11, 1823; married Eliza C. Batchelder. 6. Daniel Putnam, born March 8, 1826; married Lydia N. Dempsey. 7. Hannah Putnam, born June 2, 1828; married Dr. Bowman Bigelow Breed, of Lynn. 8. Phebe Mansfield, born May 12, 1830, died August 29, 1830. 9. Jasper Felton, (see post).

(VII) Jasper Felton Pope, youngest child of Nathaniel and Abi (Preston) Pope, was born at Danvers Center, April 4, 1832, died in Beverly, Massachusetts, January 27, 1906. His youth was spent in his home town and there he received his early education in the public schools. Later he was a student in the academy at Randolph, Vermont, and upon leaving school he returned home and worked as a clerk first in a general merchandise store at Danversport, and afterward for his brother, Ira P. Pope, a manufacturer of shoes. In 1874 Mr. Pope became a clerk in the office of Calvin Putnam, his brother-in-law, who then was engaged in a general lumber business in Danversport and Beverly, and two years afterward, in 1876, he removed his family to the latter named city. In 1880 he acquired a partnership interest in the business and the firm name became Putnam & Pope, and still later, when Mr. Pope's son, Jasper R. Pope, came into the firm, the style became J. F. Pope & Son.

Mr. Pope was a capable and reliable man of business in every respect, and showed himself worthy of the confidence and esteem of all men of business in the town and city in which he lived, and the business success of the firms with which he was connected was due to a large extent to his energy and capacity. Outside of personal concerns, Mr. Pope contributed his full share of work for the public welfare of Beverly, its people and its institutions. He was neither politician nor partisan, but he held well-grounded opinions on all public questions, whether of local or of general importance. He was a member of the Beverly board of trade, taking an active part in the work aimed to be accomplished by that body, and also was a member of the finance committee of the Lumber Mutual Fire Insurance Company of Boston. He was known as a liberal and public-spirited citizen, interested in all enterprises for the public welfare and always ready to contribute his share of either work or means to accomplish the desired object. His domestic life was always pleasant and his home was a center of comfort and hospitality.

Mr. Pope married, November 27, 1856, Sophia Jane, born in Rindge, February 11, 1831, died in Beverly, December 8, 1892, daughter of Abraham and Asenath (Partridge) Richards, of Rindge, New Hampshire. He married second, January 14, 1897, Martha Mansfield, daughter of Andrew and Sophronia (Preston) Mansfield; Mrs. Pope died July 23, 1907. Children of Jasper Felton and Sophia Jane (Richards) Pope: 1. Miriam, born February 23, 1859. 2. Jasper Richards, born August 29, 1863 (see post). 3. Elizabeth Putnam, born December 29, 1865. 4. Elsie Wilder, born October 6, 1869, died June 2, 1870.

(VIII) Jasper Richards Pope, son of Jasper Felton and Sophia Jane (Richards) Pope, was born in Danvers, August 29, 1863. He received his education in the public and high schools of Danvers and Beverly, and after completing his studies became associated in business with his father. From the time his father admitted him to partnership until the death of the senior Mr. Pope, Jasper R. was junior member of the firm, and at the present time is sole proprietor of the business. He is also serving in the capacity of vice-president of the Beverly National Bank. Mr. Pope takes an active interest in all movements for the welfare of his adopted city, and is actively connected with the Beverly Hospital. He is a man prompt in action, cordial and considerate in his intercourse with his associates and warmly attached to his friends.

Mr. Pope married, November 24, 1884, Hittie Porter, daughter of Francis A. and Caroline A. (Porter) Couch, of Salem. Children: 1. Chester Couch, born February 20, 1886, attends Harvard College, scientific course, class of 1908. 2. Ruel Putnam, born February 9, 1888, attends Harvard College, academic course, class of 1910.

POWERS The name Poer, Power and Powers, is found in English history from the times of the Norman Conquest, and one of the officers of William the Conqueror bore the name and greatly honored it in the battle of Hastings, and his name appears on the roll of that battle as preserved in Battle Abbey. Richard Poer was high sheriff of Gloucestershire 1187, and it is on record in the Herald's College that "he was killed while defending the Lord's day." Sir Roger le Poer, an "English knight," held a chief command in the army of King Henry II when he invaded Ireland for conquest in 1171, and for "distinguished services rendered" large grants of land were made to him by the crown. In the Domesday Book of St. Paul's the names of Walter Poer (Power) appears as possessing various landed rights in Ireland as a gift from the crown for services rendered in 1222. In America the name appears in "The Genealogies and Estates of Charlestown in the county of Middlesex and Commonwealth of Massachusetts, 1629-1818," prepared by Thomas Bellows Wyman, as: John Power or Powers, hosier, married Sarah and had a son Peter born in 1643. No record is found of any descendants of Peter, and as Sarah or Sally Power sells land in 1645 under power of attorney to Gaudy James, it is probable that her husband, not finding the business of hosier profitable, returned to England, where he was later rejoined by his wife and possibly son Peter who was at that time an infant. Then we have Nicholas Power, who came to the colony of Massachusetts Bay, removed to Rhode Island, where he had an only son Nicholas, and the succeeding generations were strangely limited to one male, and after several generations the lone male representative of the name failed of issue. Thomas Power, a blacksmith, appeared in Charlestown, where he was married, February 17, 1714-15, to Abigail Fosket, and they had five children, but their descendants do not appear to have been especially notable, and mostly confined to the town and city of Boston. We can therefore safely say that the progenitor of the numerous and well known families of Powers in New England trace their ancestry direct to Walter Power.

(I) Walter Power, according to a manuscript record left by the Rev. Grant Powers, of Goshen, Connecticut, from family tradition, arrived in Salem, colony of Massachusetts Bay, 1654. and married the daughter of a London goldsmith. Middlesex county records give this marriage: "ye eleventh page of ye first month 1660," Walter Power married Trial, daughter of Deacon Ralph and Thanks (or as sometimes written Thankeslord) Sheppard, at Malden in that county. Ralph Sheppard came from Stefney Parish, London (in Essex), July, 1635, with his wife Thankes. His age is recorded as twenty-nine, and that of his wife as twenty-three. They had one child Sara, aged two years, and they settled in Weymouth, removed to Malden, where he was deacon in the First Church, and died September 11, 1693, his gravestone still preserved, recording his age as ninety years. W. W. Fowler, in "Hints to Genealogists," places the English location of the Power immigrants who made a home in New England, as Essex, judging from the surnames that occur in Monant's history of Essex of families of repute who lived in that county in the fifteenth and sixteenth centuries.

Walter and Trial (Sheppard) Power settled at the time of their marriage in Concord Village, Middlesex county, the place becoming the town of Littleton, adjoining the Indian settlement of Nashobe, which property Deacon Ralph Sheppard bought of Lieutenant Joseph Wheeler. In 1694 Walter Power purchased of the Indians one-fourth of the township of Nashobe, and when he died, February 22, 1708, his remains were doubtless buried in the old Powers burial ground, as were those of his widow, who survived him many years. She was born February 10, 1641, but the date of her death is not on record. The children of Walter and Trial (Shepard) Power were: William, born 1661 (q.v.); Mary, born 1663, married Lieutenant Joseph Wheeler, January 1, 1681, died 1706; Isaac, born 1665; Thomas, 1667; Daniel, May 10, 1669; Increase, July 16, 1671; Walter, June 28, 1674; Jacob, December 15, 1679; Sarah, February 8, 1683. Walter Power used this form of the family name. It is understood in the present-day family that his son used the form Powers; that in the third generation the form of Power was observed; since then the name has been written Powers.

(II) William, eldest child of Walter and Trial (Sheppard) Power, was born in Concord Village, 1661. He married Mary, daughter of John and Hannah Bank (or Bauk), of Chelmsford. He is referred to by his father as his oldest son, and he inherited the homestead place and the Powers saw mill. He died March 16, 1710, and was doubtless buried in the Powers burial ground. Children of William and Mary (Bank) Power: John, born 168—, married Elizabeth Robbins, and died 1756; William, born 1691 (q.v.); Experience, May 10, 1693, married John Perham; Mary, April 25, 1698, married William Elder; Samuel, September 23, 1701, died at Newport, Rhode Island, 1738; Lemuel, born 1703; Ephraim, 1705, married Lucy, daughter of Isaac Powers; Walter, born 1708; Benjamin, October 10, 1711.

(III) William, second son of William and Mary (Bank) Powers, of Chelmsford, was born in Concord Village, 1691. He was married March 16, 1714, to Lydia Perham, and they lived on the westerly side of the town of Grafton, where his children were born. His wife was a native of Chelmsford. He was a cordwainer by trade. They had three children: Lemuel, born 1714 (q.v.); William, April 15, 1717, married, November 14, 1739, Remembrance Pearce; and Stephen. He died in Grafton, and after his death his widow became insane.

(IV) Lemuel, oldest child of William and Lydia (Perham) Powers, was born in Grafton in 1714; was married, January 14, 1742, to Thankful, daughter of James and Hannah (Larned) Leland, of Grafton. She was born August 16, 1724, and died in 1809. Lemuel Powers was a cooper by trade and occupation in Northbridge, Massachusetts, and he administered the estate of his father and became the guardian of his mother who was insane after his father's death. Lemuel Powers died at Northbridge in 1792, and his widow removed to Croydon, New Hampshire, and lived with her children up to the time of her death in 1809. The children of Lemuel and Thankful (Leland) Powers, of Northbridge, Massachusetts, were: Deliverance, born December 9, 1742, married John Rokes, and died 1770; Ezekiel, March 27, 1745, married Hannah Hall, and died November 11, 1808; Lydia, January 28, 1747, married Jonah Stow, of Croydon, New Hampshire, and died 1783; Prudence, 1750, married Gresham Ward, of Croydon, and died 1799; David, March 4, 1753, married twice, was a soldier in the American revolution, and died March 8, 1813; Lemuel, born in 1756, became a Baptist clergyman, and married Abigail Newland, and their daughter Abigail, born in Stillwater, New York, in March, 1798, was married February 5, 1826, to Millard Fillmore, who became the thirteenth president of the United States, and their only son, Millard Powers Fillmore, was a lawyer in Buffalo, New York; Sarah, born

1758, married twice and died 1820; Samuel, born in 1762 (q.v.); Mary, 1765, married Dean Sherman Cooper, and died June 18, 1847.

(V) Samuel, youngest son and ninth child of Lemuel and Thankful (Leland) Powers, was born in Northbridge, Massachusetts, in 1762. He was a soldier in the American revolution, having served as a private in Captain Edmund Hodges's company, Colonel Josiah Whitney's regiment, two months and seven days, although at the time he was only fifteen years of age. He marched with the regiment to Rhode Island, starting out on the day of his enlistment, May 5, 1777, and returning after his discharge, July 5, 1777. He was married, December 9, 1782, to Chloe, daughter of Deacon John and Mary Cooper, and settled in Croydon, New Hampshire. He was an officer in the state militia with the rank of colonel, and a member of the state legislature. He died in Croydon, March 9, 1813. The children of Colonel Samuel and Chloe (Cooper) Powers, of Croydon, were: Olive, born September 11, 1786, died unmarried December, 1841; Captain Obed, April 20, 1788, married Cynthia Cummings, removed to Cornish, New Hampshire, where he died; Judith, March 16, 1790, married Fry Barton, removed to the state of New York, where she had a large family; Nancy, 1792, married David Kinney, lived in Plainfield, Vermont, and died in 1829; Chloe, May 21, 1795, married Lemuel Martindale, and removed to Iowa; Captain Samuel, May 21, 1795, died unmarried December 12, 1828; Ara, February 25, 1797, married Mary Seaver, died 1865; Lemuel, March 10, 1801, died March 14, 1803; Solomon L., January 2, 1804, married Catherine Atkinson, and lived in Gettysburg, Pennsylvania; Ithamar, December 21, 1805, died unmarried November 23, 1834; Larned (q.v.), born April 20, 1808; Randilla, October 6, 1811, married Alfred Ward, of Newport, New Hampshire.

(VI) Larned, youngest son and eleventh child of Colonel Samuel and Chloe (Cooper) Powers, of Croydon, New Hampshire, was born in Croydon, April 20, 1808, married Ruby Barton, removed to Cornish, New Hampshire. He was a successful and intelligent farmer, and greatly interested in educational matters. He also took a large interest in political affairs, but always declined to accept any office. Children, born in Cornish, New Hampshire: Caroline M., 1837; Erastus B., Victoria, Samuel Leland (q.v.). Erastus became a law partner with his younger brother, Samuel Leland, after his partnership with J. H. Barton, Jr., was discontinued in 1881.

(VII) Samuel Leland, youngest son of Larned and Ruby (Barton) Powers, and of the seventh generation from Walter Power, the immigrant, Salem, 1654, was born in Cornish, Sullivan county, New Hampshire, October 26, 1848. He worked upon his father's farm, attended the district school, prepared for college at Kimball Union Academy, and Phillips Academy, Exeter, New Hampshire, and matriculated at Dartmouth College, Hanover, New Hampshire, in 1870, taught school at interims during his college course on Cape Cod, and was graduated A. B., 1874, and was winner of the Lockwood prizes for oratory and composition. He studied law in the Law School of the University of the City of New York, and in the law office of Verry & Gaskill, in Worcester, and was admitted to the Worcester bar in 1875. He commenced to practice law in Boston in January, 1876, in partnership with Hon. Samuel W. McCall, who was a classmate of his at Dartmouth, and who for many years has represented Massachusetts in congress. Mr. Powers for four years was associated with Colonel J. H. Benton, Jr., later was a partner with his brother, Erastus B. Powers, and in 1888 became counsel for the New England Telephone and Telegraph Company, and for many years devoted himself exclusively to representing corporations engaged in electrical business. In 1897 he formed a law partnership with Edward K. Hall and Matt B. Jones, which continued until 1904, when Mr. Jones retired to become the attorney of the New England Telephone and Telegraph Company, and a new partnership was formed under the name of Powers & Hall. This is one of the active law concerns of Boston, and is located at 101 Milk street.

Mr. Powers removed to Newton in March, 1882, where he has since resided, and taken an active interest in social and public affairs. He was a member of the Newton common council for three years, two years of which he was its president, and a member of the board of aldermen for one year, and for three years a member of the school board. He was nominated unanimously for congress in 1900, and represented the Eleventh Massachusetts District in the Fifty-seventh Congress, and the Twelfth Massachusetts District in the Fifty-eighth Congress, there having been a re-districting while he was serving in congress which made a change in the district which he represented. He retired voluntarily from

Paul L. Powers

congress, against the earnest protest of his district, on March 4, 1905, to devote himself exclusively to the practice of law. While in the national house he served upon the committees of judiciary, District of Columbia, and elections. He was one of the sub-committee of five appointed from the judiciary committee to frame the bill for the regulation of trusts in the Fifty-seventh Congress, and he was one of the managers appointed by the speaker to conduct the impeachment trial of Judge Swayne, before the Senate, in the Fifty-eighth Congress.

He was one of the founders and the first president of the famous Tantalus Club of Washington, and is at the present time the president of that organization. He was one of the founders and president of the Newton Club; has been president of the Channing Unitarian Club, is a trustee of Dartmouth College, vice-president of the Massachusetts Republican Club, and is the Massachusetts vice-president of the Merchants' Marine League. He is also a member of many of the leading social clubs in and about Boston.

Mr. Powers was married, in 1878, to Eva Crowell, daughter of Hon. Prince S. Crowell, of Dennis, Massachusetts. They have one son, Leland Powers, born July 1, 1890, who is now a student at Dartmouth College.

(For ancestry see Thomas Gleason 1).

GLEASON (IV) William Gleason, son of Isaac Gleason, born January 2, 1730, died February 3, 1818. He settled in Billerica, Massachusetts, and leased the college farm east of the Shawshin river and afterward bought it. This farm remained in the Gleason family until 1850, when William S. Gleason, who then owned it, sold it and removed to the village to live in a house on the south side of the Andover road. William Gleason was a taxpayer of Billerica as early as 1750. He married Mary Seger, died October 5, 1776, aged forty-five years; second, June 25, 1780, Mary Goss, widow of James Goss, and she died June 11, 1817. Children, born in Billerica: 1. William, born August 21, 1756; died young. 2. Mary, born August 17, 1758; married Mark Pitman; lived in Maine. 3. Hannah, born December 10, 1760; married Timothy Watson, son of Joseph. 4. William, born February 13, 1763; mentioned below. 5. Rebecca, born December 10, 1765; married February 28, 1786, Joseph Heywood; had Joseph, born March 14, 1800, graduate of Bowdoin College, 1821; married Maria, daughter of Hon. Judah Dana, judge of Maine supreme court. 6. Joseph, born February 5, 1768. 7. Ruth, born May 2, 1770. 8. Sarah, born August 13, 1772; married July 2, 1801, William Homer; children: William, Lucy, Augustus, Aaron and Francis. 9. Lucy, born March 21, 1776; died young. 10. Lucy, baptized July 7, 1782.

(V) William Gleason, son of William Gleason, was born at Billerica, February 13, 1763. He was brought up on his father's farm and attended the common schools of his native town. He succeeded to the homestead and was a well-to-do farmer. Besides general farming he had an excellent dairy and raised cattle, and like many farmers of that section raised hops. He was a useful and honored citizen, a prominent and devout member and for many years deacon of the Congregational church of Billerica (orthodox). He served in the state militia and held various town offices. In his later years he was a Whig in politics. He married, at Bedford, February 10 or 11, 1795, Sarah Bacon, born September 1, 1771, died December 15 or 16, 1852. Children, born at Billerica: 1. Sarah, born August 1, 1797; married June 1, 1826, Robert Ames, of Woburn; children: i. Robert Erskine Ames, born July 15, 1828, died May 12, 1906, married first, January 1, 1862, Sarah Matilda Farrington, of Methuen; second, March 1, 1874, Mary Anna Severance, of Woburn, and had by his first wife, Clara Matilda Ames, born February 26, 1864, married October 22, 1882, William Allen Prior of Woburn (had children: Allen Ames Prior, born November 19, 1890, and Ruth Tisdale Prior, born March 23, 1894); Erskine Luville Ames, born July 18, 1870, married January 1, 1896, Alversa Goodale, of Lowell, (children: Harold Farrington Ames, born December 1, 1896, Warner Goodale Ames, born September 3, 1899, and Charles Nathan Ames, born March 16, 1906). ii. Henry Lyman Ames married Charlotte E. Converse of Woburn. 2. Bertha, born February 20, 1799, died February 20, 1799. 3. William, born January 11, 1801; died March 1, 1801. 4. Mary Ann, born April 13, 1803. 5. Elizabeth, born October 8, 1805, died September 12, 1895; married December 1, 1831, Jeremiah Goldsmith, of Andover; children: i. William Gleason Goldsmith, born November 28, 1832, married March 29, 1865, Joanna Bailey Hart, and had Clara Gleason Goldsmith, born February 5, 1866, died March 4, 1873; Clarence Goldsmith, born May 29, 1874, married Ethel Peabody Southwick (had son William

Gleason Goldsmith, born February 7, 1907); Bessie Punchard Goldsmith, born November 21, 1882; ii. Elizabeth Goldsmith, born December 23, 1834, died October 12, 1854; iii. Jeremiah Goldsmith, born March 27, 1837, died in Florida, August 20, 1871, he served valiantly during the civil war. iv. Josiah Goldsmith, born October 8, 1839, died May 24, 1883; v. Albert Goldsmith, born June 11, 1842; vi. Joshua Goldsmith, born April 3, 1845, died December 29, 1851. 6. Abigail Harriet, born January 22, 1808; married April 23, 1829, George Crosby, son of Deacon Michael Crosby, of Bedford; son, Frank Crosby. 7. William Segur, born November 1, 1809; married June 1, 1842, Mary Baker; child: Sarah, born in Billerica. 8. Louisa, born February 3, 1812; married May 15, 1844. Daniel Richardson, of Woburn. 9. Izah, born and died November 9, 1814. 10. Josiah Bacon, born July 13, 1816; mentioned below.

(VI) Josiah Bacon Gleason, son of William Gleason, born in Billerica, July 13, 1816, died at Arlington, Massachusetts. He received his education in the public schools and at Phillips Academy, Andover. From early youth he worked on his father's farm, and before he came of age had saved five hundred dollars cutting timber from a woodlot that he bought. and selling the timber and wood to the Boston & Lowell railroad. He embarked in the retail dry goods business in Boston, and later returned to Billerica to enter partnership with Jeremiah Goldsmith, of Andover, in the wood and lumber business. The firm bought wood lots and cut the timber for shipyards in Boston and Medford. After two years he bought out his partner and continued in business alone until 1858. In 1845 he bought a farm of one hundred and twenty-five acres in Billerica, on the main road about one mile from the center of the village, and after 1858 devoted himself exclusively to farming, making a specialty of peaches, cranberries, apples and other fruit, and had one of the finest and most productive orchards in the county. He kept about fifteen cows and was counted among the most prosperous farmers of the town. The farm was the old Squire Crosby place, with a large house of twenty rooms, on high land, overlooking the "Stage Coach" road from Boston to Lowell and surrounded by shrubs, trees, vines and quaint old arbors. He sold the farm in Billerica 1858, when he retired from the lumber business and bought the old Captain Skilton place, in Bedford. After working this farm for nine years he sold it and bought a portion of the Simonds farm. Later he resided in Arlington, and died there at what is now 907 Massachusetts avenue. During his last years he invested extensively in real estate in Medford and Boston, and in real estate mortgages. Mr. Gleason was gifted with unusual business ability, tact and enterprise, which he evinced from early youth. He was upright, honorable and conscientious in his dealings, strong, brave, resolute, self-reliant and genial, and naturally secured a wide circle of friends. He won his competence fairly, and never failed to keep his word nor to meet every obligation. He was an honored and useful citizen. He was devoted to his home and family and greatly beloved for his sterling qualities of mind and heart. He was originally a Whig in politics and later a Republican. He held the office of highway surveyor of Bedford for a few years. He was a member of the Lexington Congregational church. He married, in Bedford, November 27. 1845, Mary Hartwell, born March 19, 1825, daughter of Deacon Amos and Louisa (Hodgman) Hartwell, of Bedford, Massachusetts. Children: 1. Henry Josiah, born March 17, 1847, died December 15, 1903; his early life was one of unusual promise and usefulness, but later ill health required a sojourn in a southern clime which failed; he then gave his fertile mind to inventions which were on the eve of perfect success, he having secured his United States patent just a few months previous to his death. 2. Frederick Eugene, mentioned below.

(VII) Frederick Eugene Gleason, son of Josiah Bacon Gleason, was born at Billerica, April 11, 1848. He attended the public schools there until ten years of age, then at Bedford, whither his parents went to live, and he took a course of study in Miss Lunt's academy. He went to Lexington with his parents and assisted his father with the farm work until 1869, when he entered partnership with his brother, Henry J. Gleason, in the meat and provision business at Charlestown, in the Waverly Market, under the old Waverly House. After two years of commercial life, Mr. Gleason returned to the farm at Lexington and worked upon it for the next five years. Then he became a farmer on his own account, buying a fifty-acre farm as the old Thurston place on Hancock street, in 1878. For fifteen years he had a dairy and conducted general farming, with some market gardening. He sold his farm and bought a small place containing seven acres of land on Hancock street, near Bedford, where he now resides, devoting his time to the care

Lewis Historical Pub. Co.

J. B. Gleason

Lewis Historical Pub Co

Mary H. Gleason

Gleason Family Group

and improvement of some thirty tenements and other property, some of which he inherited from his father, most of the property being in South Medford, Cambridge and Wakefield, including about one hundred and fifty acres of his father's homestead in Lexington. Mr. Gleason is a man of quiet, domestic tastes, and is highly respected by his townsmen. He and his wife are members of the Hancock Congregational Church, of Lexington, of which he has been a member for the past twenty-five years. In politics he is a Republican.

He married, November 23, 1885, Sarah Louise Upton, born at Lowell, May 23, 1860, daughter of Henry and Fannie (Skilton) Upton, of Lowell. Her father was in the furniture and upholstery business there. Children: 1. Henry, born October 31, 1886, died December 24, 1889. 2. Mary Hartwell, born November 10, 1887. 3. William Eugene, November 23, 1890. 4. Clarence Herbert, February 5, 1892.

FLANDERS Stephen Flanders (1), and wife Jane, early immigrants from England, were among the first settlers in Salisbury, Massachusetts, going there between the years 1640 and 1646, and Stephen died there June 27, 1684. Their children were: Stephen, Mary, Philip, Sarah, Naomi and John.

(II) John Flanders, youngest child of Stephen and Jane Flanders, was born in Salisbury, February 11, 1659, and died at South Hampton, New Hampshire, 1745. He married Elizabeth Sargent; children: Jacob, John, Ezekiel, Josiah, Philip, Jonathan, Tamsen and Hannah.

(III) Jacob Flanders, eldest child of John and Elizabeth (Sargent) Flanders, was born August 5, 1689. He went from South Hampton to Antrim, New Hampshire, prior to 1738, in which year he was chosen one of a committee formulated for the purpose of erecting a log meeting-house. He married Mercy Clough: children: Tabitha, Jacob, Jesse, Ezekiel, John, Philip, Betsey, Ruth, Hannah and Mehitable.

(IV) Ezekiel Flanders, third son and fourth child of Jacob and Mercy (Clough) Flanders, was probably born at South Hampton, but data at hand fails to mention place and date of birth. He was killed by Indians in 1756, while hunting at Newfound Lake. He married Sarah Bishop; children: Ezekiel, Enos, Sarah, Susannah, Aphia, Jemima and Benjamin.

(V) Ezekiel (2) Flanders, eldest child of Ezekiel and Sarah (Bishop) Flanders, was born at Antrim, in 1743. He erected a dwelling-house on Water street. He married Jerusha Goodwin, of Concord; children: Mary, Sarah, Martha, Susannah, Anna, Ezekiel, Lydia, Israel and Benjamin.

(VI) Benjamin Flanders, youngest child of Ezekiel and Jerusha (Goodwin) Flanders, was born in Antrim, August 19, 1782. He married Polly Walker, and the record at hand mentions but one son Walker.

(VII) Walker Flanders, son of Benjamin and Polly (Walker) Flanders, was born in Boscawen, New Hampshire, July 12 or 22, 1809. He settled in Lawrence, Massachusetts, going there when the vast hydraulic power afforded by the Merrimack river was in the early stages of its development, and establishing himself in business as a contractor and builder, was actively concerned in the building up of that splendid industrial city. He married Harriet, daughter of Thomas D. and Martha (Weeks) Nesmith, of Antrim, New Hampshire. She is of Scotch origin and a descendant in the fifth generation of Deacon James (1) Nesmith through James (2), Jonathan (3), and Thomas D. (4).

(I) Deacon James Nesmith, a Scotch Presbyterian of the north of Ireland, was one of the signers of the memorial presented to Governor Shute, of New Hampshire, in 1718, came to America the following year, and was one of the sixteen original settlers in Londonderry. He was a man of ability and integrity, who enjoyed the esteem and confidence of his fellow-townsmen, and in 1735 was chosen elder of the West Parish Presbyterian Church. He died 1767, aged seventy-five years. He was married, in Ireland, 1714, to Elizabeth, daughter of James and Janet (Cochran) McKeen. Elizabeth Nesmith died in Londonderry in 1763, aged sixty-seven. She was the mother of nine children; two of whom Arthur and James, were born in Ireland, and the former died there in infancy. The others, all born in Londonderry, were: Arthur, Jean, Mary, John, Elizabeth, Thomas and Benjamin.

(II) James Nesmith, second son of Deacon James and Elizabeth (McKeen) Nesmith, was born in 1718, just prior to the embarkation of his parents for America. He settled in the northerly part of Londonderry. Although well advanced in years at the breaking out of the revolutionary war, he entered with spirit into the struggle for national independence, responded with alacrity to the first call for minute-men, and participated in the battle of Bunker Hill. He died in Londonderry, July 15, 1793. He married Mary Dinsmore; children: James, Jonathan, Robert, Elizabeth, Mary and Sarah.

(III) Jonathan Nesmith, second son of James and Mary (Dinsmore) Nesmith, was born at Londonderry, August, 1759. In 1774, when a boy of sixteen, he secured a tract of wild land in Antrim, New Hampshire, and building a log cabin he proceeded to clear a farm. He settled there permanently in 1778. When twenty-five years old he was chosen an elder of the Presbyterian church in Antrim, and in addition to his activity in religious matters acquired prominence in public affairs, holding the office of selectman, representing the town in the state legislature for several terms, and serving on various important town committees. He was not only obliged to pay a second time for most of his land, but twice suffered the misfortune of having his house destroyed by fire. He never wavered in his religious faith, however, and when in extreme old age he found it necessary to resign his position as elder of the church, after having served in that capacity for a period of fifty years, he arose in the meeting, stretched forth with difficulty his palsied hand and solemnly invoked the divine blessing upon his successors. He died an octogenarian, October 15, 1845. In 1781 he married Eleanor Dickey, born 1761, daughter of Adam and Jane (Strahan) Dickey, of Londonderry, New Hampshire, and granddaughter of John and Margaret Dickey, of Londonderry, Ireland. She died September 7, 1818, and Elder Jonathan Nesmith married second, Mrs. Sarah Wetherbee (nee Hamlin), of Concord, Massachusetts. She was twelve years old when the Concord fight took place, and she witnessed it from the doorstep of her father's house. She died January 16, 1852, aged eighty-nine. Children of Elder Nesmith: James, Jean, Thomas D., Adam, Mary D., Maragaret, Isabel, Hon. George W., and Robert.

(IV) Thomas D. Nesmith, second son and third child of Elder Jonathan and Eleanor (Dickey) Nesmith, was born in Antrim, March 22, 1789. He inherited the homestead, and occupied it until his death, September 10, 1841. March 10, 1813, he married, first, Martha Weeks, died 1828, aged thirty-five years; February 4, 1830, he married second, Nancy Gregg. She died February 9, 1856, at sixty-three. He had children: Robert W., Jonathan, Sarah E., Miles, Harriet Frances, Martha J., Melvin, Hiram G. and Nancy R.

(V) Harriet Frances Nesmith, fifth child and second daughter of Thomas D. and Martha (Weeks) Nesmith, was born in Antrim, February 2, 1823. She became the wife of Walker Flanders, of Lawrence as previously stated.

(VIII) Frank Byron Flanders, M. D., son of Walker and Hariet F. (Nesmith) Flanders, was born in Lawrence, May 16, 1850. He fitted for college in his native city, was graduated from Harvard University with the class of 1874, and in the autumn of that year became a student at the Harvard Medical School. At the conclusion of his second year he went to the Rhode Island Hospital at Providence as an interne, remaining one year, and returning to Harvard for the completion of his studies he took his medical degree in 1878. Locating in Lawrence, he entered upon his professional career with the enthusiasm of a student, and he has ever since practiced in that city, having attained the success for which he has so diligently labored. In addition to his extensive private practice Dr. Flanders is connected with the Lawrence General Hospital. He is a member of the Massachusetts Medical Association, and also of the North Essex District Branch, of which he has served at different times as censor, councillor and president, and for many years occupied the post of secretary of the Lawrence Medical Club. Politically he is a Republican. In his religious belief he is a Congregationalist.

Dr. Flanders married, in Lawrence, June 5, 1884, Anna Lillian Niles, born in Leominster, Massachusetts, August 30, 1853, daughter of Joseph and Miriam (Hill) Niles. In common with all others in New England bearing the name, she is descended from John Niles, who was in Dorchester, Massachusetts, in 1634, and is supposed to have come from Wales. He went to Braintree, Massachusetts, and was admitted a freeman there in 1647. Joseph Niles, grandfather of Mrs. Flanders, was of Chester, New Hampshire, and Joseph Niles, her father, was born there July 10, 1814. He attended school in his native town, but by a well-selected course of reading acquired an excellent education. He began the activities of life at the age of nine years as an operative in a horn factory in West Newbury, but later engaged in the confectionery business in Lowell, Massachusetts. Later he removed to Leominster, Massachusetts, and became a comb manufacturer. His death occurred at Lawrence, Massachusetts, March 11, 1894. In

1846 he married Miriam Hill, daughter of Isaac Hill, of Mason, New Hampshire. She became the mother of five children, of whom the only one now living is Mrs. Flanders. The others were: Charles William, William Francis, Miriam Josephine and Charles Joseph.

Children of Dr. and Mrs. Flanders: 1. Eleanor, born 1885, died in infancy. 2. Miriam Nesmith, born July 18, 1886; graduate of Wellesley, class of 1908. 3. Bancroft, born July 6, 1888; died at the age of eight months. 4. William Niles, born July 26, 1889; now attending Pennsylvania Military College. 5. Richard Henry, born March 22, 1891; died December 13, 1903.

DAVIS John Davis, of Ipswich, Massachusetts, took the oath as freeman in 1638, and in 1656 bought land in Gloucester, lived several years there, and then returned to Ipswich, leaving two sons on Cape Ann—James and Jacob.

(II) James, son of John Davis, was ensign of the trainband in 1681, and was commissioned captain in 1689. In 1693 he is reported as being "very sickly" in consequence of "country service in Sir Edmund Andros's time," and in 1699 he received a grant of Straitsmouth Island "for the charge and expense he had been at and time he had spent in the late wars with the French and Indian enemy." He was selectman several years, and representative to general court eight years. By his first wife Mehitable, who died June 9, 1666, he had four children, of whom John and James grew to manhood. By his second wife, Elizabeth (Batchelder) Davis, of Wenham, he had seven children. He married third, Widow Mary Cook, who died 1725. He died May 1, 1715.

(III) John, son of Captain James and Mehitabel Davis, had three acres of upland in Gloucester, between Lobster and Hodgkins' coves, in 1684, and probably had his house there. He filled various town offices, and was lieutenant of the military company. He died March 16, 1729, aged sixty-nine years. He married Ann Haraden, who survived him as did their two sons, Benjamin and Joseph.

(IV) Joseph, son of Lieutenant John and Ann (Haraden) Davis, was supposed by Mr. Babson, in his "History of Gloucester," to have been the Joseph Davis, of Squam, who married Jemima Haskell, in 1732, and died 1753.

(V) William, son of Joseph and Jemima (Haskell) Davis, served in the revolutionary war, and for two and a half years was a prisoner in the hands of the British in Halifax, Nova Scotia, and died 1814, leaving several children noted for longevity: Betsey, lived to be ninety-three; Captain George, eighty-six; Rev. Epes, who died in Lynn, aged eighty-two; Captain William, died in Newburyport, aged seventy-five; Sally, seventy-six; and Joseph, eighty-nine.

(VI) Joseph, son of William Davis, born about 1763, was a native of Annisquam, and died in Lowell, Massachusetts, being the last of his generation. He married twice, and left three sons.

(VII) Joseph, son of Joseph Davis, born about 1800, was a fisherman, as were many of the descendants of the ancestor, John Davis. He may have carried on fishing at Cape Ann, and did so quite extensively at Marblehead, and was finally drowned on one of the trips to the Grand Banks. His wife, Sarah (Dyer) Davis, married second, William Henry Smith, of Halifax, Nova Scotia, and had a son named for the father.

(VIII) Hon. Joseph Davis, son of Joseph and Sarah (Dyer) Davis, was born in Marblehead, October 4, 1833. He was an infant when his parents settled in Lynn, in the Woodend section, where he attended the common schools. The early death of his father necessitated his going to work when he was only eleven years old. He learned the trade of shoemaking, and when about nineteen years old he began to work up stock on his own account, and his industry and energy enabled him to early make his mark in his chosen calling, in which he rapidly rose until he became one of the most extensive shoe manufacturers of Lynn. At first he was associated in business with Edward Curtin, in Broad street, and later George K. and Henry A. Pevear (sketch elsewhere in this work) were special partners with him for a period of three years. He subsequently gave to his foreman, William Henry Chase, an interest in the business, the firm then being Joseph Davis & Company. Among others associated with him at the time was William H. Wheeler in the manufacture of boots and shoes under the name of Davis & Wheeler. Later he formed the firm of Davis, Whitcomb & Company, to manufacture under contracts with the states of Maryland and Virginia. This business was very successful and reached large proportions. At one time he paid the largest yearly royalty of any manufacturer to the McKay Sewing Machine Company. In 1891 reverses overtook him and his business was practically swept away. He then associated himself with Mr. Henry C. Thacher, of Boston, and formed the Davis Boot & Shoe Company to take over the contracts for the manufacture of boots and shoes in the state penitentiary at Richmond, Virginia. He was in active control of this very successful business up to the time of his last and fatal illness. He was also officially connected with various financial institutions as president of the Lincoln National Bank of Boston for several years; director in the First National Bank of Salem; besides holding several positions of trust in Boston. He was universally respected in business circles, and was regarded as a pioneer in the larger shoe trade, of which he was a practical and progressive exponent.

In civil life Mr. Davis was also active and efficient. He was connected with the city council in 1865, when the new city hall was erected, serving upon the committee on public property, having as a coadjutor Benjamin Doak (sketch elsewhere), who was a warm personal friend. He served in the governor's council in 1881-82, and for five years was a commissioner of Pine Grove Cemetery. In politics he was a staunch Republican, and he was a candidate for the congressional nomination, dividing the Lynn delegation with Hon. Henry Cabot Lodge; both were defeated, in the convention, however, by Hon. Elisha A. Converse, who was defeated at the polls by Hon. Henry B. Lovering. Mr. Davis was a member of the Masonic fraternity, affiliated with Mt. Carmel Lodge, of Lynn. He was in early manhood an active member of the Lynn Light Infantry, Company D, Eighth Regiment. He was all his life associated with the First Universalist Church of Lynn, and it was largely through his liberality that the present splendid edifice was erected. His contribution to this church amounted to about thirty thousand dollars. He also gave liberally to the deserving needy, and all objects that appealed to him as worthy, and his extreme sympathy ever moved him to practical response to calls upon him. He was endeared to all the community not only for these kindly deeds, but for his earnest and unselfish interest in the welfare of the city and its institutions, and his public spirit and liberality in support of every measure promising improvement in municipal and community affairs. After one of his many visits to Europe, he wrote a most interesting account of his travel, experiences and impressions, which was privately printed, a volume of several hundred pages, and distributed gratuitously among his friends.

Mr. Davis married, in June, 1855, Lydia Chadwell Atkinson, of Lynn, daughter of Joseph Alley and Ruth (Mudge) Atkinson. (See Atkinson). Six children were born to Mr. and Mrs. Davis: 1. Charles Edward, died in infancy. 2. Wilbur H., born July, 1857, lives in Lynn. 3. Anna Gertrude, died in infancy. 4. Joseph Edwin, born September 11, 1859. 5. A. Lillian, born June 9, 1863, now wife of Dr. Herbert W. Newhall. 6. Florence Mudge, born August 18, 1873, wife of Alfred M. Walter, residing in Chicago, Illinois. 7. Ruth Mabel, born June 5, 1876, lives in Lynn. 8. Edith, born March 8, 1880, lives in Lynn.

Mr. Davis died in Buffalo, New York, January 24, 1897. His demise awoke profound and general sorrow at his home in Lynn, where his remains were conveyed for interment, and at the funeral a feeling tribute was pronounced by his pastor, Rev. James M. Pullma, D. D., of the First Universalist Church of Lynn, summing up the character of the deceased, the speaker said:

"A neglected and friendless boy starts out to make a place for himself in this big and busy world. He conquers his adverse conditions and wins his way, inch by inch, to a prosperous and honored estate among men. Possessed of a remarkably alert, fertile and comprehensive mind, his career is brilliant, with many striking successes, and he acquires a large confidence in the powers which have served him so well. Cheery, warmhearted and openhanded, he helps his fellows, right and left, as he goes along. In fact, his business misfortunes began with his large helpfulness to others, and his business losses grew out of his generosity of heart. At an age when most men begin to shorten sail a little, he finds himself loaded with a widely extended and embarrassed business. His struggles against his early adversities were good, but his warfare against these later misfortunes were better, rising to the point of heroism.

"He cherished one steady purpose, conceived in the very hour of defeat, to which he bent all his energies. If life was not long enough to do all that he desired, he would at least repay those who had been most disastrously involved in his misfortunes. Over and over again he returned to this purpose as the fixed determination of his soul, and in these later months it seemed to him that the consummation of this purpose was almost in sight. But his physical powers had been overtaxed in this long struggle, and today he lies dead upon the field of honorable battle, with victory only partially within his grasp. He died in sight of the promised land, meeting death as he had met the fortunes of life, with courage, dignity and faith. It is impossible not to wish that time had been granted him to achieve the desire of his heart. But as he yielded to the decree with serene composure and unshaken trust, so also must we, forgetting whatever imperfection inhered in his large nature, and cherishing the memory of his warm and tender heart, his brotherly helpfulness toward all men, and the essential and imperishable fidelities of his soul."

ATKINSON Thomas Atkinson and brother Theodore came from Bury, Lancashire, England, and settled in Concord, Massachusetts, before 1636. Thomas was made freeman, December 7, 1636, and died in November, 1646. His children were Rebecca, John, Susannah and Hannah.

(II) John, only son of Thomas Atkinson, was born in Concord, Massachusetts, about 1639-40, and after his father's death was adopted by his Uncle Theodore, of Boston, with whom he learned the trade of hatter and feltmaker, and settled in Newbury, Massachusetts, in 1662. He died before September 29, 1715. He married first, April 27, 1664, Sarah Mirick, who was mother of all his children, and who died after 1686. He married second, June 3, 1700, Widow Hannah Cheney, who died January 5, 1704. His children: Sarah, John, Thomas, Theodore, Abigail, Samuel, Nathaniel, Elizabeth, Joseph and Rebecca. Joseph, the youngest son, was killed by Indians in Maine, in 1706.

(III) John, son of John and Sarah (Mirick) Atkinson, was born in Newbury, and was a feltmaker, and passed his life in that town. In his will his father acknowledged the dutifulness of this son to him in his old age, and devised to him the house, barn and land in Newbury. He married Sarah Woodman, and died before September 27, 1744. Children, all born in Newbury: 1. Thomas, March 16, 1694. 2. John, October 29, 1695. 3. Theodore, October 8, 1698. 4. Sarah, November 6, 1700. 5. Hannah, January 11, 1702. 6. Abigail, March, 1705. 7. Joseph, October 5, 1707. 8. Mary, February 19, 1709. 9. Elizabeth, June 29, 1712. 10. Ichabod, August 13, 1714.

(IV) Deacon Ichabod, son of John and Sarah (Woodman) Atkinson, born in Newbury, August 13, 1714, died there 1803. He was a yeoman and feltmaker. He married, October 7, 1733, (published) Priscilla Bailey, died February 9, 1793. Children, born in Newbury: 1. Moses, September 22, 1734, cordwainer. 2. Matthias, January 6, 1736. 3. Miriam, March 20, 1739. 4. Abigail. 5. Hannah, September 2, 1743. 6. Anna, May 16, 1746. 7. Sarah, November 1, 1748. 8. Amos, March 20, 1754. 9. Eunice, September 18, 1759.

(V) Matthias, son of Deacon Ichabod and Priscilla (Bailey) Atkinson, was born in Newbury, January 6, 1736, died before December 26, 1815. He was a carpenter, and lived in Newbury. He married, April 10, 1766, Abigail Bayley, who survived him. Children, born in Newbury: 1. Moses, January 31, 1773. 2. Daughter, March 10, 1775. 3. Sally, May 18, 1777. 4. Joseph, April 26, 1780. 5. Eunice, October 29, 1782. 6. George, September 5, 1785.

(VI) Joseph, son of Matthias and Abigail (Bayley) Atkinson, was born in Newbury, April 26, 1780; he married, July 31, 1803, Hepzibah Alley, born in Lynn, June 5, 1785, daughter of Captain Joseph Alley, cordwainer, who married, December 13, 1781, Hannah Bacheller, and died February 10, 1832. Captain Alley was son of Joseph Alley, fisherman and cordwainer, who lived in Lynn and married, November 12, 1751, Rebecca Hall. Joseph Alley was son of Joseph Alley, born in Lynn, June 22, 1693, married first, January 14, 1724-25, Hepzibah Newhall; second, December 10, 1755, Ann Johnson. Joseph Alley was son of Hugh Alley, born October 15, 1653, and was a weaver; married, December 9, 1681, Rebecca Hood. Hugh Alley was son of Hugh Alley, born about 1608, came from London to America in the "Abigail," 1635; lived in Lynn, and owned land in Nahant; died 25, 11mo. 1673, and was survived by widow Mary.

(VII) Joseph Alley, son of Joseph and Hepzibah (Alley) Atkinson, born September 17, 1807, in Lynn, was one of the early manufacturers of shoes on a large scale in that town, but was compelled by failing health to abandon that vocation. He then bought a farm on Pine Hill and spent the remainder of his life there, conducting a fine nursery. He was a Republican in politics, and an earnest member of the Boston Street Methodist Episcopal Church. He married, May 6, 1830, Ruth Mudge; children, all born in Lynn: 1. Lydia Chadwell, married Joseph Davis. (See Davis). 2. Edward, a shoemaker of Lynn. 3. Eugene, a shoe dealer, now living in Richmond, Virginia. 4. Hannah Marie, married James Houghton. 5. Sarah E., married George Southworth.

FULLER Edward Fuller (1), immigrant ancestor, came in the "Mayflower" to Plymouth with the Pilgrims in 1620 with his famous brother, Dr. Samuel Fuller, and was one of the signers of the compact on board the ship before landing. Both he and his wife died early in 1621, leaving a son Samuel who went to live with his uncle, Dr. Samuel Fuller, and another son, Matthew, mentioned below.

(II) Captain Matthew Fuller, son of Edward Fuller, was born in England. When his parents died he went to live with friends in England and came to this country later. It is believed that he came with the wife and child of Dr. Samuel Fuller. In later years he was accounted to be "one of the first born of the colony," and had land assigned him by virtue of his primogeniture. It was the law that where no children were born to a family in this country, the right of drawing land was given to the eldest son, though he were born in the old country. Nevertheless he was classed among "the first-born of the colony." In 1642 he was granted ten acres near the farm of Thurston Clark, in Plymouth, and in the same year served as juryman. He applied for admission as a freeman, September 7, 1642, but was not allowed to qualify until June 7, 1653. He was one of the leading military men of the colony. When the first company was organized under command of Captain Myles Standish in 1643 he was appointed sergeant, and became lieutenant September, 1652. He was lieutenant, June 20, 1654, under Standish in command of fifty men organized for the proposed expedition against the Dutch of New Amsterdam, later called New York. The company was ordered to rendezvous at Sandwich, Plymouth Colony, June 29, to embark from Manonet in the barque "Adventer," owned by Captain Samuel Mayo, of Barnstable, and to join the other English colonial forces, but on June 23 news was received that peace was concluded between England and Holland and preparations for war ceased. Fuller was elected to the council of war, October 2, 1658, and was made chairman in 1671. In that year also he was lieutenant of the colonial forces in the expedition against the Indians of Saconet. He was a physician and stood well in his profession, as shown by his appointment, December 17, 1673, as surgeon general of the Plymouth Colony troops and also of the Massachusetts Bay troops. He served as captain of his company in King Philip's war and took a distinguishing part. He was a deputy to the general court as early as 1653. He lived first at Plymouth, then at Scituate, where he was admitted to the church, November 7, 1636, by letter from the Plymouth Church, and finally at Barnstable, where he was the first regular physician. His son John and some of his grandsons followed him in his profession, which he doubtless learned of his uncle, Dr. Samuel Fuller, and in turn taught to his son. He and his brother lived side by side on Scorton Neck, which was bought of the Secunke (Seeconk) Indians by Barnstable and Sandwich. The west end of the Fuller farms formed the town line between Sandwich and Barnstable. A dispute as to this boundary line caused a lawsuit, which was eventually compromised, the Fullers relinquishing their claim to certain lands granted by Barnstable, October 30, 1672, and the town of Sandwich conceding to the Fullers certain rights of way with the privilege of cutting fence stuff in Sandwich. Captain Fuller had land granted at Suckenesset, now Falmouth, and in the "Major's Purchase," Middleborough, as "first-born" rights.

He was a man of sound judgment, good understanding and courage. He was faithful to his trusts, liberal in politics and tolerant in religion. In fact he was too tolerant for his day and too frank in his speech to avoid trouble. He was indignant at the persecution of the Quakers, and was indicted for saying "the lae enacted about ministers' maintenance was a wicked and devilish law and that the devil sat at the stone when it was enacted." He admitted that he used the words and was fined fifty shillings. Yet he held the confidence of the people and received further honors and high office afterward. He died at Barnstable in 1678. He bequeathed in his will dated July 25 and proved October 30, 1678, to his wife, Frances, to grandchild, Shubael, son of Ralph Jones; to son John, and to Thomas, Jabez, Timothy, Matthias and Samuel, sons of his deceased son Samuel; to Elizabeth, wife of Moses Rowley, and Anne, wife of son Samuel; to Bethiah, wife of son John; to grandchild, Sarah Rowley, Jedediah Jones and all the rest. Also to Robert Marshall, the Scotchman. Children: 1. Mary, married, April 17, 1650, Ralph Jones. 2. Elizabeth, married, April 22, 1652, Moses Rowley. 3. Samuel, lieutenant in King Philip's war, killed March

S. B. Fuller

25, 1676. 4. John, mentioned below. 5. Ann, married her cousin, Samuel Fuller, Jr.

(III) Dr. John Fuller, son of Captain and Dr. Matthew Fuller, was born about 1645-50 and died in 1691. He resided on the paternal homestead in Barnstable on Scorton Neck, adjoining Sandwich. He was a physician of note and a prominent citizen. He married first, Bethia ———; second, Hannah ———, of Boston. His widow married second, Captain John Lothrop, of Barnstable, December 9, 1695. Children, born at Barnstable: 1. Lydia, born 1675, died in Connecticut, November 6, 1755; married, May 12, 1699, Joseph Dimock. 2. Bethia, born December, 1687, married, February 20, 1706, Barnabas Lothrop. 3. John, born October, 1689, mentioned below. 4. Reliance, born September 8, 1691, married John Prince.

(IV) Lieutenant John Fuller, son of Dr. John Fuller, was born in Barnstable, October, 1689, died there July 20, 1732, aged forty-two years. His gravestone at West Barnstable states that he was son of Dr. John. He married, June 16, 1710, Thankful Gorham. Children, born at Barnstable: 1. Hannah, born April 1, 1711; married, September 3, 1730, Matthew or Matthias Smith. 2. John, born August 3, 1714, married, October 29, 1741, Temperance Gorham. 3. Mary, born September 1, 1715, married, August 11, 1733, Seth Lothrop. 4. Bethia, born September 1, 1715, married, December 20, 1739, Joseph Bursley. 5. Nathaniel, born December 10, 1716, mentioned below. 6. Thankful, born September, 1718, married, October 25, 1739, Nathan Russell, Jr., of Middleborough.

(V) Captain Nathaniel Fuller, son of John Fuller, was born December 10, 1716. He was widely known as "Captain Nat," stern of manner, decided in opinion and of good character, though the very frank and critical historian of Barnstable families tells us that he was not very industrious and hence not prosperous. He was unlucky, however, in ways not due to idleness, for when he came home from the French and Indian war he brought smallpox with him. His wife and daughters Abigail and Thankful fell victims to the scourge; his daughter Hannah recovered. He married (first), February 22, 1739, Abigail Hinckley. He married again. He owned the western part of the homestead on Scorton Neck, about thirty-five acres on the south side of the old highway to Sandy Neck, opposite the Blossom house in Sandwich. In 1783 he sold his farm and moved over the line on Scorton Neck into Barstable. After the death of his second wife he went to live with his daughter, Hannah Smith. Children: 1. Nathaniel, mentioned below. 2. Thankful, died unmarried. 3. Abigail, died unmarried. 4. Hannah, married Matthias Smith. 5. Lydia, married Lazarus Ewer. 6. Lieutenant Joseph, died August 16, 1805, married Tabitha Jones, daughter of Josiah Jones; was an officer in the revolution.

(VI) Nathaniel Fuller, son of Captain Nathaniel Fuller, born in Barnstable or Sandwich, 1762, died at Sandwich, April 9, 1840. He married, March 18, 1791, Rachel Jones, who died at Sandwich, May 10, 1841. (Swift gives the name Ruhama Jones, town records Rachel). Children of Nathaniel and Rachel Fuller: 1. Ruhamah, born October 4, 1791, died September 5, 1840. 2. Samuel, born November 14, 1793, mentioned below. 3. James Harvey, born November 4, 1798. 4. David, born October 27, 1806. 5. Anna, born April 4, 1809.

(VII) Samuel Fuller, son of Nathaniel Fuller, was born in Sandwich, November 14, 1793. He was a sea captain. He lived at Sandwich. He married Hannah Chipman, of an old "Mayflower" family, descendant of John Howland. Children, born at Sandwich: 1. Elizabeth A., born October 10, 1823, married the Rev. Loranus Crowell; children: Elizabeth, Samuel, Abigail, Harrison, Julia and Albert. 2. Abigail F., born June 19, 1825, married Edward Pease; children: Ella, Edward, Frank and Elizabeth. 3. Sylvester Brown, born April 17, 1829, mentioned below.

(VIII) Sylvester Brown Fuller, son of Samuel Fuller, was born April 17, 1829, at Sandwich. He was educated in the public schools of his native town. He learned the trade of shoemaking, and began his career as a manufacturer at Lynn, Massachusetts, about 1870, as a partner in the firm of Haskell & Fuller. After his partner withdrew he admitted his son, Charles S., to partnership under the firm name of S. P. Fuller & Son, this name being changed later to C. S. Fuller & Company, and now (1908) conducting business under the name of The Fuller Shoe Company. The business grew from a modest beginning to large proportions, with factories at Essex, Salem and Gloucester, Massachusetts. In Salem they had a large plant on Cousins street, where they manufactured a medium McKay shoe, opening an office on Lincoln street, Boston. At this time Charles

S. Fuller assumed charge of the business, later being associated with his brother, Fred P. Fuller, but subsequently Charles S. was compelled to relinquish active business, on account of failing health, the affairs of the concern being looked after by his brother. Sylvester B. Fuller continued to live at Lynn, however, and had an attractive home on Herbert street. He had also a summer residence on Shirley Hill, Goffstown, New Hampshire, where he died July 14, 1893. He was a Republican, but never active in politics. He was a faithful and prominent member of the North Congregational Church of Lynn, of which he was one of the founders, a thoroughly upright and conscientious man, well beloved in the community in which he made his home and respected by all who knew him. From the eulogy of the Rev. Dr. Hadley, his pastor, we quote: "You all know what he was in the world of business, the home and the church. His memory you will all cherish and his good works will live after him. He has laid down the work; let us take it up with his largeness of heart and sympathy. He was always faithful in church work, as you can all testify. You also know better than I of the happy home life, his life and friendship being so rich. It seems as if a dark cloud has come over us, but we must say: 'Thy will be done.' The impress of his character and goodness was felt in the home, the church and the city."

Sylvester B. Fuller married, September 25, 1851, Mary C., born at Hadley, Massachusetts, July 9, 1831, daughter of Ansel and Sally (Johnson) Pomeroy. Children: 1. Charles S., born September 6, 1852, mentioned below. 2. George A., born November 19, 1855, married Lucy A. Burnham; two children: Sarah E., born February 16, 1880, died April 16, 1889; one child died in infancy. 3. Henry H., born August 2, 1858, died December 22, 1881. 4. Sarah E., born January 5, 1861, married, September 1, 1885, Charles S. Crosman, of Haverford, Pennsylvania; children: Marion Fuller, born October 29, 1887; Charles H., November 18, 1890; Elizabeth, June 10, 1894; Lincoln Holway, March 4, 1901, died March 17, 1902. 5. Fred P., born March 20, 1863, married, December 22, 1885, Harriet Ricker, of Lynn; children: Henry H., born January 8, 1887; Raymond, March 6, 1888; Morris Wiggin, July 23, 1891; Louise, August 6, 1895.

(IX) Charles S. Fuller, son of Sylvester Brown Fuller, was born at Amherst, Massachusetts, September 6, 1852. After graduating from the high school, as president of his class, 1872, he became associated with his father in business as hitherto related. In addition to his activity in his own business, he was deeply interested in the welfare of the city and its institutions. He was for many years vice-president of Lynn Institution for Savings and one of its board of trustees; director of Lynn National Bank for twenty-one years, up to his death; director of Lynn Safe Deposit & Trust Company; for many years clerk of the board of directors of Lynn National Bank; member of the board of managers of Lynn Home for Aged Women; acted in the same capacity for Lynn Home for Aged Men; member of board of managers of Lynn Hospital. He was prominent in the affairs of the Unitarian church, and was past president of the Unitarian Society. He was a member of the Unitarian Club of Boston and Whiting Club of Lynn. Mr. Fuller was one of the most public-spirited citizens of Lynn, and his integrity in business circles won him a host of respecting associates and friends, and his death in Lynn, December 30, 1906, was a distinct loss to that city. Although suffering great pain, with wonderful fortitude he took an energetic part in the conduct of his business affairs up to the time he was obliged to enter retirement because of invalidism.

Charles S. Fuller married, May 26, 1880, Addie G., daughter of Leonard and Lydia M. Usher. Mr. Fuller is survived by Mrs. Fuller; four sons: Lawrence W., Harold S., Charles Kenneth, Donald Wellington; one daughter, Madeline; two brothers: George A., of Lynn, and Fred P., of Salem; a sister, Mrs. Charles S. Crosman, of Philadelphia.

PRIEST This surname belongs to a curious class of patronymics, common in other languages besides English, designating offices of the church, as Pope, Cardinal, Abbot, Prior, Archdeacon, Rector, Parsons, Vicar, Deacon, Clerk, Friar, Monk, Sexton, Pontifex, Novice, etc. In some cases the origin was plainly a nickname, but in most cases, doubtless, the progenitor's office or title in the church became his family surname. Celibacy has not been a rule of the Church of England, nor of the Roman Church at all times. The first American immigrant of the Priest family was Degory, who came from Leyden, Holland, in the Mayflower. Another early settler was James Priest, of Dorchester in 1637, and of Weymouth, Massachusetts, in 1640.

Chas. L. Fuller

Lewis Historical Pub. Co.

(I) John Priest, immigrant ancestor, settled at Charlestown, Massachusetts. He owned a small farm in that town. He sold twenty acres of land near the Reading line in 1680 (recorded 1683) to Humphrey Miller. He married Sarah ——.

(II) John Priest, son of John Priest, born about 1650, died in 1704. He lived at Woborn until about 1687, then removed to the vicinity of Bare Hill, Lancaster, Massachusetts, where he had thirty acres of land. He came with John Warner and they lived together, having a sixty acre grant in common, adjoining the grant of Nathaniel Wales, later owned by James Frost. During the Indian war in 1704 he and his son John Jr. were in the Bare Hill garrison, in what is now Harvard. He died in 1704, and his inventory was dated December 21, 1704. He married, March 10, 1678, Rachel Garfield, died May 17, 1737, in her eighty-first year. His widow and son John administered the estate, the other children being under age. Children, born at Woburn: 1. Elizabeth, September 12, 1679. 2. John, November 1, 1681; sold his place in Harvard in 1738 to John Forbush; died September 29, 1756, at Bolton; married Anna Houghton; children: i. Anna; ii. Mary; iii. Abigail, baptized 1708; iv. Damaris, baptized 1710; v. Rachel, baptized 1713; vi. Hepsibah, born 1716; vii. Jonathan, born 1718; viii. Maria, born 1721. 3. Daniel, born July 19, 1686; mentioned below. Children, born at Bare Hill, Lancaster: 4. Gabriel, married Abigail ——; children: i. John, born November 21, 1717; ii. Gabriel, June 17, 1720; iii. Jeremiah, April 30, 1722. 5. Joseph; children: i. Joseph, born November 28, 1717; ii. Benjamin, February 17, 1719-20; iii. Mary, March 23, 1720-1; iv. Susanna, March 21, 1726; v. Tabitha, November 5, 1728; vi. Bathsheba, May 1, 1731; vii. Dorothy, October 11, 1733; viii. Betty, April 24, 1736; ix. John, January 13, 1737-8. 6. Mary. 7. Hannah.

(III) Daniel Priest, son of John Priest, born in Woburn, July 19, 1686, died at Lancaster, October 9, 1723. His widow Elizabeth Priest was baptized in the First church of Lancaster, September 27, 1724, with her children mentioned below. She died August, 1737, aged fifty-three years (town records), September 6, 1737, according to the records of John Secomb. A road was laid out to his house May 20, 1724. Children: 1. John, mentioned below. 2. Daniel, married, June 4, 1741, at Lancaster, Elizabeth Kilborn; lived in Lancaster. 3. Eunice. 4. Hasadiah, died at Lancaster, July 1, 1736. 5. Betty. 6. Silence.

(IV) John Priest, son of Daniel Priest, born about 1715, at Stow, Bolton or Lancaster, was baptized in First church of Lancaster with the rest of the children. He settled in Marlborough. Hudson says in his history of that town that at one time the family was numerous in Bolton, Stow and Marlborough. He married Mary ——. Children, born at Marlborough: 1. Mary, April 15, 1739. 2. Bette, March 2, 1743. 3. John, October 2, 1744. 4. Daniel, September 16, 1746; settled in Jaffrey, New Hampshire; his wife was born 1748 and died January, 1840. 5. Abraham, December 26, 1748; married Abigail White. 6. Silence, February 9, 1750; married Simon Maynard. 7. Isaac, July 2, 1752. 8. Jacob, November 17, 1753-4; mentioned below. 9. Comfort, March 4, 1758; married Jonas Wilkin. 10. Betsey, March 7, 1761. 11. Benjamin, born February 18, 1764; died October 22, 1853; married, January 15, 1786, Phebe Bruce, of Marlborough. 12. Joseph, born November 28, 1765. 13. Jonathan, October 6, 1766-7.

(V) Captain Jacob Priest, son of John Priest, born in Marlborough, November 17, 1753-4, died at Lexington, January 28, 1824, of smallpox, while on a visit, and is buried in the old cemetery at the center. He removed to Littleton, Massachusetts, about 1795, buying a farm of one hundred acres in the south part of the town near the present station of the Fitchburgh railroad. His farm is now occupied by his great-grandson, George L. Priest. He was a soldier in the revolution, a private in Captain Cyprian How's company, on the Lexington alarm, April 19, 1775; also in Captain Jonathan Rice's company, Colonel Samuel Bullard's regiment, August 17 to October 21, 1777, sent to reinforce northern army. He married first, Ann Jones, of Bolton; second, 1787, Sarah Longley, born September, 1766, died April 11, 1839. Children: 1. John Longley, born March 17, 1781. 2. Frank, February 26, 1784; died at Parishville, New York, August 7, 1850; married, 1808, at Littleton, Massachusetts, Mary Wood, born June 28, 1788, died August 15, 1874, daughter of John and Lucy (Martin) Wood. (See Wood Genealogy, by William S. Wood, published at Worcester, 1885); children: i. John, born at Pomfret, Vermont, October 18, 1809; ii. Manna Jones, born at Pomfret, November 27, 1810; iii. Maria Jones, born at Pomfret, April 26, 1812; iv. Mary Jones, born at Pomfret, March 14, 1814; v. Lucy, born at Parishville, November 15, 1816; vi. Benjamin Franklin, born at Parishville, February 20, 1818; vii. Miranda, born March 26, 1819; viii. Captain Luther, (father of Mrs. Edgar A. Newell, Odgensburg, N. Y.), born March 31, 1821; died at Martinsburg, Virginia, March 14, 1863, captain of Company E, One Hundred Sixth New York Volunteers in civil war; married first, Barbara Rose; second, January 21, 1852, Elizabeth Rose, died July 6, 1896; (children: Addie Barbara, born December 27, 1854, married, November 19, 1879, Edgar A. Newell, and had Albert P. Newell, born January 2, 1882, and William Allan Newell, born April 23, 1883; Elizabeth Cynthia, born December 2, 1858, died August 29, 1877; Rose Lucy, born January 1, 1861, married, June 26, 1890, Freeman H. Allen and had Barbara Allen, born July 20, 1891, Elizabeth Rose Allen, born January 18, 1895, died August 20, 1895, and Newell Priest Allen, born June 11, 1901); ix. Frederick, born April 28, 1823; x. Valentine Thomas, June 16, 1831. Children of second marriage: 3. Asa, born June 13, 1788; mentioned below. 4. Jacob, born March 7, 1790; mentioned below. 5. William, born August 28, 1793; died February 7, 1836; married Susanna Davis, of Acton, Massachusetts; children: i. Susan Adams, born July 23, 1825, married, October 24, 1843, John Tenney, of Acton, and had John Priest Tenney, born September 8, 1844, married, January 23, 1878, Elizabeth Appleton Moorhead, of Boston. 6. Nathan, born February 16, 1795; mentioned below. 7. Luther, born August 3, 1797. 8. Sarah, born July 2, 1802; died December 28, 1878; married first, October 22, 1829, Asa Fletcher of Westford; second, November 7, 1855, Abraham Stone, of Groton, Massachusetts, who died July 16, 1868; children of first husband: i. Asa Fletcher, born November 1, 1830, married, July 3, 1851, Isabella L. Speare, and had William Asa Fletcher, born July 14, 1862, and Walter K. Fletcher, born September 17, 1865; ii. William Fletcher, born October 18, 1832, married, January 11, 1856, Josephine L. Corser, and had Charles A. Fletcher, born August 30, 1858, died October 7, 1861, Harry K. and Herbert P. Fletcher (twins), born November 4, 1865; iii. Augustus Kimball, born October 12, 1834, married, February 16, 1861, Adelaide C. Marshall, and had Lewis Asa Fletcher, born May 19, 1871, and Lucy Fletcher; iv. Sarah Elizabeth Fletcher, born January 4, 1840; died March 3, 1903, married, October 28, 1858, James F. Wilson, and had Lucy Appleton Wilson, born August 10, 1859, married, July 20, 1890, George K. Millikin. 9. Sophia, born September 11, 1804, married Porter Tuttle, of Littleton, and had Edward H. Tuttle, unmarried, and other children.

(VI) Asa Priest, son of Jacob Priest (5), was born June 13, 1788, and died August 25, 1871. He was captain of the militia company. He married Nabby Bulkeley. Children: 1. Joseph Andrew, born August 25, 1817; died February 28, 1892; married Mary J. Bigelow; children: i. Sarah A., born April 7, 1860; ii. Mary (Minnie) J., born July 10, 1861, died August 5, 1873; iii. Frank Bigelow, of Commercial street, Boston, born June 16, 1863, married Lillian F. Malcolm, and had Malcolm, born July 23, 1890, Dorothy B., born September 10, 1891, Roger A., born January 28, 1893, and Barbara B., born October 30, 1903; iv. Edwin H., born September 12, 1865; v. George L., May 26, 1868; vi. Herbert B., February 6, 1875; vii. Benson B., December 14, 1876. 2. Sarah L., born February 25, 1819; died January 2, 1895. 3. Jane. 4. Abigail.

(VI) Nathan Priest, son of Jacob Priest (5), was born February 16, 1795, and died August 24, 1887; married, April 27, 1831, Mercy Robbins, of Harvard, Massachusetts. Children: 1. Lucy Eveline, born May 22, 1832, married James Johnson, of Troy, New York; child: i. Lilias Jean, married William Owen, of Troy, and had Lucy Owen, William Owen, Helen Owen, and Mary Owen. 2. George Sumner, born September 19, 1834. 3. Nathan Robley, born March 12, 1836. 4. Sarah Fletcher, born July 5, 1837; married, November 25, 1858, Moseley Gilson, of Groton, Massachusetts; children: i. Herbert Moseley Gilson, born October 17, 1860; ii. Fanny Ellsworth Gilson, September 4, 1861; iii. Ellen Priest Gilson, December 23, 1863; iv. Gertrude Bancroft, Gilson, October 8, 1865; v. George William Gilson, born December 31, 1870, died 1876; vi. Henry Robbins Gilson, born September 27, 1877; vii. Howard Luther Gilson, June 10, 1879. 5. William Henry, November 18, 1838. 6. John Robbins, born July 25, 1840. 7. Ellen Sophia, born August 26, 1842. 8. Adelia Caroline, born January 3, 1844. 9. Francis Davis, born January 24, 1846. 10. Jacob, born May 8, 1850.

(VI) Captain Jacob Priest, son of Jacob Priest (5), was born at Marlborough, March 7, 1790, and died at Littleton, April 18, 1869. He moved with his father's family to Littleton when he was about five years old, and attended the common schools of that town. He learned the trade of cooper. He volunteered in the war of 1812, but did not enter into active service, and worked at his trade as cooper for Ripley, the owner of Ripley's wharf, Boston. He worked on the "Chesapeake" and other American war vessels fitted out in the port of Boston. He returned to Littleton and took up farming, and in 1824, at the death of his father, with his brother Asa, succeeded to the homestead. In the early forties he removed to Acton, and after two years in farming there went to Sterling to carry on the farm of his wife's parents. Like most farmers of that thrifty day he followed his trade in winter. In 1855 he returned to Littleton, buying a farm which he conducted during the remainder of his life. He was industrious, upright and of sterling character, having the esteem and confidence of all his townsmen. He was an active and prominent member of the Unitarian church, and an officer of the society. He served on the board of selectmen of Sterling, and was captain of the Littleton militia company and was always known as Captain Jacob. He married, November 5, 1817, Eliza Porter, of Littleton, born July 21, 1796, died February 12, 1884, daughter of John and Mary (Kendall) Porter, of Littleton. Her father was a farmer. Children: 1. John Porter, born July 30, 1818; mentioned below. 2. Elizabeth Kendall, born August 20, 1821; married, April 21, 1840, Ephraim Hosmer, born November 25, 1811, died March 5, 1871, and had Joel Kendall Hosmer, born October 6, 1841, and Edmund Porter Hosmer, born September 6, 1844, died December 2, 1864. 3. Lucian Jacob, born May 8, 1830; died February 26, 1892; married, November 9, 1851, Charlotte E. Reed, of Sterling; children: i. Helen Florence, born March 19, 1853, married, September 8, 1872, Frederick Tyler Gibbs, of Cambridge, Massachusetts, (children: Lucian Everett Gibbs, born February 19, 1874, died May 10, 1898; Florence Street Gibbs, born December 10, 1876, married, November 4, 1908, Albert Orington Bullard); ii. Lottie Gertrude, born June 8, 1861, married, June 27, 1888, Huntley Sigourney Turner, of Ayer, Massachusetts, born June 12, 1863, son of John Henry and Helen Mitchell (Brown) Turner.

(VII) John Porter Priest, son of Jacob Priest, was born at Littleton, July 30, 1818, and died at Charlestown, Massachusetts. March 26, 1900. He was educated in the public schools of Littleton and at Ashby Academy. He worked on his father's farm until he was eighteen, then became station agent at Acton, Massachusetts, the first at that place on the Fitchburg railroad, remaining there until 1849, when he left to engage in the milk business in Somerville, Massachusetts. After six years of prosperous business he sold out and entered partnership with James T. Davis in the produce business at No. 1 North Market street, Boston, in the Faneuil Hall district, under the firm name of Davis & Priest. His partner enlisted in the civil war, and Mr. Priest continued the business alone for a time. Subsequently he became a salesman for the firms of Jonathan Bigelow & Company and for Bennett, Rand & Company respectively. In 1868 he engaged in the retail grocery business on his own account, with a store at the corner of Green street and Bunker Hill street, Charlestown, did business here for about twenty-five years, and then removed to the store at the corner of Polk street and Bunker Hill street. In 1898 his son Lucian, who had been associated some years with him, took over the business and Mr. Priest retired.

In his early days he was a Whig, but from the formation of the Republican party was a loyal supporter of its candidates and principles, and especially the great war president, Lincoln, in the trying days when the administration needed the firm and faithful co-operation of the business men of the country. In religion he was a Unitarian. He was a charter member of the Boston Retail Dealers' Association, of Boston. In his younger days he served in the state militia. He belonged to the Charlestown Improvement Association. Mr. Priest was a man of good judgment, of strict integrity, cautious and conservative, painstaking and industrious. He had a lively sense of humor, and a natural fund of wit that made him a pleasant companion. He made many friends both in business and social life. He married, March 29, 1842, Sarah Caroline Davis, born at Acton, November 11, 1820, daughter of Jonathan Billings and Sally (Hosmer) Davis, of Acton. Her father was a farmer. Children: 1. John Tenney, born March 13, 1843; mentioned below. 2. Sarah Eliza, born December 28, 1845; married, November 5, 1867, Thomas Warren Beddoe, of Charlestown; children: 1. Lizzie Alice Beddoe, born July 6, 1870, died July 26, 1871; ii. Carrie Delina Beddoe, born September 13, 1872, married June 30, 1897, Edward Foster Chamberlin, of East Orange, New Jersey, and had Virginia Chamberlin, born December 26, 1898, and Eleanor Warren

Chamberlin, born September 24, 1904. 3. Henry Porter, born September 23, 1852; died September 30, 1902; married, December 6, 1881, Lucia Mead Fyffe, of Manchester, New Hampshire; mentioned below. 4. Emma Caroline, born December 27, 1855; unmarried, living with her mother. 5. Dora Eveline, born April 29, 1860; died December 24, 1860. 6. Ella Davis, born June 23, 1861; died June 25, 1861. 7. Lucian Jacob, born November 3, 1865; married, November 15, 1898, Fannie De Young, of Boston; children: i. Lucian Charles, born September 18, 1899; ii. Helen Katharine, February 28, 1907.

(VIII) John Tenney Priest, son of John Porter Priest, was born at Acton, March 13, 1843. At the age of six years he moved with his parents to Somerville, Massachusetts, where he attended the public schools until 1855. He completed his schooling at Charlestown, wither his parents removed at that time and graduated in the class of 1860 from the Charlestown high school. For two years following he was clerk in the meat and provision store of Robert Wason. He enlisted in August, 1862, in Company B, Thirty-sixth Massachusetts Volunteer Regiment, going into camp immediately at Worcester. The regiment was assigned to the Second Division, Ninth Army Corps, and joined the Army of the Potomac. His first battle was Fredericksburg. Afterward the regiment was sent to Kentucky, and later to Vicksburg to reinforce General Grant's command in the spring of 1863. After Vicksburg fell the regiment moved with the army to Jackson, driving out the forces of General Johnston and investing the city. Thence the regiment returned to Vicksburg and later to Kentucky when they rendezvoused at Nicholasville, Kentucky, afterwards going to East Tennessee under General Burnside, in the Army of the Ohio. Mr. Priest took part in the battles of Blue Springs, Campbell's Station and in the Siege of Knoxville. In March, 1864, he went with his regiment to Annapolis to reinforce the army of the Potomac, and on May 6th fought in the battle of the Wilderness at Spottsylvania, May 12, on May 26 in the battle of North Anna River, and on June 3 at Cold Harbor, where he received the wound that cost him his leg. He was in the army hospital at Washington for three months and at the hospital at Boston nine months, receiving his discharge and being mustered out June 17, 1865.

He resumed business as a bookkeeper in the office of Sargent Brothers & Company, wholesale dry goods dealers and jobbers, Devonshire street, Boston, resigning that position to become city clerk pro tempore of Charlestown in April, 1871. He was elected clerk in September following, and continued in that office until January, 1874, when Charlestown was annexed to Boston. He then became assistant city clerk of Boston, continuing as such until February, 1908, when he was elected city clerk of Boston. During his long public service he has shown himself a competent, efficient and accommodating official and numbers among his friends most of the prominent men in public life in Boston and vicinity. Mr. Priest resides in Roxbury. He is a Republican in politics. He is a member of King Solomon Lodge of Free Masons, of Charlestown, which he joined in June, 1867; of Signet Chapter, Royal Arch Masons, of Charlestown; of Malden Council, Royal and Select Masons; of Hugh de Payens Commandery, Knights Templar, Melrose, Massachusetts, and Aleppo Temple, Mystic Shrine; also of the Ancient Order of United Workmen, of the Dudley Club, of Roxbury, of the Roxbury Historical Society, of Abraham Lincoln Post, No. 11, Grand Army, Charlestown, and of the Massachusetts Association of City Clerks. He married, October 14, 1875, Harriet Elizabeth Beddoe, of Charlestown, born May 23, 1851, daughter of Thomas and Harriet (Jameson) Beddoe. Her father was a painter by trade; served in the civil war. Children: 1. Warren Albert, born July 4, 1876; married, July 20, 1907, J. Edith, daughter of Myron Rounds.

(VIII) Henry Porter Priest, son of John Porter Priest, was born in Somerville, Massachusetts, September 23, 1852, and died September 30, 1902. He had a common school education. He entered the employ of the Manchester Mills Corporation in February, 1877, being employed under W. F. McConnell, engineer in charge of the surveys for the Manchester & Ashburnham railroad, which was then in contemplation. In September of the same year he entered the mill office at Manchester, New Hampshire, and won his way by successive promotions to the office of paymaster of that great corporation. He was in the employ of the company for a quarter of a century, and in all the various capacities in which he served that corporation proved a faithful and efficient worker, and won and held the respect not only of the management but of his fellow-workers as well. He succeeded J. S. Shannon as paymaster. He resigned May 30, 1901, on account of an attack of paralysis, but his resignation was not accepted until a year later. His health had been failing, however, for some time before, and his condition grew gradually worse until his death. He was a member of the First Unitarian Church and devoted to its interests attending service regularly and one of the directors of the business of the society. He was a member of the Masonic fraternity, being a past-master of Lafayette Lodge of Free Masons; of the Royal Arch Chapter, the Council of Royal and Select Masters, and of Trinity Commandery, Knights Templar, of which he was past eminent commander. He was also a member of the Odd Fellows, the Ancient Order of United Workmen, the Royal Arcanum and the New England Order of Protection. He was a man of many sterling qualities, genial, kindly, honest and sincere. Indeed, unaffected simplicity is perhaps the expression that best describes his leading characteristic. He was modest, unaffected, simple in his ways, home-loving and of strict integrity. True always to the right as he saw it, he was withal a man of strong convictions and high courage. And while he was quiet and never put himself forward into the public gaze, he had many friends and in a quiet way was a prominent club man and popular socially. He was one of the oldtime members of the Derryfield Club, was at one time president of the Calumet Club and one of the founders of the Cygnet. In all these organizations his counsel was respected and his membership prized. He was a prominent Republican, and served his district one term in the state legislature. One of his friends who knew him best is quoted by the *Manchester Mirror*: "Few people save those who knew him best, appreciated Harry Priest to the fullest extent. He was honest as the day is long and he never by word or deed did any one wrong. He had not an enemy in the world." He married, December 6, 1881, Lucia Mead Fyffe, of Manchester. They had no children.

TEBBETTS The Tebbetts family, of which Jeremiah Hall W. Tebbetts, a late resident of Lynn, was a representative, was founded in Rochester, New Hampshire, at an early date.

(I) James Tebbetts, a native and resident of Rochester, New Hampshire, was a blacksmith by trade, hard working, of sinewy common sense, and feelings remarkably strong, though scrupulously reserved from the casual glances of mere acquaintances. He died in November, 1854, aged eighty-two years. His wife, Mary (Nutter) Tebbetts, was a woman of delicate physique, but of quick sympathy and many genial, social qualities, and the memory of her life was an inspiration to her children.

(II) Noah Tebbetts, youngest son of James and Mary (Nutter) Tebbetts, was born in Rochester, New Hampshire, December 26, 1802. After the preliminary studies of the district school, he spent two or three years in the academies of Wakefield, New Hampshire, and Saco, Maine, preparing for college. He spent his freshman year at Dartmouth University, and in 1819 entered Bowdoin College, from whence he graduated in 1822. His rank at graduation was that of the third scholar. The Salutatory was assigned him at Commencement, and a Latin "Master's Oration" in 1825. Without undervaluing the importance of attention to prescribed studies, he did not confine himself to the routine of the regular course, but devoted himself also to a wide range of miscellaneous reading, and his memory was so retentive and prompt that throughout his life his college reading in poetry, history, biography and philosophy was always ready to illustrate and enforce arguments, or to enliven conversation. He was regarded as possessing a remarkably well-balanced mind, with equal tastes and capacities for the ancient languages, mathematics, metaphysics, and English literature, though as the years went on his literary enjoyments were chiefly found in Latin and English classics.

Immediately after graduating, Mr. Tebbetts began the study of law in his native village with Jeremiah H. Woodman, in whose office he remained three years, and at the end of that time, 1825, was admitted to the bar of York county, Maine, and in the fall of that year began the practice of his profession in North Parsonsfield, Maine. In the fall of 1827 he removed to the "Middle Road" Village in Parsonsfield, and became the partner of Hon. Rufus McIntire, then member of congress from Maine. His practice extended through York county in Maine, and Old Strafford (now Strafford, Belknap and Carroll) in New Hampshire. During his seven years residence in Parsonsfield, he was a member of the superintending school committee nearly all the time, and chiefly through his wise and persistent labors, the schools of Parsonsfield rose to a very high order of excellence, so that their teachers were sought for from far and wide. In November, 1834, Mr. McIntire being no longer a member of congress, and the legal business of the town being insufficient for two lawyers, Mr. Tebbetts removed with his family to his native town, Rochester, where he remained till his death. As a lawyer he was never ambitious of a reputation for managing difficult cases, and always preferred to have his own important causes argued by some other lawyer. He never favored the creation of litigation, nor allowed his clients to become involved in law, if he could keep them out of it. He steadily advanced, however, in theoretical and practical knowledge of law, and his practice grew almost in spite of himself.

As a citizen, he was early in suggesting and active in carrying out all social enterprises, even when his public spirit interfered with his private interests. He greatly enlarged the sphere and improved the character of a (social) library which he found almost extinct, and by his wise selection of books and his discriminating advice to the young who came to his office for them, he gave a permanent impulse to the literary and studious tastes of the town. In education, he continued to be the friend of progress, and did much to supersede ancient ideas by a more liberal policy, and inaugurate a generation of better school houses, better teachers and better scholars. He was for many years a teacher in Sunday schools, and occasionally a superintendent. During several summers he was the superintendent of a school in the village in the morning, and of another in the afternoon at a school house four miles away. He took an active interest in the cause of temperance very early in life, at a time when it cost something to be an open advocate of that reform. His labors in that cause were untiring throughout the town and state, and he sought by lectures and addresses to rouse his fellow citizens to prompt action in the matter. He had the rare power of denouncing vice, and endeavoring to overthrow its strongholds, without provoking the personal animosity of the vicious.

In politics Mr. Tebbetts was at first a Republican, in opposition to the Federalists, and as new distinctions arose, he was a Democrat. He was always a steadfast and conscientious politician, receiving the confidence of his party, while he did not hesitate to oppose particular measures supported by its leaders, when they seemed unwise or unfair. He had no taste for the notoriety of office, and though repeatedly urged to be the candidate of his party, in days when a nomination by the Democratic party of New Hampshire was equivalent to an election, he resolutely refused to leave the peace of private life and the duties of his professional career. In 1842, however, considerations of public duty overcame his private preferences. The contest was then very severe between the friends and enemies of the Temperance Reformation, and as the laws of the state were to be revised that year, the great struggle was for the control of the legislature, in order to regulate the penal enactments for the sale of ardent spirits. It was believed that Mr. Tebbetts alone could carry, by his personal popularity, the temperance ticket in the town of Rochester, and when this was made plain to him he consented to be a candidate for representative. The result was his election, by a large majority, in March, 1842. During two long and laborious sessions of the legislature he was a constant resident at the capitol, always in his place in the committee room to work, and in the house to vote. He was a member of two important committees, on banks and banking, and on the judiciary, and both in the committee room and in the house he was always watchful to detect and prompt to expose the elements in proposed laws, which tended to favor the few at the expense of many, while he was as ready to suggest and advocate measures that would promote the public good. In January, 1843, Mr. Tebbetts was appointed by Governor Hubbard circuit justice of the court of common pleas. In a discriminating and beautiful tribute to his memory, published a few days after his death, and understood to have been written by his lifelong friend, Hon. John P. Hale, Judge Tebbett's appointment and his character as a jurist are thus spoken of:

"Perhaps injustice is done to no one else when it is said that no appointment is recollected to have been made by the Executive of this State, within the memory of the writer, which was received with more satisfaction by the whole community than was that of Judge Tebbetts. His character, disposition and habits of thought eminently qualified him for success in the office to which he was promoted. His great integrity, his even temper, his suavity of manner, his clear perception, his modest distrust of his own powers which induced him to listen patiently and respectfully to the arguments and suggestions of others, and the clearness and distinctness with which he announced the results to which his reflections had led him, were such estimable and rare qualities for a judge, that his friends and the public had already formed, and were cherishing the most favorable anticipations of his reputation and usefulness in his judicial career. He had not the least particle of that vanity in his composition which induces some to adhere with such pertinacity and obstinacy to their own notions, however hastily formed, that the principles of law and the rights of parties must bend to conform to them. He never sank the gentleman in the judge, but always treated everyone who had occasion to transact business with him on the bench, with such uniform urbanity and kindness, that it is believed he never, even by accident, wounded the feelings of the humblest individual who approached him. He had such a rich and rare combination of those traits of character admirably adapted to his place and station, that it is believed to be far from extravagant eulogy to say that the public have suffered a loss in his death not easily to be repaired."

The following tribute was paid to the memory of Judge Tebbetts by Hon. Josiah Quincy, of Rumney, New Hampshire:

"Soon after his appointment as judge, he held a term of the court in Grafton County. At that term was the celebrated trial of Cumming for the murder of his wife. I was counsel for the prisoner. The trial was exceedingly laborious—occupying twenty-one days. Judge Tebbetts gave the charge to the jury, and discharged his duty ably, faithfully and impartially. Coming to the bench so very recently, deeply impressed with the magnitude and importance of the trial, he manifested the deepest solicitude in regard to the right of performance of his arduous duties. I believe neither the prisoner nor the government had any reason for complaint. It was a severe trial for him, but it was manifest that he possessed qualifications for the office he held of the first order. When upon the bench he was courteous in his demeanor, patient and laborious, exhibiting sound judgment and discriminating good sense, which enabled him to apply his extensive knowledge of law to the questions that were presented, with almost intuitive sagacity".

The long trial of Cumming to which Mr. Quincy alluded, left unmistakable traces upon the health of Judge Tebbetts. The tedious confinement for so many weeks in the fetid atmosphere of a court room, the continual strain of the intellectual faculties, the scrupulous anxiety of a conscientious, sensitive mind with quick sympathies and a deep conviction of the utter wrongfulness of capital punishment, completely prostrated his physical strength, which was never robust. August 19, 1844, after a very debilitating summer, he went to Gilford to hold a term of court for Belknap county. After a few days he seemed to have caught cold, and was unusually unwell. He was urged by the whole bar to adjourn the court and go home to recruit his health, but with his wonted conscientiousness and exactness in the discharge of duty, he refused, because he thought the public interest would suffer by the postponement of the causes then ready for trial. But finally it became impossible for him to hold out longer, and adjourning the court he returned home, August 30, and September 9, 1844, at the age of forty-one years and eight months, his life on earth was ended.

Judge Tebbetts married, June 3, 1828, Mary Esther, daughter of J. H. Woodman, Esq., of Rochester, New Hampshire. In his family he was all that the most sensitive affection could desire. Domestic happiness was dearer to him than gratified ambition or hoarded wealth. He sought to win the love and affection of his children, as well as to command their obedience.

(III) Jeremiah Hall W. Tebbetts, son of Judge Noah and Mary E. (Woodman) Tebbetts, was born in Rochester, New Hampshire, September 4, 1840, died March 11, 1880. He received his early education in the common schools of his native town, and later completed his studies at Exeter Academy, New Hampshire. He first worked with his brother-in-law as a carpenter, remaining a few years, and afterwards engaged in different lines of business until the breaking out of the civil war, when he enlisted and served about one year in Company I, Fifteenth New Hampshire Regiment, being with General B. F. Butler at New Orleans. He became very active in war affairs, serving as a private in two active battles, Port Hudson and Fort Donaldson, and receiving promotion in military ranks, finally becoming fifth sergeant, and later sergeant-major under General Neal Dow, and also served as adjutant. Upon his return from the war he went to Lynn, Massachusetts, and entered the Beede & Tebbetts Shoe Company as a partner, remaining several years. He later went to New York and became a partner of the Faxon Wholesale Shoe Company, located in Duane street. Subsequently, owing to ill health, he returned to Lynn, but was unable to engage in any active business, and lived retired up to his decease. He was a Republican in politics, and took a decided interest in political campaigns. He was twice elected as delegate from Lynn to the state convention at Worcester. He was a member of the Order of Free and Accepted Masons, and a regular attendant of the Unitarian church.

Mr. Tebbetts married, at Lynn, May 10, 1870, Kate P. Hood, daughter of Hon. George Hood, first mayor of Lynn, born at Lynn, July 23, 1845. Children: 1. Gertrude Hermonie, born October 22, 1871, as a teacher at Ingalls school at Lynn. 2. Mary Esther, born July 9, 1875, married Hugh K. Moore, of Lynn; child, Katherine Burgess, born May 23, 1908. 3. George Woodman, born February 19, 1877, married Ethel Morgan, of Lexington, Kentucky; they reside at Pittsburgh, Pennsylvania. 4. William Hall, born April 29, 1879, died March 31, 1903.

(For first generation see John Foster I).

FOSTER

(II) Samuel Foster, son of John and Martha Foster, baptized March 7, 1651-52, lived in Salem, where he is mentioned as husbandman. He married first, May 14, 1676, Sarah Stuard (or Stuart) and after her death he married Margaret ———. He had in all seventeen children, of whom Joseph was sixth in the order of birth.

(III) Joseph Foster, son of Samuel Foster, born Salem, March 11, 1687, died Beverly, January 28, 1750. He was a farmer and fisherman and lived in Beverly. He married, September 4, 1708, Mrs. Rebecca Groves, widow of John Groves, and daughter of Nathaniel and Margery Wallis, and by her had ten children, Samuel being fifth in the order of birth.

(IV) Samuel Foster, son of Joseph and Rebecca Foster, born Beverly, Massachusetts, August 20, 1717, died there in 1775. He married first, August 31, 1741, Mary Thorndike, who died in 1757, and he married second, November 28, 1758, Martha Bisson. Of his eight children five were born of his first and three of his second marriage: 1. Samuel, baptized May 30, 1742, died young. 2. Mary, born May 30, 1743, married, December 13, 1763, Robert Ellinwood. 3. Samuel, born March 4, 1745, married Mary Ober. 4. Lydia, born March 3, 1746, married, September 2, 1773, Josiah Thissell. 5. Paul, born July 14, 1750, married Martha Trask. 6. Josiah, born December 29, 1759, married Rachel Lovett. 7. Joshua, born May 28, 1763, died October 3, 1838. 8. Israel, born August 23, 1765, married and died before 1800.

(V) Joshua Foster, son of Samuel and Martha (Bisson) Foster, born Beverly, May 28, 1763, died there October 3, 1838. He was a mariner. He married, December 5, 1782, Sarah Ober, born in 1755, died July 8, 1825, daughter of Thomas and Abigail (Pittman) Ober. They had nine children: 1. Joshua, born September 20, 1783, married Hepsibah Pride. 2. Patty, born September 20, 1783, died June 27, 1843; married, September 11, 1803, Henry West. 3. Hezekiah, born January 29, 1786, married Betsey West. 4. Abigail, born 1787, died September 22, 1791. 5. Judith, born October 16, 1798, died April 1, 1854; married Joseph L. Foster. 6. Jonathan, born November 26, 1791, died in February, 1817, at Point Adventure. 7. Elizabeth, born September 22, 1793, married, December 31, 1818, Azor Dodge. 8. Mary, born August 9, 1796, died June 15, 1852; married, January 11, 1821, John Prince. 9. John Ober, born August 19, 1799.

(VI) Captain John Ober Foster, youngest son and child of Joshua and Sarah (Ober) Foster, born Beverly, August 19, 1799, died there May 14, 1852. He was a mariner and captain of a vessel engaged largely in coastwise trade, and after many years of seafaring life he bought and lived on the farm which now is owned by his grandson, John Henry Foster. He married (first), March 25, 1821, Hannah Foster, born 1802, died May 10, 1836; married (second), August 12, 1838, Mrs. Louisa (Woodbury) James, daughter of Samuel Lawson and Sally Emery. She was born in 1807 and died January 25, 1896. Captain John Ober and Hannah (Foster) Foster had three children: 1. Caroline E., born September 17, 1823, died August 4, 1835. 2. John O., born August 11, 1829, died 1845. 3. Henry F. W., born August 19, 1832.

(VII) Henry Francis West Foster, youngest child of Captain John Ober and Hannah (Foster) Foster, and the only one of their children who grew to maturity, was born in Beverly, August 19, 1832, and died there April 13, 1891. His business life was spent in Beverly, where he was a carpenter and joiner until the death of his father. After that he took the farm, which he had inherited from his father, and turned his attention to market gardening. He made a complete success of this business, as he did also of whatever he set out to accomplish, for he was an energetic man both in his own personal affairs and those of the town with which he was prominently identified. For many years he was a member of the board of selectmen of Beverly, also of the board of water commissioners, and at one time was district chief of the Beverly fire department. He held membership in Bass River Lodge, No. 141, Independent Order Odd Fellows, and attended the Baptist church. On March 20, 1856, Mr. Foster married Joanna H. Pierce, born January 9, 1835, died October 7, 1886, daughter of Leonard and Margaret (Lord) Pierce, of Watertown, Massachusetts. Three children were born of this marriage: 1. John Henry, born July 24, 1857, lives in Beverly. 2. Emily Esther, born October 10, 1859, married, November 28, 1878, Frank W. Plaisted, born 1855, son of William Plaisted. 3. Carrie Frances, born May 6, 1869, married, April 5, 1896, Louis Dudley Webber, born 1866, son of Henry A. and Hannah C. Webber.

(VIII) John Henry Foster, eldest child and only son of Henry Francis West and Joanna H. (Pierce) Foster, was born in Beverly, July 24, 1857. In business life he has followed the occupation of his father, that of market gardener, which he has carried on with success ever since his father's death. Mr. Foster was given a good education in the Beverly public schools, and after leaving school went to work with his father, farming and market gardening, and to-day is owner of one of the best cultivated and most productive farms in Beverly; his is the same farm which his grandfather, Captain John Ober Foster, purchased after he retired from seafaring life. Mr. Foster is something of a public man in the affairs of Beverly, but has no inclination for office, having frequently declined it. For several years he was captain of Hose Company No. 4 of the Beverly fire department. He is a member of Liberty Lodge, Free and Accepted Masons, Amity Chapter, Royal Arch Masons, and St. George Commandery, Knights Templar; member of Bass River Lodge, No. 141, Independent Order Odd Fellows, and of Golden Star Council, No. 22, O. U. A. M.

On November 22, 1881, Mr. Foster married Sadie Abbie Whitehouse, born in Beverly, September 22, 1860, daughter of Michael and Abbie (Benson) Whitehouse, the latter a daughter of Henry Benson. Mr. and Mrs. Foster have three children: 1. Louise Benson, born February 11, 1883, a graduate of Wellesley and now a teacher in Rockland, New Hampshire. 2. Sarah Gertrude, born April 28, 1884, lives with her parents. 3. Henry Franklin, born September 1, 1887, lives with his parents.

(For early generations see Nathaniel Merrill 1).

MERRILL (III) John Merrill, son of Abraham Merrill (2), was born October 15, 1673. He was called yeoman. He married first, August 7, 1708, Deborah Hazletine, of Haverhill; second, Margaret ———, who survived him. His homestead was on the Merrimac river, and he had land at Salisbury. His will, dated November 3, 1749, proved May 31, 1756, bequeathed to wife Margaret; to daughters Abigail Downer, Deliverance Williams; and the children of his daughter Deborah Brown, deceased. His sons John and Henry were executors, and were given the real estate, each to have half the homestead, and to pay all other bequests. Children, all born at Newbury: 1. Deborah, July 12, 1709; married Thomas Brown. 2. Ruth, January 7, 1710; married Christopher Annis. 3. Abigail, September 14, 1712; married Joseph Downer. 4. Elizabeth, May 4, 1714; died November 2, 1728. 5. Deliverance, March 18, 1716; married Thomas Williams. 6. John, January 13, 1717-8; married Annie Ordway. 7. Henry, June 27, 1719; mentioned below. 8. Sarah, October 22, 1721; died November 25, 1727. 9. Nathaniel, May 6, 1724; died July 10, 1727.

(IV) Henry Merrill, son of John Merrill (3), was born at Newbury, June 27, 1719. He resided in Newbury, and married Priscilla, daughter of Benjamin Lowell. They had a son Henry, mentioned below, and other children.

(V) Henry Merrill, son of Henry Merrill (4), was born about 1745. He resided in Newburyport, and married Rebecca Moulton. He was a residuary legatee with his son Samuel of the estate of his son Paul. Children: 1. Paul; will dated December 13, 1812, proved March 4, 1813; bequeathed to mother Rebecca; sister Abigail; brothers Samuel, Hardy, John and Henry, who was executor; to Paul, the two-year-old son of his brother Henry; to sister Mary Jackman and to father Henry. 2. Abigail. 3. Samuel. 4. Mary, married Joseph Jackman. 5. Hardy. 6. John. 7. Henry, mentioned below.

(VI) Deacon Henry Merrill, son of Henry Merrill (5), born February 15, 1778, died September 14, 1859, in Newburyport. He was a wool-puller and hatter, and also in the grocery business. He was active in church work and served as deacon. He married, September 3, 1803, Lydia Jackman, born December 19, 1779. (Will of son Paul calls his mother "Alice".) Children: 1. Samuel, born September 21, 1804; died while attending Yale College. 2. David Jackman, born October 6, 1806; mentioned below. 3. Henry, born June 23, 1808. 4. Paul, born August 1, 1810. Will dated October 25, 1832, bequeathing to father Henry, his mother Alice, brothers David J. (executor), Henry and William. 5. William, born April 29, 1817.

(VII) David Jackman Merrill, son of Deacon Henry Merrill (6), born in Newburyport, October 6, 1806, died there December 28, 1891. He attended the district schools and the academy in his native town and graduated in the class of 1827 from Yale College. He began the study of medicine, but his health failed and he had to abandon his studies. He taught school for a time and then embarked in the business of druggist, for which his medical learning had especially fitted him. He was successful in business and acquired a handsome property, investing extensively in real estate in Newburyport. When the civil war began he sold out his business and devoted all his time in his later years to the management and improvement of his property. In addition to the care of his own real estate he had charge of other property for various clients. He was a justice of the peace and conveyancer. In politics he was a Republican, and while a member of the school board was on the committee in charge of building the girls' high school. He was a prominent and zealous member of the Baptist church, and served for more than thirty years as its collector and treasurer. He married, September 20, 1835, Ann M. Titcomb, born January 24, 1813, at Newburyport, died September 19, 1894, daughter of Luther and Sally (Teel) Titcomb. Children: 1. Charles Griswell Gurley, born July 27, 1836; mentioned below. 2. Harriet, born February 10, 1838, died young. 3. Annie, born July 7, 1841. 4. Sarah, born May 23, 1843, died young. 5. George D., born November 28, 1846.

(VIII) Charles Griswell Gurley Merrill, son of David Jackman Merrill (7), was born July 27, 1836, at Newburyport. He attended the public schools of Newburyport and fitted for college in the high school. He was graduated from Yale College in 1861, and from the Yale Medical School in 1863. He was appointed surgeon of a Philadelphia regiment of colored troops in 1863, and remained in service to the end of the civil war. He then gave up his profession to engage in the wholesale grocery business in New Haven, Connecticut, and is at the present time manager of a wholesale grocery concern in New Haven. For many years he was United States guager in that city. In politics he is a Republican. He married May 23, 1865, Georgia A. Linsley, born 1841, daughter of Charles Linsley. Children: 1. Georgia A., born October 18, 1866; married Rev. Everett T. Root; two sons—Edward M. and Winthrop H. 2. Mabel, born January 31, 1874; married Edward C. Baldwin; one child, Grace. 3. Alice, died young.

GOODRIDGE The ancient spelling of the name Goodrich was Goodridge. This family was founded in Massachusetts in the early years of the colony by William Goodridge (1) and his wife Margaret, who settled in Cambridge and soon removed to Watertown. William Goodridge died in 1683.

(II) His eldest child, Jeremiah, was born March 6, 1637 or 1638, in Watertown, and in 1660 married Mary Adams. He was the founder of the line from which was descended Micajah Newhall Goodridge, for many years a leading citizen of Lynn, Massachusetts.

(III) Jeremiah Goodridge, son of Jeremiah Goodridge (2), and grandson of the first settler, William Goodridge or Goodrich (1), was born in 1667. He married Mary ——— and settled at Newbury, Massachusetts. Children, born at Newbury: 1. Mary, born September 27, 1704. 2. William, born July 30, 1707, married, February 3, 1735, Elizabeth Pillsbury. 3. Jeremiah, born December 26, 1708, mentioned below. 4. Ezekiel, born January 3, 1713, married, December 18, 1744, Rebecca Goodridge, daughter of Philip Goodridge.

(IV) Jeremiah Goodridge, son of Jeremiah Goodridge (3), was born in Newbury, December 26, 1708. He married there January 18, 1738, Abigail Lowell, believed to be line of James Russell Lowell. Among their children was Joseph, mentioned below.

(V) Joseph Goodridge, son of Jeremiah Goodridge (4), was born in Newbury. He was a soldier in the revolution, a private in Captain William Rogers's company, Colonel Samuel Gerrish's regiment, April 19, 1775; also in Captain William Rogers's company, Lieutenant Colonel Loammi Baldwin's regiment; also in Captain Thomas Mighill's company, Colonel Nathaniel Wade's regiment, from July 8 to October 10, 1780, reinforcing the Continental army. Joseph Goodridge Jr. was also in the service from Newbury. He married Matilda Newhall. Among their children was Bailey, born 1781, mentioned below.

M. N. Goodridge

(VI) Bailey Goodridge, son of Joseph Goodridge (5), was born in Newbury in 1781. He settled at Lynn and married in that town, March 7, 1805, Elizabeth (or Betsey) Collins. Children, born in Lynn: 1. Lucretia, born June 18, 1805. 2. Mary, born July 25, 1806. 3. Betsey, born June 2, 1808. 4. Bailey, born May 7, 1810, mentioned below. 5. Zachariah, born November 14, 1811. 6. Lydia, born April 11, 1813. 7. Abigail, born December 19, 1814. 8. Joseph, born August 1, 1818. 9. Joseph Alonzo, born May 25, 1821. 10. Marinda Ann, born January 24, 1823; only one now living; married Levi Lufkin and resides on Eastern avenue, Lynn. 11. Thirza, born January 21, 1825.

(VII) Bailey Goodridge, son of Bailey Goodridge (6), was born in Lynn, May 7, 1810. He married at Lynn, October 23, 1831, Mary Ann Newhall, a native of Lynn, daughter of Paul and Mary (Mudge) Newhall and descended from Thomas (2), the first white child born in Lynn; Joseph (3); Daniel (4); Joseph (5); Micajah (6); Paul (7). Micajah Newhall Goodridge was named after a deceased son of Paul who had been named in memory of his grandfather, Micajah Newhall, who fought at Lexington. The maternal grandmother, Mary Mudge, was descended from the following line: Thomas Mudge (1), born in England and in 1657 living in Malden; John (2), served in King Philip's war in 1675; John (3); John (4); Nathan (5), served in revolutionary war under Captain Simon Brown and is also on Ticonderoga rolls (as per Mudge memorials); Mary (6), wife of Paul Newhall. Bailey and Mary Ann (Newhall) Goodridge had five children: 1. Harriet, married George C. Collins. 2. Henry H., deceased. 3. Micajah N., see forward. 4. Mary E. 5. Augustus, in Wyoma, residing on Springvale avenue.

(VIII) Micajah Newhall Goodridge, son of Bailey Goodridge (7), was born in Lynn, November 5, 1839. He received his education in the public and high schools of Lynn, graduating from the new high school in one of the first classes and receiving his diploma in 1855 from the hands of Jacob Batchelder, the first high school principal. Like most boys of that town he learned the trade of shoe-maker, working first in the little shop of Samuel H. Frothingham. At that time the work was done by hand and all but the cutting was done in the little shoe-shops on the farms. Thenceforth for the greater part of his life he was engaged in some employment akin to or connected with this leading industry of Lynn. He preferred the mercantile life, however, and shortly after becoming master of his trade he purchased the retail store of his brother-in-law, G. Z. Collins, formerly conducted by Egbert Burrows, on Market street near Tremont, in what was then the Lynn Free Library building, and continued in that business until 1872 when he removed to Charlestown to take a position as foreman in a large shoe factory. Later he held a similar position in a factory at Claremont, New Hampshire. He then returned to Lynn to take charge of the retail department of Welman Osburne, shoe dealer and manufacurer, Lynn. He held this position until 1889, when the store was destroyed by fire. In 1890 he became associated with George Z. Collins, in the leather board business. They had leather board mills at Ashland, New Hampshire, East Tilton, New Hampshire, and Lynn, and at the time of his death was associated with George Z. Collins and Arthur J. Phillips under the firm name of G. Z. Collins & Company. He became president of the East Tilton Pulp Manufacturing Company, and remained in active business to the time of his death.

In politics Mr. Goodridge was a Republican and he was actively interested in municipal affairs though never willing to accept public office. He was a strong advocate of the cause of temperance, and was a member of Bay State Lodge of Odd Fellows, a member of the Lynn Historical Society, of the Young Men's Christian Association and one of the first members of the Athenian Debating Society, which met on Market street near Liberty, and of which the Hon. Carroll D. Wright and others of local fame were members. He was a prominent member of the Lynn Common Methodist Episcopal Church and missed but two Sundays in attendance during twenty-one consecutive years before his death, both occasions being due to illness. He was a zealous worker in the ranks and at the time of his death was treasurer of the Sunday school, secretary of the official board of this church, class leader and steward. He was for some time a member of the Methodist Social Union of Boston and director two years, and was active in the Camp Meeting Association of Asbury Grove. He was beloved by all of his associates in the church and many friends of other denominations. Mr. Goodridge died at his home on Lawton avenue, Lynn, February 22, 1902. He was an exemplary husband and father, a man of sterling principle, versatile in talent, active and enthusiastic in disposition and ever ready to lend his aid in all departments of church, city or state.

He married, in Lynn, September 13, 1865, Georgianna Frothingham, of Lynn, born in Lynn, July 22, 1843, daughter of Samuel H. and Ann Maria (Tapley) Frothingham, of Lynn. (See Tapley family). Children: 1. Samuel Bailey, born Lynn, September 10, 1866, died in infancy. 2. Harriet Leslie, born July 18, 1868, formerly a teacher in St. Albans, Vermont, now teaching in Wheaton seminary at Norton, Massachusetts. 3. Alice Melville, born July 12, 1872, married (first), O. F. Pelley, one son, Ralph Wellington Pelley; married (second), Edgar Fletcher Hodgkins, of Lamoine, Maine, resides at Waltham, Massachusetts. 4. Frederick Stanley, born August 19, 1876, graduated from Massachusetts Institute of Technology as a mechanical engineer and is now in the office of Thompson, Starett & Company of Wall street, New York City; married Ethel G. Higgins, born in Wellfleet, Massachusetts, and reared in Lynn. They reside on Hasbrouck Heights, Jersey City.

SAWYER (I) William Sawyer, immigrant ancestor, who came from England, probably from Lancashire, was in Salem as early as 1640; was a proprietor in 1642; removed to Wenham, where he was living in 1643, and later to Newbury, where he was living the next year, and where he died. He sold his house and lot March 24, 1648. He married Ruth Bitfield. Children, born in Newbury: 1. John, August 24, 1645; married February 18, 1675, Sarah Poor; died 1689. 2. Samuel, November 22, 1646; married Mary ——; died 1718. 3. Bitfield, died unmarried, aged ninety-seven. 4. Ruth, September 16, 1648; married August 27, 1667, Benjamin Morse. 5. Mary, February 23, 1649; died June 24, 1659. 6. Sarah, November 20, 1651; married January 15, 1668, Joshua Brown. 7. Hannah, February 23, 1653; died January 20, 1659. 8. William, February 1, 1655; mentioned below. 9. Francis, March 24, 1657; died February 7, 1659. 10. Mary, July 29, 1660; married June 13, 1683, John Emery Jr.; died November 3, 1699. 11. Stephen, April 25, 1663; married 1686, Ann Titcomb; died June 8, 1753. 12. Hannah, January 11, 1664; died August 28, 1683. 13. Frances, November 3, 1670.

(II) William Sawyer, son of William Sawyer, was born at Newbury, February 1, 1655, and settled there. He married, March 10, 1671, Mary Emery, born June 24, 1652, daughter of John and Mary (Webster) Emery. Her father was son of John Emery the immigrant, who settled in Newbury. Children: 1. Mary, born January 20, 1672. 2. Samuel, June 5, 1674. 3. John, March 15, 1676. 4. Ruth, September 20, 1677. 5. Hannah, January 12, 1679. 6. Josiah, mentioned below.

(III) Captain Josiah Sawyer, son of William Sawyer, was born in Newbury, January 20, 1681. Children: 1. Josiah, mentioned below. 2. Dr. Moses, born 1711; died August 25, 1778; was captain of the Newbury company; was a ship owner, and made frequent voyages to the Netherlands.

(IV) Josiah Sawyer, son of Captain Josiah Sawyer, was born in 1708, and died June 10, 1792. He was a farmer, and resided in Newbury until 1746, when he bought a farm in Southampton, New Hampshire, and removed there in April that year. He married Mary Ordway, born November 2, 1714, died March 2, 1796, daughter of Deacon John Ordway. She was much loved for her sweetness of disposition, and her universal kindness. Children: 1. Josiah, born 1737; mentioned below. 2. Israel, born 1739; married Miriam Clough; died July 19, 1821. 3. Miriam, died unmarried, September 4, 1780. 4. John, born 1745; married Abigail Shepherd; died March 19, 1796. 5. Hannah, born 1746; died September 24, 1774, unmarried. 6. Richard, born May 31, 1748; died June 22, 1818; married Elizabeth Clark. 7. Matthias, born May 31, 1748 (twin); died June 22, 1818; married Eunice Batchelder. 8. Deacon Moses, born August 2, 1750; married January 16, 1775, Ann Fitz; died April 29, 1821. 9. Tirzah, born 1758; died September 2, 1832, unmarried. 10. Molly, born 1764; died September 21, 1789, unmarried.

(V) Josiah Sawyer, son of Josiah Sawyer (4), was born in 1737, and died June 19, 1812. He settled in Deerfield, New Hampshire. He became a prosperous farmer and blacksmith. He was one of the original proprietors of Nottingham, and lived where Daniel Jones lately lived, near the line between Deerfield and Nottingham. He married Nabby, sister of Jeremiah Eastman, who surveyed the town of Deerfield. Children: 1. Josiah, removed to Guilford. 2. Jeremiah, mentioned below. 3. David, born April 14, 1666; died August 21, 1845; married first, Hannah Palmer; second, Mary Knowles; third, Mrs. Susan Chesley. 4. John, lived in Andover. 5. Israel, lived on the homestead.

(VI) Jeremiah Sawyer, son of Josiah Sawyer, married Hannah Purrington of Brentwood. He removed to Gilmanton, New Hampshire, where he died. Children: 1. John. 2. Jeremiah, mentioned below. 3. James. 4. David. 5. Nancy. 6. Miriam. 7. Lydia, married Eben Jones of Epping, New Hampshire. Jeremiah Sawyer was a soldier in the revolution, from Bradford and Cape Elizabeth, in the vicinity of which he lived. He was one of the men raised from the Fifth Company, Colonel Peter Noyes' regiment, (First Cumberland county) as returned by Captain Daniel Strout, engaged for the town of Haverhill, also Bradford, for three years. The towns of Cape Elizabeth and Bradford both claimed him in their quota, and he was finally allowed by Bradford. This does not mean that he was living there, but that he enlisted as part of the Bradford quota. He was mustered by Nathaniel Barber, muster master, of Suffolk county, July 20, 1777, in Captain Allen's company, Colonel Alden's regiment; was a private also in Captain Smart's company, Colonel Calvin Smith's regiment, 1777-9, credited to Bradford; also in Captain Nicholas Blaisdell's company, Colonel Edward Wigglesworth's regiment, and was at Valley Forge, 1777-8, was sick and reported to be dead, but recovered and joined his regiment June, 1778, and in October following was on the payroll at Providence, Rhode Island. He was in the service as late as April, 1779. The New Hampshire rolls have no record of the service of Jeremiah Sawyer.

(VII) Jeremiah Sawyer, son of Jeremiah Sawyer, was born in the vicinity of Bradford, Massachusetts, though perhaps not in that town, February 16, 1784, and died at Exeter, New Hampshire. He farmed in his youth, and learned the trade of painter. He settled in Newburyport, Massachusetts, where he engaged in business as a painter and contractor. He had a shop on Franklin street near his house and he lost all in the great fire in 1809-10. He then removed to Lee, New Hampshire, and followed farming and painting for about seven years. In 1821 he removed to Exeter, New Hampshire, and lived on a small place that he bought, located near the center of the village. In a small shop on the premises he prepared his paints and stored his materials, continuing in the business of painting until his death. He was quite religious and an active member of the church. He married Jane Chase, born February 22, 1787. Children: 1. Mary Jane, born July 2, 1808; died December 20, 1895; married, November 6, 1832, Andrew Baker Jr., of Litchfield, Maine, born August 3, 1806, died November 14, 1853; children: i. Melvina R. Baker, born June 5, 1836, married July 2, 1860, Samuel H. Green, and had Walter Baker Green, born November 11, 1861; ii. Hattie A. Baker, born December 18, 1838, married Honestus F. Senter, and had Harry Baker Senter. 2. William, married Sarah Tuck, of Brentwood, New Hampshire; their son Dr. Edward Warren was a graduate of Norwich University Medical School, Vermont, and a prominent physician. 3. Samuel, died young. 4. Samuel, married Lucy Otis; children: Lucy, Otis, Munroe. 5. Jeremiah, born at Lee, April 14, 1810; mentioned below. 6. Lydia, married Henry Hook, of Newmarket, or Brentwood. 7. Abigail, born May 1, 1821; died at Newburyport; married first, 1840, William H. Marshall; second, July, 1846, Michael C. Teel, of Newburyport; child of first wife: i. William H. Marshall Jr.; children of second wife: ii. Rebecca Marshall; iii. Jane Chase Marshall, born April 16, 1850, unmarried, resides in Newburyport; iv. Edwin Lawrence Marshall, born January 13, 1854, died August, 1907, married Laura Prescott, of Newburyport, and had Walter L. Marshall; v. Rebecca Marshall, born November, 1857, died 1859; vi. Georgianna Keeley Marshall, born July 18, 1860, married August 28, 1886, Willard Wheeler; (children: Abbie Edith Wheeler, married Frederick Thayer; George Willard Wheeler, and Arthur Wheeler). 8. Joseph.

(VIII) Jeremiah Sawyer, son of Jeremiah Sawyer, was born at Lee, New Hampshire, April 14, 1810, and died at Newburyport, January 26, 1876. He had a common school education. He removed with his parents to Exeter, where he learned the trade of carriage painting as well as his father's trade of house painter. He established himself in business at Exeter, and kept a large force of journeymen busy on his contracts. He built a residence in Exeter. In the early forties he removed to Amesbury, the home of the carriage building business of the country, and followed his trade as a carriage painter and decorator for the next six years. He worked in Boston a year, and about 1847 located in Cambridge, where he again engaged in business as a house painter and decorator with signal success. He retired from business some years before his death, and spent his last years on a small farm in Brentwood, New Hampshire. He died at Newburyport, Massachusetts, at the home of his sister. He was a very quiet, unassuming man, never taking an active part socially, owing to his somewhat defective hearing, but was studious and interested in the affairs of the world. He was an omnivorous reader. In politics he was a Democrat. In early life he joined the Baptist church. He married first, at Exeter, December, 1832, Susan Gilman Sherriff, born at Exeter, October 24, 1806, daughter of Benjamin Pierce and Martha (Gilman) Sherriff. Her father was born at Exeter, July 10, 1763; her mother June 14, 1768. Mr. Sawyer married second, Inez Evans. Children of first wife: 1. Howard Malcolm, born February 19, 1834; mentioned below. 2. Anna Elizabeth, died aged five years. 3. Sarah Ellen, born July 10, 1837; married May 5, 1861, Charles Henry Atwood, of Cambridge; child: Howard Julian Atwood, born August 24, 1866, died September 6, 1866. 4. Jeremiah Stow, born at Exeter, died at Brentwood. 5. Annie Mary, married December 31, 1863, Charles E. Wheeler, of Cambridge; children: i. Winnifred Bertha Wheeler; ii. Charles Irving Wheeler, married Emma Brown of Cambridge; iii. Bertha Howard Wheeler. 6. John Sherriff, born June 27, 1847. Two others died in infancy.

(IX) Howard Malcolm Sawyer, son of Jeremiah Sawyer, was born at Exeter, New Hampshire, February 19, 1834, and died at Medford, Massachusetts, September 7, 1902. He attended the common schools of his native town. At the age of thirteen he came to East Cambridge, Massachusetts, to work for his uncle, John L. Sherriff, manufacturer of brushes. While his father lived in Boston he attended the old Common street school and after coming to Cambridge he continued in the public schools until he graduated from the high school. He went to Chicago when he was nineteen years old, and found employment in the meat packing industry, which was then in its infancy, and had the distinction of packing the first shipment of pork sent to the eastern market from Chicago. After remaining there three years he was called home to attend his mother in her last sickness, and after her death he entered the employ of B. D. Moody, manufacturer of waterproof hats, to learn the trade. Mr. Moody formed a partnership with William H. Pettingill and Mr. Blodgett, under the firm name of Moody, Pettingill & Blodgett. Mr. Sawyer showed great proficiency in the business and rose to positions of responsibility. At the age of twenty-five he was made superintendent of the factory, and after the retirement of Mr. Moody, when the firm name became Pettingill & Blodgett, he was admitted to the firm. When Mr. Blodgett retired a few years later, the firm name became Pettingill & Sawyer. Mr. Moody afterward re-entered the firm and the name became Pettingill, Moody & Sawyer, but after two years retired, and the name of Pettingill & Sawyer was resumed. The factory was destroyed by fire August 7, 1877, and Mr. Pettingill withdrew from the firm. Mr. Sawyer continued the business, and later he and his son Charles H. Sawyer formed the firm of H. M. Sawyer & Son. In 1895 the business was incorporated under the title of H. M. Sawyer & Son, Inc., as a Massachusetts company with H. M. Sawyer president, Charles H. Sawyer treasurer. The concern does a large business, manufacturing in great variety oil clothing for the use of fishermen, sportsmen, teamsters and western farmers and cowboys. A large and increasing demand for waterproof clothing is supplied by this house.

In 1895 Mr. Sawyer established the Sawyer Belting Company as a separate corporation, with himself as president and son vice-president, to manufacture canvass waterproof stitched belting. The product of their factory has been extensively used as a substitute for old-fashioned leather belting, especially in threshing machines and machinery exposed to rain and moist conditions. This business was sold to the Rubber Goods Manufacturing Company and the plant moved to Cleveland, Ohio. It is now a part of the United States Rubber Company. In 1897 another son was admitted to the company, Lawrence T. Sawyer, and after the father's death, the third son, Ralph V. Sawyer, became active in the company.

Mr. Sawyer was an admirable type of self-made man, making his own way in business by the force of his industry and natural ability and he rose to a high position in the business world. He was well known and highly esteemed in the trade throughout the country. His goods stood the test and his house maintained the highest reputation for the quality of its product. He was not only a leader in business, but popular socially, and a distinguished Free Mason. He was made a member of old Putnam Lodge, East Cambridge, June 18, 1866; exalted in Mystic Chapter, R. A. M., Medford, May 7, 1883; received his cryptic degrees in Medford Council, R. S. M., May 15, 1890; received his degrees of knighthood in DeMolay Commandery, Knights Templar, at Boston, June 12, 1883, and was a member of Aleppo Temple, Order of the Mystic Shrine, Boston. He was also a member of Mount Vernon Lodge, No. 186, I. O. O. F., and of Mystic Lodge, Knights of Honor, West Medford. He was an active and useful citizen of Medford, though he never sought public office. He held the office of street commissioner several years, and was especially interested in good roads and parks. He took much interest and gave much of his time to the landscape gardening when Flag Staff Hill was laid out in a public park a few years ago. His residence at 4 Laurel street, opposite this beautiful spot, was built by him in the winter of 1872. In politics he was a Democrat of the old school. He was a member of the East Cambridge Baptist Church, serving on various church committees, but in his later years he attended the Congregational church at West Medford.

He married, November 29, 1859, Mary Haskell Pettingill, born Newburyport, Massachusetts, August 7, 1838, daughter of William Henry and Hannah (Johnson) Pettingill, of Newburyport. Her father was formerly a sea captain, then a railroad man, and finally in the oil clothing business with Mr. Sawyer at East Cambridge. Children: 1. Mary Ella, born September 17, 1860; married September 14, 1899, William Francis Macey, of Medford. 2. Charles Howard, born August 19, 1862; mentioned below. 3. Susan Sherriff, born November 21, 1866; died May 30, 1868. 4. William Miner, born March 12, 1870; died December 12, 1870. 5. Lawrence Taylor, born May 8, 1875; mentioned below. 6. Sarah Annie, born March 20, 1878; married, September 14, 1899, John Walter Emery, of Medford; children: i. Malcolm Sawyer Emery, born December 8, 1901; ii. Miriam Emery, born July 29, 1907. 7. Ralph Underdown, born December 8, 1880; mentioned below.

(X) Charles Howard Sawyer, son of Howard Malcolm Sawyer, was born at East Cambridge, August 19, 1862. He attended the public schools of Cambridge until he was ten years old, and the schools of Medford until he was fifteen. He began at an early age to learn his father's business and after the plant was destroyed was associated with his father in the rebuilding and management of the factory. He took charge of the shipping department, then of the counting room and when he came of age was admitted to partnership, as stated in the sketch of his father. For some years he was buyer and salesman for the firm, making the first western trip for the house when he was but nineteen years old. Since his father's death he has been president of the company, having as his department of the business the buying of stock and marketing of the product. Mr. Sawyer is also president of the Alvin Clark Sons corporation, the most famous makers of lenses and telescopes in the country. He is also president of the Rhode Island Dyeing and Finishing Company of Woonsocket, Rhode Island, organized under Rhode Island laws, a large concern engaged in finishing corduroys and velveteens. Mr. Sawyer is a prominent Free Mason. He was made a member of Mount Hermon Lodge, of Medford; exalted in Mystic Chapter, R. A. M., Medford; and received his cryptic degrees in Medford Council, R. S. M., Medford. He is a member of the Winchester Country Club, Winchester, and of the Exchange Club, Boston; president of the Monomoy Brant Club, a shooting and hunting club with a clubhouse at Chatham, Massachusetts; and belongs to the Neighborhood Club of Medford. He is president of the Medford National Bank. His home is on Wyman street, West Medford. He and his family attend the West Medford Unitarian church. He is a Republican in politics, and has served his party as delegate to various nominating conventions. In municipal affairs he believes in independence, and non-partisanship. He married, July 7, 1887, at Medford, Sarah Lizzie Simms, born at Manchester, July 3, 1863, daughter of Alexander Stowell and Sarah Jane (Livermore) Simms of Winchester. Children: 1. Howard Martin, born March 16, 1890. 2. Winnifred, October 21, 1898. 3. Charles Lawrence, October 7, 1900.

(X) Lawrence Taylor Sawyer, son of Howard Malcolm Sawyer, was born at West Medford, May 8, 1875. He attended the public schools of his native town and took a three-year course in the Medford high school. He then began to learn his father's business. He made himself familiar with every process in the manufacture of oil clothing and all departments of the business of H. M. Sawyer & Son. In 1897 he became interested in the corporation of H. M. Sawyer & Son, and later in the Sawyer Belting Company owned by his father. Soon afterward the two concerns were both incorporated under the laws of Massachusetts, and Lawrence T. Sawyer became vice-president of the H. M. Sawyer & Son company. Afterward he became treasurer and clerk of the corporation. He and his brothers share the management of the corporation. Mr. Sawyer is a resident of West Newton, Massachusetts, 266 Highland avenue. He is a director of the Medford National Bank. In politics he is a Republican, in religion a Unitarian. He is a member of the Exchange Club of Boston and the Braeburn Club of Newton. He married, May 3, 1906, Alice Louise Hurd, born at Dorchester, July 13, 1875, daughter of Edward Payson and Sarah Louise (Pope) Hurd, of Dorchester. Her father is assistant treasurer of the United Shoe Machinery Company, and is a veteran of the civil war. Child: Edward Lawrence, born July 1, 1907.

(X) Ralph Underdown Sawyer, son of Howard Malcolm Sawyer, was born at West Medford, December 8, 1880. He received his education in the Medford public schools and high school, which he left at the end of his third year to learn the business of the Sawyer Belting Company. He had four years of valuable experience in the factory before the business was sold and removed to Cleveland, Ohio. He then became associated with his father and brothers in the H. M. Sawyer & Son oil clothing business at East Cambridge, Massachusetts, and after the death of his father he became one of the owners of the business and associated with his two brothers in the management of the corporation. He is at present assistant superintendent of the plant and director of the company. He resides at 131 Mystic street, West Medford. He served a term of enlistment in the state militia, member of Lawrence Light Guard, Company E, Fifth Regiment Massachusetts Volunteer Militia. He is a Republican in politics and a Unitarian in religion. He belongs to the Neighborhood Club of Medford. He married, December 1, 1906, Marion Coburn, born March 15, 1883, daughter of Frank J. and Hannah Cushing (Haskins) Coburn, of Medford. They have one child, John Coburn, born February 21, 1908.

WELLINGTON The surname Wellington is identical with Willington, the more common spelling in the old country, though both spellings were used interchangeably by many families a few generations ago in both England and America. The history of the family extends back to the Norman conquest of England. The ancient baronial family of Willington was established at the time of William the Conqueror. It is a place-name, like that of many of the more important English surnames. The family of Willington took the name of the town. The Willington family at Umberleigh, Devonshire; at Todenham, county Gloucester; at Barchesterm Brailes and Hurley, county Warwick—all trace their ancestry to Sir Ralph de Willington, who married in the fourteenth century a daughter of Sir William Champerdowne, of Umberleigh, inherited his estates and assumed his coat-of-arms, omitting the billets: Gules a saltire vair. Crest: A mountain pine vert, fructed or. John de Wellington (or Willington) of Derbyshire, lived at or about the time of the conquest, and from him descend the baronial family mentioned above. There are parishes of this name in county Salop, county Somerset, Hereford and Northumberland. The coats-of-arms of the Wellingtons are given by Burke: Ermine a chevron sable; also ermine a chevron sable a crescent or. Crest: A demi-savage wreathed about the head and middle with laurel leaves all proper. Other Willington arms: Sable a bend engrailed cotised argent; also ermine a chevron ermine (another sable); also per pale endented argent and sable a chief or; also ermine three bends azure; also sable a bend engr. argent cotised or; also or a cross vair. The similarity of arms such as may be noted in these cited, is the best proof of relationship in old English families.

(I) Roger Willington, immigrant ancestor, planter, born 1609-10, died March 11, 1697-98, sailed from England, and probably came to Watertown at once on landing. The first record of him is the first entry of town records of Watertown, showing an allotment of land dated July 25, 1636—a grant of the great dividend allotted to the freemen and to all the townsmen then inhabiting, one hundred and twenty in number. Roger Wellington received twenty acres, now a part of Mt. Auburn cemetery, on which he built the first Wellington homestead, where he lived until 1659. Other references in town records are as follows: April 9, 1657, account of men deputed by towne to fee. To keeping of the order of hogs (the 15th) Roger Wellington is the entry 3 shillings. "Town meeting January 10, 1658, chozen to looke after the law and for the regulating of hogs and fences Roger Wellington and Thomas Straite; December 6, 1662, fined 10 shillings for insufficient fence Dated October 29, 1663." "Haveing given in an account of to rates to great diffiaction both to pastor and selectmen We have appointed Leife Burns Willy and Bond to deal with him to bring him to a more tollarable account or else to send him to the grandiary". "Att a meeting of the selectmen 30 8th Month 1662 agreed between the town & Corporall Willington that a straight line from the corner from his present fence att Eaton's house next the highway and so to the line between him and Samuel Hatchers land upon the north side of the Swampe; shall be the dividinge line between him & the Towne consented unto by the Corporall Willington owned before the selectmen by setting to his hand Signed Roger Willington". "A town meeting November 2, 1674 chozen for surveyors Corporall Willington and John Traine Senyear". "The ——— of Eaprill 79. Corporall Willington & Robt Herington with the consent of the selectmen demanded the (Cee) of the schoolhouse of Leftenant Sherman but he refused to deliver it". It is interesting to note that he was usually called Corporal. By deed dated April 4, 1657, Middlesex county registry, he purchased twelve acres of land containing dwelling house and barn which became a part of the family estate in Lexington and the home of all the Wellington ancestors. Lexington was then a part of Watertown and later Cambridge. He was admitted a freeman April 18, 1690. His will is dated December 17, 1697, and was proved April 11, 1698, "feeble by reason of age", bequeathing to sons John, Joseph, Benjamin, Oliver and Palgrave; grandchild, John Maddocks, Roger Wellington and Mary Livermore. He was selectman in 1678-79-81-82-83-84-91. He married Mary, eldest daughter of Dr. Richard Palgrave, of Charlestown, date of marriage not known. Children: 1. John, born July 25, 1638, admitted freeman 1677, farmer of Cambridge. 2. Mary, born February 10, 1641, married, May 21, 1662, Henry Maddocks; second, John Coolidge. 3. Joseph, born October 9, 1643, married first, Sarah ———; second, Elizabeth Straight. 4. Benjamin, born about 1645, mentioned below. 5. Oliver, born November 23, 1648. 6. Palgrave, admitted freeman April 18, 1690; followed the profession of his grandfather for whom he was named; married Sarah Bond.

(II) Benjamin Willington, fourth child of Roger Willington, probably born 1645, died January 8, 1710. He lived on the family estate in Lexington, and was called yeoman. December 7, 1671, he married Elizabeth Sweetman, of Cambridge. Children: 1. Elizabeth, born December 29, 1673, married John Fay, of Marlborough. 2. Benjamin, born June 21, 1676, mentioned below. 3. John, born July 26, 1678, died November 30, 1717. 4. Ebenezer, married, January 28, 1704, Deliverance Bond; settled in Lexington. 5. Ruhamah, married November 15, 1699, Deacon Joseph Brown. 6. Mehitable, baptized March 4, 1688; married, September 13, 1715, William Sherman, of Newtown, and was mother of Roger Sherman, who was named after his great-grandfather, Roger Willington. 7. Joseph, baptized January 4, 1691. 8. Roger.

(III) Benjamin Wellington, son of Benjamin Willington, born June 21, 1676, died November 15, 1738. "At towne meeting were chozen survayurs swine cattle & fences Richard Child & Benjamin Wellington". He was admitted a freeman in December, 1667. The "History of Lexington" says of him: "He was for many years one of the most popular men of the town; was assessor sixteen years, town clerk fifteen years, treasurer three years, representative three years. He was admitted to the church at Lexington, June 10, 1705. His will, dated July 13, 1708, proved January 30 following, described him as "housewright and carpenter". He married first, January 16, 1698-99, Lydia Brown, and the same year built himself a house on the family estate at Lexington; his wife died May 13, 1711. He married second, December 25, 1712, Elizabeth, widow of Samuel Phipps, and daughter of ——— Stevens, of Charlestown; she died January 17, 1729-30, aged fifty-four. He married third, Mary Whitney. Children of first wife: 1. Benjamin, born May 21, 1702, died November 15, 1738. 2. Lydia, born August 24, 1704, died August 10, 1718. 3. Kezia, born March 28, 1707. 4. John, born November 12, 1709, died September 22, 1728. Children of second wife: 5. Abigail, born July 14, 1715, married, February 19, 1734, David Munroe. 6. Timothy, born July 27, 1719, mentioned below. Children of third wife: 7. Mary, born October 20, 1732. 8. Oliver, born April 14, 1735.

(IV) Timothy Wellington, son of Benjamin Wellington, was born in Lexington, July 27, 1719, date of death unknown; his will was probated December 23, 1750. He was by trade a wheelwright and made (family tradition says) the wheels to the gun carriages of the Cambridge cannon used in the revolution. He was also a farmer, and resided on the homestead in Lexington, which remained in the family until 1895, when it was sold. He married, September 23, 1742, Rebecca Stone, born January 22, 1721, daughter of Jonathan and Chary (Adams) Stone, of Lexington, a descendant of Deacon Gregory Stone, of

Watertown. His wife survived him, and February 14, 1754, married John Dix, of Waltham. Children: 1. Benjamin, born August 7, 1743, mentioned below. 2. Chary, born July 12, 1745. 3. Timothy, born April 15, 1747, died April 18, 1809; was father of Dr. Timothy Wellington. 4. Abigail, born March 14, 1750, married, December 29, 1768, Daniel Colling, of Waltham. 5. Ruhamon, born September 4, 1751.

(V) Benjamin Wellington, son of Timothy Wellington, born at Lexington, August 7, 1743, died there September 14, 1812. He attended the district school, and early learned the trade of wheelwright, which he followed many years. His shop was across the road, just north of the house. The first house of the Wellingtons was of the old-fashioned type, where the roof slants nearly to the ground in the rear. In 1803 he built a new house. He made many of the gun carriages for the Continental army. His farm was inherited by his two sons, Peter and Benjamin. The milk raised on the farm was marketed in Boston, and it is said that Benjamin Wellington was the first man to carry milk such a distance. Wooden bottles were used, and the Charles river was crossed by a ferry. He was a member of the First Congregational Church, and was beloved for his kindly and charitable nature. In politics he was a Democrat, and served as selectman in 1717-23-25-30-32-33-36-37-85-92. He was one of the gallant company of minute-men who took part in the battle of Lexington, and was the first armed prisoner taken during the war. On this spot where he was captured, has been erected a red granite tablet commemorating the event and his gallantry. Elias Phinney, in his history of the battle, describing the march of the British towards Lexington Common on the memorable morn, says: "In order to secure persons traveling upon the road the British would send two soldiers at a considerable distance in advance of the main body with orders to secrete themselves in each side of the road and when anyone approached they would allow him to pass them so as to get between them and the troops and then rise and close in. As Benjamin Wellington was on his way to Lexington Common that morning, having been warned by the summons of Paul Revere, in climbing over a high stone wall into the highway at East Lexington he found on either side of him a British soldier. He was taken prisoner and disarmed. On being asked where he was going he replied 'Hunting.' He promised to return to his home, and as it was impossible for his captors to manage a prisoner he was allowed to go but his gun was not returned. Instead of returning home he took another way to the common and arrived before the British in time to announce their approach and take part in the fight. Thus he told a lie in order to fight in the cause of freedom." His name is given by Captain Parker in list of his company in 1775, and following in Parker's account refers to him in Twelfth campaign to the taking of Burgoyne, Sergeant Benjamin Wellington, four pounds. He was with Washington's army at Cambridge. The following story used to be told by Hepzibah (Hastings) Wellington: "When Benjamin Wellington was with Washington's army there was a time for several days that the army was practically without food. During that time Benjamin Wellington came home to find his family just ready for their dinner, but the army had to be considered so he took not only the family dinner but every edible thing in the place, and harnessing the horses carried provisions to the troops. For two days the family had only mush and milk, but such sacrifices were willingly made by them." He was in Captain John Bridges' company, Colonel Eleazer Brooks' regiment, on duty at Roxbury. He was also sergeant in Captain Samuel Farrar's company, Colonel Reed's regiment, in 1777, to reinforce the army under General Gates, and was present at the surrender of Burgoyne.

He married, December 4, 1766, Martha Ball, of Waltham (Southborough?). Children: 1. Mary, born September 22, 1767; married first, December 31, 1789, Asa Baldwin Locke; second, Abijah Harrington; children: Oliver Locke, Baldwin Locke, Abigail Locke, Mary Locke. 2. Abigail, baptized in Waltham, October 1, 1769. 3. Benjamin, baptized July 13, 1772. 4. Oliver, baptized November 13, 1774. 5. Benjamin Oliver, born August 23, 1778; died November 10, 1853; married May 20, 1811, Polly Hastings; children: i. Oliver Hastings, born February 23, 1812, died March 1, 1813; ii. Oliver Hastings, born August 19, 1813, married August 29, 1838, Charlotte Augusta Kent, of Concord, New Hampshire, and had Mary C., William A., Arthur M., and Lucy M. D.; iii. Mary Jane, born July 15, 1815, married April 17, 1845, James H. Danforth, of Boston; iv. Albert, born June 1, 1817; v. Ambrose, born April 11, 1819, married May, 1845, Lucy J. Kent; vi. Martha, born April 11, 1821, died

January, 1863; vii. Benjamin, born March 21, 1823; viii. Dorcas Ann, born April 20, 1825, married Dr. George H. Taylor; ix. Laura, born December 26, 1826, died December 30, 1843; x. Winslow, born May 16, 1829; xi. Edward, born March 3, 1831, drowned in Fresh Pond, July 6, 1852, while a member of the Lawrence Scientific School. 6. Peter, born May 31, 1781; mentioned below. 7. Richard, born July 14, 1783; died December 11, 1836. 8. James, twin with Patty, born December 12, 1785; married November 18, 1821, Susannah Jacobs, of Littleton, Massachusetts, born August 7, 1801; children: i. Edwin, born 1823; ii. Angelina, born May 20, 1824, married Darius Crosby, and had Linda, Carrie May, James Wellington and Isaac Wellington Crosby; iii. James Everett, born April 27, 1827, married October 24, 1854, Frances Jane Kilbourne, born June 21, 1829, and had Emma Kilbourne, born August 7, 1856, died March 17, 1865, Maud Kilbourne, born November 29, 1858, and Everetta Kilbourne, born September 22, 1872; iv. Adrianna, born May 27, 1829, married James H. Kidder, of Watertown, and had Osmer Wellington Kidder, Mary Wellington Kidder (married Edwin H. Baker, and had Madeline and Adrianna Baker). 9. Patty, twin with James, born December 12, 1785; married, June 28, 1821, Charles Reed, of Lexington; had Henry, not now living; she was drowned, date unknown. 10. Isaac, born December 5, 1787; married November 18, 1824, Mary Wilder Jacobs, and had Oliver, Francena, Mary Ann, Isaac Baldwin and Luther.

(VI) Peter Wellington, son of Benjamin Wellington, was born at Lexington, May 31, 1781, and died there December 5, 1869. He was brought up on his father's farm, and when his father died he and his brother Benjamin had the farm divided, each acquiring one half in separate ownership. They were progressive farmers in every sense of the word, and developed it into handsome paying properties. The raising of fruit and milk was the chief business, and the orchard was considered the finest in New England, producing about twenty-two hundred barrels of apples yearly. Benjamin owned the milk route, and numbered among his customers many of the best families of Boston. Benjamin died in 1853, and his son Winslow took his father's place, living in his part of the same double house built in 1802, Parson Clarke being present at the raising of the house, adding dignity to the occasion. At the death of Peter, in 1869, his son Cornelius succeeded to and carried on the farm until 1895, when he sold it. Benjamin and Peter Wellington married two sisters, Mary and Hepzibah Hastings. They lived together in the house now standing on their estate which they built. Henry Sandham, in his picture of the battle of Lexington called "Dawn of Liberty," has used Peter Wellington as a representative of "the embattled farmers."

Peter Wellington was a selfmade man of the highest type, working early and late, and applying every means to round out a successful life. He was strictly honest, and the closest scrutiny of both public and private life failed to reveal any dishonorable act. He was generous to a fault, and had the respect of all who knew him. Keeping himself well informed on the topics of the day, he took a lively interest in the politics of his town and country. He was a strong temperance advocate and in politics a Jacksonian Democrat, later a Free Soiler and a great admirer of Abraham Lincoln. His home was the headquarters for anti-slavery leaders, and he was a close friend of Theodore Parker, William Lloyd Garrison, Wendell Phillips, Parker Pillsbury, and other anti-slavery advocates. His house became what was known as an "underground railway" station for escaping slaves, two having been helped across the line by his son. At one time he held the office of overseer of the poor, and during his administration the rule requiring occupants of the poor farm to dress in uniform was annulled. In all his affairs of life he was strictly sincere and just, and direct in his statements. He was a member of the school committee and was road surveyor. He was a strong Unitarian, and deeply interested in the Follen church at East Lexington, owning two pews there, and serving on the building committee, but was never a regular member of any church. He was in the war of 1812, and served in a company of cavalry ordered to the northern frontier. He married, May 24, 1813, at Lincoln, Hepzibah Hastings, born May 24, 1793, died May 31, 1879, daughter of Major Samuel and Lydia (Nelson) Hastings, of Lincoln. Her father was a major of militia, selectman, and farmer. Children: 1. Henry Wakefield, born February 25, 1814; mentioned below. 2. Darius, born October 9, 1815; died February 13, 1893; married first, December 28, 1844, Hannah Duville, died July 18, 1846; second, May 1, 1853, Charlotte Chism of Boston; one child, Herbert Duville, born November 17,

1845, married June 2, 1868, Josephine Borrowscale, and had Florence D. and Herbert D. 3. Isabella, born May 23, 1817; died August 3, 1848; married April 23, 1845, Rev. Herman Snow, of Pomfret, Vermont; children: George Henry Snow, William Gray Snow. 4. Abigail, born March 29, 1819; died October 12, 1845; married January 4, 1844, James Blodgett, of Westford. 5. Caroline, born December 3, 1820. 6. Andrew, born December 23, 1822; died September 17, 1901; married January 21, 1858, Leah L. Nichols, of Hingham; children: i. Frank Goddard, born November 9, 1859, died September 4, 1860; ii. Mary Jane, born November 6, 1865. 7. Eliza, born December 6, 1824. 8. Elbridge Gerry, born July 29, 1826; died in California, October 23, 1849. 9. Cornelius, born May 23, 1828. 10. Emily, born February 24, 1830; died April 13, 1850. 11. Samuel Hastings, born August 6, 1832; died April 7, 1833. 12. Louisa Maria, born April 20, 1834; married May 24, 1863, Lucius H. Peaslee, of Boston, who died November 7, 1867. 13. Charles Austin, mentioned below.

(VII) Henry Wakefield Wellington, son of Peter Wellington, born at Lexington, February 25, 1814, died at Newton, January 21, 1899. He was brought up on his father's farm and attended the district school. At the age of fourteen, with the intention of learning the dry goods business, he entered the employ of Charles Merriam in his general store at Weston. He remained here several years, and finally bought out his employer. Later he spent one or two winters in Calais, Maine, in the interest of his business, but finally went to Boston, and was salesman for a dry goods firm there, until he started in business in the firm of Wellington, Winter & Gross, which later became Wellington Brothers & Co., his brother Cornelius having been admitted into the firm. During the time the firm was on Arch street, Mr. Wellington became the owner of a quarry of red granite at Jonesborough, Maine. The red granite from this quarry was later used in the construction of some large commercial buildings in Boston. He later sold the quarry to Governor Bodwell of Maine, a personal friend. About this time it became necessary for the dry goods firm to seek new and larger quarters, on account of increased business, and the result was the erection of the Wellington Building, at the corner of Bedford and Chauncey streets. Mr. Wellington was especially interested in having it built of the red granite quarried at Jonesborough, Maine, which was furnished by Governor Bodwell. The firm occupied their new quarters, and were one of the leading dry goods firms in the city and in New England. In 1869 Mr. Wellington became a stockholder in the Silver Lake Manufacturing Company at Newtonville, a concern making cordage of high quality, was a director of the company and later became treasurer. In 1882 the dry goods business was discontinued. While connected with this company, he was instrumental in improving the service of the life saving stations along the coast, and supplied the finest life-saving lines for their use. The great difficulty with life lines, when shot from a gun, was "kinking," and through Mr. Wellington's efforts a line was produced from his plant that met every requirement and proved to be the best ever made for the purpose.

Mr. Wellington remained in active business until his death, in 1899. On May 1, 1863, he removed to Jamaica Plain, and bought the Stephen M. Allen property, known as Allendale, and resided here until September, 1882, when he built his residence on Fairmont avenue, Newton, near the Silver Lake mill, where he died. No finer tribute could be paid to a friend than that of the address of his friend, William Lloyd Garrison, at the funeral. It sums up his character in a few words, full of feeling. He says in part: "I come to pay a brief tribute to a dear friend whose deliverance was merciful and whose memory will be cherished. His was a long life, useful and valued. * * * Mr. Wellington illustrated the virtues of self-denial, unremitting industry and excellent judgment. More than that, he was born into an anti-slavery family, hospitable to reformatory ideas, and, in the days of the great adversity, he took a manly and courageous part. He was with the abolitionists, sustaining them by word and deed, when to take such a stand implied popular reproach and mercantile disapproval. He was the valued friend and coadjutor of Garrison and Phillips. The anti-slavery lecturers found welcome in his home, and Parker Pillsbury, often his guest, held him in brotherly regard. When Boston was in subjection to the South, and fugitive slaves sought shelter among her people, his hand was extended to help them, and he shared in the counsels of the famous vigilance committee. * * * Theodore Parker, his fellow townsman, had no more devoted friend and supporter in the unpopular days than Mr. Wellington, whose theological independence was as marked as his outspoken love of freedom. He was a straightforward man, of saving common sense, with a clear head, a keen business perception, and of decisive speech. It was impossible for him to conceal opinions, or utter half-truths, because nature made him a fearless as well as an honest man. Although inheriting longevity, our friend was rarely without physical discomfort, against which he battled with courage and philosophic patience. * * * Under his habitual gravity, which a stranger might mistake for austerity, his near and dear ones found only sweetness and affection. * * * He was the founder and patriarch of the small colony on the lovely shore of the Cape, (Wiamo, Massachusetts) bound together by a common sympathy and aim. His counsel and advice were invaluable. He loved trees and flowers, his grounds and garden furnishing a perennial resource and happiness. He was tenacious of his friends, who, once approved, he grappled to his soul with hooks of steel. At an age when most men consider the time of active service ended, there came to him a business embarrassment, which he met and surmounted in a way to increase respect for his sterling character. It was an episode illustrating courage, promptness and consideration for others, that his children may well be proud to recall. Mr. Wellington was a figure to be remembered, handsome, dignified and picturesque. His individuality commanded attention, and the passer-by distinguished him from the crowd. * * * He did his own thinking, never submitting his convictions to church or party, but gravitating to fundamental principles by a law of being."

Mr. Wellington was a member of the standing committee of the 28th Congregational Society of Boston, (Unitarian) over which Theodore Parker presided. He was one of the stockholders that purchased Music Hall in order that Theodore Parker might be heard. His independence was shown in his political affiliations. He was first a Whig, later a Free Soiler, and was one of the early Republicans. Later he voted for Cleveland, and from that time remained an independent voter. He was a member of the Free Religious Society of America, of which Ralph Waldo Emerson was a member, and was a personal friend of Mr. Emerson's. He was a member of the Freedmen's Commission, and contributions in its behalf were received at his store. He belonged to the Merchants' Exchange.

He married first, at St. Mary's Church, Newton Lower Falls, June 1, 1836, Martha Small, born at Needham, November 14, 1813, died at West Roxbury, July 20, 1871, daughter of Robert and Eleanor W. Small, of Needham. Martha Small had, after the death of her father, become a member of the family of her uncle, Doctor Starr, and took his name. Mr. Wellington married second, May 16, 1872, Lydia Davenport Colburn, born October 31, 1836, daughter of John Dexter and Clarissa (Crehore) Colburn, of the Crehore family of Milton, and the Colburn family of Dedham, Massachusetts. Her father was a provision dealer at West Roxbury, and captain of militia at Dedham. Children of first wife: 1. John Ware, born November 22, 1837; married first, September 5, 1859, Jennie Howarth; second, 1869, Sarah Hall, of Maine; children: i. Emma, born June 26, 1860; died October 14, 1861; ii. Helen Frances, born March 14, 1862. 2. Henry Myron, born July 9, 1839; died April 1, 1873; lost at sea from steamship "Atlantic", in Halifax harbor. 3. Frederick Wakefield, born September 10, 1841; died November 9, 1845. 4. George Hastings, born October 3, 1844; died October 20, 1845. 5. Curtis Willard, born January 16, 1847; died January 13, 1849. 6. Caro Ware, born February 14, 1849; died August 24, 1853. 7. Louis Howard, born April 1, 1851; resides at Long Branch, New Jersey. 8. William Elbridge, born December 8, 1857; died January 27, 1872. Children of second wife, all born at Allendale, Jamaica Plain: 9. Martha Starr, born May 19, 1873; resides at 903 Beacon street, Boston, with her mother. 10. Henry Wakefield Jr., born November 11, 1875; mentioned below. 11. Anna Colburn, born March 8, 1882; resides with her mother in Boston.

(VII) Cornelius Wellington, son of Peter Wellington, was born in Lexington, May 23, 1828. He was educated in the district schools, supplemented by a course in Mt. Caesar Academy, at Swanzey, New Hampshire. After leaving school he entered the employ of George W. Torrey, wholesale grocer, as clerk. The business, which included the selling of rum, was very distasteful to Mr. Wellington, and September 8, 1846, he left his employ. He worked several years as clerk in the dry goods business; then went west, and into the lumber business at Stillwater, Michigan, where he remained a short time. After two years as clerk for Gates, Warner, Chalmers & Company, a mill machinery firm at Chicago, he returned east in 1857 and went into the dry goods business with his brother Henry W.

Wellington, and John A. D. Gross and Nathan Daniels, the firm name being Wellington, Gross & Company. In a few years the firm was dissolved and became Wellington Brothers & Company, which continued about ten years. The business was closed, and he started in with his brother Charles Wellington in the Household Art Company. While in the dry goods business he also carried on the farm at Lexington, and became interested in Jersey cattle. He imported his first herd, and the following year went abroad to the Island of Jersey, returning with a herd of fifty cattle. He made a great success in this line, and his blooded stock brought fancy prices in the markets of Boston, New York and Philadelphia. In 1895 he sold the farm and gave up the business. Later he built a fine residence on Pleasant street, which he afterwards sold. He now resides on Clark street, with his sisters, Caroline, Eliza and Louisa M. Wellington Peaslee. Mr. Wellington is a man of firm principle and high standards of living. He enjoys the esteem and confidence of his neighbors. In politics he is a Democrat in principle, but independent in action. He has been tree warden for the past seven years, and is local agent for the destruction of the gipsy brown-tail moth. He is a member of the Lexington Historical Society, of the Massachusetts Reform Club, and the Field and Garden Club, and a former member of the Liberal Union Club and the Appalachian Mountain Club. Mr. Wellington is unmarried.

(VII) Charles Austin Wellington, son of Peter Wellington, was born December 2, 1837, died unmarried February 2, 1901. He received a district school education, supplemented by a course of instruction in a private school at Cambridge. At the age of sixteen he made an engagement with a manufacturing jeweler to learn that trade. After an apprenticeship of a few years he took up and carried on the business, designing and producing only the finest goods for the then leading jewelry establishment of Boston. Because of feeble health and necessary confinement and to assist an invalid relative, he entered the crockery ware business and a short time afterward became connected with an establishment under the name of "The Household Art Company", which business was the manufacture and sale of works of art, furniture, etc., connected with which was the introduction of tiles for floors, fire places and interior and exterior decoration, at that time a new departure in decorative work and involving frequent trips to Europe, after having bought out the business from his former employer. Shortly after this, in consequence of partial failure of his eyesight, he was compelled to abandon mercantile life. He was an active member of the Lexington Historical Society, also of the Field and Garden Club. At the time of the centennial celebration in 1875 he published an edition of Phinney's history of the battle of Lexington, prefacing it by a short preface by himself. As a citizen the town was indebted to him for valuable service in various ways. Always interested in the public schools, he was at one time member of the committee who built the Hancock school house, and with the other members of that committee was instrumental in abandoning the district school buildings and transporting the children to the village centres. It was through his efforts that the statues of Hancock and Adams, ornamenting the public library, were designed and modeled by an artist instead of being cut out of granite by a quarryman. It was at his suggestion that the historical painting by Henry Sandam, now adorning the town hall, was created and there placed. Under his supervision the Hancock-Clark house was re-located, repaired and as far as possible its former appearance restored, including a reproduction of the paper originally covering the walls of its most important room. Many articles of interest now to be seen there were contributed by him, many of them his own creations. Perhaps the most important of his work was in connection with the design and erection of the Hayes fountain. That it took the form of a drinking place for man and beast was largely, if not entirely, due to him. The design of the fountain in its general outline was his also, as was the selecting and collecting of the stones necessary for the foundation, with the exception of the one stone forming the water basin for horses, that being furnished by the stone mason. He took an important part in placing memorial monuments and tablets at various points of interest about the town.

(VIII) Henry Wakefield Wellington Jr., son of Henry W. Wellington, was born at Jamaica Plain, Massachusetts, November 11, 1875. He attended a private school until eight years old, when he removed from Jamaica Plain to Newton with his parents, entered the public school and later continued his studies at Chauncey Hall School, Boston. He was prepared for college at Cutler's private school at Newton, and attended Harvard College two years, leaving to enter business with his father. He remained with the Silver Lake Company from 1895 to 1901, when he became interested with D. C. Pierce in the manufacture of lace curtains, the firm being Wellington & Pierce, a corporation under Massachusetts laws. Mr. Wellington is treasurer and director of the corporation, and is also a director of the Silver Lake Company. The firm of Wellington & Pierce is known to the dry goods business throughout the country, and has an extensive trade. Mr. Wellington resides at 65 Mt. Vernon street, Boston. In politics he is a Democrat, but has never held office. He is a member of the Harvard Club of New York city. He married June 2; 1902, May Ethel Hamblen.

TOWER

(I) Robert Tower, first ancestor to whom is traced the American family, lived in the parish of Hingham, county Norfolk, England. While the name is found in various parts of the United Kingdom at an early date, the ancestry has not been traced further. He married August 31, 1607, at Hingham, Dorothy Damon, who was buried November 10, 1629. He was buried May 1, 1634.

(II) John Tower, son of Robert Tower, was the immigrant ancestor. He was baptized at Hingham, England, May 17, 1609. He came with many others of that town to Hingham, Massachusetts, where he settled in 1637. Samuel Lincoln came with him. He became a proprietor of Hingham, and from time to time drew land with the other commoners; bought various parcels, sold a few lots. He was admitted a freeman March 13, 1638-9, and was then a member of the church. During the controversies in Hingham he took an active part, and his name figures in the proceedings before the general court in 1640-45. He deposed January 9, 1676, that he was about sixty-nine years old. He was one of the incorporators of Lancaster, but never settled there. He had an Indian deed to land in Rhode Island dated June 17, 1661, but failed after some litigation to establish his title. He bought land of Edward Wilder in Hingham by deed dated May 16, 1664, extending from what is now Main street at Cole's corner to the brook at Tower's bridge, and soon afterwards built a house thereon. Three of his sons built houses on this lot also, and some of the land has remained in the possession of descendants to the present time. The old house was torn down soon after 1800. In 1657 he was a way-warden; in 1659 constable; in 1665 he was on an important committee to lay out highways, with very full powers. He fortified his house during King Philip's war, and his sons and others formed the garrison. He was an active and enterprising man, rather illiterate perhaps, as he signed his name with a mark like a capital "T". He was frequently in court both as plaintiff and defendant. His wife signed her own name. He died intestate February 13, 1701-2, having deeded land to his children, and thus in part settled his own estate. He married, February 13, 1638-9, Margaret Ibrook, daughter of Richard Ibrook, an early settler of Hingham. She died May 16, 1700. Children: 1. John, baptized December 13, 1639; married May 14, 1669, Sarah Hardin. 2. Ibrook, baptized February 7, 1643-4; married April 24, 1668, Margaret Harden. 3. Jeremiah, baptized March 9, 1645-6; married Elizabeth Rowlands, widow, November, 1670. 4. Elizabeth, baptized October 9, 1648; married at Boston, October 9, 1667, William Roberts. 5. Sarah, baptized July 16, 1650; married ——— Curtiss. 6. Hannah, born July 17, 1652; married first, ——— Cowell; second, David Whipple. 7. Benjamin, born November 5, 1654; mentioned below. 8. Jemima, born April 25, 1660; married Thomas Gardner. 9. Samuel, born January 26, 1661-2; married December 14, 1683, Silence Damon, of Scituate.

(III) Benjamin Tower, son of John Tower, was baptized November 5, 1654, and died March 24, 1721-2. He resided in Hingham and married there, September, 1680, Deborah Garnet (Gardner), born July 5, 1657, died 1728-9, daughter of John and Mary Garnet. He inherited his father's homestead, the garrison house which he built, and which has been succeeded by one or more dwelling houses. The one now standing is or was lately occupied by the widow of William Tower, who inherited it. It was built soon after 1800. Benjamin Tower's will was dated July 2, 1717, and proved April 28, 1722. Children, born in Hingham: 1. Abigail, baptized May 22, 1681. 2. Ruth, baptized September 2, 1682; died November 2, 1682. 3. Nathaniel, born September 12, 1683; died November 24, 1700. 4. Deborah, born February 4, 1684-5. 5. Benjamin, September 2, 1686. 6. Christian, March 16, 1687-8. 7. Sarah, December 18, 1689. 8. Jael, October 26, 1691. 9. Thomas, June 27, 1693. 10. Hannah, March 14, 1694-5. 11. Peter, July 17, 1697. 12. Ambrose, mentioned below.

(IV) Ambrose Tower, son of Benjamin

Tower, was born in Hingham, in January, 1699-1700. He removed to Hull, where his eldest son was born, and later to Concord, residing in that part of the town which became the town of Lincoln. In 1733 he was before the court on account of a debt to Peter Tower, of Hingham, of fifty-eight pounds; and other records show that he was in financial difficulties. He married first, Mary ———, and second, Elizabeth ———. Children: 1. Joseph, mentioned below. 2. Ambrose, born 1727. 3. Jonathan, 1729. 4. Mary, 1731. 5. Elizabeth, 1734; died unmarried, in Concord, February 19, 1814, aged eighty. 6. Benjamin, baptized March 18, 1738-9. 7. Lydia, born November 12, 1742. 8. Sarah, born 1744; died unmarried, in Concord, May 14, 1807.

(V) Joseph Tower, son of Ambrose Tower, was born September 5, 1723, and died in Rutland in 1779. We find that one hundred and forty-one bearing the name of Tower, and whose names appear on the rosters and rolls of sailors and soldiers in the revolution, took part in the struggle for liberty, some of them responding to the alarm of April 19, 1775, at Lexington, and several bearing the name of Tower were present at the surrender of Cornwallis, at Yorktown. Joseph Tower may have been beyond the age limit, but his son Joseph was active in the struggle and died at the siege of Boston. In the early part of his life he resided in Weston and was a member of the church there. He removed to Sudbury in 1748, and resided there nearly twenty years. He afterwards resided in Princeton, Lancaster, Shrewsbury and Rutland. He was a millwright by trade, and at the time of his death owned a mill in Rutland. He married July 21, 1748, in Sudbury, Hepzibah Gibbs, born there February 25, 1730, daughter of Isaac and Thankful (Wheeler) Gibbs. She died in Waterville, New York, January 16, 1816, aged nearly eighty-six years. Children: 1. Joseph, born April 11, 1750; died 1776, in the siege of Boston. 2. Isaac, born February 2, 1752. 3. Thankful, born February 9, 1754. 4. Jeduthan, born August 7, 1758. 5. Polly, born December 17, 1760; married May 4, 1784, Abijah Potter of Brookfield. 6. Lurany, born January 4, 1763. 7. Justus, born October 16, 1765. 8. Jonas, born March 8, 1768; mentioned below. 9. John, born May 13, 1770. 10. Jotham, born January 28, 1774. 11. Joseph, born April 12, 1776; died 1780 in Rutland.

(VI) Jonas Tower, son of Joseph Tower, was born March 8, 1768, died in Petersham, Massachusetts, April 12, 1827, and is buried in the church yard there. He early learned the trade of shoemaker, and also owned a farm known as the Parmenter place, a mile south of the centre of the town. He was for many years a mail carrier, his route extending from Providence, Rhode Island, to Brattleborough, Vermont. He conveyed the mail on horseback, his residence being conveniently central between the two points. He was in Shay's rebellion. He married, February 16, 1792, Fanny Parmenter, born 1772, died October 25, 1815, daughter of John Parmenter; second, November 24, 1816, Nancy Stone, who died 1822. Children of first wife: 1. Charles, born July 2, 1793. 2. Oren, mentioned below. 3. Louisa, born January 2, 1797. 4. Fanny, born November 5, 1800. 5. Horatio, born 1803; died young. 6. Horatio N., born 1806. 7. Harriet, baptized November 9, 1817; died unmarried March 11, 1827, aged nineteen. 8. John Parmenter, baptized November 9, 1817; died in Wisconsin, 1843, unmarried, aged thirty-three. 9. Mary Ann, born August 11, 1812. Children of second wife: 10. Samuel S., born July 17, 1817. 11. Nancy, born December 23, 1818. 12. Maria, born 1821; died 1828.

(VII) Oren Tower, son of Jonas Tower, was born at Petersham, September 25, 1794, and died there December 3, 1878. He was brought up on his father's farm, acquiring the usual common school education of a farmer's son at that period, which was mostly during the winter months. He early learned the trade of house painter, which he followed more or less during his active life. He bought of his father's heirs their shares of the homestead, and settled there. He was a progressive and successful farmer, and advanced the improved methods of agriculture. His farm consisted of one hundred acres of land one mile to the westward of Petersham Common, which netted him a handsome yearly income, depending on the raising of milk and general products. He was successful as a cattle raiser. He was active in public affairs, and identified with the temperance movement in its various phases for many years, and also with other and kindred reforms. In his earlier days he was a firm and faithful Whig, but when that party went to pieces he became a Republican, and gave his earnest support to the administration of Lincoln in the trying times of the civil war. He was chairman of the board of selectmen in Petersham many years, and demonstrated special fitness for the duties of this office.

He also served the town as highway surveyor and member of the cemetery committee. He was a member of the Petersham company in the state militia when a young man. In personal character Mr. Tower had many fine and attractive qualities, making many friends, and commanding the respect of all his townsmen. A useful citizen, upright, conscientious and capable, his life was altogether exemplary and blameless. He married first, June 1, 1823, Harriet Gleason, born June 16, 1803, baptized May 3, 1808, died April 13, 1832, daughter of Joseph and Sukey (Whitney) Gleason; second, January 5, 1836, Lucy Lincoln Foster, born at Petersham, March 4, 1814, died at Pasadena, California, September 3, 1907, daughter of John and Hannah (Lincoln) Foster, of Petersham. Her father owned a sawmill and made lumber, etc. Children of first wife: 1. William Augustus, born February 26, 1824; mentioned below. 2. Harriet Ellen, born August 29, 1826; died unmarried May 28, 1855. 3. Susan Whitney, born July 22, 1828; died May 9, 1867; married January 9, 1865, Abraham G. R. Hale, of Boston; children: i. Willie Augustus Hale, born February 28, 1866, died April 4, 1866; ii. Willie Abraham Hale, born March 8, 1867, died October 11, 1867. 4. Louisa Gleason, born January 3, 1831; died unmarried July 3, 1854. Children of second wife: 5. Francis Emery, born November 30, 1836; married November 30, 1868, Ella S. Shepardson, of Petersham; children: i. Dr. Ralph Winfred, born May 24, 1870, physician, practicing at New Rochelle, New York; married, August 31, 1893, Bessie Belle West, of Bristol, Connecticut, and had Lawrence West, born July 6, 1896; ii. Maud Helen, born September 13, 1873, married, November 12, 1902, Josiah Henry Peck, of Bristol; iii. Ethel Ella, born July 25, 1876. 6. George Hammond, born September 1, 1839; died May 4, 1885; married January 22, 1873, Frances E. Farrar, of Montague, Massachusetts: child, Grace Hortense, born May 1, 1878. 7. Harriet Augusta, born April 11, 1843. 8. John Foster, born August 1, 1845; died November 18, 1849. 9. Katharine Lucy, born September 29, 1847; married April 30, 1888, Roy H. Penney, of Pasadena, California. 10. Horatio Nelson, born November 7, 1850; married December 25, 1886, Fannie Gertrude Spooner, born at Petersham, May 15, 1868, daughter of Benjamin and Fanny (Grout) Spooner; children: i. Fanny Foster, born May 24, 1889; ii. Arthur Augustus, April 17, 1892; iii. Sidney Spooner, October 30, 1895; iv. Lloyd Lysle, July 18, 1898. 11. Alfred Oren, born February 25, 1855, married, November 16, 1887, Clara Alice Shepardson, born December 28, 1870, daughter of Frank F. and Betsey Ann Lovell Shepardson; children: i. George Harold, born September 25, 1888; ii. Frank Stanley, June 2, 1890; iii. Alfred Leigh, September 12, 1892; iv. William Reginald, December 27, 1893; v. Alice Margarita, June 25, 1896; vi. Nelson Lysle, March 11, 1898.

(VIII) William Augustus Tower, son of Oren Tower, was born in Petersham, Worcester county, Massachusetts, February 26, 1824. He received his education in the common schools of his native town. Being the eldest of eleven children, he was thrown early upon his own resources, and at the age of fifteen years found employment in a country store in the adjoining town of Lancaster where, in 1845, when twenty years of age, he was admitted to partnership, this connection continuing until 1848, when he sold out to his partner and removed to Sterling, Massachusetts. In 1850 he came to Boston and entered the flour and grain business in Haymarket square, as member of the firm of Rice, Tower & Company, the first house in Boston market to establish direct communication with the west in the sale of cereal products. In 1852 the firm of Tower, Davis & Company succeeded the parent house. Unremitting attention to business impaired the health of Mr. Tower, so that in 1855, the same year in which he changed his residence to Lexington, he found it necessary to retire from active business for a time and seek a recuperation in rest and travel. During a trip south and west, while stopping in Chicago, he formed the acquaintance of George Watson, a native of Scotland, with whom he organized in Chicago the banking house of Watson, Tower & Company, which carried on an active and prosperous business until 1860. During this time Mr. Tower still held his position as head of the firm of Tower, Davis & Company in Boston, and also retained his interest as a silent partner in the firm of Davis, Whitcher & Company, which succeeded Tower, Davis & Company, until 1865. In 1860 he opened a private banking house on State street, Boston, in partnership with George E. Wilder, of Lancaster. Two years later Edward L. Giddings and Mr. Torrey were added to the firm and Mr. Wilder retired, the firm name becoming Tower, Giddings & Torrey. After a short time Mr. Torrey withdrew, and in 1867 the firm name became Tower, Giddings & Company, which still exists as a leading representative house. Subsequently his son, Augustus Clifford, who had started in business with Edward Sweet & Company of New York City, was a partner for a few years, also another son, Richard Gleason, and William Lawrence Underwood was also a member of the firm. Colonel Tower remained at the head of the firm to the time of his death. The present house of Tower & Underwood consists of Richard G. Tower, William Lawrence Underwood, Frank S. Palfrey and Charles B. Butterfield.

Railroad and banking affairs being so closely connected, naturally attracted Mr. Tower and in many of them he was prominent. From 1870 to 1873 inclusive he was president of the Concord Railroad, in New Hampshire; he was one of the founders and was a director of the National Bank of the Commonwealth since its establishment in 1871 until his death, serving as president from February, 1881, to April 4, 1882, succeeding E. C. Sherman and being succeeded by A. L. Newman; he again became president May 13, 1892, and held office for several years, and subsequently was again elected to that responsible office; during 1877-78 he was president of the Nashua & Lowell Railroad; was director of the Equitable Life Insurance Company of New York, of the Guaranty Company of North America, of the Shawmut National Bank, and was identified with the Boston Safe Deposit and Trust Company, and of the New England Trust Company; was vice-president of the Security Safe Deposit Company, and a trustee of the Boston Five Cents Savings Bank. He was a large stockholder and active in the management of other railroad properties.

He was originally an old-time Whig, but after the organization of the Republican party identified himself with it, entering with zeal and purpose into all the measures of the National government for the preserving of the Union. In 1863 he was a member of the house of representatives; was aide-de-camp on the staff of Governor Alexander H. Rice from 1876 to 1878 inclusive, with rank of colonel; in 1882 was elected to the governor's council from the third district, and served as a member of Governor Butler's council, although himself a Republican. He was a member and liberal supporter of the Follen Unitarian Church of Lexington. At the centennial celebration of the battle of Lexington, Colonel Tower not only acted as chief marshal of the parade but was also prominent in all pertaining to that well remembered event in Lexington.

From a small and modest beginning in business life Mr. Tower attained to a prominent and foremost position in business and financial circles, and everywhere his name was regarded as a synonym for integrity and honor in all his transactions. His record was as clean as it was successful, his judgment was sound and his ability grew as he faced larger questions. He was strong intellectually and he cultivated his mind constantly, and his advice in finance and business was eagerly sought and respected. Despite the multifarious cares of his busy life, he took much pleasure in his home and spent much time there. He was beloved by his family and neighbors who knew and loved him best. He was generous in giving to those in need, and he took particular interest in young men seeking an education or entering business. Mr. Tower entertained and cherished the traditions and associations of his home and ancestors, which fact is clearly demonstrated by his purchasing the old family homestead at Petersham, Massachusetts, and endowing it upon his nephew, the eldest son of his half-brother, Horatio N. Tower.

Mr. Tower was a man who entered heartily into the interests of any community where he made his home, and at Lexington his abilities as a leader were recognized. He was of genial temperament, though his almost courtly manner might have given another impression to one meeting him for the first time; he was a great admirer of the beauties of nature, and he loved animals. The horse was to him a source of delight, and touring about this section with tally-ho or drag was one of his chief enjoyments, while driving over the road from his home in Lexington to business in Boston was the habit of his life, winter and summer, going this way much oftener than by public conveyance. He never neglected business, but he frequently pushed important affairs aside that he might enjoy his ride and spend a few hours of daylight on the estate he had developed with intelligent foresight.

Mr. Tower married, at the homestead in Lancaster, April 29, 1847, Julia, daughter of Captain Austin and Sally (Wellington) Davis; Captain Davis was captain of a local militia company. Thomas Davis, father of Captain Austin Davis, was of Holden, Massachusetts; he had a long and honorable record in the Continental army during the revolution. Children of Mr. and Mrs. Tower: 1. Ellen May, born in Lancaster, February 28, 1848. 2. Charlotte Gray, born in Cambridge, February 12, 1851, died at Lexington, July 6, 1885. 3. Augustus Clifford, born in Cambridge, July 3, 1853, died at Lawrence, Long Island, December 28, 1903; he engaged in the banking business in New York City, was for a time partner in his father's firm, founded the banking firm of Tower & Sherwood in New York, which was very successful; married, June 7, 1883, Louise Greble Dreer, of Philadelphia, Pennsylvania, born July 29, 1858, daughter of Henry Augustus and Mary (Leavenworth) Dreer, of Philadelphia. 4. Richard Gleason, born in Lexington, October 11, 1857, mentioned below.

Mr. Tower died November 21, 1904, at his home in Lexington. The funeral was largely attended, many Boston friends and business associates being present. The Rev. L. D. Cochrane, of Follen church, conducted the services, which were extremely simple consisting only of appropriate scriptural selections and a prayer. Interment was in the family lot in Lexington cemetery. A forceful, progressive man, stern but kindly withal. A natural leader, although modest, and even shy. A good citizen and neighbor who made the world better for his having lived in it.

(IX) Richard Gleason Tower, son of William A. Tower, was born at Lexington, October 11, 1857. He attended the public schools of his native town and Nichols Academy. When he was twenty years old he went abroad and spent a year in study and travel. Upon his return he began to work for his father's firm, and in 1885 became a partner, and also a member of the Boston Stock Exchange. In 1893, on account of ill health, he withdrew from the firm, but two years later again became a partner. In 1905 the firm name was changed to the present name of Tower & Underwood. Mr. Tower's residence on the state road, Lexington, is one of the most imposing and beautiful in the state. Like his father he is an admirer of fine horses.

He is an Unitarian in religion, a Republican in politics. He is a member of the Middlesex Hunt Club, the Somerset Club, and the Country Club. He married September 30, 1905, Henrietta Niles Lockwood, born at Charlestown, Massachusetts, January 29, 1873, daughter of Rhodes and Henrietta (Niles) Lockwood, of Charlestown. Her father was at the head of the Davidson Rubber Company, of East Somerville. Child: 1. William Augustus, born March 6, 1907, at Thomasville, Georgia, on the old McIntyre plantation, one of the finest old places in Georgia, and now owned by Mrs. William A. Tower, and called "Boxhall."

WETHERBEE The surname Wetherbee or Wetherby is of ancient English origin, being derived from the name of a locality. The name is spelled in a great variety of ways in the early records. There is a town of Wetherby in Yorkshire. The seat of the principal family of this name in England has been for some centuries in Norfolk and its coat-of-arms: Vert a chevron ermine between three rams passant argent attired or. This is the only armorial of the Wetherby family of ancient date.

(I) John Wetherbee, immigrant ancestor, was born in the north of England about 1650. He settled first in Marlborough, Massachusetts, in the south part of the town, now the town of Southborough, and later removed to Stow, where he died in 1711. On June 7, 1684, he sold land in Stow to Thomas Ward, and August 22, 1701, he sold to Joseph Doby thirty acres with town rights. On September 20, 1706, he bought of Ruth Wheeler fifty acres of upland and eleven of meadow, and March 4, 1706, he sold land to Jacob Brown. He was called yeoman. His will was dated October 13, 1707, with codicil April 11, 1709. It was proved April 2, 1711. He married first, at Marlborough, September 18, 1672, Mary Howe, born November 18, 1653, died at Stow, June 5, 1684, daughter of John and Mary Howe, of Marlborough. He married second, Lydia Moore. Children: 1. Joseph, born at Marlborough, October 5, 1672-73, married, February 9, 1699, Elizabeth Johnson, born 1677, died September 22, 1726; children: i. Caleb, born January 5, 1700-01, married first, January 12, 1726-27, Joanna Wheeler, second, Huldah ——— and had Thomas, David, Shadrack, Nathaniel, John, Ephraim, Zaccheus, Joseph, Mary and Huldah; (Zaccheus, son of Caleb mentioned above, married Sarah Snow; children—Lucy, married Moses Morse, of Hopkinton; Martha, married Codding Wetherbee; Caleb, born April 3, 1760, died January 3, 1783; married Hepzibah Brigham and had Jabez Snow, born September 12, 1802, married, January 1, 1826, Harriet Brigham; Elijah Brigham, born January 19, 1804, married, April 12, 1829, Louisa Brigham; Nancy Maria, born October 19, 1808, died November 27, 1829; Nahum, born April

12, 1812, married, April 30, 1835, Mary Smith and had Henry Smith, born February 8, 1836; Dennis, born November 25, 1813, married first, Betsey Stowe, second, Abigail Stowe, third, Sophia Rice; John Brooks, born June 10, 1816, married Sarah Goddard; Sarah Breck, born October 26, 1818, died September 22, 1842; William Wallace, born February 21, 1821, married Elizabeth G. Brigham; David, married Ann Tyler. Catherine, married Temple Parker; Sewell, married ——— Jameson; Jabez; Jonas). ii. Thankful, born May 10, 1703, married Isaac Bellows; iii. Joseph, born February 20, 1704, married Unity Adams; iv. Hepsebah, born February 14, 1706, married Robert Sennet; v. Deborah, born December 23, 1709; vi. Elizabeth, born September 16, 1714, married Nathan Rice. 2. John, born March 26, 1675, mentioned below. 3. Thomas, born January 5, 1678, died January 23, 1712-13; married, February 20, 1698-99, Hannah Woods; children: i. Mary, born June 10, 1700; ii. Hannah, born June 3, 1702; iii. Thomas, born March 4, 1705, died June 7, 1714; iv. Silas, born July 20, 1707, died March 10, 1783, married Thankful Keyes, born 1709, died June 17, 1782, and had John Keyes, born February 28, 1743, died February 18, 1811, Lavinia (Levinah), born March 19, 1745 (married, February 1, 1780, Samuel Wilson), Lieutenant Thomas, born January 1, 1747, died May 9, 1827, Mary, born February 6, 1749, married, 1784, Leonard Brigham, Sarah, born June 14, 1753, married, November 7, 1783, Azriah Wilson, of Spencer, Massachusetts; v. Submit, born March 9, 1709-10. (John Keyes Wetherbee, son of Silas mentioned above, married, May 3, 1768, Lavinia Rand, born July 4, 1743, died June 23, 1775; children: 1. Silas, born February 20, 1769, married, June 3, 1793, Sarah Brigham and had—i. Mary, born 1796; ii. Jeremiah, born 1798; iii. Joel, born 1800; iv. Jesse Brigham, born 1807; v. Esther Louise, born 1810. 2. Danforth, born August 28, 1771, died September 18, 1794; married Lucy Stiles.) Lieutenant Thomas Wetherbee, son of Silas mentioned above, married Relief Heuston, of Dunstable, New Hampshire; children: 1. Louis, born December 2, 1770, married Huldah Wesson, daughter of Joel Wesson, of Worcester Cove, and had—i. Oliver, born July 21, 1793, married Mary Harrington; ii. Louis, born August 21, 1795, married Deborah Faye; iii. Hannah, born October 2, 1799, married, January 9, 1819, James Healey Benchley, of Providence, Rhode Island, and was mother of Henry W. Benchley, lieutenant-governor of Massachusetts; iv. Dennis Franklin, born March 14, 1814. 2. Jonathan, born March 3, 1772, married, October 30, 1796, Virtue Hemenway, born January 23, 1775, and had: i. Thomas, born April 2, 1797, married Amelia Adams, of Athol; ii. Seth, married Elizabeth Williams; iii. Levi Jennison, married Mary Hamilton; iv. Relief, married June, 1834, Nathan Craft; v. Mary Hemenway, died January 3, 1843, aged thirty-three, married Charles Stevens, of Templeton; vi. Sarah Merriam, died April 7, 1838, aged twenty-seven; vii. Susan Temple, married Luke B. Wetherbee. 3. Thomas, born February 13, 1774, died October, 1840; married, June 5, 1800, Susannah Knowlton and had—i. Calvin Knowlton, born December 9, 1801, died July 24, 1827; ii. Thomas Heuston, born June 25, 1802, married, February 22, 1824, Lois Muzzy; iii. Elizabeth, born March 3, 1804, married, May 17, 1825, Elijah A. Brigham; iv. Luke Bucklin, born December 17, 1809, married Susan Temple Wetherbee; v. Jonathan Edwin, born November 11, 1815, died December 28, 1836; vi. Susan Relief, born November, 1815. 4. Sarah, born December 10, 1775, married Joseph Merriam, of Grafton. 5. Mary, born November 1, 1777, married, May 1, 1796, Joseph Dispeau, of Grafton. 6. Silas, born January 7, 1784, married Lois D. Wheelock and had—i. Charles Silas; ii. Joseph Vernon; iii. Mary Lois; iv. Jonathan Gardner; v. Charlotte Sophia; vi. Reuben Miner; vii. Luther Brigham; viii. Persis Lucretia; ix. Lucinda Relief; x. David Thomas. 4. Ephraim, died at Boston, November 9, 1745; married first 1721, Elizabeth Hall, died June 12, 1732; second, September 18, 1732, Joanna Bellows; children of first wife: i. Ruth, born February 28, 1722-3, married July 30, 1741, Joseph Wood; ii. Ephraim; iii. Paul, died January 6, 1768; iv. Mary, born January 6, 1729-30, married July 18, 1746, Ephraim Kimball. v. Betsey; children of second wife: vi. Rachel, born April 3, 1733, married Thomas Putnam, of Charlestown; vii. Jonathan, born October 14, 1734; viii. Abigail, February 13, 1735-6; ix. Susannah, March 27, 1738; x. Abijah, April 24, 1740; xi. Joannah, September 23, 1742; xii. Samuel, April 13, 1745. (Paul Wetherbee, son of Ephraim mentioned above, married June 11, 1746, Hannah Pierce; children: 1. Ephraim, born August 24, 1747; married December 3, 1772, Keziah Pierce and had Hannah, born July 28, 1773, Keziah, born September 27,

1774, Anne, born August 24, 1782, Samuel, born November 12, 1784, Thomas, born December 3, 1786, Lucretia, born June 11, 1789. 2. Paul, born August 12, 1749. 3. Hannah, July 19, 1751. 4. Betsey, December 15, 1753. 5. David, born February 16, 1757; died January 21, 1842; married Eunice ———, and had: i. Eunice, born June 16, 1779; ii. Susannah, June 15, 1781; iii. Betsey, April 25, 1783; iv. David, March 31, 1785; v. Mary, December 26, 1787; vi. Sophia; vii. Martha, May 16, 1794; viii. John, born February 20, 1798, married Ann Upton; ix. James, born July, 1802; x. David, October 5, 1805. 6. Joel, born April 26, 1759. 7. Abijah, 1761. 8. Esther, December 3, 1763. 9. Daniel, February 16, 1766.) 5. Jonathan, born August 31, 1686. 6. David, married Mercy Brown; children: i. Edward, married April 30, 1743, Hannah Whitney, and had Mary, born June 30, 1745, Ephraim, June 5, 1747, and Edward, December 20, 1752; ii. Lydia, married August 30, 1751, Timothy Brown; iii. Joseph, married April 16, 1748, Elizabeth Whitney; iv. Silas; v. Elizabeth, born April 21, 1715; vi. Phineas, born October 6, 1716; married first Sarah ———, second, Betsey ———, and had Oliver, born April 4, 1743, Sarah, November 11, 1748, Betsey, February 11, 1753, and Israel, July 18, 1756; vii. Mary, born November 3, 1718, married ——— Stevens; viii. David, born February 28, 1722. (Silas Wetherbee, son of David mentioned above, married May 24, 1749, Betsey Brown; children: 1. Judah, born April 13, 1755; married June 19, 1781, Catherine Whitman, and had—i. Charles, born November 30, 1781; ii. Betsey, born March 8, 1783, Mehitable, December 4, 1784, Catherine, May 26, 1787, Jane, January 28, 1791, Judah, July 19, 1794, Isaac, July 17, 1796, Jacob, August 19, 1798, Anna S., November 17, 1799). 7. Ann, married June 17, 1724-5, Thomas Stow, of Concord; child: Lydia, married October 15, 1754, Samuel Dudley, of Littleton.

(II) John Wetherbee, son of John Wetherbee, was born at Marlborough, March 26, 1675, and died at Stow, where he lived and owned a farm. On June 25, 1697, he bought of Richard and Abigail Cheever twenty-five acres of land situated west of great Rattlesnake Meadow, near the Lancaster line, and nine acres in Great Rattlesnake Meadow, and other lands. John Wilson and wife Sarah, Jonathan Houghton and wife Thankful, Bezaleel Sawyer and wife Judith, and Hezekiah White, heirs of the estate of their father Josiah White, Senior, of Lancaster, conveyed to John Wetherbee, of Stow, land in consummation of a bargain, May 13, 1719. His will was dated June 6, 1720, and proved September 25, 1720, at Worcester. He married Catherine ———. Children: 1. Daniel, married Rachel ———; children: i. Oliver, born January 14, 1724; ii. Rachel, born December 18, 1726; iii. Paul, born January 2, 1729. 2. John, married, 1722, Elizabeth Whitney. 3. Hezekiah, mentioned below. 4. Josiah, married, 1729, Sarah Hall; children: i. Samuel, born August 13, 1730; ii. Samuel, June 20, 1732; iii. Sarah, June 24, 1734; iv. Ruth, died May 10, 1739; v. Hannah, died June 3, 1739; vi. Catherine, died June 3, 1739; vii. Ruth, born August 13, 1744; viii. Ethan, July 31, 1746; ix. Lucy, October 3, 1750; x. Reuben, October 3, 1750 (twin). 5. Catherine, married, 1726, Joseph Osgood. 6. Isaac. 7. Micah, born December 25, 1712. 8. Thomas, born June 10, 1715; married Elizabeth Hale, or Hapgood; children: i. Joseph; ii. Mary, died 1794, married William Whitcomb; iii. Olive, born August 5, 1745, married May 10, 1764, Jacob Whitcomb; iv. Elizabeth, born November 23, 1747, married August 22, 1766, William Wolcott; v. Sarah (twin), born August 1, 1750, married ——— Josselyn; vi. Thomas (twin), born August 1, 1750; vii. Catherine, born March 15, 1753, married February 15, 1777, John Gates; viii. Ephraim, born June 3, 1756, died January 31, 1852. (Joseph Wetherbee, son of Thomas mentioned above, married April 11, 1767, Sarah Gates, of Leominster; children: 1. Reuben, born June 8, 1773; married April 6, 1799, Rebecca Gates. 2. Joseph, born June 16, 1776; married April 12, 1800, Betsey Gates, and had: Sarah, baptized April 19, 1801, Sophronia, baptized March 13, 1803, Asa, baptized October 6, 1804, iv. Lucy Gates, baptized February 14, 1808. 3. Jonas, born August 13, 1779, married Lucy Warren; 4. Elias, born April 22, 1784; 5. Daniel, November 2, 1785.) (Thomas Wetherbee, son of Thomas mentioned above, married, 1779, Mary Gates; children: 1. Mary, born March 28, 1780; married April 14, 1807, Jonathan Sawtelle, Jr. 2. Josiah, born March 19, 1783; married November 28, 1805, Clarissa Sawtelle, and had: i. Josiah Lyman, born September 15, 1806, married first, Fannie Colburn, second, Mary Whittaker; ii. Clarissa, born April 15, 1809, died September 2, 1825; iii. Adelaide, born April 19, 1811, married Lyman Whittaker; iv. Edmund S., born January 25, 1815, married Abby G. Miller; v. Marshall, born June, 1817, married October 13, 1843, Marinda Whittaker; vi. Levi Warren, born January 3, 1820, killed. 3. Sarah, born March 14, 1786; married April 14, 1807, Solomon Wetherbee. 4. Arni, born January 21, 1793; married Mary Gates. 5. Betsey, married William Washburn.) (Ephraim Wetherbee, son of Thomas mentioned above, married October 17, 1772, Olive Gates; children: 1. Lois, born January 28, 1773; married Darius Whitcomb. 2. Thomas, born February 26, 1774; married Betsey Hale, and had Almira, Elizabeth, Alvira and Levi. 3. Dorcas, born October 11, 1775; married Jedediah Alexander. 4. Samuel, born July 17, 1777; married Hannah Ross. 5. Levi, born April 29, 1779; married Betsey Hawes. 6. Olive, born April 15, 1781. 7. Betsey, born November 14, 1783; married first, February 27, 1812, John Rogers; second, Amos French. 8. Ephraim, born April 17, 1786; married Lucy Stone, born April 29, 1788, and had: i. Mary, born August 24, 1808, married Charles B. Taft; ii. Mary, born July 23, 1810, died December 23, 1823; iii. Ariel, born October 28, 1812, married Elizabeth Colton; iv. Lucy, born October 22, 1815, married Joseph Stone; v. Otis, born November 8, 1817, married Dorothy Stone).

(III) Hezekiah Wetherbee, son of John Wetherbee, removed to Lunenburg about 1730, and was a yeoman and a prominent man of the town. He bought September 4, 1730, one hundred and twenty acres of land from Josiah Willard. His homestead was beyond Mulpus brook, and he died about 1754. The inventory of his estate was filed August 28, 1754. He married, at Marlborough, April 22, 1728, Huldah Martyn, who married second, January 12, 1773, Deacon Ephraim Pierce, of Lunenburg, and went to Rindge, where she died. She was born April 27, 1711, daughter of Thomas and Mary (Gove) Martyn. It is said that one day when her husband Hezekiah and two of the sons were absent from home to fight the Indians, she took her son John, then a year and a half old, on her back, and a child in each hand, and went through the forest at night to the garrison house, a distance of three miles. Children: 1. Benjamin, born at Marlborough, November 3, 1728; settled in Rindge, New Hampshire; married, 1755, Keziah Munroe, born October 16, 1731, died July 12, 1772; children: i. Betsey, born January 5, 1756, married Matthew Osborne; ii. Hezekiah, born June 20, 1757, at Rindge, married Lucy Hale; iii. Rachel, born January 5, 1758, married ——— Parker; iv. Benjamin, born October 2, 1762, died in the army, of small pox; v. Mary, born August 16, 1765; vi. Keziah, born July 4, 1768. 2. Thomas, born November 27, 1730; mentioned below. 3. Phebe, born February 12, 1733; died young. 4. Phebe, born July 7, 1740; married April 26, 1758, Abel Platts Jr.; children: i. Mary, born January 31, 1759, married Moses Chaplain; ii. Phebe, born November 11, 1763; iii. Sarah, born June 8, 1765; iv. Asa, born May 28, 1766, married Rebecca Bursel; v. Abel, born December 10, 1769; vi. Lucy, born April 2, 1771, married Daniel Gibson; vii. Dolly, born September 14, 1773, married ——— Carroll; viii. Ruth, born February 29, 1776, married Dr. Joel Chamberlain; ix. Aaron, born November 2, 1778; x. Abram, born March 30, 1781; xi. Huldah, born July 3, 1783. 5. Sarah, born November 17, 1742; married, 1763, Noah Dodge, of Lunenburg; children: i. Sarah Dodge, born April 20, 1766; ii. Paul Dodge, January 23, 1767; iii. Ruth Dodge; iv. Mary Dodge; v. Hannah Dodge; vi. Phebe Dodge; vii. David Balch Dodge; viii. Samuel Stillman Dodge; ix. Anna Dodge; x. Rebecca Dodge. 6. John, born September 14, 1746; died March 31, 1838; married June 23, 1773, Susannah Page, died August 21, 1840, aged ninety-three; children: i. Susannah, born November 7, 1773, died September 12, 1860, married March 4, 1795, Benjamin Foster; ii. Huldah, born November 18, 1775, died January 14, 1826; iii. John, born December 18, 1777, died April 19, 1778; iv. Jeremiah, born December 31, 1779, died August, 1863; v. Joseph, born October 8, 1781, died 1867; vi. Sarah, born January 23, 1784, married first, Enoch Breed, second, Deacon Adin Cummings; vii. Hezekiah, born May 6, 1786, died March 11, 1869, married Grace Baker; viii. Deborah, born August 11, 1788, died unmarried; ix. Phebe, born March 8, 1799, died November 10, 1837, married Moses Binney. (Jeremiah Wetherbee, son of John mentioned above, married first, Mary Pope, second, October 19, 1809, Mercy Holden, of Barre, born December 1, 1790; children, all by second wife: 1. Sarah Holden, born July 27, 1810; married William Henshaw. 2. Mary Pope, born June 12, 1812; died May, 1836; married George Washington Eddy. 3. Moses Holden, born July 5, 1814; died September 28, 1855; married Frances Hall; children: i. Mary Eddy, married Daniel Murdock; ii. Emma; 4. George W., born June 28, 1816, died June 19, 1818; 5. Susannah, born November 10, 1818; died September 14, 1820. 6. Mercy, born September 21, 1820; married Rev. Isaac K. Bronson. 7. Charles, born September 22, 1822; died July 24, 1825. 8. Eliza, born November 1, 1824; married Avery W. Gilbert. 9. Henry, born February 19, 1827; married Ellen Merrill of Westfield. 10. Seth, born November 12, 1829, married September 17, 1859, Mary Rand, of San Francisco, and had Alice, Ethel and Frank Rand. 11. Jeremiah Otis, born January 16, 1832; married January 29, 1863, Martha Trundy Lovejoy, born at Boston, April 19, 1841; children: i. Winthrop, born November 5, 1863; ii. Lila, February 11, 1866; iii. Mattie, June 23, 1868; iv. Henry (2nd), December 5, 1871; v. Nettie, August 16, 1873. 12. John Williams, born April 30, 1835; died aged two years.) (Joseph Wetherbee, son of John mentioned above, married Nancy Conant, born August 10, 1793, died April 11, 1835; children: 1. Laura, born December 20, 1810; married Smith Sunderland. 2. John, born November, 1812, married Sophia Faye. 3. Arvilla, born January 24, 1815; married Apollas Griswold. 4. Marinda Breed, born March 5, 1817. 5. Eliza Ann, born July 29, 1819; married Stephen Sylvester. 6. Harriet, born September 27, 1821; married Benjamin Stone. 7. Mersylvia, born August 24, 1824; died February 28, 1825. 8. Joseph Sylvester (twin), born May 12, 1828; married Laura M. Nutting. 9. Nancy Mersylvia (twin), born May 12, 1828; married George Godding. 10. Susan Rand, born December 1, 1832; married October 13, 1852, Anson E. Platts.) 7. Abraham, born June 5, 1752; married Joanna Sawtelle; children: i. Abraham, born August 2, 1776; ii. Benjamin, July 8, 1778; iii. Nathaniel, May 31, 1780, married March 8, 1803, Susan Hubbard; iv. John, born June 2, 1782; v. Solomon, born August 15, 1784, married Sarah Wetherbee; vi. Joanna, born August 16, 1785; vii. Thirza, born February 8, 1788; died young; viii. Thirza, born January 1, 1790, married ——— Callendar; ix. Levi, born March 3, 1782; x. Ephraim Cummings, May 15, 1793; xi. Asenath, June 5, 1797.

(IV) Thomas Wetherbee, son of Hezekiah Wetherbee, was born at Lunenburg, November 27, 1730. He owned a large farm in Lunenburg, where all his children were born, and about 1777-8 removed to Rindge, New Hampshire. He was in the revolution, in Captain George Kimball's company, and answered the Lexington alarm, April 20, 1775; in Captain Joseph Sargent's company, Colonel Josiah Whitney's regiment, pay abstract for mileage, dated June 22, 1777, ninety miles; also private same company, May 5 to July 12, 1777, company drafted from Colonels Josiah Whitney's and Stearn's regiments, marched to serve under General Spencer. He and his wife were members of the Congregational Orthodox church at Rindge, and he was a member of the standing committee from 1793 to 1800. In 1800 he removed to New Ipswich, New Hampshire. He married, (intentions dated April 22, 1756), Hannah Munroe, of Carlisle. Children: 1. Thomas, born April 7, 1757; mentioned below. 2. Daniel, born December 16, 1758; died January 3, 1845; married Hepsibah Merriam; children: i. William Burns, born January 26, 1784, married Persis Patch; ii. Daniel, born September 1, 1785, died January 11, 1813, married Polly Adams; iii. David, born February 27, 1787, married first, Harriet Keyes, second, ——— Carter, widow; iv. Mary, born September 17, 1788, married Jonathan Jones; v. Lucinda, born April 10, 1790, died February 19, 1845; vi. Josiah, born December 10, 1791; vii. Asenath, born April 25, 1800, married first John Withington, second Abel Ward. (Josiah Wetherbee, son of Daniel, married Abigail Jones, born July 12, 1786; children: 1. Isaac Josiah, born March 9, 1817; married January 3, 1837, Sarah Abigail Sheldon, born April 27, 1819, and had George Sylvester, born October 10, 1838, died October 13, 1838. 2. Marcia Maria, born June 8, 1818; married April 17, 1838, James Henry Schultz, and had: Catherine Abigail Schultz, Calista Maria Schultz, Amanda Ursula Schultz, Ellen Schultz. 3. Sylvester George, born October 3, 1822; died August 7, 1825; 4. Daniel Jones, born May 14, 1826; married August 9, 1849, Sarah Ann Gilman). 3. Hepsibah, born February 28, 1760, married Nathan Hewitt. 4. Isaac, born September 2, 1761; married Hannah Knapp. 5. Sarah, born March 30, 1763; married first, Joshua Heald; second ——— Hamblin; third, ——— Nesmith. 6. David, born May 31, 1764; married Esther Hathorne. 7. Hannah, born February 16, 1766; married Tilly Mason. 8. Lucy, born August 4, 1767; married Gregory Farley. 9. Josiah, born March 17, 1769; married Lavinia Hyde. 10. Martha, born October 10, 1771; married Benjamin Bachelor. 11. Mary, born November 14, 1773.

(V) Thomas Wetherbee, son of Thomas Wetherbee, was born at Lunenburg, August 7, 1757, and died at Ludlow, Vermont. He was educated in the district school and resided in Rindge until 1800, when he removed to New Ipswich, and afterward to Ludlow, Vermont.

He was deacon of the church. He married at Rindge, New Hampshire, June 23, 1788, Abigail Meriah Sawtelle, born January 18, 1763, daughter of Jonathan and Mary (Holden) Sawtelle. She was a school teacher at Rindge. They had twenty-one children, all but the eldest dying unnamed in infancy.

(VI) Luther Wetherbee, son of Thomas Wetherbee, was born at Rindge, New Hampshire, March 18, 1789, and died at Ludlow, Vermont, August 15, 1867. He was educated in the district school and taught in the Ludlow district school. It is related that the first day he taught in the school was exceedingly trying. The scholars were many of them as large as the teacher and did all they could to get the best of the master. They filed into the room, each with a log of wood on his shoulder, which he threw on the floor, making a woodpile in the middle of the room. The second day the same trick was attempted, but the master stood behind the door and the first pupil who entered with a log of wood was felled to the floor. The second met with a like fate, and the master had no more trouble. After teaching a short time he followed the carpenter's trade for many years, until he was obliged to give it up on account of blindness. He became blind about twenty years before his death. He was very fond of reading and was well informed in the topics of the times. He was a fervent member of the Orthodox church at Ludlow, and served as deacon many years. He belonged to the Whig party in politics, and took a lively interest in his party. He was a member of Black River Lodge, No. 85, Free Masons, at Ludlow. He married November 21, 1811, Nancy Kendall, born June 21, 1793, died May 1, 1872. Children: 1. Thomas Kendall, born November 27, 1812; died in New York, July, 1842. 2. Maria, born May 23, 1815; died February 22, 1892; married November 12, 1835, Charles Caldwell; children: i. Maria Elizabeth Caldwell, born March 25, 1837, (married July 17, 1860, William Cushing Haskins, of Medford, born February 18, 1838, died February 17, 1892; child: 1. Hannah Cushing Haskins, born July 21, 1861, married first, March 29, 1882, Frank J. Coburn, of Medford, born March 22, 1853, died November 4, 1894, son of Jonas and Sarah (Freeman) Coburn; married second, May 6, 1900, Dr. Frederick W. Jackson, of Jefferson, Maine, born September 9, 1858, son of Joseph and Arletta (Flagg) Jackson; children: i. Marion Coburn, born March 15, 1883, married December 1, 1906, Ralph Underdown Sawyer, of West Medford, and had John Coburn Sawyer, born February 21, 1908; ii. Alice Coburn, born May 20, 1884, married October 8, 1907, Winthrop Irving Nottage, of West Medford; iii. William Haskins Coburn, born March 8, 1890; and by second husband, iv. Frederick Jackson, born February 20, 1903. 2. Harriet Caldwell, born February 29, 1864, died January 19, 1869. 3. William Haskins (2nd), born January 23, 1870, died April 24, 1899, married Mabel Hutchins, of Medford, and had Elizabeth Haskins, born October 20, 1895, died July 24, 1896. 4. Alice Bemis Haskins, born July 9, 1874, died August 5, 1903, married June 28, 1900, Arthur Choate Crombie, and had twins—Elizabeth Crombie, born November 6, 1901, died September 3, 1902, and Barbara Crombie, died July 18, 1905; 5. Helen Marion Haskins, born August 6, 1876, died December 11, 1877). 3. Nancy, born October 13, 1817; died March 8, 1902; married October 29, 1839, E. S. Morgan, of South Woodstock, Vermont, born May 14, 1814; children: i. George R. Morgan, born September 26, 1848; ii. Mary M. Morgan, born January 3, 1854, married ——— Cowdray, of Vermont; iii. Homer L. Morgan, born February 29, 1856. 4. Adelaide, born September 1, 1819; died July 16, 1850; married Horace Putnam. 5. Melinda, born September 14, 1822; died June 14, 1905; married October 18, 1841, George Bent Green, of Mt. Holly, Vermont; children: i. Darius Alonzo Green, born January 24, 1843, married June 13, 1866, Harriet O. Emery, of Medford, and had Winthrop Darius Green, and George Emery Green; ii. Charles Montreville Green, born December 18, 1850, married June 29, 1876, Helen M. Ware, of Medford, and had Robert Montreville Green; iii. Luther Lorenzo Green, born October 10, 1856, married October 27, 1880, Alice J. Gill, of Medford, had two children; iv. George Wetherbee Green, born November 29, 1862, married October 18, 1888, Annie C. Bowers, had Dorothy Green. 6. Eliphalet Sawtelle, born June 21, 1823; mentioned below. 7. Tyler L., born July 21, 1825; died December 29, 1871; married Elizabeth Long, of Chester, New Hampshire, who died December 14, 1900, aged sixty-seven years. Children: Caroline L., married John F. Murphy; Melinda, married Ellsworth L. Chase. 8. Louisa, born June 30, 1828; died October 28, 1887; married Ezra H. Hatch, who died June 17, 1894, at Benton, Maine. 9. Caroline Persis, born September 23, 1830;

Eliphalet S. Wetherbee

died May 14, 1903; married March 21, 1854, William Lake Sweatt, who died December 23, 1894, aged sixty-one; children: i. Adelaide Louise Sweatt, born March 8, 1855, married December 27, 1877, Joseph Henry Eaton, of Arlington, and had Carrie B. Eaton, born February 18, 1879, died March 18, 1879, Charles S. Eaton, born January 28, 1880, (married April 29, 1903, Emma R. Withington, and had Chester Charles Eaton, born October 6, 1904, and Joseph W. Eaton, born November 25, 1907), Arthur L. Eaton, born January 17, 1882, died young, and Mildred Eaton, born January 17, 1896; died young; ii. Frederick W. Sweatt, born March 1, 1859, died November 2, 1904, married January 9, 1880, Alice Burns, of Portland, Maine; iii. Nancy Jane Sweatt, born September 14, 1861, married February 18, 1885, Charles Puffer, and had Marion Brackett Puffer, born March 6, 1890. 10. Levi Ivers, born December 6, 1833; died March 24, 1886; married March 20, 1859, Mary Ellen Cram, of Ludlow; children: i. Henry, born October 6, 1861, died October 29, 1861; ii. Minnie, born August 31, 1864, died May 17, 1900, married February 22, 1892, J. Fred McCloud, of Arlington, and had Kenneth McCloud, born August 13, 1895; iii. Walter Levi, born June 7, 1869; iv. Ivers Loring, born May 14, 1874; v. Clarence Alfred, born October 28, 1875, married August, 1904, Beatrice Maud Tutten, of West Medford, and had Beatrice Ellen, born December 20, 1905, and Evelyn, born June 15, 1907. 11. Charles I., born January 23, 1836; died August 18, 1882, crushed under his team; married Elizabeth Cole. 12. Luther, born September 3, 1840; died young.

(VII) Eliphalet Sawtelle Wetherbee, son of Luther Wetherbee, was born at Ludlow, Vermont, June 21, 1823, and died at Lexington, Massachusetts, October 23, 1906, aged eighty-three years four months two days. He attended the district school of his native town in a time-worn building where several generations of farmers' sons had learned the rudiments of an education. At ten he went to live with Charles Ives in his native town, and worked on the farm until he was twenty years old. Then he decided to seek a new field of larger opportunity than that of his native town. He sent his trunk by freight and himself walked to Boston, with the intention of going to sea, but his experience with a profane and bellicose old skipper led him to reconsider his purpose. He took his belongings to Lexington and finally found a job at Topsfield. He worked on a farm there two years, on another at Danvers three years for Rev. Mr. Tenbrook, an Episcopalian minister, and then for one year at Medford, Massachusetts, on the farm of Edwin T. Hastings, a wealthy oil merchant, of Boston. About 1848 he signed a contract with William E. Kingsbury, an enterprising market-gardener of Roxbury, Massachusetts, as superintendent. Afterward he held a similar position on the adjoining farm owned by Aaron E. Williams for the period of twenty-four years, evidence of his superior skill in this business and of the excellent relations he enjoyed with his employer. He left Mr. Williams to invest his savings in a farm of his own. In 1878 he bought the Johnson farm at North Lexington, and made a specialty of his dairy. He had a herd ranging from fifty to sixty cows of fancy stock, and owned a milk route in Roxbury. He was very successful in this venture and acquired a competence. He remained in the dairy and milk business to the end of his days. He was at one time interested as a stockholder in the Boston Lead Company. He was a typical self-made man, starting in life with but little schooling and no advantages of property or influence, and filled the humblest positions with ability. He made his way in the world by dint of quiet industry, husbanding his savings and keeping step with the advance in agricultural methods and ideas. He was essentially progressive, of sterling common sense and exceptional business ability. His personality was pleasing. He made many friends not only in business but in social life. He was thoroughly upright in all his dealings. He was brought up a Methodist and remained a member of that church all his adult years. He was treasurer and trustee of the Methodist church of Roxbury, and always an active and zealous member. In politics he was a Republican, and while interested in public affairs never was active. His chief interests was his home and his business. During the civil war he served in the Roxbury Horse Guards and did his duty in Boston in suppressing the draft riots.

He married, November 30, 1848, Eliza Massey Pike, born November 6, 1825, daughter of John and Mercy (McMillan) Pike, of Danvers, Massachusetts, descendant of James Pike, who settled in Charlestown before 1647 and removed to Reading, Massachusetts. Her father was a blacksmith. Children: 1. George Tyler, born January 2, 1850; married May 9, 1877, Mrs. Lilla (Hardway) Gurley of Marietta, Ohio, daughter of Frederick and Priscilla (Whipping) Hardway; children: i. Herbert Eliphalet, born May 4, 1878, married October 31, 1906, Lena Johns, of Wellington, Ohio. 2. Annie Florilla, born November 18, 1852; married March 24, 1880, William Hadley Whittaker, of Lexington; children: i. Bertha Esther Whittaker, born March 4, 1881; ii. Ethel Florilla Whittaker, March 28, 1884. 3. Herbert, May 7, 1856; married first, January 17, 1877, Louise Meserve, of Roxbury; second, Florence Davis, of Worcester; children of first wife: i. Alice Louise, born April 8, 1878; ii. George Meserve, born September 29, 1881, married June 19, 1901, Harriet Maud Beem, of East Machias, Maine (children: i. Vivian Beem, born September 6, 1902; ii. Richard Meserve, born April 2, 1904; iii. Hortense, born April 23, 1907). 4. Fannie, born July 28, 1861.

PEIRCE The earliest records of the Peirce family in this country relate to one Abraham Peirce, of Boston and Salem. His marriage is recorded thus: "Abraham Pierce and Isabel Witherspoon, both of Boston, Joyned in marriage March 11th 1686-7 by Rev. John Bayley, at Watertown, Mass. Recorded June 9, 1687 by L. Hammond, Clerk of the County Court, East Cambridge, Mass." They had one son, Samuel, born May 10, 1689. Abraham Peirce's name appears on the Salem town records many times. He was chosen constable in 1709, March 20, and March 24, 1711; was chosen tythingman for the ensuing year; was chosen deacon in 1713. He is several times mentionèd in land transactions. March 20, 1710, Abraham Pears and fifty others sign a petition for a new meeting house. The Abraham Peirce farm, South Peabody, Massachusetts, is on the Ipswich road, and one of the oldest in Essex county. The names of the descendants of Abraham Peirce figure conspicuously in the records of Salem, Andover and Boston. The name is spelled Pers, Pears, Pearce, Pierce and Peirce on the early records.

William Peirce, father of Isaac Newton Peirce, of this review, was born in Greenfield, Massachusetts, February 7, 1806, died in Charlestown, Massachusetts, May 22, 1883. He was the son of Proctor and Susanna (Newton) Peirce. At the age of ten years William Peirce came from his home at Greenfield to Cambridge and became an apprentice for General Samuel T. Armstrong, publisher and bookseller, in his store then known as 50 Cornhill, Boston, now (1907) Washington street. After finishing his apprenticeship with General Armstrong he engaged in business as a bookseller at 9 Cornhill, Boston, under the firm name of Peirce & Parker, where he remained until 1838-39, when he removed his business to Andover, Massachusetts. He was appointed postmaster at Andover, May 18, 1841, and to the same position at Lawrence in 1849. Retiring from these positions he was appointed to a clerkship at the custom house in Boston, which he held until April, 1854, when he was appointed clerk of the Massachusetts state prison in Charlestown. He held this position twenty-eight years and seven months, resigning in November, 1882. In 1856 he removed from Andover to Cambridge, and from the latter place to Charlestown in 1859. September 2, 1827, he was admitted a member of Park Street Church, and his wife, Ellen (Prentiss) Peirce, was admitted a member June 2, 1827; Rev. Edward Beecher was the pastor. In 1840 he took letters for himself and wife from Park Street Church, Boston, to the South Congregational Church in Andover, where he was elected clerk of the church in 1846-48, superintendent of the Sunday school, and moderator in 1850. For fourteen years Mr. Peirce took a special interest in a mission Sunday school which had been established on Bunker Hill street. He became identified with the First Congregational Church in Charlestown, where he was elected scribe on January 7, 1861, deacon of the church January 10, 1862, filling both positions until his death. He was a Mason, belonging to St. Matthew's Lodge, Andover, in which he filled the position of chaplain. William Peirce was married, June 7, 1831, at the house of Mark Weare, 21 Poplar street, Boston, by Rev. Lyman Beecher, D. D., to Ellen Prentiss, born in Cambridge, Massachusetts, July 31, 1808, died in Roxbury, Massachusetts, May 29, 1872, daughter of Jonas and Helen (Whittemore) Prentiss. During his entire life Mr. Peirce was a friend of the unfortunate, the helper to a better life of the fallen, and a true-hearted christian man.

Isaac Newton Peirce, son of William and Ellen (Prentiss) Peirce, was born in Andover, Massachusetts, "Seminary Hill", March 13, 1843, died in Newton, Massachusetts, September 20, 1907. During his boyhood years his parents moved from Andover to Cambridge, and later to Charlestown. He received his education in the public schools of Cambridge.

For many years after completing his schooling he served as bookkeeper with the Tucker Manufacturing Company, and for nineteen years was actively interested with the firm of Joel Goldthwait & Company, carpet dealers, remaining with them until the business closed December 31, 1901. He was initiated in Bunker Hill Lodge, No. 14, I. O. O. F., October 4, 1869, and served as noble grand from January, 1875, to July, 1875; initiated in Bunker Hill Encampment, No. 5, same order, December 5, 1872, served as chief patriarch of same from July, 1876, to January, 1877; admitted to third degree in Henry Price Lodge, F. A. M., May 24, 1882, and served as worshipful master from October, 1891, to October, 1893; initiated in Waverly Chapter, R. A. M., December 5, 1894; Melrose Council, R. S. M., November 20, 1893; Hugh de Payens Commandery, No. 20, K. T., March 13, 1895; admitted member of Newton Royal Arch Chapter, February 19, 1907. From the formation of the Crow Club of Charlestown in 1875 until his death he served in the capacity of secretary. During his early manhood he was a member of the Charlestown Cadets. He was a member of the Eliot Congregational Church, and his political affiliations were with the Republican party. He was a loyal and patriotic citizen, a man of high ideals in friendship, fraternity and business, and his demise was sincerely deplored by all who knew him. Isaac N. Peirce was married first, by Rev. Roscoe L. Greene, of Charlestown, Massachusetts, at the home of the bride's uncle, Wendall P. Van Kleeck, Bunker Hill street, Charlestown, January 17, 1884, to Frances Priscilla, daughter of Parker and Cynthia (de les Dernier) Lynch. She was born at Fort Lawrence, Nova Scotia, September 26, 1847, died at 39 Wildwood street, Winchester, Massachusetts, January 14, 1892, buried in Elm Avenue cemetery, Cambridge. He was married second, by Rev. Leighton Parks, D. D., of Boston, at the home of the bride's father, 277 Beacon street, to Elizabeth Brown, daughter of John and Helen (Brown) Goldthwait, of Boston, April 3, 1902. Mr. Peirce had one son by the first wife, Frederick Newton, born at 25 Green street, Charlestown, Massachusetts, February 2, 1885.

Mrs. Elizabeth B. (Goldthwait) Peirce is a lineal deecendant of Thomas Goldthwait, the ancestor of all of the name in the United States (see Goldthwait). She traces her maternal ancestry to Richard Brown (1), who came from England in the ship "Elizabeth and Dorcas", in 1634, with his brother George, who died in 1642. Richard wintered in Ipswich, Massachusetts, helping to begin that plantation. He went to Newbury and was one of the first settlers in 1635. He was admitted freeman in May, 1635. His first wife, Edith Brown, died in April, 1647. His second wife, Elizabeth (Badger) Brown, was widow of Giles Badger, and daughter of Samuel Greenleaf. He was the father of eight children. He died April 26, 1661. Richard Brown (2), born February 18, 1651, married Mary Jacques. Richard (3), born September 12, 1675, married Martha Whipple, of Ipswich, daughter of Major John and Catherine (Frost) Whipple. He was a minister of the gospel. William Brown (4), born at Newbury, January 24, 1707, married Ann Poor, daughter of Jonathan and Rebecca (Hale) Poor, of Newbury. They had ten children, among whom was Samuel (5), born December 13, 1752, married Hannah Stone. They had a son Charles (6), born February 24, 1792, married Elizabeth Chandler Hunt, at his father's mansion house, March 28, 1819, the ceremony being performed by the Rev. Daniel Dana, D. D. He settled in Boston. By an act of legislature, March 24, 1843, his name was changed to that of Charles H. Brown. Their daughter Helen, born April 29, 1826, married, July 16, 1851, John Goldthwait, and they were the parents of Elizabeth B. (Goldthwait) Peirce.

(For ancestry see Thomas Goldthwait 1).

GOLDTHWAIT (V) Ezekiel Goldthwait, son of Samuel Goldthwait (4), was born at Smithfield, Rhode Island, October 18, 1748. He received his early education in the Friends' School of his native city. His parents removed to Northbridge when he was twelve years old, and he worked with his father on the farm until April 1, 1775, when his father gave him a tract of land upon which he went to live with his young wife and on which he remained until 1784, when he bought of the heirs of Richard Derby by deed dated February 7, 1784, a farm in his father's native town, Danvers, Massachusetts, and removed thither with his family. This farm was on the Great Road from Boston to Salem and was formerly known as the Ivers and later as the Derby farm. In the purchase was included "a pew in the meeting house of South Danvers where Mr. Holt preaches and now occupied by one Joseph Flint." Ezekiel Goldthwait has left a record of some of his experiences in making the change of residence in an old account book under date of February 4, 1784. "I, Ezekiel Goldthwait of Northbridge in the county of Worcester bought a farm in Danvers and determined to move directly to it, but through disappointment through selling my farm in Northbridge as I expected I let it to Amos Flint who was on the farm when I bought it which proved an injury to me. May 3, 1784, I set out with my family (except my second son in his 9th year I left with his grandfather Adams) and I arrived in Danvers May the 5th with my family well through the goodness of God which I hope forever to remember. May 3, 1785, I brought my son Joel from his grandfather's and I saw a snow bank of considerable length in the town of Lynn." Ezekiel Goldthwait died very suddenly June 18, 1800, of a disease resembling Asiatic cholera. He was a man of many good principles and honest purposes, and was highly esteemed by all his townsmen. He married, December 3, 1772, Anna Adams, born April 8, 1754, daughter of James and Elizabeth (Dean) Adams, and twin sister of Israel Adams. The Adams family lived in that part of Sutton set off as Northbridge in 1780. Children: 1. Ezekiel, born January 1, 1774; married Polly Fuller. 2. Joel, born January 9, 1776; died unmarried January 1, 1853; was a baker at Salem, Massachusetts, his bakeshop being situated in the west part of Essex street, near the present site of Grace Church. 3. Elijah, born October 12, 1777; died at sea, May 2, 1800. 4. Prudence, born October 14, 1779; married Jonathan Wilson. 5. Beulah, born October 31, 1781; married Stephen B. Dockham. 6. Lucinda, born September 16, 1783; married first, Ezra Dodge; second, Stephen Fogg. 7. Luther, born Janu-ton City Hospital. He was a large stockholder ary 12, 1786; married Hannah Meader Lawrence. 8. Moses, born September 29, 1787; mentioned below. 9. Willard, born July 6, 1790; married Dolly Johnson. 10. Aaron, born November 6, 1793; married Christiana Peabody. 11. Anna, born March 8, 1797; died June 24, 1880; married William Johnson; no children.

(VI) Moses Goldthwait, son of Ezekiel Goldthwait (5), was born at South Danvers, Massachusetts, September 29, 1787, and died July 13, 1864. He married, May 31, 1812, Margaret G. Garney, of Marblehead, born December, 1791, and died November 17, 1875. Children: 1. Moses Jr., born August 18, 1812; married Elizabeth Barker Wormstead. 2. Margaret, born February 7, 1815; died April, 1894; married John Stevens, of Marblehead; children: John H. Stevens, Frank Stevens, Augusta Stevens. 3. Susan L., born January 1, 1817; died August 8, 1894; married John Gardner. 4. Anna A., born October 8, 1819; died April, 1863; married William Lamprell; had no children. 5. John, born July 2, 1823; mentioned below. 6. Benjamin F., born July 1, 1825; died February 23, 1904; married Elmira Porter; no children. 7. Joel, born April 4, 1831; died May 29, 1901; married Ellen A., daughter of Jasper and Lucy (Whipple) Rand; no children. 8. William Johnson, born May 7, 1834; married Mary L. Pitman.

(VII) John Goldthwait, son of Moses Goldthwait, was born at Marblehead, July 2, 1823, and died at 277 Beacon street, Boston, January 16, 1899. He attended the district schools of his native town, and when he had but just reached his teens came to Boston to begin life on his own account. After trying various occupations he became a clerk in the old commercial house of Kindmouth & Company, at the corner of Washington street and Temple Place, the present site of the dry goods house of Houston & Henderson. In 1844 Mr. Goldthwait entered partnership with Russell Bates, under the firm name of Bates & Goldthwait, on Washington street, near Cornhill, in the carpet trade, and the firm continued with marked success until the death of Mr. Bates in 1864. Shortly afterward Mr. Goldthwait also retired, and the business was continued by Joel Goldthwait, Snow & Knight. The firm became Joel Goldthwait & Company and the high reputation and prestige of the business was maintained. Joel Goldthwait had been in the employ of his brother's firm since November 1, 1847, when he began as a salesman. Both brothers were well and favorably known, not only in Boston but throughout New England, and their house stood among the foremost in the carpet trade for many years. The store of Joel Goldthwait was at 165 to 169 Washington street, the present site of the Martin building. The building at 43 and 45 Washington street, six stories high, with marble front, was erected by John Goldthwait and occupied by the business. This Goldthwait firm is the oldest in this line of business in the city. John Goldthwait was prudent and sagacious in business, straightforward, upright, self-reliant, of sound judgment and sterling integrity. His advice and counsel was often sought by other business men and

John Goldthwait

was freely given. He was an authority on subjects pertaining to the carpet and kindred business. He was a charter member of Emanuel Unitarian Church, of which Bishop Huntington was formerly the minister. Mr. Goldthwait was also a parishioner of Dr. Huntington, when he became rector of Trinity Protestant Episcopal Church, Boston. In politics he was a Republican, and at one time served the city of Boston in the common council, and for many years as trustee of the Boston City Hospital. He was a large stockholder in the old Middlesex Horse Railroad Company. He was a member of the Boston Art Club. He married, July 16, 1851, Helen Brown, born April 29, 1826, at Boston, and died May 5, 1880, at Boston, daughter of Charles H. and Elizabeth (Hunt) Brown, of Boston. Children: 1. Elizabeth Brown, born at Boston, June 12, 1852; married by Rev. Leighton Parks, D. D., April 3, 1902, to Isaac Newton Peirce, of Charlestown, Massachusetts. (See Peirce). 2. Helen Maria, born June 13, 1854; married, November 12, 1884, Simon Davis, of Charlestown, son of Silas and Mercy Elizabeth (Taylor) Davis. Children: i. Helen Goldthwait Davis, born August 21, 1885; ii. Elizabeth Goldthwait Davis, born December 16, 1888, died August 27, 1889; iii. John, born September 25, 1891; iv. Elizabeth Brown Davis, born March 10, 1898. 3. Charles Brown, born January 18, 1856; died March 30, 1897; married, December, 1893, Caroline Alexander, of Malden, Massachusetts; and had a son Crawford, born March 11, 1890. 4. John B., died in May, 1863, aged three months.

BODWELL

Henry Bodwell, immigrant ancestor, was born in England in 1654. He was a soldier in King Philip's war in 1676 and took part in the battle of Bloody Brook. His left arm was broken by a musket ball and he was surrounded by Indians, but seizing his gun in his right hand and swinging it about he mowed a swath through the savages and escaped. He was admitted a freeman in 1678. He resided in Newbury a short time and his eldest child was born there in 1682. He removed to Andover, where he was living in 1685, and finally to Haverhill, where in 1693 his father-in-law, John Emery, of Newbury, gave him and his wife a hundred acres of land. In 1712 he was living in Haverhill, a renowned hunter and a terror to hostile Indians. He is said to have shot an Indian on the opposite bank of the Merrimac, when the enemy, deeming himself out of range, was making insulting gestures. Bodwell's Ferry and Bodwell's Falls were named for him. He married, May 4, 1681, Bethia Emery, daughter of John J. and Mary (Webster) Emery, of Newbury. Sergeant John Emery Jr. came to Newbury in 1636; married Mary Webster, daughter of John and Mary (Shatswell) Webster, October 24, 1648; was a selectman 1670-73; juror 1675-76; appointed to carry the votes to Salem 1675-76; tythingman in 1679; owned eighty acres of land at Artichoke or Raspberry river, of which half was given him by his father and some of it is at the present time owned by his descendants. Emery's mill was on the site now known as Curzon's mills at Newburyport. Emery was admitted a freeman May 30, 1660; his will was dated August 3, 1793; his wife died February 3, 1709. Children of John Jr. and Mary Emery: 1. Mary, born June 24, 1652. 2. Hannah, April 26, 1654. 3. John, September 12, 1656, died July 14, 1730. 4. Bethia, October 15, 1658, mentioned above. 5. Sarah, February 26, 1660. 6. Joseph, March 23, 1663, died at Andover, September 22, 1721. 7. Stephen, September 6, 1666. 8. Abigail, January 16, 1668. 9. Samuel, December 20, 1670. 10. Judith, February 5, 1673. 11. Lydia, February 19, 1675. 12. Elizabeth, February 8, 1680. 13. Josiah, February 28, 1681, married Abigail Moody. Children of Henry and Bethia Bodwell: 1. Bethia, born June 2, 1682. 2. Mary, April 1, 1684. 3. Henry, January 27, 1685 (twin). 4. Josiah, (twin), January 27, 1685. 5. Abigail, January 15, 1686. 6. Henry, November 6, 1688; son Henry married Mary Robinson; their son Joseph married Mary How; their son Hon. Joseph Bodwell, born June 18, 1818, resided at Methuen until 1852; removed to Maine and became governor of the state; died December 15, 1887. 7. James, January 16, 1691, mentioned below. 8. Daniel, February 14, 1693. 9. Sarah, December 1, 1694. 10. Hannah, September 1, 1696. 11. Judith, April 4, 1698. 12. Ruth, December 2, 1699. 13. Infant, July 10, 1701, died young.

(II) James Bodwell, son of Henry Bodwell, was born January 16, 1691, in Andover, Massachusetts. He removed to Haverhill with his parents and later in life was of Methuen, adjoining Haverhill. He died in Methuen in 1746. His will was dated March 19, 1745, and proved July 7, 1746. He married Sarah ———. Children, mentioned in the will: 1. Stephen, mentioned below. 2. Mary, married

Timothy Myrick. 3. Hannah, married John Hibbard. 4. James Jr.

(III) Stephen Bodwell, son of James Bodwell, was born at Methuen about 1720, died in 1803 at Methuen. His will is dated November 10, 1797, and was proved July 6, 1803. He married Ruth ———. Children, born in Methuen, mentioned in his will: 1. Sarah, married Nathaniel Hibbard. 2. Ruth, married Moses Emery. 3. Lydia, married Solomon Worth. 4. Olive, married ——— Davis and had Moses Davis and Abigail Davis, of Bakerstown. 5. Mary, married Silas Brown. 6. Abigail, died unmarried 1834, mentioning in her will the children of her brother William and sisters Sarah, Ruth, Lydia, Mary, Olive; Edna was the only one surviving Abigail. 7. Abiah, unmarried. 8. Edna. 9. William, mentioned below.

(IV) William Bodwell, son of Stephen Bodwell, was born at Methuen about 1750. He was a soldier in the revolution in Captain John Peabody's company, Colonel Ebenezer Francis's regiment in 1776; also in Captain John Willey's company, Colonel Michael Jackson's regiment 1777-79, giving his age as eighteen, his height five feet, four inches, hair and complexion light and his residence Methuen. He was at West Point in the Continental service, 1779; was in Captain Abner Wade's company, Colonel Jackson's Eighth regiment in 1780. He married Sarah ———. Stephen Barker, presumably a relative of his wife, was on the committee appointed by the court to set off the widow's dower rights, in the real estate. The name has been preserved in the family. Among his children, various deeds indicate there were: 1. Zadock, mentioned below. 2. Joseph, who deeded certain land to Zadock in September, 1805. 3. John L., who deeded to Zadock September 28, 1809. 4. Isaac.

(V) Zadock Bodwell, son of William Bodwell, was born about 1780 in Methuen. He married Olive Barker, August 27, 1800. His will was dated March 7, 1839, and proved October 15, 1839, soon after his death. He lived at Bradford for a time and while there bought of Ebenezer Merrill, of Methuen, forty acres with houses and other buildings and various lots in Methuen by deed dated September 5, 1799. Children: 1. Leonard, born January 10, 1801, died August 1, 1829, in the west. 2. Nelson, born September 25, 1803. 3. Zadock, born September 2, 1805, died in the west. 4. Asa M., born March 2, 1812, died July 11, 1891, at Lawrence, Massachusetts; he was born in what is now known as the old Tarbox homestead on the Howe road in Methuen, better known as Buckly street, and his whole life with the exception of a few years in the west was spent in Lawrence and Methuen; after his birth the family removed from Methuen to Haverhill street, Lawrence, where he lived and died; in 1875 he built a spacious brick mansion on the site of the old dwelling which he moved and thereafter occupied it for his home; it was numbered 589; he was a farmer all his life; belonged to the Farmers' Grange, Patrons of Husbandry, Methuen, and of the Farmers' Alliance. 5. Nathaniel, born August 5, 1814. 6. Joseph R., born August 11, 1817. 7. George W., born November 5, 1821, veteran of civil war and was present at the capture of Jeff. Davis. 8. Stephen Barker, mentioned below.

(VI) Stephen Barker Bodwell, son of Zadock Bodwell, was born in Methuen, November 13, 1823. He was educated in the public schools. He removed to Lawrence with his father's family and lived on Haverhill street. He was by occupation a farmer. In religion he was a Universalist, and in politics a Republican. He married first, Elizabeth Dunlap; children: Stephen Byron, Albert, Leonard and George. He married second, ——— Brown; no children; married third, Aldana Spear; Stephen Byron, mentioned below.

(VII) Stephen Byron Bodwell, son of Stephen Barker Bodwell, was born in Methuen, November 18, 1846. He was educated in the public schools of Lawrence. He worked on the farm of his father on Haverhill street, Lawrence, during his youth. He enlisted in the Fiftieth Massachusetts Regiment, First Heavy Artillery, during the civil war and served three years. Afterward he worked for a time in Lowell, then engaged in the railroad business and became the road master of the southern division of the Boston & Maine railroad. Later he accepted a position as assistant superintendent of streets in Lawrence, then bought out the Wilson Building Moving Company, and about a year later he bought out a general contracting, concreting and asphalting business, in which he has been very successful. He is a member of Lanson Post, Grand Army of the Republic, of which he is quartermaster. He is a member of the Free Masons, Commandery, No. 17, Knights Templar, and of the Benevolent and Protective Order of Elks, No. 65. In politics he is a Republican and takes a keen interest in public affairs, but has never sought public office of any kind. He married, September 16, 1865, Sarah Diana Hill, born at Milton, Vermont, July 30, 1846, daughter of Warren and Nancy (Crean) Hill, of Milton. Children, born at Lawrence: 1. William, April 25, 1868, died same day. 2. Minnie Elizabeth, November 13, 1869, married, 1891, J. Allen Robbins, of Waltham. 3. Olive, November 23, 1872; married E. H. Holton.

(For early generations see John Stevens 1).

STEVENS (III) Captain James Stevens, son of Deacon Joseph Stevens (2), was born in Andover, 1685; died May 25, 1769, aged eighty-four years. He was in the French and Indian wars, 1744 to 1749, and commanded a company of Andover men in the Cape Breton expedition, taking part in the capture of Louisburg. With others of this army he petitioned for a grant of land for services, November 22, 1751, and received land in the province of Maine. He was a prominent man in his day; selectman in 1742; town treasurer 1721-29 and 1733-34. He married, March, 1712, Dorothy Frye, born 1695, died 1751. Children: James, mentioned below; Joseph; Benjamin; probably several daughters.

(IV) Ensign James Stevens, son of Captain James Stevens (3), was born in Andover, in 1720; married, 1746, Sarah Peabody, born 1728, died 1808. He raised a company in Andover and fought in the French and Indian war. He marched to Lake George as ensign at the head of his company, and died there of camp fever November 28, 1755, in his thirty-fifth year. He was in Captain Abiel Frye's company, Colonel Williams's regiment. His widow petitioned for reimbursement for the loss of personal effects in the service. Children: Jonathan, mentioned below; James; Lydia, married ——— Peters.

(V) Jonathan Stevens, son of James Stevens (4), was born in 1747, in Andover, and died there April 13, 1834, aged eighty-seven years. He was a soldier in the revolution, in the Andover company, and took part in the battle of Bunker Hill. On the anniversary of the battle he invariably invited his comrades in the fight and entertained them at his home with hearty old-fashioned hospitality, while the old veterans fought their battles over again. He was also in the battle of Ticonderoga, and a letter to his sister, dated at Pawlet, October 1, 1777, is published in the "History of Andover," (page 377). He married, December 15, 1773, Susanna Bragg, born 1755, died 1840. Children: 1. Captain Nathaniel, mentioned below. 2. William, graduate of Franklin Academy and Harvard College, 1819; many years judge of municipal court of Lawrence. 3. Isaac, philanthropist and reformer.

(VI) Captain Nathaniel Stevens, son of Jonathan Stevens (5), was born in Andover, October 19, 1786, and died March 7, 1865, at North Andover. He and his brother William were educated in the public schools and Franklin Academy. In 1804, after leaving school, he took a sea voyage to Leghorn as a common sailor before the mast, for the sake of his health and the experience. He was a trader in Andover from 1810 to 1812. He was a lieutenant of the Andover company in the war of 1812, and later was captain. The example and encouragement of his father-in-law, Moses Hale, started him in the manufacturing business. Entering partnership with Dr. Joseph Kittredge and Josiah Monroe, in 1813, he built the wooden mill on the site of the first saw mills on the Cochickawick river, the same building with brick walls instead of wooden ones being still in use as part of the Stevens mills. James Scholfield was engaged to take charge of the mill, and Mr. Stevens devoted his entire attention to manufacturing. By perseverance and energy he soon mastered in all its details the art of manufacturing cloth. He then decided to give up making broadcloth, in which he experimented first, because of the difficulty of making the goods and the uncertainty of profit, and began to manufacture flannels. He was the pioneer in the manufacture of flannel in this country. In 1828 and 1831 he bought out his partners and took entire charge of the mill and business. He was warned by well-meaning friends that he would lose his time and sink his capital. Abbot Lawrence, the importer, especially warned him that American manufacturers could not compete with the British successfully. "Take my advice," said he, one day, when Mr. Stevens carried a load of flannels to Boston, "sell out your mill and go into some other business." "Never," replied Mr. Stevens, "as long as I can get water to turn my mill wheel." Captain Stevens continued despite the discouragements of small and insufficient capital, of narrow and inconvenient quarters and of a market flooded with foreign goods, and against the advice of his friends, and won a brilliant success eventually. He lived to become one of the most wealthy, honored and influential manufacturers of the country, a leader in the woolen industry of the country, carrying on business for half a century with continuous success and increasing volume. He had the satisfaction also of seeing the industry, in which he was a pioneer, become of giant proportions in the United States; he saw American looms producing the best goods and winning a place in the markets of the world, employing millions of dollars in capital and hundreds of thousands of men. Perhaps no one manufacturer nor single individual in this country contributed more than Mr. Stevens in paving the way for the textile industries that have held the prestige of New England when she ceased to be of importance as an agricultural community. He opened the way to wealth for the nation by proving that American mills could be operated profitably. He was a remarkably shrewd and far-sighted business man, of much common sense and consummate executive ability. He had no precedents to fall back on. He had to rely on his own discretion in making goods and marketing them.

He was also generous with the wealth that came as a fruit of his enterprise and industry. He contributed to every charity within his reach, and was especially eager to contribute to the welfare and progress of his native town. He was the leading citizen of North Andover for many years. He derived much pleasure from the cultivation of the ancestral acres. He was a man of iron constitution and phenomenal industry. He used to say that he never felt fatigue until he was fifty years old. He was a member of the Merrimac Power Association, one of the founders of the city of Lawrence, which was formerly part of Andover. He believed in the value of sound learning and gave the best possible education to all of his large family. In politics he was an ardent Democrat, a loyal supporter of the Andrew Jackson administration, and formidable in debate in defending and supporting "Old Hickory." When the civil war came he was loyal to the Union, and did his utmost to support the administration in his old age. Three sons became associated with him in business in Andover, and all five became prominent manufacturers. To the sons as well as to the father the town of Andover, the town of North Andover and all the other villages in which the family has mills owe them a great debt. They have been model mill proprietors in every sense of the word.

Mr. Stevens married, November 6, 1815, Harriet Hale, born August 21, 1794, died January 29, 1882, daughter of Moses Hale, of Chelmsford, Massachusetts. Her father was a pioneer manufacturer. Children: 1. Henry H., linen manufacturer at Douglas, Massachusetts. 2. Charles A., born 1816; died at Ware, Massachusetts, April 7, 1892; began to make woolens at Ware in 1843 in partnership with George H. Gilbert; after ten years each partner continued by himself; married, April 20, 1842, Maria Tyler; represented his district in congress and in the governor's council; a Republican in politics; son Jonathan Tyler was also a prominent manufacturer of Ware. 3. Moses Tyler, mentioned below. 4. George, connected with the North Andover mills owned by his father; died in middle life. 5. Horace N., was connected with the Haverhill and North Andover mills; died in middle life. 6. Julia Maria, married Rev. Sylvan S. Hunting. 7. Catherine, married Hon. Oliver Stevens. 8. Ann Eliza, married John H. D. Smith.

(VII) Hon. Moses Tyler Stevens, son of Captain Nathaniel Stevens (6), was born in Andover, October 10, 1825. He was educated in the public schools, at Franklin Academy and Phillips Academy of Andover, taking one year in Dartmouth College. He left college to become associated in business with his father, learned every detail of the manufacture and marketing of flannel, and in 1850 was admitted to partnership by his father, under the name of Nathaniel Stevens & Son, which partnership lasted for a period of twenty-six years. The firm was dissolved in 1876, about ten years after the death of the senior partner, the business being continued by his brothers and himself separately. He then began to manufacture ladies' dress goods. In 1886 his sons Nathaniel and Samuel D. Stevens were admitted to partnership and the firm name M. T. Stevens & Sons adopted. In July, 1879, Mr. Stevens bought the Marland mills at Andover, established in 1834 by Abraham Marland, a native of Ashton parish, Lancashire, England, employing about one hundred and fifty hands and manufacturing about five hundred thousand pounds of wool yearly. The Stevens mills at Haverhill, Andover and North Andover were connected by telephone soon afterward, and the management made easier. The old mills at North Andover employ about a hundred hands, using over three hundred thousand pounds of wool yearly. The Stevens firm acquired another mill at Franklin Falls, New Hampshire. As a manufacturer of woolen goods Mr. Stevens ranks among the foremost in the country. He is president of the Stevens Linen Works, a corporation of

Webster, Massachusetts. He was conceded to be the owner of the largest private woolen establishment in the country.

Mr. Stevens was as prominent in public life as in the business world. He represented his district in the general court in 1861, and was state senator in 1868, serving on important committees. He was the first Democrat elected from his district to congress—the fifth district, formerly the eighth. In 1890 he defeated Frederick T. Greenhalge, an able and popular congressman, subsequently governor of Massachusetts. Mr. Stevens was placed on the ways and means committee and introduced the bill placing wool on the free list in the Fifty-second Congress. He was the most prominent American woolen manufacturer favoring free wool, and was a powerful factor in framing tariff legislation. He was reelected for the next term and again served on the ways and means committee. The following editorial from the influential Republican organ, the *Boston Journal,* shows his status in Congress: "Mr. Moses T. Stevens is the New England Democratic member of the ways and means committee. He holds his place securely, and the ingrate tariff reformers had better beware how they find fault with him. Their criticism will not injure Mr. Stevens; he is too strongly intrenched, but it may do harm to the Democratic party. Mr. Stevens is a tariff reformer to the extent of favoring free raw materials, and he also favors a protective duty on finished goods, i. e.: he represents what Governor Russell was protesting only two short months ago was the tariff policy of the national Democracy. Yet Mr. Stevens is now a target of sharp opposition from his party friends on the ground that he is too little of a tariff reformer to suit them and too much of a Protectionist."

Mr. Stevens has given freely to public and private charities. He contributed five thousand dollars to the Johnson high school building. He has aided the first and second parish churches generously. He is keenly interested in all that makes for the material and moral welfare of North Andover. He gave a free summer resort at Lake Cochickawick for the poor. He is a director and was formerly president of the Andover National Bank, trustee and formerly president of the Andover Savings Bank, and director of the Mutual Fire Insurance Company. In religion Mr. Stevens is a Unitarian, and is treasurer and one of the chief supporters of the North Parish church, North Andover, one of the oldest churches of New England. He was prominent in the Unitarian Club which has its home on Beacon street, Boston. He resides at North Andover.

He married, at North Andover, May 5, 1853, Charlotte Emeline, daughter of Isaac and Charlotte (Adams) Osgood. Their three sons became associated with their father as partners. Children, born at North Andover: Mary O.; Nathaniel, married Elizabeth White, of Haverhill; Samuel D.; Virginia; Helen; Moses Tyler.

SPRAGUE Edward Sprague (I), the English progenitor of this distinguished American family, was a resident of Upway, Dorsetshire, where he died in 1614. He was a fuller by trade. Earlier in life he lived at Fordington, Dorsetshire. He married and had children: Ralph, Alice, Edward, Richard, Christopher, William.

(II) William Sprague, son of Edward Sprague (I), was born in Dorsetshire, England. In Prince's Chronology we read: "Among those who arrived in Naumkeag (Salem) are Ralph Sprague with his brothers Richard and William, who with three or four more were by Governor Endicott employed to explore and take possession of the country to the westward. They traveled through the woods to Charlestown, on a neck of land called Mishawum, between Mystic and Charles river, full of Indians, named Aberginians, with whom they made peace." Hon. Edward Everett, in his address commemorative of the bi-centennial of the arrival of John Winthrop at Charlestown, said: "Ralph, Richard and William Sprague are the founders of the settlement in this place, and were persons of substance and enterprise, excellent citizens, generous public benefactors, and the head of a very large and respectable family of descendants." William Sprague remained in Charlestown until 1636, when he settled in Hingham, whither he went in a boat, landing on the east side of the cove, on a tract of land afterward granted to him by the town, and he became one of the first planters there. His house lot is said to have been the pleasantest in the town. Many grants of land were made to him from 1636 to 1647. He was elected selectman January 30, 1645, and at various later times; was treasurer in 1662; constable, fence viewer, etc., at various times. He deeded to his son Anthony, February 21, 1673, certain lands for six and thirty pounds of lawful money of New England and nine pounds in merchantable coin. His wife Millicent was admitted to the

Charlestown church, April 3, 1635. He died October 26, 1675. His will, dated October 19, 1675, bequeathed to wife Millicent; children Anthony, Samuel, William, John, Jonathan, Persis, wife of John Daggett; Johanna, wife of Caleb Church; and Mary, wife of Thomas King. He gave to Anthony the sword that was his brother Richard's. The widow died February 8, 1695-6. Children: 1. Anthony, born September 2, 1635; married Elizabeth, daughter of Robert Bartlett, of Plymouth. 2. John, baptized April, 1638; married, December 13, 1666, Elizabeth Holbrook. 3. Samuel, baptized May 24, 1640; removed to Marshfield, where he became secretary of the Plymouth colony and register of deeds before 1692. 4. Elizabeth, born 1641, baptized May 2, 1641. 5. Jonathan, baptized March 20, 1642; died July 4, 1647. 6. Persis, baptized November 12, 1643; married John Daggett. 7. Joanna, baptized December, 1645; married, December 16, 1667, Caleb Church. 8. Jonathan, born May 28, 1648; mentioned below. 9. William, born May 7, 1650; married Deborah, daughter of Andrew Lane, December 13, 1674. 10. Mary, baptized May 25, 1652; married Thomas King. 11. Hannah, baptized February 26, 1655; died March 31, 1658-9.

(III) Jonathan Sprague, son of William Sprague (2), was born in Hingham, Massachusetts, May 28, 1648. He married Mehitable, daughter of William and Elizabeth Holbook, and in 1672 they removed to Mendon. In 1675, when the Narragansett war drove the settlers from Mendon, he settled on a sixty acre lot of land left to him by his father in Providence, Rhode Island. He aided in surveying the eastern line of the colony. His was a strong, manly character, and was often honored with positions of trust and responsibility by his townsmen. He was a member of the house of deputies sixteen years between 1695 and 1714; was speaker of the house, 1703; member of the town council, 1705-12; clerk of the assembly in 1707. In 1703 he was appointed with two others to draw up rules for the procedure of the court of common pleas. The "Annals of Providence" say he was a decidedly religious man, professed the Baptist faith, and preached as an exhorter. He died in 1741. Children of Jonathan and Mehitable Sprague: 1. Jonathan, resided in Providence and Smithfield, Rhode Island, died April 22, 1764; married, November 28, 1699, Bethiah Mann, born March 12, 1683, died April 6, 1712; second, Hannah, widow of Stephen Hawkins. 2. William, born February 2, 1691; mentioned below. 3. Patience, born in Providence; married William Jenks. 4. Joanna; married John Taft, who died in 1762; she died in 1757. 5. Mary, married Daniel Brown. 6. Daughter, married Ebenezer Cook.

(IV) Captain William Sprague, son of Jonathan Sprague (3), was born February 2, 1691, and resided in Providence, Smithfield, Rhode Island. Smithfield was set off from Providence and incorporated as a town in 1730. Sprague was captain of a company in the Second Regiment of Providence in 1632. The "History of Woonsocket, R. I.," says: "For upwards of a century the Spragues were prominent actors in the religious and political history of old Springfield." He deeded much land to one cause and another, and large tracts to his children. He died in Smithfield in 1768. He married, September 16, 1714, Alice Brown, born May 31, 1691. Children: 1. Nehemiah, born January 5, 1717; mentioned below. 2. Alice (or Ales), born October 2, 1720. 3. Sarah, born February 10, 1722; married William Sly. 4. Samuel, born September 12, 1724. 5. Jetter, September 19, 1726. 6. Joshua, July 3, 1720; married Abigail Wilber.

(V) Nehemiah Sprague, son of Captain William Sprague (4), was born January 5, 1717; married, April 16, 1738, Mary Brown. Children: 1. Elias, born June 16, 1744; mentioned below. 2. Nehemiah, born January 20, 1750; died June, 1796. These brothers were farmers and both members of the Society of Friends.

(VI) Elias Sprague, son of Nehemiah Sprague (5), was born at Smithfield, Rhode Island, June 16, 1744; died in Douglas, Massachusetts, February 15, 1799. He removed to Douglas not later than 1788, at which time he deeded his homestead in Smithfield, Rhode Island, for three hundred and ninety pounds silver money, to Moses Ballou and John Coe. His will was dated March, 1798, and was proved May 7, 1799, his sons Stephen and Preserved being the executors. The inventory of the estate amounted to $5,838.52. He married Mercy, daughter of Joseph Bassett, August 5, 1764. She was sister of Alice Bassett, who married his brother, Nehemiah Sprague, Jr. Children of Elias and Mercy Sprague: 1. Jonathan, born December 9, 1765. 2. Theodate, January 4, 1768. 3. Amy, October 6, 1769. 4. Benjamin, April 10, 1771. 5. Lavinia, August 12, 1773. 6. Stephen, November 18, 1775; married Olive Seagrave. 7. Preserved, October 17, 1777; mentioned below. 8. Thankful, October 19, 1779. 9. William, June 3, 1782. 10. Alice, August 29, 1784. 11. Elias. 12. Lucina. 13. Child, unnamed.

(VII) Preserved Sprague, son of Elias Sprague (6), was born in Douglas, Massachusetts, October 17, 1777; removed to Lynn, about 1805, and there remained a resident for the rest of his life. He died December 18, 1846. He was a great-uncle of General Augustus B. R. Sprague, of Worcester; former sheriff of Worcester county, former mayor of Worcester, author of the "Sprague Genealogy" (1907). General Sprague was son of Lee and Lucia (Snow) Sprague, grandson of Jonathan and Patience Sprague, and great-grandson of Elias Sprague (6). Preserved Sprague married Joanna Trask, whose father was a man of substance, owning a mill and water power. The Trask family has been very prominent in Essex county, Massachusetts. Children of Preserved and Joanna Sprague: Lydia, Maria, Samson, Emma, William, Elijah, Benjamin, Mary, Henry, and two eldest, who died in infancy.

(VIII) Benjamin Sprague, son of Preserved Sprague (7), was born in Lynn, August 2, 1819, and was educated there in the public schools. When a young man he learned the trade of shoe making, the staple industry of his native city. In 1849 he gave up the shoe business to join the throng of gold-seekers, and made the voyage by way of the Isthmus of Panama to California, where he remained prospecting for four years. He returned to Lynn, and in 1855 began the business of shoe manufacturing in his native town. He was remarkably successful and having acquired a competence, retired from active business in 1869. Mr. Sprague has been a man of large influence and highly esteemed in the community in which he lives. He was a member of the board of aldermen from 1861 to 1865 during the trying period of the civil war. His home is at 145 Ocean street, Lynn. He married first, in 1839, Susan Emily Ireson. died 1858, daughter of Captain John and Eliza (Bulfinch) Ireson. They had six children, four of whom died in infancy. The two surviving were: 1. Charles Otis, born 1840, died 1887; married Mary Elizabeth Morrill; children: William Chase, George Everett. 2. Henry Breed, born September 27, 1854, married Laura L. Brown (see Brown family). Benjamin Sprague married second, 1867, Mary Jane, daughter of Aaron and Abigail (Eames) Pratt, of South Framingham, Massachusett. Of this marriage there was one child: Herbert, born March 19, 1872; died at age of seventeen months.

BROWN

In recent generations many of the descendants of the early families of Massachusetts have branched out in various lines of business, carved out fortunes, built up great industries, and developed a fine business talent which had been latent from lack of opportunity. Among that number was the late Joseph Gould Brown, for many years a well known resident of Lynn.

(I) Chad Brown, the ancestor, emigrated from England in the ship "Martin" which arrived in Boston, July, 1638. He was a surveyor and laid out the first house lots in Providence, of which city he was a most useful citizen, he was also a leader in the colony. In 1640 he served on a committee with three others regarding the disputed boundary between Providence and Pawtucket, and in 1642 was ordained as the first settled pastor of the Baptist church. In 1640 he with Robert Cole, William Harris and John Warner, were the committee of Providence colony who reported to them their first written form of government which was adopted and continued in force till 1644 when Roger Williams returned from England with the first charter. His name was the first of the thirty-nine signatures to this agreement. This instrument contains the arbitrary decision in which in later years, Roger Williams, in speaking of the dissensions which so disturbed the peace of the early colonists, referred to thus: "The truth is that Chad Brown, that holy man, now with God, and myself brought the remaining after comers and the first 12 to a oneness by arbitration." The exact date of his death is not known, but it is presumed he died about 1665. He was accompanied to this country by his wife Elizabeth, a son John, then eight years of age (see forward), also James, Jeremiah, Judah or Chad, died May 10, 1663, unmarried, and Daniel.

(II) John Brown, son of Chad and Elizabeth Brown, born 1630, died 1706. He married Mary, daughter of Rev. Obadiah and Catherine Holmes, of Newport, Rhode Island, where he resided at the North End in the house afterward occupied by his son, Elder James, near the junction of North Main and Randall streets. He was a surveyor of land and also surveyed for highways; was a member of the town council, and held a number of town offices. Children: Sarah, John, James, see forward; Obadiah, Martha, Mary, Deborah.

(III) James Brown, son of John and Mary (Holmes) Brown, born 1666, died October

28, 1732. He served as a member of the town council from 1705 to 1725, and from 1714 to 1718 as town treasurer; was pastor or elder of the First Baptist Church, associated with Elder Pardon Tillinghast, and in 1726 succeeded the Rev. Ebenezer Jenks, remaining its pastor until his death. He married, December 17, 1691, Mary, daughter of Andrew and Mary (Tew) Harris, granddaughter of William and Susanna Harris, also granddaughter of Richard and Mary (Clark) Tew. She was born December 17, 1761, died August 18, 1736. Children: John, James, Joseph, Martha, Andrew, Mary, Anna, Obadiah, Jeremiah, Elisha.

(IV) Elisha Brown, son of James and Mary (Harris) Brown, born May 25, 1717, died April 20, 1802. He was a prominent politician, a member of the general assembly and served as deputy governor of the colony of Rhode Island, 1765-66-67. He married Martha, born April 3, 1719, died September 1, 1760, daughter of John and Deborah (Angell) Smith, granddaughter of James and Abigail (Dexter) Angell, and great-granddaughter of the first Thomas Angell and Gregory Dexter. Children: 1. Deborah, born 1740, died July 7, 1745. 2. John, born January 28, 1742. 3. James, born April 27, 1744. 4. Jeremiah, born December 28, 1746. 5. Elisha, born June 1, 1749. 6. Isaac, born May 23, 1751. 7. Martha, born April 17, 1754, died June 27, 1755. 8. Smith, born April 12, 1756, see forward. 9. A daughter, born June 26, 1760, died aged seven days. Elisha Brown married second, February 22, 1761, Hannah, widow of Elisha Cushing and daughter of James Barker, of Newport. She was born May, 1721. One child, Martha, died at age of nine months.

(V) Smith Brown, son of Elisha and Martha (Smith) Brown, born April 12, 1756, died November 20, 1826. He married, October 12, 1785, Lydia, daughter of Samuel and Elizabeth (Barker) Gould, of Pembroke, Massachusetts, (Mrs. Sprague has their wedding certificate), and granddaughter of Isaac Barker. Children: 1. Samuel, born February 12, 1787, see forward. 2. Anna, born October 4, 1788, died June 6, 1813. 3. Gould, born March 7, 1791, died Lynn, March 31, 1857; married, November 8, 1842, Mary, daughter of Nathaniel Starbuck. 4. William D., born March 21, 1793. 5. Elizabeth, born May 10, 1795, died Lynn, November, 1823. 6. Lydia, born January 14, 1798, died Pembroke, November 22, 1883. She took an active interest in the anti-slavery society and taught for a time in the south, but later, because of failing health, returned north where she took an active part in all charitable movements. Of the thirty-five grandchildren of Elisha and Martha (Smith) Brown, eleven of whom died young, she was the youngest, but one, and the last survivor. The history of these grandchildren covers a period of one hundred and eighteen years from the birth of James in 1765 to the death of Lydia at the age of eighty-six in 1883. The *Woman's Journal* of December 22, 1883, contains the following, contributed by her nephew, William A. Brown: "She received a fair education at home and at the Friends' School, at Nine Partners, New York, where her eldest brother Samuel was a teacher and her second brother Gould, afterward so well known as the author of Brown's grammar, and a younger brother, the late Dr. William D. Brown, of Lynn, were scholars. She was a frequent contributor to the *Woman's Journal* for many years; one of the most advanced believers in the rights of woman to take her part in the management of human affairs and devoted much time, money and thought to the elevation of woman. Every benevolent, charitable and elevating object found in her an ardent supporter and firm friend, and no appeal to her kind heart was ever unheeded."

(VI) Samuel Brown, son of Smith and Lydia (Gould) Brown, born February 12, 1787, died August 19, 1868. He married, March 6, 1816, Maria, born December 1, 1792, died November 22, 1868, daughter of George Gorham and Lydia (Chase) Hussey, of Nantucket, Massachusetts, granddaughter of George and Deborah (Paddock) Hussey and of Francis and Naomi (Chase) Chase, and a descendant in the seventh generation of Tristram Coffin, one of the first proprietors of Nantucket, and its governor in 1671. Children: 1. Ann, born September 28, 1818, married, February 6, 1844, Joseph S. Barnard; he died January 21, 1885; two sons: George Albert, born January 11, 1845, and Edward Gould, born October 23, 1847. 2. Sarah Joy, born November 24, 1820. 3. Lydia Gould, born August 27, 1822, married, January 1, 1843, Nathaniel K. Randall; he died December 29, 1884; she died October 22, 1898; three children: i. Charles Franklin, born December 15, 1848, married, October 10, 1874, Mary Ann (Sterling) Doherty, of Louisiana, five children; ii. Elizabeth Chase, born March 14, 1852, died March 26, 1874; iii. Anna Gould, born September 4, 1863, died September 4, 1865. 4. Joseph Gould, born June 19, 1825, see forward. 5. Elizabeth, born August 25,

Joseph G. Brown

1827, married, October 13, 1854, Jabez Wood, of Acushnet, Massachusetts; she died June 25, 1868. 6. George Smith, born October 6, 1829. 7. William Austin, born October 11, 1832, married, May 23, 1859, Ann Maria Chase, daughter of Philip Chase; she was born October 13, 1830; residents of Lynn; four children: Samuel Gould, Abbie Chase, Alice, William Allerton. 8. Moses, born March 30, 1835, died December 28, 1861; was a graduate of the Chandler Scientific School of Dartmouth, New Hampshire, class of 1858.

(VII) Joseph Gould Brown, son of Samuel and Maria (Hussey) Brown, was born in Pembroke, Plymouth county, Massachusetts, June 19, 1825, died in Lynn, May 27, 1901. He received the greater part of his education at the district school in his own town, and this was supplemented by a course at the Friends' school in Providence, Rhode Island. After leaving school, like most young men, he felt that his energies demanded wider scope than was offered him on his father's farm, and he went to Wilmington, Delaware, where he entered into the hardware business. He gave it up, however, in 1862, and came to Lynn to engage in the manufacturing of shoes with his brother, William Austin Brown, under the firm name of Brown Brothers. Afterwards, and until the great fire of 1889, he conducted a large shoe business on his own account on the site of the present Brown building, which he erected after the destruction of a former one built by his brother and himself. In politics Mr. Brown was a staunch Republican, and was elected by that party in 1896-97 to represent wards two and four of Lynn in the state legislature. During his first term he was a member of the joint standing committee on printing, and the following year served as house chairman of that committee and also a member of the committee on liquor laws. In 1898 he served the city as an alderman from ward four and was twice re-elected. In both of these public offices Mr. Brown displayed his uncompromising fidelity to what he believed to be for the good of the people, and his successive elections to the legislature and city council indicate the esteem in which he was held by his fellow citizens. For many years, and up to the time of his death, he was one of the trustees of the Nathan Breed estate of Lynn, the duties of which he performed with faithfulness and exactness to the last. Mr. Brown's parents were Quakers, of which society he remained a lifelong member, being a constant attendant at the services, and holding the office of treasurer of the Lynn meeting until within a few months of his death, when his failing health obliged him to resign it. He was a member of the Lynn Historical Society, and was always deeply interested in everything connected with the welfare of the city of his adoption.

Mr. Brown married, December 30, 1854, Katherine Murray Bostwick, of New York, born June 14, 1832, who survives him. Her maternal grandfather was a Huguenot, whose life having been repeatedly threatened, fled with his family to America during the French revolution. Children: 1. Maria H., born March 13, 1856, in Wilmington, Delaware, married, October 29, 1878, Charles J. H. Woodbury, of Lynn; children: i. Emma Louise, born October 26, 1879; ii. Laura B., April 13, 1881; iii. Alice P., October 26, 1883. 2. Laura L., born December 21, 1858, married, October 26, 1880, Henry B. Sprague, born September 27, 1854; children: i. Howard B., born November 3, 1895; ii. Charles H., November 12, 1897. 3. Cora E., born July 18, 1863, married, January 22, 1890, Grant S. Hilton, of Swampscott; child, Adrienne C., born May 21, 1892. 4. Mary Emma, born December 9, 1864, married, March 22, 1892, Nelson A. Hallett, of Newton Centre; child, Joseph Gould, born August 6, 1894. 5. Bethany S., born January 10, 1871, in Lynn. (See Sprague).

HILTON

Edward Hilton (I), one of the pioneers in New Hampshire, was born in England. The Hilton family is of old English origin. He came with his brother, William Hilton, and Mr. David Thompson, all fishmongers from London, to begin a plantation at Piscataqua in 1623. The place of settlement was at Dover Neck, seven miles from Portsmouth, in the limits of New Hampshire. They were sent over by the proprietor of Laconia not only to fish, but to plant vineyards, discover mines, etc. Exhaustive search of the records of the Fishmongers Company of London by Charles H. Pope in 1907 failed to reveal the names of the three men, but a tax roll of London, made in 1641, brought to light by Mr. Gerald Fothergill (See New Eng. Reg. lxi), gives the name of Edward Hilton in the list of fishmongers, with the memorandum "Newe England" after it. This indicates that he had certainly been in business in London and had continued the sale and shipment of fish to a recent date. No trace of his native parish or his ancestry have been found, nor the name of his first wife. Edward Hilton was the leader of the little plantation and received the patent for the land—the Squamscott Patent, as it was called, including what is now known as Dover, Durham, Stratham and parts of Newington and Greenland, etc. The council for New England "for and in consideration that Edward Hilton and his Associates hath already sundry servants to plant in New England at a point called by the natives Wecanacohunt otherwise Hilton's Point, lying some two leagues from the mouth of the river Piscataquack * * * where they have already built some houses and planted corne, And for that he doth further intend by Divine Assistance to transport thither more people and cattle * * * a work which may especially tend to the propagation of Religion and to the great Increase of Trade" * * * convey to him "all that part of the River Pascataquack called or known by the name of Wecanacohunt or Hilton's Point * * * with the south side of the River and three miles into the Maine land by all the breadth aforesaid," etc. Possession was given in the name of the council by Captain Thomas Wiggin and others July 7, 1631. (Sup. Court files. New Eng. Reg. xxiv, 264). Part of this land was sold to individual settlers, part to the Lords Say and Brook and some to New England gentlemen. Mr. Hilton made his home after some time at Exeter and signed the petition of its inhabitants in the year 1642. In the same year he was appointed by the Massachusetts Bay government one of the local associate justices of the court, sitting with the magistrates on the highest questions and acting by themselves in cases not beyond certain limits. The general court held him to be exempt from taxation on account of this office, in 1669. He filled many other important positions and was highly honored in the colonies. The records of Exeter show that he was settled and had a house in that part of Exeter which is now South Newfields, as early as December, 1639. A large grant of land had been made to him by the Exeter authorities "on the 4 day of the 1st week of the 10th month 1639—December 4, 1639." In 1653 another grant of about two miles square, comprising the whole village of Newfields, was made to him in return for his setting up a saw-mill, and a considerable part of this later grant has remained to this day in the possession of his descendants. He was selectman of Exeter from 1645 nearly every year up to 1652. In 1657 he was one of the committee of two from Exeter to meet the committee of three from Dover to settle the bounds between the two towns by marking the line, and agreed upon the enjoyment that each town should have, of the border land. He has been called "The Father of New Hampshire." He died early in 1671. Administration on his estate was granted to his sons Edward, William, Samuel and Charles, March 6, 1670-71; the claims of two daughters were presented by Christopher Palmer; widow's dower was fixed at thirty pounds a quarter.

A possible clue to the English ancestry of Hilton is found in the record of a suit brought in the Piscataqua court by William Hilton, April 4, 1642, respecting a payment to "Mr. Richard Hilton of Norwich (Northwich)." Mr. H. F. Waters found a record at Wotten-under-edge, Gloucestershire, England, of the baptism of a child of Richard Hilton, "coming out of New England."

William Hilton came to America in the "Fortune" to Plymouth in November, 1621; his wife and children came in the ship "Anne" in 1623 and land was assigned to Hilton and family that year; he wrote soon after his arrival a letter of great historical and personal interest, published by Captain John Smith in his "New England Trialls" in the edition of 1622; he removed to New Hampshire and lived near his brother at Dover; then at Kittery, Maine, and later at York, Maine; carried on a ferry; kept a public house; was selectman, etc.; died before June 30, 1656, when his widow's second husband, Richard White, administered the estate.

Edward Hilton brought a wife to America with him, or married soon after coming, but her maiden name is not known. He married second, Jane Shapleigh, daughter of Hon. Alexander Shapleigh, agent of Sir Ferdinando Gorges in Maine, widow of James Treworgie, of Kittery, Maine. Children, all by first wife: 1. Edward, born 1626, mentioned below. 2. Captain William, born about 1628, died 1690; he married Rebecca Symmons, daughter of John Symmons, of Kittery, Maine; she died September 8, 1701, leaving sons Richard and Jonathan, perhaps others. 3. Samuel, of whom nothing further is known. 4. Charles, born 1643, died in 1683. 5. Susanna, who married, November 7, 1650, Christopher Palmer; she died January 9, 1716. 6. Sobriety, born about 1633, died January 31, 1718; married, November 20, 1651, Henry Moulton.

(II) Edward Hilton, son of Edward Hilton, was born in 1626 at Dover, New Hampshire. He removed to Exeter. He made a large purchase of Nadononamin or John Johnson, sagamore of Washucke and there dwelling, who as well for the love he bore the English generally and especially Edward Hilton, of Pascataqua, eldest son of Edward Hilton of the same Piscataqua, gentleman, and for divers other reasonable causes and considerations deeded all his lands between the two branches of the Lampreel river, called Washucke river, about six miles and a neck of land reserving half if need be of convenient planting land during grantor's life. This land is believed to be in the present towns of Newmarket, Epping and Lee, New Hampshire.

He married Ann Dudley, who was born October 16, 1641, at Salisbury, Massachusetts, daughter of Rev. Samuel Dudley, of Exeter, New Hampshire, and granddaughter of Governor Thomas Dudley, of the Massachusetts Bay colony. His wife, Mary (Winthrop) Dudley, was daughter of Governor John Winthrop, second governor of Massachusetts Bay. (See sketches of the Dudley and Winthrop families in this work). Edward Hilton died April 28, 1699. Children: 1. Winthrop, born about 1671, leader in the military affairs of New Hampshire; commander of its forces; judge of the court of common pleas; councillor of the province; killed by the Indians June 23, 1710, and buried in his own field on the west bank of the river; married Ann Wilson, daughter of Humphrey Wilson and Judith (Hersey) Wilson. 2. Dudley, resided in Exeter, now South Newmarket; was taken captive at the time his brother was killed; married Mercy Hall, daughter of Judge Kinsley Hall, of Dover, New Hampshire. 3. Joseph, born about 1681, mentioned below. 4. Jane, married Richard Mattoon, of Newmarket. 5. Ann, married Richard Hilton, son of William and Rebecca (Symmons) Hilton. 6. Mary, born 1677, died June 13, 1723; she married Thomas Bradbury. 7. Sobriety, married Jonathan Hilton, son of William and Rebecca (Symmons) Hilton. 8. Judith, died in infancy. 9. Bridget, died in infancy.

(III) Ensign Joseph Hilton, son of Edward Hilton (2), was born in 1681 and died in 1765, aged eighty-four years. He was a farmer at Exeter. He married first, Hannah Jose, daughter of Richard Jose, of Portsmouth. He married second, October 10, 1716, Mrs. Rebecca (Atkinson) Adams, daughter of John and Sarah (Merrick) Atkinson. Child of first wife: 1. Hannah, born August 11, 1710. Children of second wife: 2. Israel, born October 11, 1717, went south, settled in Virginia where he founded the town of Hilton, he was a blacksmith. 3. Ensign Joseph, born in 1720, settled in North Carolina. 4. Theodore Atkinson, mentioned below. 5. Dudley, born October 4, 1725, married Sarah Taylor and lived at Newmarket; died January 5, 1800; children: i. Dudley, lived at Parsonsfield, Maine; ii. Daniel, lived in Newmarket; iii. George, lived in Newmarket; iv. Ward, lived in Newmarket; v. Nathan, lived in Deerfield, New Hampshire; vi. Ann, married Major William Norris.

(IV) Theodore Atkinson Hilton, son of Ensign Joseph Hilton, was born at Exeter in 1721 and died there in 1765. He lived at Newmarket. He married Mary Sinclair, daughter of Richard and Katherine (Stevens) Sinclair, of Stratham, New Hampshire. Children: 1. Colonel Joseph, born in Epping, New Hampshire, June 13, 1747, died November 16, 1826; lived at Deerfield; married, in 1770, Sarah Thurston. 2. Mary, born July 16, 1749, died January 5, 1829; married, in 1768, John Marston. 3. Richard, mentioned below. 4. William, born August 15, 1759; lived in Cornville, Maine; married second, Annie Allen, of Augusta, Maine. 5. Sarah, born January 9, 1762. 6. Nathaniel, born March 17, 1764; resided at Portsmouth, New Hampshire.

(V) Richard Hilton, son of Theodore Hilton, was born at Newmarket, July 6, 1752, died at Shapleigh, Maine, where he was one of the early settlers. He settled on Hilton's Ridge in the south part of the town, where he cleared the land and built a log cabin. About 1795 he built a frame house. He was considered a prosperous farmer. He married Temperance Richards, probably born at Ossipee, New Hampshire. Children, all born at Shapleigh: 1. Winthrop, mentioned below. 2. Theodore, married at Wiscasset, Maine, Lydia Stetson. 3. Richard, born July 10, 1784, died September 7, 1868; married first, Sarah Goodrich; children: i. Joseph, born June 7, 1806, died unmarried; ii. Richard, born June 4, 1808, died September 25, 1888, married first, November 25, 1832, Nancy Dore, and second, February 23, 1842, Eunice Wentworth, born January 8, 1810, died December 21, 1882, daughter of James and Lydia (Pierce) Wentworth, and had Joseph N., born November 13, 1833, died February 26, 1846, Sarah P., born January 20, 1835, (married E. D. Whitehouse), Samuel D., born March 20, 1838, died February 23, 1846, Lydia A., born December

3, 1840, died February 19, 1846); children of second wife: i. James F., born February 26, 1843 (married, 1876, Mrs. Emma Chick Fall, born January 13, 1847, daughter of Amasa and Leonora E. Fall, of Moultonville, New Hampshire; children; i. Achsa E., born July 27, 1879, married, October 7, 1899, Frank A. Fernald, son of Tobias and Lavinia (Dore) Fernald and had Gladys M. Fernald, born September 10, 1901; ii. Newell Chick, born October 4, 1880, married, July 20, 1902, Elizabeth M. Webster, daughter of Horace F. and Ada L. Hobbs; iii. Jennie May, born August 27, 1876, married August 8, 1896, George H. Thurley, born November 9, 1872, son of George H. and Annie P. (Hanson) Thurley; iv. Richard George, born October 11, 1887, married, December 26, 1901, Elizabeth P. Johnson; v. Edward F., born August 15, 1889); ii. George Albert, born October 1, 1845, died October 12, 1884, (married, November 9, 1869, Susan Clementine Nutter, born July 26, 1847, daughter of Moses and Louisa Chick, of Tuftonborough, and had Lura May, born February 3, 1870); iii. Richard S., born December 20, 1847, died February 19, 1851; iv. Joseph F., born February 23, 1849, (married first, May 10, 1872, Mary Etta Neal, daughter of Tyler R. and Mary E. Neal; married second, July 4, 1880, Elizabeth Drake, daughter of Charles and Maria Drake); v. Smith C., born July 17, 1852, died September 18, 1875, (married, May 9, 1872, Sarah J. Bodge, born April 19, 1860, died September 5, 1898, daughter of James R. and Betsey Bodge; children: i. Emma F., born April 2, 1873, married, July 5, 1892, Fred M. Canney, born February 27, 1866, son of Henry and Sarah (Weeks) Canney, and had Karen L. Canney, born March 31, 1893, and Forest F. Canney, born July 19, 1894;) ii. Charles L., born July 5, 1874, (married, September 16, 1897, Sarah J. Hutchins, daughter of Frederick and Abbie Jane (Daggett) Hutchins); iii. Hannah, born at Rochester, New Hampshire, September, 1812, died February 15, 1866, married Smith L. Cotton, born 1805, died May 24, 1864; iv. Sarah, born at Ossipee, New Hampshire, February 18, 1820, died at Rochester, New Hampshire, January 9, 1891, married, April 27, 1847, John R. McDuffee, born March 13, 1818, died January 10, 1865, son of Seth and Lucy McDuffee, of Rochester, and had Dana H. McDuffee, born December 25, 1848, (married, September 30, 1869, Fannie Foss, daughter of Robert N. and Sarah A. Foss, of Rochester), John H. McDuffee, born August 18, 1850, John N. McDuffee, born April 7, 1861, and Herman A. McDuffee. 4. Sarah, married Thomas Shorey, born 1771, died April 10, 1864, and had David, Rebecca, Ezekiel, Sarah, Eliza, (married Thomas Appleby), Temperance, Mary, Thomas Hilton, Jason I., Thankful and Moses W. Shorey. 5. Polly or Mary, married Ichabod Shorey. 6. Temperance, baptized September 12, 1784, married Elisha Goodrich.

(VI) Winthrop Hilton, son of Richard Hilton, was born at Shapleigh, Maine, and died at Acton (Shapleigh), November 12, 1861. He was a farmer of Shapleigh and owned a farm of about two hundred acres, much of which was good timber land, adjoining that of his son Andrew. He was also a carpenter and blacksmith by trade, and had shops for both trades on his farm. In politics he was a Democrat, and attended the Union Church at Shapleigh. He was a firm believer in the Bible, which he read carefully and studiously, and he was considered an authority on scriptural matters in that section. He was upright and honorable, and a good citizen in every sense of the word. He married Mary Drew, born 1777, died January 4, 1856, daughter of Benjamin and Nancy (Savage) Drew. Her father died 1820 and her mother was said to have been the first woman who rode on horseback on the same horse with her husband into the new town of Acton, Maine. Children: 1. Nathaniel, born April 9, 1797, died March 21, 1888; married, October 5, 1828, Hannah Wentworth, born June 22, 1801, died April 13, 1884, daughter of Gershom and Abigail Wentworth, of Lebanon, Maine. 2. Sophia, born June, 1799, died unmarried November 10, 1890. 3. John, born December 5, 1802, died at St. Albans, Maine, May 25, 1889; married Maria Ricker, born August 19, 1802, died June 27, 1871; children: i. Abigail, born June 11, 1824, married Samuel Withee and had Mary R. Withee, born January 20, 1846, (married Joseph Mitchell, who died February, 1897), George Withee, born December 14, 1848, died December 15, 1850, Llewelyn Withee, born July 11, 1851, (married Flora Welch), Maria Withee, born March 27, 1853, (married Haskell Welch), Samuel Withee, born May 10, 1855, died December, 1859, and Sumner C. Withee, born February 28, 1860, (married Grace Eldridge); ii. Mary, married Samuel Hartwell and had John Hartwell, born September 21, 1847, died May, 1865, Jane Hartwell, born March 12, 1849, (married John Robinson) and reside at Palmyra,

Maine; Eliza Hartwell, born July 15, 1850, (married Belden Southard), William Hartwell, born August 10, 1852, (married Georgie Powell), Charles Hartwell, born May 12, 1854, (married Annie Gahame), Thomas Hartwell, born May 8, 1856, (married Flora Brackett), Victoria N. Hartwell, born December 8, 1858, (married Leslie Johonnott), Mary Hartwell, born May 21, 1860, died August 12, 1876, Luella Hartwell, born April 12, 1862, (married Bonaparte Forbush), Hiram Hartwell, born April 16, 1863, (married Frances Bellyea), and Leslie Hartwell, born April 10, 1869, (married Edna Battie); iii. Jane, married George Morse and had Frederick Morse, born June 17, 1851, died August 12, 1863, Ella Morse, born October 18, 1852, died October 26, 1886, Abbie Morse, born May 14, 1854, (married Frank Southard), Emma Morse, born March 12, 1856, Nellie Morse, born May 7, 1858, Frank Morse, born March 17, 1860, Jennie Morse, born March 2, 1862, died March 18, 1883, Fred Morse, born August 16, 1864, (married Belle Randlette), and Minnie Morse, born July 4, 1866; iv. Goodwin, born June 18, 1832, now resides at Fruitvale, California, married Rosella Maria Gordon, daughter of John and Rosella M. (Bateman) Gordon, and had Anson, born February 28, 1859, now practicing attorney at Fruitvale, California, (married Nancy Garside, daughter of George and Ann Cheetham, and had Harold, born June 10, 1889, and Nadine, born January 6, 1901), and Alice, born June 16, 1867, (married Edward Longley, son of Roscoe and Mary (Smith) Longley); v. Eliza, married Hiram Martin, of St. Albans, Maine; vi. Nancy, married ——— Whitney and had Wallace E. Whitney, born June 2, 1863, (married Mary Rand). 4. Joseph, born November 13, 1803, died January 19, 1861; married Jane (Bickford) Downes, widow, born November, 1807, died October 31, 1886, daughter of Moses and Lydia Bickford; child: Charles E., born April 26, 1833, died August 26, 1849. 5. James, born October 20, 1806, died December 21, 1873; married first, Jane Tash, of New Durham, and had Malvina and Jane Adeline, both died young; married second, September 23, 1855, Adeline Pike, daughter of David D. and Sarah Woodman, of Middleton, New Hampshire. 6. Nancy, married Arthur Gage, of Lancaster, New Hampshire; children: i. Eliza Gage, married Benjamin Perkins and had Charles, Laura and Albert Perkins; ii. Mary Ann Gage, married ——— Buzzell; iii. Sarah Gage; iv. Susan Gage, married William F. Derby. 7. Andrew, born September 10, 1810, mentioned below. 8. Mary, born 1812, died 1860; married Luther Drew, born 1810, died 1859; children: i. Albert Drew, born 1840, died 1856; ii. Sarah Jane Drew, born 1842, died 1848. 9. Eliza, born 1815, married Ruel Cummings and had Walter Cummings. 10. William, born November 27, 1819, died July 19, 1885; married first, Abigail Lazell, of Bellingham, Massachusetts, born April 17, 1821, died October 13, 1841, daughter of Warren and Betsey (Walker) Lazell; married second, November 9, 1842, Betsey E. Adams, born December 18, 1825, died September 3, 1894, daughter of John and Persis Wheeler, of Bellingham; child of first wife: i. Elizabeth Jane, born June 15, 1840, married, December 25, 1871, Pardon A. Cook, who with his family resides in San Francisco, California; he was born January 23, 1822, died December 22, 1901, son of Avery and Charlotte Cook, of West Wrentham, Massachusetts, and had Alvira Lizzie Cook, born March 11, 1873, died December 31, 1885, Lara Ardelia Cook, born August 23, 1874, Avie Emma Cook, born January 29, 1876, died August 10, 1876, Alice Maria Cook, born September 16, 1878, (married, June 26, 1901, Robert T. Swan), Inez Almira Cook, born January 20, 1880, (married, April 23, 1902, Dr. Paul B. Noble); children of second wife: ii. Sophia A., born October 24, 1843, died August 22, 1871, married first, March 20, 1860, John Treen, who was killed in the civil war at battle of Antietam in 1862, married second, ——— Cobb; iii. Mary A., born June 2, 1845, married, July 14, 1862, William P. Fiske, a resident of Springvale, Maine, and had Lizzie, George and Ulysses Fiske; iv. Etta M., born December 17, 1847, married, September 21, 1870, John R. Butler, born August 30, 1849, a resident of Lebanon, Maine, and had Alice M. and Ruth B. Butler; v. William H., born February 8, 1849, a resident of Milford, Massachusetts; married, June, 1873, Ida Marsh, of New Jersey, and had Lizzie H., Susie, Asa and Clarence; vi. Phebe A., born December 10, 1852, died January 17, 1873, married, December 5, 1869, Dexter L. Kennie, of Sanford, Maine, and had George and Etta M. Kennie; vii. John A., born December 17, 1855, a resident of Milford, Massachusetts; married, August 5, 1877, Alice M. Littlefield and had Grace B., born March 1, 1881, Charles S., born December 27, 1883, Evelyn, born February 11, 1886, Arthur W., born July 17, 1888, Ernest L., born January 22, 1894, and Howard E., born June 12, 1898; viii. Evelyn E., born September 2, 1859, married, May 6, 1880, William L. Godding, of Acton, Maine, born June 12, 1858, and had Raymond L. Godding; ix. Persis E., born August 19, 1861, married, July 1, 1886, Andrew J. Fernald, of North Berwick, Maine, born January 8, 1854; x. Carrie F., born May 3, 1865, married, June 23, 1884, E. Trebor, born October 27, 1862.

(VII) Andrew Hilton, son of Winthrop Hilton, was born at Shapleigh, Maine, September 10, 1810, died at Middleton, New Hampshire, December 27, 1873. He was brought up on his father's farm and besides the ordinary schooling he studied mechanics and astronomy by himself, and became a self-educated man. He was a great reader, and improved all his spare time. He learned the trade of millwright, serving his apprenticeship with Moses Paul, who later became his father-in-law. He subsequently engaged in the millwright business, taking contracts for the building of dams, the erection of mills and machinery, and doing a general business. Early in the forties he went to Havana, Cuba, to superintend mill installment, spending a year in that country. His farm was at Hilton Ridge, adjoining that of his father. It was extensive, containing about two hundred and fifty acres, being land bought of Asa Drew, Nathaniel Hilton, and part being the Prescott farm and the McCrillis farm. This farm he held for his children, who did most of the work there, as he spent most of his time in his business. He was a member of the Free Will Baptist Union Church and was a free thinker in religion. In politics he was a staunch Democrat and a warm supporter and admirer of President Jackson. He served in the state militia. He loved music and for a number of years played in the Shapleigh band. He was an earnest advocate of temperance and other reforms. He was self-possessed and at times stern and reserved in his manner, but he appreciated a joke and had a great fund of humor. Upright and honorable in every walk of life, a keen observer, a careful investigator, a useful citizen, he was a strong man in his day, possessing a wide and wholesome influence in the community.

He married Ann Eliza Paul, born at Shapleigh, Maine, October 4, 1816, died at Lewiston, Maine, October 24, 1891, daughter of Moses and Susannah (Fox) Paul. Her father was a native of Kittery, Maine, a farmer and millwright: her mother was of Lee, New Hampshire. Children, all born at Acton, Maine: 1. Mary, born January 22, 1835, died June 11, 1838. 2. John Paul, born May 3, 1836, died at Malden, Massachusetts, May 18, 1895; married, 1861, Mary Abbie Mudgett, of Acton, born September, 1835, daughter of Samuel and Nancy (Cram) Mudgett, of Freemont. New Hampshire; had no children. 3. James Madison, born February 13, 1838, mentioned below. 4. Abbie Ann, born August 3, 1839, married, December 24, 1859, Ezekiel Ancill Prescott, of Acton, born December 5, 1831, son of Ezekiel and Betsey (Worcester) Prescott: the father a native of Epping, New Hampshire, the mother of Berwick, Maine; children: i. Charles Elmer Prescott, born November 1, 1861, married, December 26, 1885, Lillian Picott, daughter of Orin Picott, of Kittery, Maine, and his wife, Melissa (Paul) Picott, of Eliot, Maine; child, Arthur Prescott, born July 9, 1888; ii. Jennie Hilton Prescott, born May 9, 1866, died May 26, 1869; iii. Marshall Leonard, born August 11, 1869, died May 9, 1894; iv. John Andrew Prescott, born March 16, 1874, died September 2, 1877. 5. Eliza Jane, born February 28, 1841, married, November 24, 1866, Thomas J. Roberts, of Milton, New Hampshire, born December 20, 1833, son of Nicholas H. and Dorothy (Hurd) Roberts; children: i. Dora Etta Roberts, born April 22, 1872, graduate of Bates College, now engaged in a clerical capacity in the Massachusetts General Hospital; ii. John Hilton Roberts, born March 9, 1875, married, January 29, 1902, Alice C. Laskey, of Milton, Maine, daughter of John S. and Sarah Abbie (Vinal) Laskey, of Dover, New Hampshire, and had Luther Hilton Roberts, born August, 1906. 6. Joseph Fullonton, born October 7, 1842, owner and proprietor of the Wiley House, at Oak Bluffs, Massachusetts, and for over thirty-five years has owned and conducted business in the stalls at 5 and 7 in the Quincy market, in Boston; married, September 26, 1866, Abbie J. Grant, born February 8, 1844, at Acton, Maine, daughter of John and Charlotte (Durgin) Grant, of Newfield, Maine: children: i. George Albert, born April 10, 1869, graduate of the Massachusetts Institute of Technology; died June 24, 1890; ii. Clarence, born July 1, 1871, died July, 1872; iii. Joseph Myron, born July 3, 1876, died March, 1877; iv. Florence, born June 3, 1878, married, June 30, 1902, Herbert Mann Chase, of Randolph, Massachusetts, now a practicing attorney of Boston, son of Dr. Augustus L. and Mary Louise (Mann) Chase, and had son, George Hilton Chase, born at Cambridge,

April 26, 1904. 7. Charles Albert, born May 2, 1856, was for several years mayor of Tama City, of Iowa, and now resides at Modesto, California, where he owns a large fruit ranch; married first, August 15, 1878, Sadie Noyes Prescott, born at Acton, October 7, 1856, died at Acton, June 13, 1879, daughter of George W. and Eliza B. Brackett, of Acton; married, second, February 6, 1883, Ida M. Rhoades, born December 20, 1856, daughter of Levi L. and Catherine McAnulty, of Pennsylvania; child of first wife, Leroy Prescott, born June 12, 1879, married, October 5, 1901, Mary Addie Coffin, and have Lucile Mary, born December 2, 1902; children of second wife: ii. Edna B., born June 14, 1884, died at Tama City, Iowa, September 10, 1884; iii. Anna C., born September 15, 1885, died October 17, 1886; iv. Charles R., born September 16, 1889; v. Fred W., born June 4, 1891; vi. Frank Drew, born October 30, 1895. 8. Luther Drew, born November 30, 1858, died at Bell Plain, Iowa, March 6, 1894; married, September 1, 1880, Clara Georgietta Prescott, born at Acton, June 10, 1860, daughter of George W. and Eliza B. Brackett; she now resides in North Carolina.

(VIII) James Madison Hilton, son of Andrew Hilton, was born at Acton, Maine, February 13, 1838, on what is known as Hilton's Ridge, where his great-grandfather settled in the south part of the town. His schooling was limited to the district school on the Ridge, supplemented by a course at the New Hampshire Institute at New Hampton, New Hampshire. From early youth he worked on his father's farm. He left home when he came of age and entered the employ of James Viles, a dealer in provisions on Cambridge street, Boston. After a short time he became a clerk in the employ of Elisha Shapleigh Stacy, dealer in meats and provisions, 6 and 8 Quincy Market, Boston, where he worked until he enlisted.

In August, 1862, he was mustered into the Eleventh Massachusetts Battery (unattached) under Captain Edward J. Jones, later attached to the Eighteenth Army Corps. He was stationed with his battery at Centerville Heights, Maryland, at the fortifications built by the Confederate generals, Johnson and Beauregard, and the battery was entrenched there from January to May, 1863, when it was relieved by the Ninth Massachusetts Battery. He received an honorable discharge and was mustered out at Boston in May, 1863. The battery was called out to quell the draft riot in Cooper street, Boston, afterward.

He returned to the provision business as a clerk for the firm of Dyer & Frost, remaining until September, 1863, when he and his brother, John P. Hilton, purchased a butter, egg and cheese business in Faneuil Hall Market and engaged in business under the firm name of J. P. & J. M. Hilton. The success that attended their enterprise warranted an extension. Accordingly they rented the cellar of E. H. Walker in the same building and sold their rights in their stall to Moses Paul. After twelve more years of successful business in the cellar store, the brothers sold their rights and removed to 38, 39, 40 South Market and 14 Chatham streets, continuing in the same line of business. In 1895 the senior partner died, and the surviving partner admitted Andrew Nimmo to the firm. After a short time this copartnership was dissolved and Mr. Hilton entered partnership with Captain Harrison Aldrich under the firm name of the Hilton & Aldrich Company, under Massachusetts corporation laws, with Mr. Hilton president and Mr. Aldrich treasurer. After three years Mr. Hilton bought out his partner and had since had his son, Everett Stacy Hilton, in partnership with him. Besides the provision business in Boston, the firm has had creameries for making butter at Tama City, Chelsea and Gladbrook, Iowa, and at Lowell, Michigan, with a total capacity of a million pounds of butter annually. The Cloverdale Creamery Company, the retail department of the Hilton-Aldrich Company, was incorporated under Massachusetts laws with headquarters in Boston, having thirty-two retail stores in Massachusetts, Rhode Island, New Hampshire and Connecticut, dealing in tea and coffee, as well as cheese, butter and eggs. The president of the company is A. P. Lee, the treasurer, Frank Herman Hilton: both being the directors. On account of ill health Mr. Hilton retired from active business in 1906, residing at 20 Cushing avenue, Belmont, Massachusetts, an estate that he bought in 1903.

Mr. Hilton had always been keenly interested in business and he was exceedingly active and industrious while in active life. He laid the foundation for a very extensive and prosperous business, and had every reason to be proud of the growth and high standing of the concerns that he founded. He was naturally domestic in his tastes and greatly devoted to his home and family. He remembered with pleasure his boyhood on the farm and tells many interesting stories of his early life. He was a member of the Tremont Temple Baptist Church of Boston, treasurer of the church and of the building, and had been deacon for the past twenty years. In politics he was a Republican, but had never been an active partisan and never sought public office. He was a member of Massachusetts Lodge of Free Masons, Boston; of Odd Fellows, Boston; of the Baptist Social Club, of Boston; of the Home Market Club, of Boston; formerly a member of the Old Produce Exchange; trustee of the Evangelical Baptist and Benevolent and Missionary Society of Tremont Temple and one of the managing committee of five of the society. Mr. Hilton died September 12, 1908.

He married, October 16, 1868, Mary Etta Frances Stacy, born at Acton, Maine, January 11, 1848, daughter of Elisha Shapleigh and Ann Maria (Hubbard) Stacy, of Acton. Her father was a provision merchant in Faneuil Hall Market, Boston. Children: 1. Everett Stacy, born at Boston, September 14, 1869, married, October 2, 1893, Augusta Gassett, born January 17, 1870, at Lunenburg, Massachusetts, daughter of Charles and Harriet Freeman; her father was born at Hancock, New Hampshire, her mother at Boston; children: i. Thelma, born at Van Wert, Ohio, November 25, 1894; ii. Leone, born at Cambridge, May 25, 1896; iii. Doris, born at Somerville, December 1, 1898. 2. Etta Frances, born at Boston, November 4, 1871, married, May 2, 1895, William Faxon Pierce, born at Cambridge, July 20, 1870, son of James Pierce, of Cambridge, and his wife Anna (Billings) Pierce, of Milford; children: i. Carl Hilton Pierce, born at Somerville, March 6, 1896; ii. Ralph Wilson Pierce, born August 29, 1900; iii. Lillian Stacy Pierce, born February 9, 1902. 3. John Paul, born at Cambridge, June 11, 1873, an officer of the Cloverdale Company. 4. Frank Herman, born at Cambridge, July 27, 1875, treasurer of the Cloverdale Company; he married, September 11, 1908, Olive Whiteley, of Kansas City, Missouri, born December 1, 1887.

TUCKER There were numerous pioneers of the Tucker family in New England during the first fifty years of its settlement, and there are evidences that many if not all of them were related. Robert Tucker came to Wentworth, Massachusetts, lived for a time at Gloucester, and finally settled in Milton. A full sketch of him appears elsewhere in this work. Richard Tucker came from Stagumbery, Somersetshire, England, and settled among the first at Falmouth (now Portland, Maine); married Margaret Reynolds, and his daughter Seaborn married Nicholas Hodge, of Portsmouth, but he left no male descendants. Richard owned mills at Newichawannock in 1657. William Tucker lived in Maine; his wife Grace was living in 1665; his estate was administered by Nathaniel Fryer in 1666.

(I) John Tucker, a fisherman of the Isle of Shoals, died in 1670, and left all his property to John Ameredith and wife Joanna.

(I) Lewis Tucker, the first permanent settler of this family, at Kittery, Maine, had brothers John and Richard. Lewis and John were early at Falmouth, but removed to Kittery. Lewis was a fisherman at the Isle of Shoals and came to Kittery about 1680. He married Sarah Gunnison daughter of Hugh Gunnison and Sarah (Tilly) (Flynn) Gunnison. He or son Lewis sold land in Falmouth in 1719, adjoining land of John Tucker. Children: Nicholas, born 1653. 2. Lewis, resided at Newcastle. 3. Hugh, married Bridget ——— and Dorcas Heard. 4. Elizabeth, married, 1727, Jethro Bragden. 5. Grace, married, May 5, 1708, Isaac Pierce, of Boston.

(II) John Tucker, son or nephew of Lewis Tucker (1), was born about 1660. He settled in Gloucester, Massachusetts. He married, May 9, 1681, Sarah Riggs. He probably had a brother Richard Tucker who married Bethia ——— and had a son in 1704 at Gloucester. His brother Lewis married on the Kittery side, and had a grant for himself and heirs of ten acres at the head of Goose Cove. Children, born in Gloucester: 1. Mary, October 5, 1682. 2. Sarah, March 14, 1685. 3. John, December 24, 1686; married, December 14, 1714, Mary Lane; twelve children. 4. William, May 11, 1690; mentioned below. 5. Thomas, July 18, 1692; drowned in Carolina, April 20, 1717. 6. Richard, May 17, 1695; married, January 16, 1718, Abigail Harvey. 7. Abigail, July 15, 1697. 8. Joseph, February 26, 1701. 9. Grace, July 27, 1706.

(III) William Tucker, son of John Tucker (2), was born May 11, 1690, at Gloucester and settled there. He married, January 8, 1713, Dorcas Lane. Children: 1. Dorcas, died young. 2. Abigail, died young. 3. Abigail. 4. William Jr., born May 22, 1721; married Patience Griggs. 5. John, mentioned below.

(IV) John Tucker, son of William Tucker

(3), was born in Gloucester, January 30, 1725; married, November, 1746, Mary Davis. Children, born in Gloucester: 1. Mary. 2. Lucy. 3. Susanna. 4. Daughter, died young. 5. John, mentioned below. 6. Nathaniel, soldier in the revolution, died June 2, 1848, aged eighty-seven years fifteen days; married, January 4, 1787, Judith Robbins, who died May 8, 1842, aged seventy-nine.

(V) John Tucker, son of John Tucker (4), was born in Gloucester, 1749-50, died January, 1831, aged eighty-two years, at Gloucester. He was a soldier in the revolution, in Captain Enoch Putnam's company (third), Colonel John Mansfield's regiment, June 8, 1775; sergeant of same company and regiment later in the year; ensign of same company 1776; lieutenant in Captain Gate's company, Colonel Rufus Putnam's regiment, in 1779. After the war he was colonel of his regiment of militia. He seems to have been commander of the privateer "Speedwell" in 1779, though this record may belong to his father of the same name. He was active in public affairs, a leading Federalist, elected seven times representative to the general court. He married, October 22, 1772, Elizabeth Elwell. She died at Gloucester, November 17, 1831, aged eighty-one; he died January, 1831, aged eighty-two. Children, born in Gloucester: 1. John, mentioned below. 2. Betsey, married Elias W. Hayes. 3. Lucy, married Colonel William Beach.

(VI) John Tucker, son of John Tucker (5), or a near relative, was born about 1780, probably in Gloucester. Many of the family here given settled before or during the revolution in New Gloucester and Pownalborough, Maine. Several were soldiers in the revolution from those towns. John Tucker was living in Pownalborough in 1784, when he was mentioned in a will. Robert Tucker, of Pownalborough, died 1798, leaving a son Richard Hawley Tucker and widow Joanna. Pownalborough adjoined New Gloucester, then in Lincoln county. Richard was from Gloucester. Lemuel Tucker, of New Gloucester, was in the revolution, as were also Samuel and William Tucker of that town, and Nehemiah of Cape Ann and New Gloucester. John Tucker settled in the adjoining town of Bath, Maine; married Rebecca ———. He was a prominent brick manufacturer in his day. Children, recorded at Bath: 1. Irean (Irene), born October 4, 1805. 2. Betsey, September 23, 1806. 3. Cordelia, January 30, 1810. 4. Nancy, August 5, 1812. 5. Lobida, August 1, 1815. 6. John Adams, March 25, 1818; mentioned below. 7. George Washington, April 30, 1821. 8. Thomas Jefferson, September 2, 1823. 9. Rebecca Madison, August 2, 1828, died July 5, 1832.

(VII) John Adams Tucker, son of John Tucker (6), was born March 25, 1818. He resided at Nashua, New Hampshire, and served as foreman in foundries at different places. He married Lucy (Watson) Howe. Children: 1. Frank E., mentioned below. 2. John, died in childhood. 3. George G., born 1849, resides in Haverhill, Massachusetts.

(VIII) Frank E. Tucker, son of John Adams Tucker (7), was born in Nashua, May 17, 1846. He was educated in the public schools, and when a lad of only twelve years of age began working at farm labor. At the age of sixteen he enlisted in Company K, Twenty-first Massachusetts Volunteers, in the civil war, and participated in the following battles: South Mountain, Antietam, Fredericksburg, Morgan's campaign, thence to Tennessee, siege of Knoxville, Wilderness, Spottsylvania, Cold Harbor, Petersburg; he was struck on the chin with a spent ball, this being the only injury he received; he was mustered out in August, 1864. He then served an apprenticeship at the trade of moulder, working at the same time at different points for eight or nine years, after which he located in Haverhill, Massachusetts, and formed a partnership with J. J. Vaughn, under the firm name of Vaughn & Tucker, furniture dealers. This connection continued for three years, at the expiration of which time Mr. Tucker purchased the interest of his partner and conducted the business alone until 1903, when he admitted his son to partnership under the firm name of F. E. Tucker & Son, which still obtains. They are conducting an extensive business, one of the largest in the city of Bradford, with annual sales of upwards of $100,000. From a very modest beginning the business has increased steadily in volume and importance, this result being achieved by steady application to business, upright and honorable transactions and a regard for the wants and wishes of his patrons. He has also devoted considerable time to the real estate business, opening up new streets, erecting upwards of twenty-five houses, and in various other ways contributing to the growth and development of the section wherein he resides. He is a Republican in politics. He is a member of Merrimack Lodge, F. A. M.; Post No. 47, G. A. R.; and General Burnside Veteran

Union. Mr. Tucker and his family attend the Congregational church.

Mr. Tucker married, November 30, 1872, Ella Chapman, daughter of Joseph Chapman, of Deerfield, Massachusetts. Children: 1. Joseph Elmer, born September 21, 1873, unmarried. 2. Lucy Belle, born March 2, 1875, married Arthur W. Durgin, of Haverhill, Massachusetts; they have one son, James Henry Durgin.

STONE John Stone, of Salem, 1636, and afterward of Beverly, Massachusetts, immigrant ancestor of the family treated in this place, was only one of several persons of the same christian and family name who were seated in the New England plantations in the early part of the seventeenth century, but this John Stone is the same referred to by various chroniclers as having embarked from London in the ship "Elizabeth" in 1635. He settled first in Salem and soon removed to Beverly, and was one of the founders of the first church there in 1667. He had a grant of lands in 1637, and it was he who with his son John kept the first ferry across Bass river, between Salem and Beverly.

(II) John Stone, son of John Stone, died in 1691, leaving a wife Abigail and several children, among them sons John, Jonathan and Nehemiah.

(III) Nehemiah Stone, son of John and Abigail Stone, was baptized May 29, 1670, and lived in Beverly. His wife's name was Lydia; children, all born in Beverly: Nehemiah, Lydia, Sarah, Jonathan, Abigail, Experience and John.

(IV) Jonathan Stone, son of Nehemiah and Lydia Stone, was baptized in Beverly, September 20, 1702, died January 11, 1750, "after a long confinement with jaundice, followed with a numb palsy and dropsy, which brought him to his end." About 1735 he went to Maine as agent for Edward Goffe, of Cambridge, and remained there until he died. After his death several of his children went elsewhere in the province, and they are mentioned in Brunswick, Berwick and other places as well as Kennebunkport. The intentions of marriage of Jonathan Stone and Hannah Lovett, of Beverly, were entered October 31, 1726, and several of their children were born in that town: Hannah, Israel, Jonathan, Elizabeth; Benjamin, who died at sea; and besides these they had other children, born in Maine: William, John, Nehemiah, and perhaps others of whom we have no record. After the death of her husband, Hannah Stone went from Kennebunkport to York in order to administer the estate. On the journey she was thrown from her horse and sustained severe injuries. She charged the doctor's bill against the estate and the same was allowed by the court of probate. One account says that she afterward returned to her former home "so lame as to be unable to walk," and that "two men carried her in a chair to her fireside."

(V) William Stone, son of Jonathan and Hannah (Lovett) Stone, was born after 1735, in Shapleigh, Maine, but lived in Berwick when he entered the service as a soldier of the revolution. The records show that he enlisted as private in Captain Philip Hubbard's company, Colonel James Scammon's Thirtieth regiment, and was in service from May 5, 1775, until August 1, 1775, three months and four days. He is again mentioned in an abstract of pay roll from July 31, 1775, to October, 1775, and on December 21 following he received an order for money in lieu of a bounty coat. He also served as private in Captain Jedediah Goodwin's company, Colonel Edward Wigglesworth's regiment, and the pay roll shows his travel allowance from Albany to his home, two hundred and eighty miles. His company was discharged November 30, 1776.

(VI) James Stone, son of William Stone, was born in Berwick, Maine, about 1781, and was a farmer there. The later years of his life were spent in Lynn, Massachusetts, and he died there December 4, 1843, aged about sixty-two years. He married Sally Trafton, of Shapleigh, Maine, and by her he had thirteen children, whose names are given here, but probably not in the order of seniority: William, Charles, Lewis, Joel, Abial; Julia, only one now living, resides in Davenport, Massachusetts; Mary, Elizabeth, Dorothy, Sarah, Susan, Belinda, Isaiah.

(VII) Isaiah Stone, son of James and Sally (Trafton) Stone, was born in Shapleigh, Maine. He was reared and educated in his native town, and when a young man was attracted to the newly discovered gold fields of California, where he remained for some time. Returning to New England he was located for a short period in Danvers, Massachusetts, whence he removed to Lynn and engaged in the manufacture of shoes, having a factory on South Common street. He was among the pioneers of that industry in Lynn. After the breaking out of the civil war he relinquished business and enlisted in the signal corps, serving with that body in the Department of the South, receiving an honorable discharge at the expiration of his term of enlistment. Upon his return from the army he resumed his trade in Lynn, that of shoemaking, and was shortly afterward appointed a special officer on the police force of that city. He remained in the department for thirty-five years, the greater part of which period he served as special watchman in the various bank buildings and at the Boston, Revere Beach & Lynn railway station. His long and faithful service in the police department was terminated by his resignation in 1899, and he spent the remainder of his life in retirement. He died in Lynn, August 21, 1904. He was widely known among the civil war veterans, being an active member of Post No. 5, Grand Army of the Republic, Lynn; he was also a member of Everett Lodge, No. 20, Knights of Pythias, and of the Gold Diggers' Association. Mr. Stone married, August 27, 1857, Catherine F. H. Ham, of Shapleigh. Children: 1. Herman E., born July 18, 1858. 2. Georgia E., born April 8, 1860, now the widow of Dr. Frank D. S. Stevens (see sketch). 3. Frank E., see forward. 4. Clarence, born September 16, 1866.

(VIII) Dr. Frank E. Stone, son of Isaiah and Catherine F. (Ham) Stone, was born in Lynn, July 16, 1862. He received his elementary education in the Lynn public schools, his secondary education at Lynn high school, and his professional education at Portland School of Medical Instruction, Maine Medical College and the Maine General Hospital. He graduated from Lynn high school, class of 1881, and in 1882 matriculated at the Maine Medical College, graduating M. D., June 25, 1885. His course at the Maine General Hospital was in the nature of the regular interneship and continued one year, but the practical experience gained there was equal to if not of greater value than a post-graduate course of study. Having completed his year at the hospital, Dr. Stone returned to Lynn and began the active general practice which has continued throughout the last twenty-two years, and which by his earnest and capable effort has placed him among the leading men of his profession in that city Few physicians in Lynn have more extended acquaintance than he, and few indeed of them have achieved greater success. In connection with professional pursuits he naturally has taken considerable interest in public affairs in the city and has served in various capacities in the city government. Since 1905 he has filled the office of city physician, and during the same period has been a member of the city board of health He is a member of the American Medical Association, Massachusetts Medical Society, Massachusetts Association of Boards of Health, Essex County Medical Society, and the Lynn Medical Fraternity. In fraternal orders he is a Pythian Knight, a Red Man, and an Essenic Knight. In religious preference he is a Universalist, and in politics a Republican.

Dr. Stone married, in Brunswick, Maine, June 25, 1889, Annie Jewell Allen, a native of Brunswick, daughter of Calvin Winchester and Aribine Louise (Jewell) Allen, the former a native of Turner, Maine, and the latter of Framingham, Massachusetts. Mr. Allen went from Turner to Brunswick when a young man, and for a time was a traveling salesman; later on he became proprietor of a drug store in Brunswick, continuing in that business many years, taking his sons as partners as they grew to manhood and eventually turning over the store and business to their management. Mr. and Mrs. Allen have three sons: Harry, Edward and Ernest; two daughters, Mrs. Dr. Stone, and Florence M. Allen, a teacher in Brunswick, Maine. Dr. and Mrs. Stone have two children: Avesia Hortense, born February 28, 1891; Ellsworth Allen, born May 10, 1892.

HOLDER The Holders of Holderness, England, are believed to be descended from one of the early naval chiefs who extended his conquests along the coast of Germany, Gaul and the British Isles about A. D. 500, the time of the invasion of Ida. Holder was a leader under Ida and his rank was the same as that of admiral of more modern times. Ida was a chief of the Angles and the first king of Bernicia and at the time of the invasion he landed his forces near Flamboro Head, Holderness, England, and there one of those in chief command under him, Holder by name, seized and held the coast between the North sea and the Humber, Yorkshire; and to the region thus fell under his control was given the name of Holderness—a name which ever since has been retained. In the centuries which succeeded the invasion by Ida and Holder others of like character followed, notably the Danes, the Norsemen, the Normans and after them the Anglo-Saxons, and in consequence of these Holderness frequently passed under new sovereignty and ultimately resulted in the survival of that which may properly be termed the survival of the fittest and the permanency of the English dominion.

Genealogy of Holder family: Holder, of Holderness, Saxon chief, who captured Holderness, England, A. D. 500: Holder, Thane during the reign of Alfred the Great, A. D. 870: Rev. George Holder, rector of All Saints, Roos, Holderness, 1588. The Rev. William Holder, D. D., born 1616, in Nottinghamshire, England, died January 27, 1697, a clergyman of distinction and author of considerable note, is believed to have been an elder brother of Christopher Holder, the immigrant ancestor of the branch of the Holder family of New England treated in these annals. He married Susannah (died 1688), daughter of Christopher Wren, dean of Windsor, and sister of Sir Christopher Wren, Bart.

Christopher Holder, American ancestor, was born in Winterburne, Gloucestershire, England, 1631, died April 13, 1688, the record of his death being as follows: "Christopher Holder, of Puddimore, in the county of Somerset, died at Ircott, in the parish of Almondsburg, 13 4mo 1688, and was buried at Hazewell." He was a most devout and conscientious minister of the Society of Friends, and for thirty-three years of his life preached the doctrine of his creed in England, America and the West Indies, and for this "offense" on the soil of New England he was persecuted and held up before the populace as an object of abhorrence, punished with severe stripes on his bare back, imprisoned and ill provided with sustenance, banished from the colony, and under sentence of his persecutors was bereft of one of his ears; yet he failed not in his duty at any time as he saw it.

Early in the year 1656 Christopher Holder sailed from England in the "Speedwell" and landed in Boston June 27 of the same year. Here he and six other persons of his own religious faith were at once subjected to persecution. Let us glance at the record: July 27, 1656, arrived at Boston and soon suffered persecution for his Quaker views. August 29, 1657, for speaking a few words "in your meeting after your priest had done, was hauled by the back of the hair of his head and his mouth violently stopped with glove and handkerchief thereunto thrust with much fury by one of your chief members." September 23, 1657, was whipped with thirty stripes "as near as the hangman could in one place, measuring his ground and fetching his strokes with great strength and advantage." October 8, 1659 was visited in prison by Mary Scott and Hope Clifton, both of whom were taken into custody for the offence, as also was Mary Dyer, who came with them to the prison. On November 22, 1659, he was sentenced to banishment from the colony under penalty of death if he should return, and as an additional punishment one of his ears was cut off. In 1673 he was again in New England and in that year was made freeman in Newport, Rhode Island. He had returned to England in the same ship in which he first came over, and on coming again he landed at New Amsterdam (New York) and in company with John Copeland made his way to Boston by way of Providence and Martha's Vineyard. On April 4, 1676, it was voted in meeting "that in these troublesome times and straits in this colony, the Assembly desiring to have advice and the concurrence of the most judicious inhabitants, if it may be had for the good of the whole, do desire at their next sitting the company and council of sixteen persons, among them Christopher Holder."

Christopher Holder married first, June 12, 1660, Mary Scott, who died October 17, 1665; children, Mary and Elizabeth. He married second, December 30, 1665, Hope, who died January 16, 1681, daughter of Thomas and Mary (Butterworth) Clifton; children: 1. Christopher Jr., born December 22, 1666, died 1720. 2. Hope, May 25, 1668. 3. Patience, February 12, 1669, died in infancy. 4. Patience, August 16, 1671. 5. John, August 20, 1672, died in infancy. 6. Content, May 22, 1674, died August 24, 1676. 7. Anne, February 29, 1676, died March 21, 1676.

Christopher Holder Jr., eldest son and child of Christopher and Hope (Clifton) Holder, born December 22, 1666, died in 1720. He married, at Hallatrow, England, February 15, 1691, Elizabeth Daniell, of Winterburne, England; two children, the first a son, born and died December 5, 1693, and John, born 1694.

Captain John Holder, son of Christopher Jr., and Elizabeth (Daniell) Holder, is mentioned in "The Holders of Holderness" as the only surviving child of his parents; that he was a mariner and master of a merchant ship sailing between Boston, the Barbadoes and English ports; and that he married and had a son Daniel, but mentions no other children, and leaves the subject with inference that there were no other children. This Daniel Holder, born 1721, was the noted Nantucket shipbuilder, and who wrote his name Daniel, although he is supposed to have been christened Daniell, taking his baptismal name from his mother's family name. In 1748, according to the authority above mentioned, he married Susannah ———, who died August 3, 1807, and by her had nine children, the seventh of whom in order of birth was Daniel, born Marblehead, Massachusetts, April 14, 1761. He married Desire Styles, of Marblehead, and had by her thirteen children, the seventh of whom in order of seniority was Nathaniel, born January 19, 1811, married, August 12, 1833, Hannah Dodge Morgan and by her had thirteen children.

Such in brief is an outline of the descent of the late Nathaniel Holder from Christopher Holder, the immigrant, through each succeeding generation of his ancestors as understood and published in various chronicles and especially in the Holder genealogy to which reference is made. But it appears according to the researches of members of the Holder family and particularly by some of the children of the late Nathaniel Holder, of Lynn, (1811-1900) that his father, Daniel, (1774-1816) was not a son of Daniel Holder, of Marblehead, (1761) who married Susannah ——— but was in fact a son of Nathaniel Holder, baptized 1732, and married 1755, Susannah Horsom; and that this Nathaniel was a son of Thomas Holder, who married in 1731 Barbara Haydon.

(I) Of Thomas Holder nothing is known previous to his marriage with Barbara Haydon, and none of the several chroniclers which purport to treat of the Holder family make any mention of his name. The Marblehead vital records give an account of his marriage, and also of the death of a Thomas Holder 1 5mo 1732. The same records also mention the marriage of Thomas Holder and Bathsheba Needham, February 11, 1721-22, but whether he is identical with Thomas Holder who married Barbara Haydon, June 29, 1731, is not known. It is safe to assume that Thomas Holder was born sometime between 1700 and 1710, and as those who claim descent from him also claim Christopher Holder the Elder as their American ancestor it is clear that Thomas must have been a grandson of the immigrant; but the records indicate that Christopher Holder Jr., was the only surviving son of his father and also that Captain John Holder was the son of the younger Christopher. From this it appears that either Christopher Holder Jr., had a son Thomas as well as a son John, or that Thomas Holder who married Barbara Haydon was of another family than that of Christopher. In his "Genealogical Dictionary" Savage mentions Nathaniel Holder, of Dorchester, 1634, but nothing further than that; and the "History of Dorchester" (1851) mentions that "Nathaniel Holder" was admitted to the church there in 1636. One writer of contemporary history speaks of a confusion of the names Holder and Holden, but from what is here written it is evident that Christopher Holder, the Rhode Island Quaker missionary, was not the first of his surname in New England. There were Haydons and Haydens too among the earliest settlers in old Dorchester, but there is nothing now obtainable which furnishes a clew to the probable ancestor of Thomas Holder who married Barbara Haydon.

(II) Nathaniel Holder, son of Thomas and Barbara (Haydon) Holder, was baptized in Marblehead, Massachusetts, October 1, 1732, and married, April 3, 1755, Susanna Horsom, who died August 3, 1807, and whose death is identical with that of Susannah ———, who is mentioned in the Holder Genealogy as the wife of Daniel Holder, of Nantucket and Marblehead. Children of Nathaniel and Susanna (Horsom) Holder (dates of birth unknown; dates of baptism given): 1. Ann, February 29, 1756. 2. Susanna, December 11, 1757. 3. Nathaniel, 1760, died young. 4. Sarah, December 20, 1761, married, June 30, 1778, Captain William Dennis. 5. Jane, 1764, died young. 6. Mary, July, 1765. 7. Nathaniel, October 4, 1767. 8. Jane, December 17, 1769, married, December 20, 1787, Lloyd Smethurst. 9. Elizabeth, June 16, 1771, married, April 15, 1798, Samuel Bowden. 10. Daniel, July 17, 1774. 11. Lydia, December 15, 1776.

(III) Daniel Holder, Quaker, son of Nathaniel and Susanna (Horsom) Holder, was born in Marblehead, Massachusetts, July 17, 1774, and died September 25, 1816. He married April 9, 1797, Desire, of Marblehead, born May 24, 1769, died October 9, 1839, daughter of Captain Richard and Desire P. Styles. Daniel and Desire (Styles) Holder are said to have had thirteen children, a record of eight of whom is found: 1. Daniel, January 26, 1799, died March 12, 1801. 2. Nathaniel, September 30, 1800, died October 15, 1804. 3. Daniel, May 5, 1802, died April 20, 1807. 4. Desire, February 28, 1804, died February 24, 1820. 5. Sally, February 24, 1806, died June 24, 1900; married Joseph Selman, of Marblehead, who died in 1873. 6. Daniel, May 14, 1808, died September 14, 1843. 7. Nathaniel, January 19, 1811. 8. Susannah, September 15, 1814, died November 20, 1899; married Isaac Abbott Allen.

(IV) Nathaniel Holder, youngest son of Daniel and Desire (Styles) Holder, was born in Marblehead, Massachusetts, January 19, 1811, died in Lynn, June 24, 1900, having attained the remarkable age of almost four score and ten years. He was of pious mind and his walk in life was in keeping with the precepts he taught during the years he devoted to the work of the ministry. He was a young man when he became a clergyman of the Universalist church and his first pastorate was in Washington, New Hampshire, where he remained a few years. Sometime after that his views changed and he became a Unitarian; he was a member of the latter church and one of its trustees for many years previous to his death. But it was as a man of business that Mr. Holder was best known in the city of Lynn, where he engaged in active pursuits nearly half a century. His young life was spent in his native town of Marblehead, where he was educated in the public schools, and after leaving school he learned the trade of baker. In 1830, when only nineteen years old, he went to Boston and started in business on his own account, remained there three years and then went to Lynn and built a bakery and residence on Commercial street. This was the real beginning of his successful business career, and as his means would allow he gradually branched out and increased his facilities for manufacture until at length he was proprietor of a large wholesale baking establishment and of a trade which was very extensive. In addition to his general bakery enterprise Mr. Holder, with excellent judgment, invested a considerable part of his unemployed capital in unimproved real estate in Lynn and its immediate vicinity. This he did in a small way at first, but before he had lived there fifteen years he owned several separate tracts of land. His first considerable purchase was made in 1844, when he bought ten acres in the vicinity of Boston street, laid it out in house lots, opened Grove street in 1845 and offered the lots for sale at public auction, the first event of its kind in Lynn, and so successful in its results that all of the lots were sold off in a single day. In the same year he opened Salem street, later laid out Linwood street from Walnut street to the Dungeon, completing one mile of it in three weeks; then opened Pine Grove avenue, Greenwood and Tapley streets. In 1848 he bought one hundred and ten acres of land on what was then known as Pine Hill, and there built his large baking establishment. The remaining portion of the purchase was laid out, improved and developed under his personal direction. In the meantime he had erected a large number of dwelling houses, and as an evidence of his public spiritedness and unselfish interest in city where he lived so long, it may be said that Mr. Holder was one of five men who purchased a tract of land seventy acres in extent and donated it for a public cemetery—Pine Grove cemetery, as now known. Mr. Holder was not in any sense a politician or seeker after political honors, although occasionally he was induced to stand as the candidate of the Republican party for local office. He served one term as overseer of the poor, was for some time a member of the school committee, and in 1853 was a member of the constitutional convention of that year. His political views inclined to independence, and he looked first at the man and at his party afterward. He himself was urged to stand for the mayoralty of Lynn, but he declined the honor, and also several other prominent offices which were offered him. At the age of seventy years Mr. Holder retired from active pursuits and turned over to his sons the management of his varied business interests.

On August 12, 1832, he married Hannah Dodge, of Salem, Massachusetts, daughter of Andrew and Rachel (Safford) Morgan. Children: 1. Sarah Selman, born July 31, 1834, died January 17, 1896; married, March 14, 1854, Charles Augustus Adams, died November 19, 1860; children: Charles Holder Adams, born December 29, 1856, died November 27, 1866; Sarah Augusta Adams, September 16, 1858, died March 10, 1859; Clara Bassett Adams, May 16, 1860, resides in Lynn. After the death of her husband Sarah Selman Holder Adams married Henry Breed, of Lynn; children: Flora Holder, Henry Lincoln, Isabel Morgan, Sarah Ellen and Emma Hawthorne. 2. Elizabeth Safford, born January 7, 1836, married, Lynn, May 7, 1855, Amos S. Adams, died Mansfield, Ohio, August 11, 1881; children: Helen Elizabeth Adams, born September 15, 1857; Florence Adams, March 24, 1860, died September 25, 1887; Annie Martin Adams, March 21, 1862, married John Henry Whipple, of Chicago; Gertrude Adams, March 26, 1868; Dr. Nathaniel Holder Adams, January 14, 1871, married Clara Rosina Melchert, in Chicago. 3. Mary Ann Morgan, born November 12, 1837, married, December 31, 1863, Andrew J. Kidder, both dead; children: Martha Richards, born April 16, 1868; Henry Worcester, January 25, 1871; Andrew Jackson, March 14, 1873, married, 1898, Helen

Arnold Bowles, who died January 20, 1901; Mary Holder, April 3, 1875; William Mudgett, January 8, 1878; Nathaniel Holder, October 19, 1880, died January 2, 1881; Luther McCutcheon, February 1, 1884. 4. Harriet Ella, born June 23, 1839. 5. William Channing, born March 7, 1841, business man of Lynn; former alderman and president of the common council; member and trustee of the Unitarian church; married, January 25, 1870, Helen Shedd; children: William Leighton, born February 26, 1871, died July 21, 1871; Henry Allen, September 4, 1872; Jesse Morgan, February 9, 1874; Mary Esther, March 28, 1875; Helen Zulette, August 6, 1876; Walter Safford, October 27, 1879; Marcellus, October 8, 1882, died April 6, 1883; Bertha, April 8, 1884. 6. Caroline Healey, born November 28, 1842. 7. Theodore Parker, born July 30, 1844, married, July 20, 1870, John Alexander Jameson; children: Hannah Holder, born May 8, 1871; Charles Smith, August 12, 1873; George Sargeant, October 14, 1874; Sarah Abbie, September 26, 1876; Arthur Lawrence, January 10, 1879; John Alexander, March 10, 1881, died July 25, 1885; Holder Morgan, August 5, 1882; Lucy Cook, December 24, 1886. 8. Langdon Healey, born March 10, 1846, former member of the state legislature; member (1907) of the board of aldermen of Lynn; married first, October 28, 1868, Ella Maria Jackson; children: Alice Josephine, born October 29, 1869; Amy Leland, June 21, 1871, married, October 15, 1890, Willard Nathaniel Morrison (had Harold Ivory, born September 5, 1891; Willard Langdon, August 27, 1892; Ella Marjorie, October 2, 1896; Hazel Amy, June 2, 1901); Healey Langdon, born March 2, 1874, died March 21, 1878; Earnest Morgan, born August 8, 1876, married, January 1, 1906, Ellen Choate; child, Kennett Morgan; Bessie Davenport, October 3, 1878, married, January 1, 1906, Frederick William Bryan; child, Louise, deceased; Everett Tracy, December 6, 1883, died May, 1905. For his second wife Langdon Healey Holder married, June 12, 1894, Anna Sophia Nutter, of Lynn. 9. Clara Bassett, born February 6, 1848, died April 21, 1891; married, July 12, 1871, Daniel Frank Bennett; children: Clara Bennett, born and died May, 1872; Frank Bennett, June 21, 1873, died November 28, 1873. 10. Nathaniel Jr., born September 22, 1849, died July 2, 1903; succeeded his father in the baking business; married, August 22, 1877, Ellen Ardelia Dow; children: Nathaniel Dow Holder, born July 21, 1878, married, June 20, 1900, Alice Inez Winslow (had Andrew Nathaniel Dow, born July 16, 1901, died August 1, 1901; and Glenna Winslow, born 1906); Andrew Morgan, June 29, 1880, died April 1, 1900; Frank Pierson, December 6, 1883, died February 1, 1908; Ralph, November 19, 1885; Clara Ethel, July 25, 1888; Lillian, July 14, 1891. 11. Emma, born September 2, 1851, died March 21, 1878; married, December 13, 1871, Jackson Locke, who died June 10, 1899; children: Sarah Sanborn Locke, born November 30, 1872, died March 15, 1878; Emma May Locke, October 7, 1875, married, June, 1899, Wilson Hiram Thorne (had Stella May Thorne, born May 19, 1900, and Wilson Hiram, born February, 1902); Sanborn Holder Locke, March 4, 1878, married, January 24, 1900, Lillian Alice Jones (had Howard Sanborn Locke, born June 3, died June 6, 1901, Clarence Morgan, Lillian May, Bernice). 12. Zulette, born July 5, 1853, died August 1, 1888. 13. Daniel, born April 1, 1855, died November 30, 1856.

McDONALD This ancient and highly respectable family name is here written McDonald instead of MacDonald for the reason that in one of the generations of the early part of the last century a MacDonald, a Scotch Presbyterian, married a McDonald, an Irish Catholic woman, and in deference to her wishes the husband adopted the Irish way of spelling the name.

(I) Ronald McDonald, a descendant of the old Scottish MacDonald family, was born on one of the northern isles of the Hebrides in Scotland, at a place called Uyst. When he was a young man, with his wife and their only child, he left his native country, crossed the Atlantic ocean and settled at Cable Head, a little to the eastward of the harbor St. Peters, on Prince Edward Island. There Ronald McDonald afterward lived and died. He was a farmer by principal occupation, an industrious honest man, and while he never succeeded in gaining a fortune in lands and money, he always lived in comfort, raised a family of ten children, educated them as well as the situation of his country home would permit, and trained them in useful occupations. The sons in the family generally took to farming and fished more or less, according to the custom of nearly all the people of that region. The eldest child was born in Scotland, and the others on Prince Edward Island, viz.: 1. Alexander, came over with his parents; farmer and shipbuilder; married and had a large family. 2.

John, was a farmer and ship carpenter. 3. Donald, was a farmer. 4. James, was a ship carpenter, one of the two sons of Ronald McDonald who left the island and remained away for a considerable time. He came to New Brunswick, Maine, worked there at his trade for a year or two and then returned to the old home and became a farmer. 5. Sarah, married Thomas Reville, and raised a large family. 6. Catherine, married Thomas Murphy, and came to the states, where he died. She afterward lived in Malden, Massachusetts, and died there. 7. Mary, never married; died 1906, aged eighty-nine years. 8. Charles, mentioned below. 9. Ronald, lived a few years in Gloucester, on Cape Ann, where several of his sons lived. They were fishermen, and three of them—Matthew, Andrew and Daniel—were lost at sea. After this misfortune the father returned to his native town and died there. 10. Andrew, always lived on the old home farm where his father settled; now is eighty-five years old. 11. Stephen, died in infancy.

(II) Charles McDonald, fifth son and eighth child of Ronald McDonald, was born about 1808 and died in 1880. He came to the states only once, and then to visit the home of his son, Captain Jerome McDonald, of Gloucester. His occupations were farming and ship carpentering, and he was a thrifty man, a good farmer and provided comfortably for his family. He married first, Mary McDonald, (not a relative) died aged twenty-eight years; second, Ann O'Hanley, a native of Prince Edward Island. Children, four by each marriage: 1. Charles, born Prince Edward Island, died in infancy. 2. John, born Prince Edward Island, died in infancy. 3. Jerome, born September 15, 1845, mentioned below. 4. Ellen, married Stephen McEachern and lived at Fairfield, Prince Edward Island. She died about 1894; children: Mary Margaret, died aged eighteen; Joseph, living at Hyde Park, Massachusetts; Emanuel, living at Hyde Park; Flora, married, and lives in Roxbury, Massachusetts; Winnie, lives on Prince Edward Island; Jerome, lives Prince Edward Island; Ellen, lives Prince Edward Island. 5. Malcolm, born Prince Edward Island, died aged twenty-two. 6. Mary, born Prince Edward Island, married Frank Bond; lives in Cliftondale, Massachusetts. 7. William, born Prince Edward Island, a farmer living on old homestead. 8. John P., born Prince Edward Island, a farmer, married twice; two children.

(III) Captain Jerome McDonald, third son and child of Charles and Mary McDonald, is a native of Prince Edward Island, born September 15, 1845, and for more than forty years has been identified with the Gloucester fisheries, although before he went to Cape Ann to live he had sailed as a fisherman from various New England ports. He was brought up on the old home farm on Prince Edward Island, where his grandfather had settled more than a century before Jerome was born, and received a good common school education, although his opportunities in that direction were somewhat limited, for he being the oldest son in the family who grew to maturity it was necessary that he do much of the work on the farm. When eighteen years old he left home and went fishing, and then began a business life which has witnessed many changes, and occasional hardships, but which resulted in ultimate success. For two years he sailed on a fishing vessel out of Cape Cod and made his first trip to the banks of Newfoundland. Later on he sailed to the West Indies, afterward returning to Cape Cod, and during the spring and summer of 1865 stayed at his old home on Prince Edward Island. In the fall of 1865 Captain McDonald went to Weymouth, Massachusetts, but soon afterward removed to Gloucester and has since been a prominent factor in the fisheries of that city. For the first five years, from 1865 to 1870, he sailed as an ordinary fisherman, but in the year last mentioned was made master of the "Eastern Light" on a trip to the Grand Banks for the firm of Maddox & Knowles. In the next year he was master of the "Midnight" for the same firm, and in the fall of 1872 engaged with Dennis & Ayer to sail the "Sarah P. Ayer" and was her master for the next two years. In 1874 Captain McDonald had accumulated money enough to purchase a half interest in the new ship "G. P. Whitman", the other half being owned by the firm of Dennis & Ayer. This ship he sailed for the following six years. Then Mr. Andrew Leighton purchased the interest of Dennis & Ayer, and Captain McDonald sailed her four years as master and part owner with his friend, Mr. Leighton. In 1885, in company with Mr. Leighton, Captain McDonald built the "Monitor", which was lost in 1886 on the coast of Fortune Bay, Newfoundland. They then built the second "Monitor" and sailed her in partnership until the death of Mr. Leighton, after which Captain McDonald purchased his interest in the "Monitor" and sailed her until 1891; then ran the

"Gladiator", "Senator", "Preceptor", and in 1901 built the third "Monitor". In 1891 he built the "Gladiator", sailed her two years, then built the "Senator" and was her master until 1898, when he quitted the sea to devote his entire time to the business management of fishing interests, which at that time had largely increased and needed his personal attention, for it was one thing to run into port with a good ship's trip of fish, but quite another thing to sell or cure it to the best advantage. In 1899 Captain McDonald built and added the "Preceptor" to his fleet, followed her with his fourth "Monitor" in 1901 and "The Actor" in 1902. His fleet of fishing vessels now comprises the "Gladiator", "Senator", "Preceptor", "Monitor" and "The Actor", and besides these ships and those before mentioned he has had a share interest in the "Elector", "Motor" and the "Mary E. McDonald", the latter having been named in allusion to his daughter, Mary Evelyn McDonald. The foregoing was the only loss Captain McDonald ever had during all his long service as a fisherman, but he was not discouraged by a single loss and on returning to Gloucester built his third "Monitor" and sailed her for the next five years with good success. Although he had an owner's interest in a fishing vessel in 1874, Captain McDonald dates his success in the fisheries from the year 1881, and gives to Andrew Leighton a full share of credit for the success he achieved during the earlier years in which he was engaged in the business. He himself started out in the business without a dollar in capital and in Mr. Leighton he had a loyal friend and helper: and they were associates together so long as the latter lived, to the profit of each of them. For many years Captain McDonald was a curer and distributor as well as producer of fish, but more recently he has sold the products of his vessels to other curers and distributors. He never made a success of salt fishing, but in fresh fishing he ranked with the most successful men in that business; in one year he was 4,000 "high line" in Gloucester.

In Gloucester, where the best years of his life have been spent, Captain Jerome McDonald is regarded as one of the substantial business men of the city, and besides his interests in the fisheries he is a considerable real estate owner, a man of sound business judgment, liberal views on matters of general and local interest, and one whose opinions have influence as well as good sense. He is a member of the Master Mariners' Association and the Fishermen's Institute of Gloucester. He is a Republican in politics, a firm supporter of the principles of his party, but never had a desire for political office.

On January 18, 1871, Jerome McDonald married Margaret, daughter of Alexander McKenzie, of Prince Edward Island. Children: 1. John James, born September 8, 1872, unmarried, lives at home. 2. George Francis, born December 18, 1873, married Mary Kane, and lives in Philadelphia, Pennsylvania, where he is a bookkeeper and accountant; children, Mary, Jerome and William. 3. Mary Theresa, born May 10, 1877, died at the age of two years, eleven months. 4. Jerome Edmund, born April 25, 1878, lives in Portland, Oregon. 5. Charles Albert, born November 21, 1880, lives in Philadelphia, Pennsylvania, an employee of the Baldwin locomotive works. 6. Mary Evelyn, born July 18, 1882, a professional nurse, lives in New York. 7. Margaret, born December 12, 1883, lives in Gloucester. 8. Joseph, born December 6, 1885, died in infancy.

ELLIS The surname Ellis comes to New England from England and has been known in America for nearly three centuries. It cannot be claimed that the earliest ancestors of the Ellis surname in the country during the first half of the seventeenth century were all of one kin, although there has been considerable speculation among the later generations of the descendants of the several ancestors in regard to the probable relationship they bear to each other.

(I) The Ellis family of the line here under consideration is descended from John Ellis, of Sandwich, Massachusetts, an Englishman by birth and parentage, but the place of nativity, the year of his birth and the exact date of his immigration to the hospitable shores of New England are not known. He was of Sandwich as early as 1641 and in 1643 he is mentioned in the town records as a person capable of bearing arms. This implies that he was a man of good report in the plantation there, a freeman, and member of the church in good standing. In July, 1657, John Ellis, mentioned as "Lieutenant Ellis", was one of the fourteen freemen of Sandwich who signed the agreement to support a minister in the town: "We whose names are hereunder written do hereby engage ourselves to pay towards the minister's support, yearly, the several sums as followeth —except as God by His Providence shall disenable us, or any of us remove out of Sandwich". To this cause John Ellis promised to pay one pound each year, there being only three of the whole number who pledged a greater sum, hence it may be inferred that he was a man of substance as well as of influence among the townsmen.

In the same year "the account of Lt. Ellis for drum, muskets &c purchased was rendered", amounting to ten pounds, six shillings, seven pence. In 1658 the lands of the town were described in accordance with an order of the court, and John Ellis Sr. and John Ellis Jr. are mentioned as property owners at that time. His name also appears in 1675, when a meeting was called by Lieutenant John Ellis and Benjamin Hammond, the constable, for the purpose of granting liberty to "any families that may be necessitated, to repair to the town garrison for safety". In the same year the name of John Ellis Sr. appears among those who could "make appear their just right to the privileges of the town" The "Annals of Sandwich" in noting events of the year 1677 state that "Mr. John Ellis, the ancestor of those of the name in this town, one of the oldest and first settlers, died this year". To this statement the author of that work adds this note: "He is called Jr., we know not for what reason. He must, we think, have been Sr. of Sandwich. There probably was one of the name older in the colony".

In 1645 John Ellis married Elizabeth, daughter of Edmund Freeman, to whom, April 3, 1637, and nine associates, the town of Sandwich was granted. He was the leading proprietor of the town. He was born in England about 1590 and came to New England in 1635, in company with his two sons, Edmund Jr., and John, the former of whom was fifteen years old and the latter eight years old at the time of their immigration. Both of them afterward married daughters of Governor Prince. He also brought with him two daughters, Alice, then seventeen, and Elizabeth, twelve years old. Alice Freeman married Deacon William Paddy, of Plymouth, the first treasurer of the colony. Elizabeth, third in the order of birth of her father's children, married John Ellis, of Sandwich. It is said of Edmund Freeman that "he was a man of consideration in England and brought with him much valuable plate: which last remark," says Mr. Freeman in his "History of Barnstable County", "we suppose was intended to be indicative of his position in society. Such, perhaps it might have been at that day, but it would be a poor criterion now. It is said, moreover, that he acted as the 'confidential agent' of certain of the 'merchant adventurers'. This would seem to be corroborated by his correspondence with Mr. Beauchampe, 'a London merchant and valuable friend to the colony', who also was brother-in-law to Mr. Freeman. Mr. Freeman was not only conspicuous in town affairs, but from 1640 to 1646 inclusive, assistant in the government of the colony. He lived to be ninety-two years old, dying in Sandwich in 1682. His sons Edmund and John also were prominent, both being deputies to the general court, and the latter, who removed to Eastham, became assistant".

Lieutenant John Ellis and Elizabeth Freeman had eight children: 1. Bennet, born 1649. 2. Mordecai, 1651, made freeman 1681, died 1715; married Rebecca Clark. 3. Joel, 1655. 4. Nathaniel, 1657. 5. Matthias (see post). 6. John, married Sarah Holmes. 7. Samuel. 8. Freeman, admitted freeman 1681; married Mercy ——— and had sons Joel, Ebenezer, Mordecai and Gideon.

(II) Matthias Ellis, fifth child of Lieutenant John and Elizabeth (Freeman) Ellis, was admitted freeman in Sandwich in 1681, and died August 30, 1748. The name of his wife is not known, but he married and had children: 1. Matthias, born 1681. 2. Freeman, 1683. 3. Mary, 1685. 4. Experience, 1687, married Stephen Churchill. 5. Malachi, 1689. 6. Remember, 1691. 7. Benjamin. 8. Samuel, 1699. 9. William.

(III) William Ellis, youngest son of Matthias Ellis, married Jane ———; children: 1. William, born 1719. 2. Experience, 1722. 3. Eleazer, 1724. 4. Thomas, 1726.

(IV) William Ellis, son of William and Jane Ellis, married Patience ———; children: 1. Thomas, born 1744. 2. Betty, 1748, married Ezra Harlow. 3. Lydia, 1750, married Thomas Clark. 4. Mary, 1753.

(V) Thomas Ellis, eldest son and child of William and Patience Ellis, was born in 1744, and married, in 1767, Jerusha, born 1745, a daughter of Israel and Deborah (Pope) Clark. Israel Clark, born 1720, married, 1741, Deborah Pope, of Sandwich, and had Josiah, Jerusha, Thomas, Thankful, Lurania, Betty, Abigail, Olive, Grace and John Clark. Israel Clark was a son of Josiah and Thankful (Tupper) Clark, whose children were Elizabeth, died young, Israel and Elizabeth Clark. Josiah Clark was a son of Thomas Clark, who married first, in 1682, Rebecca Miller and had Susannah, born 1684, married Elisha Holmes, and Thomas, born 1685. Thomas Clark married second, 1690, Elizabeth Crow and had Josiah, born 1690, Elizabeth and Nathaniel. Thomas Clark married third, Susanna Miller, and had Anna, married Gideon Ellis; Abigail, married Nathaniel Bartlett, and Sarah, born 1704. Thomas Clark, father of Josiah Clark, was a son of James Clark, born 1636, married, 1657, Abigail, daughter of Rev. John Lothrop, and had John, James, Susanna, Abigail, Joanna, Thomas and Bathsheba Clark. James Clark, father of Thomas Clark, was a son of Thomas Clark, the immigrant, who came to New England in the "Ann" in 1623 and was a merchant in Boston. He married first, before 1634, Susanna, daughter of Widow Mary Ring, and by her had Andrew, James, Susanna, William, John and Nathaniel. Thomas Clark married second, in 1664, Widow Alice Nichols, daughter of Richard Hallett. Thomas and Jerusha (Clark) Ellis had children: 1. Betsey, born 1770, married ——— Swift. 2. William, 1771. 3. Lydia, married ——— Morey. 4. Jerusha. 5. Polly. 6. Lucy. 7. Nathaniel. 8. Thomas.

(VI) Thomas Ellis, youngest son and child of Thomas and Jerusha (Clark) Ellis, married Rebecca Burgess; children: 1. Hannah, born 1803, married Joseph Harlow. 2. Elisha, 1805, (see post). 3. Betsey, 1807. 4. Lydia, 1808, married Paul Crowell. 5. Thomas, 1811, married Joanna B., daughter of Francis Ellis. 6. Anson B., married Harriet N. Howes, of Dennis. 7. Hiram. 8. Clark S., married Eliza A. Swift.

(VII) Elisha Ellis, second son and child of Thomas and Rebecca (Burgess) Ellis, was born in Plymouth, Massachusetts, 1805, and lived in that part of the town in which others of his family in earlier generations had lived, and which was named Ellisville in allusion to the family. He was a farmer and it is understood that he engaged to some extent in fishing. He lived to a good old age and was for many years a member of the Methodist Episcopal church and one of the officers of the society. Mr. Ellis died in 1892. He married Priscilla Crowell, of West Sandwich, Massachusetts, (now Sagamore); children: 1. Elisha Winslow, born 1837, passed his entire life in Manomet, Massachusetts; married Gertrude Nichols, who died September 2, 1890; two children, the first of whom died in infancy; the second was Cynthia Holmes Ellis. 2. Priscilla Ann, died in infancy. 3. Priscilla Crowell, born 1845, married Malcolm McKenzie, and had Arthur Kenneth McKenzie, James Franklin McKenzie, Susan Priscilla McKenzie and Ellis McKenzie. 4. Nathan Crowell (see post). 5. Thomas P., married Mrs. Harriet Hill and had Beatrice and Bertha Ellis. 6. Sarah Sears, married William H. Pierce and had one daughter, Alberta Williams Pierce, who died in infancy. 7. Edmund Sears, married Mary Jane Deloriea, and had Alverado Leroy, Ralph Deloriea, Edna, Ethel Vivian, Eva May and Viola Ellis. 8. Benjamin Franklin, married Eliza Townsend.

(VIII) Nathan Crowell Ellis, fourth child of Elisha and Priscilla (Crowell) Ellis, was born in Plymouth, Massachusetts, December 30, 1849, and died in Lynn, Massachusetts, January 15, 1891. He attended school in Plymouth and afterward went to Worcester, Massachusetts, where he learned the trade of machinist and became a thorough and practical mechanic. Later on he removed to Lynn, worked for a few months as a journeyman and then became a junior member of the firm of J. G. Buzzell & Company, the partners being Mr. Buzzell, George W. Emerson and Mr. Ellis. The firm engaged chiefly in the manufacture of shoe machinery and owned a number of valuable patents and also did considerable business in the way of constructing machines on special order and setting up machines in various factories. After about twelve years of successful operation the interest of the senior partner in the old firm was purchased by Mr. Emerson and Mr. Ellis and the new partnership of George W. Emerson & Company succeeded to the business. This firm was continued until the death of Mr. Ellis in 1891. He was an industrious and hardworking man, an upright citizen and an earnest member of the Methodist Episcopal church, in which he was class leader for several years. While in active business much of the hardest work of the shop fell upon him, for he was a skillful machinist and the making of machines was required to be done under his immediate supervision.

In 1875 Mr. Ellis married Linda Munroe, born in Charlton, Massachusetts, April 16, 1855, daughter of John Jordan, of Charlton, and Ellen (Royle) Jordan, the latter a native of England. Mr. and Mrs. Ellis had two children: 1. Cora Linden, born in Lynn, August 12, 1878, married Dr. John Henry Andrews, physician and surgeon in active practice in Lynn. 2. Edith Zerniah, born in Lynn, November 15, 1883.

BURCKES Thomas M. Burckes, for nearly twenty-five years a member of the police force of Lynn, Massachusetts, and incumbent of the responsible office of chief of police for the last eleven years, a naval veteran of the war of 1861-65, is a descendant of an English family of ancient origin, who have been known in New England history since the later years of the eighteenth century.

(I) Martin Burckes, great-grandfather of Thomas M. Burckes, resided for many years in Quincy, Massachusetts; later he came to Boston, where he followed the business of contractor, laying the first pavement in that city. Here he spent the remainder of his life and died at an advanced age.

(II) Martin Burckes, grandfather of Thomas M. Burckes, was born in Quincy, Massachusetts. He served as a carpenter with the rank of lieutenant on board the American ship "Hornet" under Lawrence in the naval engagement in which the British ship "Peacock" was sunk. After the war Lieutenant Burckes established a ship yard on that part of the water front in Boston which was familiarly known as "Billy Gray's wharf". He was an enterprising business man, engaged in various undertakings in the city of Boston. At the age of about fifty years he left Boston and took up his abode on a farm in Waterford, Maine, remained there about twelve years, then returned to Massachusetts and lived in Charlestown until the time of his death at the remarkable age of ninety-eight years. He married Mary Sparrowhawk, of Boston; she died in Charlestown. Their children were: 1. Martin, mentioned below. 2. Henry, who was a "forty-niner" in the gold fields of California and who died in San Francisco. 3. George, deceased. 4. James, a resident of Somerville, Massachusetts, a contractor and builder. 5. Samuel, a resident of San Francisco, California. 6. Mary Ann, married John B. Wilson; died in Boston. 7. Josephine, married David Coffin, died while visiting in southern California. 8. Barbara, married George Gibson, removed to Wisconsin, where she died.

(III) Martin Burckes, father of Thomas Mr. Burckes, was born in Charlestown, Massachusetts, 1814. He was a carpenter and contracting builder in Charlestown for many years, but the latter part of his life was spent in San Francisco, California, where he died about 1853. While living in Charlestown he married Rebecca Blanchard, who died in that city in 1869, aged about forty-seven years, and by whom he had the following named children: 1. Carrie E. 2. Thomas M., mentioned below. 3. Jennie, married Stacy Reed, of Cambridge, Massachusetts. 4. Urilda, twin, who died unmarried. 5. Nellie, twin, married Henry Whitmore, of Dennison, Massachusetts.

(IV) Thomas M. Burckes, second child and only son of Martin and Rebecca (Blanchard) Burckes, was born in Charlestown, Massachusetts, May 3, 1847. He was educated in the public schools of that city and also of Lynn, where he went when fourteen years old to live with the family of his aunt, Eleanor Snow. In the first year of the civil war he enlisted in the United States navy and served under Farragut on board the gunboat, "Aroostook", in the blockading squadron, where that worthy admiral gave such effective service to the Union cause. His naval service covered a period of one year and two months, his term of enlistment having been for one year. After being mustered out of service, Mr. Burckes returned to Lynn and found employment in a shoe factory and followed that occupation until 1884, when he was appointed special police officer on the city force. In 1885 he was made a member of the regular force by appointment of Mayor Baldwin, and after three years was promoted to lieutenant of the city police. At the end of another year he was made captain and served in that capacity nine years, then was elected chief of police, or city marshal, and has served eleven years as head of the force of the city. He is a member of Golden Fleece Lodge, Free and Accepted Masons; Bay State Lodge, No. 40, Independent Order of Odd Fellows; General Lander Post, No. 5, Lynn, Grand Army of the Republic, in which he has been commander, junior and senior vice-commander. In his political preference he is a Republican.

In 1866 Mr. Burckes married Lucy A. Clark, of Lynn, a native of Dixmont, Maine, born June 16, 1847, daughter of Meschis and Mary E. (Siders) Clark. Mr. and Mrs. Burckes have five children: 1. Charles H., married Bella S. Steeves. 2. Grace B., wife of Harry E. Southwick, of Lynn. 3. Stacy R., married Mabel Howard; two sons: Ralph and Thomas M. 4. Myron E. 5. T. Gordon.

MARTIN The surname Martin is derived from the baptismal name and is of old English origin. There are in England no less than thirty-nine coats-of-arms belonging to Martin families and fifty more to Martyn families in the United

Kingdom. Some of them have seats in Lockynge, county Berks; Bowton, county Cambridge; Bodmin, county Cornwall; Athelhampton, county Dorset, and Long Melford, county Suffolk; Plymouth, Devonshire, and in some Irish counties. An ancient armorial of this family, similar to many others Martin arms is: Argent a chevron between three mascles sable with a bordure engrailed gules. Crest: A cockatrice's head between two wings. Motto: Initium sapientiae est timor Domini.

More than a dozen of their name came to New England to make their home before 1650. Christopher Martin who came on the "Mayflower", left no descendants, his whole family being swept away by disease in the first infection. Richard Martin, an early settler at Portsmouth, New Hampshire, was one of the founders of the church there in 1671; deputy to the general court in 1672 and 1679 and speaker of the house; councillor in 1680; married, December 1, 1653, Sarah, daughter of John Tuttle, of Boston; married second the widow of John Denison and daughter of Samuel Symonds; third, Elizabeth Lear, widow of Tobias Lear, and daughter of Henry Sherburne; fourth, Mary, daughter of Benning Wentworth. George Martin, doubtless brother of Richard, and perhaps of other pioneers, came to this country in the employ of Samuel Winsley about 1639; settled in Salisbury, Massachusetts; also lived in Amesbury; blacksmith by trade; died 1686; first wife Hannah died in 1646; married second, August 11, 1646, Susannah, daughter of Richard North; she was charged with witchcraft, tried, convicted and executed at Salem, July 19, 1692.

(I) Ebenezer Martin, ancestor of the line herein treated, was born in 1741, and died at Marblehead, January 10, 1800, aged fifty-nine years. He married, at Marblehead, October 28, 1766, Prudence Merritt, who died there November 10, 1800, aged sixty-one years. Children, born at Marblehead: 1. Ebenezer, mentioned below. 2. Holbrook, baptized January 31, 1773. 3. Jane, baptized November 5, 1775. 4. Mary, baptized September 27, 1778. 5. Prudence, baptized April 29, 1781. Ebenezer Martin was a soldier in the revolution: in 1775 was in Captain Gideon Burt's company, Colonel Timothy Danielson's regiment; also a quarter gunner in Captain Edward Fettyplace's company from Marblehead in 1777.

(II) Ebenezer Martin, son of Ebenezer Martin, was born in Marblehead about 1767, died in Canada, aged thirty-three years. He was a cabinet maker by trade, and also had a farm in Marblehead upon which he raised wheat and other crops, taking them to Canada on a raft and exchanging them for various kinds of wood for use in the making up of furniture. While on one of these trips on a raft, he was seen to go over the falls and his body was never recovered. He had on his person at the time a gold watch and considerable money. He was a fine cabinet maker and was celebrated in that line. He married, November 25, 1792, Jane, baptized January 10, 1770, daughter of Elkanah and Jane (Hubbard) Hitchins, who were married, August 24, 1769. Children of Mr. and Mrs. Martin: 1. Ebenezer, baptized September 29, 1793, died in New Orleans, May 1, 1827; married Ruth Nicholds. 2. Hannah, baptized April 5, 1795. 3. Mary, baptized May 7, 1797. 4. William Phippen Merritt, born August 23, 1800, mentioned below. 5. Almira Marcella, baptized October 31, 1802. 6. George Whitfield, baptized November 4, 1804.

(III) William Phippen Merritt Martin, son of Ebenezer Martin, was born in Marblehead, August 23, 1800, died in Swampscott about 1878. He was educated in the public schools of that town, learned the trade of shoemaker and was later a shoe manufacturer, continuing for many years. He removed to Swampscott in 1842. He married second, Jemima, born in Methuen, daughter of Eben Carleton. Children, born at Swampscott: 1. Miriam Sargeant, born at Marblehead, married Samuel Clough. 2. Mary Hanson, married the Rev. David H. Sherman, of Barre, Massachusetts; children: i. Jennie Louise Sherman; ii. Mary Sherman. 3. William. Two others died in infancy. Children of second wife: Louise Carleton, deceased, and Jane Hitchins, mentioned below.

(IV) Jane Hitchins Martin, daughter of William P. M. Martin, was born at Marblehead, August 25, 1836. She was educated in a private school and in the public schools of Swampscott and the Lynn high school, graduating from the latter. She married, May 20, 1863, Captain Thomas Stanley, born at Swampscott, October 26, 1817, died aged eighty-five years. He was a fisherman and followed that vocation in his locality. He was a son of Thomas Stanley, who was born in Salem, where he was a farmer, spent all of his life and died at the age of sixty-nine years. Child of Mr. and Mrs. Stanley: Louise Carleton, born in Salem, June 1, 1865, graduate of Wheaton Seminary, a school teacher.

TUTTLE Timothy Tuttle was born in New Hampshire, and spent his life in that state. He was a descendant of an old New England family whose immigration dates to the time of the colony. Indeed, history records that four distinct families of the surname Tuttle came over from England as early as 1634-35, three of them in the ship "Planter" and the other in the "Angel Gabriel," which was wrecked off the coast of Maine in 1634. The three were John of Ipswich, Richard of Boston, and William, who went to New Haven. The survivor of the "Angel Gabriel" was John Tuttle, of Dover, New Hampshire.

Calvin Butterfield Tuttle, son of Timothy Tuttle, was born on Long Island, New Hampshire, May 16, 1851, and died in Lynn, Massachusetts, May 6, 1906. He was one of the most successful lawyers of Boston and Lynn, specializing his practice to cases involving questions of patent law, which necessitated him to relinquish his general practice in the civil courts of this commonwealth. When about eighteen years old he left his home in New Hampshire and went to New York state, remained there about two years, then came to Lynn and began a course of study preparatory to entering the legal profession. Later on, however, he entered Wesleyan University, and still later matriculated at Boston University Law School, completed the course of that institution and graduated LL.B. in 1879. He at once began practice in Lynn and soon attained an enviable prominence at the bar of the courts, and as a trial lawyer before the court and jury he was remarkably successful and came to be recognized as one of the leading men of his profession in eastern Massachusetts. He was counsel for several large industrial corporations, and as associate counsel took a prominent part in directing the affairs and operation of the great United Shoe Machinery Company. In connection with his extensive patent practice Mr. Tuttle maintained offices in both Boston and Lynn, and he was the first lawyer to take up practice under the United States patent laws in the latter city. He was one of the incorporators of what originally was known as the Hand Power Lasting Machine Company, a corporation which had its inception in Matzeliger's "nigger-head lasting machine," the later development of which was due largely to Mr. Tuttle's enterprise and business sagacity, for he saw the future possibilities to be derived from its utilization and therefore took a leading part in organizing a corporate company for its manufacture, which in the course of time became a highly important element of the consolidated corporation now known as the United Shoe Machinery Company. His best work in connection with these several enterprises was that which identified him so closely with the Shoe Machinery Company for which he secured the first patents and of which he was the chief promoter. Indeed, it was largely through his personal endeavors that the present remarkable success of that great corporation was made possible. He also was one of the principal organizers of the Expedite Heel Finishing Company, a Massachusetts corporation which ultimately merged in the United Shoe Machinery Company From what is written in the preceding, it will be seen that Mr. Tuttle must have been a very busy man in his active professional career, for otherwise the great results achieved by him would not have been accomplished. He was a man of tireless mental energy and although during the last fifteen years of his professional career he was a physical invalid, he continued the great end he had set out to accomplish until he attained the desired ultimate result and then laid aside the arduous duties of former years for needed and well earned rest. He retired from active professional pursuits in 1900, but afterward kept in close touch with concerns which he had been the chief instrument in creating and in the success of which he always took a deep interest. Mr. Tuttle for many years was an honored member of the Essex Bar Association and enjoyed an enviable standing in all professional circles. He was a member of Mt. Carmel Lodge, F. and A. M., Sutton Chapter, R. A. M., and Olivet Commandery, K. T.

He married, August 22, 1877, Anna M., of Lynn, daughter of Smith A. Morse, who was born in Sandwich, New Hampshire, came to Lynn when a young man and afterward became a shoe manufacturer. He died in Lynn at the age of eighty-three years. His wife was Ruth F. (Hiller) Morse, born in Marblehead, daughter of Captain John C. Hiller, who spent the later years of his life in Lynn, and died there at the age of eighty years. Smith A. and Ruth F. (Hiller) Morse had three children, Anna M., now Mrs. Tuttle, Mary I., and John E., now living in Connecticut. Mr. and Mrs. Tuttle had one daughter, Maud M. Tuttle, graduate of Wellesley, '06.

Joseph H. Sheldon

SHELDON The family of which the late Ex-Mayor Joseph H. Sheldon, of Haverhill, was a representative, was founded in this country by three brothers who came from England. It is supposed by some that they came over from Spain when Philip V married Queen Mary of Scotland, and about 1600 came to America. The armorial bearing, borne by the family of Sheldon of England and America: Arms—Sable a fesse argent between three sheldrakes ppr. Crest—A sheldrake ppr. Motto—"Optimun patti," "To suffer is best." The brothers—Isaac, John, William—settled in Dorchester, Massachusetts.

(I) Isaac Sheldon, eldest of the three brothers, married and was the father of four children, among whom were John (see forward), and Isaac, who removed from Windsor, Connecticut, 1654.

(II) John Sheldon, son of Isaac Sheldon, signed the Parker and Whiting agreements in Billerica in 1658, and in the same year was made freeman. The following year John and William Sheldon were granted eight acres of land; William asked for more, but after some differences between the town and himself he left Billerica. John also left and settled in Woburn for a time. On March 30, 1674, the town of Billerica granted to John Sheldon forty acres "provided there shall be an end to all differences between the Town and the Sheldons." Mr. Sheldon married, September 21, 1658, Mary (Converse) Thompson, born in England, 1622, daughter of Edward Converse and widow of Simon Thompson. One child, John, see forward. John Sheldon, Sr., died May 24, 1690.

(III) John Sheldon, son of John and Mary Sheldon, born April 24, 1660, died August 27, 1724. He was made a freeman in 1680. He married, November 20, 1690, Deborah Hill, who died 1729. Children, born in Billerica: 1. John, 1691. 2. Mary, 1692; married Peter Hunt. 3. Samuel, April 9, 1694; married, January 22, 1718, Sarah Hutchinson, died May 14, 1777. 4. Deborah, 1698, died young. 5. Hannah, 1700. 6. Godfrey, see forward.

(IV) Godfrey Sheldon, son of Deacon John and Deborah Sheldon, died 1789. He married Hepzibah Felton; five children, among whom were John, born 1732, at Beverly, and Skelton.

(V) Skelton Sheldon, son of Godfrey and Hepzibah Sheldon, married Elizabeth Walcott; children: Jonathan, Jeremiah, see forward, Amos, Hannah.

(VI) Jeremiah Sheldon, son of Skelton and Elizabeth Sheldon, was born in North Danvers, Massachusetts, June 13, 1757, died there in 1803. He married, June 5, 1781, Elizabeth Goodell, an English lady, a direct descendant on her father's side of General Israel Putnam, who commanded at Bunker Hill, June 17, 1775. She was born in Danvers, July 8, 1759, died at Wilmington, August 18, 1853, aged ninety-four. Children: 1. Elbridge G., see forward. 2. Lucinda, born August 7, 1783, married John Howard, died October 23, 1885, aged one hundred and two. 3. Samuel Holbon, born December 26, 1786, North Reading. 4. Asa Goodell, born October 24, 1788, Wilmington. 5. Harriet, born August 5, 1791. 6. Elizabeth, born December 16, 1795. 7. Jeremiah, born January 26, 1798. 8. Sophia, born August 24, 1801, married James Hathaway Milbury.

(VII) Elbridge Gerry Sheldon, son of Jeremiah and Elizabeth Sheldon, was born in Danvers, November 18, 1781, died there December 23, 1846. He married Eleanor Harding; children: Elbridge, born 1814, died June 5, 1894, at Haverhill; Samuel, born 1816; Eleanor; Samuel.

(VIII) Samuel Sheldon, son of Elbridge Gerry and Eleanor Sheldon, born in Danvers, October 16, 1819, died October 18, 1854. He married Emily B. Sleeper, born Alton, New Hampshire, November 2, 1818, died July 11, 1890. Children: 1. Joseph H., see forward. 2. Samuel H., born Haverhill, November 15, 1844, died March 25, 1884, unmarried. 3. Charles N., born Haverhill, February 27, 1847, died March 2, 1850. 4. Jesse H., born Haverhill, August 3, 1849, married Ellen Richardson, born Haverhill; one child, James Fitts Sheldon, born February 24, 1872. 5. Emily, born Haverhill, November 24, 1851, died March 12, 1852. 6. Burton, born Haverhill, May 26, 1854, drowned June 4, 1864.

(IX) Joseph H. Sheldon, son of Samuel and Emily B. Sheldon, was born in Haverhill, Massachusetts, February 12, 1843. In early life, after acquiring a practical education, he engaged as clerk in the clothing store of J. S. Wheeler, with whom he remained for thirteen years. From 1871 to 1879 he was in business on his own account on Merrimack street, Haverhill, and then associated in the same business with Frank D. Sargent, this firm continuing for several years and being succeeded by James A. Keefe. After his retirement from the clothing business Mr. Sheldon devoted himself to looking after several estates and his own real estate holdings. Honored by his fellowmen in various political positions, he discharged the trust imposed upon him, sacrificing personal business for that of his fellow citizens, and time and again refusing higher positions than those to which he had previously been elected. In the years 1882-83 he served in the board of aldermen; in 1885 was elected chief executive of the city, recalled in 1887 for another year, his administrations being without blemish and to the entire satisfaction of his constituents; in 1877 was nominated by the Democrats of the state for the position of state auditor, and from 1893 to 1899 was a member of the overseers of the poor. In social and religious circles Mr. Sheldon was equally prominent as in politics. His religious affiliations were with the First Universalist Church, of which he was a trustee for years; he was a constant attendant at church services, and gave liberally of his time and means to the support of the same. He was a member of the Merrimack Lodge of Free Masons, Mutual Relief Lodge of Odd Fellows, Haverhill Lodge of Elks, of which he was past exalted ruler, and a trustee of the Odd Fellows' Building Association. He was at one time district deputy for the Elks of Eastern Massachusetts, was a member of the Red Men and the Wachusett Club.

Mr. Sheldon married, December 27, 1866, Emily E. Jaques, born Haverhill, Massachusetts, February 26, 1843 (see Jaques). Ex-Mayor Sheldon died at his late home, 108 Main street, Haverhill, October 21, 1906, after an illness of about two months, aged sixty-three years eight months nine days. The interment was in Linwood cemetery. His death was not only mourned by his widow, but by a large circle of friends.

JAQUES The late Addison B. Jaques, for many years a widely known and valued citizen of Haverhill, traced his ancestry on the paternal side to Parker Jaques, who was instrumental in establishing American independence. The name of Parker Jaques appears as first corporal in Captain Stephen Kent's company, which enlisted July 13, 1775, discharged November 1, 1775, said company being raised for seacoast defense in Essex county, stationed at Newbury. He signed an order for wages due November 1, 1775, dated Gloucester, December 10, 1775. He served as corporal in Lieutenant John Brackett's company on the alarm of April 19, 1775, marched the following day, troop of horse, length of service nine days. He was a private in camp of Captain Jonathan Poor, March 18, 1777, six weeks service. He lived to the advanced age of ninety-four years two months, and his father attained the great age of ninety-two years, proving that the family was noted for longevity.

"Master Eliphalet Jaques," son of Parker Jaques, and father of the late Addison B. Jaques, was well known as an educator in Newbury, Massachusetts, for many years. He was a man of inventive genius and mechanical skill, as proved by the fact that on May 24, 1814, he had granted to him a patent for a washing machine, also a patent for a fountain pen, two very useful articles. He married Elizabeth Davis, born August 23, 1791, died January 8, 1864, daughter of William and Elizabeth Davis, the former born August 8, 1758, and the latter August 11, 1763. Children: William, died young. Caroline, died young. Addison B., see forward. Eliphalet Jaques died August 4; 1863, aged eighty-eight years.

Addison B. Jaques was born in Newburyport, Massachusetts, August 2, 1819 At the age of thirteen he came to old Haverhill to become a clerk in the book store of James Gale, which was kept in the Bannister block and later served in the same capacity for the Rev. Thomas G. Farnsworth, the first Universalist minister of Haverhill, who was a bookseller, and was the first commissioned postmaster of the town, in which latter responsible public service Addison B. was his assistant. In due course of time Mr. Jaques became proprietor of the book store in which his early experience was gained, and he continued in this line for several years, conducting business first in the Bannister block and afterwards in the block then known as the Currier block, on Main street, just above the Eagle House, and later as the Chase block. Subsequently he became a partner for several years in the book and stationery business with the late James V. Smiley, on Main street, the business being later sold to James A. Hale. He was successful in business, having acquired the habits of industry and frugality, and he gradually grew in favor with the people, winning their confidence to a remarkable degree. As an evidence of this fact he was elected as town treasurer and custodian of the public finances as the successor of William Taggart, in March, 1844, which office he held for twenty consecutive years and until his resignation in 1864, when he was succeeded by Calvin Buttrick. Fol-

Lewis Historical Pub. Co. L. A. Struck E. Orange N.J.

A. R. Jaques

lowing this he was elected assistant treasurer of the Haverhill Savings Bank in 1865, and the following year was elected treasurer, the successor of the venerable James Gale, and this office of great trust and responsibility he held until his resignation in 1889, a period of twenty-four years, for the express purpose of passing into comparative retirement After his retirement as an executive officer of that institution he was retained in advisory relations by being made the vice-president of the same. For one year he was a director in the Haverhill National Bank, which he resigned in 1866. He filled the office of director in the Haverhill Gas Light Company, treasurer of the Odd Fellows' Building Association, trustee of the City Hospital from the time it was founded, and was on the board of commissioners of the Haverhill city sinking fund. He also held many minor relations in various capacities where good judgment and discretion were regarded of importance. Under the city government in 1870 he was elected a member of the common council, but declined a reelection. In the voluntary associations of the city he was represented for many years. He was the owner of considerable real estate in Haverhill, erected several buildings, and in various other ways contributed to the growth and development of his adopted city. In October, 1845, he was elected a member of Mutual Relief Lodge; he was a member of Eagle Encampment of Patriarchs, in which institution he expressed great interest, and in which his counsel was often sought and held in the highest esteem; was a member of Saggahew Lodge, Free and Accepted Masons; Pentucket Social Club; and Sumner Street Universalist Society (now Kenoza Avenue Universalist Society), of which he was a much valued member.

Mr. Jaques married, June 9, 1842, Emily R. Farnsworth, of Boston, a niece of the Rev. T. G. Farnsworth, and they were the parents of two daughters: Emily E., widow of Joseph Henry Sheldon, a sketch of whom precedes this in the work; and Mary E., who died in July, 1894; she was the wife of Marlon Greene, of Amesbury, Massachusetts, and mother of four children: William A., Louis E., Harry M. and Ralph R. Greene. Mr. Jaques died at his home on Main street, September 5, 1890, and his wife died December 4, 1900.

The last rites over the remains of Mr. Jaques took place from his late residence, 108 Main street, and in accordance with the well known taste of the deceased the ceremonies were quiet and unostentatious, but solemn and impressive. Many of the prominent business men and citizens were present to share in the general sorrow. The services were conducted by the Rev. J. C. Snow, and the interment was in Linwood cemetery. The Rev. J. C. Snow spoke in substance as follows:

After referring to him as a man of simple tastes and habits, and remarking that it was the desire of the family that the services of the occasion should be void of display, he said "that his life was marked from the beginning with those characteristics which only ripened with his years into fixed habits. He was industrious, frugal and upright. Coming to this city a poor boy, at the age of thirteen, he won first the confidence of his employers and gradually rose to the favor and confidence of the general public. He was called to fill many positions of trust, of both a public and private nature. The duties of these varied positions he discharged not only with fidelity but with a certain exact and scrupulous honesty that left no possible opening for miscarriage or even suspicion. It may be said that whatever worldly fortune he won is free from all taint of dishonesty. The same spirit and temper which distinguished him elsewhere marked also his religious life. It was not demonstrative, but simple and quiet. The Summer Street Universalist Society with which he was early connected had in him a faithful supporter. No better evidence of the genuineness and strength of his religious convictions need be given than are afforded by his steady loyalty and liberality to the parish of which he was to the last an honored member. From all the other numerous associations with which he was connected would come a like tribute today. His life may well be taken as an object lesson for young men, and as an encouragement to all who would believe that integrity of conduct is not incompatible with business prosperity."

HARRIS Thomas Harris, the progenitor, was probably nephew of the first Thomas Harris, of Ipswich. Little is known of him and perhaps some facts credited to the record of Thomas Sr. and Thomas Jr. belonged to him. He lived at Ipswich, and his widow Martha married, in 1683, Samuel Burnham. Thomas Sr., who died in 1687, also had a wife Martha. Children: Thomas of Ipswich; John, mentioned below; Elinor; Aquila; Mary.

(II) John Harris, son of Thomas Harris,

was born about 1650, in Ipswich, where he lived and died. His will, dated July 16, 1714, proved November 13, 1714, bequeathed to son Thomas lands at Gloucester, excepting the lot at Pigeon Cove, and "that lot that was Law's;" to sons John and Samuel rest of land in Ipswich and Gloucester, Coxhall, (Maine), except lot at Pigeon Cove. To John he gave his gold ring and silver shoe buckles. He bequeathed also to four daughters mentioned below. He married Esther ———. Children: 1. Thomas, born in Ipswich, about 1675; married Susanna Sibley, daughter of William; she died January 15, 1705; he was in Gloucester as early as November 29, 1702, when his son John was born there; son William, born January 10, 1705, at Gloucester; he bought land at Sandy Bay, Gloucester, March, 1709, of Richard Tarr, and again in 1712 more land. 2. John, mentioned below. 3. Samuel, perhaps settled in Maine, on land inherited at Coxhall. 4. Abigail, married ——— Burnham. 5. Esther, married ——— Chapman. 6. Mary. 7. Margaret.

(III) John Harris, son of John Harris (2), was in Gloucester as early as 1711. In 1720 he had a grant of land near his home on Pigeon Hill, Gloucester. He married Maria ———. Children: 1. Thomas Jr., married Sarah Norwood. 2. Benjamin, born June 6, 1716; died September 21, 1726. 3. Hannah, born October 26, 1720. 4. Samuel, mentioned below. 5. Abigail, married ——— Grover. 6. Ann, married Jonathan Andros.

(IV) Samuel Harris, son of John Harris, was born about 1710; married at Gloucester, June 6, 1737; died before 1770. He was a fisherman. His estate was divided by deed dated July 7, 1770, signed by Thomas Harris of Gloucester, Samuel Plummer of Gloucester, as attorney for Abigail Grover and Jonathan and Ann Andros. The estate is described as belonging to their father, who inherited it from his father "John Harris of Ipswich." Samuel received land on the Cape, on the west side of Little Swamp, near his own barn, adjoining land of Caleb Poole and Jonathan Poole. Children: 1. Samuel, born about 1735; went to Maine. Amos, William and David, of New Gloucester, Maine, also appear to belong to this family. They settled before the revolution on Harris Hill.

(V) Captain Amos Harris, son of Samuel Harris (4), removed to Maine when a young man. He settled in New Gloucester. He was captain of a New Gloucester company in the Fourth Cumberland county regiment. 1776; also of second company, same regiment, 1777; and also of a detachment in Colonel Pike's command, 1779, under direction of the committee of safety at Falmouth (Portland), Maine.

(VI) Amos Harris Jr., son of Captain Amos Harris, was born about 1760. He was a soldier in the revolution from New Gloucester, Maine, a private in Captain Benjamin Parker's company, Colonel Nathaniel Wade's regiment, 1778; also in Captain Benjamin Leman's company, same regiment, later in the year, in the Rhode Island campaign. In 1790 he resided at Bakerstown, now Poland, Maine, and the federal census of that year shows that he had two sons under sixteen and three females in his family. William Harris, doubtless a brother, had three sons under sixteen and one female in his family, according to the same census. William and David Harris were early settlers of Poland, on Harris Hill, according to the local history. There was also an Amariah Harris among the early settlers of New Gloucester, adjoining Poland.

(VII) David Harris, son of Amos Harris (6), was born in Bakerstown, now Poland, and lived there on Harris Hill. He became a prosperous farmer, and followed also the trade of cooper. He was a highly respected citizen.

(VIII) Lyman Harris, son of David Harris, was born at Poland, Maine, about 1800. Children: 1. Simeon Lyman, mentioned below. 2. Albert Watson, born April 7, 1843; married, July 11, 1868, Lizzie Fuller, of London, England; child: Mabel Rose, born May 18, 1872, married, January 22, 1896, Louis E. Small, of Mexico, Maine. 3. Emma, married Amos Chadman. 4. Chase. 5. David. 6. Tristram. 7. Roscoe. 8. Abbie, married Daniel Robinson.

(IX) Simeon Lyman Harris, son of Lyman Harris, was born at Harris Hill, Poland, Maine, November 16, 1835. He received his education in the district school of his native town, and when young, was apprenticed first to his uncle, Sylvester Harris, and later to Jedediah Cook. He learned the trade of shoemaker, which he followed for a time. He owned two farms in New Gloucester, adjoining Poland, Maine, containing one hundred and fifty acres. In the early seventies he removed to Dover, New Hampshire, where he continued at farming for two years, thence removing to Madbury. About 1877, he returned to his native town and engaged in the teaming business, later taking up farming again. His farm in Poland is in the Mechanics

Falls district, about a hundred acres which he bought of Oliver Dwinell. He carries on an extensive dairy business in connection with his farm. He is a very popular man on account of his hearty good nature and friendliness. His cheerful optimism makes him a welcome visitor wherever he goes. He is a member of the Methodist church, in politics is a Republican, and has served as overseer of the poor, and has been a member of the school committee and road surveyor. He is a member of Poland Grange, Patrons of Husbandry. He married first, Clarissa, daughter of Nelson and Harriet Wight; second, Flora Etta, daughter of Oliver and Mehitable Bearce. Her father was a ship joiner, and served in the war of 1812. Children of first wife: 1. George Nelson, born February 9. 1860; married, December 22, 1885, Susie Evelyn Furbush, of North Berwick, Maine. 2. Son, died young. Children of second wife: 3. Franklin Elden, born March 9, 1864; mentioned below. 4. Frederick Lincoln, born October 17, 1865; married, February 18, 1891, Jennie Gertrude Brooks, of Portland, Maine; children: i. Levi Cutler, born September 11, 1896; ii. Ruth Annie, February 4, 1901. 5. Alberton, mentioned below. 6. Sylvia Minerva, born June 22, 1869; married, June 13, 1893, John E. Estes, of New Gloucester, Maine. 7. Jennie Grace, born May 7, 1871; married first, June 13, 1889, Stephen M. Prince, of Mechanics Falls, Maine, who died May 24, 1900; second, September 5, 1906, Frank J. Dwinal, of Minot, Maine; one child, Ralph Clyde Prince, born February 12, 1895.

(X) Franklin Elden Harris, son of Simeon Lyman Harris, was born at Poland, Maine, March 9, 1864. He received his education in the public schools of New Gloucester, Poland and Mechanics Falls, and at the early age of twelve went to work for Charles Hillman, of Poland, still attending school during the winter. Later he went to Portland, where he was employed by J. P. Hutchinson in the milk business, and remained with him for five years. After returning home he removed to Oshkosh, Wisconsin, working in the lumber business at different times for Peter Gratton, Judge Washburn and Hayward Brothers. He then went to Hillsboro, near Fargo, Dakota, and worked on the wheat farms a short time, thence going to Arkansas, where he was employed by the United States government on river improvement. Owing to the severe heat of the summers there he was obliged to give up and return to the Dakota wheat fields. Later he returned to Wisconsin and Michigan, being employed at lumbering. For some time he was in a hospital on account of injuries received from the kick of a horse, and on this account he returned east to his home in Maine. For six months he was employed by George Goodwin, grain dealer of Poland, and he subsequently went to West Medford. After a short time he went to Hope Valley, Rhode Island, to work for Edgar Swett. Returning to West Medford he bought out C. H. Dunn, a partner of his brother Alberton Harris in the milk business, the firm name being Harris Brothers. Later the firm was dissolved, he taking the Somerville route, which he still retains. He has an extensive business, with high class customers, and contracts for his milk with J. H. Prescott, of Bradford. He resides at 68 Quincy street, Medford Hillside, where he bought a house and later built a barn. He is a Republican in politics and a Universalist in religion. He was formerly a member of the Somerville and Cambridge Milk Dealers' Association. Through strict attention to business and unquestioned integrity, he has achieved success, and has the esteem and confidence of all who know him. He married, March 27, 1893, Gertrude Matilda Stuart, born at Washington, D. C., March 4, 1868, daughter of Samuel Porter and Matilda (Waterhouse) Stuart. Her father was a veteran of the civil war, employed in the war department at Washington. Children: 1. Son, died at birth. 2. Irma Gertrude, born March 20, 1904. 3. Stuart Franklin, born January 16, 1906.

(X) Alberton Harris, son of Simeon Lyman Harris, was born at New Gloucester, Maine, September 2, 1867. He attended the public schools there until the age of eight, removing with his parents to Dover, New Hampshire, attending school there two years, thence removing to Madbury and then to Poland. He attended school at Page's Mills and Mechanics Falls until he was seventeen years old, working during vacations in the shoe factory. He also worked a year in the drug store of J. C. Walker. When twenty-one years of age he went to West Medford and entered the employ of Frank A. Oxnard, a milk dealer, driving his team about seven months. He then worked for Charles C. Stevens in the same business, at Medford Hillside, for five years. On July 1, 1892, he purchased the business of Mr. Stevens and formed a partnership with C. H. Dunn. In a short time this partnership was dissolved and Frank E. Harris admitted to the firm. The brothers did a thriving business for about eight years, when the firm dissolved, Alberton retaining the Medford route and the stock in trade. He has from sixteen to forty head of the best mixed stock, and four horses. He bought his present residence of Mr. Stevens in July, 1900, and has since added a stable. He and his family attend the Universalist church at Medford. In politics he is a Republican. He is a member of Harmony Lodge, No. 68, I. O. O. F., and was formerly a member of Mount Sinai Commandery, Knights of Malta, at Medford. Mr. Harris is a man of great energy and devotes his attention to the management of the farm. He is devoted to his family, and highly esteemed by his many friends. He married, at West Medford, March 11, 1898, May Burnett, born at Cape Breton, Province of Quebec, Canada, June 30, 1871, daughter of Thomas and Mary (Christy) Burnett, of Cape Breton. Her father was a fisherman and farmer. Children: 1. Delbert Leslie, born October 18, 1898. 2. Flora Stevens, December 25, 1899. 3. Edith May, August 2, 1903. 4. Dora (twin), born April 1, 1906. 5. Doris, twin with Dora.

LINDSAY This family was of ancient Scotch ancestry, of Norman origin, the name being taken from some Norman or French location. The family probably came first to England and from there went to Scotland, where they were as early as 1116, in Roxburghshire, Fifeshire, Berwickshire and Haddingtonshire. They owned the dukedom of Montrose, and the earldoms of Balcarres, Crawford, Lindsay, and the lordship of Spynie. There were many distinguished men among the members of the family, among them David Lindsay, first Protestant Bishop of Ross, 1600, and several members of parliament; Sir John Lindsay, laird of Dunrod, Lanarkshire, John Lindsay, Anstruther, Easter, John Lindsay, of Edzell, Forfarshire, Patrick, Lord Lindsay, of the Byres, Edinburgh, Robert Lindsay, of Dunrod, Rutherglen, in 1579, Robert Lindsay, of Ruthergeln in 1617, David Lindsay, of Cupar in 1540, Sir David Lindsay, of Cupar in 1571, Sir David Lindsay, of Edgell in 1597, David Lindsay, of Brechin in 1621, David Lindsay, of Beltsanes, Forfarshire in 1593. Several of these families bore arms, as did also Alexander Lindsay, baronet, of Evelick.

(I) John Lindsay, immigrant ancestor, born in Ayrshire, Scotland, settled at Halifax, Nova Scotia. He was an officer in the British army in the revolution, and his sword was in the possession of his son John for years, and is still owned by the family. He was given a grant of a thousand acres in what is now Brookvale, Halifax county, and built a log cabin. He cleared a part of the land and carried on the farm, a large dairy being a part of his business. Later he erected a frame house, but the day before he was to move into it he died of apoplexy, while sitting in his chair. He was a Scotch Presbyterian. He married ——— Griffin. Children: 1. Sarah, died unmarried at Archat, Nova Scotia. 2. John.

(II) John Lindsay, son of John Lindsay, attended the district school at Halifax, and remained in Halifax until he was about seventeen years old, when his father was granted a farm. He went with his father to Brookvale, and received a part of the land as a wedding gift from his father. He was considered one of the best and most prosperous farmers in that section of the country, and he also did lumbering. His methods were progressive, and he was popular personally. He owned a large double house, in one half of which his son Alexander lived, and John and his son shared in the business of farming. Alexander inherited the farm, two and a half miles from the village. John Lindsay was brought up a Presbyterian, but became a Methodist in later life. In politics he was a Liberal. He married Margaret Parker. Children: 1. James, born 1809; married Mary Stuart, of Scotland, and had Anthony, Isabel, Albert, John, Jessie, and Sarah. 2. Abigail, born March 4, 1814; died October 28, 1899; married, July 4, 1832, James Hanna, of Musquodoboit; children: i. Elizabeth Hanna, born April 8, 1834; ii. John Hanna, born April 22, 1836, died July 31, 1891, married in Pottsville, Pennsylvania, Julia Teller, and had Annetta Hanna, died aged nine months; iii. James Hanna, born February 18, 1841; iv. Hugh Hanna, born September 22, 1839, died in Mobile, Alabama; v. Alexander Hanna, born May 18, 1843, married Cassie Ellis, and had Winifred Muir Hanna; vi. Margaret Hanna, born March 22, 1845, married Edward L. Howard; vii. Samuel Hanna, born April 1, 1848, married, May 27, 1886, Mary McCurdy, and had Frank Hanna, born March 26, 1887, Norma Hanna, born January 25, 1889, Grace Hanna, born November 25, 1890, William Hanna, born November 12, 1892, Victor Hanna, born January 7, 1898, and Hugh Smith Hanna, born November 17, 1903; viii. George Hanna, born February 7, 1851, married, May, 1885, Jane Sibley and had Harold Hanna, born January 19, 1888, and Anna Hanna, born December 20, 1890. 3. Thomas, born November 29, 1811; died November 15, 1889; married first, 1832, Rebecca Hanna, of Belfast, Ireland; second, 1846, Margaret Richards, of Musquodoboit; children: i. John, born August 16, 1833, married, November 26, 1855, Jessie McKenzie, and had James Alexander, born January 8, 1857 (married, January 19, 1885, Elichia H. Bosworth), Rebecca Jane, born April 23, 1859 (married, November 24, 1877, Alexander Doyle, and had Jessie Maud Doyle, Margaret E. Doyle, Frederick J. Doyle, Thomas W. Doyle, Harry W. Doyle, Lottie E. Doyle, Wilburt L. Doyle, Carrie J. Doyle, Foster H. Doyle, Frances J. Doyle, Eleanor D. Doyle and John A. Doyle), John William Dickson, born September 12, 1862, (married, July 13, 1887, Annetta Hilchey, and had Stanley James, born March 20, 1891), Thomas Warren, born August 24, 1864, (married, April 22, 1890, Mary B. Hilchey, and had Ray Dickson, Basil, Vivian, Blanchard, Harold and Jessie Laurel), Margaret, born October 1, 1869, (married, September 4, 1900, Emerson Hunt, and had Hazel L. Hunt), and Frederick, born March 17, 1873, died April 27, 1878; ii. James, married Susan Murphy, and had Everett, Myra, Lexie and Emily; iii. Hugh, married Clara Harvey, and had four children; iv. Jane Elizabeth, born May 7, 1838, married, August 31, 1868, John Wilson, of Aberdeen, Scotland, and had Charles Francis Moore Wilson, born November 3, 1869, (married Ella Munroe, of Halifax), Arthur Gordon Wilson, born February 27, 1871, (married Sarah McDonald), Florence Bertha Wilson, born September 10, 1873, Jane Oliver Wilson, born June 25, 1875, Margaret Henrietta Wilson, born October 6, 1877, and John Dickey Wilson, born January 4, 1880; v. Rebecca, born November 28, 1852, (married, September 27, 1894, Freeman Caldwell, of Gasperneaux, Nova Scotia); vi. Margaret Henrietta, married first, Charles Weaver, of Lowell, Massachusetts, and had Lindsay and Osman Weaver, married second, George Williams, of Vermont; vii. William, married Amanda Young; viii. Emily, married James Fitzpatrick, and had John, William, Mary, Emily, Nellie and Thomas Fitzpatrick; ix. (by second wife), Charles, born September 6, 1847, married, October 21, 1869, Matilda Fisher, and had Margaret Ella, born August 31, 1870, (married July, 1890, John A. Richey, and had Charles Richey, born 1891, Robert Richey, born 1893, and Jessie Maud Richey, born 1895), William George, born October 9, 1872, Sarah Gammel, born November 21, 1874, Henry, born September 13, 1877, (married, 1900, Elizabeth Wright, and had Victor, born 1903), Ethel Bessie, born November 12, 1879, (married, March 3, 1895, Gustave G. Nohl, and had Anna Nohl, born May, 1898, George Nohl, born November, 1903, and Robert Gustave Nohl, born February, 1908), John McDonald, born January 2, 1882, (married, January 2, 1907, Clara Wood, and had Edna Mae, born December 3, 1907); Angus, born April 2, 1850, married first, 1874, Jessie Fisher, who died June 10, 1891, second, November 29, 1893, Etta Beck, and had Warren, born March 11, 1875, Wallace, born February 21, 1877, Frank, born January 6, 1880, died Auguse, 1882, Frank, born July, 1883, Lloyd, born April 3, 1885, Leland, born February 15, 1887, Stanley, born March 14, 1889, (by second wife): Jessie, born September 23, 1894, Alexander, born February 18, 1899, Gladys, born June 10, 1900, Beatrice, born August 29, 1902, and Ethel, born October 17, 1905; xi. Mary, born September 15, 1855, died September 10, 1889, married, December 24, 1878, Henry Dart, and had Hadley Dart, born April, 1882, Osman Dart, born March, 1886, Angus Dart, born June, 1888, Mary Dart, born August 20, 1889, and Ernest Dart, born August, 1890; xii. Susan, born September 25, 1857, resides at Malden, Massachusetts, unmarried; xiii. Jessie, born May 17, 1863, married, April 1, 1884, Thomas Beal, of Sackville, New Brunswick, and had Carl Russell Beal, born April 2, 1885, Blanche Lindsay Beal, born January 19, 1887, Caroline Wells Armstrong Beal, born March 11, 1889, Thomas Beal, born September 6, 1890, died November 14, 1898, Ethel Beal, born January 16, 1892, died November 15, 1898, Margaret, born August 28, 1893, Lena Gladys Beal, born August 6, 1895, Jessie Mildred Beal, born February 6, 1898, and Susie Ethel Beal, born July 15, 1900; xiv. Thomas, born July 13, 1853, died March 13, 1875; xv. Blanche, born April 12, 1870, married, August 29, 1894, John Hood, of Elgin, Nova Scotia, and had Thomas Lindsay Hood, born September 12, 1895, Alexander Donald Hood, born November 12, 1898, Margaret Emily Hood, born October 1, 1901, and Florence Lavina Hood, born May 19, 1905; xvi. Alexander, born January 1, 1861, died September 1, 1898, married, December 23, 1886, Annie L. Dickey, of Lower Steweack, Nova

Scotia. 4. John, born March, 1817; died April 6, 1876; married, 1840, Margaret Hutchinson; children: i. William, born 1842; ii. John Hutchinson, born 1845, married Elizabeth Waugh, and had Margaret (married Abraham Currie) and Mabel (married Henry Shannon); iii. Francis Parker, born June 26, 1847, died unmarried March 14, 1906; iv. Robert, born April 10, 1851, married Alice Mason, of Gay's River, Nova Scotia, and had Katherine: v. Katherine Linton, born January 1, 1854, died unmarried, November 12, 1872; vi. Edgar, born May 22, 1857, married, December 18, 1882, Clara Louise Glendenning, born December 17, 1861, and had Grace Louise, born January 25, 1885, Margaret, born February 16, 1887, Elizabeth, born April 5, 1889, Lydia Carpenter, born June 3, 1891, died November 28, 1892, Mabel Lillian, born July 5, 1893, and Edgar Gardner, born February 1, 1905; vii. Joseph Howe. 5. Sarah, born 1821; died November 29, 1886; married, June 30, 1855, Alexander Stewart, of Scotland. 6. William, mentioned below. 7. Alexander, mentioned below.

(III) William Lindsay, son of John Lindsay, born at Musquodoboit, March 19, 1819, died there October 12, 1876. He went to the district school, and remained with his father on the farm until he was eighteen years old. He engaged in lumbering for a year or two in Woodstock, but returned to the farm. At his marriage he received from his father about two hundred acres of land in Brookvale, in the centre of the township—a valley farm with a stream known as Lindsay Brook, running through it. It had much wood on it, which he cut, for a time running a saw mill. He was known as a hardworking successful farmer, and had also a reputation as a good cattle raiser and trader. In person he was of medium build, and of lovable character and equable disposition. It was said that he never had an enemy. He was deeply religious, devoted to the interests of the Presbyterian church, of which he was a member, and to which he was a liberal contributor of his time and money. He took great interest in the political life of the town, and served as trustee of the school committee, overseer of roads, assessor, and selectman. He was a prominent member of the County Agricultural Society, and was in the militia. He married, February 10, 1845, Agnes Higgins, born at Musquodoboit, May 30, 1825, daughter of George and Agnes Pitt (Scott) Higgins. Children: 1. William George, born December 13, 1846; married, December 8, 1870, Isabelle McClellan, of Londonderry, Nova Scotia; children: i. Augustus, lost his life by accident; ii. Ida Belle, born August 14, 1876; iii. Charles Edgar, born January 28, 1879, married, May 25, 1904, Theresa Cruikshanks, of Ship Harbor, Nova Scotia; iv. Olla May, born July 20, 1884; v. Henry Howard, born September 13, 1886; vi. Leander Nobel, born December 20, 1888; vii. Stella Lee, born May 29, 1891. 2. Henry, born June 15, 1848; married, May, 1908, Miss Mitchel, of Musquodoboit, Nova Scotia. 3. Leander, born September 21, 1851. 4. Caroline, born October 18, 1853; married, March 28, 1876, Alexander Fraser Rhodes, of Musquodoboit; children: i. Arthur Rhodes, born January 22, 1877, died March 25, 1877. ii. Bessie Lindsay Rhodes, born January 18, 1878; iii. Edgar Allen Rhodes, born August 6, 1880, died April 30, 1896; iv. Chester Alexander Rhodes, born September 10, 1882, died December 11, 1907; v. Elida Elsie Rhodes, born May 7, 1884, married, September 25, 1907, Francis Burgess Coffin. 5. Eliza, born October 3, 1854; married, November 19, 1890, Charles Converse, of Amherst, New Hampshire, and had Agnes Fuller Converse, born October 28, 1893. 6. Melinda Margaret, born April 3, 1857; married, December 15, 1882, Adam Isaac Archibald; children: i. Carrie Mabel Archibald, born November 26, 1883; ii. Leander Lindsay Archibald, January 23, 1886; iii. Jean Braden Archibald, October 16, 1887; iv. Ernest Bayne Archibald, September 26, 1889; v. Bertha May Archibald, April 1, 1894. 7. John Augustus, born May 8, 1859; mentioned below. 8. Mary Ellen, born 1861; married, August 6, 1888, William Tupper Dickey, of Lemoore, California; children: i. Grace Willard Dickey, born September 25, 1889; ii. Bessie Tupper Dickey, September 20, 1890; iii. Leland Converse Dickey, February 22, 1893; iv. Olanta Fay Dickey, June 4, 1895; v. Leander Lindsay Dickey, March 15, 1898; vi. William Francis Dickey, August 17, 1900; vii. Harold Dickey, September 14, 1905; viii. Ellen May Dickey, September 12, 1907. 9. Arthur, born December 21, 1864; married, September 19, 1895, Frances Trent Beakes, of Trenton, New Jersey. 10. Alfred, born October 28, 1866; married, October 28, 1896, Nancy Julia Hicks, of Hanford, California; children: i. Edgar Ray, born December 8, 1897; ii. Edna Reita, June 7, 1901; iii. Osmer Newton, April 25, 1905. 11. Mortimer, died between four and five years of age. 12. Bertha, born 1866; married, December 21, 1898, Albert Murdock Higgins, of Brookvale, Nova Scotia; children: i. Edith Agnes Higgins, born September 7, 1899; ii. Ruth Beatrice Higgins, July 17, 1901; iii. Claire Linda Higgins, September 24, 1903.

(IV) John Augustus Lindsay, son of William Lindsay, was born at Brookvale, Nova Scotia, May 8, 1859. He received his education in the public schools in his native town, and remained on the home farm until a year after the death of his father. At the age of eighteen he went to Arlington, Massachusetts, and found employment with Joseph Butterfield, a market gardener. A year later he was employed by Mrs. David Fisher, who owned a large market farm on Massachusetts avenue. Here he remained eight years, taking charge of the marketing of the produce. Later he entered the employ of Daniel L. Tappan, son-in-law of Mrs. Fisher, who assumed charge of the same farm at that time, and attended to the marketing himself. Mr. Lindsay took charge of the cultivation, and has since superintended the farm. He employs some twenty-five men the year round, with the number doubled in the spring season. He has under cultivation between fifty and sixty acres, with two large greenhouses and heating plant. He makes a specialty of early small vegetables, with outside crops of onions and celery. About thirty-five acres is devoted to celery, and the output of onions reaches as much as six thousand bushels. Mr. Lindsay thoroughly understands his business, and is considered one of the best gardeners in the vicinity. He resides at 13 Belknap street, where he built his house in 1890. In politics he is a Republican, and he and his family attend the Arlington Congregational Church. He is a member of Bethel Lodge, No. 12, I. O. O. F., at Arlington, and is on the working staff of the lodge. He belongs to the Arlington Men's Club. He married, December 22, 1885, Georgianna Spencer, born at Londonderry, Nova Scotia, August 21, 1864, daughter of George Robert and Catherine (Durgin) Spencer, of Londonderry. Children: 1. Raymond Mortimer, born November 25, 1887. 2. Lillian Maud, November 7, 1890.

(III) Alexander Lindsay, son of John Lindsay (2), was born in 1822 in Musquodoboit, Nova Scotia. He received his education in the district school during the winter months, and assisted his father on the farm. He lived after his marriage in half the house on the farm, and he and his father worked the farm together. At his father's death he inherited the homestead, consisting of about three hundred acres, and he found a ready market for his produce in Halifax, doing his own selling. In 1869 he let his farm on shares and removed to Chetezcook, Halifax county, on the coast, on account of the health of his wife. Here he conducted a general store for four years. He then returned to his farm and continued there until within two years of his death, when he went to Colorado Springs. He died there March 7, 1889, and the homestead at Brookvale was sold. Alexander Lindsay was a man of high character, who was respected and loved by his neighbors. He was deeply interested in the Wesleyan Methodist Church, and served as a deacon. In politics he was a Conservative, and was trustee of the school committee, and road overseer. He was captain of the Musquodoboit militia. He married first, Charlotte Sprott Gould, born 1825, died October 8, 1882, daughter of William and Susan (Archibald) Gould, of Musquodoboit. He married second, Eliza, daughter of Alexander Scott. Children, all by first wife: 1. Sidney, born November 26, 1848; married, May 15, 1879, Auginette McCurdy; children: i. Everett R., born April 26, 1880, died August 25, 1902; ii. E. Guy, born June 27, 1884; iii. Munroe, born February 14, 1889; iv. Edith May, born January 26, 1893. 2. Parmelia, born February 16, 1851; married, January 6, 1891, Frederick Alonzo Hatch, of Somerville, Massachusetts, and had Edith May Hatch, born November 9, 1891. 3. Georgianna, born July 6, 1853; married, 1882, Howard Taylor; children: i. Austin Wylie Taylor, born July 3, 1884; ii. Czerny Lindsay Taylor, October 30, 1886; iii. Ira Garcia Taylor, June 25, 1889; iv. Ethel Neruda Taylor, September 9, 1893; v. Carl Ernest Taylor, September 15, 1895. 4. Munson Henry, born April 23, 1854; married, 1886, Jessie Kitson, born November 8, 1857; children: i. Edna Vida, born April 4, 1888, married, 1905, William Ridden, and had Ralph Rix Ridden, born May 27, 1906, and an infant, born March 15, 1908; ii. Winnie May, born June 30, 1893. 5. Susan Margaret, born September 29, 1856; married, February 16, 1882, Alexander Grant, of Pictou, Nova Scotia, born December 15, 1838, died August 17, 1898: children: i. Charlotte F Grant, born November 20, 1883, died aged two years; ii. Helen L. Grant, born February 25, 1885; iii. Charles A. Grant, born February 2, 1887, died 1905; iv. James A. Grant, born August 31, 1888, died 1906; v. John G. Grant, born January 15, 1891, died in infancy; vi. Frank M.

Grant, born January 6, 1893; vii. Harry M. Grant, born October 29, 1894. 6. Wesley, born November 1, 1857; died May 15, 1862. 7. Elliott Gould, married Rebecca Fader, of Dover, Nova Scotia. 8. Ainslee, born November 26, 1863. 9. Edith, born February 7, 1866; married, June 2, 1891, George Higgins; children: i. Eva C. Higgins, born May 3, 1892; ii. Ross G. Higgins, September 10, 1893; iii. Maud I. Higgins, December 27, 1895; iv. Walter M. Higgins, March 25, 1897; v. Edna L. Higgins, June 14, 1899; vi. Mary C. Higgins, January 21, 1901; vii. Alice G. Higgins, April 28, 1904; viii. Frank L. Higgins, July 17, 1905. 10. Libby May, born February 5, 1869; married, November 4, 1890, Edward Logan Hadley, a resident of Cambridge, Massachusetts; children: i. Harold Elliott Hadley, born March 17, 1892; ii. Ralph Gorham Hadley, December 31, 1895; iii. Margaret Cayvan Hadley, February 1, 1904.

LITTLEFIELD In the early history of the colony and subsequent province of Maine there was perhaps no single family whose representatives were more closely identified with public events or occupied a more exalted position in its civil, military and industrial life than the Littlefields. The house of one of them was the seat of colonial government for a time and the sessions of the general court were held there, and in all that was done in respect to settlement, the defense of the colonists against the ravages of hostile Indians, the conflicts in regard to sovereignty and jurisdiction and in promoting the growth of towns, the name Littlefield is associated with almost every important event throughout a period of more than a century.

(I) The founder of the Maine branch of the family on this side of the Atlantic Ocean, Edmund Littlefield, was born in England, 1591. He was knighted for bravery on the battle field, and given a coat-of-arms. He first appears in Boston, Massachusetts, 1635. He was a churchman and royalist, and on account of his political and religious opinions was refused permission to settle in any of the plantations of the Massachusetts colony, hence went to Maine and located in the colony at Wells, in that then sparsely settled region, where he, with John Wheelright, Edward Rishworth, Henry Boade and others, "entered on the land and began to make it subservient to the uses of man." His relations with Wheelright lead to the inference of a close friendship, and one authority says he was one of Wheelright's church in Exeter, and one of the combination to each of whom twenty-one acres of land was assigned under the Gorges proprietary. This church was founded by those whose theology was denounced by the dominant church in the Massachusetts colony, and as Littlefield's name does not appear in the list of those who were driven from the plantation at Boston, it is assumed that he left there before the actual expulsion took place. He built a saw and grist mill on the Webhannet river in 1641. He was one of the committee to settle boundary between Wells and Cape Porpoise, and a commission to try small causes, elected by the people for the years 1654-55-58-60-61. A family tradition is that he came over in a ship of his own building, bringing machinery for his mills. "The programme of the celebration of the 250th anniversary of the town of Wells reads: Sir Edmund Littlefield, with Rev. John Wheelright, shares the honor of founding the early settlement in Wells." The baptismal name of his wife was Annis, but her family name is not known. She died in 1678, having survived her husband seventeen years, he having died in 1661. The children: Francis, Anthony, Elizabeth, John, Thomas, Mary, Hannah, Francis. Seventy-six of his descendants were in the revolution.

(II) Francis Littlefield, eldest son of Edmund and Annis Littlefield, was born in England, 1619, acquired a university education, and has a peculiar history. It will be seen, says Bourne, that there are two children of this name, and the first Francis for some cause disappeared from his father's home in England during early childhood, probably when he was not more than six or seven years old, and that he was given up by his parents as not being alive is shown in the fact that about twelve years later another son (the last born) was given the same name. It is not known just when the elder Francis first met his parents in this country and joined the family. In 1639 he was in Exeter, New Hampshire, and then was twenty years old, but he was so far acknowledged a member of the Wheelright combination and a lot of land was assigned him. From Exeter, Francis Littlefield went to Woburn, Massachusetts, and married Jane, daughter of Ralph Hill, of Plymouth, Massachusetts, who died December 20, 1646, leaving a daughter Mary, then four days old, and who died soon afterward. Soon after the death of his wife and child he went to Dover, New Hampshire, and represented that town in the assembly in 1648. He does not again appear in the history of Wells until 1650, when he maintained a prominent position and evidently had an extended acquaintance. He kept a tavern and "because of his good moral character" was licensed to sell strong liquors. That he was a man of considerable influence is shown in the fact that he was elected representative of York in 1668, of Wells in 1675-76. He was a strong supporter of the claims of Massachusetts, and Savage speaks of him as a leader in that contest. The sessions of the general court were held in his house. He was recognized by the inhabitants of Wells as a sound man, and he lived to the good old age of ninety-three years. He may have divided his property among children previous to his death, else he died in very moderate circumstances. His personal property inventoried at twenty pounds, and he had no real estate at that time. He married second, 1648, Rebecca ———, by whom he had several children.

(III) Dependence Littlefield, son of Francis and Rebecca Littlefield, appears to have taken an active part in public affairs in Wells, and was one of those who at a town meeting held March 20, 1716, voted that "the right and property of all the common and undivided lands within the said township doth belong to and forever hereafter shall be and remain unto the persons hereafter mentioned and their heirs forever," etc. There were five Littlefields in the list of those among whom the lands referred to were proposed to be divided, and he himself was one of them. He also was one of the committee charged with the erection of a new meeting house in 1727, and was directed to see that the same "be done workmanlike to the turning of the Kee;" and when seats were assigned he and Samuel Emery were given "the liberty of cutting out a window against each of their Pues of the same bigness as the other windows."

(IV) Captain James Littlefield, son of Dependence Littlefield, gained prominence as a soldier of the French and Indian wars, and in 1744 was one of the Wells company enlisted under Colonel John Storer and embarked on board transports for the expedition against Louisburg. He was afterward advanced to the rank of captain and gave valiant service in later years. He was a man of substance, and the records showed that he owned several slaves named Scipio, Sharper, Dinah and Tom. In 1766 he was one of a committee to build a new meeting house, and when the pews were assigned he was mentioned as one of the persons who "ought to be of the first rank for pews on the floor."

(V) Captain Abraham Littlefield, son of Captain James Littlefield, spent his life in Wells and died there. In 1775 he enlisted for three months in Captain James Hubbard's company, later for five months, and subsequently served as captain in the militia and was known as Captain Littlefield.

(VI) Josias Littlefield, son of Captain Abraham Littlefield, was born in Wells, Maine, and died there. He was collector of both town, parish and county taxes. He married Sarah, daughter of Major Daniel Littlefield, who was killed in the battle of Bagaduce, aged twenty-six years; Daniel Littlefield was son of Peletiah, grandson of Captain Jonathan, great-grandson of Ensign Francis, Jr., youngest son of Sir Edmond, and great-great-grandson of Sir Edmund Littlefield. Children of Josias and Sarah (Littlefield) Littlefield: Abraham, George, Charles, Julia, Hannah, Sophia, Lydia, Horace.

(VII) Horace Littlefield, youngest son of Josias and Sarah (Littlefield) Littlefield, was born in Wells, Maine. He was educated at Exeter Academy, Exeter, New Hampshire. He was a carpenter by trade, a builder and carriage manufacturer by principal occupation as a young man, and also conducted a farm, a part of the original old homestead. He was a lieutenant in the Maine state militia, a Republican in political preference, and in religion a consistent follower of the Methodist Episcopal church. He married Dorcas Burgess Shorey, September 28, 1839; children: Elisha Jewett, William Bradbury, Susan Adelaide, Lydia, Melissa, Horace Greeley, Charles Alvin.

(VIII) William Bradbury Littlefield, son of Horace and Dorcas Burgess (Shorey) Littlefield, was born in Wells, Maine, January 24, 1842. He received his early education in the public schools of Wells, was brought up on a farm, and followed farming and milling for a number of years. Later he became a box manufacturer in Lynn, Massachusetts, a considerable real estate owner, and also in the course of time became interested in a financial way with the banking and shoe manufacturing interests of that city. In the same manner and by force of his own native capacity and enterprise, Mr. Littlefield has become closely identified with the business and social life of Lynn during his residence in the city, being extensively engaged in building operations, and he has not been an entirely passive figure in the political history of Essex county or the commonwealth of Massachusetts, although he has never sought nor desired political office of any kind. He is a Republican of undoubted quality, and for years has held a prominent place in the councils of his party in this state. In 1888 he was a Harrison elector; for several years he was a member of the Republican state committee, Lynn city committee ten years and city council three years. Among the institutions of Lynn with which he is or has been most prominently connected there may be mentioned the board of trade, of which he has been on the executive committee and also vice-president, and the board of water commissioners, of which he was chairman for seventeen years. He is part owner of the Lynn Theatre, president of the Lynn Amusement Company, vice-president of the Manufacturers' National Bank, a member of the Lynn Driving Club, the Merchants' Club, Oxford Club, Park Club and the Tedesco Country Club; a member and past grand of Bay State Lodge, chief patriarch of Palestine Encampment, No. 37, Independent Order of Odd Fellows; charter and life member of the Benevolent and Protective Order of Elks; a member of Lynnwood Lodge, International Order of Good Templars; and an attendant of the Protestant Episcopal church. Mr. Littlefield married first, at Wells, Maine, Susan Alice, daughter of Arioch and Alice (Sargent) Getchell; second, at North Berwick, Maine, Horatia Appleton, daughter of Haven A. and Lucy P. (Ricker) Butler.

LUDDEN

The Luddens of Maine are descended from the older family of the same name which has been seated in Massachusetts for more than two hundred years, and the latter in turn are without doubt descended from that James Ludden who is mentioned in our early colonial history as having been the guide and personal attendant of Governor Winthrop in October, 1632, when he travelled on foot from Plymouth to Weymouth, and in honor of whom the governor named a fording place in the North river. Through intermarriage the Maine Luddens also are descended from Peregrine White of the "Mayflower."

While there is no room to doubt the old and highly honorable lineage of the family under consideration in this place, the town and church records in some parts of Maine are so imperfect that there appears no present means by which to determine the exact relationship of Jacob Ludden and the Luddens of Braintree, Massachusetts. One of the several notable characters of the family in the colonial wars was John Ludden, of Weymouth, presumably a son of James of whom mention has been made. This John was a soldier under Captain Turner in service in the Connecticut valley during King Philip's war in 1676; and another was Benjamin Ludden, of Braintree, also a soldier of the early Indian wars and who, having in mind the uncertainty of a soldier's life in such times, made a will in 1690, with the first paragraph in these words: "I Benjamin Ludden, in New England, being now called forth as a souldier in the time of great distress for to fight the Lord's battles against the bloody enemies of the Christ and people of God in New England, namely, those Anti Christians and bloody ffrench, together with those Bloody, Martherous and Salvage Indians, And considering whether I may return again with my life to see my parents, wife, and relations, Committing my soul to God that gave it", etc.

(I) Jacob Ludden, the earliest ancestor of the immediate family here treated, was born in Turner, Maine, in 1760, hence his father, whose name is not found in any extant record, must have been one of the pioneers of that region. Jacob spent the early part of his life in Turner and removed thence to Canton.

(II) John Soule Ludden, son of Jacob Ludden, was born in Canton, Maine, September 3, 1805, and removed to Dixfield, Maine.

(III) John Mandeville Ludden, son of John Soule Ludden, was born in Dixfield, February 6, 1837, and was a farmer and prominent citizen of that town. For several years he was one of the selectmen and a part of that time chairman of the board. He also served as assessor and overseer of the poor, and as a prosperous farmer he was a member of the local grange of Patrons of Husbandry. He married Elevene J., daughter of Eleazer Carver. She died January 12, 1896, having borne her husband three children: 1. Charles Mandeville, born November 4, 1863. 2. Forest E., born October 16, 1867, at Dixfield, Maine. 3. William Elwood.

(IV) William Elwood Ludden, son of John M. and Elevene J. (Carver) Ludden, was born in Dixfield, Maine, and received his earlier education in Wilton Academy. He took up the study of law under the direction of Savage & Oakes, attorneys and counselors of Auburn, Maine, and supplemented his preliminary studies with a course in Boston University Law School, graduating in 1892. On October 10 of the same year he was admitted to practice in the courts of the state of Maine. Mr. Ludden began his professional career in Auburn, remained in that city eight years and in 1893, in connection with general practice, served as city clerk. In 1898 he removed to Boston and since that year has been an active member of the Suffolk bar. His home is in the suburban town of Saugus, for which municipality he was commissioned trial justice, February 6, 1905. He is a member of William Sutton Lodge, A. F. and A. M.; Bradford R. A. C., No. 38, of Lewiston, Maine; Lewiston Council, R. and S. M., of Lewiston, Maine; Tonoquon Chapter, No. 100, O. E. S.; North Star Lodge, No. 67, N. E. O. P.; Pejepscot Lodge, No. 1467, I. O. F.; Cliftondale Lodge, No. 193, I. O. O. F. In 1895 Mr. Ludden married Bertha G., daughter of Alfred W. and Bertha E. Hill. Mrs. Ludden died June 4, 1907, leaving one child, William Elwood Ludden, Jr., born September 10, 1901.

BRUCE Benjamin Fitz Patrick Bruce, father of the late Orsamus B. Bruce, for many years one of the best known and most popular school men in the state of Massachusetts, was born in Edinboro, Scotland, July, 1828, and reared by an aunt. While a resident of Dublin, Ireland, he was married to Helen Emmett Ennis, born in Dublin, Ireland, July, 1829; the marriage occurred at "Gretna Green", and their ages were seventeen and sixteen, respectively. William Ennis, grandfather of Helen E. (Ennis) Bruce, served as clerk to the clerk of the Crown at Dublin, and came to his death in a singular manner; the court of assizes was to sit on a very hot day in August, and he was obliged to be present; the cab failed to call for him, and he walked to the court; he was a very heavy man, of mature years, and had on a pair of new patent leather shoes; his feet became swollen and gangrene set in, from the effects of which he died. Christopher Ennis, son of William Ennis, and uncle of Helen E. (Ennis) Bruce, kept a linen draper's shop on Sackville street, Dublin, near the Nelson monument, and often used to send presents of suits of clothes to his young nephew in New York which was the admiration of Mr. Bruce's mother's acquaintances, being different in quality and style from anything in the stores in New York at that time. Mr. and Mrs. Bruce came to the United States after their marriage and settled in New York City, from whence he went to California in 1849, at the outbreak of the "gold fever", being wrecked on the way, taking nine months to reach San Francisco, going round the Horn in a sailing vessel. He sent lumps of gold home, and told in his letters many incidents of those early days of a miner's life. He died and was buried in Sonora; it was more than a month later before the family heard of his death, and nothing was ever known of what were his possessions. In those early frontier days there was little law or order; everything he had was gone, though it was known he was a successful miner. He was fond of gunning, belonging to the Sportsman's Club, the Druids, and other societies in New York City. His children, all born in New York City: 1. Robert, died in infancy. 2. Orsamus B., see forward. 3. Eugenia, deceased. 4. Mary Ann, resides in New York City, unmarried. 5. Julia, resides in New York City, married.

Orsamus B. Bruce, born in the city of New York, November 3, 1840, died in Lynn, Massachusetts, February 5, 1903. He passed his boyhood in the metropolis, obtaining his early education in the public schools, and completed his education in the Binghamton (New York) Academy, under the tuition of the famous educator, Professor D. H. Crittenden. He intended to take a college course, but the breaking out of the civil war turned him from this purpose, and he entered the Union army. Eight days after the fall of Fort Sumter he enlisted in the (Hawkins Zouaves) Ninth Regiment, New York Volunteers, equipped by the merchants of New York City. The regiment was sent to Fortress Monroe, and Private Bruce was detailed as dispatch bearer between the fortress and points nearby, and later went into the office of the regimental adjutant. Returning to Binghamton, Mr. Bruce was successively principal of a public school, superintendent of schools, instructor in New York state teachers' institutes, and head of a successful private school. He was appointed superintendent of schools in Lynn, Massachusetts, 1879, and continued in faithful service until 1901, and after retiring from the superintendency was engaged in other educational work. He was for several years secretary and was twice president of the Massachusetts Teachers' Association, was president of the Essex County Convention and president of the American Institute of Instruction, and filled all offices with dignity and skill. In all his public work he was singularly popular and useful, and few men were so widely and favorably known to teachers and school superintendents. For almost a quarter of a century he devoted himself to the children and teachers of the city of Lynn, and by them he will be remembered for many years to come. Always on the alert for better methods of instruction, he spared no pains to find and test them, devoting his vacation travels in Europe and in this country largely to personal inquiry and investigation of whatever systems promised any improvement over current practices. Many such improvements, which came into vogue after his death and were supposed to be new, had been examined, approved and recommended by him years before. So far as the matter lay with him, he brought the best there was in the world of education to Lynn. His insight into child life and his kindly and engaging manner won the love of the children, and his moral worth and personal influence upon the successive generations of pupils must be reckoned as an important factor in his chosen life work. At the funeral services of Mr. Bruce there were present the mayor, members of the city government, the school board and other city departments, as well as officials high in the councils of the state, all of whom honored and respected him, but the sentiment which expressed most effectively the loss which the city and the state sustained was represented in the large number of school teachers, who came to offer their final tribute to one who had been to them friend and counselor. Many in the vast congregation of mourners felt that their position in life, their education and their character, were due to the foresight, skill and uniform kindness of Mr. Bruce, and many felt that for all they had accomplished they were indebted largely to him. While a resident of New York, Mr. Bruce was a member of the Presbyterian church, but during his residence in Lynn he attended the First Universalist Church, in which Mrs. Bruce was the organist for twenty years.

Mr. Bruce married, in Binghamton, New York, September 6, 1864, Katharine M., daughter of Rev. Hiram W. and Katharine E. (Pease) Gilbert, of Binghamton, New York. Rev. Hiram W. Gilbert who was a Presbyterian minister, preaching in Windsor and other towns and later in Peru, New York, and also had an active part in the local Bible Society there, died in New York, 1879; his wife died in 1900. Their children: 1. Katharine M., born April 14, 1842, aforementioned. 2. Samuel Eugene, born November 15, 1859, deceased. 3. Charlotte Hortense, born August 4, 1861, deceased. Katharine M. (Gilbert) Bruce was educated in Binghamton, New York, and pursued her musical studies under Dr. William Mason, B. J. Lang, George E. Whiting and other celebrated teachers of Boston and New York. She began teaching music in a girls' school at the age of fifteen years, and played a church organ at twelve years of age in her father's church in Greene, New York. Upon coming to Binghamton she took a position as organist in the First Presbyterian Church, where she played for fifteen years, also teaching music during this time with great success, and at the time she left Binghamton for Lynn five of her pupils were playing church organs in the former city. After taking up her residence in Lynn she again took up her profession and has since maintained her usual high standard. Many of the most prominent organists in this section have taken lessons from her. She was for many years the accompanist at the great musical conventions throughout the United States, conducted by the most eminent musicians of that time, among them being Dr. William Mason, Carl Zerrahn and other prominent musicians and composers. Among her mementoes of these occasions is an autograph album, containing not only autographs, but a large number of compliments to her ability as an accompanist. When the Daughters of the Revolution was organized in Lynn, she was admitted to membership on three lines, and was regent of the chapter for three years, and has served in the state council. She is a member of the Woman's Club, of which she was president four years, also a member of the North Shore Club.

Children of Mr. and Mrs. Bruce: 1. Robert, born in Binghamton, New York, September 8, 1866; teacher of vocal music, having studied in Boston and Lynn; also conducts the music in St. Paul's Church, Lynn, where his daughter Grace M. is organist; he was for nine years a member of the old Tremont Temple Quartette of Boston, which traveled all over the country, singing baritone in this famous organization; he is favorably known in musical circles, not only as a vocalist, but as a teacher, and is a member of the Apollo Club of Boston. He resides in Lynn. He married Elizabeth Valpey, of Lynn; children: Ronald, Grace Marjorie, Donald and Robert. 2. Grace Helen, born in New York, December 3, 1868, died aged nine years. 3. Donald, born April 9, 1870, died in Lynn, aged twelve years.

HILL The surname Hill is as old as the use of family names in England. The family is widely scattered in the United Kingdom and United States and has many branches from the remotest period of history. There are many coats-of-arms. The family of this sketch settled in the north of Ireland, where King James attempted to establish a loyal Protestant settlement by grants to Scotch and English subjects early in the seventeenth century. The resulting population is still known as Scotch-Irish, though none of the Protestant settlers intermarried with the Catholic Irish. The Hill family of Carrickfergus, county Antrim, in Ulster, doubtless numbers both Scotch and English in its ancestry. This branch of the family bears a coat-of-arms, described thus: Sable with a chevron argent three discs sable, two boars heads above and one below. Crest—a greyhound sejeant. The presence of the boars' heads on the shield seems to denote a Scottish origin of the Hill family.

(I) Captain Hugh Hill was born in 1741, in Carrickfergus, county Antrim, Ireland. He was doubtless of both Scotch and English ancestry. He ran away from home when a boy and became cabin boy in the English navy. He had had no schooling, but knowing the value of knowledge gave his allowance of grog to a sailor who in return taught him the rudiments of a common school education. He left the English service and settled at Marblehead, continuing, however, to follow the sea. He married, at Marblehead, March 13, 1766, Hannah Goudey. He became a master mariner. His ship "Pilgrim" was a privateer in the American service during the revolution. He was commissioned captain September 12, 1778; also commissioned January 15, 1781, in command of the privateer "Cicero" on petition of Andrew Cabot, of Salem, and others. His valuable log books were lost in the old Hill place in North Beverly which he purchased in 1798. His wife's mother carried on the farm there. After the war Captain Hill went to Ireland with his vessel and advertised for passengers to America. He brought his father, brothers and sisters to America. At that time his father was so lame that he had to be carried. It is said that he set his brothers up in business and was the means of making them successful men in the new country. He died at Beverly, Massachusetts, February 17, 1829, aged eighty-eight years. Of him the town record of his death says: "native of Ireland and an active and successful commander of a private armed ship in the Revolutionary War."

Children: 1. Hugh, settled in Beverly, and had a family there. 2. Peter, lived in Beverly. 3. James, born 1757; mentioned below. And two daughters.

(II) James Hill, son of Hugh Hill, was born probably in Marblehead, in 1756-57, died at Beverly, May 17, 1798, aged forty-one years and six months. If this age is stated correctly in the records, his father's birth year is incorrectly given or the father must have married very early in life. The Beverly records say of his wife Elizabeth, "widow of James and a native of Ireland settled in Beverly about 1779, died December 23, 1823, aged sixty-five." She was born, therefore, about 1758, making her a year younger than her husband. James also followed the sea. He and his brothers engaged in the fishing business, owned many vessels and were highly prosperous. Children, all recorded at Beverly: 1. Hannah, born September 17, 1784, (of her the records say: "born on the passage from Ireland to this country, so says rumor, but believed not to be true (church records) died March 16, 1838, aged fifty-three." It is quite likely that she was born on her grandfather's ship on some of his trips to the old country). 2. Jane, November 16, 1786. 3. Nancy, May 28, 1789. 4. Elizabeth, July 21, 1791. 5. James, February 20, 1794; mentioned below. 6. Isabel, April 20, 1796. 7. John, December 29, 1798, died in Pedang, East Indies, December, 1821.

(III) James Hill, son of James Hill, born Beverly, Massachusetts, February 20, 1794, died November 6, 1829, aged thirty-five years, nine months, according to the Beverly records. He married, at Beverly, October 8, 1816, Sally Beckford, born February 6, 1798, died of jaundice, January 12, 1849, daughter of Captain Benjamin and Ruth (Ober) Beckford. (See Beckford sketch herewith). Children, born in Beverly: 1. James, born 1817; married Mary Curtis. 2. Nancy Stephens, June 3, 1818; married William P. Friend. 3. Benjamin Beckford, November 10, 1819; married Elizabeth Perkins. 4. Sally Beckford, October 21, 1821; never married. 5. John Beckford, September 25, 1824; mentioned below.

(IV) John Beckford Hill, son of James Hill, was born at Beverly, September 25, 1824. He was educated in the public schools of Beverly, and in 1840 was apprenticed to learn the trade of watch-maker in Salem, Massachusetts, to Edmund Currier, then the best watch-maker and clock-maker east of Boston. After four years he embarked in business on his own account in Beverly, and from 1844 to the time of his death, March 28, 1904, continued in business with uninterrupted success. He was undoubtedly for many years the best-known jeweler in this section of the county and always maintained a high reputation for excellent work and honorable dealing. At the time of his death he had been in business longer than any other man in the town of Beverly. He was prominent in public affairs, always keenly interested in the welfare of the town and county. His personal influence and public spirit effected many permanent improvements in the municipality. He was secretary and treasurer of Beverly Gas Light Company for twenty years, trustee of the Danvers Savings Bank, and later served as its vice-president. He was independent in politics and not greatly concerned with partisan affairs, but held many positions of trust and honor in the town; was assessor for a period of twenty-four years, overseer of the poor and town auditor many years. He was a member and past master of Liberty Lodge of Free Masons, of Beverly, having been master of the lodge for twelve years; member of Amity Chapter, Royal Arch Masons, and was past high priest; of St. George Commandery, Knights Templar, and was past commander of both Winslow Lewis, of Salem, and St. George Commanderies, of Beverly, Massachusetts, and had taken the thirty-third degree in Masonry. He was active in the temperance movement and a prominent member of Franklin Division, Sons of Temperance, of Beverly, and Beverly Lodge, Knights of Pythias. He was a leading member of the Baptist church of Beverly, and was clerk of the society from 1856 to 1876. He was treasurer of the Beverly Historical Society. During his later years Mr. Hill was doubtless the foremost citizen of the town, universally respected and esteemed by his townsmen. Of exemplary character, his life and example have long exerted and still exert a large and wholesome influence. He married, in 1852, Caroline Elizabeth Perkins, born Beverly, February 22, 1833, daughter of Benjamin Frankin and Elizabeth (Murray) Perkins. (See Perkins sketch herewith). Children, born in Beverly: 1. Sarah Elizabeth, born January 5, 1854; married, December 18, 1884, Theodore Taylor, of West Yarmouth, Massachusetts. 2. John Franklin, born January 10, 1856; mentioned below. 3. Benjamin Lamson, born August 27, 1858, died July 2, 1861. 4. Charles Flanders, born December 1, 1860; married June 24, 1885, Liefa Weadwell Perry, born July 19, 1861.

(V) John Franklin Hill, son of John Beckford Hill, was born in Beverly, January 10, 1856. He attended the public schools, and the Central grammar school and the Beverly high school in his native town. In 1873 he became associated in the jewelry business with his father, and in 1883 was admitted to partnership. The firm continued until dissolved by the death of the founder and senior partner, and since then Mr. Hill has conducted the business alone. Besides the mercantile interests of Mr. Hill he is director of the Beverly Co-operative Bank, and trustee of the Beverly Savings Bank. In politics he is a Democrat, a member of the board of registrars of Beverly since 1896 and of the school committee. He is a member of the Baptist church. He is a member of Liberty Lodge of Free Masons; of Amity Chapter, Royal Arch Masons; of St. George Commandery, Knights Templar, and of the Sutton Lodge of Perfection. He is well known in Masonic circles in Beverly and vicinity.

He married, November 3, 1881, Annie B. Adams, born at Beverly, July 12, 1856, daughter of Charles Adams. (See Adams sketch herewith). John F. Hill and wife have been parents of the following children: 1. Charles Adams, born June 7, 1883, died March 12, 1884. 2. Marjorie B., born April 24, 1885. 3. Karl F. A., born April 30, 1890. 4. John B., born November 1, 1897.

ADAMS William Adams, immigrant ancestor of this branch of the family, came to New England, aged fifteen, in the ship "Elizabeth and Ann," in May, 1635, and settled at Cambridge. He was admitted a freeman May 22, 1638; removed to Ipswich, and was a member of the grand jury in 1642; was selectman 1646, and died 1661. His widow was living in 1681. He probably lived in or near what is now Hamilton. Children: 1. William. 2. John, born about 1631. 3. Samuel. 4. Hannah, married, December 6, 1659, Francis Munsy. 5. Mary, married, February 29, 1660, Thomas French. 6. Nathaniel, mentioned below.

(II) Nathaniel Adams, son of William Adams, was born about 1641, and died at Ipswich, April 11, 1715. He married, June 30, 1668, Mercy, daughter of Thomas Dickinson, of Rowley. She died December 12, 1735. He was admitted a freeman May 27, 1674. Children, born at Ipswich: 1. Nathaniel, July

11, 1670; mentioned below. 2. Thomas, June 14, 1672. 3. Mercy, April 1, 1674; died June 13, 1674. 4. Sarah, July 19, 1675; married ——— Fairfield. 5. William, June 29, 1678; probably died young. 6. Mercy, March 18, 1680; married, February 4, 1703, John Smith; second, September 18, 1716, Arthur Abbott; died September 11, 1733. 7. Samuel, June 29, 1682.

(III) Nathaniel Adams, son of Nathaniel Adams, was born at Ipswich, July 11, 1670, and died August 31, 1736. He married, January, 1693, Abigail, died May 30, 1755, daughter of Caleb Kimball, of Ipswich. Children, born at Ipswich: 1. Nathaniel, March 1, 1695; died at Boston, October 25, 1712. 2. William, November 26, 1696; mentioned below. 3. Abigail, December 6, 1699; married, 1718, William Goodhue; died September 10, 1764. 4. Caleb, February 13, 1702. 5. Mercy, February 25, 1704; married, 1723, Thomas Savery. 6. Robert, October 14, 1705. 7. Anna, March 25, 1708; married, 1725, John Woodman. 8. Mary, 1714; married, 1732, Thomas Lamson.

(IV) William Adams, son of Nathaniel Adams, was born at Ipswich, November 26, 1696; married, 1716, Mary, daughter of John Warner, Ipswich. Children, born at Ipswich: 1. Mary, 1717; married, 1738, William Whipple. 2. Abigail, 1719; married, 1744, Joseph Bolles. 3. William, 1722. 4. Nathaniel, 1727; married, 1757, Ruth Bolles. 5. Sarah, 1729; married, 1750, Jacob Low, of Wenham. 6. Son, 1731; probably John, mentioned below.

(V) John Adams, son of William Adams, was born in Ipswich, 1731. He married, 1754, Mary Lamson, of Ipswich. In 1789 John and Mary Adams deeded their share in the estate of the widow Mary Potter in Ipswich to Joseph Adams. The grantees were Caleb Lamson, John Goodhue, Jr., and wife Mercy, Paul Lamson, Nathaniel Lamson, of Westborough; John Adams and wife Mary, John Rogers and wife Abigail, John Goldsmith and wife Martha, of Moultonborough. Ipswich Hamlet, part of Ipswich, later called Hamilton, was the home of this family. Thomas Adams, Stephen Adams, Joseph Adams, Asa Adams and Oliver Adams, or most of them, were brothers, sons or nephews of John Adams, all living in Hamilton about 1800. Also Samuel Adams, who married, February 4, 1794, Lydia Lamson. Isaac Adams, of Hamilton, deeded land to Stephen Adams, April 28, 1805. Stephen Adams deeded land to his brother Isaac, mariner, adjoining land of Samuel Adams, 1804. Stephen Adams married Mehitable ———. Stephen Adams deeded to Mary Adams, wife of Oliver Adams, of Hamilton, April, 1806, land there and elsewhere. Oliver Adams deeded land to John Adams, fifteen acres, March 8, 1811. Elisha Perkins also deeded land to Oliver Adams' wife Mary, in 1811. John Adams, again, deeded land to Paul Dodge, April 19, 1763, bordering on land of Samuel Lamson, evidently the homestead.

(VI) John Adams, son of John Adams, was born 1762, and died in 1838, aged seventy-six, according to Hamilton records. He was possibly a nephew of John Adams, instead of son. He was deacon of the church at Hamilton. He married, perhaps second, Mary Patch, June 26, 1804. She died at Hamilton, of dropsy, January 18, 1835, aged fifty-three. Children: 1. Son, born March 22, 1813. 2. Son John, died August 3, 1817, aged one year. 3. Child, born May 9, 1820. 4. Charles, mentioned below.

(VII) Charles Adams, son of Deacon John Adams, was born in Hamilton, Massachusetts, in 1823, and died in Sacramento, California, in 1864. He married, March 10, 1853, Anne Porter Batchelder, born September 2, 1828, daughter of Colonel Henry Batchelder. Her father was born September 24, 1793, at Beverly; married, December 3, 1815, Abigail, born April 6, 1796, died August 31, 1874, daughter of Perez Mann. Children: Clara L.; Charles H.; Annie B., born at Beverly, July 12, 1856, married John Franklin Hill, born January 10, 1856 (see Hill).

(For first generation see John Perkins 1).

PERKINS (II) Thomas Perkins, son of John Perkins, was born in England in 1616, and came to America with his parents in 1631, when he was fifteen years old. At Ipswich he owned Sagamore hill, a tract of land one hundred and seventy feet high. He exchanged this land with his brother John for a house and lot in town. After a few years he removed to Topsfield and married there, about 1640, Phebe Gould, daughter of Zaccheus Gould. She was born in England in 1620, baptized at Hemel Hempstead, September 20, 1620. Her father gave them one hundred and fifty acres of land. Thomas Perkins was chosen deacon of the Topsfield church, and was probably the first deacon. He was often selectman and tythingman, and on the committee to choose a minister. His farm was next that of his brother-in-law Redington, not far from the Newburyport turnpike. His will was dated December 11, 1685, and proved September 10, 1686. He died May 7, 1686, and his wife survived him. Children: 1. John, born 1641; married, November 28, 1666, Deborah Browning; died May 19, 1668. 2. Phebe, born about 1644; married, 1665, Joseph Towne. 3. Zaccheus, born about 1647; married Rebecca ———. 4. Martha, born about 1649; married, December 17, 1669, John Lamson. 5. Mary, born about 1651; married, October 27, 1671, William Howlett; died 1728. 6. Elisha, born about 1654; married, February 23, 1680, Catherine Towne. 7. Judith, born January 28, 1658, died unmarried before 1719. 8. Thomas, born about 1659; mentioned below. 9. Timothy, born June 6, 1661; married (first) Hannah ———; (second) Abigail ———.

(III) Thomas Perkins, son of Thomas Perkins, was born about 1659, in Topsfield, died in April, 1722. He was a weaver by trade. He received by will part of his father's farm, which it was his father's wish the brothers should conduct together. In 1718 they divided the property and separated. He was on a jury at the time of the Salem witchcraft trials, and was one of those who afterwards signed a declaration of regret for their part in the trials. He married, June 1, 1683, Sarah Wallis. Children: 1. Sarah, born January 20, 1684-85; married, January 28, 1722-23, William Makittrick. 2. Thomas, baptized December 9, 1688. 3. Hannah, baptized March 12, 1692; married David Balch. 4. Robert, born February 28, 1697; mentioned below. 5. Samuel, born November 22, 1699; married Margaret Towne.

(IV) Robert Perkins, son of Thomas Perkins, born Topsfield, February 28, 1697, died June 15, 1750. He was baptized by Rev. Mr. Capen, March 7, 1697. He married, February 24, 1719-20, Elizabeth Towne, daughter of Samuel and Elizabeth (Knight) Towne. She died November 26, 1772, "aged." Children: 1. Elizabeth, born June 7, 1723; married, August 30, 1742, Isaac Perkins. 2. Sarah, born September 9, 1725; married, February 24, 1744, Elizur Lake, Jr. 3. Rebecca, born January 12, 1726, died May 15, 1774. 4. Robert, born January 16, 1727-28; mentioned below. 5. Amos, born February 16, 1730-31; married, 1756, Keziah Kimball, of Wenham; died September 18, 1814. 6. Phebe, born February 3, 1732-33; married, December 18, 1750, Jonathan Knight. 7. Martha, born January 8, 1734-35; married (first), February 5, 1754, Archibald Dwinell; (second), April 4, 1774, Samuel Carter, of Manchester. 8. Mehitable, born February 6, 1736-37; married (first), July 2, 1761, Solomon Gould; (second) Andrew Foster. 9. Anna, born June 24, 1739; married, December 29, 1757, Thomas Gould, Jr.

(V) Robert Perkins, son of Robert Perkins, born Topsfield, January 16, 1727-28, died November 10, 1801. He was in the revolution, in Captain Stephen Perkins' company and answered the Lexington alarm, April 19, 1775. He married, probably in Ipswich, the intentions being published September 30, 1750, Hannah Cummings, of Ipswich, born 1725, died July 12, 1802. Children: 1. Ruth, born October 1, 1753; married, 1744, John Gould, 3rd. 2. Hannah, born May 17, 1755, died November 16, 1802. 3. Lydia, born August 6, 1757, died February 27, 1830. 4. Robert, born May 29, 1760; mentioned below. 5. Asa, born June 15, 1762; married Hannah Johnson. 6. Mehitable, born November 14, 1767, died December 28, 1818.

(VI) Robert Perkins, son of Robert Perkins, born Topsfield, May 29, 1760, died of consumption, January 14, 1725. He was sometimes called Captain Robert in the records. Either he or his father was in the revolution, in Captain Benjamin Adams' company, Colonel Johnson's regiment in the department of the north in 1777; also in Captain John Didge's company, Colonel Jacob Gerrish's regiment in 1778. He married, March 4, 1784, Esther Gould, who died January 29, 1817, aged sixty-three. He married (second), April 25, 1822, Hannah Perkins, born October 5, 1778, died July 19, 1855, daughter of Zebulon and Mary (Wildes) Perkins. Children, all by first wife: 1. Benjamin, born March 13, 1786; mentioned below. 2. Amos, born April 2, 1788; married Betsey Brown. 3. Esther, born January 12, 1790; married John R. Peabody. 4. Robert, born February 16, 1792, died October 9, 1814. 5. Nehemiah, born April 1, 1794; married Lydia Bradstreet. 6. Betsey, born January 8, 1798, died July 18, 1814.

(VII) Benjamin Perkins, son of Robert Perkins, born Topsfield, March 13, 1786, died April 3, 1858. He married, May 28, 1809, in Salem, intentions published April 23, Rebecca H. Ashby, of Salem, born 1791, died January 27, 1863. He was a farmer and shoemaker. Children: 1. Benjamin Franklin, born May 30, 1812; mentioned below. 2. Rebecca, baptized August 8, 1819; married (first), William Preston Dodge; (second), Elbridge Perkins. 3. Lucy Ann, married Solomon Cole. 4. Elizabeth Ashby, baptized June 1, 1823; married Benjamin Hill. 5. Edward Augustus, physician in Boston. 6. George Henry, married (first), Augusta L. Story; (second), Mary Sawyer.

(VIII) Benjamin Franklin Perkins, son of Benjamin Perkins, born Topsfield, May 30, 1812, died October 28, 1887. He married, November 5, 1832, Elizabeth Murray. He was a shoe manufacturer and resided in Beverly. Children: 1. Caroline Elizabeth, born 1833; married John B. Hill. (See sketch of Hill family herewith). 2. George Franklin, born August 28, 1834; married Harriet A. Prime. 3. Mary Ellen, born July 31, 1837; married Charles L. Dodge, of Beverly. 4. Sarah Beckford, born June 22, 1839, died unmarried, November 28, 1884.

BECKFORD (I) George Beckford, immigrant ancestor, lived in Marblehead, Massachusetts. He married, in 1666, Christian ——, born in 1649, according to her own deposition. She was granted administration of her husband's estate, June 28, 1678, and the inventory was thirteen pounds, nine shillings and six pence, the estate to remain in her hands for the bringing up of her children. Among the children were: 1. William, born in Marblehead. 2. John, born about 1674; mentioned below.

(II) John Beckford, son of George Beckford, born Marblehead, about 1674, settled in Salem. On December 8, 1717, he and his wife were baptized and received into the First Church there, with seven of their children. He married, in May, 1699, Rebecca Pinsent, daughter of William and Rebecca (Greene) Pinsent. He removed to Reading, where he died. Children: 1. George, born July 5, 1700, died May 30, 1760; married, July 30, 1722, Elizabeth Batter, daughter of Edmund and Martha (Pickman) Batter. 2. John, born September 15, 1702; mentioned below. 3. Rebecca, born February 26, 1705; married, February 6, 1722-23, John Archer; died March, 1763. 4. William, born March 4, 1706. 5. Bethiah, born February 2, 1708. 6. Benjamin, born August 30, 1711, died May, 1773; married (first), December 6, 1733, Mary Collins, daughter of Adoniram Collins; (second), 1750, Lydia, widow of James Morris. 7. Ebenezer, born May 18, 1715. 8. Priscilla, born August 8, 1717; married, May 24, 1738, David Phippen. 9. Mary, born November 22, 1719; married, May 3, 1738, Warwick Palfray; died before 1747. 10. Sarah, born December 18, 1721.

(III) Deacon John Beckford, son of John Beckford, born Salem, December 15, 1702, died January 13, 1788. He married, October 6, 1724, Elizabeth Hayward, baptized in Tabernacle Church, October 11, 1702, died October 22, 1763, daughter of Samuel Hayward. Children: 1. John, born August 2, 1725 or 26. 2. Elizabeth, born August 17, 1727; married, December 19, 1745, Jonathan Very, Jr. 3. Mary, born October 11, 1728; married, November 1, 1750, William West. 4. Samuel, born August 27, 1730. 5. Benjamin, born June 4, 1732; mentioned below. 6. Pinsent, born July 14, 1733; died before 1783; married, December 9, 1756, Deborah Ward. 7. Hannah, born October 1, 1734; married George Smith. 8. Sarah, born February 11, 1735. 9. Ebenezer, born April 8, 1737, died February, 1816. 10. Rebecca, born August 17, 1738. 11. David, born October 5, 1740; married, December 5, 1756, Sarah Frye, widow of James Odell. 12. Eunice, born December 10, 1741; married, April 10, 1759, Thomas Ropes. 13. Jonathan, born June 6, 1743; married, November 14, 1765, Sarah King.

(IV) Captain Benjamin Beckford, son of Deacon John Beckford, born Salem, June 4, 1732, died Beverly, June 5, 1799. While of Salem he married, March 29, 1753, Elizabeth Herrick, widow of Jonathan, who died May 18, 1808, of old age, aged eighty-one. The church records give the date of death as May 16. Children, born at Beverly: 1. John, born December 7, 1753. 2. Sarah, born August 1, 1755; married, November 4, 1777, John Edmunds. 3. Benjamin, born May 1, 1758; mentioned below. 4. Rebecca, born July 12, 1760; married, September 8, 1785, Asa Batchelder. 5. Eunice, born November 27, 1766; married, November 21, 1787, John Baker. 6. Elizabeth, baptized September 22, 1771; buried January 20, 1780, aged nine years.

(V) Captain Benjamin Beckford, son of Captain Benjamin Beckford, born May 1, 1758, died September 2, 1811. He was a famous sea captain, and served in the revolution. Was a member of Captain Larkin Thorndike's company, April 19, 1775. He made many voyages between Salem and Russia, and the models of some of his ships are in the Peabody Museum, of which he was a prominent member. He married, April 15, 1777, Ruth Ober, daughter of Peter, Jr., and Lucy (Woodbury) Ober, who died of dropsy, August 17, 1808, aged forty-eight. Children, born at Beverly: 1. Ruth, born 1777; married, March 13, 1800, Benjamin Chase, of Newburyport. 2. Elizabeth (twin), born September 29, 1779. 3. Benjamin (twin), born September 29, 1779; married, November 28, 1804, Elizabeth Dyson; died January 8, 1814. 4. Captain Simon (or Simeon), born January 28, 1782; married, March 7, 1807, Ruth Smith; buried November 2, 1815. 5. Ruth, born May 31, 1786. 6. John, born September 6, 1795; buried September 10, 1795. 7. Sallie, born February 6, 1798; married, October 8, 1816, James Hill (see sketch of Hill family herewith); died January 12, 1849. 8. Lucy, baptized September 8, 1799, died May 13, 1803.

GREGORY The surname Gregory or McGregory is of Scotch origin. In New England a John Gregory was an early settler at Weymouth where he died December, 1692, John Taylor being appointed his administrator. About the time of the Scotch-Irish immigration several Gregory families appear in Boston and vicinity. Patrick McGregory or Gregory died at Roxbury in 1734, leaving a widow Hannah; George Gregory, a gunsmith, died at Boston in 1730, and George Bridge was appointed administrator May 13, 1730. James Gregory, of His Majesty's ship "Sea Horse," died in 1721, and his widow, Olive (Smallpiece) Gregory was appointed administratrix December 18, 1721. This same James was probably the progenitor of the Marblehead families. He was a mariner; bought of John Smallpiece, innholder, for thirty-two pounds, ten shillings, land at Marblehead adjoining land of Isaac Turner and Samuel Read by deed dated April 5, 1720. Alexander Gregory, possibly a son of James Gregory, was a baker in Boston. His will was dated April 23, 1730, and proved June 1, 1730; his executors were Barrett Dyer and Nathaniel Green, and his only son was Alexander. Abigail, his widow, also of Boston, quitclaimed her rights to his estate April 17, 1745, and June 12, 1748, to her son Alexander Gregory, a tailor. The homestead of Alexander Gregory was on Cross street, Boston. John and Abigail (Guild) Gregory lived at Walpole, married there March 30, 1748; children: 1. Abigail, born March 28, 1749. 2. Abigail, born March 18, 1750-51; married (intention dated May 24, 1775) Jotham Morse. 3. Sarah, born June 16, 1761; married, April 26, 1787, Joseph Boyden. 4. Mille, born February 24, 1768; married, September 6, 1801, John Needham. 5. Child. 6. William.

William Gregory, of Walpole, married, March 28, 1754, Experience ———. Josiah Gregory, of the adjacent town of Medway, died 1759, bequeathing to mother Sarah, brother Daniel and wife Catherine. William Gregory, of Ipswich, died in 1711. William Gregory, of Boston, married there June 18, 1774, Mary Woodlot, and he, or another of the same name married at Boston, November 2, 1800, Elizabeth Campbell. It is not possible to trace with certainty the ancestry of the Marblehead families to these pioneers, nor to establish the relationship which must exist, on account of missing records. William Gregory, probably grandson of James Gregory, was born about 1760. He married Sarah ———, and lived at Marblehead. We have mentioned all those of the name in Massachusetts at an early date.

(I) Joseph Gregory, the first of the line herein treated of whom we have definite information, was a British soldier and a cotton weaver by trade, who came from Lancashire, England. Joseph Gregory was a blacksmith and followed that trade in Marblehead, where his death occurred at the age of fifty-six years. He married, at Marblehead, April 19, 1790, Hannah Hooper, a native of Marblehead, who there January 6, 1843, aged seventy-eight years, nine months, daughter of John Hooper, who was a son of Robert Hooper, the first ancestor. Robert Hooper was one of three brothers, two of whom settled in Maine and the third in Marblehead; Robert Hooper had two sons—Robert and John—the latter of whom was a ship chandler. Children of Mr. and Mrs. Gregory, born in Marblehead: 1. John Hooper, baptized December 1, 1793; see sketch. 2. Captain Joseph, baptized December 1, 1793, died March 9, 1824, aged thirty-three or thirty-five years; married, September 24, 1822, Ruth Roundey, then a minor. 3. Thomas, baptized December 1, 1793. 4. James, born October 27, 1796; mentioned below. 5. Ambrose Martin, baptized July 14, 1799; drowned at New Orleans, April 26, 1831; married, March 6, 1821, Eliza Bruce. 6. Hannah, baptized April 25, 1802; married, May 30, 1824, Nathaniel Brimblecom, Jr. 7. Mary Ellis, baptized June 24, 1805; married, March 26, 1826, Nathaniel Adams.

(II) James Gregory, son of Joseph and Hannah (Hooper) Gregory, was born in Marblehead, Massachusetts, October 27, 1796. He was a boot and shoe maker by trade, but became a merchant in Marblehead. He was also a pension and bond land agent, was collector of the port eight years, was a trial jus-

James J. H. Gregory

tice and auctioneer, took an active part in the political affairs of the day, was president of the Whig organization, and was a state senator two years. He married Ruth Roundy, daughter of Captain John Roundy; she was born at Marblehead, where she died aged fifty-two years. He died aged seventy-eight years. Children, born at Marblehead: 1. Mary Knight, born January 2, 1825, deceased. 2. James John Howard, born November 7, 1827; mentioned below. 3. Walter Raleigh, born September 9, 1829, died July 13, 1831. 4. Walter Raleigh, born November 17, 1831, deceased. 5. Helen Maria, born March 14, 1834; married James L. Gould, of Norwich, Connecticut. 6. Emma Brown Knight, born January 27, 1836; married Charles Griffiths, of Boston; two children: William and Arthur L. 7. Ruth Ann, born August 21, 1838; married Captain Robert Brown, now deceased, and has four children—Ruth, Annie, Gregory and Bancroft—all of whom reside in New York. 8. Hannah Hooper, born March 14, 1843; married J. Gregory Carleton, a mining expert in Marblehead, at one time of South America. 9. Arthur Elles, born January 27, 1846.

(III) James John Howard Gregory, son of James and Ruth (Roundy) Gregory, was born at Marblehead, November 7, 1827. He was educated in the public schools of his native town, pursued a two years' course at the Middlebury Academy, after which he matriculated at Amherst College, graduating therefrom in 1850. His advent into the seed business was almost by accident. He once said of his beginning in the seed business: "A man wrote to the *New England Farmer* for a nice winter squash; I heard of it and we happened to have one; my father called it "Marm Hubbard's Squash" because we got the seeds from an old lady by the name of Hubbard. I sent him some of the seeds; he tried them and so well did he like them that he wrote an article, which was published in a number of papers, describing the good points of the squash. Before I fully realized it I was getting orders for this squash seed from all parts of the United States, and also for many other kinds of seeds and soon found I was doing a thriving seed business." At first he transacted this in his home, but about the year 1883 built a store, which he enlarged from time to time, his business becoming one of the largest of the country. He sent goods to all parts of the United States and to Canada and the provinces. During the famine in India he was especially active and benevolent. He sent from his store houses large quantities of seed corn, aiding materially in the securing of a new crop for the relief of the starving people. "I had a college mate, he said, who was a missionary there and I sent him seeds of the best varieties of American vegetables. He planted and also distributed them among the people. It had such a good effect that the governor of that section of India where he was, sent for, thanked, and rewarded him, and offered him three hundred dollars a month to take charge of the agriculture of the government, but being a missionary he would not accept the offer." His extensive seed farms located in Middleton comprise over four hundred acres, and he makes a specialty of growing particular varieties for market garden purposes. During the time he was in the business he made a specialty of introducing new varieties of vegetables before unknown to the public. He has written, published and sold many thousands of copies of works on agriculture, and has lectured extensively on this subject before the colleges and seminaries throughout the northern states. Many of Mr. Gregory's clerks have been in his employ for a quarter of a century.

Mr. Gregory retired in July, 1907, from the great business he constructed during his long and active business life, and since then has devoted himself to his private concerns and charities. He has always lived modestly, notwithstanding the wealth at his command, and has taken much pleasure and satisfaction in giving away funds for southern colleges and churches and in similar good works. He has aided a number of young men to pursue a college education. He presents to every male member of the graduating classes of the colored colleges of the south a character forming book, and has awarded a fund to continue this gift for all future time. He has given books of advantage to the public, at times as many as three thousand volumes per annum, for a number of years, sending them to jails, prisons, etc. He has recently given a number of fine engravings to the schools of Marblehead and the Young Men's Christian Association, and twenty oil paintings to the different churches and chapels. He has for many years been a collector of Indian relics of which he has over two thousand, and also of shells of which he has a large collection and a thorough knowledge. Mr. Gregory has taken an active interest in public and municipal affairs. He has been one of the generous supporters of all movements of moral or material benefit to his native town. He gave the bell and clock for Abbot Hall in Marblehead. He is a Republican, and in 1876-77 was state senator, elected by the joint vote of the Prohibition and Republican parties.

Mr. Gregory married (first) Eliza C. Bubier; (second) Harriet R. Knight; (third) Sarah Lydia Caswell. Mr. Gregory has adopted four children: 1. Edgar, mentioned below. 2. James H., born Boston, 1873, educated in public schools of Marblehead, spent one year at the Massachusetts Agricultural College at Amherst, then went to South America to live with his uncle, James Gregory Carleton, a mining engineer. He enlisted in the Columbian army, being promoted through the various ranks, taking part in a number of battles, and finally being made brigadier-general. He married a Spanish girl and they are the parents of six children. 3. Annie, married Stephen Burroughs, of Long Hill, Connecticut, and has six children. 4. Laura, married Simeon Coffin, of Marblehead, and has three children.

(IV) Edgar Gregory, adopted son of James John Howard Gregory, was born at Chelsea, Massachusetts, December 12, 1869. He received his education in the public schools of Marblehead and the Massachusetts Agricultural College at Amherst, graduating from the latter in the class of 1890. He became associated with his foster-father in the seed business, and in 1901 was admitted to partnership under the firm name of J. J. H. Gregory & Son and continued thus until the senior partner and founder retired July 1, 1907. Since then Edgar Gregory has been sole proprietor though the name is unchanged. He resided at Middleton, where the seed farms were located, until 1908, when he removed to Marblehead and where the place of business is. Mr. Gregory is interested in botany, in which study he took a first prize in college. He is a Republican, and was a member of the school committee in Middleton in 1905. He is a prominent member of the Congregational church of Middleton, is a member of its standing committee and was for three years superintendent of the Sunday-school. He is a member of Philanthropic Lodge of Free Masons, of the New England Order of Protection, Elbridge Gerry Lodge, No. 303, all of Marblehead.

Mr. Gregory married, June 17, 1901, Flora Dell Stebbins, born June 14, 1871, daughter of Lafayette C. and Flora Elva (Lovett) Stebbins, of Amherst, who were the parents of one other child, Horace Canon Stebbins, born June 3, 1868. Mr. L. C. Stebbins was a soldier in the civil war; died June 19, 1872; his wife, born January 8, 1849, is daughter of Edward Ballou Lovett. Children of Mr. and Mrs. Gregory: 1. Warren Albertus, born July 17, 1893. 2. Edgar Stebbins, January 14, 1895. 3. James Capron Lovett, February 18, 1900.

(For first generation see preceding sketch).

GREGORY (II) John Hooper Gregory, son of Joseph Gregory, was baptized December 1, 1793, at Marblehead. He was educated in his native town and became a prominent citizen there. On land formerly owned by him were built the first four summer cottages at Marblehead Neck near the harbor. He sold the land April 29, 1867, and the houses were built by A. H. Dunlap, Thomas Pierson, John Blunt and George McMasters, of Nashua, New Hampshire. Mr. Gregory married, at Marblehead, 1809, Tabitha Bowden, born in Marblehead, about 1794. Children, born at Marblehead: 1. John Hooper, Jr., baptized December 17, 1809. 2. Samuel Bowden, baptized December 20, 1812. 3. Joseph, baptized February 26, 1815; mentioned below. 4. Michael Bowden, baptized April 27, 1817. 5. Hannah Hooper, baptized January 4, 1819. 6. Thomas Hooper, baptized May 13, 1821, aged two months. 7. Tabitha Angenette, baptized October 31, 1824. 8. William Doliber, baptized June 4, 1826, aged one year, six months. 9. Franklin Augustus, baptized October 26, 1828.

(III) Joseph Gregory, son of John Hooper Gregory, born at Marblehead in February, 1815, was baptized there February 26, following. He was in the fishing business, learned the trade of shipwright and was associated with his father in ship-building. He became a master mariner. He was prominent in military and political affairs also. He attained the rank of lieutenant-colonel in the Second Regiment, Massachusetts Volunteer militia, and served from 1850 to 1855. He took a lively interest in municipal affairs and was selectman for a number of years. He was upright and honorable in all his dealings, of exceptional ability, sound judgment, and strict integrity. He was a charter member of Atlantic Lodge of Odd Fellows of Marblehead. He died in July, 1873. He married, 1843, Elizabeth A. Paine, born in Marblehead, died in January, 1858, daughter of Henry Paine. Children, born in Marblehead: 1. Joseph, born March 7, 1844; mentioned below. 2. William D., born 1846; was chief officer of the clipper ship "Radiant," and was lost in the bay of Bengal in February, 1876.

(IV) Joseph Gregory, son of Joseph Gregory, was born at Marblehead, March 7, 1844. He was educated there in the public schools. He followed the sea for two years in his youth, making one voyage to China. When the civil war came he enlisted as acting master mate in the United States navy and remained in the service until October 21, 1865, when he was honorably discharged. He returned to Marblehead and followed the trade of shoemaker in various factories in his native town for a period of twenty-two years. In 1887 he was appointed inspector of customs in the Boston custom house, a position he has filled to the present time. He is a member of John Goodwin Jr. Post, No. 82, Grand Army of the Republic, and of Philanthropic Lodge of Free Masons. He has been an active and prominent member of the First Congregational Church for the past thirty years. In politics he is a Democrat, and has been chairman of the Democratic town committee. For four years he was town auditor and for the same period a registrar of voters for the town.

He married, in 1863, Hannah H. Pedrick, born in Marblehead, August 10, 1844, daughter of Captain John B. Pedrick, who was born in Marblehead in 1807, and died in California, August, 1850. Captain Pedrick was a master mariner. He married Sarah H. Johnson, who died in January, 1892; they were parents of seven children, four of whom died in infancy; those who came to maturity were: Hannah H., married Joseph Gregory; Isabella, born 1846; John J., born 1850. Captain John Johnson, grandfather of Mrs. Joseph Gregory, died in 1862.

Lafayette Gregory, only child of Joseph and Hannah H. (Pedrick) Gregory, was born in 1863. He was educated in the Marblehead public schools, and is now a partner in the firm of Joseph M. Herman & Company, Boston, manufacturers of men's shoes. He married, 1889, Caroline Goldthwait, daughter of William I. Goldthwait, of Marblehead, and they have a son, Ernest Gregory, born 1891, now a student at Amherst College.

TREFRY The surname Trefry (or Treffry) is of local or place name in derivation. There is a Manor of Treffry in the parish of Lanhydroch, Cornwall, England, and the family taking its name from this manor traces its history to a very early period. In 1620 John Treffry was eleventh in descent from Roger Treffry of this Manor of Treffry, reign of Henry III. The coat-of-arms: Sable a chevron between three trees eradicated argent. In England we also find the spelling Trevett, which is also used very infrequently as a baptismal name. This name is derived from the Manor Treffry, parish Lanhydroch, and is traced to an early period. The family removed to Fowey, where was born the gallant Sir John Treffry who, fighting under the Black Prince at the battle of Poictiers, took the French royal standard, for which he was created a knight baronet, and given augmentation of his arms—the fleur-de-lis of France. In the next century some French marauders (whether in revenge of the national disgrace or not does not appear) attacked Place House, the residence of the family at Fowey, but met a repulse at the hands of Mistress Treffry, of the period. Leland says: "The Frenchmen divers times assaulted Fowey and last most notably about Henry V. tyme when the wife of Thomas Trevry with her men repelled the French out of her house in her husband's absence, whereupon Thomas Trevry builded a right fair and strongly embattled tower in his house" ("Patronymic Brittanica").

(I) Henry Trefry (or Trevett) seems to be the ancestor of both Trevett and Trevry (or Trefry) families of Marblehead. There were many French Huguenots at Marblehead at an early date, and fishermen who spoke a patois that still lingers in the speech of that quaint old town. Trivett, Trevett, Trevery, Trifett, Trefry, and all the other spellings of the name, would have been pronounced about the same—Trefry—and there appears to be some relationship between the Trefry family mentioned below and the famous Peter family from Cornwall, England. Elizabeth Trefy, of Fowey, Cornwall, "of a family of great antiquity yielding not in quality to any in Cornwall," married William Peter, a prominent merchant, fourth son of Sir John Peter, knight, of Exeter, Devonshire, and their three sons—William, Thomas and Rev. Hugh—were eminent men in both old and New England. Rev. Hugh Peter was born in 1599 at Fowey; graduated at Trinity College, Cambridge, 1617, A. M. 1622; preached at St. Sepulchre's, London; subscribed to the stock of the Massachusetts Bay Company in 1628; became a Puritan and pastor of the English Church at Rotterdam; came to Boston, Massachusetts, in 1635, and was ordained pastor of the church at Salem and did excellent work;

returned to England as one of the representatives of the Colonies at the opening of the revolution, and became one of the foremost leaders of the parliamentary party; after the restoration was brought to trial for treason, condemned, hanged, drawn and quartered October 16, 1660. Henry Peter, a kinsman, married in 1609 Deborah Trefry, daughter of John Trefry, Esq., of Place, a lineal descendant of Sir John Trefry, mentioned above, and his son Henry Peter, imprisoned for political reasons was released through the efforts of Rev. Hugh Peter "kinsman."

(I) Thomas Trefry, immigrant ancestor, settled at Marblehead, and was a prominent citizen. He was in all likelihood descended from the Trefry family of Cornwall, and related to George Trefry who settled in York, Maine; was deputy to the general court of Massachusetts; and to Henry Trefry (Trivett, Trevett, Trevery, or Trifett as variously spelled), who was living at Marblehead from 1646 to 1674, and had a son Henry. Thomas Trefry was one of the signers of a petition for a town meeting for March 16, 1673-4, to be at eight o'clock in the morning. Marblehead then as now was inhabited principally by seafaring men, and the petition adds: "We desire it the more because we suppose the inhabitants now at home." (p. 70, Gen. Reg. 1853). Henry "Treatt" was another signer. A few years later Thomas Trefry signed a petition to the county court with numerous other Marblehead men protesting against actions begun by Erasmus James and others as agents or attorneys to the commoners or town of Marblehead. Henry "Trivitt" (same as Treatt above) was another signer. It may be added that there was a John Treby (sic) of Marblehead before 1668, probably the John Trefry of Boston who died in 1675; was aged forty-five in 1672; left no descendants and similar name is found in the colonies. (Reg. 1854, p. 163 and p. 288). (Savage Gen. Dict.). Children of Thomas Trefry: 1. Thomas, mentioned below. 2. James, married June 8, 1702, Sarah Russell. 3. Sarah (?), married November 5, 1696, Samuel Holman. 4. Benjamin (?), had son Benjamin, who died at Marblehead in 1712.

(II) Thomas Trefry, son of Thomas Trefry, was born about 1660, either in Marblehead or the old country. He lived in Marblehead. He married first, Sarah ———; second, October 14, 1692, Annas (Agnes) Dennis, who died at Marblehead, December, 1749. Child of first wife: 1. John, born June 5, 1689; perhaps. Children of second wife: 2. Thomas, born August 3, 1694. 3. Mary, baptized December 5 or 15, 1695. 4. James, Jr., born September 5, 1698, mentioned below. 5. Annas, (Agnes), born July 16, 1700. 6. John, born April 2, 1703; married Rebecca Wormstall (or Wormstead) of a prominent Marblehead family. 7. William, born May 26, 1706, baptized June 9 following. 8. Sarah, born December 15, 1709. 9. Amy, born 1712, baptized May 11, 1712.

(III) James Trefry Jr., son of Thomas Trefry, was born at Marblehead, September 5, 1698, baptized there October 9, 1698. He married, at Marblehead, June 29, 1720, Mary Tomson; second, September 26, 1738, Mary Dodd. He was called "Jr." to distinguish him from his uncle of the same name. Children, born at Marblehead: 1. James, baptized July 9, 1721. 2. Jonathan, baptized May 5, 1723. 3. Thomas, baptized August 1, 1725. 4. John, baptized January 28, 1727-8. 5. William, baptized July 12, 1730; mentioned below. Children of second wife: 8. James, baptized November 4, 1739. 9. John, baptized August 15, 1742.

(IV) William Trefry, son of James Trefry, Jr., was baptized July 12, 1730. He married, December 16, 1751, at Marblehead, Tabitha Pousland. Children, born at Marblehead: 1. William, baptized November 26, 1752. 2. James, baptized November 17, 1754. 3. Tabitha, baptized October 31, 1756. 4. John, mentioned below. 5. Mary, baptized December 14, 1760.

(V) John Trefry, son of William Trefry, was baptized at Marblehead, February 11, 1759. He was a soldier in the revolution, private in Captain James Prentiss's company, Colonel Samuel Brewer's regiment, 1777. He died August 29 or 31, 1836, aged seventy-six. He married at Marblehead, December 4, 1787, Susanna Stacey. Children born at Marblehead: 1. Susanna, baptized November 8, 1789. 2. John, baptized May 20, 1792. 3. Samuel Stacey, mentioned below. 4. Susanna, born September 11, 1796. 5. Tabby, born October 28, 1798.

(VI) Samuel Stacey Trefry, son of John Trefry, was born June 4, 1794 (church record). He was cashier of the Marblehead Bank, and one of the most prominent men of Marblehead in his day. He married, at Marblehead, November 2, 1817, Sarah (Sally) Turner. Children, born in Marblehead: 1. John, born June 2, 1818; died young. 2. Samuel Stacey Jr. (Stacey), mentioned below. 3.

Susanna Stacey, born October 1, 1822. 4. Sarah Turner, born December 27, 1824; still living at Lunenburg, Massachusetts. 5. John, born October 9, 1827. 6. Henry Gallison, born December 21, 1829. 7. Tabitha, born August 7, 1831. 8. Hannah Devereux, born March 7, 1833. 9. William Lewis, born September 7, 1835. 10. Stephen C. P. Trefry. 11. Mary Meek, born May 19, 1840. 12. Theodore, born February 21, 1843. 13. Ellen Maria, born April 17, 1844. The four last named still reside in Marblehead.

(VII) Samuel Stacey Trefry, son of Samuel Stacey Trefry, was born in Marblehead, July 5, 1820. He was educated in the public schools of his native town. He was for many years bookkeeper in the Suffolk Bank and in the Marblehead Bank. He was accountant also for the Mount Auburn Cemetery Association of Boston, and for the receivers of the Hamilton Insurance Company of Salem. In 1872 he engaged in the fire insurance business with offices at Marblehead and continued with conspicuous success to the time of his death. In politics he was a Democrat, and in religion a Unitarian. He died at Marblehead, February 2, 1882. He married, at Marblehead, November 30, 1843, Rebecca Wormstead, born at Marblehead, daughter of Benjamin and Martha (Baker) Wormstead, of Marblehead. His wife died October 28, 1863, and he married, second, Mary K. Caswell, born in Marblehead, daughter of John Caswell. Children of first wife: 1. Hannah R., married James Shepard. 2. Mary B., married Benjamin S. Phillips. 3. John H., died November, 1907. 4. William Davis Thayer: see forward. 5. Benjamin W. 6. Samuel Stacy. 7. Rebecca W., married Arthur Haines. Children of second wife: 8. Frank H., died 1896. 9. Sarah T., married Arthur R. Dinsmore. 10. Walter C.

(VIII) William Davis Thayer Trefry, son of Samuel Stacey Trefry (7), was born at Marblehead, May 10, 1852. He attended the public schools of his native town and Tufts College, where he was graduated in the class of 1878. He then studied law and was admitted to the bar at the April term of the supreme court of Massachusetts, in Essex county, 1882. He opened an office in Marblehead and practiced also in Salem, advancing rapidly in his profession. In politics he is a Republican, and he has been active in public affairs. He was chairman of the Marblehead school committee for a number of years, and he is one of the trustees and the secretary of the board of trustees of the Public Library of Marblehead. He is a trustee of Marblehead Academy and keenly interested in educational matters. In 1891 he was elected auditor of commonwealth of Massachusetts, and in January, 1892, was appointed by Governor Russell commissioner of savings banks, becoming chairman of the board. He held this office until September, 1899, when he was appointed tax commissioner and commissioner of corporations. He has filled this important and difficult position to the present time with marked ability, tact and discretion. Mr. Trefry is a member of Philanthropic Lodge Free and Accepted Masons; of Washington Royal Arch Chapter; of Salem Council, Royal and Select Masters; of Winslow Lewis Commandery, Knights Templar; of Sutton Lodge of Perfection, A. A. S. R.; of Giles S. Yates Council, Princes of Jerusalem; of Mount Olivet Chapter of Rose Croix, and Massachusetts Consistory; and an honorary member of the Supreme Council of the Northern Masonic jurisdiction for the 33d and last degree. In 1891-2-3 he was district deputy grand master of the Eighth Masonic District, and is a member of the Grand Lodge of Massachusetts. His activity and prominence in the Masonic fraternity have given a very wide acquaintance among the leading men of the state, and he is a welcome visitor and popular guest on many occasions of Masonic interest. He is a member of that society of scholars, the Phi Beta Kappa, and at the last commencement of his class, June 17, 1908, he received the degree of A. M. He is a prominent Episcopalian, and senior warden of St. Michael's Protestant Episcopal Church of Marblehead.

HOWLAND

The original Howlands in America were Arthur, Henry and John. The last named was one of the "Mayflower" number, and the others appeared in Plymouth colony in the early days of the settlement, but how and from what place in England they came from has never been definitely ascertained.

(I) John Howland held to the original faith of the Puritans, and was an officer of Rev. John Cotton's church and a stanch adherent of the Orthodox faith until his death, while Arthur and Henry were Quakers. The original painting from which the engravings of the Howland coat-of-arms in this country was made was in water colors, highly ornamented, and the following description of it was handsomely engrossed under the arms: "He beareth Sable, two bars Argent, on a chief of the second thin lions rampant of the first, and for his crest on a wreath of his colors a lion passant sable, by the name of Howland." Tradition says this was brought from England soon after the "Mayflower" came. In 1865 it was in the possession of Rev. T. Howland White, of Shelbourne, Nova Scotia. He was a grandson of Gideon White, whose wife was Joanna, daughter of John Howland, son of the Pilgrim.

John Howland's was the thirteenth name on the list, of forty-one signers of the "Compact" in the cabin of the "Mayflower" in "Cape Cod Harbor," November 21, 1620. At this time he was twenty-eight years of age, and was a member of Governor Carver's family. How this came to be is not known, but it is probable that Carver saw elements in his character which led him to supply Young Howland's wants when they left England, and caused him to be considered one of the family. That he possessed sound judgment and business capacity is shown by the active duties which he assumed and the trust which was reposed in him in all the early labors in establishing a settlement. While the "Mayflower" was yet in Cape Cod harbor, ten of "her principal" men were "sente out" in a boat manned by eight sailors, to select a place for landing. A storm drove them into Plymouth Harbor, and Plymouth was selected as the place of settlement.

The first mention of John Howland in the old Plymouth colony records is on a list of freemen, and the third in number in the governor's "councill" of seven members. In 1633 or 1634 he was an assessor; was a selectman of Plymouth 1666, and chosen deputy of the same town in 1652-56-58-61-63-66-67-70. His election June 2, 1670, was the last time he accepted public office, being nearly eighty years of age. Besides these public positions of honor and trust bestowed upon him, he was very often selected to lay out and appraise land to run highways, settle disputes, and on committees of every description. He was not only full of zeal for the temporal welfare of the colony, but gave powerful encouragement to a high standard of morals and religion, so much so that he is recorded as "a godly man and an ancient professor in the ways of Christ." It is shown that he was active in this work for Governor Bradford notes that he became "a profitable member both in Church and Commonwealth," and it appears that at the ordination of John Cotton, Jr., in 1667, John Howland "was appointed by the Church to join in the imposition of hands." He lived at what was called Rocky Nook. He died 23, 2, 1672, old style, April 23, 1673, new style. He married Elizabeth, daughter of John Tilly, who died December 21, 1687, aged eighty years, in Swanzey, Massachusetts. She was the last but three of the "Mayflower" passengers to die. They had the following children: 1. Desire, born October 13, 1623 (?), in Barnstable; married, 1643, Captain John Gorham, who was baptized at ———, Northamptonshire, England, January 28, 1621, died February 5, 1675-76. 2. John, mentioned below. 3. Jabez, died in Bristol, Rhode Island. 4. Hope, born August 30, 1629, died January 8, 1684; married, 1646, John Chipman, born Barnstable, England, 1614, died April 7, 1708. 5. Elizabeth, married first, September 13, 1649, Ephraim Hicks, of Plymouth, who died December 2, 1649; second, July 10, 1651, John Dickarson, of Plymouth. 6. Lydia, married James Brown, born 1623, died October 10, 1710; they settled in Swanzey. 7. Ruth, married, November 17, 1664, Thomas Cushman, of Plymouth, born September 16, 1637, died July 23, 1726. Thomas Cushman married second, October 16, 1679, Abigail Fuller, of Rehoboth. 8. Hannah, married, July 6, 1661, Jonathan Bosworth. 9. Joseph, died January, 1704. 10. Isaac, born November 15, 1649, died March 9, 1724; married Elizabeth Vaughn, born 1652, died October 29, 1727.

(II) John Howland, son of John and Elizabeth Howland, was born in Plymouth, February 24, 1627. He married, October 26, 1651, Mary, daughter of Robert Lee, of Barnstable. John lived for a time in Marshfield, appearing there as early as 1653, where he took the oath of fidelity in 1657. He was later an inhabitant of Barnstable (1657). He was an energetic and systematic business man, and was highly respected in the colony. In 1674 he was appointed by the court "Ensign of the Military companie of Barnstable." In 1685 he took out a license to sell cider in Barnstable. In 1689 he was selectman in that town. Children: 1. Mary, born 1652; married, 1670, John Allyn, of Barnstable. 2. Elizabeth, born May 17, 1655; married first, February, 1673, John Bursley, born 1652; second, September 14, 1691, Isaac Hamblin. 3. Isaac, born November 25, 1659, married, December 27, 1686, Ann Taylor, born December 12, 1664. 4. Hannah, born May 15, 1661; married, May 20, 1686, Jonathan Crocker, of Barnstable, born July 15, 1662. 5. Mercy, born January

21, 1663, died 1717; married, April 27, 1704, Joseph Hamblin, born November 20, 1680, died August 27, 1766. 6. Lydia, born January 9, 1665, married, March 21, 1689, Joseph Jenkins. 7. Experience, born July 28, 1668. 8. Anne, born September 9, 1670; married September 18, 1691, Joseph Crocker, born January 3, 1668. 9. Shubael, born September 30, 1672, married, December 12, 1700, Mercy Blossom, born 1678, died 1759. 10. John, mentioned below.

(III) John Howland, son of John and Mary (Lee) Howland, was born December 31, 1674, in Barnstable, Massachusetts. He married first, Abigail Crocker; second, June 11, 1719, Mary Crocker, born June 29, 1681. John Howland lived and died in Barnstable. His will was dated February 8, 1738, and proved March 29, 1738. The estate inventoried £1088, 8s. Children by first wife: 1. George Gill, born December 30, 1705; married Abigail Crocker. 2. Hannah, born February 2, 1708, died 1738, unmarried. 3. Mary, born August 11, 1711, died 1738, unmarried. 4. Joanna, born January 26, 1715; married first, April 12, 1750, James Lewis; second, December 28, 1752, John Allen, of Hingham. Children by second wife: 5. John, born February 13, 1721; graduate of Harvard College, and became a Congregational minister; died November 4, 1804; married a daughter of Rev. Mr. Lewis, of Pembroke. 6. Job, mentioned below.

(IV) Job Howland, son of John and Mary (Crocker) Howland, was born June 18, 1726, in Barnstable. He married, December 6, 1753, Hannah, daughter of Benjamin and Nancy (Howland) Jenkins, born 1733, died September 21, 1781. He died May 1, 1794, at the house of his daughter, Joannah Chapman, in Barnstable. Most of the sons and grandsons of the daughters of Job settled in Cape Cod, and many of them became master mariners. None of the sons mentioned below, though born on the Cape, settled there. Children: 1. Mary, born July 21, 1755, died June 18, 1783; married Samuel Bassett, of Barnstable. 2. John, born March 31, 1757, died June 18, 1843; married Grace Avery, June 1, 1786. 3. Shore, born December 28, 1759, died February 25, 1833; married Elizabeth Hastings. 4. Hannah, born May 20, 1762, died April 9, 1838; married first, December 11, 1783, William Chipman, born 1760, died May 11, 1786; second, June 5, 1792, Lemuel Nye. 5. Job, born July 24, 1764, died March 13, 1847; married, November 29, 1792, Mary Fisher, of Dedham. 6. Joanna, born July 28, 1766, died July 6, 1838; married, 1788, John Chipman, born June, 1762, died June, 1806. 7. Benjamin, born August 7, 1768, died ———, 1770. 8. Benjamin, born June 18, 1770, died November 11, 1825; married, June 3, 1794, Hepzibah Hastings. 9. Mehitable, born June 23, 1773, died ———, 1860; married, January 24, 1799, Heman Nye, of Sandwich, born December 23, 1773, died June 2, 1747. 10. Southworth, mentioned below. 11. Timothy, born September 17, 1777, died August 5, 1824; married, February 3, 1802, Lydia Putnam.

(V) Southworth Howland, son of Job and Hannah (Jenkins) Howland, was born March 29, 1775, in Barnstable, and died June 9, 1853. He married first, November 24, 1797, Esther, daughter of Nathan and Persis Allen, of West Brookfield, born December 18, 1780, died October 12, 1814; second, March 13, 1816, Polly, daughter of Dr. Samuel and Bertha (Avery) Ware, of Conway, born December 5, 1785, died February 11, 1870, in Conway. He learned the trade of a house carpenter with his eldest brother, John Howland, and in coming of age was employed in the erection of an elegant dwelling house in West Brookfield by the distinguished architect, Asber Benjamin, and became a prominent resident of that town. He was a man of decided convictions, and was prompt and fearless in defending them. As early as 1812 or 1814 he and his wife pledged each other not to take intoxicating drinks passed around in company, or when making calls, as was the universal custom at that time, and not long after united with a few neighbors in forming a society for the promotion of temperance. He also printed at his own cost, for distribution, an edition of a tract on the subject by the celebrated Dr. Rush. Children: 1. Southworth, died young. 2. Southworth A., mentioned below. 3. Maria, born August 22, 1802, married June 17, 1830, William Avery, of Conway, born September 16, 1705, died April 25, 1853. 4. Harriet, born July 6, 1804, died May 9, 1805. 5. Harriet, born March 18, 1806; married, March 11, 1845, Hezekiah Perry. 6. Louisa, born March 26, 1808, died September 10, 1877; married first, April 9, 1839, Galen Carpenter, of Worcester, born October 16, 1804, in Attleborough, died July 3, 1867; second, Dr. Henry O. Adams, of South Royalston. 7. Henry J., born October 26, 1810; married, November 29, 1832, Ellen Maria, widow of Horace H. Smith. 8. Harrison O., born January 28, 1813, died February 14, 1872; married, November 23, 1845, Hannah O. Bailey, of Amesbury, born March 23, 1813. Children by second wife: 9. William Ware, born July 25, 1817; married, October 14, 1845, Susan Reed. 10. Samuel, born August 2, 1819, died June 24, 1843. 11. Joseph Avery, born February 19, 1821; married, April 20, 1847, Adeline Henshaw. 12. Mary E., born August 28, 1823, died March 26, 1879; married, 1867, Edward Smith, of Enfield. 13. Elizabeth S., born April 3, 1826, died September 15, 1855, at Cincinnati, Ohio; married, February 25, 1852, Rev. H. D. Perry, of Monson.

(VI) Southworth Allen Howland, son of Southworth and Esther (Allen) Howland, was born in West Brookfield, September 11, 1800, and died October 7, 1882. He married, September 30, 1823, Esther, daughter of Captain William and Betsey (Barnes) Allen, of Plymouth, born July 13, 1801, died April 14, 1860, in Worcester. He died in Worcester, October 7, 1882. Captain William Allen was born 1775; he was a son of John Allen, who came to America about 1760, and married Esther Savery in 1768. Being a Tory he returned to England during the revolutionary war (1777). His children were: Esther, Betsey, John, William and Winslow. Southworth A. Howland learned the trade of bookbinder with Joseph Avery in Plymouth, and in the autumn of 1821 went to Worcester and entered the bookbinding and retail book trade in the firm of Dorr & Howland, remaining until 1842. From that time until 1852 he was engaged in the same business alone. He then gave his attention to the insurance business, in which he continued until his health failed. He was an active and useful citizen, an energetic worker, charitable and kind to all; a man who loved his home, and the church, of which he was a constant attendant; he was a diligent student and reader of the Bible. Children: 1. Southworth Allen, Jr., born July 5, 1826, died March 29, 1828. 2. Esther Allen, born August 17, 1828; unmarried. 3. Charles Allen, mentioned below. 4. Edward Payson, born April 6, 1834; married Elizabeth Holden, of Quincy, who died August 6, 1875; he was for many years engaged in the insurance business, and in 1885 resided in Quincy. 5. William Otis, born March 27, 1838; married, June 23, 1870, Ella F., daughter of Isaac Shepard; children: i. Shepard, born March 29, 1871, in Quincy; ii. Allen Shepard, born at Swatow, China; iii. Jehila Shepard, born in Worcester.

(VII) Charles Allen Howland, son of Southworth Allen and Esther (Allen) Howland, was born September 4, 1829, in Worcester. He received a public school and academic education. He learned of his father the trade of bookbinder, and worked with him for nearly fifteen years. He was for two years in the office of the register of deeds in Worcester. His father, having given up the book trade and become agent for a number of insurance companies, among them the Quincy Mutual, Charles A. entered the office with him. In 1857 he entered the office of the Quincy Mutual Fire Insurance Company. In 1861 the secretary of the company died, and Mr. Howland was unanimously elected in his place April 14 of that year. The company was then in its infancy and struggling for existence, but prospered finely under the new management. Its losses at the Boston fire of 1872 were nearly $460,000 and were promptly paid in full. The president and treasurer of the company, Israel M. Munroe, having died, Mr. Howland was chosen president, in April, 1885, which office he now holds. Mr. Howland has since held many positions of trust and responsibilitiy in the business circles of Quincy. He has been treasurer and one of the directors of the Citizens' Gas Light Company, trustee of the Savings Bank, and a director of the Mt. Wollaston National Bank, and is now president of that bank. He was also director of the Hingham Cordage Company. He has been justice of the peace for Norfolk county for many years. He was for a number of years superintendent of the Unitarian Sunday school of Quincy.

Mr. Howland married first, Abbie F., daughter of Israel W. Munroe, of Quincy; she died 1866. He married second, 1871, Helen Maria, born January 24, 1844, daughter of Rev. Josiah and Maria F. (Doane) Moore. Rev. Josiah Moore, a minister of the Unitarian church at Duxbury for forty-two years, was born November 27, 1800; he married, July 10, 1839, Maria Foster Doane, born November 26, 1814, in Cohasset, a daughter of Elisha Doane, a native of Wellfleet, who lived in Cohasset and married Jane Cutter, of Boston. Rev. Josiah Moore was the father of the following children: 1. James Henry, born 1840. 2. John Greenough, 1842. 3. Helen Maria, 1844; wife of Mr. Howland. 4. William Sturtevant, 1846. 5. Josiah, 1848. 6. Emily Hewes, 1851. 7. Mary Elizabeth, 1854. Rev. Josiah Moore was a son of Henry and Mary Moore, who were the parents of the following children: Henry, Nelson, Emery, Horatio, James, Caleb, Elizabeth, Hannah, Achsa, Mary and Josiah. Mr. and Mrs. Howland have two children: 1. Mabel, born January 27, 1872, in Quincy; married, June 22, 1896, Captain Francis Henry Lister, engineer commander in the British navy, performing special work in the admiralty. Their children are: i. Olive Howland, born January 20, 1898; ii. Francis Allen, born June 8, 1902; iii. Helen Roy, born April 15, 1907. 2. Charles Allen, Jr., born August 13, 1877. Mr. Howland died October 1, 1908.

REDMAN (I) John Redman, immigrant ancestor, came to Hampton, New Hampshire, about 1642, and settled as a blacksmith in the eastern part of the town. He died February 16, 1700, about eighty-five years old. He married first, Margaret ———, died May 30, 1658; second, July 23, 1673, Sabina, widow of Captain Marston. Children, all by first wife: 1. John, born 1647; mentioned below. 2. Mary, December 15, 1649. 3. Joseph, April 20, 1651. 4. Samuel, April 12, 1658.

(II) John Redman, son of John Redman (1), was born probably in Hampton, in 1647. He married, March 27, 1667, Martha, daughter of John Cass. He served as representative to the general court for five years from 1722. Children: 1. Maria, born November 12, 1669. 2. John, October 7, 1672; mentioned below. 3. Martha, December 23, 1674. 4. Joseph, December 28, 1678; died April 23, 1679. 5. Abiel, May 17, 1681; married August 7, 1700, James Gordon. 6. Mary, June 3, 1686; married James Moulton.

(III) John Redman, son of John Redman (2), was born in Hampton, October 7, 1672, and died February 9, 1718. He married, November 12, 1696, Joanna Bickford, who married second, Daniel Healey. Children: 1. Joseph, mentioned below. 2. John, March 20, 1701. 3. Martha, baptized March 8, 1712; died February 14, 1775; married Joseph Johnson. 4. Anna, baptized March 8, 1712.

(IV) Joseph Redman, son of John Redman (3), was born November 6, 1697. He married May 11, 1727, Hannah Rawlings (Rollins), who died May 4, 1758. Children: 1. Hannah, born February 1, 1728; died March 1, 1813; married first, Nathan Godfrey; second ——— Howell. 2. John, mentioned below. 3. Joseph, November 7, 1731; died October 17, 1757. 4. Patience, born December 1, 1733; married January 27, 1754, Benjamin Newman, of Newbury. 5. Tristram, born November 12, 1735. 6. Jonathan (twin), born August 3, 1740; drowned May 26, 1748. 9. David (twin), born August 3, 1740.

(V) John Redman, son of Joseph Redman (4), was born at Hampton, New Hampshire, March 20, 1701. He married Sarah, daughter of John Godfrey, and removed to Nottingham, New Hampshire, sometime after 1740. Children, (dates of baptism): 1. Benjamin, December 29, 1729. 2. Sarah, June 7, 1730. 3. Joanna, August 27, 1732. 4. John, mentioned below.

(VI) John Redman, son of John Redman (5), was baptized in Hampton, June 15, 1740, and died in Castine, Maine, August 11, 1774. He removed with his parents to Nottingham, New Hampshire, after 1740, and thence to Scarborough, Maine, and about 1770 to Castine, Maine. He settled there in the part later set off as the town of Brooksville. He married Sarah Blake (?). Children: 1. Moses, born April 8, 1763, died January 4, 1764. 2. John, born February 14, 1765. 3. Israel, baptized at Scarborough, Maine, February 16, 1767. 4. Benjamin, mentioned below. 5. Ephraim, November 10, 1770. 6. Sarah, November 1, 1772. 7. Frances, November 17, 1774.

(VII) Benjamin Redman, son of John Redman (6), was born in Nottingham, New Hampshire, November 24, 1768. He married Mary Byard, born November 30, 1768, died May 18, 1807.

(VIII) Robert Redman, son of Benjamin Redman (7), was born at Castine, Maine, July 16, 1805, died February 18, 1880. He married Sarah Smith Merrithew, born April 14, 1811, died December 24, 1885. Children: 1. Abbie D., born April 22, 1834. 2. Benjamin R., March 14, 1836, mentioned below. 3. Nancy Jane, November 11, 1837, deceased. 4. Mary Ann, July 3, 1839. 5. Sarah E., October 11, 1840, deceased. 6. Angeline, September 10, 1843, deceased. 7. Robert M., born Aprl 16, 1845, deceased. 8. Caroline J., born February 16, 1847. 9. Clara F., born March 25, 1849. 10. Varnum Rose, born September 15, 1851, died October 2, 1880, lost at sea. 11. Addie A., born April 15, 1854.

(IX) Benjamin R. Redman, son of Robert Redman (8), was born March 14, 1836, died December 13, 1905. At an early age he evinced a desire to follow the sea. His parents objected so that he complied with their wishes and helped his father on the farm until he was about twenty, at which time they gave their consent. After making a few trips he was appointed captain, in which capacity he was very successful, making some of the fastest voyages on record, one of which was crossing the Atlantic in eleven days in a sailing vessel. In 1863, his vessel, the brig "William C. Clark," was captured by the privateer "Florida" and burned, he and the crew being landed in Bermuda. At the age of forty-two he retired. Captain Redman, who was in every sense of the word a truly selfmade man, was a Unitarian in religion, a Republican in politics, and a Mason in fraternal matters. He married first, Ethelinda Chestina, daughter of Andrew P. and Philena (Parker) Gilkey (see Parker family); she died February 25, 1878. He married second, Harriet Josephine, born May 2, 1845, daughter of the Rev. James and Roxanna (Hazelton) Adams. Children of first wife: 1. Elnora Adele, born October 18, 1862; married Charles E. Williams, born January 14, 1854, master mariner, son of Captain Emory and Charlotte Williams; children: i. Benjamin Franklin, born April 29, 1882; ii. Chestina Redman, March 30, 1884; iii. Leslie Redman, June 2, 1886. 2. Walter Herman, born September 22, 1864; married Emma Violetta Platt, of Bridgeport, Connecticut; children: i. June, born June 24, 1892, died July 24, 1894; ii. Benjamin Ray, February 21, 1896; iii. Edythe, October 10, 1900. Walter Herman went to New York when a young man, and at the present time (1908) is the leading senior member of one of the largest wholesale lumber concerns in the metropolis. 3. Emerson, born June 11, 1866, died December 11, 1869. 4. Ralph Winchester, born June 15, 1868; mentioned below. 5. Infant daughter, born June 4, 1873, died September 19, 1873. 6. Blessie Chestina, born March 2, 1876, died April 8, 1879. Children of second wife: 7. James Adams, born January 18, 1888. 8. William Wason, born March 22, 1890.

(X) Ralph Winchester Redman, son of Benjamin R. Redman (9), was born June 15, 1868, at North Isleborough, Maine. He received his education in the public schools, and in his boyhood accompanied his father in several sea voyages. In 1888 he went to California and was engaged in the real estate business for a year, and he also traveled extensively in the west. He returned east and for one year was engaged in the lumber business in New York. He then removed to Dedham, Massachusetts, and established himself in the coal, ice and grain business in that town, continuing the same to the present time and achieving therein a moderate measure of success. He stands among the foremost merchants of the community, and enjoys the confidence and esteem of all who know him. He is a Unitarian in religion, a Republican in politics, and a member of the Masonic and Odd Fellow lodges. He married, July 2, 1895, Grace Derby, born July 19, 1868, daughter of Chase and Lucinda (Tirrell) Parker. Chase Parker was born July 11, 1825, died December 11, 1890, son of Chase and Betsey (Foss) Parker, of Lewiston, Maine, grandson of Abraham Parker, and great-grandson of Chase Parker, probably of Buxton, Maine. Chase Parker, Sr., was born August 20, 1792, and died in 1866. His wife, Betsey (Foss) Parker, was born in 1799, died September 4, 1867, a daughter of Major Foss, soldier of the revolution and war of 1812, who resided in Limington, Maine. Lucinda (Tirrell) Parker, wife of Chase Parker, Jr., was born May 20, 1828, daughter of Jared and Lucinda Tirrell, the former a son of Benjamin and Elizabeth (Derby) Tirrell. Children of Mr. and Mrs. Ralph W. Redman, born in Dedham: 1. Chestina Josephine, January 23, 1898. 2. Grace Parker, twin of Chestina Josephine.

PARKER The surname Parker is derived from the Latin parcarius—park keeper, or shepherd. Danes, Saxons and Normans in England all seems to have had the name in use as a surname at an early date. Parcum and de Parco are found in Domesday Book. As early as the years 900-925 in the reign of Edward I, a Geoffrey Parker is mentioned, even before the common use of surnames in England. At first the prefix Le (the) was common, and it is altogether likely that many Parker families had their origin like other families named for occupations in many different lines, distinct and unrelated. The coat-of-arms of the Brownsholme family of Parker, the pedigree of which is traced to William Le Parker, of Eztwistle, Lancashire, before 1400, and which seems most likely that to which the American line here given belongs, is: Vert, a chevron between three stags heads cabossed or. Crest: A leopard head affrontee erased or ducally gorged gules. Motto—*"Sepre aude"* (dare to be just). This coat-of-arms has descended through the Park Hall and Staffordshire lines and is now used by Sir Thomas Parker, Earl of Macclesfield, England. It is similar to the earlier coat-of-arms of the Parker family of Eztwistle and doubtless modified from that design.

(I) James Parker, immigrant ancestor, came from England before 1640 when he had settled in Woburn, Massachusetts, and he was a taxpayer there as early as 1645. He was probably related to some of the numerous other pioneers of the name located in that section of the Bay colony. Abraham Parker, of Woburn and Chelmsford, and John of Billerica and Woburn, were doubtless brothers. James Parker removed to Billerica about 1654, to Chelmsford in 1658, and to Groton in 1660. The town of Groton was divided into "acre rights," each of which entitled the owner to nearly fifty acres of the common lands when divided. Parker owned rights and further increased his holdings by purchase until he was the largest owner of land and probably the richest proprietor of Groton. He became prominent in both town and church. He was deacon of the church, and was selectman of the town from 1662 to 1699. He was town clerk for a time; moderator of all the important town meetings of his day; chairman of important committees to locate highways, lay out lots to proprietors and establish town bounds. He was representative to the general court in 1693. While living in Groton he was once elected selectman of Dunstable. He was a brave and sturdy Indian fighter, rising through the various ranks to captain of the Groton company. His home was at a distance from the present village, near Martin's pond, removed some distance from the highways, shaded and secluded, and no trace of it is left. A description of his homestead given in a recent publication doubtless belongs to a later generation of the family. A small part of the original estate was recently and perhaps is still owned by descendants in Groton. He owned a large part of the Half Moon Meadow. He died in 1701, aged eighty-three years. He married, May 1644, Elizabeth Long, daughter of Robert Long, of Charlestown, Massachusetts. He married second, Eunice ———. Children: 1. Elizabeth, born April 12, 1645, at Woburn. 2. Anna, January 5, 1646-47. 3. John, January 18, 1648, died young. 4. John, February 28, 1649. 5. Sarah, August 29, 1650, died October 15, 1651. 6. Joseph, Woburn, 1651. 7. James, April 15, 1652; married Mary Parker; he was a grantee of Billerica and was killed there by the Indians, July 27, 1694. 8. Josiah, 1655; married Elizabeth Saxon, of Boston. 9. Samuel, mentioned below. 10. Joshua, March 3, 1658, at Chelmsford; married Abigail Shattuck. 11. Zachariah, January 14, 1659, at Chelmsford. 12. Eleazer, November 9, 1660, at Groton. Thirty years after the birth of Eleazer the youngest of the family, Sarah, was born December 12, 1697, by the second wife, as shown by the will and town records. His will is published in full in Butler's History of Groton.

(II) Samuel Parker, son of Captain James Parker (1), was born in Billerica about 1657. He married Abigail Lakin, at Groton, daughter of Sergeant John and Mary Lakin, of Groton. Her father and his brother, Lieutenant William Lakin, settled in Groton with their grandfather, William Lakin, who died December 10, 1672, aged ninety years, at Groton. Children, born at Groton: 1. James, born April 28, 1686; married Abigail Prescott. 2. Robert, April 2, 1688. 3. Samuel; married Deborah Prescott. 4. John, mentioned below. 5. Abigail, August 22, 1696; married Thomas Tarbell. 6. Jonathan, married Sarah ———, and both died September 23, 1723. 7. Rachel. 8. Eunice, March 11, 1705; married, January 12, 1730, Josiah Boyden.

(III) John Parker, son of Samuel Parker (2), was born at Groton, in 1694. He married in that town, May 22, 1719, Joanna Ames. Children, born in Groton: 1. John, December 12, 1719. 2. Robert, January 20, 1720. 3. Jerusha, June 20, 1725. 4. Sarah, June 8, 1727. 5. Beulah, October 10, 1729. 6. Jonathan, December 1, 1732 (twin). 7. Relief (twin), December 1, 1732. 8. Deborah, June 4, 1736. 9. Oliver, mentioned below.

(IV) Oliver Parker, son of John Parker (3), was born February 23, 1738, at Groton. He married there, August 7, 1759, Jane Nutting. He was a soldier in the revolution, first lieutenant in Captain Asa Lawrence's company of minute-men, April 19, 1775, and was probably in the battle of Bunker Hill with Captain Prescott's company as an order for new cartridge boxes at Cambridge the day after is endorsed "Prescott." Children, born at Groton: 1. Oliver, Jr., 1760; soldier in the revolution. 2. William, November 24, 1761. 3. Stephen, February 14, 1763. 4. Mighill, February 27, 1765; settled in Isleborough, Maine. 5. Henry, November 19, 1766, died November 21, 1766. 6. Simon, August 21, 1767; settled in Isleborough. 7. Jane, March 7, 1769, died March 17, 1769. 8. Ezekiel, June 20, 1770. 9. Jonathan, September 28, 1772; mentioned below. 10. Sarah, February 20, 1775. 11. David (twin), December 2, 1779. 12. Hobart (twin), December 2, 1779.

(V) Deacon Jonathan Parker, son of Oliver Parker (4), was born in Groton, Massachusetts, September 28, 1772, died April 5, 1841. He married Hannah Holbrook, daughter of Jonathan Holbrook; second, Wealthy Dodge, who married first his brother Ezekiel Parker, and third, Zenas Lawry. He settled at Isleborough, Maine, with his brothers Ezekiel, Simon and Mighill, and perhaps others of the family. Children, born at Isleborough: 1. Jonathan, May 25, 1796, died June 10, 1723; married, May 31, 1818, Margaret Jones; their daughter Deborah, born March 14, 1823, married, December 16, 1848, William F. Veazie. 2. Silas, May 30, 1799; married, 1821, Sibyl Drinkwater; removed to Boston. 3. Lucy, August 11, 1801; married Joseph Skinner. 4. Jane, December 5, 1803; blind from birth; died unmarried, January 23, 1768. 5. Philena, April 1, 1806; mentioned below. 6. Louisa C., September 22, 1808; died young or married, December 5, 1841, Ferdinand Skinner, of Searsmont (reports differ). 7. Ellison, November 30, 1810. 8. Thomas H., April 26, 1813; married Emeline Coombs. 9. William Avery, July 1, 1815; married Caroline Veazie. 10. Sabrina, May 22, 1818; married James Warren.

(VI) Philena, born April 1, 1806, daughter of Deacon Jonathan Parker (5); married first, Jordan Veazie and second, Andrew P. Gilkey. The daughter of Andrew P. and Philena (Parker) Gilkey was Ethelinda Chestina, born May 15, 1845; married Captain Benjamin R. Redman (9). (See sketch of the Redman family).

BALKAM The surname Balkam or Balcom is of ancient English origin. The spelling in various branches of the family differs widely, the numerous possibilities of the phonetic spelling of the ancient clerk and recorder being fully realized.

(I) Alexander Balkam, immigrant ancestor, settled at Portsmouth and Providence, Rhode Island, and became a leading citizen of his day. He was in Portsmouth as early as January 31, 1664, and was probably born as early as 1635. He was a mason by trade. He was deputy to the general assembly in 1683 from Providence. He bought a tract of land twelve miles north of Providence, July 14, 1686, of Nathan Payne. He died May 4, 1711, and his will was proved July 18, 1711. His estate was settled by his widow Jane and son John, executors. His will mentions his children by name. He married Jane, daughter of William and Elizabeth Holbrook. Children: 1. Alexander, mentioned below. 2. Catherine, married Daniel Jenckes, born April 19, 1663, son of Joseph and Elizabeth Jenckes. 3. Sarah, married Timothy Sheldon, son of John; four children. 4. John, married Sarah Bartlett, born 1678, died January 30, 1739; resided at Providence and Smithfield, Rhode Island, and kept a tavern; names various relatives in his will. 5. Freegift, was insane at time of Joseph's death. 6. Joseph, born in Portsmouth, about 1660; removed to Mendon, Massachusetts, later to Douglas; married Phebe ———. 7. Hannah, married, February 22, 1716, Ebenezer Hayward; four children. 8. Samuel. 9. Deborah. 10. Lydia, married, April 14, 1701, Daniel Hix, born 1660; died March 21, 1746; five children.

(II) Alexander Balkam, son of Alexander Balkam (1), born about 1660, died at Attleborough, January 31, 1727-8. He settled in Attleborough before 1692. He took the oath of allegiance to the English crown in 1682. He was a mason by trade. He married Sarah Woodcock, daughter of William. He bought of his father-in-law twenty acres of land May 29, 1701, and another parcel of twenty acres February 17, 1707-8, of his mother-in-law, Mary Woodcock, and other heirs of William Woodcock. Children, born at Attleborough: 1. William, born September 3, 1692; married Mary Tyler. 2. Katherine, born February 7, 1694; married, February 2, 1717-8, Andrew Starkey. 3. Alexander, born April 4, 1696. 4. John, born April 29, 1699. 5. Baruck, born June 12, 1702; married Patience Blake. 6. Sarah, born February 8, 1703-4; married Richard Atwell. 7. Joseph, born February 23, 1705-6; married Mary Parmenter.

(III) John Balkam, son of Alexander Balkam (2), born at Attleborough, April 29, 1699; married Mary Grover, died January 4, 1732; married second, May 29, 1732, Sarah Grover. Children of first wife, born at Attleborough: 1. John, born July 27, 1720, baptized at Norton; married at Attleborough, Bathsheba Daggett: she married second, February 27, 1747, Henry Sweet. 2. Mary, born December 14, 1722, published April 20, 1751, to John Fisher. 3. Abigail, born June 23, 1726; married, May 18, 1749, Ebenezer Shaw. 4. Jacob, born September 29, 1728. Children of second wife: 5. Samuel, born August 31, 1734; mentioned below. 6. Bathsheba, born February 18, 1735-6; married (intentions dated February 13, 1762) Daniel Tiffany. 7. Hester, born August 16, 1737. 8. Daniel, born March 4, 1739. 9. Zilpah, born February 21, 1741-2; married (intentions dated August 6, 1763) Ichabod Shed (?). 10. Anne, born September, 1643; published January 30, 1772, to John Wetherell. 11. Hannah, born June 1, 1746; married, June 1, 1771, Thomas Norton. 12. Luce, born May 8, 1748; married (intentions dated February 16, 1776) Benjamin Grover, of Mansfield, Connecticut.

(IV) Samuel Balkam, son of John Balkam (3), born in Attleborough, August 31, 1734; married Sarah Richardson (intentions dated December 23, 1769). He removed to Plantation No. 5, in Maine, and was a soldier there in the revolution, a private in Captain Nathan Watkins's company, Colonel John Patterson's regiment, August, 1775; he was of this same company and regiment November of same year, residence then Gageborough or Partridgefield, Maine. (See p. 532, vol. i, "Mass. Sailors and Soldiers of the Revolution," and p. 243, vol. ii, same work). Children, born in Attleborough: 1. John, born November 25, 1770; mentioned below. 2. Sarah, born May 16, 1772. 3. Samuel, born June 9, 1774. Perhaps others after removing to Maine.

(V) General John Balkam, son of Samuel Balkam (4), was born in Attleborough, Massachusetts, November 25, 1770. He probably changed the form of the family name from Balcombe to Balkam. He removed with wife and four children from Plantation 5 to Plantation 4, Washington county, Maine, now the town of Robbinston. He built a fine residence at Robbinston and for many years after his death it was occupied by his family and their descendants. It was later destroyed by fire. General Balkam was one of the foremost citizens of the county, was well-to-do, and owned the first piano-forte in the town. The story of the delight of the children of the town at hearing Mrs. Balkam's playing is still told. General Balkam was a leading member and deacon for many years of the Orthodox Congregational church. He served in the state legislature, and was elected to the governor's council. He was active from his youth in the state militia, rose to the command of his regiment, and was finally commissioned brigadier-general of the state militia, and was one of the most popular and efficient of officers. His two sons were also deacons of the church subsequently, and another was a minister. The general was a staunch Democrat in politics. He married, April 23, 1795, Abigail Smith, born June 29, 1771, at Norton, Massachusetts, and died at Robbinston, October 4, 1822. He married second, Mary McLelland, of Portland, and she died November 9, 1866, aged seventy-eight, at Milltown, New Brunswick. He died at Robbinston, September 20, 1832. Children: 1. Abigail G., born at Norton, April 10, 1796; married Bryant P. Stephenson; she died June 10, 1851; children: Abigail, John, Benjamin T., Reuben M., George, Charles and Howard. 2. Deacon John Adams, born January 3, 1798, at Norton; married Mary Brewer; died March 1, 1863; she died February 5, 1884, aged eighty; children: Hannah and Charlotte. 3. George W., born January 17, 1800, in Milton, Massachusetts; died November 3, 1812. 4. Laban S., born at Robbinston, Maine, December 22, 1802, died February, 1875; married Almira Durkee; teacher and merchant; resided at Yarmouth, Nova Scotia. 5. Gilbert, born at Robbinston, October 4, 1804; married Susan O. Brewer, widow of William Brewer; died April 8, 1883. 6. Deacon Cyrus, born August 4, 1806; died December 7, 1886; married, at Calais, September 8, 1835, Adeline T. Denning; she died March 8, 1883; he was a tanner by trade; deacon of the Congregational church, and superintendent of its Sunday school; selectman and assessor, town clerk and postmaster; inspector of United States customs; children: i. Mary, born January 14, 1837; married Deacon Rufus Gates, of Robbinston, February 12, 1867, and had Helen Gates, born October 28, 1863; ii. Adeline D., born April 16, 1838, married Henry Brewer; iii. George H., October 29, 1839; iv. Ellen S., born April 24, 1842; v. Cornelia, born August 24, 1846; vi. Lucia, born November 18, 1847; vii. William D., born July 20, 1851; viii. Charlotte W., born October 20, 1852; ix. Esther D., born October 23, 1857. 7. Mary, born April 10, 1808; died March 6, 1837. 8. James Madison, born March 13, 1810, died February 25, 1863; married Harriet Palmer, daughter of a Robbinston; he was representative to the general court in 1850. 9. Rev. Uriah, born March 2, 1812; killed by a fall from his horse March 4, 1874; pastor of Congregational church, of Lewiston; and college professor; married Ellen ———. Children of second wife, all born in Robbinston: 10. Frederick G., born January 22, 1825, died April, 1857; married Susan M. Brewer, daughter of Thomas. 11. Edward H., born January 11, 1827; married Lenora, daughter of George Harris; resided at Milltown, New Brunswick. 12. Jane, born June 25, 1828, died November, 1866. 13. Horatio B., born December 10, 1829, died November 3, 1832. 14. Elizabeth G., born December 15, 1831, died December, 1854.

(VI) Gilbert Balkam, son of General John

Balkam (5), born in Robbinston, Maine, October 4, 1804, died April 8, 1883, at Jamaica Plain, Massachusetts. He married Susan (Dutch) Brewer, widow of William Brewer. She was born in Lubec, Maine. Children: 1. Stephen Brewer, born October 4, 1842; mentioned below. 2. Henry Gilbert, married first, Cora Boynton; second Annie ———; children: i. Lloyd G.; ii. Herbert. 3. Charles Herbert, died young. 4. William Frederick, married first, Emma Mills, of Boston; married second, Jennie Van Zandt; children: i. Charles, by the first wife; ii. Mary, by second wife; both deceased. 5. Sewall Drummond, married Annie Vose, of Robbinston, Maine; children: i. Arthur; ii. John; iii. Frank; iv. Ruth. 6. Mary Lee, unmarried. 7. Hannah Abigail, died December, 1907; unmarried.

(VII) Stephen Brewer Balkam, son of Gilbert Balkam (6), was born in Robbinston, Maine, October 4, 1842, and died in Hyde Park, Massachusetts, February 23, 1901. He married Alice B. Crandon, of Columbia Falls, Maine, born May 11, 1845, daughter of Joseph and Alice Bentley (Frankland) Crandon.

The following memoir of Mr. Balkam is taken from the "Hyde Park Historical Record," (vol. iii, April, 1903, written by the editor, William A. Mowry): "By the demise of Stephen B. Balkam, Hyde Park lost one of its most honored citizens, and the Historical Society one of its most useful members. Mr. Balkam was a native of Maine, that state which has furnished to the old Bay state and to the nation so many men of high character and great deeds. His birthplace was Robbinston, a town in Washington county, at the very southeastern corner of the Dirigo State. He was born October 4, 1842. He died at his home in Hyde Park, on Saturday, February 23, 1901. He had passed a busy and successful life. At the early age of seventeen he entered the employ of George Harris & Company, of Columbia Falls, where he remained about two years. He came to Boston in 1861 and accepted a position with William Pope & Sons, lumber merchants. On May 11th, 1868, he married Alice B. Crandon, of Columbia Falls, Maine, and established his home in Jamaica Plain. In 1874 he commenced business in Hyde Park, managing it for the old firm, but three years later he bought out the entire plant and stock and began business in his own name. In 1882 the firm became S. B. Balkam & Company. He moved his family from Jamaica Plain to Hyde Park in 1874, and from that time till his death, for more than a quarter of a century, he was one of the foremost men of Hyde Park, trusted and honored by everybody. He was a public-spirited citizen, alive to every interest of the town. He was a member of the board of selectmen for eight years between 1879 and 1893, and was chairman of the board two years. As a public official he was conscientious, courteous and dignified; as a private citizen simple and unassuming and in all relations he commanded in a marked degree, the respect, confidence and esteem of his fellow citizens. He was a man of good practical judgment, what Dr. Johnson called large, round-about common sense. For more than twenty-five years he was at the head of a large business in coal and lumber, always honest and always successful. He was a devoted husband, a kind and affectionate father, a good neighbor, and upright citizen and a genial Christian gentleman. Mr. Balkam was an honored and faithful member of the Congregational Church. He served the church as a teacher in the Sunday school, a deacon and a member of its prudential committee. At the memorial service held after his death it was said: 'Nor did he confine the manifestations of his Christian life to this church, nor circumscribe it within the limits of these walls. He carried the principles for which the church stands into all his daily life and associations. Whether in business or public relations or the realm of personal friendship, the same characteristics of a loyal Christain manhood stood pre-eminent. The path of right once presenting itself to him, he never swerved to the right or the left therefrom.' He was prominent in the Masonic fraternity, a Knight Templar, a vice-president of the Hyde Park Historical Society, and officer in the Hyde Park Savings Bank and in the Hyde Park Co-operative Bank. He was a lover of good music, and his happiest moments were spent at his home with his family indulging his fine musical taste, assisting in the singing or accompanying on the cello. Such in brief, was the character of Mr. Balkam. If 'an honest man' be 'the noblest work of God' surely we cannot fail to speak well of him and we ought to cherish his memory as that of a marked man, an upright character, a model for all to imitate."

Joseph Crandon, father of Mrs. Stephen B. Balkam, was born at Fairhaven, Massachusetts, July 21, 1802, and died August 21, 1883, son of Philip Crandon. He was married first to Ruth Ruggles, January, 1829. She died October 20, 1839, and he married second,

S. B. Balkam

November 3, 1842, Alice Bentley Frankland, born at St. Andrews, December 5, 1808. Children of Joseph and Ruth Crandon: i. Emily Crandon, born April 29, 1830, died November 18, 1839; ii. James Crandon, born October 10, 1831, died November 6, 1831; iii. George R. Crandon, born August 28, 1832, died about 1899; iv. Lorenzo Crandon, born December 19, 1833, died January 14, 1834; v. John H. Crandon, born March 27, 1835; vi. Stephen R. Crandon, born September 9, 1836, died about 1906; vii. Henry Augustus Crandon, born May 23, 1838. Children of second wife: viii. Joseph Crandon, Jr., born December 5, 1843, died January 20, 1908; ix. Alice B. Crandon, born May 11, 1845, at Columbia Falls, married Stephen B. Balkam, mentioned above; x. Ruth Ann Crandon, born November 11, 1846, died June 8, 1905. (See Crandon).

Children of Stephen Brewer and Alice B. (Crandon) Balkam: 1. Elizabeth Gertrude, born March 3, 1869; married, September, 1893, William Flett; children: i. Alice Gertrude Flett, born December 8, 1891; ii. Helen Hendry Flett, born May 22, 1895. 2. Charles Herbert, born November 24, 1870, at Jamaica Plain; married, September 11, 1901, Gertrude Robbins, of Charlestown; children: i. Ruth Howland, born June 21, 1902, died July 6, 1903; ii. Howland Hunnewell, born January 7, 1904, died January 25, 1908; iii. Hilda Estelle, born August 6, 1906. 3. Alice Crandon, born May 22, 1874; married, 1903, Robert T. Hathaway, of Hyde Park; had one daughter, Priscilla Hathaway, born March 23, 1906, died March 29, 1906. 4. Ralph Wilson, born November 11, 1875; married, December 29, 1901, Gertrude Savage, of Hyde Park. 5. Gilbert, born January 3, 1877, at Hyde Park; married Gertrude Mitchell; one son, Stephen, born March 13, 1907. 6. Helen, born October 20, 1878; married, May 1, 1905, Leonard Barney; one son, Wendall Robinson, born January 6, 1908. 7. Marion May, born September 2, 1885, died August 6, 1893.

CRANDON (I) John Crandon, immigrant ancestor, was born in Topsham, Devonshire, England, in 1697, and died in Dartmouth, Massachusetts, April 1, 1773. He came to this country in 1718, and lived at Boston and Dartmouth, Massachusetts. He married in Boston, November 20, 1718, Jean Best, born in Jedburgh, Roxburghshire, Scotland, in 1694, daughter of George and Margaret (Henderson) Best. She came to America in 1718 with her parents, and became acquainted with her husband in Boston, where they were married by Rev. John Cotton Mather. She died November 18, 1767. Both were buried in the old ground at Acushnet, Massachusetts. Children, born at Dartmouth and Plymouth: 1. Jean, 1722. 2. John, 1726, died in the West Indies. 3. James, married, 1749, Sarah Delano. 4. Sarah, married John Witherell. 5. Thomas, mentioned below. 6. Grace, born 1724; married John Carver.

(II) Thomas Crandon, son of John Crandon (1), was born December 15, 1728. He married, in Plymouth, June 20, 1751, Ruth Howland, daughter of Consider and Ruth (Bryant) Howland. Consider Howland was descended from John Howland, one of the Pilgrims. His lineage: Consider (4), Thomas (3), Joseph (2), John (1). Crandon died at Dartmouth, January 9, 1821. He was captain of a coast defense company in the revolution, and a prominent citizen of Dartmouth. Children, born in Dartmouth: 1. Thomas, born June 6, 1752; died January 20, 1753. 2. Joan, born October 20, 1753, died December 24, 1770. 3. James, born August 5, 1775; died August 1841. 4. Thomas, born August 12, 1757; killed by the British, in the revolutionary war. 5. Ruth, born April 22, 1760; died May 7, 1792. 6. John, born April 14, 1763, died January, 1841. 7. Benjamin, born October 22, 1765, died September 29, 1841. 8. Philip, born January 21, 1769; mentioned below. 9. Joseph, born June 11, 1771, died 1799.

(III) Philip Crandon, son of Thomas Crandon (2), was born in Dartmouth, Massachusetts, January 21, 1769, and died there January 26, 1846. He married, in 1793, Esther, daughter of Benjamin Dillingham. He resided at Fairhaven, Massachusetts. Children: John; Consider Howland; Ruth, married Lewis Shaw; Joseph, mentioned below.

(IV) Joseph Crandon, son of Philip Crandon (3), was born in Fairhaven, July 21, 1802, and died August 21, 1883. He married first, January, 1829, Ruth Ruggles, died October 20, 1839, daughter of Thomas Ruggles; second, November 3, 1842, Alice Bentley (Frankland) Small, widow of Levi Small, born at St. Andrews, December 5, 1808. Children of Joseph and Ruth Crandon: 1. Emily, born April 29, 1830, died November 18, 1839. 2. James, born October 10, 1831, died November 6, 1831. 3. George R., born August 28, 1832; died about 1899. 4. Lorenzo, born December 19, 1833, died January 14, 1834. 5. John H.

born March 27, 1835. 6. Stephen R., born September 9, 1836, died about 1906. 7. Henry Augustus Crandon, born May 23, 1838. Children of second wife: 8. Joseph, Jr., born December 5, 1843, died January 20, 1908. 9. Alice B., born May 11, 1845, at Columbia Falls; married Stephen B. Balkam (7) (see sketch). 10. Ruth Ann, born November 11, 1846, died June 8, 1905.

BROWNE (I) William Browne, probably brother of Rev. Edmund Browne, was one of the original proprietors of Sudbury, Massachusetts. He was deacon of the church, captain, and deputy to the general court in 1692. He married, November 15, 1641, Mary Bisbee (Besbeech or Bisbidge). Children: 1. Mary, born May 18, 1643; married Benjamin Price. 2. Thomas, born May 22, 1644. 3. William. 4. Edmund, November 27, 1653. 5. Hopestill, July 8, 1656; mentioned below. 6. Elizabeth, July 23, 1657. 7. Susanna.

(II) Hopestill Browne, son of William Browne (1), born July 8, 1656, died December 11, 1729. He married, November 26, 1685, Abigail Haynes, who died April 12, 1737. Children, born at Sudbury: 1. Hopestill, mentioned below. 2. Josiah, November 12, 1693.

(III) Hopestill Browne, son of Hopestill Browne (2), was born August 26, 1691, died January 2, 1737. He married Dorothy Paris, died March 24, 1725, widow of "the Reverend and unhappy Samuel Paris." Children: 1. Samuel, born October 17, 1719. 2. Hopestill, mentioned below.

(IV) Lieutenant Hopestill Browne, son of Hopestill Browne (3), was born at Sudbury, April 30, 1721. He married, December 30, 1746, Sarah Loring, born September 10, 1724, daughter of Rev. Israel and Mary (Heyman) Loring. Children, born at Sudbury: 1. Hopestill, October 27, 1747. 2. John, April 14, 1749, died young. 3. William, March 1, 1751. 4. Abigail, June 19, 1753. 5. John, April 10, 1755; mentioned below. 6. Sarah, September 23, 1760. 7. Caleb, July 16, 1764.

(V) John Browne, son of Lieutenant Hopestill Browne (4), was born April 10, 1755. He married, July 2, 1783, Alice Howe, who died April 6, 1834. He was a soldier in the revolution, in Captain Andrew Haskell's company, Colonel Thomas Marshall's regiment, 1776, and in Captain Jonathan Rice's company, Colonel Samuel Bullard's regiment, which marched to reinforce the northern army in 1777. Children, born at Sudbury: 1. Nancy, November 25, 1786. 2. Polly, December 26, 1788. 3. Israel Howe, August 1, 1791; mentioned below. 4. John, April 3, 1794. 5. Alice, December 23, 1796. 6. Newel, August 4, 1799. 7. Edward, September 7, 1802. 8. Evelina, May 15, 1806.

(VI) Israel Howe Browne, son of John Browne (5), born at Sudbury, August 1, 1791, died August 25, 1879. He married, April 14, 1816, at Malden, Lucy Bowdoin Adams, born March 17, 1790, at Hubbardston, died December 22, 1776, daughter of Reuben Adams, born 1760, and Azubah (Jones) Adams (see Adams sketch herewith). Among their children was Theodore Lyman, mentioned below.

(VII) Theodore Lyman Browne, fifth child of Israel Howe Browne (6), born August 21, 1822, at Sudbury, died September 4, 1888, at Dedham. He resided in Dedham, and was a deacon in the Congregational church and superintendent of the Sunday school. He was for many years an officer in the Norfolk county jail and later he engaged in business in the Faneuil Hall Market, Boston, in which he continued up to his death. He married, at South Acton, November 27, 1844, Elizabeth Fletcher Cole, daughter of George Browning Cole, who was born January, 1799, died June 21, 1832, and Eliza (Fletcher) Cole, born November 19, 1804, died April 26, 1883, at Dedham. Children: 1. George Edwin, mentioned below. 2. Emma Howe, born July 8, 1850; married, June 15, 1877, Dr. Ezra F. Taft. 3. Frank Fairbanks, born July 8, 1860; married May A. Morrell, in Dedham, September 19, 1883; he died June 21, 1899.

(VIII) George Edwin Browne, son of Theodore L. Browne (7), born at Sudbury, November 23, 1846, died January 14, 1908. He removed with his parents to Needham, then to South Boston, and subsequently in 1860 to Dedham, where he received his education in the public and high schools. For some years he was associated with his father in his business at Faneuil Hall Market in Boston. From his youth he had been an interested student of natural history, and at the death of his father he engaged in the business of taxidermy, and in this line achieved considerable renown and success. He was a skillful workman, and among the natural history exhibits at the World's Fair in Chicago were some prepared and mounted by him. Mr. Browne attended the Congregational church at Dedham. He married first, April 5, 1871, Emma F. Chatfield, who died July 19, 1875, leaving one child, Mabel Frances, who died December 9, 1882. Married second, May 8, 1877, Ida Florence Thomas, born at Weymouth, September 4, 1845, daughter of Colonel John Warren Thomas (see Thomas family). They have one child, Thomas Blanchard, born December 1, 1884, engaged in agricultural pursuits.

(For first generation see Henry Adams 1).

ADAMS (II) Ensign Edward Adams, son of Henry Adams (1), born in England about 1630, died November 12, 1716. He settled in Medfield, Massachusetts, where he appears as early as 1650. He was an ensign in the army. During King Philip's war his house was burned by the Indians. He was selectman, deputy to the general court from 1692 to 1702, and commissioner to end small causes. He married first, Lydia Rockwood, who died 1676. He married second, in 1678, Abigail Day, of Dedham, who died 1707. He married third, in 1710, Sarah Taylor. He had fifteen children.

(III) John Adams, third child of Ensign Edward Adams (2), born February 18, 1657, died March 1, 1751. He had a grant of land on the west side of the Charles river, "near the new mill," in 1682. He married first, in 1682, Deborah Partridge. He married second, Susanna Breck, who died in 1744. He had thirteen children.

(IV) Obadiah Adams, fifth child of John (3) and Deborah Adams, born in Medfield, January 20, 1689, died November 22, 1765. He married, April 24, 1716, Christian Sanford, who died July 21, 1777, daughter of Deacon Thomas Sanford, of Mendon. He resided in West Medway, Massachusetts, and had ten children.

(V) Nathan Adams, son of Obadiah Adams (4), was born December 30, 1723. He married, May 9, 1750, at Medway, Keziah Thompson, born November 17, 1730, daughter of Eleazer and Hannah (Daniels) Thompson. Hannah Daniels was born September 30, 1701, daughter of Joseph (3) and Rachel (Partridge) Daniels (born 1669, in Medfield). Joseph Daniels (3) was born September 23, 1666, in Medfield, son of Joseph (2) and Mary (Fairbanks) Daniels Mary (Fairbanks) Daniels was daughter of George Fairbanks, son of Jonathan Fairbanks, the immigrant ancestor of the family in America. Joseph Daniels (2) was born 1635, in Watertown, died June 23, 1715, son of Robert (1) and Elizabeth Daniels. Robert (1) died July 6, 1655, and was the immigrant ancestor of the Daniels family.

(VI) Reuben Adams, son of Nathan Adams (5), was born in 1760, in Medway; married Azubah Jones.

(VII) Lucy Bowdoin Adams, daughter of Reuben Adams (6), born March 17, 1790, died December 22, 1876. She married Israel Howe Browne. (See Browne family).

THOMAS (I) Captain John Thomas, immigrant ancestor of this branch of the Thomas family in America, settled in Braintree. The first mention of him is in the diary of Judge Sewell, of Boston, under date of January 5, 1694, which says: "Had Captain Thomas' company from Thos. Walker's to the Unkles Gate by accident." Under date of November 26, 1695, he says: "Madame Sam'l Bellingham, Captain Thomas, Mr. Willard and their wives etc dined here." He married, sometime before the latter date, Lydia Whitman, born in 1678, died 1750, daughter of Deacon Abiah and Mary (Ford) Whitman, of Weymouth. She was a beautiful woman, of great piety and strength of character. He was a wealthy man, being the second largest taxpayer in the town. He was a slave owner, and all that he possessed was of the very best quality. His estate was inventoried at twelve hundred and one pounds. He died October 4, 1714, and was buried in the old Weymouth burying ground.

(II) John Thomas, son of Captain John Thomas (1), was born February 27, 1709. He married, June 30, 1750, Silence Orcutt, born in Weymouth and died there in 1799, daughter of Benjamin and Elizabeth (Randall) Orcutt. Her father was son of William and Martha Orcutt. Her mother was daughter of John and Mercy Randall. John Randall was son of Robert and Mary (French) Randall. Robert Randall was a freeman of Weymouth in 1647.

(III) John Thomas, son of John Thomas (2), born in Braintree, June 16, 1751, died July 9, 1834. He settled in Weymouth. He was a man of good education, and was a school teacher. He was known as "Governor" Thomas. His house was situated in that part of Weymouth known as "back of the pond." The house is still or was lately standing and occupied by his grandson, Alfred Thomas. He married, December 4, 1774, Lydia Bayley, born August 1, 1755, daughter of Deacon Nathaniel and Tamer (White) Bayley. She survived her husband many years. Deacon Nathaniel Bayley was an ardent patriot in the revolutionary war; was a representative of Weymouth to the provincial congress at Watertown; the same in 1775 to the congress at Concord and at Cambridge; was a soldier in the revolutionary and French wars. Rev. James Bayley, father of Deacon Nathaniel Bayley, was born in Roxbury; graduated at Harvard College in 1719; taught a school at Andover for two years at an annual salary of forty-four pounds; he was the first minister in South Weymouth; ordained there September 26, 1723; preached forty years until his death which occurred August 22, 1763. Her mother, Tamer (White) Bayley, was born at Weymouth, January 19, 1731, died June 20, 1787, daughter of Dr. Nathaniel (4) and Sarah (Lovell) White, of Weymouth. Dr. White was an eminent physician of his day; was born at Weymouth, September 4, 1701, died November 23, 1758; graduate at Harvard College, 1725; son of Thomas and Mary White. Thomas White (3) was born August 19, 1673; married, 1700, Mary White; was distinguished in civil and military life; deacon in the Weymouth church; son of Ebenezer and Hannah (Phillips) White. Ebenezer White (2) was born at Weymouth, in 1648, died August 24, 1703; married Hannah Philips, born at Boston, November 25, 1654, daughter of Nicholas and Hannah (Salter) Philips; son of Thomas White (1), who was admitted a freeman at Weymouth, March 3, 1635-36, born 1599 in England and died 1679.

(IV) Captain Andrew Thomas, son of John Thomas (3), born November 10, 1776, died at South Weymouth, October 12, 1857. He settled in South Weymouth. He was a captain in the state militia and was aide on the staff of his brigade commander for many years. He married first, Polly Loud, born at Weymouth, November 13, 1781, died April 30, 1833, daughter of Jacob and Lydia (Joy) Loud, of South Weymouth. Married second, Deborah Whitmarsh. Married, third, Zerviah (Tower) Ager, widow of John Ager. He had twelve children, all by his first wife. Jacob Loud, father of Polly (Loud) Thomas, was a soldier in the revolution, and was son of Jacob (3) and Mary (Smith) Loud. Jacob (3) was son of Francis and Onner (Prince) Loud. Francis (2) was son of Francis (1) and Sarah Loud, of Sagadahoc, Maine. Onner (Prince) Loud, wife of Francis Loud (2), was born at Hull, in 1701, daughter of Isaac (2) and Mary (Turner) Prince, of Hull. Isaac Prince (2) was son of John and Anna (Honor) Prince. John Prince (1) was born in England, in 1610, son of Rev. John and Elizabeth (Tolderburg) Prince, of England; was a student at Oxford and was expected to succeed his father as rector of East Shefford parish in Berkshire; but he incurred the enmity of Archbishop Laud because of his liberal views, and was obliged to flee to New England in 1633; settled in Cambridge, Massachusetts, where he was a landholder in 1634; admitted a freeman March 4, 1635, and about that time removed to Hull, where he died August 16, 1676; was deputy to the general court from Hull in 1642; married, 1637, Anna Honor; married second, 1674, Anna Barstow, widow of William Barstow; was ruling elder of the church at Hull for many years. Mary (Turner) Prince, wife of Isaac Prince (2), died in 1738, aged eighty years. She was the daughter of John and Mary (Brewster) Turner, of Scituate, who was born at Leyden, Holland. Mary Brewster was daughter of Jonathan and Lucretia Brewster; Jonathan was born at Scrooby, county Notts; he came in the ship "Fortune" in 1621, his father having preceeded him to this country; married Lucretia ———. In June, 1636, was in command of the Plymouth trading house on the Connecticut river and gave the first warning of the attack of the Pequot Indians; he removed early from Plymouth to Duxbury, and was deputy to the general court in 1639-40-41 and 44; removed to New London, Connecticut, before 1649, where he was selectman, and died there before September, 1659. Jonathan Brewster was son of Elder William Brewster, who was born about 1563, at Scrooby, Nottinghamshire, and he was son of William Brewster, a favored tenant of the Archbishop of York. Elder William Brewster long resided in the house of his father, the same house at which Cardinal Woolsey made his last stop before reaching home in his final journey from court after banishment by Henry VIII, thirty years before; after honorable service with Davison, private secretary to the Queen, he abandoned political life in 1587 and was the first prominent layman to reject conformation to the Church of England; was ruling elder of the church at Scrooby and postmaster there twelve years before 1594; married first, Mary ———; fled to Holland about 1607, and was ruling elder of the church at Leyden, Holland, of which Rev. Mr. Robinson was pastor; came to New England in the "Mayflower" with his wife, his daughter Mary, and his two younger sons, and the family of his son Jonathan; settled in Duxbury and served the church twenty-three years; died at the home of his son Love April 16, 1643; left a library of three hundred volumes, sixty-four of which were classics.

(V) Colonel John Warren Thomas, son of Andrew Thomas (4), was born in Weymouth, April 1, 1815. He received his education in the public schools of his native town. He learned the trade of shoemaker and at an early age began to manufacture boots and shoes, continuing for several years. Most of his life was spent in the public service. He became interested in politics when a young man, and his zeal and activity as a Democrat soon placed him in the foremost ranks of that party. With many other prominent Democrats he joined the coalition with the Free Soilers, which was successful in Massachusetts, and he was elected representative to the general court for the Weymouth district in 1852 and to the constitutional convention of 1853. Colonel Thomas was commissioned sheriff of Norfolk county by Governor George S. Boutwell, but on the return of the Whig party to power in the following year, he was removed from office for political reasons by Governor Clifford. In 1856, the state law having been changed so that sheriffs were elected instead of being appointed, Colonel Thomas received the unanimous nomination of the Republican (Fremont) and American parties for the office of sheriff, and was elected by a plurality of three thousand votes and a majority of twenty-five hundred votes over the Democratic and (Fillmore) American candidate Edward Potter. Colonel Thomas again assumed the duties of the office of sheriff and keeper of the jail and house of correction, January 1, 1857, and soon afterward removed his residence from Weymouth to Dedham. He continued in the office until January 1, 1878, being re-elected by large majorities at each succeeding triennial election until, owing to failing health, he declined further election. His term of service by election lasted from January 1, 1857, until January 1, 1878, making with the year during which he held the office by appointment from 1852 to 1853, twenty-two years, the longest term of service of any sheriff in Norfolk county, with the exception of Sheriff Crane, of Canton, who served for a period of twenty-three years. During the long term of official service, Colonel Thomas administered the duties of his high office with rare executive ability and discretion. Selecting his subordinate officers with care and discrimination, he conducted the public business with their energetic co-operation with the greatest efficiency and won the approval of other public officers and all others who had business with the office. Thoughtful and considerate of the comfort and well being of the prisoners committed to his charge, he was able to maintain thorough discipline and at the same time to gain and hold their good-will and respect. Beginning his career as a Democrat, Colonel Thomas early became a member of the Republican party, of which he continued a firm and consistent advocate and supporter to the end of his life. Although of strong convictions and unfaltering in the support of his party, he was neither narrow nor offensive in his partisanship and he received the cordial support of Democrats as well as Republicans.

His title as colonel he won in the military service of the commonwealth, rising through the various grades in the militia to lieutenant-colonel of his regiment. His first commission, as ensign, when sixteen years of age, is in the possession of his daughter, Mrs. Browne. It reads as follows:

"His Excellency, Levi Lincoln, Governor and Commander-in-Chief of the Commonwealth of Massachusetts, to John W. Thomas, of Weymouth, Gentleman, Greeting: You have been elected on the third day of May A. D. 1831 Ensign of a company in the Second Regiment of Infantry in the First Brigade and First Division of the Militia of the Commonwealth reposing special trust and confidence in your ability, courage and good conduct, I do, by these Presents, Commission you accordingly. You will, therefore, with honor and fidelity, discharge the duties of said office, according to the Laws of this Commonwealth, and to Military Rule and Discipline. And all inferior Officers and Soldiers are hereby commanded to obey you in your said capacity; and you will yourself observe and follow such Orders and Instructions as you shall from time to time receive from the Commander-in-Chief or others, your superior officers. Given under my hand and the seal of the Commonwealth on the Twenty-sixth day of May in the year of our Lord one thousand eight hundred and thirty-one and in the fifty-fifth year of the Independence of the United States of America. By his Excellency the Governor, Edward D. Bangs, Secretary of the Commonwealth."

Colonel Thomas was a public-spirited citizen, broad in his views and liberal and generous in his disposition. Of him it may truly be said that he was the friend and supporter of all good enterprises in the community of which he was for so many years an active and influential member. He was always an attendant and later in life was a member of the Congregational church. He was a member of A. F. and A. M. He died July 20, 1888, after a prolonged and distressing illness.

He married, January, 1845, Sarah, born April 27, 1822, died January 8, 1901, daughter of Cyrus and Rachel (Haws) Blanchard. Children: 1. Ida Florence, born September 4, 1845; married George Edwin Browne (see sketch herewith). 2. Charlotte Ellen, born August 24, 1847, at South Weymouth; died January 8, 1875, at Dedham. 3. John Warren, Jr., born November 14, 1849, died March 4, 1890, in Dedham.

WILSON John Wilson was born in Scotland and removed to Nova Scotia when a young man, residing there until a short time before his death when he came to Lynn, Massachusetts, and died at the home of his son, Charles William. He was a carpenter and builder. He married in Nova Scotia, Elizabeth Newman, of English birth. Their children: Sophia, John, William, Kate, Thomas, Charles William, Elizabeth and James, all of whom were born in Nova Scotia. Of these John married and at his death left a son and a daughter. James married and also had one son and one daughter. Elizabeth married Thomas H. Reynolds, of Boston; no children.

Charles William Wilson, son of John and Elizabeth (Newman) Wilson, born in Halifax, Nova Scotia, October 19, 1826, died in Lynn, Massachusetts, October 5, 1905. His younger years were passed in his native place, where he was given a good private school education. At the age of nineteen he came to New England, landing at Gloucester, and from thence went to Boston, where he apprenticed himself to the trade of a tailor and cutter, with Charles A. Smith. Having served his time and become a thorough workman, he went to Weymouth, Massachusetts, and from there to Kingston, working at his trade in both places. In 1855 he went to Lynn and was given charge of the cutting department of Tollman & Howard's extensive department store, and when that firm failed he purchased that part of the business with which he had been connected, and subsequently became proprietor of a merchant tailoring establishment. In 1880 he retired and thereafter devoted his attention to scientific and literary pursuits, taking up departments of study in which he had long taken deep interest, but which he was unable to follow closely on account of the exactions of a mercantile life. In literature his reading took a wide range, and Shakespeare and Burns were among his favorite authors, as Booth and Forrest were his most admired interpreters of the classics in tragedy and the drama. His chief scientific study was astronomy, and he seemed to never tire or lose interest in it; and when his earlier endeavors in business life had yielded a competency, he gave his attention assiduously to this favorite pursuit. He provided himself with a good nine-foot telescope with six-inch glass, from the celebrated telescope maker Clarke, of Cambridge. His knowledge of the solar and stellar systems was self-acquired, and as he mounted successive steps of knowledge he seemed to thirst for yet deeper information. His domestic life was always surrounded by pleasant associations, and his home was a seat of comfort. He was a charter member of Golden Fleece Lodge, Free and Accepted Masons, and he was active in his interest in the work of the order. At one time he was an Odd Fellow. In religious preference he was a Unitarian, and in politics a Republican.

Mr. Wilson married, at Plympton, Massachusetts, February 14, 1853, Angeline M. Perkins, born in Plympton, 1835, died in Lynn, November 20, 1906. Children: 1. Emma Augusta, born 1855, died August 8, 1896. 2. Annie Eudora, educated in the public schools of Lynn, and well known in the social life of the city; she is a member of the Woman's Club, the North Shore Club, the Unitarian Club, being one of its board of directors; and at one time was a director of the Woman's Alliance. 3. Charles Henry Wilson, born in Lynn, February 7, 1859. In early business life he was a bookkeeper, and engaged in that and other pursuits for about twenty years; in 1895 he became interested in a hardware business in Boston, and retired about six years afterward. (See Standish and Sampson families).

STANDISH So well known to every student of American colonial history is the story of Captain Myles Standish that in the present connection it is hardly necessary to recapitulate the events of his most remarkable career during the first half century after the landing of the Pilgrims at Plymouth in 1620; but the present purpose is to trace in a brief way a single descendant line from this famous character through two generations after him to his granddaughter Lydia, who became the wife of Isaac Sampson.

Captain Myles Standish died October 3, 1656. His first wife, Rose, died in 1621, and he married second, Barbara, the mother of all his children, and who is supposed to have come to New England in the ship "Ann" in 1623. She survived him and with her sons Alexander, Myles and Josias (Josiah) was joint executor of his estate. Their children were: Alexander, married first, Sarah Alden, second Mrs. Desire Sherman; Charles, who was alive in 1627; John, who was alive in 1627; Miles, of Boston, died April 5, 1663, married, July 19, 1660, Sarah, daughter of John Winslow, and who married twice after the death of her first husband; Josias (Josiah), died March 16, 1690; married first Mary Dingley, and second Sarah Allen; Lora, and Charles.

Alexander Standish, eldest child of Myles Standish and wife Barbara, received under his father's will a full share of money, a double share of land, and also was a residuary legatee, as may be seen from the following extract from the testator's will: "I giue vnto my son & heire aparent Alexander Standish all my lands as heire apparent by lawfull decent in Ormistick Borsconge Wrightington Maudsley Newburrow Crawston and in the Ile of Man and given to mee as right heire by lawfull decent but surruptously detained from mee, my great grandfather being a vond or younger brother from the house of Standish of Standish." Alexander Standish was admitted to the freedom of the colony in 1648, was town clerk of Duxbury 1695-1700, and died in Duxbury, in 1702. He married first, Sarah, daughter of John Alden and Priscilla Mullins; second, Desire, daughter of Edward Doty and widow of Israel Holmes and William Sherman. By his wife Sarah Alden, Alexander Standish had seven children, and by his wife Desire Sherman he had four children: 1. Miles, died September 15, 1739; married Experience Sherman (or Holmes). 2. Ebenezer, born 1672, died 1748; married Hannah Sturtevant. 3. Lorah, married Abraham Sampson of Duxbury. 4. Lydia, married Isaac Sampson, of Plympton (see Sampson family). 5. Mercy, married Caleb Sampson, of Duxbury. 6. Sarah, married Benjamin Soule, of Plympton. 7. Elizabeth, married Samuel Delano, of Duxbury. 8. Thomas (by wife Desire), born 1687; married Mary Carver. 9. Desire, born 1689; married Nathan Weston. 10. Ichabod, married Phebe Ring, of Pring. 11. David killed in Duxbury, 1689, by fall of a tree.

SAMPSON In the company of Pilgrims who came to New England in the "Mayflower" was Henry Sampson, a member of the family of his uncle, Edward Tilley, and then was too young to sign the compact in the cabin of that vessel while riding at anchor in the harbor at Provincetown. However, he was enumerated in the assignment of land, 1623, in the division of cattle, 1627, and was admitted freeman of the Plymouth colony in 1637.

Abraham Sampson is believed to have been a brother of Henry Sampson, and came from England to New England about 1629 or 1630. He settled in Duxbury, and his name appears on the list of persons in that town in 1643 who were able to bear arms. He was one of the fifty-four original grantees of Bridgewater in 1645, all of whom then lived in Duxbury, but it does not appear that he ever settled in Bridgewater. He was surveyor of highways in Duxbury in 1648, constable in 1653, and was made freeman in 1654. He was still living in 1686. His wife, baptismal name not known, was a daughter of Samuel Nash, lieutenant of the Duxbury company. He was frequently engaged in the military service of the colony, and was an officer in nearly all of the expeditions; was sheriff or chief marshal for more than twenty years, beginning in 1652. One authority says that he had a second wife, but does not give her name; and there is no record of the settlement of his estate, the Duxbury records previous to 1666 having been destroyed by fire, hence there is no way by which to ascertain the names of all of his children, of whom there were several. The names of four sons are known, for they grew to maturity and had families, as follows: 1. Samuel, born about 1646; married Esther ———. 2. George, born 1665; married Elizabeth ———. 3. Abraham, born about 1668; married Sarah Standish. 4. Isaac, born 1660; married Lydia Standish, sister of Sarah.

Isaac Sampson, youngest son of Abraham Sampson, was born in Duxbury, in 1660, and died September 3, 1726. He was one of the first settlers in Plympton, and his house stood on the north side of the road leading from Plympton green to Durham's neck. His wife was Lydia Standish, daughter of Alexander

Standish and granddaughter of Captian Myles Standish (see Standish family). Isaac Sampson and Lydia Standish had children: 1. Isaac, born April 18, 1688; married first, Sarah ———; second, Elizabeth ———. 2. Jonathan, born February 9, 1690; married Joanna Lucas. 3. Josiah, born June 5, 1692; died March 29, 1731; unmarried. 4. Lydia, born April 22, 1694; unmarried; lived in Plympton, 1734. 5. Ephraim, born May 8, 1698; married Abigail Horrel. 6. Peleg (twin), born November 12, 1700; married Mary Ring. 7. Priscilla (twin), born November 12, 1700; married Jabez Fuller. 8. Barnabas, born February 12, 1704-5; married Experience Atkins.

Jonathan Sampson, second son and child of Isaac and Lydia (Standish) Sampson, was born in Plympton, Massachusetts, February 9, 1690, and died intestate February 3, 1768. He spent his entire life in Plympton, and lived in the house where one of his descendants dwelt nearly one hundred years after his death. He married, September 28, 1721, Joanna Lucas, who survived him ten years and died January 1, 1768; children: 1. Mary, born July 26, 1722, died December 31, 1812; married Nathan Perkins, of Plympton. 2. Joanna, born July 31, 1723, died single in Plympton, January 22, 1784. 3. Priscilla, born April 14, 1726; married Joseph Perry, of Plympton. 4. Abigail, born April 12, 1727; married Jabez Prior, of Duxbury. 5. Jonathan, born April 23, 1729; married Deborah Bradford. 6. Bethiah, born April 22, 1731; married Joseph Sampson. 7. Josiah, born January 23, 1733-4, died aged about fifteen years.

Mary Sampson, eldest child of Jonathan and Joanna (Lucas) Sampson, was born in Plympton, Massachusetts, July 26, 1722, and died there December 31, 1812; married Nathan Perkins, of Plympton, and had children, among them a son Josiah Perkins, born 1751, and lived in Plympton on the Jonathan Sampson homestead place. He married Deborah, daughter of Elijah Bisbee, and his wife Deborah Sampson, the latter born March 14, 1724-5, died October 25, 1815, daughter of George Sampson and Hannah Soule, granddaughter of George Sampson and his wife Elizabeth ———, and great-granddaughter of Abraham Sampson, the immigrant ancestor of the branch of the Sampson family purposed to be treated in this place.

Elijah Bisbee, father of Deborah Bisbee, who married Josiah Perkins, was born March 20, 1720, and died September 28, 1804. He was a son of Elijah Bisbee, born January 22, 1692, at Pembrooke, Massachusetts, and his wife Eleanor Pierce, whom he married June 14, 1719. The Elijah Bisbee last mentioned was a son of John Bisbee, born in Hingham, Massachusetts, in 1647, died September 4, 1826, and his wife Joanna Brooks, died August 17, 1726. John Bisbee was a son of Elisha Bisbee, of Scituate, Massachusetts, and his wife Hannah ———. Elisha Bisbee was a cooper by trade, although in his will he calls himself "glover." In 1643 his name was on the list of those in Scituate able to bear arms, and in 1644 he is mentioned as keeper of a ferry and tavern. His children were Hopestill, born 1645; John, 1647; Mary, 1648, married Jacob Beals; Martha, married Jonathan Turner; Elisha, born 1654, died 1715; and Hannah, born 1656, married, 1687, Thomas Brooks. Thomas Bisbee, father of the Elisha Bisbee last mentioned, came from Sandwich, England, with six children and three servants, and settled in Scituate as early as 1634. He was admitted freeman of the Plymouth colony January 2, 1637-8. In the early records his name appears as Besbeach, Besbetch, Besbitch, Besbege and Beesbeech, as well as Bisbee. In one of Rev. John Lothrop's entries in the church records of Scituate this mention is found: "Goodman Besbitch joyned the Church in Scituate, April 30, 1637; and was invested into the office of Deacon February 22, 1637-8." He was of Duxbury in 1638, representative of that town in 1643, but he afterward lived in Marshfield.

Josiah Perkins and Deborah Bisbee, of whom mention is made in a preceding paragraph, had children, and among them a son Josiah Perkins; married Deborah Hall, and had a daughter Angeline Perkins, born 1835; married, in Plympton, Massachusetts, February 14, 1853, Charles William Wilson, born in Halifax, Nova Scotia, October 19, 1886, died in Lynn, Massachusetts, October 5, 1905 (see Wilson family).

(For preceding generations see Elizabeth Cutter 1).

CUTTER (III) William Cutter, son of Richard Cutter (2), was born at Cambridge, Massachusetts, February 22, 1649-50, and was baptized at the Cambridge church. He and his wife were admitted to the church July 28, 1700, and his family Bible is still in existence. He resided in that part of the town called Menotomy, on the banks of the stream flowing from Lexington through Arlington to the Mystic river. Here he received from his wife's father an acre of land, and added to it by purchase April 10, 1684. He built the house bought by his son John, which stood on the site of the present residence now or lately of his descendant, Cyrus Cutter. This land was the west corner of the Rolfe homestead. When he sold the house to his son, he removed to what was no doubt the home of the Rolfes, in a house which was built in 1671. William Cutter inherited his father's estate, and was a housewright by trade. He was also a farmer, and dealt largely in real estate. He owned a mill on the banks of the stream near his house. He married Rebecca Rolfe, daughter of John Rolfe, of Newbury and Cambridge, who came to New England about 1670. She married second, June 3, 1724, John Whitmore, and gave six pounds towards a communion service for the Menotomy church in 1739. She died November 23, 1751, aged ninety years. William Cutter made his will June 1, 1722, and it was proved April 29, 1723. Children: 1. Elizabeth, born March 5, 1680-1; married, April 12, 1705, John Harrington, Jr.; died February 8, 1749-50. 2. Richard, November 13, 1682; married, August 20, 1706, Mary Pike. 3. Mary, January 26, 1684-5, died April 6, 1685. 4. Hannah, May 20, 1688; married, June 17, 1708, Ephraim Winship; died April 9, 1764. 5. John, October 15, 1690; married Lydia Harrington; died January 21, 1776. 6. Rebecca, January 18, 1692-3; married, January 18, 1710-11, Lieutenant Joseph Adams; died January 12, 1717-18. 7. William, 1697; married Anne ———. 8. Samuel, June 4, 1700; mentioned below. 9. Sarah, baptized October 18, 1702; married Ebenezer Cutter; died February 4, 1788. 10. Ammi Ruhamah, baptized May 6, 1705; graduate of Harvard 1725; physician and surgeon in the revolution.

(IV) Samuel, son of William Cutter, was born June 4, 1700, and baptized September 15 following. He was executor and heir of his father's estate, and lived in the house on the site of the late William Whittemore's residence on the road to Winchester and Woburn Westside, within the Charlestown limits. He died September 27, 1737, intestate, and his tombstone is near the centre of the Menotomy graveyard. He married, November 10, 1720, Anne Harrington, daughter of John and Hannah (Winter) Harrington. They owned the covenant at Cambridge church, September 17, 1721, and were admitted members September 29, 1723. His widow owned the covenant at the founding of the Menotomy church September 9, 1739, and married second, March 31, 1743, Nathaniel Francis, of Medford. She died December 31, 1777. Children of Samuel and Ann Cutter: 1. William, born September 10, 1721, died April 27, 17—. 2. Esther, February 15, 1723-4; married, August 6, 1741, Stephen Prentice. 3. Samuel, baptized March 31, 1728, died young. 4. Anne, born January 30, 1730-1; married, May 3, 1750, Walter Dickson. 5. Rebecca, March 3, 1732-3; married, October 26, 1749, Jason Dunster. 6. Hannah, February 27, 1734-5; married, March 21, 1754, Joseph Tufts, Jr. 7. Samuel, January 21, 1736; mentioned below.

(V) Lieutenant Samuel Cutter, son of Samuel Cutter, was born January 21, 1736, and died April 7, 1791. The sentiment on his gravestone at Arlington reads:

"A sov'reign God, who set my bounds,
Did quickly take my breath,
Be ready then each hour you live
To meet an instant death."

He resided on the homestead. He was in the revolution, and fought at the battle of Bunker Hill June 17, 1775, and was ensign of Captain Isaac Hall's company, Colonel Thomas Gardner's regiment. This regiment was stationed in the road leading to Lechmere's Point, East Cambridge, and late in the day was ordered to Charlestown. On arriving at Bunker Hill, General Putnam ordered part of it to assist in throwing up the defenses, while Captain Harris' company was stationed at the rail fence. On the way while descending the hill, Colonel Gardner was mortally wounded. July 6, 1775, the company was stationed at Prospect Hill, and before the close of the year Cutter was commissioned lieutenant. On April 7, 1791, while going up the eastern slope of Winter Hill in Somerville, on his way home in a cart with a barrel of tar, an accident to the cart threw him headlong to the road, the heavy tar falling upon him, and he was instantly killed. He married, April 28, 1757, Susanna Francis, born November 28, 1734, died December 19, 1817, daughter of Ebenezer and Rachel (Tufts) Francis, of Medford. Children: 1. Samuel, born January 30, 1758; mentioned below. 2. William, July 15, 1759; married first, April 29, 1783, Hannah Cutter; second, November 9, 1818, Lydia Cutter, widow; died November 28, 1846. 3. Susanna, March 12, 1761; married, November 16, 1783, Thomas Whittemore; died October 10, 1818. 4. Francis, April 15, 1763; married, December 29, 1782, Susanna Whittemore; died March 6, 1807. 5. Ezekiel, December 24, 1764; married first, Abigail (Oakes) Stacy, widow; second, Margaret (Averill) Mitchell, widow; married first, 1789, Abigail Brown Bowman; second, February 3, 1805, Anna Frost; died December 10, 1824. 7. Abigail, January 19, 1769; married, January 21, 1787, Samuel Cutter; died October 17, 1803. 8. Anne, June 19, 1771; married, February 2, 1796, William Whittemore, died October 27, 1849. 9. Adam, April 12, 1774; married Sally Putnam; died April 11, 1855. 10. Edward, June 9, 1775, died August 2, 1778. 11. Washington, June 18, 1777; married first, March 16, 1800, Elizabeth Robbins; second, January 26, 1823, Anna Fillebrown.

(VI) Samuel Cutter, son of Lieutenant Samuel Cutter, was born January 30, 1758, and died in Charlestown, now Somerville, in April, 1820. He was a farmer in Menotomy, now Belmont, and afterwards at Prospect Hill, Somerville. He took part in the revolution, and took a musket from the hands of a British sergeant on the retreat from Concord. This musket is or was lately owned by Fitch Cutter, of Somerville. He was adjutant of the militia and an esteemed member of the church and of the Masons. He married, September 29, 1780, Rebecca Hill, who died February 9, 1847, aged ninety, daughter of Abraham and Susanna (Wellington) Hill. Children: 1. Samuel, born July 22, 1781; married first, February 17, 1805, Eunice Carter; second, November 10, 1835, Rachel Ireland; died April 7, 1854. 2. Edward, January 13, 1783; married, April 8, 1808, Elizabeth Nutting; died February 7, 1862. 3. Rebecca, January 29, 1786; married Isaac Waitt. 4. Susan Francis, May 17, 1790; married Nehemiah Wyman, died 1863. 5. Fitch, March 22, 1791; mentioned below. 6. Sophia, January 25, 1794; married Moses Whitney, October 27, 1816. 7. Ebenezer, died April 22, 1796, aged ten days. 8. Anna, born May 23, 1799, died same day. 9. Ebenezer Francis, March 13, 1801; married, May 13, 1827, Eliza Ann Edmands; died April 22, 1857.

(VII) Fitch Cutter, son of Samuel Cutter, was born March 22, 1791. He was engaged in brickmaking and farming in Somerville, where he lived after his fourth year. In 1812 in the war he was stationed at Chelsea Bridge on duty with the artillery to defend the United States navy yard from an expected incursion of the British fleet. About 1822 he went on a voyage to Cadiz, Spain, in a merchant vessel. He married first, April 5, 1818, Lucy Hathon, who died December 7, 1848, aged fifty-three, daughter of Ebenezer Hathon, of Jaffrey, New Hampshire. He married second, November 14, 1850, Mary J. (Fiske) Mitchell, widow, of Somerville, who died Noyember 25, 1859, aged forty-seven. He married third, September 19, 1860, Mary C. (Ellis) Cannan, widow, of East Boston. Children of first wife: 1. Edmund Fitch, born May 13, 1819; married, November 20, 1845, Charlotte Maria Watson, and resided in Boston; children: i. Alexander DeWitt, born July, 1847, died August 16, 1849; ii. Chester Guild; iii. Nina, married December 29, 1887, Hollis Bowman Page, and died September, 1889; other children, died young. 2. Ebenezer Francis, born December 13, 1821; died March 9, 1828. 3. Samuel, born October 12, 1823; died August 15, 1825. 4. Samuel Henry, born August 12, 1826; mentioned below. 5. Ebenezer Francis, born May 26, 1830; removed to Indianapolis, Indiana, and was captain in the infantry under General Grant at Vicksburg in the civil war. 6. Lucy Sophia, born August 29, 1833; married, October 20, 1858, Rufus Baker; died March 26, 1866. 7. Charles Edward, born September 16, 1835; married, November 5, 1860, Jennie Fox, of Porter, Maine; children: i. Lillian Estelle, born July 1, 1862; ii. Charlotte Evelyn, born November 27, 1865; iii. Jennie Mabel, born December 12, 1867. 8. Martha Bowman, born May 10, 1838; married, November 14, 1860, J. Foster Clark, and resided at Titusville, Pennsylvania. Child of second wife: 9. Frederic Webster, born October 9, 1852; died February 28, 1853.

(VIII) Samuel Henry Cutter, son of Fitch Cutter, was born August 12, 1826. He married, December 9, 1847, Harriet S. Blanchard, daughter of Reuben K. and Mary G. (Edmands) Blanchard, of Charlestown. Children: 1. Fitch Henry, born April 15, 1849. 2. Charles Kimball, born March 15, 1851; mentioned below. 3. John Goodnow, born November 6, 1852; died September 2, 1854. 4. Effie, born July 3, 1855 (twin). 5. Ettie (twin), born July 3, 1855; died July 28, 1855. 6. Minnie, born February 20, 1858. 7. Ida, born February 20, 1858 (twin). 8. Lucy, born September 24, 1860. 9. Benjamin Russ, born May 24, 1867.

(IX) Dr. Charles Kimball Cutter, son of Samuel Henry Cutter, was born in Somerville, March 15, 1851. He attended the public schools of his native city and graduated from the high school under George L. Baxter, principal, who still holds the same position. The present submaster of the school, Frank M. Hawes, was for four years classmate and roommate of Dr. Cutter at college. Dr. Cutter entered Tufts College, where he was graduated with the degree of A. B. in 1873. He studied his profession in the Harvard Law School and received his medical degree with the class of 1876. Since that time Dr. Cutter has enjoyed an extensive and profitable practice in Charlestown and Somerville, Massachusetts. While in college he began a somewhat notable career as a teacher. He began as substitute for several weeks in the Somerville high school and the Foster grammar school, Winter Hill, Somerville. He was an instructor for a year in the Greenfield high school and also taught in the high schools of Bedford, Massachusetts, of Woodstock and Strafford, Vermont. His teaching was in addition to his college work, and left him no leisure. Yet the extra burdens of those student years undoubtedly contributed much to his success in his profession through the formation of habits of industry, of persistent attention to the duty in hand, and of great concentration of mind and purpose when necessary. Evidently his ability as a teacher was beyond the average, for his services were in much demand. He was made principal of the old Franklin Evening School, Washington street, Boston, just above Dover street, in 1874 while a student in the Medical School, and he continued in this position until 1880 during the early years of his practice. Dr. Cutter was a capable and successful instructor and he has good reason to take pride in the letters from prominent educators and school officials commending his work. And the doctor's interest in education has never diminished. His acquaintance with other teachers and scholars has continued. From 1876, when he began to practice, until 1879 his office was at the corner of Main and Franklin streets, Charlestown. He moved then to 200 Franklin street and remained there until May 1, 1890, when he bought the brick house at 208 Main street and remained until 1893. Since then he has made his home in Somerville, in a house he bought at the corner of School and Medford streets, but has continued his office in the Main street building, Charlestown. For ten years he served as physician and surgeon at the Charlestown Free Dispensary and for many years has been on the board of physicians of the Winchester Home for Aged Women and treasurer of the Charlestown branch of the Associated Charities, giving much medical advice and assistance in the work. He is a member of the Middlesex South District Medical Society, which he represents on the Council of the Massachusetts Medical Society. To him is largely due the changing of the rules in the society, so that women physicians were allowed to join. He was a constant and earnest advocate of the admission of female members and the wisdom of the change in the rules has been abundantly proved by experience. Dr. Cutter was surgeon in the Spanish-American war and had charge of the examination of recruits for the regular army from Boston from April 20, 1898 to June 30, 1899, when he received an honorable discharge from the service. Dr. Cutter is as much of a medical student as ever. The demands of his practice and other interest do not prevent his studying the current literature of his profession and continuing his own researches. When Dr. Cutter left Charlestown the *Enterprise* said: "The recent removal of Dr. Charles K. Cutter from this district to the suburbs of Somerville is felt as a distinct loss in a social way by the old families in the district who have long regarded the eminent physician and his lady as fixtures in the social firmament. Dr. Cutter's patients, however, find comfort in the knowledge that he will not relinquish his practice here and will continue his office hours at the Main street building practically as heretofore. For the past seventeen years Dr. Cutter has been a well known personage in the district. Graduating from the Harvard Medical School in 1876, he came to Charlestown in July of the year and has ever been classed among its active and progressive men."

He is a member of various fraternal orders. He became a member of John Abbot Lodge of Free Masons in 1873, and of Howard Lodge of Odd Fellows in 1875. He is one of the founders and charter members of Joseph Warren Council, Home Circle; a charter member of Monument Council, Royal Arcanum; member of the Windrow Castle, Knights of the Golden Cross; and a director of the Charlestown Club. Dr. Cutter is a member of the Universalist church and was formerly superintendent of the Charlestown church. In politics he is a Democrat.

SWAN Benjamin Franklin Swan, son of Henry Swan, was born at Arlington, Massachusetts, in 1829, and died at San Francisco, California, January 9, 1900. He had a common school education in Arlington, and assisted his father in the poultry business. He went to work for Nathan Robbins, a poultry dealer, driving his team to Boston, and gathering stock from farmers of the district. When he was twenty years of age the gold fever broke out, and he was one of those early "Forty-niners" who braved countless dangers to go overland to California. When he had accumulated quite a fortune, he returned and married, taking his wife to California with him, by way of the isthmus. In 1866 he returned to Arlington, where he lived several years, but finally returned to California. Like all "Forty-niners" money came easily and went as it came, and he made and lost three large fortunes. He was for a long time interested in stocks, and was a member of the Pacific Stock Exchange at San Francisco for years. During his last few years he suffered from a severe kidney trouble, which terminated in a heart affection, causing his death, January 9, 1900, at San Francisco. He was a man of strong qualities and superior intellect, energetic in business. He was a member of the Congregational church at Arlington. In politics he was a Republican. He was a member of Hiram Lodge of Masons, at Arlington. He married, April 8, 1863, Elizabeth Thaxter, of Arlington, who died June 25, 1885, aged thirty-nine years, nine months. Children: 1. Benjamin Franklin, mentioned below. 2. James Thaxter, born April 4, 1867; married, October 9, 1889, Alice Gertrude Tappan, of Arlington, Massachusetts.

Benjamin Franklin Swan, son of Benjamin Franklin Swan, was born at San Francisco, California, August 14, 1864. When he was quite young his parents removed to Arlington, Massachusetts, their former home, where he received his education in the common schools, graduating from the grammar school and going two years to the Cotting high school. During these two years he worked after school hours in Dodge's Pharmacy. Then his desire to learn the business impelled him to give up school and after spending two and one half years in the Pharmacy, he entered the wholesale drug business of Gilman Brothers, 50 Franklin street, Boston, as clerk. Strict attention to business soon led to promotion, and today he occupies a position of trust, being buyer and salesman for the firm. Gilman Brothers is one of the old established firms in Boston, and went through the big fire in 1872. Mr. Swan purchased in 1892 a house at 68 Evans street, Dorchester, where he resides with his family. Since 1906 he has been a member of the Church of the Epiphany (Episcopal) in Dorchester. He was one of a committee of five to start that society, and has always been a leader in the church, and is treasurer of the society. In politics he is a Republican. He is a member of the church club. He was formerly a member of the Arlington Boat Club, being captain of the first club bowling team that was entered in inter-club competition. He married, October 11, 1892, Sophia Priscilla Rudolf, of Dorchester, born May 8, 1864, daughter of John George and Priscilla Couch (Collings) Rudolf, of Lunenburg, Nova Scotia. Her father was a sea captain and a prominent Free Mason, a descendant of the old family of Von Rudolphs, of Germany. Children: 1. Franklin Rudolf, born February 22, 1897. 2. Ernst Thaxter, August 6, 1900; died September 22, 1900. 3. Evelyn Elizabeth, born September 14, 1903.

PACKARD (I) Samuel Packard, immigrant ancestor, came to New England with his wife and one child in the ship "Diligent," of Ipswich, John Martin, master, in 1638. He came from Windham, a small hamlet, near Hingham, county Norfolk, England. He settled in Hingham, Massachusetts, and removed about 1660 to Bridgewater, held office there in 1664, and was licensed to keep an ordinary in 1670. His sons, and probably he himself, were soldiers under Captain Benjamin Church, in King Philip's war, 1675-6. His will was dated 1684. Children: 1. Elizabeth, born probably in England; married, 1665, Thomas Alger, of West Bridgewater. 2. Samuel, Jr., born in Hingham; married Elizabeth Lathrop. 3. Zaccheus, mentioned below. 4. Thomas, born in Hingham; living in Bridgewater in 1673. 5. John, born in Hingham. 6. Nathaniel, married a daughter of John Kingman. 7. Mary, married Richard Phillips. 8. Hannah, married Thomas Randall. 9. Israel. 10. Jael, married John Smith. 11. Deborah, married Samuel Washburn. 12. Deliverance, married Thomas Washburn, brother of Samuel, mentioned above.

(II) Zaccheus Packard, son of Samuel Packard (1), was born in Hingham, and died in Bridgewater, August 3, 1723. He married Sarah, daughter of John Howard, of West Bridgewater. Children, born in Bridgewater: 1. Israel, mentioned below. 2. Sarah, born August 19, 1682; married, July 27, 1704, Captain Josiah Edson; died 1754. 3. Jonathan, born December 7, 1684; married first, December 24, 1719, Susanna Hayward; second, Abigail ———. 4. David, born February 11, 1687; married, December 17, 1712, Hannah Ames; died November 3, 1755. 5. Solomon, born

March 20, 1689; married, November 16, 1715, Sarah Lathrop; second, Susanna Kingman; third, October 5, 1760, Dorothy, widow of Mark Perkins. 6. Deacon James, born June 2, 1691; married, June 7, 1722, Jemima Kieth; died November 24, 1765. 7. Zaccheus, Jr., born September 4, 1693; married, October 21, 1725, Mercy Alden; died 1775. 8. John, born October 8, 1695; married, 1726, Lydia Thomson; died June 3, 1738. 9. Captain Abiel, born April 29, 1699; married January 11, 1723, Sarah Ames; died 1776.

(III) Israel Packard, son of Zaccheus Parkard (2), was born in Bridgewater, April 27, 1680. He married first, 1703, Hannah ———; second, November 20, 1735, Susanna, daughter of Daniel Field, of West Bridgewater. Children: 1. Seth, mentioned below. 2. Mehitable, born 1705; married first, 1725, John Ames; second, 1727, Samuel West. 3. Sarah, born 1707. 4. Eliphalet, 1708. 5. Hannah, 1710; married ——— Phillips. 6. Zerviah, born 1713; married Benjamin Washburn. 7. Israel, Jr., born 1717; married Ruth Field; died 1752. 8. Robert, born 1722; married, 1749, Lydia Titus; died about 1753.

(IV) Seth Packard, son of Israel Packard (3), was born in 1703. He married, about 1727, Mercy Bryant. He died in 1788. Children: 1. Sarah, born August 25, 1728. 2. Lucy, July 26, 1731. 3. Mehitable, March 28, 1733. 4. Mercy, May 20, 1735. 5. Isaac, September 22, 1737. 6. Mary, November 28, 1739. 7. Joshua, April 20, 1741. 8. Seth, Jr., March 12, 1743. 9. Abigail, March 17, 1746. 10. Abner, mentioned below. 11. Jonathan, September 27, 1751. 12. Jerusha.

(V) Abner Packard, son of Seth Packard (4), was born April 9, 1749. He married Elizabeth ———. He was a soldier in the revolution, sergeant in Captain John Callender's company, commanded by Lieutenant William Perkins, Colonel Richard Gridley's regiment of artillery, 1775; also captain in Colonel Gridley's regiment later in 1775. He was then of Milton, Massachusetts. Children: 1. William, mentioned below. 2. Elisha.

(VI) William Packard, son of Abner Packard, was born at Milton, Massachusetts, November 18, 1773. He married Lucy Turner, who lived to the advanced age of ninety-six years. Children: 1. Lucy Ann (Newcomb), born December 6, 1806. 2. Margaret, April 6, 1807; married ——— White. 3. Rosamond, July 12, 1809. 4. Lydia, February 10, 1811; married ——— Savill. 5. William Henry, October 7, 1812. 6. Elizabeth, January 2, 1814; died young. 7. Elizabeth, January 3, 1816; died young. 8. Elisha, mentioned below. 9. Emily, married ——— Marsh. 10. Louisa, married ——— Stowe. 11. Colonel Abner B., born November, 1821; died 1902. 12. Abigail, married ——— Dunbar. 13. Sarah, married ——— Burrill. There were eighteen children in all, of whom eleven grew to maturity.

(VII) Elisha Packard, son of William Packard, was born January 23, 1818, in Quincy, Massachusetts. He married Lucy Newcomb. Children, born in Quincy: 1. Elisha, Jr., mentioned below. 2. Francesca, married William N. Eaton; children: Minnie Francesca Eaton, Lucy Eaton, Annie Eaton, Edith Eaton, Grace Eaton.

(VIII) Elisha Packard, Jr., son of Elisha Packard, was born in Quincy, June 8, 1844. He was educated in the public schools of his native town and studied for the ministry, but before completing his course was attracted to a business career. He engaged in the manufacture of type metal, and remained in that business for a period of forty years, becoming one of the best known and most highly respected men in his trade. Since 1906 he has represented the firm of E. W. Blatchford, of Chicago, manufacturers of type metals, with his headquarters in Boston. Mr. Packard is considered among the most expert judges of type metal. The introduction of typesetting machines in the newspaper and printing offices of the country has enormously expanded the trade in metals of this kind.

Mr. Packard is an active and prominent Republican. He was a member of the common council of the city of Quincy in 1898-99 and 1900-01, and was twice the nominee of his party for mayor. His record in the legislative body of the city was irreproachable. Many improvements of great importance were due in large measure to his energetic advocacy. He was the prime mover in securing the system of free transfer on the street railways; greatly improved the sidewalks and street crossings throughout the city, and brought about a better standard of road-building and street-lighting in the city. He was chairman of the committee on state and military aid during the Spanish-American war, and did excellent work in that department. He made an enviable record as chairman of the committee on finance and public buildings, effecting economy as well as progress in that department. He was a pioneer in the movement to abolish grade crossings in Quincy; his influence and rousing arguments stirred the people to action and brought about a greatly needed reform, though against the firm opposition of the conservative, standstill element and various individual interests of much strength. He is a prominent member of the Protestant Episcopal Church of Quincy, active in the various charities and benevolences of that parish, and has been vestryman or warden for more than twenty-five years. Mr. Packard is upright, honorable and capable in business life, active, enterprising and public-spirited citizen, of engaging manner and pleasing personality, sound judgment and sterling common sense.

He married, June 30, 1867, Charlotte Holbrook Beale, born June 30, 1849, daughter of Joseph and Susanna H. (Adams) Beale. (See Beale family). Children, born in Quincy: 1. Elisha B., born August 20, 1872; died January 18, 1873. 2. Susan Adams, born February 22, 1876; married, June 4, 1900, Charles Lewis Greene; child, Mary Virginia Greene, born April 6, 1901. 3. Dr. Abner Beale, born June 29, 1882; graduate of Harvard Dental School, now favorably known and successfully practicing in Quincy; a vestryman of the Quincy Protestant Episcopal Church.

BEALE The surname Beale is of ancient English origin. Great variations in the spelling have been found even to the present time. We find in the early records Beal, Beale, Beals, Beales and Biell used interchangeably, besides many others. Hingham, Massachusetts, is the chief seat of the family. John Beal, a shoemaker, came there in 1638 with wife, five sons, three daughters and two servants from Hingham, England; was admitted a freeman March 13, 1638-9; was proprietor and deputy to the general court; married Narazeth Hubbard, daughter of Edmund, Sr.; second, March 10, 1659, Mary Jacob, widow of Nicholas. He died April 1, 1688, one hundred years old. It is a well authenticated fact that John Beal, Jr., who also came to Hingham, was a younger brother of the same name. Many similar cases are found, and doubtless many more exist where proof is wanting, where two children in the same family have the same names. John, Jr., died in 1658. He made his will October 26, 1657, when about to go to England, and bequeathed to his father Edmund Beal, England. Thomas Beal, of Cambridge, left no children; died 1661, aged sixty-three. William Beal of Marblehead had a numerous family.

(I) Benjamin Beale, of Boston, appears to be a relative of the Hingham family, but very little is known of him. He married Bathshua ———. But one child's birth was recorded in Boston. John and Susanna Beale, of Boston, had a daughter Martha, born March 29, 1683, in Boston. John and Benjamin were doubtless brothers or near relatives. Children: 1. Mercy, born July 17, 1672. 2. Benjamin, Jr., mentioned below. Perhaps others.

(II) Benjamin Beale, son of Benjamin Beale (1), was born in Boston or Seetomb, about 1676. He married Anne ———. Children, born in Braintree, formerly part of Boston: 1. Bathshua, April 13, 1701. 2. Benjamin, December 22, 1702; mentioned below. 3. Mary, April 17, 1709. 4. Abigail, October 11, 1704.

(III) Lieutenant Benjamin Beale, son of Benjamin Beale (2), was born in Braintree, December 22, 1702. He married Abigail ———. Children, born in Braintree: 1. Benjamin, May 21, 1741. 2. Joseph, mentioned below. 3. Peter, July 11, 1745. 4. Abigail, March 22, 1746. 5. Hannah, September 17, 1748. 6. Mary, July 15, 1750. 7. Nathaniel, January 30, 1753.

(IV) Joseph Beale, son of Lieutenant Benjamin Beale (3), was born in Braintree, May 21, 1743. He married Lilly ———. Children, born in Braintree: 1. Joseph, born May 12, 1769. 2. Peter, born January 30, 1771. 3. Samuel Davis, born March 23, 1773. 4. Theodocia, born December 9, 1775. 5. Lilly, born October 30, 1776. 7. Jonathan, mentioned below. Probably others born in Quincy.

(V) Jonathan Beale, son of Joseph Beale (4), was born in Quincy, Massachusetts, about 1780. He married Maria Swift. Children, born at Quincy: 1. William, born April 27, 1789; married ——— Holbrook. 2. Jonathan, born December 25, 1790; died young. 3. Thomas Swift, born March 3, 1793. 4. Captain Jonathan, born December 20, 1794. 5. Peter, born January 26, 1797. 6. Benjamin, born November 7, 1798; married Salome Dillingham Gibbs, of Sandwich; children: i. Benjamin Franklin, married Emma Russell; ii. Albert Seymour; iii. Salome Isadore, married George R. Spurr; iv. Marion Gibbs, married John Oliver Holden; v. Walter Gibbs, married Ida Whitcomb; vi. Nathan Gibbs, married Isabel Blackwell. 7. Joseph Swift, born September 9, 1800; mentioned below. 8. Maria A., born July 3, 1803; died July 19, 1856. 9. Cynthia Ann, born March 2, 1805; died unmarried. 10. Caroline, born May 1, 1807.

(VI) Joseph Swift Beale, son of Jonathan Beale, was born in Quincy, September 9, 1800, and died April 3, 1882 (?). His father's home, where he was born, was in Quincy, near the Milton line. The old house was burned shortly before he was born. He married Susanna H. Adams. Children, born in Quincy: 1. Joseph, married Frances Messinger; children: Joseph Henry, Emily Adams, Mary McKenzie, Agnes, Lillian, Arthur, Edith. 2. Jonathan, went west and died there; married. 3. Sarah Ann Adams, married Frederick M. Severance; children: Carrie Severance, married Samuel Shaw; Clara Severance, married Samuel Chase; Mabel Severance; Russell Severance. 4. James Adams, married Ellen Homer; children: Inez; Frederick. 5. Caroline, married Granville S. Webster; children: Grace, married Hervey Varney; Alice. 6. George Washington, married Sarah Hobbes. 7. Samuel G., married Emma Peterson. 8. Annie M., born 1844; unmarried. 9. Charlotte, born June 30, 1849; married Elisha Packard (see Packard family).

BARRETT William Barrett, of Cambridge, Massachusetts, tailor, was living there in 1656 and bought a house and land in Dunster street, near to the college building. He was a selectman in 1671 and 1681, served as lieutenant during King Philip's war, and died May 19, 1789. He married first, August 9, 1656, Sarah, daughter of Elder Richard Champney. She died August 21, 1661, and he married second, May 19, 1662, Mary, daughter of John and Phebe Barnard; married third, October 8, 1673, Mary, daughter of Nathaniel and Patience Sparhawk; married fourth, Margaret Bartlett, who survived him. His children: 1. Lydia, born September 17, 1657. 2. William, August 15, 1659; died young. 3. John, February 6, 1661. 4. Mary, January 11, 1663. 5. William, May 3, 1665. 6. Edward, February 8, 1668. 7. Samuel, February 8, 1670. 8. Bartholomew, April 6, 1672; died young. 9. Margaret, May 4, 1676. 10. Thomas, January 25, 1678. 11. Bartholomew, April 12, 1681. 12. Lydia, May 14, 1683.

(II) William Barrett, son of William and Mary (Barnard) Barrett, was born in Cambridge, May 3, 1665, and died about 1730. He was a tailor and lived on the homestead with his father. He married Hannah, daughter of Daniel Cheever; children: 1. William, baptized January 16, 1696-97; died young. 2. Hannah, baptized March 6, 1696-97; died young. 3. Elizabeth, baptized 1699. 4. Hannah, born 1700. 5. William, baptized May 30, 1703. 6. John, July 9, 1706. 7. Daniel, born February 28, 1707-08.

(III) William Barrett, son of William and Hannah (Cheever) Barrett, was born May 30, 1703, and was a cordwainer, living on the old homestead in Dunster street, Cambridge, until about 1737, when he sold the property to his son-in-law and then probably removed to Boston. The baptismal name of his wife was Mary, but her family name does not appear. Children: 1. William, born November 30, 1728. 2. Jonathan, February 6, 1730; died young. 3. Hannah, October 14, 1731. 4. Daniel, November 12, 1733; married his cousin Elizabeth, a daughter of Daniel Barrett. 5. Samuel, August 3, 1735. 6. Mary, May 15, 1737; died young. 7. Mary, baptized February 11, 1739. 8. Joshua, baptized January 25, 1741. 9. Jonathan, baptized June 25, 1741. 10. Caleb, baptized June 27, 1745. 11. Hannah, baptized February 8, 1747.

(IV). William Barrett, son of William and Mary Barrett, was born November 30, 1728, probably in Cambridge, and died in Boston. He married, in Boston, June 21, 1758, Abigail Bradford, and at the time of their marriage his age is mentioned as about twenty-eight, and his wife about three years his junior. They had ten children, all born in Boston: 1. John, twin, March 21, 1759. 2. Thomas, March 21, 1759. 3. William, August 28, 1760. 4. John Spencer, July 26, 1762. 5. Daniel, twin, September 20, 1764. 6. Samuel, twin, September 20, 1764; died young. 7. Samuel, October 5, 1766. 8. Benjamin, September 17, 1768. 9. Nathaniel, February 27, 1770. 10. Smith Freeman, May 13, 1772.

(V) William Barrett, son of William and Abigail (Bradford) Barrett, was born in Boston, August 28, 1760. Little is known of him except that he was a soldier of the war of 1812-15, and died in the service. He married, March 24, 1798, Hannah Turner Sumner, born Boston, July 24, 1778, died in Melrose, Massachusetts, August 22, 1858, daughter of Samuel and Elizabeth (Shedd) Sumner, of Boston. (See Sumner). She survived her husband and married (second) Amos Ruddock. She was a most devout and exemplary member of the Methodist church, having been received in full communion March 3, 1811; and in the church edifice in East Boston is a beautiful window, a memorial of her true christian character and womanly worth. William and Hannah Turner (Sumner) Barrett had two children: 1. William, Jr. 2. Samuel Sumner Wilton.

(VI) Samuel Sumner Wilton Barrett, son of William and Hannah Turner (Sumner) Barrett, was born in Boston, May 9, 1809, and died in Melrose, Massachusetts, in 1896. He first learned the trade of carpenter and joiner, later became a machinist, and for several years was employed by the Tuft Printing Press Manufacturing Company. After a time he adandoned mechanical work and was employed as superintendent in the service of the Cunard Steamship Company, Boston. Still later he was appointed station master of the Boston & Maine railroad at Melrose, whither he removed from Boston in January, 1855, and held that position for the next twenty-five years, until he retired from active pursuits. It may be mentioned here that after his marriage Mr. Barrett changed his name to Sumner Foster Barrett, and ever afterward was so known. During Governor Lincoln's administration he held the rank of captain of the watch. He married, in Boston, February 28, 1831, Hannah Barrett Sumner, born Beverly, Massachusetts, February 26, 1811, daughter of John Witt and Déborah (Hogan) Sumner, of Beverly (see Sumner). Children, all born in Boston: 1. Albert Brown, born January 25, 1832. 2. Amos Ruddock, July 29, 1833. 3. Sumner Foster, November 1, 1835; died young. 4. Charles Lewis, December 30, 1838. 5. Sarah Ann, July 17, 1843; died young. 6. Frank Sumner, September 25, 1850. Mr. Barrett and his sons were Masons.

(VII) Albert Brown Barrett, eldest son and child of Sumner Foster (formerly Samuel Sumner Wilton) and Hannah Barrett (Sumner) Barrett, was born in Boston, January 25, 1832. He received a good early education in Boston public schools and the famous Dummer Academy, Byfield Parish, Newbury, Massachusetts. After leaving school he became a machinist in the East Boston shops of the old Eastern Railroad Company, beginning his business career in 1849, first as machinist apprentice and continuing afterward as journeyman and practical workman. From the latter position he was advanced to that of foreman of the machinist department, later became master machanic for the Boston & Maine Railroad Company, successor to the Eastern, and finally was advanced to the still more responsible position of general inspector for the Boston & Maine Company, which he held until his retirement from active pursuits, March 1, 1908. In religious preference Mr. Barrett is a Unitarian and in politics a Republican. He is a member of various subordinate Masonic bodies, past master of Mt. Tabor Lodge, F. and A. M., and a charter member and past commander of William Parkman Commandery, K. T. He married, March 30, 1854, in East Boston, Ellen Hall, born Marshfield, Massachusetts, December 28, 1835, daughter of Luke and Alice (Carver) Hall. Children: 1. Sarah Ellen, a graduate of the Boston grammar and high schools; not married. 2. Emma Sumner, a graduate of South Portland (Maine) high school; married Dr. Frank Henry Carter, and had Philip Barrett, Margaret Pillsbury, Doris Eloise, Elsee Carver and Constance Carter. 3. Isadora, a graduate of Somerville grammar school and Melrose high school; not married.

(VII) Amos Ruddock Barrett, second son of Sumner Foster and Hannah Barrett (Sumner) Barrett, was born in Boston, July 29, 1833, died May 11, 1895. He was educated in the schools of Boston, learned the trade of machinist and then that of locomotive engineer, and went to Wisconsin about 1854 as an engineer, remaining for several years. Upon his return east he was employed as superintendent of engineers for the Eastern railroad of Massachusetts, later entering the employ of the Atchison, Topeka & Santa Fe railway as division master mechanic, located in Arizona. He remained with that line eight years, after which he returned east as master mechanic of the Worcester & Nashua railroad, and finally was master of rolling stock of the Boston & Maine system, holding that position up to his decease. He was a member of the Masonic fraternity. He married first, November 2, 1858, Eliza Jane Gardiner, of Saco, Maine; children: 1. Carrie Anna, born November 12, 1863; died young. 2. Fred Sumner, born April 8, 1867; mentioned below. Married second, November 6, 1890, Lucy Anna Milliken, of Bucksport, Maine. No children.

(VII) Charles Lewis Barrett, fourth son of Sumner Foster and Hannah Barrett (Sumner) Barrett, was born in Boston, December 30, 1838. He was educated in the schools of Boston and Melrose, and in 1858 went to Haverhill, Massachusetts, to learn the shoe business, residing there from then to the present time. In the civil war he enlisted in Company G, Forty-second Regiment, Massachusetts Volunteers, was with General N. P. Banks at New Orleans, Louisiana, and Galveston, Texas, taken prisoner and confined in Houston prison, Texas, paroled but not exchanged, sent to Ship Island and later home;

was mustered out August 20, 1863. He is a Royal Arch Mason. He married, May 23, 1865, Hannah Elizabeth Chace, of Haverhill, Massachusetts; she died May 8, 1875; no children. Married second, February 25, 1889, Isabelle C. McDonald, of Melrose, Massachusetts. No children.

(VII) Frank Sumner Barrett, youngest son and child of Sumner Foster and Hannah Barrett (Sumner) Barrett, was born in Boston, September 25, 1850, and gained his education in the grammar and high schools of that town, and Phillips Academy, Andover, Massachusetts. When a young man he learned the trade of machinist, later became a mechanical draughtsman and worked in that capacity for several years. He then engaged with a large Boston wholesale thread house and for the next twenty years represented the interests of that concern in Chicago. While living in the middle west he became much interested in amateur photography and indulged and cultivated his tastes in that direction until he attained a degree of proficiency which entitled him to recognition among the leading artists of that profession; and thus it was that in 1902 he returned east and settled in Winthrop, Massachusetts, where in 1904 he became a professional photographer in that town. He is a Master and Royal Arch Mason and both his wife and himself are members of the Unitarian church. In 1872 he married, in Boston, Frances E., born Charlestown, Massachusetts, daughter of George H. and Sarah M. (Bird) Morse, both descendants of old New England stock. Mr. and Mrs. Barrett have children: 1. Sidney Foster, born July 19, 1875; died aged three months. 2. Ernest Laurence, born November 24, 1895.

(VIII) Fred Sumner Barrett, only livng child of Amos Ruddock Barrett was born in East Somerville, Massachusetts, April 8, 1867. He was educated in the schools of East Somerville, learned the trade of locomotive engineer, which line of work he is following at the present time in the employ of the Boston & Maine railroad. He resides in Worchester, Massachusetts. He married, April 7, 1892, Agnes Child Hicks, of Worcester. Children: 1. Frances Jennette, born September 23, 1897. 2. Mildred Alice, November 28, 1899.

SUMNER Roger Sumner, of Bicester, Oxfordshire, England, husbandman, died 1608; married, 1601, Joane Franklin, who married (second) 1611, Marcus Brian, of Merton, who died 1620. Roger and Joane (Franklin) Sumner had one son.

(II) William Sumner, only son of Roger and Joane Sumner, born Bicester, England, 1605, came to New England and settled in the plantation at Dorchester, Massachusetts, 1636; was made freeman, 1637; selectman, 1637, and for more than twenty years afterward; magistrate to try small causes, 1663 to 1671; one of the feoffees of the school land, 1663 to 1680; clerk of the trainband, 1663 and afterward; deputy from Dorchester to the general court, 1658, 1666-70, 1678-81, 1683-86. He died December 9, 1688. Married, in Bicester, England, 1625, Mary West, died in Dorchester, June 7, 1676; children: 1. William. 2. Joane, born Bicester, married Aaron Way, of Dorchester. 3. Roger, 1632. 4. George, 1634. 5. Samuel, Dorchester, May 18, 1638. 6. Increase, Dorchester, February 23, 1643.

(III) William Sumner, son of William and Mary (West) Sumner, was born in Bicester, England, and died in Boston, Massachusetts, 1675. He was a mariner, lived first in Dorchester and afterward in Boston. Married Elizabeth, daughter of Augustine Clement, of Dorchester; she died before 1687; ten children, the first two of whom were born in Dorchester and the others in Boston: 1. Elizabeth, 1652, died 1728; married Joshua Henshaw. 2. Mary, 1654, died 1706; married first, Nicholas Howe; married second, John Trow. 3. William, February 9, 1656. 4. Hannah, June 10, 1659; married John Goffe, of Boston. 5. Sarah, February 14, 1662, died February 12, 1736; married first, ———; second, Joseph Weeks. 6. Experience, September 22, 1664; married Thomas Gould. 7. Ebenezer, October 30, 1666; soldier in the Phipps expedition to Canada, 1690. 8. Deliverance, March 18, 1669, married Ebenezer Weeks. 9. Clement, September 6, 1671. 10. Mercy, January, 1675, died young.

(IV) Clement Sumner, son of William and Elizabeth (Clement) Sumner, was born in Boston, September 6, 1671; married, May 18, 1698, Margaret Harris; children, all born in Boston: 1. William, March 18, 1699. 2. Ebenezer, September 1, 1701. 3. Margaret, December 7, 1702, died same day. 4. Margaret, July 18, 1705; married William Jepson, of Boston. 5. Elizabeth, October 8, 1707; married John Bennett, of Boston. 6. Samuel, August 31, 1709. 7. Benjamin, May 28, 1711.

(V) Ebenezer Sumner, son of Clement and Margaret (Harris) Sumner, was born in Boston, September 1, 1701, died there December

26, 1783; married, October 8, 1723, Elizabeth Cox; children, born in Boston: 1. Elizabeth, October 11, 1724. 2. Susannah, September 13, 1726; married Ephraim Abraham Foster. 3. Ebenezer, 1728, died young. 4. Samuel, December 22, 1730. 5. Ebenezer, March 25, 1733. 6. Clement, 1735. 7. Mary, March 26, 1739, married Joseph Ingraham. 8. Rachel, 1741.

(VI) Samuel Sumner, son of Ebenezer and Elzabeth (Cox) Sumner, was born in Boston, December 22, 1730, and died at Port Royal, February 26, 1783. He lived in Boston and married first, Bethia, daughter of Benjamin Clough, of Boston; married second, Elizabeth Shedd, who died December 28, 1810. Two children by first wife and eight by second marriage, all born in Boston: 1. Benjamin Clough, April 14, 1755. 2. Samuel, August 22, 1758. 3. Elizabeth, July 20, 1765, died same day. 4. Sarah, died November 10, 1769. 5. Elizabeth, November 10, 1768, died 1836. 6. Rebecca, 1770, died 1775. 7. Joseph Shedd, November 10, 1771, died June 27, 1776. 8. Bethia Clough, 1773, died 1776. 9. Hannah Turner, July 24, 1778, died Melrose, August 22, 1858; married, March 24, 1798, William Barrett, of Boston, who died in service during the war of 1812-15. (See Barrett). 10. Bethia Clough, August 24, 1779; married Jabez Knight.

(VII) Benjamin Clough Sumner, son of Samuel and Bethia (Clough) Sumner, was born in Boston, April 14, 1755, and died in Beverly, Massachusetts, June 21, 1807. He married, in Beverly, Mary Witt; children, born in Beverly: 1. Mary Clough, March 9, 1784, died March 1, 1849; married Nathaniel Hogan, of Beverly. 2. Benjamin Clough, March 13, 1786, died at sea November, 1803. 3. John Witt, February 18, 1788. 4. Samuel, September 8, 1789. 5. William Clough, August 5, 1791. 6. Sarah, January 6, 1794. 7. Ebenezer, April 5, 1796. 8. Rebecca H., July 16, 1798, died Melrose, January 12, 1871.

(VIII) John Witt Sumner, son of Benjamin Clough and Mary (Witt) Sumner, was born in Beverly, February 18, 1788, and died there July 3, 1828. He married first, Deborah Hogan, and second, Elizabeth Legro. Three children by first wife and three by second wife, all born in Beverly: 1. Hannah Barrett, February 26, 1811; married, February 28, 1831, Sumner Foster Barrett, of Melrose. (See Barrett). 2. Anna Black, June 2, 1812; married Daniel Poor, of Bradford. 3. John Witt, March 15, 1815, died East Boston, 1851; married Hannah Arbuckle. 4. Eliza Cleaves, November 5, 1820; married William Elliott, of Topsfield. 5. Rebecca Haskell, March 21, 1822, died October 11, 1824. 6. Rebecca Haskell, April 24, 1825; married, June 20, 1844, Edward R. Fiske, of Worcester.

HALL (I) John Hall, immigrant ancestor of this family, according to family tradition was born in Wales. He settled in Barnstable, Massachusetts, about 1640, and his name appears on the list of those able to bear arms in 1643. He removed to Yarmouth in 1653 or even earlier, locating in that part now forming the town of Dennis, and his descendant, Josiah S. Hall, was recently living on the original homestead. He must have been closely related to George Hall, who had lands assigned to him in Duxbury before 1639; who was of Taunton on the list of those able to bear arms in 1643 and town officer in 1645; whose will was dated October 26, 1668; bequeathing to wife Mary, sons John, Samuel and Joseph, daughters Charity and Sarah, and to William Evans. Hall's house in Barnstable was near the site of the new court house. He owned a small tract near Cooper Pond, and a great lot of forty acres at Indian Ponds. He bought his house and lands of General James Cudworth, and sold to James Nagle when he removed to Yarmouth. He settled, about 1651, on a farm of one hundred and forty-seven acres in Conny Furlong, at Nobscusset, a short distance from the meeting house. He also owned fifteen acres of upland west of Coy's Pond, and twelve acres of meadow in that vicinity. He was a constable in Barnstable in 1647; surveyor of highways at Yarmouth in 1653; on the grand inquest 1657 and 1664. He was a man of eminently distinguished moral worth, we are told, and of religious character. He died at an advanced age in 1694. His will was dated July 15, 1694, and was proved August 25, 1696, bequeathing to sons Samuel, Joseph, William, Benjamin, Elisha, John, Nathaniel and Gershom. He was buried on the homestead. Of his children we have the following record: 1. Samuel, married Elizabeth Pollard; he died without issue, mentioning his seven brothers in his will; his widow married second, April 27, 1799, Nathaniel Jones. 2. John, see forward. 3. Joseph, baptized July 3, 1642. 4. Benjamin, born 1744; baptized July 14, of that year; died July 23, 1744. 5. Nathaniel, baptized February 8, 1746. 6. Gershom, baptized March 5, 1648. 7. William, baptized June 8, 1651. 8. Benjamin, baptized May 29, 1653. 9. Elisha, born 1655.

(II) Deacon John Hall, son of John Hall (1), was born about 1637; died at Dennis, Massachusetts, October 14, 1710, according to record on the gravestone. He was deacon in the church; selectman in 1685; and had a pew in the meeting house as early as 1672. He resided at Yarmouth. He married Priscilla Bearse, born March 10, 1643, died March 30, 1712, daughter of August Bearse, of Barnstable, who came from Southampton, England, at the age of twenty years, sailing in the ship "Confidence," April 2, 1638. They had children, all born in Yarmouth: John, 1661, died young; Joseph, see forward; John, 1666; Priscilla, 1668; Priscilla, February, 1671; Esther, 1672; Mary, March 1, 1674; Martha, May 24, 1676; Nathaniel, September 15, 1678, married Widow Jane Moore, removed to Lewiston, Pennsylvania.

(III) Deacon Joseph Hall, second son and child of Deacon John (2) and Priscilla (Bearse) Hall, was born in Yarmouth, Massachusetts, September 29, 1663, died January 29, 1737. He settled on the farm of his father in Dennis, and was deacon of the church in Yarmouth. He was appointed a member of the committee to confer about getting a new meeting house in 1716; was deputy to the general court in 1715-6; selectman in 1701, and for twenty-eight years altogether. He married first, February 12, 1690, Hannah Miller, born April 19, 1666, died August 23, 1710, daughter of Rev. John Miller, the first minister of Yarmouth; children: 1. Hannah, born February 30, 1691; married, November 22, 1715, Ebenezer Crocker. 2. Priscilla, born March 28, 1693. 3. Margery, born February 24, 1695. 4. Joseph, born August 6, 1697. 5. Daniel, see forward. 6. Josiah, born August 12, 1701. 7. David, born August 6, 1704. Mr. Hall married (second) Mary, daughter of ——— Faunce and widow of John Morton. She died May 31, 1761, at the age of eighty years. They had children: Mary, born March 31, 1712; Peter, born May 19, 1715; John, born January 30, 1717; Bethsheba, born July 5, 1719.

(IV) Daniel Hall, second son and fifth child of Deacon Joseph (3) and Hannah (Miller) Hall, was born in Yarmouth, July 15, 1699, and died October 14, 1768. He was representative to the general court for four years, 1735 and later; selectman, 1757; and deacon of the Yarmouth church. He married first, May 18, 1721, Lydia Gray, of Harwich, Massachusetts; second, Sarah Downs; third, Rebecca Bangs. His children, all born in Yarmouth, were: Daniel, Jr., born August 6, 1722; David, born March 6, 1724; Lot, March 18, 1725; Joshua, born May 5, 1737; Atherton, see forward; Peter, born February 10, 1750; Samuel, born March 7, 1752, removed to Ashfield in 1777. He also had two sons and seven daughters, of whom the names are not known.

(V) Atherton Hall, son of Daniel Hall (4), was born in Yarmouth, Massachusetts, March 7, 1748. He was a prominent citizen of his day, being selectman in 1786 and representative to the general court three years, 1751-4. He married Ruth Crowell, born in Yarmouth, September, 1749, and they had children: 1. Atherton, see forward. 2. Peter, born November 14, 1772; married Polly ———; children: Alran, born September 25, 1794; Joseph, February 10, 1797; Joshua, March 4, 1799; Polly, June 5, 1801; Peter, February 8, 1803; John C., March 25, 1804; Sabina, February 14, 1805; Rebecca, October 21, 1807; Bradford, March 21, 1810; Henry, February 22, 1812; Daniel, March 17, 1814; Aguley, September 10, 1816; Benjamin, June 21, 1819; John C., September 8, 1823. 3. Sarah, born September 30, 1774; married Isaac White; children: Polly, born October 14, 1798; Ruth, June 7, 1801; Sarah, November 27, 1802; Mira, September 29, 1804; Lydia, May 3, 1806; Isaac, December 29, 1807; Rebecca, December 29, 1809; Bartlett, September 25, 1811; Joseph, October 21, 1813. 4. Lydia, born October 8, 1776; married Gideon Hallet; children: Edmund, born August 20, 1798; Atherton, October 10, 1799; Ruth, February 13, 1801; Lydia, August 31, 1802; Gideon, April 16, 1804; Freeman, November 24, 1805; Russell, December 12, 1807; Marsene, November 26, 1809; Sebina, October 30, 1811; Phila Ann, July 19, 1813; Otis; Howes; Mary, November 3, 1819. 5. Ruth, born July 13, 1778; married Israel Nickerson; children: Ruth H., born April 22, 1809; Hiram, February 6, 1811; Mehitable P., May 26, 1812; Caroline, December 25, 1813; Keziah, November 12, 1815; Sophia, May 26, 1817. 6. Mehitable, born August 4, 1780; married Newson Perry; children: Mehitable, born May 18, 1801; Newson, April 28, 1803; Ruth, March 4, 1805; Mira Ann, July 2, 1807; William B., September 2, 1810; Daniel, May 17, 1813; Ralph, September 2, 1815; Hilyard H., February 25, 1818; Daniel W., January 14, 1821. 7. Elizabeth, born January 3, 1783; married Ezra Ide; children: Esther, born October 15, 1804; Hiram H., January 31, 1806; Russell B., August 6, 1807. 8. Rebecca, born February 18, 1785; married Isaac Gorham; children: Emily, born August 20, 1812; Diantha, March 18, 1814; Irvin, February 4, 1816; Jane, October 26, 1817; Charles, March 10, 1818; Hannah, December 7, 1820; Jason, March 25, 1822; Atherton, May 29, 1824; Hiram, September 21, 1827; Rebecca, September 27, 1829. 9. Desire, born January 8, 1788; married Vine Carpenter; children: Infant, born July 17, 1808; Harriet, July 18, 1811; an infant, January 1, 1813; Sophia, July 19, 1814; an infant, June 26, 1816; Pamela, January 4, 1818; Grant, January 26, 1820; Almira, December 25, 1823.

(VI) Atherton Hall, eldest child of Atherton (5) and Ruth (Crowell) Hall, was born in Yarmouth, Massachusetts, November 4, 1770, and died November 21, 1848. His farm was in Dennis, as incorporated June 19, 1793, from the old town in Yarmouth. He married, January 29, 1795, Olive Hallet, born April 16, 1775, died October 10, 1854; children: 1. Edward, see forward. 2. Sally, born May 5, 1798; died June 25, 1803. 3. Atherton, born October 29, 1800; died September 15, 1881. 4. Olive, born April 19, 1803; died October 31, 1853. 5. Hiram, born May 29, 1806; died February 20, 1887; married, 1831, Silence Sophronia DeWitt, born April 27, 1809, died February 26, 1893. 6. Sally, born October 9, 1808; died September 21, 1859. 7. Harriet, born December 5, 1811; died March 13, 1815. 8. Nathan Hallet, born June 22, 1815; died October 13, 1862; married, July 12, 1847, Elizabeth Smith, born November 21, 1818, died September 26, 1898; children: Jennie Elizabeth, born September 1, 1849, died September 2, 1883; and Fannie Smith, born January 21, 1859. 9. Eliza Jane, born March 21, 1818; married, February 14, 1839, George Ranney, born February 7, 1813, tenth child of Elijah and Lydia (Crawford) Ranney. 10. Ebenezer, born October 16, 1820, died February 19, 1898; married, December 30, 1847, Betsey Miller, born February 16, 1821, died January 9, 1900, daughter of John and Betsey (Robinson) Miller; children: Charles Atherton, born November 8, 1848; Henry Augustine, born September 21, 1850; Florence Amelia, born December 2, 1852.

(VII) Edward Hall, eldest child of Atherton (6) and Olive (Hallet) Hall, was born December 20, 1795; died March 13, 1889. He married first, October 28, 1819, Orpah Goodell, born in West Westminster, Vermont, July 26, 1797, died November 30, 1845. Children: 1. William Goodell, born August 15, 1820, died August 24, 1896; married, at Ashby, Massachusetts, May 20, 1846, Mary Russell Haskell, born January 17, 1821, died January 15, 1906; children: Frances Jane, born April 13, 1847, died May 30, of the same year; Georgiana, born May 8, 1848, died July 3, 1851. 2. Mary, born February 19, 1823; died August 12, 1825. 3. Julia Ann, born November 27, 1824; died September 16, 1901; married, January 21, 1846, Daniel Campbell, born in Westminster, Vermont, March 8, 1820, died at Saxton River, February 3, 1898, son of Edward Raymond and Clarissa (Chamberlin) Campbell; children, the five elder born in West Westminster, the others at Saxton River: Charles Hamilton, born December 31, 1846, died August 28, 1848; Flora Elizabeth, born May 1, 1848; Julia Alice, born November 23, 1849, died August 4, 1851; Edward Raymond, born September 27, 1853; William Hall, born June 7, 1856, died March 24, 1904; Harriet Julia, born January 11, 1859; Clara Orpah, born October 5, 1861; Mary Ellen, born May 9, 1867. 4. Mary, born February 25, 1827; died April 27, 1890; married, October 13, 1857, Henry Holmes, born in Grafton, Vermont, February 5, 1806, and died in same town, August 27, 1871. They had one child: George Henry, born in Grafton, May 1, 1860; died at Bellows Falls, Vermont, January 23, 1893. 5. Edward Bangs, born November 13, 1828; died July 15, 1893; married, October 30, 1851, Ellen Narcissa Buxton, died June 6, 1889; children, all born at West Westminster: A daughter, born March 17, 1855, died April 13, same year; Herbert Edward, born December 25, 1856, died in Danvers, Colorado, December 19, 1899; Willis Henry, born December 23, 1860, died in Fresno, California, August 26, 1895. 6. Josiah, born February 5, 1835; married, November 29, 1865, Delia Elizabeth Adams, born in Montague, Massachusetts, November 12, 1846, fourth child of Amos and Sarah (Whitney) Adams; children: George Warren, born in Greenfield, Massachusetts, December 25, 1866; Carrie Luella, born in Greenfield, Massachusetts, September 25, 1868. 7. Nathan, born March 7, 1837; died August 11, 1875; married, November 30, 1865, Laura Bugbee, born April 26, 1846, died January 10, 1872; one child: George Edward, born in Brattleboro, Vermont, August 2, 1868; married, September 30, 1902, Anna Copeland Ames, daughter of Frank M. and Catherine H. (Copeland) Ames; children: Catherine Ames, born in New York City, May 24, 1904, and Alice Ames, born in Watertown, New York, September 6, 1905. 8. Hiland, born August 1, 1841; married February 12, 1868, Julia Ann Britton, born in Neosho, Missouri, July 29, 1850, tenth child of George Washington and Catherine Ann (Moody) Britton; children; Edward Clay, born in Neosho, Missouri, November 18, 1868; Myrtle Pearl, born in Greenfield, Missouri, April 30, 1874.

Edward Hall married second, May 12, 1846, Mrs. Frances A. Wheeler, whose maiden name was Tuttle. She was born in Grafton, Vermont, March 15, 1811, and died February 11, 1905. She married first, November 27, 1834, Holland Wheeler, born in Westmoreland, New Hampshire, April 3, 1796, died October 10, 1842. They had children: Kirke W., born August 15, 1835, died June 25, 1904; and Holland, Jr., born April 19, 1837. Mrs. Hall was a daughter of Daniel and Lucretia (Hapgood) Tuttle, who were married in 1808. The former was born at West Springfield, Massachusetts, June 5, 1788, and died June 6, 1861; his wife was born at Bellows Falls, Vermont, June 12, 1792, and died March 19, 1871. They had children: Quarters Morgan, born August 28, 1809, died March 19, 1877; Frances Adeline, who married Mr. Hall; Adeline; Daniel Atwater, born July 4, 1815, died July 17, 1882; Caroline Matilda, born August 18, 1817; Lyman Hapgood, born October 28, 1819, died October 3, 1841. By his second marriage Mr. Hall had children: 1. Alfred Stevens, born April 14, 1850; married first, October 18, 1876, Martha Annette Hitchcock, born November 3, 1849, died September 26, 1887, daughter of Josiah Hubbard and Martha Ann (Chamberlin) Hitchcock. The former was born October 1, 1818, died March 7, 1866; his wife was born January 30, 1823, and died July 2, 1886. They married September 8, 1842, and had children: Sherman Josiah, born September 9, 1844, died February 25, 1862; Martha Annette, who married Mr. Hall; Abbie Frances, born September 13, 1856, died April 8, 1862; Frank Ellsworth, born October 28, 1864, died July 2, 1882. By this marriage Mr. Hall had children: Francis Chamberlin, born September 23, 1878, and Helen Annette, born January 15, 1883. Mr. Hall married (second), April 10, 1895, Delia Rebecca Ranney, born December 21, 1854, only child of Henry Porteus and Frances Augusta (Hamblen) Ranney, the former born January 30, 1829, the latter born August 20, 1833, died November 19, 1903. 2. Solon Goodridge, born September 11, 1852; married, September 23, 1884, Libbie Fowler Clarkson, born in Dundee, Illinois, April 2, 1860, seventh child of David and Jeanette (Crichton) Clarkson.

BEALS Beal (or Beals) is an English surname of great antiquity, derived from the name of a place. It means literally a narrow pass. The Scandinavian giant Beli, from whom the name may descend, was slain by Freyr. The French form de la Beale is found in the Hundred Rolls in the thirteenth century. There is a hamlet of this name in the detached portion of Durham, England, and the family is numerous in Herefordshire and Northamptonshire. Their coat-of-arms: Argent a chevron between three pheons sable, the two in chief lying fesseways point to point. Another ancient coat-of-arms of this family was derived from William Beale, portreeve of Maidstone in the fourteenth century; his descendant, Sir John Beale, of Farmington Court, Kent, was high sheriff of county Kent in 1665. Arms: Sable on a chevron or between three griffons heads erased argent. As many estoiles gules. Crest: A unicorn's head erased or semel of estoiles gules.

(I) John Beal, immigrant ancestor, came from the parish of Hingham, county Norfolk, England, where he was born, 1588, to Hingham, Massachusetts, with his wife, five sons and three daughters, and two servants. This fact is stated in so many words on the town clerk's records by Daniel Cushing, fourth town clerk of Hingham. He had a grant of land at Hingham, Massachusetts, September 18, 1638, six acres for a house lot on what is now South street, near Hersey street. He was a shoemaker. He was admitted a freeman in 1639, and was deputy to the general court in 1644-59. He married first, Nazareth Hobart, born in England, about 1600, died at Hingham, September 23, 1658, daughter of Edmund and Margaret (Dewey) Hobart. He married second, March 10, 1659, Mary, widow of Nicholas Jacob; she died at Hingham, June 15, 1681. In noticing his death, David Hobart, son of Rev. Peter Hobart, made full record "April 1, 1688, my uncle John Beal died suddenly." Judge Sewell also made a record on the same date, "Father Beal of Hingham died aged one hundred years." His will was dated September 27, 1687, and bequeathed to his children and grandchildren. Children, all by first wife: 1. Martha, born 1620, married, March 16, 1640, William Falloway, of Plymouth; second, June 29, 1649, Samuel Dunham; died April 26, 1690. 2. Mary, born 1622, married, December 30, 1647, James Whiton, of Hingham; died

December 12, 1696. 3. Sarah, born 1625, married, March 22, 1648-49, Thomas March; second, September 5, 1662, Edmund Sheffield, of Braintree; died at Braintree, November 9, 1710. 4. John, born about 1627. 5. Nathaniel, born 1629. 6. Jeremiah, born about 1631, mentioned below. 7. Joshua, born about 1633. 8. Caleb, born 1636. 9. Rebecca, baptized at Hingham, February, 1640-41, died December 13, 1686. 10. Jacob, born October 13, 1642.

(II) Jeremiah Beals, son of John Beal (1), was born in England about 1631. He came with his parents to America, and settled in Hingham. He was a blacksmith; was constable, 1672; selectman, 1671-73-84; deputy to the general court 1691-92-1701. He resided on Bachelor street, near Main street, near the meeting house of the First Parish, but late in life removed to East street, near Hull street. He married, November 18, 1652, Sarah Ripley, born in England and died in Hingham, June 29, 1715, daughter of William Ripley. He died August 10, 1716, aged eighty-five years. Children, born at Hingham: 1. Jeremiah, May 13, 1655. 2. John, March 8, 1656-57, mentioned below. 3. Sarah, July, 1659, married, January 21, 1679-80, John Lane. 4. Lazarus, September 7, 1661. 5. Phebe, March 2, 1663-64, died July 12, 1665. 6. Mary, May 6, 1666, married, December 23, 1702, John Orcutt, of Bridgewater. 7. Elizabeth, May 16, 1669, married, December 29, 1708, Ephraim Lane.

(III) John Beals, son of Jeremiah Beals (2), was born in Hingham, March 8, 1656-57, and died December 30, 1735, in his seventy-ninth year. He resided on East street, at Rocky Nook. He married, about 1686, Hannah ———, who died April 27, 1762, aged ninety-three years. His will was dated May 7, 1734, and proved January 27, 1735-36. Children, born at Hingham: 1. Sarah, October 12, 1687. 2. Ruth, 1690, married, 1718, Richard Cobb; died May 14, 1719. 3. Infant, died young. 4. Infant, died young. 5. Hannah, October 14, 1695, married, November 15, 1722, Caleb Marsh. 6. Lydia, April 10, 1697, married, December 25, 1718, David Lincoln. 7. Deborah, June 22, 1699, died November 14, 1711. 8. John, December 30, 1700. 9. Daniel, June 1, 1703, married, October 15, 1724, Elizabeth Tucker. 10. Samuel, February 2, 1704-05, mentioned below. 11. Stephen, September 16, 1707. 12. Mary, May 7, 1710, married, November 20, 1729, Thomas Waterman.

(IV) Samuel Beals, son of John Beals (3), was born at Hingham, February 2, 1704-05, died 1750. He settled at East Bridgewater, on the Eleazer Kieth place. He married, 1725, Mary, daughter of Elnathan Bassett. Children, born at Bridgewater: 1. Samuel, 1726, married, 1745, Elizabeth Blackman; settled in Medford; children: David and Samuel. 2. Nathan, 1727, married Bathsheba ———. 3. Daniel, 1729, married Mehitable Byram, daughter of Joseph Byram, and settled in Medford. 4. Jonathan, 1730, mentioned below. 5. Joseph (twin), 1733. 6. Benjamin (twin), 1733, married Sarah ———; settled at Medford. 7. Seth, 1736. 8. Mary, 1742. 9. Joseph, 1743.

(V) Jonathan Beals, son of Samuel Beals (4), was born 1730, died 1813, aged eighty-three. He married, 1751, Abigail Harlow, who died 1779, aged fifty. He married second, Abigail (Snow) Edgerton, widow of John Edgerton, and daughter of James Snow, in 1780. He removed with his brothers to Mendon (now Medford), Massachusetts. Children, born in Bridgewater: 1. Joseph, 1752, removed to Abington. 2. Azariah, 1753, mentioned below. 3. Abigail, 1755, married, 1779, Josiah Hull. 4. Jonathan, 1758. 5. Hannah, 1760, died young. 6. Hannah, 1762, married, 1780, Noah Hull. 7. Molly, 1770, married, 1793, Bela Reed.

(VI) Azariah Beals, son of Jonathan Beals (5), was born at Bridgewater, Massachusetts, 1753. He removed to Cummington and Plainfield, Massachusetts, residing in the latter place during the revolutionary war, and later moved to Pharsalia, New York. He had extended service in the revolution; was in an independent company under Captain Joseph Trufant, 1775; in Captain Thomas Nash's company, Colonel Solomon Lovell's regiment at Dorchester Heights, 1776; under the same captain in Colonel Josiah White's regiment, at Hull, 1776-77; in Captain Thomas Nash's company, Colonel David Cushing's regiment, 1777-78, in Rhode Island in Captain Nathan Alden's company, Major Eliphalet Cary's regiment, in Rhode Island, 1778. He married, at Bridgewater, 1776, Bathsheba Bisbee, born April 21, 1753, died March 24, 1844. Children: 1. Daniel, born 1779, probably died young. 2. Ezra, born February 20, 1781, married, January 29, 1807, Lucena ———, born January 4, 1789; children: i. Bathsheba, born March 16, 1808; ii. Delilah, November 28, 1809; iii. Ralph, May 11, 1812, died April 1, 1834; iv. Orphia, June 26, 1814; v. Badoura, September 12, 1816; vi. Horatio, January 23, 1819; vii. Rush, March 1, 1821; viii. Leroy, September 17, 1823; ix. Horace, June 16, 1829. 3. Rox-

Erl V. Beals

anna. 4. Levi, born May 18, 1789, mentioned below. 5. Patty.

(VII) Levi Beals, son of Azariah Beals (6), was born May 18, 1789, died August 31, 1861, at Moline, Illinois. He was brought up on his father's farm, and learned the trade of a tanner, which he followed for some time. He also learned the trade of shoemaker. From Pharsalia, New York, where his marriage occurred, he removed to Moline, Illinois, where he made his home until his death. He was a man of excellent judgment, and was prominent in the town. He married Catherine Smith, who died December 30, 1833. Children: 1. Morell Bisbee, born September 18, 1822, mentioned below. 2. Pattie M., born August 28, 1826, married Horatio Beals, of Bear Lake, Pennsylvania; one child. 3. Austin M., born September 22, 1828, married Julia Wells, of Meadeville, Pennsylvania. 4. Charles James, born July 12, 1832, died June 6, 1865; married, December 24, 1853, Henrietta Prosser, born March 10, 1837, died January 26, 1884, of Girard, Pennsylvania; children: i. Bird Prosser, born October 17, 1855, married Ida V. Blood, of Monroe, Ohio; had Marie Henrietta, July 26, 1889; Prosser Blood, February 9, 1890; Gilson Willis, October 10, 1892; Cary Chamberlain, September 26, 1894; Edith Cornelia, April 2, 1896; ii. Mary Jane, born December 25, 1857, married, November 21, 1878, Edgar R. Skinner, of Ohio; children: Charles Lothrop, born September 25, 1880, married, September 10, 1907, Levia M. Bond; Homer Burden, December 1, 1882, married, December 25, 1906, Ella M. Griffey, one son, Robert Edgar, born September 16, 1907; Ruth Henrietta, born October 20, 1885, married, February 28, 1907, John Lee White, one son, Albert Noble, born April 2, 1908; Edgar Prosser, born July 20, 1890; Lois Trayne, born January 9, 1896; iii. Charles Bartlett, born May 7, 1859, died March 20, 1901; iv. Emma Ruth, born August 20, 1861, married, April 4, 1894, Charles H. Dixon, of Cleveland, Ohio; children: Charles H., Jr., born April 23, 1898, died April 29, 1898, and Lelia Alberta, born April 28, 1899, died same day.

(VIII) Dr. Morell Bisbee Beals, son of Levi Beals (7), was born in Pharsalia, New York, September 18, 1822, and died at Muskegon, Michigan, November 26, 1889. He fitted for college in his native town, and graduated at Williams College at the age of twenty-five. He studied medicine and took an allopath degree. He went west and taught school several years, being teacher and school superintendent at La Crosse, Wisconsin, Iowa City, Iowa, Moline and Rock Island, Illinois, also several years at Flint, Michigan. In 1868 he became interested in the theory and practice of homeopathy, and in 1877 he received a diploma from the Hahnemann College in Chicago. He located at Muskegon, Michigan, where he built up a large general and surgical practice, and remained there until his death. He was a scholarly man, of fine intellect, one of the foremost teachers of his day, and a powerful public speaker, although he was not generally speaking a public man. He was a close follower of the Swendenborgian religion for forty years, having become acquainted with the works of Swedenborg while at college, and always admired and studied them. He was a member of the Masonic order, and was a Republican in politics. He married Caroline Wells, born October 25, 1827, died in New Mexico, June 7, 1897, daughter of Joab and Edna (Long) Wells, of Meadeville, Pennsylvania. Her father was a farmer. Children: 1. Dr. Guy William, born March 21, 1853, resides in Hillsboro, New Mexico; married Ida M. Morrish, of Flint, Michigan; children: i. Pattie, born October 31, 1889; ii. Ethel, June 13, 1891; iii. Morell Morrish, June 6, 1893; iv. Carolyn, June 30, 1895; v. Arthur Carroll, September 24, 1898, died May 23, 1901. 2. Ella Gertrude, born April 18, 1855, unmarried. 3. Jessie, born November 22, 1857, deceased. 4. Jessie, born November 25, 1859, unmarried. 5. Carl Morell, born May 10, 1865, died February 2, 1908; married Emma Quick, of Lake Valley, New Mexico; children: i. Kenneth Bisbee, born September 13, 1902, died April 28, 1906; ii. Carlton Madison, April 27, 1904; iii. Guy Morgan, May 28, 1906. 6. Caroline. 7. Erl Vinton, born June 17, 1867, mentioned below. 8. Archie Bisbee, born December 12, 1869, unmarried.

(IX) Erl Vinton Beals, son of Dr. Morell Bisbee Beals (8), was born at Topeka, Kansas, June 17, 1867. At the age of four he removed with his parents to Moline, Illinois, where he attended the public schools, later removing to Ovid, Michigan, and thence to Muskegon, same state, where he received the greater part of his education, going to the high school until 1886. He then became reporter for the *Muskegon Chronicle*, where he remained ten years. He became interested in type-setting machines before any practicable machines were on the market and later turned his attention to the problem of improving the machinery for type-setting. In 1891, when he took up the work seriously, there were several type-setting machines on the market. The Thorne machine set type and distributed it again by an ingenious device. The Mergenthaler machine casts each line separately, and after using the slugs the metal is melted and used again. The monotype machine, which in later years has become a strong rival of the linotype, casts each letter separately and is used extensively in book work. The Rogers and Mergenthaler companies each had devices advantageous to the other's machine, and finally the Mergenthaler obtained a monopoly of them. Since 1893 the Mergenthaler company has equipped almost every newspaper office of importance in the United States and many foreign countries with its machines, changing the whole character of the press, enormously increasing the size of newspapers. The *New York Sun* uses the the monotype machine. The original type-setting machines have not held their own in the race—the type-casting machines have the field. Mr. Beals studied the problem of simplifying the mechanisms which require skilled machinist's care all the time, and which are costly to make and to keep in repair. The linotype costs from three to four thousand dollars, and some offices have more than fifty of these machines in use. He secured the financial support of such men as Chief Justice Charles D. Long, Colonel Frank J. Hecker, of the Panama Commission, and M. S. Smith, of Detroit, where he began his experimenting. He has developed a machine entirely different from all others, more efficient, less complicated and less expensive. He had the machine well worked out in 1897 when he came to Boston to complete it, the mechancial facilities for developing the more complicated parts being obtainable best in that city. After two years in Boston he made his home in Arlington, Massachusetts, occupying the Piper estate. In 1901 he purchased the Sampson estate, which overlooks the city of Boston and its harbor. He has converted a portion of the buildings into a laboratory and workshop for his experiments, and installed an electrical plant that lights all his buildings and supplies power for his shop. His machinery is of the most delicate and expensive sort. The three floors of his laboratory have an area of four thousand square feet. The Beals machine, which was placed on the market a year later, has at least double the capacity of any other machine for setting or casting type. It is operated entirely by electricity. The keyboard has the one-magnet system, a device of Mr. Beals that is being applied to church organs, typewriters, leather measuring machines and similar mechanisms. Mr. Beals has also invented an area-meter for measuring leather sides, a device that is indispensable to tanners and concerns buying large quantities of leather. This machine is built by the Beals Area-meter Company, a corporation organized under state of Maine laws. Mr. Beals is a follower of the Swedenborgian religion, and a radical thinker. In politics he is a Republican. He married, June 27, 1899, Marguerite (Bammel) Cook, born July 4, 1860, adopted daughter of John and Mary (Franauer) Bammel, of Marine City, Michigan. Her father was a farmer and stationary engineer.

(For first generation see Nicholas Worthington 1).

WORTHINGTON (II) Jonathan Worthington, of West Springfield, Massachusetts, eldest son of Nicholas Worthington (1), married first, February 19, 1708, Elizabeth, daughter of John and Sarah (Bliss) Scott, of West Springfield, died September 18, 1743; second, March 21, 1744, Experience Fowler. Children by first wife: 1. Elizabeth, born February 17, 1710, married, January 3, 1730, Samuel Gaylord, of Hadley; he died 1759. 2. Margaret, born February 2, 1712, married, December 1, 1733, Jonathan Purchase, of Wallingford, Connecticut. 3. Jonathan, see forward. 4. Nicholas, born July 26, 1717, died February 23, 1720. 5. William, born January 16, 1720, married, about March 21, 1743, Sarah Rogers, who died December 17, 1804. 6. Amy, born November 3, 1725, died February 20, 1743. Children by second wife: 7. Olive, born April 10, 1750. 8. Beulah, born April 7, 1752, died in infancy. 9. Beulah, born April 2, 1754.

(III) Jonathan Worthington was born June 17, 1715. He married Mary Purchase. He lived at Agawam, Massachusetts, and died there. Children: 1. Jonathan, see forward. 2. Eleanor, born October 27, 1746, died July 22, 1749. 3. Amy, born July 6, 1749, in Agawam, married, December 10, 1772, Lieutenant Jube Leonard, born March 12, 1747, son of Benjamin and Thankful Leonard. Amy Leonard died April 26, 1813, at Agawam, and her husband September 22, 1820, at Agawam. 4. John, born July 25, 1751, in Agawam, married first, January 20, 1774, Eunice Ferre, born September 6, 1752, at Springfield, Massachusetts, died May 16, 1780, daughter of Aaron and Eunice (Choplin) Ferre; second, Polly Leonard; third, September 30, 1794, Betsey Potter. John died April 15, 1815, at Agawam. 5. Eleanor, born July 23, 1754, married, August 15, 1771, Stephen Bodurtha, born March 22, 1746, son of Jonathan and Joanna (Frost) Bodurtha. 6. Hulda, born August 23, 1756, married, July 10, 1774, Isaac Cooley, who died June 5, 1782. 7. Seth, born August 18, 1760, was killed by Indians near Fort Stanwix (near Roscoe, New York) during revolutionary war. 8. Margaret, born September 30, 1763. 9. Eunice, twin to Margaret, born September 30, 1763; married Major Gad Warriner, born January 29, 1762, in West Springfield, Massachusetts, son of Hezekiah and Persis (Hitchcock) Warriner.

(IV) Jonathan Worthington, of Agawam, Massachusetts, was born there March 31, 1744. He received upon the division of the land in West Springfield (now Agawam), Massachusetts, lot number one, which was east of Darby brook to the main road, also number twenty-one, which was south of number one. He afterward purchased from the Indians a piece of land one mile square, situated in the south part of the town. In 1894 his grandson Henry lived on the same land, and part of it has been held by the family ever since. He married first, January 11, 1770, Mary Burbanks, born 1750, died May 10, 1794; second, June 5, 1795, Mrs. Sybil Cotton, died March 29, 1803; third, February 26, 1804, Lorena Chapin. He died August 14, 1809. Children of first wife: 1. Lucy, born August 26, 1772, married, November 25, 1787, Captain Eli Ball, of Agawam, born April 2, 1764, son of Moses Ball. She died April 20, 1838, at Agawam; he died May 26, 1844, at Agawam. 2. Amos, born October 19, 1774, at Agawam, married, June 22, 1798, Dezier Gallup, born November 20, 1773, in Groton, Connecticut, daughter of Benjamin and Bridget (Palmer) Gallup. Amos remained engaged in business in Agawam until 1847, when he moved to Cincinnati, Ohio, where he died January 31, 1852; his widow died in 1862. 3. Ambrose, born April 16, 1777, at Agawam, married, May 6, 1801, Ruth Chapin, born November, 1778. They lived for thirty years in Agawam and then moved to Bloomfield, New York, where he died December 15, 1854. She died there August 22, 1831. 4. Jonathan, see forward. 5. Mary, born July 15, 1782, at Agawam, married, October 21, 1802, Roderick Morley. 6. Margaret, born October 30, 1784, married, January 6, 1805, Samuel Smith, of Groton, Connecticut, born June 9, 1772, son of Captain Samuel and Abigail (Woodmansee) Smith. They lived at Suffield, Connecticut, where both died, he October 4, 1828, and she April 25, 1829. 7. Fanny, born August 18, 1787, married, April 17, 1823, Benjamin Austin, of Kirkland, Ohio. 8. Seth, born January 5, 1790, died young.

(V) Jonathan Worthington, of Agawam, Massachusetts, was born September 2, 1779, at Agawam, Massachusetts. He married first, December 26, 1803, Phebe Smith, born January 6, 1781, died May 17, 1809, at Agawam, daughter of Captain Samuel and Abigail (Woodmansee) Smith: second, June 2, 1811, Fanny Smith, born April 29, 1784, died May 7, 1855, in Groton, Connecticut, sister to Phebe. He died February 26, 1870, at Groveland, New York, and was buried at Agawam. Children of first wife: 1. Samuel Smith, born November 10, 1805, died in infancy. 2. Henry, born August 3, 1807, in Agawam, married, May 6, 1835, Henrietta Kenton, born August 13, 1814, in Oxford, England, daughter of William and Henrietta (Kayne) Kenton. Both Mr. and Mrs. Worthington were living in 1892, residing on the old homestead at Agawam. The land came to the grandfather of Henry upon the division of land in West Springfield, now Agawam. Children by second wife: 3. Miner, born September 17, 1812, married, May 30, 1838, Nancy I. Flower, who was born April 5, 1813, died May 9, 1883. 4. Job, born June 24, 1815, in Groton, Connecticut, died March 30, 1878; married, September 16, 1846, Eliza J. Warner, of Groveland, New York, born 1822, in Geneseo, daughter of David and Hannah (Welton) Warner. 5. Roland, see forward. 6. Solomon, born April 3, 1820, in Agawam, married (first), October 16, 1850, in Groveland, New York, Nancy L. Pray, born 1826, in Groveland, daughter of James Pray, of Groveland. She died August, 1852. He married (second), April 18, 1854, in New York, Matilda W. Westfall, born 1829, daughter of George Westfall, of New York. 7. Phebe S., born June 4, 1822, in Agawam, married, October 24, 1867, Gilbert L. Deane, of East Groveland, New York, born December 23, 1840, in Allen, New York, son of Apollos and Wealthy (Lincoln) Deane. 8. Jonathan Hiram, born February 2, 1825, in Agawam, died in Cleveland, Ohio, September 11, 1854. 9. Fanny Smith, born November 9, 1829, in Agawam, married, July 26, 1854, Amos Beach, of Cedarville, Ohio, born 1828, in Aurora, New York, son of Jabez and Abigail (Gates) Beach.

(VI) Hon. Roland Worthington, of Boston, Massachusetts, was born in Agawam, September 22, 1817. He received his education in the district schools of his native place, and from the early age of twelve until he attained his twentieth year was employed in various capacities, supporting and educating himself as he went along. In March, 1837, he went to Boston, and found employment in the counting-room of the *Daily Advertiser*. For six years he had the valuable experience of association with the business department of that paper, which, with Nathan Hale as its editor, was indisputably the leading daily of New England, both in points of enterprise and influence. In 1843, in order to recuperate his failing health, he crossed the Atlantic, and made a journey up the Mediterranean, touching at various points, and enlarging his knowledge of Europe by actual observation. Returning to this country he then passed a winter at the south, where he acquired a practical insight into the political and social conditions of that section, which proved valuable to him as the great questions which culminated in the civil war developed themselves. In June, 1845, having returned to Boston with fully-renewed health, he took charge of the *Daily Evening Traveller*, with whose history his name has been inseparably connected. The first number of the *Daily Evening Traveller* appeared on April 1, 1845; it was a four-page sheet, about fourteen by twenty, bearing the imprint of Upton, Ladd & Company as the publishers, but that firm very soon afterwards relinquished all connection with it. Its originators and first editors were Rev. George Punchard and Deacon Ferdinand Andrews. They projected it as a strictly Orthodox paper, devoted to the zealous advocacy of the temperance cause. Rev. Mr. Punchard was popularly spoken of as "the bishop of the Orthodox churches of New Hampshire," in which state he had been preaching with marked ability and power. Mr. Worthington brought with him, from his experience on the *Advertiser*, a large fund of practical wisdom as a publisher, and a natural endowment of creative and originative faculty besides, and these were dominating factors in the development of his new enterprise. Mr. Worthington's name is identified with some notable steps in the progress of journalism. The newspaper life of Boston, at the time he first entered it, was a very stately and slow-going affair. All the dailies of the Hub, save the *Mail* and *Times*, were six-penny sheets, and newsboys were not permitted to cry any of them for sale on the streets. Their very rigid ideas of what dignity required confined them to circulations acquired "by subscription only." In August, 1848, Daniel Webster was announced to address a meeting to his neighbors at Marshfield on the political issues of the hour. Mr. Worthington engaged Dr. James W. Stone, a well-known and expert stenographer of that time, to go to Marshfield and report Mr. Webster's address in full. Early the following morning an extra was on the streets of Boston, and had an immense sale. Large editions were rapidly called for, and the newsboys of Boston cried it lustily all day long. From the *Traveller's* report it was sent especially to the *New York Herald*, and from that time on till the organizing of the Press Association, the *Traveller* was the Boston correspondent of the *New York Herald*. Mr. Worthington was obliged to seek a personal interview with the president of the Eastern Railroad in order to obtain a permit for a boy to go upon the ferry-boat in the afternoon to sell his evening paper. He persisted in the innovation, however, and by another energetic stroke made it a permanent feature of the newspaper business. When the news of the French Revolution of 1848 and the dethronement of Louis Philippe arrived at New York, it was sent by telegraph to the Boston reading-room. Mr. Worthington got out extras as quickly as his press facilities would allow, and his press-room was kept at the high pressure point of activity until late in the evening, satisfying the demand for this startling piece of foreign intelligence. Another feature of newspaper offices, which is now stereotyped by general use, but the initiation of which in Boston belongs also to Mr. Worthington, is the staring placards, or bulletins, giving the brief heads of the latest news of the day.

Mr. Worthington was one of the earliest of the Free Soilers of Massachusetts, and is remembered by all the survivors of "the men of '48" as a staunch and steadfast member of the little band of men who at that early date foresaw and welcomed the conflict with the slave power, and who were in fact the advance guard of the great Republican party, which was twelve years later to take the destiny of the nation into its keeping. When the Republican party was organized, Mr. Worthington, in common with his brother Free-Soilers, at once joined it, and carried his paper with him, though this last step cost him a conflict of opinion with Editor Andrews, who was strongly disposed to follow the lead of Daniel

Webster's famous speech of the seventh of March, 1852. It was wholly due to Mr. Worthington's inflexible attachment to the Free-Soil idea that Mr. Andrews's views were overruled and the *Traveller* held true to the policy which made it one of the most fearless and ablest exponents of the Republican creed. Mr. Manton Marble then became managing editor of the paper, filling the position with signal ability until Samuel Bowles joined the paper in 1857. Mr. Bowles was the managing editor from April 13 until August 10 following; his connection with the paper was brief and brilliant. Mr. Bowles entered upon the project of uniting the *Atlas*, the *Bee*, and the *Chronicle*, with the *Evening Traveller* and founding upon the consolidation a great quarto, modelled after the *New York Tribune*, to be supported by the highest literary talent, and to be first-class in every respect, but this scheme failed utterly. Mr. Bowles was succeeded by Joseph B. Morss, who put upon its columns many years of solid and effective work. The war for the Union came and the price of the paper was advanced to four cents, and later to five cents a copy. Mr. Reuben Crooke followed Mr. Morss as managing editor, and he sustained the paper's reputation as a champion of sturdy Republicanism in politics, and kept it on the right side in all the moral reform movements of the time.

The *Traveller* showed a truly remarkable foresight in discussing the political situations. In 1860 it was the first paper to suggest, as the successor of Governor Banks, the man who became the great war governor of the Commonwealth. In 1879 it brought forward the name of Hon. John D. Long for the office of governor, and against the united and strenuous opposition of the other Republican dailies of Boston it urged Mr. Long's nomination upon the convention, and he was nominated and elected. In 1882 it warned its party against the nomination of Mr. Bishop, and the following year, against every other Republican paper in Boston, it insisted that Hon. George D. Robinson was the wisest nomination that could be made against Governor Butler; the party came near to making another nomination, but at the eleventh hour the advice of Mr. Worthington was taken, Mr. Robinson was nominated and subsequently elected. Again and again it foretold the national overthrow of Republicanism if the feud of 1880-81 was kept up. When the Chicago convention was about to meet in June, 1885, the *Traveller* appealed most earnestly to the New England delegates to join the Arthur column early and secure the defeat of Mr. Blaine, whose candidacy it plainly intimated would, in its belief, be perilous to the party at the polls. Mr. Blaine and the party suffered national defeat. This is a remarkable record of political far-sightedness and the credit of it belonged to Mr. Worthington, who laid down its course and inspired its utterance. A keen and close observer of the current of public affairs, with a strong faculty for perceiving the practical points in a political situation, his judgment gave the paper a singular pre-eminence as a sound and safe political guide. Although writing but little himself he was a very ready and correct critic of good writing, and always drew around him, by an instinctive appreciation of literary talent, an editorial corps of capable and accomplished writers. Always a warm admirer of Hon. Chester A. Arthur, he sturdily championed him against the hostile criticism of the so-called half-breed presses, at the time of his nomination for the vice-presidency. Without solicitation President Arthur tendered to Mr. Worthington the office of collector of the port, in April, 1882. A bitter opposition was made to his confirmation by Senator Hoar, purely on political grounds, but the appointment was confirmed by a very large majority, and even those who then opposed it later conceded that he proved a most efficient collector, conducted the business of the office with an eye single to the service of the government and the business community which had to do with the custom house, and never allowed partisan considerations to interfere with the management of the large force of employees under his orders. It is doubtful, indeed, if true civil service reform has been carried out more perfectly in any government office in the country than at the Boston Custom House under Collector Worthington. His term expired in May, 1886. He was also a member of the house of representatives of Massachusetts and alderman of the city of Boston.

Mr. Worthington married, April 25, 1854, Abbie Bartlett Adams, born 1825, in Roxbury, Massachusetts, daughter of James and Mary (Williams) Adams, of Hardwich, Vermont, and Roxbury, Massachusetts, respectively. Children: 1. Julia Hill, born March 5, 1855. 2. Roland, Jr., born November 10, 1858, drowned July 11, 1908 (see below); married, June 12, 1902, Edith Louise Johnson, born in Somerville, Massachusetts, July 4, 1879; one child, Theoda, born January 22, 1907. 3. Edward Adams, born 1860, died 1862. 4. Fannie

Smith, born August 1, 1862; married, October 11, 1898, Daniel Staniford, of Roxbury, Massachusetts.

The following tribute to Roland Worthington, Jr., who came to his death by drowning, was from the pen of a friend:

"Roland Worthington, son of the collector, was a Roxbury school-boy, and caring not for a college career went into the office of the *Boston Traveller*. Being an observing youth, with a bent toward machinery, he laid in a store of knowledge which proved its value later. He inherited from his father a soundly balanced mind. A lover of nature in all its aspects, he was, at first, in contact with men, reserved even to bashfulness, but after his father's death and the responsibilities of his position fell upon him, his strong qualities of head and heart were asserted. He developed rare tact in the management of business affairs, and in that of the building bearing his father's name, on State street, manifested such practical knowledge of details and discrimination as to tenants, that the building became one of the most desirable for offices in the city.

"Tolerant almost to a fault of the shortcomings of others he was equally firm in his treatment of such when convinced of their unworthiness. Later in his life he went beyond his building to mingle in the larger affairs of men and by energy, sagacity and enterprise prevented one of the largest and most solid corporations of our country from being captured by stock jobbers and watered out of existence. He gained thereby not only the praise and esteem of its president, but also of the directors whom he had awakened to the gravity of the situation.

"He died in the prime of life, both respected and beloved, just as he was impressing himself upon the community as a man of marked business ability, just and yet merciful, keen in his perceptions, loyal and true."

(For ancestry see Reginald Wentworth 1).

WENTWORTH (XXIII) Ephraim Wentworth, son of Ephraim Wentworth, died at Dover, New Hampshire, February 24, 1776. He married February 11, 1724-5, Martha Grant, of Berwick. He and five children (Mary, Grant, William, Ephraim and Martha) were baptized August 24, 1740. On March 6, 1778, William Wentworth and wife Hannah, of Somersworth, Reuben Wentworth and wife Eleanor, and Ephraim Wentworth and wife Phebe, of Rochester, deeded their rights in their father's estates to their brother, Spencer Wentworth. On June 30, 1778, Daniel Kimball and wife Martha (Wentworth), gave a similar deed, and July 9, 1778, Daniel Heard and wife Anna (Wentworth) did the same. Children of Ephraim and Martha Wentworth: 1. Mary. 2. Grant, in Captain Gerrish's company, 1760. 3. William, born October 20, 1730; mentioned below. 4. Ephraim, baptized August 24, 1740. 5. Martha, baptized August 24, 1740; married Daniel Kimball. 6. Spencer, born October, 1734. 7. Reuben. 8. Anna, married September 28, 1768, Daniel Heard, of Dover.

(XXIV) William Wentworth, son of Ephraim Wentworth, was born October 20, 1730. He fought at the battle of Bunker Hill, and served throughout the revolution. There was some controversy in 1781 between the towns of Wakefield and Somersworth as to which town his service belonged. He married Hannah, daughter of Ichabod and Abigail Hayes, of Madbury, New Hampshire, granddaughter of John Hayes, the immigrant. She was born January 5, 1734, and died August 11, 1808. He died October 20, 1798. Children: 1. Mary, born October 8, 1756; married October 1, 1793, John Varney. 2. Ichabod, born February 25, 1759; mentioned below. 3. William, born August 15, 1761. 4. Abigail, born June 2, 1764; married George Yeaton, of Wolfborough. 5. Martha, born August 21, 1766; married June 7, 1787, James Varney, of Milton. 6. Sarah, born September 26, 1769; married January 1, 1793, Dudley Burnham. 7. Ephraim, born June 16, 1773. 8. Hannah, born March 22, 1778; married Jeremiah Cook, of Milton.

(XXV) Ichabod Wentworth, son of William Wentworth, was born February 25, 1759, and died April 16, 1834. He was admitted to the church at Rochester, July 4, 1790. He married first, Marcy Wentworth, born October 7, 1764, died January 23, 1790, daughter of his uncle Ephraim Wentworth. He married second, March 10, 1791, Keziah Cook, of Somersworth, born January 14, 1763, died April 4, 1833. Children of first wife, born at Rochester: 1. Jonathan, November 21, 1787. 2. Abigail, February 1, 1789; married August 30, 1835, Jonathan Howe, of Milton. Children of second wife: 3. Marcy, born January 16, 1791; married, November 16, 1808, James Cook, of Rochester; died January 2, 1851. 4. Martha, born April 4, 1793; married October 30, 1814, Elihu Hayes; resided at Exeter; died January 18, 1871, at Milton. 5. Ichabod H., born December 14, 1795; mentioned below. 6. William, born October 30, 1797. 7. Keziah, born January 14, 1799; married April 2, 1817, Joshua Gray, of Farmington. 8. Joseph C., born September 24, 1801.

(XXVI) Ichabod H. Wentworth, son of Ichabod Wentworth, was born December 14, 1795, and died at Milton, New Hampshire, July 19, 1872. He resided in Milton, and was representative to the state legislature in 1846 and 1847. He married, December 18, 1817, Peace Varney, died July 30, 1873, aged seventy-seven years, nine months, daughter of Aaron and Mary (Clement) Varney. Children: 1. Hiram, born November 12, 1818. 2. Eli, mentioned below.

(XXVII) Eli Wentworth, son of Ichabod H. Wentworth, was born in Milton, February 19, 1821, and died July 18, 1863, at Millville, Mississippi. He was quartermaster of the Sixth New Hampshire Regiment of Volunteers in the civil war, and died in the service, and his body was brought to Milton for interment. He lived at Milton, New Hampshire, and was a prominent citizen. He was a manufacturer of boots and shoes. He represented his district in the state legislature four years and the state senate. He was an active and influential Republican. He was a prominent member of the Baptist church and superintendent of its Sunday school. He married, July 23, 1843, Mehitable Jane Howe, daughter of Jonathan Howe. After his death she lived at South Milton. Children: Clara Anna, born November 26, 1844; married May 26, 1865, Daniel S. Burley (see Burley); Charles Walker, born April 21, 1853, resides with his sister.

BURLEY The surname Burley is an ancient English family name. The most common spellings of this name in the early records are Burley, Burleigh, Burly, Birle, Birley, Birdley and Burdley. No less than nineteen branches of this family in England have coats-of-arms.

(I) Giles Burley, immigrant ancestor, was an inhabitant of Ipswich, Massachusetts, as early as 1648, and was born in England about 1640. He was a commoner at Ipswich in 1664. He was a planter, and lived eight years on what was later called Brooke street, owning division lot No. 105, situate on Great Hill, Hogg Island. His name was spelled Birdley, Birdly, Burdley and Budley, in the Ipswich records, and his name as signed by mark to his will is given as Giles Berdly. He bequeathed to his wife Elizabeth, (called elsewhere Rebecca), his sons Andrew, James, John, and an uncle whose name is not given. Theophilus Wilson was executor; Deacon Knowlton and Jacob Foster, overseers; Thomas Knowlton, Sr., and Jacob Foster, witnesses. Soon after his death in 1668 his widow was granted trees for a hundred rails and one hundred posts, June 13, 1668. She married second, February 23, 1669, Abraham Fitts, of Ipswich. Children: 1. Andrew, born at Ipswich, September 5, 1657; married Mary, daughter of Governor Roger Conant. 2. James, born February 10, 1659; mentioned below. 3. Giles, born July 13, 1662. 4. John, born July 3, 1662 (twin); died February 27, 1681.

(II) James Burley, son of Giles Burley (1), was born at Ipswich, February 10, 1659, and died in Exeter, New Hampshire, about 1721. He married first, May 25, 1685, Rebecca, daughter of Thomas and Susannah (Worcester) Stacy. She died October 21, 1686. Her mother was a daughter of Rev. William Worcester, of Salisbury. His sons Joseph, Giles, Josiah and James made a written agreement in 1723. Children: 1. William, born in Ipswich, February 27, 1692-3; mentioned below. 2. Joseph, born April 6, 1693. 3. Thomas, born April 5, 1697. 4. James, born 1699. 5. Josiah, born 1701; died 1756; married Hannah Wiggin. 6. Giles, born 1703; married December 9, 1725, Elizabeth Joy, of Salisbury.

(III) William Burley, son of James Burley (2), was born in Ipswich, February 27, 1692-3. He was at Newmarket, New Hampshire, in 1746. Children: 1. John, born at Ipswich, December 18, 1717; died November 18, 1776; married first, February 11, 1740, Sarah Hall; second, December 15, 1757, Elizabeth Chesley. 2. William, born 1721; died at Candia, New Hampshire, June 18, 1801; married Olive ———. 3. Andrew, married Martha ———. 4. Jacob, mentioned below.

(IV) Jacob Burley, son of William Burley (3), married Abigail ———. His will was dated at Newmarket, July 17, 1776. Children: 1. Mary, born at Newmarket, October 21, 1752; died March 12, 1828; was blind from infancy, and lived with her brother Jacob. 2. Lucy, married in Newmarket, March 17, 1777, Solomon Huntress. 3. Abigail, married Joshua Sanborn. 4. Jacob, born June 23, 1756; mentioned below. 5. Jonathan, born 1757; died at Wakefield, New Hampshire, May 24, 1814; married Sarah Haley, of Epping.

(V) Jacob Burley, son of Jacob Burley (4),

was born June 23, 1756, and died February 13, 1828. He resided in Newmarket, and was a highway surveyor, 1784-7, tythingman 1785, selectman 1788-9, and auditor 1790. He was in the revolution, and was at the surrender of Burgoyne. He married, May 20, 1779, Sarah, daughter of Josiah and Judith (Tuttle) Burley. Children: 1. Abigail, born August 16, 1781; died June 2, 1856; married January 19, 1804, Trueworthy Chamberlain. 2. Jacob, born November 17, 1783; mentioned below. 3. Josiah, born March 30, 1787; died September 20, 1832; married June 13, 1812, Margaret M. Newcomb, of Machias, Maine. 4. John, born February 27, 1790; died July 23, 1872; married February, 1814, Betsey Page. 5. Judith, born November 6, 1793; married first, her cousin Asa Sanborn; second, Colonel Isaac Freeman. 6. Ezra, born June 18, 1796; died June, 1878; married, 1819, Lucy Hyde. 7. Henry, born August 23, 1801.

(VI) Jacob Burley, son of Jacob Burley (5), was born in Newmarket, November 17, 1783, and died September 30, 1840. He was a farmer and blacksmith, and resided in the homestead in Newmarket. He married first, Mary Chamberlain, sister of Trueworthy Chamberlain, of Brookfield, New Hampshire. He married second, Lois Mather, born at Lee, New Hampshire, July 26, 1798, died April 21, 1848. Children of first wife: 1. Jasper H., born April 5, 1811; married January, 1845, Harriet S. Hayden, of Quincy, Massachusetts; children: i. Jasper H., born October 20, 1852, died young; ii. Jasper M., August 27, 1857; iii. Mary C., February 22, 1859. 2. Frederick Plumer, born December 25, 1814; mentioned below. 3. Mary Chamberlain, born June 7, 1817; died unmarried, September 5, 1840. Children of second wife: 4. Reuben Mathes, born January 8, 1822; married Olive B. Littlefield. 5. Jacob Chamberlain, born August 17, 1831. 6. John, born October 13, 1840; married Ada Jane Perkins; children: i. Lois Maude, born February 13, 1869; ii. Mabel, April 27, 1871; iii. Ada Gertrude, August 9, 1875; iv. Jacob, May 29, 1878.

(VII) Frederick Plumer Burley, son of Jacob Burley (6), was born in Newmarket, December 25, 1814. He removed from Newmarket to Middleton, New Hampshire, in 1843, and from there to Union. He married, January 16, 1839, Martha J., daughter of John and Hannah (Gilman) Burley. Children: 1. Daniel Smith, mentioned below. 2. Eli, died young. 3. Ellen. 4. Charles P., died young. 5. Elizabeth S., married Jacob B. Stevens.

(VIII) Daniel Smith Burley, son of Frederick Plumer Burley (7), was born in Newmarket, New Hampshire, June 10, 1843. When he was two years old his parents removed to Middleton, New Hampshire, where he was educated in the public schools. He worked at farming in his youth. When the civil war broke out he enlisted in Company I, Third New Hampshire Regiment of Volunteers, in August, 1861, under Captain Rall Carlton. He served three years, and was in all the engagements in which his regiment participated for fifteen months, being then transferred to the signal corps with the rank of sergeant. He took part in all the battles and skirmishes in which the Tenth Corps was engaged, and during the siege of Morris Island and Fort Sumter was continuously under fire for months. He was honorably discharged August 24, 1864. He was for a time a partner in a boot and shoe firm in business at Pittsburgh, Pennsylvania. He was in Boston for a time, then located in Newburyport, where he began in the manufacture of boots and shoes in a small way. He was successful, however, and gradually enlarged his factory and increased its capacity until he became one of the leading manufacturers of the city. Shrewd and far-sighted, industrious and enterprising, his success was due to his own abilities and efforts in the face of many difficulties and discouragements. The reputation of Mr. Burley and his shoes is high throughout the shoe trade of the country. Mr. Burley has been an exemplary citizen, active in works of charity and benevolence and in the Congregational church, of which he is a prominent member and has been for many years a deacon. He is president of the Young Men's Christian Association, of Newburyport. No man has taken a keener interest or a larger share in the various movements for the welfare and improvement of the city than he. No man in the city is better known or more generally loved and honored than he. Mr. Burley was president of the National Bank of Wolfeborough, New Hampshire, and director of the Ocean Bank of Newburyport, and of the Mutual Insurance Company, of Boston. He always has had an office in Boston, since he began manufacturing shoes and has large acquaintance and varied interests there. He is a staunch Republican, but has never taken active part in political campaigns and has declined to take public office. He is a member of the Dover (New Hampshire) Lodge of Masons; of the Chapter, Royal Arch Masons; of the Council, Royal and Select Masters, and of the Knights Templar. He is also an Odd Fellow. He was a member of no clubs and preferred the domestic pleasures of his beautiful home to any others. His health failed late in 1907, and for months he has been confined to his bed.

He married, May 26, 1865, Clara A. Wentworth, born at Milton, New Hampshire. (See Wentworth family). They had several children, all of whom died young, the one of longest life dying aged four years and a half.

ALLEN The various Allen families of New England are the progeny of different immigrants. The family mentioned below is descended from an early settler in Kittery, Maine, who came from England. John Allen was mentioned in the court records of Kittery of 1655, showing that he was residing there at that time. Whether or not he was an immigrant cannot be accurately ascertained.

(I) Robert Allen, perhaps son of John, was of English origin. He received a grant of land in Kittery in 1671, and lived a short distance below Sturgeon creek. He died in 1701, and his son Francis was appointed administrator of his estate. He married Hannah, daughter of John and Lucy White, of Kittery, where her father was an early settler. Children of Robert and Hannah (White) Allen: 1. Robert, probably married, 1700, Sarah, widow of John Lary, daughter of George Lydston. 2. Francis, see forward. 3. Anna, married, Nathaniel Fernald, September 10, 1702. 4. Elizabeth, married John Cole, September 23, 1700. 5. Mary, married Timothy Robinson, of Dover, 1692. 6. Lydia, married Joseph Catlin, of Dover.

(II) Francis Allen, son of Robert, was born in Kittery, where his will was proved in 1744 or 1749. He married Hannah, daughter of Jabez and Hannah (Curtis) Jenkins, and granddaughter of Reynolds (or Reginald) Jenkins, who was born in England in 1608, and was in the service of John Winter at Richmond's Island from 1634 to 1639. Children of Francis and Hannah (Jenkins) Allen: 1. Francis, mentioned below. 2. Hannah, born August 10, 1699, married Samuel Hill, December 23, 1721. 3. Robert, born October 4, 1701, died young. 4. Anna, married Ephraim Tibbetts, of Dover, November 6, 1722. 5. Elizabeth, born December 30, 1705, died young. 6. Elizabeth, born February 6, 1708-9; married Daniel Meader, of Dover, June 22, 1727. 7. Robert, born July 24, 1710, died 1761; married, December 10, 1730, Catherine Furbish. 8. Mary, born July 19, 1712; married Timothy Robinson, of Dover, July 24, 1730. 9. Jabez, born August 19, 1715. 10. Lydia, July 12, 1717. 11. Eliza, March 12, 1719-20.

(III) Francis Allen, son of Francis (2), was born in Kittery, about 1697, and died prior to 1759. He resided in one of the famous old block houses erected by the early inhabitants as a means of protection against the savages, and the four succeeding generations mentioned in this article were born there. This block house was demolished in 1853. September 17, 1824, he married Mary Pettigrew, born October 12, 1707, daughter of Francis and Elizabeth (Ball-Hammons) Pettigrew. Her father was of French origin, and her mother, who married second, Edward Hammons, was daughter of John and Joanna Ball, of Kittery. Children of Francis and Mary (Pettigrew) Allen: Elijah, see forward; Jedediah; Ezekiel.

(IV) Elijah Allen, son of Francis, was born in Kittery, probably about 1716, and died 1765. He was a tanner by trade, and followed that occupation in connection with farming. He married first, Elizabeth Reed, of Salem, Massachusetts; second, December 7, 1760, Elizabeth Jenkins, widow of Jabez Jenkins, daughter of Ebenezer and Abigail (Hill) Dennett. Elizabeth was born October 22, 1721, and was a descendant of Hugh d'Anet, who was of Norman origin, said to have come into England with William the Conqueror, and many of the name of Dennett in England trace their lineage back six centuries or more. Elijah Allen's children, by first marriage: 1. Jabez, died young. 2. Ephraim, mentioned below. 3. Jacob, born in Kittery, was a revolutionary soldier and a pensioner; was a farmer and lived in North Berwick; reared a large family, and died an aged man. Children of Elijah by second marriage: 1. Elizabeth, born August 22, 1762, married James Neal, Jr., of North Berwick, Maine. 2. Sarah, born January 1, 1764, married James Varney, of Dover, New Hampshire, January 3, 1793.

(V) Ephraim Allen, son of Elijah by first marriage, was born August 16, 1750. He was a tanner and a farmer. In his religious belief he was a Quaker, as were his father and mother. He married Lillis Brown, of Smithfield, Rhode Island; children: 1. Aza, see forward. 2. Anna, born in Kittery, October 30, 1782, married Samuel Breed, of Lynn, and died there aged eighty-nine years. 3. Hannah, born in Kittery, and resided there nearly up to her death, but died in Lynn unmarried. 4. Content, born in Kittery; married Nathaniel Jenkins, and died in Madbury, New Hampshire. 5. Lydia, born May 24, 1791, married Nathan Hanson. 6. Lavina, born in Kittery, 1793; married Benjamin Breed, of Lynn. 7. Sabina, born in Kittery, died young. 8. Moses, died young.

(VI) Aza Allen, son of Ephraim, was born in that part of Kittery now Eliot, December 29, 1780. After concluding his education he taught school and also taught navigation. He was a surveyor of considerable note, and for many years did nearly all the surveying for the town; served as town clerk several years; was regarded as a talented man, and was thoroughly devoted to his home and family. He was originally a Whig in politics, later supported the Anti-slavery movement, in 1844, and voted for the Liberty party candidate for president, James G. Birney, of Ohio. He married, 1821, in North Berwick, Maine, Lydia, daughter of Joshua (5) and Patience (Rogers) Buffum. She was a descendant in the sixth generation of Robert (1) and Tamson Buffum, who came with their children from Yorkshire or Devonshire about 1638, settling in Salem, Massachusetts, and the line of descent is through Caleb (2), Caleb (3), Joshua (4), and Joshua (5). Children of Aza and Lydia (Buffum) Allen: 1. Statira P., deceased; married Stillman Estes. 2. Matilda B., deceased; married Charles H. Breed, of Lynn. 3. Caroline M., died in Eliot, Maine. 4. Walter B., of whom more later. 5. Martin Read, resides upon the old homestead in Eliot. 6. Mary Ann, died young. 7. Ellwood, died young. 8. Ellwood (2d), died 1875, aged thirty-seven years.

(VII) Walter Brown Allen, son of Aza Allen, was born January 17, 1828, in Eliot, Maine, in the old block house, which had been the birth place of at least five generations of the Allen family. He received his preliminary education in the public schools of his native town and at a Friends' boarding school in Providence, Rhode Island, now known as the Moses Brown school. Possessing a natural ability for mechanical pursuits, he adopted the carpenter's trade, which he followed in Lynn for about three years, and then established himself as a contractor and builder in that city. At the age of twenty-six years he was awarded the contract to erect a church at East Saugus, although considered by some of his contemporaries as being too young for such an undertaking. He completed the work successfully, however, and a few years since had the satisfaction of attending the ceremony commemorating the fiftieth anniversary of its dedication and was one of the speakers on that occasion. During his long and unusually active business career covering a period of more than fifty years, he has erected numerous business blocks and residences, which attest the substantial character of his work. When young he acquired a good knowledge of surveying under the direction of his father and has often found opportunity to apply it to advantage. For several years he has devoted a large part of his time to the care of his real estate, which consists of valuable city property. In 1862, after serving several years in the capacity of ward officer, Mr. Allen was elected a member of the common council, serving two years, and for the three succeeding years was a member of the board of aldermen. He was a member of the City Hall building committee, and during the three years of its construction served as its secretary. For seven years from 1869 he was annually elected a member of the school board, and he also is an ex-member of the Massachusetts legislature. Through all his political career he never failed of an election when nominated, a conclusive fact of his popularity, and has voted at every national, state and city election up to the present time (1908), fifteen times for president and fifty-seven times for governor. Being strongly anti-slavery, his first presidential vote was cast for John P. Hale, of New Hampshire, the Free Soil candidate. He was enthusiastically active in the Fremont campaign in 1856, and was a member of the Republican city committee in 1860, the first Lincoln campaign.

Mr. Allen is a member of the Friends' church, of Lynn; a charter member of Lynn Historical Society, life member of Essex County Agricultural Society, charter member of Old Men's Home Corporation, member of Old Ladies' Home Corporation, member of Lynn Board of Trade, and for many years director of the Saugus Mutual Fire Insurance Company. Early in the history Mr. Allen became identified with the Houghton Horticultural Society, a local institution which has for its object not only the encouragement of the cultivation of fruit and flowers, but the planting of ornamental trees and the efforts that tend to raise the standard of civic pride. He served as president of this society for ten years. About thirty years ago Mr. Cyrus M. Tracey originated the idea of obtaining a portion of the Lynn woods for the purpose of

Walter B. Allen

having a public park for the city. Mr. Allen was then a member of the Houghton Horticultural Society, and he endorsed and entered heartily into this movement with Mr. Tracey and others, assisting financially and otherwise toward the object which soon grew into popular favor and eventually resulted in the city taking an active part in the matter and obtaining the land for the beautiful park now known as Lynn Woods Park. Mr. Allen went to Maine and from the woods of the old Allen homestead he took up a number of trees of different varieties, brought them to Lynn and planted them in the new park where they have since continued to flourish. Among them were some Norway pines which are now over fifty feet high.

Mr. Allen married, October 14, 1858, Eliza M. Fry, daughter of Homer and Patience (Boyce) Fry, of Lynn, and sister of the late Brigadier-General Charles Coffin Fry (see Fry). Children: 1. Carrie M., born in Lynn, July 25, 1859, educated in Lynn and Providence; married, 1883, Louis A. Aldrich, of Lynn; he died 1886; one child, Florence Buffum Aldrich. 2. Walter Frank, born October 12, 1863, educated in Lynn common and high school, one year at Moses Brown school at Providence, Rhode Island, after which he became engaged at the carpenter's trade with his father for a time, then entered the furniture business as a dealer and is now a manager of the sales department of a large furniture house in Boston; he married Annie Decator, of Malden; children: Francis Ellwood, Elizabeth Gertrude, Albert D. Allen. 3. Charles Edward, born July 3, 1869, educated in Lynn, after which he began in the electrical business in a small way, later working up to a position where he formed the company of Sampson & Allen; he died November 30, 1901.

On October 15, 1908, Mr. and Mrs. Allen celebrated the fiftieth anniversary of their marriage, upon which occasion there were present their two children, four grandchildren and some three hundred guests from all over the New England states; among the number were twelve who had been present at their marriage fifty years before. The presents were numerous, and the occasion one to be long remembered.

FRY Brigadier-General Charles Coffin Fry (deceased) was born in Lynn, Massachusetts, May 31, 1842, son of Homer Fry, of Bolton, Massachusetts, and Patience (Boyce) Fry, a native of Lynn. Like the majority of those of his name in New England he may have been a descendant of General Joseph Fry, founder of Fryeburg, Maine, who was born in Andover, Massachusetts, in April 1711; was an ensign in the army that captured Louisburg in 1745; colonel in the British army at the capture of Fort William Henry by Montcalm in 1747; attained the rank of brigadier-general in the revolutionary war and died in Fryeburg in 1794. Charles Coffin Fry's parents and ancestors were members of the Society of Friends.

Charles Coffin Fry was educated in the public schools of Lynn, and after graduating from the high school he entered the shoe business with which he was connected for a number of years. Later he was employed by the Lynn Gas Light Company, of which he became treasurer in 1880, and still later served in the same capacity for their successors, the Lynn Gas and Electric Light Company. In 1862 he enlisted in the Eighth Regiment Massachusetts Volunteer Infantry for service in the civil war, and was appointed corporal. He served in the department of North Carolina, under General John C. Foster; was subsequently with the army of the Potomac in Maryland, with which he continued until the expiration of his term of enlistment in 1863. From 1865 to 1874 he served as first lieutenant of Company I, Eighth Regiment Massachusetts Volunteer Militia; was adjutant of same regiment, 1874-75; major of Seventh Battalion 1876-77-78; adjutant of Eighth Regiment, 1879-80-81, and assistant adjutant-general Second Brigade, 1882-97. He was in the latter year retired, at his own request, with the rank of brigadier-general, having rendered efficient military service both to the state and to the nation for a period of thirty-two years. His devotion to the Massachusetts militia was second to no other interest, and he emphasized this in a most graceful manner by writing an able and comprehensive "History of the Second Massachusetts Volunteer Militia." In politics General Fry was a Republican, and his marked ability in various directions made him an exceedingly eligible candidate for public offices. His long and honorable service in behalf of the city began in 1876 as city auditor, and for the two succeeding years he acted as city marshal. In the years 1896-97-98 he was a member of the common council; was a member of the board of aldermen 1899-1900 and 1901, and president of that body the latter year. For five years he served upon the committees on finance, and for various periods upon the committees on education, ordinances, public grounds, water supply, license, the police and fire departments. For many years he was an active member of Mt. Carmel Lodge, F A. M.; Sutton Chapter, R. A. M.; Zebulon Council, R. S. M.; Olivet Commandery K. T.—all of Lynn; LaFayette Lodge of Perfection; George F. Yaters Council, Princes of Jerusalem; Mt. Olivet Chapter, Rose Croix; Massachusetts Consistory; and Aleppo Temple, Order of the Mystic Shrine; Grand Commandery of Knights Templar, of Massachusetts and Rhode Island; Grand Encampment of the United States, and an honorary member of the Most Supreme Council, Northern Masonic Jurisdiction, Thirty-third degree. His official Masonic record is as follows: Worshipful master of Mount Carmel Lodge, 1876-77; eminent commander Olivet Commandery, 1882-83; right eminent grand commander of Knights Templar of Massachusetts and Rhode Island, 1893-94; president of Massachusetts Union of Knights Templars Commanders, 1896-97. He was a member of the Park Club, of Lynn, and its president for the years 1892-93-94; the Oxford Club of that city; and a comrade of General Lander Post No. 5, Grand Army of the Republic. General Fry died March 31, 1901. He was unmmaried.

PEARSON Deacon John Pearson (1), immigrant ancestor, came to New England from county Essex, England. He settled at Rowley, Massachusetts Bay, and became a leading citizen. He was a town officer in 1649 and was elected to various positions of trust and honor. A pious and godly man, he was elected the first deacon of the Rowley church. He was admitted a freeman in 1647, and was a deputy to the general court in 1678 and afterward. He married Dorcas ——— who survived him. He made a will, but it is not extant. The widow Dorcas declined administration May 19, 1694, the son John also declined July 28 following and the sons Jeremiah and Stephen undertook the charge and gave bond August 6 following. The inventory is dated January 11, 1693-94, shortly after his death. Children, born at Rowley: 1. Mary, May 26, 1643. 2. John, December 27, 1644. 3. Elizabeth. 4. Samuel, July 29, 1648, resided in Newbury; married ——— Poor and D. Johnson. 5. Dorcas. 6. Mary, February 17, 1651-52. 7. Jeremy, October 25, 1653. 8. Sarah. 9. Joseph, August 21, 1656. 10. Benjamin, born April 6, 1858, mentioned below. 11. Phebe, April 13, 1660. 12. Stephen, 1663. 13. Sarah, May 6, 1666.

(II) Benjamin Pearson, son of Deacon John Pearson (1), born in Rowley, April 6, 1658, died in 1731. He married, 1680, Hannah Thurston. Children, born in Rowley: 1. Hannah, 1681. 2. Phebe, 1682. 3. Daniel, 1684. 4. Ruth. 5. Abigail, 1689. 6. Benjamin, 1690, died 1774. 7. Sarah, 1691. 8. Jedediah, 1694. 9. Mehitable, 1695. 10. Jonathan, 1699. 11. David, 1702, mentioned below. 12. Oliver, born in Newbury, 1704. 13. Bartholomew.

(III) David Pearson, son of Benjamin Pearson (2), born in Rowley in 1702, was a resident of Newbury, Massachusetts. Children: 1. Eliphalet, born 1752, died 1826; resided at Byfield, Newbury, graduate of Harvard College in 1773, professor of Phillips Academy, Andover, 1778-86, professor of Hebrew at Harvard 1786-1806, ordained 1806, earliest professor at Andover Theological Seminary; died at Greenland, New Hampshire, 1826; one son Henry B. 2. Joseph, mentioned below. 3. Dr. Abiel, born 1756, at Byfield, resided at Andover; died 1827. 4. Jesse, born 1762, removed to Pittsburg, Pennsylvania, in 1790; married ——— Plummer; son Samuel, born 1806; son Frank M., resided in Washington, D. C. 5. Ebenezer. 6. Mary, married ——— Jewett.

(IV) Joseph Pearson, son of David Pearson (3), was born in Newbury in 1755. He was a soldier in the revolution in 1775 in Captain Jacob Gerrish's company, Colonel Moses Little's regiment.

(V) Joseph Pearson, son or nephew of Joseph Pearson (4), born in Andover, September 5, 1792, and died there July 15, 1841. He married, October 24, 1814, Sally F. Pearson, born September 25, 1789, died February 11, 1853. Children, born at Andover: 1. Sarah J., born September 23, 1816, married George Pearson. 2. Hannah T., born February 21, 1818, married Albert Bancroft and lived on the homestead. 3. Joseph James, born February 5, 1820, mentioned below. 4. Mary E., born December 29, 1822, married Herbert Currier.

(VI) Joseph James Pearson, son of Joseph Pearson (5), born in Andover, February 5, 1820, died January 11, 1894. He was educated in the district schools of his native town, and spent his youth on the homestead helping his father. He sold his share in the estate to his sisters after his father died and hired a farm in Andover on a twenty-year lease. He bought the farm on which his sons are now living and greatly improved it. The house was built in 1855, and a small barn. He attended the old South Congregational church. He married, at Boston, in 1845, Dorcas Ricker

Residence of George H. Pearson, Andover, Mass.

Chadwick, of South Berwick, Maine, born October 11, 1824, died December 14, 1901. Children, born in Andover: 1. George Henry, October 12, 1848, mentioned below. 2. Fred J., June 11, 1855; has always resided on the homestead and has charge of the milk route owned by the family. 3. Frank J., June 11, 1855, twin brother of Fred J.; married Charlotte Ward; he died October 25, 1905; remained on the homestead all his life.

(VII) George Henry Pearson, son of Joseph James Pearson (6), was born in Andover, October 12, 1848, on what is known as Sunset Place farm, then under lease by their father. He was educated in the public schools. He began in early youth to work on the farm and continued with his father as long as he lived. Since the death of his father in 1894 the farm has been carried on by Mr. Pearson and his two brothers, one of whom has since died. The farm to which the family removed in 1865 consists of two hundred acres of land and is known as the High Hill farm. They do general farming, dealing to some extent in wood and lumber, and having an extensive dairy and milk route. They have some forty cows in their dairy. Mr. Pearson is a Republican in politics, and a Congregationalist in religion. He married, March 14, 1895, Margaret Warcup, born October 6, 1869, at Leeds, Province of Quebec, Canada. They have no children.

(For early generations see John Hill 1).

HILL

(III) Joseph Hill, son of John Hill, was born about 1657, according to deposition he made September 27, 1682, that he was about twenty-five years of age. He was then a constable. In 1685 he sold to John Smart a farm at Oyster River, which he had bought of his father. John Hill. He married first, in Kittery, Maine, about 1688, Catherine Knight, and settled in Dover, where he bought land of Job Clements in 1689. He sold this, and a grant which he had received from the town in 1694, to John Downing, in 1699. Exception is made in the deed to "a rod square, where my former wife and children are buried." He married second, before 1699, Susanna, daughter of Christopher Beedle. In 1696 he bought land at Long Reach, in Kittery. His will was dated January 30, 1712-3, and proved July 1, 1713. Children: 1. Samuel, mentioned below. 2. Joseph, married July 17, 1725, Sarah Dennett. 3. John. 4. Elizabeth, married December 9, 1714, John Emerson. 5. Hannah, married August 5, 1720, Thomas Hutchins. 6. Abigail, married January 30, 1723-4, Thomas Ham. 7. Catherine, married Edward Ordway, of Haverhill. 8. Mary, married, January 20, 1732-3, Samuel Jackson, of Portsmouth. 9. Dorcas, married, 1729, Joshua Remick. 10. Sarah, married March 2, 1727, Nathaniel Jackson, of Portsmouth.

(IV) Samuel Hill, son of Joseph Hill, married December 23, 1721, Hannah, daughter of Francis and Hannah (Jenkins) Allen. He was a Friend. He inherited land on the upper side of Cammock's Creek, in Eliot. His will was made in 1764 and proved in 1775. Children: 1. Joseph mentioned below. 2. Isaac, married first, Lydia Roberts; second, Elizabeth Estes. 3. Simeon, married, 1745, Rebecca Austin. 4. Miriam, married, 1751, Nathaniel Austin. 5. Ruth, married ——— Spinney. 6. Huldah, married May 9, 1744, Moses Sawyer. 7. Jerusha.

(V) Joseph Hill, son of Samuel Hill, removed in 1773 to Beech Ridge, in Berwick, Maine. He married first, 1744, Miriam Sawyer; second, Mary Breed. Children: 1. Stephen, commander of a privateer; died at sea. 2. Miriam, died young. Children of second wife: 3. Mark, lived on Beech Ridge. 4. Amos, mentioned below. 5. Abner, married Susanna Thayer; removed to New York. 6. John, born April 15, 1770; died in Vermont, in 1840. 7. Sarah, married Ephraim Gary, of Sanford. 8. Lydia, married William Frost, of Sanford. 9. Miriam, married Stephen Staples. 10. Daughter, married Joseph Winslow, of Windham, Maine.

(VI) Amos Hill, son of Joseph Hill, was born at North Berwick. He married December 30, 1790, Mercy, born March 8, 1771, daughter of Timothy and Abigail (Hussey) Varney. Children, as recorded in Dover, where dates vary a little from those given in the record at North Berwick: 1. Lebbeus, born January 28, 1792; died January 22, 1816. 2. Oliver, born September 26, 1794; removed to Sandwich, New Hampshire. 3. Comfort, born February 26, 1796; married Amasa Varney, of Dover, New Hampshire. 4. Sarah, born May 7, 1798; married Benijah Varney, of Dover. 5. Mary, born April 4, 1800; married Jedediah Felch, of Sandwich, New Hampshire. 6. Isaiah Breed, born November 18, 1804, died in Melrose, Massachusetts. 7. Mercy, born March, 1807, died in Lynn, Massachusetts. 8. Timothy Varney, born December 28, 1808; died in North Berwick. 9. Abner, born March 6, 1810; mentioned below. 10. Huldah, born March 22, 1814; died November 16, 1814.

(VII) Abner Hill, son of Amos Hill, was born in North Berwick, Maine, March 6, 1810. He received a common school education, and at an early age went to Lynn, Massachusetts, where he worked on the farm of George Hood, the first mayor of Lynn. This farm was one of the best in Lynn, and was famous for its orchards and gardens. During the time that Mr. Hill worked here he started the first milk route in Lynn, building up a large trade and was very successful. Some years later Mr. Hill left Mr. Hood's farm and went to Derry, New Hampshire, where he purchased a farm, and carried it on under the most improved methods. After seven years he was burned out, losing all, and removed again to Lynn. He bought several acres of farm land, which is now used for circus grounds. Here he remained the rest of his life, running the farm with success. The farm was considered one of the best in the town, and was developed by his own hard work and good management. He was a man known widely and highly respected. He died in Lynn, 1867. In politics he was Republican, but never held office. He was of the old Quaker faith, but owing to his marriage out of this faith, he was according to the customs of the Quaker denomination "read out of church," after which he attended the Methodist church. He married, in Lynn, Martha Ann, daughter of Abner and Mary (Richardson) Hood. Her father was born in Nahant and her mother in Lynn. They had four children: 1. Charles G., died 1892. 2. Edwin L., mentioned below. 3. Henry M. (twin), married Ellen Porter, of Lynn; children: Henry, Melville and Mabel. 4. Hermoine Adelaide (twin), married Franklin Pike, of Lynn; he died in Saugus, December 2, 1905; children: i. Mary Adelaide, married John Honeywell, she died in Lynn, 1892; ii. John Henry, born in Lynn, married Mary Lavery, of Philadelphia; children: James, George, John, Frank, Mary, Sydney and Ellen; iii. Martha Ann, born Lynn; married Henry E. Wrigley, of Newark, New Jersey; had Hermoine and Robert R.

(VIII) Edwin Libbeus Hill, son of Abner Hill, was born in Lynn, December 3, 1838. When he was eight years old he removed to Derry, New Hampshire, with the family and attended school there. When he was sixteen he was apprenticed for three years to learn the trade of shoe cutting in Lynn. He worked at his trade several years, and then began to manufacture boots and shoes on his own account. His shop was in the old Union Block at first, and he employed five journeymen. He sold out his business after a few years and returned to the bench and worked as a cutter in Doherty's factory, Bubier's and Spinney's. In 1865 he established himself in the retail milk business in Lynn, and continued with uninterrupted success for a period of seventeen years. He was one of the most successful men in this line of business in the city of Lynn. After he disposed of his milk route he devoted his time and attention to real estate, buying and selling much property and acquiring through business and investment a handsome competence. He has been retired from active business since 1875 at Lynn. In politics Mr. Hill is a Republican, and has always taken a lively interest in municipal affairs. He has been a useful citizen in the various walks of life. In religion he is a Methodist. He married, at Manchester-by-the-Sea, 1866, Charlotte Rust, born at Manchester, daughter of William Choate and Eliza (Lee) Rust, of Gloucester, Massachusetts. Her mother was born in Manchester. Children, born in Lynn: 1. Clara Benton, married Elvin Varney, of Dover, New Hampshire, an electrician; child, Gladys. 2. Lilla Lee, resides at home, unmarried. 3. Josephine, married Fred O. Richmond, of Lynn; she taught in the public schools of Lynn eight years. 4. L. Gertrude, resides at home, unmarried.

William Rust, father of Mrs. Hill, was born in Gloucester, but removed when very young to Manchester-by-the-Sea, and became a fisherman. He then learned the trade of cabinet maker and followed it throughout his active life in Manchester, where he died. In politics he was a Republican, in religion Orthodox. Children, born at Manchester: 1. William C. Rust, lives at Manchester. 2. David Rust, died in Minnesota. 3. George Rust, died at Manchester. 4. Charles Rust, lives in Philadelphia, Pennsylvania. 5. Ann Eliza Rust, married Joseph Lee, of Manchester, and later of San Diego, California, where his widow resides; children: i. Josephine Lee, died young; ii. Lottie A., married William H. Morse, of Holliston, Massachusetts, now of San Diego, California.

(For preceding generations see Barnard Hutchinson 1).

HUTCHINSON (XVI) Nathaniel Chickering Hutchinson, son of Osgood and Hannah (Fuller) Hutchinson, was born in Francistown, New Hampshire, July 3, 1811, died in Lynn, Massachusetts, October 15, 1875. He married, October 27, 1833, Rebecca J. Lyons, born in Marblehead, Massachusetts, and died in Lynn, August 11, 1904, daughter of Captain John and Rebecca (Selman) Lyons, of Marblehead. Rebecca J. Lyon Hutchinson was the oldest member of the Congregational church. Nathaniel Chickering and Rebecca J. (Lyons) Hutchinson had four children, all born in Lynn: 1. William Henry, born March 25, 1834, died March 23, 1902. 2. George, born March 13, 1837, died January 31, 1861. 3. James, born July 7, 1848; died young. 4. Abbie Jane, died August 3, 1900; married Frank Robinson.

(XVII) William Henry Hutchinson, son of Nathaniel Chickering and Rebecca J. (Lyons) Hutchinson, was born in Lynn, Massachusetts, March 25, 1834, and died in that city March 23, 1902, after a long, honorable and entirely successful business career. When old enough to work he learned the trade of painting with his father, who himself was a practical workman in that line, and when he attained his majority purchased his father's interest in the business and carried it on for several years. Gradually, as his means would permit, he branched out in other mercantile lines and established what afterward became one of the largest concerns in the general hardware and builders' material trade in Essex county, while he came to be regarded as one of the most capable and progressive men of Lynn. In addition to his interests in Lynn, which he always kept under personal supervision, Mr. Hutchinson made considerable investments in other enterprises, and was for a number of years senior partner of the firm of Hutchinson & Kimball, coal dealers in Brockton, Massachusetts. He took a commendable interest in public affairs in Lynn, although not in the sense of being a politician. He was a member of the city council in 1890-91, alderman in 1892-93, and again in 1899, and was a representative from Lynn to the lower house of the general court in 1894-95. While in the legislature he was a member of the committee on banks and banking and on parishes and churches. He was a director of the Lynn National Bank and a trustee of the Lynn Safe Deposit and Trust Company, vice-president of the Asbury Grove Camp Meeting Association, and a consistent member of the Boston Street Methodist Episcopal Church of Lynn, and chairman of its board of trustees. Mr. Hutchinson always found relief from business cares in his favorite recreation of hunting and fishing, and he was a true sportsman, having hunted nearly every kind of game in this country, always in proper season and never did he permit his enthusiasm as either hunter or fisherman to indulge in the wanton killing of game of any kind. He loved the pleasures of travel, and his trips and excursions took him over the whole country and even across the Atlantic ocean. Only a few years before his death he visited the Holy Land, and many parts of Europe were quite familiar to him. Mr. Hutchinson married Jane Howard Howes, daughter and one of ten children of Samuel Howes, who was born in Anson, Maine, and who married Sarah Abbot, who was born in Sidney, Maine. Four children were born of this marriage.

(XVIII) W. Howard Hutchinson, eldest child of William Henry and Jane Howard (Howes) Hutchinson, was born in Lynn, Massachusetts, February 4, 1860, received his education in the public and high schools of that city, and after leaving school began his business career as clerk in his father's store. In 1902, after the death of his father, he assumed the entire management of the business for the estate, and still continues in that capacity. He is a member of various subordinate Masonic bodies, the lodge and chapter, also of Olivet Commandery, Knights Templar, and is a Republican in politics. He married Mary Nellie Black, of Lynn. By a former marriage Mr. Hutchinson has one child, Marion J. Hutchinson, born April 23, 1885.

(XVIII) Samuel Chickering Hutchinson, son of William Henry and Jane Howard (Howes) Hutchinson, was born in Lynn, February 15, 1864, was educated in the Lynn schools and after leaving school began a clerkship in his father's store which continued about eighteen years. In 1900 he organized the Hutchinson Lumber Company, secured its incorporation and became its president, treasurer and general manager. The company was founded largely with his capital, and he is its principal stockholder as well as its active managing head. Mr. Hutchinson is a business man, with little time or inclination for political participation, although he is a strong Republican. He is a member of Golden Fleece Lodge, Free and Accepted Masons, and other subordinate bodies of the order, and also is a Knight Templar. He married Mabel Abbot, who was born in Lynn, January 13, 1873, daughter of Frederick Everett and Eunice Maria (Bassett) Abbot, the former born October 23, 1836, died March 9, 1903, and the latter born March 30, 1843. Mr. and Mrs. Hutchinson have no children.

(XVIII) Jennie Howes Hutchinson, only daughter of William Henry and Jane Howard (Howes) Hutchinson, was born in Lynn, December 1, 1865, and married, May 26, 1886, Rufus Henry Kimball, who was born in Bridgewater (now Brockton), Massachusetts, April 5, 1854. Mr. and Mrs. Kimball have two children, Howard Hutchinson Kimball, born in Lynn, September 1, 1887, and Marjorie Kimball, born in Lynn, September 10, 1894.

(XVIII) James Abbot Hutchinson, son and youngest child of William Henry and Jane Howard (Howes) Hutchinson, was born in Lynn, Massachusetts, May 20, 1874. He was educated in the public and high schools of that city and graduated from Yale College A. B., 1896. His business career was begun as a clerk in the office of Keck, Mosser & Company, dealers in leather, where he remained between one and two years and later he continued with the successor firm of William F. Mosser & Company until 1902. In the year last mentioned Mr. Hutchinson secured a clerical position with the Boston house of Vermilye & Company, bankers and brokers, and continued in the employ of that firm five years. Two years of this time was spent in the Boston branch office, where he had charge of the office of McKay & Company, and about two and one-half years in the New York city office of Vermilye & Company. In March, 1908, Mr. Hutchinson began business in Boston on his own account as broker and bond dealer, but maintains his residence in Lynn. He married, May 11, 1905, Mary Knowlton Whiton, who was born in Plainfield, New Jersey, February 17, 1878, daughter of John Milton and Mary Elizabeth (Bond) Whiton, of Boston. Mr. and Mrs. Hutchinson have two children, James Abbot, Jr., born in Plainfield, New Jersey, January 25, 1906, and John Whiton, born in Plainfield, April 9, 1907.

CHASE The surname Chase is undoubtedly derived from the French *Chasser* (to hunt). The ancestral seat in England was at Chesham in Rockinghamshire, through which runs a rapidly flowing brook or river, the Chess.

(I) William Chase, immigrant ancestor, came from England with Winthrop in 1630. Thomas and Aquila Chase, who settled at Hampton, New Hampshire, in 1639, were brothers, and perhaps cousins of William Chase, the first comer. The record of Rev. John Eliot, the Indian Apostle, of "such as adjoined themselves to this church," the first church of Roxbury, has this entry: "William Chase, he came with the first company, bringing with him his wife Mary and his son William." The maiden name of his wife is not known. The son William was about seven years old at the time of migration. The father applied for admission as a freeman October 19, 1630. He was a town officer at Roxbury. He served against the Narragansetts in 1645. He removed to Yarmouth, Massachusetts, in 1638, and died there. His will was dated May 4, 1659, and states that he was aged. It was proved May 13, 1659. He bequeathed to his wife Mary and two sons, Benjamin and William. His daughter Mary was buried at Barnstable, October 28, 1652. The early records of the town of Yarmouth were destroyed by fire, so that it is impossible to give the dates and birth of all his children.

(II) William Chase, son of William Chase, was born in England about 1623 and removed with his father's family to Yarmouth in 1638. He died there February 27, 1685. Children, born at Yarmouth: 1. William, married first, Hannah Sherman; second, December 6, 1732, Priscilla Perry. 2. Jacob, married Mary ———. 3. John, married, 1674, Elizabeth Baker. 4. Elizabeth, married, May 27, 1674, Daniel Baker. 5. Abraham, married Elizabeth ———. 6. Joseph, married, February 28, 1694, Sarah Sherman. 7. Benjamin, married, September 21, 1696, Amy Borden. 8. Samuel, mentioned below.

(III) Samuel Chase, son of William Chase, was born in Yarmouth and married, in 1699, Sarah Sherman, daughter of Samuel and Martha (Tripp) Sherman. Children: 1. Phebe, born January 22, 1700; married, December 6, 1720, Edward Slead. 2. Martha, February 24, 1702, married first, June 5, 1722, Ezekiel Fowler; second, May 11, 1749, Samuel Bowen. 3. Susanna, April 7, 1704, married, July 5, 1726, William Buffinton. 4. Elisha, May 5, 1706, married first, October 20, 1726, Elizabeth Wheaton; second, January 16, 1746, Sarah Tucker. 5. Samuel, January 20, 1710, married, August 13, 1730, Abigail Buffum. 6. Eleazer, April 27, 1711, married, May 26, 1730, Ruth Perry. 7. Philip, August 20, 1715, mentioned below. 8. John, December 8, 1720, married, January 18, 1744, Lydia Luther. 9. Sarah, married Daniel Baker.

(IV) Philip Chase, son of Samuel Chase, was born in Yarmouth, August 20, 1715. He married, November 18, 1735, Hannah Buffum. He resided in Swansea, Massachusetts. He had a son Samuel, mentioned below.

(V) Samuel Chase, son of Philip Chase, was born probably at Swansea, about 1755, and died March 20, 1825, at Lynn, Massachusetts. He was a cordwainer by trade, and belonged to the Quaker church at Lynn. He married there, September 27, 1780, Alice, who died July 15, 1817, daughter of John and Hannah Mower. Children, born at Lynn: 1. Thorndike, March 1, 1782, married (intentions dated October 22, 1807) Betsey Pierce, of Bolton. 2. Phebe, October 1, 1784, married, May 10, 1812, Samuel Carter. 3. Mary, February 26, 1788. 4. John, February 26, 1790, died October 27, 1791. 5. John, March 26, 1792, mentoned below. 6. Lydia, August 15, 1795, died October 6, 1797. 7. Philip, November 27, 1798, married, September 10, 1828, Roxanna Wilkins.

(VI) John Chase, son of Samuel Chase, was born at Lynn, March 26, 1792. He was a Quaker. He married first, Mary Pierce, of Bolton. He married second, intentions dated November 22, 1817, Esther Myrick, of Charlestown. She died March 29, 1824, and he married third, intentions dated October 24, 1824, Sarah, born June 16, 1816, daughter of James and Sarah (Wells) Lakeman (Lynn records). He was educated in the public schools of Lynn, and learned the trade of shoemaker. He built a shop of his own on High street, and made shoes the remainder of his life, having worked at a bench in the shoe shop, a period of seventy years. He was a Whig in politics, later a Free Soiler, and then joined the Republcan party, taking an active interest in city affairs. Late in life he joined the Methodist church. Children: 1. Mary Pierce, born at Bolton, October 19, 1813, died October 4, 1835. 2. Esther, born at Lynn, October 3, 1823, married Walter Sisson; one son, Walter. 3. John Henry, born August 27, 1825, died September 13, 1825. 4. Andrew Clarkson, born August 28, 1826, married first, Lucy Jewett, of Ipswich; two children: Ida and Alice. 5. Wesley Fillmore, born March 27, 1828, mentioned below. 6. Alice Lucilla, born September 10, 1830, died May 10, 1833.

(VII) Wesley Fillmore Chase, son of John Chase, was born at Lynn, March 27, 1828, died November 16, 1908. He was educated in the public schools. He began to work with his father at the shoemaker's trade at the age of twelve years and continued in his employ until he was twenty-four. He then worked at shoemaking for two years at Wood End, Lynn. He returned to the city and was for seven years employed in the boot and shoe factory of B. F. Spinney and afterward in the factories of Mr. Kimball, of Joseph Davis for ten years and Brewer & Parker, where he worked until 1904, when he retired. In politics he was originally a Whig, but was a Republican from the time that party was organized until his death, performing much active work. He attended the Methodist church at Lynn. He was identified with the hand tub firemen's brigade, and was a member of the City of Lynn Veteran Firemen's organization, besides belonging to other fraternal organizations. He married, June 27, 1852, Mary A. Parrott, of Lynn, born August 1, 1834, daughter of William and Mary (Palfry) Parrott, of Salem. Children, born in Lynn: 1. John W., born December 12, 1853, resides in Lowell, Massachusetts; with the Goodale Drug Company of that city; married Marie Wallace, of New York. 2. Charles Wesley, June 10, 1855, died aged six years. 3. Charles Wesley, March 30, 1866, died in infancy. 4. Addie May, May 29, 1867; married Frank Lewis Cass, of Rockport, Massachusetts. Mr. Cass came to Lynn when young; he was educated in the public schools; learned the leather business with the firm of John B. Alley & Company, of Boston. Later he was in the employ of Frank Hilliard, of Lynn. Since 1893 he has been a partner of the firm of Breed & Cass, manufacturers of cut soles, Lynn. In politics he is a Republican, and in religion reared a Quaker. Children: 1. May W. Cass, born October 3, 1889. 2. Anna S. Cass, April 2, 1891. 3. Charles F. Cass, April 8, 1893, died May 25, 1894. 4. Hazel L. Cass, February 12, 1897. 5. William R. Cass, September 10, 1898. 6. Florence A. Cass, May 21, 1900, died January 8, 1901.

WILLSON (I) John Willson, immigrant ancestor of this family, was one of the numerous Scotch-Irish pioneers of this name who came to New England from the north of Ireland, after 1718. He lived in Upton, Worcester county, near the Scotch-Irish settlement of Hopkinton in Middlesex, where many Scotch-Irish located. Later in life he returned to the north of Ireland, and died there December 29, 1774. He married Jane (maiden name not known). Children: 1. Robert, born February 2, 1729; mention below. 2. Jane, born March 18, 1730-1, at Marlborough; married Joseph Stewart. 3. John, Jr., born December 3, 1732, at Marlborough; settled at Putney, Vermont; married first, Lucy Stewart, May 10, 1757; second, Molly Graham. 4. Joseph, born at Upton, August 6, 1737. 5. Elizabeth, born March 24, 1739, at Upton; married Joseph Lyttle, May 29, 1764. 6. Mary, born at Upton, October 17, 1742; married Abraham Hunter, February 27, 1764.

(II) Robert Willson, son of John Willson, was born in Ireland, February 2, 1729. According to family tradition he came over from Ireland when forty weeks old, with his parents. He was a cordwainer (shoemaker) by trade and a farmer, a sturdy, upright man. He was very anxious that his grandson should become a minister, but died before his wish was fulfilled. Both grandson and great-grandson were preachers. He died at New Braintree, April 16, 1801, aged seventy-two years. He lived in New Braintree for many years. He married Martha Dunlap, a native of the north of Ireland, who died July 9, 1808. Children, born in New Braintree: 1. Joseph, January 16, 1762; mentioned below. 2. Samuel, January 8, 1764.

(III) Joseph Willson, son of Robert Willson, was born in New Braintree, January 16, 1762, and died there June 3, 1844. He was educated in the common schools of New Braintree, and followed farming there, and in the adjacent town of Leicester, where he lived for a short time. He was a member of the Congregational church (orthodox) and a useful and influential citizen. He married, April 18, 1782, Sarah Matthews, at New Braintree. She was born October 3, 1763, and died June 16, 1802. Children, born at New Braintree: 1. Luther, mentioned below. 2. Melissa, died April 21, 1795.

(IV) Rev. Luther Willson, son of Joseph Willson, was born in New Braintree, April 26, 1783. Much of the matter relating to the life of Rev. Luther Willson and his son, Rev. Edmund Burke Willson, some of which will be quoted, is taken from a memoir of the latter by Robert S. Rantoul, in the Essex Institute Historical Collections for 1895. Luther Willson attended the public schools and Leicester Academy, of which he became principal in course of time, and from which no less than thirty of his descendants have received their education in good part. He prepared for college Governor Emory Washburn, Judge Charles Allen, and many other men who became distinguished in later life. "But not content to follow this career, he fitted himself for the pulpit, and in due time received a license to preach. He had been trained in the strict morality and in the rigid dogma of the century that had closed. But the period was one of mental activity and growth, and Luther Willson was not long in finding out that to conserve what was priceless in the former did not require him to cherish what was worthless in the latter. He had left his ancestral home for the Congregational parish in Brooklyn, the county seat of Windham county, in eastern Connecticut, and here he had grown to be respected and loved. Upon the close of the war of 1812-15 differences of dogma began to assert themselves in the New England Congregational polity, which culminated in a few years in the liberal religious or so-called Unitarian movement. In 1817 Luther Willson was tried for heresy and was convicted, against the protests of a majority of his parishioners and of the eminent theologians of the day who were in sympathy with him. Aaron Bancroft, of Worcester, the historian's father, was among them. Luther Willson was forced by the Consociation of Churches of Windham county to give up his pulpit, and in 1819 found him established over a broader and more independent congregation at Petersham in his native county, but not before he had accepted from Dr. Channing an invitation to pay him an extented visit at the famous parsonage in Boston, and had received from the hand of the great reformer, in recognition of his sturdy manhood, the gift of a watch which remains an heirloom amongst his descendants." The fine old Unitarian meeting house at Petersham, still well preserved, is a landmark of the town. Paul Revere's foundry furnished the bell on the rim of which is cast these lines: "The living to the church I call and to the grave I summon all." He had a long and eminently successful pastorate in Petersham. He died there November 20, 1864. "He was of that limited order of men rare enough always—men of whom the world owes its best—men who are able to make sacrifices cheerfully in behalf of their convictions. Born in the bracing air of the high table-land of central Massachusetts, at the close of the Revolution, and baptized in the spirit of those stirring times, Luther Willson seems to have been, like Jackson and Calhoun and Greeley and many more of our conspicuous men, of Scotch-Irish lineage." He married first, November 30, 1806, Sally Bigelow, born in Waltham, Middlesex county, Massachusetts, daughter of Abijah Bigelow, who was a soldier in the revolution in the battle of Lexington when but nineteen years of age, and when eighty years old went west, where he died twelve years later, after founding with his family the settlement called Bigelow's Mills. The immigrant ancestor of the Bigelow family was among the early settlers of Watertown, of which Waltham was formerly a part. Sally (Bigelow) Willson died in Petersham, January 29, 1826, and Luther Willson married second, December 5, 1827, Fidelia Wells. Children of first wife: 1. Martha Amelia, born November 20, 1807; married September 4, 1831, Aaron Brooks, Jr.; children: i. James W. Brooks, born at Petersham, August 7, 1833; ii. John Brooks, April 29, 1836; iii. Abbie N. Brooks, August 4, 1839; married John Fiske, the historian; iv. Martha W. Brooks, March 27, 1842. 2. William Cowper, born at Leicester, Massachusetts, December 29, 1809; married June 30, 1851, Sara O. Hastings; children: i. William C., born at Ogdensburg, New York, March 12, 1853; ii. Charles H., April 21, 1857. 3. George Campbell, born in Leicester, December 16, 1811; married September 27, 1837, Arethusa Parkhurst; children: i. William P., born December 28, 1838; ii. Juliana, August 19, 1841; iii. Helen, August 20, 1845; iv. George L., November 1, 1848; v. Eugene B., October 18, 1852; vi. Edmund B., June 16, 1855. 4. Sarah Matthews, March 24, 1814; died December 11, 1814, in Brooklyn, Connecticut. 5. Joseph, born October 1, 1816, in Brooklyn, Connecticut; married first, June 3, 1846, Elizabeth O. Weed; children: i. Lucy A., born at Petersham, April 13, 1847; ii. Edmund H., born at Keene, New Hampshire, September 1, 1849; iii. Mary Jane, born at Bellows Falls, August 25, 1851; iv. Joseph Spencer, born at Petersham, March 21, 1856. 6. Zibiah Nelson, born at Brooklyn, September 1, 1818; married August 9, 1837, Joseph L. Partridge; children: i. John N., born at Leicester, September 28, 1838; ii. Joseph L. Partridge, born at Leicester, March 11, 1845; iii. Edward Lassell Partridge, born at West Newton, September 27, 1853. 7. Edmund Burke, born August 15, 1820; mentioned below. 8. Lucy Williams, born at Petersham, August 27, 1822; married January 3, 1849, Charles C. Burr. 9. James, born at Petersham, August 11, 1824, died young. Children of second wife: 10. Frederick Matthews, born at Petersham, April 17, 1830; married April 17, 1856, Mary Arms. 11. Mary Bigelow, born at Petersham, April 7, 1832; married June 13, 1860, George A. Southgate. 12. Sarah Wells, born September 18, 1834; died young. 13. Sarah, born March 4, 1837, never married. 14. Catherine Wells, born May 3, 1841; died young.

(V) Rev. Edmund Burke Willson, son of Rev. Luther Willson, was born in Petersham, August 15, 1820, and died at Salem, Massachusetts, June 13, 1895. "The scenes and duties of school and farm-yard, the simple sports and pastimes of rural New England, filled his opening years. No special event, destined to give direction to the future, marked his young career. An unconquerable diffidence, an affectionate temperament, a deep resentment of wrong done to others, a lively appreciation of music and a keen enjoyment of fun, a quick moral sense, a tender, sympathetic heart, a healthy, well-balanced mind, a manhood that never flinched, and a stalwart independence of character which could by no means be subordinated, for it was part and parcel of his religious nature—these were the furnishings with which Mr. Willson started out to make his way in life. His health was not robust. This interfered with prospects opening before him both at Harvard and at Yale, and led to his retirement from the latter college, on his father's injunction, when he had been there but a single year. But ultimately, under the rugged but congenial tutelage of a dairy farm, his health became confirmed, and while he wavered then, as he did later in life, between the pulpit and the teacher's desk, he at last betook himself under the influence of Henry Ware to the School of Divinity at Cambridge and there received a degree in course with the class of 1843. Ten years later he received from Harvard the honorary degree of Master of Arts, and at the annual visitation of the Divinity School in June, 1874, Mr. Willson was selected as the essayist of the day, and read an address before the Association of the Alumni of the School which earned high praise. He had entered the Divinity School in the summer of 1840, a youth of twenty. An admiring classmate, Rev. Joseph H. Allen, D. D., has said of him as a student: "Candor, modesty and a clear intelligence; a companionable temper, genial and sunny, and a certain grave maturity of character; a mental temperament sound rather than robust, disclosing a rare intellectual quality coupled with a still rarer humility of spirit and deep self-distrust—these were traits as clearly written then on that winning face of his, we have read them in all the decades since—traits perhaps favored by training in a rural academy, which in some points may compare to advantage with the hothouse culture some immature natures undergo in college life." Mr. Willson was ordained the first week of January, 1844, at Grafton, Massachusetts, as minister of the First Unitarian Church. From 1835, when he left Yale, he had been a teacher in Leicester Academy, Westford Academy, in Littleton and Petersham, Massachusetts, in Brooklyn and New Haven, Connecticut, and elsewhere, alternating teaching and study. His first school was at Canterbury, Connecticut, when he was but fifteen years old, and was attended with the usual rough experience looked for when a delicate and ambitious boy was set to master pupils older and larger than he.

But from the time his pastorate at Grafton began, he devoted his entire time and energy to his duties. "Every faculty of his being was consecrated to life-long ministrations of love and peace," said Mr. Rantoul. "Self-distrust seems, indeed, to have been recognized then as always, by those who knew him well, as the stumbling-block in his career. And, judging from the frequency with which he was approached with flattering offers throughout his professional life, it would seem that the public to which he ministered was much more alive than he to the very exceptional fibre and quality of his mind. His views of the pulpit function, though never extreme, were wholly untrammeled and somewhat peculiar to himself. No man should enter the pulpit, he thought, who was not charged with an evangel —conscious of a message. The society which invited his ministrations must respect his earnestness and trust his delicacy. It was not without a meaning that we have built the pulpit higher than the pews. If the utterances of the pulpit were to be dictated by the judgment of the pews, the preacher's highest value must fail of being reached."

His first publication was an historical sermon preached in December, 1846, based upon a study of his parish records. In 1854 he was orator at the exercises to celebrate the centennial of the incorporation of the town of Petersham. Of his address the *Christian Examiner* said at the time of its publication: "It is simple, chaste and graceful in its diction; full, but not redundant in its materials; as enthusiastic as it ought to be for such an occasion and from a son of the town. With prudent but rather provoking discretion, he has refrained from sketching some characters which gave him ample chance for humorous description." The State Historical Society of Wisconsin made him a corresponding member at this time; Bancroft, the historian, assured him in an autograph letter of the pleasure he derived from reading his address at Petersham, while ten years later the *New England Historic Genealogical Register* was holding up this rare production of Mr. Willson's pen as a model for future essays in local history.

Mr. Willson remained at Grafton until 1852. His years in that pastorate were active and fruitful. He took a leading part in the great and momentous struggle for the present free school system of Massachusetts. The public schools were assailed by the Calvinists, as they have been later, by Catholics, because religion is not taught in them. "It as a godless system, so they thought, in that it leaves religion to the home, welcomes the children of the State as the common progeny of that grand old mother —our beloved Commonwealth—who counts them neither Greek nor Jew, barbarian, Scythian, bound or free, but only a precious brood all given her to cherish and advance alike, and which concedes to parents of whatever sect the natural right to indoctrinate their offspring as they will. From evangelical pulpits and from lyceum platforms the advocates of the system were ruthlessly denounced as atheists, as infidels, and as false lights, threatening to mislead the people they professed to serve. But Mr. Willson never wavered in his course; neither at Grafton, where his position on the school committee cost him many friends, at West Roxbury where he became the superintendent of schools, nor afterward at Salem, where he was conspicuous in resisting the enforced observance of Protestant rites in non-sectarian schools as impolitic and unfair." The whole school system was in its experimental stage. Time has justified the stand of Mr. Willson and the system is now well intrenched in popular favor. Scarcely a day passed that he did not visit school in Grafton during term time.

The slavery issue was even more incessant in its call to disagreeable and discouraging duties in the years before the war. Mr. Willson stood in the foremost rank of the foes of slavery. "So clear were his utterances, so searching his clarion tones, so unmistakable the quality of his courage, and his determination to put the interests of the country before any of his own that when Theodore Parker, a few years later, left West Roxbury for the wider field he found in Boston, the inclination of the parish turned toward Mr. Willson, and a successful effort was made to secure his service there. Other pulpits had before invited him. On leaving the Divinity School he had been called to Templeton in his native county, and Meadville too, a seminary of Unitarian theology—an appeal not easy to resist—had at that time swung open her hospitable doors, with offers from the Huidekoper household of pulpit aid and of the freedom of their rare accumulation of books."

He began the West Roxbury pastorate in 1852, and found a congenial congregation. Among other men of his flock of kindred ideas of education, slavery and other questions of the day, he found George R. Russell, who remained a lifelong friend. His sermon on "The Rendition of Anthony Burns," the runaway slave, was published and elicited widespread praise from the anti-slavery camp, and condemnation from the pro-slavery element of the country. Secretary William H. Seward, then active in public life, in the United States Senate, wrote to Mr. Willson: "Your sermon came to me this morning and was immediately read, and it excited a glow of feeling such as in early life the first dramatic picture of suffering virtue produces. Indeed, sir, although it is without art, it is wonderfully, wonderfully eloquent." Theodore Parker wrote: "I thank you heartily for your brave, noble words * * I know what it costs to preach faithfully on such matters." Dr. Gannett and Senator Charles Sumner also commended the sermon. He continued at West Roxbury, resisting all other calls that came frequently, until in 1859 he accepted the call to Salem. Even then he had to leave a congregation that made a unanimous appeal for him to remain. He was invited to come to Hingham, to become colleague of Rev. Dr. Dewey, Boston, and to help build up the liberal faith at Albany, New York. When he left West Roxbury, where he had been superintendent of schools, he received a very flattering testimonial from the teachers. After he was settled at Salem, he was content to stay in that field of labor to the end of his days, refusing to be persuaded to enter new fields. In 1865 a determined effort was made to have him come to Ithaca, New York, a point of exceptional importance on account of Cornell University, but he stayed at his old post. The anti-slavery feeling ran higher. After the convictions of John Brown and his men, a public meeting was called at Salem to raise money to pay the expenses of the trial and interment of John Brown and his convicted raiders. Mr. Willson was the only Salem clergyman to take part. Ralph Waldo Emerson, John A. Andrew, James Freeman Clarke, John G. Whittier and Wendell Phillips were the other speakers. "Clergymen were not numerous at that time who cared to test the hold they had on the affections of their people by taking part in a gathering like that. Neither this nor any subsequent demonstration of his invincible purpose to be free in thought and act, whether made in behalf of co-education in schools, or against the compulsory requirements therein of religious forms, or on the selection of a president, a governor or a mayor, or on any other debated question, be it political, sectarian, social or moral, which for the time being might disturb the public mind—themes on the most stirring of which Mr. Willson never hesitated to be heard—nothing from that time forth ever availed to interrupt, for a day, the perfect accord between the pastor and his flock." When the civil war broke out, he was a staunch supporter of the federal government, and when he was chosen chaplain of the Twenty-fourth Regiment Massachusetts Volunteers, then at St. Augustine, Florida, without his knowledge, he felt constrained to accept the duty in the field. In order that both he and his people might act without constraint he resigned his pastorate, but instead of accepting the resignation, his parishioners made up a generous purse to facilitate his departure and bade him a tearful God-speed. He went by steamer from New York, passing so near the beleaguered city of Charleston that he could see the church spires and the flashes of light as the cannons were fired and the shells exploded. He went ashore at Beaufort, South Carolina, in search of men of his regiment in the hospitals there. He found several and was welcomed by the sufferers. Two on his list had died. He took up his work at St. Augustine with zeal. On the first anniversary of the Emancipation Proclamation he addressed the freedmen. His quarters were in a shambling, two-story parochial school-house without stove or fire-place, attached to a deserted Episcopal Church of St. Augustine, rededicated to the service of the Union army under the name of Trinity Parish Church. In the early days of 1864 the regiment was bivouacked in the spring rains, in a ploughed field within three hours march of the rebel capital and operating against the railroad, the telegraph and the turnpike wagon-trains between Petersburg and Richmond. Voices could be heard in the still night from the Confederate rifle pits; newspapers, coffee and tobacco were exchanged between the armies; the spires of Richmond were in sight. During an engagement on May 24, Lieutenant Clough of his regiment was killed and many were wounded and killed. He was under fire for ten days or more. Picket duty and incessant digging in the trenches as the line advanced toward Richmond, when not actually fighting, prevented the holding of preaching services and finding there was little for him to do as chaplain, he finally resigned, and came home, bringing the regimental flag to the State House, after running the gauntlet of the rebel raid on General Franklin.

"For the thirty years during which he survived the war, Mr. Willson grew steadily in the appreciation of his neighbors and, as the generations marched along, came to be regarded as a Nestor and a Patriarch among men. No gathering was complete without his presence; no feast, no social function wholly happy, without his blessing. Sects forgot their dogmas in recognition of his noble manhood, and when the national convention of the Methodist Episcopal body met in Salem, Mr. Willson was the choice of the Salem pastors to extend their welcome. His was for years the most potent voice in the county conference of his own denomination, and there he received that spontaneous homage which should attend desert. When the Unitarian body, which had achieved a vantage-ground by defying hierarchy in all its forms, and by insisting on the right of private judgment, attempted to rid itself of some obnoxious members whose private judgment led them to results unpalatable to the sect at large, Mr. Willson stood like a rock against the innovation and at the national conference in 1872 which sat at Boston, and planted himself in a position which he lived to see adopted by the national Unitarian conference of 1894 at Saratoga; but which, when he espoused it, cost him the criticism usually meted out to men who dare to stand alone, and called forth an expression of contempt from the New England organ of the denomination itself."

Mr. Willson's field of labor was always larger than his parish. He served eight years on the school board of Salem; was a member of the board of control of the Home for Aged Women and for several years its manager; trustee for fifteen years of the Plummer Farm School—one of the only two clergymen ever appointed to that board. He was one of the corporators of the Salem Savings Bank. No other man has been asked more than once to deliver the Memorial Day oration at Salem, but Mr. Willson was thrice honored in this way. When the Salem Light Infantry Veteran Corps in April, 1886, observed the quarter-century of the departure for the field, he accepted an invitation to march as chaplain for the day, and he marched as chaplain at every subsequent parade until his death. He had been a resident member of the New England Historic Genealogical Society since 1859 and finally became its vice-president for Massachusetts. He had been president of the Salem Athenaeum since 1886. He was a member of the Essex Institute from the time of his coming to Salem, and keenly interested in its work. He contributed memoirs of John Lewis Russell, John Clarke Lee and Charles Timothy Brooks. He became president of the Institute in 1893. He wrote an admirable sketch of the ecclesiastical history of Salem for Hurd's "Essex County History," and a sketch of the North Church and Parish printed by the society in a memorial volume. Mr. Willson was representative to the general court from Salem in 1883-84, serving as chairman of the committee on education and of the committee on parishes and religious societies, and exerting a large and wholesome influence on legislation. He was an officer of many of the local charitable organizations.

"And so" says Mr. Rantoul, "this rare and admirable man rounded out his full half-century of duty in the church and on the thirty-sixth anniversary of his installation here—a day to which, year after year, for a whole generation, he had looked forward with a manly pride—this noble man, gazing into the upturned faces of the people he had served so well—some born and grown, some mellowed and grown older under his gracious charge—moved by the tender memories of those gone before—and speaking at the altar words of benediction which he meant to be his last—faltered and fainted at his post and, lingering a little, passed away. At his simple funeral the needy and the humble bore testimony by their presence that they had lost a friend, and mourners of every station felt their kinship for an hour at his bier. The clergy of the town forgot their differing creeds and made known their sorrow in a formal vote." "A conservative by instinct, whose face was ever turning toward the future; a devotee of progress" wrote Mr. Rantoul, "who adored and reverenced the past; hopeful without optimism, cautious without timidity; a balanced thinker, broad enough to know that there is a reverse to every shield, and that the sphere of truth has sides beyond the ken of any single eye; gentle with the erring; human nature could not sink so low as to escape the recognition of his yearning heart; an ardent patriot, an unflinching friend, a speaker who weighed his words, a pastor whose every word was instinct with the spirit of the man who spoke; uttering the fitting word, be it at the bed-side, at the marriage altar, or at the open grave; in every demonstration of thought and feeling genuine; winning all trust; walking in daily fellowship with all that is fine and high in nature; broad as charity in all things; keenly alive to the terrible deficiencies of the hour, but equally assured of what Whittier has called 'the steady gain of man,' Mr. Willson was the citizen, the neighbor, the pastor, the friend, such as no community can surrender without a pang." * * "To me—to all of us—Salem will be a little less than Salem, now that he is gone—honor a little rarer—beauty and grace of soul something less a tangible reality, something more an evanescent dream—the world without his sunny smile something poorer—life itself something less worth living!"

We quote from the *Christian Register:* "Mr. Willson was a man so fresh in his thought and so youthful in spirit that it was difficult to believe that he was seventy-five years old. Only six of our ministers had longer settlements. He kept himself always abreast of the new thought and the new literature of his time. He was one of the old-fashioned gentlemen, kindly, courteous and unassuming in his demeanor, but resolute in his purpose. During the many years of his ministry in Salem he had grown to be an important part of the life of the city as well as of that of his parish. Naturally, it happened in the changes which passed over this old community that many members of the older families drew together under his administration; and he came to represent in a peculiar degree the old-fashioned, cultivated, self-respecting, dignified life of one of the oldest cities of New England. In a singular way, without conscious purpose or ostentation, Mr. Willson carried on the traditions of the older clergy."

We select from a multitude of tributes written and spoken after his death the beautiful words of Rev. Francis Tiffany, who knew him long and well: "No lamp in an alabaster vase ever shone through more translucently than through his speaking eyes, mobile features and responsive mien shone the vibrations of the light and love within. As youth, mature man, and in old age, he was dowered with the rare gift of personal beauty, a beauty not only lighting up his expressive countenance, but revealing itself in the delicate finish of limb and overflowing in the exquisite courtesy of his manners. Spared to the ripe age of seventy-five, the beautiful Indian summer of his life was steeped in a rich, golden sunshine and haloed with a poetic atmosphere that visibly transfigured him into a living, breathing exemplar of the merit of the saints. His mere passing along the streets had grown to be a public benediction. A shrewd judge of character, a keen and amused dissector of human weaknesses, a sure discerner too of hidden traits of excellence—business men enjoyed talking over with him the events of the day and the characteristics of leading politicians, educators and divines. All the more they respected his spiritual appeals, for the force and penetration of his practical, every-day sense. Under the glove of silk there was the hand of steel."

Mr. Willson married, May 8, 1844, Martha Ann Buttrick, born at Framingham, Massachusetts, July 20, 1817, died in Salem, November 7, 1891, daughter of Stephen and Patty (Wheeler) Buttrick. (See Buttrick family). Children: 1. Sophia Edgell, born in Grafton, March 1, 1845; married Francis H. Lee; no children. 2. Martha Buttrick, born at Grafton, November 3, 1847. 3. Lucy Burr, born at Grafton, November 13, 1849; never married. 4. Alice Brooks, born August 5, 1851; never married. 5. Robert Wheeler, born at West Roxbury, July 20, 1853; married December 14, 1881, Annie Downing West; living in Cambridge, Massachusetts. 6. Edward Russell, born in West Roxbury, April 21, 1856; married 1882, Anne LeMoyne Frost; he died September 9, 1906; children: i. Amey L., born in Providence, Rhode Island, October 30, 1883; ii. Martha Buttrick, born August 16, 1885.

BUTTRICK (I) William Butterick, immigrant ancestor, was born in England, in 1617. The name is spelled often Buttrick also. He came from Kingston-on-Thames, county Surrey, embarking May 9, 1635, with Rev. Mr. Bulkeley, later the minister at Concord, Massachusetts, and Thomas Brook, who also settled at Concord, on the ship "Susan and Ellen." He stated his age as sixty-eight in 1684. He settled in Concord, was admitted a freeman May 26, 1647. He removed to Chelmsford, and was one of the committee appointed to invite the pastor of the church at Wenham to remove to Chelmsford, in 1654. John Hastings called William Butterick his son-in-law, a term used for stepson. His home at Concord was on the west bank of the Concord river, in the upland about a quarter of a mile from the North Bridge. Having served as sergeant of militia, at the age of sixty-five he petitioned to be excused from that office. He died June 30, 1698.

aged about eighty-two years. His will, dated March 1, 1687, proved June 28, 1698, bequeathed to eldest son John a house he had built in Stow; to son Samuel lands at Concord; to daughter Sarah Barrett and to children of all three. He married first, 1646, at Concord, Sarah Bateman, died July 17, 1664; second, February 21, 1667, Jane Goodnow, of Sudbury, daughter of Thomas Goodnow. Children, all by first wife: 1. Mary, born September 19, 1648; died November 1, 1648. 2. William. 3. John, born September 21, 1653; married Mary Blood; settled in Stow. 4. Samuel, born January 12, 1654-5; mentioned below. 5. Edward, born January 6, 1656-7; died January 15, 1656-7. 6. Joseph, born October 29, 1657; killed in the Sudbury fight with the Indians, April 21, 1726. 7. Sarah, born July 27, 1662; married John Barrett, of Chelmsford. 8. Mary, born June 17, 1664; died April 21, 1665.

(II) Samuel Butterick, son of William Butterick, was born at Concord, January 12, 1654-5, and died August 8, 1726. He succeeded his father on the first homestead in Concord. He was a soldier in King Phillip's war, 1675-6, and his son Jonathan drew a lot of land at Narragansett No. 6 (Templeton, Massachusetts) in payment for his services, granted by the general court June 24, 1735. Samuel married, 1677, Elizabeth Blood. Children, all born at Concord: 1. Elizabeth, August 25, 1679. 2. Samuel, Jr., January 31, 1681-2; settled at Charlestown, New Hampshire; married Mercy Hett, born 1680. 3. William, April 15, 1683; died September 16, 1711. 4. Sarah, November 21, 1687; died October 7, 1746; married May 7, 1713, John Flint. 6. Deacon Jonathan, mentioned below.

(III) Deacon Jonathan Butterick, son of Samuel Butterick, was born at Concord, April 24, 1690, and died there March 23, 1767. The Butterick house stood near the North Bridge, and is now or was lately owned by Major John Butterick, his son. Before this old house and to the eastward is Battle Lawn, lately so-called, where the militia and the minute-men formed preparatory to the march to the bridge, and near it the detachment of regulars under Captain Parsons passed on the way to and from the home of Colonel James Barrett. Battle Lawn is marked by suitable inscribed tablets. Deacon Jonathan was followed to his grave, according to the inscription on his monument, by his widow and thirteen well-instructed children. He married, 1717-8, Elizabeth Wood. Children: 1. Samuel, born November 16, 1718; died January 14, 1814; married, 1744, Lucy Wheeler. 2. Mary, born April 18, 1720. 3. Captain Jonathan, born January 30, 1721-2; died May 18, 1775; married July 14, 1756, Mary Brown. 4. Joseph, born January 9, 1723-4; died December 29, 1803; married July 23, 1751, Sarah Brown. 5. Nathan, born September 27, 1725; died December 25, 1812; married December 12, 1757, Grace, daughter of Joseph and Sarah Wheeler. 6. Elizabeth, born August 21, 1727; married December 21, 1753, Charles Flint. 7. Abigail, born August 21, 1729. 8. John, born July 20, 1731; mentioned below. 9. Rachel, born November 12, 1733. 10. Ephraim, born February 15, 1735-6; died April 15, 1785, unmarried. 11. Daniel, born April 3, 1738; died February 24, 1843. 12. Lois, born June 2, 1740; died April 27, 1783, unmarried. 13. Sarah, born August 10, 1742; died July 12, 1827. 14. Willard, born November 12, 1746; married November 22, 1769, Esther, daughter of John and Esther Blood.

(IV) Colonel John Buttrick, son of Deacon Jonathan Butterick, was born in Concord, July 20, 1731, and died May 16, 1791. He was a prominent citizen in town and military affairs before the revolution, and held the rank of major when the revolution began. He was in command of the American forces at Concord, April 19, 1775. Shattuck, the historian of Concord, says: "His name will be handed down to posterity with distinguished honor for the noble stand he took, and the bravery he manifested in leading a gallant band of militiamen on to meet the invading enemy at North Bridge and for beginning the first forcible resistance to British arms. He returned the fire, saying: 'Fire, fellow soldiers, for God's sake, fire,' and discharged his own gun the same instant." The inscription on his monument reads: "In memory of Colonel John Buttrick, who commanded the militia companies which made the first attack upon the British Troops at Concord, North Bridge, on the nineteenth of April, 1775, having with patriotic firmness shared in the damages which led to American Independence, he lived to enjoy the blessings of it, and died May 16, 1791, aged sixty years. Having laid down his sword with honor, he resumed the plough with industry; by the latter he maintained what the former had won. The virtues of the parent, citizen and Christian adorned his life and his worth was acknowledged by the grief and respect of all ranks at his death." During the summer of 1775 he was major in the regiment of Colonel John Nixon, at the siege of Boston; was commissioned lieutenant-colonel of Colonel John Robinson's regiment, August 1, 1775; was colonel of volunteers, acting as captain of a company in Colonel Reed's regiment at the taking of Burgoyne, serving from September 28, 1777, to November 7 following, and his company was detached from Colonel Brooks' regiment to reinforce General Gates to the northward. He was in the Rhode Island campaign in 1778, when his regiment was detached to reinforce the Continental army. His house was on the hill west of Flint's Bridge, and was occupied lately by Captain Francis Jarvis. His gun is still in the possession of the family, and his tobacco box is at Antiquarian Hall, Concord. He married, June 24, 1760, Abigail Jones. Children, born at Concord: 1. Colonel John, October 8, 1761; died September 11, 1825; married first, December 10, 1795, Lydia Wheeler; second, December 9, 1813, Hannah Wheeler. 2. Levi, October 11, 1762. 3. Jonas, November 17, 1764. 4. Abigail, December 8, 1766. 5. Esther, August 8, 1768. 6. Anna, September 19, 1770. 7. Stephen, August 25, 1772; mentioned below. 8. Phebe, October 17, 1774. 9. Horatio Gates, March 4, 1778. 10. Silas, May 15, 1780.

(V) Stephen Buttrick, son of John Buttrick, was born at Concord, August 25, 1772, and died April 17, 1828. He settled first on No. 3, third range, Hancock county, Maine, and his three eldest children were born there. He removed to Framingham, Massachusetts, in 1814, and occupied the Wheeler farm. He was deacon of the Baptist church. He married December 6, 1801, Patty Wheeler, born December, 1776, daughter of Abner Wheeler, of Lincoln. She died May 6, 1827. Children: 1. Eliza W., born May 8, 1828; married Rev. George Noyes, of Brookfield, and later a professor at Harvard College. 2. Rebecca, born January 16, 1807; died unmarried. 3. Abner W., born June 24, 1809; settled in Lowell. 4. John A., born April 14, 1813; teacher in Medford, Massachusetts, 1834-38; settled in Lowell, Massachusetts, March, 1839; was city treasurer, 1843-47; cashier of the Appleton Bank 1847-78; state senator 1855-6; representative to general court; died March 3, 1879, while an officer in the City Institution of Savings in Lowell, Massachusetts; married Martha Parkhurst, of Chelmsford. 5. Benjamin W., born June 11, 1815; died November 4, 1836. 6. Martha Ann, born July 20, 1817; married, May 8, 1844, Rev. Edmund B. Willson. (See Willson family). 7. Alden, born January 22, 1820; settled in Lowell. 8. Harriet Newell, born May 6, 1822; died August 20, 1825.

WYMAN The origin of this surname is Saxon or German, although the American families are descended from English stock of ancient pedigree. The English family Wymond is evidently of the original stock, as the coat-of-arms is the same. The German spelling was Weymann, and the spelling varies, some of the forms being Wiman, Wymant, Wymond, Wimond, etc.

(I) Francis Wyman, the early English ancestor, lived in the parish of Westmill, county Hertford, where he died in 1658. He was a farmer and a man of some property. His will, dated September 15, 1658, proved February 14, 1659, bequeathed to wife Jane; to sons Francis and John Wyman, "who are beyond the sea, ten pounds apiece of lawful English money" to be paid to them if they be in want and come over to demand the same. The sons never had the legacies, both being prosperous citizens of Woburn, Massachusetts. He also bequeathed to his sister, Susan Huitt, widow. He left his homestead to his son Thomas, who was likewise the residuary legatee. He married, at Westmill, May 2, 1617, Elizabeth Richardson, doubtless related to the three brothers who with Wyman were founders of Woburn. She was buried June 22, 1630, and he married second, Jane ———, who was buried in July, 1656. He was buried September 19, 1658. Children, all by first wife: 1. Thomas, baptized at Westmill, April 5, 1618; married Ann Godfrey; settled in New England. 2. Francis, baptized February 24, 1619; settled in New England. 3. John, baptized February 3, 1621; mentioned below. 4. Richard, baptized March 14, 1623. 5. William, baptized August 31, 1628; buried July, 1630. (See page 46, vol. li, N. E. Register).

(II) John Wyman, son of Francis Wyman, was baptized at Westmill, Hertfordshire, England, February 3, 1621, and was the immigrant ancestor. He was one of the early settlers at Charlestown, in New England. His name appears on the records as early as 1640, together with his brother Francis, who is associated closely with him through life. He was a subscriber at Charlestown in December, 1640, to town order for Woburn, which was set off from Charlestown. He removed to Woburn soon after, and his name is on the county tax list there under date of September 8, 1645. He was a tanner by trade. He was admitted a freeman May 26, 1647. He deposed in court, December 18, 1660, that his age was about thirty-nine years, which would make his birth and baptism closely correspond. He died May 9, 1684. He married, November 5, 1644, Sarah Nutt, daughter of Miles Nutt, an early settler at Watertown who removed to Woburn. She married second, Thomas Fuller, of Woburn, August 25, 1684. Children: 1. Samuel, born September 20, 1646; died young. 2. John, Jr., born March 26, 1648; died 1676. 3. Sarah, born April 15, 1650; married December 15, 1669, Joseph Walker, of Billerica; died January 26, 1669. 4. Solomon, born February 26, 1651-2; died September 22, 1725. 5. David, born April 7, 1654. 6. Elizabeth, born January 18, 1655-6; died November 21, 1658. 7. Bathsheba, born October 6, 1658; married Nathaniel Fay, of Billerica, May 30, 1677; died July 9, 1730. 8. Jonathan, born July 13, 1661. 9. Seth, mentioned below.

(III) Lieutenant Seth Wyman, son of John Wyman, was born in Woburn, August 3, 1663, and settled there. He married, December 17, 1685, Esther Johnson, who died March 31, 1742, daughter of Major William Johnson. He died October 26, 1715. Children, born at Woburn: 1. Seth, September 13, 1686; mentioned below. 2. Esther, October 25, 1688. 3. Sarah, January 17, 1690-1; married Caleb Blogget. 4. Jonathan, November 5, 1693; died January 19, 1693-4. 5. Susanna, June 30, 1695. 6. Abigail, February 6, 1698-99; married January 19, 1725, Timothy Brooks; died March 16, 1780. 7. Love, February 14, 1701-02; married Josiah Wyman.

(IV) Ensign Seth Wyman, son of Lieutenant Seth Wyman, was born in Woburn, September 13, 1686, probably on the old Wyman place, in what is now the west part of Burlington, a farm bequeathed to his father by the immigrant ancestor Wyman. He was in the famous Lovewell fight with the Indians in 1725, and had the conduct of his company after the commander was shot. He was one of the nine who escaped serious wounds out of the thirty-three in the company. We quote from the history of Woburn: "At Lovewell's fight he greatly distinguished himself by his self-possession, fortitude and valor. All his superior officers having been killed or mortally wounded early in the engagement, he had the command of our men almost the whole time of its continuance, and by his prudent management and courageous example was doubtless mainly instrumental under God for preserving so many of them as there were from being utterly cut off. Seeing them in danger of becoming dispirited in the contest in view of greatly superior numbers and other advantages of the enemy, he animated them to action (it was afterward reported by Eleazer Davis, who was one of them) by assuring them that the day would be their own if their spirits did not flag, and so encouraged by these exhortations and so briskly did they fire in consequence that several discharged their muskets between twenty and thirty times apiece." Immediately after the return of the survivors Wyman was honored by Lieutenant Governor Dummer, commander-in-chief of Massachusetts, with a captain's commission. He also received from his fellow citizens in testimony of the public appreciation of his valor, a silver-hilted sword, but did not live long to enjoy the honors that came to him. To encourage volunteers to enlist against the Indians, the general court offered four shillings wages per day in addition to the bounty of one hundred pounds for every scalp. Many enlisted and marched under command of Captain Wyman and others, but the extreme heat and illness effectually stopped their progress. Several died on their return, among them Captain Wyman, September 5, 1725, in his thirty-eighth year. After his death his wife's father adopted the children. Seth Wyman married, January 26, 1715-6, Sarah Ross, of Billerica, who died November 5, 1727, daughter of Thomas Ross. Children: 1. Seth, born November 5, 1715. 2. Ross, born August 16, 1717; married first ——— Jefts; second, April 10, 1751, Dinah Taylor; third 1761, Sarah Haggett, widow. 3. Peleg, born August 20, 1719. 4. Hezekiah, August 5, 1720; mentioned below. 6. Sarah, September 20, 1722.

(V) Hezekiah Wyman, son of Captain Seth Wyman, was born in Woburn, August 5, 1720. He was a soldier in the French and Indian war, and was in General Wolfe's army at the battle of Quebec. Tradition has it that he pointed out the secret path that led to the Heights of Abraham, by which the British and Americans were led to the plateau, met the French on equal footing and conquered the city. In recognition of his services in this campaign he was granted a manor in New York, but never claimed his grant, and it was finally taken up by squatters. When the revolution came he marched with his company on the Lexington alarm and took part in the fighting at Concord, April 19, 1775. When he died he bequeathed outside his family the gun he carried on that eventful day, but it is now in

Isaac Wyman

the possession of his grandson, Isaac Chauncy Wyman, of Salem. He was fifty-five years old at the time of the battle, and lived but a few years afterward. A picture of him, seated upon a white horse, is preserved in the public library at Woburn. His home was in Cambridge, Massachusetts, in later years. He married Sarah Reed, of Woburn. Children, born in Woburn: 1. Hezekiah, March 21, 1747. 2. Seth, March 17, 1749; died young. 3. Seth, February 17, 1750; removed to Maine. 4. Daniel, March 6, 1752. 5. Sarah, May 12, 1754. 6. Isaac, mentioned below.

(V) Isaac Wyman, son of Hezekiah Wyman, was born in Woburn, December 12, 1756. He died about 1836, in Salem, Massachusetts. He was an active and influential patriot in revolutionary days, and a distinguished military figure. He was with his father in the battle of Concord, and rose step by step to the rank of colonel of a cavalry regiment, or horse troops, as they were called. After the war he became a merchant in Boston for seven years, then removed to Keene, New Hampshire, and for three years was engaged in manufacturing pearlash and dealing in lumber and wood. He returned to Salem, Massachusetts, then the busiest seaport of New England, and bought the property at Forest River, South Salem, formerly owned by his wife's family, the Ingalls of Salem. He demolished the old buildings, including the house, the mill and the dam, and constructed a new house and flour and grain mills. He also engaged in the manufacture of dyestuffs. The logs for his dyes were imported from the East Indies. He also had a large trade in wool, buying this commodity of the farmers, who had many sheep at that time. He had the wool sorted, picked and baled for export to England. He also went into the blacklead business, manufacturing graphite, but after a time sold this branch of his business to Colonel Frank Peabody, who developed it to large proportions. The graphite business that he founded is known at the present time as the Forest River Mills, and the excellence of the products of the mill was well-known to the trade. The founders of the Dixon Crucible Company, of Jersey City, New Jersey, (Jule and Frank Dixon) learned their trade in Wyman's mill. The name of Dixon and lead pencils are associated together wherever writing is done.

Colonel Wyman acquired military habits of arbitrary thought and action during the war, and was rather austere and stern. In business he commanded, and his word was law; he asked for no advice from his employees and he took none from anybody. Though he never voted, he was a Whig in sentiment and doubtless a Federalist in the day of that party. He was public-spirited and a strong and influential citizen of Salem. He had sound judgment and prospered in his affairs. In all his varied undertakings he was successful and he was enterprising, almost speculative in his ventures, according to the ideas of his contemporaries. He was essentially a constructor of business, always a leader of men and affairs. Like most of the Continental army officers, he was a Free Mason. He married, July 2, 1820, Elizabeth Ingalls, born in Lynn, January 19, 1789, daughter of Henry Ingalls, an officer at one time of the famous frigate "Constitution." Her mother was Susan (Brown) Ingalls (see Ingalls), a native of Salem. The family is in some doubt as to whether the children were born in Salem or Marblehead, as the farm extended into both places, and at the time the children were born the process of tearing down the old buildings and building new ones was going on. Though some of the children may have been born in Marblehead, none of the births are recorded. Children: 1. Sarah, died in infancy. 2. Susan, died about 1888, in Salem. 3. Isaac Chauncy, born January 30, 1827; mentioned below. 4. William Burnett; married Elizabeth Adams; he was educated in Bradford Academy and at the Friends' School at North Weare, New Hampshire; fitted for the profession of civil engineer, but followed farming at Marblehead most of his life; was for about two years in the produce business in Boston; Republican in politics and Episcopalian in religion; died in Marblehead; children: i. Elizabeth, married William Stanley Phillips, now of Colorado; she is dead; ii. Susan B., married Daniel Dickinson; reside in Marblehead.

(VI) Isaac Chauncy Wyman, son of Isaac Wyman, born January 30, 1827, is not only one of the few surviving sons of revolutionary soldiers, but has the distinction of having had his paternal grandfather of the revolutionary service. He was educated in the public schools and at Princeton University, where he was graduated in 1848 with the degree of A. M. Of the one hundred and four members of that class but four survive (1908)—Rev. Dr. Wall, of New York; Chancellor Pinckney, of New Jersey; Roscoe Field, of Memphis, Tennessee; and Mr. Wyman. He studied his profession in the Dane Law School of Harvard University, graduating in 1851. He was admitted to the bar the same year, and later admitted to practice in the Federal courts. He began to practice in Boston, making his home in Cambridge. He was associated with United States District Attorney Benjamin F. Hallett, who was once chairman of the Democratic national committee. While with him he prosecuted the last case of piracy ever tried in Massachusetts. The ship "Wanderer," was engaged in the slave trade between African and Cuban ports, also running cargoes of slaves into Mobile. Her captain and owner, Oakes Smith, a native of Maine, and graduate of Bowdoin college, finally escaped from prison and was never recaptured. At that time the United States made no appropriation for assistant district attorneys or for detective work necessary in prosecuting criminal cases successfully. Gathering evidence and all this work devolved on Mr. Wyman, who acted as assistant district attorney. He even went out on the streets and did detective work in the most lawless part of the north end, where his life would have been in danger had his errand been known. When Mr. Hallett's son took over his father's practice, Mr. Wyman associated himself with Charles G. Thomas, one of the old-fashioned lawyers, whom he induced to engage in admiralty cases. There were but few lawyers making a special study and practice in this line of work at that time. Hardy Prince, John C. Dodge, Judge Benjamin R. Curtis, and occasionally Sydney Bartlett and Charles G. Curtis, together with Richard H. Dana, Sr., had all of the business. Judge Sprague was district judge at that time, and Judge Woodbury was on the circuit bench. This admiralty practice presented interesting points of law and procedure, and Mr. Wyman followed it from choice. His firm had a remarkable record of losing less than a half-dozen cases out of two hundred. After leaving Mr. Thomas, Mr. Wyman continued alone with his office on School street, Boston. He gradually drifted into the banking business, and in course of time became president of the Marblehead National Bank, an office he has held for more than fifty years. He is also interested in real estate, not only in Massachusetts but in divers sections of the country and to some extent in mining property in Colorado. While he was in Hallett's office, the Secretary of War came to consult Mr. Hallett about purchasing a new site for the United States courts, and during the visit Mr. Wyman purchased the old Masonic Temple on Temple Place for $75,000. The proof of his foresight in this speculation is found in the fact that some years later the property was sold for four hundred thousand dollars. In politics he is a Republican, but has never accepted public office. In religion he is an Episcopalian. He is a member of the Masonic order. An interesting anecdote that he tells is of his first meeting with an Indian. It was during the last Sioux uprising in the eighties, when he with a friend and a scout were on the plains. The scout suddenly noticed an Indian camp ahead. At this time the Sioux were especially cruel and warlike, and the scout turned to the party at once and advised a rapid retreat. "Have they seen us?" asked Mr. Wyman. "Yes," replied the scout. "Well, my knowledge of human nature tells me that to run would be to court trouble, so I am going on," said Mr. Wyman. After futile wrangling on the part of the scout, Mr. Wyman and his companion insisted on proceeding. After riding fifteen miles the party approached the Indians. An Indian detached himself from the camp and party and waved a red blanket, a sign that he wanted one of the party to advance alone. Wyman selected himself for the task and found, instead of a war-like party, only a camp of squaws and old men who were scared more than the white men. After making the Indians presents of tobacco and other articles, Wyman and his party proceeded on their way.

INGALLS The name of Ingalls is supposed to be of Scandinavian origin, derived from Ingislld. During the ninth century the Scandinavian pirates often descended upon the east coast of Great Britain, and in after years many of this nationality settled here, especially in Lincolnshire. The name appears in England as Ingall, Engle, Ingolds and Ingles, and the following coats-of-arms are recorded: Ingles—Gules, three bars gemelle or, on a canton argent five billets en saltire sable. Crest, a lily springing from a crown. Motto: Humilis ex corona. Also, Ingle: Ar., two chevrons sable, on the chief of the second a lion passant of the first Crest, a hand erect issuing out of a cloud, holding a sword, blade waved, perpendicular. The earliest record found is that of a will of Henry Ingalls, grandfather of Edmund the immigrant, and made in 1555, he probably having been born about 1480. The next record is the will of Robert, the father of Edmund, made in 1617. The name of Ingalls is still common in England, and signifies "By the power of Thor." The Domesday Book records a Baron Ingald, a tenant of King William at Rersbi and Elvestone, Leicestershire, in 1080. This Baron came from Normandy.

(I) Edmund Ingalls, immgrant ancestor, son of Robert and grandson of Henry Ingalls, was born at Skirbeck, Lincolnshire, England, about 1598. He came to Salem, Massachusetts, in Governor Endicott's company in 1628, and with his brother Francis and four others settled in Lynn, where they were the first settlers. His name is found often on the records of the town, and he was a prominent citizen. Once he was fined "for bringing home sticks in both his arms on the Sabbath day." In March, 1648, while travelling to Boston on horseback, he was drowned in the Saugus river, owing to a defective bridge. His will was proved September 18, 1648. He married Ann ———. Children: 1. Robert, mentioned below. 2. Elizabeth, born 1622; died June 9, 1676; married Rev. Francis Dane, of Andover. 3. Faith, born 1623; married Andrew Allen. 4. John, born 1625; married Elizabeth Barrett. 5. Sarah, born 1626; married William Bitnar. 6. Henry, born 1627; married first, Mary Osgood; second, Sarah Farnum. 7. Samuel, born 1634; married Ruth Eaton. 8. Mary, married John Eaton. 9. Joseph, died young.

(II) Robert Ingalls, son of Edmund Ingalls, was born in Skirbeck, Lincolnshire, England, about 1621, and came to New England with his parents. He was a farmer at Lynn, and inherited his father's farm. He was admitted a freeman in 1691. On January 1, 1685-6 he deeded most of his estate to his sons Robert, Nathaniel and Samuel, they to support the widow and pay the other heirs. He was buried January 3, 1698. He married Sarah, daughter of William Harker. She died April 8, 1696. Children: 1. Hannah, born September 20, 1647; died June, 1684; married May 2, 1673, Henry Stacey, of Salem. 2. Robert, born February 9, 1649; married Rebecca Leighton. 3. Samuel, born September 22, 1650; married Hannah Perkins. 4. Sarah, born July 4, 1654; died January, 1688-9. 5. Elizabeth, born 1657; died November 2, 1681; married, 1680, Samuel Hart, Jr. 6. Nathaniel, born about 1660; mentioned below. 7. Eleazer, born 1661; married Mary Hendley. 8. Ruth, born about 1663.

(III) Nathaniel Ingalls, son of Robert Ingalls, was born at Lynn, about 1660. He resided at Lynn, and was a farmer. He married Anne ———. His will was dated July 12, 1735, and proved January 9, 1737. Children: 1. Nathaniel, born December 25, 1692; married Tabitha Lewis. 2. Sarah, born April 14, 1693; married Samuel Ingalls. 3. Ruth, born June 29, 1695; married, 1711, John Berry. 4. Joseph, married Rebecca Collins. 5. William, married Zeruiah Norwood. 6. Henry, mentioned below. 7. Maria, married Samuel Berry, of Salem. 8. Tabitha, married, 1723, John Williams. 9. Hannah, married, 1735, Daniel Hitchings. 10. Jacob, married Mary Tucker.

(IV) Henry Ingalls, son of Nathaniel Ingalls, was born at Lynn, and died there. He married, December 26, 1734, Sarah Richards.

(V) Amos Ingalls, son of Henry Ingalls, was born in 1739, at Lynn, and died there October 20, 1819. His will was made in 1811. He married, March 31, 1768, Mary Ingalls, daughter of Jacob and Mary (Tucker) Ingalls. Children, born in Lynn: 1. Henry, mentioned below. 2. Abigail, married John Watts. 3. Mary, married August 23, 1789, James Bickford.

(VI) Henry Ingalls, son of Amos Ingalls, was born in Lynn, where he lived and died. He married April 5, 1790, Susanna Brown. Children, born in Lynn: 1. Amos, December 19, 1787. 2. Elizabeth (twin), January 19, 1789; married July 2, 1820, Isaac Wyman, of Marblehead (see Wyman family). 3. James (twin), January 19, 1789; married Lorana Withey. Children of Henry and Sarah Ingalls: 4. Sarah, born May 23, 1792; died September 3, 1872; married October 11, 1812, John Withey. 5. Charles, born November 19, 1799; married Hannah Shaw. 6. Mary, born October 28, 1803; married September 28, 1819, John Mudge, of Lynn.

DENNEN Members of this family still vary in the spelling of the surname. The two prevalent forms are Denning and Dennen. The first immigrant of the name was William Denning, who in 1634 was in the employ of William Brenton, of Boston. William Denning was admitted to the church March 23, 1634, and was a proprietor in Boston, December 14, 1635. He died January 20, 1653-4. His will, proved January 31, 1653-4, bequeathed to wife Ann, son Obadiah in England, and to kinswoman, Mary Powell.

(I) Nicholas Dennen, immigrant ancestor, born in England, 1645, died at Gloucester, Massachusetts, June 9, 1725. He may have been a nephew or a close relative of William mentioned above. Both were doubtless mariners, and the surname is very uncommon. All the old Colonial families of this name may be traced to this Gloucester progenitor. His children were probably born before he came to Gloucester and their mother may have died in the old country. He married first, Eme, daughter of John Browne, who was one of the first settlers in Maine, and was living in Pemaquid within three or four years after the Pilgrims landed at Plymouth; he was the first man in New England to have an Indian deed recorded, buying his land at Pemaquid from Samoset, the Indian, who said "Welcome Englishmen," to the Plymouth settlers; the deed is dated July 15, 1625. Nicholas Dennen married second, at Gloucester, November 25, 1697, Sarah Paine. Children: Nicholas, Jr., William, and George; all mentioned below.

(II) Nicholas Dennen, son of Nicholas Dennen, was born about 1675. In 1724 he had a grant of land where his house was then located. He was doubtless a seafaring man. He married first, December 1, 1699, Elizabeth Davis; second, January 4, 1732, Ann Fuller. He, his wife Elizabeth, his daughters Margaret and Hannah, were baptized May 9, 1725, in the Gloucester church. Children: 1. Elizabeth, born 1703; married November 7, 1723, Daniel Gordon. 2. Nicholas, born 1706. 3. Eme, 1711. 4. Margaret, born 1714, married November 9, 1736, Thomas Boffet. 5. Hannah, 1717. 6. Nicholas, October 12, 1732.

(II) William Dennen, son of Nicholas Dennen, was born about 1680. He settled in Gloucester, and had a house west of Fresh Water Cove. He married first, December 5, 1706, Hannah Paine, and second, Susanna ———. Children, born in Gloucester: 1. Sarah, baptized 1710. 2. William, Jr., born 1713; died young. 3. Mary, 1715. Children of second wife. 4. William, baptized 1727. 5. Elizabeth, born August 9, 1729. 6. Samuel, mentioned below.

(II) George Dennen, son of Nicholas Dennen (1), was born about 1686. He was a seafaring man, and was lost on a voyage to the Isle of Sables, in August, 1716, aged thirty. He married, March 20, 1708, Hannah, sister of Richard Byles. His widow lived in the west precinct of Gloucester. Children: 1. Job, settled in Gloucester. 2. James, had children born in Gloucester. 3. George, married November 21, 1738, Mary Eveluth; had sons Francis, George, Simeon and Joseph, who was born May 6, 1752; married second, October 16, 1773, Molly Haskell, and served throughout the revolution. 4. Joseph. 5. Hannah.

(III) Samuel, son of William Dennen, was born in Gloucester, November 12, 1732, and died 1798. As Samuel Denning he appears on return dated Gloucester, April 9, 1759, of men enlisted or impressed for his Majesty's service in Col. William Allen's regiment to be put under command of Gen. Amherst, for the invasion of Canada; age 26; residence Gloucester; enlisted April 2, 1759; reported in King's navy; took oath of fidelity, etc. (Mass. Arch., vol. xcvii, p. 101). Also on muster roll not dated, for seamen in His Majesty's service on board "Neptune," discharged by order of Vice Admiral Saunders; service from April 2, 1759, to November 10, 1759; reported in council warrant of January 19, 1760; service up the St. Lawrence. (ibid, vol. xcvii, p. 305). Samuel Dennen married, in Gloucester, March 14, 1754, Keziah Bray, of an old family of that section. They resided in Gloucester until late in life, when he removed to Poland, Maine, where both of them died. Children, all born in Gloucester: 1. Abigail, 1756. 2. Job, 1760; in the revolution, from Bakerstown, Maine. 3. Mary, 1762. 4. Sarah, 1764. 5. George, 1769; mentioned below. 6. Simeon, 1770. 7. Abigail, 1774. The descendants residing in Gloucester have spelled the name in many cases Dennen, while those in Poland use more often Denning.

(IV) George Dennen, son of Samuel Dennen, was born in Gloucester, in 1769, and died April 26, 1833. He married, 1792, Ellena Rollins, born 1770, died May 7, 1837. The records are from the family Bible of J. K. Denning, who lives in the family homestead at Mechanic Falls, Maine. Children: 1. Samuel, born September 26, 1793; mentioned below. 2. Stephen, November 28, 1794. 3. Hannah, 1796. 4. Ruth, 1799; died young. 5. Ruth, born about 1800. 6. Bathsheba, 1801. 7. George, 1803. 8. Job, 1805. 9. Moses, 1806. 10. Rhoda, 1808. 11. James, 1810. 12. Jacob, 1812. Job had the homestead at Poland, which descended to his son, James K. Denning, the present occupant.

(V) Samuel Dennen, son of George Dennen, was born at Poland, Maine, September 26, 1793, and died June 17, 1864, at Oxford, Maine. He married, at Poland, March 27, 1816 Marion Mitchell, born October 11, 1796, at Shirley, Maine, died September 22, 1872. Children: 1. Eleanor R., born February 23, 1818, died May 28, 1906. 2. Basheba, born March 22, 1819; married. 3. Emeline, born April 3, 1821; married January 31, 1843, Mr. Pratt. 4. Stephen, born March 29, 1823; married; died November 6, 1874, at Springfield, Massachusetts. 5. Britannia, born February 21, 1825; died young. 6. Job Cushman, born June 18, 1826; mentioned below. 7. William C., born May 20, 1829; married. 8. Hannah, born February 11, 1831; married. 9. Augustus, born November 9, 1833, at Shirley, Maine; married, in California. 10. Samuel F., born August 16, 1836, in Shirley; married. 11. John W., born July 16, 1838; married. 12. Charles O., born March 16, 1841. 13. Eugene L., born December 19, 1845, in Greene, Maine; married.

(VI) Job Cushman Dennen, son of Samuel Dennen, was born in Poland, Maine, June 18, 1826, and died November 5, 1892. He was a soldier in the civil war. He married first, Martha Brewster, of Leeds, Maine; second, Harriet Low Berry, born 1842, at Leeds, died February 24, 1904, daughter of Amos and Mary (Curtis) Berry. Child of first wife: 1. Clara Ella; married Horatio Gammon. Children of second wife: 2. Mary Jane, died young. 3. Hollis Ellsworth, born at Braintree, February 28, 1862. 4. Charles Russell, born May 30, 1864; married first, Alice Stubbs, of Yarmouth, Maine, and had Helen M., Earl and Paul; married second, Eliza Dwinnell, widow. 5. Bertram.

(VII) Hollis Ellsworth Dennen, son of Job Cushman Dennen, was born at Braintree, February 28, 1862. His childhood and youth were spent in Oxford and Mechanic Falls, Maine, and he received his education in the public and high schools of the latter town. At an early age he assisted his father in the management of the farm, where he remained until the death of his father. He then removed to Waltham, Massachusetts, and engaged in the real estate and insurance business, which he has conducted successfully up to the present time. He is a Republican in politics, and has served two terms as alderman of Waltham. He is a prominent Free Mason, a member of Tyrian Lodge, at Mechanic Falls, Maine, where he was master of the lodge for three years. He is an active member of the Methodist church, and has been superintendent of the Sunday school several years. He married, November 22, 1882, Mary Gertrude Harding, born at Mechanic Falls, Maine, July 24, 1866, daughter of Nathaniel and Helen A. (Perkins) Harding. (See Harding). Children: 1. Ralph W., born May 18, 1884. 2. Barbara L., July 6, 1890. 3. Doris H., January 9, 1901.

HARDING The surname Harding is derived from the very ancient personal name Hardin, of Gothic origin, in use at a very early period in Germany, Scandinavia and Britain, even before the coming of the ancient feudal system. Several men bearing this name are mentioned in Domesday Book (1086) and several localities bearing this name or its derivities like Hardington. There were no less than six immigrants of this surname in Massachusetts before 1650—Abraham, who left many descendants; Elizabeth who settled in Boston; George, of Salem, of whom nothing further is known; John, of Weymouth; Robert, of Boston, who left no issue in this country. Some connections existed between the patentee of Maine, Captain Robert Gorges, and the Harding family. A kinsman, Sir Robert Gorges, married Mary, daughter and heir of William Harding.

(I) Martha Harding, widow, the immigrant ancestor, was in Plymouth as early as 1632. She died in 1633, leaving her son Joseph to the care of John Doane, probably her brother. It is believed that her husband came to Maine in 1623 with Governor Gorges, and when the colony was abandoned he took refuge at Plymouth, but he may have died before his family removed to Plymouth. It appears that the widow had previously committed her elder son, John, to the care of John Doane. Children: John, Phebe, married, 1634, John Brown; Winifred, married, 1639, Thomas Whiton; Joseph, mentioned below.

(II) Joseph Harding, son of Martha Harding, was born about 1635. He was given into the care of Deacon John Doane by his mother, and lived with his guardian during his minority, at Duxbury and Eastham, Massachusetts. About 1650 he came to Braintree, taking possession apparently of lands inherited from his father and from time to time his name is found in the probate records from 1650 to 1660. He married, April 4, 1660, Bethia, daughter of Josiah and Elizabeth (King) Cook, of Eastham, formerly of Plymouth, and grantee of Little Compton, Rhode Island. Joseph settled early at Eastham. Children, born at Eastham: 1. Martha, December 13, 1662. 2. Mary, August 19, 1665. 3. Joseph, July 8, 1667. 4. Josiah, August 15, 1669. 5. Maziah, November 1, 1671; married Hannah ——. 6. John, October 9, 1673; died June 4, 1697, without issue. 7. Nathaniel, December 25, 1674; mentioned below. 8. Joshua, February 15, 1676; married June 26, 1702, Sarah Smith. 9. Abiah, January 7, 1679-80; married September 24, 1713, Rebecca Young. 10. Samuel, September 1, 1685; married August 28, 1707, Elizabeth Eldred.

(III) Nathaniel Harding, son of Joseph Harding, was born at Eastham, on Cape Cod, December 25, 1674; married, March 20, 1700-1, Hannah Collins; second, November 30, 1725, Hannah Young. His widow was appointed administratrix August 12, 1741. He settled in Truro. Children, born at Truro: 1. Thankful, April 3, 1703. 2. Nathaniel; mentioned below. 3. Jonathan, died 1752; married Huldah ———; second, Abigail ———; lived at Truro. 4. David (?), died 1742. 5. Lot, born 1723; lived in Truro. 6. Ruth, about 1724; died April, 1742. Children of second wife: 7. Martha. 8. Sarah. 9. James. 10. Anna. 11. Mary.

(IV) Nathaniel Harding, son of Nathaniel Harding, was born in Truro, about 1705. He was a yeoman in his native town. His will, dated February 9, 1748, bequeaths to wife Mercy (executrix), and was proved July 7, 1748. The inventory amounted to 1,481 pounds, fifteen shillings. Children, born Truro: 1. Ephraim, mentioned below. 2. Jesse, March 27, 1736. 3. Nathaniel, died intestate, 1757. 4. Elizabeth. 5. Samuel. 6. Hezekiah. 7. Nehemiah.

(V) Ephraim Harding, son of Nathaniel Harding, was born in Truro, about 1734. He had a large family of sons, some of whom removed to Bath and New Meadows, Maine. Children: 1. Nathaniel, mentioned below. 2. Nehemiah, settled in Bath, progenitor of a prominent family there. And others.

(VI) Nathaniel Harding, son of Ephraim Harding, was born in Truro, about 1760. He married ——— Collins, of an old Truro family, and lived in his native town. Children: 1. Ephraim. 2. Nathaniel, mentioned below. 3. Benjamin, died in truro. 4. Richard, Jr., settled in Maine. 5. Jedediah, died at sea, January 1, 1810; children: i. Clarissa, born 1799; ii. Hannah, 1801; iii. Lydia, 1803; iv. Samuel Dyer, 1806, married Eliza Burr, of Leicester, Massachusetts; v. Ephraim, 1808.

(VII) Nathaniel Harding, son of Nathaniel Harding, was born in Truro. His brother Richard and perhaps Ephraim also settled in Maine. He married Betsey Dyer. He was a master mariner, and was lost at sea. Children: 1. Jedediah, mentioned below. 2. Betsey, married Rev. Sargeant, a baptist minister.

(VIII) Jedediah Harding, son of Nathaniel Harding, was born about 1810. He settled in Andover, Oxford county, Maine. He married Dorcas Taylor. Children: Harriet; Joel; Nathaniel, mentioned below; William; Charles; Lizzie; Alfred; Malinda; George; Fred; Julia; Augustus.

(IX) Nathaniel Harding, son of Jedediah Harding, was born in New Sharon, Maine, October 27, 1839. He was a member of Company A, 12th Maine Regiment, enlisted at Andover, Maine, September 19, 1861, and re-enlisted in same company, New Orleans, in 1863, and served until the close of the war. He was wounded at the battle of Winchester, under Sheridan, and was confined in a hospital at Philadelphia almost a year. He was made sergeant soon after enlisting, and continued in that rank as long as he was in service. He married Helen A. Perkins, daughter of Lewis and Eliza Jane Buxton (Waite) Perkins. His wife was born April 13, 1845, and died October 12, 1906. Children: 1. Mary Gertrude, born at Mechanic Falls, Maine, July 24, 1866; married Hollis Ellsworth Dennen (see Dennen). 2. Francis E., born April 4, 1874; married Ernest Tilton, of Everett, Massachusetts. 3. Edgar, born August 23, 1881; married Blanche Rafuse.

WARDLE (I) James Wardle, progenitor of this family, was an Englishman. He married Margaret ———.

(II) James Wardle, Jr., son of James Wardle (1), was born in England at Stayley Bridge, near Manchester, in 1792-93, and died at Valatie, New York. He came to America about 1816 and settled at Valatie. He was an expert cotton spinner and was one of the first to engage extensively in the manufacture of cotton goods in this country. He began as a manufacturer in partnership with Mr. Benjamin Baldwin, of Valatie, and later he removed to Stockport, New York, where he manufactured cotton goods on a large scale until 1841 when he met with reverses and went out of business. He lived at Pittsburgh, Pennsylvania, for a time, but returned to Valatie and died there. He married, at Ghent, Columbia county, New York, June 13, 1826, Mary Swift Van Buren, born January 1, 1804, daughter of Abraham Van Buren, of Philadelphia. (See Van Buren). Children: 1.

Robert Lawton, born June 6, 1828; mentioned below. 2. Sarah Elizabeth, December, 1830.

(III) Robert Lawton Wardle, son of James Wardle (2), was born in Valatie, New York, June 6, 1828. He lived in New York state until twelve years of age and then went with his mother to live in Philadelphia, where he received his education in the private schools and under the tuition of his mother. He worked at various trades during his active life, principally wood-working, however, in which he was especially skillful. He is now living with his son, Harry L. Wardle, at Dedham, Massachusetts. He married Mary Caroline Simson, born December 24, 1833, daughter of George Washington and Caroline (Wetherell) Simson, of Boston. The Simson family was one of the early families of Massachusetts. George W. Simson married Caroline Wetherell, November 7, 1825; he died February 2, 1832; he was a son of Benjamin and Phebe (Todd) Simson, who were the parents of seven children, as follows: Warner, Joshua, George W., Freeman, Mary, Almira and Roxy Simson. Caroline (Wetherell) Simson was the daughter of George and Lydia (Hunt) Wetherell, and granddaughter of George and Lydia (Phillips) Wetherell. The Wetherell family is one of the oldest in Massachusetts; direct descendant of William who was the first settler, being of Norton, Massachusetts; he was born in England and admitted a freeman at Plymouth in 1658. Children of Mr. and Mrs. Wardle: 1. Minnie Caroline, born February 15, 1858, married, January 1, 1884, Melvin N. Royal; children: Arthur and Roselle A. 2. Walter Lawton, born May 4, 1859, married, March 31, 1884, May Belle McGregor, daughter Mabel. 3. Harry Leonard, mentioned below. 4. Alice M., born October 26, 1875, married Harry H. Barrett; daughter Beatrice Barrett.

(IV) Harry Leonard Wardle, son of Robert Lawton Wardle (3), was born in Boston, September 2, 1861. He was educated in the public and high schools of Dedham and the Massachusetts College of Pharmacy in Boston. When he was sixteen years old he entered the employ of B. F. Smith, druggist, in Dedham as clerk and remained in his employ until he came of age, when he bought the business of his employer and has carried it on successfully to the present time, a period of more than twenty-five years. Mr. Wardle is a leader in business circles, a citizen of much influence and popularity. He is a past master of Constellation Lodge, Ancient Free and Accepted Masons; past high priest of Norfolk Chapter, Royal Arch Masons; Hyde Park Council, Royal and Select Masters; Cyphas Commandery, Knights Templar; Aleppo Temple, Nobles of the Mystic Shrine. He is a member of the Protestant Episcopal church of Dedham. He married, June 26, 1884, Aurilla F. Heath, daughter of William Welch and Julia (Merrow) Heath. (See Heath family herewith). Children: 1. Robert Heath, born September 18, 1888. 2. William Heath, May 28, 1899.

HEATH

(I) Bartholomew Heath, immigrant ancestor, was born in England in 1615 and died in Haverhill, Massachusetts, January 15, 1681. He settled first in Newbury, but removed to Haverhill about 1645. He was a proprietor there in 1646. He deeded land March 12, 1668-69, to his sons John, Joseph and Josiah Heath. He deposed in 1657 that he was about forty-one years old. The inventory of his estate was dated March 28, 1682. His brother, John Heath, also of Haverhill, died January 17, 1674-75, mentioning Bartholomew in his will, dated December 28, 1674. Bartholomew married Hannah Moyce, daughter of Joseph Moyce, the immigrant. She died at Haverhill, July 19, 1677. Children: 1. John, born August 15, 1643, mentioned below. 2. Joseph, mentioned below. 3. Joshua, born February 12, 1646-47, died August, 1647. 4. Hannah, born September 3, 1648, died November 9, 1668. 5. Josiah, born September 4, 1651. 6. Elizabeth, born March 19, 1653-54, died January 28, 1654-55. 7. Benjamin, born August 8, 1656, died June 29, 1657. 8. Elizabeth, born September 5, 1658, died February 11, 1659.

(II) John Heath, son of Bartholomew Heath (1), was born August 15, 1643, at Haverhill; married, November 14, 1666, Sarah, daughter of William Partridge. He died at Hampton, New Hampshire, September 21, 1706; his widow Sarah died there July, 1718. Children, all born at Haverhill: 1. Bartholomew, September 2, 1667, married, January 23, 1690-91, Mary Bradley; killed by the Indians, August 4, 1704; left five children born 1691-1700 at Haverhill. 2. Elizabeth, March 1, 1669-70, died December 9, 1683. 3. Hannah, May 3, 1673. 4. John, March 14, 1674-75, mentioned below. 5. Martha, November 3, 1677. 6. Nehemiah. 7. Rachel, July 23, 1682, married Samuel Stevens. 8. Ann, June 30, 1684. 9. Sarah, April 22, 1688.

(III) John Heath, son of John Heath (2), was born in Haverhill, March 14, 1674-75, married, January 12, 1696-97, Frances Hutchins. Their first child, Samuel, was born April 25, 1698.

(II) Joseph Heath, son of Bartholomew Heath (1), was born in Haverhill, married, June 27, 1672, Martha Dow; he died December 1 or 18, 1672. She married second, December 2, 1673, Joseph Page, son of John Page (1), and third, March 19, 1688-89, at Haverhill, Samuel Parker, son of Joseph (1). Joseph Heath had but one child: Joseph, mentioned below.

(III) Joseph Heath, son of Joseph Heath (2), was born March 23, 1673, and married, in 1697, Hannah Bradley. They had nine children between 1698 and 1718 at Haverhill. Among them was Samuel, mentioned below.

(IV) Samuel Heath, son of Joseph Heath (3), was born in Haverhill, September 8, 1698. He married Elizabeth ———. Children, born in Haverhill: 1. Moses, November 11, 1725. 2. Samuel, February 18, 1727. 3. Susanna, September 26, 1729. 4. Stephen, May 4, 1731. 5. Daniel, February 25, 1733-34, mentioned below. 6. Hannah, March 19, 1735 (twin). 7. Elizabeth (twin), March 19, 1735, died April 9, 1735. 8. Elizabeth, March 1, 1736-37.

(V) Daniel Heath, son of Samuel Heath (4), was born in Haverhill, Massachusetts, February 25, 1733-34. He settled in Plaistow, New Hampshire, the adjoining town, and married, about 1753, Elizabeth Call. He was a soldier in the revolution from Plaistow, in Captain Jesse Page's company, Colonel Abraham Drake's regiment in 1777; also in 1778-79 in Captain Ezekiel Gile's company. Among his children was Daniel, born January 22, 1764, was also a soldier in the revolution, enlisting from New Chester (now Hill) New Hampshire, in 1780, and his age is given as sixteen at that time. (Vol. 3, p. 96, N. H. Rev. Rolls).

(VI) Daniel Heath, son of Daniel Heath (5), was born in Plaistow, New Hampshire, January 22, 1764, died in Enfield, July 4, 1828. He removed to New Chester, New Hampshire, and Enfield. His revolutionary service is given above. He married first, a Miss March, of Newburyport, New Hampshire; children: Jonathan, Daniel, David, Eben, Holland, Ichabod, Dorset, mentioned below; Lydia and Sarah. He married second, Rhoda Black, a native of Newburyport, Massachusetts, by whom he had two children: Rhoda and Charlotte. He married third, ———.

(VII) Dorset Heath, son of Daniel Heath (6), was born in Enfield, New Hampshire, February 9, 1800, died there February 23, 1872. He was a farmer in Enfield. He married Sarah Welch, born July 8, 1804, in Canaan, New Hampshire, and died January 24, 1883, in Lebanon, New Hampshire. Children, born at Enfield: 1. Augustus, married Melissa Babbett. 2. Olivia, married first, William Huse; second, ——— McMurry. 3. Alzena, married William Currier; children: William, Elbridge, Nellie and Mabel Currier. 4. Horace, married Julia Morgan; child, Jennie. 5. Alvira, died young. 6. William Welch, mentioned below. 7. Aurilla, died young. 8. Ellen, died young. 9. Belle, married Elbridge Currier. 10 and 11. Children, died in infancy.

(VIII) William Welch Heath, son of Dorset Heath (7), was born in Enfield, May 24, 1831, died February 26, 1870. Married Julia Merrow, born 1833 and died April 12, 1887, daughter of Reuben and Pamelia (Wiswall) Merrow. Her father was born in Maine in 1800, and her mother in the same year. William W. Heath was educated in the public schools of his native town. He came to Dedham, Massachusetts, in 1866, and was employed for a number of years as conductor on the Boston and Providence railroad, now the New York, New Haven and Hartford. Child: Aurilla F., born May 19, 1861, in Lowell, Massachusetts, married, June 26, 1884, Harry Leonard Wardle. (See Wardle).

VAN BUREN

It was not a custom among the early Dutch settlers on Manhattan island and in New Netherlands to have recognized surnames previous to the conquest of their possessions in America by the Duke of York, soon after the middle of the seventeenth century, except in cases where by some special distinction one was placed in a position of pre-eminence, and then the patronymic assumed or acquired usually had relation to the particular event which placed the possessor in a more exalted station than his fellows or, which more frequently was the case, in allusion to the village or municipality in which he lived or from whence he came or the seat of abode of his ancestors in Holland. And when family names were assumed they usually were accompanied with the prefix Van, which is Dutch for of or from. Thus doubtless it was with the second generation of the Van Buren family, the progenitor of which was Cornelis Maessen, Maes or Maas being the christian name of his father, and the suffix sen or se signifying son. This manner of patronymic was the custom not only with the Dutch, but with some other European peoples. To illustrate: Marten, the eldest son of Cornelis Maessen, made his will in 1703, and wrote his name "Marten Cornelissen van Beuren," meaning Marten son of Cornelis from Buren.

(I) Cornelis Maessen, the immigrant, son of Maes and ancestor of perhaps the oldest family of the Van Buren surname in this country, probably came from the village of Buren, in the province of Gelderland, Holland, or was a native of that place. In the summer of 1631 he sailed for America in the ship "Rensselaerwyck," with his young wife Catalyntje Martense (daughter of Marten), and brought with them at least one child, a son Marten, who afterward made oath that he was born in Houten, a small village not far from Buren. A second son Hendrick was born on the passage. Cornelis Maessen settled on a farm on the east side of Hudson river, a short distance below Greenbush, at a place called Papsknee, the land being leased to him by Killian Van Rensselaer, who had large estates granted him in the present counties of Albany and Rensselaer, and to which had been given the name of Rensselaerwyck. The grant had been made on condition that the lands be occupied and improved by actual settlers. The rental for the first few years was at about one-tenth of the product raised by each settler, and thus in 1644 Van Rensselaer received from Cornelis Maessen one hundred bushels in wheat, oats, rye and peas, indicating a yield of about one thousand bushels. Cornelis Maessen and his wife both died in 1648, and it is recorded that they were buried on the same day. He evidently died intestate and before any of his children had attained full age, for in 1657 they were under guardianship of Teunis Dirksen (Van Vechten) and Cornelis Teunissen (Bos), who also were appointed trustees of the estate. The latter came over in 1631 with Cornelis Maessen as his farm hand, afterward became a trader and at one time was commissary at Fort Orange (Albany). The estate of Cornelis Maessen consisted in part of property in New York, described as "a house and plantation at the North River on the Island of Manhattan next to Wouter Van Twiller and Thomas Hall." This farm was purchased October 24, 1646, from Volckert Evertsen, and afterward was sold by the trustees to Rutger Jacobsen for fifteen hundred guilders ($600). It was located between Christopher and Fourteenth streets and probably fronted North river. Cornelis and Catalyntje (Martense) Maessen had five children: 1. Marten. 2. Hendrick, born in 1631, on passage to America. It is said that he lived "very quietly," on lands inherited from his father or in that vicinity. During the Indian outbreak in 1663 he was a soldier of the garrison at Fort Cralo, near Papsknee. 3. Maes Cornelisse, who for some reason adopted the name of Bloomingdael; and the American Bloomingdales of the present day trace their ancestry to this son of Cornelis Maessen. 4. Styntje (Christina) Cornelisse, married, 1663, Dirck Wesselse (Ten Broeck) a merchant and trader, who became prominent and rich; was recorder of Albany under the charter granted in 1686, mayor, 1696-98, and major in Colonel Pieter Schuyler's regiment, in 1700. 5. Tobias, supposed to have died without issue. It may be said here that of the sons of Cornelis Maessen all except Maes and possibly Tobias, of whom little is known, adopted the surname of Van Buren.

(II) Marten Cornelise Van Buren, son of Cornelis Maessen, and who for some reason acquired the name of "Black" Marten, deposed in 1660 that he was born in Houten, in the province of Utrecht, Holland, not far from the town of Buren from which the family derives its name. He was born in 1629 and died November 13, 1703. In 1662 he owned a house and barn, with some other property, "this side of Bethlehem," which he afterward sold to Gysbert Cornelise Van Den Bergh. In 1675 he leased half of Constapel's island, below Albany, and in 1683 both he and his wife were members of the Dutch Church in Albany, having become members probably in 1682. In 1700 he was captain of a company of Colonel Schuyler's regiment. His will, dated April 10, 1703, was admitted to probate June 7, 1710. He married (first) Maritje, daughter of Pieter and Marritje Quackenbosch, and married (second) May 7, 1693, Tanneke Adams, widow of Pieter Winne. Marten Cornelise had seven children: 1. Cornelis Martense, married September 22, 1689, Ariantje Gerritse (Van Der Bergh), and had a son Tobias, ancestor of the Van Burens of Ulster county, New York. After the death of Cornelis, his widow Ariantje married Coenraad Elmendorf, of Kingston, New York. 2. Cornelia, married September 22, 1689, Robert Teuwise (Van Deusen). 3. Pieter. 4. Marritje, married (1) March 14, 1695, Jans Teuwise (Van Deusen); (2) December 20, 1702, Cornelis Gerritse (Van Der Bergh). 5. Marten, died October, 1740; was freeholder at Rensselaerwyck in 1720; married (1) about 1700, Judikje Barentse; (2) July 14, 1719, Maria Van Der Bergh; had seven children by each wife. 6. Catalina, married Jonathan Jans Witbeck. 7. Magdalena.

(III) Pieter Martense Van Buren, son of Marten Cornelise Van Buren, was born about 1670, and died before 1743, when his four eldest sons are mentioned as freeholders at Kinderhook. In 1695 both he and his wife were admitted to the Dutch Church in Albany as from Kinderhook, where he probably settled at the time of his marriage. The farm he occupied there joined that of Pieter Vosberg, who had married Jannetje, sister of Ariaantje Bernetse. He was a freeholder at Kinderhook in 1720. There is no record of his will and it is probable that he died intestate. He married January 15, 1693, Ariaantje Berentse, daughter of Barent and Eytje (Ida) Meindersen. The record of baptism of their nine children in the Dutch Church in Albany is as follows: 1. Cornelis, May 14, 1693; married September 8, 1724, Maria Litner. 2. Barent, January 20, 1695; married December 29, 1719, Maria Winne. 3. Marritje, March 8, 1696; probably died unmarried. 4. Tobias, November 7, 1697; married January 10, 1721, Anna Goes. 5. Eytje, January 7, 1700; married October 21, 1719, Marten Vosburg. 6. Marten, December 28, 1701. 7. Cornelia, August 24, 1707. 8. Ephraim, March 11, 1711. 9. Maria, December 18, 1715.

(IV) Marten Pieterse Van Buren, son of Pieter Martense and Ariaantje Barentse (Meindersen) Van Buren, was baptized in the Dutch Church, Albany, New York, December 28, 1701, and married November 7, 1729, Dirckje Van Aelstyne, born April, 1710, daughter of Abraham Janse and Marritje (Van Deusen) Van Aelstyne, who married January 17, 1694. Marten and Dirckje (Van Aelstyne) Van Buren had seven children: 1. Marritje, baptized January 18, 1730; died young. 2. Pieter, baptized October 27, 1731; died young. 3. Pieter, baptized July 22, 1733; married 1766, Catharine Quackenbosch, and were sponsors at the baptism of their nephew, Martin Van Buren, eighth president of the United States. 4. Marritje, baptized April 6, 1735; died young. 5. Abraham, baptized at Albany, February 27, 1737. He owned a small farm at Kinderhook, and in connection with farming pursuits kept tavern in his large house. During the revolution he was captain of a company in Colonel Abraham Van Alstyne's regiment of New York troops. He married Maria Goes, widow of Johannes Van Allen, and by her had five children: Dirckje, born 1777, died October 18, 1865; Jannetje, baptized January 16, 1780; Martin, baptized December 15, 1782, eighth president of the United States; Lawrence, born Kinderhook, 1783, died July 1, 1868, (farmer at Kinderhook; major in the American army during the war of 1812-15; presidential elector, 1852); Abraham, baptized May 11, 1788, lawyer at Hudson, New York. 6. Ariaantje, baptized March 4, 1739. 7. Marritje, baptized October 2, 1743. 8. Marten, baptized 1748.

(V) Marten Van Buren, son of Marten Pieterse and Dirckje (Van Aelstyne) Van Buren, was baptized at Claverack-on-Hudson, in 1748. He married twice; first, September 10, 1761, Hendrikje Van Buren; married second, August 8, 1774. He had five children by his first wife: 1. Barent, born August 29, 1762. 2. Margarita, June 3, 1765. 3. Teunis, May 3, 1769. 4. Maria, July 21, 1774. 5. Abraham, April 16, 1782.

(VI) Abraham Van Buren, son of Marten and Hendrikje Van Buren, was born near Albany, New York, April 16, 1782, and became a prominent and wealthy merchant of Philadelphia, Pennsylvania. He married three times, and by wife Mary (Swift) Van Buren had children: 1. Mary Swift, born January 1, 1804; married in Ghent, Columbia county, New York, June 13, 1826, James Wardle (sometimes written Wardwell) (see Wardle). 2. Philip. 3. Henry.

(For ancestry see Thomas Low 1).

LOW (II) John Low, second son of Thomas and Susannah Low, was born probably in Ipswich, and died there about 1695, leaving an estate inventoried at about one hundred, sixty-five pounds. He was a malster succeeding to the business formerly carried on by his father, and continued it until about the time of his death. He married first, December 10, 1661, Sarah, daughter of John and Elizabeth Thorndike, of Beverly; second, Dorcas ———. By wife Sarah he had five children, and one child by wife Dorcas: 1. John, born April 24, 1665. 2. Elizabeth, October 10, 1667. 3. Margaret,

January 26, 1669. 4. Dorcas, November 3, 1673. 5. Martha, September, 1679. 6. Hannah, July 13, 1685.

(III) John Low, sometimes called John, Jr., first son of John and Sarah (Thorndike) Low, was born in Chebacco Parish, Ipswich, April 24, 1665, and married, in 1690, Johannah ———; children: 1. John, February 22, 1691; married, 1713, Anna Annable. 2. Thomas, March 5, 1692. 3. Hannah, February 1, 1693-4. 4. Nathaniel, November 15, 1695; married Abigail Riggs. 5. Johanna, January 4, 1698.

(IV) Thomas Low, son of John, Jr., and Johannah Low, was born in Chebacco Parish, Ipswich, March 5, 1692, and married (intentions) September 30, 1721, Abigail Fellows, born 1688, youngest but one of six children of Joseph Fellows, of Ipswich, who is mentioned as entitled "to certain rights of commonage in 1664, and was a voter in town affairs in 1679," made freeman, 1682, and died in 1693. He married August 19, 1676, Ruth ———, and had sons Joseph and William, and daughters Mary, Ruth, Sarah and Abigail. Joseph Fellows was son of William Fellows, who was granted common rights in Ipswich in 1641, and died before November 27, 1677. The name of his wife does not appear, but he left sons Ephraim, Samuel, Joseph and Isaac, and daughters Mary, Elizabeth, Abigail and Sarah. Thomas and Abigail (Fellows) Low had children, and if more than two their names do not appear in the Ipswich records. They had Daniel, baptized January 16, 1725-6, and Aaron baptized January 7, 1727-8.

(V) Daniel Low, son of Thomas and Abigail (Fellows) Low was born in Chebacco Parish, Ipswich, and was baptized there January 16, 1725-6. He married (published) Octo- 27, 1748, Ruammi (or Ruami) Andrews, who was baptized in Chebacco Parish, August 31, 1729, daughter of Deacon John Andrews, born Chebacco, February 2, 1675-6, and married (published) January 4, 1706-7, Elizabeth Story. Deacon John Andrews was son of Ensign William Andrews, born about 1649, in Chebacco, and married October 21, 1672, Margaret Woodward. Ensign William Andrews was son of Lieutenant John Andrews, carpenter and yeoman, born in England about 1618, and was of Ipswich, (Chebacco) as early as 1642. His wife's name was Jane. Daniel and Ruammi (Andrews) Low had (Ipswich vital records) children: 1. Daniel, born September 13, 1749. 2. Ruami, September 7, 1751. 3. Abigail, March 11, 1753; died young. 4. Abigail, baptized March 17, 1754. 5. Simons (or Symonds), born May 27, 1756.

(VI) Daniel Low, son of Daniel and Ruammi (Andrews) Low, was born in Chebacco Parish, Ipswich, now Essex, September 13, 1749, and died in Salem. He married, January 1, 1774, in North Church, Salem, Mary Luscom, the ceremony being performed by Rev. Dr. Thomas Barnard. They had six children: Hannah, Polly, Abigail, Susan, Richard and one other.

(VII) Richard Low, son of Daniel and Mary (Luscom) Low, was born in Salem, about 1800. He married Margaret Brown; eight children: Adeline, Samuel, Mary and Daniel, and four others who died young.

(VIII) Daniel Low, son of Richard and Margaret (Brown) Low, was born in Salem, February 13, 1842. He is a merchant, head of the firm of Daniel Low & Company, jewelers and silversmiths, the largest establishment of its kind in Essex county, and one of the most extensive in all respects in New England. Mr. Low married April 12, 1866, Eliza J. Stevens, born in Searsmont, Maine, October 7, 1842, daughter of Ebenezer and Eliza J. (Currier) Stevens (see Stevens). Children: 1. Seth Frederick, born Salem, July 17, 1867; married Florence, daughter of Daniel Stevens, a native of Newburyport, Massachusetts, and resident of San Francisco, California. 2. Harry Chamberlain, born August 5, 1870; married Mabel Chipman, had Daniel Story and Carolyn Low. 3. Florence, born November 28, 1875; married Harlan P. Kelsey, had Harlan Low Kelsey, born November 1, 1904, and Seth Low Kelsey, 1906.

STEVENS The Stevens family of the line here considered is not believed to have any connection with those of Salisbury and Amesbury, and appears to have been a distinct offshoot of an English family of that surname which in the first half of the seventeenth century became seated in Gloucester on Cape Ann, whence in later years its descendants migrated to other parts, some of them to New Hampshire, others to Maine, and perhaps still others to various towns east of the Hudson river.

(I) William Stevens, ship carpenter, was among the first permanent settlers in Gloucester, and became famous for his mechanical skill, his inflexible integrity, and his service in various public capacities. He came to New England before 1632 and probably lived for a time in the vicinity of Boston. He was in

Salem in 1636, was made freeman there in 1640, and in 1642 appears in Gloucester as one of the commissioners appointed by the general court for ordering town affairs; and it is believed that because of his prominence and influence and the efficient discharge of his duties in whatever capacity he received the unusual grant of five hundred acres of land lying between Chebacco and Annisquam rivers. He also had a grant of six acres on the "Meeting-house Neck," but his house was at the "Cut, near the Beach," where he had eight acres of land. He was selectman several years, commissioner for ending small causes, town clerk, and four years representative to the general court. He is said to have built a number of vessels of superior quality, one of which was the "Royal Merchant," "a ship of 600 tonns." He was a member of the general court in 1665, when the colonial government made a strong protest against the action of the commissioners sent over by the king for the purpose of directing legislation in the colony, and because of his declarations at that time he was arraigned for trial before the court in Salem in 1677. According to the testimony of four Gloucester witnesses, he was shown to have said "that he would bear no office within this jurisdiction, nor anywhere else, where Charles Stewart had anything to do; that he cared no more for Charles Stewart than any other man, as king; and that he abhorred the name of Charles Stewart as king." For this offence of "lese majeste" he was punished with a sentence of imprisonment for one month, a fine of twenty-five pounds, besides costs, and to be deprived of his privileges as freeman. Soon afterward his wife in a petition to the general court represented that he was deranged and herself aged and having a family. There is no record of his death or the settlement of his estate, for he again "grew to poverty," having mortgaged part of his lands in 1667 and never recovered them. This took away the five hundred acres granted him, as is mentioned in a preceding paragraph. Another portion of his lands, including a new house, was deeded in trust to his sons James and Isaac for the use and benefit of their mother Philippa, who died August 31, 1681. Besides these sons he had a daughter Mary, who married John Coit, and a daughter Ruth, who married William Glover.

(II) James Stevens, son of William, had a grant of land on Town Neck, near Trynell Cove, in 1658. He married Susannah, daughter of Sylvester Eveleth, December 31, 1656, and died March 25, 1697, leaving an estate of nearly two hundred and forty pounds. It is supposed that he was a shipwright, and the records show that he filled many of the most important offices in the town, deacon of the church, officer of militia, selectman in 1667 and from 1674 to 1691, and for ten years represented Gloucester in the general court. He had eleven children, of whom William, Samuel, Ebenezer, David, Jonathan, Mary (married Francis Norwood) and Hannah were living at the time of the death of their father. His children: 1. William, born March 10, 1658. 2. James, died young. 3. James, February 4, 1661; died probably September 7, 1688. 4. Isaac, August 15, died December 20, 1664. 5. Samuel, December 5, 1665. 6. Isaac, died 1668. 7. Ebenezer, September 20, 1670. 8. Mary, June 13, 1672; married Francis Norwood. 9. Hannah, April 9, 1675. 10. David, November 5, 1677. 11. Jonathan, March 7, 1679.

(III) Ebenezer Stevens, son of Deacon James and Susannah (Eveleth) Stevens, was born in Gloucester, September 20, 1670, and is believed to have been identical with Major Ebenezer Stevens, of Kingston and Salisbury, New Hampshire, one of the foremost men of that province in his time and in whose honor Stevenstown is named. "No name was given the granted township in the conveyance by the Masonian proprietors, but the grantees with one accord, without formal action, designated it is 'Major Stevenstown,' which in the course of time was abbreviated and called Stevenstown." In his "History of Gloucester," the author, Mr. Babson, speaking of Ebenezer Stevens says that he was born in 1670 and is supposed to have married widow Mary Day in 1723; that no children are recorded as having been born to him, and that he died about 1757; but in his "Notes and Additions" to Mr. Babsons's original work, Mr. Perley corrects the error of the former writer in stating that Ebenezer Stevens married and died in Gloucester, Mr. Babson having confused him with another person of the same name. Mr. Perley himself says that he cannot trace Ebenezer Stevens beyond 1699, when he was at sea. It is very well known that several of Deacon James Steven's sons went from Gloucester to New Hampshire and were prominently identified with the early civil and military history of that region; and there are many circumstances which tend to confirm the belief that Major

Stevens is identical with the son of Deacon James and Susannah (Eveleth) Stevens, of Gloucester and Cape Ann.

There appears to have been two persons of the name Ebenezer Stevens among the grantees of Stevenstown, the "Major" and the "Colonel," while still another is mentioned in the early records, although not as a proprietor; and he was known as the "Captain." They in fact represented three generations of the same family, the "Major," his son the "Colonel," and his grandson the "Captain." Major Stevens was a very prominent man in Kingston history, for several years member of the assembly, four or five years speaker of the house, and a soldier of the early wars with the French and Indians. In 1710, when Captain Gilman went with a company in pursuit of the Indians who killed Colonel Hilton's men, Stevens was his guide, although in Colonel Potter's narrative it is stated that "Ebenezer Webster, grandfather of Daniel Webster, was the pilot" of the avenging party. Major Stevens died November 1, 1749. The place and date of his birth are not mentioned in any New Hampshire references, and in the "History of Salisbury" the author says "we are not able to ascertain the date or the place of his birth," which statement tends to confirm the belief that he was in fact a son of Deacon James Stevens, of Gloucester. Major Stevens married December 5, 1710, Elizabeth Colcord, who died November 20, 1769; children: 1. Benjamin, February 3, 1713. 2. Colonel Ebenezer, June 14, 1715. 3. Hannah, June 25, 1718. 4. Mary, May 23, 1721. 5. Samuel, May 21, 1724. 6. John, March 9, 1729.

(IV) Samuel Stevens, son of Major Ebenezer and Elizabeth (Colcord) Stevens, was born in Kingston, New Hampshire, May 21, 1724, and is mentioned with his father and elder brother Colonel Ebenezer, among the proprietors of Stevenstown, in 1749. He married first, December 15, 1748, Shuah Fifield, died January 30, 1751, at the birth of her only child; second, January 29, 1752, Hannah Morrell. He had children: 1. Samuel, born January 30, 1751. 2. Ebenezer, December 4, 1752. 3. Benjamin, January 10, 1754. 4. Moses, April 28, 1756. 5. Shuah, April 13, 1757, died young. 6. Sarah, twin, March 27, 1759. 7. Shuah, twin, March 27, 1759. 8. Joshua, November 3, 1761. 9. Daniel. 10. Hannah, 1764. 11. Peter, 1766. 12. Edward, February 8, 1768.

(V) Ebenezer Stevens, son of Samuel and Hannah (Morrell) Stevens, was born in Kingston, New Hampshire, December 4, 1752, and married Polly Stevens, born June 11, 1757. They had two children and probably others whose names are not found. They had Ebenezer, born November 1, 1782, died September 28, 1851, and Benjamin, born April, 1788, died in Farmington, Maine, October 1, 1835. His widow went to Belfast, Maine, and was known to the family as "Aunt Ben," she married again a Mr. Palmeter.

(VI) Ebenezer Stevens, Jr., son of Ebenezer and Polly Stevens, was born in Gilmanton, New Hampshire, November 1, 1782, and died in Montville, Maine, September 28, 1851. He was one of the very first settlers in the vicinity of Montville, and lived there more than forty years. He was universally esteemed and will long be remembered for his many excellent traits of character, especially for that humane and benevolent disposition which made him the friend and benefactor of those around him in times of mental distress or pecuniary want. He married January 17, 1809, Ursula Judkins, born March 7, 1789, daughter of Benjamin and Ruth (Choate) Judkins and granddaughter of Joel and Mehitable (Calkins) Judkins. Ebenezer and Ursula (Judkins) Stevens had ten children: 1. Ebenezer 3d, born December 11, 1809. 2. Ruth, October 29, 1811, died April, 1863. 3. Moses, July 22, 1813. 4. Samuel S., January 14, 1815. 5. Abigail G., January 22, 1818, died 1841. 6. Rhoda M., June 21, 1820, died August, 1853. 7. Daniel, died February, 1886. 8. Frederick A., May, 1825, died 1838. 9. Ursula, June 2, 1827. 10. George W. August 4, 1830; married (1) November 30, 1857, Harriet Shepley, (2) June 11, 1868, June Stevens.

(VII) Ebenezer Stevens, 3d, son of Ebenezer Jr. and Ursula (Judkins) Stevens, was born December 11, 1809, and married August 27, 1835, Eliza J. Currier. Their daughter, Eliza J. Stevens, born Searsmont, Maine, October 7, 1842, married April 12, 1866, Daniel Low, of Salem (see Low).

BROWN The town of Kilmarnock, in Ayrshire, Scotland, is situated about twenty miles from the city of Glasgow and lays of the Kilmarnock water. For many years the town was famous for the manufacture of "Kilmarnock cowls", and afterward became noted for the superior quality of its immense output of carpets. For many years the town was a principal center for skillful weavers and drew its population of workmen from all the country about and also from the cities.

Among those who went to the factories of Kilmarnock from Glasgow was one Robert Brown, who was born about the year 1815 and died in 1854, at the age of thirty-nine years. He was a carpet weaver, and after his apprenticeship spent the remaining years of his life at his trade; but died when still a young man, and left a family of several children to the care of his widow. Her name before marriage was Margaret Glover, and they were married in Kilmarnock. Both of them were devout Presbyterians and their children were brought up in that faith. When the children of the widow Brown were old enough to work they were put out to learn trades, and when they became practical workmen, capable of earning good wages, they set about locating themselves in a place which provided better living than the factories of Kilmarnock and Glasgow, and thus it was that Hugh Brown, second son and fourth child of Robert and Margaret, left Glasgow and came to America about the year 1870. He was followed within a few years by others of the family, and in 1872 the mother herself came over with her youngest son and two of her daughters, one daughter and one son having died before she left Scotland for America. Those of the children who came to New England may be mentioned as follows: 1. James, the eldest child, came about 1872, and has spent the greater part of his business life in the vicinity of Providence, Rhode Island, where he is a machinist. 2. Janet, the eldest daughter, came in 1872. She married Edward Bateson, who died, and she now lives with her daughter in Worcester, Massachusetts. 3. Mary, the second daughter, came in 1872. She married, in Glasgow, George Muir, and died in Providence, Rhode Island, leaving children. 4. Hugh, the fourth child, came to this country in 1870, and was the first of the family to cross the Atlantic. In Scotland his home was in Glasgow, and in New England he lived first in Worcester, then in Boston, later in Gloucester, where he was employed by his youngest brother, William G. Brown, and he died in Everett, Massachusetts. He married Mary Hair, and had children. 5. Margaret, the third daughter, never came to America. She was born in Kilmarnock and died in Glasgow, in 1869. She married David Tyndall, but had no children. 6. Robert, the next child in order of birth, died when young. 7. William Glover, the Gloucester merchant, mentioned below.

William Glover Brown, youngest child of Robert and Margaret (Glover) Brown, was born in Kirkfieldbank, Scotland, April 26, 1854, and was an infant when his father died. After his death his widow left Kilmarnock and returned to Glasgow, and there William was sent to the day school until he was about twelve years old, when he was put in the office of a tradesman as message boy, and later on, as he grew more familiar with the work of his employer, he went into the sales department as clerk, and worked there until 1872, when he came with his mother and her two daughters to New England.

Mr. Brown was a young man of eighteen years when he arrived in New England, but even then he had gained a fair understanding of the dry goods trade and the duties of a clerk in the sales department, and therefore he easily secured a position with the house of Callendar, MacAuslan & Troup, merchants, of Providence, where he was employed during the next eight years; and these were profitable years for the young salesman and enabled him to gain a good knowledge of business methods in a large New England mercantile establishment, and also to lay by a small sum of money with which to start in business for himself. He proved himself a capable and trustworthy employee, but even then had higher ambitions than a future life behind the counter in a salesroom, and shaped his course to the end of being himself proprietor of a mercantile house; but it is a question whether Mr. Brown then had any idea whatever that he would become the head of an establishment so extensive as his great department store in Gloucester, larger by far than any other on Cape Ann, and one of the largest in Essex county; and this great business enterprise he has built up within the last fifteen years.

Having worked as a clerk for his Providence employers for eight years, Mr. Brown opened a small dry goods store in Milford, Massachusetts, in partnership with Mr. J. S. MacDonald. They remained together from 1880 until 1883, when he bought out his partner's interest in the business and continued it alone about two years more. In 1885 he moved his stock to Gloucester and opened a store in a small building on the south side of Main street. Five years later the demands of increasing trade made it necessary to find more ample store space, and in 1890 he moved to his present location on the north side of Main street; but since then he has enlarged the capacity of his store some four or five times, and

W. G. Brown

his small dry goods shop of 1885 has developed into an extensive modern department house, and he himself to-day stands at the head of the most successful mercantile establishment on Cape Ann, and this position the result of his own personal effort and capable business management. In Gloucester, Mr. Brown is regarded as one of the leading business men of that city, one of its most enterprising and public spirited citizens, and a man of strict integrity of character and moral worth. He was brought up under Presbyterian influences and religious teaching, and is a regular attendant at the services of the Congregational church of Gloucester. Mr. Brown is a director in the City National Bank of Gloucester; a vice-president of Gloucester Co-operative Bank; president of the Commonwealth Club of Gloucester; vice-president of the James H. Tarr Company of Gloucester; director in the Snowden Mills Corporation of Providence; director in the Gloucester Fresh Fish Company; director in the Adams Clock Company of Boston; member of various Masonic bodies—the blue lodge, chapter and commandery; also of the Scots Charitable Society of Boston, and of the Ancient and Honorable Artillery Company of Boston.

On October 31, 1884, Mr. Brown married Minnie S. Russell, of Worcester, Massachusetts, daughter of James Russell, of that city. Two children have been born of this marriage: 1. William Glover Brown Jr., born September, 1886, now a student at Dartmouth College. 2. Margaret Murdock, born September, 1888, a graduate of Gloucester high school, now attending Rogers Hall School, at Lowell, Massachusetts.

(For ancestry see Samuel Packard 1).

PACKARD (VII) Colonel Abner B. Packard, son of William and Lucy (Turner) Packard (6), born in Quincy, Massachusetts, November 21, 1821, died there October 17, 1902. He was educated and reared to manhood in his native town. He was early taught habits of industry and economy by his parents. In 1842 he founded the business of manufacturing various kind of type metals and refining dross, etc., at Quincy. In this undertaking he met with immediate and marked success. He was sincere and punctual in all his affairs, and by all with whom he had business dealings he was regarded with high esteem, and it may be correctly said that at the time of his death he had left the impress of his individuality upon a wide community, and to his family the priceless heritage of an honored name. Mr. Packard was in the militia when a young man, and was promoted through the various grades to the rank of colonel. He responded to the first call for troops when the civil war broke out in April, 1861, and served at the head of his regiment, the Fourth Massachusetts Infantry. During his long and useful career, he always strove to do his duty as a citizen, and frequently gave of his time and substance to promote the material as well as the social interests of the town. He served as vice-president and for many years was a member of the board of directors of the National Mt. Wollaston Bank, and was also vice-president of the Quincy Electric Light and Power Company. Politically he was a Democrat, and took an earnest interest in public affairs, but never sought or held public office. Colonel Abner B. Packard married, October 31, 1849, Elizabeth A. Newcomb, born November 1, 1830, daughter of Lewis and Mary Elvira (Page) Newcomb (See Page family). Children: 1. Abner, born September 20, 1850, died September 29, 1851. 2. Frank Clare, born June 6, 1852, mentioned below. 3. Lizzie Lee, born August 3, 1854, died March 14, 1861. 4. Ella Marie, born July 26, 1857, died March 12, 1861. 5. Lucy Newcomb, born May 15, 1861, died 1861. 6. Walter M., born June 23, 1862, mentioned below.

(VIII) Frank Clare Packard, son of Colonel Abner B. Packard (7), was born at Quincy, June 6, 1852. His educational training was obtained under private tuition. He began early to take up the practical duties of life, at the age of twenty became engaged with his father in the manufacture of inks and extracts. In this undertaking he met with well merited success, and about 1900 he engaged in the manufacture of extracts on his own account at Quincy, continuing in this line of pursuit until after the death of his father, October 17, 1902, soon after which time he became associated with his brother, Walter M., in the type metal manufacturing business, and the management of his father's estate. Not unlike his worthy sire, he is progressive and enterprising, and is regarded as a good and useful citizen. He is a member of Rural Lodge, Free and Accepted Masons, of Quincy; St. Stephens Chapter, South Shore Commandery, Knights Templar, Aleppo Temple, Mystic Shrine; Lodge No. 80, I. O. O. F., of Quincy; the Ancient and Honorable Artillery Company and many others. He has been actively identified with the fire department of the town for over thirty-five years, and during this time has served as assistant chief, and for one year was chief of the department. He married, March 31, 1875, Lucy C. Newcomb. Their children are: 1. Alice Gertrude, born July 7, 1879, married, June 6, 1903, Henry P. Miller; one son, Clare Lewis Miller, born March 30, 1906. 2. Bertha Haskell, born June 13, 1882, married, February 5, 1908, Joseph C. Morse.

(VIII) Walter M. Packard, son of Colonel Abner B. Packard (7), was born in Quincy, June 23, 1862. He acquired his early educational training under the tuition of his aunt, Lydia Savil, and after attending the Adams Academy at Quincy for some time he entered upon a four years' course in Harvard College, after which he spent two years in the Harvard Law School. He then became identified with his father's manufacturing interests, and since his death in 1902 has been associated with his brother, Frank Clare, in the manufacture of type metal and the management of the interests of his father's estate. Politically he is a Democrat. Walter M. Packard married, March 26, 1886, Carrie Fuller Litchfield, born December 13, 1869, daughter of Elwood M. and Clara Alice (Harris) Litchfield (see Litchfield family). Children: 1. Minnie, born October 2, 1887, now a student of the class of 1907 at Wellesley College. 2. Elvira Francisca, born July 8, 1889, now a student at the Boston University, class of 1911. 3. Ruth, born September 10, 1890, a graduate of the Quincy high school. 4. Dorothy, born May 16, 1892, a student in the Quincy high school.

PAGE

Nathaniel Page (1), immigrant ancestor, was probably a brother of Nicholas Page who settled in Plymouth colony. He bought land and settled in Billerica in the part now in Bedford, Massachusetts, by deed from George Grimes under date of 1688. In the same year he was appointed sheriff of Suffolk county by Governor Joseph Dudley. He married Joanna ———. He died April 12, 1692; his will is dated April 11, 1692, and was proved May 9, 1692. He owned land at Dedham, Squabauge, Worcester and Billerica. Children: 1. Nathaniel, born about 1679, mentioned below. 2. Elizabeth, married John Simpkins. 3. Sarah, married Samuel Hill. 4. James, died young. 5. Christopher, born 1690.

(II) Nathaniel Page, son of Nathaniel Page (1), was born about 1679, probably in England, and died in Bedford in 1755. He married first, November 6, 1701, Susannah Lane, born October, 1661, died January 17, 1714-15, daughter of Colonel John and Susanna (Whipple) Lane, who died August 4, 1713. Colonel John was son of Job Lane, born 1620, died August 23, 1697, and Hannah (Rayner), his wife, who died April 30, 1704. Nathaniel Page married second, in 1748, Mary Grimes. Children, born at Bedford: 1. Nathaniel, born September 4, 1702. 2. John, born October 11, 1704, mentioned below. 3. Christopher, born July 16, 1707. 4. Susannah, married Samuel Bridge, of Lexington. 5. Joanna, born 1714, married Josiah Fassett.

(III) John Page, son of Nathaniel Page (2), born in Bedford, October 11, 1704, died February 18, 1782. Although advanced in years he took an active part in the battles of Lexington and of Bunker Hill, and aided in the capture of six regulars April 19, 1775. He is credited on the state rolls with service in Captain Abishai Brown's company, Colonel John Nixon's regiment (Fifth Middlesex) at Cambridge in June, 1775; and with the same company for a short time in 1776. He married, December 31, 1730, Rebecca Wheeler, of Concord, who died July 12, 1755, aged forty-three years. He married second, January 15, 1756, Amittai Fassett, who died December 25, 1771; third, June 3, 1773, Rachel Fletcher, widow of Joseph Fletcher. He was a man of large frame and stature, and a prominent citizen of Bedford. Children, born in Bedford: 1. John, born September 2, 1733, settled in Hardwick. 2. James, born May 12, 1735. 3. Eben, born June 3, 1737. 4. Susanna, born 1739, died young. 5. Timothy, born June 11, 1741. 6. Nathaniel, born June 20, 1742. 7. Rebecca, born August 23, 1743, married Solomon Cutler. 8. Mary, died young. 9. Joanna, born June 15, 1746, married Samuel Reed. 10. Sarah, born June 8, 1747, married Josiah Beard. 11. Elizabeth, born August 3, 1748, married Micah Reed. 12. Susanna, born June 12, 1750, married Amos Haggett. 13. Samuel, born August 1, 1751, resided in New Hampshire. 14. Mary, died young.

(IV) Nathaniel Page, son of John Page (3), born June 20, 1742, died July 31, 1819. He was one of the minute-men of Bedford, April 19, 1775, and cornet and standard bearer at the Concord fight that day. He was credited with service in Lieutenant Moses Abbott's company of Bedford minute-men. He married, December 10 or 15, 1774, Sarah Brown, who died August 22, 1839, daughter of James Brown. Children, born at Bedford: 1. Nathaniel, born October 25, 1775. 2. Sarah, born May 22, 1777. 3. Timothy, born January 29, 1779. 4. John (twin), born March 3, 1781. 5. Benjamin (twin), born March 3, 1781, mentioned below. 6. Christopher, born December 10, 1784 (twin). 7. Thomas (twin), born December 10, 1784. 8. Thaddeus, born May 1, 1788. 9. Ruhamah, married Jonathan Lane.

(V) Benjamin Page, son of Nathaniel Page (4), born in Bedford, March 3, 1781, died April 8, 1855. He settled in Boxborough, Middlesex county, Massachusetts. He married, September 9, 1804, Mary Penniman, who died July 25, 1805. Their daughter, Mary Elvira, born February 25, 1805, married Lewis Newcomb, who was born in 1800. Elizabeth A. Newcomb, daughter of Lewis and Mary Elvira (Page) Newcomb, born November 1, 1830, died at Quincy in 1893 or 1894, married Colonel Abner B. Packard (See sketch of the Packard family herewith).

LITCHFIELD Lawrence Litchfield (1), immigrant ancestor, was born in England, and is progenitor of all the old families of this name in America. He was a member of the Boston Artillery Company as early as 1640, but soon afterward made his home in Scituate. He was on the list of men able to bear arms in Barnstable in 1643. In 1645 he returned to Scituate. His widow Judith married William Dennis. She testified March 20, 1657-58, that her husband on his death-bed consented that John Allen, of Scituate, might adopt his son, Josiah or Josias Litchfield. Children: 1. Lawrence, resided at Barnstable and Scituate. 2. Remembrance, married ——— Lewis. 3. Dependance, born February 15, 1646, at Scituate. 4. Josiah, born in 1647, mentioned below.

(II) Josiah (or Josias) Litchfield, son of Lawrence Litchfield (1), was born in 1647 at Scituate. He was given by his father at the time of his death to John Allen who left him a legacy in land at Scituate, June 2, 1663. He married, February 22, 1671, Sarah Baker, daughter of Rev. Nicholas Baker, pastor of the First Church of Scituate. Josiah was a leading citizen in town and church; was deputy to the general court and held other offices of trust and honor. Children, born at Scituate: 1. Hannah, born December 24, 1672. 2. Sarah, born September 25, 1674. 3. Josiah, born January 10, 1677, married, 1712, Mary Griggs. 4. Nicholas, born February 7, 1680, mentioned below. 5. Experience, born May 25, 1683. 6. Judith, born April 25, 1687. 7. Samuel, born February 4, 1690, married, 1712, Abigail Buck; second, Fear Turner.

(III) Nicholas Litchfield, son of Josiah Litchfield (2), was born in Scituate, February 7, 1680. He was a prominent citizen of his native town; deputy to the general court from 1738 to 1741. He married Bathsheba Clark, daughter of Thomas Clark, who came to Scituate from Plymouth about 1674, and probably granddaughter of Thomas Clark, mate of the "Mayflower." Children, born at Scituate: 1. Experience, born November 20, 1705, died January 6, 1706-07. 2. Josiah, born December 20, 1706, mentioned below. 3. Nicholas, born March 10, 1707-08, died 1787. 4. Bathsheba, born May 8, 1709. 5. James, born July 12, 1711, died about 1734; married, July 12, 1732, Ruth Tilden. 6. John, born 1712, married, July 17, 1750, Lucy Cady. 7. Israel, born 1714, married Penelope Burden, of Providence, Rhode Island; second, Phebe Hunt, of Hampton, Connecticut. 8. Eleazer, born 1715, married Desire White. 9. Susanna, born 1717. 10. Isaac, born 1719, married, 1743, Lydia Cowing; second, 1758, Hannah Hersey. 11. Thomas, born 1721, married, 1750, Lydia Coe.

(IV) Josiah Litchfield, son of Nicholas Litchfield (3), born December 20, 1706, married, July 4, 1732, Susanna Morey. Children, born in Scituate: 1. Lot, born April 23, 1733 (name changed later to Josiah). 2. James, born November 12, 1734, married Rachel Mansfield. 3. Jonah, born August 30, 1738. 4. Susanna, born March 24, 1740. 5. Daniel, born March 7, 1742, mentioned below. 6. Samuel, born February 14, 1744, married, May 29, 1766, Samuel Stockbridge, Jr. 7. Penelope, born February 17, 1746, married Ephraim Littlefield. 8. Bathsheba, born April 9, 1749. 9. Jacob, born March 12, 1750. 10. Deacon Israel, born July 7, 1753, mentioned below. 11. Lot, born November 16, 1755, married, 1777, Rachel Littlefield.

(V) Captain Daniel Litchfield, son of Josiah Litchfield (4), was born in Scituate, March 7, 1742. He was a prominent citizen in the town and militia. He married, April 20, 1765, Sarah Whitcomb. Children, born at Scituate: 1. Elijah, born June 3, 1767. 2. Bethia, born February 14, 1769. 3. Thankful, born October 23, 1772. 4. Silas, born July 17, 177—, married Polly Briggs. 5. Azotus, born November 12, 177—, married Mercy Pratt. 6. Josiah, born March 6, 177—, married Abigail Litchfield. 7. Zintha, born August 16, 1782. 8. Thankful, born July 18, 1785. 9. Daniel, born July 10, 1788, mentioned below.

(V) Deacon Israel Litchfield, son of Josiah Litchfield (4), was born in Scituate, July 7, 1753. He was a "much enlightened and respected" citizen. He was deputy to the general court in 1778; member of the state convention to frame a constitution in 1779. He was a soldier in the revolution, a sergeant in Captain Samuel Stockbridge's company, Colonel Bailey's regiment, on the Lexington alarm; also clerk of Captain Hayward Peirce's company, Colonel John Cushing's regiment (Second Plymouth County) in the Rhode Island campaign December, 1776. He prepared a genealogical tree of the Litchfield family and is credited with Rev. Abner Morse with great accuracy in his work. He married, March 26, 1778, Sarah Cass. He died in 1840. Children, born in Scituate: 1. Sibyl, April 6, 1780, married Hector Stockbridge. 2. Zoa, born February 19, 1782, married Paul Merritt. 3. Festus, born October 1, 1783, married Penelope Stockbridge. 4. Enos, born December 17, 1785. 5. Enos, born August 25, 1788. 6. Milton, born January 20, 1791, mentioned below. 7. Harvey, born August 6, 1793, died young. 8. Sophia, born August, 1797, married Thomas Litchfield. 9. Serissa, born April 14, 1803, married Rowland Bailey; second, ——— Read. 10. Alfred, born November 8, 1804, married Mary Cole.

(VI) Captain Daniel Litchfield, son of Captain Daniel Litchfield (5), was born July 10, 1788. He married Hannah Litchfield. Children, born at Scituate: 1. Priscilla Vinal, born October 30, 1807, died young. 2. Seth, born December 25, 1808. 3. Catherine, born January 1, 1811, married Alfred Clapp. 4. Priscilla, born December 24, 1812, married Isaac Litchfield. 5. Liba, born February 21, 1815. 6. Josiah, born September 5, 1816, married Harriet Pinson. 7. Lillie, born November 7, 1818, married Sumner Litchfield; mentioned below. 8. Olive, born December 31, 1820, married Israel Barnes. 9. Daniel, born August 28, 1823. 10. Otis, born March 15, 1826.

(VI) Milton Litchfield, son of Israel Litchfield (5), was born January 20, 1791, at Scituate. He married Abigail Otis. Children, born at Scituate: 1. Sumner, born January 15, 1821, mentioned below. 2. Winnett Atkins, born September 1, 1823.

(VII) Sumner Litchfield, son of Milton Litchfield (6), was born in Scituate, January 15, 1821. He married Lillie Litchfield, mentioned above, born November 7, 1818, daughter of Captain Daniel and Hannah (Litchfield) Litchfield. Children: 1. Sumner Otis, who married Salome Stoddard and they had one child, Frank Webster. 2. Milton Gray, married Sarah W. Stoddard. 3. Elwood M., born May 8, 1847, mentioned below.

(VIII) Elwood M. Litchfield, son of Sumner Litchfield (7), was born on the old Litchfield homestead, May 8, 1847. He married Clara Alice Harris, daughter of William F. and Clara Clarissa Chapman. Children: 1. Carrie Fuller, born December 13, 1869, married Walter M. Packard (See sketch).

TITCOMB The name Titcomb probably originated from the parish of Tidcombe, in county Wilts, England. Some members of the family claim the following coat-of-arms; Or, a bend azure, between two foxes' heads, erased gules. Crest, a dexter arm couped above the elbow, armed garnished or, the hand grasping a broken lance gules.

(I) William Titcomb, immigrant ancestor, came to New England in the ship "Hercules", from London. He had taken passage on the "Mary and John", which sailed March 24, 1634, but was detained and came a month later. He settled in Newbury, and was one of the original proprietors who had grants of eighty acres or less. He was admitted a freeman June 22, 1642; was selectman 1646, and at other times; representative to the general court, 1655. He took an active part in the church controversy in Newbury, and was fined four nobles for his action in supporting Mr. Woodman, together with several others. He died September 24, 1676, of "fever and ague". In a will made six days before his death he bequeathed to his wife and eldest son. He married first, Joanna Bartlett, died June 28, 1653, daughter of Richard Bartlett, Sr., of Newbury; second, March 3, 1654, Elizabeth, probably widow of William Stevens, and daughter of ——— Bitsfield. Children of first wife: 1. Sarah, married Thomas Treadwell, of Ipswich. 2. Hannah, died young. 3. Mary, married John Poore, of Newbury. 4. Mellicent, died aged seventeen. 5. William, died aged eleven. 6. Penuel, married Lydia Poore. 7. Benaiah, married Sarah Brown. Children of second wife: 8. Elizabeth, married Samuel Bartlett. 9. Rebecca, married Nathaniel Treadwell. 10. Tirzah, married first, Thomas Bartlett; second, James Ordway. 11. William, mentioned below. 12. Thomas, married Mary Dam. 13. Lydia, married Jonathan Clark. 14. Ann.

(II) Sergeant William Titcomb, son of William Titcomb (1), was born August 14, 1659, and died February 4, 1740. He married May 15, 1683, Ann Cottle, died August 15, 1847, daughter of William and granddaughter of Edward Cottle, of Salisbury. Children: 1. Jedediah, married Elizabeth Boardman. 2. Joanna, married Michael Hodge. 3. Daniel, married January 1, 1718-9, Ann Wingate; died 1758-9. 4. Sarah, married Deacon Moses Pearson. 5. Elias. 6. Joseph, mentioned below. 7. Benjamin, twin with Joseph. 8. Moses, died young. 9. John. 10. Mary, 11. Colonel Moses, married Miriam Currier.

(III) Captain Joseph Titcomb, son of Sergeant William Titcomb (2), was born March 30, 1698. He was a prominent man, and held many offices in church and state. He married, October 3, 1721, Ann Smith. Children: 1. Sarah, married John Ropes, of Salem. 2. Henry, mentioned below. 3. Mary, married ——— Lowell. 4. Benjamin. 5. Oliver, married Anna Osgood. 6. Joseph, married first, Hannah Hale; second, ——— Wyatt. 7. John, died young. 8. Anna. 9. Elizabeth, married Ebenezer Lowell. 10. Eunice, married Jonathan Dole. 11. John, married Sarah Titcomb. 12. Abigail.

(IV) Henry Titcomb, son of Captain Joseph Titcomb (3), married his cousin Mary Titcomb. Children: 1. Enoch, mentioned below. 2. Elizabeth. 3. Mary. 4. Lucy, married ——— Thompson. 5. Joseph. 6. John Smith. 7. Henry, married Abigail Whitmore. 8. John Berry.

(V) Honorable Enoch Titcomb, son of Henry Titcomb (4), was born December 6, 1752, and died August 13, 1814. He was a merchant in Newburyport. He was town treasurer for twenty-eight successive years; notary public, justice of the peace, a member of the council that framed the state constitution, a member of the state legislature during the early days of the state, and senator for a long term of years. He was in the revolution, commissioned brigade major July 3, 1778, and served in Rhode Island from July to September under Brigadier General Jonathan Titcomb. He was a deacon in the First Presbyterian Church. He married Ann, daughter of Ephraim and Mary Jones, of Portland, Maine. Children: 1. George, mentioned below. 2. Luther, married Sarah Teel. 3. Edward. 4. Nancy, married Moses Chase; had son John. 5. Francis, died aged thirty-seven; married Sally Dodd; was a silversmith. 6. Salina, went west; married Greenleaf Dole. 7. Fanny, married Moses Lord, who was postmaster many years.

(VI) George Titcomb, son of Hon. Enoch Titcomb (5), was born February 21, 1785, at Newburyport, and died there December 4, 1863. He was educated in the public schools of his native town and started to learn the printer's trade. On account of trouble with his eyes, he had to change his vocation, however, and turned to teaching school, and followed that profession for a period of fifty years. He was especially noted for his skill in penmanship and his success in teaching the art of penmanship. He had a night school for writing, for many years, in addition to his duties in the public schools. He was of the strictest integrity and sterling character, kindly and charitable. He was active in St. Paul's Protestant Episcopal Church, and for many years warden. He was a Whig and later a Republican in politics, and always keenly interested in the affairs of his native city, but never sought public office. He married Catherine DeBlois Tracy, born at Newburyport, November 12, 1794, died March 13, 1875, daughter of John and Margaret (Laughton) Tracy. Children, born at Newburyport: 1. Ann S., February 22, 1820; married George W. Hale, of Newbury; children: Catherine A.; Edward A., who is a box manufacturer in Newburyport. 2. Catherine, born March 16, 1822; married Jacob F. Hodskins, born 1818, at Newburyport, died January 9, 1890; a jeweler by trade; child, Emily Agnes Hodskins, born 1851, died 1876, married Charles F. Foy. 3. George J., born April 8, 1824, served in the civil war in an artillery company under General Benjamin F. Butler; never was heard from after the war, and must have been killed. 4. Margaret, born September 23, 1826; unmarried. 5. Mary, died in infancy. 6. Elizabeth, died in infancy. 7. Patrick Tracy, born 1834; died 1839. 8. Selina Jane, born May 19, 1835, unmarried. 9. Henry L., born June 24, 1837, died July 27, 1852.

BROWN Elder John Browne, Salem, was admitted freeman there in 1637, and joined the church the same year. He was a man of substance and influence, mariner and merchant, and carried on an extensive trade along the coasts of Maryland and Virginia. On July 8, 1660, he was chosen ruling elder of the church, then being absent on a voyage, and he accepted the office on condition that he be allowed to attend to his business in Virginia during the following winter. He was chosen to this office at the special request of Rev. John Higginson, the pastor elect, in his answer to a call to the Salem church: "There is but one thing I would commend unto ye congregation that you would think seriously of a Ruling Elder, for though I should not be unwilling to doe it wt ye Lord shall enable me, yet I am not free to undertake church work without ye assistance of a Ruling Elder the place being great, the people many, and ye work like to be much, especially in such times as these". So Mr. John Browne was nominated and after due consideration "was chosen by the church by general consent". In the church records for March 3, 1661, it is written: "It pleased God to return home our Elder Mr. Browne in safety from Virginia in ye 3d mth, notwithstanding the casting away of his vessel and goods to his great loss, and great danger he was in afterwards by ye Indians which preservation & danger was related by himself and for which solemn thanks were rendered to ye Lord in ye congregation". And again: 1664. 5th, 4th mo.: "Elder Browne, upon his return from Virginia this Spring, finding by experience his occasions such as he could not attend to ye work of an elder with the constancy and expence of ye time yt ye work of it did require, and professing a need of attending his calling as a seaman, wherein he was to be much absent from ye Church, he desired ye church yt they would dismiss him from his office, yt he might with more freedom of spirit attend the necessary duties of his calling, ye church after some time of consideration, consented to his desire, and accordingly, on ye 5th day of the 4th mth. he was dismissed from his office." In his "Annals of Salem" Mr. Felt says that Elder Brown afterward resumed the office and held it until his death.

Elder John Browne and his sons—Jonathan, John and James—were large traders to Virginia and Maryland, and had large possessions there, which were mostly lost by the untimely death of his son James, and through which Elder Browne became involved in some trouble; yet he left a good estate at his own death. The name of his wife does not appear, and it is probable that she came with him from England. She was living in 1667 and died before 1683. Elder John died before November, 1685, the date on which his will was probated. Jonathan, the eldest son, was engaged in commercial trade with Maryland and Virginia, but became financially involved and died insolvent about 1667. John, the second son, was baptized in Salem July 16, 1638, and was a master mariner. He married Hannah, daughter of Rev. Peter Hobart, of Hingham.

(II) James Browne, youngest son of Elder John Browne, was baptized in Salem July 4, 1640, and met death by violence in Maryland, where he had a plantation and trading station. The jury summoned to investigate the circumstances of his death returned a verdict that he had died by his own hand—*felo de se*—but afterward it was discovered that he had been murdered by a negro. He married 5th 7mo. 1664, Hannah, daughter of Henry Bartholomew, one of the eminent men of the colony, several times deputy to the general court, member of many colonial and town commissions, an officer of the troop of horse, and a man of large property. He died in 1692, aged ninety-two years. After the death of James Browne, his widow married, March 8, 1679-80, Dr. John Swinnerton, a noted Salem physician, and whose house adjoined that of Elder Browne. By her second husband Hannah had one child, Mary, born December 24, 1681. Children of James and Hannah (Bartholomew) Browne: Bartholomew, born March 31, 1667; Elizabeth, January 26, 1670; Hannah, March 9, 1672; James.

(III) James Browne, son of James and Hannah (Bartholomew) Browne, was born in Salem, May 23, 1675. He was a mariner in early life, and in 1717 bought of George Trask, blacksmith, for forty pounds, land near Browne's pond in Salem, now a part of South Danvers, and became a husbandman. There is a tradition in the family that James Browne was once captured by Captain Kidd's pirate crew, but escaped from the ship and swam ashore. He married, February 22, 1698-9, Elizabeth, widow of Samuel Nichols, and daughter of John and Alice Pickering. She was born 7 7th mo. 1674, and had a daughter Elizabeth by her first husband. By Samuel Browne she had sons James, Samuel, John and William; daughters Mary and Hannah.

(IV) Samuel Brown, son of James and Elizabeth (Pickering-Nichols) Browne, was baptized November 3, 1706. In 1728 he received from his father a deed of twenty acres of land in Salem, including a dwelling house, barn and outhousing, with a provision that the grantee "shall duly improve the premise according to the rules of good husbandry, and shall pay to his father and Mother Elizabeth, or the longest liver of them, during their natural lives, the full half part of the produce, and also pay to his sister Mary, wife of Samuel King, * * * within two years after the decease of his Father and Mother, fifty pounds, in good bills of the Province, or in Silver money, at eighteen shillings pr. oz; on failure the premises become the property of his father and his heirs". Samuel Brown married, January 7, 1728-9, Mary Porter, of Salem (one record says Wenham); children (dates of baptism): 1. Edith, May 3, 1730. 2. Mary, November 15, 1730. 3. John, February 5, 1732-3. 4. Anna, February 2, 1734-5. 5. Huldah, January 25, 1738. 6. Apphia, May 18, 1740. 7. Samuel, December 26, 1742. 8. William, December 16, 1744. 9. Asa, January 18, 1746-7. 10. Amos, May 14, 1749. 11. Hannah, December 15, 1751. 12. Ezra, December 8, 1754. 13. Nathan, August 28, 1757.

(V) Captain Asa Brown, son of Samuel and Mary (Porter) Brown, was baptized January 18, 1746-7. He was Captain Asa Brown of Beverly, who was sergeant in Captain Israel Hutchinson's company of minute-men from that town that marched to Cambridge on the Lexington alarm, April 19, 1775, and served two days. He married July 26, 1796, Sarah Traske, died April 16, 1841; children: 1. Saloma, baptized May 12, 1797. 2. William Trow Trask, April 19, 1798. 3. Israel, January 22, 1799. 4. Asa, March 19, 1801. 5. John, April 18, 1803. 6. Samuel, September 1, 1804. 7. Sullivan, April 21, 1806. 8. Hannah, July 11, 1808. 9. Amos, June 12, 1810.

(VI) John Brown, son of Captain Asa and Sarah (Traske) Brown, was born in Beverly, April 18, 1803, and was a farmer. He married, June 6, 1832, Sarah F., daughter of Captain Samuel Wilkins; children, (dates of baptism): 1. Sarah Elizabeth, June 20, 1838; married Ansel Webster. 2. Harriet Locke, June 20, 1838, married Francis H. Hovey. 3. Mary, June 20, 1838. 4. Martha. 5. Lucy Masury, September 6, 1841. 6. John, died in infancy. 7. John Adams, September 6, 1841. 8. Charles E. 9. George B.

(VII) George B. Brown, son of John and Sarah F. (Wilkins) Brown, was born in Beverly, Massachusetts, July 4, 1852, and received his education in the public schools of that town and in the famous Dummer Academy. After leaving school he learned the trade of a mason, and followed that occupation as a journeyman until 1878, when he removed to Ipswich and for a number of years carried on business as a builder and contractor. After the Boston fire he built and rebuilt many buildings in that city, and he also has erected several substantial buildings in Lynn, Amesbury and in other places. He was foreman of construction work on the Danvers asylum. In 1881 Mr. Brown changed his occupation and started in business as a miller and dealer in flour and feed and is still so engaged. He married first, Ada J. Dole, who died September 11, 1879, aged twenty-five years two months; second, November 29, 1883, Lottie F. Lake, of Topsfield, Massachusetts, daughter of Henry Lake. Mr. Brown had three children, all born of his first marriage and all now deceased, viz.: 1. Clarence W., born February 9, 1894, died same year. 2. Malcolm, born December 13, 1897, died May 22, 1898. 3. Elizabeth, born November 22, 1900, died July 22, 1901.

PRIOR Thomas Prior, so far as known the first of this surname in New England, was in Scituate in 1634; he died there in 1639. His sons, Daniel and John, who came from England in 1635, settled in Duxbury, as also did his son Joseph. Benjamin Prior, of a later generation of the Duxbury family, married, December 9, 1697, Bethia Pratt. Their son Benjamin, of Duxbury, who was a tanner by trade, married, November 7, 1723, Deborah Weston; he died December 3, 1766. His son Benjamin, second, born October 23, 1740, married, January, 1765, Sarah Soule, daughter of Joseph and Mercy (Fullerton) Soule. Joseph Soule was a son of Joshua Soule (3), who was son of John Soule (2), and grandson of George Soule (1), one of the "Mayflower" Pilgrims. Their son Benjamin, third, married and was the father of four sons: Jabez; John, was lost at sea with his father in a severe storm, the father being a fisherman; Hiram and William, the other two sons, were boys when their father was lost at sea; they were "let out" for some years, and William learned the trade of ship carpenter.

William Prior, son of Jabez and Sarah (Holmes) Prior, was born in 1805, died March 1, 1881. After working at the trade of ship carpenter for a time, he was a master of a fishing vessel, and was one of the pioneers in the fish catching and marketing trade of Boston, having brought to this market with his fleet many million of fish annually. The later years of his life were employed in agriculture, upon the Myles Standish farm in Duxbury. He married Amanthis Peterson, born July 10, 1807, died January 2, 1894, daughter of Daniel and Bethia (Weston) Peterson, and granddaughter of Joseph and Rebecca (Delano) Peterson, of Cape Cod, living and dying, possibly in Duxbury. Amanthis (Peterson) Prior was a woman of a rather high education for her day, and was known locally for her more than ordinarily bright mind; in early life she was a Wesleyan Methodist, but later became a Spiritualist, in the ranks of which sect her father and she became very prominent and knew personally some of its foremost followers. Children of Daniel and Bethia (Weston) Peterson: 1. Daniel, married Phebe Moore, children: i. Ellis F., married first, Martha Parker and had four children: Abbie, Emma, Sarah and Charles; married second, Julia Fitzgerald and had two children: George and Emily. ii. Sarah, married John Haskell, for years a very well known theatrical man; no children. iii. Hannah, unmarried. iv. Stephen, married Elizabeth Ray, of Nantucket; children: Lillian, Emma, Florence, Henry. v. Seth, deceased, married Julia ———, who resides in South Boston; no children. vi. Jerusha, married Lieutenant Fillbrick. vii. Alexander, married but had no children. viii. Elizabeth, married a Mr. Whitney, one daughter, Mattie Whitney. Daniel and Phebe (Moore) Peterson spent the early years of their life in Duxbury, but in later years moved to Boston, where their deaths occurred. 2. Hannah. 3. Amanthis, aforementioned as the wife of William Prior. 4. Jerusha. 5. George. Children of William and Amanthis (Peterson) Prior: 1. William, Jr., married first, Abbie Torrey, three children: i. William H., married Edna Walker, no children; ii. Charles Olden; iii. Harry, died young. 2. George Peterson, see forward. 3. Bethia Weston, died 1858; she was the wife of William K. Turner, now of California; they had one child, William J. Turner, who married Zilphia E. Brewster, children: Sarah W., William P., Leslie C., Marcia B., Bethia A., and Emily and Edith, twins, the latter deceased. 4. Sarah H., married Parron H. Prior, deceased; left children: Bethia I., Eunice E. and Parron H. Jr. 5. Edwin, died April 15, 1877; married, in Duxbury, Wealthy S. Freeman; he left one son, Arthur E., who married Edna E. Foster, one child, Louise F. Prior.

George Peterson Prior, son of William and Amanthis (Peterson) Prior, was born in Duxbury, Massachusetts, August 17, 1836, died August 29, 1908. Leaving school at the age of fourteen, he became cook on his father's fishing vessel. Thereafter, taking his turn at all the employments of the crew of such craft, he became a thorough seaman, and at the age of twenty-one was master of a vessel. Having spent eighteen years in that occupation, he obtained employment with Parron H. Prior, who was then engaged in the wholesale fish trade at 30 Commercial Wharf, Boston. In 1884 he engaged in the same business as a member of the firm of Prior & Ingalls. His experience, acquired in fishing and in Parron H. Prior's employment, enabled the firm to advance rapidly and to prosper when other firms failed. The house was successfully conducted until 1899, when the National Fish Company, in which Messrs. Prior and Ingalls were important factors, was formed. This corporation dissolving in July, 1901, the firm resumed their business under their former name, Prior & Ingalls. Mr. Prior was a very public-spirited and generous man, contributing liberally of his time and means to all worthy causes. Mr. Prior was the owner of a handsome house, equipped with everything necessary for the comfort of its inmates, and the beauty of its surroundings, which bespeak the exercise of a refined taste, add to the attractiveness of the place.

Mr. Prior married Lydia Ann Sampson, born in Duxbury, December 16, 1839, daughter of Captain Elisha and Ann (Weston) Sampson, who were the parents of ten children, as follows: 1. Lydia Ann, aforementioned as the wife of George P. Prior. 2. Lucy W., wife of Edgar Loring, of Duxbury; children: Mabel, Fannie W., Harry B., Florence, Waldo F., Edward W. and Albert O. 3. Laura J., wife of John A. Soule, of California; two children: Fannie E. and Edward F. 4. Julia, deceased; was wife of George Atwell, of Duxbury; children: Amanda G., Elmer E., Hattie, Grace and Florence. 5. Abbott, a resident of Marshfield; married Lydia Sampson and had twins, dying in early infancy, and Anna, wife of George Lane, of Stoughton, Massachusetts. 6. Clara, unmarried, residing with her sister, Mrs. George P. Prior. 7. Silvia, wife of Joshua Paulding, of Marshfield, Massachusetts; children. Ella T., John B., Arthur, Clifton, Alphia, Russell, Isabelle T. and Frederick. 8. Simeon, unmarried. 9. Elisha, married Mary Bragdon and has two sons, Frank and Howard. 10. Caleb, accidentally drowned when a child five years old. Captain Sampson was a well known seafaring man of the Cape, being master of several trans-Atlantic liners, among them being the good ship "Martha". He sailed vessels in about every quarter of the globe. He was successful in his pursuit, following this occupation throughout the greater part of his active career. His death occurred at his home in Duxbury, 1876. His wife, who survived him, died at the home of her daughter, Mrs. George P. Prior, in Winthrop, 1898, at the age of eighty-one years. Children of Mr. and Mrs. Prior: 1. Georgianna, residing in Newton, Massachusetts; widow of J. Walter Hamilton; children: Estelle Louisa, Easter Locke and Easter Irving, pupils of the public schools, and Georgianna, died aged six years. 2. Cordelia, wife of Wilbert Wilson Freeman, a successful hardware merchant; they are residents of Winthrop, Massachusetts. 3. Anna Weston, wife of William Munday; children: Alice Abbott, Forrest Prior and Georgia Leslie; of these Forrest Prior Munday married Louisa Clark, of Winthrop, and have a child, Dorothy; Mr. and Mrs. Munday reside in Winthrop. 4. George Herbert, married Fannie Frothingham Robbins, residents of Winthrop.

TAYLOR

General Thomas Taylor was born in Quincy, November 26, 1790, and died there January 1, 1838. He lived in that part of Braintree known as The Farms. He was a prominent member of the First Congregational Church (Unitarian) at Braintree, and owned pew 48 in that structure. He commanded the East Company of militia at Quincy, rose to the command of his regiment, and finally received a general's commission. He was active in public affairs, and one of the best known and most useful citizens of the town. He married Ann Adams, born February 11, 1800, died March 29, 1883, daughter of Thomas and Ann (Capen) Adams; her father was baptized August 2, 1772, died June 4, 1842, married thrice; her mother, Ann Capen, his first wife, born 1776, died May 24, 1806. Deacon Ebenezer Adams, father of Thomas (6), was born at Braintree, March 15, 1737, died 1791; married Mehitable Spear, born 1737, died 1814. Captain Ebenezer Adams, father of Deacon Ebenezer Adams (5), was born December 30, 1704, died 1769; married Ann Boylston, born 1706, died February 18, 1770. Joseph Adams, father of Captain Ebenezer Adams (4), was born at Braintree, 1654, and died February 12, 1736-7; married Hannah Bass, born June 22, 1667, died October 24, 1705; daughter of John and Ruth (Alden) Bass, and granddaughter of John and Priscilla (Mullins) Alden; and all their descendants are eligible to the Mayflower Society. Joseph Adams, father of Joseph Adams (3), was born in England, in 1626, died December 6, 1694; married Abigail Baxter, who died August 27, 1692. Henry Adams, father of Joseph Adams (2), was the immigrant. (See Adams). Children of General Thomas and Ann (Adams) Taylor: born at Quincy: 1. Edmund Billings, born June 7, 1818: mentioned below. 2. Thomas, born May 4, 1820. 3. Charles, born August 4, 1822, lives in Quincy. 4. Henry, born November 20, 1824. 5. George (twin of Henry), born November 20, 1824; died August 10, 1825. 6. Annie A., born May 18, 1828. 7. George Washington Beale, born August 19, 1831. 8. Joseph, born May 26, 1837, died December 27, 1838.

(VIII) Edmund Billings Taylor, son of General Thomas Taylor (7), was born in Quincy, June 7, 1818. He married, May 2, 1844, Abigail Billings Faxon (see Faxon family). Children of Edmund Billings and Abigail Billings (Faxon) Taylor: 1. Edmund Faxon, born February 7, 1845; died May 31, 1902; married Sarah Bragdon Seward; children: Edmund S.; Marion; Blanche M. 2. Joseph Adams, born December 14, 1847; died November 8, 1871. 3. Maria Davenport, born October 12, 1851, died 1854. 4. Abbie Frances, born November 11, 1853; married Thomas Fenno, born June 29, 1855, in Quincy, son of Thomas Glover and Elizabeth Hardwick Fenno. 5. Alice Maria, born January 14, 1858; married E. Frederick Carr, born August 8, 1855, son of Joseph and Sarah Jane (Frederick) Carr; children: i. Bradbury Taylor Carr, born September 29, 1880, died October 27, 1880; ii. Florence Frederick, December 6, 1881; iii. Janet Faxon, March 12, 1883; iv. Sidney Taylor, June 18, 1884; v. Wallace Bradbury, June 29, 1886. (See Thatcher).

FAXON

(I) Thomas Faxon, immigrant ancestor, born in England about 1601: came to New England with his wife Joane and three children, before 1647. His name first appears at Dedham, when his daughter Joanna was married to Anthony Fisher, Jr., September 7, 1647. He settled at Braintree, Massachusetts, and was a prominent citizen there. He was selectman in 1670-72, and deputy to the general court from Braintree in 1669. He married second, September 5, 1670, Sarah, widow of William Savill, of Braintree. He died November 23, 1680. Children: 1. Joanna, born about 1626 in England; married, September 7, 1647, Anthony Fisher, Jr. 2. Thomas, born about 1628-9 in England; married April 11, 1652, Deborah, daughter of Richard Thayer. 3. Richard, mentioned below.

(II) Richard Faxon, son of Thomas Faxon (1), was born in England, about 1630. He came with his parents to New England, and married Elizabeth ———. He died December 20, 1674. Children; 1. Elizabeth, born March 26, 1655; died April 3, 1673. 2. Mary, born September 7, 1656; died September 14, 1657. 3. Mary, born December 19, 1657. 4. Sarah, born March 13, 1659. 5. Josiah, born September 8, 1660; mentioned below. 6. Thomas, born August 2, 1662; married Mary Blanchard. 7. Lydia, born September 1, 1663; died 1663. 8. Hannah, born September 1, 1663 (twin); 9. Ebenezer, born December 15, 1664; died March 27, 1665. 10. Richard, born June 21, 1666. 11. John, born April, 1667; died April 12, 1668. 12. Joseph, born August 26, 1669; he died before 1674. 13. Abigail, born September 18, 1670.

(III) Josiah Faxon, son of Richard Faxon (2), was born September 8, 1660, in Braintree. He married Mehitable Adams, of Medfield, born March 20, 1665, daughter of Edward and Lydia Adams. Children, born in Braintree: 1. Josiah, born May 23, 1690; married January 13, 1717, Deborah Thayer. 2. Thomas, born February 8, 1692; married May 22, 1716, Ruth Webb. 3. Lydia, born November 30, 1695; married November 20, 1722, Benjamin Richards. 4. Mehitable, born June 14, 1698; married April 3, 1733, Ebenezer Whitmarsh. 5. Edward, born May 6, 1700; married first, January 30, 1746, Hannah Blanchard; second, December 7, 1749, Mercy Wells. 6. Elizabeth, born April 7, 1702; married May 12, 1722, Benjamin Hayden. 7. Eliashib, born March 10, 1704; mentioned below. 8. Sarah born June 3, 1706; married December 16, 1725, Joseph Thayer.

(IV) Eliashib Faxon, son of Josiah Faxon (3), was born in Braintree, March 10, 1704, and died in 1761. He married, February 17, 1726-7, Elizabeth Crane, born January 17, 1702, daughter of Ebenezer and Mary Crane of Milton, Massachusetts; they were married by Rev. Peter Thacher, who was the first minister of Milton, Massachusetts. He was a cordwainer and tanner. He and his wife were members of the First Congregationalist church of Braintree. He removed to Pembroke, Massachusetts, where he died in 1761. Children: 1. Elisha, born November 10, 1727; mentioned below. 2. Elijah, born November 24, 1731; married December 28, 1752, Beulah Wild.

(V) Elisha Faxon, son of Eliashib Faxon (4), was born in Braintree, November 10, 1727. He removed with his father to Pembroke, and later to Halifax, Massachusetts, where he resided until his death in 1776. He served in the early part of the revolution. He married, April 12, 1749, Sarah Allen, who died before 1774, probably daughter of Benjamin and Deborah Allen. Children; 1. Elizabeth, born November 24, 1749; died young. 2. Sarah, born 1751; married, 1770, Stephen Washburn. 3. Elisha, born November 23, 1753; mentioned below. 4. Mary, baptized June 6, 1756; married September 15, 1777, Jonathan Curtis. 5. Samuel, born July 10, 1758; married December 11, 1783, Priscilla Thomas. 6. Allen, born September 1, 1761; married October, 1791, Margaret Smith. 7. Benjamin, born May 12, 1764; married first, December 20, 1787, Ruth Bryant; second, January 8, 1792, Rebecca Stone. 8. William, born 1769; married first, March 23, 1794, Wealthy Watson; second, October 16, 1803, Phebe Lawrence. 9. Susanna, died young. The last two children were probably born in Halifax.

(VI) Elisha Faxon, son of Elisha Faxon (5), was born in Pembroke, November 23, 1753 and died July 17, 1826. He was a soldier in the revolution in Captain John Bradford's company, Colonel Theophilus Cotton's regiment, and served twenty-six days after the Lexington alarm, April 19, 1775. He enlisted then in Captain Wadsworth's company with the rank of sergeant. He was a farmer, and was for some time captain of the Halifax Light Infantry. He married Sarah Cushing, born August 4, 1760, died October 27, 1845, daughter of Noah Cushing, of Hingham, and later of Halifax, Massachusetts. Children: 1. Sarah, born January 28, 1781; married October 30, 1803, Abijah Haskell. 2. Sophia, born November 11, 1782; died April 15, 1858. 3. Thomas Cushing, born November 2, 1784, married September 16, 1817, Hannah E. Hunt. 4. Welthia, born January 29, 1787; married June 12, 1806, Ichabod Howland. 5. Mercy, born October 9, 1788-1789; married 1814, Robert Byram. 6. Darius, born January 30, 1792; died November 27, 1794. 7. Oren, born August 2, 1794; mentioned below. 8. Harriet, born May 7, 1797; married Moses Standish. 9. William, born January 7, 1801; married first, July 31, 1825, Mary Ann Howard; second, October 2, 1851, Clarissa Seaman.

VII) Oren Faxon, son of Elisha Faxon (6), was born in Halifax, Massachusetts, August 2, 1794, and died March 14, 1873. He married June 29, 1817, Theodora Billings Mann, born August 12, 1795, daughter of Nathaniel and Abigail (Billings) Mann, of Scituate. Her mother was daughter of Edmund Billings of Braintree (See Billings) and Theodora (Dyer) Billings. Theodora Dyer was daughter of Joseph and Jerusha (Gulliver) Dyer. Jerusha Gulliver was a daughter of Jonathan and Theodora (Thatcher) Gulliver, and who was a granddaughter of Rev. Peter Thatcher. Rev. Peter Thatcher was born at Salem, July 18, 1651, and was the first minister at Milton. He married first, Theodora Oxenbridge, daughter of Rev. John Oxenbridge. He married second, Frances, only daughter of Hezekiah Woodward, vicar of Bray, England. Rev. Thomas Thacher, of Westham, county Sussex, England, father of Rev. Peter, married first, Elizabeth, daughter of Rev. Ralph Partridge, of Duxbury, Massachusetts. He married second, Margaret, daughter of Henry Webb, and widow of Jacob Sheafe. He was the first pastor of Old South Church, Boston, installed February 16, 1670. Rev. Thomas Thacher was born May 1, 1620, son of Rev. Peter and Anne Thacher, was descended from John Thacher, sheriff of England.

Children of Oren and Theodora Faxon: 1. Oren Jerome, born October 15, 1818; married December 27, 1849, Mary Ann Matilda Goodrich. 2. Abigail Billings, born April 24, 1820, at North Bridgewater, now Brockton; married May 2, 1844, Edmund Billings Taylor (See Taylor family). 3. William Thomas, born March 1, 1823; died September 27, 1848. 4. Edward, born October 12, 1824, (twin); married first, June 9, 1850, Eliza Pope; second, June 22, 1870, Lucretia Porter. 5. Edwin, born October 12, 1824, (twin); married March 18, 1852, Hannah L. Gaffield. 6. Maria Davenport, born October 19, 1826; married January 13, 1848, Edwin Wood, of Quincy, died May 9, 1851. 7. Harriet Minerva, born June 30, 1828. 8. Theodore Cushing, born March 16, 1831; married October 11, 1853, Margaretta A. Little. 9. Alice, born January 11, 1835; married September 10, 1863, Charles E. Tileston. 10. Son, born and died March 10, 1836. 11. Charles Cushing, born July 25, 1839; died August 8, 1839.

THACHER "Thacher is a name of high antiquity in the Isle of Thanet, and this county, Kent" (Ireland's "History of Kent"). John Thacher, married Margarette, daughter of Sir Goddard Oxenbridge, was son of John Thacher, who was sheriff of the counties of Surrey and Sussex, in the 36th year of Henry VIII, son of Thomas Thacher of Westham, county Sussex, probably ancestors of Rev. Peter Thacher, of Old Sarum, born 1588, died 1640. Rev. Thomas Thacher, his son, by wife Anne (supposed Allwood), born May 1, 1620, came to New England with his uncle Anthony Thacher, in 1635; married first, Elizabeth, daughter of Rev. Ralph Partridge, of Duxbury, (May 11, 1641); married second, Margarette, daughter of Henry Webb, and widow of Jacob Sheafe; installed first pastor of Old South Church, Boston, Massachusetts, February 16, 1670. His son, Rev. Peter Thacher, by Elizabeth, was born at Salem, July 18, 1651, and became the first settled minister of Millton, Massachusetts. His wife was Theodora, daughter of Rev. John Oxenbridge, by his second wife, Frances, only daughter of Hezekiah Woodward, Vicar of Bray. Rev. John's first wife was Jane Butler, and his third was widow Susanna Abbott, who survived him. Bathshua Oxenbridge was doubtless daughter by his first wife. The children of Rev. Peter Thacher and Theodora were: Theodora, Bathsheba, Oxenbridge, (born 1680, died 1772), Elizabeth, Mary, Rev. Peter of Middleboro, John, Thomas, John 2d, Rev. Peter of Milton, married second, Susanna, widow of Rev. John Bailey, and third, Elizabeth, widow of Rev. Jonathan Gee. He died December 27, 1727. Rev. John Oxenbridge, born January 30, 1609, son of Daniel Oxenbridge, M. D., and grandson of Rev. John Oxenbridge (and wife Mary), "the preacher," a supposed descendant of Sir Goddard Oxenbridge. Sir John Gresham married a Thacher. Rev. John Oxenbridge's descent from Edward III, is as follows: Son of Daniel Oxenbridge and Katherine Harby, daughter of Thomas Harby (son of William, son of Thomas) and Katherine Throckmorton, daughter of Clement Throckmorton, (descended from John de

Throckmorton, A. D., 1130), who was son of Sir George Throckmorton and Katherine, daughter of Sir Nicholas Vaux, descendant of Lord Harold de Vaux, A. D. 1066. Clement Throckmorton's wife was Katherine Neville, daughter of Sir Edward Neville, son of Sir George Neville, son of Sir Edward Neville and Lady Elizabeth Beauchamp, daughter of Richard Beauchamp, Lord Abergarenny, and Isabel Spencer, daughter of Thomas de Spencer and Constance Plantaganet, daugh- of Edmund, Duke of York, and Isabel (daughter of Peter, King of Castile), and son of Edward III Plantaganet, King of England, and Phillippa, daughter of William, Earl of Hainault, and Jane de Valois, descended from the kings of France.

On a broad gravestone in King's Chapel burying ground, are the names and dates of death of Revs. John Oxenbridge, John Cotton and John Davenport, all of whose homes were on the opposite side of Tremont street, Boston, between Beacon street and Pemberton square, covered largely by Houghton and Dutton's store. It is probable that Rev. Thomas Thacher, first pastor of the Old South Church, and his second wife Margarette, are interred in the same ground. An old portrait of him hangs under the sounding-board in the Old South Church, and in the Old State House collection of relics is a watch which was presented to Rev. Peter Thacher of Milton by the maker, in London, England, over two hundred years ago.

"This knightly family (Oxenbridge) of Sussex is *heire* by descent to (this) Aland of Winchelsea, and beareth his arms" (Leland). They first resided in the parish of Iden and took their name from that estate. They rose into importance in the early part of the fourteenth century."

BILLINGS (I) Roger Billings, immigrant ancestor, was born in England, in 1618, and died at Dorchester, Massachusetts, November 15, 1683 (gravestone), aged sixty-five years. He settled early in Dorchester, and was a proprietor of the town and in 1640 a member of the church. He was admitted a freeman May 10, 1648. He was a carpenter as well as a farmer. The widow Ann Gill calls him "brother" in a paper dated July, 1683. He married first, Mary ———, and second, Hannah ———, who died May 25, 1662. His will is dated November 15, 1683, and November 13, 1683, proved December 13, 1683, bequeathing to his wife; to Joseph, son of his deceased son Joseph; to son-in-law James Penniman; daughter Mary who married Samuel Belcher; Nathaniel Wale's daughter Elizabeth; John Penniman, Nathaniel Wale's wife and Deacon Tomson's wife; daughter Mary Mels; sons Ebenezer and Roger Billings; cousin Alexander Marsh and various grandchildren. Child of first wife: 1. Mary, born August 10, 1643; died December 4, 1643. Children of second wife: 2. Mary, married ——— Mels. 3. Hannah. 4. Ebenezer. 5. Roger, born November 18, 1657. 6. Elizabeth, born October 27, 1659. 7. Zipporah, born May 21, 1662; died October 8, 1676. 8. Jonathan, died January 14, 1677.

(II) Roger Billings, son of Roger Billings (1), was born in Dorchester, Massachusetts, November 18, 1657. He married Sarah, daughter of Stephen and Hannah Paine of Braintree, January 22, 1678. Children, born in Dorchester: 1. Hannah, born January 21, 1679. 2. Joseph, born May 27, 1681. 3. John, born March 10, 1683; mentioned below. 4. Roger, born January 9, 1684. 5. William, born July 27, 1686. 6. Sarah, February 27, 1688. 7. Stephen, August 27, 1691. 8. Moses, November 20, 1696. 9. Ann, August 4, 1698. 10. Abigail, February 15, 1700. 11. Elizabeth, June 11, 1702. 12. Isaac, July 9, 1703.

(III) Major John Billings, son of Roger Billings (2), was born in Dorchester, March 10, 1683. He was captain before 1731, and major, according to the town records, in 1733. He married Mary ———. Children, born at Dorchester: 1. Abigail, born February 1, 1727-8. 2. John, born August 22, 1729. 3. Edmund, born May 30, 1731; mentioned below. 4. Samuel, born August 26, 1733.

(IV) Edmund Billings, son of Major John Billings (3), was born in Dorchester May 30, 1731. He married Theodora Dyer; (see Faxon). He settled in the adjacent town of Braintree, Massachusetts. Children, born in Braintree: 1. Joseph Dyer, born March 23, 1759. 2. Edmund, born July 30, 1761, died young. 3. Theodora, born February 1, 1763. 4. Jerusha, born May 17, 1765. 5. Abigail, born February 15, 1767; married June 5, 1786, Nathan Mann. 6. Edmund, born July 1, 1769, mentioned below. 7. Jonathan Gulliver, born October 24, 1775. 8. Eunice, born November 30, 1777.

(V) Colonel Edmund Billings, son of Edmund Billings (4), was born in Braintree

July 1, 1769. He was a prominent citizen of Braintree, now Quincy, Massachusetts. He did not marry and died on the homestead in Quincy.

HARRINGTON This surname is one of our old English patronymics, and was known in England several hundred years before Robert Harrington crossed the Atlantic ocean and sat down in the plantation at Watertown in the colony of Massachusetts Bay. From there his descendants have spread out, increased and multiplied until now they are a numerous family in almost every state in the federal union. And there are descendants of this same immigrant ancestor known by other names, for in the early parish and town records there are frequently found the Harrington, Herington, Arrington and Errington surnames, which are merely different forms of spelling Harrington and are due to the fact that our Puritan forefathers who kept the parish and town records were not schooled in the art of spelling and set down family names phonetically rather than according to correct orthography.

(I) Robert Harrington, immigrant ancestor of the family here considered, was born in England, about 1616; sailed for New England in the ship "Elizabeth" in 1634, and first appears in the plantation at Watertown as one of the proprietors in 1642 and 1644. He took the oath of fidelity in 1652, was admitted freeman in 1663, and was a mill owner, having lands given him by Deacon Thomas Hastings, with whom he came over and who by reason of the interest he showed in the welfare of the young man is believed to have been a relative. Robert Harrington appears to have been a person of considerable importance in the town, was selectman fifteen years and evidently a man of substance as well as influence. He died May 11, 1707, aged ninety-one years. On October 1, 1647 or 1648, he married Susanna, daughter of John George, who died June 1, 1647, and Anna Goldstone, born 1632, died July 6, 1694. Their children: 1. Susanna, born August 18, 1649, married February 9, 1671, John Cutting. 2. John, born August 24, 1651, married November 17, 1681, Hannah Winter and he died August 24, 1741. 3. Robert, born August 31, 1653, died young. 4. George, born November 24, 1655, killed by Indians at Lancaster, 1675-76, during King Philip's war. 5. Daniel, born November 1, 1657, died April 19, 1728. 6. Joseph, born December 28, 1659, admitted freeman April 18, 1690. 7. Benjamin, born January 26, 1661-62, died 1724. 8. Mary, born January 23, 1663-64, married John Bemis. 9. Thomas, born April 20, 1665. 10. Samuel, born December 18, 1666. 11. Edward, born March 2, 1669. 12. Sarah, born March 10, 1670-71, died November 28, 1710; married Joseph Winship Jr. 13. David, born June 1, 1673, died March 11, 1675.

(II) Edward Harrington, eleventh child of Robert Harrington, was born in Watertown, March 2, 1669, and was a farmer. He married first, March 30, 1692, Mary Occington, and second, May 24, 1727, Anna Bullard, widow of Jonathan Bullard, of Weston. His children: 1. Mary, born January 2, 1692-93, married first, December 7, 1710, Daniel Rogers, died November 5, 1711, married second, January 3, 1716-17, Joseph Grant. 2. William, born November 11, 1694, died February 27, 1751-52. 3. Mindwell, born June 19, 1697, died October 14, 1700. 4. Joanna, born August 16, 1699, married, May 25, 1720, John Tainter. 5. Edward, born June 17, 1702, died December 6, 1792. 6. Samuel, born August 3, 1704. 7. Nathaniel, born June 25, 1706. 8. Francis, born June 11, 1709. 9. Susanna, born September 9, 1711, married, November 25, 1731, Samuel Barnard.

(III) Nathaniel Harrington—"Master" Harrington—son and seventh child of Edward and Mary (Occington) Harrington, was born in Watertown, Massachusetts, June 25, 1706, graduated from Harvard College in 1728 and was a noted teacher in his day and generation. He married, first, August 4, 1747, Mary Kemball, died July 15, 1760, daughter of Henry Clarke, descendant of Uriah Clarke, who married Martha Pearce; he was made freeman in 1685 and he married second, March 29, 1762, Rebecca Clarke. Children, all of first marriage: Mary, born May 18, 1748, married October 6, 1773, John Stimpson; Nathaniel, born August 1, 1750, graduated Harvard College in 1769, a physician, died in Jamaica; Peter, born May 4, 1752, married February 9, 1775, Anna Hammond; Catherine, born August 6, 1755; Charles, born May 19, 1759.

(IV) Charles Harrington, youngest son and child of Nathaniel and Mary (Kemball), Harrington, was born May 19, 1759, and died in 1817. He removed from Watertown to Salem, Massachusetts, soon after the revolution. He was a tanner and currier by trade and carried on that business with gratifying success during the early part of his career. He also did a large and profitable business as a packer of pork and opened a large export trade in that line until the French war, during which he suffered serious losses in vessels and cargoes by French spoliations. Mr. Harrington married Mary Bond, born in Watertown, January 26, 1761, died July 24, 1827, daughter of Jonas Bond, farmer, who lived on the old Bond homestead place, and who married in 1753, Ruth Harrington. Ruth Harrington was daughter of Joseph Harrington, born 1690, son of Daniel Harrington, born 1657, and grandson of Robert Harrington. Jonas Bond was a son of Jonas Bond Esq., of Watertown, who married December 4, 1718, Hannah, daughter of Nathaniel, son of Henry Bright, born in England in 1609 and grandson of Thomas Bright, of England, and Mary (Coolidge) Bright. Jonas Bond last mentioned, born December 10, 1691, died in September, 1768, was appointed justice of the peace by Governor Shirley, and represented Watertown in the general court from 1738 to 1750, with the exception of a single year. He was a son of Colonel Jonas Bond, Esq. and Grace (Coolidge) Bond, his first wife. Colonel Bond held a justice's commission more than twenty-four years and was frequently called "the marrying squire" on account of the great number of marriage ceremonies performed by him during his term of office as justice of the peace. He was a member of the military expedition sent to Canada under Sir William Phipps in 1690, and later was commissioned lieutenant colonel of militia. Colonel Bond, born 1664, died 1727, was a son of Captain William Bond, the immigrant, born England 1625, died 1695, who settled in Watertown before 1649-50, and whose first wife, the mother of all of his children, was Sarah, daughter of Nathaniel Biscoe, "the rich tanner" of Watertown. Charles and Mary (Bond) Harington had children: 1. Charles, born January 29, 1782. 2. Artemus, October 14, 1784. 3. Ruth, August 25, 1789. 4. Jonas B., August 22, 1792. 5. Leonard Bond, July 29, 1803.

(V) Leonard Bond Harrington, youngest son and child of Charles and Mary (Bond) Harrington, was born in Salem, Massachusetts, July 29, 1803, and died in that city March 6, 1889. His father having removed to Salem after the close of the revolution, the boy passed his school days in that city. At the age of thirteen years he shipped for a voyage to South America, but an experience with yellow fever and the horrors of a shipwreck checked his ambition for the life of a mariner, and he went to Roxbury to learn the trade of tanner and currier. He worked several years as a journeyman, and in 1829 with the money he had saved from his wages established himself in business in Salem and quickly laid the foundation of what subsequently became the largest and most successful leather manufactory in New England. He devoted himself closely to business, and his honor and industry were of the sterling old-fashioned quality. He manufactured heavy wax leather principally, and the hides never were hurried in the process. During the civil war his business interests became more widely extended and increased immensely in volume. For many years he kept a regular patronage and he was one of the few manufacturers who could afford to wait for and get his own price. He acquired great wealth, but his nature was thoroughly unselfish and he was a man of broad and liberal generosity. He took a deep interest in Salem and his opinion and advice were much sought. He never aspired to public office, and in political preference originally was a Whig and afterward a Republican. In religious faith he was a Universalist and an influential member of the church of that denomination in Salem. During the later years of his life he attended services at the First Unitarian church. He always was a friend of the poor and ready to give a struggling young man a friendly lift. At the time of his death he was president of the Bertram Home for Aged Men, Salem, and a trustee of the Salem Public Hospital, taking an active interest in both institutions. He was a shrewd and able financier and for many years was president of the Asiatic National Bank of Salem, vice-president of the Salem Savings Bank and a director of the Naumkeag National Bank. He also was a director of the Mechanic Hall Corporation, and for twenty or more years was engineer of the Salem fire department in the old days when brawn and muscle had not been supplemented by steam and mechanical appliances. Mr. Harrington was a man of most exemplary habits and of remarkable physical strength and energy. Until within a very short time before his death he had been regularly to his place of business in Salem, and to the bank, and even in his eighty-fifth year he continued his visits to Boston for his daily round in the leather center about High and Congress streets. He was one of the original founders of the "Salem Senate," and informal association of Salem leather manufacturers. On January 8, 1831, Leonard Bond Harrington married Margaret G. Hersey, of Roxbury, a superior woman and one who did much to encourage and assist her husband in his business plans and operations. Children: 1. Henry, born January 6, 1832, died June 18, 1898. 2. Mary, wife of George Goodhue of Salem. 3. Leonard, born September 4, 1842. 4. Child who died in infancy.

(VI) Leonard Harrington, son of Leonard Bond and Margaret G. (Hersey) Harrington, was born in Salem, Massachusetts, September 4, 1842, and died there March 4, 1888. He was educated in the Salem schools and from the time he married until his death he always maintained a comfortable home in that city. On September 15, 1862, at the age of twenty-one years, he enlisted in Company A of the Fiftieth Massachusetts Infantry, Salem Light Infantry, for nine months, and served one year under General Banks, and took part in the siege of Port Hudson. In 1863, at the end of one year in the service, Mr. Harrington was mustered out and returned to his home in Salem. He had performed a soldier's duty faithfully and fortunately escaped without wound or serious illness while in the army, but the hardships of soldier life in the far south, in a region where climatic diseases were prevalent, affected his general health in later years and proved a contributing cause of his untimely death. His father had urged him not to enlist and offered to provide a substitute to take his place in the ranks, but the young man felt it his duty to go and share the fortunes of war with his comrades of the Salem Light Infantry, many of them his companions of boyhood days. When the men of Company A took the train for New York City, whence they were to sail for the south, the elder Harrington went with them and on Thanksgiving day, 1862, was host of the entire company at a complimentary dinner, at which also a number of military officers and a few invited guests were present. But that was only one of the characteristic kindnesses for which the elder Harrington was noted, and he always took much pleasure in doing something that would contribute to the comfort and enjoyment of others. Leonard Harrington was like his father in many respects, a capable, successful business man, and his life—all too short at best— was characterized by the same straightforward honesty, good judgment and generous spirit that marked his father's career and gave him such prominence in trade circles throughout the country; and like his father the son was a man of kind impulses, quiet domestic habits, benevolent disposition, and nowhere did his generous nature display to better advantage than within the sacred precincts of home, at the fireside, in his love of family and unselfish devotion to their comfort, and in his loyalty to friends, and in his loose pursestrings for the relief of distressed persons and the appeals of deserving charities. Mr. Harrington was a comrade of Phil Sheridan Post, No. 34, Grand Army Republic, and a member of the Colonial Club. He frequently attended post meetings, occasionally was seen at club, but he always felt that when released from the cares of business his most enjoyable place was home, with wife and daughter, to both of whom he was entirely devoted, and they to him in equal, generous measure. In business life Mr. Harrington was a manufacturer and jobber of leather, for many years in partnership with John Cummings, under the firm style of Jno. Cummings & Co., with tannery and factory at Woburn and principal sales offices in Boston. The destruction by fire of the firm's extensive plant at Woburn resulted in heavy financial losses and removal to Boston in 1873, but did not affect the stability of the concern in business circles.

On December 4, 1871, Leonard Harrington married Ellen Langmaid, a woman of admirable qualities of mind and heart and whose greatest pleasure is found in contributing to the happiness of those about here. She was born in Salem, daughter of John Pousland and Rebecca Morrison (Taylor) Langmaid, granddaughter of Thomas and Grace (Pousland), Langmaid, and a descendant on both sides of good old New England stock (see Langmaid family). Mr. and Mrs. Harrington had one daughter, Mable Cummings Harrington (now Mrs. Mabel Cox), born in Salem, January 12, 1874.

(VI) Henry Harrington, son of Leonard Bond and Harriet G. (Hersey) Harrington, was born in Salem, January 6, 1832, and died there June 18, 1898. He was given a good education in the public schools, and after leaving school apprenticed himself to the trade of watchsmith and jeweler with Daniel Smith, a famous old watchmaker and clockmaker of Salem, with whom he served out his time; but instead of continuing the business which he had set out to learn, he readily agreed to his father's request that he become associated in the extensive leather business of which the latter was the founder and principal head, and make that his vocation in life. From that time Mr. Harington was actively indentified with the leather business in Salem and Boston until the death of his father, in 1889, and a little later on he retired from active pursuits. He was a good business man and gained an extended and favorable acquaintance in trade circles throughout the leather markets of the east. He was a Republican and for two years a member of the city council of Salem, but he had no particular love for politics and by far preferred the quiet pleasures of home to any honors which public office might bring or to the social life of the club. Both he and his wife were earnest members of the First Unitarian church of Salem and took a deep interest in the institutions of the society and its work. On February 7, 1877, Henry Harrington married Lydia Frye Nichols, daughter of Daniel Frye and Lydia Foster (Cheever) Nichols, of Salem (see Nichols family). No children were born of this marriage.

(V) Jonas Bond Harrington, son of Charles and Mary (Bond) Harrington, was born in Watertown, Massachusetts, August 22, 1792, and died in Salem. According to the recollection of his son, he received his early education in the public schools in Watertown and South Danvers and was a young man when he removed to Salem, then the chief center of commercial activity in New England. Unlike some of his brothers he chose farming as his vocation and was hardly less successful in accomplished results, for he was an enterprising, thrifty farmer and therefore gained a competency. He became a man of influence as well as of means, and while he never was ambitious of political honors he was always a firm advocate of the principles of the old Whig party. The several members of his family were regular attendants at the services and nearly all of them were members of the South Congregational Church of Salem. Mr. Harrington married Margaret Bishop, of Salem, born February 6, 1792, died July 6, 1856. Children: 1. Charles, born September 28, 1815, died August 15, 1895. 2. Margaret, September 7, 1817, died July 6, 1904. 3. William, August 9, 1819, died April 6, 1900. 4. Augustus, May 1, 1822, died August 7, 1906. 5. George, December 29, 1823, died January 3, 1897. 6, Eliza W., September 13, 1825, died August 19, 1841. 7. Samuel B., April 4, 1827, died November 11, 1860. 8. Richard D., February 13, 1829. 9. Francis, September 20, 1832, died September 4, 1903. 10. Mary B., October 1, 1836, died April 19, 1908. 11. Jonas W., May 10, 1839, died September 11, 1840.

(VI) Richard Downing Harrington, son of Jonas Bond and Margaret (Bishop) Harrington, was born February 13, 1829, and as a boy attended schools in South Danvers, as then known, but which now is Peabody. In 1845, then being sixteen years old, he went into a machine shop to learn the trade, with the view of making that his occupation in life, but in the course of a few years his attention was turned into other channels and he took to the sea; but the years he spent at the bench in the machine shop when only a boy served a useful purpose and his knowledge of mechanical work proved of much value to him in later years. In 1849 Mr. Harrington's father bought for him an interest in a deep sea vessel for the merchant service and in her he sailed a voyage to the Pacific coast which took one hundred and eighty-five days between Salem and San Francisco, by way of Cape Horn. He stayed in California during the next three years, engaged in mining, working as a clerk and for a time serving as a member of a vigilance committee, the latter being perhaps the most strenuous duty he was called upon to perform while on the coast. But this act of generosity on the part of his father Mr. Harrington never has forgotten, and it always has seemed to him that his father must have had it in mind that the experiences his boy would receive in the part ownership of a merchant ship and sailing her for a six months' voyage to California at a time when the "gold fever" was at its zenith, would furnish him an education which never could be gained in any school of whatever grade or character; and so it proved, and even to this day Mr. Harrington is conscious of the fact that his life in California was the most useful object lesson in practical experience that he could have received, and that he owes a debt of gratitude to the kind parent which should endure to his children and grandchildren for generations to come. Mr. Harrington returned to Salem in 1852 and soon afterward became partner with his brother in the firm of Charles Harrington & Company, manufacturers of leather, doing business on an extensive scale, with tanner-

Richard Harrington

ies in Peabody and Salem and a large wholesale house in South street, Boston. The firm became in time one of the most widely known concerns in the country and its business was very heavy as well as highly successful; for it is a fact that the name Harrington in connection with the manufacture and sale of leather—and several of that name were so engaged for more than half a century—always stood as an equivalent for integrity and character, and was so recognized in all business and trade circles throughout the country. Mr. Harrington retired from the leather business in 1892, and since that time has devoted his attention to the management of his real estate and other invested interests. He is among the heaviest taxpayers of Salem, hence naturally has always taken an earnest interest in whatever best promotes the growth of the city and the welfare of its institutions in every direction. In his earlier years he was a member of the Salem Cadets, that famous old military organization. He is a trustee of the Corporation of Harmony Grove cemetery, a member of Fraternity Lodge, No. 118, Independent Order Odd Fellows, a Republican in politics, and Unitarian in religious preference. His leisure hours are devoted to reading, his tastes inclining to historical subjects, and in his comfortable home in Munroe street, Salem, may be seen a valuable collection of relics and family treasures, each possessing its own interesting history and association.

In 1854 Mr. Harrington married Ellen, daughter of Nathan and Ursula K. (Chapman) Millett, of Salem. Children: 1. Ella H., married Walter C. Harris, of Salem, and has four children, Eleanor C., married Thomas Sanders, of Peabody; Richard H., Sophia O. and Mary B. Harris. 2. Caroline B., now dead. 3. Mary, wife of J. T. Eustis.

IVES

In the Gaelic and Welsh, Iver or Ives means a "chief" or a "leader," and in the Danish Ives means "zeal," "fervor." The surname Ives also comes from the ancient town of St. Ives in the county of Huntingdon, England. Ivar or Iver, familiar to Scotchmen as Mac Iver, came to the Normans from the northern lands whence they were sprung, and with them into England. Lyson in his "Environs of London" gives the families of Eve and Ive great antiquity in the parish of Pancras, and mentions that A. D. 1252 Henry III granted leave to Thomas Ives to "enclose a portion of the highway adjoining to his mansion at Kentefetonne." He also says that in the church is the tomb of Robert Eve and Laurentia, his sister, daughter of Francis, son of Thomas Eve, clerk of the crown.

In the "Index of Tenants" in the time of William the Conqueror who held their lands immediately from the crown, ordinarily styled "tenents in capite" is found the name of "Iveri, Rogerus de." "This Roger," says the authority before quoted from, "was the son of Walerande Ivery, who held one knight's fee in the bailiwick of Tenechelbrai in Normandy, by the service of cupbearer to the duke, and three other fees within the said liberty, as also eight fees and a half of the town and castle of Ivery. He enjoyed the same honor of cupbearer to William, king of England, which his father had done to him while duke of Normandy."

The family of Rogerus de Ivery descended from one Rudulph, half brother of Richard the first duke of Normandy, who killed a monstrous bear when hunting with his brother the duke, and was by him rewarded for that service with the castle of Ivery, on the river l'Evre, and from thence comes the title of de Ivreio. (Parochial Antiquities). Says Bradsley's "English Surnames," "Ivo de Usgate was bailiff of York, 1271; now we have the simple Ive or Ives, and the more patronymic Iverson, Iveson, Ivison and Ison."

"John Ives, of Saham Tonye, was seized of a manor called Woohhows manor, with its appurtenances in Ovington, Saham Tonye, Braddenham, Carbrooke, Tottingham, Traxton and Stanfforde in the county of Norfolk, and after his death the premises descended to Thomas Ives as son and next heir. The said John died October 23, 10th Elizabeth (1568), at Saham, and the said Thomas Ives was nineteen years and nine months old and no more." (Gleanings from English Records about New England Families, Waters).

"Thomas Ives, yeoman, has livery," etc.; "Thomas Ives, yeoman, Ickford, Bucks, 30 October, 1653, proved 21 February, 1653; wife Joane, sons Thomas, John, Robert, daughter Joane Coales, niece Joane Lee, dau. of Lettice Lee; John, Thomas, William, Zachary and Anne Ives, Richard and Thomas Coles, my seven g————ch'n; Richard and Thomas Coles, overseers." (Ibid).

(I) It is from out of these English families of the surname Ives that doubtless came the immigrant ancestor of the particular branch of the Ives family proposed to be treated in these annals. In 1668 Thomas Ives was in Salem, Massachusetts, for in that year he was in court there, and gave his age as twenty years; hence he was born in 1648, somewhere in England, and he died at Salem in 1695, as letters of administration were granted August 5, 1696, to his widow Elizabeth, who was his second wife. He married (first), April 1, 1671, Martha Withe, and (second), about 1679, Elizabeth Metcalf, born Ipswich, Massachusetts, about 1645, daughter of Thomas and Abigail Metcalf, and granddaughter of Captain Joseph Metcalf, born in England, 1605, died in Ipswich, 1665, and his wife Elizabeth, whom he married in England. By his wife Martha Withe Thomas Ives had three children and by his wife Elizabeth Metcalf four children: 1. Elizabeth, born Salem, February 12, 1672, died July 21, 1673. 2. Thomas, born Salem, March 31, 1674, settled in Marblehead, Massachusetts. 3. Deborah, born Salem, December 8, 1675. 4. Joseph, baptized March, 1683. 5. John, baptized March, 1683. 6. A daughter (Elizabeth) baptized December 4, 1687; married John Philpot, his second wife. 7. Benjamin, born about 1692, see forward.

(II) Captain Benjamin Ives, youngest child of Thomas Ives, was born in Salem about 1692 and died in 1752. He was baptized in the First Church of Salem, August 9, 1702, and in his business life was a master mariner and afterward a tanner. He was a man of considerable consequence in the town, the owner of a tract of land in the vicinity of Very's plain, and appears to have accumulated a large property for his time, his estate having inventoried at more than twenty-three hundred pounds. On January 2, 1717-18 Captain Ives married Anne Derby, born December 10, 1695, daughter of Roger Derby and his second wife, Elizabeth (Haskett) Derby. Roger Derby was born in Topsfield, Devonshire, England, in 1643, and immigrated to New England in 1671, arriving at Boston on July 17, with his first wife, Lucretia Hilman (or Kilman). They afterward removed to Ipswich, where in January, 1672-73, he bought two acres of land and a dwelling house. In the deed of conveyance from Philip Fowler he is mentioned as "Roger Darby sope boyler." Captain Benjamin and Anne (Derby) Ives had nine children: 1. Anne, born March 20, 1719. 2. Benjamin, born November 2, 1720, died December 26, 1767; married October 12, 1743, Elizabeth Hale, daughter of Colonel Robert and Elizabeth (Gilman) Hale, of Beverly, Mass. 3. Samuel, born December 22, 1722, died about 1750; married July 4, 1745, Mary Berry. 4. Elizabeth, born July 5, 172-, married Richard Lee, his second wife, and after his death married Josiah Gilman, of Exeter, New Hampshire. 5. Mary, born about 1728, died June 4, 1794; married, July 12, 1750, John Crowninshield, son of Clifford and Martha (Hillard) Crowinshield, and grandson of Dr. John Kasper Richter von Kronenshelt and Elizabeth Allen his wife. 6. Abigail, mentioned in her father's will, June 19, 1752. 7. John, born about 1732, see forward. 8. Martha, married, November 23, 1760, Daniel Cheever. 9. Margaret, married Peter Cheever.

(III) John Ives, youngest son of Captain and Anne (Derby) Ives, born in Salem, Massachusetts, about 1732, died October 1801. He married, March 13, 1755, Sarah Ward, born in Salem, March 1, 1734, died there October 18, 1801. She was a daughter of Miles and Elizabeth (Webb) Ward, and granddaughter of Joshua and Hannah (Flint) Ward. Deacon Miles Ward was born in the county of Kent, England, in the town of Hurne, and probably came to America with his father. John and Sarah (Ward) Ives had three children: 1. William, born in Salem, Mass., November 25, 1756, see forward. 2. Sarah, baptized in the Tabernacle Church, Salem, October 2, 1757; married, about 1779, William Brewer, mariner, born in 1750 and died at sea in 1795. 3. John, baptized in the Tabernacle Church, Salem, July 22, 1759; married, May 19, 1781, Elizabeth Newhall, who survived him and married for her second husband, August 11, 1785, Jeremiah Emmerton.

(IV) Captain William Ives, eldest son and child of John and Sarah (Ward) Ives, born in Salem, Massachusetts, November 25, 1756, (town records); November 25, 1761, (family Bible), but according to the parish records was baptized in the Tabernacle Church, Salem, May 2, 1756. He was a seafaring man, became a member of the Salem Marine Society, October 31, 1795, and died at Savannah, Georgia, April, 1814. He married, September 12, 1790, Polly Bradshaw, born September 14, 1768, died in Salem, December 3, 1820, daughter of Stephen and Polly (Mansfield) Bradshaw. Captain William and Polly (Bradshaw) Ives had five children, all born in Salem, Massachusetts: 1. William, born February 15, 1794, died there December 12, 1874; married, May 12, 1824, Lucy Gardner. 2. John Mansfield, born

July 8, 1798 (perhaps 1799), died July 29, 1883; married, September 23, 1827, Lois Alley Southwick. 3. Stephen Bradshaw, born April 12, 1801, see forward. 4. Mary Mansfield, born May 14, 1803, died January 21, 1887. 5. Benjamin Hale, born November 7, 1806, (town records), 1805 (family Bible); died Salem, January 26, 1837; married, October 29, 1833, Lydia Ann Harraden.

(V) Stephen Bradshaw Ives, third child and third son of Captain William and Polly (Bradshaw) Ives, born in Salem, Massachusetts, April 12, 1801, died in that city, July 31, 1883. He served an apprenticeship of seven years to the trade of printer and bookbinder, and on attaining his majority began business on his own account. In January, 1823, he formed a partnership with his elder brother, William, and established the *Salem Observer*" and also "The Old Corner Bookstore," both of which proved very successful ventures, and the latter of which survived for more than three score years. Having disposed of his interests in Salem, he afterward established a business in Boston for the importation and sale of fancy goods, and when he finally retired from active pursuits this latter business was turned over to his sons. During the course of his business career he was identified with various interests and institutions of Salem, where he always made his home. He was a director in several corporations, took an active part in municipal affairs, and frequently was connected with the city government. In 1858 he was president of the common council and at one time was a member of the lower house of the state legislature.

Mr. Ives was married twice. His first wife, whom he married May 16, 1826, was Mary Perkins, who was born in Salem, April 1, 1825, and died there July 4, 1873. She was a daughter of David and Harriet (Fabens) Perkins, and a descendant of the seventh generation of John Perkins, of Ipswich, Massachusetts, the immigrant ancestor of that branch of the Perkins family of New England. For his second wife Mr. Ives married, May 31, 1876, Harriet Perkins, a sister of his first wife. She was born in Salem, November 26, 1808, and died in Philadelphia, Pennsylvania, December 23, 1886. By his first wife Mr. Ives had ten children: 1. Stephen Bradshaw, Jr., born March 9, 1827, died February 8, 1884; married (first), in January, 1848, Mary Eliza Burnham; married (second) widow Constance (Telford) Farmdale, of England. 2. David Perkins, born July 13, 1828, married, December 21, 1854, Sarah Shreve Calef, daughter of John and Elizabeth (Shreve) Calef. 3. Henry Perkins, born April 15, 1830, married, October 2, 1856, Adeline Simes Jones. 4. Edward Lang, born October 13, 1832, died September 8, 1834. 5. Mary Elizabeth, born April 9, 1835. 6. Margaret Perkins, born August 26, 1836, married, in 1863, Charles Sewall, son of Levi and Mary Ann Sewall; children: Grace Sewall, (twin), born September 1, 1866; Alice Sewall (twin), born September 1, 1866, died the same year; Edward Lang Sewall, born July 29, 1867, died July 22, 1876; Elizabeth Sewall, born September 5, 1868, died December 4, 1876; Stephen Ives Sewall, born November 11, 1876, died November 29, 1876; Charles Sewall, Jr., born July 11, 1877. 7. George Augustus, born September 13, 1839, married, October 10, 1866, Clara Thorndike Rand, of Beverly, Massachusetts. 8. Caroline Louisa, born September 10, 1842, died August 7, 1844. 9. Cornelia Allen, born July 27, 1844; married, June 29, 1871, Frederick Manton Osborne, and had two children: Frederick Brace Osborne, born August 18, 1872; Ethel Bradshaw Osborne, born May 15, 1876. 10. Caroline Louisa, born October 27, 1847; married, October 11, 1871, Frank Augustus Langmaid, born in Salem, November 5, 1847, and had six children (see Langmaid family).

(For first generation see Thomas Nichols 1).

NICHOLS (II) Thomas Nichols, son of Thomas Nichols (1), was born in Amesbury, October 16, 1670. He married first Jane Jameson, second (published April 30, 1721) Judith Hoage. He had eight children by his first and two by his second wife, all born in Amesbury: 1. Anna, May 1, 1694 (or 1695); married, 1718, Samuel Colby. 2. Jonathan, December 13, 1697; married (probably) January 16, 1718-19, Mary Challis. 3. Mary, October 11, 1701; married April 10, 1718, Ralph Blaisdell, Jr. 4. Esther, September 11, 1703; married January 24, 1723-4, Ichabod Colby. 5. Thomas, June 20, 1706. 6. David, October 26, 1709. 7. Rachel, March 10, 1712. 8. Stephen, November 15, 1717. 9. Ebenezer (by second wife) March 28, 1722. 10. Benjamin, October 8, 1723.

(III) David Nichols, son of Thomas and Jane (Jameson) Nichols, was born in Amesbury, October 26, 1709, and was lost at sea in 1756. He married in 1730, Hannah Gaskill. The Gaskills were a notable family in early colonial history, whose immigrant ancestor was Edward Gaskill, the Salem ship carpenter and owner of a right of twenty acres of land in that town in 1636. He had a wife Sarah, and children: Samuel, Daniel, Sarah and Hannah, born between 1639 and 1648. Samuel Gaskill, son of Edward and Sarah, was born in Salem in 1639, and was a Friend (Quaker), perhaps one of the leaders of that sect in the town, for he was instrumental in the building of the first meeting house for the Friends in Salem, and for the "sin" of being a Quaker he and his wife were punished by Salem magistrates, the charge against them being that they "did attend Quaker meetings." He also helped in erecting the second meeting house of his people in Salem, in 1718. His wife was Provided (Providence) Southwicke, whom he married 30 10 mo. 1662. Their children were Samuel, Hannah, Edward and Provided. Samuel Gaskill, son of Samuel and Provided, was born in Salem, 23 11 mo. 1663, and died after September 1, 1725. He owned four rights of common land in the two lower parishes of Salem. He married Bethiah, daughter of Thomas Jr. and Hannah Gardner; children: Samuel, Nathan, Jonathan, Hannah (married David Nichols), Content, Sarah, and four others, names not mentioned. Children of David and Hannah (Gaskill) Nichols: David, Samuel, Jonathan, Ichabod, Thomas, Nathan, Sarah.

(IV) Thomas Nichols, son of David and Hannah (Gaskill) Nichols, was born probably in Salem. He married Hannah Pope; children: Stephen, blacksmith, born 1770, died November 14, 1846; Ichabod, born 1772, died March 1, 1847; David, Hannah, Jonathan, Abigail and one other.

(V) Jonathan Nichols, son of Thomas and Hannah (Pope) Nichols, was born in Somersworth, New Hampshire, 1781, and died in Salem, September 25, 1848, aged sixty-seven years. He married first, Lydia, daughter of Daniel Frye; second, Elizabeth Rodman.

(VI) Daniel Frye Nichols, son of Jonathan and Lydia (Frye) Nichols, was born in Salem, and married there Lydia Foster Cheever. Their children: Benjamin; George, born 1829; Daniel A., May 22, 1831, lives in Salem; Lydia Frye, married Henry Harrington (see Harrington family); Jonathan, born 1842, died November 15, 1848; Henry Clay, lives in Salem.

LANGMAID

There is a tradition which runs to the effect that sometime during the first half of the seventeenth century three Langmaid brothers came to New England from the mother country. Another tradition in the family is that the Langmaids are of ancient Scotch origin and the New England branches are descendants of Scotch ancestors. Such traditions, however, are not always well grounded and while genealogists neither confirm nor deny the tradition concerning the "proverbial" three immigrant brothers, it appears to be reasonably well settled that the Langmaid family of the line here under consideration is of English ancestry. The surname Langmaid is classed with our English patronymics which are derived from localities, and originally comprised the two words, lang and mede, the former an equivalent for long and the latter for meadow, from which antiquarians reason that the name was first applied to a person or family whose habitation stood in proximity to a long meadow; and hence Langmaid is only one of the modified forms of Longmede, or Longmeadow, the latter having become virtually obsolete.

(I) William Langmaid is believed to have been the immigrant ancestor of the family here treated, and although the ships' lists of passengers from English ports do not mention his name, nor the names of either of his supposed immigrant brothers, there is reason to believe that he came to America through the agency of the Mason proprietary, under which settlement on the Piscataqua river in New Hampshire was begun as early as 1631, and was continued at intervals by later arrivals for many years. It is not probable, however, that William Langmaid was living in New Hampshire previous to 1675, for according to the best information obtainable he must have been born about 1650. The names of his wife and all of his children are not known, but among the latter are found the names of John and Samuel.

(II) Samuel Langmaid, son of William Langmaid, is given by one of the descendants of William as next in line, but no definite information concerning him is obtainable. The period of his life is believed to have been in the last quarter of the seventeenth and the first half of the eighteenth century. In 1696 he is mentioned in the list of ancient names in New Castle and Sandy Beach for all male persons "from the age of 16 years and upwards" to take the appointed oath of allegiance.

(III) Samuel Langmaid, son of Samuel Langmaid, was born probably about 1710, and is supposed to have lived in the vicinity of Rye, Hampton and Chichester, although in the towns last mentioned there is no record of his family so as can be ascertained.

(IV) John Langmaid, son of Samuel Langmaid, was born about 1745-50, and spent the later days of his life in Chichester, New Hampshire, which for more than a century and a half has been a principal seat of residence for families of that surname. No less than five Langmaids were among the New Hampshire men enlisted for service during the revolution, and the records furnish the names of Harvey, Henry, John, Joseph and Stephen, who were in the American army during that contest. A John Langmaid was in Colonel McClary's regiment that went to Bennington to join General Stark's army in 1777, and was paid six pounds, thirteen shillings, nine pence for that service. He also was a private in Captain Sanborn's company of Colonel Thomas Evans' regiment at Saratoga, and is credited with service from September 8, to November 30, 1777. The town records of Chichester are very imperfect and not all of the old families are mentioned in such books as are found, but among the children of John Langmaid were Richard and Polly, twins, born September 3, 1777; William, December 5, 1779; Mehitable, January 21, 1782; Samuel, May 26, 1784; Thomas, September 29, 1785.

(V) Thomas Langmaid, son of John Langmaid, born in Chichester, New Hampshire, September 29, 1785, died in 1845, aged sixty-one years, having spent his entire life on a farm in that town. He married, April 5, 1812, Grace Pousland, of Beverly, Massachusetts, who survived him and afterward went to live in Pembroke, New Hampshire, where she died in 1873, aged seventy-seven years. They had thirteen children, all born in Chichester: 1. Lucinda, April 2, 1813, died 1842, aged thirty years. 2. Eliza Ann, August 17, 1815, died in Pembroke, 1867. 3. John P., April 24, 1817; 4. Thomas D., October 24, 1819, died in Chichester, 1848. 5. Mary M., August 24, 1821, died in Salem. 6. Hannah, March 8, 1824, died Wayland, Massachusetts, 1899. 7. Alfred A., November 14, 1826, died Ipswich, 1905, a soldier of the civil war. 8. Charles A., September 13, 1828, died Chichester, 1849. 9. James F., April 25, 1833, died Granite Falls, Minn., 1902. 10. George W., February 4, 1835, died Salem; soldier of the civil war. 11. Frank, 1836, died 1865, aged twenty-nine years. 12. Ira W., November 22, 1837. 13. Warren B., born 1840, veteran of the civil war, lives in Cochituate, Massachusetts.

(VI) John Pousland Langmaid, son of Thomas and Grace (Poulsand) Langmaid, born in Chichester, New Hampshire, April 24, 1817, died in Salem, Massachusetts, December 24, 1904, after a business career of more than forty years and one which was rewarded with gratifying and well earned success. At the age of sixteen years he left home and went to Boston, where for about one year he was employed at the State Reform School. After that he returned to Chichester, married, and soon afterward started in mercantile business in Concord, New Hampshire. As a merchant in the capital city of New Hampshire Mr. Langmaid soon found himself established in a satisfactory business, but a disastrous fire destroyed his stock, at serious loss to himself. Soon afterward he removed to Salem and for the next twenty years was an employee in David Buffum's planing mill. Having at length accumulated a small capital and a fair knowledge of the lumber business he started a lumber yard on Austin's dock on Lafayette street, removing thence to Derby street, nearly opposite Salem Hospital, and soon afterward to what for almost half a century has been known as Langmaid's wharf in Derby street. As his sons came of age they were taken into partnership with their father, and for more than thirty-five years the firm name of J. P. Langmaid & Sons has been well known in business and trade circles in Salem and Essex county. In many respects Mr. Langmaid was a remarkable man. He possessed splendid courage and never yielded to obstacles or disappointments; for had he been differently constituted it is doubtful if his business life would have been so successful after the loss of his store in Concord and the twenty years of hard daily work as a mill hand which followed before he had earned sufficient capital to start in business again. And besides being a tireless worker, even after he had gained a competency, he also was a thoroughly honest man, frugal in his habits, yet liberal in providing for the comforts of home and family, and for the education and business training of his sons. He enjoyed a large acquaintance among business men, and was respected wherever he was known. During the later years of his life he withdrew from active connection with the lumber business and turned its management over to his sons, knowing that its affairs were in safe hands. For many years he was a member of the Congregational church, a liberal contributor to its maintenance and also to the charitable work of the society; the beautiful memorial organ in memory of his father and mother in the Wesley Methodist Episcopal Church is his voluntary and generous gift, and he himself frequently attended services in that church.

Mr. Langmaid married Rebecca Morrison Taylor, who died in 1888. She was born in Derry, New Hampshire, daughter of Robert Taylor whose wife was Dolly Colby, daughter of Isaac Colby. Robert Taylor was a son of David Taylor, born August 10, 1735, married Margaret Kelsey and had seven children. David Taylor was the fourth son of Matthew Taylor and his wife Janet, who was one of the first settlers of Londonderry, New Hampshire. It is probable that both of them were born in Ireland, but they were of Scotch descendants, their ancestors having been compelled to flee from Scotland because of religious persecution, being Protestants, and found refuge in the north of Ireland. Matthew and Janet Taylor had six sons and two daughters: John, Matthew, William, David, Adam, Samuel, Sarah and Janet. John Pousland and Rebecca M. (Taylor) Langmaid had three children: 1. Ellen L., married Leonard Harrington (see Harrington family). 2. John Henry, died in Paris, France, May 19, 1900 (see forward). 3. Frank A., see forward.

(VII) John Henry Langmaid, son of John P. and Rebecca M. (Taylor) Langmaid, was born in Salem, and received a good early education in the public schools of that city. After leaving school he began working with his father, and when he attained his majority was taken into partnership and given an interest in the lumber business. When his younger brother came into the firm the business was thereafter carried on under the style of J. P. Langmaid & Sons, and was so continued for the next thirty-five years, and after the father had retired from active pursuits the sons John H. and Frank A. succeeded to the proprietorship and continued the business as in former years. John H. Langmaid early proved himself to be a capable business man, and his worth as a man of integrity and high character was known in all business circles in Salem: and besides that desirable recognition he was one of the popular men in the city, not in a political sense, for he had no ambition in that direction, but rather as a genial companion and local friend, interesting in conversation of pleasing manner and appearance, always ready to do a favor and lend a helping hand, and there was nothing in his nature that was mean or narrow. And as he was in this respect in his business and social life, so he was at home, and there perhaps, the pleasing traits of his loyal character were most clearly manifested, for he was entirely devoted to his family, and in turn was almost idolized by them. The death of his only daughter in 1894 affected him so seriously that to the day of his own death he had not become reconciled to his loss.

Mr. Langmaid was not a clubman, nor member of any fraternal orders. In politics he was a Republican, and in religious preference a Unitarian. In the early part of the year 1900 he went abroad and died in Paris on May, 1900. His wife, whom he married September 5, 1871, was Ella Webber Lambert, who was born in Salem, May 8, 1847, daughter of Porter and Julia (Daland) Lambert, granddaughter on her mother's side of Robert and Mary (Welcome) Daland,* and a descendant of the seventh generation of Benjamin Daland (sometimes written Deland and Dealand), who was an early settler in Beverly, Massachusetts. Robert Daland probably was a son of John Daland and Elizabeth Tucker, his first wife. John Daland is mentioned in several published works as "Capt. John Daland, master mariner," but this is a mistake, for he never followed the sea. He is mentioned too as having married first, Hannah Dove; second, Elizabeth Tucker; third, Mary Fowler. He in fact married first, Elizabeth Tucker; second, ——— Rust, and third, Mary Fowler. His father was Benjamin Dal-

*The following letter is preserved:

SALEM, JUNE 6, 1799.

TO ROBT. DELAND.

Dear Sir: We are all well and are hoping to hear of your welfare your Marm has been very much concerned about your health for my part I hope you will keep a good heart and brave out every difficulty, times is very dull here. Write by every opportunity, take good care of yourself and not lay about deck nights.

Should you have the misfortune to be taken short let that nor anything else trouble you that you could not avoid. Keep up your spirits and do the best you can, be always obliging to your superiors and there is no fear but you will do well. You will hear to the Captain in respect to your adventure as he knows best what to bring home. I fain would write more but have nothing to write upon a line from you would be very acceptable much more so with your good health. Should you receive these you certainly will write the first opportunity. I conclude with all our best respects hoping you are well at this present time.

Your friend, Thorndike Deland.

P. S. My best respects to Capt. Osborn.

To Rob't Deland on board Sch. Molly—at Tunete Martinique. per favor Capt Bachelor.

J. H. Langmaid

and, who married Hannah Cook, and whose father George Daland, of Beverly, married Catherine, daughter of George Hodges of Salem.

Mr. and Mrs. Langmaid had one daughter, Bertha Ray Langmaid, born in Salem, October 16, 1874, died in Clifton, Massachusetts, September 19, 1894. She was of the fifth successive generation of Dalands who were members of the First Unitarian Church of Salem.

(VII) Frank Augustus Langmaid, son of John F. and Rebecca M. (Taylor) Langmaid, was born in Salem, November 5, 1847, and received his education in the public schools of that city and also in Boston. He began work even before leaving school, and about the first remunerative work he found was to run errands, and later on he was given a place as clerk in a store. When his father left Buffum's planing mill and set up in the lumber business, Frank A. was given work in yard and office at three dollars per week, later on received five dollars per week, and when he reached his majority he was taken into the firm of J. P. Langmaid and Sons, of which he is now sole surviving member, and sole proprietor of the business, except that his own sons have a partnership there, but the old firm name of J. P. Langmaid & Sons is still retained. Like his father, Mr. Langmaid is a capable, reliable and straightforward business man, and as he himself was trained in business methods, so in turn has he trained his own sons who are associated in business with him. He is a prudent man both in speech and action, of quiet tastes, and much prefers the companionship of family and his comfortable home to the enjoyment of club associations or the excitements of political activity. Yet with all, he is counted among the public spirited and substantial citizens of Salem and takes an earnest interest in whatever measures are proposed for the welfare of the city and its people.

On October 11, 1871, Mr. Langmaid married Caroline Louisa Ives, born in Salem, daughter of Stephen Bradshaw and Mary (Perkins) Ives (see Ives family). Six children have been born of this marriage: 1. Mary Perkins, born in Salem, February 22, 1873, educated in public and high schools; married, October 12, 1896, A. Lawrence Peirson, of New York; children: Abel Lawrence, born August 3, 1897; Rebecca, born August 5, 1901; Charles Lawrence, born January 3, 1903; Elizabeth, born August 12, 1907. 2. Harry Taylor, born in Salem, August 24, 1874, educated in Salem public and high schools; engaged in business with his father until he went to Sion, Canada, where he is proprietor of a general merchandise store; married, February 22, 1906, Corsia Whittaker, born in Kentucky. 3. Alice Ives, born in Salem, February 8, 1876, died February 1, 1890. 4. John Frank, born in Salem, February 7, 1880, educated in Salem public and high schools, graduated from Harvard College, A. B., 1902; A. M., 1903; instructor in chemistry at Harvard, also at Case School, one year; was chemist to Sun Oil Company at Marcus Hook, Pennsylvania, now with father; married, June 24, 1906, Sally, daughter of Charles Odell, of Salem, and has one child, John Frank, Jr., born April 24, 1907. 5. Stephen Ives, born in Salem, July 31, 1884, graduated from Harvard College, A. B., 1906; A. M., 1907; now engaged in business with his father. 6. Bradshaw, born in Salem, December 21, 1889; Harvard student.

EATON There were persons of distinction among the English families of the surname Eaton, and among the New England descendants of that ancient house in every generation from the time of the immigrant ancestor there have been men of distinction and high character equal perhaps to that of their European forbears, although on this side of the Atlantic we find none of the name who have placed their chief reliance for character and worth on the coat of arms "or a fret azure" so much as on personal endeavor and individual achievement. The family of the Eaton surname whose pedigree is traced here, begins its history in New England with John and Anne Eaton, the former of whom is mentioned in some chronicles as John Eaton of Haverhill and in others as John Eaton of Salisbury, both in the colony of Massachusetts Bay. He came of the old English family of the same name, and while there is room for the belief that his ancestors were of the same kin with those of Sir Peter, baronet, the fact is not easily established. The immigration registers and ship's lists of passengers give no account of the departure of John Eaton and his family from England, neither is it known exactly when they arrived in this country, nor the name of the ship in which they took passage; but they came, John Eaton and his wife and six children, and sat down in one of the plantations in the Massachusetts

Bay colony, in or sometime previous to the year 1639.

(I) John Eaton first appears on the proprietors' books of Salisbury in 1639-40, and several grants of land to him were made between 1640 and 1646. A tradition which has run in the family for more than a century and a half is to the effect that he had a brother and a cousin in the colony about or soon after the time of his arrival, but the researches of more recent investigators seem to dispel the theory. One of the grants of land to John Eaton was that made on the "26th of ye 6th mo. 1640, 2 acres, more or less, for his house lotte, lying between the house lotts of Mr. Samuel Hall and Rolfe Blesdale"; and another was his "planting lotte," granted "the 7th of the 9th mo. 1640, containing pr estimation six acres more or less, lying uppon ye great neck," and his house was built near the "great neck bridge, on the beach road." It is interesting to note in this connection that in 1890 the old homestead property was still owned and in possession of descendants of the immigrant. Late in 1646 John Eaton conveyed the property to his son John, and then moved with the other members of his family about fifteen miles up the Merrimack to Haverhill, and there spent the remaining twenty-two years of his life. In 1646 he was chosen grand juror, and also one of five prudential men of Salisbury. He was a husbandman, and the records mention that he also made staves. He died in Haverhill, October 29, 1668, aged about seventy-three years, hence he was born about 1595. He married Anne, born about 1617, and all of their children were born in England. She died February 5, 1660, and he married second, November 20, 1661, Phebe, widow of Thomas Dow, of Newbury, Massachusetts. She died in 1672. John and Anne Eaton had children: 1. John, born 1619; married Martha Rowlandson, of Ipswich, Massachusetts. 2. Ann, born about 1622, died in Haverhill, December 13, 1683; married June 25, 1645, Lieutenant George Brown, who married second, March 17, 1684, widow Hannah Hazen of Rowley. 3. Elizabeth, born about 1625; married December 1, 1648, James Davis, of Haverhill; ten children. 4. Ruth, born about 1628; married December 9, 1656, Samuel Ingalls; lived in Ipswich. 5. Thomas, born about 1631; married first, Martha Kent; second, Eunice Singletery; lived in Haverhill. 6. Hester, born about 1634, died young.

(II) John Eaton, eldest child of John and Anne Eaton, was born in England in 1619, and died on the old homestead in Salisbury, Massachusetts, November 1, 1682. He went to Salisbury with his father in the winter of 1639-40, and when the latter removed to Haverhill, in 1646, he deeded his house and property "on the neck" to his son John who lived there until his death. He was a planter and cooper, as he describes himself in his will, and he appears to have become possessed of a large estate in lands which he gave to his son, making ample provision for each, the homestead going to his eldest son John. About 1644 John Eaton married Martha, daughter of Thomas Rowlandson Sr., of Ipswich, and sister of Rev. Joseph Rowlandson, who graduated from Harvard college in 1652, the only member of his class. The Rowlandsons came from England, and it is believed that they were acquainted with the Eatons before coming to this country. Martha, wife of John Eaton, survived him about thirty years, and died in July, 1712, "a woman of great age and of great excellency of character." Children: 1. Hester, born August, 1645, died 1649. 2. John, born about 1646; married Mary ———; lived in Salisbury. 3. Thomas, born January 17, 1647; married Hannah Hubbard; lived in Salisbury; she was a descendant of William Hubbard, "an eminent inhabitant" of Ipswich. 4. Martha, born August 12, 1648; married first, Benjamin Collins, of Salisbury, second, Philip Flanders, of Salisbury. 5. Elizabeth, born December 12, 1650; married January 7, 1673, Dr. John Groth, who was admitted to practice medicine in 1679. 6. Ann, born December 17, 1652, died June 12, 1658. 7. Sarah, born February 28, 1655; married May 6, 1675, Robert Downer, of Salisbury. 8. Mary, born December 9, 1656, died January 1, 1657. 9. Samuel, born February 14, 1659; a mariner. 10. Joseph, born March 1, 1661; married Mary French; lived in Salisbury. 11. Ephraim, born April 12, 1663; married Mary True; lived in Salisbury.

(III) Captain Joseph Eaton, son and tenth child of John and Martha (Rowlandson) Eaton, was born in Salisbury, March 1, 1661, and died there January 13, 1743. His house was in that part of the town known as Sandy hill, where his houselot comprised three acres of land given him by his father, but he had much other land and is said to have bought and sold land quite extensively for his time, and to have gained an honest competency through his dealings. He was a joiner by trade, and built many houses and other buildings in the town, and he also was captain of militia and a man of considerable influence in public affairs. Captain Eaton was a famous hunter and trapper, and at certain seasons of the year went with companions as far east as Brunswick, Maine, and on his return home he would entertain his family and friends with ancedotes of his frequent excursions. These stories aroused an adventurous spirit in his sons, and three of them afterward sought their fortunes down in the wilds of Maine. They were not adventurers, however, but sturdy pioneers, men of courage and determination, Indian fighters in defense of home and family, and one of them fell a victim of Indian rapacity, while the son of another received a wound, and was made prisoner and carried away into captivity. In the history of Brunswick, Maine, it is written as a matter of tradition that one Jacob Eaton went there from Salisbury, Massachusetts, about 1680, or earlier, with one Michael Malcom, and were trappers and traders with the Indians; that they bought lands from the Indians which included the territory now comprising the town of Brunswick, and laid claim to title. The story is not without foundation, though essentially incorrect in many respects, and is the outgrowth of the hunting excursions which furnished recreation for Captain Eaton's hunting parties. If a purchase was made from the Indians, as might be inferred if what has been termed as the "Eaton claim" had any foundation in fact, the grant doubtless was secured by Captain Eaton himself rather than his son Jacob, and at a period much later than 1680, for the captain then was less than twenty years old and his son Jacob was not born until 1703. Whatever truth there may have been in the story that the Eatons ever seriously laid claim to title to the lands of Brunswick is not now known, but there is no evidence that an Indian deed was ever executed, or presented as a foundation of the so-called claim; but if family tradition be true the worthy captain possessed a sufficiently keen sense of humor to narrate to his friends the story of having acquired title to Indian lands by verbal cession, if such had been the case.

Captain Eaton married first, December 14, 1683, Mary French, of Salisbury, who died July 12, 1726, ten children. The intentions of his second marriage were recorded in November, 1726, and he married soon afterward Mary Worster (or Worcester) of Bradford, Massachusetts, who died September 2, 1759. His children, all born of his first marriage: 1. John, born August 23, 1684, died December 12, 1684. 2. John, born October 18, 1685; married Esther Johnson, of Kingston, New Hampshire; lived in Salisbury. 3. Samuel, born December 7, 1687; married Mary Malcom; removed to Brunswick, Maine. 4. Joseph, born August 14, 1690; married Mary French; lived in Newbury, Massachusetts. 5. Benjamin, born February 14, 1693; married Sarah Merrill; lived in Salisbury. 6. Moses, born May 18, 1695; was killed by Indians near Brunswick, Maine, 1722. 7. Mary, born April 9, 1697; married January 14, 1715, Benjamin True, of Salisbury. 8. Nicholas, born September 12, 1699; married Mercy Walton; lived in Salisbury. 9. Sarah, born May 20, 1701; married June 30, 1726, David Buswell, of Bradford, Massachusetts. 10. Jacob, born April 16, 1703; married first, Sarah Plummer; second, Sarah Malcom; lived in Topsham, Maine.

(IV) Samuel Eaton, third son and child of Captain Joseph Eaton and Mary French his first wife, was born in Salisbury, December 7, 1687, and is mentioned in the history of Brunswick as having come from Salisbury "early in the last century and built a house on the corner of Bank and Maine streets." But the author of the history just mentioned is mistaken in saying of this Samuel Eaton that "one of his children, Samuel, was a soldier in Fort George in 1722," for the Samuel Eaton of Fort George and the colonial wars was Samuel the elder son of Captain Joseph, and the pioneer of the family in Maine. He inherited a love of exploration and "to gratify it he plunged into the forests of Maine and finally settled in what is now Brunswick." He is the Samuel Eaton who figured so conspicuously in what has been called Lovewell's war, which began in 1722, and it was he whom Captain Gyles (or Giles) sent from Fort George to Colonel John Harmon at Georgetown, Massachusetts, with a letter tied up in an eelskin and concealed in his hair. When it was unsafe for him to travel by land he took to the water and swam, and thus reached his destination in safety. During the same war Moses Eaton, brother of Samuel, was taken prisoner (June, 1722), tortured and mutilated, and finally was carried to Point Pleasant and was killed by his savage captors.

Samuel Eaton married, about 1715, Mary, daughter of John Malcom, first of Salisbury and afterward of Brunswick. John Malcom was one of the companions of Captain Joseph Eaton on his hunting expeditions from Salisbury into Maine, and it was he who with Eaton is said to have taken part in purchasing the Indian title to what now is Brunswick, although the history of Brunswick ascribes that action to one Michael Malcom. It is not known that John Malcom took part in the colonial wars, although one or more of his sons entered the service. The names of all of Samuel Eaton's children are not known, but it is stated (on the authority of the late Martin Eaton) that he had two sons, Enoch and Daniel; and a daughter Mary. Enoch Eaton was drowned when a boy.

(V) Daniel Eaton, son of Samuel and Mary (Malcom) Eaton, was born in Brunswick, Maine, in 1722, and through him are descended many of the Brunswick Eaton families. Little is known of his family life and there is no present record by which we may learn of his marriage, the name of his wife and their children, except John. But there is a clear account of a part of the service of Daniel Eaton as a soldier of the French and Indian war. Early in May, 1757, while John Malcom and Daniel Eaton were going to Maquoit for salt hay, they were attacked by Indians. Malcom escaped, but Eaton received a bullet wound in the wrist, was captured and taken to Canada and held there about a year. His captor was the Indian chief Sabattis, who sold his prisoner for four dollars. Many years after this event, about 1800, the old chief again visited Brunswick, met his former prisoner and was shown the mark of the bullet wound on his arm; and seeing the scar Sabattis said, "That long time ago; war time too."

(VI) John Eaton was a son of Daniel Eaton, but other than this fact little is known of him, except that he married Jane Grant, and had children, among them sons Martin, John and David, and a daughter Jane.

(VII) Martin Eaton, son of John Eaton, was born in Brunswick, Maine, in 1796, and died in South Durham, Maine, in 1888, having attained the remarkable age of ninety-two years. He was a substantial farmer, living first in Brunswick and afterward for many years in Webster, Maine, but later returned to Brunswick in order that his children might have the benefits of the better schools of the latter town. Mr. Eaton married, April 27, 1834, Phebe Winslow, of Durham, born January 31, 1805, daughter of William Winslow, founder of the town of Winslow, Maine, and one of the foremost men of his time in the province. Children of Martin and Phebe (Winslow) Eaton: 1. Sarah Jane, born May 30, 1835, died June 8, 1906; married, October 17, 1879, George P. Day, of South Durham, Maine. 2. William Winslow, born May 20, 1836; married, July 12, 1865, Agnes H. Magoun. 3. Rebecca Annie, born July 18, 1837; married, April, 1878, George Richardson. 4. Abigail Stewart, born October 10, 1838, died July 13, 1839. 5. Martha Ellen, born October 8, 1839, died February 4, 1872; married, December 8, 1864, James Clark. 6. Alonzo Jones, born January 10, 1841; a soldier of the civil war, and died August, 1905, of disabilities contracted in service; married, March, 1861, Elizabeth M. Lyon, who died in 1906. 7. Lucinda Maria, born January 10, 1841, died November 2, 1842. 8. Edward R., born May 29, 1843; died October 30, 1861, while in service in the first year of the civil war.

(VIII) Dr. William Winslow Eaton, eldest son and second child of Martin and Phebe (Winslow) Eaton, was born in Webster, Maine, May 20, 1836, and for more than forty years has been prominently identified with the professional and civil life of Danvers, and of Essex county, Massachusetts. When Dr. Eaton was a boy living down in Maine his father removed from Webster to Brunswick that his children might have every opportunity to gain a better education than was afforded in the common schools in Webster, and William attended the public schools in Brunswick, and later finished the course of the high school and was graduated. But this was not enough for him for he had determined to obtain a higher education and to that end fitted himself for college, entered Bowdoin for the classical course and graduated with the degree of A. B. in 1861; and best of all, he accomplished this course wholly through his own persevering effort, maintaining himself and paying his own tuition rates from the day of matriculation to commencement day when the dean of the faculty handed him his coveted and honestly deserved diploma. In 1865 he received the degree of M. A. from the same institution. While making his course in college Dr. Eaton had begun the study of medicine under the competent preceptorship of Dr. Isaac Lincoln of Brunswick, but after graduating he taught in the Bridgton high school one year and at the same time continued his preliminary medical studies more definitely than before, taking his first and second courses of lectures in 1861 and 1862 in the Maine Medical School, although for very good reason he did not receive his diploma in medicine until something like two years later. The interval of years, however, was not without value from the standpoint of practical medical and surgical experience, although for the time the young aspirant was compelled to lay aside his text books and didactic studies for the more practical surgical duties of the hospital tent and the battlefield.

On June 6, 1862, Dr. Eaton enlisted from Brunswick, Maine, in the Sixteenth Maine Volunteer Infantry Regiment, and on June 27, 1862, was appointed hospital steward. He was promoted to assistant surgeon January 25, 1863, and to surgeon, with rank of major, November 25, 1864, having served as acting surgeon from May 1, 1864. His regiment was organized at Augusta, Maine, and was there mustered into the service of the United States for a period of three years or during the war, on August 14, 1862, Colonel Asa W. Wildes commanding. The regiment left Augusta on August 19 for Washington City, arriving there August 21, and the next day crossed the Long Bridge into Virginia, being assigned to Forts Cass, Woodbury and Tillinghast. On September 7 it was withdrawn from the forts and ordered to active duty in Maryland. At Gettysburg only two officers and fifteen men remained able for duty at the close of the three days' battle, out of 248 who went into action. Surgeon Eaton was captured there on July 1st, and remained in charge of the Lutheran Church Hospital until July 4th, when after the advance of the Union forces he rejoined his regiment. He was always to be found at his post, performing the arduous duties of an army surgeon in the field with efficiency and skill, caring for the sick and wounded of his command, often under most unfavorable conditions, and achieving a most creditable record, whether in camp, hospital, or on the field of battle. While a prisoner he ministered to sick and wounded rebels, as well as his own comrades. In this connection it may be noted that he still retains a fragment of his regimental flag, which, when capture was inevitable, was torn to pieces by the color-bearer, and distributed among the men to prevent it falling into the enemy's hands. While in winter quarters at Mitchell's Station, in December, 1863, he received from Secretary of War Stanton a leave of absence to admit of his completing his professional studies in the New York Hospital and Medical School, receiving the degree of M. D. from New York University on March 4, 1864. During this course he sat under the instruction of the eminent D. Valentine Mott and other noted physicians and surgeons. Surgeon Eaton was honorably discharged from service at Augusta, Maine, June 5, 1865, by reason of end of war.

After being mustered out of service, Dr. Eaton returned to his old home in Brunswick, where he married, but did not practice there. His professional career was begun in South Reading, Massachusetts, (now Wakefield), where he was induced to locate in answer to the urgent request of his old regimental chaplain, with whom he was visiting after returning from the front. After two years' residence in South Reading Dr. Eaton removed to Danvers and has engaged in active and successful general practice in that locality since 1867, a period of more than two score years. He maintains an office in Salem as well as in Danvers, although his home is in the latter town, and his practice, while general, has its special side and he is an electro-therapeutist of wide reputation. It is doubtful if there is any professional man in Essex county with a more extended and favorable acquaintance than Dr. Eaton, and few whose endeavors in professional life have been rewarded with better success or more substantial results. In 1865 he became a member of the Essex County Medical Society and the Massachusetts Medical Society, and besides he holds membership in various other organizations of men of his profession, among them the Maine Medical Society, the American Medical Association and the American Electro-Therapeutic Society, of the latter of which he is a former vice-president, and also he is ex-president of the Essex South District Medical Society, and ex-vice-president of the Massachusetts Medical Society. He became a member of the board of U. S. examining surgeons for pensions, June, 1889, and still occupies that position. He is an interesting but not prolific writer. One of his best professional monographs is one on "The Use and Abuse of Alcohol," and he is author of a "History of the Physicians of Danvers," which has been published; and a concise and accurate "History of the Sixteenth Regiment Maine Volunteer Infantry," his old command.

Dr. Eaton is a Mason of long standing, having first become a member of Army Lodge, No. 8, F and A. M., while in service at the front in 1864. He is affiliated with Amity

Lodge, of Danvers; was a charter member and past master of Mosaic Lodge, of Danvers; is a charter member of Holton Chapter, R. A. M., of Danvers; also member of Salem Council, R. S. M., Winslow Lewis Commandery, No. 18, K. T., of Salem, of which he has been prelate for sixteen years; and member of Sutton Lodge of Perfection, A. A. S. R., of Salem; and Aleppo Temple, Mystic Shrine, Boston. He is a comrade of Ward Post, No. 90, G. A. R.; was its second commander, serving two terms; and for thirty-eight years has been annually installed in his present position of surgeon. In his life in Danvers he has been for many years variously identified with the best interests and institutions of the community, and while he has never aspired to political honors, he has taken an active part in the interest of good citizenship and the general welfare. He has filled several offices of minor importance, and for fifteen years served as member of the school committee, of which he was at one time chairman. He was a trustee of the Peabody Institute; and for twenty-two years has been president and a trustee for twenty-seven years of the Walnut Grove Cemetery Corporation, still holding both offices. He is a member of the Danvers Scientific Society. He is one of the organizers of the Danvers Improvement Society, was its first vice-president, and for eighteen years president, which position he yet occupies. This Society was formed with the idea of beautifying the roads, walks, shade trees, railroad station, etc., of the city. The Society, without any means in the treasury, purchased for five thousand dollars, which has been paid, a tract of land of twenty-five acres, which is proposed to turn over to the town as a beautiful park bordering on Porter river for a quarter-mile wide, with landscape scenery, river view, etc., all graded and beautified, besides thousands of dollars expended in improvements. This will be turned over to the town, to be enjoyed as a public park forever. Dr. Eaton delivered the address at the Memorial Institute at the time of the death of General Grant, and has made addresses on several Memorial Days.

On June 25, 1865, Dr. Eaton married Agnes Hirst Magoun, born in Carlisle, England, January 5, 1842, who came to the United States when a child. She died in Danvers, July 14, 1904. Children of Dr. and Mrs. Eaton: 1. Elbert, born August 8, 1866, died May 31, 1880. 2. Susan Wilhelmina, born April 2, 1870. 3. Harold P., born January 2, 1881, died May 2, same year. 4. Marion Agnes, born June 19, 1882.

(For preceding generations see Allen Breed I.)

BREED-HACKER (VII) Nathan Breed, son of James and Hannah (Alley) Breed, was born January 28, 1794, died July 15, 1872. He was one of eleven children: Huldah, James, Hannah died young, Hannah, Mary, Nathan, Content, Lydia, Keziah, Isaiah and Sarah. From both parents he inherited sterling qualities of character, and a liking for business from his father, who was a tallow chandler and maker of soaps, and whose house was located about where the entrance of Bowman place now leads from Broad street, being called one of the oldest, and his shop stood upon the site of the drug store across Bowman place. Nathan Breed, who was the founder of the shoe industry in Lynn, and for many years one of its most prominent and extensive manufacturers, began business by purchasing small pieces of stock of Micajah Burrill and making them up into children's sizes of shoes. The period of his activity included the years from about 1830 to the introduction of shoe machinery. The shoes were not actually made at the factory, that is, put together, but the soles were cut there and likewise the uppers. The shoes were then put out to be bound by the women, and then made by the men, sometimes the two tasks being done by husband and wife. This was the beginning of the little "ten-footer" shoeshops which as a result soon became abundant throughout this and adjacent towns, and the making was largely done in them, when not done in the kitchen, after the fashion of an earlier day. The making was also put out to people in other states as well as Massachusetts, this building up the formerly well-known "shoe express" business, the carriers taking large cases of cut stock away, and returning the made-up shoes. Mr. Breed's product went into every state in the Union and sometimes into Canada.

One of Mr. Breed's foster industries was located at St. Louis, where he assisted a former employee, John C. Abbott, to go into business under the firm name of Hood & Abbott. They later extended their sale business to Nashville, Tennessee. Mr. Breed's business was one of such extent that he came in time to leave it largely to trusted assistants, while he devoted his grand energies to larger interests. He would come to the factory in the morning, look over the simply kept books,

Nathan Breed

draw the required checks, and then depart for the day. A strictly temperance man himself, he would allow no stimulants used in his factory or by his men if he knew it. Out of the proceeds of this business Mr. Breed built largely for the prosperity of the town. With it there grew up other and collateral lines of business, such as the making of boxes, which was first made a really important business or trade by James N. Buffman. These Mr. Breed purchased largely in advance, as he did his leather stock, usually attending to this part of his business in person. Likewise, he would keep his workmen employed during the dull winter season, and even solicited sales from buyers, giving them the advantage of reduced prices and extended time if they bought and thus introduced business methods by which he reaped the benefit by a direct increase of his trade. The buyers always came to the factory and no salesman went on the road to solicit trade, nor was such a thing known as selling by sample. Mr. Breed often advanced money to his women employees and friends for the purchase of the new sewing machines, which were then being introduced, and later on, these were applied to the shoemaking industry, for stitching purposes, this being a source of additional income to the women employees who often left their bank books with Mr. Breed, so that the safe at the factory became a sort of small savings bank repository.

In due course of time Mr. Breed desired to build for himself a house suited to his growing needs and public spirit, and accordingly purchased, from his father the property across Broad street, removing the ancient homestead to Silsbee street, where it now stands somewhat altered, and giving his father a life use of it, with such income as it might bring, and also in another house he already owned next to it. The new house he built was the well known "mansion house" which stood back from Broad street until removed to its present and less influential site to the rear of Bowman place. In its prime it was a place of great beauty, with a famous old garden. As his business increased, Mr. Breed invested largely in real estate, owning land in Lynn Woods, also upon Chestnut street, where many of the shade trees are the work of his beauty-loving hand, upon Exchange and Spring streets, and from Broad back to Farrar. He purchased land running back from Union street at the rear of the present Sagamore Hotel, and planted it with mulberry trees, being interested in the then craze for raising silk worms, there being a silk mill at West Lynn. When the industry waned, he cut a street through his land and named it Mulberry street. He owned at one time the "Quaker Pasture" off the present Union street and Burchstead place, now thickly settled with dwellings and business blocks, and when the cut was made for the Eastern Railroad through "Smith's Field", he displayed his wisdom and sagacity by securing the diggings to fill in the low portions of his tract and thus made it better building land. With his brother Isaiah he was instrumental in having Oxford street cut through to meet High street, and thus benefited not only himself but the property owners in that section. As a member of the Sagamore Hotel Corporation, he withdrew when he learned of the intention to establish a bar in the house, and likewise withdrew from the movement to cut through Central avenue when he learned that a theatre was likely to be built upon that thoroughfare, thus attesting to his unyielding allegiance to principle above profits. He was also a stern opponent of the slave trade and never cared whether his adversary in an argument upon the subject was a customer, past or prospective. He never signed any real estate paper for let or leasage but what he had the clause included that the land or buildings thereon should never be allowed to hold or harbor the sale of intoxicating liquors or the business of gambling or betting in any recognized form. For thirty-six years Mr. Breed held the office of director of Lynn Mechanics', later the First National Bank, and the Essex Trust Company; for a long period was trustee of the Lynn Institute for Savings, of which he was one of the founders; and director of the Lynn Gas Light Company, of which he was one of the founders, five other men being associated with him in this enterprise, which is at present one of the most extensive in Eastern Massachusetts.

Mr. Breed was a member of the Society of Friends and always took a deep interest in the affairs of that denomination. The "Reading Meetings" were frequently held at his house, and under the guidance of a goodly company of older Friends, the young folks listened to readings from books written by Friend authors, or at least highly approved by Friends, and thought to be instructive as well as entertaining. Scripture was read, and Mr. Breed, with beautiful dignity, would call on some elderly man to offer prayer, and the latter portion of the meeting was sometimes entirely given up to religious exercises. Mr.

Breed was sterling and loyal to his convictions, and though of great dignity and reserve, his impression upon his generation was for lasting good. The mansion which he built across from his shop and which cost ten thousand dollars, was specially planned for the entertainment of Quaker guests, who were welcome at all times, but who came in large numbers from all parts of the country at the time of the quarterly meetings. The house had seventeen bed rooms, all of which were at the disposal of the guests. His charities were far spread, but performed in a quiet and unostentatious manner, known better by the recipients than by the public. At his death he bequeathed fifty thousand dollars to establish a school and asylum for the destitute children of Lynn, a most noble and worthy philanthropy.

Mr. Breed was a man of quiet, unassuming manner, of even temperament, cordial and considerate in his intercourse with his associates and warmly attached to his friends. His capacity for business was large and was increased by his systematic and quiet methods. He was always master of himself, saw clearly the end he had in view and pursued it with a direct and persistent aim. He was a man of clear judgment and marked sagacity in affairs, prompt in action but not hasty in reaching conclusions. While firm in his opinion he was tolerant of the opinions of others, and his whole life was an illustration of the refined amenities which large experience and a wise philosophy of living may produce in a bright and kindly nature. To have known him well one must have known him in his own home and in the intimacies of private life. Those who knew him there can never forget the sunny even temperament, the kindly nature and the warm and generous instincts of the man.

Mr. Breed married, October 27, 1819, Mary E. Sweet. Children: 1. Moses Sweet, born October 21, 1820, died February 1, 1862; he married, December 7, 1841, Deborah Phillips, and had one son Charles, deceased. 2. Sarah Sweet, born December 20, 1821, see forward. 3. Lucy Jones, born March 10, 1824, died January 1, 1846; married, November 15, 1843, Henry M. Hacker. 4. Mary Sweet, born April 12, 1826, died January 26, 1907; married, December 15, 1847, William Bradford, the great artist and explorer who was known throughout the world and was the first American to lecture before the English Geographical Society; his pictures were purchased by the leading Americans and Europeans; one of his largest paintings, representing the Arctic regions, which was twelve feet long and five feet high, was purchased by the Duke of Argyle's son, Lord Walter Campbell; two children: i. Esther H., deceased; ii. Mary E., who now resides in their home at Fair Haven, Massachusetts; Mr. Bradford died April 25, 1892. 5. James Edward, born September 14, 1827, died May 7, 1828. 6. Hannah Emily, twin of James Edward, died November 10, 1833. 7. Catherine B., born November 7, 1830, married, November 17, 1847, Henry M. Hacker, her brother-in-law; children: Lucy B., Nathan B., Henry Marriott Jr., Nathan, Arthur M., Charles, Katherine, Mary B.; of these children the second, fourth, fifth and sixth are deceased.

At the time of the death of Nathan Breed, 1872, all of the papers of that day—The *Lynn Transcript*, *Lynn Record* and *Lynn Semi-Weekly Reporter* contained notices of Mr. Breed in which they said: "One of our most enterprising and successful business men has passed away. He held for many years a prominent place in the business circles of the city, and took an active part in all of its affairs of a business and religious nature, and we mourn the death of a man who was a devoted friend and safe adviser." The directors of the First National Bank passed appropriate resolutions in which they said: "We learn with deep sorrow of the decease of Nathan Breed who for nearly forty years has taken an active part in the business affairs of this bank and done so much to assist in establishing its credit as one of the foremost banking institutions of Eastern Massachusetts".

(VIII) Sarah Sweet Breed, eldest daughter of Nathan and Mary E. (Sweet) Breed, was born December 20, 1821, died July 24, 1906, at the ripe age of eighty-four years. She married, November 15, 1843, W. Alfred Hacker, of Philadelphia; he was of a Salem family, but had lived from early manhood in the Quaker City. Later he removed to Worcester, Massachusetts, where he engaged in the coal business, building up a large trade and there spent the remainder of his life; he died in 1877, aged sixty-two years. Children: 1. William, died aged seventeen years, six months, having a remarkable military record; he was captain in the military school in Worcester, later enlisted in the United States service as second lieutenant, was promoted to first lieutenant, then captain and just previous to his death was made lieutenant-colonel, the papers having been made out. 2. Mary E., married Howard Porter, both deceased. 3.

Edward H., who was a slipper manufacturer in Lynn, later superintendent of a factory; married, February 20, 1879, Elizabeth Stratton Ross; he died at forty-nine years of age. 4. Alfred Rowland, retired oil, stock and cotton broker, residing in New York City. 5. Sarah H., a resident of Lynn.

It was characteristic of Mrs. Hacker that when she came to woman's estate, she should become an ardent Abolitionist like her father. She threw herself into the movement and when the war broke out she gave a son to the cause. By this time she was a resident of Worcester, Massachusetts, and there she did true womanly service on the sanitary commission. Soon after the war Mrs. Hacker returned to Lynn, and here took up her residence. Her interest in her fellows was in no way abated, and she was eager to lighten the lot of her own sex. In 1869 she was the prime mover in organizing the Women's Union for Christian Work, of which she was vice-president for seventeen years and its inspiring genius. In 1886-87 it became a part of the work of the Associated Charities. Up to the last Mrs. Hacker took an interest in the organization, and at the present time her daughter, Sarah H., fills her place. Early in the seventies Mrs. Hacker, along with others, sought to establish a hospital in Lynn. It was carried on for several years, but owing to lack of funds and the conflicting ideas of the two schools of medicine it was given up, but it served a valuable service, giving an impetus to the movement which resulted in establishing the present Lynn Hospital. She was possessed of a brilliant intellect; her moral and spiritual qualities were equal to her intellect, and the service she rendered humanity was a service of no mean significance. She was always a great reader, and the range of her reading was wide and varied as became a woman of her intelligence and interests. Books of history and travel, works of biography and belles-lettres, all good poetry and fiction, the current magazines and the daily papers, all seemed necessary to serve her taste. She did not neglect religious works; her habit was to read a passage and then to think about it—to turn it over and over in her mind until she had got all the marrow out of it. These intellectual spiritual interests she kept up to the very day of her death, and in this way she learned the secret of eternal youth. The following is from the pen of the Rev. Samuel B. Stewart, who had known her long and intimately:

"The life she led was thoughtful, earnest, beautiful in virtue. No one could meet her but to feel one's self in the presence of a woman of true refinement and culture. Her bearing was that of a disciplined mind and conscientious motive. She was as brave and outspoken as she was tender, kindly and sympathetic. She seemed to me to represent the best that it is our privilege to aspire to and to admire, not only in private but in public. In matters of religion she kept abreast the prophecy and the inspiration of the hour, true in every sense to the best spirit of the venerable body of Friends with which her early life was intimately associated, and to which she remained loyal. Much of the traditional theology was now to her a dead letter, and she was frank in the expression of her dissent; at the same time she was appreciative of the feelings by which the human family, in its various divisions of belief, through education and association, is affected. Her mind and heart were stayed by the spiritual realities that are our common inheritance".

(VIII) Mary, third daughter of Nathan and Mary E. (Sweet) Breed, was born in Lynn, April 12, 1826. Like her sister Sarah, the early life in the home—where they met men and women of distinction not only of this country but from abroad (for Nathan Breed's hospitality was great, and the exciting time of those anti-slavery days, as Nathan Breed's house was one of the stopping places of the "underground railroad" for the negro)—she learned that broad outlook on life and helpfulness for others that distinguished them both. On December 12, 1847, she married William Bradford, who afterwards became the "distinguished artist of the frozen north," and whose paintings are in many private homes and public institutions both in America and England. He was the first American to lecture before the Royal Geographical Society of England, and was introduced by Lyndall, and spoke of his experiences in the far North. It was during the Civil War that Mary Bradford, with Elizabeth Comstock, the Quaker preacher, visited many of the camps and hospitals in the South, ministering alike to the needs of the Blue and the Grey, comforting the sick and dying, and taking messages for the wives and mothers of the poor wounded soldiers. The quiet hour with the immortal Lincoln at the White House, about three weeks before his death, when they came from the battlefield at Winchester at his request, his great heart, his pity for the sorrows of mankind, as he knelt with them and asked

God's blessing on the work he had to do, was an experience never to be forgotten. While she hated wrong, she had an intense sympathy for the wrongdoer, and did what she could to bring them to a right way of living. She was always trying to help somebody, both in public ways and individual cases. She accompanied her husband twice to England, where she met many titled and distinguished people—the Duke and Duchess of Argyle, Baroness Burdett-Coutts, Lady Jane Franklin, Lord Alfred Tennyson and others. Mr. Bradford's studio was in New York City, where he died in 1892, but his home was in the lovely old town of Fairhaven, Massachusetts, the home of so many artists. Here his wife spent the last years of her life with her devoted daughter Mary, and where the daughter still lives. Another daughter, Esther, died in childhood.

WHEDON Thomas Whedon, immigrant ancestor, born in England, about 1635, seems to be the only early immigrant of this surname, sometimes spelled Wheadon. Some authorities think that Weedon and Wheaton were of the same family, but no definite proof is afforded. Whedon settled in New Haven, Connecticut. He was a young man at the time of his coming, and had just entered an apprenticeship with John Meigs to learn the trade of tanner, and came with Meigs from England, sailing from Southampton about 1647. He was of age, and took the oath of fidelity and allegiance prescribed by the English crown in 1657. He removed to Branford, Connecticut, where he was one of the proprietors before 1667, and he joined the New Compact of the settlement in lieu of that which had governed those who went away to form a new settlement in New Jersey. He married, May 24, 1661, Mary Ann Harvey, and died in 1691, leaving a widow and five children. Children: 1. Thomas, born May 31, 1663; mentioned below. 2. Sarah, born April 23, married Samuel Elwell. 3. Esther, born January 26, 1668; married at Branford, Edward Johnson. 4. John, born about 1671. 5. Hannah, born about 1675.

(II) Thomas Whedon, son of Thomas Whedon (1), was born in Branford, Connecticut, May 31, 1663. He was admitted to the Branford church in 1691. He married Hannah ———, who was admitted to the church March 7, 1687-8. He was a farmer, and at his death about 1707 left a goodly estate. Children, born at Branford: 1. Hannah, about 1686. 2. Abigail, about 1688. 3. Thomas, 1691; mentioned below. 4. John, 1694, joined church September 28, 1718. 5. Nathaniel, 1697. 6. Rebecca, 1701. 7. Jonathan, 1704. 8. Martha (posthumous), 1706-7.

(III) Thomas Whedon, son of Thomas Whedon (2), was born at Branford, Connecticut, in 1691. His father died when he was a boy of sixteen. He lived at Branford and Easthampton, Connecticut. He married Eunice Servaine. Elizabeth, who seems to have been his second wife, died at Easthampton, September 3, 1746. His children were: Eunice; Dorcas; Thomas; Elizabeth; Daniel, see forward; Jehiel; Ephraim.

(IV) Daniel Whedon, son of Thomas Whedon (3), was born in 1726. He married Abigail Granger, and resided at Easthampton, Connecticut. Children: 1. Sarah, married Jedidiah Darrow. 2. Lucretia, married Samuel Root. 3. Grace, married Henry Hughes. 4. Denison, mentioned below. 5. Abigail, married ——— Hopson. 6. Asenath.

(V) Denison Whedon, son of Daniel Whedon (4), was born in Easthampton, about 1750. He married Mary Parish (also spelled Parrish and Paris). His children were: Betsey; Abigail; Daniel, mentioned below. He removed when a young man to what was then Charlotte county, New York, now in the state of Vermont, and settled in Bennington or vicinity. In the New York State Revolutionary records we find him credited with service in the Charlotte county regiment along with Edmund, Ansell, David and Daniel Whedon. Daniel was doubtless his father and the others his brothers. Edmund Whedon settled at Pawlet, Vermont, in 1787, and his descendants are still living there; was a constituent member of the Baptist church, which was organized in his house in 1791; was a substantial citizen who contributed much to the upbuilding of the village of West Pawlet, building some of the first mills; removed to Cayuga county, New York, and lived to an advanced age. Ansel Whedon, brother of Edmund, soldier in the revolution, settled in Pawlet, Vermont; died 1826, aged sixty-two years; his widow Rachel in 1837, aged seventy-one; children: i. David, had his uncle Edmund's homestead; ii. Ansel Jr., married Jane Allen; iii. John, married Lovice Harndon, daughter of Joshua; iv. Samuel, married another daughter of Joshua Harndon, and removed to Illinois; v. Rachel, married Washington Z. Wait, of Hebron, New York; vi. Lorene, married Rev. Archibald Wait; vii. Agnes.

(VI) Daniel Whedon, son of Denison Whedon (5), was born in that section of New York, now Vermont, about 1775. He married Clarissa Root. They resided in Hebron and Munsville, New York. Children: 1. Hiram, mentioned below. 2. Alvah, father of Oscar Whedon, of New York. 3. Daniel Denison, the well known Methodist divine, commentarian and author, born in Geddes, near Onondago, March 20, 1808.

(VII) Hiram Whedon, son of Daniel Whedon (6), was born in Hebron, New York, in 1798, and died in Ann Arbor, Michigan, May 28, 1881. He lived for a time in Stockbridge and Rome, New York, but passed his last years with his son William in Ann Arbor. He married first, Margaret Avery; second, Flora Stoddard; third, Abigail Lyman; fourth, Anna Parmalee. Children of first wife: 1. Daniel Avery, born 1823. 2. William Wesley, mentioned below. Margaret Avery, first wife of Hiram Whedon, was descended from Christopher Avery (1), the emigrant, through Captain James (2), John (3), William (4), John (5), John, Jr. (6), Robert (7), who married Lydia White. On the maternal side she was descended from William (1) White, the Mayflower Pilgrim, through Peregrine (2), (born on the Mayflower), Daniel (3), Cornelius (4), Daniel (5), and Lydia (6). She was born January 27, 1763; died March 24, 1847.

(VIII) William Wesley Whedon, son of Hiram Whedon (7), was born in Rome, New York, October 17, 1827. He removed to Ann Arbor, Michigan, with his uncle in 1849. His uncle, Rev. D. D. Whedon, D. D., was one of the four professors of the literary department of the University of Michigan. William entered the dry goods business as partner to David Godfrey. In 1853 he embarked in business as a dry goods dealer at Chelsea, Michigan, and continued there for a period of twelve years. He was a member of the Chelsea Methodist Episcopal church, and an official during his residence there. In 1865 he returned to Ann Arbor and entered into a partnership with A. J. Sutherland, under the firm name of Sutherland and Whedon, real estate and insurance brokers. He was always active in town and church affairs. He was a prominent member of the Methodist Church at Ann Arbor, and held several offices in that parish. He was especially interested in the education of the young, and for twenty-three years was a member of the school board, during most of the time being secretary. He died March 24, 1907, at Ann Arbor, Michigan. He married September 11, 1849, Helen Mar Turner, born September 15, 1831, daughter of Robert and Caroline (Ellis) Turner. Her father, Robert Turner, was born at Glastonbury, Connecticut, July 22, 1803, died at Saginaw, Michigan, May 20, 1893; married, at North Orange, Massachusetts, March 12, 1829, Caroline Ellis; children: i. Henry E. Turner, born April 1, 1830; ii. Helen Mar, mentioned above; iii. Montilia R., born 1833, died 1834; iv. Susanna M. Turner, born October 11, 1835; v. Sarah Turner, born January 21, 1843. Her mother, Caroline Ellis, born September 11, 1807, died at Saginaw, Michigan, November 1, 1896, daughter of Seth and Susannah (Cheney) Ellis, granddaughter of Seth and Elizabeth (Rawson) and great-granddaughter of John and Thankful (Baker) Ellis. John Ellis, born 1727, died 1814, his wife died in 1797. (See Rawson sketch). Captain William Henry and Mercy (Risley) Turner were the parents of Robert Turner. Captain Turner was born in 1764, and died July 25, 1810. His wife's lineage is: Mercy (6), Reuben Risley (5), Job Risley (4), Samuel (3), born 1681, married Rebecca Gaines; Richard Risley Jr. (2), married Mary Hills (?); Richard Risley (1), married Mary Steele (?). Children of Captain William Henry and Mercy Turner: i. William H. Turner; ii. James Turner; iii. Chauncey Turner; iv. Alanson Turner; v. Robert Turner, mentioned above; vi. Sanford Turner; vii. George Turner; two daughters died in infancy. Captain William Turner, a master mariner, father of Captain William Henry Turner, was drowned near Glastonbury, Connecticut.

The children of William Wesley and Helen Mar (Turner) Whedon: 1. Helen Margaret, born 1852, died 1883; married Dr. W. J. Webb. 2. Caroline, born 1854, died in childhood. 3. William Turner, born July 20, 1859; mentioned below. 4. May, born 1863; married 1889, Dr. T. C. Phillips, of Calumet, Michigan, now residing in Milwaukee, Wisconsin. 5. Susa, born 1868; married Charles W. Coan, September 5, 1907, now residing in Brooklyn, New York. 6. Sara, twin with Susa, instructor in English ~~literature,~~ high school, Ann Arbor.

(IX) William Turner Whedon, son of William Wesley Whedon (8), was born in Chelsea, Michigan, July 20, 1859. He attended the Ann Arbor public and high schools, and graduated from the University of Michigan with the class of 1881. He then came east and entered the employ of Lyman Smith's Sons, sheepskin tanners and manufacturers, Boston and Norwood, Massachusetts. In 1891 he became a member of the firm. In 1901, when his company was consolidated with the firm of Winslow Brothers under the name of Winslow Brothers and Smith Company, he became factory sales manager of the company, a position he has filled to the present time. Mr. Whedon has been a trustee of the Morrill Memorial Library of Norwood for a number of years; for nine years was secretary of the Norwood Business Association and Board of Trade, from 1896 to 1905, and was president two years, 1905-7; also is a member of the executive council of the Massachusetts State Board of Trade. He is vice-president of the Norwood Literary Club, and president of the Norwood Choral Society since its organization. He was editor and manager of the *Norwood Review* for several years, and is a regular contributor to the columns of its successor, the *Norwood Messenger*. He is vice-president of the Old Home Week Association. He is a member of the Congregational church. He is prominent in the Masonic order, a member of Orient Lodge, of Norwood; of Hebron Chapter, Royal Arch Masons, Norwood, and for years its secretary; of Cypress Commandery, Knights Templar, of Hyde Park. He is also a member of Lambda Chapter of Beta Theta Pi college fraternity. He resides on Bullard street, Norwood.

He married first, Mildred S. Knowlton, of Ann Arbor, Michigan, daughter of Ernest J. and Roxanna Knowlton. She was born in South Lyons, Michigan, 1860, and died March 9, 1897, at Norwood. (See Knowlton sketch). He married second, Florence (Barker) Loomis, widow of Henry Loomis, daughter of Captain Joshua P. Barker. She is a descendant of a long line of Barkers who for several generations were notable officers in the British army, and on her grandmother's side is a direct descendant from the English house of Stuarts. She had one daughter, Elizabeth Loomis, by her first marriage. Children of first wife: 1. Helen Knowlton, born March 2, 1891. 2. Florence Mildred, May 4, 1895.

(For preceding generations see Edward Rawson 1).

RAWSON (III) David Rawson, son of William Rawson (2), was born December 13, 1683. He inherited the homestead at Braintree. He was a persevering business man, with much force of character. He died at Braintree, April 20, 1752. He married Mary Gulliver, daughter of Captain John, of Milton. Their graves are near that of President John Quincy Adams, at Quincy, formerly Braintree. Children, born at Braintree: 1. David, September 14, 1714, married Mary Dyer. 2. Jonathan, December 26, 1715; married Susanna Stone. 3. Elijah, February 5, 1717; married Mary Paddock. 4. Mary, May 20, 1718; married Captain Joseph Winchester. 5. Hannah, April 2, 1720; died July 24, 1726. 6. Silence, June 12, 1721; died August 17, 1721. 7. Anne, July 30, 1722; married Samuel Bass. 8. Elizabeth, November 30, 1723; married Peter Adams. 9. Josiah, January 3, 1727; mentioned below. 10. Jerusha, December 21, 1729; married Israel Eaton. 11. Lydia, January 17, 1731; married Samuel Baxter. 12. Ebenezer, May 31, 1734; married Sarah Chase.

(IV) Josiah Rawson, son of David Rawson (3), was born at Braintree, January 3, 1727. He settled first in Grafton, Worcester county, then in Warwick, Franklin county, Massachusetts. He died February 24, 1812. Children: 1. Josiah, born 1751; married Elizabeth Barrows. 2. Simeon, born 1753; married Ama Holden. 3. Abigail, born November 14, 1755; married Joshua Garfield; lived at Royalston. 4. Mary, born November 23, 1757; married David W. Leland. 5. Anna B., born October 11, 1759; married Thomas Leland. 6. Jonathan B., born 1761; married Livonia Robinson. 7. Lydia, born 1763, died aged eighteen. 8. Elizabeth, born 1765; mentioned below. 9. Lemuel, born January 18, 1767; married Sarah Barrows. 10. Amelia, born 1769; (The Rawson Genealogy has her married to Seth Ellis). 11. Hannah, born 1771; died in Warwick. 12. Secretary, born September 19, 1773; married Lucy Russell.

(V) Elizabeth Rawson, daughter of Josiah Rawson (4), was born in 1765, at Grafton or Warwick, Massachusetts. She married Seth Ellis, and resided in Orange, Massachusetts. Caroline Ellis, daughter of his son Seth Jr., married March 12, 1829, Robert Turner, at Winchester, New Hampshire, and their daughter Helen M., born September 15, 1831, at Claremont, New Hampshire, married September 11, 1849, at Munsville, New York, William Wesley Whedon. (See sketch). On her mother's side Caroline Ellis was sixth in direct descent from William Cheney, immigrant ancestor from England in 1635 to Roxbury, Massachusetts, and her grandfather, Ebenezer Cheney, fought in the revolution, and in 1779 was stationed at Fort Ticonderoga.

P. M. Neal
Aged 96

KNOWLTON (I) Captain William Knowlton, immigrant ancestor, was born in England, and was himself part owner of the vessel in which he came to this country. He died on the voyage, and is said to have been buried in what is now Shelburn, Nova Scotia. He married Ann Elizabeth Smith. Their four sons became prominent in early colonial history in Massachusetts Bay: 1. John, born 1610; married Margery Wilson; settled at Ipswich; a shoemaker by trade. 2. William, born 1615; mentioned below. 3. Deacon Thomas, born 1622. 4. Samuel.

(II) William Knowlton, son of Captain William Knowlton (1), was born in England, in 1615, and died in 1655. He was a brick mason by trade. He settled in Ipswich, Massachusetts Bay, in 1641 and sold land in 1643. The account of his estate was presented to the court by his brother Thomas in 1678, according to Pope's "Pioneers of Massachusetts," but this account was probably that of his son's estate. He was a member of the First Church of Ipswich. Children: 1. Thomas, born 1640; married Hannah Green. 2. Nathaniel, born 1641; married Deborah Grant. 3. William, born 1642, removed from Ipswich to Norwich, Connecticut. 4. John, born 1644; married Bethia Carter. 5. Benjamin, born 1646; married Hannah Mirick. 6. Samuel, mentioned below. 7. Mary, born 1649; married Samuel Abbe.

(III) Samuel Knowlton, son of William Knowlton (2), was born in Ipswich, Massachusetts, in 1647; married Elizabeth Witt.

(IV) Rice Knowlton, son of Samuel Knowlton (3), was born in Ipswich, 1670, and died 1760; married Mary Dodge, of Ipswich, January 2, 1699. Children: 1. Paul, born 1703. 2. Rice, born January 27, 1705; mentioned below. 3. Bethia, 1709. 4. Mary, 1716. 5. Churchill, 1720. 6. Deborah, 1723. 7. Abraham, 1725.

(V) Rice Knowlton, son of Rice Knowlton (4), was born in Ipswich, January 27, 1705; married Lydia Woodbury, of Ipswich, November 25, 1727. Children, born at Ipswich: 1. Benjamin, December 10, 1728; mentioned below. 2. Francis, May 4, 1732. 3. Joseph, August 12, 1734. 4. John, 1737. 5. Rice, 1740.

(VI) Benjamin Knowlton, son of Rice Knowlton (5), was born December 10, 1728, at Ipswich. He married, at Westford, Massachusetts, 1750, Phebe Wright. Children: 1. Phebe, born 1751. 2. Benjamin, born September 26, 1753; mentioned below. 3. Henry, born 1756. 4. Lydia, 1758. 5. Esther, 1761. 6. Sarah, 1764. 7. John, 1766. 8. Eunice, 1769. 9. Bethia, 1771. 10. Hannah, 1776.

(VII) Benjamin Knowlton, son of Benjamin Knowlton (6), was born September 26, 1753; married Abigail Wright. Children: 1. Abigail, born June 22, 1777. 2. Charlotte, 1778. 3. Benjamin, 1780; mentioned below. 4. Amos, 1783. 5. Lucy, 1786.

(VIII) Benjamin Knowlton, son of Benjamin Knowlton (7), was born in 1780; married at Sangerfield, New York, May 31, 1803, Lucy Campbell. Children: 1. Ursula, born 1804. 2. Charlotte, born 1806, died in infancy. 3. Benjamin, born 1809. 4. Charlotte, 1811. 5. Emeline, 1813. 6. Oliver Jerome, born 1816. 7. Ernest J., 1818; mentioned below. 8. Mariah, 1822.

(IX) Ernest J. Knowlton, son of Benjamin Knowlton (8), was born in 1818; married at Ypsilanti, Michigan, March 17, 1850, Roxanna A. Potter, born June 1, 1831, at Ellesburg, New York, daughter of Ichabod and Amanda (Streeter) Potter. Her father was the son of Abel and Margaret (Green) Potter. Abel Potter was a soldier in the revolution, and was wounded in the Rhode Island campaign. Children: 1. Jerome C., born 1850; married Adele Pattengill. 2. Ida M., born 1853; married Judge V. H. Lane. 3. Mildred S., born 1860; married William T. Whedon. (See sketch).

NEAL Hon. Peter Morrell Neal, who had the distinction of having served the city of Lynn four consecutive years as its war mayor, a faithful, patriotic citizen, who had fairly earned the right to the title of Honorable, and who was familiarly known in the most respectful use of the sobriquet as Lynn's "Grand Old Man", was born at Doughty's Falls, North Berwick, Maine, September 21, 1811, and died April 13, 1908, at the home of his son, William E. Neal, of Lynn, thus closing an unusually long and useful life. He was descended from hardy old colonial stock, members of which have filled many places of honor and trust in the gift of the people of the Pine Tree State.

That the Neal family is of ancient origin in England is attested by the fact that reference is made to them in records of the reign of Edward IV (1461-83), and among them was Richard Neale, Knight, one of the justices of common pleas and lord of Prestwould, who died in 1485. The name has been subjected to a wide range of orthography. The Neals of Leicestershire and Northamptonshire are either descended from Sir Richard or from the same source, as their coat-of-arms consisting of "three greyhounds heads-erased-collared-and-ringed" was the same as that borne by the judge just referred to. Thomas Neale (1519-96) was professor of Hebrew at the University of Oxford and a distinguished author. John Neal, Esq., of Dean, Bedfordshire, married Anne, daughter of Henry Cromwell, the latter a cousin of Oliver Cromwell, lord protector of England, and their son John, who married Mary Lawes, of Norwich, emigrated to New England, settling in Salem, Massachusetts. He was a near relative, if not a brother, of Francis Neale, who was appointed a magistrate for Maine in 1660, and was a man of influence in Concord and vicinity. In 1670 he represented Falmouth in the general court. At the breaking out of Indian hostilities in 1675 he removed to Salem, where he was admitted to citizenship in the following year, and his death occurred there subsequently to July, 1699. About 1670 he married Elizabeth, daughter of Samuel and Jane Andrews, who were passengers in the "Increase" from London in 1635. There is also a record stating that Francis Neale married a daughter of Arthur Macworth, but whether or not this referred to Francis Sr. or Francis Jr. cannot be definitely determined. Francis Sr. had two sons: Francis Jr., died in 1693, and Samuel, who survived him. He also left two daughters. Francis Neale Sr. was the ancestor of many of the Neals of York county, Maine.

(I) The ancestors of the Neal family here under consideration were two brothers, John and James, who came to America and settled in Maine, the former in the parish of Unity. He married Joan ———. Children: 1. Mary, married Samuel Miller, 1693. 2. Amy, in 1699 was taken captive by Indians; after her release she married, 1706, Samuel Johnson. 3. Andrew, mentioned below. John Neal died February 18, 1704.

(II) Andrew Neal, son of John and Joan Neal, inherited the entire homestead. He married, about 1694, Catherine, daughter of William Furbish. He died in 1739. Children: 1. Katherine, born December 4, 1695, married, September 22, 1714, Nathaniel Austin, of Dover. 2. John, born October 18, 1698, mentioned below. 3. Andrew, born May 4, 1701, died 1757; married Dorcas Johnson. 4. Hannah, born May 28, 1704, died young. 5. Rebecca, born January 20, 1706-07. 6. Mary, born August 17, 1708, married, January 12, 1726, Benjamin Hill. 7. James, born May 4, 1711, died August 31, 1730.

(III) John Neal, son of Andrew and Catherine (Furbish) Neal, was born October 18, 1698, died in 1755. He married, intention published June 29, 1728, Patience Johnson, of Hampton, born November 23, 1709, daughter of Edmund Johnson. She survived him. Dow says she married Ebenezer Godfrey, and he may have been her second husband. Children: 1. John, born August 25, 1729, died September 12, 1729. 2. Mary, born December 24, 1730, died August 20, 1736. 3. Abigail, born May 23, 1732, married, November 28, 1757, Alden Warren. 4. Rebecca, born January 6, 1735, died April 14, 1737. 5. Mary, born July 24, 1736, married, January 18, 1755, Tristram Warren. 6. Patience, born January 24, 1738. 7. John, born August 17, 1741, married, November 27, 1765, Elizabeth Hubbard. 8. Andrew, born March 12, 1742-43. 9. James, named in his father's will in 1752, mentioned below. 10. Edmund, named in will; married Jane Came, of York, 1775.

(IV) James Neal, son of John and Patience (Johnson) Neal, resided in Berwick, Maine. He married, in Wells, Maine, Jean Hubbard, intention published July 25, 1778. Children: 1. John, settled in South Berwick, in "the wilds of Maine". 2. Elijah, mentioned below.

(V) Elijah Neal, son of James and Jean (Hubbard) Neal, was born in North Berwick, Maine, about 1785. He married, July 30, 1807, Comfort Morrell, born January 3, 1788, daughter of Peter and Hannah (Winslow) Morrell (see Morrell family). They lived at Doughty's Falls, North Berwick, where their son, Peter Morrell, mentioned below, was born, and James. Elijah Neal was a blacksmith and ironworker by trade and manufactured carriages. He spent his life in North Berwick where he died at an advanced age.

(VI) Peter Morrell Neal, son of Elijah Neal, was born September 21, 1811. He received a part of his early education in the public schools of his native place, and at the age of fifteen was enrolled as a pupil in the Friends' School in Providence, Rhode Island; this was supplemented by attendance at the North Berwick Academy, from which institution he was graduated. In 1832 he opened a private school in Portland, Maine, where he remained until 1842, when he accepted the principalship of the North Berwick high school, a position which he held until 1850, when, owing to ill health, he relinquished it and removed to Lynn, in which city he established his home. He built a house in what was then Beech street, now Washington, where he resided for several years, when he built another in the adjoining lot where they resided until the death of Mrs. Neal, January 6, 1903. He became actively identified with the business, social and political life of the city, and subsequently became its chief executive. On coming to Lynn Mr. Neal formed a partnership for the carrying on of the lumber business with Philo Clifford, which was continued until 1859, Mr. Neal carrying on the business alone until 1863, when he formed a partnership with Nehemiah Lee, to whom he sold out a year later. Shortly afterward he built a new wharf on what is now Washington street, opposite Tudor, and started in there as an individual. Here he continued until his retirement from active life in the latter eighties.

At the time of Mr. Neal's birth, Maine was a province of Massachusetts, and his first vote, cast in 1832, was for Henry Clay, presidential candidate for the Whig party. He afterward joined the Free Soil party and later, upon the formation of the Republican party, he was its first candidate for the office of representative. His political activity began soon after coming to Lynn, when he was elected a member of the common council from ward four. Later he was chosen a member of the school committee and was for a time chairman of that body. On January 6, 1862, he was inaugurated mayor, and was re-elected to that office the three following years, serving throughout the civil war, and of all the famous war mayors of Massachusetts cities none could take a higher rank than he. Mr. Neal's record as the city's war mayor is one that will never be forgotten. There were stirring times during his administration of the affairs of the city, and his was a familiar figure on the streets of Lynn, and ever since that time his name has been held in grateful remembrance by not only the soldiers, but those who were associated with him in the municipal affairs of his time. He was constant in his devotion to the interests of the soldiers and their families, and many times visited the army and the hospitals. His labor for the soldiers' and widows' pensions from the government, for which services he would never receive compensation, although many times urged to do so, was noteworthy. The Mexican, Civil and Spanish wars took place during his life and he took an active interest in them all. In 1870-71 he was a member of the house of representatives, and in 1876 was a member of the state senate from the first Essex district. It was a source of great pride to Mr. Neal that his grandson, Charles Near Barney, Esq., was nominated and elected to the office of mayor of the city of Lynn in 1906, upon which occasion the Hon. Peter M. Neal, although ninety-five years of age, was the guest of honor and took an active interest in all the proceedings.

After his retirement from active life, some Mr. Neal for some time devoted his well earned leisure to Biblical research which he began in his schoolmaster days, and never wholly abandoned during his mercantile career. He also kept close track of the doings of the world about him, and throughout the declining years of his life manifested a keen interest in all affairs pertaining to the city over which he was once mayor. His last appearance in public was at the recent anniversary of the Friends Society on Silsbee street, when he was called upon for a few remarks, and though greatly fatigued by the exertion of reaching the meeting house, spoke at some length in a reminiscent vein that was highly entertaining to those who heard him. He was revered and loved by every citizen of Lynn, and it may truly be said that he was one of nature's noblemen, upright, honest and ever ready to recognize the rights of others. In private and public life he was the soul of honor and often sacrificed much personal gain that his principles might remain unprofaned. Too much cannot be said of the splendid life of Mr. Neal, and his name will go down in local history as one to be held among those in the list of Lynn's famous men. Mr. Neal was a member of several societies, among them being the Old Boys of Ward 4, of which organization he was elected the perpetual president at the meeting held in Lynn Woods in the summer of 1904. He was also one of the trustees of the Friends' school.

In September, 1836, while a schoolmaster in Portland, Maine, Mr. Neal married Lydia Cobb, the ceremony taking place in a little Quaker meeting house in Portland, Maine. She was born March 26, 1815, at Parsonfield, Maine, daughter of Edward and Phoebe (Pope) Cobb, and a descendant of Henry Cobb who came from England to Plymouth in 1629. Her parents moved to Parsonfield from Portland temporarily, fearing that the English soldiers would destroy that city as they did at the time of the revolutionary war, but they returned to Portland as soon as they believed all danger to have passed. On her mother's side Mrs. Neal traced her descent to Joseph Pope, who came to Salem in the "Mary and John" in 1634. Edward Cobb joined the Society of Friends when a young man, and his wife was born a Friend, thus their daughter Lydia was a birthright member of the Society and all her life one of its active workers. Mrs. Neal was educated in Portland, and for a short time was engaged in teaching in that city. She always took a strong interest in religious and educational work and in the various activities of women in the city of Lynn. She served for years on the committee of the Friends' school in Providence, Rhode Island, and from time to time held various positions of trust in the Society of Friends. She was one of the charter members of the Lynn Woman's Club, and at the close of her life was on the honorary list of that organization. No younger woman took a more genuine interest in the various activities with which she was connected than did Mrs. Neal, but while always willing to assist in any work she sought no recognition or advancement and never desired office. The center of Mrs. Neal's life was always her own home. During the sixty-six years of their married life there existed between husband and wife that true companionship which makes the real home life. Her interest in her husband's activities, her wide search for the knowledge to be gained from reading and conversation and her kindly interest in the old and young, made her, even to the end of her long life, younger in spirit than many women of half her years. Her death occurred January 6, 1903, after an illness of less than two weeks. Although in the eighty-seventh year of her age, she was up to that time in the full enjoyment of all her faculties and possessed the same keenness of intellect and graciousness of manner which characterized her in younger days and won for her the love and admiration of all who knew her. Children of Mr. and Mrs. Neal were: Edward Cobb, of Lynn; Mary Louise, wife of William Mitchell Barney, of Lynn; Ellen M., wife of John E. Cheney, of Boston; William E., married Harriet Louise Schofield; one daughter, Louise. Their grandchildren are: Rev. Edward Mitchell Barney, Lydia Louise Barney, of Lynn, former Mayor Charles Neal Barney, of Lynn, Herbert Neal Cheney, of Boston and Louisa Neal. Their great-grandchildren are: Josephine Cheney, of Boston, and Virginia and Stuart Neal Barney, daughter and son respectively of former Mayor Barney.

With simple ceremony which coincided with his ideas of life and in accordance with the spiritual devotion of the church of which he was a member, the Society of Friends, the last words were spoken over the remains of the late Peter M. Neal and the body laid to rest. The funeral services were held at the Friends' Church, Silsbee street. Besides the friends and relatives of Mr. Neal there were present the members of the Lynn city government, ex-mayors of the city, members of the board of aldermen, common council, school board, department boards, many of the older residents of the city, over eighty years of age, who had been associated with the departed in business and social life, and a large delegation from General Lander Post, No. 5, Grand Army of the Republic, many of whom were the "boys of '61," who left Lynn in the defense of their country under the first administration of Lynn's war mayor. Remarks in eulogy of the life and work of Mr. Neal were made by Augustine Jones, of Newton, a friend of Mr. Neal, and who was formerly stationed in Lynn; John Elwood Paige, also a firm friend of Mr. Neal; senior vice commander of the Grand Army of the Republic; and J. L. Parker, who spoke in part as follows: "The death of Hon. Peter M. Neal brings to the comrades of General Lander Post a profound sorrow. They recall his services to the men who fought to preserve the Union; his unfailing thoughtfulness for the sick and wounded; his ready helpfulness for the families of those who went to the front; his tender sympathies for those called to mourn the loss of loved ones; how he spoke words of encouragement when the prospect of success was clouded; how he rejoiced when victory was perched upon the Union banners. His devotion to his country never faltered and his affection for those who stood between the loyal hearts he represented and the enemies of their country never failed. A fine example of sturdy manhood, governed by high virtues, patriotic in his devotion to public duty, of unswerving rectitude in private life, ever the good citizen, recognizing his responsibility and never shirking it, he has gone to his reward, full of years and honors, blessed with strength of days and the commendation of his fellow citizens." The Rev. Mary E. Miurs, pastor of the church, also delivered a eulogy, which was in part as follows: "The public life of Peter M. Neal was an open book, so clean it needs no words of mine, indeed I can add no words to make it more complete. After he had in his generation served the counsel of God, he fell asleep."

"Here lies God's noblest work—A man.
A friend to truth with a soul sincere. A statesman,
Who broke no promise, served no private end.
With honor clear, betrayed no friend".

MORRELL (I) John Morrell, immigrant ancestor, born 1640, settled at Cold Harbor, now Eliot, Maine, in 1666. He had a grant of land in 1668. He was a mason by trade, and was licensed to keep a ferry and ordinary in 1686. He was living in 1720, when the last record of him appears. He married Sarah, daughter of Nicholas and Elizabeth Hodson. Children: 1. Nicholas, born 1667; married Sarah Frye. 2. Sarah, married first, August 4, 1701, George Huntress; second, Thomas Darling. 3. John, mentioned below. 4. Edah, married April 27, 1702, Jonathan Nason. 5. Hannah, married John Tidy. 6. Abraham, married Phebe Heard. 7. Elizabeth, married February 3, 1698, Samuel Drown.

(II) John Morrell, son of John Morrell, married December 16, 1701, Hannah, daughter of Peter and Mary Dixon. His will was dated in 1756 and proved in 1763. His wife died December 20, 1765. Children: 1. John, born July 30, 1702; married Ruth Dow. 2. Thomas, born August 20, 1705; probably died young. 3. Peter, born September 16, 1709; mentioned below. 4. Jedediah, born August 29, 1711; married first, December 5, 1734, Elizabeth Jenkins; second, October 20, 1737, Anna Dow; third, January 28, 1762, Sarah Gould; died 1776. 5. Richard, born September 23, 1713; not named in will. 6. Keziah, married ——— Roberts. 7. Mary, married William Gerrish, of Berwick.

(III) Peter Morrell, son of John Morrell, was born September 16, 1709, and died November 11, 1801. He married first, October 10, 1734, Sarah Peaslee, of Hampton, who died June 19, 1780; second, Elizabeth Sawyer. He resided at North Berwick. Children: 1. Thomas, born February 19, 1733; married February 25, 1754, ——— Johnson. 2. John, born May 10, 1734; married September 24, 1757, Sarah Winslow. 3. Sarah, born March 23, 1736; killed by Indians, at North Berwick, May 9, 1748. 4. Stephen, born April 10, 1737; married October 27, 1761, Elizabeth Winslow; second, June 4, 1788, Sarah Austin. 5. Jacob, born February 6, 1739; married October 27, 1760, Elizabeth Huston. 6. David, born December 14, 1740; married December 31, 1766, Sarah Lewis. 7. Jonathan, born July 9, 1742; died June 15, 1743. 8. Ruth, born January 4, 1744; married May 24, 1762, Samuel Winslow. 9. Peaslee, born September 25, 1748; married first, July 14, 1768, Phebe Chadbourne; second, Peace Ricker; third, Jane (Emery) Frost, widow. 10. Peter, born May 5, 1753; mentioned below.

(IV) Peter Morrell, son of Peter Morrell, was born May 5, 1753, and died January 1, 1819. He was a lawyer and farmer at North Berwick. He married, at Falmouth, February 26, 1776, Hannah Winslow, died October 3, 1807. Children: 1. Elizabeth, born April 15, 1777; married May 1, 1800, Jacob Sawyer. 2. Lydia, born March 29, 1779; married March 14, 1799, Oliver Austin. 3. Sarah, born April 4, 1781; married April 4, 1799, Thomas Stackpole. 4. Theodate, born May 29, 1783; died October 25, 1801, unmarried. 5. Hope, born August 16, 1785; married January 6, 1814, James Harvey; died March 22, 1865. 6. Comfort, born January 3, 1788; married July 30, 1807, Elijah Neal (see Neal family). 7. Lovina, born January 5, 1790; died November 14, 1872, unmarried. 8. Hannah, born March 21, 1792; died March 14, 1870. 9. Guliela Maria, born June 22, 1794; died August 8, 1794. 10. Benjamin, born July 14, 1795; died March 23, 1796. 11. Peter Winslow, born March 12, 1797; married first, Lois Whitney; second, Ruth (Hersey) Frothingill, widow. 12. Asa, born June 3, 1799; married Cynthia Dow.

NEWHALL The Newhall family of the line here treated comes of the English branch which was seated in Cheshire, and was itself descended from the ancient Newhalls so closely associated with events in the time of the Conqueror. All writers of Newhall genealogy (and they have been many) agree that Thomas and Anthony Newhall were the immigrant ancestors in America, and that they landed in Salem in the colony of Massachusetts Bay in the year 1630. It is with Thomas Newhall and a single line of his descendants that we have to deal in this place.

(I) Thomas Newhall, immigrant ancestor, was born in England, and came with his brother, Anthony Newhall, to Lynn about 1630. Thomas Newhall married Mary ———, who died September 25, 1665. He died at Lynn, May 25, 1674. His will was dated April 1, 1669, and filed June 30, 1674; he bequeathed various parcels of real estate to his children. He had land at Rumney Marsh,

Gaines Neck and Lynn. His son Thomas was executor of his will. The estate was appraised at one hundred and seventy-three pounds. Children: 1. Susanna, born about 1624, died February 7, 1682; married Richard Haven. 2. Thomas, born about 1630, mentioned below. 3. John, married first, Elizabeth Leighton; second, July 17, 1679, Sarah Flanders. 4. Mary, born about 1637, married Thomas Brown.

(II) Thomas Newhall, known as Ensign Thomas, son of Thomas Newhall (1), said to have been the first white child born in Lynn, died April 2, 1687. He married, December 29, 1652, Elizabeth, daughter of Nicholas Potter; she was buried in Lynn, February 22, 1676-77. His executor, John Newhall, filed his will in Suffolk county. His estate was valued at six hundred pounds. He was ensign in the military company. His homestead adjoined land of Benjamin Potter, bounded on the common northerly and on the country road or highway southerly. Children, born in Lynn: 1. Thomas, born November 18, 1653, married Rebecca Greene, of Malden. 2. John, born December 14, 1655, died January 20, 1738; married Esther Bartram, of Lynn. 3. Joseph, born September 22, 1658, mentioned below. 4. Nathaniel, born March 17, 1660, married Elizabeth Symonds. 5. Elizabeth, born March 21, 1662, drowned in April, 1665, in a pit near the father's house. 6. Elisha, born November 3, 1665, buried in latter part of February, 1686-87. 7. Elizabeth, born October 22, 1667. 8. Mary, born February 18, 1669. 9. Samuel, born January 19, 1672, married Abigail Lindsey. 10. Rebecca, born July 17, 1675, married Ebenezer Parker, of Reading.

(III) Joseph Newhall, son of Thomas Newhall (2), was born in Lynn, September 22, 1658, died January 29-30, 1705-06, while he was on the road from Lynn to Boston during a great snow storm. He was a prominent citizen, holding many positions of honor and trust, was representative to the general court in 1705-06, and was called Ensign Newhall. He left a considerable landed estate. He married Susanna Farrar, born March 26, 1659, daughter of Thomas and Elizabeth Farrar, of Lynn. Children: 1. Jemima, born December 31, 1678; married Benjamin Very. 2. Thomas, January 6, 1680. 3. Joseph, February 6, 1683-84; married Elizabeth Potter. 4. Elisha, November 20, 1686; married Jane Breed. 5. Ephraim, February 20, 1688, mentioned below. 6. Daniel, February 5, 1690; married Mary Breed. 7. Ebenezer, June 3, 1693; married Elizabeth Breed. 8. Susanna, December 19, 1695; married Joseph Breed. 9. Benjamin, April 5, 1798; married Elizabeth Fowle. 10. Samuel, March 9, 1700. 11. Sarah, July 11, 1704; married Thomas Burrage.

(IV) Ephraim Newhall, son of Joseph Newhall (3), was born in Lynn, February 20, 1688, married there, December 12, 1716, Abigail Denmark, who died September 10, 1753.

(V) Ephraim Newhall, son of Ephraim Newhall (4), was born about 1718. He married, June 11, 1745, Abigail Newhall, who was buried at Lynn, August 23, 1777. Children, born at Lynn: 1. Rufus, mentioned below. 2. John, married, June 22, 1790, Mary Bachellor.

(VI) Rufus Newhall, son of Ephraim Newhall (5), was born May 7, 1747, died December 31, 1815. He married, December 26, 1787, at Lynn, Keziah Breed, who died there March 8, 1849, aged eighty-three. Children, born at Lynn: 1. John, born August 22, 1788, mentioned below. 2. Archelaus, July 23, 1790. 3. Keziah, August 13, 1792, died May 10, 1815. 4. Eliza, December 24, 1794. 5. Anna Rowell, October 16, 1797, died September 27, 1815. 6. Rufus, October 16, 1800. 7. Abigail, August 29, 1802. 8. Enos, August 27, 1804, mentioned below. 9. Clarissa Ingalls, October 1, 1806, died January 1, 1833. 10. Nathan Beed, January 21, 1808, died May 12, 1847. 11. James, July 27, 1810, died August 29, 1810.

(VII) John Newhall, eldest son of Rufus Newhall (6), was born in Lynn, August 22, 1788. He was called Junior to distinguish him from other older John Newhalls. He was a farmer in Lynn, residing at the corner of what is now Broad and Atlantic streets, in a house which is still standing. He was among the substantial fathers of his day and time, and in addition to his tillable land he owned a large amount of wood land. He took an active part and interest in all agricultural matters, and was for many years an active member of the Essex Agricultural Association. He owned a large farm in the vicinity of Broad and Atlantic streets, and the latter street was by him cut through and laid out and he sold a number of building lots on either side of it, and he also owned and sold considerable land on what is now the boulevard. He was formerly a Whig and later a Republican in politics, and held the office of overseer of the poor. He also was one of the owners of the two whaling ships—"Nimus" and "Commodore Presle"—which for a number of

Wm O. Newhall

years sailed out of Lynn. He was a member of the Society of Friends. He married, November 26, 1817, Delia Breed, daughter of Samuel and Theodate Breed, of Lynn. Children born at Lynn: 1. Ann, born August 29, 1818, died July 4, 1830. 2. Avis, January 28, 1820, died June 19, 1829. 3. Edward, July 22, 1822, died June 12, 1905. 4. Harriet, August 20, 1824, died December 24, 1824. 5. Charles, August 26, 1826, died October 20, 1867. 6. William Oliver, November 9, 1828, mentioned below. 7. Anna, August 15, 1831, died September 30, 1833.

(VII) Enos Newhall, son of Rufus Newhall (6), was born on Atlantic street, Lynn, August 27, 1804, died 1870. He followed the occupation of farming throughout the greater part of his active career, and in all respects proved himself to be an exemplary citizen. He married Eliza Flanders, of Boscawen. New Hampshire, whose death occured in 1894. Children: A child who died in infancy. 2. Franklin Enos, born December 9, 1835, mentioned below.

(VIII) William Oliver Newhall, youngest son of John (7) and Delia (Breed) Newhall, was born November 9, 1828, at the corner of Broad and Atlantic streets, Lynn, died April 4, 1908. He received his education in the Lynn schools and the Moses Brown boarding school in Providence, Rhode Island, of which he was later a member of the school committee for more than a quarter of a century. He left school at the age of eighteen, and immediately began his business career in a shoe factory, which line of work he followed for a quarter of a century, and after his retirement acted in the capacity of trustee of estates and in looking after his own property. He developed a part of the old farm and built some houses, among them being his late residence on Atlantic street. He was the first vice-president and trustee of Lynn Institution for Savings, was for many years treasurer of the Lynn Home for Aged Women, holding that position at the time of his death, and trustee of the Home for Aged Men. He was a life-long member, and a minister for many years, of the Society of Friends in Lynn, and held a prominent position in its councils. He served as clerk of the New England yearly meeting for twenty years or more, and was one of the most widely known and respected of this denomination. He was a Whig and Republican in politics. He was a man of sterling integrity, and endeared himself to his friends by his kindly interest and ready sympathy. He had a wonderfully retentive memory of men and events, and a fund of anecdotes of the experiences of his early life. He married, at West Falmouth, on Cape Cod, October 23, 1856, Mary Elizabeth Boyce, daughter of Jonathan and Deborah (Dillingham) Boyce, and their children are: 1. William Boyce, born January 13, 1860, is a florist, having three greenhouses in Lynn; he is a yachtsman and is commodore of the Lynn Volunteer Yacht Club. 2. Mary Alice, born October 19, 1861, married Edmund F. Buffington, of Fall River, who is engaged in the coal business there; one child, Gertrude Elizabeth Buffington, born July 10, 1892. Mrs. William O. Newhall died April 27, 1906.

(VIII) Franklin Enos Newhall, son of Enos Newhall (7), was born December 9, 1835, in Lynn, in the old house built by his father about the year 1832. He was educated in public schools, and for many years followed the shoe trade, which proved highly remunerative. He is now leading a retired life, enjoying the rest and ease which should follow a live of activity and usefulness. He married Hannah Elizabeth Goldsmith, born October 22, 1836, died April 9, 1895. She was a native of Lynn. Their children were: 1. Frank E., born April 24, 1860. 2. Fred W., mentioned below.

(IX) Fred W. Newhall, son of Franklin Enos Newhall (8), was born in Lynn, December 29, 1864. He attended the public schools of Lynn, completing his studies at the age of sixteen. His first employment was in the newspaper business, and for the past two decades he has been engaged as a newsdealer, conducting a stationery store at No. 224 Lewis street, Lynn. He is a member of East Lynn Lodge, No. 207, Independent Order of Odd Fellows; Lynn Encampment, No. 58; Sagamore Tribe, No. 2, Improved Order of Red Men, and Knights of the Golden Eagle. He is a Republican in politics, in which he has taken an active part, having been a delegate to a large number of conventions. He was a member of the city council four years. He married, in March, 1889, Mary E. Thomas, of Swampscott, daughter of the late Henry and Mary (Twining) Thomas. One child, Lillian G., born April 23, 1890.

(For ancestry see preceeding sketch.)

NEWHALL (IV) Samuel Newhall, son of Joseph Newhall (3), was born in Lynn, March 9, 1700. He married Keziah Breed, of Lynn, December 8, 1724. She was the daughter of Samuel Breed, who died in 1755. Samuel

Newhall was adopted in his youth by an uncle, Thomas Farrar, who in his will, dated June 5, 1730, proved January 11, 1733, bequeathed the bulk of his estate to Samuel Newhall and Richard Hood, another kinsman. Samuel's will, dated July 28, 1768, proved October 1, 1770, bequeathed to sons, Pharaoh, Abijah and Daniel; to daughters Anna Estes, Elizabeth, Sarah, Lydia Johnson, Abigail Purinton, Rebecca Chase and Ruth Newhall; also his brother, Elisha Newhall. His death is entered on the Friends' records as October, 1770. This record gives the date of his wife's death as October 9, 1749. Children, born in Lynn: 1. Anna, October 27, 1725; married as his second wife, Matthew Estes. 2. Elizabeth, March 7, 1727-8. 3. Sarah, August 20, 1730; married Abner Jones. 4. Lydia, January 14, 1732-3; married Nehemiah (?) Johnson. 5. Pharaoh, February 15, 1733-4; mentioned below. 6. Abijah, February 15, 1736-7. 7. Abigail, March 4, 1738, married Samuel Purinton, of Danvers. 8. Daniel, February 4, 1740-1. 9. Rebecca, October 28, 1743; married Abner Chase, of Salem. 10. Ruth, October 12, 1746.

(V) Pharaoh Newhall, son of Samuel Newhall (4), was born in Lynn, February 15, 1733-4; married, April 24, 1764, Theodate Breed, born December, 1733. (See Breed family). He was a blacksmith by trade, and in religion a Friend, as were many of the family of earler and later date. His name is supposed to have been a corruption of the surname Farrar of his paternal grandmother. His wife died in Lynn, September 9, 1810, and he died in September 15, 1821. His will, wherein he is styled Pharaoh Newhall, of Lynn, yeoman, dated December 30, 1816, and proved October 2, 1821, mentions grandsons Abner, Austin and Thomas F. Newhall; his son Winthrop, to whom he gave a lot called Leighton Field; son Silvanus to whom he gave a lot laid out to Joseph Newhall; and son Samuel. Children born in Lynn: 1. Samuel, born March 9, 1765; married Sarah Phillips. 2. Abner, born September 24, 1767, died August 8, 1769. 3. Winthrop, born June 6, 1769, mentioned below. 4. Abner, born July 19, 1771; died August, 1802, at Portsmouth, New Hampshire. 4. Silvanus, born July 18, 1773, married Lydia Gove. 6. Theodate, born February 6, 1776, married Manuel Austin. 7. Francis, born September 23, 1778, died November 29, 1787.

(VI) Winthrop Newhall, son of Pharaoh Newhall (5), was born in Lynn, Massachusetts, June 6, 1769, and died there August 19, 1852. He was a tanner by trade, and for many years carried on a successful tanning business, his vats and tanyard being located on the west side of Market street, near the present railroad crossing. He married, January 12, 1794, Elizabeth Farrington. Children: 1. Francis S., born April 30, 1795. 2. Henry, March 10, 1797, mentioned below. 3. Eliza, January 12, 1799, died young. 4. Eliza, April 25, 1800. 5. Sophia, May 9, 1806. 6. Lydia, January 10, 1810. 7. Horace, August 30, 1813.

(VII) Henry Newhall, son of Winthrop Newhall (6), was born in Lynn, Massachusetts, March 10, 1797, and died July 15, 1878. In partnership with his brother, Francis Newhall, he continued his father's business, adding to it the manufacture of morocco of which he made a specialty until he retired from active labor and business on account of failing health. He filled with ability and fidelity several municipal offices. He was a director of the Leighton Bank, which became the Central National Bank, from October 7, 1850, under its two charters to January 11, 1876, the longest continuous service on the board of directors; and on the death of his brother Francis, succeeded February, 1858, to the office of president, a position that he likewise held until he resigned January 11, 1876. His early opportunities for schooling were limited, but he made the most of them, and through observation and study acquired an excellent liberal education. Early in life he joined the Unitarian church, which was incorporated in 1822. He married, December 8, 1829, Ann Atwell, who was born February 26, 1809, and died February 13, 1863. Among their children were: 1. Sarah C., married Benjamin J. Berry. 2. Henry Pickering. 3. Charles Atwell. 4. Charles Henry.

Zachariah Atwell, father of Ann (Atwell) Newhall, was born November 1, 1779, and died in January, 1847; married Anna Bredeen, of Malden, Massachusetts, who was born July 17, 1778, and died June 8, 1864. Zachariah Atwell, father of Zachariah (6), was born October 9, 1755, and died November 6, 1836. William Atwell (4), father of Zachariah Atwell (5), was born about 1730, and died November 5, 1806; was a soldier in the revolution from Lynn, a private in Captain Gallusha's company, Colonel Benjamin R. Woodbridge's regiment, 1775; also in Captain John Devereux's company, Colonel Jacob Gerrish's regiment; discharged July 3, 1778. Nathan

Eng'd by A.H. Ritchie

Henry Newhall

Atwell (3), father of William (4), married, November 27, 1729, Anna Ramsdell. John Atwell (2), father of Nathan (3), married, June 19, 1693, Margaret Max. John Atwell, father of John (2), was the immigrant; born in England, settled first in Maine; married there, and about 1690 removed with his family to Lynn, Massachusetts.

Henry Newhall was one of the most prominent and intelligent citizens of his generation in Lynn. He was associated in business with his older brother, Francis S. Newhall, in the morocco trade and leather manufacturing, in which they followed to some extent in the footsteps of their father, who was a tanner by calling. The business which the brothers controlled was one of the largest in the town, and they maintained head offices in both Boston and Lynn, also for a short time having a branch office in New York City. In 1850, owing to ill health, Henry Newhall retired from the firm and for several years spent most of his time in travel, both in his own country and abroad, in the hope of recuperating. When his brother Francis died, however, he succeeded him in the presidency of the Leighton (later the Central National) Bank, established by himself and brother Francis in the year 1858, and served as such until he retired. He was a director of this bank from 1850 to 1876, shortly before his death. He was then nearly eighty years old, and his long hold upon important business affairs was but one indication of the strength and vigor of an intellect remarkable in every way. Many members of the family have been noted for ability in the management of large interests, and undoubtedly he inherited his most marked traits from a line of ancestors whose achievements were matters of pride to those of the name. His own qualities were developed in the care of large business ventures, in which the fortunes of others as well as his own were involved, in the discharge of numerous public trusts, and in thoughtful study of the questions of his day, to which he gave much attention. He was not solely a business man, but a student and philosopher as well, and his influence in the community was exercised in many ways. He was a very useful citizen, identified with everything which concerned the life of the town, though not so much as an office holder, but rather as the promoter and encourager of worthy objects. His friendly and genial disposition made many things possible under his management which might have failed in the hands of one less esteemed or less respected. Under the old town government he held a number of offices, and he was one of the first commissioners of the Lynn city hall and city debt sinking funds. His advice was often solicited, in business matters of various kinds, and there were few of the progressive concerns of the day with which he did not have some connection. Thus he was identified with and a trustee of the Lynn Institution for Savings and a director of the Lynn Gaslight Company, the old Mechanics Insurance Company, the Lyceum Hall Association, of which he was president, as he was also of the Exchange Hall Association, and he was one of the benefactors of the Lynn Public Library.

Mr. Newhall was an omniverous reader. In fact, there was little of worth in the current literature of his day that escaped him, and few men in active business life find as much time as he did for his wide range in the fields of history, politics, biography and fiction. His interest was comprehensive, his understanding and appreciation of books unusually keen, and his judgment in culling and retaining the best worthy of a profound scholar. But most of his reading and study was determined by his absorbing interest in human life and affairs, the things that came to him in his daily intercourse with men. While he fed his mind on the best in literature he had that independence of thought and spirit which made him hold to his own convictions, the results of his own experience, and he lacked neither the mind to form those opinions nor the language to express them. But though he spoke with the earnestness and sincerity which made him positive and plain to a remarkable degree, his real kindliness of heart and shrewd knowledge of human nature made it impossible for him to give offense intentionally or to be guilty of riding roughshod over the opinions of others, for whom he was always considerate. His words had weight and influence wherever he was known, yet it was a matter of common remark that he never thrust his opinions upon others, nor attempted to give advice unsolicited. His wide experience, reading and travel, acting upon a mind naturally quick and strong, and a temperament optimistic in its views of the inherent honesty and ambition of human nature, made him a most agreeable and interesting companion. His conversation and society were welcomed everywhere.

Mr. Newhall was very public-spirited, and always kept abreast of the times on the important issues of the day. He was a strong advocate of anti-slavery from the beginning of the movement, and when that cause was very unpopular. By nature he was prudent and conservative, not cautious in upholding principles which might win him personal unpopularity, but careful about adopting unsound or inefficient doctrines until he had weighed them in his own mind and determined their worth. He believed in progressive reform, and was always willing to support worthy movements in that direction. Indeed, he believed in fair play to all, and was anxious to give others the same independence of thought he claimed for his own right, listening to arguments for honest causes, whether they appealed to his sympathies or not. He retained his activity of intellect and clearness of judgment to the last, and when sickness impaired his physical abilities he met the affliction with all his old-time serenity and cheerfulness, his patience and sweetness of disposition then, as ever, drawing around him a circle of admiring friends. He was as companionable to the young as to the old, and enjoyed the society of young people to an extent which proved the youthfulness of his spirit even to his last years.

Of Quaker descent, Mr. Newhall had much of the gentleness and forbearance which characterize that kindly sect, but his religious convictions were not so much the effect of tradition and early training as of conscience and reasoning. He was one of the leaders in the liberal movement in his town which eventually brought about the formation of the Unitarian Society, which he supported consistently and liberally. His whole life was governed by the principles of justice and honor which are the highest expression of the Christian faith, and which in him found a worthy and intelligent advocate.

(VIII) Charles Henry Newhall, son of Henry Newhall (7), was born in Lynn, January 18, 1846. He received his education in the Lynn schools and the Chauncey Hall School, Boston, and upon its completion he was for some time connected with the firm of George W. Keene, abandoning this business in order to associate himself with several firms in the financial world. For many years he was a director of the Lynn Gas and Electric Company, and in 1882 he was elected its president: he was also vice-president of the Central National Bank, a stockholder in the Lynn News Publishing Company, a director and member of the executive committee of the Security Trust Company and a trustee of the Five Cents Savings Bank. He was a director of the Lynn Mutual Fire Insurance Company from June 7, 1887, until his death. At a meeting of the directors of this company called shortly afterward, suitable resolutions were passed. Mr. Newhall was also a trustee of the Lynn Hospital, the Lynn Home for Aged Women, the Lynn Home for Aged Men, Home for Aged Couples, the Lynn Public Library, the Pine Grove Cemetery Association and the Second Congregational Unitarian Church. In addition to these he was identified with a number of trust companies and savings institutions of Boston. Mr. Newhall, after an illness of about eleven weeks, passed away April 23, 1908. His will is an admirable testimony to his kindness. In it he bequeathed one hundred and twenty-two thousand dollars to charitable and other institutions and servants who were long in his employ, the remainder being divided between relatives, who were also generously remembered. He married (first) Helen, daughter of John Swasey, of Boston, and several years after her death married (second) Elizabeth, daughter of Nathaniel White, of Concord, New Hampshire, who also passed away. By neither marriage were there any children, the only near relative surviving Mr. Newhall being a sister, Mrs. Benjamin J. Berry.

Mr. Newhall was undoubtedly the greatest philanthropist the city of Lynn has yet produced and his good works are beyond accounting. His purse was ever open for the benefit of those in need, yet there was no ostentation in his charity. The extent of his private charities can never be known, as his labor in behalf of others was so constant and unremitting that it is a marvel that he found the time to look after his large and ever increasing personal interests. Mr. Newhall was an ideal citizen, broad-minded, public spirited, tactful and persistent, and he carried through many projects where others would have failed. Unselfishness was one of his chief characteristics: he was willing and ready to share his personal prosperity with the citizens of Lynn and he accepted every opportunity to give to the public the benefit of any advantages which his able management has secured. Of a naturally open hearted and lovable disposition, he unconsciously demanded from friends, business associates and employes their respect and admiration. His unfailing interest in the public good, his example as a faithful citizen and his philanthropic work in the field of public and private necessity will never be forgotten.

(For ancestry see Thomas Newhall 1.)

NEWHALL (IV) Thomas Newhall, son of Joseph and Susanna (Farrar) Newhall, was born in Lynn, January 6, 1680. He married, December 12, 1707, Mary, (probably his cousin), daughter of John and Esther Newhall. He married second, December 12, 1717, Elizabeth Bancroft, of Lynn. Thomas Newhall was a farmer, and in a deed of 1731 was called "cloathier." He lived on the north side of the Reading road, running from Salem through Peabody and Lynnfield to Wakefield. He died November 30, 1738. His children Jeremiah, born November 4, 1708; Esther, September 1, 1710; a daughter (stillborn) March 22, 1719; Jonathan, September 13, 1721; Thomas, February 18, 1723-24; John, March 20, 1726; James, October 29, 1729; Amos, March 1, 1730-31; Asa, August 5, 1732.

(V) Asa Newhall, son of Thomas and Elizabeth (Bancroft) Newhall, was born in Lynnfield, August 5, 1732, and lived to be nearly eighty-two years of age, dying May 1, 1814. He married, November 21, 1769, Sarah, born 1746, daughter of Jonathan Tarbel Sr., of Lynnfield. She survived her husband, and died November 3, 1843, at the great age of ninety-seven years, nine months and twenty days. Asa Newhall in 1764 bought what was formerly the farm of Jedediah Newhall, lying on both sides of the road from Lynn to Lynnfield, a little below its intersection with the Salem and Reading road, containing about one hundred acres, which had once belonged to Joseph Newhall, father of Jedediah, and before him to the first Joseph Newhall, grandfather of this last purchaser. To this he added by other purchases until he became the owner of a farm of two hundred and fifty acres, besides numerous outlying lots. He was at the battle of Concord, 1775, and also subsequent battles. His children: Asa Tarbel, born June 28, 1779; Sarah, July 7, 1781; Mary, May 6, 1786.

(VI) Asa Tarbell Newhall, only son of Asa and Sarah (Tarbell) Newhall, was born in Lynnfield, June 28, 1779, died December 18, 1850. He married, (intentions published September 20, 1807), Judith Little, of Newbury. In August, 1807, he received from his father the farm above described, the father also conveying to him a bill of the cattle and farm equipments, the son in return giving his father a bond for the possession of this estate during the natural life of the parent and for the support of father and mother, and after the father's death for the payment of certain sums to his two sisters, Mrs. Sarah Sweetzer and Mrs. Mary Moulton. Mr. James S. Newhall has a copy of this document and all through it the title "my honorable father" and "my honorable mother" is used. Mr. Newhall was bred a farmer, and followed his occupation all his life. He was a close observer of the operations of nature, and brought to the notice of others divers facts of much benefit to the husbandman. He delivered one or two addresses at agricultural exhibitions, and published several papers which secured marked attention and elicited profitable discussion. His mind was penetrating, producing a happy mingling of the practical and the theoretical, and he had sufficient energy and industry to produce results. He was liberal in his views, courteous in his manners, and by his sound judgment and unswerving integrity secured universal respect. In his earlier manhood he was somewhat active in political affairs, and proved himself judicious and trustworthy. He was a member of the constitutional convention of 1820, and a senator in 1826, and a representative in 1828. He was master of Jordan Lodge of Danvers (now Peabody), and presided at all stated meetings of the lodge during the Morgan excitement and was later district deputy grand master of this district. This was the only lodge in the state which did not surrender its charter at this time. He was the father of nine children; who came to maturity: Joshua L., born May 18, 1808; Asa T., December 20, 1809; Thomas Bancroft, October 2, 1811; Hiram, born October 12, 1812, died April 25, 1813; Sallie M., born May 3, 1815; Eunice A., May 14, 1817; Judith B., May 17, 1819; Caroline, October 5, 1821; Hiram L., August 5, 1824; Elizabeth B.

(VII) Thomas Bancroft Newhall, third son of Asa T. and Judith (Little) Newhall, was born in that part of Lynn which is now Lynnfield, October 2, 1811. He was fitted for college at Phillips Academy, Andover, Massachusetts, and Lynn Academy, and graduated from Brown University in 1832, the year in which he came of age. He studied law in offices in Danvers and Boston, and at the Harvard Law School, and was admitted to the bar at the March term of the court of common pleas, 1837. Early in the next month he established himself in practice in Lynn, and soon drew to himself a large and influential clientele. He continued in active practice for a half century, and this occupation, with the discharge of duties in public and private life, with which he was honored, made his life active, useful and honorable. He was a member of the first Lynn city government, was appointed postmaster by President Harrison, in 1842; in 1849, on the establishment of the Lynn police court, received the appointment of judge, and remained in that office until 1866, when he resigned; served as a member of the school board, and as chairman of that body; also upon the water board; and in 1853 was elected mayor, but declined to accept the office. He served as commissioner for some of the city's sinking funds, as city solicitor, and for several years was a member of the state board of health. He was for years president of the Lynn Five Cents Savings Bank, and for twenty-three years president of the Lynn Mutual Fire Insurance Company, and had also been a manager of the Home for Aged Women. He was a member of the Lynn Bar Association. For many years he was a trustee of the Unitarian church. Judge Newhall died September 25, 1893. He married, May 10, 1842, Susan S. Putnam, of Salem, and their children were: James Silver, born August 13, 1843; Susan Agnes, born July 19, 1845, died August 29, 1845; Thomas Bancroft, born December 12, 1846; died September 15, 1847; Thomas Little, born December 31, 1851, died September 2, 1862; Caroline P., born January 27, 1860, married John A. Heath, of Boston.

(VIII) James Silver Newhall, eldest child of Judge Thomas Bancroft and Susan S. (Putnam) Newhall, was born in Lynn, August 13, 1843. He obtained his education in the public schools in that town, discontinuing his studies when he was about seventeen years of age. He then went to live with his grandfather, Jacob Putnam, and learned the leather business with him and his uncle, G. F. Putnam, of Salem, it being the old-fashioned heavy leather business. He was so engaged for thirteen or fourteen years, until he was about thirty-two years of age, when he went west. After three or four years absence he returned, and engaged in the retail coal business in which he continued till 1899. He has occupied various responsible positions in public life, and in semi-public institutions. He was a member of the city government, in Salem, for two years. On January 1, 1905, he was elected president of the Lynn Mutual Fire Insurance Company, after having been a director for several years; and is one of the vice-presidents of the Lynn Five Cents Savings Bank, a director in both the Central National Bank and the Security Safe Deposit and Trust Company. He is a member of the Second Congregational (Unitarian) Church, and has been its treasurer since 1881. In politics he is a Republican. He is affiliated with various Masonic bodies: Starr King Lodge, F. A. M.; Washington Chapter, R. A. M.; and Olivet Commandery, K. T. He is a member of the Lynn Historical Society, Sons of the American Revolution, and the Society of Colonial Wars. He is president of the Home for Aged Women, also Home for Aged Men.

Mr. Newhall married, October 26, 1871, Marion Wentworth Clarke, born in Sydney, Australia, March 7, 1853, daughter of Frederick W. and Ellen Augusta (Brimblecom) Clarke, formerly of Gilmanton Corner, New Hampshire. Children of Mr. and Mrs. Newhall: 1. Ellen Augusta, born August 24, 1872, married, November 22, 1900, Larkin E. Bennett; reside in Wakefield; children: James Stephen Bennett, born March 1, 1905; Everett Newhall, born August 23, 1907. 2. Susan Putnam, born January 20, 1874, married, October 7, 1901, William Gerry Keene; resides in Lynn; one son, William Gerry Keene, Jr., born September 14, 1907.

Frederick W. Clarke, father of Mrs. Newhall, was born at Northwood, New Hampshire, September 23, 1818, and died at Netherwood, New Jersey, February 19, 1892. He was American consul at Sidney, New South Wales, appointed by President Pierce, and held the office eight years. He was the son of Jonathan Clarke Jr., of Northwood, and grandson of Jonathan Sr. Joseph Clarke, father of Jonathan Sr., was son of John Clarke (1). Ellen Augusta Clarke, mother of Mrs. Newhall, was born in Lynn, May 16, 1818, daughter of Colonel Samuel Brimblecom by his second wife, Eleanor, daughter of Jonathan and Mary (Perry) Newhall. Susanna Lane, who married Jonathan Clarke Sr., in 1773, was born in Stratham, in 1750, daughter of Deacon Samuel and Mary (James) Lane. Deacon Samuel Lane, a member of the Fourth Provincial Congress, held at Exeter, New Hampshire, May 17, 1775, was eldest son of Deacon Joshua Lane (3), of Hampton, and his wife, Bathsheba (Robie) Lane. Deacon Joshua Lane was the son of William and Sarah (Webster) Lane, of Boston, Massachusetts, and Hampton, New Hampshire, and grandson of William Lane (1), the immigrant, who was in Boston as early as 1650. Charlotte Johnston, who married Jonathan Clarke Jr., was a daughter of Nathaniel Johnston, a soldier in the revolution, descendant of Ensign Stephen Johnston, an early proprietor and householder of Andover, Massachusetts. Lineage: Nathaniel (5), Zebediah (4), Zebediah (3), Francis (2), Stephen (1). Stephen Johnston married, in 1661, Elizabeth Dane. Their daughter Elizabeth was imprisoned six months on a charge of witchcraft. Sarah Hawke, who married Francis Johnston, was tried for witchcraft and acquitted. Sarah Webster, wife of the second William Lane, was a daughter of Thomas Webster, immigrant ancestor of Daniel Webster, the orator. Mrs. Newhall is also ninth in descent from Thomas Newhall (1).

(For ancestry see Thomas Newhall I.)

NEWHALL (IV) Daniel Newhall, son of Joseph Newhall (3) and Susanna (Farrar) Newhall, born in Lynn, February 5, 1690, married (intentions published November 20, 1713) Mary, daughter of Allen and Elizabeth (Ballard) Breed. His will proved November 27, 1752, mentions his wife Mary and children Jacob, Josiah, Elizabeth, Jemima, Allen, Daniel, Nathaniel, Joseph, Mary and Rebecca. The widow of Daniel died January 1, 1775, in her eighty-fourth year. In a notice of her death published in the *Essex Gazette*, she is said to have left eleven children, sixty-six grandchildren, thirty-two great-grandchildren—in all, one hundred and nine descendants.

(V) Josiah Newhall, son of Daniel Newhall, born 1717, married, December 24, 1740, Hannah Newhall, born October 13, 1722, in Lynn. Josiah is made by the "History of Lynn," to be a son of John, who is of uncertain father, but a grandson of Thomas Newhall (2). Josiah Newhall was a cordwainer, and lived in that part of town now called Lynnfield, where he died October 29, 1789, in his seventy-third year. His wife Hannah died January 27, 1806. Children: Daniel, born November 15, 1741; John, October 29, 1743; Josiah, November 5, 1745; Hannah, August 28, 1747; Lydia, September 25, 1749; William, May 22, 1751; Joel, February 19, 1753; Nathaniel, November 25, 1754; Micajah, October 18, 1756; Jacob, September 16, 1758; James, May 26, 1760; Hannah, July 30, 1762; Susan, August 3, 1764.

(VI) William Newhall, son of Josiah Newhall, born May 22, 1751; married, September 2, 1773, Martha Mansfield; children: Mary, born May 22, 1774; Martha, January 28, 1778; Hannah, September 6, 1780; Elizabeth, August 31, 1782; Nathaniel, July 18, 1784; William, August 3, 1786; Robert, February 17, 1788; Josiah, January 7, 1790; Sally, January 17, 1792; Frederick, August 1, 1795.

(VII) Nathaniel Newhall, third son of William and Martha (Mansfield) Newhall, was born in Lynn, July 18, 1784. He was a manufacturing shoemaker in a small way, as was usually the case in those days. He was engaged in the express business, and is said to have established the first express between Boston and Lynn. He was a teacher of music, and conducted what was known as the old-fashioned singing school. He was a member of and much interested in the South Street Church and spoke much in its public meetings, and with much acceptance to the people. He married, in Lynn, April 22, 1806, Patty, daughter of Captain William Chadwell, an officer in the revolution. Children: William H., born August 11, 1807; Elvira, August 27, 1811; Fletcher, November 15, 1816; Ezra Mudge, July 4, 1819; Elliott, June 6, 1822; Ruth; Nathaniel Addison; Martha Maria, November 21, 1824; Sarah Ellen, October 17, 1831; the two latter are living.

(VIII) Elliott Newhall, son of Nathaniel and Patty (Chadwell) Newhall, was born June 6, 1822, in Lynn; he died February 25, 1904. He learned the shoemaker's trade, and followed it in Lynn until he became station agent of the old Eastern railroad, at the Commercial street station in West Lynn. He continued in this position for some years, and then became station agent at Saugus Center, under Mr. Hornby, and here he continued for the remainder of his active life, which carried him well up into the 70s. He was a member of the South Street Church, Lynn. He married, June 8, 1845, Ellen Handy. Their children: Henry Elliott, born August 1, 1846; Emma E., resides in Saugus in the old homestead.

(IX) Henry Elliott Newhall, only son of Elliott and Ellen (Handy) Newhall, was born in Lynn, August 1, 1846. His primary schooling was obtained at the Center street school, under Master Upton and John Batchelder, where he attended until he was about fourteen years of age, when he left school. In 1860 he entered the dry goods store of Caldwell & Merritt, and remained about one year.

He then went into the hardware and notion store of Lucius H. Peck, where he remained for a few months only. Upon President Lincoln's first call for three months men at the outbreak of the rebellion, he entered the City Bank as clerk, taking the place of Richard Nichols, who had responded to the call for troops. Although a boy of only seventeen, he did the work of his predecessor, in the bank, with entire satisfaction to its officers. It became a national bank, 1864, and moved into its news quarters, 1868, and he continued with the bank until December, 1870, when he entered Oberlin (Ohio) College, and was a student there one year. In 1871, at the request of the Lynn Five Cents Savings Bank, he returned to Lynn and took the position of first clerk in that bank, in which capacity, and when but twenty-five years old, he practically took entire charge, and has so continued to the present time. He is one of the trustees of the bank, and was elected treasurer in May, 1880. During his connection with the bank he has seen its assets increased from one and three-quarters millions to six millions dollars. Giving his sole attention and best thought to the institution of which he has been treasurer for twenty-seven years, he has registered a dual success in making the bank one of the most substantial of its kind in eastern Massachusetts, and for himself a successful career. Mr. Newhall has never been active in politics. While he has usually voted the Republican ticket, his tendencies have been strongly towards independence in his political action. He married Florence M. Davis, daughter of Henry A. Davis, of Lynn. No children.

(For ancestry see Thomas Newhall I.)

NEWHALL (III) Lieutenant Thomas Newhall, son of Ensign Thomas and Elizabeth (Potter) Newhall, was born 18 9mo. 1653, removed to Malden about the time of his marriage and bought a farm there. He was a weaver as well as husbandman, lieutenant of the militia, selectman of Malden in 1700 and three times afterward. He died July 3, 1728, and is buried in the old burying ground in Malden. In November, 1674, he married Rebecca, daughter of Thomas and Rebecca (Hills) Greene, of Malden. The father of Thomas Hills, (father of Rebecca) was Joseph Hills, Esq., of Malden and Newbury, a man of much prominence, representative, speaker of the house, an active and energetic magistrate, elder of the church, and compiler of the laws of the colony. Rebecca, wife of Thomas Newhall, died May 25, 1726, having borne him nine children: Elizabeth, Thomas, Hannah, Daniel, Lydia, Samuel, Martha and Elisha.

(IV) Daniel Newhall, son of Lieutenant Thomas and Rebecca (Greene) Newhall, was born in 1685, probably in Malden, where his father married and died, and where several of the Newhalls were settled about the beginning of the eighteenth century. He was an innkeeper, a man of considerable consequence in the town, and on one occasion showed himself capable of defending the dignity of his house as well as the safety of his person. The history of Malden contains several interesting incidents in connection with his life in the town. He died in Malden, February 23, 1760, aged seventy-five years. He married, January 8, 1706-07, Sarah, daughter of John Fosdick, of Charlestown. She was born June 11, 1686-87, died December 12, 1763, having survived her husband about three years and evidently continued the tavern formerly kept by him. Their children born in Malden were: Daniel, December 12, 1707; Sarah, November 27, 1711, married Thomas Burditt; John, May 12, 1714, married Dorothy, daughter of Thomas Newhall; Nathan, October 26, 1719, married Tabitha Waite, of Malden.

(V) Daniel Newhall, son of Daniel and Sarah (Fosdick) Newhall, was born in Malden, December 12, 1707, and removed to Leicester, Massachusetts, soon after his marriage with the daughter of Deacon Upham. He bought land in the northeast part of the town and is supposed to have spent the greater part of his life there. He married, December 26, 1728, Tabitha Upham, of Malden, and by her had several children, the names of five of whom are known, although they may have had others whose names are not found in the somewhat imperfect records. The eldest child was born in Malden and the others in Leicester: Tabitha, September 28, 1730, married, August 9, 1750, Nathanial Garfield; Daniel, 1734, married, April 17, 1755, Elizabeth Stebbens; Elizabeth, December 15, 1737, said to have married Stephen Proctor, of Danvers; Phineas, September 28, 1742; Samuel, August 15, 1744, married ——— Reed, of Conway.

(VI) Colonel Phineas Newhall, son of Daniel and Tabitha (Upham) Newhall, was born in Leicester, September 28, 1742, and although he lived in that town until after the revolutionary war, he probably died in Shelburne or in that locality in the Connecticut valley. Accounts concerning him are somewhat meagre, but he is mentioned by one writer as having kept tavern on the old North County road in Leicester for many years. He was a soldier of the revolution and won an adjutant's commission in that war. His record as given in the public archives is about as follows: Corporal in Capt. Thomas Newhall's company of militia which marched to Cambridge, April 19, 1775; service seven and one half days: March 28, 1776, mentioned in list of officers chosen by the several companies in Colonel Samuel Denny's (First Worcester county) regiment of Massachusetts militia; said Newhall recommended as adjutant of said regiment; also official record of the ballot by the house of representatives, dated April 22, 1776, chosen adjutant of first Worcester county regiment; appointed by the governor's council and commissioned April 23, 1776. He was called colonel, probably by reason of his connection with the state militia after the close of the war, but there is no proof that he was mustered as such. His occupation was that of tavern keeper, and he appears to have lived in various localities, being mentioned as of Conway and Shelburne Falls. The history of Deerfield speaks of his marriage in that town and mentions him as of Shelburne Falls at that time. He married, September 21, 1763, Lydia Wilson, who died December 30, 1803, aged fifty-seven years. He had a son Joseph born in 1765, probably his eldest child, and Artemas and Persis; and some accounts state that there were other children than those mentioned, born later than 1769, among them Phineas, David, James, Nathan, Samuel, Esther and Sally; although we have no positive proof of a son Phineas it is more than reasonably sure that there was such a child in the family, born in Conway or Shelburne or Deerfield.

(VII) Phineas Newhall, Jr., was born in 1776, in one of the Connecticut valley towns, and lived, according to one narrative, in Shelburne and Conway, Massachusetts, and Waterbury and Stowe, Vermont. Other than this little appears to be known of him except that he was a farmer, and raised a large family. In March, 1804, he married Wealthy Willis Newcomb, born Deerfield, December 22, 1783, died in May, 1855. She was a daughter of Rev. Ebenezer Newcomb, whose wife was Wealthy Willis, granddaughter of Benjamin and Mary (Everett) Newcomb, great-granddaughter of Jonathan and Deborah Newcomb, great-great-granddaughter of Peter and Sarah (Cutting) Newcomb, and great-great-great-granddaughter of Francis Newcomb, who was born in England about 1605, came to New England in 1635 with his wife Rachel and lived first in Boston and later in that part of Braintree which then was called Mt. Wollaston and now Quincy. Phineas and Wealthy Willis (Newcomb) Newhall had ten children: 1. Relief, born December 30, 1804, married in November, 1825, J. B. Bigelow, of Conway. 2. Emily, May 6, 1806, married, in 1829, Emery Sherman. 3. Wealthy Willis, October 23, 1809, married, January 23, 1826, Ira Hudson. 4. Anna, 1811, married Charles Field, of Conway. 5. Alvah O., March 23, 1815, died June, 1838. 6. Sarah, February 4, 1817, married, December, 1845, T. P. Sargent. 7. Joseph, March, 1819, married, 1842, Ruth Dwinnell. 8. Artemas, March, 1821, married, 1848, Luceba Munn. 9. Solomon Newcomb, September 12, 1824, see forward. 10. James, October 30, 1827, married October, 1850, Amanda Sargent.

(VIII) Solomon Newcomb Newhall, son of Phineas and Wealthy Willis (Newcomb) Newhall, born in Vermont, September 12, 1824, died Danvers, Massachusetts, April 12, 1876, after an active and useful but all too short business life. His occupation was that of a farmer, to which he gave close attention for many years and in which he gained gratifying success; and he always was a man of high character, strong convictions, and there was that about him in his bearing, manner and conversation which suggested the old type of the Puritan whose highest ideal was freedom of conscience, justice, and right. His religion was carried into his daily life and never was put aside for any other consideration whatever. He was a strong Methodist, a devout worshipper in the sanctuary and a devoted christian husband and father within the home circle; among men his walk was honest, and sincerity in all things was one of his marked characteristics. Mr. Newhall continued to live in Vermont until after the marriage of his eldest daughter and then took up his residence in Danvers. He married, October 2, 1845, Clarissa H. Guptill, born Waterbury, Massachusetts, September 18, 1828, daughter of Thomas and Olive (Goodwin) Guptill. Five children were born of this marriage: 1. Fidelia Emily, born Stowe, December 7, 1846. 2. Lurana B., born Stowe, November 29, 1848, lives in Salem. 3. Alvah T., born Stowe, October 29, 1851, married Mary Thom and lives in Salem. 4. Ireneus

E., born Stowe, October 19, 1855, married Clara Smith and lives in Salem. 5. Milo A., born Stowe, January 8, 1866, married Joan Turner and lives in Salem.

(IX) Fidelia Emily Newhall, daughter of Solomon N. and Clarissa H. (Guptill) Newhall, born December 7, 1846, married, November 30, 1869, Matthew Robson. Four children were born of this marriage.

Matthew Robson was born in Tyrone, Ireland, February 22, 1833, son of Matthew and Eliza (Beattie) Robson, and a descendant of Scotch ancestors. His father was a man of superior educational attainments, a pedagogue of note and experience and a strict disciplinarian. In April, 1854, having just attained his majority, Matthew Robson, the younger, came to America, landed at St. John, New Brunswick, and after a year came to Salem. His immediate purpose at that time was to gain a practical knowledge of the leather business and his ultimate purpose was to engage in the manufacture of leather. Ten years later, in 1865, the Robson Leather Company began operations in Salem, a small plant at first and gradually increasing its capacity with the growing demand for its product until it ranked with the leading industries of its kind in the east.

This brief narrative covers in a cursory way the history of the Robson Leather Company for a period of about thirty-five years, but in this place it is hardly necessary to speak of the success which has rewarded the efforts of the man who started the business with small means and comparatively little practical experience at the close of the late civil war, built it up and grew up with it until the time of the merger in 1899, when it became a considerable factor in the operations of the American Hide & Leather Company. Since that consolidation of interests Mr. Robson's ostensible relation to the greater corporation has been that of resident manager at Salem, but by reason of the fact that he is recognized as one of the very best authorities on the manufacture of leather in this country and also on the leather trade in general, his actual service to the company is something more than local manager. And besides his connection with the American Hide & Leather Company he is variously interested in several of the institutions of Salem, being vice-president and a director of the Mercantile National Bank; a trustee and member of the investment committee of the Salem Five Cents Savings Bank; president for many years of the Young Men's Christian Association, and a generous contributor in its behalf and in support of its work. He is a consistent member of the Wesley Methodist Episcopal Church, president of its board of trustees, and that society too has received substantial benefactions at his hands as well as the various charitable and benevolent institutions of the city.

On November 30, 1869, Matthew Robson married Fidelia Emily Newhall. Their children: John Caldwell, born August 21, 1871; Arthur Lawrence, August 17, 1874, died November 10, 1900; Alice, born February 6, 1880; Miriam, November 26, 1885.

(For ancestry see Thomas Newhall 1 and Daniel Newhall 4.)

NEWHALL (VII) Josiah H. Newhall, son of William (6), and Martha (Mansfield) Newhall, was born in Lynn, January 7, 1790, died November 7, 1842. He was a highly respected and useful citizen, and for many years continued to fill the most responsible offices in the town. He was a representative, and a senator in 1832-33. He lived and had his business at the east end of the common. He was for many years one of the most extensive shoe manufacturers in the town, and in all his business relations enjoyed the utmost confidence of those with whom he dealt. In manners he was dignified and courteous, and he was excelled by none for integrity of character and purity of life. For many years he was a prominent member of the First Methodist Episcopal Church, and active in benevolent enterprises. He was one of the charter members of Mt. Carmel Lodge, Free and Accepted Masons, of Lynn. He married (first), March 19, 1811, Lydia Johnson, who bore him children: Robert, died in infancy. Elizabeth. Martha, died in infancy. Harrison, see below. He married (second), in 1832, Clarissa Martin, who bore him children: Charles M., died in infancy. Josiah H., who was a Methodist clergyman, died October 13, 1866; he married Anna Maria Lee Shepard, who was the first white child born in Oregon, her father, Rev. Cyrus Shepard, being a missionary among the Indians. Their daughter, Clara Traxler, now resides in Eugene, Oregon.

(VIII) Harrison Newhall, son of Josiah H. Newhall, was born October 18, 1819. He completed his studies in the common schools of Lynn in 1832, and later this knowledge was supplemented by attendance at Lynn

Academy, Bradford Academy and Wesleyan Academy at Wilbraham. In 1840, after completing his educational course, he engaged in the shoe business with Hon. Thomas P. Richardson, and this connection continued until the firm was dissolved in 1842. He continued alone in the same line of business until 1870, during this interval occurred the first strike in the shoe shops of Lynn. He admitted his son, Israel Augustus, as a partner, in 1870, which relationship continued until 1875. He was prosperous in his undertakings and was enabled to accumulate a competence for his declining years. In 1849 he was the last treasurer of the town and in 1850, the first year of the city government for Lynn, he served as a member of the board of assessors, and in 1858 was elected a member of the board of aldermen, and of the 1858 board of aldermen he has been for many years the sole survivor. He served for many years in the capacity of trustee for the Lynn Institution for Savings, Lynn Five Cents Savings Bank, and Wesleyan Academy of Wilbraham, which he and all his children attended; he was also a director of the Leighton Bank, now Central National Bank, serving for a period of fifteen years. For over half a century he has been a member of the First Methodist Episcopal Church, and for many years acted as chairman of the board of stewards. Although beyond four score years and ten, the scriptural allotted term of man's life, he is in possession of most of his faculties, and quite often is at the office of his son. During his lifetime he has witnessed many changes, notable among which was the unusual prosperity that marked the year 1836, and the panic of 1857 when a large number of the great business concerns failed. Mr. Newhall has always resided in the house in which his birth occurred, and in the community he is justly esteemed for his sterling integrity of character. He married, April 13, 1842, Martha Mudge Perkins, who died September 19, 1889. They were the parents of three children: Israel Augustus. Loranus Campbell, see forward. Howard Mudge, see forward.

(IX) Loranus Campbell Newhall, second son of Harrison and Martha M. (Perkins) Newhall, was born in Lynn, Massachusetts, June 11, 1849. He attended the common and high schools of Lynn, Chauncy Hall School of Boston, and later Wesleyan Academy, Wilbraham. He began his business career in the shoe business of his father, continuing up to 1875, in which year his father retired from active pursuits, when he assumed the management of the business and continued to conduct the same until 1890, when he turned his attention to the life and accident insurance business, which he still continues, with office in Boston. He married, October 29, 1878, Susan E. Felt, born in North Reading, Massachusetts, July 18, 1857. Three children: Ida N., married George W. Russell, of Kearsage, New Hampshire. Walter H., a resident of West Virginia, interested in coal business. Ralph P., student of Lynn high school.

(IX) Howard Mudge Newhall, third son of Harrison and Martha M. (Perkins) Newhall, was born in Lynn, Massachusetts, in same house as his father, May 7, 1854. He was reared in his native city, educated in its high schools, and pursued advanced studies at Wesleyan Academy, Wilbraham, and Wesleyan University, Middletown, Connecticut. He began his business career as superintendent of his brother's shoe factory, where he continued until 1886, when he engaged in the real estate and insurance business, his last occupation. In addition to his real estate business he acted as trustee of estates. He was also United States attorney for, and cashier of the Baxter Leather Company, Limited, of London, England, with offices in Boston, Massachusetts. He was secretary of Lynn Historical Society, clerk of Lynn Hospital, member of board of management of Lynn Home for Aged Men, also Lynn Home for Aged Women, member of Council of Associated Charities, one of the vice-presidents of the Lynn Board of Trade, treasurer of Bay State Historical League, and member of Sons of American Revolution. He married, January 20, 1880, Kittie May Knox, of Methuen, Massachusetts, daughter of Otis and Martha (Furbush) Knox, born October 9, 1855. Mrs. Newhall is a member of the Daughters of the American Revolution and of ladies' clubs and charitable societies in Lynn. Mr. Newhall died December 25, 1908.

(For ancestry see Thomas Newhall 1 and Daniel Newhall 4.)

NEWHALL (VI) Micajah Newhall, son of Josiah (5) and Hannah (Newhall) Newhall, was born October 18, 1756. He married, June 10, 1779, Joanna Farrington. Children: Josiah S., born November 10, 1780. Micajah, July 25, 1784. Paul, February 17, 1786. Otis, January 16, 1788. Sarah, August 17, 1789. Ellis, August 17, 1791, died 1792. Ellis (2d), March 7, 1793. Joanna, February 2, 1795. Hannah,

April 8, 1797. Susanna, October 25, 1799. William, January 13, 1802. Lydia, September 2, 1804.

(VII) Paul Newhall, son of Micajah and Joanna (Farrington) Newhall, was born February 17, 1786. He married, March 15, 1808, Mary Mudge. Children: Alden, born January 30, 1809. Mary Ann, April 20, 1811. Joanna, April 19, 1814. Warren, born in Baltimore, Maryland, April 27, 1816. Lucy Blish, born October 20, 1818. Lydia Mudge, April 14, 1822. Lucian, October 13, 1824.

(VIII) Lucian Newhall, youngest child of Paul and Mary (Mudge) Newhall, was born at the corner of South Common and Church streets, West Lynn, October 13, 1824. He was educated in the Lynn public schools and academy, and on completing his studies entered the shoe manufactory of his father. He later established a business of his own, 1847, he being one of the first to locate in the central part of the city, and took as partner Charles B. Tebbetts. The establishment was located on the corner of Spring and Exchange streets, where they built up an extensive business, the success being achieved entirely through their own efforts and sagacious management. Having amassed a competency Mr. Newhall retired in 1875. He was active in community affairs, served as director in the Lynn Gas Company, and was interested in various other enterprises. He was especially interested in having the woods preserved for the purpose of public parks, and assisted in raising a fund for this purpose, to which he gave liberally, and was later appointed by Mayor Harwood one of the Metropolitan park board, upon which he served with great energy until his death, May 17, 1898. He was generous and public-spirited, assisting in all good works. He was a man of strong convictions and nobility of character. Before the organization of the Republican party he was an earnest opponent of human slavery, and when that party came into existence he at once identified himself with it and gave it his earnest support. He was also a strong advocate of the temperance movement. He was a consistent Christian, and a devoted member of the Unitarian (Second Congregational) church. He traveled extensively, having crossed the Atlantic three times. While in England, on one of these trips, he obtained the plans for the beautiful home which he afterward built at the corner of Ocean and Nahant streets, where his widow and daughter now reside. He was a large owner of real estate in the city of Lynn.

He married, first, in 1858, Esther Nichols, of Malden; she died in 1882. Married, second, December 11, 1884, Emma D. Ireson, daughter of Benjamin and Harriet (Choate) Ireson, and one daughter was the issue, Margery Choate, born October 29, 1885, now residing at home. Benjamin Ireson was senior member of the firm of Ireson & Ingalls, flour, grain and lumber merchants, also built the wharf, and was interested in agricultural pursuits. He was born in Lynn and died there in 1873, aged seventy-three. Benjamin and Harriet (Choate) Ireson were the parents of nine children, two of whom died in infancy. Julia, the eldest, died at the age of sixty; the surviving members of the family are: H. Isabel, resides with Mrs. Newhall; Helen M.; Anna, who married Amos B. Tapley; Adelaide, who married F. W. G. Lewis; Emma D., who married Mr. Newhall, as stated above; Katherine Choate.

(For ancestry see Thomas Newhall 1.)

NEWHALL (VIII) Charles Newhall, son of John (7) and Delia (Breed) Newhall, was born August 26, 1826, and died October 20, 1867. He was a farmer in Lynn all his life. He married November 26, 1856, Hester C. Moulton. Children: John Breed, born September 17, 1857; died young; Hattie C., born June 15, 1859, died in infancy; Avis Ella, born February, 1861; John Breed (2d), October 1, 1862; Hattie C., September 7, 1864.

(IX) John Breed Newhall, younger son of Charles and Hester C. (Moulton) Newhall, was born in Lynn, October 1, 1862. He was educated in the Lynn grammar and high schools, graduating from the latter in 1880, at the age of eighteen. He then entered Harvard, from which he was graduated in 1885, and in 1888 graduated from the Harvard Law School. After a year in the office of a leading Boston lawyer he entered upon practice on his own account. He has confined himself closely to his profession, and has achieved a large measure of success. While his practice has been of a general character, he has had much to do with the settlement of estates, and has acted in the capacity of trustee for a number of the largest estates in and about Lynn. At the same time he has rendered much service to the community in various public and semi-public capacities. He was for three years (1890-92 inclusive) a member of the Lynn common council, and during the last two terms president of that body, and member of the school committee *ex officio,* and was a

Lucian Newhall

member of the Lynn school board in 1901, 1902 and 1903, and chairman in the latter year. In 1893, 1894 and 1895 he was a representative from Lynn in the lower house of the legislature, in the first term serving on the rapid transit committee, and in the second term on the committees on election laws and rapid transit. For a number of years he has been a trustee of the Lynn Institution for Savings. He was secretary of the Lynn Board of Trade in 1891, and a trustee of the Lynn Public Library in 1891 and 1892. He is a Republican in politics, and was president of the Young Men's Republican Club of Ward Four, Lynn, in 1897, and a member of the Republican Club of Massachusetts. He is a member of the leading social club of Lynn, the Oxford, the University Club of Boston, and the Pi Eta fraternity of Harvard. He is a member of the First Universalist Church of Lynn. He married, December 6, 1893, Gertrude J. Cutler, of San Francisco, California. Children: Hester Moulton, born October 19, 1894; Avis E., September 1, 1896; Frances Ella, November 12, 1898; Charles Boardman, June 8, 1902.

(For ancestry see Thomas Newhall 1.)

NEWHALL (VII) Archelaus Newhall, second son of Rufus (6) and Keziah (Breed) Newhall, born July 23, 1790, died in Lynn, Massachusetts, about 1862. He was educated in the schools of Lynn, acquiring thereby a practical knowledge which qualified him for his active career. In early life he was a fisherman and farmer, later learning the trade of shoemaker, which occupation he followed throughout his lifetime. He was a member of the old Whig party, very active in town affairs, and was also a member of the old Quaker church. He married Ann Brown, and their children were: 1. George, born in Lynn, died in Lynnfield; married Harriet Elsworth, a native of Rowley, Massachusetts. 2. Lucy Ann, born and died in Lynn; married William Henry Searles, of Rowley, Massachusetts. 3. John Warren, see forward. 4. Samuel, born Lynn, resides there unmarried.

(VIII) John Warren Newhall, second son of Archelaus and Ann (Brown) Newhall, was born in Lynn, Massachusetts. After completing his education in the schools of Lynn, he served an apprenticeship at the trade of shoemaker, which line of work he followed until the breaking out of the civil war, when he enlisted as a private in Company F, Eighth Massachusetts Regiment, September 17, 1862, serving until August 7, 1863. He re-enlisted August 19, 1864, in Company L, Heavy Artillery, and was discharged June 17, 1865. Since the war Mr. Newhall has been unable to engage in any business, he having lost his eyesight as a result of sunstroke received while in the service. He attends the Universalist church of Lynn, and casts his vote for the candidates of the Republican party. He married, in Lynn, January 21, 1852, Mary S. Skilton, of Lynn, daughter of William and Sarah (Spinney) Skilton, of Lynn. Children: 1. Addie Maria, born Lynn, married James A. Minor, of Milford, Massachusetts. 2. George L., born Lynn, deceased; married Harriet Pixley, of New Hampshire; children: Warren A., Sadie F., Addie; they had other children who died young. 3. Sarah F., born Lynn, married Thomas J. Ready, of Andover, Massachusetts; children: Frank N., Hermonie, Reginald and Raymond.

NEWHALL Rufus F. Newhall, a late resident of Lynn, Massachusetts, who for many years prior to his decease was an invalid, also being deprived of his eyesight, which afflictions he bore with remarkable patience, traced his ancestry through eight generations to Thomas Newhall, the immigrant of this name, who came to America and settled in Lynn, Massachusetts, in 1630; Thomas (2), the first white child born in Lynn, 1630; Joseph (3), born in Lynn, 1658; Thomas (4), born January 6, 1680, who shortly afterward removed to Lynnfield, where the succeeding generations down to the father of Rufus F. Newhall were born, and which is consequently known as the Lynnfield branch of the Newhall family. Thomas (4) died in Lynnfield, November 30, 1738. His son Amos (5), born 1730, died 1765. His son William (6) born in Lynnfield, February 9, 1750, died 1823, was a soldier of the revolution. His son Amos (7), born August 28, 1775, in Lynnfield, died February 18, 1821.

(VIII) Allen Breed Newhall, son of Amos (7), was born May 18, 1813, in Lynnfield, where he obtained his early education and learned the shoemaker's trade, which he followed in winter, and farming in summer. In 1849, during the California gold fever, he went to the Pacific coast, subsequently returning home, but again going to California, and returning across the plains. He died in Sacramento, California, August 9, 1872. He married, April 30, 1835, Augusta Viles, who was born in Lynnfield, and died December 10, 1893, in Lynn. Children: 1. Helen Augusta, born in Lynnfield, August 1, 1836, died in California. 2. Mary W., born July 12, 1836. 3. Elizabeth B., born May 19, 1838; married Mr. Farrar, of Brooklyn, New York; now deceased. 4. Hannah Viles, born October 5, 1840; married Eugene Putnam, of Lynn. 5. Rufus Franklin, born August 19, 1842; see forward. 6. Caroline Elizabeth, born July 8, 1844; married Albert Mansfield, of Wakefield. 7. Allen Putnam, born May 10, 1849. 8. Charlotte Cox, born March 12, 1852; married George S. Monroe, of Lynnfield, now deceased. 9. Bertram Breed, born June 25, 1857.

(IX) Rufus Franklin Newhall, fifth child and eldest son of Allen Breed and Augusta (Viles) Newhall, was born in Lynnfield, Massachusetts, August 19, 1842. He attended the common schools of his native town, and completed his studies at the seminary at Topsfield, Massachusetts. During his early manhood he took up his residence in Lynn, engaging in the grocery business with Eugene A. Putnam, his brother-in-law. He subsequently turned his attention to the milk business, which proved a profitable undertaking, and continued in this until he relinquished it in order to accept the position of foreman in the livery stable of L. B. Usher, in which capacity he continued up to 1895, when on account of failing health he retired from active pursuits. He was a man of sterling character, faithful in the discharge of his duties, both public and private, and in the community in which he resided he was ever held in the highest esteem. He was an attendant of the Universalist church, and his wife of the Methodist church, both contributing toward the support of those bodies and of their various benevolences. He was a member of Bay State Lodge and Palestine Encampment, Independent Order of Odd Fellows.

Mr. Newhall married, April 2, 1888, in Lynn, Mrs. Mary E. Buzzell, born in Monroe, Maine, September 9, 1853, daughter of John M. and Rhoda (Grover) Buzzell. Her father was a native of Maine, and died at the age of seventy-two years; her mother was a native of Salem, Massachusetts, and died in Lynn, aged sixty-five years. Mrs. Newhall was the youngest of eight children, two of whom are now (1908) living: Mrs. Newhall, and Mrs. Martha Rogers, widow of Lyman Rogers, of Lynn. Rufus F. Newhall died at Lynn, May 1, 1903.

SWAIN

William Allen Swain, a venerable and representative citizen of Lynn, honored by all who know him, for his sterling integrity, upright character, executive ability displayed in the management of his business, and high culture and probity, was a native of Pittsfield, New Hampshire, born October 27, 1823, son of Rev. William Swain.

Rev. William Swain was born in Brentwood, New Hampshire, where the family had long resided, his grandfather, Dudley Swain, a tanner and currier, having lived there, dying an aged man. Rev. William Swain was reared and educated in his native town, then removed to Pittsfield, where he remained until 1827, when he removed to Chichester, where he passed the remainder of his life. He cultivated a farm, upon which he resided, and on Sundays preached three sermons, often riding from six to ten miles on horseback to the different small towns where he ministered. He knew by memory every word of the new testament, and in a biography of him it was said: "Should the New Testament be destroyed, the Rev. William Swain could be depended upon to compile a new one verbatim from memory." He was prominent in the town, held the office of selectman, also other offices, and took an active interest in all town affairs. He died at the age of seventy-seven years. He married Sallie Drake, born in Brentwood, a direct descendant of Sir Francis Drake, and a daughter of Abraham Drake. She died a fortnight after her husband, and at the same age. She reared twelve children, of whom only two are now living: 1. Susan, married E. Winslow Bowker, of Cambridge, who is now deceased; her only child, a son, died June 11, 1908, aged forty-six years. 2. Mary Ann, married Herbert Sanborn, now deceased; she resides in Chichester, New Hampshire; seven children.

William Allen Swain, son of Rev. William and Sallie (Drake) Swain, when four years of age, accompanied his parents to Chichester, New Hampshire, where he passed his youth, and acquired a practical education. Later he learned the trade of carpenter, becoming an expert in that line. In 1866 he removed to Natick, Massachusetts, where for a time he followed the business of contractor, achieving well merited success. In 1883 he visited California, and spent three years in the south and west, visiting all points of interest and note, and deriving therefrom a vast amount of pleasure and recreation. In 1886 he returned to Natick, Massachusetts, where he followed

R. Frank Newhall

William A. Swain

Isaac Newhall

his trade and contracting until 1893, when he removed to Boston, where he remained until 1895, engaged in the real estate and insurance business. In 1895 he took up his residence in Lynn, which was thereafter his home, taking an active interest in all that pertains to its welfare and progress. He retired from active business in 1906. During his residence in New Hampshire he served for a time as justice of the peace, under appointment by Governor Gilmore; and in 1861 was recruiting officer under Adjutant General Colby, serving two years. In 1877, while residing in Natick, Massachusetts, he served as a member of the board of assessors. In Lynn he was nominated for school committee, alderman, councilman, representative and senator. His nomination for the latter position was announced in a circular by the senatorial district committee, in which it was said: "This nomination was wholly unsought or even unknown to Mr. Swain. The convention gave him a unanimous nomination by acclamation. A committee was appointed to inform Mr. Swain of his nomination and ask him to accept the same. With reluctance he has consented to be our standard bearer. We cannot say too much in his favor. He is a man of sterling integrity, and one of long business career, positive in views, and takes great interest in the affairs of our city."

In politics, Mr. Swain was a Democrat. He attended the Methodist church for many years, and served as a trustee of St. Luke's Protestant Episcopal Church, Lynn. He joined the fraternity of Odd Fellows in 1845, and remained a member until his lodge lapsed. On October 27, 1903, Mr. Swain celebrated his eightieth birthday anniversary, having lived well past the scriptural alotted period of three score years and ten. Upon that occasion he was presented, by the members of St. Luke's Church, a magnificent gold-headed cane, the presentation address being made by James A. Elliott, who said among other things, "The head of this cane is of pure gold, a fitting symbol of your true character; and its richness is a fit token of that crown of glory which awaits you in the other world." Mr. Swain died November 8, 1908. Mr. Swain married, June 22, 1893, Lucy B. Newhall, of Lynn, daughter of Isaac Newhall, who was a descendant in the seventh generation of Thomas Newhall, the immigrant (see Thomas Newhall 1, and Samuel Newhall, 4).

(V) Daniel Newhall, son of Samuel Newhall (4), born February 4, 1740-1, died at Lynn, November 15, 1793. He was a Quaker also. He was a cordwainer by trade. His will, dated March 1, 1785, proved December 3, 1793, bequeathed to sons Estes and Daniel, to daughter Lydia the legacy given to his deceased wife by her father, William Estes; appointed Pharaoh Newhall and Henry Oliver guardians of his minor children. His widow Elizabeth died February 18, 1822, leaving will proved April 2, 1822, bequeathing to her sisters Priscilla Bowers, Hannah Adkins, Deborah Robinson, brother Elijah Dodge and sons-in-law (i.e. stepsons) Estes and Daniel Newhall and daughter-in-law Lydia Pope. Daniel Newall married first, Hannah, daughter of William Newhall. She died November 27, 1781, and he married second, May 20, 1789, Elizabeth Dodge, of Boston. Children of first wife: 1. Estes, born September 9, 1770, married Hepzibah Wing and Miriam Philbrick. 2. Deborah, born December 5, 1772, died August 17, 1783. 3. Lydia, born March 16, 1775; married James Pope, of Salem, March 1, 1794. 4. Daniel, mentioned below.

(VI) Daniel Newhall, son of Daniel Newhall (5), was born in Lynn, November 21, 1778. In religion he followed the example of his ancestors and adhered to the Society of Friends. He married, June 6, 1805, Mary Bailey, of Hanover, Massachusetts, at Pembroke. She was also of Quaker ancestry and became an eminent preacher of that sect. Children born at Lynn: 1. John Bailey, May 3, 1806. 2. George P., August 23, 1808. 3. Hepzbiah, June 20, 1810. 4. Joseph, May 10, 1812. 5. Isaac, January 4, 1814; mentioned below. 6. Henry, February 10, 1816. 7. Mary Bailey, April 28, 1818; died June 17, 1845. 8. Lucy, November 15, 1820.

(VII) Isaac Newhall, son of Daniel Newhall, was born in Lynn, January 4, 1814, and died there February 22, 1879. He early engaged in the shoe business, becoming one of the most extensive and successful manufacturers in Lynn, and kept up with the progress of the age along that line until he withdrew and turned his attention to the real estate business, conducting his operations in his native city. He became a large land owner in the section where Mrs. Swain now resides, owning seventy-five acres now thickly covered with buildings. He took an active part in all the affairs of his day, and was instrumental in advancing the welfare and prosperity of the city, at all times interested in its municipal affairs, and serving as a member of the board of aldermen in 1851 and 1875. A number of the enterprises and institutions of Lynn are due to his efforts, particularly the street railway built to Glensmere. During the last few years of his life he was a great sufferer from neuralgia, which he bore with remarkable patience and fortitude, no complaint ever falling from his lips. He was twice married, and at his death was survived by his widow and five children.

CALDWELL Tradition has it that the Caldwells have been seated in England for several centuries, and that some of its later branches drifted into Scotland and ultimately back again into England, settling in the vicinity of Nottingham. For many generations previous to the immigration of any of its representatives to New England the surname was common in England, Scotland, Ireland and France. In England, according to "Patronymica Brittanica," it is derived from "Coldwell," and the armorial bearings are wells, fountains, sea waves and fishes, each suggestive of water. In the Scotch the name is written "Cold-wold," meaning the hazelwood or divining rod, the latter being a symbol of authority, and as such was hung for a long time in a conspicuous place in the Bavarian court rooms. In "Domesday Book" the name is spelled Cauldeuuelle.

The Caldwells came to this country from England, Scotland and Ireland in the early times of the colonies, and located in New England, New Jersey and the south. The family of the particular line here treated comes of the English branch, and had for its immigrant ancestor John Caldwell, born in England, 1624, was in Boston in 1643 and settled in the plantation at Ipswich, in the colony of Massachusetts Bay in 1654.

(I) John Caldwell's name first appears in the records of the general court of Massachusetts in 1643, when he was nineteen years old: "October, 1643. Rich'rd Collecot, Edward Fuller, John Cauldwell and Richard Smith, were appointed to fetch the Cattle from Providence." He was a husbandman, although he learned the trade of weaving, as did two of his sons. He became possessed of several tracts of land in Ipswich, some by purchase and others by grant as the lands of the town were divided among the inhabitants. He was a commoner in 1664, admitted freeman in 1677, and in 1691 was appointed "searcher and sealer and viewer of leather," but refused that office "as not being capable threw business & otherwise." He made his will June 20, 1692, and died July 7, following. His estate was inventoried at two hundred twenty-one pounds sixteen shillings four pence. He married Sarah Dillingham, born in Ipswich, April, 1634, daughter of John and Sarah Caly (Calley) Dillingham. Her father died when Sarah was less than a year old and her mother two years later, 1636, and she was brought up under the care of Mr. Saltonstall and Mr. Appleton, with the maternal admonition that she be "religiously educated, if God gave her life." The Dillinghams were of an old English family of yeomen, and John, father of Sarah, came from Leicestershire, England, in 1630, with the younger John Winthrop. His name was frequently written with the prefix "Mr.," indicating something of his position in the colony. He was admitted freeman 1631, served as juror same year, was appointed to hear and determine small causes 1633, and in 1634 received a grant of lands in Ipswich. He became a man of influence in that town, being frequently entrusted with important duties, and at his death gave to his only child, Sarah, all of his estate in lands and goods, except "such pticuler legacyes as hereafter are named." Children of John and Sarah (Dillingham) Caldwell: 1. John, died February 27, 1721-2; married May 1, 1689, Sarah, daughter of Deacon Jacob Foster and Martha Kinsman, his first wife, and granddaughter of Reginald Foster, who came from the northern part of England in 1638, and was an early inhabitant of Ipswich; children: Martha, born August 28, 1690; John, August 19, 1693; Jacob, February 26, 1694-5; Sarah, July 16, 1696-7; Abigail, May 14, 1700, died November 1, 1700; Anna, born January 18, 1702; William, January 17, 1708. 2. Sarah, born April 2, 1658; married June 9, 1684, Joseph, son of Captain John Ayers; children: Sarah, born August 5, 1685; Elizabeth, January 28, 1687; John, February 26, 1692-3; William, September 13, 1696; Benjamin, December 16, 1700. 3. Anna, born August 23, 1661, died September 4, 1721; married John Roper, of Ipswich, a man of considerable wealth and prominent in public affairs. 4. William, died February 19, 1695; he was a cooper, and also followed the sea. In 1694, "being bound to sea, and calling to mind ye uncertain estate of this transitory life," he made a will disposing of his property worth a little more than fifty-six pounds. 5. Dillingham, born March 6, 1666; (see post). 6. Nathaniel, born October 18, 1669, died December 13, 1738; married February 12, 1703, Abigail Wallingford; he was a weaver, and had a comfortable home, although he followed seven of his ten children to the grave. Children: Abigail, born November 8, 1705, died young; John, born November 19, 1708. died December 19, 1792; Abigail, born July 7, 1710, died young; Nathaniel, born October 3, 1711, died September 4, 1733; Abigail, born June, 1713, died young; Sarah, born February 27, 1715, died August 31, 1733; Mary, born May 26, 1717; Anna, born August 23, 1719; Martha, born June, 1721, died May 1722; Hannah, born June, 1724. 7. Mary, born February 26, 1671, died April 2, 1709; married, March 5, 1696, Jacob Foster, son of Deacon Jacob and Abigail (Lord) Foster, and grandson of Reginald Foster. Children: Jacob, born May 9, 1697; William, May 11, 1699; Mary, March 9, 1701; Abigail, September 27, 1703; Israel, March 3, 1706-7. 8. Elizabeth, born October 15, 1675, died May, 1752.

(II) Dillingham Caldwell, third son and fifth child of John Caldwell, the immigrant, born in Ipswich, Massachusetts, March 6, 1666, died there May 3, 1745, aged seventy-nine years. He was a weaver, and tradition says he was proficient at the trade, for on May 14, 1691, he made an agreement with William Parsons of Boston that he should be taught by the latter the art of making sloas and harnessess used in weaving. He was twenty-five years old when learning his trade in Boston and afterward in Ipswich was one of the most influential men of the town. He married first, Mary Lord, died October 21, 1698, having borne her husband two children; he married second, Mary Hart, born August 25, 1665, died September 19, 1748, eldest child of Lieutenant Thomas Hart of Ipswich, and Mary Norton his wife. Lieutenant Hart was first a corporal and afterward a lieutenant of the Ipswich company of foot, representative in 1693-4, selectman, and one of the committee appointed to obtain a plan and superintend the building of a new meetinghouse in Ipswich, 1700. He had six sons and two daughters. He was the eldest of three children of Thomas Hart of Ipswich and Alice his wife, 1641, and the elder Thomas Hart was a tanner, his tanyard having been devised in his will to his two sons, Thomas and Samuel. Dillingham Caldwell had two children by his first wife and six by his second wife: 1. Mary, born November 3, 1695, died October 3, 1698. 2. Daniel, born August 30, 1698, died October 23, 1698. 3. Mary, born June 9, 1700, died July 7, 1700. 4. Daniel, born October 5, 1701; (see post). 5. Mary, born September 28, 1703; married, March, 1725, Jeremiah Lord, and had Mary Lord, Sarah Lord, Elizabeth Lord (married John Potter), Jeremiah Lord, Lydia Lord (married Benjamin Kimball) and Ebenezer Lord. 6. Sarah, baptized July 8, 1705, died young. 7. Sarah, baptized September 3, 1707; married August 13, 1737, Nathaniel Hart, (3d), she being his second wife; had by him two children; Mary; Sarah, born 1740, died January, 1805. 8. John, baptized May 10, 1710, died young.

(III) Daniel Caldwell, eldest son and fourth child of Dillingham and Mary (Hart) Caldwell, born in Ipswich, October 5, 1701, died there April 18, 1759. He was prominent in the public affairs of the town, and the records frequently mention his name with "gentleman" added, indicating affluence as well as influence. He also is styled sergeant and ensign, showing his connection with the militia. He held several town offices, being hayward 1734, hayward and fence viewer 1741, hayward and field-driver 1742, surveyor 1746 and 1748, and fence viewer 1752. He worshipped in the south parish meetinghouse, and gave seventy-two pounds toward the erection of the first church edifice there in 1747. His estate was appraised at five hundred thirty-two pounds fourteen shillings eleven pence, and was divided between the widow and their sons Daniel and John, his only children that survived him. He married (published) January 17, 1723, Elizabeth Burley, born August 25, 1700, died December 29, 1769, daughter of Cornet Andrew Burley and Mary Conant his wife, the latter a great-granddaughter of Roger Conant, the early planter of Gloucester and Salem, and one of the famous characters of his time in New England colonial history. Cornet Burley was impressed for the expedition against the Narragansett Indians in November, 1675, and in 1687 he had land granted him for a brickyard at Jeffries' neck. He was the eldest of three sons of Giles and Elizabeth Burley, the former of Ipswich in 1648, commoner in 1664, and died before September 29, 1668. Daniel and Elizabeth (Burley) Caldwell had eight children: 1. Daniel, baptized February 7, 1724-5, died December, 1798; married April 12, 1749, Hannah Burley, his cousin, who died January 24, 1770; no children. 2. Elizabeth, baptized December 22, 1728, died February 13, 1729. 3. Elizabeth, baptized April 19, 1730, died April

25, 1730. 4. Andrew, died September 25, 1738. 5. Mary, baptized July 20, 1735, died August 8, 1735. 6. Mary, baptized September 26, 1736, died October 21, 1736. 7. John, baptized October 5, 1740, (see post). 8. Andrew, baptized July 1, 1744, died young.

(IV) John Caldwell, next to youngest child of Daniel and Elizabeth (Burley) Caldwell, born in Ipswich, October 5, 1740, died February 20, 1825. He was a blacksmith by trade, and devoted much of his time to anchor making, at which he did a considerable business. During the revolution he was frequently drafted for service, but from the fact that he had a family of nine small children at home he prudently procured and paid a substitute to take his place in the ranks. The intention of marriage of John Caldwell and Sarah Haraden was published December 17, 1762. She was a daughter of David Haraden, an early settler on Cape Ann and progenitor of one of the prominent old families of the town of Gloucester. John and Sarah (Haraden) Caldwell had children: 1. Sarah, born March 12, 1765, died October 13, 1838. 2. Elizabeth, born August 27, 1766, died November, 1770. 3. John, born May 20, 1768, (see post). 4. Daniel, born June 5, 1770, died November, 1804. He was one of the crew of twelve Ipswich men lost from brig "Sally," in a wreck on Ipswich bar, November, 1804. He married, September 28, 1797, Eunice Lord; two sons: Daniel, died at age of twenty years, and buried with military honors by Denison Light Infantry, of which he was a member; and David Haraden, born October 9, 1804, died January 18, 1867. He was Captain Caldwell, and spent the later years of his life in Danvers, Massachusetts. 5. Elizabeth, born August 17, 1772, died January 6, 1838; married John Grow, of Marblehead; daughter, Eliza Grow, became wife of Charles Dodge, of Ipswich. 6. Hannah, born October 18, 1774, died January 21, 1811. 7. Mary, born July 25, 1776, died January 26, 1861. 8. Susanna, born August 11, 1778, died March, 1844. 9. Lucy, born November, 1782, died April, 1868.

(V) John Caldwell, elder son and third child of John and Sarah (Haraden) Caldwell, born in Ipswich, May 20, 1768, died in Burrillsville, Rhode Island, May 11, 1820. He lived in various towns in Massachusetts and Rhode Island, and had children born in Concord, Marlborough, Lancaster and Boston. He married Susannah Robinson, born December 24, 1768, died in Bolton, Massachusetts, February 26, 1814. They had children: 1. John, born Concord, Massachusetts, October 13, 1788; married Sarah Whittles, of Dunstable, New Hampshire. 2. James, born Marlborough, Massachusetts, May 3, 1791; (see post). 3. Mary, born September 2, 1792; married September 25, 1819, J. C. Hardenburgh, of Providence, R. I.; children: Nancy Hardenburgh, born September 24, 1820, married Horatio L. Holmes; John Caldwell Hardenburgh, born May 15, 1822; Fayette Hardenburgh, born August 3, 1824, married Anna Clarke, of Providence; Charles Hardenburgh, twin, born May 21, 1826, married Abbie Wing; Augustus Hardenburgh, twin, born May 21, 1826; Willington Hardenburgh, born August 14, 1828, married Abby Clarke; Frank Hardenburgh, born December 22, 1830, married first, Anna Marshall, second, Emma Emery; Mary Hardenburgh, born February 16, 1833, died December 4, 1869; Henry Warren Hardenburgh, born May 4, 1836, married Rebecca Smith. 4. Eunice, born September 29, 1794, died June, 1873; married Daniel Ross, born February 4, 1781; children: George C., born June 1, 1816; Levi S., September 24, 1817; Abby and Sarah, twins, October 17, 1821; Charles, September 6, 1822; Warren, June 24, 1825; Augustus, August 28, 1827; Harriet, February 14, 1830. 5. Daniel, born November 10, 1796, died Broomfield, Illinois, May, 1866; married Abigail Wallace Goodwin, born Charlestown, Massachusetts, 1801; children: Rev. William Edward, born June 6, 1825; Alabia Elizabeth, born 1828; Martha Ann, and Francis Rhoades. 6. Susanna, born January 17, 1799; married Theodore Bigelow, of Boston. 7. Sally, born July 12, 1801, died Burrillsville, Rhode Island, August 3, 1818. 8. William, born October 6, 1803, died young. 9. Lydia, born Lancaster, April 3, 1806, died young. 10. Jeremiah, born June 21, 1808, died Providence, Rhode Island. 11. Adaline, born Boston, March 11, 1811, died September 22, 1811.

(VI) James Caldwell second son and second child of John and Susannah (Robinson) Caldwell, born in Marlborough, Massachusetts, May 3, 1791, died in Ipswich, November 10, 1874. His wife, Mary Kimball, was born May 4, 1792, and died February 8, 1873. She was a daughter of Abraham Kimball, first husband of Mary Sutton (Mary Sutton's second husband was Nathaniel Rust), was a daughter of Richard Sutton and Elizabeth Foster, his first wife, and a granddaughter of William and Susanna Sutton. By her marriage with

Col. Luther Caldwell

Nathaniel Rust, Mary Sutton became mother of Rev. Richard Sutton Rust, DD., LL. D. James and Mary (Kimball) Caldwell had three children to grow up: 1. Colonel Luther, born September 17, 1822 (see post). 2. Susan, born January 4, 1824, died January 5, 1895; married James P. Jewett. 3. Mary Elizabeth, born 1826, died July 5, 1843.

(VII) Colonel Luther Caldwell, only son and eldest child of James and Mary (Kimball) Caldwell, was born in old Ipswich, the home of his ancestors for six generations previous to his own, where his immigrant ancestor settled nearly two centuries before he was born, and died in Washington, D. C., after a long, brilliant and honorable career in the varied fields of military life, journalism, literature, politics, on the rostrum and in official station. In whatever capacity he was called to serve he acquitted himself well, and fairly earned a reputation which may well be called national, for his was a familiar name and his a familiar figure in governmental military circles and national politics, on the platform in his strong advocacy of temperance reform throughout the states of the union and in England, where he went as an advocate and speaker.

His earlier years were spent in his native town and he received his education during the winter sessions and working out during the summer months, and thus learning the lesson of self-reliance and personal independence. He attended in turn the public schools in his native town; Breed's Hill Academy, Maine, Tilton (N. H.) Seminary; and Smith Sisters' School in Connecticut. On leaving school he learned the trade of painting, and later gained a practical knowledge of photography, when that art first came into existence. and practiced it for some time. A little later he was a journeyman mechanic in the employ of the New York and Erie railway company at Piermont, New York, where he then lived, and therefore it is not surprising that afterward, when his own abilities had won for him a higher station in the activities of life, he was ever practically mindful of the interests of laboring men and was looked upon as their champion and loyal friend in the time of need.

Almost from the time when he first took up his residence in the "southern tier" in New York State, Colonel Caldwell became interested in public affairs, and while going through with the routine of daily labor was very much alive to the march of events. He possessed in unusual degree that strong New England sense which always has had much to do in directing affairs of government, and it is not surprising that he aspired to a position which would bring him more immediately in contact with public men and public events. To the attainment of this end he directed his energies, and in 1858 we find him filling the position of clerk in the office of the state engineer and surveyor, and in 1859 he was secretary of the commission for adjudicating the claims of soldiers of the war of 1812-15. These appointments, however, were the outgrowth of others which preceded them. In 1857 he had an appointment as deputy clerk of the assembly, the annual session of the lower house of the legislature, a temporary clerkship which continued only to the close of the legislative session, perhaps three or four months. In the latter capacity he served during the sessions of 1857, 1859 and 1860, and during the remaining months of the year performed the duties of clerk first in the state engineer's office and afterward with the commission before mentioned. But in this connection it is important to state that the office of deputy clerk of the New York assembly calls for the performance of far more than mere clerical duties, and its incumbent is required to possess an understanding of legislative usages, parliamentary rules, and the manner and form of legislative bills; and almost daily he was called upon to read before the house the full text of bills offered for passage, and it so happened that Luther Caldwell was found to be one of the most clear, accurate and reliable readers who ever arose before the house.

It was the fortunate quality, together with his known worth as a man of unquestioned integrity and his sterling Republican principles, and also his ability to uphold them on the platform, that won for him recognition in the councils of the Republican party and placed him among the leaders of that party in the state. In 1859 he was reading secretary of the Republican state convention, and performed the same duties in the convention of 1860, and afterward from 1865 to 1868, inclusive. During the intervening years he was temporarily out of politics, but when he reappeared in the state convention in the fall of 1865 he was greeted as Major Caldwell.

Colonel Caldwell was a delegate to the Republican national convention that nominated Mr. Lincoln for the presidency in 1860, and next year he entered the Union army to maintain and make permanent the principles for which Mr. Lincoln stood and for which he was "raised up of God" to establish and make perpetual. In 1861, at the outbreak of the war, Colonel Caldwell formed one of the companies of the Seventeenth New York Infantry, the first regiment that marched through Baltimore after the attack on the 6th Massachusetts Infantry under Colonel (now General) Jones, and the regiment that captured the first fieldpiece taken from the Confederates by the Army of the Potomac, to which the 17th was attached. On the organization of his company Colonel Caldwell was commissioned lieutenant, subsequently was promoted captain, and still later received from Governor Reuben E. Fenton of New York, the rank of major. In the army throughout the two years' term of enlistment he was prompt in the performance of every duty and never ordered his company into any action where he did not lead the men.

In June, 1864, the 17th Regiment was mustered out of service, and very soon after Colonel Caldwell purchased a half interest in the *Elmira Daily Advertiser*, which soon became the leading paper in the southern tier of New York state, a reputation it maintained for many years afterward. He later purchased the entire plant of the *Advertiser* and was editor in chief several years and in the editorial chair soon won recognition as an able writer and newspaper man, indeed one of the strongest in western New York; and with his journalistic career he soon again became closely identified with state and national politics. In 1867 he was elected clerk of the assembly, in 1868 was reading secretary of the Republican national convention held in Chicago that nominated General Grant for the presidency, and on that occasion it was his distinguished privilege to call the roll of states upon Grant's unanimous nomination. He also was second on the committee of which General Hawley, late of Connecticut, was chairman, to inform General Grant of his nomination.

During these years of journalistic and political activity Colonel Caldwell appeared upon the platform in every important campaign and was regarded as one of the most powerful and effective speakers in the service of both the Republican state and national committees; and it was because of his worth as an exponent of party principles that he was chosen to fill the important and difficult office of clerk of the assembly in 1867. The office was worthily bestowed in that year, and as evidence of the ability with which he performed its duties we may be permitted to quote an article which appeared in the *New York Tribune* soon after the close of the legislative session of that year: "Major Caldwell proved during the session just closed that as an executive officer for a large body he is unexcelled. Thoroughly posted in parliamentary rules he has, besides a knack of doing business quickly and thoroughly, a voice that would fill the largest hall in that state, and any one at all acquainted with the deliberations of a legislative body knows how valuable this is to the members."

In the same connection the following letter to the *Rochester Democrat* will be of interest: "I cannot close this letter without paying my tribute of respect to the clerk of the house, Major Caldwell, whose prompt and efficient discharge of his duties, coupled with his courtesy and kindness to members and to all with whom he came in contact, made him not only a most popular officer with the members, but also made him a host of warm and enthusiastic friends among outsiders at the capital. I doubt whether a more accomplished and popular officer ever filled the clerk's desk at Albany. That he is likely to be chosen clerk of the coming constitutional convention without competition is a just and deserved tribute to his worth as a gentleman and an officer." At the adjournment of the legislature he received the thanks of the house and a gold watch valued at $500 for the faithful and able performance of his laborious duties.

But it was perhaps as secretary of the constitutional convention of 1867-8 that he became most conspicuously and widely known as an efficient political man and unsurpassed as an assistant of deliberative bodies. The duties of secretary of the convention he performed in a most prompt and satisfactory manner, and it was afterward said of him that as chief clerk of a legislative body he was without an equal in the state or the country.

From 1864 to 1870 Colonel Caldwell was editor and proprietor of the *Elmira Advertiser*, and as was only natural during his residence in that city he took an active part in public matters and in connection therewith was soon called upon to perform important duties in the municipal government. In 1871 he was elected alderman and served two years as member of the common council. In 1872 he led the independent Republican movement in support of Mr. Greeley's candidacy for the presidency, and while actuated by motives of right and honest convictions of duty he nevertheless became alienated from that element of republicanism which placed party advantage above all other considerations. But in 1873 he entered the field as the mayorality candidate of the Liberal Republicans and Democrats of Elmira and contested successfully against George M. Diven, concededly the strongest nominee for that office that the republican party had ever placed at the head of its city ticket. Colonel Caldwell was elected over his opponent and served as mayor of Elmira in 1873-4. During this time he was a member of a number of clubs, including the Tuttle Club of New York.

Later on he became prominently identified with the cause of temperance reform under what has been termed the Murphy movement and promulgated its doctrine throughout this country and also in some parts of England; and no more powerful temperance orator and advocate than he ever appeared on the platform in that righteous cause in this country, either before or after him. In 1889 he was appointed chief of the bond division of the postoffice department in Washington and filled that position until 1893. The remaining years of his life were devoted to literary pursuits, travel and the enjoyment of the comforts earned by years of honest and earnest endeavor. Although the scene of his public career was laid chiefly in localities outside of his native state he never lost interest in old Ipswich and the friends and acquaintances of earlier years. In 1869 he erected there the substantial structure since known as Caldwell block, and so far as possible he spent the summer seasons in that vicinity and in the city of Lynn, where he maintained his home. His latest contribution to literature was a memorial of Anne Bradstreet, America's earliest poetess, which was published in 1898.

Early in life Colonel Caldwell became a member of the Methodist Episcopal church in Ipswich, and never departed from the faith, although he afterward united with the church of the same denomination in Lynn. While living in Elmira he was identified with various institutions of that city, and was a charter member and past commander of Post No. 6, G. A. R.; a trustee and liberal supporter of the Southern Tier Orphans' Home; a Mason of high standing and at one time president of the board of trustees charged with the erection of a Masonic Temple in Elmira; member of the firm of Lormore Bros. & Co., wholesale grocers, and he also held a considerable interest in the Wycoff Wooden Pavement Company, and himself was patentee of two of its devices.

Colonel Luther Caldwell married first, January 27, 1846, Almira Flint of Sudbury, Massachusetts, daughter of Jeremiah Flint. She was born January 27, 1829, and died in Swansea, Wales, February 3, 1888, while traveling with her husband. She was the mother of all of his children. He married second, December 11, 1890, in Cincinnati, Ohio, Sarah Maria Newhall of Lynn, Massachusetts, daughter of Isaac and Sarah (Graves) Newhall, of Lynn. (See Swain and Newhall). His children: 1. Susan Velina, born October 22, 1846; married Henry Cushing, of Aurora, Illinois; in Washington, D. C. 2. Luther Sutton, born February 8, 1848, in Elmira, New York; married Emeline Goodwin, of Ipswich. 3. Louis Dillingham, born April 22, 1850; married Eliza J. Sigison, of Elmira; resides there. 4. Mira Elizabeth, born February 11, 1860, in Albany, New York; resides in Lynn, Massachusetts. Colonel Luther Caldwell died January 17, 1903.

FRAZIER It is said by one of the recognized authorities of the origin of family surnames that the names Frazier and Fraser are derived from the French "fraise", signifying a strawberry, and hence "the well known heraldic object is explained" The same authority also says that "the French word probably was derived from the fragrance of the fruit, as was the Latin 'fragaria'". (Chamber's Encyc.)

It will hardly be questioned that Frazier and Fraser represent different ways of spelling the same surname, and while both may have come from the same root, it is not always safe to attribute continental origin to a name so distinctively Scotch as that of Frazier (or Fraser), and one which has been known in the history of that people for perhaps ten or more centuries. Fraser is taken more frequently than Frazier as the form of the name in ancient Scotch history, and while there were several apparently distinct families a similarity of arms—there were many of distinguished rank among them—leads to the conclusion that originally they were of the same house.

"Oliver Fraser", says "Burke's Peerage", "13th Thane of Man, married Elizabeth, daughter of Henry, Thane of Glenlyon; he lived about 1110". And again, "Sir Simon Fraser married King Robert Bruce's sister Jane. In the reign of Alexander III, Sir Simon, son of Sir Bernard Fraser, was appointed, together with Sir Francis Fraser and William Fraser, archbishop of St. Andrews and Lord Chancellor of Scotland, auditors of the competition for the crown between Bruce and Baliol". (Burke's Peerage.)

In the succession of those who came down from Oliver Fraser, 13th Thane of Man, in one generation after another were many of the christian name Hugh, but there is nothing by which we may connect the descendants of Oliver with the ancestor of the branch of the American family of Fraziers intended to be treated in this place, although such connection may have been possible notwithstanding the different spellings of the surname.

The immigrant ancestor of the Frazier family here considered was Hugh Frazier (I), a native of Boleskine, Inverness, Scotland, born in the year 1761, the son of Scotch parents and a descendant of Scotch ancestors. He was a soldier of the revolution, on the side of the mother country, and came to America in 1775 with the Seventy-first Regiment of Infantry of his majesty's troops. His service was continuous to the time he was taken prisoner and held at Taunton, Massachusetts, until exchanged. He was discharged from the British army in 1783, and next appears in Taunton after the overthrow of the British dominion in America, devoting himself to the peaceful arts of his trade, for he was a blacksmith. He was a member of the Protestant Episcopal church. His wife, Prudence (Wilbore) Frazier, was born in 1764, died December 24, 1851, aged eighty-seven years. They had one son, Hugh Frazier, Jr., see forward.

(II) Hugh Frazier, Jr., son of Hugh and Prudence (Wilbore) Frazier, born Taunton, August, 1790, died May 24, 1870, aged almost eighty years. He was a farmer during the early part of his life, and afterward was a shoemaker in Lynn. He was an industrious, thrifty man and acquired considerable property in lands in that part of Lynn which is now Western avenue. In religious preference he was a Baptist, and in politics a Republican. He married, November 29, 1812, Delia Hudson, born November, 1793, died April 14, 1878, having borne her husband ten children: 1. John Hudson, born July 14, 1813, died January 26, 1814. 2. George Washington, born December 1, 1814, died December 13, 1886; married, April 17, 1836, Lydia Carl. 3. Delia M., born October 24, 1816, died May 30, 1860; married December 1, 1840, William Hoyt, who died June 25, 1864. 4. William A., born September 8, 1818, died January 6, 1885; married, June 26, 1861, Sarah E. Carlton. 5. Lyman Barney, born August 3, 1821, see forward. 6. Eliza Jane, born August 5, 1823. 7. Harriet, born May 3, 1826, died November 9, 1893. 8. Charles F., born October 20, 1829, died November, 1874; married, September 18, 1856, Sarah A. Emmerton. 9. Louisiana, born September 20, 1833, now living in the old homestead. 10. Lydia E., born September 9, 1836, died January 12, 1895.

(III) Lyman Barney Frazier, fourth son and fifth child of Hugh and Delia (Hudson) Frazier, was a native of Lynn, Massachusetts, and for many years one of the leading business men of that city. He received his early education in public schools, but left his books when thirteen years old and went into a shoe shop, where he gained a practical knowledge of the shoemaking business in the workshop and there laid the foundation of his later successful career in the capacity of manufacturer. In the course of time he started a factory and thereafter was identified with the shoe industry of Lynn until 1872, when his works were destroyed by fire. After this Mr. Frazier turned his attention to other pursuits and became a stockbroker, as sole proprietor at first and afterward as senior member of the firm of Frazier & Tewksbury, stock brokers, with offices in Boston, where he was a member of the stock exchange. Throughout the period of his active business life he was variously identified with the interests of Lynn and took a commendable interest in public affairs. He was a director in the City National Bank, member of the Unitarian church, and in politics a firm Republican. But his interest in political affairs was chiefly that of a citizen and taxpayer, although at various times he was elected to office in the municipal government of the city.

Mr. Frazier married three times. His first wife, whom he married September 29, 1846, was Mary Elliott Ayer, daughter of John and Sophia (Elliott) Ayer; she was born in Haverhill, Massachusetts, October 29, 1825, died in Lynn, November 24, 1855; he had by her three children: Mary E., William H., who married Josephine Batchelder and had a son Charles, and Lyman Rhoderick, who married Caroline Batchelder and had two children, Elliott and Emma Frazier. His second wife, whom he married June 28, 1858, was Emma E. Munroe, daughter of Colonel Timothy Munroe. She died in Lynn, May 12, 1868. One child was born of this marriage: Elbridge M., who married Nellie Nichols and had four children (Lyman B., Donald Nichols, Emma Marjorie and Kathleen Frazier). For his third wife Mr. Frazier married Maria B. Newhall, who

Lyman B. Frazier

Lewis Historical Pub Co.

Eng^d by W. T. Bather

Francis S. Newhall.

died February 25, 1908; she was a daughter of Francis Stewart and Lydia (Burrill) Newhall, and granddaughter of Winthrop and Elizabeth (Farrington) Newhall, (see Samuel Newhall 4).

NEWHALL (VII) Francis Stewart Newhall, (see Winthrop Newhall 6), eldest son and child of Winthrop and Elizabeth (Farrington) Newhall, born Lynn, April 30, 1795, died in that city February 2, 1858. In many respects he inherited the traits of his ancestors, who were largely members of the Society of Friends, and while he never sought to depart radically from the teachings of his parents he himself became Unitarian in religious affiliation. In business life he was perhaps more successful than any other of the family in generations before his own, and for many years was prominently identified with the business and industrial history of Lynn, and later on he engaged in mercantile pursuits in the city of Boston, dealing extensively in leather, his trade being chiefly with the larger concerns. His business career was begun as a tanner, and afterward was continued at Market street, Lynn, in the manufacture of morocco and other fine grades of leather, at first as sole proprietor and later in partnership with his brother Henry. However, he eventually retired from manufacturing and established himself as a leather dealer in Boston, an undertaking which proved highly successful and yielded him a large fortune. In Lynn he was variously identified with the best interests and institutions of the city and of his means gave generously to worthy charities, but always in such a way as not to attract attention to himself. Together with his brother, Henry Newhall, he established the Leighton Bank, and was president of it till his death. This was one of the first institutions of its kind in the city, and held a high place in financial circles. In his business transactions with men he always spoke directly to the subject in hand and never in meaningless or idle words. He was a good man in every sense and made the best use of the talents with which nature endowed him, and he was greatly respected in the city in which he lived so long and in which he died. On February 23, 1818, Mr. Newhall married Lydia Burrill, born May 3, 1797, died March 30, 1881, daughter of Thompson and Lydia Burrill, and by whom he had six children: 1. Eliza, born May 5, 1819, married John G. Warner, died 1897; (see Warner family). 2. Persis, born September 6, 1820, resides in Louisville, Kentucky; married James E. Breed; he died February 2, 1857. 3. Henry Francis, born January 15, 1823, died July 20, 1902. 4. Lydia Ann, born June 12, 1825, resides in Lynn. 5. Maria Burrill, born December 23, 1827, married, October 26, 1870, for his third wife, Lyman Barney Frazier, she died February 25, 1908, aged eighty years. (See Frazier family). 6. George Thompson, born December 22, 1832, mentioned below.

George Thompson Newhall, son of Francis S. and Lydia (Burrill) Newhall, born December 22, 1832, was reared and educated in Lynn. He began as a clerk with his father, and later the firm name was changed to Francis Newhall & Sons. This continued for some years when he retired from this business and was later associated with the United States marshal's office for a time, after which he entered the newspaper business in Lynn, which he followed till his death, July, 1897. He was active in the political affairs of Lynn, being a Republican, and serving a number of years in the city council. He was a member of the militia, captain of the Lynn Light Infantry, and April 1, 1861, when the war broke out, enlisted in the three months service and was commissioned as captain of Company D, April 19, 1861, and after his discharge he re-enlisted in the nine months service as captain. He was a constant attendant of the Unitarian church. He married, 1859, Harriett C. Trask, born in New Hampshire, daughter of John Trask, a shoemaker by trade, who spent his last years in Lynn, where he died an aged man. Mrs. Newhall is the only one living of three children. She has had three children: 1. Francis Stewart, an assistant bank examiner, with offices in Boston. 2. Grace W., married Joshua B. F. Breed, and resides in Louisville, Kentucky. 3. Frederick, who was born, reared and educated in Lynn, and has been for a number of years connected with R. L. Day & Company, bankers and brokers of Boston.

BEMIS Joseph Bemis, immigrant ancestor, born in England, 1619, came to Watertown, Massachusetts, as early as 1640, and died there August 7, 1684. He was accompanied by his sister Mary, who married at Watertown, March 20, 1644-5, William Hagar. Joseph Bemis was selectman of Watertown 1638-72-75. He was a blacksmith as well as farmer. His will was dated August 7, and proved October 7, 1684. His widow administered the estate, which was divided November 18, 1712, soon after her death. Children, born in Watertown: 1. Sarah, born January 15, 1642-3; married John Bigelow. 2. Mary, born September 10, 1644; married Samuel Whitney. 3. Joseph, Jr., twin, born October 28, 1647, buried November 4, 1647. 4. Ephraim, twin, born October 28, 1647, buried November 4, 1647. 5. Martha, born March 24, 1649. 6. Joseph, Jr., born December 12, 1651; died at Westminster, August 7, 1684. 7. Rebecca, born April 17, 1684; married John White, and second, Thomas Harrington. 8. Ephraim, born August 25, 1656, settled at Windham, Connecticut. 9. John.

(II) John Bemis, son of Joseph Bemis, born in Watertown, August, 1659, died October 24, 1732; married first, at Watertown, about 1680, Mary, daughter of George and Susanna Harrington, second, January 1, 1716-17, Mrs. Sarah, widow of Jonathan Phillips, born November 16, 1663, died February, 1703-4, daughter of Nathaniel Holland (baptized 1638) and his second wife, Sarah Hosier. The second wife of John Bemis was born in Watertown, November 30, 1662, and died before 1726. He married third, at Watertown, May 30, 1726, Judith (Jennison) Barnard, born at Watertown, August 13, 1667, died there, daughter of Ensign Samuel Jennison, born 1645, died October, 1701, and his wife, Judith Macomber, who died March 1, 1722-3. She was the widow of James Barnard. John Bemis owned land in Marlborough before April 26, 1701, when he sold it. Children of first wife: 1. Beriah, born June 23, 1681; died in Weston, February 10, 1701-2; married Daniel Child. 2. Susanna, born December 24, 1682; died November 15, 1703; married John Hastings. 3. Joseph, born November 17, 1684, died 1738. 4. John. 5. Mary, born September 24, 1688; married Isaac Stearns. 6. Samuel, born 1590; died in Spencer, August, 1766. 7. Lydia, born 1692; married Jonathan Fiske. 8. Hannah, born October 9, 1694; died October, 1700. 9. Isaac, born 1696, probably died young. 10. Jonathan, born November 17, 1701. 11. Abraham, born November 26, 1703. 12. Susanna, born December 3, 1705; married John Vilas. 13. Hannah, born December 3, 1705; married John Flagg.

(III) John Bemis, son of John Bemis, born in Watertown, October 6, 1686; married first, May 8, 1710, Hannah, born January 25, 1690-1, daughter of Daniel Warren, born October 6, 1653, and his wife, Elizabeth (Whitney), born June 9, 1656. He married second, April 2, 1713, Anna, born June 9, 1690, daughter of Samuel Livermore, born 1640, died 1690, and his wife, Anna (Bridge) who was born 1646 and died August 28, 1727. After John Bemis died, his widow married, December 5, 1769, Josiah Smith. Child of John and Hannah: 1. John. Children of John and Anna Bemis: 2. Anna, born April 29, 1714; married Samuel Fiske and second Hopestill Bent. 3. Josiah, born February 9, 1715-6. 4. Abraham, born December 27, 1717. 5. Grace, born November 5, 1719. 6. Lydia, born April 5, 1721; married Capt. Jonas Dix. 7. Abijah, born March 16, 1722-3; died at Paxton, June 19, 1790. 8. Elisha, born March 20, 1725-6. 9. Elizabeth, born March 23, 1727-8. 10. Nathaniel, born May 6, 1730. 11. Susanna, born April 3, 1732; married Elisha Garfield. 12. Phinehas, born March 24, 1734.

(IV) John Bemis, son of John Bemis, born at Watertown, February 11, 1711-2; married, February 16, 1731-2, Hannah, born April 28, 1715, daughter of Capt. Daniel Warren, born April 30, 1686, and wife, Hannah (Bigelow). He was surveyor of highways, and a soldier in the French war, 1656. Children, born in Watertown: 1. John, born August 28, 1732. 2. Timothy. 3. Anna, September 30, 1736. 4. Elizabeth, born January 17, 1738-9; died July 16, 1750. 5. Lydia, born June 10, 1741. 6. Abigail, born September 1, 1743; died July 25, 1750. 7. Nathaniel, born March 12, 1745. 8. Sarah, born September 27, 1748; married Elisha Cox. 9. Henry, born January 28, 1750-1. 10. Jeduthan, born June 10, 1753; married Polly Staples, of Sudbury. 11. Mary, born May 16, 1755; married William Corey. 12. Daniel, born March 5, 1758; married Patty Winch.

(V) Nathaniel Bemis, son of John, was born in Weston, March 12, 1745. He was a soldier of the revolution, private in Capt. Miles' company of Col. Jonathan Teed's regiment, October 4, 1743. He married a daughter of Elisha and Anna Cox of Weston. They had six children: 1. Lucy, born August 5, 1766; married Jonas Billings. 2. Nathaniel, May 8, 1770. 3. Lot, August 5, 1772. 4. Polly, November 22, 1777. 5. Elisha, January 22, 1780. 6. Charles, January 9, 1785.

(VI) Charles Bemis, son of Nathaniel, was born January 9, 1785, and spent probably nearly all his life in Maine. He was a carpenter by trade and afterward a successful builder and contractor. He married, December 20, 1807, Betsey Jones, who was born December 24, 1781, daughter of Lieut. Eli Jones, born

1756, died May 9, 1811, (a revolutionary soldier) and who married Anna Brown. Charles and Betsey (Jones) Bemis had children: 1. Emily Jones, born November 29, 1808; married William Dudley. 2. Charles Winslow, May 15, 1811; married first, April, 1835, Eliza Hanley; second, 1846, Lucy Heywood; third, November, 1850, Emily Coggen. 3. Dexter, May 3, 1813; a farmer of Hillsboro, Massachusetts; married Mary Jones and had Mary J., Sarah E. and Abbie A. 4. Eli Emery, July 17, 1815. 5. Betsey Jane, December 24, 1817; married Leander Ballard. 6. Royal, October 1, 1820; married Mary Ann Bond. 7. Luke, November 10, 1822, now dead; was a contractor and builder at Waltham, Massachusetts, and accumulated a fortune. 8. John, June 26, 1825.

(VII) Eli Emery Bemis, son of Charles and Betsey (Jones) Bemis, was born in Weston, Massachusetts, June 17, 1815, on the old Bemis homestead farm. He was an energetic farmer and when not employed with the cultivation of his acres he turned his attention to contract work. He was a man of quiet habits, but he possessed remarkable energy in business matters, and was withal a public spirited and progressive citizen. He married Eliza Leman; children: 1. Emery Leman, born in Weston and died there, aged sixty-five years; married Abbie Lind and had Jennie, now dead, and Minnie. 2. Eliza Leman, married ——— Parsons; both dead. 3. Isidora Ophelia, married Dennis Eldridge and owns and occupies the old Bemis family homestead in Weston. 4. John Leman.

(VIII) John Leman Bemis, son of Eli Emery and Eliza (Leman) Bemis, was born on the old home farm in Weston, July 28, 1844, lived there until he became of age, then bought a farm of his own and occupied it until 1872, when he removed to Winthrop, Massachusetts, where he now lives. When he settled in Winthrop he purchased a small tract of land near the center of the town and set up in the milk business, but after a few years sold out his milk route and removed to Chicago to take the position of purchasing agent for the Swift Packing Company, with which concern he was connected in one way and another and in one place and another for the next ten years, four years of which time was spent on the Pacific coast, when he had intended to begin business on his own account. However, having spent about twenty years in Chicago and the west, Mr. Bemis returned to Winthrop in 1891, and has since devoted his attention to the milk business, selling his product in bulk. He has a very pleasant home and with his family enjoys the comforts of life and the fruits of years well spent. On November 27, 1866, he married Frances Underwood, born in Lincoln, Massachusetts, April 27, 1847, daughter of Moses and Sophronia (Whitney) Underwood, both born in Lincoln, her father in 1789 and her mother December 13, 1808. They lived and died on the old Underwood house farm, which had been settled by the Underwoods during the time of the colony. Moses Underwood was a soldier of the war of 1812-15, and a man of great physical strength; and it is said of him that such was the power of his voice that he could make himself heard a full mile away. It is said too that when the custom house in Boston was in process of erection he was selected to drive the great team of eighty yoke of oxen required to haul the large granite columns from the quarries in Quincy to the site of the building.

Mr. Underwood's father, Moses Underwood, was one of the early settlers of Lincoln, a minute-man in 1775, who fought the British at Arlington and Lexington and continued in service two years. It is said that his daring in battle was remarkable, always in the thickest of the fight, and that on one occasion, when almost completely surrounded he used his old musket with such effect that he cut his way out and left several of the enemy lying on the ground. His whole life was spent in Lincoln, when he was a man of much prominence. His wife was Sarah Pierce, who also came of one of the old New England colonial families. Moses Underwood, last mentioned, was a son of Joseph Underwood, who was born in Lincoln and married a Gage, and Joseph Underwood was a son of Moses Underwood, born in Lincoln and a son of Moses Underwood the immigrant, who came from England to America in the first half of the seventeenth century and was among the early planters of Lincoln. The lands set off to him were cleared by his own hand and the farm which he made to yield its first crop continued in possession of his descendants through one generation to another until the year 1902, when its last remaining acres passed into other hands.

The children of Moses and Sophronia (Whitney) Underwood: 1. Martha, died young, result of accident. 2. Mary, married Albert McCleary, and now is a widow. 3. Moses, lives in Waltham, Massachusetts, retired; married first, Mrs. Mary A. Warren, whose family name was Hill; married second, Tilley Crane. 4. Lydia, married Hiram Garfield of Weston, and died by accident. 5. Sarah, married William Harrington and now is a widow, living in Minneapolis, Minnesota. 6. Sophronia, married Frank Farnsworth and lives in Waltham. 7. Frances, wife of John Leman Bemis. 8. Addie Sophronia, died at the age of six years.

John Leman and Frances (Underwood) Bemis have two children. Their son, Clarence Leman, born in Winthrop, September 6, 1869; lives in Chicago and is employed by the Swift Packing Co.; married Belle Byrnes, born Chicago, October 23, 1871, and has two children, Clarabelle, born September 7, 1893, and Ruth Leman, born August 4, 1896.

RAWSON Many of the family of this name have so demeaned themselves as to bring honor upon themselves and those so fortunate as to bear this cognomen. The industry and high character of the Rawsons have always been conspicuous virtues, and they have ever enjoyed the respect and esteem of their contemporaries. Their record is long and honorable, telling of men moral to a remarkable degree, independent in thought and action, patriotic and brave, prominent in the communities where they dwelt, and often leaders of their fellows.

(I) Secretary Edward Rawson, immigrant ancestor, was born at Dillingham, Dorsetshire, England, son of David and Margaret (Wilson) Rawson, the former of whom was a citizen and merchant tailor of London, England, and the latter a sister of the Rev. John Wilson, minister at Boston. In 1637, at the age of twenty-two, Edward Rawson left his native land for the new world, settling in Newbury, Massachusetts, where he was one of the grantees and proprietors. He was active and prominent in public affairs, and served in the capacity of second town clerk of Newbury; notary public and register, serving from April 19, 1638, to 1647; was selectman of the town; commissioner to hear and determine small causes; deputy to the general court from Newbury from 1638 nearly every year until 1650; clerk of the house of deputies 1645-46-49. He had a special grant for his services to the general court—a tract of fifteen hundred acres near the Narragansett country. In company with Joseph Hills he revised the laws of the province. He succeeded Increase Nowell, who had been secretary of the colony since the beginning in 1636. Edward Rawson was chosen May 22, 1650, and after that made his home in Boston, residing on Rawson lane, so called until changed to Bromfield street, and he owned some acres bordering on the Common. He was re-elected annually to his position until 1686, a period of thirty-six years, when Sir Edmund Andros came into power. Mr. Rawson and his wife were members of the church of which the Rev. John Wilson was pastor, and after the death of the latter named Mr. Rawson became one of the twenty-eight disaffected persons who left the First Church and united to form the Third or Old South Church in May, 1669. He became the agent or steward of an English Society for the Propagation of the Gospel among the Indians in New England, in 1651. He countersigned the warrant sent to Massachusetts for the arrest of the regicides, Goffe, Whalley and Dixwell, but the arrests were never made. The one blot on his good record was his participation in the persecution of the Quakers, then a fashionable custom. His salary as secretary was at first twenty pounds a year, later sixty pounds. He was subsequently elected recorder of Suffolk county. His family Bible is now or was lately in the possession of R. R. Dodge, of East Sutton, Massachusetts, having descended through this line: John Rawson Young (6), Anna (5), David (4), David (3), William (2), Edward (1). Edward Rawson was an efficient officer, and a useful and distinguished citizen. He died August 27, 1693, and administration was granted to his son William. The warrant to distribute the estate was dated April 6, 1695; a partial account was dated January 14, 1722. Edward Rawson married Rachel, daughter of Thomas Perne, granddaughter of John and ——— (Grindal) Hooker, the latter of whom was a sister of Edmund Grindal, archbishop of Canterbury in the reign of Queen Elizabeth. Children: 1. Daughter, married and remained in England. 2. Edward, graduate of Harvard, 1653; settled in Horsmonden, Kent county, England, 1655. 3. Rachel, married, January 18, 1683, William Aubrey. 4. David, born May 6, 1644, went to England. 5. Perne, born September 16, 1646, married the Rev. Samuel Torrey. 6. William, born May 21, 1651, married, July 31, 1673, Anne Glover. 7. Susan, died in Roxbury in 1654. 8. Hannah, baptized October 10, 1653, died May 27, 1656. 9. Rebecca, born October 19, 1654, died young. 10. Rebecca, born May 23, 1656. 11. Elizabeth, born November 12, 1657, married Thomas Broughton. 12. Rev. Grindal, born January 23, 1659, mentioned below.

(II) Rev. Grindal Rawson, son of Edward and Rachel (Perne) Rawson, was born in Boston, Massachusetts, January 23, 1659, died February 6, 1715; a stone suitably inscribed marks his burial place in Mendon. He was graduated at Harvard in 1678, and after receiving his first degree, Bachelor of Arts, was invited by his brother-in-law, the Rev. Samuel Torrey, to come to his house and study divinity. He proved an apt pupil and was advised to enter the ministry. He preached his first sermon at Medfield, and for two months after that was heard in various churches until October 4, 1680, when he accepted the invitation to fill the pulpit at Mendon, Massachusetts. He preached there until April 7, 1684, when he was permanently settled as minister of the town. He married Susanna, daughter of the Rev. John Wilson, of Medfield, sister of Dr. John Wilson, granddaughter of the Rev. John Wilson. They were distant relatives. She died July 8, 1748. Children: 1. Edward, born November 21, 1683. 2. Edward, born 1684, died May 26, 1685. 3. Susanna, born October 31, 1686, married, 1719, Benjamin Reynolds. 4. Edmund, born July 8, 1689. 5. Wilson, born June 23, 1692, mentioned below. 6. John, born October 1, 1695, married Mercy Hayward. 7. Mary, born June 22, 1699, married, April 9, 1724, Joseph Dorr. 8. Rachel, born September 6, 1701, married Samuel Wood. 9. David, born October 25, 1703, died January 18, 1704. 10. Grindal, born September 6, 1707, married Dorothy Chauncey. 11. Elizabeth, born April 21, 1710.

Rev. Cotton Mather, classmate and friend of the Rev. Grindal Rawson, in his preface to his sermon preached at the funeral of the latter, quotes the language used by President Urian Oakes at Commencement in 1678 when he conferred degrees on the class of that year. Following is a translation: "The third somewhat high-sounding, in Grindal Rawson, sprung likewise from a most illustrious stock, for his honored father holds a high place in the state; the very pious and orthodox John Wilson, a truly Apostolic man, was his great-grandmother's brother, and the Right Rev. Edmund Grindal, sometime archbishop of Canterbury, a most saintly man and in the archbishopric little less than a Puritan, his great-great-grandmother's brother, and may God grant that in learning, holiness and excellence of character he may resemble both Wilson and Grindal". Mr. Mather himself said: "We generally esteemed him a truly pious man and a very prudent one, and a person of temper and every way qualified for a friend that might be delighted in. We honored him for his industrious oversight of the flock in the wilderness which had been committed unto him and the variety of successful pains which he took for the good of those to whom God had therefore exceedingly endeared him. We honored him for his intellectual abilities which procured frequent applications to him and brought him sometimes upon our most conspicuous theatres. And we usually took it for granted that things would be fairly done where he had an hand in the doing of them. We honored him for his doing the work of an evangelist among our Indians of whose language he was a master that has scarce an equal and for whose welfare his projections and performances were such as render our loss herein hardly to be repaired. Such services are Pyramids". Dr. Metcalf said of him: "He was an excellent scholar and eminent divine". His reputation as a theologian was of such a character that the general court sometimes preferred grave and serious questions of ecclesiastical polity to him for decision. In 1698 he visited the Indian tribes of the Province with the Rev. Samuel Danforth, of Taunton. He was appointed chaplain to the forces going to Canada. He wrote the pamphlet entitled "Confession of Faith", published in English and Indian. His Artillery Election sermon in 1703, and Election sermon May 25, 1709, were published.

(III) Wilson Rawson, son of the Rev. Grindal and Susanna (Wilson) Rawson, was born in Mendon, Massachusetts, June 23, 1692, died December 1, 1726. He was a farmer at Mendon. He married Margaret Arthur, of Nantucket, May 4, 1712; she died November 14, 1767. Children: 1. Wilson, born August 13, 1713, at Mendon, mentioned below. 2. Priscilla, born December 17, 1715. 3. Mary, born May 12, 1717, died June 22, 1717. 4. Grindal, born July 13, 1719. 5. Edward, born April 2, 1721, married Mary Morse. 6. Stephen, born April 2, 1722. 7. Paul, born April 9, 1725, married Phebe Gardner. 8. John, born January 23, 1727.

(IV) Wilson Rawson, son of Wilson and Margaret (Arthur) Rawson, was born at Mendon, August 13, 1713, died at Upton, 1778, where he had settled many years previously. His will was dated July 5, 1778, and filed December 2 following. He married Abigail Temple, of Harvard (intention dated December 24,

1737). Children: 1. Wilson, born October 24, 1738, died March 15, 1744. 2. Caleb, born April 23, 1741. 3. Abigail, born June 9, 1743, married ——— Whitney. 4. Joshua, born April 12, 1746. 5. Mary, born March 2, 1748. 6. Wilson, born February 20, 1752, soldier in the Revolution. 7. Joshua, born April 1, 1755. 8. Artemas, born 1759, mentioned below.

(V) Artemas Rawson, son of Wilson and Abigail (Temple) Rawson, was born at Upton, Massachusetts, 1759, died at Upton, March 27, 1815. He was a farmer in Upton. During the Revolutionary war he served as a private in Captain Ezra Wood's company on the Lexington alarm; also in Captain Benjamin Farrar's company, Lieutenant-Colonel Nathan Taylor's regiment, at the Rhode Island campaign of 1776. He married, November 25, 1779, Dorcas Bachelor, of Grafton. Children, born at Upton: 1. Levi, born January 19, 1781. 2. Asenath (given Marcena in the genealogy), born July 13, 1782. 3. Emma, born January 25, 1784. 4. Artemas, born September 13, 1785, mentioned below. 5. Phila, born May 11, 1787, (also given Philanda). 6. Dorcas, born and died 1790. 7. Mark B., born March 3, 1793. 8. Dorcas B., born March 2, 1795, married William Brooks. 9. Nathaniel Ward, born April 11, 1797, died January 30, 1818.

(VI) Artemas Rawson, son of Artemas and Dorcas (Bachelor) Rawson, was born in Upton, Massachusetts, September 13, 1785, died at Lynn, Massachusetts, November 29, 1869. After completing his duties at the common school, he aided with the work on his father's farm and also served an apprenticeship at the trade of shoemaking. For a few years he followed his trade in his native town, then moved to Paris, Maine, where he continued to make shoes, after the custom of the times, and also conducted a farm there, both occupations proving highly successful. Later he removed to Ordway, Maine, where he purchased a small farm, and during the winter months manufactured shoes. In 1859 he removed to Arlington, Massachusetts, retiring at that time from active labor and business. He was a member of the Methodist Episcopal church, formerly a Democrat and later a Republican in his political views, and in early manhood was a member of the state militia. He married, February 3, 1816, at Paris, Maine, Dorcas Rice, and lived there until 1832. Children: 1. Solon, born October 29, 1817. 2. Aurelia P., born July 22, 1819. 3. Warren, born July 18, 1821. 4. Mary, born October 18, 1823. 5. William, born May 1, 1826. 6. Dorcas B., born May 1, 1829, died March 1, 1891. 7. Miranda, born June 17, 1831. 8. Ann E., born June 25, 1833, died August 26, 1871. 9. James, born July 6, 1835. 10. Van Buren, born July 17, 1839, died September 16, 1869. 11. Elbridge M., born November 12, 1840, mentioned below. 12. S. Greenleaf, born December 10, 1842, died March 5, 1865.

(VII) Elbridge Marcellus Rawson, son of Artemas and Dorcas (Rice) Rawson, was born at Oxford, Maine, November 12, 1840. He received his education in the common schools of his native town, working on his father's farm. At the age of seventeen he came to Lynn, Massachusetts, where he served a three years' apprenticeship in the trade of carpenter with Daniel Hyde. At the breaking out of the civil war, desirous of showing his patriotism and loyalty to country, he offered his services for the defense of the Union, and enlisted as a private in the Fifteenth Massachusetts Battalion, Company I, Captain William D. Chamberlain. The company left Boston May 10, 1861, for Fortress Monroe, where the company was later merged into the Twenty-ninth Massachusetts Regiment, in Sumner's Second Army Corps, Richardson's First Division, Meagher's Second Brigade. The regiment remained at Fortress Monroe until November, 1861, at which time General McClellan took command of the army, and the Twenty-ninth went into winter quarters at Newport News, joining McClellan's forces in the spring of 1862, just before the battle of Fair Oaks, and was in the battle May 31 and June 1, 1862. He was through the Pennsylvania campaign and marched to reinforce Pope, where the Second Corps covered his retreat. The regiment was in the battle of South Mountain, September 14, 1862, and Antietam, the 17th. The regiment soon went into winter quarters at Fredericksburg, and the following spring joined Burnside's Army of the Ohio, Potter's Ninth Army Corps, Ferraro's First Division, Christ's Second Brigade, the regiment under command of Colonel Ebenezer W. Peirce. The corps went to Paris, Kentucky, when it was ordered to reinforce General Grant at Vicksburg, and while en route met Jackson and drove him out. The regiment later went to East Tennessee and was at the siege of Knoxville. Subsequently came to Annapolis, Maryland, where the corps was reorganized, and later was in the battles of the Wilderness and Spottsylvania, after which was sent back to Washington, and May 24, 1864, was mustered out of service. While at the battle of the Wilderness Mr. Rawson was wounded and laid in hospital about six weeks.

After returning from the war Mr. Rawson took up his residence in Lynn, Massachusetts, where he entered the employ of his old employer, Daniel Hyde, as a journeyman carpenter, remaining several years. In 1872 he removed to Boston, where he worked at his trade for N. W. Morrison, and when the Simmonds block was erected he became superintendent of that building, remaining in that service twenty-nine years, discharging the duties pertaining thereto in a highly creditable and efficient manner, and thereafter led a retired life as far as active business pursuits was concerned, enjoying to the full the consciousness of years well spent and duties faithfully performed. In 1883 he erected a fine residence in Brookline, in which he made his home, and in 1886 erected another at No. 52 Harrison street (nearby). He was reared in the faith of the Methodist church, but in later years attended the Unitarian church at Brookline. He was a Republican in politics. He had the distinction of belonging to the oldest lodge of Masons in the country, St. John's of Boston, having joined it in November, 1880. He was a member of St. Andrew's Chapter, Royal Arch Masons, joining in 1880; Boston Commandery, Knights Templar, 1880; John A. Andrews Post, No. 15, Grand Army of the Republic, at Boston. Mr. Rawson married, October 5, 1878, Emma Rice Vose, born November 1, 1835, daughter of Royal and Mary Ann (Sanford) Vose. Royal Vose was a mason contractor.

OSGOOD John Osgood (1), born in Wherwell, Hampshire, England, 1595, came to New England from Andover in the mother country and was first of Ipswich, then of Newbury and before 1645 was settled in Andover, Massachusetts, being the second settler in that town. He was made freeman in 1639, one of the founders of the first church there in 1645, and the first representative from Andover to the general court in 1651. His will bears date April 12, 1650, and was admitted to probate November 25, 1651. His wife Sarah, whom he married in England, survived him more than fifteen years, and died April 8, 1667. Their children were: Sarah, John, Mary, Elizabeth, Stephen, Hannah, and perhaps Christopher and Thomas.

(II) Captain John Osgood, son of John and Sarah Osgood, was born in England about 1631 and came to New England with his parents. He was captain of the militia, selectman, representative to the general court, and died in Andover in 1693. He married, November 15, 1653, Mary, daughter of Robert Clement, who came from Coventry, Warwickshire, England, about 1652. Mary was charged with witchcraft in 1692, indicted, but was not punished. She bore her husband twelve children: John, Mary, Timothy, Lydia, Peter, Samuel, Sarah (died young), Mehitable, Hannah, Sarah, Ebenezer and Clement.

(III) Lieutenant John Osgood, son of Captain John and Mary (Clement) Osgood, was born in Andover, September 13, 1654, died April 22, 1725. He was a man of consequence in the town, constable, 1684, selectman, 1685, and seven times afterward, lieutenant of militia, surveyor, 1693, deacon of the church from 1719 until his death, 1725. He married, October 16, 1681, Hannah Ayers, born August 2, 1662, died September 6, 1735, daughter of Peter and Hannah (Allen) Ayers. Their children were: John, Ebenezer, Nathaniel, Jeremiah (died young), Jeremiah, Daniel, William, Hannah, Benjamin, Samuel and Josiah.

(IV) Nathaniel Osgood, son of Lieutenant John and Hannah (Ayers) Osgood, was born January 6, 1686-87, and died in Salem in 1756. He was a shoemaker and lived in Salem. He married, March 27, 1710, Hannah, daughter of John and Sarah (Pickering) Buttolph, and granddaughter of John and Alice (Flint) Pickering. Their nine children were: Hannah (died young), Hannah, Nathaniel, John, Benjamin, Mary, Jeremiah, William and Sarah.

(V) Nathaniel Osgood, son of Nathaniel and Hannah (Buttolph) Osgood, was born in Salem in 1716, and died June 6, 1799. He married, October 6, 1745, Hannah Babbridge, and had two children, Christopher and Polly.

(VI) Christopher Osgood, son of Nathaniel and Hannah (Babbridge) Osgood, was born in Salem, October 26, 1748, died March 4, 1828. He married, April 21, 1772, Mary Shepard, born in Salem, February 23, 1750, died May 9, 1832, daughter of Thomas and Susanna (Pike) Shepard. They had eleven children, all born in Salem: 1. Nathaniel, October 12, 1773, died February, 1776. 2. Polly, October 5, 1775, died March 3, 1855. 3. Nathaniel, July 6, 1777, died November 17, 1849. 4. Christopher, January 13, 1780, died July 21, 1798. 5. Sukey (Susan), September 8, 1781, died July 16, 1860. 6. John B., November 7, 1783, died December 27, 1853. 7. William B.,

April 7, 1785, died April 2, 1834. 8. Henry, January 29, 1787, died June 24, 1820. 9. Betsey, May 20, 1789, died 1834. 10. Jeremiah, June 3, 1791, master mariner, living in 1825. 11. Abigail P., June 11, 1794, died March 25, 1816.

(VII) Betsey Osgood, daughter of Christopher and Mary (Shepard) Osgood, was born in Salem, May 20, 1789, died there in 1834. She married Willard Williams, who was born in Salem and died May 21, 1835. They had three children: 1. Henry Willard Williams, born Boston, 1821, entered the medical profession; studied abroad, and practiced many years in Boston, where he has attained a high rank in medical circles and is recognized as an ophtholmologist of splendid experience and rare skill. He married Elizabeth Lowe, of Jamaica Plains, Massachusetts. 2. Abigail Osgood Williams, born Boston, 1828, lives in Salem. 3. Mary Elizabeth Williams, born Boston, 1830, died in Salem.

Willard Williams was employed in a minor capacity in the Suffolk Bank, Boston, where he was a young man, and continued in the service of that great financial institution until the close of his life, but he was advanced from time to time through various grades of promotion to a position of responsibility and gave faithful service in whatever capacity to which he was appointed. He was a firm old-line Whig, but had little time to devote to political affairs. He was a pious man, an earnest member of the Congregational church and took deep interest in promoting the work and influence of the society in general. His daughters, Abigail Osgood and Mary Elizabeth, were educated in select schools in Boston and early in life show decided inclination for art studies and work. They were encouraged in this and previous to the death of their father applied themselves diligently and intelligently to their tasks under the instructions of the best artists in Boston. After their father's death they went abroad and lived in Italy for the next sixteen years, studying, painting independently from the best works of the most famous masterpieces, and also devoted considerable attention to collecting rare art treasures, both for exhibition and sale, and when at length they returned to Boston their art studio was furnished with numerous valuable paintings from their brushes and many others which had been selected with intelligent and scrupulous care from various parts of the old world. Having lived many years in Boston, the Misses Williams removed to Salem and there continued their work, but perhaps less zealously than in earlier years; and since the death of Miss Mary Elizabeth her sister Abigail Osgood has kept up her own work with occasional periods of rest. She is a highly cultured and most interesting woman, and has surrounded herself with many of the choicest gems of her art.

PAIGE

It is sometimes surprising when searching the great genealogical libraries of New England to discover how little has been written of some of the most prominent families of the region, whose surnames have been known in all generations from the early colonial period to the present time. This appears to be true of the family treated in this place, the immigrant ancestor of which landed on the shore of the new world within the next twenty years following the landing of the Pilgrims on historic Plymouth Rock.

(I) Nicholas Paige (Page), was the ancestor of the family here considered. He was of Welch birth and parentage and first appears in New England history as one of the earliest settlers in what now is Hampton, New Hampshire, about the year 1638. This is about all that is known of him.

(II) Amos Paige was a son of Nicholas Paige, but there is no further account of him, the period of his life, his marriage, or the names of his children, with one exception.

(III) Theophilus Paige, son of Amos Paige and grandson of Nicholas Paige the immigrant, was born about the year 1707, and spent perhaps the greater part of his life in Kensington, New Hampshire, where he died June 12, 1782, aged seventy-five years. He married Hannah Dow, who survived him and died in 1786; children: 1. Daniel; see forward. 2. Enoch, married Ruth Peaslee; settled in Berwick, Maine. 3. Nathan, married Molly (or Mary) Brown; lived in Kensington, New Hampshire. 4. Samuel, married first, Patience Gove; second, Mary Johnson, and died in 1769.

(IV) Daniel Paige, eldest son of Theophilus and Hannah (Dow) Paige, was born in Kensington, New Hampshire, and about 1772 removed thence to Weare, New Hampshire, where he afterward lived. In the records of the latter town he is mentioned as a Quaker from Kensington who "settled on law lot 23, range 6, Bear hill." He died comparatively young, leaving two sons and three daughters. One of his grandsons became an eminent physician. He married Mary Peaslee, born in 1736, daughter of Joseph and Martha (Hoag) Peaslee, and granddaughter of John and Mary (Martin) Peaslee. John Peaslee was a son of Dr. Joseph and Ruth (Barnard) Peaslee, and grandson of Joseph Peaslee, who with his wife Mary came from England in 1638, settled first in Newbury, Massachusetts, and in 1641 was living in Colchester (Salisbury) Massachusetts. In 1645 he was one of thirty-two landholders in Haverhill, Massachusetts, which in 1641 was a part of old Colchester, but now is within the boundaries of New Hampshire. He is mentioned in the old records as "a preacher and gifted brother." and also as "a self-educated physician of much repute." Daniel and Mary (Peaslee) Paige had children: 1. Hannah, married Moses Green. 2. Ruth, born 1765; married Moses Osborn. 3. Sarah, married Joseph Hussey. 4. John, born 1767, died 1848; married Hannah Paige; eight children. 5. Daniel, born in 1772.

(V) Daniel Paige, youngest child of Daniel and Mary (Peaslee) Paige, was born in Weare, New Hampshire, 1772, and died 1855. He was a farmer, and in his religious views appears to have departed somewhat from the faith of his fathers, for he was one of the men of Weare who were instrumental in erecting the Universalist Church in that town. He married Comfort Hoag, born 1775, died 1850. Comfort Hoag was a daughter of Joseph Hoag, who settled in the south part of Herkimer, New Hampshire, and who married, 1768, Hephzibah Hoag, daughter of Jonathan Hoag and Comfort Stanyan. Joseph Hoag was son of Nathan Hoag, who married Martha Goodwin, grandson of Jonathan Hoag whose wife was "Ebenezer" Emery, and great-grandson of John Hoag, who was born in England or Wales in 1641, and came to this country in 1643 with his father's family, an account of which will be found elsewhere in this work. Daniel and Comfort (Hoag) Paige, had children: 1. Sarah, born 1798; married Moses Wheeler. 2. Joseph, born 1801. 3. Anna, born 1804; married George Nichols. 4. Daniel, born 1808; married first, Elizabeth Nichols; second, Mary Jones. 5. Jonathan, born 1812; married first, Eleanor Locke; second, Mary Willard; third, Mary Shaw.

(VI) Daniel Paige, fourth child of Daniel and Comfort (Hoag) Paige, was born in Weare, New Hampshire, in 1808, and died in 1873, in Peabody. He married first, Elizabeth Nichols, who died in 1838; second,

Mary Jones, the mother of his children: 1. James J., born in 1844. 2. Moses B., born 1846. 3. Martha L., born 1850.

(VII) Moses Bailey Paige, second son and child of Daniel and Mary (Jones) Paige, was born in Weare, New Hampshire, in July, 1846, and for the last more than thirty years has been actively identified with the business life of the town of Peabody, Massachusetts. When about ten years old he went from Weare to Winthrop, Maine, where he received his education and afterward became a farmer, which occupation he followed until 1872, when he removed to Peabody. Mr. Paige was a farmer in Peabody for a short time after he went to live in that town, and afterward found employment in the pottery and earthenware works of Charles Worthen. In 1876 he himself became proprietor of the works and at once proceeded to enlarge its capacity and improve its facilities for producing superior wares. Not only once, but several times during his personal ownership of the plant, Mr. Paige made material improvements in and about the factory and placed it on a foundation where in addition to the pottery wares he at first made, the works have been made to produce an excellent quality of crockeryware in general. Under his capable management the concern became a highly profitable enterprise, and whatever the M. B. Paige Company is to-day is the result of his own effort and industry. In 1906 the M. B. Paige Company was incorporated, and since that time Mr. Paige has been its president and general manager.

On July 18, 1893, Mr. Paige married Mrs. Eliza Wilkinson, widow of Robert H. Wilkinson (born January 29, 1854, died September 22, 1884), and daughter of Nathan Holt Poor and Abigail Morrill, his first wife; Wilkinson issue: Edward Poor Wilkinson, born August 5, 1884, died October 16, 1884. Mr. and Mrs. Paige have one child: James Edward Paige, born in Peabody, June 23, 1896.

RUTTER

The Rutter family of England has an ancient and honored history. Nicholas Rutter, probable ancestor of the American emigrant, bore arms: Gules three garbs and chief a lion passant argent or mullet for difference. Nicholas Rutter lived at Holcot, Gloucestershire. The Rutter family of Kingsley Hall, county Chester, bears similar arms: Gules three garbs or, on a chief azure lion passant guardant argent. Apparently the same family in

Cheshire, Gloucestershire and Stratford-on-Avon, county Warwick, has arms: Gules a lion passant in chief and three in base argent. But one other coat-of-arms of the Rutter family is given by Burke, that of the family at Exeter in Devonshire, and differing from these just described.

(I) John Rutter, immigrant ancestor of the Sudbury family of this surname, born in England, 1616, came to America in the ship "Confidence," sailing from Southampton, April 24, 1638, with other passengers who settled in Sudbury, Massachusetts. Rutter was listed with several other young men as "servants" of Peter Noyes, who was making his second trip, but tradition tells us that he was not really in the employ of Noyes, though many young men worked their passage and were called servants in the ship's papers. Rutter was a carpenter by trade. He settled in Sudbury, and was a proprietor of that town in 1640. He contracted with the selectmen February 17, 1642, to "sett, sawe, hew & frame" a house—the first meeting house. Several acres were given him by the town in acknowledgment of services, perhaps in connection with this contract. He was a selectman in 1675. He and his descendants resided for many years on South street, East Sudbury, (now Wayland) and the old homestead of Joseph Rutter, which was a name found in the family from the earliest generation, was lately occupied by James A. Draper. In this house General Micah Maynard Rutter, was born in 1779, son of Joseph Rutter, Jr. Another descendant of note was Dr. Joseph Draper, graduate of Williams College, principal of the high schools at Saxtonville and Milford, surgeon in the Union army in the civil war, practicing physician in South Boston, who died in 1885. He was the son of Eunice (Rutter) Draper, daughter of Joseph Rutter, Jr., and Ira Draper. Dr. Draper well represented the John Rutter family, which as a race was noted for purity and uprightness of character. He is buried in the old burying ground at Wayland. Another grandchild of Joseph Rutter, Jr., is Mrs. A. S. Hudson, (L. R. Draper), formerly principal of the Wadsworth Academy at South Sudbury, and of high schools at Lincoln, Wayland and Marlborough, Massachusetts. John Rutter married, November 1, 1641, Elizabeth Plympton, who came in the ship "Jonathan" in 1639, probably sister of Thomas Plimpton, of Sudbury, also called a servant of Peter Noyes, who was killed by the Indians in King Philip's war. She died May 5, 1689. Children: 1. Elizabeth, born October 6, 1642. 2. John, born February 7, 1645; married March 12, 1690, Hannah Bush. 3. Rebecca, born February 28, 1647. 4. Thomas, born April 6, 1650; mentioned below. 5. Joseph, born May 1, 1656; died March 17, 1691, at Sudbury.

(II) Thomas Rutter, son of John Rutter (1), was born in Sudbury, April 5, 1650. He married, October 15, 1689, Jemima Stanhope, born June 24, 1665, died September 28, 1748. he resided at Sudbury. Children, born there: 1. Elizabeth, September 1, 1690. 2. Mary, April 7, 1693. 3. Jemima, December 2, 1695; married Joshua Heminway. 4. Anna, May 22, 1698. 5. Sarah, May 3, 1701. 6. Joseph, mentioned below.

(III) Joseph Rutter, son of Thomas Rutter (2), was born at Sudbury, September 25, 1703. He married (possibly second wife), April 28, 1743, Mary Willard. Children, born in Sudbury: 1. Mary, April 8, 1744. 2. Eunice, October 5, 1745; died June 17, 1764. 3. Thomas, born February 14, 1748; married June 24, 1773, Abigail Heard; was a soldier in the revolution. 4. Joseph Jr., mentioned below. 5. Jemima, May 4, 1756.

(IV) Joseph Rutter, son of Joseph Rutter (3), was born in Sudbury, March 28, 1752. He married Eunice Maynard, of an old Sudbury family. He resided on the homestead at Wayland. Children: 1. Micah Maynard, mentioned below. 2. Eunice, married Ira Draper.

(V) General Micah Maynard Rutter, son of Joseph Rutter Jr. (4), was born in East Sudbury, March 4, 1779, and died at Wayland (formerly East Sudbury) May 8, 1837. For many years he was a deputy sheriff of Middlesex county. He served in the Massachusetts militia many years; was colonel of First Regiment, Second Brigade, Third Division, Massachusetts, 1816 to 1826 inclusive; brigadier-general Second Brigade, Third Division, 1829 to 1834 inclusive. He was a member of the Massachusetts house of representatives ten years, and also served as state senator. He was a member of the Masonic fraternity, receiving the degrees in Middlesex Lodge and demitting to Monitor Lodge, and was exalted in St. Paul's Royal Arch Chapter, April 22, 1828. He was a patriotic, public-spirited man, and interested in all matters that concerned the welfare of the town and commonwealth. He married, October 13, 1805, Nancy Plympton, of Wayland. Children, born in Wayland: 1. Micah Maynard, Jr., born May 1, 1806, mentioned below. 2. Adelaide, never married. 3. Josiah, born March 2, 1813. 4. Susan, married ——— Pierce; children: Edward and Charles Pierce. 5. Eliza Jane, never married. 6. Susan. 7. Nancy P. 8. Adeline.

The following appeared in a local paper at time of the death of General Micah M. Rutter: "In Wayland, on Monday evening last, Hon. M. M. Rutter died. Wayland, his native town, will long feel a sincere regret for his loss; for he was benevolent and kind, indulgent and upright in all his relations in life. He was truly a friend to mankind in its broadest sense. For more than twenty years he was called by the voice of the people to represent them in one or the other branches of our state legislature, and his variety of acts and transactions, both in private and a long public life, will bear prominent and durable testimony to the integrity of his purpose, unbending and unyielding from a steady course of unflinching conscientious rectitude. In fact he was one of the noblest works of God—an honest man. His family to whom he was endeared by the strongest ties of domestic attachment survive to bemoan his loss from their familiar and happy circle, though recollections of his worth will long live and play in the memory, and cherish them onward to join him in Heaven."

(VI) Major Micah Maynard Rutter, eldest son of General Micah Maynard Rutter (5), was born at Wayland, May 1, 1806, died at Newberne, North Carolina, November 8, 1870. He married, May 1, 1829, Harriette Gibson, born at Boston, June 6, 1810, baptized at Hollis Street Church, July 1, 1810, and died at Wayland, November 21, 1870, daughter of John Gibson (see Gibson). Children: 1. Micah Maynard, born at Newton, Massachusetts, June 25, 1830; married, January 31, 1854, Martha Bartlett Glover, born at Orano, Maine, May 26, 1836, died at Methuen, December 8, 1896. Children: i. Jesse Maynard, born at Lawrence, December 31, 1858, married, March 4, 1897, Agnes Walker, daughter of Archibald and Janet (Walker) Gall, of Niel, East Lothian, Scotland. ii. Clara Minta, born at Lawrence, November 6, 1861, unmarried. 2. Harriet Gibson, born at Newton, May 4, 1834, died at Wayland, July 4, 1889; married, November 28, 1854, George A. Rice, of Wayland, where he was born August 21, 1822, died July 20, 1888, son of Samuel and Dorcas (Heard) Rice, descendant of Deacon Edmund Rice, who came to Sudbury from Barkhamstead, England, and was a pioneer of Sudbury in 1639, through Rice lineage: George A. (7); Samuel (6); Ezekiel (5), soldier in the revolution; Eliakim (4); Elisha (3); Thomas (2); Deacon Edmund Rice (1).

Eliakim Rice (4), son of Elisha Rice (3), was born at Sudbury, February 27, 1709, and lived there. He married, May 14, 1730, Mehitable, daughter of Daniel and Mehitable Livermore of Weston. Children, born in Sudbury: i. Mehitable, born September 10, 1731. ii. Daniel, born December 29, 1733. iii. Eliakim, born April 4, 1736. iv. Betty, married Ebenezer Johnson. v. Ezekiel. Ezekiel Rice (5), son of Eliakim Rice (4), was born in Sudbury, December 21, 1742; died January 23, 1835, at Wayland, formerly East Sudbury. He married, October 27, 1768, Eunice Cutting; she died at Wayland January 3, 1833; children: i. Susanna, born at Sudbury, September 10, 1769. ii. Ezekiel, born August 16, 1771, at Sudbury. iii. Eunice, born February 27, 1778, at East Sudbury. iv. Samuel, born August 12, 1783. v. Abel, born at East Sudbury, August 16, 1788. Samuel Rice (6), son of Ezekiel Rice, was born at East Sudbury, August 12, 1783, and lived at Wayland, where he married, June 15, 1815, Dorcas Heard, who died December 13, 1828; children, born at Wayland: i. Samuel L., August 14, 1818; died May 10, 1836. ii. George A., August 21, 1822. iii. Frederick D., November 13, 1827; died April 26, 1852. George Alonzo Rice (7), son of Samuel Rice, was born in Wayland, August 21, 1822; married January 6, 1848, Mary Bent, died August 16, 1849, daughter of William. He married second, Harriet Gibson Rutter. (See Rutter family). The only child of George A. Rice was Nellie Rutter Rice, born at Wayland, April 22, 1856, married, August 20, 1890, David Fuller Fiske, who was born in Dedham, February 7, 1836, enlisted in the civil war July 20, 1861, in Company H, Thirteenth Massachusetts Regiment Volunteers, and was mustered out August 1, 1864; Mrs. Fiske is regent of Wayside Inn Chapter, Daughters of the American Revolution. 3. William Frederick, born August 31, 1836, mentioned below. 4. George Henry, born at Wayland, November 21, 1841, married (second), January 15, 1881, Mrs. Olive Meserve; no children; residence, Franklin, Maine. 5. Helen Eliza, born at Wayland, August 22, 1847, died at Boston, March 14, 1879; married, January 3, 1864, Essex Saunders Abbott, of Lawrence; children: i. Essex Saunders, of Haverhill, born at Lynn, March 11, 1870, unmarried. ii. Vivian Irving, of Boston, born at Lynn, November 2, 1871, unmarried. 6. Edward Everett, born at Wayland, January 30, 1851; see forward. 7. Hon. Charles Gibson, born at Wayland, January 28, 1853; see forward.

The following obituary notice was published in the *Waltham Sentinel:* "Micah M. Rutter, who died in New Berne, North Carolina, on the 8th instant, was a native of Wayland, where he was born in 1806. Early in life he commenced business in West Newton as a trader, where he resided for a number of years, and where he is still remembered by the older inhabitants as a genial companion and an active business man. He afterwards moved to Cambridgeport. The discouragements incident to an unsuccessful mercantile career in time clouded his prospects and palsied his energies. Since the close of the war he has resided in North Carolina, a few miles out of New Berne, in a country thinly populated and mostly by negroes. To them he made himself quite useful and received their confidence and affection by his readiness to aid and advise them in their new duties and relations. His friends and relatives here will be glad to know that his 'last of earth' was cared for by the Masonic Fraternity of which he was a member, who rendered to the dying and the dead every needed service. The news of his death reached his friends here on the day of its occurrence by telegraph from the officers of the Lodge at New Berne. It is pleasant to know that there is one organization which from a fraternal sympathy and above all sectional and party ties can minister to the wants of a stranger in a strange land."

Major Micah M. Rutter was a man of excellent reputation, and respected by all who knew him. He was generous, large-hearted and benevolent, and many were the deeds of kindness performed by him. He exemplified in his life and daily walk the characteristics that make up the perfect man, and in all relations, whether of a public or private nature, faithfully performed the duties and obligations devolving upon him. Although his business career was not successful from a financial point of view, still he left behind him a name for honesty and uprightness, which is far better than great riches.

(VII) William Frederick Rutter, son of Major Micah Maynard Rutter (6), was born at Cambridge, Massachusetts, August 31, 1836. He was educated in the public schools, and learned the trade of machinist. He entered the employ of the Pemberton Mills, Lawrence, in 1858, and has lived since then in Lawrence. In 1866 he left the Pemberton Company to work for the Lawrence Gas Company. In 1869 he embarked in business on his own account, in the plumbing and steam heating business, on Appleton street, on the site of the old post-office. He was prosperous and accumulated a competence, retiring from active business, April 1, 1907. Mr. Rutter is president of the Broadway Savings Bank of Lawrence; president of the Bellevue Cemetery Association; director of the Merchants' National Bank; trustee of the Old People's Home. In politics he is a Republican; in religion he and his family are attendants of the Baptist church. He is a man of sterling character, and is held in the highest esteem by his townsmen. He married, December 27, 1860, Ann Maria Turner, born at Ellsworth, Maine, November 11, 1839, daughter of Thomas and Margaret (Lindsey) Turner, granddaughter of James Turner: Children: 1. William Frederick, Jr., born June 29, 1863, died at Hope, Kansas, January 1, 1895; married, (first) November 5, 1885, Ida A. Peabody, born at Salem, New Hampshire, March 2, 1866, died at Jacksonville, Florida, March 23, 1890; one child, William Peabody, born June 5, 1888; married (second), November 10, 1891, Ina Eliza Emery, born in Lawrence, July 30, 1869; children: i. Sylvia Josephine, born December 19, 1892, died September 4, 1893. ii. Walter Frederick, born August 18, 1894. 2. Annie, born February 30, 1865, died July 5, 1865. 3. Carrie Maria, born November 14, 1866, married, December 18, 1888, Elias E. Grimes, of Lawrence, Massachusetts, born September 13, 1866; children: i. Bertha Adeline, born March 9, 1890. ii. Mildred Louise, born December 20, 1892. iii. Carolyn R., born November 6, 1902. 4. Adeline, born 1868, died same year.

(VII) Edward Everett Rutter, son of Major Micah Maynard Rutter (6), was born in Wayland, Massachusetts, January 30, 1851, and spent his boyhood on the farm and was educated in the public schools of his native town. At the age of eighteen years he went to Lawrence, Massachusetts, to learn the plumbing and steam heating business in the employ of his brother, William F. Rutter, who afterward admitted him to partnership, and the firm continued until his death, July 23, 1902. He died at his home in Lawrence, and is buried in Bellevue Cemetery in that city. He was a skillful mechanic and a business man of

E. E. Rutten

Lewis Historical Pub Co.

sound judgment and strict integrity. In national politics Mr. Rutter was a Democrat; in municipal affairs he was independent. He was a member of the Winolancet Lodge of Red Men, of Lawrence. He married, November 5, 1890, Hannah Clara Rogers, born November 27, 1854, daughter of Francis and Hester Ann (George) Rogers. (See George family). Mrs. Rutter spent her youthful years in Iowa, and was educated in the public schools of Fort Atkinson, in Fayette Academy, and in the Medical School of Boston University, where she was graduated in the class of 1879. She began to practice her profession as soon as she came to Lawrence, March 5, 1879, and has continued to the present time with the utmost success. She is a member of the Gynecological and Surgical Society of Massachusetts, the Medical Society of Boston, the Homoeopathic Society of Massachusetts, and the Twentieth Century Society. Mr. and Mrs. Rutter had two children, born in Lawrence: Everett, February 14, 1893, and Harriet Esther, November 13, 1897.

Francis Rogers, father of Mrs. Hannah Clara Rogers, was born in Vermont in 1803, and died in Iowa, November 23, 1879. He resided in Lowell, Orleans county, Vermont, removed to Fort Atkinson, Iowa, where he was one of the first settlers, then to Missouri, returning to Iowa, where he passed the remainder of his life. He married in Lowell, Massachusetts, February 4, 1843, Hester Ann George, daughter of Josiah George Jr., of Sanbornton, New Hampshire. (See George family). They were married by Mr. Ebenezer Fisk. Children: 1. Martha George, born November 7, 1843; married Warren Ripley, of Cambridge, Massachusetts; she is now a practicing physician at Minneapolis, Minnesota. 2. George Henry, born August 30, 1845; married, 1870, Mary Metcalf; he is now a ranchman in Idaho, formerly in Audubon county, Iowa. 3. Benjamin Franklin, born September 15, 1850, a grocer at Lawrence, Massachusetts; married June 24, 1880, Harriet Frances Moulton. 4. Dr. Hannah Clara, born November 27, 1854, married Edward E. Rutter, of Lawrence, Massachusetts. (See Rutter family).

RUTTER (VII) Hon. Charles Gibson Rutter, son of Major Micah Maynard Rutter (6), was born in Wayland, Massachusetts, January 28, 1853. He was educated in the district schools of his native town, and his youth was spent on the farm until he was seventeen years old, when he left home and began an apprenticeship at the machinist's trade in the shops of Davis & Furber, at North Andover, Massachusetts. Two years later he found employment at Lawrence in the machine shops of the famous Pemberton mills. He worked for eight years in this position and acquired most valuable experience in the making and repairing of mill machinery. He was for five years after that in the employ of the Russell Paper Company of Lawrence. He left to accept the position of master mechanic for the Lippitt Woolen Company at Woonsocket, Rhode Island, but after a few years was called back to Lawrence by the Russell Paper Company to take the position of foreman and the superintendence of the steam plant of that corporation. He filled this position with signal ability, to the entire satisfaction of his employers from 1887 to 1900, when he resigned.

Mr. Rutter has had a notable public career. While living in Woonsocket he was elected chief of the fire department and filled that office two years. Upon his return to Lawrence he was appointed a member of the board of fire engineers by Mayor Lewis P. Collins, and in 1892 was reappointed for a term of three years by Mayor Henry P. Doe. Mr. Rutter is a Democrat in politics and has been active in his party. He was elected mayor of the city for 1894 and again for 1895, and served with ability. His administration was clean, businesslike and honorable. He resigned his position with the Russell Paper Company to accept the office of chief engineer of the fire department, a position for which he was admirably fitted by training and experience, as events have shown. He received his first appointment from Mayor James F. Leonard, was reappointed by Mayor Grant, and has been reappointed annually since by succeeding mayors. He is a member of Monadnock Lodge, I. O. O. F., and a past noble grand. He and his family attend the Baptist church. He married Ophelia A. Frost, daughter of Ira W. and Susan B. (Dunlap) Frost, of Canaan, Maine. They have an adopted daughter, Marion Stewart Rutter, born April 17, 1893.

GIBSON John Gibson, immigrant ancestor of this distinguished family, was born in England, 1601, and died in Cambridge, Massachusetts, 1694. He came to New England as early as 1631 and settled in Cambridge. He was admitted a freeman May 17, 1637. His home lot was granted in the west end of the town, August 4, 1634. It was located between Harvard and Brattle Squares, in what is now an important business district, and extended to the Charles river. His house stood at the end of what is now Sparks street, not far from Brattle street, on the road to Watertown, and was built before October 10, 1636. He was doubtless a member of Rev. Mr. Hooker's church, and belonged later to the succeeding society of First Church, February 1, 1636, under the pastorate of Rev. Thomas Shepard. He held minor town offices. His wife and daughter accused Winifred Holman, widow, and her daughter of witchcraft, and the charge not being sustained, they were sued for damage by the Holmans. For particulars of this interesting case, see "History of Holman Family." The Gibsons paid a small fine. John Gibson married first, Rebecca ———, who was buried December 1, 1661, at Roxbury; second, July 24, 1662, Joan, widow of Henry Prentice, a pioneer at Cambridge. Children, all by first wife: 1. Rebecca, born in Cambridge, 1635; married Charles Stearns, of Watertown; thought she was bewitched by the Holmans. 2. Mary, born May 29, 1637; died at Roxbury, December 6, 1674; married John Ruggles. 3. Martha, born April 29, 1639; married November 3, 1657, Jacob Newell of Roxbury. 4. John Jr., born about 1641; mentioned below. 5. Samuel, born October 28, 1644; died at Cambridge, March 20, 1709-10.

(II) John Gibson, son of John Gibson (1), was born in Cambridge, about 1641, and died October 15, 1679. He married, December 9, 1668, Rebecca Harrington, born in Cambridge, daughter of Abraham and Rebecca (Cutler) Harrington (or Errington, as it was spelled and perhaps pronounced). Her father was a blacksmith, born at Newcastle-on-Tyne, England, and died in Cambridge, May 9, 1677. Her mother died in Cambridge, 1697. John Gibson settled in Cambridge, on the homestead deeded to him by his father, November 30, 1668. He also was involved in the trial of his family for calling the Holmans witches, and had to acknowledge his error in court or pay a fine. He took the cheaper course. He was a soldier in King Philip's war, under Captain Thomas Prentice. He was in the Swanzey fight June 28, 1675, and in the Mt. Hope expedition later; also in Lieutenant Edward Oakes' troop scouting near Marlborough, March 24, 1675-6, and in Captain Daniel Henchman's company, September 23, 1676, which marched to Hadley in early summer time. He was possibly the John Gibson in Captain Joshua Scottow's company at Black Point, near Saco, Maine, September, 1677, where the garrison was captured the following month by the Indians. He was admitted a freeman October 11, 1670, and held a number of minor offices. He died of small pox when only thirty-eight years old. Children of John and Rebecca Gibson: 1. Rebecca, born at Cambridge, October 4, 1669; died at Woburn, June 10, 1698, unmarried. 2. Martha, married twice. 3. Mary, married at Concord, October 17, 1700, Nathaniel Gate of Stow. 4. Timothy, mentioned below.

(III) Timothy Gibson, son of John Gibson (2), was born at Cambridge, 1679, and died at Stow, July 14, 1757. His grave is in the lower village graveyard in the eastern part of Stow. He married first, at Concord, November 17, 1780, Rebecca Gates, of Stow, born in Marlborough, July 23, 1682, died in Stow, January 21, 1751, daughter of Stephen Jr. and Sarah (Woodward) Gates. He married second (published November 30) 1755, Mrs. Submit Taylor, of Sudbury, died at Stow, January 29, 1759, in her seventy-fifth year. Both wives are buried by his side. Deacon Gibson was brought up by Selectman Abraham Holman, of Cambridge, son of William and Winifred Holman, who were involved in the lawsuit with his parents and grandparents. In 1689 the Holmans removed to Stow and he went with them, living in the family until 1703, when they removed to the northwest part of Sudbury and settled on the Assabet river, on a sixty acre farm bounded on the west by the Stow line, on the east by the road from Concord to Jewell's mill. Holman died in 1711. Gibson was a prominent citizen of Sudbury and owned land also at Lunenburg, laid to him and his son Timothy. Neither ever lived at Luenburg, however, but John, Arrington, Isaac and Reuben, his younger sons, settled there, and all were noted as men of great personal prowess. He removed to Stow between December 6, 1728, and February 24, 1731-2, and was selectman there in 1734-35-36 and 39. His homestead in Stow lay on the south slope of Pomciticut Hill and was deeded ten years before his death to his son Stephen and was passed down in the family until 1823. This farm is now in the town of Maynard, which was formed from Sudbury and Stow in 1871. Children: 1. Abraham, born 1701; mentioned below. 2. Captain Timothy, born January 20, 1702-3. 3. Rebecca, born in Sudbury, March 19, 1703-4; married May 4, 1727, Joseph

Farnsworth, of Groton. 4. Captain John, born April 28, 1708; settled in Lunenburg. 5. Sarah, born October 27, 1710; married first, Thomas Willard, of Harvard. 6. Samuel, born August 27, 1713; died April 11, 1746. 7. Stephen, born March 14, 1715; died young. 8. Arrington, born March 22, 1717; died at Luenburg, July 15, 1795, aged seventy-eight years. 9. Deacon Stephen, born at Sudbury, June 16, 1719, died at Stow, October 23, 1806; married Sarah Goss. 10. Isaac, born at Sudbury, April 27, 1721; lived at Stow and Fitchburg, and Grafton, Vermont, (originally Tomlinson, New Hampshire and Vermont), where he died June 1, 1797. 11. Mary, born June 14, 1723. 12. Captain Reuben, born February 14, 1725; married Lois Smith; died July 27, 1800.

(IV) Abraham Gibson, son of Deacon Thomas Gibson (3), was born in Stow, 1701, and died there November 8, 1740. He married Mary Wheeler, born at Stow, November 5, 1707, died there January 15, 1793, daughter of Deliverance and Mary (Davis) Wheeler. Her father was born at Cambridge in 1663, and died at Stow, February 4, 1716; married May 28, 1691, Mary Davis, born at Concord, October 3, 1663, and died at Stow, June 27, 1748, daughter of Lieutenant Simon and Mary (Blood) Davis. Children of Lieutenant Simon and Mary (Blood) Davis: 1. Deliverance Davis, born June 5, 1691; settled in Stow, was selectman, assessor and treasurer. 2. Thomas Davis, baptized June 27, 1697. 3. Ephraim Davis, born 1702. 4. Mary Davis, above mentioned. Deliverance Wheeler was son of Thomas Wheeler, who died at Concord, December 10, 1676; married Ruth Wood, daughter of William and Mary Wood. He was captain of the second troop of horse, and by order he acted as escort July 27, 1675, to Captain Edward Hutchinson into the Nipmuck country. He was wounded August 2, 1675, in the ambuscade at Quaboag. He wrote an account of the expedition. Children: 1. Alice Wheeler, died March 17, 1640-1. 2. Nathaniel Wheeler, died January 16, 1676-7. 3. Joseph Wheeler of Stow. 4. Ephraim Wheeler, died February 19, 1689. 5. Thomas Wheeler, died January 9, 1676-7. 6. Deliverance Wheeler, above mentioned. Mary (Davis) Wheeler was descended on her mother's side from Simon and Dolor Davis of Cambridge.

Abraham Gibson was a namesake of Abraham Holman, with whom his father lived so many years. He removed from Sudbury to Stow. He was in Captain Nathan Bridgam's company, 1725; was assessor, 1733-4; constable, 1735-6; selectman 1732-33-39 and 40. His widow married Deacon Daniel Hapgood, who was a selectman of Stow. Children of Abraham and Mary Gibson, born at Stow: 1. Mary, born August 20, 1725, married Ezekiel, son of Deacon John and Abigail (Dudley) Davis (6), Ezekiel (5), Dr. John (4), Dr. Simon (3), Lieutenant Simon (2), and Dolor Davis (1). Among their children was Captain Isaac Davis who was killed at Concord Bridge, April 19, 1775. 2. Rebecca, born January 27, 1728; married Ensign Ephraim Hapgood. 3. Abraham, born August 26, 1730; died young. 4. Sarah, born August 26, 1732; married Peter Conant, of Stow. 5. Abraham, born June 25, 1735; mentioned below. 6. Ephraim, born October 23, 1737; died young. 7. Lieutenant Ephraim, born January 21, 1740; died at Ashby, 1825; married, 1761, Lucy Wyman, daughter of Ezekiel and Abigail (Wyman) Wyman; soldier in the revolution, in Captain Samuel Stone's company, Colonel William Prescott's regiment.

(V) Lieutenant Abraham Gibson, son of Abraham Gibson (4), was born at Stow, June 25, 1735, and died at Lunenburg, September 9, 1813. He resided at Stow, Concord and Fitchburg. He married (intention published January 13, 1760) Esther Fox, born at Concord, July 23, 1743, baptized at First Parish Church, July 24, 1743, and died at Rindge, New Hampshire, April 30, 1803, daughter of Thomas and Rebecca (French-Carey) Fox. Thomas Fox (4) housewright, was born at Concord, June 8, 1706, and died at Concord, July 30, 1759. He married Mrs. Rebecca (French) Carey, who died at Concord, November 22, 1745, daughter of Joseph and Elizabeth (Knight) French, of Bedford, and widow of James Carey. Samuel Fox (3) father of Thomas Fox (4), was born at Concord, September 11, 1670, and died there January 15, 1734. He married June 13, 1693, Ruth Knight, died at Concord, September 21, 1741, daughter of Jonathan and Ruth (Wright) Knight of Concord. Eliphalet Fox (2), father of Samuel Fox (3), died at Concord, August 15, 1711. He married October 26, 1665, Mary Wheeler, born at Concord, September 6, 1645, died December 24, 1678, daughter of George and Katherine Wheeler, pioneers in Concord in 1635-8. Thomas Fox (1) settled in Concord 1640 and was admitted a freeman there May 29, 1644. See sketch of Fox family elsewhere.

Lieutenant Gibson was in early life a schoolmaster, and taught in Lunenburg, but returned to Stow to the homestead. He afterward removed to Concord and about 1768 to Fitchburg. He resided on a farm of one hundred and fifty acres on the east slope of Pearl Hill. On March 25, 1786, he deeded part of the farm to Jeremiah Kinsman, of Ipswich. Lieutenant Gibson was a soldier in the French and Indian war, in Captain Abijah Hall's company, Colonel Willard's regiment, at Crown Point; also in the revolution, in Captain Ebenezer Wood's company, Colonel Asa Whitcomb's regiment, April 19, 1775. Children: 1. Thomas. 2. Esther, born at Concord, April 25, 1762; died at Grafton, Vermont, November 1, 1825. 3. Mary, born February 2, 1764; married William Wyman. 4. Rebecca, born November 15, 1765, married John Priest. 5. Sarah Gardner, born at Concord, September 5, 1767, married first, ——— Rosendell; second, Ebenezer Winter Calef. 6. Abraham, born September 1, 1769, died July 10, 1816; married first, Frances Davis; second, Mrs. Susan (Norcross) Spurr. 7. Lucy, born May 19, 1771; married June 30, 1795, Peter Adams. 8. John.

(VI) John Gibson, son of Abraham Gibson (5), was born at Fitchburg, March 20, 1776, and baptized at the First Church of Boston, April 25, 1776. He died at Boston, July 14, 1825, and is buried on Boston Common, in a tomb built by himself and his brother Abraham, "No. 89, Abraham and John Gibson's Tomb, 1800." He married at Boston, October 22, 1795, Phebe Low, baptized at Hollis Street church, January 30, 1797, and died at Boston, January 2, 1838, aged sixty-two. He was a leading business man of Boston, and was highly esteemed for his executive ability and thorough business qualifications. He was a distiller, and resided at No. 10, Warren street, near Hollis Street Church, of which he was a prominent member. Children: 1. Esther Fox, born January 14, 1797; married Warham Priest. 2. Phebe Low, born 1799; married Robert Bradford. 3. Abigail Pope, baptized July 1, 1810; died October 8, 1818. 4. John Fox, baptized July 1, 1810; died young. 5. Harriette, mentioned below. 6. Mary Ann, born May 25, 1813; died in New York City, January 10, 1853; married September 10, 1835, Asa Stone Crosby, a native of Shrewsbury, Massachusetts. 7. William Fox, born December 19, 1815; lost at sea; unmarried.

(VII) Harriette Gibson, daughter of John Gibson (6), was born at Boston, June 6, 1810, and baptized at the Hollis Street Church, July 1, 1810. She married May 1, 1829, Major Micah Maynard Rutter. (See Rutter family).

GEORGE The surname was a personal name, meaning originally farmer or earthworker in Greek, and has been in use from ancient times in England. Gideon George (1), progenitor of this family, sailed from England about 1680, with his wife and son Gideon. He settled in Salem, Massachusetts. One account says that he was from Yorkshire, another that he was from the city of Norwich, England. Children: 1. Gideon. 2. John, born on the voyage; mentioned below.

(II) John George, son of Gideon George (1), was born on the voyage, about 1680. He settled in Haverhill, Massachusetts. He signed the petition for a school house in the northeastern part of the town in 1711. He was drowned while attempting to cross the Merrimac river on the ice, February 27, 1715. He married, about 1700, Ann Swadock, who died February 7, 1763. Children: John Swadock, mentioned below; William; Augustine; Elizabeth; Gideon, born May 27, 1712, married, April 14, 1737, Elizabeth Jewett, had grandson named King.

(III) John Swadock George, son of John George (2), was born in Haverhill, December 25, 1702. The middle name was then extremely rare, and the writer knows of no other case as early as this in the colonies. Not till after the revolution did the practice become customary. One must believe, therefore, that the mother held her own family in high esteem. John Swadock George married three times. His third wife was Sarah Ash, born in Haverhill, March 11, 1728. Children: Josiah, mentioned below. Others by first and second wives. Children of third wife: 1. Austin, born 1763; married Sally Bradbury. 2. Nathaniel Ash, born October 16, 1769; married Apphia Moores, of Haverhill; settled in part of Greenfield now Bennington, New Hampshire. 3. Abigail, married Benjamin Moody. And two others.

(IV) Josiah George, believed to be son of John Swadock George (3), was born about 1740-50. He was a soldier in the revolution, in Captain Richard Weare's company, Third New Hampshire Battalion; enlisted in the Continental service April 1, 1777, and died September 20, 1778, then of Captain Isaac Frye's company, Colonel Alexander Scammell's regiment. This company was from Haverhill and vicinity. George was of Hampton in 1777, and perhaps proprietor of the historical George Tavern at Hampton Falls. The history of Hampton states that his wife and infant were burned to death when his house was burned. His son Josiah rescued two sisters. The home was at Hampton or New Hampton, New Hampshire. Children: 1. Josiah, Jr., mentioned below. 2. Two sisters.

(V) Josiah George, son of Josiah George (4), was born about 1765-70. He was apprenticed to Nathaniel Piper, of Sanbornton, New Hampshire, after his father's death. He married, about 1793, Peace Hodgdon, of Northfield, and they settled on a farm between the turnpike and the old road to New Hampton, lot 47, Second Division. He died of palsy, March 25, 1847. His wife was born November, 1774, was baptized by Rev. John Crockett, in 1801, in the Free Will Baptist Church, at New Hampton, and died at the home of her son, September 13, 1858, aged eighty-three years, ten months. Children, born at Sanbornton: 1. Charlotte, born September 24, 1792, (adopted); married Jonathan Cate, of Canterbury. 2. Josiah, born September 9, 1794; married Eliza Hanaford; second, ——— Miller, of Ryegate, Vermont. 3. Hannah, born August 31, 1796; married Chase Hodgdon. 4. Polly, born April 3, 1799; died unmarried, November 30, 1850. 5. Edmund Hodgdon, born March 7, 1801. 6. Mehitable, born February 23, 1803; married Josiah E. Morrison, of Bridgewater. 7. King, born November 12, 1804, farmer at Reading, Massachusetts. 8. Olive, born September 15, 1806, died of quinsy, August 23, 1818. 9. Benaiah Sanborn, born July 11, 1808; died January 20, 1829. 10. Hester Ann, born January 19, 1810; mentioned below. 11. Huldah S., born May 27, 1812; married John Plummer. 12. John Kezer, born November 12, 1816; teacher in Arkansas.

(VI) Hester Ann George, daughter of Josiah George, Jr., (5), was born January 19, 1810, at Sanbornton, New Hampshire. She married February 4, 1843, Francis Rogers. (See Rogers).

(For ancestry see John Rutter 1).

RUTTER (VI) Josiah Rutter, son of General Micah Maynard Rutter, born in Wayland, March 2, 1813, died September 3, 1876, in Waltham, Massachusetts. He was educated in the public schools of his native town and at Harvard College, where he was graduated. During his boyhood he worked on his father's farm, and after leaving college taught school for some years in Wayland and Brighton. He was the first teacher in the high school at Waltham. In the meantime he studied law and was admitted to the Massachusetts bar, entering the legal practice in Waltham and Boston. He was trial justice in Waltham for eighteen years, and served twenty years on the school committee of the town, fourteen years of which he was chairman of the board. He was elected as representative to the general court, and served two terms. He was active in church work also, and was a member of the First Parish Unitarian Church of Waltham. He served on the parish committee for a number of years. He was a man of considerable literary attainment, and naturally gifted in writing, and his productions as an author were remarkable for their purity of style. On July 4, 1876, he delieved the centennial oration at Waltham. He was a frequent contributor to the local press. He married Abigail Eliza Baldwin, born at Brighton, April 15, 1821, died at Waltham, May 14, 1889, daughter of Henry and ——— (Brackett) Baldwin. Children: 1. William B., born November 9, 1848, died November 24, 1888. 2. Frederick Plympton, born August 16, 1851; mentioned below. 3. Francis Josiah, born September 8, 1854, died January 28, 1894; married Fanny Howe and had Francis W. and Katherine. 4. Nathaniel Plympton, born 1857, died July 9, 1907; married Elizabeth Lang, and had Robert, Josiah and Elliott.

The following is an extract from the obituary notice of Mr. Rutter in the *Waltham Free Press:* "Mr. Rutter has held many positions of public trust through a long series of years, enjoying in large measure the confidence of his fellow townsmen, who likewise frequently turned to him in seasons of intellectual requirement as to one whose ready pen and voice could be depended upon. For many of the closing years of his life Mr. Rutter was not apparently closely connected with either of the great political parties. Neither of them seemed to have his full confidence and sympathy, so we judge in part from the leading editorials in the *Sentinel,* which have been understood as from his pen. But while evincing a lack of confidence in some leading men, his words were ever for an honest government, and for the subsidence of partisan feelings."

(VII) Frederick Plympton Rutter, son of Josiah Rutter, was born at Waltham, August 16, 1851. He was educated in the public and high school of Waltham. He began his business career in the employ of Phineas Upham in the dry goods business. He was next employed by the firm of Clark, Maynard & Company, of Waltham, remaining with them seven years. At this time he and his brother, William B. Rutter, formed a partnership and engaged in the coal business, later selling out to J. A. Wellington & Company. Mr. Rutter remained as manager for the Wellington Company for four years, when the business was again sold to W. A. Hunnewell, who in turn sold it to the Waltham Coal Company, incorporated July 2, 1894. Mr. Rutter has been president of the company since its incorporation. He has always been interested in town affairs. He has served on the cemetery board for seven years, four as chairman. In 1897, when he was appointed as an assessor, he relinquished his office on the cemetery board, and has remained on the board of assessors up to the present time. He is a member of the First Parish Unitarian Church, and of the parish committee. He is past master of Monitor Lodge of Free Masons, of Waltham. He married Minnie Holden Upham, born August 22, 1852, daughter of Samuel O. and Sarah (Maynard) Upham. (See sketch). Children: 1. Abby Baldwin, born October 20, 1879. 2. May, died young.

UPHAM The surname Upham is derived from the Anglo-Saxon words *Up* and *Hame,* signifying a home, dwelling or village. At first the final "e" was used, but was finally dropped. The first mention of the surname in England occurs in a deed in 1208 of land to the church of St. Maria de Bradenstock, by Hugo de Upham. Upham is also a place name given to various villages and parishes in England and Ireland.

(I) John Upham, immigrant ancestor, was probably of Somersetshire, England, and came to New England in the company with Rev. Joseph Hull, known as Hull's colony, in 1635. With him were his wife Elizabeth, (probably Webb) aged thirty-two; Sarah Upham, probably his sister, aged twenty-six, and his children—John, Jr., aged seven; Nathaniel, five, and Elizabeth, three. They settled at Weymouth, where he was admitted a freeman September 2, 1635. In 1636 he drew land at Weymouth, and added to it from time to time by purchase and by drawing. He was a prominent figure in the colony from the outset, and was one of the six who treated with the Indians for lands at Weymouth. He was appointed a commissioner to try small causes. He was selectman in 1645-46-47, and a deputy to the general court. He removed to Malden about 1648, and was elected selectman there in 1651-52-53. He was a commissioner also for Malden. In August, 1671, he married second, ——— Holland—probably Katheryn, widow of Angell Holland. He was moderator of town meetings in Malden in 1678-79-80. He was deacon of the church twenty-four years. He and his son were interested in the settlement of Worcester at the time of King Philip's war. He died February 25, 1681, aged eighty-four years. Children: 1. John, born in England, 1627. 2. Nathaniel, born in England, May 23, 1629-30; married Elizabeth Steadman, March 5, 1661-2; died March 20, 1661-62; widow married, 1669, Henry Thompson. 3. Elizabeth, born 1632; married Thomas Welch, and had thirteen children; died January 12, 1705-06. 4. Phineas, born probably 1635; mentioned below. 5. Mary, married John Whittemore; died June 27, 1677. 6. Priscilla, married Thomas Crosswell, and had twelve children; died December 8, 1717.

(II) Lieutenant Phineas Upham, son of John Upham, was born in 1635, at Weymouth, or during the voyage from England. He bought land in Malden in 1663, and resided there. In 1673 he surveyed a road from Malden to Cambridge, and in 1672 he first became interested in the settlement of Worcester, with other Malden settlers. He drew a lot of fifty acres July 8, 1673, in consideration of his services in promoting the colony. The grant was confirmed in April, 1675. He was commissioned lieutenant in September, 1675, in King Philip's war. The forces met the Indians in battle December 19, 1675. In this fight, which is known as the storming of Fort Canonicus, or the battle of the Great Swamp Fort, he was mortally wounded, and with other wounded was carried to Wickford from the field of battle. He was sent to Rhode Island, January 6, 1675-76, and later was sent to his home in Malden. The march from Rhode Island is called the "Hungry March." There was much suffering from lack of food and the horses were killed and eaten on the way. In October, 1676, he died. The general court made a special appropriation to pay the cost of his long illness and gave the widow ten pounds, as she was left with seven small children to support. The Upham genealogy says of him: "In battle Lieutenant Upham exhibited the character of a brave man and patriot, purchasing with mortal wounds the palm of victory, and the government was not unmindful of his great sacrifice; but bore testimony upon the records to the long and good services he did to the country and the great loss sustained by his friends in his death." He married, April 14, 1658, Ruth Wood, died January 18, 1696-97, aged sixty, widow of Edward Wood, who died in Charlestown, August 20, 1642. Children: 1. Phineas, born May 22, 1659. 2. Nathaniel, born 1661. 3. Ruth, born 1664, died December 8, 1676. 4. John, born December 9, 1666; married Abigail Hayward, of Howard. 5. Elizabeth; married, October 28, 1691, Samuel Green. 6. Thomas, born 1668; mentioned below. 7. Richard, born 1675.

(III) Thomas Upham, son of Lieutenant Phineas Upham, born in Malden, 1668, died November 26, 1735, in his sixty-seventh year. His gravestone marks his grave at Wakefield, formerly Reading. He resided on the homestead in Malden, which was annexed to Reading in 1727, and is now Wakefield. He married first, in 1693, Elizabeth Hovey, of Topsfield, who died February 16, 1703-04, aged thirty-two. He married second, October 2, 1704, Mary Brown, of Reading, who died 1707. He married third, Ruth (Cutler) Smith, born 1688, died May 17, 1758, daughter of Thomas Cutler, of Reading, who was a descendant of John Cutler, of Hingham, in 1637, and widow of John Smith, of Charlestown. Children of first wife: 1. Thomas, born 1694; mentioned below. 2. Elizabeth, born 1695; married, 1726, Joseph Woolson. 3. Abijah, born 1698. 4. Nathan, born 1701. Child of second wife: 5. Josiah, born 1705. Child of third wife: 6. Joseph, born April 14, 1712.

(IV) Thomas Upham, son of Thomas Upham, baptized at Topsfield, November 18, 1694, died September 25, 1729-30. He and his wife were members of the church at Malden in 1721. He was a miller by trade, and bought lands in Weston in 1724, near James Spike's and the Four Mile Brook. He married first, Ruth Smith, daughter of John and Ruth Smith. She died in Weston, in 1722, aged twenty-eight. He married second, in 1723, Elizabeth Bullard, died 1753, widow of John Bullard. Children of first wife: 1. Ruth, born August 31, 1716, at Charlestown, baptized at Reading, October 4, following; married, March 2, 1736, David Green; died August 11, 1755. 2. Thomas, born June 30, 1718; mentioned below. 3. Jabez, born at Weston, died 1720. Child of second wife: 4. Elizabeth, born 1723-24; married, 1753, Abijah Fisk; married second, 1775, Colonel John Trowbridge.

(V) Thomas Upham, son of Thomas Upham, was born in Charlestown, June 30, 1718. He resided in Weston and was a farmer. He was a pious man, and a deacon of the church. It is said that it was his custom during a thunder storm to assemble the farm help and the family in the large kitchen of the house and to read the Bible and offer prayer while the storm lasted. He died on a communion Sunday, of apoplexy, October 17, 1780, aged sixty-two. The following poem appears on his gravestone:

"Here the clay form in hope to rise,
Of Dea. Thomas Upham lies;
Sixty-two years measured his race,
Thirteen of which in deacon's place,
With other trusts he did sustain;
But God ordains the wise and just,
Like other men must mix with dust."
Composed by his pastor,
Parson Kendall.

He married first, in 1740-41, Ruth Hammond, of Waltham, died June 2, 1749. He married second, March 18, 1750, Susanna Myrick, who died January 22, 1772, aged forty-five. He married third, September 17, 1772, Martha Williams, of Newton, who died at Pembroke, New Hampshire, aged ninety-two. Child of first wife: 1. Ruth, born September 3, 1742; married, April 1, 1762, Noah Norcross; married second, Josiah Myrick. Children of second wife: 2. Susanna, born September 21, 1751; married, May 20, 1773, Joseph Russell. 3. Thomas, born July 21, 1762, died January 10, 1776. 4. Lydia, born February 7, 1765; married Micah Fisk, February 5, 1789. Children of third wife: 5. Nathan, born June 20, 1773; mentioned below. 6. Amos, born October 4, 1774, died unmarried, July 1, 1803. 7. Jonathan, born January 4, 1776; married Mehitable Whiting. 8. Thomas, born March 1, 1777; married, October 7, 1800, Sarah Fanning. 9. Ephraim, born November 3, 1778, married Hannah Cushman. 10. Patty (Martha), born December 9, 1780—posthumous—married Ezra Fuller.

(VI) Nathan Upham, son of Thomas Upham, born in Weston, June 20, 1773, died June 16, 1812. He resided two years in Waltham, engaged in the manufacture of paper, and then returned to the homestead at Weston. He married, November 22, 1798, Lydia Dix, of Waltham, who died in Framingham, August 18, 1872. Children: 1. Amos, born in Waltham, June 18, 1800; married, March, 1825, Elmira Hobbs. 2. Charles, born in Waltham, November 9, 1801; married Elizabeth Curtis. 3. Otis, born about 1802, in Waltham; mentioned below. 4. Nathan, born in Weston, April 27, 1804; married Mary R. Bradlee. 5. Eliza Dix, born in Weston, June 10, 1808; married Joseph Curtis; married second, Phineas Upham. 6. Thomas, born August 14, 1811; married Clarissa Ellenwood.

(VII) Otis Upham, son of Nathan Upham, was born about 1802. He married Mary Cary. Children: 1. Samuel Otis, born January 21, 1824; mentioned below. 2. Mary Jane, born November 10, 1825. 3. Martha Maria, born August 26, 1828. 4. Charles Lewis, born August 12, 1831. 5. George Lewis, born December 14, 1833. 6. Charles Frederick, born December 17, 1836. 7. Esther Elizabeth, born December 10, 1839. 8. Lydia Ann, born August 22, 1841. 9. Henry Harrison, born May 12, 1843. 10. Edward Payson, born December 19, 1845.

(VIII) Samuel Otis Upham, son of Otis Upham, born in Waltham, January 21, 1824, married, May 23, 1849, Sarah Maynard, at Waltham, born Sudbury, March 6, 1824, daughter of Warren Maynard. Children: 1. Frederick W., born May 6, 1850; married Elizabeth Rice; children: Samuel R. and Roger M. 2. Minnie Holden, born August 22, 1852; married Fred P. Rutter (see sketch). 3. Emma; married J. A. Higgins; child, Mildred Higgins. 4. Frank, born January 14, 1859; unmarried.

OSBORNE This family is one of the oldest and withal one of the most respectable of the many that became seated in the ancient town of Salem within the ten years next following the landing of the Pilgrims; and in the mother country as well as in New England they who bore the Osborne surname were noted for respectability and high moral character. The Yorkshire Osbornes were also an ancient people, and genealogists have given them great antiquity in countries of Europe. In various records the name is found written Osborne and Osborn in the same general family, the use or disuse of the final letter being merely a matter of taste.

In the records of Essex deeds (iii, p. 292) is found the following conveyance which gives some light in respect to the place of abode of the Osbornes in England:

"May 24, 1670. Bezaliell Osbourne of South Hampton, within the precincts of East Riding of Yorkshire, Eng., attorney to Friswiel Mulford of East Hampton of said riding (as in an instrument bearing date May 14, 1670, more fully doth appear) sendeth greeting: That said Bezaliel Osborne in consideration of a valuable sum paid by Antipas Newman of Wenham, Mass., preacher of the word of God, deed him a farm of 100 acres of upland and 10 of meadow, according to the grant of Salem, many years ago unto William Osborne, then husband of the said Friswiel Mulford, lying in Wenham, Mass.—with consent of her husband John Mulford—that the said Bezaliel Osbourne by virtue of his power of attorney from Friezwood Mulford his mother and John Mulford her husband has lawful authority to grant, etc.

Thomasin Collacut, Joseph Osbourne, wit.

"Signed, BEZALIEL OSBOURNE."

(I) William Osborne, of Salem, colony of Massachusetts Bay, Puritan, immigrant ancestor of a notable family, first appears there in 1630, was made freeman May 22, 1639, having been granted on June 4, 1636, with Ananias Concklane, an acre of land each for a houselot, near Strongwater brook; and besides his houselot William Osborne had another grant of ten acres of land.

In speaking of William Osborne, of Salem, in his "Genealogical Dictionary," Savage says that by wife called (in Felt's list of church members, 1641) Frezwith or Freesweed, had no children born there, but after his removal to Dorchester the town records there mention that by wife Frodisword he had Recompense, born May 26, 1644, at six o'clock p. m. The same authority also states that this Recompense Osborne graduated from Harvard College in 1661; that at Braintree he had: Hannah, born August 24, 1646, Bezaliel, born March 8, 1650, "and others afterward at Boston, by wife called in the records Fredswith, and in the Providence records by wife called Freesword, he had Joseph, born April 6, 1652, and Jonathan, born November 16, 1656. Further, says Savage, he was a merchant and died in middle life; that the inventory of his property, made April 29, 1662, shows over one thousand pounds, "well for that time." His widow married John Mulford, of South Hampton, Yorkshire East Riding, and in 1670 "sold to Rev. Antipas Newman, of Wenham, that 110 acres granted to Osborne."

From what is stated above it will be seen that William Osborne left Salem sometime after 1642, and lived in Dorchester at the date of birth of his son Recompense; that soon afterward he was in Braintree, where he had children born, and still later was in Boston, where, it is said, other children may have been born. He ultimately removed to Rhode Island and died there. It may be said, however, that the foregoing record of the immigrant's children cannot be taken as correct in all respects and that at least one of them, William, is not mentioned there. Mr. Austin, author of "One Hundred and Sixty Allied Families," himself an Osborne by descent, gives Wapping, England, as the birthplace of William, and the date about 1640. It has been asserted that William Osborne, the second, was a son of William and Frizwiel Osborne, but it seems impossible that he could have been born in England about 1640 (or 1644, as some accounts have it) for his father had then been ten years in New England, and his places of abode during the years subsequent to his landing in Salem are satisfactorily shown—therefore the only reasonable assumption is that he was born in Salem or possibly in Dorchester. (See footnote, where Recompense is called eldest).

(II) William Osborne, son of William Osborne, the immigrant, was born about 1640, died in Salem January, 1728-29; will proved February 5, 1730. He married, March 17, 1672, Hannah, born 1640, died about 1721, daughter of Captain John Burton, of Salem, who was a tanner there as early as 1637, and according to well authenticated accounts came from England to New England by way of the Barbadoes, from which it may be assumed that he was transported to the island in one of the ships sent there with political or religious prisoners, and thence made his way to the colonies in New England. Being a sympathizer with the Friends, he evidently found little real comfort or safe refuge from religious persecution, for in 1658, charged with the "heinous" crime of being a Quaker, he and Josiah Southwick were arrested at Dedham while on their way to Rhode Island to provide an abiding place for their families in that locality. They were soon released and went on to Rhode Island, remained there less than two years and then returned to Salem. Children of William and Hannah (Burton) Osborne: 1. Samuel, born April 27, 1675, see forward. 2. John, August 27, 1677. 3. Hannah, October 2, 1679; married November 26, 1701, John Trask, Jr. 4. William, May 3, 1682; married February 8, 1710, Margaret Derby.

(III) Samuel Osborne, eldest child of William and Hannah (Burton) Osborne, was born in Salem, April 27, 1675, and died about 1750. He married first, Ellinor Southwick, who was born June 25, 1674, died 10mo. 26d. 1702, daughter of Daniel and Esther (Boyce) Southwick, and granddaughter of Lawrence and Cassandra Southwick. Lawrence Southwick came in the "Mayflower" in 1629; was made freeman in Salem in 1639; had land given him in 1637; was a glassblower by trade, although a farmer by principal occupation. In the same year the town made grants of land to the "glassmen," and in 1641 the general court voted that if the town of Salem would loan the glassmen the sum of thirty pounds it would be repaid out of the next rate and the glassmen should repay the town the sum advanced them "if the works succeed, when they are able." How long this primitive industry was maintained does not appear, but it was operated for some time, and probably was the first of its kind in the country. In 1658 Goodman Southwick and his wife Cassandra and their son Josiah were imprisoned for being Quakers, and were confined in the Boston jail twenty weeks. They frankly admitted that they were Friends, and were fined, but being unable to pay were subsequently released and banished from the colony.

Samuel Osborne married second, 6mo. 30d. 1705, Sarah, daughter of Abraham Clark, of Oyster River. He had four children by each wife: 1. Samuel, born 2d mo. 4th d., 1697. 2. Elizabeth, 1st mo. 14th d. 1699. 3. Hannah, 11th mo. 14th d., 1700. 4. Joseph, 10th mo. 26th d., 1702. 5. Thomas, 4th mo. 1st d., 1706. 6. Sarah, 11th mo. 4th d., 1707. 7. Mary, 7th mo. 27th d., 1709. 8. Isaac, 2d mo. 13th d., 1711.

(IV) Joseph Osborne, son of Samuel and Eleanor (Southwick) Osborne, was born 8 mo., 26, 1702, and died after November 17, 1780, will proved December 4, 1780. He married first, Rachel Foster, died before 1734, and second, Sarah Gardner. Children: 1. Joseph, born August 6, 1726; see forward. 2. Rachel, baptized September 29, 1734. 3. Ginger, baptized September 29, 1734. 4. Eunice, baptized December 19, 1736. 5.

NOTE—Probate Court, Suffolk Registry of Deeds, Boston. William Osburne, administration of his estate granted his late wife and relict (26th August, 1662) in behalfe of her selfe and five children. "10 Sept. 1662, on the motion of Mr. Richard Collecott in behalf of freesweed Osborne widow and her five children it being alleadged that the *eldest* sonne Recompense was brought up in learning and had tooke one degree and therefore desired that he might have but a single portion with the rest.' The Court allowed that the widow shall, after all debts be payd and satisfied, be allowed one cleere third part of the estate * * * and that the rest of the estate to be divided amongst the five children part and parcel alike. (From "Pioneers of Mass" by Pope) (William Osborne, merchant, Hingham, propr 1635). William Osborne Salem propr., town officer, freeman May 22, 1639; went to Braintree to become of the Iron Works; son at Braintree [Recompense] born at Dorchester May 26, 1644, being born at the home of his brother.

Israel, baptized May 27, 1739. 6. Mehitable, baptized November 15, 1741; married first, February 9, 1764, Ezra Porter; second, Sylvester Proctor. 7. Abel, baptized August 18, 1745, died young. 8. Abel, baptized November 9, 1746; married Lydia, daughter of Gideon Foster, Sr. 9. Aaron, born November 15, 1742, died February 8, 1803; married March 24, 1774, Lydia Proctor.

(V) Joseph Osborne, eldest son of Joseph Osborne, was born in Salem, 8 mo. 26, 1726, and died July 9, 1804. He married January 6, 1756, Mary Proctor, born December 13, 1733, died January 6, 1791, a descendant of John Proctor, a witchcraft martyr. Children: 1. Joseph, born January 5, 1757, died August 27, 1829; married first, Mary Shillaber; second, Judith Francis. 2. Sylvester, November 10, 1758, died October 2, 1845; married first, Susanna Southwick; second, Elizabeth Poole; third, Mrs. L. W. Sanders. 3. Rachel, January 31, 1761, died December 27, 1813; married Jonathan Howard, born August 10, 1783, died March 22, 1826. 4. Jonathan, August 30, 1763, died July 29, 1833; married Susanna Smith. 5. John, November 22, 1765; see forward. 6. Daniel, September 10, 1768, died February 11, 1826; married Mehitable Proctor. 7. Amos, April 2, 1773, died June 21, 1836; married Nancy Fowler. 8. Mary, August 14, 1779, died June 1, 1850.

(VI) John Osborne, fifth child of Joseph and Mary (Proctor) Osborne, was born in Danvers, (formerly Salem prior to 1752, Danvers until 1855, South Danvers until 1868, and since that Peabody), Massachusetts, November 3, 1845. He married, March 22, 1784, Lydia Southwick, descendant of Lawrence and Cassandra, born November 1, 1766, died January 7, 1834. Children: 1. Betsey, born June 23, 1785, died April 16, 1869; married November 3, 1805, Jonathan Dustin. 2. Lydia, April 8, 1787, died September 25, 1869; married May 23, 1807, Samuel Stanley, died September 11, 1818. 3. Henry, July 4, 1789, died December 23, 1855; married February 4, 1810, Betsey Snow. 4. Miles, May 16, 1792, died March 23, 1793. 5. Miles, March 6, 1794, died January 30, 1873; married first, December 17, 1820, Eliza Poor; second, Sally Brown. 6. Kendall, July 22, 1796; see forward. 7. Polly, January 25, 1799 died November 28, 1800. 8. Polly, February 4, 1801, died September 13, 1879; married October 27, 1822, Henry Poor. 9. Franklin, born February 9, 1803, died December 16, 1883; married October 2, 1828, Nancy Poor Jacobs, born 1804, died November 17, 1885, daughter of Benjamin and Sally (Poor) Jacobs. 10. Susanna Southwick, May 22, 1805, died July 22, 1891; married July 31, 1827, Samuel Cheever, born Salem, December 8, 1799, died Peabody, July 8, 1876, son of Samuel and Deborah (Osborn) Cheever (Deborah Osborn 5, George Osborn 4, William 3, William 2, William 1). Susanna Southwick (Osborn) Cheever's children: Serena Dustin Cheever, born November 27, 1828, died July 4, 1850, married June 18, 1849, Angevine Ferguson, born October 9, 1822, died February 12, 1854; Eliza Sutton Cheever, born May 17, 1830, married May 4, 1851, Louis Osborn, born January 5, 1829, died September 25, 1872; John Osborn Cheever, born February 10, 1835, married Georgiana Ferrin, November 5, 1867. 11. John, born July 18, 1807, died July 19, 1814.

(VII) Kendall Osborn, sixth child of John and Lydia (Southwick) Osborn, was born July 22, 1796, and died October 16, 1875. He married first, Sally Bushby, born July 17, 1798, died February 19, 1849, daughter of Asa and Lydia (Wilson) Bushby; second, June 5, 1851, Susan, born December 20, 1807, daughter of Sylvester Osborn. Children: 1. Sally, born April 17, 1825. 2. Caroline, March 18, 1827. 3. Kendall, May 1, 1829. 4. Benjamin G., March 26, 1831. 5. Louisa, July 7, 1833. 6. Lyman, April 2, 1835.

(VIII) Lyman Osborn, youngest child of Kendall and Sally (Bushby) Osborn, was born April 2, 1835. He married, January 6, 1859, Maria T. Perley, born January 29, 1839, daughter of Proctor Jefferson and Lydia H. (Perkins) Perley (see Perley).

(IX) Lyman Perley Osborn, only child of Lyman and Maria T. (Perley) Osborn, was born September 22, 1860, and married October 4, 1892, Elizabeth Cheever, daughter of Louis and Eliza Sutton (Cheever) Osborn.

(III) John Osborne, second son and child of William and Hannah (Burton) Osborne, was born in Salem, August 27, 1677, died August, 1744. He married first, May 9, 1704, Mercy, born 1676, daughter of Daniel and Esther (Boyce) Southwick; second, May 7, 1713, Hannah, daughter of Caleb and Hannah (Pope) Buffum, and granddaughter of Robert and Tamasin (Thompson) Buffum of Salem. Robert Buffum was a farmer and trader, and both he and his wife were Friends, frequently fined for not attending the regular established church and were punished because they were Quakers. John Osborne had children: 1.

Esther, born March 27, 1705; married April 17, 1726, Jonathan Marsh, of Sutton. 2. John, July 28, 1707, died August, 1760. 3. Mercy. 4. Hannah, January 18, 1717; married March 21, 1735, Jonathan Southwick, of Mendon. 5. Jacob, September 4, 1719.

(IV) Jacob Osborne, son of John Osborne, was born September 4, 1719, at Salem (now Peabody), died between April 20 and December 6, 1773. He married Anna, daughter of Daniel and Ruth Purington. Children: 1. Elijah, born 1747; married, October 13, 1770, Susannah Buffum. 2. Jacob, born March 29, 1750; married Abigail Simpson; removed to Epping. 3. Joshua, born 1756, died January 28, 1794; married, February 7, 1778, Susannah Codner. 4. Micajah, born 1759. 5. Caleb, born May 1, 1760; see forward. 6. John, born 1763, died November 16, 1819; married widow Rebecca Roberts, who died July 30, 1824. 7. Damaris, born November 5, 1767; married first, William Endicott; second, Samuel Endicott, cousin of William. 8. Nannie, never married.

(V) Caleb Osborne, son of Jacob and Anna (Purington) Osborne, was born in Danvers, May 1, 1760, and died there May 4, 1827. He married, in Danvers, June 30, 1785, Hannah Trask, born June 29, 1766, died September 28, 1844, daughter of Amos and Hannah (Goldthwaite) Trask, and a descendant of Thomas Goldthwaite, Ezekiel Cheever the schoolmaster, Captain William Trask, Edmund Batters and Hannah, daughter of William and Hannah (Burton) Osborne. Caleb and Hannah (Trask) Osborne had children: 1. Hannah, born May 26, 1786, died May 5, 1803. 2. Caleb, August 19, 1788, died June 18, 1789. 3. Abigail, February 10, 1790, died same day. 4. Mehitable, August 3, 1791, died October 26, 1795. 5. Caleb, November 20, 1796. 6. Amos, February 12, 1794; married Lavinia White. 7. Hetty, June 3, 1800, died young. 8. Jacob, August 2, 1802, died November 1, 1804.

(VI) Caleb Osborne, son of Caleb and Hannah (Trask) Osborne, was born November 20, 1796, and died September 5, 1872. He married, May 25, 1820, Elizabeth Galeucia, born December 13, 1799, died July 29, 1886, daughter of Jacob and Sally (Newhall) Galeucia, the former a son of Daniel and Hannah (Lindsley) Galeucia. Hannah Lindsey was daughter of Captain Eleazer Lindsey, a descendant of Thomas Maule. Daniel Galencia was lieutenant in Captain Lindsey's company, and on account of the ill health of the latter officer he left the service and the command devolved on "Captain" Lieutenant Galeucia. Sally Newhall was born December 9, 1774, died April 18, 1846, daughter of Nathaniel Newhall, a Revolutionary soldier (son of Joseph 5, Joseph 4, Joseph 3, Thomas 2, Thomas 1). Caleb and Elizabeth (Galencia) Osborne had children: 1. Caleb Warren, born April 4, 1821, died June 5, 1894. 2. Hannah, June 7, 1823, died February 10, 1889; married October 1, 1846, James Wilson. 3. Louis, January 5, 1829, died September 25, 1872; married May 4, 1851, Eliza Sutton Cheever. 4. Jacob, December 25, 1830; married July 31, 1853, Hannah Richards Ferrin. 5. Elizabeth, July 7, 1835, died July 31, 1837. 6. Elizabeth, November 10, 1839, died October 25, 1861; married November 25, 1860, Lieutenant Charles Boardman Warner, of Company H, Nineteenth Massachusetts Volunteers, killed at battle of Fair Oaks, Virginia, June 25, 1862, aged twenty-seven years three months.

(III) William Osborne, son of William and Hannah (Burton) Osborne, was born May 3, 1682, and died September 29, 1771. He married February 8, 1710, Margaret Derby, born August 14, 1693, died July 11, 1765, daughter of Roger and his second wife, Elizabeth (Haskett) Derby. Children: 1. William, born August 18, 1711, died July 6, 1712. 2. Stephen, October 16, 1712. 3. Elizabeth, December 10, 1714. 4. William, February 12, 1716. 5. Benjamin, May 31, 1718. 6. Margaret, September 13, 1719. 7. Jonathan, about 1722. 8. Richard, died 1765. 9. Abigail, born 1733. 10. Benjamin, June, 1735.

(IV) William Osborne, son of William and Margaret (Derby) Osborne, was born February 12, 1716, and died in 1765. He married November 3, 1737, Elizabeth Tucker, born 1719, died January 17, 1809. Their children: George, William, Margaret, Elizabeth.

(V) George Osborne, son of William and Elizabeth (Tucker) Osborne, was born in Salem, in 1738, and died there June 17, 1808. He married Deborah Stearns, descendant of Samuel Appleton, Richard Jacobs and Simon Willard, and by her had children: 1. Deborah, baptized 1771, died in infancy. 2. Deborah, born November 27, 1772, died June 4, 1850. 3. George, married, in 1795, Eliza Deland, and died October 16, 1800; lost at sea; father of Dr. George Osborne, Sr., of Danvers, now Peabody.

(VI) Deborah Osborne, daughter of George and Deborah (Stearns) Osborn, married November 4, 1794, Samuel Cheever, (his third wife,) and bore him children: 1. Deborah Cheever, born March 9, 1796; married Timothy Wellman. 2. Samuel Cheever, December 8, 1799, died June 8, 1876; married July 31, 1828, Susan Southwick Osborn. 3. Margaret Cheever, November 26, 1802; married David Wright. 4. Rebecca G. Cheever, April 8, 1808, married ——— Tirrell. 5. George Osborn Cheever, July 4, 1804, died December 26, 1829. 6. Sarah Ring Cheever, January 13, 1806; married Joseph Hanson.

PERLEY (I) Allan Perley, the immigrant, was born in Wales, England, in 1608, and came to America with Winthrop's fleet in 1630, settled in the plantation at Charlestown, Massachusetts Bay colony, removed thence to Ipswich, where he died December 28, 1675. It appears, however, that before settling in Ipswich he had returned to England, and was there in 1635. He was made freeman in 1642, grand juror in 1660, and evidently was a person of considerable importance in the town, his manner, character and influence and his home with its furnishings indicating social position and gentle birth. He married, 1635, Susanna Bokesen (sometimes written Bokensen), who survived him about sixteen years and died in Ipswich, February 11, 1692; children: John, Samuel, Thomas, Nathaniel, Sarah, Timothy and Martha.

(II) Thomas Perley, third son and child of Allan and Susanna (Bokesen) Perley, was born at Ipswich in 1641. Prior to 1667 he went to Rowley, where he was admitted freeman 1677, and in 1684 settled in Boxford, where he became a prominent resident. He served as constable in 1688; selectman 1690-94-99, 1701-04-09; representative to general court 1689-90-93, 1700 and 1702; served as grand and petit juryman and was frequently chosen moderator of town meetings. He also served on numerous town committees, notably the one formulated in 1701 to receive the deed of the town of Boxford from the grandsons of the old sagamore, Masconnomet, also those appointed to organize the first religious society, erect the first meeting house, and he assisted in establishing the boundary line between Boxford and Topsfield. In addition to his extensive agricultural interests he aided in promoting the iron-moulding industry, which was begun in Boxford as early as 1669. He was also a member of the local militia and attained the rank of lieutenant. He died in Boxford September 24, 1709. July 8, 1667, he married Lydia Peabody, born 1644, daughter of Lieutenant Francis and Mary (Foster) Peabody, of Topsfield, the former of whom was of Great St. Albans, England, and emigated in 1635, being a fellow passenger with Allan Perley on the latter's return from his visit to the old country. Mary Foster (or Forster), wife of Lieutenant Francis Peabody, was a daughter of Reginald Foster, a representative of a distinguished Scotch family mentioned by Sir Walter Scott in both "Marmion" and "The Lay of the Last Minstrel." Children of Thomas and Lydia (Peabody) Perley: Thomas, Jacob, Lydia, Mary, Hepzibah and Sarah. The mother of these children died April 30, 1715. She was admitted to the church in Boxford by letter from the church in Rowley, February 1, 1702.

(III) Jacob, second son and child of Thomas and Lydia (Peabody) Perley, was born in Rowley, about 1670. He accompanied his parents from Rowley to Boxford, and acquired possession of the estate located on the north side of Baldpate pond, which in after years was owned and occupied by Augustus M. Perley. The original dwelling which he erected stood a few rods north of the present barn, and he lived there until 1736, when he removed to Bradford, Massachusetts. In his will he is mentioned as a housewright. In 1710 he with others was granted liberty to erect and operate a sawmill in Boxford, and while living there he participated actively in local public affairs, serving as constable in 1705; selectman 1708-12-29-32; surveyor of highways 1706; moderator, 1729-31; also on various town committees, and was town treasurer from 1713 to 1721. In 1705 he joined the local militia company as sergeant, was promoted to cornet in 1717; was commissioned lieutenant in 1724, and served with credit in Captain Lovewell's expedition against the Indians. He died at Bradford, 1751. Lieutenant Jacob Perley was three times married, and it is a somewhat singular coincidence that two of his wives were named Lydia Peabody, which was also the maiden name of his mother. On December 6, 1696, he married Lydia, daughter of Captain John and Hannah (Andrews) Peabody, of Boxford, born there March 9, 1673, and died there in 1707-08, having been admitted to the church with her husband some four years previously. He married second, May 9, 1709, his first wife's cousin, Lydia Peabody, born in Boxford, February 4, 1683, daughter of Joseph and Bethia (Bridges) Peabody. She died April 30, 1732. He married third, in 1733, Mrs. Mehitable Brown, nee Stafford, a widow, who had previously been married twice, first to John Hovey, and second to Ebenezer Brown of Rowley. She died intestate at Bradford, probably in 1754, as on March 22 of that year her son Samuel Hovey was appointed her administrator. Jacob Perley was the father of seven children, namely: Lydia, Jacob, Nathan, Francis, Moses, Isaac and Hannah.

(IV) Jacob Perley, son of Jacob and Lydia (Peabody) Perley, was born in Boxford, Massachusetts, September 19, 1700, and died in 1750. He married May 28, 1729, Sarah Morse, born in March, 1708, died after 1763, daughter of Benjamin and Susanna Morse of Newbury; children, all born in Boxford: Isaac, Jacob, Benjamin, Sarah and John.

(V) Lieutenant Benjamin Perley, third son and child of Jacob and Sarah (Morse) Perley, was born in Boxford, February 10, 1735, and died in Dunbarton, New Hampshire, in 1816. He then was eighty-one years old, vigorous in body and mind, and he met death in his own house, which had taken fire, while he was endeavoring to extinguish the flames. He was a soldier and patriot of the revolution and at the battle of Lexington was lieutenant of Captain William Perley's company of minute-men. In 1777 and again in 1780 he was a member of the war committee of Boxford to furnish and equip men for the service. In 1781 or 1782 he removed from Boxford to Topsfield, lived there until 1789 then returned to his native town and in 1791 removed to Dunbarton, New Hampshire, where he died. He was a man of considerable prominence in town affairs, possessed a good property, and in some records is mentioned as "gentleman." He was hogreeve in Boxford in 1765 and again in 1791, constable in 1770, selectman and overseer of the poor in 1774 and three times afterward, moderator and warden in 1776, sealer of weights and measures in 1767 and six years afterward, tythingman in 1772 and twice afterward, one of the committee of seven to regulate prices in 1779, and in 1781 was one of the two townsmen appointed to instruct the representative to the general court regarding the duties of his office. He married first, January 2, 1759, Hannah Clark, born in Topsfield, May 9, 1735, died about 1771, daughter of Jacob and Mary (Howlett) Clark of Boxford; second, October 12, 1773, Apphia Andrews, of Danvers. He had six children born of each marriage: Mary, Dorothy, Rebecca, Benjamin, Hannah, Paul, Apphia, Anna, John, Sarah, Betty and Jacob.

(VI) Lieutenant John Perley, son and ninth child of Lieutenant Benjamin and Apphia (Andrews) Perley, was born in Boxford, May 29, 1779, and died in Salem, October 15, 1816. He went with his father's family from Boxford to Dunbarton, but afterward returned to Massachusetts, settled in Salem, and was proprietor of a hotel at the corner of Essex and Beckford streets. In 1810 he was chosen lieutenant of the Salem Artillery Company, and in one record is mentioned as "late lieutenant in the U. S. army." He married, December 6, 1801, Mehitable Proctor, born December 19, 1775, died August 31, 1852, daughter of Sylvester (a descendant of John Proctor, witchcraft martyr) and Mehitabel (Osborn) (Porter) Proctor; children: Proctor Jefferson, John Andrews, Mehitabel, Elbridge Gerry (died in infancy), Eliza Ann, Elbridge Gerry and Jacob.

(VII) Proctor Jefferson Perley, eldest child of Lieutenant John and Mehitabel (Proctor) Perley, was born in Salem, June 17, 1802, and died there February 16, 1841. He was a painter by trade. He married May 23, 1828, Lydia Herrick Perkins, born in Essex, Massachusetts, December 6, 1804, and died in South Danvers, (now Peabody), November 29, 1889, having survived her husband almost half a century. She was daughter of Abraham and Mary (Burnham) Perkins. Proctor Jefferson and Lydia Herrick (Perkins) Perley had children: Mary Wilder, Lucy Secomb, Elbridge Gerry and Maria Taylor.

(VIII) Maria Taylor Perley, youngest child of Proctor Jefferson and Lydia Herrick (Perkins) Perley, was born in Peabody, January 29, 1839, and married there, January 6, 1859, Lyman Osborn, born in Peabody, April 2, 1835, son of Kendall and Sally (Bushby) Osborn (see Osborne family).

UPTON The Upton family ancestry in England is traced back to the time of William the Conqueror, and the ancient manuscript of the De Uppton family of Cornwall is still in existence, though partly illegible, at the ancient seat of the family in Westmoreland. The English branch of the family traces an unbroken line of descent from John Uppeton de Uppeton, Cornwall. The family has spread widely through Wales, Scotland and Ireland, as well as England.

(I) John Upton, who came to New England about 1652, was the immigrant ancestor. There is a tradition that he came from Scotland. He may have been one of the Scotch prisoners taken by Cromwell at Dunbarton, September 3, 1650, or at Worcester in 1651.

The last named battle was fought near the town of Upton, England, the seat of the ancient family. Cromwell took seventeen thousand Englishmen and Scotchmen prisoners in these two battles, and many of them were sent to the American colonies. There is a tradition that the name of his wife was Eleanor Stuart, and that she too was Scotch. He settled in Salem Village, now Danvers, Massachusetts. He seems to have refused to join the Puritan church, and that may indicate that he was Scotch and a Presbyterian. He did not take the freeman oath until it had been modified. He was admitted a freeman April 18, 1691. The first record is of date December 26, 1658, when he bought land of Henry Bullock, some time of Hammersmith (the Lynn iron works at Saugus). He paid four pounds for forty acres in Salem. He bought land of Daniel Rumboll of Salem, April 6, 1662, adjoining his farm. His homestead was near the line of the present town of Danvers, half a mile from the present line of Lynnfield, one mile south of the Ipswich river, and two miles west of the Newburyport turnpike. It is two miles and a half from the site of his later residence in North Reading. His neighbors were the Popes, Gardners, Flints, Walcotts and Smiths. He bought and sold considerable land in the vicinity. Active, energetic and successful, he began with no capital and accumulated a handsome estate. Among his holdings was a tract of land in West Peabody which he purchased from the Indians, and this at his death was divided between his six children; a portion of it is still owned by his descendants. He died July 11, 1699, aged about seventy-seven. The will was dated November 16, 1697, and proved July 31, 1699. He used a fleur-de-lis for a seal, and in his will tried to entail his estate, but the laws of the colony effectually prevented him. Children: 1. John, born 1654. 2. Eleanor, 1656. 3. William, 1658. 4. James, September, 1660. 5. Mary, 1661; died 1663. 6. Samuel, born October, 1664; mentioned below. 7. Ann. 8. Isabel, born January 3, 1666-7; died 1689. 9. Ezekiel, born September, 1668. 10. Joseph, April 9, 1670. 11. Francis, July 1, 1671. 12. Mary.

(II) Samuel Upton, son of John Upton, was born in October, 1664, and lived on the homestead in Danvers, which he had inherited jointly with his brother William. For at least half a century the two brothers occupied the same house, on Wood Hill, and until 1708 they held property together. At this time the real estate was divided. He owned land in Danvers, North reading and Middleton. He and his brother had a negro servant whom they freed in 1717. They sat together in the meeting house, as did their wives. Their seats in the meeting house indicated that they were both prominent in the community. Samuel Upton conveyed all his real estate to his son Benjamin, March 26, 1740, on consideration of nine hundred pounds in province bills. His design was to carry out his father's purpose in entailing the estate. The property was kept in the family as late as 1849, if not to the present day. He married January 14, 1702-3, Abigail Frost, of Danvers, baptized August 3, 1707, at the church in Danvers, probably on owning the covenant. Children: 1. Samuel, born June 30, 1704; married Ruth Whipple. 2. Abigail, born 1705. 3. Nathaniel (twin), baptized March 27, 1709; married Mary Eaton. 4. Jemima (twin), baptized March 27, 1709; married Israel Eaton. 5. Anna, baptized April 6, 1712. 6. Benjamin, baptized May 10, 1713; married Sarah Swinnerton. 7. Eunice, baptized April 24, 1715; married ——— Twist. 8. Amos, baptized October 20, 1717; mentioned below. 9. Lois, married ——— McIntyre. 10. Noah, baptized September 17, 1721.

(III) Deacon Amos Upton, son of Samuel Upton, was baptized in Danvers, October 20, 1717, and died October 6, 1780. He resided in the north parish of Reading, about a mile northeast of the present meeting house, in a house still (or lately) standing. He was deacon of the church there under Rev. Daniel Putnam and Rev. Eliah Stone from February 18, 1762, until his death. He was a man of great energy and stern Puritan principles. He was frequently in offices of trust: was surveyor of highways in 1750-56 and 61; selectman 1764-66 and 68; assessor and parish clerk in 1769; moderator of North Reading parish, 1767-72-74 and 78. His will is dated May 24, 1780, and proved October 3, 1781. He married December 5, 1739, Sarah, daughter of John Bickford of Salem. She was admitted into full communion to the church at Danvers, March 28, 1756, and died in North Reading, November 17, 1818, aged ninety-nine years seven months. Children: 1. Amos, born October 3, 1742; married first, Edith Upton; second, Joanna Bruce; third, Hannah Haskell. 2. Benjamin, born May 7, 1745; mentioned below. 3. Sarah, born November 22, 1748; died young. 4. Eunice, born December 2, 1751; married first George Upton; second,

——— Richardson. 5. Nathaniel, born November 28, 1753; married first, Sarah Flint; second, Jerusha Upton. 6. Sarah, born April 9, 1757; married January 10, 1782, Job Bancroft. 7. Rebecca, born June 28, 1761; married February 24, 1785, Ephraim Pratt, of North Reading. 8. Eliab, born 176—; died young. 9. John, born June 12, 1768; married Hannah Hart.

(IV) Benjamin Upton, son of Deacon Amos Upton, was born in North Reading, May 7, 1745, and died there August 12, 1827, aged eighty-two. He was a prominent citizen; was justice of the peace, parish clerk in 1783, and moderator to annual parish meeting same year; also moderator in 1801 and for eleven years following; was deputy to general court. Rev. James Flint, in a letter written in 1844, says of him: "Benjamin Upton, Esq., an able man, that thought well of himself * * * somewhat stern and opinionated, of unquestioned integrity, and held in respect by his fellow citizens," etc. He was rigorously orthodox in his religious views and delighted in religious discussion, always holding his own ground. He married first, December 20, 1770, Rebecca Putnam, born January 18, 1752, daughter of Deacon Daniel Putnam. She died September 13, 1785, and he married second, Elizabeth (White) Cowley, a descendant of Peregrine White, who was born in November, 1620, the first child of European parents born in New England, son of William White, one of the "Mayflower" company. Children of first wife: 1. Benjamin, born May 12, 1773; married Abigail Kilham. 2. Daniel Putnam, born August 12, 1775; married Hannah Bruce. 3. Rebecca, born 1778; died young. 4. Rebecca, born September 22, 1780; married David Preston. 5. Ebenezer, born January 14, 1783; married Polly Putnam. 6. Elisha, born August 14, 1785; died young. 7. Elijah (twin), born August 14, 1785; mentioned below. Children of second wife: 8. Elisha Cowley, born January 14, 1788; married Irene Flint. 9. Edward, born March 31, 1789; married Betsey Davis.

(V) Elijah Upton, son of Benjamin Upton, was born at North Reading, August 14, 1785, and died March 25, 1860, at Brattleborough, Vermont. He was a tanner and currier by trade, and in 1809 engaged in the manufacture of glue. In both departments he did a large business and accumulated a handsome fortune. He was an invalid for many years before his death, and removed on account of his health to Brattleborough, Vermont. Elijah Upton in his youth was apprenticed to Captain Dennison Wallis and was in partnership at different times with Joseph Tufts and Caleb I. Frost. He was the first man in town to manufacture glue, and built up a large trade. He had a great inventive faculty and was constantly making improvements in the manufacture and improving his plant. He dealt quite extensively in real estate. He was a liberal giver to public charities in which he was interested, among the chief being temperance reform and missionary work. He married first, July 2, 1809, Phebe Wood, born in South Danvers, March 23, 1787, died there July 12, 1821; second, November 9, 1821, Ruth (Harrington) Downing, died June 1, 1843. Child of first wife: 1. Elijah Wood, mentioned below.

(VI) Elijah Wood Upton, son of Elijah Upton, was born February 24, 1811, in Peabody, formerly South Danvers, and died there in 1881. He received a good academical education and supplemented his studies by European travel. Some years before his father's death, Elijah Wood Upton took upon himself the management of the glue business, as his father was not in good health. In 1847, with Theophilus and Nathaniel Walker, he built and put in operation the Danvers Bleachery. Under his management the business grew to large proportions. He was president of the Warren Bank in Peabody, and dealt largely in real estate. He married first, September 12, 1832, Louisa King, born in South Danvers, October 27, 1809, died at Boston, January 15, 1847, daughter of Ebenezer and Betsey (Upton) King; second, June 14, 1848, Lucy Elizabeth Winchester, born in Danvers, January 8, 1821. Children of first wife: 1. Maria Louisa, born August 4, 1833, married Charles B. Farley. 2. George, born July 8, 1837; mentioned below. 3. Mary Annette, born April 5, 1843; died April 23, 1843. Children of second wife: 4. Phebe Wood, born February 23, 1849; died May 12, 1849. 5. Edgar Wood, born April 27, 1851; married January 28, 1873, Elizabeth G. Evans. 6. Francis Robbins, born July 26, 1852. 7. Henry Bancroft, born August 26, 1854; died December 18, 1864. 8. Sarah Frost, born March 27, 1856. 9. Mary Ann, born July 22, 1861; died August 25, 1868.

(VII) George Upton, son of Elijah Wood Upton, was born in South Danvers, now Peabody, July 8, 1837, and died January 26, 1883. He was educated in the public schools and Groton Academy. He learned the business in which his father and grandfather had been so prominent and successful, and became a partner in the firm of Upton & Company, with his father and D. Webster King. This firm was afterward dissolved, and the original business was continued by George Upton alone. He inherited the business ability of his father, and achieved even greater success, enlarging the plant and facilities, and increasing the output of the factories. He held a high position in the manufacturing and commercial world, and was held in esteem as a farsighted, upright and conscientious citizen. In politics he was a Republican, and in religion a Unitarian. He married, September 6, 1860, Marian Cloutman, born in Boston, daughter of John and Margaret (McKay) Cloutman. Children: 1. King, born April 12, 1862, mentioned below. 2. Roger, born in Peabody, September 15, 1873. He began his education in the home schools, and at the age of twelve went to Europe, where he was a student until he was seventeen. Returning home, he completed his studies at Harvard University. He is now clerk and assistant treasurer of the American Glue Company. He married, in 1899, Elizabeth Phebe Key Lloyd, born in Maryland, daughter of Colonel Edward Lloyd; children: Lloyd, born July 26, 1900; Edward, March 18, 1902; Dorothy, August 23, 1903.

(VIII) King Upton, son of George Upton, was born in Peabody, April 12, 1862. He was educated in the public schools of his native town, and later in Paris, Allen's Academy, Newton, Massachusetts, and Massachusetts Institute of Technology. He entered his father's establishment, thoroughly learned the business, and became associated with him in his various enterprises. On the death of the father, in 1883, he became managing trustee of the estate and acted as such until 1894, when the estate was settled, and the business passed into the ownership of Marian C. Upton, King Upton and Roger Upton. A few months later it was sold to the American Glue Company of New Jersey, of which D. Webster King was president, and King Upton vice-president. This corporation, organized in 1894, took over not only the glue business of the Upton estate, but that of the D. Webster King Company, the Pennsylvania Glue Company and the Illinois Glue Company, King Upton being chief owner in the two last named corporations. In 1900 the American Glue Company purchased the Boston Flint Paper Company, the Union Sand Paper Company, and the sand paper business of Wiggin & Stevens. Two years later it also acquired the Cape Ann Isinglass Company, and in 1906 the American Glue Company, organized under Massachusetts laws, took over from the New Jersey corporation all the glue and other business owned thereby. As now constituted, the American Glue Company of Massachusetts, of itself or through subsidiary companies, owns and operates nineteen different plants in Maine, New Hampshire, Massachusetts, Connecticut, New York, Pennsylvania, Indiana, Illinois and Iowa, and has stores in Boston, New York City, Philadelphia, Chicago and St. Louis, and is the largest corporation in the country engaged in the manufacture, purchase and sale of glue and gelatine, sand paper, garnet paper and cloth, emery paper and cloth, isinglass, hair and fertilizer. The business also includes the mining of garnet and other minerals used in the manufacture of its products. The main office of the corporation is in Boston, and its officers are: Jesse P. Lyman, president and treasurer, who organized and successfully developed the G. H. Hammond Company and the Hammond Packing Company, and was a prime factor in the formation of the National Packing Company, of which he was president for several years; King Upton, first vice-president, who is in charge of the manufacturing plants, and is recognized as one of the most expert glue manufacturers in the country; Everett J. Stevens, second vice-president, ex-mayor of Malden, and for several years a member of the Massachusetts legislature; Roger Upton, before mentoned, clerk and assistant treasurer; B. L. M. Tower, general counsel. George Upton, son of King Upton, is also connected with the business, in the technical branch of the work. The present large factory at Peabody is built near the site of the original building, and is called "The Upton Factory," or "Plant No. 1." This (1908) is the centennial year of the glue business owned by the Upton family in Peabody, developed from small and unpretentious beginnings into a large industry of national importance and international fame. The utilization of by-products and waste materials has been a remarkable incident in the growth of this business. Not only the concentration of capital, but the production of new machinery, the discovery of new chemical and mechanical processes, and the most modern and economical methods of manufacture and distribution, have been important factors in the great expansion and prosperity of this establishment.

Mr. Upton is affiliated with Starr King

Lodge, Free and Accepted Masons; Washington Chapter, Royal Arch Masons; and is a member of the Eastern Yacht Club, the Boston Yacht Club, the Corinthian Yacht Club, the Portland Yacht Club, and the Chicago Athletic Association. In politics he is a Republican. He resides in Marblehead. He married, in April, 1883, Annie Dane, born in Salem, daughter of Joseph F. Dane. They have one child, George, born March 23, 1884, mentioned above.

TILTON William Tilton, immigrant ancestor, was born in England, and settled first in Lynn, Massachusetts, prior to 1640. He was "freed from training, but to keep his arms fixed," according to an order dated April 30, 1646, indicating that he was past middle age. He died in the early part of 1653. His widow Susannah presented his will for probate in May, 1653. She married (second) Roger Shaw, of Hampton, New Hampshire, whither she took her youngest son by her former husband, Daniel Tilton. We find the record also of John Tilton at Salem in 1641, when the wife of his son John was presented to the court for opposing infant baptism. Children of William and Susannah Tilton: 1. Abraham, married Mary Cram, daughter of John. 2. Samuel, married, December 17, 1662, Hannah Moulton. 3. Daniel, mentioned below.

(II) Ensign Daniel Tilton, son of William Tilton (1), was born in Lynn, 1646-47; married, December 23, 1669, Mehitable Sanborn, daughter of William and Mary Sanborn, of Hampton. He settled on what is known as the Akerman place on Hampton Falls hill, and died at Hampton, February 10, 1715. In 1667 the town of Hampton made him a grant of land "in case he would sit down as blacksmith," and he and his descendants carried on the blacksmith business continuously in the town for one hundred and fifty years, down to the time of the death of Captain Stephen Tilton in 1821. Daniel bore the title of ensign of the militia in 1696, and was in command of a garrison at Hampton. He was a member of the executive council and general assembly in 1693-95 and 1702, during his last year being speaker of the house. He was again member of the assembly in 1709-11 and finally in 1714, when he requested dismission "being infirm and antient." Daniel was the progenitor of the Tiltons of New Hampshire. Children of Daniel and Mehitable: 1. Abigail, born October 28, 1670, married Christopher Shaw; she died October 4, 1759. 2. Mary, born March 9, 1673. 3. Samuel, born February 14, 1675. 4. Joseph, born March 19, 1677, mentioned below. 5. Mercy, born May 25, 1679, married Samuel Elkins, son of Eleazer. 6. Daniel, born October 23, 1680. 7. David, born October 30, 1682, died May 26, 1729; married Deborah Batchelder. 8. Mehitable, born October 2, 1687, married, May 14, 1708, Joseph Lawrence. 9. Hannah, born April 27, 1689, married Nathaniel Hedly. 10. Jethro, married Mary ———. 11. Josiah.

(III) Captain Joseph Tilton, son of Ensign Daniel Tilton (2), was born in Hampton, March 19, 1677; married (first) December 26, 1798, Margaret Sherburne, and (second) Elizabeth Hilliard. Children: Sherburne, John, mentioned below; Mary, Margaret, Jonathan, Joseph.

(IV) John Tilton, son of Captain Joseph Tilton (3), was born in Hampton, January 4, 1702. He resided at Kensington, New Hampshire. Children: John, mentioned below; Jeremiah, David, Nathaniel, Joseph.

(V) John Tilton, son of John Tilton (4), born in Kensington, New Hampshire, 1736, died January 21, 1818, aged eighty-two years. He settled in that part of Gilmanton, now Gilford, New Hampshire, near Meredith. He married, May 19, 1761, Hannah Clifford, who died March 28, 1824, aged eighty years. Children born at Gilmanton: Samuel, Elizabeth, Nathaniel, Judith, Hannah, Abigail, Mary, John, Richard, David, mentioned below; Sarah, Dolly.

(VI) David Tilton, son of John Tilton (5), was born in Gilmanton about 1765. He settled in Gilford with his brothers, Nathaniel and Samuel. According to the federal census of 1790 Nathaniel had a son over sixteen and two females in his family; Samuel had three sons under sixteen and seven females in his family. David had two sons under sixteen and two females (doubtless wife and daughter) in his family. He married Sarah Foster, born December 30, 1767, daughter of Hon. Abiel Foster, born Andover, Massachusetts, August 8, 1735; married, May 15, 1761, Hannah Badger, daughter of General Joseph Badger, of Gilmanton, New Hampshire. Abiel Foster married (second) Mary Rogers, born November 1, 1745, died March 12, 1813, daughter of Dr. Samuel and Hannah (Wise) Rogers, of Ipswich, descendant of John Rogers, of Dedham, England. Abiel Foster fitted for college, graduated at Harvard in

1756; was minister at Canterbury, New Hampshire; chief justice of the court of common pleas, Rockingham county; congressman in 1789-91 and 1795-1803; once president of the New Hampshire senate; a man of integrity, virtue and great usefulness, having the confidence and favor of all men; a personal friend of Washington who gave him a miniature of himself—a precious heirloom of the family; died February 6, 1806. David and Sarah Tilton settled in Meredith, New Hampshire. Children: Joseph Badger, born July 3, 1788, died September 18, 1788. Joseph Badger, mentioned below.

Captain Asa Foster, father of Hon. Abiel Foster, was born at Andover, June 16, 1710; married, October 26, 1732, Elizabeth Abbot, born October 21, 1712, died July 4, 1758, daughter of John. He married (second) 1763 Lucy Rogers Wise, of Ipswich, born 1723, died October 17, 1787, daughter of Major Ammiruhamah Wise. Asa Foster was a captain in the regiment of Colonel Ebenezer Nichols in the French war, 1758; was on the committee of safety and correspondence in 1776; owned one hundred and sixty acres of land in Canterbury, New Hampshire; a very prominent citizen.

William Foster, father of Captain Asa Foster, was born at Rowley, now Boxford, in 1670; married, July 6, 169—, Sarah Kimball, born September 19, 1669, died November 6, 1729, daughter of John and Sarah Kimball; married Margaret Gould; removed to Andover, Massachusetts, 1697-98, and died there.

William Foster, son of Reginald, father of William just mentioned, was born in England in 1633. Married, May 15, 1661, Mary Jackson, born February 8, 1639, daughter of William and Joanna. He lived at Rowley on the site of the old Dean Andrews place.

Reginald Foster, the immigrant, has a sketch elsewhere in this work.

(VII) Joseph Badger Tilton, son of David Tilton (6), was born in Meredith, New Hampshire, about 1790. He married, December 22, 1819, at Gilford, New Hampshire, Sally P. Robertson (or Robinson), of Meredith. (By Rev. William Blaisdell). Child, Daniel Lambert, mentioned below.

(VIII) Daniel Lambert Tilton, son of Joseph B. Tilton (7), born in Meredith, New Hampshire, in 1824, died in 1882. He married Ellen M. Jennings. They lived in Boston. Children: 1. Ella, married Frank B. Roundy; children, Grace E. Roundy, Anna M. Roundy. 2. Walter Francis, mentioned below.

(IX) Walter Francis Tilton, son of Daniel Lambert Tilton (8), was born in Boston, April 26, 1857. He resided in Chelsea in his youth and attended the public schools of Chelsea and Boston. He began at an early age as clerk in the wholesale millinery store of Sleeper, Fisk & Company, Boston, and was advanced step by step to positions of greater trust and responsibility in this concern. When the firm was re-organized under the name of J. K. C. Sleeper & Company, he became a partner. In 1892 he entered partnership with Elmer E. Clapp and established the well-known firm of Clapp & Tilton, wholesale milliners. This firm occupies the quarters at 12 Summer street, Boston, formerly occupied by the firm of J. K. C. Sleeper and Company, and its business has grown until it ranks as the largest and most progressive concern east of New York in this line of business. Mr. Tilton has always taken an active part in the public affairs of the town of Norwood, where he resides. He is an active an influential Republican, serving many years on the Republican town committee and often being elected delegate to the nominating conventions of his party. He is a member of the executive board of the Norwood Business Association; is director of the Norwood National Bank. He is a member of the electric light commission of Norwood. He is an active member of the Norwood Universalist church, and has served for a number of years on its parish committee. He is a prominent Free Mason, belonging to Orient Lodge; to Hebron Chapter, Royal Arch Masons, of which he is treasurer, and to Hyde Park Commandery, Knights Templar.

He married, April 26, 1883, Anna M., daughter of Francis E. and Emeline Francis (Whiting) Colburn. (See Whiting sketch). Children: 1. Mabel Frances, born April 29, 1886. 2. Arthur Colburn, born December 31, 1887.

COBB

Elder Henry Cobb the "Mayflower" passenger on her second trip from England, came presumably from Kent, and was in Plymouth in 1629, in Scituate in 1633, where he was deacon in the First Church of Scituate, Mr. John Lothrop, minister, and he removed with the minister and some members of his congregation in 1639 to the Indian place known as Mattacheese on Cape Cod, and they there, under authority of the colony court, given June 4, 1639, established the First Church of Barnstable, of which he was a deacon up to April 14, 1670, when he was made a ruling elder, and he was afterward known and his name was written Mr. Henry Cobb. He was an original grantee of the town and was for several years deputy to the colony court. He married Patience, daughter of Deacon James Harch, in 1639, and she died in 1648, after having had by him seven children; he married second, Sarah, daughter of Samuel Hinckley, December 12, 1649, and by her had eight children. He died in 1679. His children were: John, born in Plymouth, June 7, 1632; James, Plymouth, January 14, 1634; Mary, Scituate, March 24, 1736; Hannah, Scituate, October 5, 1639; Patience, 1642; Gershom, January 10, 1444-5; Eleazer, March 30, 1648; Mehitable, September, 1652; Samuel, October 12, 1654; Sarah, January 15, 1658; Jonathan, April 10, 1660; Sarah, March 10, 1662-3; Henry, September 3, 1665; Mehitable, February 15, 1667, and Experience, September 11, 1671. Of these children, John lived in Taunton and Plymouth; Mary married Josiah Dunham, being his second wife; Hannah married Edward Lewis, May 9, 1661; Patience married Robert Parker, 1667; Gershom removed to Middleboro; Mehitable (1) died in infancy; Sarah (1) died in infancy; Sarah (2) married Deacon Samuel Chipman, December 27, 1686; Henry, born 1665, is referred to below; his elder brother James married Sarah Lewis and became the progenitor of the Sylvanus Cobbs and of Cyrus and Darius Cobb, noted preachers, authors and artists, the line being through James 3, James 4, Sylvanus 5, Ebenezer 6, Rev. Sylvanus 7, the writer; Sylvanus 8, Cyrus and Darius (twins) 9, born August 6, 1834, the former of whom is an artist.

(II) Henry Cobb, of Barnstable, youngest son of Elder Henry and Sarah (Hinckley) Cobb, was born September 3, 1665. He married, April 10, 1690, Lois Hallet; children: Gideon, born April 11, 1691; Eunice, September 18, 1693; Lois, March 2, 1696, and Nathan, 1700. He removed to New London county, Connecticut, and was prominent in the early history of the county. He purchased land in the proposed society of Voluntown in May, 1719, and May 14, 1724, he petitioned the authorities for a meeting house site and was deacon in the newly organized church. In 1731 he purchased from Governor Saltonstall his large grant of land, which he divided into farms and sold to settlers. Previous to 1740 he connected himself with the church organized by the society of Mortlake, and his wife also joined the society, and he was assigned a prominent pew in the new church. His son Gideon was captain in the militia and, like his father, he took a prominent part in church affairs and was appointed on important committees at various times to settle difficulties with the older neighboring societies that disputed the rights of their domain, and he was finally influential in securing the union of the Plainfield and Windham associations. He was appointed guager and packer, and also a highway surveyor at the town meeting held in 1761 for the erection of the new society of Hanover out of territory occupied by the Canterbury Society. The line of ancestry is traced through Gideon Cobb to Thomas Cobb, who was a resident of Carver, Massachusetts, and he was father of Andrew B. Cobb, who was born at Carver, married Lydia Morton Eddy, granddaughter of Captain Joshua Eddy, a revolutionary soldier, and a descendant from Samuel Eddy, of Middleborough, Massachusetts Bay Colony, 1624. Mr. and Mrs. Cobb resided at Hartford, Connecticut.

Henry Eddy Cobb, son of Andrew B. and Lydia M. (Eddy) Cobb, was born in Hartford, Connecticut, June 21, 1839, died at his home on Bellview avenue, Mt. Ida, Newton, Massachusetts, February 2, 1908. He removed with his parents to Newton, Massachusetts, where he received his school training in the best grammar and high schools to be found in the Commonwealth of Massachusetts, which is synonymous with the best in the English speaking world. At the age of fourteen he entered the Newton Bank in the capacity of messenger, clerk and general utility boy, thereby gaining valuable experience which aided him in later years. He later entered the office of Potter, White & Bailey, wholesale shoe commission merchants in Boston, but his inclinations led him to the financial rather than the commercial, and he engaged permanently in the business of banking, the exchange of stocks, bonds and other securities. His first connection was with R. L. Day & Cobb, general bankers and stock auctioneers in Boston, and he thus became a familiar figure on the floor of the Stock Exchange. This training was an essential factor in the formation of the firm of Brewster, Bassett & Company, and later of Brewster, Cobb & Estabrook, bankers and brokers, of which firm he was the senior member at the time of his withdrawal from active financial life in January, 1896. He was no speculator in the general acceptance of the term, and the capital accumulated during his business career and placed in well established conservative securities. He was a generous distributor of the wealth he accumulated, and while his charities were unostentatious, they were liberal and continuous throughout his entire lifetime.

The city of Newton, in which he was brought up and in whose schools and business institutions he received his boyhood training, was the especial object of his concern and his first public service was on the board of education, on which he served one year. In 188? he was appointed a member of the board of aldermen to fill the vacancy caused by the death of Edward W. Cate for the first ward, and he was re-elected the following year. In 1896 he was elected the eleventh mayor of the city of Newton and was re-elected the following two years, being the second mayor in twenty-five years to receive a third term re-election to that office, his last two nominations being made by the unanimous voice of the convention. He was instrumental in the adoption of a new city charter which was put into force in 1898, and it is largely due to his wise forethought and untiring and persistent efforts that the construction of Commonwealth avenue through the city, the widening of Washington street and the abolishing of all grade crossings within the city limits were each brought to a successful completion, and these three improvements consummated under his administration were the principal monuments to his successful official conduct of municipal affairs. In 1898, on surrendering the office of mayor to Hon. Edward B. Wilson, his associates in the City Hall who aided him in making his administration so great a success, presented him with a silver pitcher as a slight token of their regard and as an acknowledgement of his successful inauguration of the increased powers and responsibilities imposed by the city charter on the executive officer.

He was an early member of the Newton Club, and served as president from 1890 to 1896. He also served as president of the Newton Home for Aged People, and is a trustee of Wellesley College and of the New England Conservatory of Music. Dartmouth College conferred on him the honorary degree of Master of Arts by virtue of his interest in educational matters and of educational institutions in general. He held membership in the Eliot Congregational Church of Newton, his services being both faithful and helpful, and was a member of the Congregational Club of Boston. His initiation into the mysteries of the Masonic fraternity was through the Winslow Lewis Lodge, Free and Accepted Masons, and he was advanced to the Royal Arch Chapter and Gethsemane Commandery, Knights Templar, of Newton. His club and Masonic positions as well as his official position in the city government made him influential in both civic and social life, and his honors were carried with the instinct and bearing of the true gentleman who made himself an equal with his associates in all walks of life. His position as president of the Claflin Guard Veteran Association of Newton made him a familiar figure in the counsels of that military organization, and his military inheritance made him an honored member of the Sons of the American Revolution.

Henry Eddy Cobb married May 11, 1864, Hattie M. Cooley, of Norwich, Connecticut, who is a direct descendant from Elder Brewster of the Mayflower Company, 1620. Children: Morton Eddy, of Newton Centre; Lucy Ely and Helen Minerva.

COOK (I) Captain Aaron Cook, immigrant ancestor of this family, was born in England in 1610. He settled in Dorchester, Massachusetts, as early as 1634; some authorities fix the date as 1630. He was admitted a freeman May 6, 1635. He had a grant of land in Windsor, Connecticut, July 5, 1636, and in 1653 had a grant at Massacoe, on both sides of the river next above the falls. He became discouraged by the controversy in the church, and in 1661 removed to Northampton, Massachusetts, with others. Thence he went to the adjacent town of Westfield, where he was a tavern keeper; proprietor 1667 and afterward, deputy to the general court in 1668. He was a man of great energy, a devoted friend of the regicide judges, Goffe and Whalley, while they were in this country, resided in his neighborhood. He was captain of his company, and in 1653 was chosen commander of ten Connecticut towns in the war against the Dutch of New York. In 1687 he was commissioned major by Governor Andros. He sat in the county court at Springfield and heard the famous witchcraft case against Mary Webster. He died September 5, 1690. His inventory, filed December 26, 1690, in Connecticut, shows three hundred acres in Hartford, land at Windsor, etc. Nathaniel Cook, of Windsor undoubtedly a relative, may have been brother. Both left many descendants in the vicinity of Hartford. He married ——— Ford, daughter of Thomas; second, Joanna Denslow, who died April, 1676, daughter of Nicholas and Elizabeth Denslow; third, December 2, 1676, Elizabeth Nash, baptized January 3, 1647, died September 3, 1687, daughter of Major John and Elizabeth (Tapp) Nash. He married fourth, October 2, 1688, Rebecca (Foote) Smith, born 1634, died at Hadley, April 6, 1701, daughter of Nathaniel and Elizabeth (Denny) Foote, of Wethersfield, and widow of Lieutenant Philip Smith, of Hadley, Massachusetts. Children of first wife: 1. Nathaniel. 2. Joanna, baptized August 5, 1638. 3. Aaron, baptized February 21, 1640; married Sarah Westwood; resided at Hatfield, Massachusetts. 4. Joanna, baptized February 21, 1640; married Simon Wolcott. 5. Miriam, baptized March 12, 1642-3; married November 8, 1661, Joseph Leeds. 6. Moses, baptized November 16, 1645; married November 25, 1669, Elizabeth Clark; killed by Indians at Westfield; widow married Lieutenant Job Drake. Children of second wife: 7. Samuel, baptized November 21, 1650. 8. Elizabeth, baptized August 7, 1653; married Samuel Parsons, of Northampton. 9. Noah, baptized June 14, 1657; died June 1, 1699; married Sarah Nash. 10. John, mentioned below. And probably others.

(II) John Cook, of Middletown, Connecticut, was born as early as 1655, and died January 16, 1704-5. While we have no record of birth, the proof seems sufficient to place him among the children of Aaron, rather than as nephew or more distant relation. He settled at Middletown, below Hartford, where he died January 16, 1704-5. His estate was valued at 331 pounds, two shillings, three pence in the inventory, March 5, 1704-5, made by Thomas Ward, William Ward and Joseph Johnson. His will was dated August 1, 1698, bequeathing to son John two hundred acres at Cockingchange; to Mary, silver spoons; to son Daniel his house and homestead; to Sarah a feather bed; and to an expected child one hundred acres of land. His widow Hannah was executrix. Children: 1. John, was of age in 1704. 2. Mary, also of age in 1704. 3. Daniel, born 1690; mentioned below. 4. Sarah, born 1692. 5. Ebenezer, born 1697-8.

(III) Daniel Cook, son of John Cook (2), was one of the original grantees of Tolland, Connecticut. The only other Daniel Cook in that section was the son of Nathaniel, of Windsor, of about the same age. But we can prove that this Daniel was not living (dying without heirs) by the division of the estate of a sister. Daniel Cook was grantee in the original deed from the trustees of land at what became the town of Tolland, dated May 11, 1709. His name was on a petition of inhabitants dated May, 1718. There were then but three towns in what is now Tolland county—Mansfield, settled in 1703; Hebron, settled in 1709; and Coventry, in 1709. Tolland was first settled about 1713, and adjoins Coventry. Daniel Cook was appointed by the town to take care of the ordination of the first minister, Rev. George Steele, June 19, 1723. The farm of Josiah Goodrich adjoined that of Cook, who with two others was appraiser of the estate of Jacob Bacor (Baker) July, 1742. The Cooks of Coventry were all doubtless his descendants. Among his children we have good authority for placing: 1. Daniel, Jr., born in Tolland. 2. Jesse. 3. Jonathan (?), married Martha Woodward; children, born in Coventry: i. Stephen, December 24, 1743; ii. Silas, February 17, 1745-6; iii. Jonathan, June 13, 1748; iv. Hannah. 4. Josiah, mentioned below. 5. Moses. 6. Shubael.

(IV) Josiah Cook, son or nephew of Daniel Cook (3), was born about 1730, in Tolland, probably; died at Alstead, New Hampshire, July 2, 1807. He married first, Huldah Bassett; second, at Coventry, Connecticut, August 1, 1762 (as per town records) Lucy Demone or Deman (generally Damon, as now spelled). Children, born at Coventry: Huldah, April 23, 1765; Lucy, June 23, 1767; Captain Josiah, mentioned below.

(V) Captain Josiah Cook, son of Josiah Cook, was born at Coventry, October 16, 1770. He settled at Alstead, New Hampshire, and became a prominent citizen and deacon of the Alstead Congregational church. He married Sarah Emerson, of Haverhill, Massachusetts. Children, born at Alstead: 1. John, October 9, 1792; mentioned below. 2. Arva, May 3, 1795; married Rhoda Willard. 3. Benaiah, November 20, 1800; married Rebecca Harrington. 4. Polly, July 3, 1798; married Elisha Kittridge. 5. Sarah, February 15, 1803; married Erastus Doolittle, of Boston.

(VI) Captain John Cook, son of Captain Josiah Cook, was born in Alstead, New Hampshire, October 9, 1792. He was a farmer and stock raiser. Later he settled at Bellows Falls, Vermont, where he died March 1, 1872, aged seventy-nine years. He rose to the rank of captain in the state militia of New Hampshire. In religion he was a Congregationalist;

in politics an old-line Whig, as long as that party existed. He married at Springfield, Vermont, Eunice Parker. Children: 1. Philetta, born March 16, 1819; died unmarried. 2. Ezra Parker, mentioned below.

(VII) Lieutenant Ezra Parker Cook, son of John Cook, was born in Alstead, January 18, 1820, and died October 31, 1881. He had a common school education, and worked at farming in his youth. He became a stage driver, and continued until the railroads were built along the Connecticut river, when he entered the employ of the railroad company as baggage master between Boston and Burlington, Vermont. During his later years he held a position as stationary engineer. He attained the rank of first lieutenant in the state militia of Vermont in a regiment known as the Green Mountain Guards. He died in 1881, aged sixty-one years, his wife, Mary Lucretia Tracy, of Woodstock, Vermont, dying the same year, aged fifty-four. He was a Universalist in religion. In early life he was a Whig in politics, but followed the majority of Whigs into the Republican party before the civil war.

(VIII) George Ward Cook, only child of Ezra P. Cook (7), was born at Plymouth, Vermont, May 13, 1850. He attended the district schools, the graded schools of Bellows Falls, later Powers Institute, Bernardston, Massachusetts, and then took a commercial course in Comers's Commercial College, of Boston. He began his business career in the lumber business of Tarbell, Tolman & Company, having charge of the locks and canals and later as book keeper in the hardware store of Arms & Wilson, Bellows Falls, Vermont. Then he became connected with the Vermont Farm Machine Company in 1872, being one of the incorporators, and continued with that company until 1880, advancing in the meantime to the position of secretary and acting treasurer. In 1880 he became bookkeeper for Hon. Moses How, in the manufacture of boots and shoes in Haverhill, Massachusetts, and later on his own account. He was employed afterward as financial manager in the clothing store of Warren Emerson, Haverhill, Massachusetts, and later established a store on his own account.

In 1876 Mr. Cook established the excursion and ticket business that made his name famous all over the world. Wherever tourists go, the name of Cook is known. He has an office in Old South Building, Boston, and in other leading cities of the country. Mr. Cook was instrumental in securing the Massachusetts exhibit at Jamestown, Virginia, and also on procuring the ten thousand dollar appropriation from the states of New Hampshire and Vermont for the same purpose. He is a man of public spirit, ready to co-operate in all movements to benefit the city of Haverhill, in which he lives. He introduced the use of the electric light in Haverhill, and organized the present Board of Trade of that city. He has invested extensively in Haverhill real estate, and built many houses in that city. He is a member of the American Forestry Association, the National Rivers and Harbor Congress, also the National Good Roads Congress, being one of its secretaries; and the Atlantic Deeper Water Ways Association. He belongs to Mizpah Lodge and Haverhill Encampment, Independent Order of Odd Fellows; to many Masonic bodies, up to the thirty-third degree, Scottish Rite; and is a member of the Ancient and Honorable Artillery Company of Boston; the Vermont Association of Boston; and the Hannah Dustin Association (of which he is secretary), being a descendant of the Dustin family. He is president and treasurer of Cook's Hotel and Tourist Company, and of the Merrimac River Steamboat Company; president of the Merrimac River Improvement Company, the Vermont Association of Haverhill, and the New Hampshire Association of Haverhill. He is the promotor of the Boynton Bicycle Railroad and other electric systems, also petitioner for charter for lock-dam and canal at Mitchell's Falls, on the Merrimac river, to benefit navigation to Lawrence and create electric power. Mr. Cook has an international reputation, and is especially well known and popular among the railroad men of New England, and the travelling classes. He is also known as a newspaper editor and publisher, being interested in several publications. He is also deeply intested in literary lines and lectures. He brought the late Henry M. Stanley, African explorer, to Haverhill, to lecture, and was a close friend of George Francis Train. He is himself a lecturer, using screen views to illustrate his public work, in forestry and navigation. In politics he is a Republican, and in religion a member of the North Congrational Church. He served as justice of the peace and notary public for many years.

Mr. Cook married June 30, 1877, Hattie Berson Emerson, born in Haverhill, August 2, 1856, daughter of Master Luther Emerson. Their only child, Gladys Emerson, was born in Haverhill, November 7, 1894.

Geo. Ward Cook

DENNETT The Dennett family is of Norman origin, and Hugh D'Anet is said to have come to England with William the Conqueror. The Dennett family is numerous in England, and there are many who can trace their lineage back six centuries or more. One branch of the family lived in the Isle of Wight, and were farmers. Another family was the owner of Woodmancote, county Sussex, holding an estate of six hundred acres for several centuries. John Leighton Wade Dennet, born May 24, 1802, was a late owner, and had a son of the same name. This family had a coat-of-arms. John and Alexander Dennet, brothers, came from England to Portsmouth, New Hampshire, between 1660 and 1670. John Dennet resided at Portsmouth, and was a carpenter. He was admitted a freeman May 15, 1670, and died May 5, 1709. His will was dated March 17, and proved August 1, 1709. He married Amy ———. Children: 1. John, born December 15, 1675. 2. Amy, April 9, 1679; married John Adams. 3. Joseph, July 10, 1681. 4. Ephraim, August 2, 1689.

(I) Alexander Dennett, immigrant ancestor mentioned above, born about 1639, died in Newcastle, New Hampshire, 1698. He came to New England with his brother John, and settled in Portsmouth. Children: 1. Alexander, mentioned below. 2. Mehitable, died March 12, 1733. 3. Samuel, died March 12, 1733. 4. Joseph, married Sarah Low, November 6, 1734. 5. Annie, married Samuel Jackson, December 28, 1738.

(II) Alexander Dennett, son of Alexander Dennett, was born about 1670. He settled in 1681 in what is now Eliot, Maine, where he lived for a time, and had a grant of land in 1694. He married first, Mehitable, daughter of Gabriel Tetherly; second, Esther Cross, who married second, Anthony Rowe. He died June 7, 1773, in Portsmouth. He was a blacksmith by trade, and carried on business in Portsmouth many years, accumulating considerable property for those days. At one time it was said that he was the richest man in Portsmouth, and the inventory of his estate was but about fifty pounds. He died in Portsmouth, in 1733. Children: 1. Moses, mentioned below. 2. Samuel, died July 15, 1759. 3. Ebenezer, born about 1692; married Abigail Hill. 4. Susanna, married November 18, 1724, Joshua Downing. 5. Mehitable, married ——— Stewart. 6. Elizabeth, married Enoch Sanborn. 7. Sarah, married Joshua Weymouth, October 13, 1720.

(III) Moses Dennett, son of Alexander Dennett, was born about 1690, in Portsmouth, and died July 15, 1749. He married, February 11, 1723, Lydia Furnel, of Kittery, Maine. Children: 1. David, born March 15, 1727, in Newington, New Hampshire; married, 1772, Dolly Downing; died January 18, 1788. 2. Charles, born April 21, 1729, mentioned below. 3. Lydia, born April 16, 1731; died November 13, 1736. 4. Anna, born August 2, 1733; died May 5, 1736. 5. Elizabeth, born December 20, 1735; died December 11, 1736. 6. Moses, born January 17, 1737; died December 27, 1739. 7. Lydia, born February 25, 1738; died December 27, 1738. 8. Mary, born July 31, 1740; died January 5, 1746. 9. Ruth, born 1742; died January 5, 1748.

(IV) Charles Dennett, son of Moses Dennett, was born April 21, 1729, and died April 6, 1763. He married, September 13, 1753, Harriet Nutter. Children: 1. Mary, born 1756; died January 1, 1775. 2. Moses, born 1758; mentioned below. 3. Hannah, born in Barnstead, New Hampshire, 1760; married Jonathan Perkins, of Louden, New Hampshire.

(V) Moses Dennett, son of Charles Dennett, was born in 1758, and died December 28, 1810, in Barnstead, New Hampshire. His homestead at Barnstead was on high ground looking towards Gilmanton. He removed there from Portsmouth about 1769, and was a tailor by trade. His house of logs stood on the spot now occupied by his descendants. For a considerable time after moving there he brought all his provisions on horseback from Dover, following a blazed trail through the forest. The house stood deep in the woods and in his absence he usually left a small boy with his wife. At one time the boy, becoming tired of the lonely life, ran away to his home in Dover, leaving Mrs. Dennett alone in her cabin for several days and nights to be entertained by the howling wolves and the bleak storms of winter. Moses Dennett had an excellent farm, which has descended for four generations to the present occupants. He was in the revolution, in Colonel Dike's regiment, enlisting September 8, 1777, discharged December 15, 1777. He married Betsey Nutter. Children, born in Barnstead: 1. Polly, 1782 (?), married Francis Blake; died 1862, in Dorchester. 2. Hannah, born 1784; married John Nutter, of Stratham; died 1859. 3. Annie, born 1786; died March 27, 1807. 4. Charles, born November 8, 1788; married November 1813, "Mappy" Ham, of Rochester;

died March 4, 1867. 5. Oliver, born November 6, 1790; mentioned below. 6. Olive, born February 6, 1793; married 1812, William H. Newell; died August 25, 1878. 7. Mark, born November 5, 1795; died May 10, 1843. 8. Elizabeth, born November 28, 1799; married first, Abijah Ross; second, ——— North; died in Lowell, Massachusetts, January 7, 1873.

(VI) Oliver Dennett, son of Moses Dennett, was born in Barnstead, November 6, 1790, and died there July 11, 1865. He was brought up on his father's farm, and also assisted him in his work as a tailor. He received his education in the district school, and at the age of twenty-two went to fight for his country in the war of 1812. After the war he returned home and took charge of the farm, assisting his father at his trade as before. He was very popular among his townsmen, and was for many years justice of the peace. He served as selectman, and was a Republican in politics. He married April 11, 1810, Eunice Seward, of Barnstead. Children, born in Barnstead: 1. Moses, March 23, 1817; married October 7, 1839, Elizabeth Frank, of Illinois. 2. George Seward, December 7, 1818. 3. Mark Alexander, October 9, 1820; married October 31, 1842, Hannah Foss, of Pittsfield; died April 4, 1900, at Gilmanton. 4. Elizabeth Ann, born October 3, 1822; married December 10, 1842, John Lyford Pickering. 5. Lucia A., born November 15, 1824, married August 23, 1849, Hiram Lee; died March 5, 1875. 6. Charles, born October 15, 1826; married December 29, 1863, Kate G. Watson; died 1904. 7. Maria J., born July 27, 1828; married September 10, 1851, Lafayette Moore. 8. Miranda E., born October 31, 1830; married April 19, 1854, Philemon C. Parsons. 9. Mary W., born October 1, 1832; married December 25, 1850, Freeman Higgins, of Gorham, Maine. 10. Oliver Augustus, born March 7, 1837; married June 8, 1870, Fannie Hopkins of West Lebanon, New Hampshire. 11. Laura, born June 27, 1839, married June 22, 1862, James Emerson, M. D., of Gardner, Massachusetts. 12. John Plumer, born May 27, 1841. 13. Herbert Enos, born March 7, 1844; mentioned below.

(VII) Herbert Enos Dennett, son of Oliver Dennett, was born in Barnstead, March 7, 1844. He married November 17, 1869, in Gloucester, Massachusetts, Alice Howard Battles, born at Graniteville, South Carolina, August 12, 1858, daughter of Benjamin Porters and Lucretia (Olds) Battles. Her father was born in Boston, and her mother in Norwich, Vermont. Benjamin P. Battles was a cotton manufacturer. Children of Herbert Enos Dennett: 1. Lyford Guy, born December 6, 1871; mentioned below. 2. Oliver Max, born March 27, 1874; married June 1, 1893, Mabel Hart, of Belmont; children: i. Kenneth, born November 22, 1898; ii. Helen, May 26, 1900; iii. Dorothy, November 2, 1901; iv. Donald, December 23, 1903; v. Frances, February 10, 1905. 3. Roger Herbert, born July 21, 1876; graduated from Harvard Medical School; is in practice in New York City; April 12, 1905, he married Agena Villette Wheeler, of Brooklyn, New York; two children: Alice, born June 10, 1906; Nancy W., January 18, 1908. 4. Howard Scott, born in Boston, October 1, 1878; is a broker in New York City; he married Mabel Hammond Brett, August 27, 1902; children: Margaret, born June 13, 1903; Mary Hammond, March 22, 1905; Cynthia, September 8, 1906. 5. Eunice, born in Boston, January 16, 1880; married Clarence Walton Eaton, October 16, 1907; resides in New Bedford, Massachusetts. 6. Keith, born in Boston, April 22, 1884, died December 29, 1887. 7. Minot Savage, born in Belmont, Massachusetts, June 4, 1888.

(VIII) Lyford Guy Dennett, son of Herbert E. and Alice Howard (Battles) Dennett, was born in Rockport, Massachusetts, December 6, 1871. He attended the public schools of Belmont, Massachusetts, graduating from the high school. He studied his profession in the Law School of Boston University, and was admitted to the bar at the age of twenty-two years. He entered partnership with William P. Foster, under the firm name of Foster & Dennett, and continued until the firm was dissolved on account of the ill health of the senior partner, in 1904. Since then Mr. Dennett has practiced alone. He has taken high standing in the legal profession and is well known in Suffolk and Middlesex county. He resides in Waverly, Massachusetts, and has offices in Boston. He is a Republican in politics, and a Unitarian in his religion. He is a member of the Blue Lodge of Free Masons. He married, December 6, 1894, Mabel Ellis, who was born September 8, 1871, daughter of Lucius and Grace Gurnsey Ellis, of Belmont, Massachusetts. Children: 1. Jessie, born in Belmont, September 14, 1897. 2. Ellis Howard, born September 3, 1900. 3. Theodore Norris, born in Belmont, May 24, 1904.

BERWICK James Berwick, an active factor in the growth and development of Norwood, a member of the Norwood Press Company, is a native of Halifax, Nova Scotia, born February 18, 1840, son of James and Lucy Charlotte (Anderson) Berwick, of Scotch ancestry.

James Berwick (father) was born at Orkney Islands, in 1808, son of William and Ellen Berwick. James Berwick was a sea captain, and was lost at sea about the year 1852. He married Lucy Charlotte, daughter of John and Margaret (Bauer) Anderson. The parents of John Anderson were natives of Glasgow, Scotland, from whence they came to America, settling in Pennsylvania, near Philadelphia. John Anderson was drafted into the Colonial army, but after a raid by the Colonial army on his mother's property she urged him to join the British army, which he eventually did, and at the close of the war he was retired as adjutant and drew land in Nova Scotia, where he settled. He was a friend of Major Andre. Four children were born to Mr. and Mrs. Berwick: William Anderson; James, see forward; Ellen Margaret; Emily Lucy, died November 3, 1905, married Stuart C. Miller; children: Stuart B., Malcolm D., Mildred A. and Lawrence G. Miller.

James Berwick was reared and educated in Halifax, remaining there until fourteen years of age, when he came to the United States and settled at Cambridge, Massachusetts, where he worked in the office of the *Cambridge Chronicle* for seven years. He then entered the employ of John Wilson of the University Press, later working for his son. For eighteen years he was in the employ of the firm of Rockwell & Churchill, and in 1884 formed a partnership with George H. Smith in the printing business and press work. In December, 1894, they moved their business to Norwood, Massachusetts, in order to secure larger and more adequate facilities for the conduct of their business. In 1903 this was incorporated under the name of Berwick & Smith Company, printers. Its extensive plant comprises a building four hundred and eight feet in length, and eighty-one feet in width, one story in height, except the central part, which is two stories, projecting beyond the wing fronts, and surmounted by a tower. The walls are fifteen feet in height, and the numerous windows, of unusual width, ascend to the ceilings. The walls are of brick, and the floors of concrete. All portions of the building are kept scrupulously clean. The presses are largely Huber and Cottrell, but some other makes are also used. Mr. Berwick supervises the printing plant, while Mr. Smith occupies himself with the office business. A spur track from the railroad leads to the doors of the establishment, so that loading and unloading are readily accomplished. Mr. Berwick has organized for the benefit of the employees of the house, an athletic club and a benefit association. He is chairman of the electric light commissioners of the town of Norwood. He is affiliated with the Masonic fraternity, and is an independent in politics.

Mr. Berwick married, in 1865, Georgianna Jones, who died in 1897, daughter of Benjamin Jones. Children: Walter J., born 1867, married Clara Rich; Emily Florence, married Albert T. Olsen.

HAYWARD There are various traditions in regard to the ancestry of the New England Haywards previous to the immigration of Thomas and William Hayward, who appear to have been in some manner related, and one tradition is that the ancestors of these immigrants went from Denmark and settled in Ireland; and another tradition runs to the effect that the founders of the families in this country were in some manner induced to go on board a ship just before sailing and were brought here and bound out to farmers in order to secure payment of their passage money. But whatever may have been these old traditions the probable truth is that the Haywards are an English family and may have originated there with the conquest of the Danes. In the records the name is found written Hawared, Haywood, Heyward, Heywood, Haiward and Hayward, and one branch of the family after many years from the time of the ancestor changed its name to Howard.

(I) Thomas Hayward, progenitor of the numerous family of that name in Bridgewater, Massachusetts, was of English birth and ancestry, and came to America from Aylesford in the same ship with John Ames, and settled in Duxbury, Massachusetts, before 1638. He was made freeman there in 1646, and afterward was one of the original proprietors and first settlers of Bridgewater. He made his will in 1678, died in 1681, and then was a widower. He left children, but the records are imperfect, because of lack of dates and correct spelling of baptismal names. However, so far as appears to be known the children of Thomas Hayward were sons Thomas, Nathaniel, John, Joseph and Elisha, and daughters Mary and Martha.

(II) John Hayward, son of Thomas, was called "John of the Plain," to distinguish him from John Haward, both of which names had the pronunciation of "Howard." His home was "on the plain between the late old Mr. Jonathan Capeland's and the old powder house," where his son-in-law, Nathaniel Brett, afterward lived. His estate was settled in 1710. He married Sarah, daughter of Experience Mitchell; children: 1. Sarah, born 1663; married, 1683, Nathaniel Brett. 2. John, 1667. 3. Joseph, 1669. 4. Mary, 1672; married 1698, William Ames. 5. Thomas, 1674. 6. Benjamin, 1677. 7. Susanna, 1680; married, 1702, Thomas Hayward. 8. Elizabeth, 1683; married, 1717, Edmund Rawson. 9. Benoni, 1686; married first, Hannah Gould, second, Hannah Page. 10. Mary, 1687.

(III) Deacon Thomas Hayward, son of John and Sarah (Mitchell) Hayward, was born in Bridgewater, in 1674, and lived on the southerly side of Matfield river, within the bounds of East Bridgewater, where his father-in-law Brett lived before him. In 1706 he married Bethiah, daughter of William Brett, and by her had five children: 1. Alice, born 1707. 2. Bethiah, 1715; married, 1741, Arthur Harris. 3. Mary, 1719; married, 1745, Samuel Dunbar. 4. Seth, 1721. 5. Phebe, 1725; married Josiah Washburn.

(IV) Seth Hayward, son of Deacon Thomas and Bethiah (Brett) Hayward, was born in 1721, lived in South Bridgewater, and died there in 1778. He married, in 1748, Tabitha Pratt, died 1789, daughter of Joseph Pratt, Jr.; children: 1. Azariah, born 1749. 2. Sarah, 1752; married, 1774, Noah Whitman. 3. Solomon, 1754. 4. Bethiah, 1757. 5. Charity, 1760; married David Benson. 6. Ruth, 1764.

(V) Solomon Hayward, son of Seth and Tabitha (Pratt) Hayward, was born in Bridgewater in 1754; married, in 1782, Zerviah Washburn; children: 1. Solomon, born 1783; married, 1807, Betsey Bates. 2. Martin, 1784. 3. Joseph, 1786. 4. Silas, 1788. 5. Nahum, 1790. 6. Seth, 1792. 7. Betsey, 1794. 8. Almarine, 1796. 9. Lewis, 1798. 10. Lavinia, 1800. 11. Luther, 1802.

(VI) Martin Hayward, son of Solomon and Zerviah (Washburn) Hayward, was born in Bridgewater, in 1784, and while his name appears in the published records among the children of Solomon and Zerviah, there is no further account of him.

(VII) Captain Linus Hayward, son of Martin, was born about 1821. In 1861, soon after the outbreak of the civil war, he entered the service and was commissioned second lieutenant of the Forty-eighth Massachusetts Infantry, January 18, 1864; promoted first lieutenant March 2, 1864; captain August 8, 1864; and was honorably discharged and mustered out of service July 14, 1865. He married Ruth Alger; children: George E., Martin and Susan Hayward.

(VIII) George E. Hayward, son of Captain Linus and Ruth (Alger) Hayward, was born in West Bridgewater, March 21, 1846, and for many years was engaged in mercantile pursuits, first as a general grocer and grain dealer, afterward becoming a shoe cutter. He is now retired from active pursuits and devotes his attention to his real estate interests, which are quite large. Mr. Hayward married Susan A. Holmes, who died in 1903. They had seven children: Lillian, died in infancy; Merton E., Elmer C., George B., Walter E., Evelyn A. and Carrie L. Hayward.

(IX) Walter Edwin Hayward, son of George H. and Susan A. (Holmes) Hayward, was born at Elmwood, Massachusetts, March 26, 1878, and was given a good education in grammar and high schools. In 1897, at the age of nineteen years, he began his business career as office boy and messenger in the office of the Brockton Street Railway Company. Four years later, in 1901, he was made cashier of the company in Brockton, and in 1903 was advanced to the position of travelling auditor and general cashier for the several lines operated by the company. This office he filled to the satisfaction of his employers and with credit to himself until 1907, when he left the company's service and on October 1 of the same year became auditor of the Ipswich Hosiery Mills, Ipswich, Massachusetts. In November following he was made agent for the operating company and still serves in that capacity. In 1901 Mr. Hayward married Maud Messick, daughter of Amos Messick, of Brockton.

(For first generation see John Symonds 1).

SYMONDS

(II) James Symonds, son of John Symonds, was born in 1663, probably in England. He was a joiner by trade. He settled in the section known as Northfields, Salem, near Marblehead, and there his descendants lived for many generations. He died intestate, and his son John was administrator. His farm at Salem was bought of Henry Lunt, bounded by land of James Boyce, John King and Caleb Buffum. He married, November 20, 1661, Elizabeth Browning, daughter of Thomas. Children: 1. Mary, born November 1, 1662; married December 3, 1685, Edward Norris. 2. Ruth, born February 19, 1664. 3. John, July 8, 1666. 4. James, October 14, 1670; died young. 5. Elizabeth, March, 1673; died young. 6. James, April 14, 1674. 7. Benjamin. 8. Thomas; mentioned below. 9. Elizabeth, died young. 10. Joseph. 11. Sarah. 12. Elizabeth, died young.

(III) Thomas Symonds, son of James Symonds, was born in Salem, Northfields, about 1680. He bought lands at Northfields, inherited others; bought marsh land of Abigail, only daughter of Joseph Williams, April 10, 1719. Just before his death he deeded land to his family, June 16, 1747, to William Lynde; July 13, 1747, to Samuel Symonds, Sr.; August 14, 1749, to Benjamin Symonds, Sr., and May 13, 1751; also October 26, 1751, and May 9, 1752, to son Nathaniel. All this land was at Northfields. His will, dated February 27, 1752, bequeathed to wife Elizabeth and children, mentioned below. Children, born at Salem: 1. Thomas, blacksmith, resided at Reading, Massachusetts; married Hannah ———; conveyed his rights in his father's estate at Northfields, Salem, to brother Nathaniel, January 16, 1760, a fifth interest. 2. Samuel. 3. Benjamin, whose son John was appointed his administrator. 4. Joseph. 5. Nathaniel, mentioned below. 6. Elizabeth, married ——— Trask. 7. Mary, married ——— Osgood. 8. Ruth, married ——— Osgood.

(IV) Nathaniel Symonds, son of Thomas Symonds, was born in 1723, at Salem. He was a potter by trade. His homestead was at Northfields, adjoining land of Benjamin Osgood, Elizabeth Symonds and Jonathan Symonds. As mentioned above he was given land by his father October 26, 1751, and May 9, 1752. He married Elizabeth ———. He deeded his homestead to his son William, August 8, 1781. Children: 1. Nathaniel, 3d., (?) soldier in the revolution. 2. William, mentioned below. Perhaps other children. Nathaniel Symonds was a soldier in the revolution from Salem, a private in Captain Thomas Barnes's company, Colonel John Mansfield's (Nineteenth) regiment, under Lieutenant Colonel Israel Hutchinson, 1775-76.

(V) William Symonds, son of Nathaniel Symonds, was born in Northfields, Salem, about 1760. He died intestate in 1802. A William Symonds of Salem served in the revolution on the brigantine "Massachusetts," Captain John Fish, 1777, from Salem. William Symonds was a potter by trade, and lived at Northfields. He married Elizabeth ———.

(VI) William Phipps Symonds, son or nephew of William Symonds, was born in Salem about 1780. He married Peggy Ropes, also a native of Salem. Children: 1. William Phipps, Jr., married Nancy ———. 2. Benjamin Ropes, mentioned below. 3. Timothy. 4. George, drowned in North River. 5. Margaret, died unmarried. 6. Calvin. 7. Ephraim. 8. James. 9. Joseph.

(VII) Benjamin Ropes Symonds, son of William Phipps Symonds, was born in Salem, 1801, and died there in 1862, aged sixty-one years five months five days. He was educated in the district schools of his native town and learned the trade of shoemaker. In later years he established a retail grocery business at North Salem, and was a successful and prominent citizen. He was a member of the Tabernacle Congregational Church. In politics he was first a Whig, later a Republican, but held no public offices. He married Eliza Shatswell, also a native of Salem, who died in 1842. Children, born in Salem: 1. Benjamin Ropes, November 22, 1829; married Sarah C. Fillebrown; he died in 1890. 2. Thomas S., born December 3, 1832; mentioned below. 3. Joseph, born July 3, 1835; married Flora Kimball. 4. Eliza, born 1842; married Henry M. Bixby.

(VIII) Thomas S. Symonds, son of Benjamin Ropes Symonds, was born in Salem, December 3, 1832. He was educated in the public schools of North Salem. At the age of fifteen he went to sea on coasting voyages. In 1849 he drove a delivery wagon for his father's grocery business. He again went to sea, and in 1850 and 1851 made the voyage to the East Indies and South America in the ship "Siam" of Salem. Then he went to California in a clipper ship, returning to Brooklyn, New York, with a cargo of guano from South America, then shipped on the barque "Argentine" of Salem, Captain George Upton, to South America. He shipped as second mate on the ship "Juniper" on a voyage to Rio Janiero, from Philadelphia, returning with a cargo of coffee. Next he was second mate of the ship "Derby," Captain Hudson, making a voyage first to San Francisco, later to Hong Kong and Calcutta, eighteen months from home. He became first mate of the ship "Ashburton" of Boston, to Savannah, in 1858, with a cargo of ice. He then engaged with his brother Benjamin, who was a grocer. The store was then at the corner of Bridge and North streets, and later was located at North and Federal streets. In 1868 he bought his brother's interests and continued the business until 1906, when on account of failing health he retired. He is one of the best known business men of the city. He attends the Universalist church. In politics he is a Republican, and was a member of the common council of Salem in 1890-91. He was for three years an assistant engineer of the Salem Fire Department. He is a member of Essex Lodge of Odd Fellows. He married first, May 6, 1858, Eliza R. Jordan, born in 1837, died 1867; second, 1869, Sarah F. Cross, born 1851, daughter of Charles B. Cross. Children of first wife: 1. Alice. 2. Annie G., married John S. Ives, Jr. 3. William A., lives with his father. 4. Florence, adopted by Charles S. Buffam and wife. Children of second wife: 5. Sarah, married Charles L. Smith. 6. Nellie G., lives with father. 7. Eva S., married Herbert A. Stone. 8. Bessie, married George E. Millett. 9. Walter, died in infancy.

VERY Bridget Very, born about 1600, was a member of the First church in Salem, in 1648. She lived with her son Samuel, on the north side of Cedar pond, and the brook running from it, about sixty rods from the almshouse in Danvers, where they owned a large tract of land. There her descendants lived for a century afterward, as is shown by various deeds, wills, and other records as well as by family tradition. Perhaps the greater part of her descendants, however, removed to Salem, leaving pursuits of husbandry to become seamen, for many of the name have been shipmasters in Salem, famous mariners some of them. While living in Salem, Bridget Very married a second husband, Edward Giles, who was admitted to the first church in 1636, and by whom she had children, Mehitable, Remember, Eleazer and John Giles, who lived largely in Gloucester and Beverly; the oldest stone in the South Danvers graveyard is that which bears the name of James Giles, grandson of Bridget (Very) Giles. Bridget Very died before 1680. Her children born of her first marriage were: Samuel, 1619; Mary; Thomas, 1626, died 1694.

(II) Samuel Very, son of Bridget Very, born 1619, died in 1683-84. He appears to have been his mother's chief mainstay and supporter until her second marriage. He was a soldier of King Philip's war and took part in the historic Narragansett expedition. For his services in that war he received a grant of land on "Sowhegin" river, but it is not known that he ever occupied his possessions there. His farm in Salem was much larger than his mother's which it adjoined. He left his homestead to his son, Samuel, who in 1769 gave it to his wife, Abigail (Pepper) Very, and her children. In 1793 John, George, Amos and William Very sold to Nathaniel Nurse "all their right to the estate of their honored father, Samuel Very, deceased." Samuel Very married Alice, daughter of John and Frances Woodice (Woodis) and had children: Samuel, born before 1659; Thomas; Jonathan, born 1659; died 1769; Joseph, 1661, died 1663; Isaac, 1663; Joseph, 1664, died 1694; Hannah, 1666; Mary, 1668; Benjamin; John, died 1720; Sarah; Elizabeth.

(III) Jonathan Very, son of Samuel and Alice (Woodice or Woodis) Very, born 1659, died 1769. He was a cordwainer. He married, in 1718, Mary Symonds, daughter of James Symonds, who was son of James Symonds, and the latter a son of John Symonds, 1636. Children of Jonathan and Mary (Symonds) Very; Mary, married a Symonds; Abigail, married a Cook; a daughter, name not found, married a Pratt; Elizabeth, married a Cheever; Martha, married a Pickman; Bethiah, married an Archer; Jonathan, Jr.

(IV) Jonathan Very, Jr., son of Jonathan and Mary (Symonds) Very, was born in Salem and died there, aged about seventy-eight years. He was a teamster and had his house in St. Peter street, near the corner of Church street. His house was taken down a year before the "great fire of 1859." He married, December 19, 1745, Elizabeth Beckford (sometimes written Bickford), born Salem, August 17, 1727, daughter of Deacon John and Elizabeth (Hayward) Beckford. Deacon Beckford, born September 15, 1702, died January 13, 1788, was a son of John and Rebecca (Pinsent) Beckford. John Beckford, born in Marblehead, about 1674, was a son of George Beckford, who lived in Marblehead and of whom little is known other than that administration on his estate was granted June 28, 1678, to his widow Christian, who according to her own deposition was born in 1649. Jonathan, Jr. and Elizabeth (Beckford) Very had nine children, all born in Salem: Elizabeth, 1747; Jonathan, 1748, died young; Jonathan, 1750;

James, 1752, died young; Nathaniel, about 1755; Samuel, 1759; Sarah, 1762; James, 1763; Abigail, 1766.

(V) Samuel Very, son of Jonathan and Elizabeth (Beckford) Very, born 1759, died January 21, 1832. He married (first), May 5, 1782, Abigail Crowninshield, born 1760, died September 20, 1792. She was a daughter of John and Mary (Ives) Crowninshield, and grandson of Dr. John Kaspar Richter von Kronenshelt, the latter the immigrant ancestor of the family of his surname in America. He came of an old Saxon family and it is said traditionally that while a student at the College of Leipsic he became involved in a quarrel with a fellow student and was compelled to flee to this country. He settled in Boston in 1688 and was a celebrated physician there and in Lynn for many years. Among his patients was Elizabeth Allen, of Lynn, daughter of Jacob and Elizabeth (Clifford) Allen, whom he married in 1694. He lived in Lynn a few years and then returned to Boston. By his marriage with Abigail Crowninshield, Samuel Very had four children: Samuel, baptized March 5, 1785, died April, 1813; John Crowninshield, baptized March 6, 1785; Abigail, married Theodon Eames; Jonathan, married Susan Peabody. Samuel Very married (second), September 26, 1793, Mary, widow of Robert Rantoul, and daughter of Andrew and Mary (Lambert) Preston. Andrew Preston, born in Beverly, was a son of Randall and Susanna Preston. By his marriage with Mary (Preston) Rantoul, Samuel Very had one child, William Randolph, who was baptized in the East Church (Unitarian), Salem, July 29, 1794. For his third wife Samuel Very married, May 28, 1797, Martha Cheever, who was baptized in the Tabernacle Church, Salem, June 4, 1769. She was a daughter of Peter and Martha (Osgood) Cheever. Martha was Peter's second wife, his first wife, Margaret Ives, being a cousin of Samuel Very's first wife (see Cheever family). By his wife Martha, Samuel Very had five children; Elizabeth, married, September 28, 1826, John Felt; Nathaniel, mentioned below; Harriet, died unmarried; Martha, married, August 30, 1827, Nathaniel Horton; Mary Ann, married Joseph Gomes.

(VI) Nathaniel Very, son of Samuel and Martha (Cheever) Very, born Salem, about 1798, died there in 1848. He was a shipsmith by trade, following that occupation all his life, and he also appears to have taken considerable interest in the affairs of the old Salem fire department, serving many years as engineer. In political preference he was an old line Whig, and nothing could shake his faith in that party and its principles. He was a member of the Unitarian (Barton Square) Church. On September 9, 1821, Nathaniel Very married Esther Gilbert Ward, who died in Salem, 1868, daughter of Ebenezer B. Ward, of Salem. They had four children: 1. Esther, married George L. Page; both now deceased; one child living, Florence Page. 2. Abbie W., married Samuel Smith, of Salem; both now deceased; three children living: Mary, Samuel and Abbie Smith. 3. Martha C., married Benjamin M. Perkins. 4. Nathaniel O., born March 9, 1838.

(VII) Nathaniel Osgood Very, only son of Nathaniel and Esther Gilbert (Ward) Very, was born in Salem, March 9, 1838. He was educated in the public schools of that city, and began his business career as clerk in a dry-goods store in Salem when he was about eighteen years old. About three years later, when he attained his majority, he was given employment by Mr. Lemuel B. Hatch in his coal office, and with the exception of a few months during the year 1862, he continued in that position until 1885, when he himself succeeded to the proprietorship by purchasing Mr. Hatch's interest in the business. On May 27, 1862, Mr. Very enlisted in the Salem Cadets and went with that command to Fort Warren, Boston Harbor, where the Cadets were on garrison duty until discharged, October 11, 1862. From 1885 until 1905, when he sold out and retired, Mr. Very was actively engaged in business in Salem, and even from the time when he was clerk for Mr. Hatch and practically in charge of his coal business, he has been looked upon as one of the substantial, conservative and thoroughly reliable business men of Salem. He enjoys a wide acquaintance among business men and always has felt a deep interest in the welfare of the city, and while he never has taken an active part in political affairs, never had a desire for public office of any kind, he has always tried to do his full duty as a citizen and taxpayer in promoting the interests of his native city, its institutions and its people. In politics he is a Republican, and in religious preference is Unitarian.

Mr. Very married, March 26, 1863, Elizabeth Ann Hatch, born in Hanson, Plymouth county, Massachusetts, May 2, 1836, daughter of Lemuel B. and Ann C. (Thomas) Hatch, of Hanson (see Hatch family). Mr. and Mrs. Very have one son, Nathaniel Thomas Very, born Salem, August 14, 1865, married Caroline L. Howarth, a daughter of Austin S. and Miriam (Howard) Howarth. He entered his father's coal office soon after leaving school, and was connected with the coal business until 1905. He is a member of the Second Corps Cadets (Salem, Massachusetts), and during the Spanish-American war was stationed with other members of his company and corps at Marblehead, Massachusetts. He is first lieutenant of Company A.

HATCH Elder William Hatch, of Sandwich, Kent, England, was born there, and a merchant, and was of Scituate, Massachusetts, before 1633. Soon afterward he went to England, and returning to this country in March, 1635, in the "Hercules" of Sandwich, brought with him wife Jane, five children, six servants and much goods of various kinds. He sat down again in Scituate, where he was a merchant, a man of considerable consequence in the plantation, ruling elder of the second church in Scituate, 1644, lieutenant of militia, and otherwise a man of influence as well as substance. In 1637 he was presented at court for trespass, and the punishment meted out to him therefor was that he "reap the crop thereupon this year, and leave the land." In 1638 he had granted him "an Island called the Old Island (afterward Hatches island) lying on the southwest side of the North river, containing about 20 acres." In 1638 he was a juror at the trial of three men charged with killing an Indian, in 1638-9 was surveyor of highways; one of a committee to provide for war against the Indians, 1642; elected lieutenant "for trayning their men," 1643. Elder Hatch died November 6, 1651. He married, in England, Jane ———, who survived him and afterward married Elder Thomas King, who succeeded Elder Hatch in his church office. Elder William Hatch had children, all born in England; Jane, Anne, Walter, Hannah, William and Jeremiah.

(II) Jeremiah Hatch, son of Elder William and Jane, was made freeman 1658, and frequently served on juries of inquest and trial; was selectman 1672 to 1675, and 1679 to 1686; deputy to general court 1676, and five times afterward; grand juror, 1657; commissioner to assist in dividing common lands, 1662-3; elected constable in 1674, but declined to serve. He lived near his brother Walter, with whom for a number of years he carried on ship building. His will is dated 1703-4, and was admitted to probate March 16, 1712-13. He married, about 1657, Mary, daughter of John Hewes, "the Welshman;" children, all born in Scituate: 1. Mary, 1658. 2. Jeremiah, 1660. 3. Joanna, 1662. 4. Mercy, 1665. 5. John, 1666-7. 6. Lydia, 1669. 7. Phebe, 1671. 8. Thomas, 1672. 9. James, 1674. 10. Anna, 1677. 11. Deborah, 1678-9. 12. Israel, died before 1702. 13. Elizabeth. 14. Joseph, died 1748-9.

(III) James Hatch, son of Jeremiah and Mary (Hewes) Hatch, was born in Scituate, May 4, 1674, and died May, 1741, leaving a will in which provision is made that his wife Abigail shall have "all his indoor movables, ten bushels of corn yearly during life, the keeping of a cow winter and summer, the great room in the house, and the keeping of a pig in the pasture." He lived in that part of Scituate which was set off to Hanover, and appears to have owned considerable land and to have bought and sold quite extensively, but it does not appear that he was active in town affairs. He married about 1696, Abigail ———; children: 1. James, born November 19, 1698. 2. Phebe, June 14, 1701, died young. 3. Abigail, May 19, 1704. 4. Shadrack, May 26, 1706.

(IV) James Hatch, son of James and Abigail Hatch, was born in Scituate November 19, 1698, and lived in Hanover, where he was a husbandman. Little else is known of him except that he bought lands in 1741 and 1743, married Anna ———; children: 1. James, born February 22, 1732. 2. Experience, born 1739, died 1820; married April 19, 1759, Seth Freeman.

(V) James Hatch, son of James and Anna Hatch, was born in Hanover, February 22, 1732, and died in Pembroke, February 11, 1824. In Pembroke records he is called captain, but the character of his military service does not appear. He married first, January 27, 1763, Mary Moore, born September 17, 1746, died June 6, 1777, daughter of Thomas and Mary Moore, of Pembroke; second, January 29, 1784, Sarah Cushing. Children, all born in Pembroke, and of his first marriage: 1. Polly, May 27, 1764; married April 11, 1782, Joseph Barstow; removed to Vermont. 2. Phebe, May 1, 1766, died April 5, 1799; married March 7, 1785, Joseph Torrey. 3. Charlotte, March 1, 1768, died February 11, 1831; married May 28, 1786, Williams Collamore. 4. Anna, October 11, 1770, died May 11, 1799. 5. James, November 3, 1773. 6. Betsey, May 12, 1774, died November 4, 1780. 7. Nathaniel, November 12, 1777, died October 11, 1780.

(VI) James Hatch, son of James and Mary

Lemuel B. Hatch

(Moore) Hatch, was born in Pembroke, November 3, 1773, and died July 7, 1811. He is called a "refiner of iron." He married, June 29, 1794, Orpah Bonney, born May 12, 1777, died February 8, 1810, daughter of Lemuel and Lucy Bonney. Lemuel Bonney, born January 15, 1737, died December 7, 1803, son of Ezekiel and Hannah Bonney. Lemuel and Lucy Bonney married December 3, 1761, and had four children: Lemuel, born June 19, 1767; Luther, February 9, 1769; Lucy, September 4, 1772; Orpah, May 12, 1777. James and Orpah (Bonney) Hatch had children: 1. James, born March 3, 1796. 2. Luther, about 1798, died North Bridgewater, November 29, 1818. 3. Nathaniel, July 4, 1800, died July 2, 1864. 4. Calvin, December 11, 1803; lived at East Bridgewater, and was a cabinet maker and carpenter; married June 4, 1829, Zelpha W., born March 14, 1809, daughter of Benjamin and Betsey (Willis) Palmer. 5. Lemuel Bonney, twin, August 31, 1806. 6. Lewis, twin, August 31, 1806. 7. Orpah Bonney, February 8, 1810; married November 5, 1830, David R., son of David and Abiah Green.

(VII) Lemuel Bonney Hatch, son of James and Orpah (Bonney) Hatch, was born in Hanson, Massachusetts, August 31, 1806, and died in Salem, Massachusetts, March 1, 1885. For several years he was superintendent in a woolen mill in Hanson, and about 1840 removed to Salem and began a successful career as dealer in wood and coal. He continued in business many years and on retiring was succeeded by his son-in-law, Nathaniel O. Very. He also took an active and commendable interest in public affairs in Salem and was regarded as one of the leading men of the Republican party in the city. He served in various capacities, notably as overseer of the poor, member of the board of aldermen, and although earnestly urged to stand as the candidate of his party for the mayoralty of the city he steadfastly refused the proffered honor. Although he was always a firm and unyielding Republican, Mr. Hatch never felt any particular desire for public office, but as a loyal citizen and considerable taxpayer he regarded it a duty to the city as well as his party to give some service for the public welfare. This he did, and whatever capacity he consented to serve in the municipal government he performed the duties of his office with the same scrupulous care which always marked his business life in respect to personal concerns; and he was just as honest as he was careful, and the entire people of the city without distinction of party appreciated the man for his known character and worth. Mr. Hatch married June 14, 1835, Ann C. Thomas, born November 2, 1812, daughter of Ira and Betsey (Cushing) Thomas; children: 1. Elizabeth Ann, born May 2, 1836. 2. Charles Francis, November 14, 1841. 3. Thomas Cushing, January 12, 1847.

(VIII) Elizabeth Ann Hatch, only daughter of Lemuel Bonney and Ann C. (Thomas) Hatch, was born in Hanson, Massachusetts, May 2, 1836, and married March 26, 1863, Nathaniel Osgood Very, born March 9, 1838; children, both born in Salem: 1. Annie Osgood, January 20, 1864, died July 31, 1864. 2. Nathaniel Thomas, August 14, 1865 (see Very family).

(VIII) Charles Francis Hatch, son of Lemuel Bonney and Ann C. Hatch, was born in Salem, November 14, 1841. He received his education in the public schools of that city, enlisted there for naval service during the civil war, and for the last thirty years has been proprietor of the Nonpareil Oil Company, of Boston. He lives in Everett, Massachusetts. His naval record from 1863 is written as follows: "Was in the war of the rebellion; first ordered to sloop-of-war "Savannah," then to gunboat "Queen;" executive officer of the tinclad "Glide;" pro tem duty on board monitors "Catskill" and "Ironsides;" at close of war ordered to special duty as executive officer and clerk of naval station at St. Paul de Leander, southwest coast of Africa; resigned in 1869." Mr. Hatch married January 17, 1865, Mary Dodge, born August 1, 1847, daughter of Charles P. and Mary Dodge. Children: 1. Mary Frances, born January 18, 1867. 2. Bessie Alberta, July 20, 1869.

(VIII) Thomas Cushing Hatch, youngest child of Lemuel Bonney and Ann C. (Thomas) Hatch was born in Salem, January 12, 1847, and died October 15, 1865. He was cavalryman in the United States service in 1864, engaged in duty on the Canadian border, and his death was in a measure caused or hastened by hardships and exposures encountered while on duty there.

(For ancestry see Henry Way 1.)

WAY

(V) William Way, son of Ebenezer and Mary (Harris) Way, was born in New London, May 15, 1720, and married May 3, 1765, Mary Lathrop.

(VI) George Way, son of William and Mary (Lathrop) Way, was born in New London, Connecticut, June 18, 1771. He married

December 5, 1773, in New London, Sarah Douglas, a descendant of the distinguished family of Douglas of Scotland, whose representatives of that surname have for centuries figured conspicuously in English, Scotch, Welsh and American history. Sarah Douglas was a cousin of the American statesman, Stephen A. Douglas, and the late Arthur Truman Way, of Salem, Massachusetts, grandson of Sarah, is said to have borne a striking resemblance to the famous statesman. The children of George and Sarah (Douglas) Way were George, Sally, Gordon, Rhoderic, Joseph, Lucy, Emily, Christopher and Truman.

(VII) Truman Way, son of George and Sarah (Douglas) Way, was born in Lempster, New Hampshire, February 22, 1811, and came to Salem, Massachusetts, June 30, 1849. On September 20, 1857, he left that city and for the next fifteen years was supervising engineer in railroad construction in New York state, Canada and the west. He lived several years in Indianapolis, Indiana, where he was connected with the operation of the Eastern railroad, and died there March 14, 1889. Mr. Way was admitted to Essex Lodge, F. and A. M., July 1, 1856, but had already taken his degrees in Canada. He married Sarah L. Boynton, of Cornish, Maine; children: Emily; Oliver D., ex-alderman of Salem, married Lucy Varney; Ellen, married Thomas Stewart; William, married Belle Crawford; Arthur Truman.

(VIII) Arthur Truman Way, son of Truman and Sarah L. (Boynton) Way, was born in Salem, March 21, 1855, and died in that city March 10, 1908. He was a child of less than two years when his father went west, and his youth was spent chiefly in Indianapolis, Indiana, where he was educated in the public schools and graduated from the high school. When about sixteen years old he returned to Salem, and there set out to gain a thorough and practical knowledge of the leather business. Soon after 1890 he started in business for himself, occupying the Riley, the Braden and the Leonard Harrington factories, securing the latter factory in 1895 and afterward carrying on an extensive and very successful business there. Mr. Way was counted among the most capable and successful business men of Salem, and in social, fraternal and political circles he was one of the most popular men in the city. But he was not a politician and never sought political advancement, although he served two years as member of the board of aldermen. In Freemasonry he attained the highest degree conferred on craftsmen. He was past master of Essex Lodge, F. and A. M.; past high priest of Washington Chapter, R. A. M.; past illustrious master of Salem Council, R. and S. M.; past eminent commander of Winslow Lewis Commandery, K. T., of Salem; and past thrice potential grand master of Sutton Lodge of Perfection, A. A. S. R. For several years he was grand lecturer of the Grand Chapter of Royal Arch Masons of the jurisdiction of Massachusetts, and deputy grand high priest of the same body, and acting grand high priest during the illness of the incumbent of that office; and he discharged the duties of his position with dignity and much credit. In 1907 he had the high distinction of being deputy grand master of the Grand Lodge of the jurisdiction of Massachusetts, and in that capacity officiated at the laying of the corner stone of the Pilgrim monument at Provincetown, assisted by President Theodore Roosevelt. Mr. Way also was second lieutenant commander of Massachusetts Consistory (32) A. A. S. R. At the annual conclave of the Supreme Council of Scottish Rite Masons of the northern jurisdiction of the United States, held in September, 1907, he was elected a 33d degree Mason. He also was a member of the Ancient and Honorable Artillery of Massachusetts, an honorary member of the Salem Cadets, and an active member of the Salem and Colonial clubs of Salem. On October 12, 1886, Arthur Truman Way married Sarah Pearson Nye, born October 17, 1855, daughter of Joseph Warren and Susan Abbie (Rhodes) Nye (see Nye). Mrs. Way is a woman of culture, refined tastes and social position. Before her marriage she was for fourteen years a teacher in the public schools of Lynn, and for nine years a member of the choir of the Washington Street Baptist Church, Lynn. Mr. and Mrs. Way had two children—Eleanor Varney and Jessie Nye Way.

NYE For the origin of this ancient family we must look to Denmark, for according to history and tradition about the middle of the thirteenth century there came one who settled in Fredericksborg bailiwick and Slangerup parish, in the Sjelland section of Denmark, and who is said to have been a descendant of Harold Blautand through his daughter who married the famous Swedish hero Styribiorn, son of Olaf, king of Sweden.

(I) Lave Nye, son of this descendant of the royal house of Sweden, became bishop of Roskilde, in the Sjelland section, 1316.

(II) Sven Nye is mentioned in 1346 as the heir of his father, the bishop of Roskilde.

(III) Marten Nye was declared in 1363 the heir of his father in Tudse.

(IV) Nils Nye, son of Marten Nye, is mentioned in 1418 as possessing land in Tudse, which he then deeded to his son.

(V) Bertolf Nye is mentioned in 1466 as son of Nils Nye of Tudse. He had sons James and Randolf, the former of whom on account of a duel fled to England, accompanied by his brother Randolf, and settled in Wiltshire, removing afterward to Hampshire.

(VI) Randolf Nye settled in Sussex, 1527, and held land in Uckfield. His son William is mentioned as having inherited land of his father, Randolf of Uckfield.

(VII) William Nye, son of Randolf, married Agnes, daughter of Ralph Tregian, of Ballance-Horned, Hertfordshire, studied for the ministry, and became rector of the parish church of Ballance-Horned.

(VIII) Ralph Nye, son of William, became heir to his father in Uckfield and Ballance, 1556; married, 1555, Margaret Merynge, of St. Mary, Woolchurch, and had five children.

(IX) Thomas Nye, son of Ralph and Margaret, married, 1583, Katherine Poulsden, of London, and had four children, the youngest of whom was Thomas Nye, father of the immigrant ancestor and progenitor in America of the family of this surname intended to be treated in these annals.

(X) Thomas Nye, son of Thomas and Katherine, married for his second wife, 1619, Agnes Rye, and had two sons—Benjamin, the immigrant, and Thomas.

(I) Benjamin Nye, first son of Thomas and Agnes, was born at Bidlenden, Kent, England, May 4, 1620, came in the "Abigail" to Lynn, Massachusetts, in 1635, and went to Sandwich, Massachusetts, in 1637. He is mentioned as able to bear arms, 1643; contributed toward building a mill, 1654, and toward building a meeting house, 1655; surveyor of highways, 1655; took the oath of fidelity, 1657; grand juror, 1658 and 1668; constable, 1661; trial juror, 1662. He fulfilled other offices of greater or less importance, and appears to have discharged their duties with fidelity. He married, October 19, 1640, Katherine, daughter of Rev. Thomas Tupper, who came in the "Abigail," 1635, and went to Sandwich. They had children: 1. Mary. 2. John. 3. Ebenezer. 4. Jonathan, born November 20, 1649. 5. Mercy, April 4, 1652. 6. Caleb. 7. Nathan. 8. Benjamin, killed by Indians at Rehoboth, in King Philip's war, 1676.

(II) Jonathan Nye, son of Benjamin and Katherine (Tupper) Nye, was born in Sandwich, November 20, 1649; took the oath of allegiance, 1678; served as grand juror, 1681; selectman, 1698. He married first, Hannah ———; second, Patience Burgess; children, four by his first and ten by his second wife: Jabez, Sarah, Joanna, Ichabod, Jonathan, Patience, Joseph, Benjamin, Thomas, Abigail, Isaac, Mary, David, Zervia.

(III) Joseph Nye, son of Jonathan and Patience (Burgess) Nye, was born in Sandwich, November 16, 1675, and died before May 4, 1750. He lived in Sandwich, and probably was a husbandman, for he was possessed of considerable land as well as personal property. He married December 10, 1741, Mary Bodfish, of Barnstable, born June 17, 1719, daughter of Joseph and Thankful (Glish) Bodfish; children, born in Sandwich: 1. Joseph, October 10, 1742. 2. Sylvanus, August 16, 1744. 3. Samuel.

(IV) Dr. Samuel Nye, son of Joseph and Mary (Bodfish) Nye, was born in Sandwich, March 29, 1749, and died August 31, 1834. He graduated from Harvard College in 1771, and settled for practice in Salisbury, removing thence to Newbury, and was there at the beginning of the revolutionary war. The military records of the state mention his service as follows: Samuel Nye, Newbury, doctor; descriptive list sworn to in Suffolk county, June 9, 1780, of the officers and crew of the ship "America," commanded by Capt. John Somes; age 27 years; stature, 5 feet 6 inches; complexion dark; residence, Newbury. Under his first commission as surgeon Dr. Nye served from June 18 to August 9, 1780, but from August 16, 1778, to May 29, 1779, he was surgeon on board the ship "Vengeance," Captain Wingate Newman, commander. After the war Dr. Nye returned to his practice in Newbury and in connection with professional employments served in various official capacities. In 1774 he was a member of the committee of safety and correspondence, town clerk 1786-87, and served as selectman of the town for ten years. On April 22, 1783, Dr. Nye married Abigail Bachelder, who survived him and died in Salisbury, May 22, 1848, aged ninety-four years: children: 1. Abigail, born March 21, 1784; married May 29, 1804, Fessenden Clark. 2. Samuel, April 24, 1785, died July 25, 1816. 3. Joseph Proctor, November 11, 1786. 4. Clarissa, June 2, 1788. 5. James, August 17, 1792, died September 8, 1793. 6. Mary Ann, October 4, 1794, died October 26, 1794.

(V) Joseph Nye, son of Dr. Samuel and

Abigail (Bachelder) Nye, was born in Salisbury, November 11, 1786, and died there April 4, 1842. Little else is known of him except that his wife's name was Sallie, and that their children were all born in Salisbury: 1. Joseph, died October 31, 1822. 2. Samuel, died October 13, 1822. 3. John P., died October 21, 1822. 4. Joseph Warren, born January 24, 1816. 5. Dr. James M., died April 21, 1872; married June 29, 1842, Hannah C. Peasley, of Amesbury, who died July 6, 1898. Dr. Nye lived in Lynn.

(VI) Joseph Warren Nye, son of Joseph Proctor and Sallie Nye, was born January 24, 1816, at Salisbury Point. His mother died when he was four years old, and he was brought up in the family of her parents; and while living with them he became acquainted with Whittier, the poet. He learned the trade of cabinet making with John Woodbury, of Lynn, his great-uncle, and in 1855 located at East Princeton, Massachusetts, but after a few years returned to Lynn and carried on business there until the time of his death, November 21, 1901. He married June 1, 1841, Susan Abbie, daughter of Ezra Rhodes, of Lynn; children: 1. Ezra Warren, born 1843, died March 6, 1863. 2. Abbie Augusta, born 1848, died August 4, 1849. 3. Ida Frances, married June 14, 1871, Christopher D. Chadwell. 4. Annie Augusta, died September 30, 1908. 5. Sarah Pearson, born October 17, 1855; married October 12, 1886, Arthur Truman Way, who died March 10, 1908 (see Way). 6. Eleanor Porter, born April 9, 1858, died January 25, 1860.

KNOWLES (I) Richard Knowles, immigrant ancestor, was born in England, and settled first in Cambridge, Massachusetts. He removed soon to Hampton, New Hampshire, where he died February 1, 1682. Very little is known of him. Children: 1. James, born at Cambridge, November 17, 1648. 2. John, mentioned below.

(II) John Knowles, son of Richard Knowles, was born probably in England, about 1638. He removed, according to Hampton history, from Cambridge to Hampton, and married there, July 10, 1660, Jemima, daughter of Francis and Isabella (Brand) Asten. He took the oath of allegiance in December, 1678, and died at Hampton (north), December 5, 1705. He bought of Giles Fifield a house and lot of ten acres, and also six acres of marsh. His homestead is now or was lately owned by his lineal descendants. He was blind for ten years before his death. Children: 1. John, Jr., born February 6, 1661; mentioned below. 2. Ezekiel, born August 19, 1663; died December 11, 1666. 3. James, born November 20, 1665; died February 1, 1682. 4. Simon, born November 22, 1667; married Rachel ———; second, Rachel Joy. 5. Joseph, born June 11, 1672, died young. 6. Sarah, born April 17, 1676; married Robert Drake; died June 8, 1742. 7. Hannah, born April 18, 1678; died September 12, 1769; married William Locke.

(III) John Knowles, son of John Knowles, was born at Hampton, New Hampshire, February 6, 1661. He resided on the homestead where his father settled. He married Susanna ———, died October 17, 1745, aged eighty-two years. Children: 1. John, born May 14, 1686; married Tryphena Locke. 2. Ezekiel, born June 29, 1687; mentioned below. 3. Amos, born about 1689; married Abigail Dowse; died February 24, 1746. 4. Reuben, born 1691. 5. Abigail, born December 3, 1695; married Ephraim Marston; died January 22, 1727.

(IV) Ezekiel Knowles, son of John Knowles, was born June 29, 1687, at Hampton, and resided at Hampton and Rye. He married at Hampton, January 31, 1712, Mary, daughter of David Wedgewood. Children, born at Rye: 1. Hannah, March 1, 1713. 2. Nathan, baptized May 27, 1716; married Hannah Clifford. 3. Mary, born November 2, 1718; married John Lane. 4. Amos, November 4, 1722; mentioned below. 5. David, September 1, 1725; married Deborah Palmer.

(V) Amos Knowles, son of Ezekiel Knowles, was born at Rye, New Hampshire, November 4, 1722, and died at Candia, New Hampshire, in 1809, aged eighty-seven years. He settled at Candia, and was a farmer. He married, October 11, 1744, Libby ———. Children, born at Rye or Candia: 1. Nathaniel, 1745; soldier in the revolution. 2. Lydia, 1747. 3. Ezekiel, 1749; in the revolution. 4. Isaac, 1751. 5. Amos, 1755; in the revolution. 6. Elizabeth, 1755; died young. 7. John, 1759; in the revolution. 8. Elizabeth, 1761; married Benjamin Palmer. 9. David, mentioned below. 10. Seth, born at Candia, April 12, 1766; married June 14, 1789, Anna Emerson.

(VI) David Knowles, son of Amos Knowles, was born in 1764, in Rye, New Hampshire. According to the federal census of 1790 he was living at Starling Plantation, Maine, Lincoln county. He settled at Corinna, Maine.

(VII) Loel Knowles, son of David Knowles, was born at Corinna, Maine, about 1801, and died in 1886. He was a farmer, and lived the greater part of his life in his native state, and was one of the most enterprising and progressive men of Corinna. He was an active and consistent member of the Methodist Episcopal church. He married Rosamond Wilkinson, a native of Maine also, daughter of William Wilkinson, a farmer in Corinna. Children, born at Corinna: 1. Flora, June, 1853; married N. S. Johnson, of Corinna. 2. Lilly, September 9, 1860; died March 14, 1906. 4. Loel L., mentioned below. 5. Raymond L. The personal names Loel and Lilley were common among the older families of Reading, Massachusetts.

(VIII) Loel L. Knowles, son of Loel Knowles, was born at Corinna, Maine, July 4, 1855. He was educated in the public schools of his native town. For many years he has conducted a prosperous grocery business in Haverhill, Massachusetts, established by him in 1876. He stands high in the confidence of business men in Haverhill and vicinity, and is highly respected by his townsmen. He is a member of Mutual Relief Lodge of Odd Fellows. He married second, 1884, Flora E. Clark, of Corinna. Child by first wife: 1. Arthur L., born February 11, 1880; lives in Haverhill. Children of second wife: 2. Raymond L., born February 21, 1885; mentioned below. 3. Edna B., September 4, 1891.

(IX) Raymond L. Knowles, son of Loel L. Knowles, was born February 21, 1885. He was educated in the public schools of Haverhill, Massachusetts. He was first employed for a time in a broker's office in Boston. In 1904 he was appointed teller of the Pentucket Savings Bank, and in 1905 he was chosen to his present position of treasurer of the bank. Mr. Knowles has the sort of personality that is well fitted for a responsible and important position. He has made many friends by his courtesy and kindness both for the bank and for himself. He is a member of the Pentucket Club, of Haverhill. In politics he is a Republican. He is unmarried.

SHEPPARD Opinions are divided as to whether the Sheppards are of Scotch or English ancestry; but they were among the earliest settlers of this country, not only in the New England states but also in the colony of New Jersey. Shourds, in his "History of Fenwick's Colony," says that they emigrated from England probably as early as 1683, and after remaining in Shrewsbury for a few years finally located in what is now Cumberland county, on Penn's Neck, a small peninsula bounded on the north by the Cohansey river and on the south by a small creek named Back creek. Here, on September 29, 1690, the three brothers James, Thomas and John Sheppard bought of Jonathan Walling one hundred and fifty acres apiece, on which they settled and in the region of which their descendants have lived for centuries. Their brother David had previously bought another place near there, and the descendants of all four brothers are very numerous throughout all that part of New Jersey. James Sheppard died in 1690, leaving two daughters, and his brothers were his executors; David died in 1695, leaving a wife and seven or eight children; Thomas Sheppard apparently moved up into Monmouth county; John Sheppard is treated below.

(I) Besides the one hundred and fifty acres he purchased at first, John Sheppard bought one hundred and fifty acres more adjoining, and then gave the whole of this property to his eldest son Dickason Sheppard, at the same time buying another three hundred and eighty-five acres for himself "near Cohansey and adjoining Edmund Gibbons." He died intestate in 1710, leaving seven children: Dickason, David, John, Enoch (died 1717), Job, treated below; Margaret, married Thomas Abbot; and Hannah, who married first, Timothy Brook, Jr., and second, Obadiah Holmes.

(II) Job Sheppard, son of John, was born 1706, and died March 2, 1757, of smallpox, and was buried in Salem, having been for many years the first pastor of the Baptist church at Mill Hollow. By his wife Catherine he had thirteen children: Elnathan, married and lived in Hopewell township, near the old Cohansey church; Job, treated below; Belbe, 1737 to 1764, who lived and died at Alloways creek; Elizabeth, died young; Jemima, married, but died without issue; Daniel, married and lived in Salem, and had one child, Daniel; Kerenhappuch, who lived in Lower Alloways Creek township; Rebecca, who became the first wife of Jonathan Bowen, and had one child that died in infancy; Catherine, died about sixteen years of age; Cumberland, married Amy Matlack, of Gloucester county, and had several children; Martha, married Isaac Mulford, of Hopewell township, and had one child; Keziah, married William Kelsay, and went west; Ruth, died unmarried, about twenty-two years old.

(III) Job, second son of Job and Catherine

Sheppard, was born July 6, 1735, lived at Hopewell, near Bowentown, Cumberland county, and married Rachel, daughter of Thomas Mulford, of Cumberland, and had seven children, one of whom was Job, treated below.

(IV) Job, son of Job and Rachel (Mulford) Sheppard; served in the war of 1812, and was buried at Red Bank, New Jersey. He married Sarah, daughter of William Kelsey, who was a captain and paymaster in the American revolution. Among his children was William Kelsey Sheppard, treated below.

(V) William Kelsey Sheppard, son of Job and Sarah (Kelsey) Sheppard, was born in Greenwich, Cumberland county, about 1810. He was a farmer and resided in Greenwich all his life, and owned a large farm there. He married, in 1831, Sarah Ewing Fithian, born 1809, daughter of Charles Beatty and Mary (Ewing) Fithian. Mary Ewing was daughter of Enos Ewing; and Charles Beatty Fithian was son of Joel and Elizabeth (Beatty) Fithian, and grandson of Samuel and Phoebe Fithian. Elizabeth Beatty was daughter of Charles and Ann, daughter of John Reading, a descendant of one of the earliest Quaker settlers of Burlington; and granddaughter of John Beatty and Christiana Clinton, a cousin of Governor George Clinton, of New York. William Kelsey and Sarah Ewing (Fithian) Sheppard had children: Joseph; Jemima; Joel Fithian, treated below; Catharine; Lewis, a colonel in the civil war; Ruth, married Mr. Evans; Robert; William; Belle, and Mary.

(VI) Joel Fithian Sheppard, son of William Kelsey and Sarah Ewing (Fithian) Sheppard, was born in Greenwich, New Jersey, 1835. He was educated in his native town, and apprenticed to a ship carpenter. He went to sea, and later became master of a vessel, and followed the sea for fourteen years. During the civil war he twice ran the blockade of the Potomac. His brothers and first cousins fought under the Stars and Stripes, while not a few distant relatives were with the Confederates. In 1869 he went into the coal business, locating in East Braintree, Massachusetts, and later in Quincy. He is a Republican in politics, and in 1870 was representative to the general court. He was for a time president of the Co-operative Bank. He is a member and past master of Delta Lodge of Free Masons; of the Royal Arch Chapter, of which he has been high priest; and South Shore Commandery, Knights Templar. He has always been interested in church work, and has been an active member of the Congregational Church, first at Weymouth, later at Braintree. He married in 1856, Hannah A. Wallen, born 1838, and has children: Charles G., married Mary Perkins, and has one son, Willard Perkins; Eben Wallen, treated below; Ella W., married Dr. William Gallagher, and has one daughter, Rebecca Gallagher; Ida E., married B. H. Davidson, and has one daughter, Irene Davidson.

(VII) Eben Wallen Sheppard, son of Joel Fithian and Hannah A. (Wallen) Sheppard, was born in Greenwich, New Jersey, May 7, 1860. He was educated in the public schools of Braintree, Massachusetts. In 1882 he came to Quincy to engage in the retail coal business in partnership with his father and brother. He is a well known and highly respected business man of Quincy. He is a Republican, and was representative from his district in the general court in 1899, 1900 and 1901. He is a member of the Union Congregational Church of Weymouth, but attends the Bethany Congregational Church of Quincy. He is a director of the Quincy Co-operative Bank. He is a member of Rural Lodge of Free Masons; of St. Stephens' Chapter, Royal Arch Masons; of South Shore Commandery, Knights Templar; and of Aleppo Temple, Order of the Mystic Shrine. He married Fannie M., daughter of Asa and Mercy (Clapp) Pratt. Children: Joel Fithian, graduate of Cornell University, class of 1907; Carl R., student in Cornell, class of 1908, married Charlotte B. Van Buren; Oliver Leeth; and Mercedes. (See Pratt).

HANSON The surname Hanson is of very ancient origin, and was handed down by the Flemings to the English speaking people. The root of the name is Hans, which is only one of the abbreviations of the original Johannes, and from the latter we derive the familiar Hansons, Hankins, Hankinsons, Hancocks and others. The Hanson ancestry in the old world has been traced back through the several generations for centuries, even to the time of Roger de Rastrich, 1251, reign of Henry III, in the wapentake of Morley, Yorkshire, England; and thence to Hugh de Rastrich; thence to John de Rastrich; thence to John de Rastrich; thence to Henry de Rastrich; thence to John de Rastrich, called "Henry's son" and then Hanson; thence to John Hanson; thence to John Hanson, whose son, John Hanson, was an immediate ancestor of the particular family of that surname in America of which this narrative is intended to treat.

(I) Thomas Hanson, immigrant, was born in England, came thence to New England, and was at Dover, New Hampshire, in 1639. In 1658-9 he had a grant of a hundred acres of land near Salmon Falls, was made freeman in 1661, lived at Cochecho in 1664-5, and died in 1666. "Old widow Hanson," as the record reads, was killed by Indians, June 28, 1689. The baptismal name of his wife was Mary, but her family name does not appear. Children being Thomas, born about 1643; Tobias, about 1640; Isaac, born at Dover; and Timothy.

(II) Tobias Hanson, son of Thomas and Mary Hanson, was born about 1640, and was killed by Indians May 10, 1693. He lived in Dover, and was taxed there from 1662 to 1672. His wife, whose name does not appear, was made prisoner by Indians, June 28, 1689. Children: Tobias, Jr.; Joseph; Benjamin.

(III) Tobias Hanson, Jr., son of Tobias, was born at Dover, about 1675, and was one of the first of his family to espouse the faith of the Society of Friends, or Quakers, as they were called, and punished because they were such. He married first, Lydia Cheeney; second, Ann Lord. He had two children by his first and eight by his second wife: 1. Benjamin. 2. Elizabeth, married Samuel Buxton. 3. Mercy, born August 4, 1699; married Stephen Varney. 4. Tobias, born 1702. 5. Judith, February 7, 1703; married Samuel Twombley. 6. Joseph, January 10, 1704, died September 5, 1758; married first Rebecca Shepard; second, Sarah Scammon; third, Susannah Burnham. 7. Nathaniel. 8 .Isaac, married Susanna Canney. 9. Samuel. 10. Aaron.

(IV) Tobias Hanson, son of Tobias and Ann (Lord) Hanson, was born in Dover, in March, 1702, and died August 27, 1765. He was a farmer and a devout Friend, and both of his wives were Friends, as well as all of his children. He married first, December 22, 1728, Judith Varney, born April 11, 1710, daughter of Ebenezer and Mary (Otis) Varney; second, October 21, 1750, Sarah Fry (Frye), daughter of William Frye. Children: 1. Anne, married ——— Cortland. 2. Mary, married Jedadiah Varney. 3. Elizabeth, married Reuben Tuttle. 4. Aaron, born about 1740, removed to Rochester, New Hampshire, and was one of the proprietors of that town. 5. Patience, June 12, 1743; married Benjamin Meder. 6. Moses, February 3, 1744-5. 7. Mercy.

(V) Moses Hanson, son of Tobias and Sarah (Frye) Hanson, was born in Dover, February 3, 1744-5, and at the time of his marriage was living in Rochester, New Hampshire. He married Mary Hanson; children: Timothy, Moses, Lydia and Catherine, and one other child.

(VI) Moses Hanson, son of Moses and Mary (Hanson) Hanson, was born probably in Rochester, New Hampshire, although the record of his birth is not found. His brother Timothy was born in 1787, and Moses is believed to have been a year or two his junior. He was a minister of the Society of Friends, a very pious and exemplary man and worthy leader of the meeting. He married Mary Varney, and lived in Farmington, where both died. Children, all born in Farmington: 1. Jane, married William Penn Hussey, of North Berwick, Maine, and had William P. and Charles F. Hussey. 2. Gilman, married late in life. 3. Huldah, married Horace C. Ware, of Salem, Massachusetts. 4. Job Varney, born November 7, 1825. 5. John, born November, 1830; married, 1860, Isabella Whipple, born April 7, 1827, daughter of Joseph Whipple, who at one time was lieutenant-governor of Rhode Island, and whose wife was Alice Knight. Mary Varney, who married Moses Hanson, was a daughter of Caleb and Huldah (Hussey) Varney. Caleb Varney was born in Rochester, New Hampshire, but before marriage purchased the old Varney homestead in Farmington, which then contained eighty acres of land. His children were William, Job, John, Mary (married Moses Hanson), Hannah, and one other who died in infancy. Caleb Varney was son of Ebenezer Varney, who married Mary Otis, and was himself a son of Humphrey Varney by his second wife, Mrs. Sarah (Starbuck) Austin. She was a daughter of Elder Edward and Catherine (Reynolds) Starbuck, and had married twice before she became the wife of Humphrey Varney. Humphrey Varney was eldest son of William Varney, who came to America from England about the middle of the seventeenth century and settled at Ipswich, Massachusetts. He afterward lived in Gloucester, removing thence to Dover, New Hampshire, and still later to Salem, Massachusetts, where he died leaving children—Humphrey, Sarah, Rachel and Thomas.

(VI) Job Varney Hanson, son of Moses and Mary (Varney) Hanson, was born November 7, 1825, and for many years was engaged in extensive mercantile and milling enterprises in Salem and Danvers. He carried on business in partnership with his brother John, having a large general mercantile store in Salem and a flouring and grain mill in Danvers. They were energetic, capable and straightforward business men and enjoyed a very high reputation in all trade circles. On December 9, 1862, Job Varney Hanson married Jane Moore, born Salem, May 12, 1827, daughter of Robert Moore, who was born in Northampton, England, and who married Philadelphia Pepper, also of English birth and parentage. Mr. and Mrs. Hanson had children: 1. Horace Ware, born Salem, October 31, 1866; unmarried. 2. Annie Moore, born Salem February 12, 1868; married October 16, 1889, Benjamin Franklin Nason of Salem, and have four children: David Varney, born February 27, 1891; Mildred, August 14, 1892; Edith H., June 12, 1895; Mary M., October 30, 1903.

ALLEN Warren Allen (1) was born, lived and died in Cornish, Maine where he followed farming for his occupation all his active years. He married Mary Ann (Goodwin) Dinsmore. Children, born at Cornish: 1. Franklin H. (M. D.), fitted for college in the public schools and entered Bowdoin College, changing after a year to Ann Arbor University, Michigan, where he studied one year; then entered Bowdoin Medical School, where he was graduated in the class of 1876; he began to practice medicine immediately in Farmington, New Hampshire, removing after one year to Ayers Village, where he was located several years; settled finally in Haverhill, Massachusetts, however, and continued in successful practice until his death in May, 1904. 2. Atwood M., resides in Springvale, Maine. 3. Jethro G., real estate agent at Springvale, Maine. 4. Mary E., deceased; married Henry C. Welch, of Springvale, Maine. 5. George Edwin, born May 10, 1863, mentioned below. 6. Charles Howard, a merchant at Lynn, Massachusetts. 7. Jacob S., died aged three years, nine months, nine days.

(II) Dr. George Edwin Allen, son of Warren Allen (1), was born in Cornish, Maine, May 10, 1863. He attended the public schools of his native town, and studied for his profession in the Boston Medical College, receiving the degree of M. D. in the class of 1883. He and his brother, Dr. Franklin H. Allen, both studied also under Dr. Ivory Brook, of Springvale, Maine. After receiving his degree Dr. George E. Allen located in Bradford, Massachusetts, since annexed to the city of Haverhill, and he has been practicing in that place to the present time, enjoying an excellent patronage and standing high in his profession. He is a member of the New Hampshire Medical Society, Massachusetts Medical Society, American Medical Association, New England Therapeutic Association and the American Therapeutic Association. He is affiliated with the Essex North District Medical Society. He is medical examiner for the Metropolitan Life Insurance Company and several other insurance companies and orders. He is a member of the medical staff of the Haverhill City Hospital. He is a prominent member of the Masonic Order, belonging to Saggahew Lodge, Free Masons, of Haverhill; Haverhill Council, Royal and Select Masters; Pentucket Chapter, Royal Arch Masons; Haverhill Commandery, Knights Templar. He is a member and past noble grand of Mizpah Lodge, No. 151, Odd Fellows, and past chief patriot of Haverhill Encampment and has the rank of major in the Canton Eagles. He is also a member of Palestine Lodge, Knights of Pythias; Passaquai Lodge, No. 27, Red Men, the Essenic Club and the Junior Order of American Mechanics. In politics he is a Republican; he was superintendent of schools while in New Hampshire and member of the board of health of Bradford several years.

He married, November 8, 1885, Nellie M. Smith, of Auburn, New Hampshire, daughter of Richard G. and Martha J. Bixby. Children: 1. George Edgar 2d., born January 1, 1888, now a student in Dartmouth College. 2. Mildred Beatrice, born February 7, 1891, of the class of 1908, Haverhill high school.

CUNNINGHAM It is said by distinguished antiquarians and others who have made exhaustive studies of the origin of our European families that the Cunninghams of England, Scotland and Ireland, and of course of their descendants in America, are all sprung from the ancient family of that surname whose clansmen were seated in Ayrshire, Scotland, as early as A. D. 1200. An ancient tradition runs to the effect that the first Cunninghams who emigrated from Scotland to Ireland were two of six brothers who won fame in the wars fighting under the standard of King James of Scotland, who afterward became James I of England. The records show several of that surname among the first grantees of estates in Ireland through the favor of that monarch.

As early as 1610 John Cunningham, of Crawfield, Ayrshire, received a grant of one thousand acres of land in county Donegal, Ireland, and in the same year James Cunningham, laird of Glangarnocke, had two grants, one of one thousand and the other of two thousand acres, and Cuthbert Cunningham, of Glangarnocke, a grant of one thousand acres, all in the precinct of Portlagh, county Donegal; and one Alexander Cunningham, of Powton, gentleman of Sorbie, Wigtonshire, Scotland, had lands granted him by royal patent in the precinct of Boylagh, county Donegal.

There is reason for the belief that Glangarnocke in Ayrshire was the original seat of the Cunninghams, and history furnishes much that is interesting concerning the emigration and settlement of these Scotch Cunninghams full three centuries ago. They were there many long years before others of their countrymen sought refuge in the north part of Ireland under the compulsion of religious persecution; and after the end of about another century many of their descendants came to America. In the course of time too the descendants of these Scotch emigrant brothers became scattered throughout the counties and precincts of Ireland, and by frequent intermarriages in generations one after another they ultimately came to be regarded as of the native families of that country. The Cunninghams are frequently spoken of as a Scotch-Irish family, Scotch by ancient ancestry, and Irish by long continued residence, intermarriage and adoption of national customs.

(I) The particular Cunningham family under consideration here is descended from one of the three Scotch brothers mentioned in preceding paragraphs, although by reason of lapse of centuries there probably is no certain means by which to trace that descent through the many succeeding generations to the time of the earliest ancestor of the family of whom we have a definite knowledge. He was Michael Cunningham, of Killalo, county Clare, who was undoubtedly a descendant of one of these three brothers. He was a sturdy tiller of the soil, and a man of good repute in the precinct.

(II) Daniel Cunningham, the immigrant, son of Michael Cunningham, of county Clare, was born in Killalo in 1835, and came to this country in 1861. He landed at New York, came to Boston and afterward settled in Saugus, Massachusetts, where he was a farmer all his life. He died in that town December 20, 1904. He married Mary Kehoe, daughter of Maurice Kehoe, of Carlow, in the county of Carlow, and Katharine (Cavanagh) Kehoe, of Carlow, descendant of the Cavanaghs of House of Bouns in that county. They had three children: 1. John M., died at Saugus. 2. Maurice F., see forward. 3. Mary R., who married Henry A. Comack.

(III) Maurice F. Cunningham, son of Daniel and Mary (Kehoe) Cunningham, was born in Saugus, November 8, 1869, and received his early education in the public schools of that town, graduating from the high school with the class of '84. In connection with his later business life he took up the study of law and made the course of the Young Men's Christian Association Evening Law School, Boston, then passed the prescribed examination, and in February, 1907, was admitted to practice in the courts of this commonwealth, and in 1908 was admitted to practice in United States courts. He is a member of the bar of Suffolk and Essex counties. During the ten years preceding admission to the bar, Mr. Cunningham has been junior member of the real estate and insurance firm of Stokes & Cunningham, of Saugus, through whose enterprise and stirring business qualities the beautiful village of Cliftondale has been built up and made one of the most desirable places of residence in the suburbs of the metropolitan district of the city of Boston. Mr. Cunningham is a member of the Nanepashemet Club of Saugus, Malden Lodge, No. 965, B. P. O. E., Santa Maria Council, No. 105, K. of C., of Malden, Massachusetts, and member and first master workman of Benoni Lodge, No. 169, A. O. U. W. In 1904 he married Henrietta F., daughter of John J. Donahue, of Malden, and has two children: Charles Carroll, born June 30, 1905, and Helen Frances, born September 30, 1907.

TAPLEY This surname is common in England, though there are many variations in spelling, such as Tapleigh, Topley, Topping, Toppan, Tapling and Topling. It is believed to be derived from a place name in Cheshire, England. Branches of the family lived in Marldon and Paignton, near Exeter, England, in the early part of the seventeenth century. The earliest record of the family found is dated 1553, of a John Tapley, of Dawlish, England. There are two Tapley coats-of-arms: Gules on a fess between three escallops argent a lion passant azure. Also: Gules on a fess between three crosses crosslet fitchee argent a lion passant azure.

(I) Gilbert Tapley, immigrant ancestor, was born in England, 1634; died in Salem April 17,

1714. He settled first at Salem before 1665. Like most of the settlers on the north shore of Massachusetts at that time, he was a fisherman. He was in Beverly, Massachusetts, as early as 1676, when he bought a house and half an acre of land of Lieutenant Thomas Gardner, of Pemaquid, by deed dated November 26 that year. His wife was admitted to the church in Beverly, January 6, 1674, and their three children were baptized in that town January 3, 1674. He removed to Salem very soon afterward. He was called of Salem in a deed dated December 7, 1677, when he bought of Major Thomas Savage, of Boston, half an acre of land "on ye neck of land neire Winter harbour" (Salem). The deed mentions a stone wall enclosing the lot. He bought a house and land December 13, 1678, of Henry Bartholomew, located near the causeway to Winter Island. He lived for many years afterward on this property, at the site of the old Juniper house on Salem Neck, near the causeway to Winter Island. The settlement at this point was the first made in the town. The cattle of the pioneers were pastured on Winter Island on the Sabbath. In 1680 he was one of the petitioners for a new church at Salem; in 1681 was constable, and in 1686 a juryman. From 1690 to 1714 he kept an ordinary, or tavern and doubtless gave up the sea and fishing. His tavern was sold when the estate was settled by his grandson Joseph Tapley, and became the property of John Abbot. He married Thomasin (Tamsin) ———, born 1632, died at Salem, November 6, 1715. Children: 1. Gilbert, born August 26, 1665; mentioned below. 2. Joseph, March 10, 1668; died before his father. 3. Mary, April 4, 1671.

(II) Gilbert Tapley, son of Gilbert Tapley, was born at Salem, August 26, 1665, and died at Salem, in 1710. He married first, April 10, 1686, Lydia Small, of Salem; second, August 21, 1707, Sarah Archer, of Salem. His widow Sarah was appointed administratrix of his estate, November 6, 1710. Children, born at Salem: 1. Mary, born November 4, 1689. 2. Joseph, born July 30, 1691; mentioned below. 3. Lydia, born March 10, 1696-7. 4. Gilbert, born July 13, 1699, baptized at the First Church, of Salem, November 19, 1699.

(III) Joseph Tapley, son of Gilbert Tapley (2), was born at Salem, July 30, 1691. He succeeded his grandfather as tavern-keeper in Salem, and continued for a number of years. From 1718 to 1735 he was not taxed for real estate. He was engaged also in the fishing trade. The records indicate that for many years before his death he was an invalid. He married, November 27, 1712, Margaret Masury, of Salem. Children: 1. Gilbert, born May 6, 1722; mentioned below. 2. John, born about 1728. 3. Lydia, married a French or British officer, and went to England, according to family tradition. 4. Elizabeth (?).

(IV) Gilbert Tapley, son of Joseph Tapley, was born in Salem, May 6, 1722, and died at Danvers, May 6, 1806. He is buried in the old Preston burying ground at Danvers. At the age of twenty-five he removed to Danvers, formerly Salem Village, and was the progenitor of all the Danvers family and of the Lynn families of this surname. He was a housewright by trade. His house on Buxton Lane which he bought of Joseph Subley in 1767 with sixty-seven acres of land, is still standing. He was constable in 1765, highway surveyor 1766-78-79-80-82. He was an active member of the First Church of Danvers, and in 1785 was on a committee to propose plans for the new meeting house. He was one of the founders of the Social Library, the predecessor of the public library, in 1794. He owned land in Andover, Middleton, Lynn, Danvers, and had large tracts in Fitchburg and Sterling in Worcester county from 1775 to 1800. He sold his pew in the north parish church in 1800. A characteristic story is told of him in the Essex county history. While driving a heavy load of ship timber with three yoke of oxen in the west part of Danvers, after a heavy fall of snow that made turning out difficult, he met a character famous in his day as "King" Hooper. "Turn out!" shouted Hooper. "Can't do it; the load's too heavy," said the old man, "let your man take one of these shovels and we'll soon make room." "No, half the road's mine and I'll wait till I get it." "All right," was the complacent answer, and slipping the pin out, he unhitched his team and drove his oxen home, leaving the loaded sled effectually blocking the narrow road. He was a soldier in the revolution, lieutenant in Captain John Putnam's company that marched to Lexington, April 19, 1775, and he was again on the alarm list in 1778. He served on various important town committees during the revolution. His will was proved June, 1806. He married first, June 6, 1747, Phebe Putnam, died May, 1770, daughter of John and Lydia (Porter) Putnam, and sister of Dr. Amos Putnam; second, March 11, 1771, Mrs. Mary (Flint) Smith, widow of Nathaniel Smith; third, June 6, 1799, Mrs. Sarah Abbott Farrington, of Andover, where she died January 19, 1823. Children, born at

Lewis Historical Pub. Co.

Danvers: 1. Amos, October 15, 1748; mentioned below. 2. Daniel, December 6, 1750; married May 5, 1774, Mary Tarbell. 3. Phebe, August 20, 1753. 4. Joseph, April 10, 1756. 5. Aaron, January 25, 1758; died December 18, 1776, soldier in the revolution. 6. Asa, September 11, 1761. 7. Elijah, December 14, 1765. Child of second wife: 8. Sally, born October 19, 1771.

(V) Amos Tapley, son of Gilbert Tapley, was born at Danvers, October 15, 1748. He was one of the most active and prominent citizens of Danvers, serving on the school committee from 1787 to about 1811; highway surveyor 1777-91-93-1802-3-12-16; selectman and assessor 1787-88-89-91-97-99-1805-7-8-9; tax collector 1787-88-89; tithingman 1780. He was a member of the standing committee of the First Church of Danvers, and built his pew in the meeting house. He was a soldier in the revolution, sergeant on the Lexington alarm, in Captain Samuel Flint's company, Colonel Timothy Pickering's regiment, and later in 1775; second lieutenant in Captain John Pool's company, Colonel Jonathan Cogswell's regiment, 1776; second lieutenant in Captain Asa Prince's company, Eighth Essex Regiment; first lieutenant in 1778, resigned May 4, 1778. He built the present Joel Kimball house at Danvers Center, in 1784. He died intestate September 6, 1835, and was buried in the old Preston burying ground, where a tablet to his memory was erected by his grandson, Amos Preston Tapley. James Berry administered his estate. He married May 9, 1772, Hannah, daughter of Lieutenant John and Hannah (Putnam) Preston. Children, born in Danvers and all baptized in the First church: 1. Hannah, born April 26, 1773. 2. David, born May 6, 1775. 3. Phebe, born August 28, 1777. 4. Eunice, born June 1, 1780; died December 24, 1781. 5. Amos, born November 4, 1782, mentioned below. 6. Moses, born November 8, 1784. 7. Betsey, born May 14, 1787. 8. Aaron, born July 6, 1789. 9. Daniel, born July 14, 1791. 10. Philip Preston, born July 22, 1793; died on voyage from New Orleans to Boston, June 8, 1819. 11. Ede, born August 17, 1790; married April 23, 1839, Dr. D. A. Grosvenor. 12. Rufus, born October 16, 1800.

(VI) Amos Tapley, son of Amos Tapley, was born at Danvers, November 4, 1782; died at Lynn, September 1, 1830. He was a housewright by trade. He married, February 24, 1814, Elizabeth Lye, born at Lynn, March 9, 1788, died May 30, 1841. Children, born at Lynn: 1. Eunice Ann, March 14, 1815; died April 3, 1837. 2. Amos Preston, March 25, 1817; mentioned below. 3. Henry Massey, March 3, 1820.

(VII) Amos Preston Tapley, son of Amos Tapley, was born March 25, 1817, at Lynn, and died in Boston, March 18, 1905. He was educated in the Lynn public school. His business carreer began when he was fourteen in the boot and shoe house of Joseph Pierce, Broad street, Boston. Here he continued as clerk for a few years, when, in partnership with Daniel Bingham, the bookkeeper, he purchased the business and continued it under the name of Bingham & Tapley until the business depression made it necessary for the firm to compromise with its creditors. In 1846 Mr. Bingham retired and Mr. Tapley continued the business, and, although under no legal obligation to do so, he surprised his creditors after a time by paying from his own resources the balance of the firm's indebtedness, covering the difference between the dividend paid and the amount of the original claim, including interest. Subsequently Mr. Tapley admitted his son, Henry F. Tapley, into partnership, under the name of Amos P. Tapley & Company, and the business still continues under that name. Mr. Tapley was one of the strong financiers of Lynn, and for years a vital force in the boot and shoe jobbing trade, his house being one of the oldest if not the oldest jobbing house not only in Boston but this country. Although nearly eighty-eight years of age he was at his office every day until one week prior to his death. Mr. Tapley was one of the organizers of the City Bank of Lynn, chartered by the state in 1854, and was the guiding spirit in this bank until 1858, when upon the resignation of John C. Abbott, Mr. Tapley became its president and continued in that position for thirty-five years, during which time the bank was removed to its present quarters and its name changed to the National City Bank of Lynn. His resignation as president of the bank was reluctantly accepted January 10, 1893. He was for many years one of the commissioners and chairman of the board of Pine Grove cemetery, and an officer in the Lynn Five Cents Savings Bank, and in addition to his other responsibilities, he acted as trustee for a number of large estates. He was at one time interested in the lumber business at the old Commercial street wharf. In connection with the shoe trade, Mr. Tapley exercised a progressive spirit and was interested in the adoption of the McKay sewing machine, and during the existence of this corporation he served on the executive committee. At the time of his death he had been connected with the wholesale shoe business continuously longer than any other man in the country. Mr. Tapley was brought up in the First Congregational Church of Lynn, but the Unitarian faith early appealed to him and he became connected with the First Church of Boston, then under the pastorage of the Rev. Nathaniel L. Frothingham. While residing in Lynn, 1844-87, he attended the Second Congregational (Unitarian) Church, but upon his return to Boston became connected with the First Church. Charitable, without ostentation, his benefactions were liberal and widely scattered; inspiring confidence and affection, his friendships were lasting. He possessed rare good sense, and his advice and counsel were often sought and freely given. Absolutely faithful, confidential positions of great responsibility came to him unsolicited. Mr. Tapley married first, at Lynn, December 15, 1842, Adeline E., daughter of James and Betsy Fuller; she died in Lynn, December 19, 1851. Married (second), June 23, 1856, Anna Sarah, daughter of Benjamin and Harriet (Choate) Ireson. Child by first wife: Henry Fuller, born Boston, November 2, 1843. Child by second wife: Alice Preston, born Lynn, May 27, 1857.

(VIII) Henry Fuller Tapley, son of Amos Preston and Adeline E. (Fuller) Tapley, born Boston, November 2, 1843. Removing at an early age with his parents to Lynn, he has since resided there. He was educated in the schools of Lynn, and after completing his studies in 1862, entered the Boston store of his father, becoming later a partner, and since the death of his father he has conducted the business alone. Active, energetic and progressive, he is connected with the following Lynn institutions: Vice-president of Five Cents Savings Bank; director of Central National Bank; director of Security Safe Deposit & Trust Company; director of Mutual Fire Insurance Company; director of Manufacturers' and Merchants' Mutual Fire Insurance Company; trustee of Public Library, Hospital, Home for Aged Women, Home for Aged Men; commissioner of Pine Grove cemetery; vice-president of New England Shoe and Leather Association; a former vice-president of National Shoe Wholesalers' Association of the United States; was also former president of the New England Shoe Wholesalers' Association. By birth a Unitarian, he has continued in that faith and is prominent in the counsels of his home church. The strenuous life of modern times requires relaxation; present civilization is showing the value of a fad. Among those appealing to Mr. Tapley is the gathering of a fine private library and the collecting of rare prints. Much of his leisure is devoted to this, and membership in the leading private, historical and collecting clubs of the country has made possible the acquirement by him of many limited editions, scarce volumes and prints.

He married, in Lynn, June 26, 1867, Ida Jane, born in Lynn, July 22, 1844, daughter of Joseph N. and Eliza A. Saunderson. Children: 1. Adaline Elizabeth, born May 18, 1869, married, February 26, 1896, Charles Henry Stephenson; resides in Lynn; children: i. Preston Tapley, born November 6, 1897; ii. Ruth, July 8, 1900; iii. Henry Dexter, September 5, 1901. 2. Edith, born October 23, 1870; married, April 14, 1897, George Richardson Beardsell, formerly of Hudson, Michigan; resides in Lynn; children: i. Editha, born January 13, 1899; ii. George Richardson, Jr., February 26, 1900; iii. Barbara, August 15, 1906; iv. Henry Tapley, October 30, 1907. Joseph N. Saunderson, father of Mrs. Tapley, was born in Medford, January 25, 1801, passed away 1871. At an early age he removed to Lynn, and like all boys of his generation early learned a trade, which in his case was that of shoemaker. Mastering the mechanical part, he became a successful shoe manufacturer, and so continued for many years. At the age of fifty, obliged by failing health to give up the confinement of an indoor life, he took a long rest and partially recovered his health; he then devoted a portion of his time to the care of estates as executor. He was for many years connected with the Lynn Institution for Savings, of which he was president. He was also a director of the First National Bank of that city, and first secretary-treasurer of the Lynn Gas Company. In religion he was a Unitarian, and was always a church goer.

HUSE Abel Huse (1), immigrant ancestor, was of Welsh ancestry. He came from London in 1635; settled among the pioneers at Newbury, Massachusetts, and was admitted a freeman May 15, 1642. He married first Eleanor ———. He married second, May 25, 1663, Mary (Hilton, alias Downer) Sears, widow of Thomas Sears, of Newbury. Mr. Huse died at Newbury, March 29, 1690, aged eighty-eight years, being born accordingly in 1602. Children of second wife: 1. Ruth, born February 25, 1664. 2. Abel, born February 19, 1665; men-

Henry F. Tapley

tioned below. 3. Thomas, born August 9, 1666, married Hannah ———; children: i. Mary, born March 23, 1691; ii. Israel, born October 23, 1693; iii. Ebenezer, born January 16, 1696; iv. James, born June 29, 1698; v. Hannah, born November 5, 1700; vi. Ruth, born February 14, 1703. 3. William, born October, 1667; married, 1699, Anne Russell; children: i. Anne, born May 22, 1700; ii. William, born October 30, 1701. 4. Sarah, born October 8, 1670. 5. John, born June 20, 1672. 6. Amy, born September 9, 1673; died May 18, 1675. 7. Ebenezer (a daughter according to the town records), born August 10, 1675. 8. George, of Salisbury; perhaps son of first wife; married Mary Allen; children: i. William, born June 27, 1672; ii. Solomon, born January 2, 1674-75; married Mary Calef, of Boston, in 1700.

(II) Abel Huse, son of Abel Huse, was born in Newbury, Massachusetts, February 19, 1665. He married Judith Emery, born February 5, 1673, daughter of John and Mary (Webster) Emery, and granddaughter of John Emery. Abel Huse, died in Newbury, March 11, 1758, aged ninety-three. Children: 1. John, born October 31, 1694. 2. Abel, born November 18, 1696. 3. Stephen, born November 16, 1702; graduate of Harvard College in 1728; married Judith Emery, widow of Daniel Emery; removed to Haverhill, Massachusetts. 4. Samuel, born March 30, 1705. 5. Judith, born February 13, 1709. 6. Sarah, born March 29, 1712, married Caleb Kimball. 7. Mary, born March 16, 1716; married Enoch Davis. 8. Nathan, mentioned below.

(III) Dr. Nathan Huse, son of Abel Huse, was born in Newbury, Massachusetts. He became a well-known physician of Amesbury, Massachusetts, "who practiced a great many years in the West Parish." He died April 23, 1809, in his ninety-third year. He married, December 5, 1738, Rachel Sargent, born February 23, 1721, daughter of Joseph and Elizabeth (Carr) Sargent, of Amesbury. Her father was a member of the "Snowshoe" military company. Thomas Sargent, father of Joseph Sargent, born 1643, was lieutenant in the train band, son of William Sargent, the immigrant, of Salisbury. Children of Dr. Nathan Huse, born in Amesbury: 1. Sargent, born August 22, 1739, soldier in the revolution. 2. Elizabeth, born February 25, 1741. 3. Hannah, born January 12, 1742. 4. Nathan, born February 13, 1747, died young. 5. Joseph, born March 2, 1749, mentioned below. 6. Ebenezer, born December 25, 1750. 7. Rachel, born May 6, 1755. 8. Sarah, born February 19, 1757. 9. John, born December 31, 1758. 10. William, born August 22, 1760. 11. Nathan, born August 8, 1769.

(IV) Joseph Huse, son of Dr. Nathan Huse, was born in Amesbury, March 2, 1749. He removed to Sanbornton from Amesbury before 1782, and was the first of the brothers who located in that town. His house was northeast of the square, lot 41, first division. He was a soldier in the revolution. He married first, Abiah ———; second, Mrs. Pease, daughter of Daniel Morrison, and widow of the first settler on the Dearborn Taylor place (No. 26, second division) where he finally settled and died July 10, 1827, aged seventy-eight. His wife died December 12, 1824. Mr. Huse built and owned the first mills at North Sanbornton and bequeathed them to his nephew. His mill house stood near the house of Thomas Webster, lately the postoffice. His only child was John, Jr., mentioned below.

(V) John Huse, Jr., son of Joseph Huse, was born in Sanbornton. He married Mary Carter, of New Hampton, New Hampshire, October 4, 1796. He resided at Sanbornton several years where the late Jonathan Taylor lived, west of his father's house. He removed to Littleton, New Hampshire. Children: 1. Simeon, resided in Coventry, Vermont. 2. Joseph, went west. 3. Daniel, mentioned below.

(VI) Daniel Huse, son of John Huse, Jr., according to the best authority available, married Sarah Day. He was certainly descended from these ancestors. They settled in Enfield, New Hampshire and had five children, among whom was Timothy, mentioned below.

(VII) Timothy Huse, son of Daniel Huse, was born in Enfield, New Hampshire, September 18, 1821. He was educated in the public schools, and learned the trade of carpenter. He engaged in business as a carpenter and builder when a young man, and followed that calling all his life, with much success. He settled in Haverhill, Massachusetts, and built many important buildings in that city. His death occurred there. Mr. Huse was a Republican in politics. He was a prominent and active member of the Congregational church of Haverhill, a man of high character and unusual ability, of strict integrity and wide influence for good in the city in which he lived. He married in 1844, Angeline Gordon, daughter of Jesse and Harriet (Connor) Gordon. She survives him and lives at the old home in Haverhill, well known and highly respected by her many friends and neighbors. Children: 1. Frank G., born August 24, 1846. 2. Edward E., born July 20, 1848. 3. George H., born July 11, 1850, died September 8, 1850. 4. Harriet S., born June 30, 1851, died August 14, 1851. 5. Mary S., born February 1, 1854. 6. Walter L., born April 6, 1855. 7. Charles Herbert, born February 12, 1858. 8. George Johnson, born April 3, 1862; died August 24, 1862.

BLANEY This name is also spelled in the early records of Essex county Blaner, Blano, Blany and Blarney. The first of this name in America was John Blaney (1), born about 1630. He was a planter, and lived in Salem as early as 1659. He married first, Hannah King, of Lynn, alias Salem, being that part of Lynn which is now Swampscott, July 11, 1660; she died about 1676. He married second, Elizabeth, widow of Thomas Purchase, of Lynn, November, 1678; she died before 1696. He was living as late as 1709. Children, born in Salem: John, Daniel, Henry, Hannah; Joseph, mentioned below; Elizabeth and Sarah.

(II) Joseph Blaney, son of John Blaney, was born in Salem, October 2, 1670. He was a shipwright, and lived in Hingham until 1697, when he settled in Lynn. He married, January 16, 1693-94, Abigail Andrews, of Hingham, born January 6, 1669-70, died December 10, 1765. He died January 16, 1726-27; in his will he gave to the poor of the First Parish in Lynn twenty pounds, to be distributed by the deacons. Children: Joseph, Hannah, Benjamin, Jedediah; Jonathan, mentioned below; and Ambrose.

(III) Jonathan Blaney, son of Joseph and Abigail (Andrews) Blaney, was born in Lynn, January 6, 1703-04, died September 8, 1757. He was a yeoman, and lived in Lynn. He married Hannah Gray, of Lynn (published October 7, 1736). Children: Joseph, mentioned below; Mary, Abigail and Hannah.

(IV) Joseph Blaney, son of Jonathan and Hannah (Gray) Blaney, was of age in 1765. He was a yeoman, and lived in Lynn. He married first, November 24, 1763, Anne Cox, of Salem: second, Hannah Hanford, of Salem (published November 12, 1797). Children: Jonathan, Martha, Anne, Joseph, mentioned below. Joseph Blaney died March, 1826, in Lynn.

(V) Joseph Blaney, son of Joseph and Anne (Cox) Blaney, was born May 9, 1777, died April 20, 1826. On July 12, 1830, Joseph Blaney, with three others, left Swampscott in the schooner "Finback," for a fishing trip. When about twelve miles southeast of Minots Lodge they anchored, and each taking a dory left the vessel, and when some distance apart began to fish. In a short time their attention was attracted toward Mr. Blaney who was standing up in his dory waving his hat. They saw that a hugh shark was in the dory and was making vigorous efforts to get back into the water; suddenly the boat was overturned, and Mr. Blaney, boat and shark disappeared. The boat soon came to the surface bottom up, but Mr. Blaney was never seen afterward, and it is supposed he was devoured by the shark. The old Blaney house, situated on Humphrey street, Swampscott, near Black Will's cliff, was built by Captain Ralph King in 1641, and was occupied by John Blaney in 1660. Joseph Blaney married October 29, 1803, Ruth Phillips, who died June 23, 1854. Children: 1. Benjamin, born August 9, 1804, died January 8, 1847; married Sarah Abbott. 2. Alice, born September 9, 1805; married Nathaniel Blanchard. 3. Jonathan P., born March 20, 1808; married Sally Rhodes. 4. Ann, born December 11, 1810, died January 26, 1890. 5. Joseph Ingalls, born July 22, 1813. 6. James Phillips, born December 11, 1815. 7. Elbridge G., mentioned below.

(VI) Elbridge G. Blaney, son of Joseph and Ruth (Phillips) Blaney, was born in Swampscott, February 3, 1822, died October 29, 1902. He married, August 25, 1850, in Marblehead, Anna V. Bessom, born December 11, 1831, in Marblehead, daughter of William and Maria (Van Blunk) Bessom. Children: 1. Elizabeth B., born September 21, 1851, married first, July 11, 1867, Benjamin H. Phillips, of Marblehead; one son, Amos; married second, Henry Ireland, of Nashville, Tennessee, her cousin; one child, Susie, born September, 1881; married third, in Brooklyn, New York, John Ellison, of Lynn, a native of Sweden. 2. Amos P., born July 9, 1853, died October 24, 1854. 3. Elbridge G., born July 21, 1856, died October 31, 1858. 4. Elbridge G., mentioned below. 5. Annaurilia, died aged four years.

(VII) Elbridge G. Blaney, son of Elbridge G. and Anna V. (Bessom) Blaney, was born in Swampscott, December 4, 1859. He attended the common schools of his native town, after which he learned the trade of wood worker with the firm of Stephen N. Breed & Company of Lynn, where he was employed until the great Lynn fire, November 12, 1889, at which time the plant of this firm was destroyed. He then took up the business of florist at his home on Burrill street, Swampscott, where he has resided since the age of four years, and where he is still conducting a very successful business. He is a member of Swampscott Lodge, and Palestine Encampment, I. O. O. F. In politics he is a Republican. He married, March 28, 1881, Jessie F., daughter of Jonathan and Sarah J. (Winch) Leach. One child, Harold C., born April 4, 1883, married, September 19, 1900, Susie G., daughter of Joseph and Eliza (Gordon) Stone, of Marblehead. Children: 1. Jessie E., born March 15, 1902. 2. Edith G., June 6, 1903.

AMERIGE The Amerige family, represented in the present generation by Dr. Charles W. Amerige, a practicing physician, a specialist, with offices in the city of Boston, was founded in this country by Morris Amerige (1), a native of Germany, who emigrated to this country at the age of fifteen, shipping as cabin boy, he thinking that there were greater possibilities for advancement in the new than in the old world. He settled in Boston, and two of his brothers, who came to this country about the same time, settled in Philadelphia; they became lawyers and gained renown for themselves along the line of their profession. Morris Amerige was a sugar refiner by trade, gaining a lucrative livelihood for his family. He married Sarah Brown, of Saugus, Massachusetts. Children: 1. George, went to California in 1849, was married but left no children; died in San Francisco, California. 2. William, went to China, was a sail maker and mate in a vessel, made many trips back and forth; he was a bachelor; died in Necco, China. 3. Charles, worked in a tinshop in Boston; died at the age of eighteen. 4. Mary, married John Odion and (second) Charles Bond; by the latter she had one son, Charles H. Bond, who died July 3, 1908. 5. Henry, married three times; by his second wife had two children, both of whom died; by his third wife had five children: Ella, George, Alfred, Hattie and Edward. 6. Francis, see forward.

(II) Francis Amerige, youngest son of Morris and Sarah (Brown) Amerige, was born on Prince street, Boston, August 16, 1820. He worked as printer on the *Boston Post* when a young man, and later went to Saugus and learned the art of making shoes with his uncle, Solomon Brown, and he followed this trade in a shop on his premises until he retired at the age of seventy, since which time he has enjoyed a well-earned rest. He is at the present time (1908) eighty-eight years of age, having lived far past the scriptural allotted time of three score years and ten. He married Belinda Burrill, whose birth occurred in Malden, Massachusetts, and who died in Saugus, January, 1896. She was one of five children, the other members of the family being Warren, who served his country in the war of 1812; Charles; Ellen, married Stephen Danforth, of Saugus, but moved to Goffstown, New Hampshire, and died there; Eliza, married Henry I. Fisk, of Waltham, Massachusetts, and died there. Children of Mr. and Mrs. Amerige: 1. William H., married Lina Lockwood; resides in Lynn; served three years in the civil war under General Grant; is now employed in the navy yard. 2. Judge George M., graduate of the Boston University of Law; judge of the district court for fourteen years; was with the Boston Marine Underwriters for forty years, serving as their secretary at the time of his death, January 17, 1905; he married Mary L. Hawkes, who survived him as did also two sons, George M. and Henry. 3. Frank W., married Lizzie King and died leaving one son, George. 4. Henry, married Mary Babbitt and died leaving two children, Edith and Arthur; Edith married Varnum Merrithew, died April 27, 1908, leaving two sons, Leslie and Henry Merrithew, all reside in Saugus. 5. Charles W., see forward.

(III) Dr. Charles W. Amerige, youngest son of Francis and Belinda (Burrill) Amerige, was born in Cliftondale, town of Saugus, Massachusetts, May 27, 1855. He was educated in the public schools of Saugus, and graduated from the Indiana College of Medicine, Indianapolis, Indiana, 1882. He has been a practicing physician since his graduation, a period of twenty-six years, and is now a specialist, with offices at No. 74 Boylston street, Boston. Previous to becoming a physician he was engaged in the real estate business, contracting and building, and some of the finest and most costly buildings in Saugus, both public and private, stand as monuments to his skill and ability along that line. He served the town of Saugus in the capacity of building inspector one year and as assessor three years, acting as chairman two years and secretary one year. He was brought up in the Methodist faith, and attends the church of that denomination. He was a charter member of Cliftondale Lodge, Independent Order of Odd Fellows, and was its first noble grand. He is a member of the Grand Lodge of the same order of the state of Massachusetts, also the Knights of Pythias and Red Men.

Dr. Amerige married, June 27, 1903, Lida W. Briggs, born in West Winfield, Herkimer county, New York, February 7, 1862, daughter of Daniel Bowen and Ruth W. (Scott) Briggs, granddaughter of Archibald and Harriet (Moulton) Briggs, and great-granddaughter of James Briggs, who with his two brothers fought in the revolutionary war. Her grandparents were pioneers in settling New York state, coming from Willimantic, Connecticut, in a two-horse lumber wagon with their furniture in the spring of 1816 and settling on what is now known as Briggs Hill in the town of Winfield. Her father was the proprietor of a bookstore at Utica, New York; he died April 13, 1907, at the residence of Dr. Amerige, at the age of nearly eighty-four; he and his wife were the parents of four children: Lida W. (Mrs. Amerige); George B. Briggs, a produce dealer in St. Louis, Missouri; he married and is the father of two children: Harry and Zoe Briggs; Mrs. Hattie M. Peter, of Butte, Montana, mother of three children: Ira, Cora and Ruth Peter; Mrs. Zoe C. Johnson, of Macedon, New York, who is the mother of one child, Halford H. B. Johnson. Mrs. Amerige received her education in the district school and academy of West Winfield, and later in New York City, where she graduated from the Normal College in June, 1881. She has been a teacher and writer, being author of the novel "Words That Burn" and contributor of articles and short stories to various papers. She is a member of the League of American Pen Women, of Washington, D. C.

COLE Thomas Cole, immigrant ancestor, in England, is believed to have come in the ship "Mary and John," sailing March 24, 1633. He settled in Salem as early as 1649. The will of William Cole, of Hampton, New Hampshire, perhaps a brother, was filed at Salem, proved April 14, 1663. Thomas Cole bought a house and land at Marblehead Neck, February 14, 1665, of Philip Cromwell. The will of Thomas Cole was dated December 15, 1678, and proved April 27, 1679. The will of his widow, Ann Cole, was dated November 1, 1679, and proved May 2, 1681. Children: Abraham, mentioned below; John.

(II) Abraham Cole, son of Thomas and Ann Cole, was born in Salem about 1645, died 1715. He signed the Salem protest against imposts in 1666. He removed to Hampton, but returned to Salem. He was a tailor by trade. He married, at Salem, June 11, 1670, Sarah Davis, who was accused of witchcraft during the delusion in 1692, but was never tried. Her will was dated July 2, 1717. His will was proved December 31, 1715. Children, born at Marblehead: 1. Samuel, born May 11, 1671, died June, 1671. 2. Sarah, August 29, 1672. 3. Abraham, Jr., January 6, 1674, died young. 4. Isaac, June 6, 1677, died young. 5. Elizabeth, married ——— Jeffords. 6. Samuel, May 19, 1687. 7. Thomas, mentioned below. 8. Abraham.

(III) Thomas Cole, son of Abraham and Sarah (Davis) Cole, was born about 1689. He married (first), November 4, 1706, Susanna Sikes, of Beverly; second, June 10, 1710, ———; third, January 5, 1718-19, Elizabeth Mathews or Mahews, of Marblehead. Children: 1. Elizabeth, baptized November 29, 1819. 2. William, mentioned below.

(IV) Captain William Cole, son of Thomas and Elizabeth Cole, was born about 1730. He purchased land of Eben Hawkes, of Windmill Hill, Marblehead, May 29, 1758. He married, at Marblehead, December 1, 1757, Ruth Lee, died July 23, 1798; died in 1774. Children, born at Marblehead: 1. William, mentioned below. 2. Richard, baptized February 15, 1761. 3. John, baptized September 15, 1765. 4. Elizabeth, baptized December 13, 1767.

(V) Captain William Cole, son of Captain William and Ruth (Lee) Cole, baptized January 14, 1759, died, according to his gravestone, August 12, 1808. He married, February 12, 1788, Elizabeth Tutt, died October 30, 1850, aged seventy years. Children, born at Marblehead: 1. William, baptized December 7, 1788, lost October 1, 1830, from schooner "Panther," on the Grand Banks. 2. Richard, mentioned below. 3. Elizabeth, baptized June 19, 1792. 4. John, baptized June 28, 1795. 5. Samuel Horton, baptized December 13, 1801, died February 24, 1817.

(VI) Richard Cole, son of Captain William and Elizabeth (Tutt) Cole, was baptized June 19, 1791. He married, December 12, 1815, Abigail Call, died July 29, 1830, aged thirty-eight; second, October 17, 1830, Miriam Call. Children, born at Marblehead: 1. Child, died October 6, 1826. 2. Child, died aged thirteen months. 3. John, born September 25, 1827, mentioned below. 4. Benjamin, born 1831, died August 14, 1832, aged fourteen months.

John Pilling

5. Richard, born 1834, died December 4, 1835, aged one year, four months. 6. Richard, died November 30, 1839.

(VII) Captain John Cole, son of Richard and Abigail (Call) Cole, born at Marblehead, September 25, 1827, died July 22, 1902. He was educated in the public schools of his native town. When a young man he learned shoemaking, like most of the youth of his day. He also followed the sea in seasons of fishing, sailed around Cape Horn in 1849 and landed in California at time of gold fever, and rose to the rank of master mariner. He became captain of the merchant vessels "Aberdeen" and "Hollyhead," commanding the former when only twenty-one years old, and later he commanded the ship "Blackwall." In 1879 he abandoned a seafaring life and settled in his native town. He established a coal and wood business there in 1882 and became a prosperous merchant, continuing up to his death. In politics he was a Republican; for three years served as selectman of the town and chairman of the board one year. He was a member of Philanthropic Lodge, F. A. M., many years, and its treasurer from 1880 until his death; a member of Washington Chapter, R. A. M., of Salem; Atlantic Lodge, I. O. O. F.; Neptune Lodge, Knights of Pythias. In religion he was a Unitarian. He married, in 1855, Sarah Trefry, born in Marblehead, daughter of Thomas Trefry. Children, born in Marblehead: Hattie Bishop; Richard Thomas, mentioned below.

(VIII) Richard Thomas Cole, son of Captain John and Sarah (Trefry) Cole, was born in London, England, January 6, 1870. He crossed the ocean when six weeks of age, and landed in Marblehead at the age of eight weeks. He again sailed with his father, starting at age four, and after visiting England, Australia, South America, Germany and principal seaboard cities of America, come to Marblehead at the age of nine. He attended the public schools there and Hickock's Short Hand School and Business College, Boston. He began work for the American Radiator Company as bookkeeper and continued five years. He was then for several years traveling salesman for the firm of E. T. Burrowes Company, of Portland, Maine, manufacturers of screens. In 1906 he returned to Marblehead, Massachusetts, and since then has been engaged in the coal and wood business under the name of the Gilbert & Cole Company. He is a member of Philanthropic Lodge, Free and Accepted Masons. He married, September 12, 1897, Jane Green Wilson, born in Marblehead, daughter of Francis B. and Mary Jane Wilson.

PILLING John Pilling, son of Marmaduke Pilling, and descendant of an ancient English family of this name, was born in Yorkshire, England, March 11, 1838. He was educated in his native place. In 1857 he came to America, working first in Delaware, removing thence to Salem, New Hampshire, where he learned the trade of shoemaker in the factories. He rose to places of responsibility, and in 1867 was in a position to begin manufacturing on his own account, which he accordingly did in the old White building on Washington street, Haverhill, Massachusetts. Later he established his shoe business in a brick building which he erected for his use, and built up a large and flourishing business. The building was destroyed by fire February 19, 1882, but Mr. Pilling immediately rebuilt and forty days later was again manufacturing shoes. He was a leading manufacturer in one of the foremost shoe towns of New England, and was one of the best known and most highly respected business men of the city of Haverhill for some twenty years. He removed his business to Lowell in 1888, which was continued in the city until his death, July 8, 1903; he still resided at Haverhill. He was succeeded by his sons, who continued the business. He invested extensively in Haverhill real estate and built and acquired a large amount of renting property. Mr. Pilling was generous with his wealth and set an excellent example in his benevolence. He gave liberally to every charity and movement that appealed to him as worthy, and none knew the full extent of his giving. He was a man of strictest integrity and exemplary character, and was a useful citizen and a public benefactor, both in Haverhill and Lowell. He was a member of the Merrimac Lodge of Free Masons, and an active member and liberal supporter of the Christian Church of Haverhill. He was a steadfast Republican in politics. Pilling street was named in his honor.

Mr. Pilling married Eliza E. (Messer) Pettengill, born at New London, New Hampshire, February 5, 1829, daughter of Frederick Messer, and widow of Horace Pettengill. After the death of Mr. Pilling she resided in the old home at Haverhill until the property was bought by the city for school purposes, when she removed to Bartlett street, Mt. Washington. She was a member of the Haverhill

Christian Church, for many years a teacher in its Sunday school, and in every respect a woman of the finest Christian character. At her death she donated the Bartlett street property to the Christian Church of Haverhill, for use as a parsonage, the new dormitory to the Young Men's Christian Association, and gave liberally, in sympathy with her husband's wishes, to many other charities. The children of Mr. and Mrs. Pilling are: Eugene, born January 30, 1861, died 1889; John B., born February 16, 1863; Fred A., born February 5, 1868; Ernest, died in infancy.

John B. Pilling was educated in the common schools at Haverhill, after which he entered his father's shoe factory and there learned every detail of the business. He married, November 6, 1888, Delia I. Kelley. To them was born, September 3, 1894, one daughter, Ruth E.

Fred A. Pilling married, April 15, 1890, Martha Rapp, now deceased. To them was born April 25, 1891, one son, John W. Afterward he married December 24, 1894, Belle V. Buchanan, his present wife.

When the Pilling shoe business was moved to Lowell, it was incorporated under the laws of Massachusetts as John Pilling Shoe Company, John Pilling being its first president and treasurer, he, together with John B. and Fred A. Pilling, constituting its board of directors. Upon the death of John Pilling, John B. Pilling became its president and treasurer, and has since served in that capacity. At the present time (1908) John B. and Fred A. Pilling, are in active management of the John Pilling shoe business at Lowell, having one of the most modern factories in this section of the state. The brothers are thoroughly practical business men and have inherited the sterling business qualities so forcibly effectuated by their father, and to this is largely due the success which has continually crowned their efforts.

CLARK The first ancestor of this family of whom we have information was Jonathan Clark, grandfather of William Paige Clark, who was born in Hopkinton, New Hampshire, 1779, died 1825, aged forty-six years. He was a farmer at Weare, New Hampshire. He married Sarah Paige, born 1785, of North Weare, who died, his widow, May 8, 1883, aged ninety-eight years. Children: 1. Lois, born 1803. 2. John P., 1805. 3. William, 1810, married Delia Purington. 4. Martha, 1812. 5. Jacob, 1817. 6. Sebastian S., 1820. 7. Bailey, died in Ohio when a young man. Sarah (Paige) Clark traced her ancestry to John Paige (1), born in Dedham, England, 1586, came to New England in 1630 and settled in Watertown, Massachusetts. Samuel Paige (2), son of John and Phebe Paige, born in 1633, lived in Salisbury, Massachusetts. Joseph Paige (3), eldest son of Samuel Paige, was born in 1667, married and had sons. John Paige (4), son of Joseph Paige, was born June 17, 1696, married Mary Winslow, 1720, and they lived in South Hampton and also in Salisbury, Massachusetts. Colonel Samuel Paige (5), son of John and Mary (Winslow) Paige, served in the revolutionary war, Captain Nathan Hutchins's company, Colonel Joseph Cilley's regiment; it was the first New Hampshire regiment in General John Sullivan's brigade and saw service under Washington at Trenton and Princeton; was at Ticonderoga four months and twenty-four days. He married Eleanor Stevens. John Paige (6), son of Colonel Samuel and Eleanor (Stevens) Paige, also served in the revolutionary war; he married Hannah Barnard, and they were the parents of Sarah Paige, aforementioned as the wife of Jonathan Clark.

(II) William Clark, son of Jonathan and Sarah (Paige) Clark, was born at North Weare, New Hampshire, 1809, was burned fatally, August 25, 1835, at the early age of twenty-six years. He followed the occupation of farming in his native town. He married Delia, born 1808, died 1889, daughter of Elijah and Delia (Brown) Purington, in Weare, New Hampshire. Her grandfather and great-grandfather, both named Elijah Purington, lived in Weare on land settled by her great-grandfather who was born in Hampton, New Hampshire, 1730, and who married Dolly Green, sister of Isaiah Green, who also settled in Weare. They belonged to the Society of Friends. Mr. and Mrs. Clark were the parents of one child, William Paige, see forward.

(III) William Paige Clark, only son of William and Delia (Purington) Clark, was born in North Weare, New Hampshire, March 17, 1834, died April 12, 1896, very suddenly, in Lowell, Massachusetts. He accompanied his mother to Pelham, New Hampshire, 1837, and there acquired his education. In 1852 he went to Lowell, Massachusetts, and was there engaged as clerk in a store. He removed to Lawrence, Massachusetts, 1863, and there engaged in the wholesale country and produce business, continuing until his decease. He was also president of Lawrence National Bank at time of death, discharging the duties pertaining thereto with ability and efficiency, his long and active career as merchant thoroughly qualifying him for this position of trust and responsibility. He was a member of Trinity Congregational Church, and in politics was a Republican, serving as alderman of Lawrence in 1876. Mr. Clark married, June 3, 1866, at Lowell, Massachusetts, Elizabeth Atwood, born February 28, 1838, in Pelham, New Hampshire, daughter of Alvah and Lydia (Atwood) Gage, the former of whom was born 1796, a farmer in Pelham, New Hampshire, and the latter born 1802. Mr. and Mrs. Gage had three children: Lydia, born 1831; Betsey, 1833; Elizabeth, mentioned above. Children of Mr. and Mrs. Clark: 1. Kate Marion, born October 25, 1869, married, January 24, 1893, George Warren Hamblet, born at Dracut, Massachusetts, May 4, 1865; children: i. Helen Elizabeth, February 22, 1894; ii. Marion Clark, December 10, 1896; iii. Theodore Clement, October 30, 1898; iv. Katherine Gage, September 6, 1900; v. George Warren, Jr., January 17, 1904; vi. William Paige Clark, January 17, 1907. 2. Alice Gage, born July 24, 1871.

COLBY Anthony Colby, founder and American ancestor of one of the prolific families in New England, came in Winthrop's fleet in 1630 and his name appears as ninety-third on the list of members of the church. He came from the eastern coast of England, and was driven by religious persecution to seek a home in the new world. He appears in Cambridge, Massachusetts, in 1632, on his marriage with Susannah Sargent, but in 1634 removed to Salisbury, and thence in 1647 to the west side of Powow river, in what now is Amesbury. He was recorded as a planter and received land in the first division in 1640 and 1643. He was one of the first commoners in Amesbury, had grants of land in 1654 and 1658, and his widow in his right in 1662 and 1664, he having died in Salisbury, February 11, 1661. His widow, Susannah, married, in 1663, William Whittridge or Whitred, and was again a widow in 1669. She died July 8, 1689. Anthony Colby's children were: John, Sarah, Samuel, Isaac, Rebecca, Mary, Thomas, and one other died young.

(II) Samuel Colby, of Amesbury and Haverhill, planter and innholder, was born in 1639. He was a soldier of King Philip's war and served under Captain Turner in the Falls fight, March 18, 1676. He married, before 1668, Elizabeth, daughter of William Sargent. Samuel Colby had a grant of land in Amesbury in 1659, again in 1662; was townsman then in 1660; lived in Haverhill in 1668, 1672, 1674, and probably in 1677, although he was in Amesbury in 1676, perhaps for the safety of his family during the war in which he took part. He took the oath of allegiance and fidelity in Amesbury in December, 1677, and was representative from there in 1689. His will bears date July 2, 1716. His widow Elizabeth died February 5, 1736-37. According to the Amesbury records they had five children: 1. Dorothy, born about 1668; married William Hoyt. 2. Elizabeth, June 1, 1670, died young. 3. Samuel, March 9, 1671. 4. Daughter, April 2, 1672. 5. Philip, probably married, May 1, 1703, Annie Webster.

(III) Samuel Colby, son of Samuel and Elizabeth (Sargent) Colby, was born in Amesbury, March 9, 1671, was called "junior" before 1716, and afterward was called "senior." He married Dorothy Ambrose, who was appointed, September 29, 1746, administratrix of his estate, which was divided about 1748-50. They had eleven children, born in Amesbury: 1. Elizabeth, December 7, 1694, married John Rowell. 2. Keziah, May 11, 1697, married first David Currier; second, Jacob Bagley. 3. Samuel, April 19, 1698, "oldest son." 4. Ambrose, May 11, 1700. 5. Enoch, November 7, 1702; removed to Chester, New Hampshire. 6. Susanna, August 15, 1705, married Micah Hoyt. 7. Obadiah, July 15, 1706. 8. Dorothy, May 25, 1708. 9. Hezekiel, March 25, 1710. 10. Ruggles, June 10, 1711. 11. Abigail, April 29, 1713.

(IV) Samuel Colby, of Amesbury, son of Samuel and Dorothy (Ambrose) Colby, born Amesbury, April 19, 1698, married there October 23, 1718, Anna Nichols, born May 1, 1694-95, daughter of Thomas and Jane (Jameson) Nichols, and granddaughter of Thomas and Mary Nichols, the former of whom was in Amesbury as early as 1665 (see Nichols family). Children: 1. Samuel, December 30, 1720. 2. Moses, June 26, 1723, married Mary Sargent. 3. Aaron, October 13, 1726. 4. Gideon, May 13, 1729. 5. Barzilla, October 22, 1731, married (first) Elizabeth Plummer, (second) Miriam Worthen. 6. Lydia, June 26, 1735.

(V) Gideon Colby, son of Samuel and Anna (Nichols) Colby, born Amesbury, May 13, 1729, was by trade a carpenter and joiner. He was a soldier of the colonial army during the French and Indian war in 1755, taking part in the campaign of that year and again during the year 1758. He married, April 29, 1747, Elizabeth Tucker, of Amesbury, who died May 9, 1792. They had eight children, all born in Amesbury: 1. Winthrop, October 19, 1749, married, 1778, Abigail Nichols. 2. Aaron, October 15, 1751. 3. Gideon, August 9, 1753, soldier of the revolution. 4. Sarah, March 25, 1758. 5. Elizabeth, April 24, 1760. 6. Anna, June 8, 1762, died young. 7. Molly, June 5, 1767. 8. Anne, December 9, 1774.

(VI) Aaron Colby, son of Gideon and Elizabeth (Tucker) Colby, born Amesbury, October 15, 1751, was a cooper by trade. He also was a soldier of the revolution, his service record being as follows: Private in Captain Matthias Hoyt's company of minutemen that marched on the Lexington alarm, April 19, 1775; served nine days; private in Captain Timothy Barnard's company of Colonel Moses Little's seventeenth regiment; muster roll dated August 1, 1775; enlisted June 1, 1775; service eight months five days; also mentioned in company return dated October 9, 1775, age twenty-three years; private Captain Eliphalet Badwell's company of Colonel Edward Wigglesworth's regiment; pay abstract for mileage from Albany home in December, 1776; also return of men enlisted to serve in the continental army from Essex county, credited to Amesbury, February 11, 1778; residence Amesbury; joined Captain Blaisdell's company of Colonel Wigglesworth's regiment for term of eight months to expire January 10, 1778; also served in same company and regiment by enlistment May 24, 1777, one month seven days; reported as having been referred payment of wages due previous to July 1, 1777, by Jonathan Trumbull, paymaster general at Albany, on account of not joining the regiment at Peekskill before said date; roll certified at Boston. Aaron Colby married, May 2, 1776, Mary Hoyt, daughter of John Hoyt (John 4, Joseph 3, John 2, John 1), by whom he had five children, born in Amesbury: 1. Molly, (Mary) August 5, 1777. 2. Anne, April 16, 1779. 3. John, 1780. 4. Thomas, November 29, 1781. 5. Moses, April 17, 1786.

(VII) Deacon John Colby, son of Aaron and Mary (Hoyt) Colby, born Amesbury, 1780, died Salem, where the greater part of his life was spent. He was a ship caulker by trade and also could turn his hand to ship carpentry, and there found profitable employment so long as he was able to work. He was a very pious man, for many years deacon of the Second Baptist Church, Salem, a conservative old-line Democrat in political affiliation, and at one time was a selectman in Salem. He had eight children, all born in Salem: 1. John B., who was lost overboard from the steamship "Rhode Island" while on a voyage from New York to San Francisco. 2. William, born March 8, 1816, married Susan S. Roberts. 3. Francis W. 4. James T. 5. Sarah M., married Edward Dalton. 6. Eliza Ann, married George W. Bruce. 7. Caroline, married David Ruff. 8. Ella, married Daniel Lord.

(VIII) James T. Colby, son of Deacon John Colby, born in Salem, died in San Jose, California, where he was owner of a fruit farm. His young life was spent in Salem, where he attended the town school, and afterward worked for several years in his father's ship yard. In 1849 he followed the tide of westward emigration to the Pacific coast, at the time when the so-called "gold fever" was attracting thousands of adventurous young men to that far distant region. He continued to live in California, and at the time of his death was somewhat extensively engaged in fruit raising. Like his father, Mr. Colby was a firm Democrat, and in religious preference was a Baptist. His wife, Elizabeth (Clemmons) Colby, was born in Salem and died there. They had four children, all born in Salem: 1. Sarah, married Freeman Baston and removed to California; one child, Freeman Baston, Jr. 2. Rebecca, married Lawrence Palmer and removed to California. 3. John Anderson, of Salem. 4. William, now dead, married a daughter of Hezekiah Sleeper, of Salem.

(IX) John Anderson Colby, son of James T. and Elizabeth (Clemmons) Colby, was born in Salem, February 19, 1846. He was only a child when his brothers and sisters went to live with their parents in California, and then he was taken into the family of John Anderson, his uncle, by whom he was brought up, educated and put to useful and profitable employment. Mr. Colby remembers with kindest regard his uncle and aunt, both of whom treated him with affectionate and almost parental consideration. They set him in the right pathway in life and provided for his comfort in every way. Mr. Colby always has made his own way in business life, having early learned glue-making and has always followed that occupation, with satisfactory results to himself and his family. He is a Republican, but not an active partisan, and for many years has been a member of Company H, Eighth Regiment, Massachusetts Volunteer Militia. Mr. Colby married Annie Fitzpatrick, of Salem,

John Mitchell Anderson

and has two children: 1. Annie, born Salem, October 15, 1885, married L. W. Tate. 2. Mary, born Salem, March 24, 1887, lives with her parents.

John Anderson, referrred to above was born in Marblehead, April 12, 1812, and died August 8, 1900. He resided in his native town until 1857, there receiving his education in the common schools, and then located in Salem. He learned the business of glue and soap making, and carried it on very successfully in Marblehead, on a street which still bears his name. Upon locating in Salem he erected a large glue factory at 90 Highland avenue, which he successfully conducted for several years. He was at one time engaged in the shoe business with John W. Reynolds, the firm name being Anderson & Reynolds. While a resident of Marblehead he was captain of the Glover Guards. In Salem he was a member of the common council in 1872, and for many years a director in the Mercantile National Bank. He was prominently connected with the Universalist Church of Salem. He was an Odd Fellow, having joined Fraternity Lodge on April 26, 1859. On May 8, 1836, he married Rebecca Clements, a native of Salem, but at the time of her marriage was living in Marblehead. This union was childless, but Mr. and Mrs. Anderson adopted a nephew, John Anderson Colby.

(For early generations see preceding sketch).

COLBY

(IV) Ensign Enoch Colby, son of Samuel and Dorothy (Ambrose) Colby, born November 7, 1702, died in Chester, New Hampshire, between January 5, 1779, and August 30, 1780. He is said to have been of Hampton, but his name appears on the tax list in Hampton Falls, 1727. He was a member of the militia company and its ensign (lieutenant) and possibly may have been out in the early French wars. His first wife was Abiel, daughter of Benjamin Sanborn, one of the grantees of Chester, son of Lieutenant John Sanborn. In 1723 Benjamin Sanborn, of Hampton, in consideration of affection conveyed to Enoch Colby, also of Hampton, one half of his right in Chester, with the house on said right. Enoch Colby married (second), 1748, Sarah Sargent. Ensign Colby removed to Chester about 1728, and his name first appears on the records as surveyor of highways in 1730. He died before August 30, 1780, the date his will was admitted to probate. Enoch Colby had ten children: 1. Enoch, born probably in Hampton. 2. Sarah, died May 30, 1810; married William Turner, one of the earliest settlers in Candia, New Hampshire. 3. Dorothy, born January 5, 1730, died 1816; married (first) David Worthen, (second) Jacob Chase. 4. Jethro, born May 8, 1733, married Elizabeth Bartlett. 5. Susannah, born August 22, 1735, married ——— Blake. 6. Abiel, born July 10, 1741. 7. Abigail (by second wife), born December 19, 1749, married James Towle. 8. Mary, born November 9, 1756, married Benjamin Long. 9. Elizabeth, born June 27, 1758, married John Wilson. 10. Judith, born August 10, 1760, married Joseph Long.

(V) Enoch Colby, eldest son and child of Enoch and Abiel (Sanborn) Colby, was born probably in Hampton, and settled in Candia, New Hampshire, on the south end of lot 39 (third division). He married Abigail Blaisdell, and of their sons three were soldiers of the revolution. They had eight children: 1. John, a soldier of the revolution, died at Valley Forge. 2. Jethro, soldier of the revolution, served in Rhode Island; died after his return home, on the "dark day" in 1780. 3. Enoch, soldier of the revolution, married Lydia Worthen and settled in Thornton, New Hampshire; was representative, senator and councillor five years, 1813-1817. 4. Nehemiah, died 1840; lived on the old homestead; married Mary Rowe. 5. Abner. 6. Samuel. 7. Abigail, married John Colby, of Amesbury. 8. Mary, died 1780.

(VI) Samuel Colby, son of Enoch and Abigail (Blaisdell) Colby, born in Chester, New Hampshire, died in Vermont, probably in Derby. He married Ruth French and soon afterward settled in Thornton, New Hampshire, where some of their children were born, probably Nehemiah, Sarah, Moses, Ruth and Emily. In 1798 Mr. Colby and his wife started out to make a new home in Vermont, both riding on the same horse, Ruth mounted behind her husband. They went to Derby and were among the earliest settlers there, and at least one son was born there or in the vicinity. From Derby the family became much scattered, one son, Moses, going to Stanstead county, Canada.

(VII) Samuel Colby, son of Samuel and Ruth (French) Colby, was born in Vermont, perhaps in Derby, although possibly in Putney or Brattleboro, for reliable data of the family in that region are indeed meagre. He married Rebecca Eaton, who was born in Boston (north end) and whose mother was a Revere (of the same family as Paul Revere, on whose lap as a child Rebecca's mother frequently sat). Leaving his Vermont home when he was a young man, Mr. Colby went to Boston and for a short time engaged in the grocery business, but soon abandoned mercantile pursuits for the sea. As a seaman he soon demonstrated his ability to handle a vessel, and being a young man of good habits and thoroughly reliable he was made chief mate and sailed as an officer until 1835, when he applied for and received a license as pilot for Boston harbor. At the time of his death he was one of the oldest pilots in point of years of service engaged in guiding vessels in and out of the harbor, and as proof that he was not wanting in either skill or courage, it may be stated that in March, 1840, he rescued the "Newburyport" from a very perilous position and during a heavy gale ran her between Egg Harbor Ledge and the Boston Light, through that narrow channel where only light craft were attempted to be sailed; but he took the chance—the only chance left him—and brought her through safely into the harbor. For this daring piece of seamanship Mr. Colby was presented with a magnificent solid silver service by the underwriters of Boston. Samuel and Rebecca (Eaton) Colby had five children: 1. Adelaide, now Mrs. Augustus Hooper, of Somerville, Massachusetts. 2. Walter C., now of Everett, Massachusetts. 3. Samuel K., deceased. 4. Eben Clarence. 5. Simeon, lives in Everett.

(VIII) Eben Clarence Colby, son of Samuel and Rebecca (Eaton) Colby, was born in Boston, July 17, 1852. He graduated from the Elliott school, July 21, 1868, and later on took a course of practical study in Eaton's Business College, Boston, and for the next several years was employed in clerical work in Boston. On returning to Boston he became connected with the wholesale house of Claflin, Larrabee & Company, dealers in dry goods, remained there six years and then, having a decided preference for outdoor life, he became proprietor of a milk route in Everett and developed it into a large and successful business enterprise. He engaged in the milk business from about 1875 to 1900, then sold out and was appointed milk inspector of Everett. This office he still holds, having been reappointed for another term; and during his incumbency of office Mr. Colby has succeeded in effecting the removal of many evils of long standing and by his conscientious work has earned the gratitude and appreciation of the people of the city in which he lives. He had some knowledge of municipal affairs in Everett before taking his present office, and in 1894-95-96, was a member of the city council. He is a Republican in politics, and member Republican city committee, ward 5, and being a citizen and considerable property owner he appreciates the fact that whatever best promotes the public welfare naturally advances his personal interests. Mr. Colby is an influential member of the Universalist church (Broadway), a past grand of Howard Lodge, Independent Order of Odd Fellows, Charlestown; ex-governor of the Order of Pilgrim Fathers; and a member and for twenty-two years financial secretary of Franklin Lodge, Ancient Order of United Woodmen.

He married Hattie Speary Martin, born in Wayne, Maine, daughter of Jerome D. Martin, born in Craftsbury, Vermont, and Almira Townsend (Foss) Martin, his wife, born Leeds, Maine, daughter of Ephraim Foss, who married Harriet Townsend. Mr. and Mrs. Colby have one son, Fred Martin Colby, born Everett, in June, 1884, married Bertha Frances Reilly, and has one daughter, Constance Colby, and a son, Parker Martin Colby, born June, 1908. Fred M. Colby is connected with the American Loan and Trust Company, Boston, transfer clerk. He was a member of Everett common council two years, 1905-06.

WILSON The surname Wilson is one of the most common and widespread in England, Scotland and Ireland. It is derived, of course, from *Will* and *son*, in the same way as Johnson, Jackson, Davidson, etc., and, like those surnames, there were doubtless hundreds of progenitors of unrelated families that assumed the surname when the custom became general in the twelfth century or earlier. Many of this name have won distinction. There are numerous coats-of-arms borne by Wilsons of the higher classes. In Scotland the Wilsons were numerous in Renfrewshire, Elginshire, Fifeshire, Lanarkshire, and were found in other counties also at an early date. During the frightful persecution of the Scotch Presbyterians, one of this family suffered martyrdom. In 1685 James II, an avowed Roman Catholic, became king of England, sworn to maintain the Established Church (Episcopal), but his accession brought no relief to the persecuted Covenanters in Scotland and Ireland. An Episcopal farmer named Gilbert Wilson had two daughters—Agnes, aged thirteen, and Margaret, aged eighteen. These girls attended conventicles and had become Presbyterians. Arrested and condemned to death, their father succeeded in procuring the pardon of the younger by paying one hundred pounds sterling, but the elder, and an old woman named Margaret MacLaughlin, were bound to stakes on the seashore that they might be drowned by the rising tide. After the old woman was dead and the water had passed over Margaret Wilson's head, the latter was brought out, restored to consciousness, and offered life if she would take the abjuration oath. But she said: "I am one of Christ's children, let me go." She was then once more placed in the sea, and her sufferings ended by death.

In the north of Ireland the crown granted to William Willson, of Suffolk, England, two thousand acres of land in the precinct of Liffer (barony of Raphoe) county Donegal, about 1610. In 1611 Willson bought two thousand acres granted to Sir Henry Knight. His residence is given as Clarye, in Suffolk, and his Irish agent was Chris. Parmenter. He brought over some English settlers. This Englishman may never have settled there himself. In 1619 we find a Scotchman named Stephen Wilson (also Woolson), a tenant of John Cunningham, precinct of Portlough, county Donegal, Ireland. There were doubtless other Scotch from time to time settling in Ulster. Few surnames are more numerous than Wilson in Ireland. In 1890 there were 366 births of children of this name, 287 being in the Ulster counties of Antrim, Armagh, Down, Tyrone, Londonderry and Fermanagh, indicating a population of about 18,000 of this name in Ireland at the present time. In 1689 one of these Scotch Wilsons living in Enniskillen became famous. July 1st, Lieutenant MacCarmick, in whose company James Wilson was a soldier, made a stand against the Duke of Berwick, an illegitimate son of King James, at the head of a detachment of Irish, six hundred dragoons on foot and two troops of horse. Governor Hamilton, his superior officer, failed to keep his promise to support MacCarmick, and his little company was fairly cut to pieces, his son slain at his side, and he was taken prisoner. But thirty escaped. Among these was a brave soldier named James Wilson. Surrounded by a number of dragoons he was assailed by all at once, some of them he stabbed, others he struck down with his musket, and several he threw under the feet of their own horses. At last wounded in twelve places, his cheeks hanging over his chin, he fell into a bush. There a sergeant struck him through the thigh with a halbert; but Wilson, exerting all his strength, pulled it out and ran it through the sergeant's heart. By the assistance of this halbert he walked back to Enniskillen. He was afterwards cured of his wounds and survived for thirty years." Whether descended from him or not, the Wilson family of Enniskillen, mentioned below, may well pride in this exploit.

(I) John Wilson was born in the parish of Enniskillen, county Fermanagh, Ireland. He became a wealthy farmer, and was always known familiarly among his townsmen as "Jack" Wilson. He was a citizen of prominence, and a strict Episcopalian in religion. He married Catherine Wilson. Among his children were: 1. James Alexander, mentioned below. 2. Alexander. 3. John. 4. Andrew.

(II) James Alexander Wilson, son of John Wilson (1), was born in Enniskillen, Ireland, in 1783. He attended the parish school and was well educated for his day. About 1800 he came to America, and was employed at first in Philadelphia, and in New Jersey. After he had accumulated some means he returned to his native land and bought a large farm. Later he bought more land and settled each of his sons on farms. He was a successful farmer and became a leading cattle trader in the county, amassing considerable wealth. He raised flax and farm produce. His farm was at White Hill, a part of the township of Enniskillen. He left a large amount of property, which his children inherited. He was called "Yankee" Wilson, after he returned from America, a name which clung to him the rest of his life. He was a member of the parish church and brought his family up in the Episcopal faith. He married first, ——— Armstrong; second, Mary, daughter of William Johnson, of Enniskillen. Children: 1. John, a farmer at Enniskillen; married Catherine Lettimer, born 1825, died December 2, 1898, daughter of George and Dolly (Morfitt) Lettimer, of Enniskillen; children: i. James, born March 3, 1855, married March 15, 1880, Caroline Maria McManus, of Arlington, Massachusetts, and had Hattie, born March 3, 1881 (married September 21, 1904, Henry F. Ireland), George Lattimer, born October 4, 1883, William Andrew, born December 8, 1889; ii. George, born April 3, 1857, married October 7, 1885, Ellen Sproul, died October 2, 1892, daughter of James and Sophia (Robinson) Sproul, and had John Alexander, born March 14, 1887, Florence, born December 19, 1888, died January 3, 1890, (twins), born June 22, 1890, died July 13, 1890, Henry (twin), born June 22, 1890, died August 4.

1890; iii. John, born August 3, 1859; iv. William Henry; v. Robert, born October, 1865; vi. Andrew, born August 18, 1868, married December 25, 1896, Nellie King, of Arlington; vii. Mary Jane, born May 14, 1873, married February 10, 1908, C. A. Cheney. 2. Katherine, married Thomas Hodgdon, of Enniskillen; had Mary Ann Hodgdon, married John Morfitt of Enniskillen. 3. Frances, married Thomas Morfitt, of Enniskillen; children: i. Mary Morfitt. ii. Catherine Morfitt; iii. Latishie Morfitt; iv. Frances Ann Morfitt; v. Margaret Morfitt; vi. Becky Jane Morfitt. 4. William, born June 11, 1832, mentioned below 5. Ann, married Robert Johnson; children: i. John Johnson, married Maria Sheridan, of Enniskillen, and had Robert, Ann Jane, Margaret, William, Thomas, John and James Johnson; ii. Mary Johnson, married William Reynolds, of Swanland Bar, Ireland, and had Samuel, Annie, Robert, Hugh, John, Margaret, James, Jane, Eliza and William Reynolds. 6. Alexander, born March 20, 1815. 7. Robert, married Ellen Sheridan, of Enniskillen, and had Mary Ann, Margaret, Tilly, William, James and Robert Wilson. 8. James, married first Mary Jane Farley of Arden Moore, Ireland; second ——— Johnson.

(III) William Wilson, son of James Alexander Wilson (2), born at White Hill, Enniskillen, Ireland, June 11, 1832, died at Arlington, Massachusetts, November 27, 1891. He was educated in the parish school of his native town and worked at home until he became of age. He came to America, landing in Boston July 1, 1854. He found employment at market gardening with Henry Frost, of Belmont, where he remained a year. He was next employed by Josiah Locke of Winchester, driving a market wagon to Boston, for five years. About the time he was married he bought of Dr. R. L. Hodgdon thirty-two acres of land in the northwest part of Arlington. He was employed by Dr. Hodgdon for three years as foreman on his farm, and then engaged in market gardening on his own farm. Until 1880 he conducted his farm with great success, when he leased it to Robert Dinsmore, and bought the Childs farm at East Lexington, and was associated with his son James in the same business. In his later years his eyesight was inpaired, and about two years before his death he retired and lived on his farm there, where he died November 27, 1891. He was a faithful member of St. John's Episcopal Church at Arlington, serving as vestryman and warden, was one of the charter members and largely instrumental in its erection and a generous contributor to its charities. He was a man much respected in the community and beloved by his family. In politics he was a Republican. He married, in Boston, January 22, 1858, Ann Irwin, born at Enniskillen, Ireland, March 19, 1822, died at Arlington, October 3, 1899, daughter of John and Jane (Johnson) Irwin, of Florence Court, county Fermanagh, Ireland: Children: 1. James Alexander, born November 5, 1859; mentioned below. 2. Mary Jane, born January 25, 1861; married September 9, 1891, Joseph Dickson, of Arlington; children: i. Thomas Wilson Dickson, born November 23, 1892; ii. Annie Dickson, July 12, 1894; iii. Eliza Dickson, April 4, 1896; iv. William Henry Dickson, September 6, 1897; v. Margaret Jane Dickson, August 25, 1898; vi. Ralph Wardlaw Dickson, October 9, 1900.

(IV) James Alexander Wilson, son of William Wilson (3), was born at Arlington, November 5, 1859. He was educated in the public schools of his native town and in the Cotting high school. He remained with his father in Arlington, and a year in East Lexington, and subsequently accepted a position as salesman for the commission house of A. L. Andrews. After two years he engaged in the grocery business at Arlington Heights for three years. At this time he returned with his father to the farm and spent the next eight years at market gardening, then leasing the place to Archibald McCoy. The following three years Mr. Wilson was the buyer for the wholesale produce house of R. P. Puffer, 3 Richmond street, Boston, and travelled through all parts of the United States and Canada, on business for the firm, which had a large Montreal trade. Being anxious to return to farming again, he returned to Arlington and resumed work on the place, where he has since remained. He is a successful gardener, cultivating about twenty of the thirty-two acres, making a specialty of lettuce. He is a member of St. John's Episcopal Church, and has served as vestryman and treasurer of the society. In politics he is a Republican. He is a member of Shawmut Tribe, No. 4, I. O. R. M., having been transferred from Pomona Tribe, No. 7, of Arlington. He is also a member of the Men's Club of Arlington. He married, March 24, 1885, Lillie Flora Elliott, born at Montreal, Canada, November 26, 1864, daughter of James and Annie (McLean) Elliott. Children: 1. Annie Rebecca, born December 29, 1885; married November 5, 1906, Frank Bernard Needham, of Arlington; had Frank Wilson Needham, born May 7, 1907. 2. William Elliott, born July 22, 1887; died August 24, 1897. 3. Edna Gertrude, born October 22, 1891; died April 2, 1895. 4. George Skermish, born November 30, 1894. 5. James Norman, born November 2, 1896; died November 22, 1897. 6. Walter Bolton, born September 11, 1899. 7. Ernest Irving, December 17, 1901. 8. Lillie Flora, May 10, 1905. 9. Grace McLean, September 4, 1907.

(For first two generations see James A. Wilson 2).

WILSON (III) Alexander Wilson, son of James Alexander Wilson (2), born at White Hill, Enniskillen, Ireland, March 20, 1815, died at Tewksbury, Massachusetts, October 9, 1901, aged eighty-six years. When a young man he came to America and remained a short time, then returning to his native town again. After a short stay he returned to Boston and was employed in the hostelry of Charles Adair as foreman. He made another trip to Ireland with his wife, but soon came back to Boston and was employed at the Tremont House as butler, being in that position for about eight years. Later he had a similar position at the Revere House. He always retained the confidence of his employers, and did everything well. He was ever thoughtful of others, and generous to a fault, an upright and honorable citizen. He was a member of St. John's Episcopal Church at Arlington. He married Martha Monahan, born at Enniskillen, May 4, 1833, died at Lexington, Massachusetts, November 25, 1889, daughter of John and Martha (Willis) Monahan, of Enniskillen. Children: 1. John E., born December 4, 1855; died February 14, 1889; married September 6, 1885, Ellen Frances Goff, of Arlington; children: i. Albert Everett Goff, born February 1, 1886; ii. Herbert Sumner Goff, April 11, 1887; 2. Mary Frances, married first, ——— Eldrige; second, John Murphy. 3. James Alexander, born March 8, 1859; mentioned below. 4. William Henry, born November 5, 1865; married February 29, 1899, Alice A. Frybe, of Sussex, New Brunswick; children: i. Martha, born October 13, 1899; ii. Albert Edward, January 27, 1901; iii. William Henry, June 13, 1903; iv. Kathleen, February 8, 1905; v. Francis Robert, October 6, 1907. 5. Robert, born January 9, 1869; married October 3, 1893, Jennie M. Edmunds, of Milwaukee, Wisconsin; had Kathlyn Scott, born January 23, 1903.

(IV) James Alexander Wilson, son of Alexander Wilson (3), was born at Enniskillen, Ireland, March 8, 1859. He attended the parish school of Enniskillen, living with his grandfather on the farm, and working there until he was eighteen years old. He then came to America and was employed at market gardening by his uncle William at Arlington, where he remained until he was of age. He leased the farm of Dr. Francis Brown, in East Lexington, and began market gardening on his own account. The venture was successful from the start, and the business steadily increased. He soon bought the fifteen acre farm of the Brown heirs, February 27, 1903, and has conducted it successfully ever since. He makes a specialty of celery. Mr. Wilson has built up a large and lucrative business, and is counted one of the most successful in his line. He belongs to St. John's Episcopal Church of Arlington, and has been a vestryman. He is a member of the Boston Market Gardeners' Association, and has served on various committees of the organization. In politics he is a Republican. He married, November 16, 1887, Margaret Chambers, born at Huntington, Canada, December 16, 1862, daughter of James and Jane (Heuston) Chambers. Children: 1. Walter Harrison, born October 3, 1888. 2. Martha Jane, June 28, 1891. 3. James Ernest, September 25, 1893. 4. William Stanley, August 22, 1897. 5. Doris Elizabeth, May 10, 1900. 6. Marion Chambers, May 14, 1907.

JOHNSON (I) William Johnson was born in Enniskillen, Ulster province, county Fermanagh, Ireland. He died on his farm there about 1836. He was brought up on his father's farm and educated in the nearby district school. He became a prosperous farmer and owned a farm of twenty or thirty acres in the southeast part of the township, it being free land. He raised large amounts of oats, barley, flax and farm produce, selling his grain in the nearby towns of Irwinstown, Pettigoe, Dunquin and Enniskillen. His cattle, horses and sheep which he raised also were marketed in these towns. He was a man highly respected in the community, of positive opinions but sound good sense. He belonged to the Episcopal church and to the Order of Orangemen. In politics he was a Liberal. He married Rosanna Muldoon, daughter of John Muldoon, of Corlaught, Ireland. Children: 1. Joseph, married Katherine Sullivan; children: i.

Mary Hannah, married, September 22, 1880, Charles E. Meade, of Greenwich, Connecticut; ii. William; iii. Jane; iv. Elizabeth; v. Alice Meade. 2. John, died young. 3. Irving, born April 16, 1835; mentioned below. 4. William, unmarried; resided in Ireland.

(II) Irving Johnson, son of William Johnson (1), was born at Corlaught, Ireland, April 16, 1835. He attended the district school until he was fourteen years old, walking a mile and a half to the school house, which was situated in the nearby parish of Adneveigh. At the age of fifteen he came to America, where his brother Joseph had already settled, having come some time previously. After a forty-two days voyage on the ship "Castelian," he arrived in New York City August 4, 1850, and went to Greenwich, Connecticut, where he joined his brother, who was employed by Silas D. Meade on his farm. Here he remained two years, and then worked for Silas Husted on his farm for a year, and the following eight months for a Mr. Savage. Going to New York city, he was employed on the estate of James Donaldson on Fifth avenue. For two years he worked for the street railroad in New York as conductor, and then entered the dry goods establishment of Stebbins, Hoyt & Co. at 43 Barclay street. He remained with them until 1858, when he came to Boston, and was employed at market gardening by William Adams on his farm at Winchester. Afterwards he worked for Samuel Butterfield, a prominent market gardener of Arlington, and was his foreman for ten years. At this time his employer died, and Mr. Johnson managed the farm four years for the widow. He then leased the William Hill farm of thirteen acres at Belmont, and engaged in market gardening on his own account for five years. He removed to Arlington and leased the Butterfield estate on which he had worked, and conducted it up to 1897. He purchased his present farm in Lexington, October 15, 1897, removing his family there the following December. He bought also an eighty-acre farm in the town of Stoneham, known as the Richardson estate, and his son Joseph had the care of this place. He later sold this property to Captain Mareus B. Buford, a retired naval officer. Mr. Johnson conducts a successful business at market gardening, making a specialty of lettuce, celery and onions, with spring growth of cucumbers under glass. His produce is sold to Allen Hurd & Company, commission merchants of Boston, his son, Frederick W. Johnson, being the selling agent. Mr. Johnson is a man of sterling character and is highly esteemed by his townsmen. He is of the Episcopal faith and served as vestryman at St. John's Church at Arlington. He is a Republican in politics, but never held office.

He married, September 13, 1855, Esther Irwin, born in Enniskillen, Ireland, June 6, 1830, died at Lexington, July 29, 1907, daughter of John and Jane (Johnson) Irwin; (see Irwin family sketch herewith). Children: 1. Sarah Jane, born June 19, 1856, died September 11, 1857. 2. William James, born March 23, 1858, died April 4, 1858. 3. Harriet Emily, born March 14, 1859, unmarried. 4. Joseph Henry, born September 1, 1861, unmarried. 5. Frederick William, born August 25, 1863, married, August 12, 1889, Jennie Chambers, of Huntington, Province of Quebec, and had Alice M., born December 12, 1890, died April 19, 1901; Frederick William, Jr., born January 5, 1892. 6. Annie Irwin, born July 1, 1865. 7. Everett Hale, born January 16, 1868, died June 29, 1869. 8. Jennie Esther, born February 3, 1870, married, April 12, 1893, Nelson Hayden, of Ferrisburg, Vermont, and had Irving Nelson Hayden, born January 7, 1897.

IRWIN The Irvine, Irving or Irwin family of Scotland, Ireland and England, is descended from William de Irwin whom Robert Bruce appointed armor bearer and on whom he conferred, besides a grant of land comprising the forest of Drum, his own coat-of-arms when Earl of Carrick: the three holly leaves now found in the coats-of-arms of all the Irwins, Irvines and Irvings, of this family, his descendants. From the Irvines of Drum, county Aberdeen, Scotland, we find the late chief Alexander Irvine, the Irvines of Lenturk, Hilltown, Kingcausie, Fortrie, Murthill Cutts, etc., all being descendants. Some branches of the family in Ireland retain the old spelling Irwin, others use the more common Irvine. Sir Gerard Irvine was created a baronet (29 Charles II) of Castle Irvine, county Fermanagh. Burke says of the Irwin family in Ireland: "The Irwins of Tauragoe have maintained a position of great respectability amongst the gentry of the county of Sligo, since their settlement in Ireland, but from which branch of the Scottish Irwines or Irvings they descended has not been ascertained." The peculiar name of Crinus borne by members of the family is traditionally derived from Krynin Abethnae, second husband of the mother of Duncan, King of Scotland, to whom and his descendants that monarch granted the privilege of bearing a thistle as a crest. John Irwin, who married a daughter of Colonel Lewis Jones, of Ard-na-glass, held a commission in the parliamentary army in which his father-in-law also served, and accompanying Cromwell to Ireland, settled at Sligo.

Alexander Irwin, son of John Irwin, lived at Sligo; married a sister of ——— Griffiths, Esq., of Ballincar, and aunt of Colonel Griffiths, who was father of Anne, countess of Harrington and of Lady Rich. Of their six sons all died without issue except the eldest, John, mentioned below.

Colonel John Irwin, son of Alexander Irwin, born about 1680 in Sligo, died in 1752. He married (first) Lady Mary Dilkes, widow, of county Cork, and had no children. He married (second) Susanna Cadden, of the ancient Cavan family, and had children: 1. Lewis Francis, mentioned below. 2. Letitia, married Captain Thomas Webber, of the Fourth Horse, and had a son and daughter. 3. Margaret, married Robert Browne, Esq., of Fortland, county Sligo.

Lewis Francis Irwin, son of Colonel John Irwin, resided at Tauragoe, county Sligo, Ireland, where he was born in 1728 and died in 1785. He married, in 1766, Elizabeth Harrison, only sister of the late John Harrison, Esq., of Norton Place, Lincolnshire, England. She died in 1815, aged eighty-two. Children: 1. John, mentioned below. 2. Crinus, took holy orders; became archdeacon of Assoy; married, in 1807, Amy, eldest daughter of Mr. Justice Chamberlain, judge of the King's bench in Ireland; two sons: John Lewis and Lewis Chamberlain. 3. Elizabeth, died in 1822; married Robert Jones, of Fortland. 4. Mary, married Rev. Schuchhurgh Upton, of Templeton family. 5. Beatrice Susanna, married Benjamin Agar, Esq., of Brockfield, Yorkshire.

John Irwin, son of Lewis Francis Irwin, born about 1770, succeeded his father at Tauragoe, Calloony. He was colonel and high sheriff in 1822. Of the county Fermanagh family mentioned above, we find at present the representative is John Arthur Irwin, Esq., of Derry Gore. He was high sheriff in 1887; justice of the peace. He was born January 1, 1854, son of Edward Irwin, who was high sheriff in 1863; justice of the peace; married Hannah Baynes. The seat of this family has been and is Derrygore, Enniskillen, county Fermanagh, Ireland. The coat-of-arms, a mural crown gules between three holly leaves proper; upon the escutcheon is placed a helmet befitting his degree with a mantling gules, double argent. Crest: upon a wreath of the colors a mailed arm fessways holding in the hand a thistle and a holly leaf all proper and charged on the arms with a crescent gules. The motto: Nemo me impune lacessit. (No one attacks me with impunity).

Similar coats-of-arms are borne by Thomas Angelo Irwin, justice of the peace, county Cumberland, England, born April 10, 1832. Practically the same arms are borne by the Irvines of Banshaw from the remotest period. The Irvines of Castle Fortagh, Scotland, and in fact most of the families of this name bear arms with the holly; crest with the thistle somewhat varied but much alike and establishing kinship clearly enough.

(I) John Irwin, progenitor of the family recorded below, was of the Fermanagh family as described above, and resided at Florence Court, county Fermanagh, Ireland. He was probably born about 1720.

(II) John Irwin, son of John Irwin (1), was born at Florence Court, county Fermanagh, about 1760; was educated there in the parish schools, and was brought up on a farm. He became a prosperous farmer in his native place, owning a sixty acre farm in free land, raising sheep, cattle and horses, large quantities of flax and all kinds of produce, and employing many hands. He was accounted a man of wealth at the time of his death. He was a member of the Royal Order of Orangemen in Florence Court. He married (first) Esther Bracken; (second) Margaret Brown. Children of first wife: 1. John, mentioned below. 2. Richard, married Annie Carr. 3. Thomas, died unmarried. 4. Jane, married John Belford. Children of second wife: 5 James, married Mary Montgomery. 6. Edward, married Margaret Graden. 7. Christopher, married Katherine Jones. 8. Sarah, married Robert Manley. 9. Mary, married Thomas Burley.

(III) John Irwin, son of John Irwin (2), was born at Florence Court in 1788. He received his education in that parish and was an apt student. He worked during his youth on his father's farm. After his marriage he leased a twenty-five acre farm of the Lord of Enniskillen and lived upon it all the remainder of his life. He raised general farm produce and much flax; horses, cattle and sheep. He was yeoman and forester for Lord

Enniskillen. His children, Margaret and Richard Irwin, after his death conducted the farm until they left for America in 1865. John Irwin was of large and powerful physique; jovial and amiable in disposition; making many friends. He served in the military company under Lord Enniskillen. He died in 1856. He was a faithful parishioner of the Church of England; member of the Royal Order of Orangemen.

He married Margaret Johnson, who died in 1865, daughter of William and Jane (Wilson) Johnson. Her father was a farmer and weaver. Children: 1. John, married, February 6, 1858, Mrs. Jane (Armstrong) Price, of Arlington, Massachusetts; both deceased; no children. 2. William, born at Enniskillen. 3. Ann, married William H. Wilson. 4. Esther, married, September 13, 1855, Irving Johnson (see sketch of the Johnson family herewith). 5. James, married Mary Lunney. 6. Thomas, died young. 7. Henry, died young. 8. Jane, died young. 9. Margaret, married, July 30, 1865, George S. Drummond. 10. Richard. 11. Thomas, married Mary Jane Clark and had William and Mary.

GRAHAM

The surname Graham is used interchangeably with Graeme in Scotland, and the history of the family would fill a volume of itself. The name is also spelled Graemes, Grahames, and Grimes. According to Scotch genealogists, who as Camden tells us, "think surnames as ancient as the moon," this illustrious patronymic is derived from Greme, who was regent of Scotland during the minority of Eugene II, commencing A. D. 419, and had many engagements with the Britons, and by forcing that mighty rampart they had reared up between the rivers Forth and Clyde immortalized the name so much that to this day that entrenchment is called Graham's Dyke. Collins, who gravely states this, finds no record however of the family earlier than the time of King David I, about 1125, when the name was written De Graeme, which shows local origin—that is, the surname was taken from a place named Graham or Graeme. Graeme indeed is merely the Scotch pronunciation, spelled simply. The termination shows the word to be of old English origin, and the family in Scotland is traced to William de Graham, who settled in Scotland in the twelfth century. The only place of the name in South Britain is near Kesteven, Lincolnshire. The name is found in the Hundred Rolls (vol. 1, p. 288) in England in the twelfth century. But the name is one of the most distinguished and prolific in Scotland. Of the forty-six Graham coats-of-arms, all but one are Scotch, and the other is borne by a Scotch family settled in Ireland. Many of the Scotch armorials are like this ancient one: Argent on a chief sable three escallops. The Duke of Montrose uses it quartered with others. The Irish family bears: Argent an escallop sable on a chief of the last three escallops of the first. Crest: A hand in fesse couped proper holding a fleur-de-lis or. Before 1150 the family is found in Linlithgowshire, Forfarshire, Perthshire, Stirlingshire, and Dumfriesshire. The family possesses the dukedom, marquisates and earldom of Montrose; marquisate of Graham and Buchanan; earldoms of Airth, Kincardine, Monteith and Strathern; viscountcies of Dundas, Dundee and Preston; lordships of Aberuthven, Kilpoint, etc.; barony of Esk, etc. Hanna says the family is of reputed Norman origin, which agrees with the statement of the local origin of the name and that the progenitor came through England.

The Irish branch of the family was founded by Sir George Graham and Sir Richard Graham, knights, who received a grant of two thousand acres of the confiscated lands of the Irish Catholic precinct of Tullaghah, county of Cavan, in 1610, by the English crown. In 1619 we find an Archibald Graham in the precinct of Fewes, county Armagh, in Ulster, a tenant of John Hamilton; also in precinct of Strabane, county Tyrone, John and Thomas Graham (Gryme) as tenants. In 1619 we find that Sir George and Sir Richard Graham (then spelled Grimes) had a stone "bawn" built, containing a little house. The family became numerous and is still numerous in the Protestant counties of Ulster—Antrim, Down, Tyrone, Armagh and Monaghan, as well as in many other sections of the country. It is estimated that there are ten thousand of the name in Ireland in 1908, of whom about seven thousand are in the counties named.

(I) Andrew Graham, of this Scotch-Irish family, was born, lived and died in county Donegal, Ireland, province of Ulster. He was a prosperous farmer. He was a member of the Established Church, and a man of very strong religious convictions. Children: 1. Andrew, married Sarah Lytle; had Richard, Andrew, William, Margaret and Mary. 2. John, married first, ——— Dinsmore; second, Mary Scott, of Kellymard, Ireland; children by first wife: i. Jane, married George Johnson; ii.

John; children of second wife: iii. Robert; iv. James; v. Elizabeth, married Edward Leslie; vi. Mary, married William Crowley; vii. Catherine; viii. William; ix. Isabel, married Richard Love. 3. Isaac, had child Margaret, married Robert Hawks. 4. James, born March, 1801; mentioned below. 5. Elizabeth, married David Ray; had Margaret and Richard Ray, and a daughter died young. 6. Richard, was a prominent Free Mason in his native county; married Ann Love; children: i. John, married Sarah Colvin; ii. William; iii. Richard, married Isabel Graham; he lost his life by accident while horseback riding, 1866; iv. Robert, married Sarah Graham; v. Margaret, married John Colvin; vi. Mary Jane, married ——— Love. 7. Catharine, married Thomas Knox; one child.

(II) James Graham, son of Andrew Graham (1), born at Lackan, Donegal county, Ireland, March, 1801, died August 20, 1887. He was brought up on his father's farm, and at an early age learned the trade of blacksmith, serving an apprenticeship of seven years, in the nearby parish of Lackey. After he had become proficient in his trade he returned to his native town, bought a farm of eleven acres, and erected a blacksmith shop. He followed his trade all his life, and in later life his son William worked with him. He carried on the farm and raised the usual farm produce and flax. He made plows at his shop for all the surrounding country, and was a good carriage smith, wheelwright and an expert chain maker. He was an enterprising man, and his good nature and democratic character were factors in his business success. He was a member of the Episcopal church, and conscientious and upright in all his dealings. He was a Liberal in politics. He was a member of Donegal Lodge, thirty-second degree, Masons. He married Margaret, daughter of Richard Freeborne, of Lackan. Children: 1. Richard, married Isabel Erwin, of Drimlask; had Ann Jane and Margaret. 2. William, born 1828; died December 9, 1901; married Bess Patterson, of Timmond, Ireland; children: i. James, married Frances Spence, and had Charlotte and one other child; ii. Margaret, married Addison Twining, of Wintersport, Maine; iii. Mary Ann, born April 7, 1867, died May 31, 1904, married William Hammond, and had Mary Hammond, born October 4, 1888; iv. Robert, married Christina Watson; v. Elizabeth, born July 12, 1871, married October 3, 1890, Henry Barrett, of Woburn, Massachusetts, and had Lillie Maud Barrett, born October 3, 1891, William James Barrett, born August 25, 1892, Florence Graham Barrett, born March 24, 1894, Ida Pearl Barrett, born February 28, 1896, Alice Elizabeth Edna Barrett, born September 19, 1901, Henry Roosevelt Barrett, born September 16, 1904, and Robert Barrett, born May 26, 1906, died young; vi. William, born August 30, 1877, married April, 1904, Jessie Sterling. 3. Elizabeth, died aged eighteen. 4. Margaret, died aged two. 5. Margaret, married Andrew Ray, of Arnagassan, Ireland; children: i. Andrew Ray, Jr., married Jane Love; ii. Margaret Ellen Ray, married Andrew Corrigan, and had Margaret Ellen, Henry, Richard, Robert, Andrew, Alfred, Elizabeth, Ernest, Ernest Given and Matilda Corrigan; iii. James; iv. Robert Wellington. 6. James, born November 15, 1840; mentioned below. 7. John, married first, Sarah Ray; second, Ann Love; children by first wife: i. James, married first, Margaret J. Graham, and had Robert, married second, Jennie B. McCue, and had James Warren, Thelma Boyd, and two other children; ii. Annie, married Frank Turner, of Woburn, Massachusetts, and had Edna May and Margaret Knowd Turner; iii. Joseph, married Isabella Graham, and had Mabel Jane; iv. Margaret; children of second wife: v. John. vi. Jane; vii. Alexander; viii. William; ix. Isaac. 8. Isaac, married Katherine McCue; children: i. James William, married Mabel McCrea; ii. John, married Isabel Graham; iii. George; iv. Margaret Jane, married James Graham, of Woburn, and had Robert; v. Sarah; vi. Catherine, married Benjamin Davey and had two children. 9. Sarah, married Robert Graham, of Moyen, Ireland; children: i. Annie, married John Ray and had Sarah, Robert, James and Ray, and an adopted daughter, Lilly Ray; ii. Margaret, married James Kee. 10. Frank, married Maria A. Arthur; children: i. James Freeborne, married Flora McDonald; ii. Frank Hood, married Rebecca Graham; iii. John Edward, married Elizabeth B. Hawthorn, of Malden, and had one child. 11. Mary Ann, married December 21, 1874, Adam Busteed of Woburn, and had one child, Lillian May, born April 19, 1877, married July 8, 1902, Edward D. Hart, of Woburn, and had Edward Dexter Hart, born September 16, 1903, and Charles Ward Hart, born April 27, 1907.

(III) James Graham, son of James Graham (2), was born at Lackan, county Donegal, Ireland, November 15, 1840. He attended the parish school at the little stone schoolhouse at Tullynaught, under Master Robert Maxwell, an old pensioner of the crown. At the age of fifteen he began to drive a team for his father, carrying lumber from Donegal to Pettigo. At the age of twenty-one he came to America, landing at New York city, and was employed in a brick yard at Newburg, N. Y., remaining there three months. He subsequently came to Woburn, Massachusetts, and was employed on the farm of John Cummings, and for a number of years was engaged at training high-bred horses for the leading turfmen of New England. Mr. Graham many times drove trotting horses in the races at Lexington and Concord; and also had charge of marketing produce in Boston, and later became superintendent of the market gardening for Mr. Cummings. He also had charge of the milk raising, and was in his employ for thirty-eight years. In the fall of 1897 he retired from active labor and bought his present property on Main street, North Woburn, known as the old Chadburn place. Mr. Graham is a type of the sturdy, upright, conscientious Scotchmen that have come to America and helped to build the nation. Honest, openhearted and kindly, he has the confidence and esteem of his neighbors to a marked degree. He is zealous in support of the Protestant Episcopal Church, of which he is a member and for many years has been a vestryman. In politics he is a Republican. He was made a member of Mt. Horeb Lodge of Masons, at Woburn, April 2, 1879, and is a member of True Blue Lodge, No. 119, Loyal Order of Orangemen, at Woburn. He married, January 31, 1863, Elizabeth Given, born August 27, 1844, daughter of Robert and Eleanor (Porter) Given. Children: 1. William Gage, born December 25, 1863; married, at Woburn, April 2, 1884, Louise H. Hartwell; children: i. James Ephraim, born October 12, 1884; ii. Ruby Wyman, November 22, 1886; iii. Elizabeth Given, November 21, 1888; iv. Josephine Louise, January 16, 1893. 2. John Given, born May 23, 1867; mentioned below. 3. Elizabeth Given, born May 14, 1873; died April 22, 1876. 4. James Robert, born September 15, 1877; married November 9, 1897, Agatha Anderson, of Bridgton, Nova Scotia; children: i. James; ii. Elizabeth Marion, born July 26, 1901; iii. James Raymond, October 6, 1907. 5. Sarah Cummings, born November 8, 1880; married John Thomas Davey, of Prince Edward Island, and had James Grafton Davey and Victor Graham Davey.

(IV) John Given Graham, son of James Graham (3), was born at Burlington, Massachusetts, May 23, 1867. He received his education in the public schools, graduating from the Cummings grammar school and attending Warren Academy for one year. He was employed by his father on the John Cummings farm, of which he was superintendent, and continued until he was thirty years old, becoming an expert gardener. In 1887 he embarked in business on his own account. He bought the old Thurston farm on Burlington street, Lexington, consisting of fifty acres, with house and other buildings. He has thirty acres under cultivation, using five hundred or more sash in starting his plants. He raised all kinds of produce, finding his market in the commission houses of Boston. His land has a southern exposure, and is very favorably situated for this sort of cultivation. Mr. Graham has also a fine dairy consisting of twenty-five head of Holstein cattle. Though quiet and retiring in manner, Mr. Graham is well known and highly respected in the community. He is a member of the Protestant Episcopal Church of Our Redeemer, Lexington. In politics he is a Republican. He is a member of Mount Horeb Lodge of Free Masons, Woburn; of True Blue Lodge No. 119, Loyal Order of Orangemen, Woburn, and holds the office of director in that body. He was formerly a member of Woburn Phalanx, Company G, Massachusetts Volunteer Militia, of which he was corporal and sergeant. He married, December 11, 1889, Catherine Graham, born February 24, 1868, daughter of Richard and Isabel (Graham) Graham. Her father was a farmer at Lackan, Ireland. Children, born at Woburn: 1. James Harold, born May 26, 1891. 2. Isabel Elizabeth, born November 13, 1892. 3. John Cummings, born August 4, 1894, in Lexington. 4. Sarah, born May 10, 1899, died August 8, 1899. 5. Catherine Dorothy, born May 27, 1905

HUMPHREY (I) Mr. John Humphrey, immigrant ancestor, was a member of the Massachusetts Bay Colony. Winslow says in his history: "July, 1634, Mr. Humphrey and the lady Susan, his wife, one of the Earl of Lincoln's sisters, arrived at Boston, bringing military supplies, sixteen heifers given by Mr. Richard Andrews to the plantation, one for each of the ministers and the rest to the poor, etc., and messages from people of quality who desired to come over." He had a grant of land at Saugus, March 6, 1632-3. He was a distin-

James Graham Elizabeth Given, Graham

guished magistrate. He brought with him two thousand pounds, but died poor in 1653. He was called a very useful ruler by Governor Winthrop. He was admitted a freeman May 25, 1636. He had a sad experience in regard to some of his children in 1641; was appointed by the general court, June 2, 1641, sergeant major general. Administration was granted to his son Joseph, December 13, 1661. The court gave him a grant of three hundred acres which he sold. In 1662 there was litigation over his estate in the Essex Court, some of the Humphrey grants, as stated in the Marblehead history, were in what is now Marblehead. The general court voted May 6, 1635, "to improve the land between Clifte and Forest River and dispose of it to the inhabitants of Marblehead as they stood in need of it, the only charge to the purchaser being enough to recompense him (Mr. Humphrey) for the labor and costs bestowed upon it." In March, 1636, the general court agreed that Mr. Humphrey's land should begin at the Clifte in the way to Marblehead, which is the boundary between Salem and Lynn, and "so along the line between the said towns to the rocks one mile by estimation, to a great red oak from which the said marked tree all under and over this rock upon a straight line to the running brooke by Thomas Smyth's house all the which said ground we allow him (Humphrey) for his owne and soe from Thomas Smyth's to the sea." The site of the village of Marblehead was selected near his farm. He was granted land beyond Forest River. In 1636 the general court appropriated four hundred pounds for the erection of a college, and Humphrey was on the committee and the site was selected at Marblehead. But later the college site was fixed at its present location in Cambridge. Children: 1. Theophilus, baptized January 24, 1636-37. 2. Thomas, baptized August 26, 1638. 3. Joseph, baptized April 5, 1640. 4. Lydia, baptized April 25, 1641. 5. Dorcas, born about 1632. 6. Sarah, born about 1634.

(III) Elizabeth Humphrey, wife of ——— Humphrey (probably Edward, son of Joseph), was a member of the Marblehead church, and as such her children were baptized without mention of the name of her husband, who was unquestionably grandson of John Humphrey (1), and son or nephew of Joseph Humphrey (2) Children, baptized in Marblehead: 1. Edward, March 11, 1687-8; married Eunice ———. 2. Henry, March 11, 1687-8. 3. Stephen, died young May, 1688; baptized same date as two preceding. 4. William, baptized September 23, 1688. 5. Coombs, mentioned below.

(IV) Coombs Humphrey, son of ——— and Elizabeth Humphrey (3), was baptized at Marblehead, Massachusetts, April 16, 1693. He married, April 4, 1717, Bethia Poland, of Ipswich (by Rev. Samuel Wigglesworth). Children, born at Marblehead: 1. Bethia, October 30, 1718. 2. William, baptized April 22, 1722; mentioned below. 3. Elizabeth, baptized October 4, 1724, died young. 4. Samuel, baptized July 17, 1726. 5. Elizabeth, baptized June 29, 1729.

(V) William Humphrey, son of Coombs Humphrey (4), was baptized at Marblehead, April 22, 1722. He was a member of the Second Congregational Church (now Unitarian). He married, September 26, 1745, at Marblehead, Rebecca Brown. Children, born in Marblehead: 1. Rebecca, baptized July 20, 1746; died young. 2. William, baptized July 17, 1748; married February 11, 1772, Miriam or Mary Le Crow. 3. Benjamin, baptized March 4, 1750; married April 28, 1775, Jemima Gale 4. Samuel, baptized March 15, 1752. 5. John, baptized November 11, 1753; mentioned below. 6. Rebecca, baptized November 14, 1756. 7. Amos, baptized June 13, 1760; married October 24, 1782, Martha Hale. 8. Bethia, baptized November 21, 1762; married November 20, 1783, Samuel Gale. 9. Sarah, baptized March 31, 1765; married February 12, 1785, Charles Florence.

(VI) John Humphrey, son of William Humphrey (5), was baptized at Marblehead, November 11, 1753. He was a soldier in the revolution, a corporal in Captain William Hooper's company, July 17, 1775, at Marblehead, and again in 1776, February 29 to March 31, on coast duty. (See p. 497, vol. 8, Mass. Soldiers and Sailors). He was a benefactor of the academy with Samuel Sewell and others in 1778-9. He married twice and both wives are buried by his side, all three having gravestones in the Green Street burial ground, Marblehead. He married first, February 26, 1776, Mary Caswell, died February 8, 1786, aged twenty-nine years; second, Mercy (or Marcia) Eaton, May 25, 1786. She was born in 1768, daughter of Israel and Mary Eaton. He died August 18, 1801, aged forty-seven years, according to the gravestone, and his widow died July 13, 1803. Children: 1. John, born May 25, 1787; died February 14, 1848; married first, Eliza Doliber, August 5, 1826; she died August 24, 1827, and he married second, November 11, 1830, Hannah D. Bridges, who died March 7, 1881; child of first wife: i. Caroline E., born June 15, 1827; died September 16, 1827; children of second wife: ii. John, born September 25, 1831; iii. George B., September 23, 1833; iv. Caroline E., October 16, 1838; v. Edward B., September 6, 1842, died October 22, 1843; vi. Henry, September 11, 1845, died September 24, 1845. 2. Mary, May 13, 1789; died July 22, 1874. 3. Marcia, born June 25, 1791; married William Orne. 4. Sally, born July 2, 1793; died June 18, 1858. 5. Louisa, born August 28, 1795; died August, 1881. 6. Harriet, born September 5, 1797; died November 22, 1858. 7. George Washington; mentioned below.

(VII) George Washington Humphrey, son of John Humphrey (6), was born in Marblehead, January 1, 1800, and died August 1, 1875, at Needham, Massachusetts. He married Betsey Hill Devereux, born May 8, 1798, Marblehead. Children: 1. George H., born June 17, 1822; mentioned below. 2. Eliza Ann, Leach, born December 22, 1824; married Charles Merriam. 3. John Devereaux, born January 22, 1828; married Hannah Rogers, of Marblehead, daughter of John Rogers; children: Hannah Eliza, Mary Ellen, John D. 4. Joseph, born January 8, 1830; died October 11, 1873; married June 26, 1854, Charlotte Elizabeth Vaughan, of New York; children: i. Joseph Vaughan, born September 23, 1855, in New York, and died October 26, 1856; ii. Richard V., born May 20, 1857, in Brooklyn, died April 20, 1880; iii. George W., born August 14, 1860, at Brooklyn; iv. Charlotte Bauscher, born October 17, 1862; v. John Van Cleve, born February 5, 1864, died March, 1865; vi. Arthur Vaughan, born April 30, 1867. 5. Mary E., born March 27, 1832. 6. William Eaton, born March 1, 1836, died June 22, 1866.

(VIII) George H. Humphrey, son of George Washington Humphrey (7), was born June 17, 1822, at Marblehead, died December 12, 1898, at Needham, Massachusetts. He was by occupation a bookbinder. He married Clarinda T. Noyes, born in Minot, Maine, April 17, 1828, daughter of Daniel and Rachel (Simmons) Noyes. Children: 1. George Washington, born November 1, 1848, mentioned below. 2. Mary Eliza, born October 25, 1852, at Roxbury. 3. Henry Devereux, born June 20, 1861, mentioned below. 4. Anna Walker, born March 17, 1863.

(IX) George Washington Humphrey, son of George H. Humphrey (8), was born November 1, 1848. He was educated in the public schools of Roxbury and Cambridge. When he was thirteen years old he went to work as clerk in the shoe store of Thomas Moseley, for whom he worked a year. He then worked two years in the Suffolk National Bank of Boston. In July, 1866, he entered the employ of Roberts Brothers, publishers, and continued for thirty-four years. After leaving the Roberts firm he worked as bookkeeper for Hardy, Pratt & Company. In 1901 he started in business for himself, with a book store on Brattle street, Boston, his present business. He married Ellen Thatcher Follansbee, born at Brooklyn, New York, March 29, 1851, daughter of Alonzo and Nancy Sherman (McIntosh) Follansbee. Children: 1. Ralph Devereux, born November 7, 1882, died July 4, 1904. 2. Marion Louise, born March 5, 1886.

(IX) Henry Devereux Humphrey, son of George H. Humphrey (8), was born at Jamaica Plain, West Roxbury (now Boston), June 20, 1861. He was educated in the public and high schools of Dedham. He established his present real estate and insurance business, and has been very successful in the same. In politics he is a Republican, and he has been representative from his district to the general court three years, 1894-5-6; member of board of assessors three years, 1898-99-1900; member of the board of selectmen of Dedham for five years, and its chairman four years. In 1906 he was elected treasurer of Norfolk county, an office he now holds. Mr. Humphrey has been secretary of Constellation Lodge of Free Masons for many years. He is president of the Dedham Board of Trade, and of the Ancient Society in Dedham for Apprehending Horse Thieves, membership in which is valued at present entirely for social reasons. Mr. Humphrey is a member of the Dedham Congregational Church. He married first, Lena R. Witham, of Gloucester, Massachusetts, daughter of Sidney and Susan Witham; second, Margaret Davidson, of Somerville, Massachusetts. Children: 1. Edith, born September 19, 1900. 2. Margaret, born June 20, 1903.

(For early generations see John Humphrey 1, and William Humphrey 5.)

HUMPHREY (VI) Amos Humphrey, son of William Humphrey, was born at Marblehead, Massachusetts, 1760, and baptized there November 30, 1760. He was a soldier from Marblehead in the revolution, a private in Captain John Devereux's company, Colonel Jacob Gerrish's regiment, 1778; also on guard duty,

1778, at Winter Hill, in Captain Simeon Brown's company, Colonel Gerrish's regiment. He married, October 24, 1782, Martha Hale, born June 6, 1764, died June 20, 1849. Children, born at Marblehead: 1. Amos, Jr., June 12, 1784; died August 27, 1857. 2. Martha, August 27, 1786, died May 3, 1814. 3. William, May 1, 1791; died July 14, 1868; married December 28, 1815, Lucy Gallison, died August 1, 1843; children: i. William, born October 2, 1816, died April 10, ——; ii. Lucy, born November 10, 1818; iii. Martha, born September 17, 1821. 4. Edward, born July 26, 1793; died March 19, 1877. 5. Rebecca, born August 27, 1795; died April 19, 1876. 6. Richard, mentioned below.

(VII) Captain Richard Humphrey, son of Amos Humphrey, born February 11, 1809, at Marblehead, died there April 26, 1880. He married Margaret Thompson, who died in 1883. He was a master mariner for many years. Children, born at Marblehead: 1. Edward T. 2. Richard, mentioned below. 3. Samuel T. 4. Sarah.

(VIII) Richard Humphrey, son of Richard Humphrey, born in Marblehead, 1835, died July 2, 1870. He was a heel contractor in the shoe manufacturing business in Marblehead for a number of years, and afterward for many years superintendent of the boot and shoe factory of William H. Boynton. He was a Democrat in politics and a Congregationalist in religion. He married Mary E. Hooper, born in Marblehead, 1840, died November 24, 1881, daughter of John P. Hooper. Children, born at Marblehead: 1. Martha B., 1859. 2. Richard, Jr., 1861. 3. Herbert, mentioned below. 4. Mary A., 1867. 5. Richard, Jr., September, 1870.

(IX) Herbert Humphrey, son of Richard Humphrey, was born at Marblehead, February 2, 1863. He attended the public schools of his native town, leaving when but eleven years old to earn his living in a shoe factory. He returned to school for a short time, and then worked in the shoe factories of Marblehead until 1884 when he went to Beverly, where he followed his trade in the shoe factories of that town until 1897. Since then he has resided in Marblehead and been engaged in business on his own account. In partnership with John D. Paine, under the firm name of Humphrey & Paine, he started to manufacture boots and shoes, and their business grew rapidly to large proportions. In 1906 the partnership was dissolved, and since then Mr. Humphrey has continued manufacturing alone. He has just erected one of the largest and best equipped factories in this country, and is at present turning out five thousand pairs of shoes daily. Even in the heart of the shoe manufacturing world this output is remarkable, placing Mr. Humphrey among the leading manufacturers of the country. He stands high in the business world, having shown extraordinary business ability, energy, integrity and uprightness. He affords an excellent example of the self-made men of New England and illustrates the possibilities in the field of manufacturing for the youth of to-day. In politics he is an Independent, and a Congregationalist in religion. He is a member of the Order of American Mechanics; of Atlantic Lodge, No. 55, Odd Fellows; of Philanthropic Lodge of Free Masons; of Salem Chapter, Royal Arch Masons; of Salem Council, Royal and Select Masters; and of Winslow Lewis Commandery, Knights Templar. He is a trustee of the Masonic building fund, which is soon to be used to erect a Masonic building in Salem to cost $250,000. He married, March 25, 1884, Martha W. Graves, born in Marblehead, daughter of John and Caroline S. Graves. Children: 1. Gerald, born May 13, 1885; died June 19, 1885. 2. Leonard, born July 2, 1886; now superintendent of his father's shoe factory. 3. Bert, born July 16, 1888; died November 24, 1900. 4. Beatrice Mae, born April 3, 1891. 5. Herbert, Jr., born October 24, 1899. 6. Gordon Hale (twin), born October 3, 1901. 7. Gertrude H., (twin), born October 3, 1901.

LANE

The surname Lane is of the same class as Woods, Pond, Field, Hill, coming into use as a surname at a very early date. The personal name modified by the designation "In the Lane," "By the Lane," "In Lana" "Ad Lanam" may be found in medieval documents. The Lane family of Kings Bromley claims to be of Norman origin, descending from a Sir Reginald de Lane of the Twelfth century. Many of the English branches of the Lane family have coats-of-arms.

(I) William Lane, immigrant ancestor, born in England, came probably from the western part of England. He was a resident of Dorchester, Massachusetts, as early as 1635. He received grants of land there in 1637. His will, proved July 6, 1654, mentions children, but no wife. Children, all probably born in England: 1. Elizabeth, married Thomas Rider. 2. Mary, married first Joseph Long; second,

Joseph Farnsworth. 3. Anis, or Avith, married Thomas Lincoln. 4. George, mentioned below. 5. Sarah, married Nathaniel Baker; died at Hull, August 19, 1695. 6. Andrew.

(II) George Lane, son of William Lane (1), was an early settler in Hingham, and at the first division of land, September 18, 1635, was granted a house lot of five acres; also had a grant of ten acres at "Nutty Hill" and thirteen shares in the common lands. He was a shoemaker, and resided on what is now North, near Beal street. He was selectman in 1669 and 1678. He died June 11, 1689. His will was dated October 16, 1688, and proved August 20, 1689. He married Sarah Harris, died at Hingham, March 26, 1694-5, daughter of Walter and Mary (Frye) Harris. Her father came to Weymouth in 1632. Children, all born in Hingham: 1. Sarah, born March, 1637-8; married, 1655, James Lewis. 2. Hannah, born February 24, 1638-9; married December 23, 1665, Thomas Humphrey. 3. Josiah, born May 23, 1641. 4. Susannah, born June 23, 1644; married December 23, 1665, William Robbarts. 5. Elizabeth, born 1646; married Walter Poor. 6. John, born January 20, 1647-8. 7. Ebenezer, born August 25, 1650; mentioned below. 8. Mary, born April 11, 1653; married ——— Ellis. 9. Peter, born July 21, 1656.

(III) Ebenezer Lane, son of George Lane (2), was baptized in Hingham, August 25, 1650, and died December 12, 1726. He resided on the homestead, and was called yeoman. He was assigned the second seat in the west gallery of the new meeting house, January 5, 1681-2. He was one of Captain Johnson's company in King Philip's war. His will, dated January 8, 1722-3, proved December 27, 1726, mentions wife Hannah, sons Ebenezer and Peter as joint executors, daughters Sarah Leavitt, Susannah Lane, and grandson Abraham Leavitt. He married, December 27, 1688, Hannah Hersey, born February 13, 1668-9, died March 31, 1745, daughter of William and Rebecca (Chubbuck) Hersey, of Hingham. Children, born in Hingham: 1. Hannah, February 13, 1689-90; married, August 23, 1714, Abraham Leavitt. 2. Sarah, December 4, 1692; married January 24, 1712-3, Elisha Leavitt. 3. Ebenezer, December 11, 1694; mentioned below. 4. Peter, May 25, 1697. 5. Susanna, December 4, 1699; married, December 31, 1724, Jonathan Studley.

(IV) Ebenezer Lane, son of Ebenezer Lane (3), was born December 11, 1694, in Hingham, and died May 30, 1777. He was a farmer, and resided on High street, Hingham, near Nutty Hill. In his will, dated August 3, 1774, proved July 4, 1777, he bequeaths to wife Mary; to son Ebenezer house and land at Cohasset, and to son Josiah the homestead at Hingham; to daughters Mary French, Delight Lincoln and Sarah Stodder. He married, the intention published November 16, 1717, Mary Leavitt, born February 18, 1695-6, died September 11, 1777, daughter of Israel and Lydia (Jackson) Leavitt, of Hingham. Children, all born in Hingham: 1. Ebenezer, June 24, 1720. 2. Mary, June 16, 1723; married, January 3, 1744-5, Daniel French. 3. Sarah, April 20, 1726; married, October 22, 1744, Simon Stodder. 4. Lydia, August 29, 1727; died August 25, 1746. 5. Abigail, baptized September 8, 1728. 6. Delight, born May 16, 1734; married, January 4, 1757, Elijah Lincoln. 7. Josiah, July 6, 1736; mentioned below. 8. Elizabeth, July 1, 1739; died August 15, 1746.

(V) Lieutenant Josiah Lane, son of Ebenezer Lane (4), was born in Hingham, July 6, 1736, and died August 13, 1813. He was a farmer, and resided on High street, Hingham. He was a soldier in the revolution, second lieutenant in Captain Enoch Whiton's company, April 19, 1775, on the Lexington alarm; also in Captain Byram Lincoln's company March 4, 1776. His will was dated April 8, 1805, and proved September 6, 1813, his sons Leavitt and Josiah being executors. He married, November 27, 1760, Lucy Tower, born February 17, 1741-2, died December 1, 1807, daughter of Peter and Patience (Gardner) Tower, of Hingham. Children, all born in Hingham: 1. Leavitt, May 26, 1761; mentioned below. 2. Lucy, April 22, 1767; married, November 29, 1787, Stephen Marsh, Jr. 3. Lydia, November 2, 1768; married, March 24, 1788, Benjamin Wilder. 4. Peter, July 13, 1772. 5. Josiah, baptized May, 1776.

(VI) Captain Leavitt Lane, son of Lieutenant Josiah Lane (5), was born in Hingham, May 26, 1761, and died at Hanover, Massachusetts, July 15, 1840, aged seventy-nine years. He was a soldier in the revolution, private in Captain Baxter's company, in the Rhode Island campaign of 1778; also in Captain Joseph Baxter's company, Colonel McIntosh's regiment, General Lovell's brigade, in secret expedition of 1778 to Rhode Island: he was in Continental army 1780 and 1781. He was also a shipmaster in the service during the revolution. He married, November 9, 1786, Elizabeth, daughter of Job and Judith (Whiton) Loring. She was born in Hingham, September 15, 1766,

S. Cushing Lane
U.S.N.

and died at Hudson, New York, October 17, 1834, aged sixty-eight years. He resided on the paternal homestead, High street, Hingham. Children, all born in Hingham: 1. Betsey, April 5, 1787; married, March 2, 1809, Samuel Torrey, of Weymouth, and died 1870, aged eighty-three years. 2. Leavitt, October 15, 1788, was master of schooner "Independence," and was lost at sea in the summer of 1812 on a return voyage from Lisbon. 3. Lydia, December 1, 1790; married, December 26, 1810, Lebbeus Stockbridge, of Hanover; she died 1869, aged seventy-eight. 4. Quincy, January 16, 1793. 5. Sarah, September 12, 1795; died unmarried, at Weymouth, January 12, 1860; aged sixty-four. 6. Lucy, October 7, 1797; married December 23, 1818, William Gordon, of Hudson, New York. 7. Marcus, April 10, 1800. 8. Andrew, born March 3, 1803, removed west; resided at Cattaraugus county, New York. 9. Alfred, born March 3, 1803, settled in Poughkeepsie, New York. 10. Peter, born October 1, 1805; mentioned below.

(VII) Captain Peter Lane, son of Captain Leavitt Lane (6), was born October 1, 1805, and died December 26, 1886. He was for many years master of his own vessel, owned a number of whaling crafts, and was well known in marine circles. He married, January 2, 1831, Deborah Cushing, born January 24, 1813, died September 13, 1884, daughter of Seth Cushing, born January 18, 1769, married September 18, 1794, Joanna Cushing, of Hingham, who was born September 19, 1773. Children of Peter and Deborah Lane: 1. Edwin, died at sea. 2. Webster, married first, Charlotte Portington, of New York; second, Sarah Jane Hagan. 3. Seth Cushing, mentioned below. 4. Joanna Alden; married Frederick Cate; children: i. Frederick W.; ii. Dora L.; iii. Hawthorne A.; iv. Harold W.; v. Lawrence.

(VIII) Seth Cushing Lane, son of Captain Peter Lane (7), was born in Weymouth, Massachusetts, September 29, 1838, and died March 14, 1879, at the comparatively young age of forty years and some months. Yet his life was one of conspicuous usefulness and highly honorable. He was educated in the Weymouth schools, and under the private tutorship of Principal Z. L. Ferris, of the high school, by whom he was instructed in mechanical engineering. For three years he was an apprentice under Samuel Flagg, of Worcester, and there gained a thorough and practical knowledge of mechanics. In 1862 (the second year of the civil war period) he passed a highly satisfactory examination before the examining board of the navy department, in Philadelphia, and was assigned to the steamer "Michigan," on Lake Erie, on which he served one year; he served for some time on the U. S. S. "Cimerone" and "South Carolina." He was then transferred to the monitor "Montauk," engaged in blockading service off Charleston harbor, South Carolina, and also bombarding Forts Sumter and Moultrie and other of the rebel defences on twenty-eight different occasions. Later he was assigned to special duty at the Charlestown (Massachusetts) navy yard. At the close of the war he resigned, having then the rank of third assistant engineer, under warrant from Hon. Gideon Welles, secretary of the navy. In 1867 he located at Ellsworth, Kansas, during the construction of the Pacific railroad, there erecting the United States Hotel, and otherwise devoting his enterprise to the upbuilding of the embryo town. After a residence there of three years he went to Bridgeport, Connecticut, where he engaged in a wholesale and retail business in partnership with J. H. Willis, formerly of Weymouth, Massachusetts. He gave himself to the cares and responsibilities of this important business so closely that the confinement sowed in his system the seeds of disease, and after a period of seven years he returned to his father's home in 1877, and where he resided during the remainder of his life. Primarily devoted to his naval and business duties during his active years, he developed qualities which well fitted him for public life, and while a resident of Bridgeport, Connecticut, he served most creditably and efficiently as a member of the board of councilmen. With his family he attended the Universalist church, and while in Bridgeport he served for some years as a member of the board of trustees. He was a highly regarded member of the Masonic fraternity, and his lodge attended his funeral, sent resolutions of condolence to the bereaved family, draped its charter, and inscribed a page of its record book to his memory. His pastor, Rev. Anson Titus, who conducted the funeral services, made special reference to the noble and generous characteristics of the deceased, which made him friends in whatever circle he moved; to his service for his country during the war days; and emphasized the fact that in all his relations with his fellows he left the precious legacy of a useful and honorable life.

Mr. Lane married, October 18, 1867, Sarah Eleanor, daughter of David Radcliffe and Eleanor Maria (Brown) Cloudman, of Gorham, Maine (see Cloudman). Children: 1. Georgianna Cushing. 2. Carleton Cushing, married, December 15, 1905, Susan Godfrey, daughter of Samuel Adams and Jessie (Godfrey) Morse, and they have one child, Eleanor, born July 26, 1908, at Brookline, Massachusetts.

PARTRIDGE (I) Captain John Partridge lived in Navestock, England. Although he may never have lived in this country, he had an account in the general court October 17, 1649, with Captain Clarke (see Pope). Children: 1. John, born 1620; mentioned below. 2. William, 1622. 3. Margaret, 1628.

(II) John Partridge, son of Captain John Partridge (1), was born in Navestock, England, 1620. He was the immigrant ancestor. He came to Medfield, Massachusetts, from Dedham, in 1653, probably accompanied by his brother William and his sister Margery. He had a share in the division of land in Dedham, March 7, 1652. John and William Partridge had house lots in Medfield, on "The Bachelor's Roe," now North street, and both signed the proprietor's agreement. John was selectman, and clerk of the market in 1672. His house and barn, with a quantity of grain and several head of cattle, were burned at the time of the Indian raid in 1676. He married, December 18, 1655, Magdalen Bullard, died December 27, 1677, daughter of John and Magdalen Bullard, early of Watertown and later of Medfield. He died May 28, 1706, and his will was proved June 25 following. Mention is made of sons John, Eleazer, Samuel and Zachariah; daughter Rachel, wife of Theophilus Clark, and three grandchildren, Eleazer and Obadiah Adams, and Hannah Rockwood. Children: 1. John, born September 21, 1656; mentioned below. 2. Hannah, April 5, 1658; died March 8, 1680; married, April 2, 1679, Joseph Rockwood. 3. Deborah, August 16, 1662; married April 4, 1681, John Adams. 4. Eleazer, February 20, 1664; died November 8, 1736. 5. Abiel, June 13, 1667; died July 2, 1667. 6. Experience, June 13, 1667 (twin); died July 5, 1667. 7. Rachel, July 12, 1669; died December 1, 1717; married, September 25, 1670, Theophilus Clark. 8. Samuel, February 22, 1671; died December 12, 1752. 9. Zachariah, July 2, 1674; died September 23, 1716. 10. Mary, died February 15, 1677.

(III) John Partridge, son of John Partridge (2), was born in Medfield, September 21, 1656. He settled in 1681 in that part of Medway which is now Millis. He was one of the first to take up his residence in that part of Medfield lying west of the Charles river, and was active in having it set off as Medway in 1713. In 1710 he was chosen master of a school established for residents of the west side; was interested in church affairs, and chosen deacon of the Medway church. He was present at Deerfield when news was received of the return of the captives taken at the Deerfield massacre, and is said to have himself made a copy of Benjamin Waite's letter announcing their arrival at Albany, which, in company with John Plympton, Jr., he brought to Medfield and delivered to Rev. John Wilson, by whom it was forwarded to the governor of the colony. He married first, December 24, 1678, Elizabeth Rockwood, born in Medfield, April 3, 1657, died July 22, 1688, daughter of Nicholas and Margaret (Holbrook) Rockwood; second Elizabeth Adams, born in Medfield, March 18, 1666, died August 14, 1719, daughter of Jonathan and Elizabeth (Fussell) Adams; third, April 17, 1721, Hannah Sheffield, born in Sherborn, April 18, 1663, died July 19, 1754, daughter of William and Mary Sheffield. He died in Medway, December 9, 1743. His will was proved September 4, 1744. Children by first wife: 1. Elizabeth, born September 13, 1679; died April 25, 1706; married, December 22, 1701, Ebenezer Daniel. 2. Mary, February 26, 1681; died February 14, 1754; married November 25, 1706, Ebenezer Lawrence, of Wrentham. 3. John, about 1683; died September 6, 1756. 4. Benoni, May 25, 1687; mentioned below. Children of second wife: 5. Jonathan, November 25, 1693. 6. Hannah, March 16, 1696; died October 12, 1751; married May 7, 1713, Jeremiah Daniel. 7. Deborah, March 1, 1698; died August 30, 1740; married February 21, 1703, Israel Kieth. 8. James, October 8, 1700; died March 9, 1769. 9. Sarah, January 8, 1702; married March 13, 1723, George Adams. 10. Stephen, April 16, 1706; died March 10, 1742.

(IV) Benoni Partridge, son of John Partridge (3), was born in Medfield, (now Millis) May 25, 1687, and died December 26, 1769. He was one of the proprietors of the town at its incorporation in 1713, and resided in the new grant which became West Medway, and his children were born there. The farm was divided equally between his sons Timothy and Moses. He was a member of the first church of Medway. He married July 14, 1708, Mehitabel Wheelock, born in Medfield, September

10, 1689, died January 20, 1761, daughter of Samuel and Sarah (Kendrick) Wheelock, and granddaughter of Ralph Wheelock, founder of Medfield. Children: 1. Preserved, born March 13, 1709; mentioned below. 2. Thomas, November 28, 1711. 3. Seth, March 17, 1713, died August 5, 1786; married Ruth Holbrook. 4. Joseph, August 22, 1715; died 1753. 5. David, May 22, 1718; died August 4, 1741. 6. Mehitabel, April 24, 1720; died August 4, 1741. 7. Samuel, June 24, 1722; died September 7, 1741. 8. Sarah, September 27, 1724; married, March 24, 1756, Samuel Fiske. 9. Timothy, January 18, 1727; died September 18, 1787. 10. Eli, June 3, 1729. 11. Moses, August 28, 1733; died October 6, 1804.

(V) Preserved Partridge, son of Benoni Partridge (4), was born in Medfield, March 13, 1709. Soon after his marriage he settled in Holliston, and was also in Milford as early as 1750 and as late as 1754. He removed as early as 1761 to Cumberland county, Maine, and settled near Gorham. In 1764 his name appears as a tax payer of Stroudwater, now a suburb of Portland. He was in the colonial service in 1755. He married November 10, 1737, Catherine Armstrong. Children: 1. Nathan, born August 3, 1738; died in Westbrook, Maine, 1786; was in the revolution; married January 1, 1781, Anna Conant, of Falmouth. 2. Bathsheba, born August 19, 1740; married 1761, Uriah Nason, of Gorham, Maine. 3. Jesse, born August 29, 1742; died December 21, 1795; was in the revolution; married first, Lydia Bailey; second Rebecca ———. 4. Catherine, born August 26, 1744; died March 24, 1832; married 1766, Timothy Cloudman (see Cloudman). 5. David, born January 26, 1747; married Mary Conant; was in the revolution. 6. Jotham, baptized July 27, 1750; was in the revolution; married ——— Bailey. 7. Azuba, baptized December 18, 1752; married Joseph Quimby. 8. Rosina, married Nathan Quimby. 9. Zipporah, born 1757; married Eliphalet Watson. 10. Rhoda, died unmarried.

CLOUDMAN (I) Thomas Cloutman (or Cloudman, as the name is commonly spelled at the present time) was the immigrant ancestor. Th "History of Gorham, Maine," (McClellan) states that he and his brother John came in September, 1690, to America from the highlands of Aberdeen, Scotland, landed at Plymouth and settled at Marblehead, where they worked as ship-carpenters for about ten years. Tradition says also that "the brothers were noted for their strength and stalwart forms, also for their large Roman noses, were members of the Society of Friends, of strict integrity and sound christian character." But the vital records of Salem give the birth of a daughter of Thomas and his wife as early as 1681, and we fail to find anything of the brother John. But Thomas had a son John, born according to the records at Salem, named perhaps for an uncle. The wife of Thomas Cloutman was Elizabeth. Children: 1. Edward, mentioned below. 2. William, went to Dover, New Hampshire. 3. Mary, born August 12, 1681, at Salem, died young. 4. Thomas, born January 23, 1683, the first settler at Marblehead; married there October 3, 1723, Widow Mary Mully; children, born at Marblehead: i. Mary, baptized October 20, 1709; ii. Thomas, born August 22, 1711; iii. John, baptized May 23, 1714; iv. Joseph, baptized March 30, 1718. 5. John, born June 14, 1685, doubtless the John presumed to be an immigrant in the history of Gorham. 6. Mary, born at Salem, May 13, 1691. 7. Joseph, born September 19, 1693, at Salem.

(II) Edward Cloutman (Cloudman), son of Thomas Cloutman (1), was born possibly in Scotland, about 1670. He settled early in life in Dover, New Hampshire, and married there April 22, 1698, Sarah Tuttle, of a celebrated Dover family. Among their children was Edward, mentioned below.

(III) Edward Cloudman, son of Edward Cloudman or Cloutman (2), was born in Dover, New Hampshire, February 15, 1714-15. He removed to Falmouth at the age of twenty-two years, and there married April 16, 1738, Anna Collins, who came from Philadelphia, Pennsylvania, she was a daughter of Timothy and Sarah Collins. After his marriage he went to Presumpscot Lower Falls, where he had charge of the first saw mill ever built there. The mill was built by Colonel Westbrook, Samuel Waldo and others in 1735. Mr. Cloudman is said to have been a tall and very strong man, weighing about two hundred and twenty pounds. It is said that he was accustomed to throw all the boards from the medium sized pine logs to the brow of the mill and over, and that he was able to break off pieces of pine board "like chunks of cheese." He was accustomed to run the mill at night, and one night in 1741 when alone, he saw an Indian, who twice attempted to fire at him. Cloudman hurled the bar used for placing the log on the carriage at the Indian, killing him instantly. He then threw the body into the wheel pit and went home. The next night the Indians burned the mill. Cloudman and his wife and son packed their goods in a canoe and paddled down the river to what is now Stroudwater. In 1745 he went to Gorham and bought the thirty acre lot No. 7, where the late Daniel Billings lived, near Fort Hill. Early in the morning of April 19, 1746, a party of Indians entered the settlement and after killing William Bryand, they surprised Mr. Cloudman as he was sowing wheat in his field, and after a hard struggle overpowered him and took him to Canada, where he was placed in the fortress at Quebec. He and a man named Robert Dunbar planned to escape. They saved a part of each day's rations, and one stormy night made good their escape, October 23. This is the last that is known of them. They never reached home, but were probably drowned crossing Lake Champlain, as the next summer two skeletons with their clothes on their backs were washed ashore. In the pocket of one was a compass, identified as belonging to Cloudman. His widow married second, Abraham Anderson, of Windham, Maine; she was for seven years a resident in the Gorham garrison. Edward Cloudman had children: 1. Timothy, mentioned below. 2. Sarah, born February 5, 1742; married, April 20, 1760, Eli Webb, of Gorham.

(IV) Timothy Cloudman, son of Edward Cloudman (3), was born at Presumpscot Lower Falls, and after his mother's second marriage lived with her at Windham. He was like his father strong and daring, and was accustomed to go in neighborhood scouts against the Indians. He was with Anderson and a boy named Winship when Manchester shot the famous chief, Poland. He was at that time a boy of fifteen, and fired at the Indians with the gun his father had picked up in the saw mill, when he killed the Indian. He married, July 24, 1766, Catherine Partridge, died March 24, 1832, aged ninety-one, probably of Marblehead. They settled on the farm at Gorham, and built a log house and a "hovel" for the cow. The house stood a little east of the present house, and the uneven ground still marks the site of the cellar. The place produced only hay enough to winter one cow. Timothy worked often in the saw mill at Horse Beef Falls, and his wife used to send the two little boys down the river with their father's dinner, armed with a razor for protection from the Indians and wild beasts. Timothy Cloudman died October 22, 1830, aged ninety-one. Children: 1. Betty, born May 3, 1767, married, November 1, 1789, Barnabas Bangs, and had a daughter Susan Bangs, and two sons, Barnabas and Thomas, who joined the Shakers, Barnabas became an elder of their church. 2. Nancy, born May 7, 1769, died 1779, she married a Mr. Maxfield. 3. Edward, born July 5, 1771, went to New Hampshire, he married ——— Johnson. 4. Nathan (twin), born July 29, 1773, married Eunice Sweet in 1802 and removed to Stetson. 5. Jesse Partridge (twin), born July 29, 1773, mentioned below. 6. John, born February 20, 1776, married first, July 2, 1800, Elizabeth Cobb; second Sarah Cobb, sister of his first wife. 7. Polly (Mary) born July 13, 1779, married, December 1, 1808, Caleb Graffam. 8. William, born September 16, 1780, married, 1804, Sarah Hamblen, daughter of Hannah (Whitney) Hamblen. 9. Thomas, born August 20, 1783, married, 1808, Martha Gilpatrick. 10. Solomon, born December 4, 1785, was a Baptist preacher in Cornish, Maine. 11. David, born September 16, 1788, resided in Portland; married Susan Greenleaf, of Newburyport, Massachusetts.

(V) Jesse Partridge Cloudman, son of Timothy Cloudman (4), was born in Gorham, Maine, July 29, 1773, and died January 25, 1848. He lived on a hill near the river, a little east of the house where his sons Solomon and Edward now reside. He married, in March, 1798, Hannah Swett, of Standish Neck. She died August 7, 1815, and he married second, August 22, 1822, Mrs. Sarah (Bacon) Burton, who died March 23, 1869, aged eighty-two, widow of Thomas Bacon, and daughter of William Burton. Children of first wife: 1. Nathan, born August 12, 1799; married March 29, 1826, Elizabeth Gallison, born January 27, 1802, died June 8, 1877, daughter of John and Abigail (Winslow) Gallison, the latter born in the house built by Governor Edward Winslow; she died in 1836; she was a daughter of Hendri and Abigail (Bourne) Winslow, and she resided in Mansfield, Massachusetts; Nathan Cloudman died in Windham, June 17, 1869. 2. David Radcliffe, mentioned below. 3. Eunice, born July 7, 1801, died unmarried, February 27, 1885. 4. Sarah, born February 20, 1803, married, December, 1826, Moses Stiles; died in Westbrook, March 10, 1859. 5. John Tying Smith, born November 24, 1805, married in Saco, Maine, December, 1827, Mary G. Waterhouse; died in Westbrook, Maine, January 15, 1852, had one child, George H. 6. Susan, born August 12, 1807, married, 1830, Bartholomew Johnson, of Pownal. 7. Josiah, born June 10, 1809, married first, May, 1833, Susan Babb, of Sacarappa, Maine; second, November, 1840, Huldah Estes, of Gorham, Maine, died in Westbrook. 8. Abraham A., born February 14, 1811, died in 1897, married December, 1840, Betsey Smith, of Standish, Maine. 9. William, born May 13, 1813, unmarried; lived in California, died 1898. 10. Daniel B. (twin), born August 6, 1815, married in Bath, May, 1853, Martha Spencer, of Turner, Maine; died December 15, 1853, in Westbrook. 11. Moses (twin), born August 6, 1815; died October 19, 1815. Children of second wife: 12. Hannah Swett, born May 30, 1823, died March 18, 1897; married, February 25, 1849, Levi Estes, who died October 13, 1907, aged eighty-six years. 13. Lucretia A., born January 13, 1826, died July 17, 1826. 14. Solomon B., born March 27, 1827, married first, November 22, 1854, Lucy Sweetser, of Yarmouth, Maine; she died October 17, 1880, aged fifty-six years; married, second, Maria Trott; she died April 9, 1900, aged fifty years. 15. Edward T., born December 29, 1829, married, June 3, 1868, Sarah J. Haskell, of Windham, Maine, who died November 26, 1904, aged sixty-seven years.

(VI) David Radcliffe Cloudman, son of Jesse Partridge Cloudman (5), was born in Gorham, May 19, 1800, and died January 1, 1877, at Little Falls, Maine. He married January, 1832, Eleanor Maria Brown, of Charlestown, Massachusetts, born August 10, 1813, died July 15, 1896, daughter of Captain William and Eleanor (Mann) Brown. Her father was born January 6, 1777, and died January 30, 1853; married February 19, 1809, Eleanor Mann, born December 5, 1783, died August 4, 1827; he married second, October 9, 1823, Sarah Brackett, who died September 8, 1855. Amos and Elizabeth (Babb) Brown were the parents of Captain William Brown. Children of David R. and Eleanor Maria (Brown) Cloudman: 1. Eliza Ann, married Lewis H. Kingsbury, of Wellesley (formerly Needham), Massachusetts: children: i. Ella L., married Joseph Peabody; ii. Harry M., married Catherine Carey; iii. Albert L.; iv. Mary Eleanor. 2. Andrew Hamlin, born November 16, 1834, died January 28, 1835. 3. Marcellus Copeland, married Helen W. Bates, of Weymouth; children: i. Helen A., married Ralph Sweetland, of Natick, Massachusetts, where they now reside; ii. Marcellus Emmons; iii. Harry Radcliffe, married Ida Fisk. 4. Sarah Eleanor, married Seth Cushing Lane (see Lane). 5. William Henry, married Margaret J. Sayres; children: i. Mortimer M., married Maud Hamlin; children: Carolyn, Eleanor and Margaret; ii. Belle W., married Guy Vassar Dickinson; iii. William Henry, Jr.

FLOYD In the early parish and town records the surname Floyd is found variously written Floid, Flood, Fludd and Fluds, as well as Floyd, but it cannot be said that those who now bear the surviving names Floyd and Flood are descendants of a single immigrant head. The records show several Floyds having the baptismal name John who were settled in New England previous to the year 1650, and who may be regarded as contemporaries in respect to the periods of their lives. Later researches have cleared away much of the obsecurity which surrounded the identity and relationship of the several Johns, and our present records of descendants of one of these John Floyds may be accepted as established beyond reasonable question of doubt, although it is now impossible to assert that Captain John Floyd of Rumney Marsh was the son of John and Anne Floyd of London and Boston of whom the "Aspinwall Notarial Records" says: "1646. John and Anne Floyd of Scituate mercht granted a tre Atturney to Mr. Chr: Rogers head of the New Inne hall in Oxford & Mr. John Ffreeman of London mercht to take all Legacies wch are or shalbe due unto his wife by the decease of any of her brethern or frends. Also to receive a debt of six pounds due from Samuel Greaves & to compound &c: & to appeare before al Lords &c to doe say pursue implead pesecute &c." Savage says John Floyd of Scituate, 1640, was of Boston, 1653, and next year was fined five shillings for receiving Mrs. Pacey (Governor Dudley's daughter) into his house as an inmate, had a son Nathaniel, "as Deane says, but he strangely mistakes him for a member of the London Society for Propagating the Gospel in Foreign Parts."

The first definite knowledge we have of the immigrant ancestor of the family here under consideration is that he was of Lynn, where also lived Joseph Floyd, 1635, who sold out his possessions there 1666, and removed to Chelsea, and from the fact that John Floyd also lived first in Lynn and afterward in Chelsea it is fair to assume that they may have been of kin; but when they came into the country no record furnishes any clear light and a search of the emigration books in which are supposed to be found the ships lists of immigrants does not reveal their names.

In speaking of John Floyd of Scituate, merchant, to whom reference has been made, the recent work, "Pioneers of Massachusetts," says: "John Floyd, citizen and haberdasher of London; his wife Anne gave power of attorney, 28 6mo 1640, for the care and maintenance of their son Thomas, apprenticed to Arthur Howland of Duxbury, planter. He came to New England and resided at Scituate. Gave letters of attorney, 4 9mo 1646, for collections in England. Released his servant, Jane Douglas, October 26, 1647; removed to Boston; sold his house and lands November 28, 1655."

(I) Captain John Floyd, progenitor of the family here considered, lived in Lynn, Massachusetts, where the births of five of his children are recorded. Savage says that he owned much land and was distinguished for his services as captain against the Indians in 1690. In a deposition made in 1680 his age is given as "44 yeers or thare abouts," from which it appears that he was born sometime between 1634 and 1638. He was taxed in Chelsea in 1681, and is mentioned as grantee in the second Indian deed of lands in 1685. He took the oath of fidelity in 1674, and was constable for Rumney Marsh in 1681. He is mentioned as a man of intelligence and an officer of merit in the Indian war of 1690, where "he sailed against the enemy at the eastward," an account of which appears in the narrative of the Indian troubles at York, Maine. May 27, 1690, Captain John Floyd was ordered to gather the troops under his command and advance toward Piscataqua, and June 10 sixty soldiers were added to his command and stationed at Portsmouth, New Hampshire. On July 6 his force fought the Indians at Wheelwright's pond (then Dover, now Lee, New Hampshire) but was compelled to retire with a loss of sixteen men. He engaged the enemy again at Casco (Portland), Maine, in September, 1690. In King Philip's war he was lieutenant under Captain Henchman, 1676, and was credited to Malden. The records are full of accounts of his military services, and in 1689 he received a letter from Governor Andros in relation to the mutinous conduct of the troops in his command. The governor said: "fforasmuch as you have given me to understand that Severall of yr Souldiers undr yor Command have in a Mutinous Manner contrary to yor Ordr left & Deserted their Service & Station att Saco River & are marching towards this place, * * * You are therefore forthwith to Repair to yr sd Station & by the Way to Command & March back any of yr sd Souldiers you shall meete with" and "there Remain till further Ordrs." On March 14, 1700-1, the general court resolved "That Twenty Pounds be granted in full of Accts of Capt. John Ffloyd," for his services "during the time of Sr. Edmond Andros's Government."

In June 1692, Captain John Floyd was brought under the fanatical accusation of witchcraft. A warrant was issued for his arrest and testimony was given against him at Salem, but it does not appear that he was tried on this purely imaginary charge: "Phelpses daughter complayned her (Abigail Faulkner of Andover) afflicting her: but she denyed that she had any thing to doe with witchcraft: she sd Ffalkner had a cloth in her hand, that when she squeezed in her hand ye afflicted fell into grevous fits as was observed: ye afflicted sayd Dan'll Eames and Captain ffloyd was upon that cloth when it was upon ye table."

Captain Floyd was surveyor in Rumney Marsh, 1681 and 1698; surveyor, 1684; tythingman, 1685 and 1695. He married Sarah, daughter of John Doolittle, who died in 1681, and whose name appears on the tax list of Rumney Marsh for 1674, he being the largest taxpayer in the district. He was constable 1653 and 1671; surveyor 1663; tythingman 1680. His name is found on a Lynn petition in 1643, and in 1658 he received a small legacy under the will of Edward Holyoke; was overseer of the mill of William Burnell of Pullen Point in 1660 and held other offices of trust. In 1667-8 he bought thirty-five acres of land, with "a new house," on the Malden side of the line. He died in 1701, and Sarah, his widow, died June 16, 1717. Children: 1. Sarah, born 24 12m 1661. 2. Hugh, born 10 7m 1663. 3. John, born 20 12m 1664. 4. Joseph, born March 15, 1666. 5. Joana, January 3, 1668. The foregoing is taken from the Lynn vital records, and differs somewhat with the record printed in the recent history of Chelsea, which is as follows: Hugh, born September 10, 1663, died November 17, 1730; John, born 1665, died January 7, 1723-4; Joseph; Noah, 10 mo. 1670; Daniel, born 28 10mo 1675. He also left two daughters, Sarah, wife of Nathaniel Upham, of Malden, and Mrs. Jonathan Hawkes, wife of Jonathan Hawkes who kept the tavern in the house now standing and lately occupied by Mr. Tewksbury.

(II) Ensign Hugh Floyd, son of Captain John and Sarah (Doolittle) Floyd, born in

Lynn, Massachusetts, September 10, 1663, died in Chelsea, November 17, 1730. He was a yeoman, and with his mother administered his father's estate. He inherited lands from his father and acquired other tracts by purchase and in time possessed a large property. He and his wife were members of the Malden church, and in 1724 took letters to the church in Rumney Marsh. He was constable 1688 and 1709; surveyor 1694; tythingman 1705 and 1712. In his will, dated August 28, 1730, provision was made for his wife Elinor (Eleanor), and after bequests to his daughters his real estate was divided among his four sons. His negro man Richard was to serve each of the sons in turn a year and then receive his freedom. He married Eleanor ———, but the date of their marriage does not appear, nor the dates of birth of their children. Children: 1. Joanna, married by Rev. Cotton Mather, June 11, 1706, to Edward Tuthill. 2. Sarah, married by Rev. Thomas Cheever, March 25, 1713, to Francis Leath, Jr. 3. Elinor, married May 30, 1717, John Leath. 4. Benjamin, married by Rev. Thomas Cheever, November 28, 1726, to Sarah Eustice. 5. Samuel, married February 8, 1727-8, Johanna Floyd. 6. Hugh, see forward. The Malden records mention two other children of Hugh and Eleanor: Ebenezer, born February 21, 1690, and Mary, born July 22, 1698.

(III) Hugh Floyd, son of Ensign Hugh and Eleanor Floyd, born May 13, 1704, died in September, 1789. He was a farmer, and acquired several considerable tracts of land. In 1746 he sold a forty-two acre tract of pasture land for two thousand pounds (old tenor) and in 1749 he and his wife joined in a conveyance of sixty acres of improved land, with mansion house and other buildings, wherein the consideration was mentioned in the deed as eleven thousand (old tenor). The records of deeds and other instruments relating to land transactions show his name more frequently perhaps than that of any other member of his family before him, yet at the time of his death he was not a man of large means, having no lands in Chelsea, while the total value of his property as shown by the inventory made by Joshua Cheever and James Stowers was only a little more than eleven pounds. In 1724 Hugh Floyd and his wife Mary were dismissed from the Malden church to that at "Rumney-marish," and were received into full communion. He made valuable donations to the church in Chelsea, and appears to have promised a similar gift to the Malden church, but the latter was not carried out according to the original intention of the donor. He married, April 29, 1729, in Boston, Mary Baker, born May 19, 1706, daughter of Thomas and Mary (Lewis) Baker, of Lynn, granddaughter of Thomas and Mary Baker, and great-granddaughter of Edward and Joan Baker, of Lynn. Hugh and Mary (Baker) Floyd had children (record in Chelsea): 1. Mary, born 5 3 mo 1730. 2. Eleanor, born 27 8mo 1731. 3. Hugh, Jr., born 2 2mo 1732. 4. Peter, born 6 6mo 1734. 5. Hannah, born 27 12mo 1735. 6. Susannah, born 26 11mo 1737. 7. William, born 27 6mo 1739. 8. Stephen, baptized November 22, 1741. 9. Andrew, baptized December 25, 1743.

(IV) Hugh Floyd, Jr., son of Hugh and Mary (Baker) Floyd, born in Chelsea, 2d 2d mo, 1732, died there August 6, 1800. He was a farmer, and in 1798 lived on the so-called Cogan farm in Chelsea. He was a soldier of the revolution and in May, 1781, was voted bounty by the town to enter the Continental army under General Washington. The records show that June 5, 1781, the town gave a note of eighty pounds to the father of Hugh Floyd, Jr., in part payment of his enlistment, and on June 8 paid the elder Floyd ten pounds more. His military services included four enlistments—private in Captain Sprague's company from Chelsea that marched on the alarm of April 19, 1775, and served until May 16, 1775. Name enrolled with soldiers from Suffolk county for nine months from date of arrival at Peekskill, New York, agreeable to resolves of congress, April 20, 1778; returns as received of Jonathan Warner, commissioner, by Captain John Santford, of Colonel Malcolm's regiment; also list of men returned as mustered by Henry Rutgers, Jr., deputy muster master at Fishkill, August 1, 1778; reported as arrived at Fishkill, June 27, 1778. Private in Captain Perez Cushing's company, Colonel Craft's regiment of artillery; service forty-seven days; company reported as Boston militia stationed at Hull, July 26 to September 11, 1777. Private in Captain Robert Davis's company of Colonel Freeman's regiment; service thirty-seven days; company raised for a secret expedition to Rhode Island; service to December 4, 1777. In 1759 Hugh Floyd married Rachel Floyd, born 1739, daughter of Samuel and Joanna (Floyd) Floyd, and granddaughter of Hugh and Eleanor Floyd. Nine children were born between 1760 and 1780, among them Hugh, born April 23, 1760; married, 1785 (published) Abigail Fern (or Fairn) of Lynn. Rachel, born July 25, 1762; admitted to full communion in the church in 1783. David, see forward.

(V) David Floyd, son of Hugh and Rachel Floyd, born in Chelsea, June 7, 1767, died in Winthrop, Massachusetts, August 1, 1842. In 1807 he bought of Samuel Sewall, of Marblehead, for $1550, a tract of twenty-six acres of upland and marsh on the west side of the Salem turnpike, and in 1848 conveyed the same with five acres of additional to his own son David, receiving therefore $2500. He was a farmer by principal occupation, an active and energetic man in whatever he undertook. In 1825 he removed to Winthrop and afterward lived in that town. In both towns he took a prominent part in the public affairs. In Chelsea his home was in North Chelsea (now Revere), Massachusetts, and there he was selectman from 1804-06, 1811, 1815-19, and again 1821-22. In Winthrop he held the same office frequently between the years 1826 and 1841. Mr. Floyd was an upright man and consistent member of the church in Chelsea and also in Winthrop, having been admitted to communion March 30, 1817. He married, November 6 (December 6) 1798, Hannah Tewksbury, baptized 1779, daughter of John, Jr., and Anna (Bill) Tewksbury (see Tewksbury family). Of this marriage there were born six sons—Deacon David, Henry, John, Thomas, Edward and Philip Payson; and three daughters—Hannah, Lucy and Mary Hall.

(VI) Deacon David Floyd, eldest son of David and Hannah (Tewksbury) Floyd, was born in Revere, 1808. He was reared to young manhood in the section now known as Winthrop, and then became a successful farmer and large land owner, having secured possession of that valuable property known as Winthrop Highlands which at the present time (1908) is mostly covered with beautiful and substantial houses. His foresight was not only marked by this particular possession, but by others as well in that beautiful seabound town of Winthrop. In 1852, when the town was set off from Revere and the organization was effected, he took an active interest in its organization, at once becoming prominently identified with its official life, having been elected one of the first selectmen and serving on this board for many years. He was also for a number of years a member of the board of school commissioners. His political faith was of the most marked and decided nature, being a Republican from the organization of that party, having previously voted with the Whigs. If there was one thing that marked his life's history more than another, it was his very liberal and generous nature combined with strong spiritual uprightness. For over half a century he was a pillar in the Congregational church of Chelsea, serving all these years as one of its deacons, and of his substance he gave unstintingly to both the church and needy, frequently being imposed upon by the unscrupulous but never allowing this to change his sweet and generous temperament. The latch-string of his house was always out to his friends, and his purse strings were always loosened to those who appealed to him for material aid. When on May 14, 1905, Deacon Floyd died, there were many who felt his loss in the town, church and the community in general, as "Uncle Floyd" was a man who had no enemies and his friends were legion.

Deacon Floyd married, in Winthrop, Sallie Tewksbury, born in the town of Revere, now Winthrop, August, 1814, died December, 1893, daughter of Washington and Hannah Benard (Floyd) Tewksbury, and granddaughter of James and Mary (Sargent) Tewksbury. The Tewksbury family was one of the oldest in that section of the state. James Tewksbury was born on what is known as Pullen Point about 1744, died there November 7, 1800. He married Mary Sargent, a native of Malden, Massachusetts, who lived to be over ninety years of age, dying in Winthrop, daughter of John Sargent, one of the very early settlers of Winthrop and prominent in his day. James and Mary (Sargent) Tewksbury were the parents of seven children, namely: James, John, Samuel, William, Sally, Polly and Washington. Washington Tewksbury, father of Sallie (Tewksbury) Floyd, was born in what was then North Chelsea or Revere, now Winthrop, 1784, died 1857. When a young man he went to sea and for some years was an active seafaring man, but later he decided to lead a more quiet and domestic life, and accordingly abandoned the romance of the ocean and took up the occupation of farming in Winthrop, at which he continued up to the time of his death, meeting with great success in his undertaking. He married Hannah Benard Floyd, a native of Winthrop, born 1779, died in August, 1857. They were the parents of children: 1. George Washington, born 1810, died in August, 1894; married Jane Waite, of Malden, who died in 1904. 2. Samuel, married Catharine Kimball, of Salem, who died in 1898. 3. Sallie, aforementioned as the wife of Deacon David Floyd. 4. Hannah, born March 20, 1819, married

Thomas Belcher, of Winthrop. Deacon David and Sallie (Tewksbury) Floyd were the parents of the following children, although probably not in the order of their birth: 1. Viola, died in infancy. 2. Lucius, born November 18, 1834, was a carpenter and builder, now retired from active labor; he was a prominent figure in Winthrop, having held about all the public offices in the gift of the people, which he filled with much satisfaction. He married first, Mrs. Eliza Crosby, nee Treeworthy or Trueworthy, who died in middle life; she was the mother of one child by her former marriage, Charles Crosby, now a carpenter in Winthrop; married second, Mary Richardson, of New York, who bore him one daughter, Alma, wife of Robert Cobb, a carpenter of Winthrop. 3. Henry Otis, born in Winthrop, September 18, 1836, died 1881, respected by all the citizens of the community; he married first, Philena Proctor, who died a comparative young woman and left one daughter, Carrie, now wife of ——— Parker, and they reside in Winthrop. 4. David Albert, born October 15, 1838; see forward. 5. Philip Payson, born October 13, 1840, died in Winthrop, March 24, 1902, leaving many close friends among the best families of Winthrop; he was a mechanic; was for many years foreman for the forestry department of the Standard Oil Company; he married Abbie F. Allen, a native of New Hampshire, sister of the wife of D. Albert Floyd; she died in Winthrop, February 14, 1897, leaving two children: Charles Payson, who is connected with the firm of Rhoades & Ripley, merchants of Boston; he married Edna Richardson, four children: Walter, Leland, Myrtle and Allen R.; Millie, wife of Ernst Griffin, a carpenter and builder of Winthrop; one child, Sidney R. Griffin. 6. Benjamin Tappan, see forward. 7. Willard Frank, a prominent citizen of Melrose, California, where he is associated extensively in business, also officially; married Maggie Ling, one child, Chester. 8. Ephraim Buck, a carpenter and builder of Winthrop; married Sarah Wyman, of Point Shirley, three children: George E., Frank, Ella, died at the age of eighteen years. 9. Alma V., widow of Edward Durham, who died in 1890; Mrs. Durham resides on Locust street, Winthrop; she has one son, Howard Durham. 10. Sallie Levina, died at the age of two and a half years.

(VII) David Albert Floyd, son of Deacon David and Sallie (Tewksbury) Floyd, was born on the old homestead in Winthrop, October 15, 1838, and was reared and educated there. At the age of eighteen, the sea having a great fascination for him, he engaged in that line of work, continuing for a period of five years, during which time he had a varied experience. He then accepted a position which was offered him by the Beacon Oil Company (later absorbed by the Standard) and was with them several years, but not approving of the cutting down system of the Standard Oil Company he resigned from his position and accepted one in the office of Sheriff Seavy of Suffolk county, and was attached to that office in the county court house for eighteen years, chiefly as watchman, and during this period became closely acquainted with a large circle of people having business at court, and held a very high place in the estimation of his superiors and also made many friends among the people he met. Upon his resignation from the sheriff's office, he accepted a minor position with the Lynn & Revere Beach railroad. In connection with this work he serves in the capacity of town constable, having been appointed to this office thirteen years ago, 1895, and acts as an administrator of a large estate, which important duties occupies a great portion of his time, they being performed in a highly creditable and efficient manner. Mr. Floyd is a member of the Blue Lodge, Ancient Free and Accepted Masons, of Winthrop. He attends the Baptist church of which his wife is a member.

Mr. Floyd married, in Hillsboro, New Hampshire, October 29, 1863, Carrie Augusta Allen, born in West Medford, Massachusetts, November 17, 1839, removing to Hillsboro when five years of age. She is a daughter of John and Susan (Teele) Allen, both natives of Hillsboro, who led exemplary lives and who lived to a ripe old age; John Allen (father) was a farmer by occupation; he was a son of John and ——— (Danforth) Allen, also natives of the state of New Hampshire. John and Susan (Teele) Allen were the parents of the following named children: 1. Abbie, deceased, who was the wife of Philip Payson Floyd, a resident of Winthrop. 2. Carrie Augusta, wife of D. Albert Floyd. 3. James, resident of Dorchester, Massachusetts, engaged with Rhoades & Ripley, Boston merchants; married Hattie Teele. 4. Charles H., died at the age of forty-five. 5. Mary G., wife of Ellis J. Pitcher; resides in Weymouth, Massachusetts. 6. Florence, wife of M. Austin Belcher, a successful contractor of Winthrop. Mr. and Mrs. D. Albert Floyd have two sons: 1. James A., born May 31, 1870, unmarried, resides at home. 2. Ellis A., born July 23,

1874, unmarried, now engaged with the Boston Belting Company.

(VII) Benjamin Tappan Floyd, son of Deacon David and Sallie (Tewksbury) Floyd, was born in Winthrop. He was for many years a successful market gardener of Winthrop, and a man in whom every person who knew him held in highest respect, and who is still closely allied with the interests of the place as one of its representative citizens, having in later life been engaged in contract work for the town and state. He married, in the town of Revere, Adaline Pierce, a native of Revere. She has been a woman who has made her good influence felt and who is still very energetic and active, both physically and mentally. Their children are as follows: 1. Nelson, see forward. 2. Alvira, unmarried, resides at the old homestead. 3. Emma, unmarried, for some years has been connected with the Clark Publishing Company of Boston. 4. Florence, a bookkeeper with the American Soda Fountain Company of Boston. 5. Everett, died at the age of two and a half years.

(VIII) Nelson Floyd, son of Benjamin Tappan and Adaline (Pierce) Floyd, was born on the old homestead in Winthrop, November 24, 1866. He was reared and educated in his native town. He married, in Winthrop, November 29, 1893, Edith L. Crosby, a native of Charlestown, born 1872, coming to Winthrop when young with her parents, Elijah E. and Abbie (Tarbox) Crosby, the former of whom was born on Cape Cod and the latter in Maine; they now reside in Winthrop. Mr. and Mrs. Floyd have had two children: 1. Everett N., born May 14, 1895, died January 9, 1897. 2. Mildred, born January 25, 1900.

(VI) Thomas Floyd, fifth son of David (5) and Hannah (Tewskbury) Floyd, was born in Revere and later moved on what was then known as Floyd's Hill, the farm being a part of what has became the government barracks and known as Fort Banks. This property was known as the old David Floyd estate, and was marked for its beauty of location and marine scenery, also the scene of many of the births of this large and interesting family. He was reared to manhood on the old farm, and was probably best known as a famous gunner, his marksmanship being unerring. He was known as the Daniel Boone and Kit Carson of Massachusetts. He met in Boston Hannah Bourne Sturgis, who some time afterward became his wife. She was the daughter of Samuel and ——— (Bourne) Sturgis, members of well known Boston families. One of the daughters of Samuel Sturgis became the wife of the well known and wealthy Joshua Bates, of the firm of Baring Brothers, bankers, London, England, and in whose honor Bates Hall of Boston was named. Mr. and Mrs. Floyd became active citizens of the town of Winthrop, and lived to enjoy life among their friends there for many years. They were closely allied with the Methodist Episcopal church, and of their substance contributed liberally toward any worthy cause. They were the parents of the following named children: 1. Almira, born in Winthrop, April 9, 1833, became the wife of Lorenzo Chamberlain Tewksbury, born in Winthrop, August 16, 1823, who is living at the present time (1908), the oldest native resident of the town as well as the oldest living member of the Methodist Episcopal church in Winthrop, and who, except for his hearing, is in good health of mind and body; his wife Almira died 1907. 2. Captain William B., a retired seaman; married Augusta Wilson, of Malden; they are both living and enjoying life in Winthrop. 3. Thomas, Jr., see forward.

(VII) Thomas Floyd, youngest son of Thomas and Hannah B. (Sturgis) Floyd, was born in Winthrop, November 3, 1838. His early life was spent in Winthrop, and his education was that acquired in the public schools. He inherited one of the characteristics of the family, love of the sea, and his brother being a sea captain, he directed his energies to that line of work and accordingly joined his brother, who was sailing coasting vessels, and worked his way up from man before the mast until he became a second mate, in which capacity he served for some time, after which he turned his attention to farming, achieving therein a large degree of success, and accumulating a large landed property. In addition to his agricultural pursuits, he has built up a substantial real estate business, disposing not only of his own property at advantageous prices, but creating a demand for the property of others, and thus working for the general welfare and advancement of the town. When the war broke out he responded nobly to the call for troops to suppress the rebellion, joining Company I, Sixtieth Regiment, Massachusetts Volunteer Infantry, Captain D. H. Boynton, at Haverhill, Massachusetts, and went to the front, but after a short period of time impaired health compelled him to abandon the life of a soldier and he was honorably discharged. He served in the capacity of town collector twelve years, as assessor fifteen years, which latter office he still fills, and his careful and impartial judgment of values has made him a valuable officer. He was also for a term a member of the board of selectmen; in 1871 he was sent to the state legislature, and again in 1881-82, and served with earnestness and fidelity on a number of committees, including fisheries, public buildings and woman suffrage. He is a member of Theodore Winthrop Post, No. 35, Grand Army of the Republic, of Chelsea. His beautiful home, located on the crest of Floyd's Hill, overlooks beautiful Fort Banks and the bays around Boston, and the charm of scenery is enhanced by the liberality and hospitality of its owner.

Mr Floyd married, January 1, 1861, in Revere, or what was then known as North Chelsea, Mary Pierce, who died December 21, 1897, aged fifty-nine years and eight months, after many years as an invalid from paralysis, since which time Mr. Floyd has led the life of a widower. Mrs. Floyd, who was a member of the Methodist Episcopal church, was a daughter of Royal and Mary (Hall) Pierce, early residents of North Chelsea, where they led pure, upright lives and where their deaths occurred. Mr. and Mrs. Floyd had three children, namely: 1. Edgar Lincoln, died at the age of three and a half years. 2. Thomas Sturgis, born December 20, 1869, educated in the schools of Winthrop, learned the trade of carpenter and builder, and since attaining manhood has conducted business on his own account to some extent and with a certain degree of success. He is unmarried. 3. May L., born December 29, 1873, unmarried, was from childhood interested in music, and after graduating from the New England Conservatory of Music and also from a musical school in Germany, she became an instructor and has devoted her life to her art; she has taught many classes in the east and west and is highly successful in her line of work.

(VI) Edward Floyd, son of David and Hannah (Tewksbury) Floyd, born in Chelsea, Massachusetts, 1809, died in Winthrop. He was about sixteen years when his father removed from Chelsea to Winthrop, and in after years he became one of the leading men of the town, filling with credit a number of offices of local importance and throughout his life enjoying the respect of all of his fellow townsmen. He married Lucretia Tewksbury, born in Winthrop, daughter of John W., and granddaughter of Andrew Tewksbury, both prominent men and descendants of good old New England revolutionary stock. Children of Edward and Lucretia (Tewksbury) Floyd: 1. Adelaide M., lives in Winthrop. 2. Charlotee, now Mrs. Scoville, of Malden. 3. David; David; see forward. 4. Lucy A. 5. Harriet.

(VII) David Floyd, son of Edward and Lucretia (Tewksbury) Floyd, was born in Winthrop, Massachusetts, and for more than forty years has been closely identified with the civil and business life of his native town, and since 1889 has been senior member of the firm of Floyd & Tucker, real estate dealers in Boston and Winthrop., A native of Winthrop, educated in the public schools there and widely acquainted throughout the town, he naturally has always taken an active and earnest interest in whatever might tend to promote the public welfare, and indeed it may be said that in all measures proposed for the promotion of local interests and institutions he generally has been one of the leading spirits in each enterprise and a valuable factor in accomplishing the desired result. His own business interests are large and have been built up on foundations laid by himself, and as he has been abundantly successful in personal enterprises, so too has he been called upon by his fellow townsmen to serve in various official capacities in the interest of the public welfare; and he has given freely to this end of both his time and means. He is a Republican in politics, loyal in his allegiance to the party and one of its most influential adherents in Suffolk county. He served eleven years as town treasurer of Winthrop, six years as assessor, two years, 1877 and 1878, as representative to the general court, and for the last twenty-five years has been treasurer of the sinking fund commssion of the town.

Mr. Floyd is a member and present chairman of the board of trustees of the Dean Winthrop House, an historic landmark of the town and which recently has been occupied by the Winthrop Improvement and Historical Society. He was largely instrumental too in the preservation of the "old Bill house," another of the historic old houses of Winthrop. He is a trustee of Chelsea Savings Bank, the Winthrop Co-operative Bank, and is a Royal Arch Mason and a member of the Royal Arcanum.

David Floyd married, in Winthrop, Belle A. Seavey. Her great-grandfather, Joseph Floyd, born in Rye or New Castle, New Hampshire, served in the revolution in Captain Parsons's company, doing duty largely in Massachusetts, with the rank of sergeant. Children of Sergeant Seavey: 1. Samuel, born 1783, came to New Hampshire when a young man; was a farmer in East Concord, where he died aged sixty-five years; he was twice married; by his second wife, Nancy Stevens, he had children: i. Theodore H., twice married; ii. Adoniram B., married ———; iii. Gilman S.; iv. Charles Fred, father of Mrs. David Floyd; v. Augusta. 2. William Seavey, born 1791, spent most of his life in East Boston, where he was a prominent ship carpenter and a man of affairs. Charles Fred Seavey, son of Samuel and Nancy (Stevens) Seavey, was born in 1821, on his father's farm, East Concord, New Hampshire. On reaching manhood he came to Boston, and engaged in his trade as carpenter and builder. About 1863 he settled in Cambridge, where he died in 1881. He was widely and favorably known in Boston and vicinity. He was a Democrat in politics. He married Emily Eastman Fernald, born in Cambridge, who survived her husband, and died at the home of her son, Sheriff Seavey, April 28, 1908. She was great-granddaughter of Captain Ebenezer Fernald, of revolutionary fame; granddaughter of Jacob Fernald, and daughter of Joseph Fernald, a soldier of the war of 1812. Children of Charles Fred and Emily Eastman (Fernald) Seavey: 1. Belle A. Seavey, became wife of David Floyd. 2. Fred H., born April 1, 1854. He was liberally educated, and from early manhood has been prominent in public affairs, having been elected as a Republican four times to the high office of sheriff of Suffolk county—a most notable distinction.

(VII) Sumner Floyd, son of Philip Payson Floyd (6), was born in Winthrop, November 14, 1845. He received such education as was afforded by the public schools, and from the time he attained manhood his association has been continued with his native town, and his interest in the welfare of the community has never waned. His occupation is that of undertaker and embalmer. He has rendered valuable service in various important positions—for twenty-one years he was town clerk, his service beginning when the town had one hundred and fifty voters, increased more than tenfold when he retired from that office; was elected tax collector when twenty-one years of age; and served a term of six years on the school committee, and a like period on the sinking fund committee. He married first, in Gloucester, Massachusetts, Melissa J. Fleming, born in Gloucester, where she was reared, having come of parentage who had been identified with New England and Massachusetts for many years. While yet in the prime of life she died, in 1884, aged thirty-two years. She left two children: 1. Carl Sumner, born November 8, 1878, lives in Winthrop; is chief clerk of eighth division, Boston Elevated railway; married May Perry. 2. Lulu M., wife of Wiley S. Young, treasurer and head bookkeeper for Richards & Company, Sudbury street, Boston; children: Sumner Edward, Dorothy Elsie. Sumner Floyd married second, in Cambridge, Ada Estelle Whicher, born in Alfred, Maine, February 27, 1850; no children. Mr. Floyd is a Republican in politics, and he and wife are Methodists in religious belief.

BUCKLEY This surname is a place name of ancient English origin, and was originally spelled, in the time of King John, in 1199, Buclough, and later Bulclough. It signifies "a large mountain." There have been many and are still variations in spelling. Bulkeley is the one most commonly used, other forms being Bulkley, Bulkly and Buckley.

Baron Robert de Bulkeley (1) lived in the time of King John (1199-26). Baron William de Bulkeley (2) married a daughter of Thomas Butler. Baron Robert de Bulkeley (3) married Jane, daughter of Sir William Butler. Baron William de Bulkeley (4) married, 1302, Maud, daughter of Sir John Davenport. Baron Robert de Bulkeley (5) married Agnes ———. Baron Peter de Bulkeley (6) married Nicola, daughter of Thomas Bird. Baron John de Bulkeley (7), of Houghton, married Arderne Fitley. Baron Hugh de Bulkeley (8) married Helen, daughter of Thomas Wilbraham. Baron Humphrey de Bulkeley (9) married Grisel Moulton. Baron William de Bulkeley (10), of Oakley, married Beatrice, daughter of William Hill. Baron Thomas de Bulkeley (11) married Elizabeth, daughter of Randelle Grosvenor. Rev. Edward de Bulkeley (12) was born at Ware, Shropshire, England. He was admitted to St. John's College, Cambridge, April 6, 1560, and was curate of St. Mary's, Shrewsbury, in 1565; prebend of Chester; prebend of Litchfield about 1580; rector of All Saints, Odell, in the Hundred of Willey, Bedfordshire, where he died and was succeeded by his eldest son Peter, mentioned below. He married Almark Irlby (or Islby), of Lincolnshire.

(XIII) Rev. Peter Bulkeley, son of Rev. Edward Bulkeley, was born January 31, 1582-3, at Odell, Bedfordshire, England. He entered St. John's College, Cambridge, at the age of sixteen, March 22, 1604-5; fellow 1608, with M. A. degree, and "said, but on doubtful authority, to have proceeded bachelor of Divinity." He succeeded his father as rector of Odell. He was known to be a non-conformist, but "the Lord Keeper Williams, formerly his diocesan, and his personal friend, desired to deal gently with his non-conformity" and connived at it, as he had at his father's for twenty years, but when Loud became primate of England in 1633, Mr. Bulkeley was silenced and with no hope of reinstatement. He therefore sold his estate and sailed for New England in 1635, at the age of fifty-two, with his children, on the ship "Susan and Ellen." His wife Grace, aged thirty, was enrolled on the ship "Elizabeth and Ann," but it is probable that she sailed with her husband. There is a tradition in the family that while on the voyage, the wife Grace apparently died. Unwilling to have her body buried at sea, the husband pleaded with the captain to keep it until they reached port. As no signs of decay appeared, he consented, and on the third day symptoms of vitality appeared, and before land was reached animation was restored. Though carried from the ship an invalid she recovered and lived to a good old age. Rev. Peter Bulkeley settled first in Cambridge and the next year with twelve others began the settlement of Concord. Three years later he received a grant of three hundred acres of land at Cambridge. He was teacher of the church at Concord of which Rev. John Jones was pastor, and was installed pastor April 6, 1637. He is always spoken of as the first minister of Concord. He brought with him from England about six thousand pounds, most of which he spent for the good of the colony. He was a learned and pious man. He wrote several Latin poems, some of which Cotton Mather, in his "Magnalia," quotes, as a part of the sketch of his life. He also published a volume in London in 1646, entitled "The Gospel Covenant," made up of sermons preached at Concord, and an elegy on his friend, Rev. Hooker. He was among the first to instruct the Indians, and the singular immunity of Concord from Indian attack was largely credited, by tradition, to his sanctity and influence. He died at Concord, March 9, 1658-9. There is a large tablet to his memory near the open square at Concord. His will, dated April 14, 1658, with codicils of January 13 and February 26 following, was proved June 20, 1659. Before his death he gave many books to the library of Harvard College. He married first, about 1613, Jane, daughter of Thomas Allen, of Goldington. She died at Odell, in 1626, and he married second, about 1634, Grace Chetwoode, born 1602, daughter of Sir Richard and Dorothy (Needham) Chetwoode, of Odell. She died April 21, 1669, at New London, Connecticut, at the home of her son. Children of first wife, born in England: 1. Edward, June 17, 1614; came to New England before his father; died January 2, 1696. 2. Mary, baptized August 24, 1615; died young. 3. Thomas, born April 11, 1617; married Sarah Jones; settled in Fairfield, Connecticut. 4. Nathaniel, born November 29, 1618; died 1627. 5. Rev. John, born February 11, 1620; graduated at Harvard with the first class. 6. Mary, born November 1, 1621; died 1624. 7. George, born May 17, 1623. 8. Daniel, born August 28, 1625. 9. Jabez, born December 20, 1626; died young. 10. Joseph (probably), born 1619. 11. William, of Ipswich, in 1648. 12. Richard. Children of second wife, born in New England: 13. Gershom, December 6, 1636; mentioned below. 14. Elizabeth, born probably 1638, married Rev. Joseph Emerson. 15. Dorothy, August 2, 1640. 16. Peter, August 12, 1643.

(XIV) Rev. Dr. Gershom Bulkeley, son of Rev. Peter Bulkeley, was born at Concord, December 6, 1636, and died December 2, 1713. He graduated at Harvard College in 1655, as a fellow of the college. In 1661 he became the minister of the Second Church at New London, Connecticut, and in 1666-7 removed to Wethersfield, where he was installed as pastor. In 1676 he asked for dismissal on account of impaired health, and he thereafter devoted himself to the practice of medicine and surgery, in which he achieved much success and reputation. He was an ardent student of chemistry and philosophy, and master of several languages, and was also an expert surveyor. During his pastorate in 1675 he was appointed surgeon to the Connecticut troops in King Philip's war, and placed on the council of war. The court gave orders to have him taken especial care of. At one time the party to which he was attached was attacked by a number of Indians near Wachusett Hill, Massachusetts, and in the fight he received a wound in the thigh. His monument in the Wethersfield cemetery says of him: "He was honorable in his descent, or rare abilities, excellent in learning, master of many languages, exquisite in his skill, in divinity, physic and law, and of a most exemplary and Christian life." His will was dated May 28, 1712, and proved December 7, 1713. He married, October 26, 1659, Sarah Chauncey, born at Ware, England, June 13, 1631, died June 3, 1699, daughter of Rev. Charles Chauncey, president of

Harvard College. Children: 1. Catherine, born about 1660; married Richard Treat. 2. Dorothy, born about 1662; married, July 5, 1693, Lieutenant Thomas Treat; died 1757. 3. Dr. Charles, born about 1663. 4. Peter, married, March 21, 1700, Rachel Talcott; lost at sea. 5. Edward, born 1672; mentioned below. 6. Rev. John, born 1679.

(XV) Captain Edward Bulkeley, son of Rev. Gershom Bulkeley, was born in 1672, and died at Wethersfield, August 27, 1748. His tombstone contains a rough sketch of the Bulkeley coat-of-arms. He was collector 1703; selectman 1708; was admitted an attorney in June, 1711. He married, July 14, 1702, Dorothy Prescott, who died November 30, 1760, in her eighty-first year, daughter of Jonathan Prescott. Children: 1. Charles, born March 25, 1702-3. 2. Elizabeth, born January 24, 1704-5; married Joseph Smith. 3. Sarah, born February 8, 1706-7; married Joseph Stowe. 4. Rebecca, born February 2, 1708-9; married Isaac Treat. 5. Peter, born 1710-11; died young. 6. Peter, born March 11, 1711-12; mentioned below. 7. Gershom, born July 28, 1714. 8. Dorothy, born September 11, 1716; married Thomas Curtis. 9. Jonathan, born September 11, 1718. 10. Abigail, born 1720; married John Marsh. 11. Lucy, born 1723; married Charles Butler.

(XVI) Peter Bulkeley, son of Captain Edward Bulkeley, was born March 11, 1712, and died April 4, 1776. He was appointed justice of the peace for Hartford county in May, 1775, and resided at Wethersfield. He married first, April 2, 1741, Abigail Curtis, who died November 27, 1762, in her fifty-fifth year; second, January 26, 1769, Christian Smith, who died (probably) December 22, 1802. Children: 1. Joseph, born January 28, 1742. 2. Abigail, born April 13, 1743; married Nathaniel Miller; died April 14, 1834. 3. Oliver, born December 5, 1744; died at sea, April, 1776. 4. Solomon, born March 21, 1747; mentioned below. 5. Dorothy, born July 17, died 28, 1749. 6. Justus, born December 24, 1752.

(XVII) Solomon Bulkeley (or Buckley), son of Peter Bulkeley, was born at Wethersfield, March 21, 1747, and died March 4, 1790, aged forty-three. He married, June 6, 1776, Martha Williams, daughter of Moses Williams. She married second, March 6, 1796, Elizur Goodrich. Solomon was in the revolution, and a pensioner in Hartford county, 1832; was in Captain Hart's company, Colonel Erastus Walcott's regiment, 1776, which was one of three regiments to guard the lines at Boston until the Continental army was established; was in Captain John Chester's company at the time of the Lexington alarm, April 19, 1775. Children: 1. Sally. 2. James, perhaps the James who died January 11, 1860, aged eighty-two. 3. Oliver, mentioned below. 4. George. 5. Martha. 6. Nancy. 7. Brazilla.

(XVIII) Oliver Buckley, son of Solomon Buckley, was born in Wethersfield, Connecticut, about 1780-90. He removed to Maine, and settled in what was then the town of Westbrook, now part of the city of Portland, Maine. He was a manufacturer. He married Sally Humphrey. Children: 1. Nancy G., born 1806; died 1904, aged ninety-eight years; married ——— Stevens; their son Alfred A. Stevens resides in Portland. 2. Mary Ann. 3. Charles S., mentioned below. 4. Oren.

(XIX) Charles S. Buckley, son of Oliver Buckley, was born in Westbrook, Maine, about 1810; died in 1866, aged fifty-six years. He was educated in the public schools of his native town. He was in business for many years at Augusta, Maine, and afterward at Chicago, Illinois, where he died. His body was brought home and buried in Pine Grove Cemetery, Portland. He was a pioneer in sending out the very popular and profitable tin-peddler outfits. These carts were owned by itinerant merchants. They were huge red carts devised with Yankee ingenuity to hold everything used in the household. The interior was devoted to tinware; the outside to brushes, brooms, mops, pails and huge bags in which the peddler stored the rags collected of thrifty housewives in payment for the tinware. The rags, especially in war time, were in great demand for making paper and the business was developed greatly in that time, and is still conducted in rural sections of the country. At one time Mr. Buckley had sixty carts on the road. He married, and had children: Laura; Charles M., mentioned below; Henry; Oliver; Sumner; Sadie.

(XX) Charles M. Buckley, son of Charles S. Buckley, was born in Westbrook, Maine. He received his education in the public schools of his native town and at Westbrook Seminary at Deering, Maine. In the early days of gold discoveries in that section he went to the Black Hills, Dakota, and prospected there for several years, suffering the hardship and dangers of frontier life. He had varying success in mining. After a few years he returned to Maine, thence to Chester Harbor, Nova Scotia, near Halifax, where he established a large lobster-packing industry, conducting it

Lewis Historical Pub. Co.

with marked success for a number of years. His knowledge of the tinsmith trade, acquired in his youth, stood him in good stead in this business, in which a practical knowledge of making and sealing the cans is essential. After he retired from this business he came to Boston to live with his son and spent his last years there. He died in February, 1902. In politics he was a Democrat. He was a member of the Masonic Blue Lodge and Clarke Lodge of Nova Scotia. He had superior business ability and achieved great success in his undertakings. He was universally respected by all who knew him, and esteemed alike by business associates and employees. He married, at Portland, Maine, Carrie Johnson, born in Portland, 1845, died at Portland, aged fifty-four years, a descendant of one of the old and estimable colonial families of New England; of Scotch descent, being closely related to George B. McClellan. Children: 1. William A., born June 25, 1863, mentioned below. 2. Paul E., November 9, 1865, resides at Alton, New Hampshire, where he conducts a stove and tinware business; is unmarried. 3. Son, who died in infancy.

(XXI) William A. Buckley, son of Charles M. Buckley, was born in Portland, Maine, June 25, 1863, died in Winthrop, Massachusetts, June 5, 1908. He was educated in the public schools of Portland and at the Elliot Business College of Burlington, Iowa. During his boyhood he worked as clerk in the gents furnishing store of Charles Curtis, of Portland, and followed this line of work until about 1882, in which year he took up his residence in Boston, Massachusetts, where he was employed as traveling salesman for C. B. Young, a merchant in upholstering supplies, serving in that capacity until 1889, when he resigned to engage in the life insurance business in partnership with his uncle, O. H. Buckley, continuing under the firm name of O. H. & W. A. Buckley until 1894, when W. A. Buckley purchased the business and became general manager of New England for the Provident Savings Life Assurance Company of New York. About 1902 he was made assistant superintendent of agencies for the United States. For the past seven years he resided in Winthrop, with office at 24 Milk street, Boston. He was well and favorably known to the insurance men of New England and his ability was universally recognized. He was prepossessing in appearance, attractive in personality and winning and persuasive in his speech and manner. He knew human nature well; he attracted friends and enjoyed good society. Of strict integrity and honor in business, of strong character and decided opinions, he was a natural leader among men. In politics he was a Republican, but he never sought office. Mr. Buckley was a prominent Free Mason, a member of Charity Lodge, the chapter, council and commandery of Knights Templar; and Aleppo Temple, A. A. O. N. M. S. He was also a member of Winthrop Yacht Club, New York Club, Arkwright Club and Republican Club of New York City. His beautiful residence was on Washington Avenue overlooking Chrystal Bay, in Winthrop, where he had invested largely in real estate, and had a principal part in the development and progress of the town.

Mr. Buckley married, December 25, 1888, in Burlington, Iowa, Mary E. Mellinger, born in that city, 1862, daughter of Samuel E. and Emeline A. (Marshall) Mellinger (see Mellinger sketch herewith). Her parents were born in Lebanon county, Pennsylvania. She was educated in the public schools of her native place and of Geneva, Illinois, where she made a study of the fine arts. Her home shows many specimens of her skill. Her mother belonged to the family made famous by the great chief justice of the supreme court, John Marshall. Children: 1. Ruth Virginia, born December 20, 1889. 2. William A. Jr., December 24, 1894. They reside with their mother in Winthrop.

MELLINGER The surname Mellinger is of German origin. The immigrant ancestor came among the early settlers of Pennsylvania, and for several generations the family continued to speak and write the German language. According to the federal census of 1790, nine families of this name were living in the province of Pennsylvania, all doubtless related. The heads of these families were Abraham, Anthony, Benedict, Frederick, Jacob Esq., John, Martin, Melchior and William. The principal seat of the family was in Lancaster county; Abraham Mellinger lived in 1790 in Warwick township, and William and John in Cocalico township. Lebanon county was set of from Lancaster county at a later period, in 1816. At that time even the German language still prevailed.

(I) John Mellinger, son of John or William Mellinger, mentioned above, was born March 4, 1790, in Lancaster, now Lebanon county, Pennsylvania. He was educated in the German tongue, but attended an English school for three months. He learned the trade of weaver and became an inventor and promoter. He had a patent on the loom on which coverlets were made. He was a Democrat to the time of the civil war, afterwards being a staunch and faithful Republican. He enlisted in the war of 1812 as a drummer boy from Baltimore, Maryland. In religion he was connected with the Dunkards in early life, but after his removal west in 1836 was a Methodist. He married, in Lebanon, Barbara Rohland, a native of that town. Children: 1. Maria, mentioned below. 2. Susannah; married John Miller. 3. William S., married Jane Black; settled at Monongahela City, Pennsylvania; drilled a military company when a youth; is said to have served in the Mexican war; served throughout the civil war and rose to rank of major; was killed after the war; was state senator of Pennsylvania. 4. Lydia S., married William M. Patten, of Butler, Pennsylvania. 5. John J. R., married Elizabeth Patten, of Butler City, Pennsylvania; enlisted from that town as private in the civil war. 6. Jeremiah A., married Margaret Johnson; lived at Butler; raised a company and commanded it in the civil war.

(II) Maria Mellinger, daughter of John Mellinger, was born in 1811; married George Eba, born April 11, 1808. George Eba was of old German stock. The name is also spelled Eby and Eaby, and the family is descended from the immigrant Theodorus Eby, a Mennonite in religion, born in Switzerland, took refuge in the Palatinate and finally came to America, about 1715, settling on Mill Creek. George Eba was a carpenter and contractor; a member of the German Lutheran Church in early life, later of the Methodist Episcopal Church; Democrat in politics until 1840, Whig until that party went to pieces, and afterward a Republican; enlisted in 1861 and went to Pittsburg to be mustered in, but was rejected on account of his age. Children: 1. Mary Ann Eba, died young. 2. William Henry Harrison, mentioned below. 3. Mary Ann Eba. 4. Mellinger Winfield Scott Eba; served in Eighth Iowa Regiment; killed under General Lyon in Missouri. 5. Mary Anna Eba, died young. 6. George Washington Eba; was a member of the Eleventh Pennsylvania Regiment; was wounded in the Seven Days Fight before Richmond, taken prisoner, exchanged, but died of his wounds and the exposure. 7. Thomas Jefferson Eba; served in One Hundredth Pennsylvania under General Benham, at James Island, South Carolina.

(III) William Henry Harrison Eba, son of George and Maria (Mellinger) Eba, was born November 5, 1831, at Lebanon, Pennsylvania. He moved with his parents in 1836 to Monongahela City, Washington county, same state, and was educated in the common schools and Monongahela Academy. He began to work in a cigar factory, but after a year concluded to learn stove and hollow-ware moulding. He served four years' apprenticeship at this trade, receiving in wages five dollars a month the first year; eight dollars a month the second year, twelve the third year and twenty the fourth. A few months before his time expired the works were destroyed by fire. He found employment as second clerk on a steamboat plying between Pittsburg and Wheeling, West Virginia. In July, 1852, he removed to Kentucky, landing at Catlettsburg, July 3, and becoming salesman there in the general store. In 1892 he removed to Ashland, Kentucky, where he is now living. For fifteen years he was a book-keeper for the A., C. & I. railroad, in the machine shop department. He was originally a Whig, now a Republican. He was mayor of Ashland one term; is at present city truant officer. He enlisted in Company I, Fifth West Virginia Regiment; was promoted sergeant-major, March, 1862; first lieutenant. He declined the post of adjutant after being acting adjutant two months. He was commissioned a month later by Governor Pierpont captain of Company F, same regiment. Ninety or more of the men of his company were born in Wayne county, West Virginia, while two were from North Carolina. He was in various engagements, but none of the great battles of the war. Once his shoulder-strap was shot off, but he was never wounded. He is a member of the Good Fellowship Brotherhood and of the Methodist Episcopal Church. He married, October 9, 1856, at Catlettsburg, Greenup (now Boyd) county, Kentucky, Amanda Lydia Henderson, born July 18, 1832, in Cabell county, Virginia, daughter of Duncan and Mary (Wentworth) Henderson. Children: 1. Charlotte Culver, born July 14, 1857; died October 20, 1857. 2. Amelia Maria, born February 15, 1859; died June 18, 1860. 3. Edward Everett, born March 31, 1861; died April 25, 1882, graduate of the high school in 1879.

(I) William Mellinger, brother of John Mellinger, was born in Lebanon county, Pennsylvania, 1798, and died June 22, 1869, at Burlington, Iowa. He had a common school education. He was a tin and iron merchant. In politics he was a Republican and in religion a Methodist. He married Elizabeth ———, born September 8, 1802; died February 20, 1880, in Burlington. Children: 1. Mary, born December 15, 1825; died September 8, 1899, at Burlington, Iowa. 2. Sarah, born May 13, 1825; died April 1, 1899. 3. Samuel E., born October 10, 1827; mentioned below. 4. Lydia, born August 1, 1830; died June 21, 1898, at Burlington. 5. Louisa, born February 14, 1834; lives in Burlington. 6. William, born March 4, 1837; lives at Keithsburg, Illinois. 7. Henry, born February 18, 1842; died October, 1894, in Keithsburg.

(II) Samuel E. Mellinger, son of William Mellinger, was born October 10, 1827, at Shaferstown, Lebanon county, Pennsylvania. He lives in Burlington, Iowa. He was educated in the common schools and the Annville Academy at Annville, Pennsylvania. He began his business career in 1845 and has continued to the present time. He manufactured tin, iron, stoves and hardware. He became the owner of various woolen mills, paper mills and lumber mills, a wheel factory and tannery. In later years he has had an extensive ranch and raised horses and cattle. He has invested in real estate all the way from Texas to Canada and at the present time has large holdings. He was first a Whig, then a Republican in politics. He is a member of the Independent Order of Odd Fellows. He and his family attend the Methodist and Congregational churches. He married at Annville, Pennsylvania, April 14, 1852, Emeline Amanda Marshall, born June 23, 1828, at Annville, daughter of Dr. John Gloninger and Elizabeth (Behm) Marshall. Dr. Marshall, his father and two of his sons, were graduates of the Philadelphia Medical College; also his brother Jacob Marshall, of Reading, Pennsylvania, who was minister plenipotentiary of the United States on a foreign mission at one time. Dr. Marshall and his son each raised a company in the civil war —one at Lebanon, the other at Annville. The children of Samuel Mellinger were all educated in the Burlington high school. Children: 1. Mary Jane, born January 10, 1853: now deceased. 2. Frank Marshall, born September 25, 1854; lives in Burlington; engaged in real estate and insurance business; married Lulu Ann Stubbs, of Mount Pleasant, Iowa; children: Frank Stubbs, born December 2, 1864; Mabel Emeline; Grace Sarah; Delia Marie. 3. Marshall Eba, born November 27, 1857; lives near Boise, Idaho, a farmer; married Ida Yaley; children: Clarence; Ida May; Mary Viola. 4. Elizabeth Barbara, born December 31, 1859; married Clarence Lincoln Waggoner, of Decatur, Illinois, banker; children: Arthur Waggoner; Carl Waggoner; Park Waggoner; Marshall Waggoner. 5. Mary Emma, born May 28, 1862; married William Albert Buckley, of Boston (see Buckley family). 6. Ida Belle, born December 2, 1864; married William Henry Sheldon, Percival, Iowa, grain buyer and dealer in farm implements; no children. 7. Charles Gloninger, born December 11, 1867; lives at Anaconda, Montana, book-keeper; married Grace Bosworth, of Boston; children: Marion; son unnamed, married.

QUINN

The Quin or Quinn family is of ancient Irish origin. Aeneas (or Aongus) Ceannathrach, a younger brother of Blad, one of the royal family of O'Brien, (see No. 92 p. 108 of the third edition of O'Hart's Irish Pedigrees), was the ancestor of O'Cuinn or Muintir Cuinn, of Munster; anglicized O'Quin, Quin, Quain, and Quinn. The Earl of Dunraven is a descendant and the most prominent member of this large and widely distributed family. The lineage is traced without a break in this branch of the family, according to O'Hart, for one hundred and thirty or more generations, and is well authenticated apparently for more than a thousand years.

(I) Peter Quinn was born in Pound Town, county Clare, Ireland. He was a farmer all his life. He married and among his children was Martin, mentioned below.

(II) Martin Quinn, son of Peter Quinn (1), was born in Pound Town, county Clare, Ireland. He was a farmer all his life. He married and had children: 1. Peter, was in this country for some time and went back unmarried. 2. John, never came to this country. 3. Martin, lives in Lawrence and is a motorman. 4. Mortimer, see forward.

(III) Mortimer Quinn, son of Martin Quinn (2), was born in the parish of Pound Town, county Clare, Ireland, July 16, 1871. He was educated in the schools of his native parish and spent his youth there. He left home in March, 1890, and came to Andover, Massachusetts, where for the next six years he worked in the mill. Then he came to Lawrence, Massachusetts, and engaged in real estate and is the owner of several nice properties. He has been prosperous in business. He is an independent Democrat in politics, and a Roman Catholic in religion, attending St. Mary's Church. He married, April 18, 1900,

Mary Riley, born May 4, 1860, daughter of John and Ann (McCaffery) Riley. They have no children. Children of Mr. and Mrs. Riley: 1. John, died aged twenty-one, in Ireland. 2. James, came to Lawrence at twenty-six years of age; is unmarried. 3. Mary, born 1860, mentioned above. 4. Patrick, born 1869, working in Boston as a brewer; married Miss A. Riley; children: Annie, Lucy, Margaret. 5. Annie, unmarried. 6. Barnard, residing in Boston. 7. Bennie, residing in Boston. 8. Frank, was a farmer all his life.

GOGGIN

Edward Goggin, well known as a contractor and builder in Lawrence, Massachusetts, and vicinity, is a descendant of an honored family of Ireland. Patrick Goggin, father of Edward Goggin, was a farmer in Ireland.

Edward Goggin was born in county Cork, Ireland, 1856, and worked on the farm of his father for some years. He was also employed on a steamer for a time. At the age of sixteen years he emigrated to the United States, and came to Lawrence. He found employment in the Pacific Mills, where he remained for some time. He then entered into a business partnership with Thomas John Farrel, in the building and contracting line, in which they met with a good share of success. For the last five years, since the death of Mr. Farrel, Mr. Goggin has been carrying on the business alone. His political affiliations are with the Democratic party, and he is a member of the Catholic church. He married, February 7, 1891, Catherine O'Brien, born in Waterford, Ireland, February 6, 1872, and came to this country in September,.1886. She is the daughter of Walter O'Brien Mr. and Mrs. Goggin have had children: Patrick William, January 14, 1893; Edward Walter, October 16, 1894; John Joseph, born November 8, 1896; Mary Ellen, August 30, 1898; Rose Anna, January 14, 1901; Agnes Catherine, October 25, 1903, died August 14, 1905; Frances Alice, twin of Agnes Catherine.

DOOLEY

Michael Dooley, for many years identified with business affairs in Lawrence and its vicinity, now living in retirement, represents the second generation of his family in the United States.

Michael Dooley, father of Michael Dooley mentioned above, was born in Ireland and died in Lawrence, Massachusetts. In Ireland he had followed the occupation of farming. He emigrated to Canada with his family, settling for a time in Quebec, then migrating to Lawrence, where he spent the remainder of his life. Children: 1. James, resides in North Andover; married Etta Ryan, of North Andover; children: Helena and James. 2. Bridget, married Charles A. Bradley, of Lawrence, real estate dealer. 3. John, of Lawrence. 4. Michael, see forward.

Michael Dooley, whose name heads this sketch, was born in county Limerick, Ireland, September 25, 1831. He was about sixteen years of age when he came to this country with his parents, and after living five months in Quebec, Canada, came to Lawrence, where he obtained a position as a hat finisher, he having learned that trade. After a time he turned his attention to building, and followed that line for a number of years until he retired from all active business life. Politically he is a Democrat, and he is a member of the Catholic church. He married Anna Edith Ryan, born in Ireland, February 7, 1837, came to this country in 1855, daughter of Thomas Ryan, a farmer. Mr. and Mrs. Michael Dooley have had children: 1. James Joseph, born August 10, 1864. 2. Annie Maria, January 10, 1866. 3. Mary Frances, February 12, 1868. 4. Bridget Helena, September 29, 1869. 5. Ellen Maria, December 4, 1871. 6. John Joseph, April, 1874. 7. Anguin Xavier, June 18, 1877. Mrs. Dooley died October 28, 1907.

MURLEY

John Murley, son of Daniel and Ellen (Kenney) Murley, and grandson of Martin Murley, was born September 5, 1842, in the city of London, England. He is descended from an ancient Irish family. His father was born in the city of Cork, Ireland, came to America from England, and died in 1862, in Lawrence, Massachusetts. John had a common school education and learned the trade of plasterer when a young man. He was eighteen years old when he came to America, landing at New York city, where he worked for three years at his trade. He removed to Lawrence, Massachusetts, in March, 1865, and has lived there ever since. He has been in business as a plasterer and mason, and is among the successful men of his line. He invested his savings from time to time in Lawrence real estate, and since he retired from active business in 1900, has been occupied with the care and improvement of his real estate. He owns and rents a number of houses. Mr. Murley is distinctly domestic in his tastes and belongs to few societies and organizations. He has been a member of the Ancient Order of Hibernians for thirty-five years, and is also a member of the Father Matthew Total Abstinence Society. He is a firm and consistent advocate of total abstinence, and he has exerted a good influence upon the community in his stand for temperance and morality.

Mr. Murley married, September, 1878, Helen O'Hearn, who was born in county Cork, Ireland, July 8, 1851, daughter of John O'-Hearn, a native of Ireland. Mr. and Mrs. Murley have no children. They are devout and loyal members of the Immaculate Roman Catholic church, and liberal contributors to their parish. Their home is at 10 Lexington street, Lawrence, Massachusetts.

LEONARD Owen Leonard was born in England of an ancient English family. He married Anna Smith, who was born in England, the daughter of Edward and Mary (Lynch) Smith. The family came to America about 1850 and settled in Haverhill, Massachusetts, where they resided the remainder of their days.

(II) Owen Leonard, son of Owen Leonard (1), was born in England. He came to America in his youth, landing in 1857 in New York city, where he learned the trade of marble cutter. From New York he came to Boston and thence about 1867 to Haverhill, Massachusetts. Here he entered the employ of Calvin Weeks, the marble cutter, and remained in this concern for a period of eighteen years. He was industrious and frugal, and wisely invested his savings in real estate in the city of Haverhill. His property increased in value with the growth of the city, and under his careful management produced for him an ample competence. For the past fifteen years the care and development of his real estate had engrossed all the time of Mr. Leonard, who is looked upon as an expert judge of the value of real estate. He is a useful citizen of sterling character, enjoying the respect and confidence of his townsmen to an unusual degree. In politics he is a Republican, but has taken no active part. In religion he is a Roman Catholic.

He married Mary E. Carney, born in Ireland. Children: 1. Mary E., born June, 1883, educated in the public and high schools of Haverhill and the State Normal school, and has been for the past four years a teacher in the public schools of her native city. 2. Alice E., educated in the public and high schools of Haverhill and in the State Normal school; married John Gorman, of that city. 3. John S., born November, 1886, educated in the Haverhill schools, employed at present at his trade of leather cutter, Haverhill.

DIGNAM Peter Dignam, late an esteemed resident of Lawrence, Massachusetts, was born in Ireland, October 8, 1821, and received his education in his native land. His father died when he was very young, and he found his way to England where he learned the art of nail sorting, in which he acquired great proficiency. Later he emigrated to America, settling in Lawrence, where he was one of the first workers in the Pacific Mills. He was active in business life until about five years prior to his death, when he retired. His political affiliations were with the Democratic party, in whose affairs he was an active worker. He was an earnest and prominent church member, of the Catholic persuasion, and took a great interest in financial matters. His death, which occurred January 30, 1898, was a particularly affecting one. He had left his home to attend Mass, and as he entered his pew in the church, laid down his glasses and prayer book and knelt in prayer, and while thus engaged his spirit passed away. His death was deeply deplored.

Mr. Dignam married, February 20, 1851, Catherine Masteison, of Woonsocket, who was also a native of Ireland. They had children: Edward, born August, 1852, died 1895; Michael, born November 27, 1853; James, born August, 1855, married Delia Landers, of New Bedford; Joseph T., born February 7, 1857, married Mary McCarthy, of Valley Fall, Rhode Island; Sarah Ann, born May 14, 1859; Catherine, born November 29, 1860, married John H. Parant, died 1895; Peter, Jr., born November 30, 1862; Francis, died young.

CAMPOPIANO Geremia Campopiano, son of Joseph and Maria-Giavanna Campopiano, grandson of Domènico, and great-grandson of Joseph Campopiano, was born September 27, 1863, in Marzanoa Appio, Provincia-di-Caserta, Italy. He received his education in the schools of his native place, and during his youth worked with his father on the farm. He joined the tide of immigration for America July 9, 1888, and upon reaching this country made his home first in Providence, Rhode Island, where he worked in various mills and foundries. He removed to Lawrence, Massachusetts, August 4, 1893, and found employment there in the great Washington mills. He embarked in business on his own account in 1903 as a real estate and insurance broker in Lawrence, and received from the governor of the commonwealth an appointment as notary public. He prospered and December 23, 1905, extended his business by engaging in the wholesale and retail liquor trade in Lawrence, continuing to the present time. He is one of the most influential and capable Italian-American citizens of the city of Lawrence. He was the founder of the Christopher Columbus Society of Lawrence, June 10, 1895, and was its president for the first five years. He is a member of the Benevolent and Protective Order of Elks. In religion he is a Roman Catholic.

He married, August 18, 1892, in Providence, Benedetta Leonardo, born January 29, 1872, daughter of Angelo Leonardo. Children: 1. Ciro, born May 6, 1893. 2. Joseph, born January 30, 1894. 3. William, born August 25, 1896. 4. Consiglia, born August 23, 1898.

SLEE The surname Slee, or Sly, is identical with Sleigh, according to "Patronimica Britannica." Originally it was doubtless a nickname, and implied unusual ability and cleverness, in accordance with the ancient meaning of the word sly. Shakespeare used Sly as a surname in "The Taming of the Shrew." The name appears as early as 1273 in the Hundred Rolls, at least twice—Richard Sle and John le Slege. The seat of the family in ancient times down to the present was Ashe, in Derbyshire. The coat-of arms of the Derbyshire family: Gules a chevron between three owls or. Other branches of the Sleigh family bore similar arms. One coat-of-arms belongs to the family spelling the name Slee: Vert a one-masted galley with oars in action sails furled or flags gules. Crest: A chapeau sable with a plume of three ostrich feathers in front. A family of Sley lived in Derbyshire, bearing the similar arms to the Sleighs of that county. A Slie family also bore the same arms.

(I) Samuel J. Slee, a descendant of the ancient English Slee, or Sly, family, was born in Liverpool, England, and was employed there during his active life as an officer in the British custom house. He married Alice Ivy. Children, born at Liverpool: Samuel J., mentioned below; Richard B.; Edwin; William Henry; Emily; Alice; Lily.

(II) Samuel J. Slee, eldest son of Samuel J. Slee, was born in Liverpool, England, May 22, 1827. He began early in life to follow the sea, and in course of time rose to the rank of master mariner and became owner of the vessel he sailed. After coming to this country he lived at Salem, Massachusetts, and at Philadelphia, Pennsylvania. He married Lydia Anderson, born March 17, 1833, in Halifax, Nova Scotia, daughter of James H. Anderson, a native of Scotland. She died July 21, 1892, and he died May 21, 1876. Their first two children were born in Salem, the others in Philadelphia: 1. Samuel J. 2. Lydia L., married at Salem, George W. Barnes, then of Philadelphia, now of Washington, District of Columbia. 3. Alice L. A., married Harry J. Bright, of Washington, D. C.; she is deceased. 4. Richard Boardman, resides in Washington. 5. James Henry, resides in Washington. 6. Charles Ackley, mentioned below. 7. Annie E.; married Dr. E. K. Harriman Gerow, of New York City. 8. Lillie A.; married Roscoe Wall, of Washington. 9. Amy A.; married Clarence Shraeder.

(III) Captain Charles Ackley Slee, son of Samuel J. Slee, was born in Philadelphia, August 9, 1867. He was educated in the public schools. He removed to Massachusetts and learned the drug business, and remained in it until 1891, when he entered the fire insurance office of the Hon. W. D. T. Trefry, of Marblehead, and has continued to the present time in this line, having assisted in building up a large business. He has also established a real estate agency in Marblehead, and by close application and strict attention to detail has developed an extensive and prosperous business. His thorough knowledge of the value of property in Marblehead and vicinity, his personal integrity and special attitude for this line of work, his wide acquaintance and popularity, have brought him to the front rank of fire insurance and real estate men of Essex county. He has taken a lively interest in public affairs, and has been honored with various positions of trust and responsibility. He was a member of the Marblehead school committee from 1904 to 1908 and its secretary for two years and a half. He was a member of the building committee in charge of the erection of the Samuel Rhoads, Jr., school house. He is a Democrat in politics, and has been secretary of the town committee and delegate to various nominating conventions of his party. He is a member of Philanthropic Lodge of Free Masons, and The Old Guard of Massachusetts. He is a member of St. Michael's Protestant Episcopal Church, has been vestryman, and since the death of Hon. Samuel Rhoads, Jr., has been the parish clerk. His military career is as follows: On January 9, 1891, he enlisted in the Second Corps of Cadets, and was discharged August 11, 1892. He was later in Company C, Eighth Regiment Massachusetts Volunteer Militia, of which he was elected second lieutenant, September 11, 1893; first lieutenant, March 27, 1896; and captain, October 30, 1896. He resigned his commission November 8, 1897. While he was in command, the Marblehead company had the pleasure of entertaining the officers of the United States cruiser "Marblehead." In military circles, in the Masonic order, in the church, in public life, Captain Slee has made many friends through his characteristic kindliness, courtesy and good nature. He married, September 5, 1889, Bella H. Gilley, born in Marblehead, daughter of Eben and Marietta Winslow Gilley, of Marblehead. Their only child is Ackly Roads, born June 14, 1892.

(See Hill family elsewhere in this work).

HILL The Hill family was among the first settlers of Madbury, New Hampshire, formerly part of Dover, where the family was established very early by John Hill. William Hill, Jr., the first in Madbury, was a taxpayer there as early as 1743. He married, August 21, 1729, at Dover, Patience Drew. His father, William Hill, born 1679, in Dover, married before 1723, Judith ———.

(I) Joseph Hill, descendant of John Hill, of Dover, and of William Hill, of Madbury, New Hampshire, mentioned above, was born at Madbury, New Hampshire, April 10, 1782. He married Sally Perkins, born in Dover, April 16, 1790. He settled in Newfield, Maine. Children: Joshua Perkins, born April 15, 1810, mentioned below; Joseph Shephard, John Quincy, Moses, Morris S., Rebecca, Huldah, Sarah, Almira, Aaron.

(II) Joshua Perkins Hill, son of Joseph Hill (1), born in Newfield, Maine, April 15, 1810, died May 24, 1904, at Methuen, Massachusetts, aged ninety-four years, one month and nine days. He settled in Pelham, New Hampshire. He married, in Pelham, March 17, 1836, Marian Richardson, who died in Methuen in 1860. He married, second, at Lynn, Massachusetts, December 25, 1862, Carrie A. Gowen. Children of first wife: 1. Joshua Eliot, born in Rockport, Massachusetts, May 16, 1838, carpenter, residing in Medford Hillside, Massachusetts; married, in Medford, Massachusetts, February 23, 1860, Sarah Louise Osgood. 2. Joseph Shepard, born April 2, 1844, at Methuen, Massachusetts, a hatter by trade; died unmarried in 1903. 3. Thomas Cummings, born in Methuen, October 15, 1845, a carpenter by trade, residing in Methuen; married, in 1869, Julia Pressey, who died July 4, 1871; married, second, December 25, 1871, Mrs. Elizabeth Merrill, who died February 27, 1880. 4. John Quincy Adams, born June 11, 1848, mentioned below. Children of second wife: 5. Charles F., born in Methuen, September 28, 1863, member of the city fire department, Providence, Rhode Island; married, September 15, 1886, in Medway, Massachusetts, Frances Ruthford. 6. Carrie M., born in Methuen, April 15, 1865, unmarried. 7. Sarah E., born in Methuen, February 18, 1867, married, June 16, 1888, Arthur G. Hopkins, of Worcester, Massachusetts. 8. Morris S., born in Methuen, February 28, 1869, resides in Pleasant Valley, Methuen; a farmer; married, January 1, 1896, Mabel Shetler. 9. Mary P., born in Methuen, September 8, 1871, married, at Lawrence, December, 1891, Orren Everett Lowell. 10. Dolly Ann, born in Methuen, July 6, 1875, married June 22, 1907, in Lowell, Frank Davis. 11. Eben, born in Methuen, January 20, 1878, resides with brother Morris; married, October 26, 1904, in Providence, Clara Butler. 12. Sherburne, born February 22, 1882, married, September 26, 1907, Martha ———, in New York City.

(III) John Quincy Adams Hill, son of Joshua Perkins Hill (2), was born in Methuen, June 11, 1848. He was educated in the district school of Methuen. At the age of eleven years he began to work for his father on his milk route, and at the age of sixteen enlisted in Company C, Fifth Regiment, Massachusetts Volunteer Militia, under Captain George F. Barnes, and served his term of enlistment in the civil war. Soon after the war he engaged in the teaming business, established an ice business on Mystic pond, and with the exception of two years has been in the ice business to the present time. At present he is in partnership with his nephew, Bennie E., son of his brother, Thomas Cummings Hill. Mr. Hill has been a dealer in wood and lumber for many years. He has cut much timber in Salem, New Hampshire, an adjoining town. Mr. Hill is also a stockholder in the Elk River Milling Company,

Minnesota, and is a director and vice-president. He is a member of Hope and of Rebekah lodges of Odd Fellows; Hancock Lodge of Free Masons, of which he is a past master; Colonel William B. Greene Post, No. 100, Grand Army, of which he has been commander; Knights of Pythias of Methuen; Methuen Grange, Patrons of Husbandry; Association of Veteran Firemen; of the Home Club. In politics he is a Republican. He is an attendant of the Universalist church. He married, December 13, 1871, Sylvia Cordelia Crofut, born November 8, 1849, at New Fairfield, Connecticut, daughter of Nathan B. and Julia (Brisco) Crofut. Her mother was a native of Newton, Connecticut. Her father was born November 12, 1800, in Danbury, Connecticut, and died July 23, 1877. Mr. Crofut was a hatter by trade, a maker of fur and wool hats. He spent nine years in farming in Illinois, returning to Methuen in 1871, and followed his trade until within three years of his death, when his health prevented him. He was a Universalist in religion, and a faithful member of the church and regular attendant upon its services.

JOHNSON

Samuel Allen Johnson, sheriff of Essex county, Massachusetts, has served in that position continuously since 1892, and has been connected with the sheriff's office altogether for over thirty years. His eminent fitness for its duties has been demonstrated in the discharge of many important commissions. He is a native of Salem, born July 31, 1847, son of Samuel S. and Elizabeth (Allen) Johnson, and is descended on both sides from old New England stock.

On the paternal side Mr. Johnson belongs to the Johnson family of Stafford Springs, Connecticut, the progenitor of which in America was John Johnson, who was from Boston or vicinity in the county of Lincoln, England, coming to this country with Governor Winthrop. He brought with him his wife and family, and settled in Roxbury, in which town he became a man of considerable distinction. In 1630 he was chosen constable, was many times a representative in the Colonial Assembly, etc. Isaac Johnson, son of the settler, came with his father to this country and to Roxbury; was made a freeman in 1635; was captain of artillery company; representative, etc. He was killed in the great Swamp fight, Dcember 19, 1675. He married Elizabeth Porter. Nathaniel Johnson, son of Isaac, born in 1647, married in 1667, Mary Smith. He became one of the first settlers of what is now Woodstock, Connecticut, which town was settled by Roxbury families in 1686-87, and was then called New Roxbury, and was prominent in the affairs of the new town. It is likely that Samuel Allen Johnson, of Salem, is descended from this source.

One Aholiab Johnson, son of John, and descendant of the emigrant, born March 18, 1762, was twice married— first, September 22, 1785, to Hannah Bacon, who died in Stafford, September 15, 1796; second, April 19, 1798, to Dolly Converse, of Stafford.

The Johnson family of Stafford, Connecticut, it is said originated in Scotland, and through every generation from the first in the town has displayed those traits which have contributed to the success of the native-born of that country in every locality and position in which they are found. We have further record of these Johnsons, as follows:

One Nathaniel Johnson married first, Huldah Hammond (marriage of Vernon town record); second, Martha Washburn, daughter of Solomon and Martha (Orcutt) Washburn, of Bridgewater, Massachusetts.

Ebenezer Johnson, son of Nathaniel, born in Stafford, Connecticut, April 9, 1759, died there April 2, 1817. He married Mary Edson, born June 22, 1767, who died January 5, 1848. They were farming people of Stafford, and reared a large family, which became connected by marriage with many of the oldest and best families of New England. Their children were: Clarissa, born February 7, 1785; Celia, September 23, 1787; Mary, October 26, 1788; Cyril, July 24, 1791; Marcia, November 20, 1793; Selinda, December 29, 1798; Nathaniel, October 15, 1801; Timothy Edson, June 1, 1804; Louisa, August 27, 1807; Ebenezer Joy, May 28, 1810. (N. B. It is likely Nathaniel first named descended from John, of Roxbury).

On the maternal side Sheriff Johnson is descended from Chester Allen, son of one of the first settlers of Sturbridge, and Anna Rice, of Belchertown. Of the Allen family we have the following record:

(I) James Allen came to Dedham about 1637, and took the freeman's oath in 1647. He went to Medfield with the first thirteen settlers, and drew his house lot on South street. In 1638 he married at Dedham, Ann Guild, who died in 1673. He died in 1676.

(II) Joseph Allen lived in the north part of Medfield. He was twenty-one years of age in 1673, and then had a grant of land. He married, in 1673, Hannah Sabin.

(III) Daniel Allen, born in 1681, settled in Pomfret, Connecticut, and his brother David, born in 1683, settled in Ashford, Connecticut.

(III) Joseph Allen (2), born in 1676, settled on North street, in Medfield. In 1701 he married Miriam Wight.

(IV) Moses Allen, son of Joseph (2), born in 1708, went to Sturbridge, as did also his brother Aaron, who was born in 1715. He was in Sturbridge in 1740. He had previously lived in Dedham.

(III) Nehemiah Allen, son of Joseph and grandson of James, was born in 1699, and married Mary Parker. They were in Sherborn, 1723-1741, and in Sturbridge in 1745.

The town of Sturbridge was originally settled by a company of emigrants, chiefly from Medfield and a few other towns in that vicinity, and in about 1729, as a grant was made from its settlement in September of that year. This was for a time called New Medfield. There were forty-two original proprietors to the town when the grant was made, and soon thereafter Nehemiah and Moses Allen were among others admitted into partnership.

Samuel Allen Johnson received his literary education in Wisconsin, attending the public schools of Beloit, and fitting for college at the Beloit College Preparatory School. He also took part of a course at that college, as a member of the class of 1869, but was obliged to relinquish his plan of pursuing the full course because of failing eyesight. Soon after leaving college, Mr. Johnson began the study of law in the office of Todd & Converse, in Beloit, continuing thus for about a year, after which for two years he traveled in the far west and in Europe. In the autumn of 1870 he returned to Salem, and again took up the study of law, with Hon. William D. Northend, being admitted to the bar of Essex county, October 3, 1871. After that he remained in the office with Mr. Northend, until May, 1872, when he formed a partnership with Dean Peabody, at that time one of the leading practitioners of Lynn, Massachusetts, for legal practice. Mr. Peabody has since served many years as clerk of the courts of Essex county. Mr. Johnson was in practice in Lynn until May, 1875, when a severe and prolonged illness caused his withdrawal from professional labors, and he sought health and strength in Colorado, where he remained until July, 1876. Returning to his old home in Salem, he decided to abandon his profession on the advice of his physician, who told him it would not be wise to attempt to follow his chosen calling if he expected to keep his health. The following December he took an appointment as deputy sheriff, serving as such until he was elected sheriff in 1892. He was engaged much of the time as special sheriff, and his record of service has been irreproachable and highly satisfactory to all concerned. He has held no other elective office, nor has he ever sought such preferment.

Mr. Johnson was lieutenant colonel and commander of the Second Corps of Cadets of Salem, of which body he was a member for over twenty-five years, having joined in April, 1874. He has passed through all the various grades up to the rank of lieutenant colonel, being retired with the rank of colonel, given him unsolicited by Governor Wolcott. He is also an active member of various fraternal organizations, being especially well known in the Masonic order as a member of Essex Lodge, Washington Royal Arch Chapter, Winslow Lewis Commandery, and Sutton Grand Lodge of Perfection, all of Salem, as well as Aleppo Temple, Mystic Shrine, of Boston. He also belongs to Essex Lodge, Independent Order of Odd Fellows, also having been a member of Naumkeag Encampment; to John Endicott Lodge, Ancient Order United Workmen; and to Naumkeag Tribe, Improved Order of Red Men. In political connection he is a staunch Republican.

On November 17, 1872, Mr. Johnson was married to Eliza A. Fitz, daughter of Daniel P. Fitz, of Salem. She passed away February 1, 1885, the mother of two children: Nellie M., born September 2, 1873, married Alfred J. Paul, of Boston, a wholesale jeweler, member of the firm of Paul & Company, they have one child Barbara; Chester Allen, born March 28, 1879, married Florence Webb, of Saratoga Springs, New York, he is receiving teller of the old Colony Trust Company, Boston. On October 5, 1886, Mr. Johnson married (second), Miss Lily J. Shannon, of New York City, and they have one child, Mary Hilda, born January 30, 1891.

ROWE The surname Rowe or Roe is very ancient, derived in the same way as Doe, Stagg, Hinds, and from the use of John Doe and Richard Rowe as anonymous legal persons, it is likely that the name was pretty common at an early date.

(I) John Rowe, immigrant ancestor, born in England, came to Gloucester, Massachusetts, before 1651, and settled in that part known as the farms. He bought land there in 1651 of Thomas Drake, and was the first settler in a lonely and isolated spot. He had difficulties with his townsmen, however, and seems far from satisfied with his farm, for June 26, 1656, he was presented in court for "saying if his wife were off his mind he would set his house on fire and run away by ye light and ye devil should take ye farme and speaking the same a second time added he would live no longer among such a company of hellhounds." For thus relieving his mind he was fined twenty shillings and ordered to make a confession at the next town meeting in Gloucester. He died March 9, 1662. His inventory amounted to two hundred and five pounds sixteen shillings ten pence. His widow Bridget married November 14, 1662, William Coleman; she died May 2, 1680. Children: John, Hugh.

(II) John Rowe, son of John Rowe, was born about 1640; died at Gloucester, September 25, 1700. He inherited part of his father's homestead, and lived there. He married first, September 27, 1663, Mary Dickinson, who died April 25, 1684, daughter of John Dickinson, of Salisbury; second, September, 1684, Sarah, daughter of Abraham Redington, who mentions her in his will. She died at Gloucester, February 15, 1701. Children, born at Gloucester: 1. John, April 6, 1665, died November, 1680. 2. James, born December 25, 1666. 3. Thomas, November 26, 1668; married January 8, 1696, Sarah Brown. 4. Mary, February 11, 1670. 5. Elizabeth, May 21, 1673. 6. Stephen, November 26, 1675; mentioned below. 7. Samuel, March 26, 1678. 8. Ebenezer, August 19, 1680; died September 24, 1692. 9. Andrew, born December 31, 1683; died August 15, 1700. 10. Benjamin, born August 1, died October 24, 1685. 11. Sarah, born March 28, 1689, died August 21, 1700. 12. John, born December 20, 1691; died August 29, 1700. 13. Rebecca, born July 21, 1694.

(III) Stephen Rowe, son of John Rowe, was born in Gloucester, November 26, 1675; married there, July 6, 1699, Martha Low, who died December 4, 1718; second, April 28, 1731, Elizabeth Cumey, who lived to a great age. Of his fifteen children, eleven were living at the time of his death. Children, born at Gloucester: 1. Susanna, married August 19, 1717, William Millbury. 2. Sarah, died young. 3. Stephen, died young. 4. Martha, married November 29, 1723, Benjamin Boynton. 5. Sarah, married December 7, 1735, John Winnery. 6. John, died young. 7. Stephen, born December 25, 1709; married December 31, 1731, Mercy Day. 8. Elizabeth. 9. John, mentioned below. 10. Thomas. 11. Joseph. 12. Benjamin. 13. David. 14. Jonathan.

(IV) Lieutenant John Rowe, son of Stephen Rowe, was born in Gloucester, June 28, 1714; died October 2, 1781. He settled at Sandy Bay, Gloucester. He was a lieutenant of the Gloucester company in 1755, and served in the French and Indian war. He married first, November 11, 1736, Mary Baker, died about 1752, daughter of Jabez Baker; second, June 16, 1752, Abigail Langsford, who died of small pox, December 15, 1779. Some accounts say he had sixteen children, and Babson states that the births of ten are to be found on the town records. Those given and known are: 1. Ebenezer, died young. 2. Jabez, died young. 3. Daniel, mentioned below. 4. Jabez, born July 1740. 5. John, born 1747; captain in the revolution; was with his son John in battle of Bunker Hill; was taken prisoner during the revolution; afterward major of militia. 6. Ebenezer, born August 13, 1750, resided at Georgetown, Maine. 7. Isaac, born December 31, 1751. 8. Lucy, baptized at Boxford, November 16, 1752 (residence of parents, John and Abigail, given as Cape Ann).

(V) Daniel Rowe, son or nephew of John Rowe, was born at Gloucester, and lived in that part now the town of Rockport, Massachusetts. He appears to be the Daniel Rowe who served in the revolution in the Continental army for nine months, enlisting December 8, 1779, and credited to the town of Gloucester, the return being dated at Boxford, near which Rowe seems to have lived. He was also in Colonel Michael Jackson's regiment (Eighth Essex County). He married Mary Knutchford, born in Rockport, daughter of Stephen K. Knutchford, a native of London, England, who died in Rockport, then Gloucester, married Mary Andrews. The family tradition has it that the father of Stephen Knutchford was an English lord, and that Stephen, the eldest son, was bought a commission in the English navy. He came to America on the admiral's ship, and when the vessel was at Gloucester was ordered by the admiral to go ashore and forage for vegetables and fruit. Knutchford refused to obey, and by order of the admiral had his shoulder straps cut off and was rowed ashore stern first—a signal disgrace in the English navy. It was during the revolution, and at the first house he inquired for the Continental army, and received his reply from the girl whom he married subsequently. He enlisted and fought to the end of the revolution in the American army. After the war he returned to Gloucester, cleared a small farm there, married and for many years taught the village school. The story is a charming bit of colonial romance, and doubtless correct in the essentials. In his garden Knutchford had an excellent orchard of fruit trees and he raised fowls. His children were: i. Thomas Knutchford; ii. John Knutchford; iii. Stephen Knutchford; iv. William Knutchford; v. Mary Knutchford, married Daniel Rowe, mentioned above; vi. Sallie, married William Tarr; vii. daughter, married ——— Dennison. Daniel Rowe was a member of the Congregational church. He was a fisherman by trade, and was in the employ of one man for a period of forty years.

Children of Daniel and Mary (Knutchford) Rowe: 1. Daniel, married Sophia Poole; lived in Boothbay, Maine; followed the sea, going on foreign trips in winter and on fishing trips in summer; died at sea. 2. Mary, married George Wainwright, of Rockport. 3. Lucy, married Nathaniel Foster. 4. Susan, married first, Huston Oakes; second, Thomas O. Marshal. 5. Charlotte, married Moses Poole. 6. Stephen Knutchford, mentioned below.

(VI) Stephen Knutchford Rowe, son of Daniel Rowe, was born in Rockport, formerly Sandy Bay, in Gloucester, lived and died there. He married Hannah Poole. He was educated in the common schools of his native town. He followed the sea in his younger days, on fishing trips mainly. He kept a general store in Rockport, and in his absence the business was managed by his wife. He learned the trade of carpenter, and stone cutter, but ill health prevented him following either trade. He was a well-known and very influential citizen, a Democrat in politics, tax collector many years. He was one of the founders and principal supporters of the Universalist church at Rockport, though his wife remained a member of the Congregational church. Children: 1. Charlotte, died young. 2. William Turner, mentioned below.

(VII) William Turner Rowe, son of Stephen Knutchford Rowe, was born in Rockport, January 26, 1840. He was educated for the most part in Ezekiel Bradstreet's school in his native town. He began at the age of twelve to follow the sea as a fisherman, summer and winter. In 1880 he removed to Beverly and took up the trade of shoemaking, not wishing to have his sons become fishermen. He has worked in the various shoe factories of Beverly to the present time. He is interested in public affairs, a Jeffersonian Democrat, in political belief, holding to the righteousness of a tariff for revenue only. He is a Unitarian in religion. He has held no public offices aad delongs to no lodges or secret organizations. He resides in North Beverly. He married, in 1863, Mary Augusta Griffen, born at Annisquam, daughter of Moses L. and Sarah E. (Butler) Griffen. His wife died at Beverly June 2, 1905. Children: 1. William Augustus, born July, 1865, at Lanesville, on Cape Ann; educated in public schools of Gloucester and Beverly; went to live with his grandfather in Lynn at an early age; was for a time in the bicycle and hardware business, now in the automobile business in Beverly; a Congregationalist in religion; married first, Alice Ayres of Lynn; second, Etta Alexander; residing at North Beverly; child of first wife, Alice. 2. George Ellis Rowe, mentioned below.

(VIII) George Ellis Rowe, son of William Turner Rowe, was born September 23, 1867, in Lanesville, and educated in the public schools of Gloucester and Beverly. He learned the trade of shoemaker. He was employed by the firm of Millett, Woodbury & Company, the largest shoe manufacturers of the town of Beverly, rose to a position of responsibility in the business and was finally admitted to partnership. He is interested in municipal affairs, a Republican in national politics and a citizen of influence and public spirit. He is a member of Liberty Lodge, Free Masons, of Beverly; of the Chapter, Council and Commandery. Mr. Rowe married, November, 1889, Martha Ellen Bell, daughter of Samuel and Mary Elizabeth (Pickett) Bell, of Beverly, and granddaughter of John Bell, also of Beverly. Children, born at Beverly: 1. Martha Pickett, born September 7, 1890. 2. Phillip Kendall, born March 16, 1898. (See Bell).

BELL Robert Bell, immigrant ancestor, came to Beverly, Massachusetts, when a young man and married there November 7, 1717. But one child is recorded, Samuel, mentioned below, but he was doubtless the father also of John Bell, of Beverly.

(II) Samuel Bell, son of Robert Bell, was born at Beverly, Massachusetts, April 27, 1719.

(IV) John Bell, grandson of Samuel Bell,

was born April 2, 1795. He married, December 1, 1814, Betsey Friend, who died February 12, 1849. Children, born in Beverly: 1. Elizabeth, April 5, 1815, married November 30, 1837, Luther Wallis. 2. Mary, February 26, 1817; married, May 6, 1843. 3. Caroline, February 27, 1819; died June 20, 1827 or 28. 4. John, February 10, 1823; married November 21, 1841, Mary Ann Baker; children: i. John William, born March 24, 1842; ii. Emmeline, born January 17, 1847; iii. Caroline, born October 17, 1849. 5. Augusta, born March 23, 1823; married August 12, 1845, Elnathan Dodge, of New Boston, New Hampshire. 6. Ann Maria, born March 14, 1825. 7. Samuel, born June 8, 1827; died June 21 following. 8. Samuel, born July 21, 1828, mentioned below. 9. George Walcott, born January 9, 1831. 10. Caroline, born July 27, 1833; died October 3, 1849. 11. William Henry, born July 27, 1835. 12. Caroline, baptized July 2, 1837. 13. Clarissa Friend, born October 9, 1838.

(V) Samuel Bell, son of John Bell, was born at Beverly, July 21, 1828, and died in his native town. He married Mary Elizabeth Pickett, born 1832, at Beverly, daughter of Josiah and Mary (Cressey) Pickett. Her mother was born September, 1799, and died June 9, 1879. He was a shoemaker by trade. He attended the First Universalist Church Death cut short his promising career and he was sincerely mourned. Children of Josiah and Mary Pickett: i. General Josiah Pickett, born November 21, 1822, distinguished in the civil war; postmaster of Worcester; died 1907; ii. John William, born December 30, 1824, married Susan H. Tucker; iii. Charles, born December 12, 1826; iv. Mary Howard, born February 3, 1830, died September 25, 1833; v. Sarah Frances, married Dewing Southwick; vi. Mary Elizabeth, married Samuel Bell, mentioned above; vii. Martha, married James H. Kendall; viii. George Augustus, married Agnes C. Munsey; ix. Hepzibah Ann, married Charles L. Woodbury and Charles Friend.

Thomas Pickett, father of Josiah, was born at Beverly, June 27, 1750; sailmaker by trade; married Miriam, daughter of Samuel and Mary Striker; she died in Beverly, August 23, 1839. Thomas Pickett (3) father of Thomas Pickett (4), was baptized July 17, 1719-20, and was lost at sea about 1753; married Sarah Trevett, granddaughter of Henry Trevett, of Marblehead, the immigrant ancestor. John Pickett (2), father of Thomas (3), was born about 1680; died May 1763, a fisherman and shoreman, of Marblehead; married, January 17, 1704, Elizabeth Kelley, daughter of John and Grace Kelley; second, October 31, 1721, Elizabeth Savory. The immigrant ancestor of the Pickett family was Nicholas Pickett, who came to Marblehead as early as 1670; married a daughter of John Northay.

Children of Samuel and Mary Elizabeth (Pickett) Bell: 1. Charles. 2. Mary Ella, died aged twenty-one years. 3. Frank. 4. Arthur, married Mary Gately. 5. Frederick, born July 17, 1864; married Lucy F. Slater, June 9, 1887; she was born March 14, 1865, and died March 9, 1889; child: i. Mary Elizabeth; he married second, September 30, 1890, Elizabeth K. Slater and had: ii. Lucy Slater, born August 1, 1891; iii. Bessie, married Edwin Dodd; iv. Sadie, deceased; v. Martha, married George E. Rowe (see Rowe); vi. Willis, married ——— Caldwell; vii. Samuel P., married Cora Flanders.

VAUGHN Ira Vaughn (1), with whom this narrative must begin, and of whom no other record appears, is said to have been born in New Vineyard, Maine, and was a wheelwright by trade, owner of a gristmill, and a reasonably successful man in a business way. It is said too that he was a musician of considerable talent for his time and generation, one who could make a good instrument as well as good music; a bass viol made by him a century or more ago is still in the possession of one of his descendants. The name of the immediate ancestor of Ira Vaughn has been a source of perplexity to genealogists as well as to various of his descendants, and various theories and suggestions have been offered respecting the subjects. By reason of circumstances, residence and various relationships it has been assumed that he was born in New Vineyard, but this may be an error, and whether so or not there is reason for the opinion that he may have been born in Vermont and of kin to the three brothers—Benjamin, John and James Vaughan, the famous soldiers of the revolution, the first of whom enlisted in Shoreham, 1778, in Captain Gideon Ormsby's company, Colonel Ira Allen's regiment. In 1781 all three of these brothers were in Captain Jacob Odell's company, Colonel Allen's regiment. If this theory is correct Ira Vaughn was a grandson of Christopher Vaughan, Jr., who was born in East Greenwich, Rhode Island, 1710, son of Christopher Vaughan, born in England, about 1615, and was of Watertown, Massachusetts, 1633, and afterward of Providence, Rhode Island. Ira Vaughn married first, Abigail Luce Johnson, who died May 21, 1830; second, January 18, 1831, Emely Johnson, by whom he had one son, Joseph Warren Vaughn; married third, Mary Cutts, born July 22, 1810, and by her had two children: 1. Elisha Cutts, born in New Vineyard, December 6, 1840, went to Tacoma, Washington; married in 1862, Mary L., eldest daughter of Captain William Took, a '49er on the Pacific coast, and one of the pioneer traders on the Columbia river and Puget Sound. 2. Ira, Jr., born in New Vineyard or Farmington, Maine.

(II) Joseph Warren Vaughn, only son of Ira and Emely (Johnson) Vaughan, was born in New Vineyard or Farmington, and died in Salem, Massachusetts. He changed the family name from its original form of Vaughan to Vaughn, after his removal to Peabody. He was a natural mechanic, and his inventive genius ultimately gained him a fortune, although when he first came to Massachusetts he was for some time proprietor of a grist mill in Peabody. After leaving the mill he turned his attention to mechanical pursuits, chiefly to the invention of appliances and machines designed to overcome certain difficulties constantly met with in the manufacture of leather, and which he believed could be removed by mechanical devices. His first notable success in this direction was in the construction of a putting-out machine, the returns from which enabled him to establish the Vaughn Machine Company, of Peabody, which afterward under the capable management of his sons was developed into an industry of large proportions and ultimately passed to the ownership of the Turner Tanning Machinery Company. But this is only a single one of Mr. Vaughn's several patented devices which gave him a wide reputation and yielded a fortune in return for his patient and intelligent efforts, and as well had the effect to practically revolutionize the leather manufacturing process. He seemed to enjoy the successful operation of his machines fully as much as their substantial returns, and while he came to be recognized as an inventor of remarkable genius, his prominence never had the effect to make him vain of his achievement, and he always was the same agreeable companionable man as in the days when he worked at the bench to gain a livelihood. During the civil war he served a nine months' enlistment in a Maine regiment, and was a comrade of the Grand Army of the Republic. In religious preference he was a Baptist, in politics a Republican, and a member of North Star Lodge, F. and A. M., of New Portland, Maine. Mr. Vaughn married first, Martha Cutts, daughter of George and Anna (Metcalf) Cutts (see Cutts); second, Dolly C. Robbins, of Pittston, Maine. Children, all born of his first marriage: 1. Mary Emily, November 19, 1857; married Melville Woodbury; lives in Beverly. 2. Maria Frances, born in North Portland, Maine; married John Rollins, and had Oliver H. Rollins. 3. George Cutts, born in Anson, Maine; married Annie Groce, and had Dwight W., G. Parke and Gordon; married second, Bessie Dane, and had two children. 4. Ira. 5. Charles Parker; married Fannie W. Thomas, and had Catherine Nelson and Barbara Thomas. 6. Martha.

(III) Ira Vaughn, more frequently known in military circles as Major Vaughn, is a native of New Portland, Maine, born August 9, 1864, son of Joseph Warren and Martha (Cutts) Vaughn. His younger life was spent chiefly in Peabody, Massachusetts, where he attended the public schools, and where after attaining his majority he acquired an interest in the business of the Vaughn Machine Company, and after the death of his father the company and its plant passed to the ownership and management of his sons and continued in successful operation until 1901, when it was sold. About the same time Major Vaughn and his brother Charles purchased the Dungan Hood & Company leather manufacturing establishment in Philadelphia, and have since operated its extensive business, with principal offices and sales department in Boston. Major Vaughn is a thorough business man, with a wide acquaintance in leather manufacturing and trade circles in general, and he also enjoys a large acquaintance among officials of the administration department of the state government, especially in connection with affairs of the Massachusetts volunteer militia. As aide-de-camp on the staff of Governor Guild, with the rank of major, he has been always a participant in the functions which fall to the lot of staff officers of rank on public occasions. He was reappointed November 30, 1908, by Governor Draper. For many years he was a member of the Second Corps Cadets, Salem, first as quartermaster, then paymaster and afterward as captain of Company C. He is a 32d degree Mason; member of Essex Lodge F. and A. M., past high priest, Washington Chapter, R. A. M.; past master, Salem Council, R. and S. M.; past commander, Winslow Lewis Commandery, No. 18, K. T.; member of Sutton Lodge of Perfection, A. A. S. R.; member of the Salem Club, and member and president of the Colonial Club. On October 9, 1890, Mr. Vaughn married Hannah Nelson Thomas, of Peabody, Massachusetts. Their children: 1. Joseph Warren, born in Salem, November 9, 1892, died April 27, 1900. 2. Olive, born in Salem, November 3, 1901.

CUTTS (I) Robert Cutts, one of three immigrant brothers—John, Richard and Robert—came to America from England with their sister Anne before 1646. Robert went first to the Barbadoes, West Indies, and sailed thence for New England, where he lived for a time at Great Island (Portsmouth), New Hampshire, and from there removed to Kittery, Maine. In the West Indies he married Mary Hoel, a young English woman, and by her he had children: Richard, Elizabeth, Bridget, Sarah, Mary, Robert.

(II) Richard Cutts, son of Robert and Mary (Hoel) Cutt, married, 1686, Joanna, daughter of Thomas and Lucia (Treworgye) Wills; children: 1. Robert, born November 13, 1687. 2. Elizabeth, November 25, 1689. 3. Mary, February 18, 1697, died young. 4. Thomas, April 15, 1700. 5. Bridget, December 13, 1702. 6. Lucia, April 23, 1705. 7. Edward, July 9, 1707. 8. Samuel, September 21, 1709. 9. Joseph, April 22, 1713. 10. Joanna, April 14, 1715.

(III) Deacon Thomas Cutts, son of Richard and Joanna (Wills) Cutt, was born April 15, 1700. He was the first deacon of the Congregational church in the middle parish of Kittery, which was built in 1749; and he outlived half of his children, dying in 1795, aged ninety-five years. His descendants are spoken of as the Spruce creek branch. He married, April 23, 1724, Dorcas, daughter of Judge Joseph and Hannah (Stover) Hammond; children: 1. Mary, born April 30, 1726. 2. Lucy, May 26, 1728. 3. John, August 28, 1730. 4. Thomas, November 23, 1732. 5. Robert, September 19, 1734. 6. Joseph, August 2, 1736. 7. Hannah, April 23, 1740. 8. Samuel, September 20, 1744.

(IV) Samuel Cutts, son of Deacon Thomas and Dorcas (Hammond) Cutts, was born September 20, 1744, and married October 15, 1767, Sarah, daughter of Judge John and Mary (Plaisted) Hill; children: 1. Mary, born July 30, 1768, died September 17, 1855; married first, Enoch Billings; second, Jabez Bradbury. 2. Sarah, March 23, 1770, died December 21, 1860; married December 5, 1803, William Stevens. 3. Hannah, July 11, 1772, died November 17, 1854; married first, Robert Clark; second, Philip Fowler. 4. Thomas, born March 30, 1775. 5. Samuel, August 2, 1777, died October 1, 1853; married November 2, 1806, Catherine Woodward. 6. Elisha, August 1, 1780, died 1841; married, 1802, Hannah Hooper. 7. Robert, November 14, 1782, died December 23, 1810. 8. Betsey, January 20, 1785, died July 1, 1869; married April 23, 1807, Joseph Flitner. 9. Dorcas, August 23, 1787, died July 3, 1879; married July 8, 1816, Isaac Lapham. 10. Abigail, September 23, 1790, died April 25, 1870; married October 20, 1810, ——— Jackson.

(V) Thomas Cutts, son of Samuel and Sarah (Hill) Cutts, was born March 30, 1775, and died March 2, 1857. He married, November 30, 1797, Sarah, daughter of Oliver and Margaret (Burns) Colburn; children: 1. Samuel, born October 21, 1798, died 1864; married December 26, 1823, Dolly Bray. 2. Thomas, July 3, 1800, died June 2, 1819. 3. Dorcas, May 15, 1802; married December 29, 1824, Joseph Luce. 4. William, August 19, 1804, died September 27, 1850; married September 12, 1830, Rachel Jackson. 5. Abigail, May 31, 1806; married December 11, 1823, Sewell Rand. 6. George, May 24, 1808. 7. James, August 11, 1810; married January 28, 1834, Olive Colburn. 8. Sarah Ann, August 12, 1812, died June 2, 1888, married February, 1834, Oliver Robbins. 9. Oliver, March 5, 1815, died February 16, 1885; married August 4, 1840, Hannah Cutts.

(VI) George Cutts, son of Thomas and Sarah (Colburn) Cutts, was born May 24, 1808, and married April 2, 1829, Anna, daughter of John and Sarah (Fletcher) Metcalf; children: George B., John, Oliver, Sarah and Martha.

(VII) Martha Cutts, daughter of George and Anna (Metcalf) Cutts, married Joseph Warren Vaughn, his first wife (see Vaughn).

(V) Elisha Cutts, son of Samuel and Sarah (Hill) Cutts, was born August 1, 1780, died October 1, 1853, and married, in 1807, Hannah Hooper; children: 1. Robert, born August 24, 1804; married Anna Dorr. 2. Enoch Billings, October 4, 1806; married Lucretia Gray. 3. William, May 16, 1808; married Elizabeth Aldrich. 4. Mary, July 22, 1810. 5. Sarah Ann, October 5, 1815, married Oliver Cutts. 7. Elisha, January 21, 1819; married Eliza Lincoln. 8. Samuel.

(VI) Mary Cutts, daughter of Elisha and Hannah (Hooper) Cutts, was born July 22, 1810, and married Ira Vaughn (see Vaughn).

WASHBURN This family name is derived from two simple words—wash, which applies to the swift moving current of a stream, and burn or bourne, a brook or small stream. It has been said of the family, whose origin is in England, carrying a coat-of-arms, that the posterity of John Washburn, who was the first emigrant to locate in New England in 1632, "will seldom find occasion to blush upon looking back upon the past lives of those from whom they have descended. Fortunate indeed may the generations now in being, esteem themselves, if they can be sure to bequeath to their posterity an equal source of felicitation." In this illustrious family have been found some of our nations's greatest characters, in public and private life, statesmen and military men in all of the American wars. Maine, Vermont, Massachusetts and Winconsin have all had governors from the Washburn family, and three brothers served as congressmen from three states at the same time, and all with much ability. Authors and college graduates may be found to a score or more, who have left their impress upon the world. In England a John Washburn was the first secretary of the council of Plymouth, and was succeeded in office in 1628 by William Burgess; but it is not known that he was identical with John Washburn, of Duxbury, in 1632; nor is it known that the New England Washburns, the descendants of John, were of kin to William, Daniel and John Washburn who had land on Long Island as early as 1653, but whose names soon afterwards disappeared from the records there.

(I) John Washburn, immigrant ancestor, settled in Duxbury, Massachusetts, in 1632. In that year he had an action in court against Edward Doten. He was a taxpayer in 1633. In 1634 he bought of Edward Bompasse a place beyond the creek called Eagle's Nest. He with his sons John and Philip were on the list of those able to bear arms in 1643. He and his son John were among the original fifty-four proprietors of Bridgewater in 1645. They bought the lands of the old Sachem, Massasoit, for seven coats of one and a half yards each, nine hatchets, twenty knives, four moose skins, ten and a half yards of cotton cloth. The transfer was signed by Miles Standish, Samuel Nash and Constant Southworth. He died at Bridgewater in 1670. John Washburn married Margery ———. Children: 1. John, mentioned below. 2. Philip, born 1624, died unmarried.

(II) John Washburn, son of John Washburn, was born in England in 1621, and married Elizabeth Mitchell, daughter of Experience Mitchell, as shown by a letter from Thomas Mitchell, who made his will in 1686, dated Amsterdam, July 24, 1662, to his Uncle Experience. John Washburn sold in 1670 his house and lands at Green's Harbor, Duxbury, which his father had given him. His son John was executor of his will in 1679, and John Tomson and Edward Mitchell were overseers. Children: 1. John, married Rebecca Latham. 2. Thomas, mentioned below. 3. Joseph, married Hannah Latham and resided in East Bridgewater. 4. Samuel, married Deborah Packard. 5. Benjamin, died on the Phipps expedition to Canada; nuncupative will executed in 1690. 7. Mary, married, 1694, Samuel Kingsley. 8. Elizabeth, married first, James Howard; second, Edward Sealey. 9. Jane, married William Orcutt Jr. 10. James, married Mary Bowden. 11. Sarah, married, 1697, John Ames.

(III) Thomas Washburn, son of John Washburn, resided in Bridgewater near the present site of the Bazell & Perkins works. He married, first, Abigail Leonard, daughter of Jacob Leonard. He married, second, Deliverance Packard, daughter of Samuel Packard. His will was made in 1729. Children: 1. Nathaniel. 2. Thomas. 3. Timothy, mentioned below. 4. Hepzibah, married, 1708, John Hutchinson. 5. Patience, died before 1708. 6. Deliverance, married, 1719, Ephraim Jennings. 7. Elizabeth, married, 1701, Josiah Conant.

(IV) Timothy Washburn, son of Thomas Washburn, was a tanner by trade. He resided in Bridgewater and bought land in 1720 at Poor Meadow of Ebenezer Washburn Jr. He married Hannah ———. Children, born at Bridgewater: 1. Timothy, mentioned below. 2. Hannah, born 1724. 3. Mary, born 1725.

(V) Timothy Washburn, son of Timothy Washburn, was born in Bridgewater, 1721, and went in 1740 to Kennebunkport, Maine. He settled in that part of the town which is now Arundel. He married Sarah Miller. Children, born at Kennebunkport: 1. David, mentioned below. 2. Alexander, lost at sea. 3. Joseph, married Mary Miller. 4. Sarah, married Amni Hooper. 5. Margaret, married Samuel Hutchins. 6, Mary, married Daniel

Lord. 7. Sarah, married George Hooper. Perhaps other children.

(VI) David Washburn, son of Timothy Washburn, was born in Kennebunkport, Maine, about 1750-60. He had a son Timothy, mentioned below.

(VII) Timothy Washburn, son of David Washburn, born about 1780-90, married Jane ———. Children: 1. David Washington, born January 3, 1818, mentioned below. 2. Sarah Ann, May 19, 1819. 3. Mary Jane, September 14, 1820. 4. Ralph E., April 17, 1822. 5. Thomas, April 17, 1824. 6. Tobias W., May 29, 1827. 7. Francis W., February 4, 1831. 8. Susan E., November 3, 1832. 9. Francis M., April 4, 1835. 10. Harriet E., July 26, 1836.

(VIII) David Washington Washburn, son of Timothy Washburn, was born in Kennebunk, Maine, January 3, 1818, died in Somerville, Massachusetts, June 3, 1886. He went to Somerville when a young man, and there became a practical brick maker. In a few years he started in business for himself at first in Somerville and later in Everett, and carried on a constantly increasing and successful business all his life. He is remembered as a straightforward man in his dealings with others, and he held the respect of all. In politics he was first a Whig and later a Republican. He and his family attended the Congregational Orthodox church. He married Elizabeth Green, of Otisfield, Maine. Children, born in Somerville: 1. Charles Francis, died young. 2. George Franklin. 3. Charles Francis, mentioned below. 4. Wilbur David.

(IX) Charles Francis Washburn, son of David W. Washburn, was born in Somerville, April 7, 1855. After leaving school he began work in his father's brick yard, and later acquired an interest in the business. At his father's retirement from business, he and his brother, George Franklin Washburn, became sole owners, and have since carried it on with gratifying success. Mr. Washburn has taken considerable interest in political affairs, and has served on the board of aldermen and the board of public works in Everett. He is president of the Everett Co-operative Bank, and a member of the Glendon Club. He is a member of the Free Masons, Knights Templar, Independent Order of Odd Fellows and Red Men. By religious preference he is a Universalist. He married, June 16, 1879, Lucy M. Littlefield, born in Lyman, Maine, April 20, 1851, daughter of Israel and Henrietta (Kimball) Littlefield, of Lyman. Children: 1. Lucy M. 2. Octavia A., died aged three. 3. Etta. 4. Chester A., mentioned below.

(X) Chester A. Washburn, son of Charles F. Washburn, was born in Somerville, May 10, 1881. He attended the public and high schools of Everett and fitted for college at the Frye School, Boston. He began to study medicine at Tufts Medical School, but left after a time on account of ill health. He resumed his study of medicine in Boston University Medical School and finally at the Hahnemann Medical College, of Chicago, Illinois, where he was graduated with the degree of M. D. in the class of 1908. He has taken a year's course at Harvard Medical School in the class of 1909. He married, April 8, 1908, Albertha M. Hopkins, at Chicago, daughter of Fred and Catharine M. Hopkins, of Lowell, Massachusetts.

DAY

Captain Elias Harry Day, one of the famous old mariners of New England who sailed for many years from Maine seaport towns, was born in Freeport, Maine, in 1792, and died there about 1866. He was a descendant of Anthony Day, immigrant, a passenger in the ship "Paule," which sailed from London, England, in 1635, bound for Virginia. Where he spent the first ten years after landing in this country never has been made clear, but in 1646 he appears in Gloucester, Massachusetts, where he bought lands, spent the remaining years of his life and died in April, 1707, aged ninety years. His wife, Susan (Machette) Day, bore him six sons and one daughter. In 1736 four descendants of Anthony Day, grandsons or possibly great-grandsons, went from Gloucester to Maine and were among the founders there of the town of New Gloucester. They were Ezekiel, Eliphalet, Timothy and Pelatiah Day, and from them have sprung nearly all of the Days of Maine; but the most careful examination of published records fails to reveal the name of Captain Elias Day's father, while the researches of members of his family have yielded no satisfactory results.

Captain Elias H. Day early took the sea and was master of a ship sailing from Portland at the age of seventeen years. He was a deep sea sailor and during the thirty years of his life as mariner he visited nearly every important European port. Finally he quit the sea, purchased a farm at or near Freeport and there spent his remaining years. He married Sarah Randall, who survived him and died at the age of eighty years. Their children were: Elias H., Augusta A., Enos E., Maria S., Elizabeth E., Rebecca A., Ellen E. and Susan F., only one of whom, Mrs. Ellen E. Stoddard, of Deering, Maine, is now living.

Captain Elias H. Day, son of Captain Elias H. and Sarah (Randall) Day, was born in Freeport, Maine, in 1835, and died in Wilmington, Massachusetts, January 28, 1908. Like his father, he was a master mariner and followed the sea thirty-five years, sailing from Portland. He was placed in command of a vessel when only seventeen years old and was about fifty-five when he followed his father's example and took to farming, although he took up his home in Wilmington. He married Sarah J. Morse, of Livermore Falls, Maine, who survived him and by whom he had six children: William H., of Portland, Maine; Frank E., of Everett, Massachusetts; Ernest A., of Boston; Mary S., now Mrs. Berry, of Cumberland Mills, Maine; Minnie R., now Mrs. Black, of Everett, Massachusetts; Eugenie A., now Mrs. Chandler, of East Boston, Massachusetts.

Frank Edward Day, son of Captain Elias Henry and Sarah J. (Morse) Day, was born in Freeport, Maine, December 25, 1868, received his education at Westbrook high school, Westbrook, Maine, and was a boy of eighteen years when he left home for Boston to make a start in his business career, his only available capital at the time being his bicycle, which was turned into cash, and thirty-five dollars. However, he made a start, by opening a lunch room, later sold out to good advantage, then bought a larger establishment of the same kind, sold that and soon became engaged in a rather extensive business in buying and selling restaurants and dining rooms and lodging houses in the city. Still later he became proprietor of an office and sign cleaning business operating with modern machines and apparatus, and this he has carried on with excellent success for the last fifteen years. In 1897 Mr. Day took up his residence in the suburban city of Everett, where he now lives and is one of its large taxpayers. He is a Republican in politics but takes no active part in public affairs, for he is a very busy man with his large property and other business interests. He married Maud Coleman, of Centerville, Cape Cod, daughter of John F. and Emma F. (Nickerson) Coleman, and granddaughter of Captain F. W. Coleman, of Centerville. Mr. and Mrs. Day have four children: Minnie F., born Boston, September 16, 1894; Lillian M., born Boston, January 26, 1896; Frederick Edward, born Wilmington, June 30, 1901; Frank Coleman, born Everett, June 7, 1906.

Mr. Day and his wife have for several years been interested in church work and Mr. Day's name can be found on the list as one of the large contributors toward the building fund for a new Methodist church, of which he is at present one of the trustees.

DOWNING Dennis Downing, immigrant ancestor, was born in England about 1615-20. He settled in Kittery, Maine, and was one of the signers of the submission to the jurisdiction of Massachusetts in 1652. He was a blacksmith by trade. He was living in 1690. Children: 1. Dennis Jr., killed by the Indians at Kittery, July 4, 1697, the same time as Major Charles Frost whose body was dug up by the Indians and suspended from a stake the night after his burial; he had a grant of land March 16, 1694, laid out December 21, 1709, to his brother, Joshua Downing, at Beaver Dam. 2. John, mentioned below. 3. Joshua, born 1644, married, 1675, Patience Hatch, daughter of Philip and Patience Hatch; second, Rebecca Trickey, widow of Joseph Trickey and daughter of William and Rebecca Rogers; children: i. Joshua, married Sarah Hall; ii. Elizabeth, married Jonathan Woodman; iii. Sarah, married Jonathan Mendum; iv. Alice, married Richard Downing, April 24, 1709.

(II) John Downing, son of Dennis Downing (1), was born about 1635. He was before the court 1653 for disobeying his father. An Elizabeth Downing, possibly his wife, deposed August 8, 1738, then aged eighty-eight years, that she had lived at Scarborough sixty-four years before, viz: in 1674. From various deeds and documents we have the names of his children: 1. Benjamin. 2. Richard, of Portsmouth, 1697. 3. John, mentioned below. 4. Anne. 5. Alice. 6. Joanna.

(III) Captain John Downing, son of John Downing (2), was born in 1658-59, died September 16, 1744. He had a seat in the Portsmouth meeting house in 1697 and with his brother Richard and son John, was October 26, 1715, a charter member of the church at Newington, New Hampshire, where they settled. He was chosen elder of the Newington church, January 19, 1724. He married Susanna Miller, daughter of John Miller, of Arundel, Maine. He and wife Susanna deeded September 10, 1725, land at Cape Porpoise to son Benjamin. Their son John was mentioned. By a quitclaim deed April 18, 1720, the heirs of John Miller deeded their interests in his estate to John Downing Sr., April 18, 1720. The deed is signed by Benjamin and Jeremiah Miller, Daniel and Hannah Q———.

(IV) John Downing, son of Captain John Downing (3), was born about 1690. He had a seat in the Newington meeting-house in 1715 and was one of the organizers of the church. He married Elizabeth Harrison, of Newington, daughter of Nicholas and Mary (Bickford) Harrison. She owned the covenant and was baptized May 15, 1740, at Newington. He was a representative in the legislature in 1756 and served on a committee to adjust the boundaries of Newtown. Children: John, called *Tertius* (third), mentoned below; Alice, baptized April 1, 1722; Ruhama, born July 27, 1718; perhaps others.

(V) John Downing, 3d, son of John Downing Jr. (4), was born about 1715. He joined the Newington church in full communion, March 28, 1736. He was a trooper in Captain Joseph Hanson's company, August 5, 1745, in the old French and Indian war, commanding a squadron of scouts. He married Patience ———. Children, born at Newington: 1. John, mentioned below. 2. Samuel, baptized January 4. 1740-41.

(VI) John Downing, son of John Downing (5), was born about 1739 in Newington. He married, August 1, 1765, Mary Downing. He owned the covenant in the Newington church in 1767. He lived in Newington and Somersworth. There is a tradition that he had a brother in Salem, Massachusetts, and another in Dowington, Chester county, Pennsylvania. Children: 1. John, baptized in Newington, January 11, 1767. 2. Alice, baptized May 22, 1768. 3. Elizabeth, baptized July 15, 1770. The three preceding were born at Newington. 4. Samuel, mentioned below. Perhaps others born at Somersworth.

(VII) Samuel Downing, son of John Downing (6), was born about 1782 in Somersworth, New Hampshire. He settled in Middleton, New Hampshire. He married Mary Ann Davis, daughter of Zebulon Davis, of Alton, New Hampshire. Children: 1. John. 2. Patience, married Peter Cook and lived at Wakefield, New Hampshire. 3. Samuel H., born 1814, mentioned below. 4. Maria, married ——— Pike. 5. Jeremiah. 6. George. 7. Adeline, married Andrew Green and lived in Maine.

(VIII) Samuel H. Downing, son of Samuel Downing (7), was born at Middleton in 1814 and died in 1904. He married, in 1836, Eliza A. Whitehouse, born 1818, died 1875, daughter of Amos Whitehouse. He was a farmer in Middleton. Child, Amos Warren, mentioned below.

(IX) Amos Warren Downing, son of Samuel H. Downing (8), was born in Middleton, New Hampshire, March 31, 1838. He received a common school education in his native town. He removed to Haverhill, Massachusetts, where he is at present engaged in the fire insurance business. He is president of the Haverhill Co-operative Bank. He is a member of the Saggahew Lodge of Free Masons of Haverhill; of the Royal Arch Masons; Royal and Select Masters and of Haverhill Commandery, Knights Templar. He is independent in politics and has held the office of overseer of the poor in Haverhill for two terms. He and his family attend the First Baptist Church of Haverhill. He married, October 30, 1859, Susan Abigail Grace, born 1835, daughter of Captain Robert Grace, of New Durham, New Hampshire. Children, born at Haverhill: 1. Nellie Grace, August 24, 1862, died young. 2. Irving G., June 20, 1866, married, December, 1896, Eva Lucretia Bartlett; child, Rachel Downing, born March 15, 1904. 3. Albert Warren, May, 1869, died November 29, 1872.

CASWELL The surname Caswell is identical with Cassell and is also spelled Casewell. Many of the early Massachusetts families of this name were descendants of Thomas Caswell, of Taunton, a settler in that town before 1643 when his name appears on the list of men able to bear arms; died in 1697, leaving a large family of children. The surname is of ancient English origin. About the same time that Simon Caswell appears in Marblehead we find a William Caswell settled at Kittery, Maine, also a port that attracted sea-faring men; William married Mary Mitchell, daughter of Robert and had six or more children at Kittery. He may have been brother; it is likely that he was a near relative of Simon, mentioned below.

(I) Simon Caswell, immigrant ancestor, was doubtless born in England. Henry Caswell, probably a brother, possibly his father, was a merchant of Boston and Marblehead; bought land with buildings of Abraham Howard, of Marblehead, in the town May 25, 1736, and February 10, 1741, and had other deeds and mortgages of land in Marblehead. Simon was a fisherman at Marblehead. Among his children were: 1. John, mentioned below. 2. Grace, baptized August 4, 1728. 3. Thomas, baptized August 23, 1730. 4. Samuel, married, December 21, 1748, Remember Greeley.

(II) John Caswell, son of Simon Caswell, was born probably in England about 1715. He came with his father Simon and settled in Marblehead. He married, November 29, 1742, at Marblehead, Elizabeth Savage. He was a fisherman and shoreman. He was a member of the Puritan Church and deeded pew 55 in the new meeting house—a wall pew on the southwest side of the church, December 31, 1773, to his son, Simon Caswell. He bought land of Mary Yakley including the mansion house of the late John Yakley, of Marblehead, and half the orchard. Children, born at Marblehead and date of baptism: 1. Simon, August 17, 1744. 2. John, October 20, 1745, married, February 8, 1767, Elizabeth Seavey. 3. Samuel, September 27, 1747, mentioned below. 4. Tabitha, October 1, 1749. 5. Richard, November 18, 1750. 6. Tabitha, October 22, 1752. 7. Elizabeth, October 15, 1754. 8. Hannah, August 8, 1756. 9. Grace, October 22, 1758. 10. William, November 16, 1760, died intestate 1800-01.

(III) Samuel Caswell, son of John Caswell, was baptized September 27, 1747, at Marblehead. He was a soldier in the Marblehead company in the revolution, served in the continental army and late in life was granted a pension. He died at Beverly in 1804. He married first, Sarah ———, and second, Hannah Legrow, January 31, 1779. She drew a pension as his widow ($65.33 per annum), and at her death, July 4, 1849, left four children—John, William, Robert R. and Thomas M. Children: 1. Anna, baptized at Marblehead, May 28, 1780, buried July 7, 1805, at Beverly, aged twenty-four. 2. Thomas M., baptized at Marblehead, February 16, 1783, mentioned below. 3. Samuel, baptized September 12, 1784, died at Gloucester in 1847. 4. John, baptized November 4, 1787. 5. Philip, born November 29, 1789. 6. William, baptized September 4, 1791, cordwainer, died 1868. 7. Robert R., mentioned in probate records.

(IV) Thomas M. Caswell, son of Samuel Caswell, was baptized at Marblehead, February 16, 1783. He settled at Wenham. He married, November 27, 1798, Sally Porter, of Wenham, who died November 5, 1848, aged seventy-four years, at Wenham. Children: 1. Mary, born December 23, 1799. 2. Ebenezer Porter, born January 13, 1804. 3. Joseph D., mentioned below.

(V) Joseph Dodge Caswell, son of Thomas M. Caswell, was born in Wenham, Massachusetts, 1822. He was a tailor, wheelwright, shoemaker and farmer in Wenham and Beverly, Massachusetts. He married, April 23, 1843, Eliza Hull, who died April 2, 1890, aged sixty-eight years, four months, twenty-four days. Children: 1. Joseph W., born June 13, 1844. 2. Edward F., December 17, 1845, died December 30, 1907. 3. Winfield Scott, January 29, 1848, mentioned below. 4. Julia A., April 19, 1850, died October 23, 1850. 5. Augusta, September 30, 1851. 6. Caroline, February 14, 1853, died September 3, 1866. 7. Otis, August 9, 1855. 8. Pierce, July 17, 1857, died September 10, 1866. 9. Sarah E., July 14, 1860, died October 20, 1861. 10. Sarah E., May 17, 1863, died August 26, 1866. 11. Nelson, May 3, 1865, died May 24, 1865.

(VI) Winfield Scott Caswell, son of Joseph Dodge Caswell, was born at Wenham, January 29, 1848. He attended the public schools of Wenham, completing his studies at the age of sixteen. In 1864 he enlisted in Company E, Second Unattached Infantry, Massachusetts Volunteer Militia, and was discharged in Beverly, November, 1864. He then engaged in farming and shoemaking until about 1883, and then began the manufacture of shoes in Marblehead under the firm name of Phillips & Caswell, continuing until 1889, and since that time has been engaged in looking after his property interests. He married, March 1, 1870, Harriet A., daughter of Andrew J. Bowden, of Marblehead, Massachusetts. Children: 1. Frederick P., born July 3, 1871, mentioned below. 2. Nellie, April 4, 1874, married John H. Smith, of Marblehead. 3. Louis B., April 8, 1876, married Ida Melzard, of Marblehead. 4. Annie, born October 8, 1882, died April 29, 1891. 5. H. May, born November 20, 1883, married Ernest Cronk, of Maine.

(VII) Frederick P. Caswell, son of Winfield Scott Caswell, was born at Marblehead, Massachusetts, July 3, 1871. He was educated in the public schools of his native town and at Bryant and Stratton Commercial College, Boston. In 1894 he became a clerk and bookkeeper for Humphrey & Twisden Coal Company of Marblehead and filled this position with such fidelity and efficiency that he was made general manager of the Humphrey Coal Company in July, 1899. In partnership with Louis D. Weber he became one of the owners of the business in July, 1907. The company carries on a large retail business in wood and coal, and is in a flourishing condition. Mr. Caswell is a member of Neptune Lodge, No. 31, Knights of Pythias; master of Elbridge Gerry Commandery, Knights of Malta, and member of the M. A. Pickett Association. In politics he is a Republican, and is a prominent member of the Republican Club of Marblehead.

BLAISDELL Ralph Blaisdell first appears in York, Maine, about 1637-40, and removed thence to Salisbury, Massachusetts, where he had land granted him in 1640-41 and again in 1644-45. In 1642-43 he bought the rights of John Harrison, and died somewhere between 1648-50. He was a tailor by trade and appears to have filled some minor town offices. His wife was Elizabeth ———, who survived him and administered his estate. She died in Salisbury, "about ye middle of August, 1667." Children: 1. Henry, born about 1632. 2. Sarah, 17 7mo. 1640, in Salisbury. 3. Mary, 5 1mo. 1641.

(II) Henry Blaisdell, only son of Ralph and Elizabeth Blaisdell, was born about 1632 and died between 1705 and 1707. He was a tailor and husbandman and lived in that part of Salisbury which was set off to form Amesbury. He took oath of fidelity in 1667, was made freeman in 1690 and had several grants of land. He married, first, about 1656, Mary Haddon, who died in 1690 or 1691; married, second, before 1702, Elizabeth ———. He had nine children, all born of his first marriage: 1. Ebenezer, 7 8mo. 1657, died August 10, 1717; married Sarah Colby. 2. Mary, May 29, 1660, married Robert Rawlins. 3. Henry, mentioned below. 4. Elizabeth, about 1665, married John Huntington. 5. Ralph, about 1667, died 1691. 6. Lieutenant John, May 27, 1668, died 1733; married widow Elizabeth Hoyt. 7. Sarah, November 11, 1671, married Stephen Flanders. 8. Jonathan, October 11, 1676, died before November 28, 1748; married Hannah Gimson (Jameson). 9. Samuel, died October 3, 1683.

(III) Henry Blaisdell, son of Henry and Mary (Haddon) Blaisdell, was born in Salisbury, April 28, 1663, died before March 11, 1707-08. He was a tailor and lived in Amesbury, where he had a garrison house which was used by the settlers as a refuge against Indian attacks. He married, first, before 1686, Mary ———; married, second, about 1691, Hannah Colby, widow of Thomas Colby, and whose family name was Rowell. She died August 9, 1707, and he married, third, October 23, 1707, Dorothy Martin, who survived and married, March 7, 1709-10, Thomas Ayers, of Haverhill. Henry and Mary Blaisdell (first wife) had three children, all born in Amesbury: 1. Henry. 2. Mary, married Samuel Clough, husbandman, of Amesbury. 3. John, born February 4, 1686-87, mentioned as "second son."

(IV) Henry Blaisdell, son of Henry and Mary Blaisdell, was first a cordwainer and after 1713 is mentioned as a "doctor of Physics." About 1715 he removed from Amesbury to Chelmsford and was progenitor of Chelmsford Blaisdells. He died in the winter of 1735-36, his will dated January 7, 1735-36, being probated March 18, following. He married, first (published) May 7, 1709, Martha Bartlett, of Haverhill; married, second, before 1720, Lydia Parker, who survived him and married, before 1739, ——— Spaulding. Henry Blaisdell had nine children, two born in Amesbury and seven in Chelmsford: 1. Henry, April 11, 1710. 2. Martha, September 22, 1713, died young. 3. Mary, August 27, 1720, married, about 1741, Dr. Jonathan Stedman. 4. Lydia, May 7, 1723, married Henry Gould, of Concord. 5. Anna, April 7, 1725, married John Ball. 6. Ann, March 3, 1727, married Oliver Hildreth, of Andover. 7. Sarah, March 23, 1729-30, married Joseph Haywood. 8. John, November 23, 1732. 9. William, June 6, 1735.

(V) Henry Blaisdell, son of Henry and Martha (Bartlett) Blaisdell, was born in Amesbury, April 11, 1710. He was a "shipwright" and "caulker" and after 1739 lived in Boston. He is supposed to have died September 17, 1794, and although no record of his marriage is found, he is believed to have been the Henry Blaisdell who by wife Sarah had daughter Sarah, born in Chelmsford, February 10, 1735-36, and other children probably born in Boston.

(V) John Blaisdell, son of Henry and Lydia (Parker) Blaisdell, was born in Chelmsford, November 23, 1732, and died in the "Army of the Havannah." He married, August 5, 1756, Mary Sawyer, of Newbury, who survived him and married, second, Benjamin Wallingford, of Rowley, west parish. John and Mary (Sawyer) Blaisdell had one son, John Sawyer Blaisdell, born Chelmsford, November 3, 1757, lived in Newbury, Rowley and

Boxford; married Jane Adams, of Rowley, and had two children, both daughters who died very young.

(V) William Blaisdell, son of Henry and Lydia (Parker) Blaisdell, was born in Chelmsford, June 6, 1735, and lived in that town. He married Sarah ———, and had several children, two sons having served during the revolutionary war. His children whose births are recorded in Chelmsford as follows: 1. William, November 30, 1756. 2. Henry, November 23, 1760. 3. Aaron, November 2, 1762, probably married, November 29, 1787, Olive Byam. 4. Lydia, May 13, 1768. 5. Isaac, May 17, 1770.

(VI) Henry Blaisdell, who may have been the son of Henry Blaisdell (5), the "shipwright" and "caulker," who went from Chelmsford to Boston, or the son of William Blaisdell (5) last above mentioned, was born in Chelmsford and spent his life in that town and Boston, although no account of him is found in any of the published records, which are incomplete and imperfect, and information from members of the family is very uncertain.

(VII) Jacob Clough Blaisdell was born in 1822, in Chelmsford or Boston, and died in the latter city after an active and successful business career of about twenty or twenty-five years. As a boy just out of school he first found employment as apprentice to one Gurney of South Abington, Massachusetts, a manufacturer of tacks, steel shanks and railroad spikes, which then were worked out by hand at the anvil. Having served out his term he continued with Gurney for sometime afterward and then went to Somerville and began business on his own account. And it appears that he was something of a mechanical genius as well as a practical workman, for he soon invented a machine for heading and pointing spikes, the first device of its kind in use and one which was found to work satisfactorily to the great advantage and profit of its inventor who soon found himself engaged in an extensive business as senior partner of the firm of Blaisdell & Page and still later of the successor firm of Blaisdell & Tobey. In 1866 Mr. Blaisdell went to Bath, Maine, and started in business in that city, but in the course of a few months he was compelled by sickness to return, and he died in Boston during the same year, in the prime of his life. His wife, whom he married in Boston, was Margaret C., daughter of John Lawler, and who died in that city in 1871, having borne her husband two children: 1. Mary Elizabeth, born Somerville; married ——— Sarger and lives now in Fall River, Massachusetts. 2. James M., now of Lynn, Massachusetts.

(VIII) James Munroe Blaisdell, son of Jacob C. and Margaret C. (Lawler) Blaisdell, was born in Somerville, Massachusetts, in 1861, and as a boy was sent to the public schools in Boston and afterward found opportunity to attend an evening school in the city, for he was only about nine years old when it became necessary for him to do some kind of work for his own support. His first work was in the Jordan Marsh Company, then as cash boy afterward in the same capacity with Shepard, Norwell & Company, then with A. Stowell, jeweller, and still later with M. C. Warren, hardware dealer at Dock square. He next found employment with John Peck & Son, undertakers, with whom he continued as assistant for some time and then for the next three years worked for the Union Casket Company. In 1882 he left Boston and engaged in business with J. W. Darcey, undertaker and funeral director in Lynn. In 1892 Mr. Blaisdell became himself proprietor of an undertaker's business in Lynn and has so continued to the present time. He is a capable business man and takes a commendable interest in public affairs in the city, having served continuously for eight years as member of the school committee. He is a Republican in politics, member of the Methodist Episcopal church, Golden Fleece Lodge, F. and A. M., Kearsarge Lodge, No. 217, I. O. O. F., Fraternity Encampment, No. 17, P. M., and of Peter Woodward Lodge, No. 72, K. P.

Mr. Blaisdell married Emeline L. Downing, of Lynn, daughter of George H. and Emeline S. (Call) Downing, of Salem. Mr. Downing came from Baltimore, Maryland, to Lynn more than half a century ago and was for many years a skilled workman in making "hand turned" shoes in the best shoe factories of the city. He married Emeline Call and had five children, all of whom were born in Lynn and still live there. They are William, George, Emeline L., Phebe and Abbie Downing. James M. and Emeline L. (Downing) Blaisdell had eight children, all born in Lynn: 1. Maud, died young. 2. Harold C., died aged nine years. 3. Lawrence C. 4. Leonard C. 5. Florence G. 6. Arline. 7. James Reginald. 8. Clarisse.

(For early generations see Philip Pevear 1).

PEVEAR (IV) Joseph Pevear, son of Daniel Pevear (3), was born at Hampton Falls, New Hampshire, about 1795. He was a farmer in his native town, and after his death his premises were occupied by Samuel L. Pevear, son of Samuel, and he finally sold it to Alexander Short, who came from Newburyport. Children, born at Hampton Falls: 1. Mark, settled at Lynn. 2. Stephen, settled in Lynn. 3. Sewell Brown, mentioned below. 4. Warren B., resided at Hampton Falls. 5. Sylvester, settled in Brentwood, New Hampshire; was a soldier in the civil war and was severely wounded, losing the sight of one eye; was in the Eleventh New Hampshire Regiment with his brother, Sewell B.

(V) Sewell Brown Pevear, son of Joseph Pevear (4), was born in Hampton Falls, New Hampshire, 1840. He was educated there in the public schools, and raised on the farm of his father. He enlisted in the civil war in Company I, Eleventh New Hampshire Volunteer Infantry, served under General Burnside, and was detailed to guard duty in front of General McClellan's tent on the night that the order was received relieving him (General McClellan) of command, he being superseded by General Burnside. He served three years and was discharged at the close of the war. He settled after the war in Lynn, and was engaged extensively in the leather business in that city until his death in 1901, in Massachusetts. He was a member of the Bay State Lodge, I. O. O. F., also of the I. O. R. M.; he attended the Boston Street Methodist Episcopal Church; was a member of no clubs, finding his enjoyment in his home with his wife and children. He married Sarah Helen Stephens, born in Raymond, New Hampshire, daughter of John Stephens. She died in 1907. Children: 1. Everett Sewell. 2. Eveline Florence, married Charles de Chantell, born Boston, July 2, 1866, in business with Mr. Pevear; children: Charles Sewell, died young; Charles Sewell, 2d., born 1895. 3. Helen M., married John Newhall; resides on Lincoln avenue, Saugus. 4. Norman W., at same address.

(VI) Everett Sewell Pevear, son of Sewell Brown Pevear (5), was born in Hampton Falls, New Hampshire, in the old Pevear homestead February 7, 1863. He removed with his family to Lynn in 1865, when he was a child, and attended the public schools of Lynn. Until he was twelve years old he spent his summers on his grandfather's farm in Hampton Falls. At the age of fifteen he left school to begin work for his father, who was engaged in the leather business at Lynn. He followed that until 1889, when Mr. Pevear established himself as a contractor in Lynn, building bridges, sewers, mason work of all kinds. He first acted as a superintendent and had charge of the work on the Hawks Brook Reservoir for the city of Lynn water works. He then on his own account built four miles of sewers for the town of Wakefield, Massachusetts, did the rock excavation for the Salem line of the Boston & Northern railroad, and he built for the city of Lynn the Little river conduit from Stony Brook to Saugus branch railroad. Since that time his business has steadily increased and he has at times kept as many as two hundred men, being one of the largest contractors in Lynn. Among his other work he has constructed nearly all the sewers in the city. He keeps from thirty to forty horses and has a complete equipment for all work in his line. He is an attendant of the Boston Street Methodist Episcopal Church. In politics he is an active member of the Republican city committee from ward five. He is a member of Kearsarge Lodge, No. 217, Odd Fellows; Fraternity Encampment, also the Montowampate Tribe of Red Men. He is one of the best known and most substantial men in his line of business in the city of Lynn, and is highly esteemed by his townsmen for his public spirit, business ability, success and exemplary character.

Mr. Pevear married, December 2, 1884, Abbie Helen Crocker, born in Taunton, Massachusetts, daughter of Elbridge and Almeda Warren (Spencer) Crocker. Her father was born in New Bedford, Massachusetts, and died in Taunton; he was foreman in an iron foundry in Taunton for many years Her mother died in North Dighton, Massachusetts; she was a daughter of Thomas Spencer, who came to America from England and settled in Taunton, where he married Almeda Merriam Blanchard, a native of New Hampshire, who lived to the ripe old age of eighty-six. Mr. and Mrs. Pevear have no children.

(For first generation see John Swan 1).

SWAN (II) Ebenezer Swan, son of John Swan (1), was born November 14, 1672, died July 27, 1740. He married, March 2, 1698, Elizabeth Bruce, of Woburn. Children: 1. Elizabeth, born March 29, 1699, married, January 8, 1724, Ezra Skinner, of Norton. 2. Sarah, born February 26,

1701, married, December 14, 1727, Ephraim Cook, of West Cambridge, Massachusetts, died March 24, 1748. 3. Ebenezer, born March 23, 1704, mentioned below. 4. Mary, born March 4, 1706-07, died 1750, unmarried. 5. Samuel, born April 5, 1711, married Sarah Patten; died June 19, 1750. 6. William, born January 31, 1713-14, married, April 13, 1743, Ruth Polley, of Medford, Massachusetts; married (second) ——— at New London, Connecticut.

(III) Ebenezer Swan, son of Ebenezer Swan (2), was born March 23, 1704, and died April 23, 1752. He married, September 12, 1728, Bathsheba Grant, of Watertown. Children: 1. Peter, born January 6, 1729. 2. Ebenezer, born November 18, 1730, mentioned below. 3. Benjamin, born April 20, 1733. 4. Joseph, born February 16, 1735-36, married, January 26, 1764, Jannet MacCloud. 5. Bathsheba, born February 15, 1737-38, died August 26, 1805, unmarried. 6. Mary, born January 29, 1738-39, died July 22, 1740, 7. Joshua, born June 28, 1743, married, July 20, 1762, Sarah Cutler; died in April, 1777. 8. Mary, born April 3, 1745, died August 1, 1747.

(IV) Ebenezer Swan, son of Ebenezer Swan (3), was born November 18, 1730, and died August 8, 1798. He married in January, 1757, Mary Mansur, of Watertown. Children: 1. Peter, baptized February 19, 1758, died young. 2. Ebenezer, baptized January 25, 1761, mentioned below. 3. Peter, born May 12, 1763, chairmaker, died February 21, 1822, unmarried. 4. Gershom, born March 18, 1766, chairmaker; married, January 4, 1787, Cherry Hill; died October 10, 1827. 5. Timothy, born August 16, 1769, married Lydia Munroe, of West Cambridge; died December 12, 1813.

(V) Ebenezer Swan, son of Ebenezer Swan (4), was born at West Cambridge, Massachusetts, (Menotomy) and baptized January 25, 1761. He was brought up on his father's farm and received the usual education of a farmer's son of that period. He continued farming all his life. It was his house that his grandsons, Henry and Harrison Swan, moved to the rear of the present Swan block when it was built in the seventies. He was a soldier in the Revolution, being a private in Captain Alexander Foster's company, Colonel Thomas Carpenter's regiment, in Rhode Island in the summer of 1778; also in Captain Joshua Walker's company, Colonel Samuel Denny's regiment, in 1779, three months to reinforce the Continental army; also in Captain Abraham Andrew's company, Colonel Cyprian Hows's regiment, July 27, 1780, to October 30, 1780, detached from Middlesex county for the same purpose. He was a stern man, very strict in the management of his home. He was a member of the First Church. He died February 3, 1814. He married, October 9, 1791, Sally Adams, of Waltham, Massachusetts. They had one child, Henry, born 1792, mentioned below.

(VI) Henry Swan, son of Ebenezer Swan (5), was born at West Cambridge, Massachusetts, 1792, and died March 15, 1846. He was educated in the district school, going during the winter months, and helping his father on the farm, where he stayed until he was of age. He early started in the poultry business. Nathan Robbins, afterwards a leading poultry dealer, worked for him. He carried on this business all his life. In those days, before vessels could be supplied with ice, live stock was carried to be killed en route. He made a business of supplying outgoing vessels with poultry and hogs, some of which was furnished by nearby farmers. His house was on a three acre plot, which was his share of the Swan property. He was a man six feet tall, of slender build, and like his father was very stern and decided. He was an Orthodox Unitarian, and a Whig in politics. He was in the War of 1812, and served at Fort Independence. His widow received a pension during her life. He died of consumption March 15, 1846.

He married, August 27, 1815, Elizabeth Parker, of West Cambridge, born in 1793, died October 29, 1884, daughter of David and Elizabeth (Tufts) Parker. Children: 1. Sally Ann, born 1816, married (first), September 11, 1842, Daniel Peirce, of Lexington, and (second), Frederick Fiske, of Holliston; died without issue in 1889. 2. Elizabeth, born March 23, 1818, died October 22, 1878; married, September 4, 1842, Eli Simonds, of Lexington; children: i. Alice Parker Simonds, born June 8, 1843, married, April 6, 1871, James H. Wright, of Concord, and had Harry Simonds Wright, born November 5, 1885, who was married June 6, 1905, to Harriet Martha Roberts and had Harry Simonds Wright, born July 2, 1907. ii. William Henry Simonds, born November 1, 1844, married (first), May 3, 1877, Jenny Garty, of Concord, Massachusetts, who died March 20, 1891; he married (second), July 14, 1892, Winifred B. Thorndyke, of Rockport, Maine. Child of the first wife. Frank Herbert Simonds, born April 5, 1878, married, December 25, 1902, Mary Gledhill, and had Katharine Garty Simonds, born November 26, 1906; children of the second wife: Margaret Simonds, born July 31, 1895; Ruth Thorndyke Simonds, born May 31, 1897. iii. Frank H. Simonds, born May 12, 1848, died February 22, 1878, married, March 23, 1877, Eliza Maria Emery, of Lexington, and had Gertrude Naomi Simonds, born October 31, 1877. 3. Henry, born August 24, 1822, mentioned below. 4. Hannah Adams, born May 19, 1824, died August 8, 1891; married, March 24, 1841, John J. Brown, of Lexington; children: i. Henrietta Brown, died young; ii. Henry Brown, died young; iii. Ida Florence Brown, born November 7, 1849, married, September 9, 1868, Frank E. Richardson, of Arlington, Massachusetts, and had Alice Brown Richardson, born August 3, 1872, who married, December 2, 1900, Dr. Charles W. W. Miller, of Philadelphia, Pennsylvania; iv. Charles Adams Brown, born December 2, 1851, died March 1, 1907. 5. William Parker, born February 24, 1827, died August 24, 1848. 6. Benjamin Franklin, born 1829, mentioned below. 7. Harrison, born January 9, 1832, mntioned below. 8. Gershom, born June 19, 1834, died August 2, 1893; married, June 9, 1864, Mary Ward Harrington, of Lexington, who was born November 24, 1834, and died September 6, 1884; children: i. Charles Ward Swan, born July 24, 1866; ii. Elizabeth Bowen Swan, born November 16, 1869, died July 22, 1870. 9. Ellen Parker, born March 3, 1838, died March, 1906; married, June 4, 1865, William Mullet, of Brighton, Massachusetts. 10. Ebenezer Willard, born August 4, ——; died June 9, 1891; married (first) Octavia Bragdon, of East Boston, Massachusetts; (second), in 1850, Emily Hutchins, of North Kennebunk, Maine; (third), Caroline Cushing, of Framingham, Massachusetts; (fourth), Nellie E. (Hallett) Tidd; children of the second wife: i. Emma Hutchins Swan, born September 25, 1852, married, March 22, 1875, James S. Southgate, of Worcester, Massachusetts, and had Freddie Swan Southgate, born February 29, 1876, died February 26, 1877; Edna Southgate, born July 10, 1877; Alfred Willard Southgate, born September 27, 1878; Herbert Ralph Southgate, born December 22, 1879, married, March 20, 1907, Helen May Trim; Stewart Swan Southgate, born July 15, 1887. Children of the third wife: ii. Allston DeWitt Swan, married Hattie Morse; iii. Harry Everett Swan; iv. Dr. Roscoe Wellesley Swan, married Elizabeth Prentice; v. Bertha Cushing Swan, married John Kennedy.

(VII) Henry Swan, son of Henry Swan (6), was born at West Cambridge, August 24, 1822, and died October 1, 1895. He was educated in the West Cambridge common schools until sixteen years of age, assisting his father on the farm until early manhood. He then entered the employ of Joshua Robbins, a poultry dealer, where he remained until about 1846, doing much of the selling for Robbins. Then he started a business of his own, having good success, selling poultry in the Boston market. After a time he opened a stall, No. 18, in Faneuil Hall market, where he was associated with Sullivan B. Newton under the firm name of Swan & Newton, afterwards Swan, Newton & Co., where he continued up to the time of his death. The firm continues under the same, the present partners being Kidder, Richardson and Newton. Sullivan B. Newton died September 30, 1907. In 1876 the general appearance of Arlington Center was improved by the removal of the old Swan house and erecting on a portion of the lot the westerly half of Swan's block by Henry and Harrison Swan, owners of the property. Two years later another and larger section was added, the upper part being finished as a public hall. Within a short time this was leased to the trustees of the Robbins Library, and was used as a library and reading room until the new library was built.

Henry Swan and his brother Harrison were associated in the real estate business in Arlington, buying out the heirs of the old Swan homestead, which had been held by the Swan family since 1650. The old house bore many evidences of its extreme age. It was made of cedar timbers, and when it was taken apart for removal, several bullets were found embedded in the timbers. Henry Swan was a man who enjoyed the confidence of his fellow citizens to a remarkable degree. Upright and honorable, his word was as good as his bond, and he had many friends. He was a member of the Universalist church, serving on the parish committee, and was superintendent of the Sunday-school for twenty-two years. He was a public-spirited man, and held several town offices. He was a Republican, and had held the offices of selectman and overseer of the poor. He was a member of the school committee for twenty-five years. He belonged to Hiram Lodge of Masons, the Boston Chamber of Commerce, and was also a director of the Arlington Five Cents Savings Bank.

He married, May 10, 1846, Lydia Ann Frost, daughter of John and Lydia (Winship) Frost, of West Cambridge, who was born March 19, 1825, and died August 21, 1904. Children: 1. Henry Oscar, born August 1, 1848, died October 11, 1851. 2. Lizzie M., March 16, 1851, died July 18, 1860. 3. Annie Florence, July 3, 1853, died September 30, 1900, unmarried. 4. Nellie Hortense, January 18, 1858, married, April 29, 1885, Rev. Charles Arthur Knickerbocker, of Arlington, and had Henry Swan Knickerbocker, born June 5, 1888. 5. Gracie Greenwood, October 3, 1859, married, April 22, 1891, Shirley C. Ingraham. 6. Harrie, May 6, 1863, died March 12, 1864.

(VII) Harrison Swan, son of Henry Swan (6), was born at Arlington, Massachusetts, January 9, 1832. He was educated in the common schools of his native town, attending school until he was seventeen years of age, the last four years going only during the winter months. He then entered the employ of his brother Henry, who was a poultry dealer, and became a salesman for him until about 1854. Then he went to Lowell, Massachusetts, and became a salesman for the wholesale provision house of Smith & Waite, at Fletcher & Dutton streets, remaining about two years. After returning and working for his brother another year, he started in business for himself, making daily trips to Boston market with his poultry until September 25, 1871. At this time he took stall, No. 1, basement, No. 3, New Faneuil Hall market, in company with Nathan A. Fitch, under the firm name of Swan & Fitch. The firm continued the business successfully until January 12, 1885, when Mr. Fitch sold his interest in the firm to Mr. Swan, and bought out the business of George C. Boynton, at stall No. 10. Mr. Swan then admitted George H. Valpey to the business under the name of Swan & Valpey, poultry and game. Mr. Valpey remained in the firm four years, retiring September 29, 1888, later acquiring the business of George H. Scoville, stall No. 8, butter and eggs. Since the retirement of Mr. Valpey Mr. Swan has conducted the business alone, occupying the same stall in which he began business in 1871. Mr. Swan has been a member of the Arlington First Baptist Church since 1867, and has served on its standing committee. He is a Republican.

He married, January 29, 1857, Rebecca Monroe Walton, born at Lexington, Massachusetts, October 23, 1834, daughter of Jonathan and Eliza (Locke) Walton, of West Cambridge. Children: 1. Hattie Maria, born November 27, 1861, married, September 18, 1882, Wesley E. A. Legg, of Boston; children: Harry Wesley, Marion Edith, Vera Mildred, Edward Raymond Legg. 2. Elizabeth Walton, born June 17, 1864, died April 17, 1865. 3. Mildred Eliza, born April 17, 1867, married, February 17, 1897, Rev. Jonas Hamilton Woodsum, of Hyannis, Massachusetts, native of Boston; children: Mildred Munroe, born May 5, 1902; Hamilton Swan, March 5, 1905, died September 25, 1906.

(VII) Benjamin Franklin Swan, son of Henry Swan (6), was born at Arlington, Massachusetts, in 1829, and died at San Francisco, California, January 9, 1900. He had a common school education in Arlington, and assisted his father in the poultry business. He went to work for Nathan Robbins, a poultry dealer, driving his team to Boston, and gathering stock from farmers of the district. When he was twenty years of age the gold fever broke out, and he was one of those early "Forty-niners" who braved countless dangers to go overland to California. When he had accumulated quite a fortune, he returned and married, taking his wife to California with him, by way of the isthmus. In 1866 he returned to Arlington, where he lived several years, but finally returned to California. Like all "Forty-niners" money came easily and went as it came, and he made and lost three large fortunes. He was for a long time interested in stocks, and was a member of the Pacific Stock Exchange at San Francisco for years. During his last few years he suffered from a severe kidney trouble, which terminated in a heart affection, causing his death, January 9, 1900, at San Francisco. He was a man of strong qualities and superior intellect, energetic in business. He was a member of the Congregational church at Arlington. In politics he was a Republican. He was a member of Hiram Lodge of Masons, at Arlington. He married, April 8, 1863, Elizabeth Thaxter, of Arlington, who died June 25, 1885, aged thirty-nine years, nine months. Children: 1. Benjamin Franklin, mentioned below. 2. James Thaxter, born April 4, 1867; married October 9, 1889, Alice Gertrude Tappan, of Arlington, Massachusetts.

Benjamin Franklin Swan, son of Benjamin Franklin Swan, was born at San Francisco, California, August 14, 1864. When he was quite young his parents removed to Arlington, Massachusetts, their former home, where he received his education in the common schools, graduating from the grammar school and going two years to the Cotting high school. During these two years he worked after school hours in Dodge's Pharmacy. Then his desire to learn the business impelled him to give up school and after spending two and one half years in the Pharmacy, he entered the wholesale drug business of Gilman Brothers, 50 Franklin street, Boston, as clerk. Strict attention to business soon led to promotion, and today he occupies a position of trust, being buyer and salesman for the firm. Gilman Brothers is one of the old established firms in Boston, and went through the big fire in 1872. Mr. Swan purchased in 1892 a house at 68 Evans street, Dorchester, where he resides with his family. Since 1906 he has been a member of the Church of the Epiphany (Episcopal) in Dorchester. He was one of a committee of five to start that society, and has always been a leader in the church, and is treasurer of the society. In politics he is a Republican. He is a member of the church club. He was formerly a member of the Arlington Boat Club, being captain of the first club bowling team that was entered in inter-club competition. He married, October 11, 1892, Sophia Priscilla Rudolf, of Dorchester, born May 8, 1864, daughter of John George and Priscilla Couch (Collings) Rudolf, of Lunenburg, Nova Scotia. Her father was a sea captain and a prominent Free Mason, a descendant of the old family of Von Rudolphs, of Germany. Children: 1. Franklin Rudolf, born February 22, 1897. 2. Ernest Thaxter, August 6, 1900; died September 22, 1900. 3. Evelyn Elizabeth, born September 14, 1903.

MERRILL Major Merrill, a descendant of one of the leading families and earliest settlers of Salisbury and Amesbury, Massachusetts, was born in Lewiston, Maine. He was educated in the common schools, and followed farming during his active years. He married Sarah Stevens, born at Auburn, Maine. Children, born in Auburn: Stephen Stetson, Samuel Parker, Samuel Parker, George Henry, Seba Stevens, mentioned below; Major B., William T., Sarah M., Carrie, Martha.

(II) Seba Stevens Merrill, son of Major Merrill, was born in Auburn, Maine, December 22, 1843. He was educated in the public schools of his native town, and learned the trade of shoemaker. He worked for the firm of Roak & Packard, manufacturers of boots and shoes at Auburn, for a period of twenty years. In 1870 he came to Lynn and from 1883 to 1899 was in the employ of Mark J. Worthley, manufacturer of boots and shoes of that city. In 1899 he established the summer hotel at Middleton known as Maplehurst, and has conducted it with great success to the present time. The hotel has twenty-one rooms and its dining room seats fifty or more. It is located on a forty acre farm which has apple, peach and pear orchards and various small fruits. Besides the hotel there is a cottage used as an annex, containing twelve beds. The hotel is extremely popular, the surrounding country is very attractive, and the boating and bathing excellent. Mr. Merrill is a member of the Odd Fellows, and has taken all the degrees of the order outside of the Grand Lodge. He is also a member of Mount Carmel Lodge, Free Masons; Sutton Chapter, Royal Arch Masons; Olivet Commandery, Knights Templar; Aleppo Temple, Mystic Shrine, of Boston; Middleton Lodge, Improved Order of Red Men. In politics he is a Republican, and has been selectman of the town of Middleton. He is a member of the Congregational church. He is fond of travel and has visited all parts of the United States. In 1908 he made a trip to Cuba.

Mr. Merrill married Almeda Conant Mitchell, daughter of Benjamin Mitchell, of Auburn, Maine. Three children, two died in infancy; the surviving child is Clara Etta, born at Auburn, married Walter N. Durgin, of Northwood, New Hampshire; child, Bessie L., born September 19, 1887.

BREEN Hon. John Breen, son of Patrick and Margaret (Heffernan) Breen, was born in Tipperary, Ireland, June 20, 1842. His parents were in comfortable circumstances at the time of his birth, but four years later were evicted from their farm, owing to religious and political disturbances that presaged the troublous times of the Irish movement in 1848. The family came to America in 1847, and after temporary residence in various places settled in Lawrence, Massachusetts, in April, 1853. Mr. Breen attended the public schools and was fitted for college in a private school. He entered St. Charles College, Ellicott Mills, Maryland, but on account of ill health had to abandon his college course before graduating. Afterwards he attended a private school and Comer's Commercial College, Boston. He was an enthusiastic Fenian, and after graduating from Comer's, while employed as a bookkeeper in the commission house of E. H. Walker & Company, he was ordered to Ireland by General Thomas F. Burke, a leader in the Fenian organization. He went in December, 1867, and, evading the detectives and police reached Liverpool, and followed his instructions faithfully in Manchester and in Dublin, where he went to prepare the people of Ireland for their part in the insurrection already planned. The treachery of Curydon, the informer, rendered all his plans abortive, and after persistent efforts and many hazardous attempts to release a companion imprisoned in Dublin (Daniel Donovon, of Lawrence, Massachusetts), he gave up further efforts and in 1868 returned to America. Soon afterward he engaged in the undertaking business in Lawrence with a very limited capital, but he made up in energy and self-sacrifice what he lacked in money, and was soon well-established and prosperous in business.

Mr. Breen has been active in politics and a man of large influence and usefulness in the Democratic party. He was a member of the common council in 1876-77, resigning during his second year to accept an appointment on the board of fire engineers. He was elected mayor of Lawrence for the years 1882-83-84, thus enjoying the distinction of being the first Roman Catholic or Irish-born mayor of any city in New England. Notwithstanding many adverse circumstances causing a general business depression during his term of service, Mayor Breen's three years of administration were conspicuous for efficient management of municipal affairs. He has been rightly designated one of the most energetic and successful executives the city has had. Mr. Breen is one of the vice-presidents of the Irish National League. He was elected to the board of water commissioners in 1884, and was for many years chairman. He was regimental inspector of rifle practice in Twelfth Company, Ninth Regiment, National Guard, intending to go to Cuba, but was notified that inspectors were not acceptable. He then immediately raised a company of volunteers, called the Twelfth Massachusetts Provisional Company. On the 24th day of June, 1898, he was commissioned captain by Governor Roger Wolcott. On July 17, 1899, was commissioned quartermaster of the Ninth Regiment Infantry, Second Brigade. On April 15, 1899, was honorably discharged from the Provisional Company. Mr. Breen has been and is a member of the school board for twenty-five years, is vice-chairman of the school board, and in 1907 was elected for three more years; he has handed all his children their diplomas.

He married, in Boston, April 1, 1872, Nancy Jane Brackett, daughter of Daniel G. and Roxanna (Tuttle) Brackett, of Danville, New Hampshire. Her great-grandfather was in the War of 1812, and was governor, as was also her other great-grandfather, Governor Tuttle. Her grandfather, William Hanover Brackett, served in the civil war. She is a descendant of Hannah Dustin. Children of Hon. John and Nancy J. (Brackett) Breen are: 1. Charles Francis, born April 15, 1874, married Louisa Bruns. 2. John Joseph, October 24, 1875. 3. Arthur, died at the age of eight months. 4. Margaret Mary. 5. Louise Patrick, died in infancy. 6. Helena C.

KNOWLES Knowles is an ancient English surname, sometimes spelled Knollys, and branches of the family are found in many of the English counties. During the period of the Commonwealth Thomas Knowles came from England to Killeighy and Knockabowlea in the county of Cork, Ireland, and married Dorothy Busteed of that county and they became the ancestors of a large family of Knolles and Knowles in Ireland. Several immigrants came from England to America before 1650. Richard Knowles settled in Plymouth. Rev. John Knowles, a Puritan minister, was in Boston as early as 1638; was sent to Virginia with Rev. William Thompson to plant churches of the New England type there; returned to Bristol, England, before 1655.

(I) David Knowles was born in Bradford, Yorkshire, England, May 1, 1824. He was educated and learned his trade in his native town. He came to America and followed his trade as jeweler.

(II) David Benjamin Knowles, son of David Knowles (1), was born June 26, 1864, at Lawrence, Massachusetts. He was educated in the public schools of his native town and then learned his trade as jeweler in his father's store, Essex street, Lawrence. He became associated in business with his father and succeeded to the business when his father retired. He is a well known and successful business man. In politics he is independent and he has devoted all his time to business, preferring not to mix politics and business. He is a member of the Free Masons, Odd Fellows, Knights of Pythias, Royal Arcanum. He attends the

Protestant Episcopal church. He married, October 3, 1891, Josephine Brackett, born March 12, 1873, in Maine, daughter of John and Adeline (Hanson) Brackett. Her father is a farmer. Children, born in Lawrence: 1. Clifford, born July 15, 1893. 2. Helen, March 15, 1895. 3. Russell, March 28, 1899. 4. Leslie, September 14, 1901.

STANLEY Rufus Stanley entered mercantile life in Portland, Maine, became a prosperous grocery merchant and was one of the most prominent business men of that city.

Charles Rufus Stanley, son of Rufus Stanley, was born in Portland, August 10, 1845. His preliminary studies were pursued in the Portland public schools, including the high school, and he completed his education at the West Brook (Maine) Seminary. His business training, began in his father's store in Portland, was continued in Boston, where he remained for two years, and returning to his native city he succeeded the elder Stanley in the wholesale grocery business, which he conducted successfully for a number of years. Selling his Portland establishment he removed to Lawrence, and purchased in company with his brother the brewery on Oxford street of George Bilbrook, and an extensive and profitable business was built up under the firm name of the Stanley Brewing Company. That concern continued in business until 1890, when the brewery was sold to an English syndicate and Mr. Stanley retired from active business pursuits. His death, which was both sudden and untimely, occurred January 24, 1893, and its announcement was received with sincere regret by his business associates, who held him in high esteem. A Democrat in politics he occupied a prominent position in the councils of his party, by which he was regarded as an eligible candidate for some of the most important city offices, including the mayoralty. He was a Master Mason and a Knight Templar; also affiliated with the Benevolent and Protective Order of Elks, and as a leading member of the Home Club he manifested his interest in the welfare of that organization by the presentation of a magnificent picture at the dedication of its new quarters in the Odd Fellows Block. In his religious belief he was an Episcopalian and attended Grace Church. Mr. Stanley married Nellie Maria Swett, daughter of John R. Swett, of Windham, Maine, who was the father of two other children: Frank Howard and Mary Louise. Mrs. Stanley is the mother of two children: Henry Rufus, and Helen, who is the wife of Irwin Wilder Sargent, a well-known attorney at law of Lawrence.

PRATT Tradition relates that the progenitor of this family was John Plat, or Platt, who fled from France from some political persecution, and became an armor-bearer to the King of England, and his name was subsequently spelled Pratt. Both names have the same significance derived from the Latin root word *Pratum*, a meadow.

(I) Henry Pratt, the progenitor was a nonconformist minister, and for preaching the Gospel contrary to the rules of the Established Church was imprisoned at the same time that over four hundred religious teachers were confined in damp and gloomy jails in England for the same offence. While thus incarcerated he managed to communicate with the distressed family by writing to them with blood drawn from his arm for the purpose. Whether he died in jail, as many of these devout and wretched prisoners did, or was released. Among his children were: 1. Joshua, came to Plymouth in ship "Anne," 1623; was admitted a freeman in 1633; constable and messenger January 1, 1633-4; juror and commissioner; administration granted to widow Bathsheba, October 5, 1633-4; widow married August 29, 1667, John Daggett. 2. Phinehas, mentioned below.

(II) Phinehas Pratt, son of Henry Pratt (1), was the immigrant ancestor. He was one of a company of about sixty sent to Massachusetts to found a colony by Thomas Weston, a London merchant, who was first a friend and chief promoter of the Plymouth Colony, and then a rival. Pratt with nine others sailed from England in the ship "Sparrow," arriving at Damariscove Island in May, 1622. He with others left the vessel in a shallop, and after touching at several places on the coast landed in the latter part of May at Plymouth. About July 1st, the ships "Charity" and "Swan," two other vessels sent out by Weston, also arrived; and subsequently a party left Plymouth in the "Swan" and commenced the settlement at Wessaguscus, in the present town of Weymouth. Pratt was one of this company. The head man of the colony was Richard Greene, a brother-in-law of Weston, but he, dying in a subsequent visit to Plymouth, was succeeded by John Sanders. These settlers began with little provision. "They neither applied themselves to planting of corn, nor taking of fish, more than for their present use; but went about to build castles in the air and making of forts, neglecting the plentiful time of fishing. When winter came their forts would not keep out hunger, and they having no provision beforehand, and wanting both powder and shot to kill deer and fowl, many were starved to death, and the rest hardly escaped." The survivors of the little colony were then really in the power of the Indians; and they were indebted to the courage, adroitness and endurance of Phinehas Pratt for their deliverance and their lives. In the winter of 1623 the Indians matured a plan to cut off the English, both at Wessaguscus and Plymouth, in one day. Pratt, then about thirty-two years of age, had seen some of his companions die of starvation; and learning in his intercourse with the Indians of this scheme of massacre for the rest, resolved to send intelligence of it to Plymouth. When all others had refused to go he determined to go himself. He was closely watched by the Indians, but by a subterfuge effected his escape. He was closely pursued and narrowly escaped capture, reaching Plymouth, March 24, 1623, wellnigh exhausted. His story corresponded with the intelligence received from Massasoit, and hence Captain Myles Standish and his party started on their expedition to kill Pecksuot and Wittewamut. Standish was successful, and though his act was simple murder, it was effective. The head of the Indian chief decorated a pole at Plymouth, and the plot was frustrated by the death of the two sachems. Pratt was too exhausted to return with Standish. On regaining his strength he went to Piscataqua and was in skirmishes with the natives at Agawam and at Dorchester. He says: "Three times we fought with them; thirty miles I was pursued for my life, in a time of frost and snow, as a deer chased by wolves." Pratt settled at Plymouth when the Wessaguscus colony broke up. His brother was also an inhabitant, and he shared in 1624 in the distribution of cattle and of lands in 1623, being classed with the settlers who came with his brother on the ship "Ann." He was a joiner by trade.

In 1648 Pratt purchased the place at Charlestown, Massachusetts, on which he lived the rest of his life. In 1658 he shared in a division of lands. In 1662 he presented to the general court of Massachusetts Bay what he termed "An History," called "A Declaration of the Affairs of the English People that first inhabited New England." This narrative is preserved in the publications of the Massachusetts Historical Society, and is of surpassing interest. Under the date of May 7, 1658, is the following record of the general court: "In answer to the petition of Phinehas Pratt of Charlestown, who presented this Court with a narrative of the straits and hardships that the first planters of this Colony under went, in their endeavors to plant themselves at Plymouth and since, whereof he was one, the Court judge it meet to grant him three hundred acres of land, where it is to be had, not hindering a plantation." This land was laid out in the wilderness on the east of the Merrimack river, near the upper end of Nacooke Brook. In October, 1668, Pratt, then nearly eighty, presented another petition to the general court, in which he states that he "was the remainder of the forlorn hope of sixty men," that he was now lame; and he requested aid "that might be for his subsistence the remaining time of his life." The Court refused to grant his petition. The Charlestown records a few months later, show the following charitable, January 25, 1668-9: "Ordered constable Jon. Hayman to supply Phineas Pratt with so much as his present low condition may require." At this time Pratt was regarded with uncommon interest. Winslow's "Relation," which had been in print for forty years, referred to him as one of Weston's men who came to Plymouth "with his pack on his back," and "made a pitiful narration of their lamentable and weak estate and of the Indian carriages;" Morton's "Memorial," printed in 1669, stated that Pratt had "Penned the particulars of his perilous journey and some other things relating to this tragedy" of Weston's Colony; Hubbard and Increase Mather mention his service. Pratt's will is dated January 8, 1677, bequeathing an estate valued at forty pounds sixteen shillings to wife Mary and son Joseph. He died April 19, 1680. His gravestone is still preserved. On the right of a centre design is the figure of a spade and pickaxe crossed, and on the left hand a coffin and crossbones. The manuscript of Pratt's Declaration, for many years lost in the state archives, was found and published by Richard Frothingham in 1858. It consists of three folio sheets sewed together, one half of which appears to have been torn off after they were thus arranged. Hence a portion is lost. The manuscript is torn at the edges and portions of the writing are obliterated. He married Mary, daughter of Diggory Priest and his wife Sarah, who survived her first and second husbands and married third, Cuthbert Cuthbertson, or Godbert Godbertson, as he was sometimes called, a pious Hollander who joined Robinson's church at Leyden, and came to Plymouth in the ship "Ann." Priest died in the "great sickness," January 1, 1621. He was one of the signers of the compact on board the "Mayflower," having left his wife and children behind. His wife Sarah was a sister of Isaac Allerton, who was chosen assistant governor with Bradford, 1621-24, and was perhaps the wealthiest as he was one of the most influential of the Plymouth colony. Priest married her when she was a widow. He was admitted a citizen of Leyden, Holland, in November, 1615, Isaac Allerton "guaranteeing for him" upon his admission to civic rights in that city. During 1619 Priest's deposition was taken there, in which he says he was forty years old. Sarah, widow of Diggory Priest, had two daughters by him—Sarah and Mary. The daughter Sarah married John Come (or Coombe) who is styled "gentleman" in the Old Colony records; her name is frequently spelt Sara, or Zara. Cuthbertson was a widower when he married Mrs. Sarah Priest, who had twice been a widow, her first husband's name being Vincent, of London. Cuthbertson had a son Samuel by a previous marriage. The historians are mistaken in asserting that Pratt married a daughter of Cuthbertson; she was his stepdaughter. Hence all the descendants of Pratt are of "Mayflower" stock by descent from his wife. The proof is unquestionable. Pratt was on the list of those able to bear arms in 1643. His wife survived him about ten years. Children: 1. John. 2. Samuel, slain in the Pawtucket fight, March 26, 1676. 3. Daniel. 4. Peter, died before 1738. 5. Joseph, married February 12, 1674-5, Dorcas Folger; died December 24, 1712, at Charlestown. 6. Aaron, born about 1654, mentioned below. 7. Mary, probably wife of John Swan; she died February 11, 1702-3. 8. Mercy, married ——— Perry.

(II) Aaron Pratt, son of Phinehas Pratt (1), was born about 1654, in Charlestown, and died February 23, 1735. He was a farmer, and about November 28, 1685, removed to that part of Hingham known as the first division of land of Conohasset, consisting of eighteen acres of upland. He built a house two stories high, with gable roof, the lower story of stone, the upper of wood. The windows were of a small diamond pattern of glass known as "quarrels"—inserted in leaden sashes. The farm has always remained in the family. He married first, Sarah Pratt, born May 31, 1664, died July 22, 1706, daughter of Joseph and Sarah Pratt; second, September 4, 1707, Sarah Cummings, widow, daughter of ——— Wright. She died December 25, 1752, aged eighty-four years, "lamented by all who knew her." Children: 1. Henry, a blacksmith, settled in Newton. 2. Daniel, blacksmith, settled in Needham. 3. Aaron, born March 21, 1690; mentioned below. 4. John, a tanner, settled in Taunton. 5. Jonathan, a farmer, settled in Cohasset. 6. Moses, a mariner. 7. Sarah, married ——— Weebs. 8. Mercy, married Samuel Orcutt, of Hingham.

(III) Aaron Pratt, son of Aaron Pratt (2), was born March 21, 1690, and died March 28, 1767. He was a farmer, and resided in Cohasset, and built his house in 1729. He left his heirs one thousand acres of land in Hingham, and three hundred in the province of Maine. He married Mary Whitcomb, who died September 3, 1776. Children: 1. John, born 1729; married August 19, 1775, Bethia Tower. 2. Aaron, married ——— Collier. 3. Thomas, mentioned below. 4. Joseph. 5. Samuel; died unmarried. 6. Mary, married Job Tower. 7. Sarah, married Jessaniah Nichols.

(IV) Thomas Pratt, son of Aaron Pratt (3), was born at Cohassett, November 25, 1736, and died October 18, 1818. He resided at Cohasset. He was a soldier in the revolution, in Captain Peter Cushing's company, Colonel Solomon Lovel's regiment, December, 1776; company raised in Hingham and Cohasset; served at Hull. He married his cousin Sarah, daughter of Rev. Jonathan and Abigail (Pratt) Neal. Children, born at Cohasset: 1. Benjamin, December 1, 1766; died September 25, 1855. 2. Abigail, February 17, 1768; died February 9, 1856. 3. Sarah, January 25, 1769; died March 6, 1835; married Benjamin Briggs. 4. James, October 22, 1770; died January, 1795; married Elizabeth L. Burrill. 5. Thomas, died young. 6. Thomas, April 25, 1773; died November 20, 1865; married Lucy Turner. 7. Betsey, August 4, 1775; married Caleb Mann. 8. David, May 7, 1777; died September 15, 1812, unmarried. 9. Alice, July 18, 1778, died November 14, 1867; married Captain William Kilburn. 10. Job, December 1, 1779; died January 7, 1853; married first, 1801, Lucretia Oakes; second, Patience Cole; third, 1841, Mary Howe. 11. Henry, born October 16, 1781; died September 25, 1852; married, December 2, 1818, Clara Stockbridge. 12. Phinehas, born January 23, 1783; mentioned below. 13. Eleazer, born January 10, 1785; died August 21, 1849; married October 16, 1808, Mary Jones.

(V) Phinehas Pratt, son of Thomas Pratt (4), was born at Cohasset, January 23, 1783, and died at Boston, February 7, 1825. He was a housewright, and removed to Boston about 1800. Children: 1. Phinehas Neal, born September, 1808; died April 14, 1886. 2. Sarah, died young. 3. Sarah Ann, married ——— Woodbury. 4. William Henry. 5. Maria Alice. 6. Caroline Elizabeth. 7. Asa Thomas, mentioned below.

(VI) Asa Thomas Pratt, son of Phinehas Pratt (5), was born December 10, 1820. He married Mercy Clapp, born in Weymouth, August 25, 1820. Among his children was Fannie M., who married Eben W. Sheppard. (See Sheppard).

CHEEVER The common ancestry of most of those who are known to have borne the surname Cheever in New England in colonial times is most clearly shown by the public records, and may be briefly referred to here. Bartholomew Cheever, of Boston, cordwainer, in his will dated October 21, 1693, probated December 28, 1693, mentions his brother Daniel and his cousins Ezekiel Cheever, schoolmaster, and Richard Cheever. Daniel Cheever, of Cambridge, husbandman, in his will dated April 30, 1698, admitted to probate June 21, 1704, speaks of his brother Bartholomew Cheever, of Boston, deceased. Peter Cheever, of Salem, glover, in his will dated July 15, 1699, probated August 7, 1699, calls Samuel Cheever, of Marblehead, (son of Ezekiel) his cousin. Administration on the estate of Abraham Cheever, of Boston, was granted to Joshua Atwater, 1669-70, his brother Bartholomew Cheever having declined to act.

(I) Peter Cheever, of Salem, glover, whose will was admitted to probate August 7, 1699, was a cousin of Rev. Samuel Cheever, of Marblehead, whose father was Ezekiel Cheever; and from this it is clear that the father of Peter Cheever was a brother of Ezekiel, although the name of Peter's father is not known; neither is it known whom this Peter married. The Salem records give an account of the marriage of a Peter Cheevers and Lydia Haly, February 19, 1669, and of that marriage there was born Peter and Samuel Cheevers, twins, October 29, 1678. It is known, however, that Peter Cheever, of Salem, glover, did marry and have children, one of whom was a son Peter.

(II) Peter Cheever, son of Peter Cheever last mentioned, was born probably in Salem, but little else is known of him. He lived in Salem, married and had children, and it is possible that he may have been the Peter Cheevers, who married June 29, 1695, Mary Mackmallin, although there is no satisfactory proof of the identity of these two Peters. The records show that Peter and Mary had a son James, born in Salem May 1, 1696, but none other of their children are recorded there. The "Driver Family" genealogy gives the succession of these Peters from Peter, of Salem, glover, from whom we may be assured of the correctness of the line of the family here under consideration; but the compiler of that work does not assume to give the names of wives of the Peter Cheevers of the first and second generations. It is known, however, that Peter Cheever (2) had a son Peter, and it is probable that he had other children besides him.

(III) Peter Cheever, son of Peter last mentioned, was born probably in Salem, and is the same Peter Cheever who in 1746 bought of Benjamin Lynde, Esq., a piece of land which from the description of its boundaries must have been at the corner of what now is Brown and Winter streets, where his son Samuel afterward built a tannery. According to "Driver Family," Peter Cheever married Margaret, daughter of Captain Daniel and Margaret (Luscomb) Caiton, and among their children was a son Peter.

(IV) Peter Cheever, son of Peter and Margaret (Caiton) Cheever, was born about 1735, and died about 1801, and then was of Andover, Massachusetts. He married (first) Margaret, daughter of Captain Benjamin and Anne (Derby) Ives; married (second) December 23, 1762, Martha, daughter of Samuel and Martha (Walker) Osgood. He had two children by his first wife and seven children by his second wife: 1. Anna (Nancy), baptized December 9, 1759; married (first) Samuel Cook; (second), William Merriam. 2. Margaret, January 3, 1762; married John Flynt. 3. Peter Osgood, March 18, 1764. 4. Samuel, September 8, 1765. 5. Martha, June 4, 1769; married Samuel Very, of Salem. 6. Abigail, married James Perkins, of Salem. 7. James, baptized December 22, 1771. 8. Benjamin. 9. Nathaniel.

(V) James Cheever, son of Peter and Martha (Osgood) Cheever, was born in Lynn, Massachusetts, in 1767, and was a farmer, living during at least a part of his life in that part of the old town of Lynn which was set off to form the town of Saugus. He married May 19, 1791, Margaret Willson, and by her had eight children, born as follows: 1. Lucy, March 29, 1792. 2. William, October 24, 1795. 3. Lois, March 4, 1797. 4. James, October 16, 1803. 5. Benjamin, August 6, 1806. 6. Elma, July 16, 1808. 7. Asa, September 12, 1812. 8. Lot, October 22, 1814.

(VI) Lot Cheever, son of James, was born October 22, 1814, and died January 2, 1892. He was a cordwainer, and is so mentioned in the record of his marriage with Olive Dale Guilford, of Salem, born September 6, 1820. Children: 1. David H., born May 19, 1838. 2. Edward N., July 1843, died September following. 3. Francis Wilson, July 13, 1843, died April 4, 1844. 4. Margaret, March 1, 1840, died August 17, 1840. 5. Charlotte, July 23, 1847, died January 7, 1894. 6. Fernando Wood, December 18, 1854. 7. Mary L., July 14, 1861, died July 16, 1862.

(VII) David H. Cheever, son of Lot and Olive Dale (Guilford) Cheever, was born in Saugus, Massachusetts, May 19, 1838, and like his father was a cordwainer, or shoemaker, and for several years was foreman of a factory for the manufacture of shoes. He enlisted in 1861, at Malden, as private in Company K, Seventeenth Massachusetts Volunteer Infantry, was promoted sergeant, and served an enlistment of three years. He was mustered out of service in 1864, then returned to his former home and resumed work as shoemaker. He married, January 1, 1860, Mary E. Poland; children: 1. Frederic C., born November 8, 1860. 2. Josephine A., December 16, 1867, married Henry C. Russell, formerly of Lynnfield, now of Malden, and a produce merchant of Boston; has one child, Eugene Russell, born December 8, 1905. 3. Archie C., November 26, 1872; married Alice Cowdrey, of Lynn, and has one child, Frederic H., born January 15, 1904.

(VIII) Frederic C. Cheever, son of David H. and Mary E. (Poland) Cheever, was born in Saugus, Massachusetts, November 8, 1860, and received his education in the public schools of that town, afterward taking a business and commercial course in Boston. For the next five years he was bookkeeper in a Boston wholesale house, and in 1884 left that position to become proprietor of a laundry in Lynn. In the following year he went to Wakefield, Massachusetts, and in company with Charles H. Cox established a steam laundry in that town, continued the business until 1890, when the firm dissolved. Mr. Cheever then returned to Lynn, and has since carried on a large laundry establishment in that city. He is a well-known figure in fraternal circles, member of William Sutton Lodge, F. and A. M., of Saugus; Sutton Chapter, R. A. M., of Lynn; Mt. Olivet Commandery, K. T., of Lynn; and Aleppo Temple, A. A. N. M. S., of Boston; he is a member of the Nanepashemet Club, of Saugus; the Sons of Veterans, of Saugus; Danvers Country Club, the Oxford Club, of Lynn, and of the Bay State Automobile Club of Boston. Since 1904 he has been a member of the Saugus board of water commissioners, and he also is a member of the finance committee of the same town.

Mr. Cheever married, June 9, 1885, Kate M. Hasty, born in West Durham, Maine, January 6, 1864, daughter of Daniel Hasty, born Scarboro, Maine, November, 1818, died March 28, 1864; married Catherine Moses, born West Durham, December 31, 1823, died May, 1895.

WOODS Samuel Woods was one of the first settlers in the region which includes the present towns of Shirley, Groton and Pepperell in Massachusetts, and was the ancestor of a numerous line of descendants who in later generations became scattered throughout the New England states, notably Massachusetts, New Hampshire and Maine. Samuel Woods was living in Shirley as early as 1662, and was one of the proprietors of that town, having a grant of eleven acres of land. By his wife Alice, whose family name does not appear, he had six children whose names are found recorded: 1. Thomas, born March 9, 1663. 2. Elizabeth, September 17, 1665. 3. Nathaniel, March 27, 1667-8. 4. Mary, August 2, 1670. 5. Abigail, August 19, 1672. 6. Hannah, July 18, 1674, died September 29, 1703.

(II) Nathaniel Woods, son of Samuel and Alice Woods, was born March 27, 1667-8, and married about 1693, Alice ———. Their children: 1. Nathaniel, born October 19, 1694. 2. Daniel, August 10, 1696. 3. John, March 4, 1698. 4. Isaac, February 20, 1699-1700. 5. Bathsheba, April 5, 1702. 6. Hannah, March 16, 1704. 7. Phebe, February 13, 1705-6, died young. 8. Aaron, May 26, 1707. 9. Moses, July 6, 1709. 10. Reuben, April 11, 1711. 11. Phebe, March 13, 1713. 12. Jonathan, June 4, 1716.

(III) Jonathan Woods, youngest son and child of Nathaniel and Alice Woods, was born June 4, 1716, and probably was among the first of the Woods colony that went into the province of New Hampshire, although the year of his emigration and the place of his settlement in that region are not known. With others he took up his abode in a new and sparsely settled region at a time when unfriendly Indians were frequently devastating the new settlements, and to escape their depredations the settlers were compelled to seek safety in the vicinity of well defended towns. Children: 1. Mary, born January 31, 1738-9. 2. Jonathan, April 3, 1741, died young. 3. Phebe, February 14, 1742. 4. Joseph, May 4, 1745. 5. Rachel, March 30, 1746. 6. Jonathan, May 5, 1749. 7. Alice, February 14, 1750. 8. Levi, born May 10, 1753.

(IV) Joseph Woods, son and fourth child of Jonathan and Mary Woods, was born May 4, 1745, and is mentioned as one of the early settlers of Mason, New Hampshire, where during the period of his residence he appears to have been a person of considerable importance. He eventually went into the adjoining province of Maine, and it is probable that he may have lived there before settling in Mason. He married Mary Waugh; children: 1. Joseph, born October 27, 1782. 2. Samuel, October 6, 1784. 3. Polly, May 27, 1786, died young. 4. Sally, April 19, 1790. 5. Polly (Mary), March 7, 1792. 6. Betsey, April 19, 1798.

(V) Joseph Woods, eldest child of Joseph Woods, is believed to have been born in Standish, Maine, and he died October 6, 1840. According to family recollections his occupation was farming, but the history of North Yarmouth in noting some of the principal events of that region mentions a serious fire that destroyed the old Jenks tavern and several other buildings. In speaking of Joseph Woods the writer of that history has this to say: "Joseph Woods' cabinet shop and dwelling house in the rear were consumed. He probably was the most industrious man in the town. Early and late he might be found in his shop. He manufactured mahogany furniture and made the coffins for the dead. During his life the fashion was changed of painting coffins black to a light red color. He was an ardent pioneer of the abolitionists and an active member of the Baptist church."

It may also be said that Mr. Wood was more than an "ardent pioneer of the abolitionists;" he was a man who advocated strict temperance in all things, and he practiced in his daily life the principles he so earnestly professed. It is said of him that he never ate white bread, never drank tea or coffee, but throughout the period of his usual life ate only brown bread, pork and baked potatoes and drank only sweetened water.

On one occasion the neighbors assembled at the "raising" of his barn, and then he shattered the old established custom of opening the cask of rum which always had been considered an indispensible requisite of the raising; but notwithstanding the absence of the liquor the frame was raised, for the people of the town knew the upright character of the man and respected his adherence to principle regardless of traditions or customs. Besides being a temperate man Mr. Woods was a very pious man and one of the pillars of the Methodist Episcopal church. His wife was Elizabeth (or Lydia) Radcliffe, who survived her husband more than twenty-five years. The town records mention her death in these words: "Elizabeth Woods, widow of the late Joseph Woods, died February 10, 1875, aged eighty-six years, eight months." Their children were: Chandler, Joseph, Wesley, John, Benjamin, Greenleaf, Mehitable, Lydia, Betsey, Amanda, Ann, child, name unknown.

(VI) Benjamin Woods, fifth child of Joseph and Elizabeth (Radcliffe) Woods, was born in Unity, Maine, January 24, 1828, and when twenty-one years old was attracted to the gold fields of California, having the honor of being a "forty-niner" and one of the pioneers of placer mining at Sacramento on the Pacific slope, where he remained several years. Upon returning to Maine he became a farmer and was one of the prominent men of the town. He served as selectman of Unity, and like his father was a devout member of the Methodist Episcopal church. He married Angeline Holmes, born in Freedom, Maine, July 11, 1837, daughter of George Holmes, of Freedom. Children: 1. Lindley R., born October 16, 1856. 2. Wesley F., October 7, 1859. 3. Franklin B., August 23, 1861. 4. Laura Jane, June 7, 1865; lives in Everett, Massachusetts. 5. Lyrtle B., November 13, 1873; married William B. Pickering; lives in Everett, Massachusetts.

(VII) Franklin Benjamin Woods (baptized Benjamin Franklin Woods), third child and third son of Benjamin and Angeline (Holmes) Woods, was born in Unity, Maine, August 23, 1861, and for the last nearly forty-five years had engaged in mercantile business in Everett, Massachusetts. In 1878, when less than seventeen years old, he left home and began working for his cousin, John W. Plaisted, with whom he learned plumbing, sheet-iron working and furnace and stove repairing. Ten years later, in 1888, he went to California and worked at his trade about one and one-half years in Los Angeles and Pasadena, and returned to Everett in April, 1890. Four years later he began business on his own account and since that time has been numbered with the substantial men of the town. Mr. Woods is a member of the congregation of the Congregational church, is a master Mason, an Odd Fellow, and in politics is a Republican. He also is one of the trustees of the Everett Savings Bank. He married, 1889, Desdemona Hunt, born in Ivesboro, Maine, daughter of John Hunt, whose home was on Acre Island, off Lincolnville. Mr. and Mrs. Woods have two children: Angeline and Helen, both born in Everett.

BROWN John Browne, of Burrough Stamford, Lincolnshire, England, was chief magistrate of the city, 1376-1377. John Browne (2), son of John, lived in Stamford and had children. John Browne (3), son of John (2), was a draper and merchant at Calais, was alderman, chief magistrate of the city, and on his death in 1442 was buried in All Saints' Church, which he built for the parish at his own cost. John Browne (4), son of John Browne and Margaret his wife, was born in Stamford, about 1410, and was a draper and merchant, alderman three years, and died before 1470. His wife was Agnes. Christopher Browne (5), son of John Browne (4), was born in Stamford, lived there and at Tolthorpe. He married first, Grace Pinchbeck; second, Agnes ———, of Bedingfield, Norfolk; third, Elizabeth ———. Christopher Browne (6), son of Christopher, was born about 1460-70, and lived at Swan Hall, Hawkedon parish, Suffolk, England, and was church warden, 1564. Christopher Browne (7), son of Christopher, was born at Swan Hall, about 1490, was church warden there in 1564, and his children were born there. Thomas Browne (8), son of Christopher, was born at Swan Hall, about 1510-20, and married Joan ———.

(I) Abraham Browne, the immigrant, son of Thomas (8) and Joan, was born at Swan Hall about 1590, and was one of the first planters at Watertown, Massachusetts, in 1631-2, where he was selectman 1636-43. In 1634 he and Robert Selley were appointed to survey all the lots that were granted, and they were made conservators of all the timber trees, none of which could be cut without their consent. He was one of seven freeman who in 1635 were appointed "to divide every man his property of meadow and upland that is ploughable, the rest to be commoan." He was highway surveyor the same year, and laid out many of the highways, some of which are still in use. He was appointed, October 7, 1641, on a committee to lay out a thousand acres granted to the military company of Boston at its organization. His will was proved October 1, 1650. His first homestall was east of Mt. Vernon, between the present town of Watertown and Harvard Square. His second homestall was bounded by the present Harvard street, Main street and Pleasant street, and was lately and may be now the only case where land granted to the first settlers in Watertown is still held by lineal descendants. There is an engraving of the old house published in Bond's Watertown history. His widow Lydia married, November 27, 1659, Andrew Hodges, of Ipswich. She died at Watertown September 27, 1686. Children of Abraham and Lydia Brown: 1. Sarah, born in England, married December 16, 1643, George Parkhurst, Jr. 2. Mary, born in England; married April 10, 1650, John Lewis, of Charlestown and Malden. 3. Lydia, born at Watertown, March 22, 1632-3; married Lieutenant William Lakin, Jr., of Groton. 4. Jonathan, born Watertown, October 15, 1635. 5. Hannah, born Watertown, died March 5, 1638-9, an infant. 6. Abraham, born March 6, 1639-40, died 1667; bought land at Groton; married February 5, 1662-3, Mary Dix, who married second, in 1668, after Abraham's death, Samuel Rice, of Sudbury.

(II) Jonathan Brown, son of Abraham Browne, was born October 15, 1635, at Watertown, Massachusetts. He married, February 11, 1661-2, Mary Shattuck, daughter of the immigrant, William Shattuck, of Watertown. She was born August 25, 1645, and died October 23, 1732, aged eighty-seven years. She is buried in the Waltham graveyard. His will was dated February 19, 1690-91, and proved April 7, 1691. Up to this generation Bond says that the name generally was spelled with the final "e." The sons of Jonathan dropped this letter. Children of Jonathan and Mary Brown: 1. Mary, born October 5, 1662; married May 22, 1682-3, John Warren; married second, Samuel Harrington. 2. Elizabeth, born September 19, 1664; married March 25, 1687, Daniel Benjamin. 3. Jonathan, born October 25, 1666, died young. 4. Patience, born March 6, 1668-9; married March 5, 1686-7, James Bigelow. 5. Abraham, born August 26, 1671, died November 27, 1729. 6. Samuel, born October 21, 1674. 7. Lydia, born March 31, 1677; married January 18, 1698-9, Benjamin Wellington. 8. Ebenezer, born September 10, 1679. 9. Benjamin, born February 27, 1681, died in 1753. 10. William, born September 2, 1684; died October 28, 1756.

(III) Deacon Benjamin Brown, son of Jonathan Brown, was born at Watertown, February 27, 1681, and died March 11, 1753. He married February 27, 1702-3, Ann, daughter of Captain Benjamin Garfield, son of Edward Garfield, Jr., of Watertown. They settled at Watertown Farms, now Weston, in the part that subsequently became Lincoln. He was deacon of the church there, elected April 20, 1715, and was an influential man in church and town affairs. Children of Deacon Benjamin Brown: 1. Anna, born March 2, 1703-4; married December 24, 1724, Josiah Jones, Jr.; settled in Stockbridge. 2. Benjamin, born February 10, 1705-6. 3. Elizabeth, born January 13, 1707; married December 29, 1726, John Billings, of Concord. 4. Mary, born January 10, 1709-10; married December 6, 1730, Nathan Upham. 5. Mehitable, born February 9, 1711-12, died April 22, 1725. 6. Ephraim, born 1714. 7. Lydia, born February 23, 1715-16; married February 18, 1738-39, Joseph Upham, of Reading. 8. Joseph, born Weston, February 17, 1718. 9. Deliverance, born November 11, 1720, married March 31, 1743, Daniel Fiske, of Sturbridge. 10. Tabitha, born August, 1723, died September, 1723. 11. Timothy, born December 18, 1724; married Rebecca Farrar.

(IV) Ephraim Brown, son of Deacon Benjamin and Anne (Garfield) Brown, was born April 8, 1714, and was admitted to the church in Spencer October 6, 1754. He married February 21, 1755, Hannah Edmunds, who died in 1799.

(V) Ephraim Brown, son of Ephraim and Hannah (Edmunds) Brown, was born February 8, 1763, and died March 28, 1842. He married Elizabeth Boardman, born July 27, 1768, died October 2, 1824. Their children: 1. Increase Howe, born January 16, 1793, died in November 1869. 2. Ephraim, born November 12, 1795, died February 28, 1851. 3. Asa, born October 31, 1797, died April 7, 1868. 4. Elizabeth, born January 13, 1800, died April 6, 1878. 5. Thomas, born July 16, 1802, died March 24, 1889. 6. Rhoda, born October 1, 1805, died March 4, 1892.

(VI) Increase Howe Brown, son of Ephraim and Elizabeth (Boardman) Brown, was born in Ipswich, Massachusetts, January 16, 1793, and married June 8, 1820, Eliza (or Elizabeth) Harris. (The records mention that on October 28, 1830, Increase Howe Brown married Mary W. Gerry, and it is possible that she may have been his second wife). Mr. Brown was engaged in business in Marblehead. The Marblehead records show that he had three children born in that town: Increase Howe, baptized 1824; John Harris, baptized August 5, 1827; child, died January 8, 1837, age seventeen days.

(VII) Increase Howe Brown, son of Increase Howe and Eliza (Harris) Brown, was born in Marblehead, Massachusetts, and was baptized there July 4, 1824. For a time he was in the dry goods business in partnership with his father, later was in Boston, and still later received an appointment in the treasury department at Washington, D. C. His wife Catherine T. was a daughter of Major Joseph W. Green, of Marblehead. They had two children.

(VIII) Henry Brown, son of Increase Howe and Catherine T. (Green) Brown, was born in Lynn, Massachusetts, November 26, 1847, and received his early education in the public schools at Melrose, Massachusetts. When only a boy he began working in the millinery establishment of W. Heckle & Company, of Boston, running errands and doing such other work about the store as a boy of his years could do, but it was a real beginning at useful employment and soon led to something more profitable in the way of returns. In the course of time he was given a clerkship in the store, and in 1865 went to Providence, Rhode Island, and for the next five years filled a still more responsible position as salesman In 1870 he returned to Boston and became connected with the importing house of H. C. Cook, and two years later, in 1872, he was made foreign buyer for the house. In connection with the duties of his position of buyer of imported goods Mr. Brown went to various European cities twice each year to study foreign manufactures and goods in his line and also to make purchases for the house he represented. However, in 1880 he himself became proprietor of the business in Boston and has since carried it on with gratifying success. On August 22, 1871, Mr. Brown married Ellen M. Hawkins, daughter of Albert M. Hawkins, of Providence, Rhode Island. Children: 1. Henry E., born August 4, 1872, now appraiser in United States custom house, Boston. 2. Frank, born November 29, 1873. 3. Maud E., born August 7, 1875. 4. Robert, born January 19, 1877. 5. Carl, born September 22, 1879. 6. William O., born February 23, 1881, died December 10, 1883. 7. Hope, born April 17, 1887. 8. Kenneth, born June 5, 1889.

SWEENEY Patrick Sweeney, deceased, for many years well and favorably known in the business and social world of Lawrence, Massachusetts, was a descendant of an honored family of Ireland His father, John Sweeney, was a farmer in Ireland.

Patrick Sweeney was born in county Cork, Ireland, in 1841, and died in Lawrence, Massachusetts, July 22, 1899. He was about twenty-five years of age when he came to this country, where for a time he followed the occupation of stone dressing. Considerations of health compelled him to abandon this occupation and he became a cloth dresser in the Pacific Mills. For eight years prior to his death he was the proprietor of a store which he conducted very successfully. He was a Democrat in politics, and his religious affiliations were with the Catholic church, of which he was a devout member. He was also a member of a number of the church organizations. He married, November 28, 1882, Elizabeth Ann Sullivan, born in 1862, daughter of Colanus and Margaret (Collins) Sullivan, who were the parents of seven children. Colanus Sullivan came to Lawrence from Ireland, and worked as a dyer for five years preceding his death in 1887. Mr. and Mrs. Sweeney had children: Joseph Henry, born January 15, 1885; Jeremiah Francis, September 11, 1886; George Cornelius, July 27, 1890; Mary Constance, April 5, 1893; and Elizabeth, who died December 18, 1896.

SLAVIN The Slevin family is one of the ancient Ulster families. O'Hart in his Irish Pedigrees gives the family of Sleven, as it is sometimes spelled as among th numerous families that trace their descent from Colla da Chrioch, most of whom are Protestants in the north of Ireland. Colla da Chrioch was one of the three sons of Eochaidh Dubhlen, so-called from the fact that he was brought up in Dublin. The father of Eochaidh was Cairbre-Lifeachar, the 117th Monarch of Ireland, son of Cormac Art. O'Hart gives his pedigree to the remotest antiquity, including the 117 kings. Branches of the Slavin family settled in Scotland, but the seat of the family remains to day in Ulster. In 1890 eleven Slavins were born in Antrim county, Ulster and but three in all the rest of Ireland, while most of the Slevens also lived in Ulster.

(I) William Slavin, the progenitor, was born in Scotland and lived there all his life. He was a Protestant in religion.

(II) Blyth Slavin, son of William Slavin (1), was born in Scotland. He was educated in his native parish and learned the trade of weaver. When a young man he came to America and settled in Lawrence, Massachusetts, where he found employment in the famous Pemberton Mills, at his trade as weaver. He married Marion Morrison. Children: Agnes, Marion, William, Mary, Margaret, Marion, Hugh, Isabel.

(III) William Slavin, son of Blyth Slavin (2), was born in Scotland, July 17, 1837, and died in Lawrence, Massachusetts, January 17, 1899. He received his schooling in his native town and learned the trade of painter. He came with his father and the family to Lawrence in 1855. He followed his trade as a painter, as journeyman and contractor all his life. He was successful in business, careful, prudent and shrewd. In 1862 he enlisted in the Fourth Massachusetts Regiment of Volunteers in the civil war, in Captain Roland's company, and served his term of enlistment. In politics he was a Republican, in religion a member of the Protestant Episcopal Church. He married, September, 1857, Margaret Cochran, who was born in Scotland, October 9, 1834. She comes of an ancient Scotch family. The Cochranes were located in Renfrewshire and Ayrshire before A. D. 1300, and this family possesses the earldom of Dundonald and the lordship of Cochrane. Children of William and Margaret Slavin; born in Lawrence: 1. William, October 27, 1858; died October 27, 1858. 2. Christina, born February 6, 1860. 3. Margaret, July 27, 1861; died July 8, 1864. 4. Marion, born February 12, 1863; died 1905. 5. Mary, born March 4, 1865. 6. Albert M., October 15, 1869. 7. Thomas, 1870. 8. Charles Henry, October 24, 1874.

JOHNSON The surname Johnson represents one of the oldest New England family names, and has been known in English history since a period antedating the Norman conquest. Among those who bore it in some of the generations preceding and following the planting of the English colonies on this side of the Atlantic ocean were persons high in the royal favor, men famed in the wars and of the nobility, with coats-of-arms, titles and other evidences of high position. But all of these things were put aside when the tide of emigration set toward the new world to begin anew the settlement and development of another region.

(I) The particular branch of the Johnson family intended to be treated in this place begins with Richard Johnson, the immigrant, who was born in England in 1612, came to America with Sir Richard Saltonstall in 1630, and settled in the plantation at Watertown, Massachusetts, where he was made freeman in 1637. In the same year he moved to Lynn and located on a farm at the eastern end of the common, a part of the land then owned by him being the site of the city hall. He died August 26, 1666, aged fifty-four years. The name of his wife was Alce, probably Alice, and it may be assumed that he married after coming to New England, for at that time he was only about eighteen years old. Savage mentions his children as Samuel, Elizabeth, Abigail, Daniel.

(II) Lieutenant Samuel Johnson, son of Richard Johnson, the immigrant, was a soldier in King Philip's war, serving as cornet, 1676, and won the rank of lieutenant. For his services he received in 1685 a grant of land from the general court, and lived to enjoy his possessions until 1723, having attained the age of eighty-two years. He was representative to the general court in 1703 and 1708. He married, January 22, 1664, Mary Collins, and she had nine children: 1. Mary, born January 11, 1665, died at the age of three months. 2. Samuel, born November 18, 1666, died young. 3. Mary, born May 25, 1669. 4. Hannah, born May 15, 1671. 5. Elizabeth, born December 16, 1672. 6. Richard, born November 8, 1674, mentioned below. 7. Ruth, born March 6, 1676. 8. Samuel, born March 18, 1678. 9. David, January 31, 1689.

(III) Deacon Richard Johnson, second son and sixth child of Lieutenant Samuel and Mary (Collins) Johnson was born in Lynn, Massachusetts, November 8, 1674, died September 26, 1754, and his will was dated March 8, 1753, proved October 7, 1754. He was prominently identified with town affairs, town clerk in 1722 and for several years afterward, representative to the general court from 1720 to 1724, and afterward in 1731 and 1732. For many years he was a leading member of the church known as the Tunnell Meeting House, and at the time of his death and for several years previous one of its deacons.

Deacon Johnson married Elizabeth Newhall, July 3, 1705, who was born in Lynn, May 12, 1678, died March 8, 1749-50. She was a daughter of John Newhall, born Lynn, February 14, 1655, died January 20, 1738, and his wife, Esther Bartram, born Lynn, April 3, 1658, died September 28, 1728. He was a bricklayer and was generally known as John Newhall Tertius. His father, Thomas Newhall, is said to have been the first white child born in Lynn (1630). He married, December 29, 1652, Elizabeth Potter, and of their ten children John was second in order of birth. Thomas Newhall was the elder of two sons of Thomas Newhall and his wife Mary ———, the last mentioned Thomas being the immigrant ancestor of a prominent branch of the family of that surname in New England, Richard and Elizabeth (Newhall) Johnson had four children: 1. Mary, born February and who settled in Lynn in 1630. Deacon 25, 1706-07, married, 1727, Solomon Newhall. She died September 28, 1743, having borne her husband seven children: Richard, born October 14, 1727, married Lydia Williams; Ezra, born January 5, 1729-30, married December 12, 1751, Elizabeth Peck; Hulda, born July 18, 1732, married June 26, 1753, Jacob Alley; Timothy, born September 15, 1735; Jerusha, born October 17, 1737, died February 23, 1738; Elizabeth, born August 2, 1742; Solomon, born September 28, 1743, died February 7, 1744. 2. Samuel, born March 17, 1708-09. 3. Joseph, twin, born May 20, 1715. 4. Benjamin, twin, born May 20, 1715, died May 24, 1716.

(IV) Joseph Johnson, third child of Deacon Richard and Elizabeth (Newhall) Johnson, was born in Lynn, May 20, 1715. In 1736 he married Ann Legree, whose family name is mentioned in the town records as Legree, Legory and also Legery. Their children: 1. Benjamin, born August 13, 1737, died October 15, 1740. 2. Mary, born November 9, 1739. 3. Benjamin, born November 21, 1745. The names of these children are taken from the published vital records of Lynn.

(V) Benjamin Johnson, third child of Joseph and Ann (Legree) Johnson, born in Lynn, November 21, 1745, died there November 12, 1810. He was an earnest man in all that he undertook to accomplish and his energies were always directed in right channels. To him perhaps more than to any other person belongs the credit of planting the first seeds of the Methodist Episcopal society in Lynn. While journeying in the south he had made an acquaintance of the Rev. Jesse Lee, the famous apostle of Methodism, and it was through the urgent request of Mr. Johnson that Mr. Lee was induced to visit Lynn and proclaim to the townsmen there the teachings of the new doctrine. Mr. Lee began his preaching in Benjamin Johnson's barn in the latter part of 1790 and gained so many followers and converts to his faith that February 20, 1791, a Methodist Episcopal society was formed in Lynn. The first meeting house of the society was raised on June 21 following, and on June 26 the new edifice was dedicated. Throughout the entire time during which this preliminary work was in progress Mr. Johnson was earnestly engaged in all that took place and it was largely through his efforts and influence that the house of worship, the first of its denomination in Massachusetts, was erected; and until the day of his death he was one of the chief supporters of the church of which he was the principal founder.

Mr. Johnson married first, January 3, 1764, Lydia Richards, who died October 19, 1773; children: 1. John Legree, born March 30, 1766; see forward. 2. Benjamin, born December 4, 1767. 3. Joseph, born August 11, 1770. Mr. Johnson married second, January 27, 1774, Lydia Breed; she died March 23, 1776; children: 4. Lydia, born June 23, 1775. 5. Holton, born July 5, 177—. Mr. Johnson married third, September 29, 1776, Rachel ———, who died August 22, 1811, aged fifty-nine years; child, Rachel, born September 6, 1780.

(VI) John Legree Johnson, eldest son and child of Benjamin and Lydia (Richards) Johnson, born in Lynn, March 30, 1766, died there November 20, 1829. He married, first, September 11, 1791, Anna Burchstead, who died May 2, 1794, having borne her husband two children. He married, second, September 28, 1794, Sarah Rogers and by her had five children. His children were as follows: 1. Anna, born November 8, 1792, died October 29, 1793. 2. Benjamin Burchstead, born April 25, 1794. 3. John Rogers, born June 29, 1795. 4. Legree, born May 17, 1796. 5. Anna, born April 15, 1797. 6. Sarah, born May 20, 1798. 7. Holton, born October 19, 1801.

(VII) Benjamin Burchstead Johnson, second child and only son of John Legree and his first wife, Anna (Burchstead) Johnson was born in Lynn, April 25, 1794. He married, first, April 30, 1818, Harriet Newhall, who died April 15, 1879. He married, second, Rebecca ———, who died October 24, 1848. His children: 1. Mary Ann, born March 20, 1819, married Captain Joseph M. Rowell. 2. Harriett, born February 21, 1821, married William Wright. 3. Henry A., born August 10, 1823. 4. Sarah Rogers, born May 9, 1825, died young. 5. Edwin Holton, born May 21, 1826. 6. Sarah Rogers, born September 27, 1829, married S. S. Ireson. 7. Ruth Maria, born August 30, 1832, married Isaac Call. 8. Almira, born April 20, 1838. 9. Antoinette, born October 22, 1839, married M. N. Warren Page. 10. Horace Lyman, born January, 1842. 11. Benjamin Legree, born October 12, 1844.

(VIII) Edwin Holton Johnson, eldest son of Benjamin Burchstead and Harriet (Newhall) Johnson, his first wife, born in Lynn, May 21, 1826, died at his home in that city, March 22, 1894, which latter event marked the termination of a business career as successful as it was honorable, and all the deserved result of his own personal effort and industry. Mr. Johnson was educated in the Lynn public schools and graduated from the grammar school in 1842. After leaving school, being sixteen years old at the time, he secured employment in a shoe factory and soon became a practiced workman, having a good understanding of the mechanical part of the work in the shop and a fair knowledge of the management of the business in general. In 1854, after twelve years in the capacity of employee, he started in business on his own account and soon became proprietor of a shoe manufactory that gave employment to two hundred workmen. From the outset his business life was successful, and at its close he was possessed of a competence and, still better, he enjoyed the respect and confidence of a wide circle of friends and acquaintances. But while always a busy man, Mr. Johnson was not selfish with his time and means, and for many years took a commendable interest in public affairs in Lynn and was identified with several of the best institutions of the city.

In 1867 he represented the sixth ward in the board of aldermen, and while in that office was largely instrumental in securing much needed improvements in the old Lynn burying ground. He had little inclination for political office, but as a loyal citizen and large taxpayer willingly contributed his share of service for the public welfare. At the time of his death he was secretary of the Lynn Mutual Fire Insurance Company. He seems to have inherited from his worthy great-grandfather

E H Johnson

something of his loyal devotion to the Methodist Episcopal church and its institutions and charitable dependencies, and throughout the period of his business life it was his invariable custom to set aside one-tenth part of his annual income for charitable and benevolent purposes. He was a member of the board of trustees of Wilbraham Academy, an educational institution of high standing at Wilbraham, Massachusetts, conducted under the management of persons of influence in the Methodist Episcopal church. He was a trustee also of the corporation of Boston University, and of the First Methodist Episcopal church in Lynn. Each of these institutions at various times were made recipients of unsolicited gifts from his hands, and the society of his church in Lynn will ever remember him with gratitude on account of the handsome parsonage which stands near the church edifice which was erected at his personal expense. In addition to these benefactions he gave freely from his purse for various worthy causes of which the public at large never heard, and he also voluntarily assisted a number of young men in obtaining an education, those especially who sought to enter the ministry of the Methodist Episcopal church.

Mr. Johnson married twice. His first wife, whom he married November, 1857, was Grace Oliver, of Malden. She died in 1887, and he married, second, August 23, 1893, Lizzie Bishop, of Bristol, New Hampshire. One child, Margaret, who died in infancy.

WARNER The surname Warner is of ancient English origin, and the family has had many distinguished representatives for many years in England. More than twenty families of the name in England have coats-of-arms. Important branches of the Warner family have had their seats in Kent, Norfolk, Suffolk, Warwick and Yorkshire, England, Ayrshire, Scotland, and in Ireland.

(I) William Warner, immigrant ancestor of this branch of the Warner family, is believed to be son of Samuel Warner, of Boxstead, county Essex, England, and was doubtless born in England as early as 1580. He settled in Ipswich, Massachusetts, and was a proprietor as early as 1635. He was a planter; was admitted a freeman May 2, 1638. The date of his death is not known, but he was living October 29, 1654. Children: 1. Daniel, married Elizabeth Dane. 2. John, mentioned below. 3. Abigail, born in England, married Thomas Wells; died July, 1671.

(II) John Warner, son of William Warner (1), was born in England about 1615; he embarked on the ship "Increase" from London in 1635, giving his age as twenty. He settled in Ipswich; he was one of the first settlers of Brookfield in 1670, was one of three who took the Indian deed for the town December 19, 1673, was one of the principal citizens, removing in 1676 on account of the war to Hadley, where his son Mark had already settled. He probably died at the home of some of his children in 1692. John Warner married first, ———; second, Priscilla, daughter of Mark Symonds, about 1655. Children of first wife: 1. Samuel, born about 1640. 2. John, born about 1643, mentioned below. 3. Mark, born 1646, died at Northampton, Massachusetts, May 31, 1738, aged ninety-two. 4. Nathaniel, born about 1650, was a resident of Brookfield in 1673, died in Hadley, January 15, 1714. 5. Daniel, born about 1653, died in Ipswich, June 8, 1659. Children of second wife: 6. Joseph, born August 15, 1657, died June 18, 1658. 7. Mehitable, born April 16, 1659, died at Hadley, June 12, 1678. 8. Daniel, born April 16, 1661, died 1668. 9. Eleazer, born November 13, 1662, died at Hadley, May 8, 1729. 10. Priscilla, born 1664, married Thomas Cummings, of Dunstable, Massachusetts, December 19, 1688.

(III) John Warner, son of John Warner (2), was born about 1650 in Ipswich, and settled when a young man in Springfield, Massachusetts, removing from Hadley where his eldest child was born. He was a soldier in King Philip's war and was wounded in battle. He was a deputy to the general court. His will was dated 1718. He married first, April 2, 1674, Lydia Boltwood, daughter of Robert Boltwood; she died January 26, 1682. He married second, August 31, 1683, Sarah Warner, who died January 24, 1687. He married third, January 24, 1688, Sarah Ferry, who died July 25, 1689. He married fourth, November 26, 1691, Rebecca Cooley, widow of Obadiah Cooley, Jr.; she died October 18, 1715. John Warner died January 21, 1725. Children: 1. Lydia, married Josiah Beeman. 2. Priscilla, born April 4, 1677, married Edmund Bement. 3. John, born February 22, 1678, resided in Enfield and Suffield, Connecticut. 4. Ebenezer, born February 16, 1681, mentioned below. 5. Mary, born January 15, 1682, died January 29 following. Children of second wife: 6. Nathaniel, born August 19, 1684. 7. Child born October 1, died October

18, 1685. Child of fourth wife: 8. Child born May 2, 1695.

(IV) Ebenezer Warner, son of John Warner (3), was born in Springfield, February 16, 1681. He had a grant of twenty acres of land on the south side of the Little Wachogue path on South End hill, Wachogue, Springfield, March 9, 1724-25. He was at various times hogreeve, tithingman, and held other town offices. He married, about 1720, Mary ———. Children, born in Springfield: 1. Mary, born September 1, 1721. 2. John, born November 19, 1723. 3. Lydia, born February 28, 1726-27. 4. James, born July 21, 1731. 5. Lois, born March 1, 1733-34. 6. Ebenezer, born July 11, 1736, mentioned below.

(V) Ebenezer Warner, son of Ebenezer Warner (4), was born in Springfield, July 11, 1736. He removed to Marblehead, where he died May 15, 1790, the records stating his place of birth, and giving his age as fifty-five. He was a seafaring man. He married, at Springfield, October 8, 1761, Elizabeth Cook, who died December 11, 1800, aged fifty-nine years, four months, at Marblehead. Among their children were John, mentioned below. Hannah, born September, 1767-68, died July 23, 1787, at Marblehead, aged nineteen years ten months.

(VI) Captain John Warner, son of Ebenezer Warner (5), was born about 1770. He was a mariner and was lost at sea in the schooner "Jachin" which was last heard of when she sailed from Marblehead, January 23, 1822. He married, October 24, 1805, Rebecca Patten, who died August 27, 1825, aged thirty-five. At the death of both father and mother, the son Richard was adopted by Deacon Richard Homan. Children: 1. James Madison, baptized January 15, 1809. 2. John Cook, born November 23, 1806, died January 12, 1810. 3. William, was adopted by Captain William Story. 4. John Gerry, born November 11, 1811, mentioned below. 5. Child, name not given in records, died October 25, 1821, aged five years. 6. Richard Homan, baptized September 4, 1825. 7. Elizabeth, married John Florence. Of the above named James M., William and Richard made their homes in the west.

(VII) John Gerry Warner, son of John Warner (6), was born November 11, 1811, baptized in Marblehead, December 1, 1811. He was educated in the district schools of his native town and learned the trade of shoemaker. He removed to Boston and engaged in the wholesale boot, shoe and leather trade, conducting a large and flourishing business to the time of his death, in 1847, at the early age of thirty-six years. He married Eliza Newhall, who died in 1892, aged seventy-five years, daughter of Francis Stewart and Lydia (Burrill) Newhall, and a descendant in the ninth generation of Thomas Newhall (see Newhall family). Her mother was a descendant in the seventh generation from George Burrill, immigrant, who settled in Lynn, Massachusetts, in 1630. Children of John Gerry and Eliza (Newhall) Warner: 1. Helen Story, born 1839, died 1897, unmarried. 2. Eliza Frances, born November 13, 1842, married Howard Perley, of Lynn. 3. John Gerry, mentioned below.

(VIII) Captain John Gerry Warner, son of John Gerry Warner (7), was born in Boston, September 27, 1846. He attended the public schools of Lynn, Massachusetts, completing his education at the Chauncy Hall School, Boston. He began his business career as clerk for the firm of John B. Alley & Company, leather dealers, Boston. Afterward he was salesman for various firms in the leather and shoe finding business in Boston, and finally with the firm of Dunbar, Hobart & Whidden, later merged into the Atlas Tack Company, manufacturers of tacks, nails, etc. He was with this house for a period of twenty-one years. In 1898 he embarked in business in partnership with Albert and Percy F. Munsey in the Munsey Shank and Counter Company for the manufacture of leather board, steel shanks, etc., with a factory in Lynn. In company with Albert J. Lyons and Percy F. Munsey Mr. Warner incorporated the Lyons Counter Company, January 1, 1901, for the manufacture of sole leather moulded counters. In 1905 Mr. Warner organized the Warner-Robertson Company, of which he was elected president, and his son, Stewart C. Warner, secretary. This company manufactures moulded counters, turns, welts and box toes for shoe manufacturers, with factory in Lynn. The high standard of their goods and the enterprising management of the company have combined to put this concern among the leading dealers in shoe findings. Mr. Warner has been singularly successful in his business ventures. He has not only a thorough knowledge of his business, but the good judgment, industry and persistence necessary to conduct a manufacturing concern successfully.

In November, 1864, when but eighteen years of age, he enlisted at the time of the civil war as private in Company D, Captain W. H. Merritt, Eighth Massachusetts Volunteer Infantry, Colonel B. F. Peach, Jr. He continued in this company and regiment, being promoted through the various grades until he became captain of his company in 1875. In 1878 he resigned his commission as captain and accepted the appointment of paymaster of the regiment, a position he held until 1896 when he resigned and was placed on the retired list. He has been a member of the Ancient and Honorable Artillery Company of Boston since 1896 and held various offices in that body. He is also a member of the Oxford Club of Lynn, the Lynn Historical Society, the Howard Council, Royal Arcanum, of Boston, the Sons of the American Revolution and the Old Guard of Massachusetts. He is a member of the Unitarian church, in the work of which he takes an active part. In politics he is a Republican.

Captain Warner married, October 5, 1875, Ellen Louisa Kettell, born in Worcester, Massachusetts, January 10, 1843, daughter of Deacon John P. and Elizabeth F. (Wheeler) Kettell. Children: 1. Winthrop Kettell, born September 23, 1879, died at the age of seven years. 2. Stewart Gerry, born April 21, 1881, member of class of 1904, Lawrence Scientific School, Harvard University; now secretary of the Warner-Robertson Company; married Florence E. Bartol, of Lynn, descendant of the Bartol family of Marblehead; child, Marguerite, born May 16, 1907.

HINDS The surname Hyne, Hine, Hinds is variously spelled. It is derived from the trade or occupation, like many other English surnames. A Hyne, Hine or Hind was a tiller of the soil, peasant farmer. The surnames Haynes, Haines, Hine and Hinds, may have had different origins, but for a long time the spellings were used interchangeably in England and America, and it is not possible to separate the families by the surnames. In fact, nine different ways of spelling their name are still found among the descendants of James Hinds, the immigrant mentioned below.

(I) James Hinds, the first settler, born in England, came to Salem, Massachusetts, as early as 1637. About the same time came also two brothers, William and Richard, of Hinds, many of whose descendants spell their names, Haines, Haynes, Haine and Hayne. They owned a farm together, selling it in part June 29, 1648, and William gave a letter of attorney November 25, 1647, to Thomas Haynes, merchant, of London, for collection at Danes Balle, Bedfordshire. James and these two were believed to be related, perhaps brothers, and the records indicate London and Bedfordshire as the English home of the family. He was admitted a freeman, March, 1637-8, and sold land in Marblehead in 1649. He was a member of the Salem Church April 25, 1637. He removed to Southold, Long Island, New York, and died there March, 1652-3. He was a cooper by trade. His widow Mary married second, June, 1656, Ralph Dayton, of Southold. Hinds made his will March 1, 1652-3, bequeathing to wife Mary, eldest son John, and other children not named in the will. Children: 1. John, born August 28, 1639; mentioned below. 2. James, born August 2, 1641. 3. Benjamin, baptized August 26, 1643. 4. Mary, baptized February 19, 1646. 5. James, baptized December 27, 1647-8. 6. Jonathan, baptized April 11, 1648. 7. Sarah, baptized April 11, 1648, (twin). 8. Thomas, baptized March 4, 1651.

(II) John Hinds, son of James Hinds, was born August 28, 1639, and died at Lancaster, Massachusetts, March 20, 1720. He resided in Lancaster, removing there from Woburn in 1676, or soon afterwards, and his house was a garrison house under John Moore, April 20, 1704. For a short time he lived in Brookfield, but went back to Lancaster, where he died. His will was dated March 8, 1719-20, in Lancaster. He married first ———; second, February 9, 1681-2, Mary Butler. Child of first wife: 1. James, resided at Lancaster. Children of second wife: 2. John, born January 19, 1683, mentioned below. 3. Jacob, born at Brookfield, 1685. 4. Hannah. 5. Hopestill, born October 22, 1713. 6. Deborah. 7. Enoch, born October 30, 1717. 8. Experience, born November 18, 1718.

(III) John Hinds, son of John Hinds, was born in Brookfield, January 19, 1683, and died there October 10, 1747. He married Mrs. Hannah (Whitaker) Corliss, of Haverhill, born September, 1691. She married third, June 18, 1749, Oliver Heyward, who died at Brookfield, September 24, 1764. She was the heroine of a historical incident in Haverhill while living in the home of Mr. Rolfe, in which she saved the lives of his children. At her death she left thirteen children, all by John Hinds; eighty-two grandchildren, and seventeen great-grandchildren. John Hinds was on a committee of five, January 23, 1728, to divide Brookfield into four parts. He built a mill on Horse Pond, Brookfield, as early as

1738, and sold it to his son Seth. He was in Captain Thomas Buckminster's company in August, 1748, in the garrison at Fort Dummer. He made his will May 10, 1749, and mentions nine children. He resided at Lancaster until 1719, and in Brookfield afterward. Children: 1. Anna, born June 10, 1710. 2. John, born August 31, 1711. 3. Frances, born December 14, 1713; married Seth Bannister. 4. Mary, born February 12, 1716; married November 20, 1734, Joseph Bannister. 5. Seth, born April 3, 1718. 6. Jonathan, born October 23, 1720; died July 6, 1738. 7. Dinah, born October 14, 1722. 8. Corliss, born April 28, 1724; mentioned below. 9. Rachel, born August 25, 1726; died July 31, 1738. 10. Tryphena, born April 23, 1728, married Edward Wright. 11. Cornelius, born March 17, 1730; died July 7, 1738. 12. Submit, born July 27, 1732; died August 1, 1738. 13. Susannah, born December 17, 1733.

(IV) Corliss Hinds, son of John Hinds, was born in Brookfield, April 28, 1724, and died there in 1821. He was constable in 1768, and on the Committee of Safety from 1780 to 1789. From March to December, 1756, he was a member of Captain Solomon Keys's company, and was also a member of Captain Nathaniel Wolcott's company. He married first, September 6, 1742, Janet McMaster, of Brookfield. He married second, in 1809, Jennie McCullar. Children, all by first wife: 1. Cornelius, born March 17, 1743. 2. Anna, born October 7, 1744. 3. Rachel, born May 26, 1746. 4. Corliss, born April 10, 1748. 5. Susannah, born March 15, 1750. 6. Submit, born April 18, 1752. 7. Howard, born March 6, 1755; mentioned below. 8. Forbes, born May 25, 1759. 9. Catherine, born April 15, 1760. 10. Jesse, born September 7, 1764.

(V) Howard Hinds, son of Corliss Hinds, was born in Brookfield, March 6, 1755, and died at Worcester in 1850. During the last years of his life he was afflicted with blindness. He married, April 8, 1778, Anna Paine Hinds, born 1759, died November 19, 1821. Children: 1. Molly, born July 1, 1779; died August 22, 1782. 2. Anna, born September 12, 1780. 3. Calvin, born June 30, 1783, mentioned below. 4. John, born January 23, 1786. 5. Polly, born July 17, 1788. 6. Warren, born August 10, 1790. 7. Lydia, born May 22, 1793. 8. Cheney, born June 29, 1796. 9. Zenas, born February 11, 1799; died February 20, 1800. 10. Achsah, born May 15, 1801.

(VI) Calvin Hinds, son of Howard Hinds, was born in Hubbardston, Massachusetts, June 30, 1783, and died at Holden, October 21, 1857. He married first, at Barre, December 1, 1805, Susannah Clark, born May 31, 1785, died September 1, 1820, daughter of Joseph and Phebe (Rice) Clark. He married second, December 8, 1826, Mrs. Betsey (Lyon) Woodward. He was killed by the falling of a tree while cutting wood. Children, all by first wife: 1. Lucretia, born April 29, 1806. 2. Dorothy Quincy, born February 23, 1808. 3. Lowell Leland, born January 5, 1810. 4. Alanson Gibson, born February 26, 1812. 5. Eliza, born January 15, 1814. 6. Martin, born September 24, 1815. 7. Calvin P., born September 1, 1817. 8. William Augustus, born April 2, 1819; mentioned below.

(VII) William Augustus Hinds, son of Calvin Hinds, was born in Barre, April 2, 1819, and died at Worcester, January 21, 1876. He was a veteran of the civil war. He married in Boston, October 25, 1841, Rebecca Lougee, born March 10, 1818, died April 29, 1892, daughter of Hugh and Betsey (Parsons) Lougee, of Parsonfield, Maine. Chilrden: 1. Annie Jeanette, born May 25, 1842; married George H. Gregg (see Gregg family). 2. Emma Augusta, born July 25, 1844. 3. Calvin Parkman, born April 10, 1848. 4. William Augustus, born January 21, 1850; died December 20, 1852, in Boston. 5. Frank Clark, born April 23, 1852. 6. William Herbert, born June 6, 1856. 7. Ida Josephine, born July 11, 1859; died young.

GREGG The surname Gregg, or Greig, is ancient Scotch origin, and the family is found in the early history of Scotland in Fifeshire and other counties. Among the Scotch Presbyterian ministers sent to Ireland in 1645 to preach to the Scotch settlers in Ulster was Mr. John Greg, who was located at Carrickfergus. In July, 1648, he represented the Irish Presbytery in the Assembly of Scotland as commissioner; the assembly returned an answer by him and appointed to supply the pulpits in Ireland four more clergymen. Symon Greig was a member of the Scotch Parliament from Cupar as early as 1478. The first of the family in Antrim, Ireland, of whom we have record is William Gregg of Glenarm Barony in 1653. One of the "Ejected Ministers" on the list dated 1661 as published by Dr. Reid was John Gregg of Newtown Ards, County Downs, a Scotch Presbyterian. Early in 1670 this same minister who is the same man mentioned above as among the first to preach Presbyterianism in Ireland, was requested by his brethren in the ministry "to endeavor the composing a History of the Beginning and Progress of the Gospel" in the north of Ireland; but he died in July of the same year and the task devolved on Rev. Andrew Stewart Kirkpatrick, in his "Presbyterian Loyalty" says: "Mr. John Greg, Presbyterian minister in Newton, and Mr. Andrew Stewart, Presbyterian minister in Donaghadee, were men of great sagacity, judgment and veracity, as many yet alive can testify."

(I) Captain James Gregg, immigrant ancestor, was born about 1670, in Ayrshire, Scotland, and was twenty years old when his parents removed to Ulster Province, Ireland, and settled in the parish of Mulasky, county Antrim. He had been apprenticed at the age of fourteen to learn the trade of tailor and had just completed his time when he removed to Ireland with his father's family. There he immediately established himself in business and was very successful as a linen draper. One day Janet Cargill came to his shop to order her wedding dress. The romance that followed, embellished perhaps by some imaginative details of tradition and the author, is thus described in an article published half a century ago in the Nashua (New Hampshire) *Gazette*: "When she came into the shop he recognized her as a person he had seen, but had no particular acquaintance with her; he saw at once that she was very beautiful and interesting person, and had a most captivating smile on her countenance, and at the same time discovered that there was a shade of melancholy, which plainly told that some unseen affliction was preying upon her mind." After taking her measure and receiving her instructions, she very politely bade him adieu, and turned to go out of the door when he spoke to her in a tremulous tone of voice and said: "My dear friend, I am almost tempted to envy Mr. Lindsey his happiness." This unexpected salutation came upon her like a shock of electricity, and suddenly an effusion of tears burst from her eyes, while the tumult in her bosom choked her utterance, and she was silent a few moments until her emotion had somewhat subsided. At length she mustered fortitude enough to reply and said: 'My dear friend, if I could have my wishes realized, Mr. Lindsey would be the envious man and you would be the person envied.' This modest reply was too plain to be misunderstood, and it broke the ice at once and opened the way for a full explanation. Then they conversed freely on the subject, when she told him her story very candidly and said to him: 'I am now published to Mr. Lindsey, an old gentleman who is said to be respectable; he is three score and ten and I am eighteen. My father, Mr. Cargill, is under pecuniary embarrassment and is indebted to Mr. Lindsey to a large amount and he has taken advantage of this circumstance to induce me to accept his hand. My parents are intimidated and see no way to extricate themselves from this situation but by consenting to an unhallowed connection. Consequently, they had been worried with their pressed circumstances, I have with painful reluctance given my consent. And now, my dear friend, if you feel willing to relieve me from my deplorable situation, with honor both to yourself and me, I will cheerfully consent to any measures which you may think proper.' The result of this interview was the firm agreement to elope under cover of evening shadows and have the marriage performed by a curate in a neighboring parish, which was done to their mutual joy and satisfaction. Mr. Gregg and his young wife settled in the parish of Mausky where he pursued his business to good advantage; went extensively into the business of bleaching linen cloth and in the course of a few years accumulated a handsome property. In the year 1718 Mr. Gregg, with fifteen families from the same place, embarked on board a vessel commanded by Captain Crowningshield, of Salem, bound for America. They landed late in the season at Casco Bay, where they tarried the winter, and in the month of April came to Nutfield, now Derry, where they made a permanent settlement."

Janet Carhill was doubtless sister of Marion (Cargill) wife of Rev. James MacGregor, the minister, and of David Cargill who was one of the most important figures in the colony of Nutfield, subsequently the town of Londonderry, New Hampshire, owning the first saw mills, fulling mill and grist mill, a man of much ability, and property, honored frequently with positions of trust and responsibility. Captain Gregg and wife came with the first Scotch-Irish in accordance with the petition to Governor Shute from the Presbyterians of the north of Ireland and was with the party from this company who attempted a settlement at Cape Elizabeth, Casco Bay. He returned to Massachusetts, in the spring, and became one of the first eighteen settlers of Nutfield. During the winter there was much suffering from cold and lack of food and many of his poorer fellow-immigrants owed much to the kindness and generosity of Captain Gregg. He was chosen captain of the first military company of Londonderry, and was one of the foremost citizens of the town as long as he lived. He held various town offices. Children: 1. William, a surveyor, married Janet Rankin; children: James, Hugh, Naomi and Frances. 2. John, mentioned below. 3. Samuel, married Mary Moore; children: James, John, David, Margaret, Mary and Elizabeth. 4. Thomas, married Ann Leslie. 5. Elizabeth, married James Moore.

(II) John Gregg, son of Captain James Gregg, was born in Antrim, Ireland, about 1700. He married Agnes Rankin, also of Scotch Irish stock. Children, born at Londonderry: 1. James, married Mary McCurdy; had five sons and three daughters. 2. Hugh, married Sarah Leslie, sister of wife of Deacon James McPherson (or Ferson); settled in New Boston, New Hampshire. 3. John. 4. William, married Barbara Aiken; children: Ebenezer, William, Jane, Rosanna and Elizabeth. 5. George. 6. Samuel, mentioned below. 7. Joseph, married Susanna Aiken; children: John, Nathaniel, Joseph, David A., Anne, Margaret, Barbara, Susanna, Elizabeth, Jane and Sarah. 8. Benjamin had children—John, James, Lettice and Jane. 9.10. Elizabeth, Janet, twins.

(III) Major Samuel Gregg, son of John Gregg (2), was born in Londonderry, in 1738. He was a substantial citizen. Besides farming he manufactured spinning wheels and flax wheels. He was selectman of Peterborough 1768 to 1771, and later, and was on the committee of safety in 1779, during the revolution. He resided at Londonderry until about 1760, afterward at Peterborough. He was sergeant in the French and Indian war in 1759, and fought at Montreal under General Wolfe. He was commissioned major when the revolution came, and with two hundred men whom he enlisted hastened to Boston, arriving the day after the battle of Bunker Hill. He married Agnes Smiley, born 1743, died February 2, 1803, aged sixty years. Children, born at Londonderry: 1. John, February 23, 1764. 2. Hugh, November 22, 1765; mentioned below. 3. Sarah, November 7, 1769; married General David Steele. 4. Samuel, October 25, 1772. 5. George, March 15, 1775; married Sally Moore. 6. Ann, November 14, 1778; married ——— Gregg. 7. Mary, January 27, 1782. 8. Elizabeth, October 21, 1785; married William Hutchins.

(IV) Hugh Gregg, son of Major Samuel Gregg, was born in Londonderry, November 22, 1765. He (or his son or nephew of the same name) settled in Watertown, Massachusetts, when a young man. He married Betsey Howe, whose father was a cooper in Boston. Children: Charles, Mary Ann, Alexander.

(V) Alexander Gregg, son of Hugh Gregg, was born in Watertown, June 1, 1816. He married, December 8, 1839, Anna Maria Fuller, daughter of Eben Fuller. He was for years engaged in the cabinet making and furniture trade, and finally engaged in the undertaking business at Watertown. Children, born at Watertown. 1. Celia, 1841, married Frank Pattee. 2. Charles, married Emma L. Leonardson; child: Waldo H. 3. George H., June 19, 1845; mentioned below. 4. Alice, married Warren L. Rockwell; children: Winthrop and Abbott Rockwell. 5. Albert, married Fannie Gill (deceased).

(VI) George Herbert Gregg, son of Alexander Gregg (5), was born at Watertown, June 19, 1845. He received his educational training in the public schools of his native town, and under the careful guidance and tuition of his father; he was reared to habits of industry and economy. During his early manhood he acquired a thorough knowledge of the cabinet making trade and the undertaking business, in his father's establishment at Watertown, and not unlike his worthy Scotch ancestors, he acquired to a marked degree traits of fearlessness, nobility, modesty, untiring industry, and astute business judgment, which stood him in good stead during his active and useful career. He did much by his enterprise towards advancing the material as well as the social interests of his native town. He was public spirited and took an active interest in the town affairs, though he never held or sought public office. His acts of benevolence and kindness were many, and given with unstinted liberality. He was broad and forbearing in his religious views, and always had a kindly and sympathetic word for all. Mr. Gregg was prominent in Masonic circles. He was a member of Pequossette Lodge, Free and Accepted Masons, at Watertown; of Newton Chapter Royal Arch Masons; the Royal and Select Masters; of Gethsemene Commandery, Knights Templar; of Aleppo Temple, order of the Mystic Shrine; also of Pequossette Lodge, American Mechanics, of Watertown, and Watertown Lodge, Ancient Order of United Workmen. He was a member of the Newton Club, the Watertown Club, the Old Colony Club, the Massachusetts Undertaker's Association, and an honored member of Isaac S. Patten Post No. 51, Grand Army. During the civil war Mr. Gregg proved his loyalty and patriotism, and for some time was on duty at the Watertown Arsenal at Watertown, New York. He was a valued citizen, a loving husband, and an indulgent father. He died at his home in Watertown, February 6, 1907, and it has been correctly said that he left the impress of his individuality upon a wide community, and the priceless heritage of an honored name to his family. In his religious beliefs he was an Episcopalian, and he was one of the organizers of the church of the Good Shepherd, at Watertown, of which he was a member and served for a number of years as its first treasurer.

George Herbert Gregg married, June 19, 1873, Annie Jeanette Hinds, born May 25, 1842, daughter of William A. and Rebecca (Lougee) Hinds. Children: 1. Maud Georgette, born October 14, 1874, died October 27, 1874. 2. Frances A., born June 7, 1876, died November 30, 1876. 3. Walter Hinds, born December 17, 1881; see forward.

(VII) Walter Hinds Gregg, son of George Herbert Gregg (6), received his elementary educational training in the private school of Miss Spear, at Newton, and at a private school at Belmont, where he attended for some time. He then entered Phillips Exeter Academy, where he was prepared for college. He did not however enter upon a college course, and instead entered his father's office and undertaking establishment at Watertown, and under the parental tuition learned all the technical as well as the practical features of the business. Since his father's demise, in 1907, he has succeeded to the management of the enterprise, which is the leading one of its kind in Watertown, and the high standard of efficiency which his father had so thoroughly established has been well maintained by the son. He is an active member of Pequossette Lodge, Free and Accepted Masons; Newton Royal Arch Chapter; Gethsemene Commandery, Knights Templar; Aleppo Temple, Mystic Shrine; and Lafayette Lodge, Independent Order of Odd Fellows, at Watertown.

SMITH

Henry Smith, the ancestor of this branch of the Smith family, came to America from England in 1637 with his wife Elizabeth and his two eldest sons. He settled first in Dedham where, as stated in the records of that town, he was burned out in 1641. He went to Medfield, Massachusetts, in 1651-52, and took up his house lot on South street. He served on the board of selectmen for thirteen years. He died in 1687 and his wife in 1670. Children: 1. John, born in England, was in Dedham in 1660; later went to Medfield where he owned a house on Canal street; in 1667 he is mentioned as being in Taunton, and later in Marlboro; he married Lydia ———. 2. Seth, born in England, died in 1682; married, 1660, Mary Thurston. 3. Daniel, born 1639. 4. Samuel, see forward. 5. Joseph, born 1643, died 1661.

(II) Samuel Smith, fourth son of Henry and Elizabeth Smith, was born 1641, probably in Dedham. He inherited his father's house lot and property in Medfield. He married, in 1669, Elizabeth Turner, who was killed by the Indians in an attack upon the town. He married, second, Sarah, widow of John Bowers. He died in 1691 and his widow in 1704. Children by first wife: 1. Elizabeth, born 1670, died 1671. 2. Elizabeth, born 1671, died 1704; married, 1692, Eleazer Partridge. 3. Samuel, see forward. Children by second wife: 4. Sarah, born 1678, died 1769; married, 1701, Matthias Evans; married, 1726, Henry Harding. 5. Henry, born 1680, died 1743; married, first, 1703, Deborah Pratt, who died 1706; married, second, 1708, Mary Adams, who died 1725; married, third, 1730, Ruth Barber. He served on the Medfield board of selectmen in 1737. 6. Daniel, born 1682, died 1704. 7. Nathaniel, born 1684, married, first, 1705, Mary Clark, who died 1717; married, second, 1717, Lydia Partridge. 8. Abigail, born 1686, died 1725; married, 1705, John Fisher. 9. Mary, born 1688, married first, 1706, Henry Plimpton; married, second, 1732, Jabez Pond, of Dedham; married, third, 1750, Joseph Wright. 10. Prudence, born 1691, married, 1711, Joseph White, of Mendon.

(III) Samuel Smith, eldest son and third child of Samuel and Elizabeth (Turner) Smith, was born in 1674. He was deacon of the church, and filled many other positions of trust in Medfield. He served twenty-one years on the board of selectmen, nine years as town clerk, and some time as town treasurer. He was also a representative to the general court. He married, in 1695, Elizabeth Adams. He died in 1742 and his widow in 1753. Children: 1. Eleazer, born 1696, died 1768; married, 1729, Sarah Turner, who died 1763. 2. John, born 1699, died 1699. 3. Samuel, see forward. 4. Hannah, born 1703, died 1744; married, 1725, Benjamin Plimpton; married, second, Jonathan Metcalf. 5. Elizabeth, born 1705, died 1785; married, 1727, Nathaniel Cutter, of Medway. 6. Jonathan, born 1708, died 1708. 7. Elisha, born 1710, died 1710. 8. Lydia, born 1712, died 1795, unmarried.

(IV) Samuel Smith, third son of Samuel and Elizabeth (Adams) Smith, was born in 1700. He served six years on board of selectmen in Medfield. He married Silence ———. He died in 1763 and his widow in 1778. Children: 1. Keziah, born 1722, died 1777; married, first, 1738, Isaac Boyden; married, second, 1772, John Cutter. 2. Abigail, born 1724, married, 1747, Samuel Allen, of Wrentham, son of Eleazer Allen. 3. George, see forward. 4. Silence, born 1728, married, 1750, John Turner. 5. Elizabeth, born 1730, married, 1751, Moses Hartshorn. 6. Samuel, born 1732, died 1778, probably unmarried. 7. Hannah, born 1732, died 1732. 8. Abel, born 1734. 9. Seth, born 1736, died 1786; married, 1759, Drusilla Lyon, of Walpole, daughter of Peter Lyon; she died 1816.

(V) George Smith, eldest son of Samuel and Silence Smith, was born in Medfield in 1726. He received from his father, during his lifetime, some portion of his estate. He was constable in 1752. He married, in 1751, Mercy Metcalf, of Wrentham. He died probably in 1798. Children: 1. Eliphalet, born 1751. 2. Susanna, 1753. 3. George, 1755. 4. Silence, 1757. 5. Titus, see forward. 6. Lydia. 7. Rogers, 1761, in Wrentham. 8. Samuel, 1764, in Wrentham.

(VI) Titus Smith, second son and fifth child of George and Mercy (Metcalf) Smith, was born in Medfield in 1759, died 1805. He married, 1782, Atarah Hamant, who died in 1856. Children: 1. Titus, born 1783, died 1789. 2. Lucretia, 1785, died 1867; married, 1805, Seth Chenery. 3. Polly, 1787, died 1813; married, 1806, James Clark. 4. Olive, 1790, died 1880; married, 1811, David Clark. 5. Asa, 1792, died 1793. 6. Clark, 1795, married, 1821, Caroline Morse, who died in 1878. 7. Atarah, 1797, died 1865; married, 1824, Marcus Gilmore. 8. Thomas, 1799, died 1878; married, 1825, Eliza Wadsworth, of Dover, Massachusetts. 9. Abigail, 1801, died 1829. 10. Titus, 1803, died 1843; married, 1832, Abigail Bennett, of Roxbury, Massachusetts. 11. George M., see forward.

(VII) George M. Smith, youngest son of Titus and Atarah (Hamant) Smith, was born in Medfield, 1806, died in 1883. He married Joanna Harding in 1830. Children: 1. Jason, see forward. 2. Angelina E., born 1835.

(VIII) Jason Smith, son of George M. and Joanna (Harding) Smith, was born in 1832 and died in April, 1870. He was reared in Medfield and afterward moved to Milford, Massachusetts, where he became a machinist. He was very prominent in Masonic circles and in the Knight Templar Commandery of that town. He was a member of the Universalist church. He married, first, Elizabeth Mason Heath; married, second, Frances Isabella Murdock. Child by first wife: George Harding, see forward. Child by second wife: Charles House, married Hannah Elizabeth ———; children: Isabella Frances, born June, 1894, and Ethel Maud, January, 1899.

(IX) George Harding Smith, son of Jason and Elizabeth M. (Heath) Smith, was born at Milford, Massachusetts, February 18, 1859. He was reared in Medfield and educated in the public schools. He was for a number of years engaged in the furniture business, acting in the capacity of bookkeeper and confidential clerk of a large furniture house in Boston. In 1884 he entered into partnership with James Berwick, a sketch of whom appears in this work, in the printing business, Mr. Berwick being an excellent pressman, serving his time in Cambridge, and afterward being employed in good offices in Boston. They selected as a site for their plant the pretty village of Norwood, fourteen miles southeast of Boston, to which place two firms of Boston printers, J. S. Cushing & Company and Berwick & Smith, determined to remove, there establishing an office with more light and better sanitary conditions than they could obtain in the city, and in a town where workmen and workwomen could live at less cost and in a better way than would be possible in any metropolis. The necessary buildings completed the two firms removed their presses and other material thither, and began work under new conditions. The building is of brick, one story high except in the middle. Its length is four hundred and eight feet and its width eighty-one feet. The central part is two stories, with a tower still higher, which also projects from the front of the building. The north wing is appropriated by J. S. Cushing & Company, and the south wing is occupied by Berwick & Smith, who confine themselves to presswork. Mr. Berwick, a master of his art, attends to the problems of the printing department, while Mr. Smith who is a man of excellent business qualifications, is occupied with financial matters. To carry on business in the way they intended the two firms were organized as a corporation under the laws of Massachusetts, entitled the Norwood Press, for the purpose of holding real estate and buildings in the town of Norwood for their mutual benefit; otherwise, the concerns will continue to operate their respective businesses as heretofore.

Mr. Smith married, December 2, 1886, Laura Huntington Brown, daughter of Henry Sanders and Lucretia Richardson (Janes) Brown. Children: 1. Dorothy Elizabeth, born April 2, 1888. 2. Henry Sanders, October 20, 1889. 3. George Harding Jr., January 17, 1894. 4. Laura Huntington, March 5, 1898.

Mrs. George Harding Smith is descended through her grandmother, Laura Huntington Sanders, from the Rev. Dr. David C. Sanders, born in Sturbridge, 1768. Her father and mother were both of Medfield, Massachusetts, stock, though residents of Sturbridge before their marriage. His father was Michael, son of Daniel Sanders, who married in 1715 Sarah Metcalf, born 1683, daughter of Michael and Elizabeth (Bowers) Metcalf. Michael Metcalf was born 1650 and was son of John Metcalf, who was born at Norwich, England, 1622, and fled to this country from religious persecution, settling in Dedham, where he was the founder of the Metcalf family. Michael Sanders married Azubah Clark, and died in 1773.

Rev. Dr. David C. Sanders graduated from Harvard College in 1788. In 1789 he was made preceptor in the Cambridge high school. He studied theology with Dr. Prentiss, of Medfield, taught the North school there in 1790, and was licensed to preach in the same year by the Dedham Association. He married Nancy, daughter of Dr. Jabez Fitch, of Canterbury, Connecticut. He was ordained pastor of the church in Vergennes, Vermont, in 1794. In 1798 he preached the election sermon. He was elected president of the University of Vermont in 1800, and received the degree of D. D. from Harvard College in 1809. In 1814, the buildings, being occupied by the American troops, his family left Burlington, May 14, the British flotilla appearing before the town and bombardment being expected. In September of the same year he came to Medfield. He was a member of the convention for the revision of the constitution in 1820-21. The first historical sketch of that town was prepared by him and delivered as a sermon in 1817. After the division of the church and the organization of the Orthodox Congregational church he resigned his ministry. He was representative to the general court in 1832-33-34-35, served on board of selectmen repeatedly, and was on the school committee for a number of years. He died in 1850, and his wife in the same year.

The following are taken from a sermon preached by the Rev. John Arthur Savage, of the First Congregational Church of Medfield, on the occasion of the two hundredth and fiftieth anniversary of the incorporation of the town of Medfield, Massachusetts. "Some ten months after the death of Dr. Prentiss, pastor of the Congregational church at Medfield, a call was unanimously extended to the Rev. David C. Sanders, D. D., to become pastor of this church. The call was accepted and Dr. Sanders was installed and began his ministry here in May, 1815. He was a man of eminent learning and talent, and his pastorate in Medfield marks an epoch in the history, not only of this church, but of the whole religious life and Congregational faith of this town. Dr. Sanders was forty-seven years of age when he settled here, and had been the pastor of Congregational churches in the cities of Vergennes and Burlington, Vermont. In October of 1800 he had been made president of the University of Vermont, which position he held some fifteen years, and until in the course of the War of 1812 the American troops took possession of the college buildings as winter quarters, thereby necessitating the suspension of the work and practices of the institution. Dr. Sanders was then in the prime of middle life and manly and scholarly strength. He had already published one book and some twenty discourses, and Harvard, his alma mater, had honored him with the doctor's degree. But the breaking up of the college in Burlington was a great interruption in his career and a heavy blow to his ambitions. He left Burlington with his family and, as has been said, settled here in the spring of 1815. His parents and grandparents had originated in this town; here in his youth he had studied divinity under the venerable Dr. Prentiss; here he had preached his first sermon after being licensed as a minister by the Dedham Association in 1790. Dr. Prentiss had baptized him and admitted him to communion. Naturally enough his heart and hopes turned this way when, after the disaster that had come to the college in Burlington, your ancestors invited him unanimously to become the successor of Dr. Prentiss.

"He entered vigorously upon his work in this pulpit and parish, and was soon famous as a preacher in all this region of country. He was in demand at dedications, ordinations, installations, and on nearly all public occasions of importance. But the ministry of Dr. Sanders in this place had fallen upon evil times. The very year in which he settled here was the year that witnessed the breaking out of the controversy in the Congregational churches of New England between Trinitarians and Unitarians. That year Dr. Morse read the copy of Belshaw's 'Life of Lindsey' that had been sent from England to Harvard College, and 'the vail was torn away'. In less than four years from the time John Lowell had written and published his vigorous pamphlet entitled 'Are you a Christian or a Calvinist'? Dr. Channing had preached his famous Bathmore sermon, and the first parish in Dedham, mother of this church and here at your side in the neighboring town, had been rent in twain in a manner peculiarly exasperating. Controversy and division were in the air and in the pulpits and in the hearts of the people. It was inevitable that Medfield should breathe the spirit of the hour and enter strenuously into the conflict. Dr. Sanders foresaw the coming strife and division, and worked faithfully and anxiously to prevent controversy and ward off a schism in his church. And as a matter of fact, the actual division did not come until after Dr. Lyman Beecher had in May, 1827, visited the town and preached a sermon in this pulpit at the request of the deacons and 'without the consent of the pastor'. Dr. Beecher's avowed purpose was the defense and promotion of a stricter orthodoxy. There were at that time many disciples of Channing in this parish, as the sequel plainly proved. On the other hand, there were also a goodly number of zealous and conscientious evangelical believers. Dr. Sanders, appreciating the situation and wishing to allow freedom of thought and to maintain peace and union, avoided controversial themes and always used the time-honored church covenant, in receiving members, that had been used by Dr. Prentiss and his predecessors. But all these precautions and efforts to harmonize conflicting elements were unavailing, and not long after Dr. Beecher's visit the actual and permanent division of the parish occurred. Seventeen members withdrew from the church of the First Parish, and February 6, 1828, organized the Second Congregational Church of this town. Those were followed by nineteen others that same year among whom were some of the best members in the church, including, with others, the widow and two daughters of Dr. Prentiss. The large majority that remained in the First Church and Parish then seemed to insist that the preaching and the covenant should be more distinctly Unitarian. In this Dr. Sanders did not sufficiently comply with their wishes, and on March 2, 1829, a vote was passed by the parish dissolving the pastoral relation at the request of the pastor himself. This vote took effect on the 24th of the following May".

Children of Rev. Dr. David C. Sanders: 1. Laura H., born 1798, died 1870; married, 1818, Slade D. Brown, of New York, who was born in Porter, Rhode Island, January 10, 1794, son of David and Mercy (Slade) Brown. David Brown was born in Swanzey, Massachusetts, 1769; his wife was born there October 19, 1767. Mary Brown, sister of Slade D. Brown, was born in Hartford, New Hampshire, August 27, 1795. Slade D. and Laura H. Brown had two children: Henry Sanders, see forward. Helen Maria, married Robert Roberts, died 1876 in Framingham. 2. Miranda W., married, 1822, Amos Parker, of Concord, New Hampshire. 3. Henry F., born 1804, was a physician, died 1835. Besides these one son and four daughters died in childhood.

Henry Sanders Brown, son of Slade D. and Laura Huntington (Sanders) Brown, was born May 27, 1820. He married, October 2, 1848, Lucretia Richardson Janes, born 1826, died 1879, daughter of Walter and Lucretia (Richardson) Janes. Children: 1. Walter Janes, died young. 2. Helen Sanders, unmarried, resides on old Sanders homestead in Medfield. 3. Laura Huntington, married, December 2, 1886, George Harding Smith.

STONE Gregory Stone, immigrant ancestor, was baptized in Great Bromley, county Essex, England, April 19, 1592. According to his own deposition, made September 18, 1658, he was born in 1591 or 1592, his age at that time being given as about sixty-seven years. His age at death, November 30, 1672, was given as eighty-two. He was born, therefore, in all probability, in 1591, and was the son of David and Ursula Stone, grandson of Simon and Agnes Stone, all of England. His father was not Rev. Timothy, as formerly supposed. He had a brother, Simon, who also emigrated to America, sailing in the ship "Increase", April 15, 1635; settled in Watertown; was admitted freeman May 25, 1636; was a town officer and deacon; died September 22, 1665. Various other immigrant settlers have been erroneously supposed to be brothers of Gregory. Rev. Samuel Stone, of Hartford, Connecticut, was not a brother.

Gregory Stone was admitted a freeman with his brother Simon, May 25, 1636. He was a proprietor of Watertown, but resided most of his life in Cambridge, Massachusetts. He had some famous orchards for his day. His farm was on the present site of the Botanic Gardens of Harvard University. He was one of the most prominent men of his day; deputy to the general court; was deacon of the church and served thirty-four years, being the last survivor of the original membership; was a civil magistrate and one of the governor's deputies. His will, proved December 14, 1672, mentions his wife Lydia, and her children by a former husband—John Cooper and Lydia Fiske; his sons, Daniel, David, John and Samuel; daughter Elizabeth Porter; daughter Sarah, wife of David Merriam; grandson John, son of David Stone. Gregory Stone married in England, July 20, 1617, Margaret Garrad, born December 5, 1597, died August, 1626, in England. He married, second, Lydia Cooper, widow, who died June 24, 1674. Her son by her former husband was John, married Anne Sparhawk; her daughter Lydia married David Fiske. Children of Gregory and Margaret Stone: 1. John, born July 31, 1618, mentioned below. 2. Daniel, baptized July 15, 1620, settled in Cambridge, Massachusetts; married Mary ———; was a physician. 3. David, baptized September 22, 1622, resided at Cambridge; married thrice —Elizabeth ———, Dorcas ——— and Hannah ———. 4. Elizabeth, born 1624, baptized October 3, buried in Nayland, England. Children of Gregory and Lydia Stone. 5. Elizabeth, baptized March 6, 1628, married Anthony Porter. 6. Samuel, baptized February 4, 1630, died September 27, 1715; resided at Watertown; married, second, June 7, 1655, Abigail ———. 7. Sarah, baptized February 8, 1632, died 1677; married, July 12, 1653, Joseph Merriam. The foregoing were all baptized in the church at Nayland, England.

(II) John Stone, son of Gregory Stone (1), was baptized at Nayland, England, July 31, 1618, died at Cambridge, Massachusetts, May 5, 1683. He removed to Sudbury with the early settlers; was a proprietor there and shared in three divisions of the common lands. He bought of the Indians at Natick, May 15, 1656, ten acres of land on the south side of the Sudbury river, and his purchase was confirmed by the general court in 1656, together with another grant of fifty acres of land for special services, etc. He added to the tract that he already owned in what is now the village of Saxonville, in Framingham, until he owned a very large stretch of land. He built his house where the present railroad station is located in Saxonville. He also built the first house in the present village of Cochituate, then part of Sudbury, now in the town of Wayland. He built in all six houses in Sudbury and Framingham, and built the first mill in Framingham, in 1659, at the falls now known as Stone's Mills; a cord mill, and his son Daniel, built there the first saw mill. He was elected fence viewer in 1654; town clerk in 1655; and was admitted a freeman in 1665. In 1645 he sold his house in Sudbury to John Moore and was the first to build his house in Framingham. He located also without having a grant, at Otter Neck, on the west side of Sudbury in 1646-7. He married in 1638 Anne Howe, born in England, daughter of Elder Edward and Margaret Howe, both natives of England. Children: 1. Hannah, born June 6, 1640, married, July 1, 1658, John Bent. 2. Mary, married, first, Isaac Hunt; second, April 30, 1681, Eliphalet Fox. 3. Daniel, born August 31, 1644. 4. David, October 31, 1646, married Susanna ———. 5. Elizabeth, 1650, married, 1678, Samuel Stow. 6. Margaret, October 22, 1653, married, January 11, 1695, William Brown. 7. Tabitha, May 20, 1655, married, November 3, 1674, John Rice. 8. Sarah, September 2, 1656, married Jacob Hill. 9. Nathaniel, May 11, 1660. mentioned below. 10. John, non compos mentis. 11. ———, died young. 12. ———, died young.

(III) Nathaniel Stone, son of John Stone (2), was born in Framingham, Massachusetts, May 11, 1660. He lived near the present site of the Saxonville Mills. He was a prominent citizen; selectman for several years and honored with other positions of trust and responsibility. He died in 1732. He married, April 25, 1684, Sarah Wayt, of Malden. Children: 1. Nathaniel, born October 15, 1685. 2. Ebenezer, April 16, 1688. 3. Jonathan, March 24, 1690. 4. Isaac. 5. John, April 13, 1702, maried Elizabeth Stone, daughter of Samuel Stone, of Sudbury, and resided at Rutland. 6. Mary, December 19, 1705, married ——— Coggin. 7. Sarah, October 12, 1708, married ——— Carter. 8. Hezekiah, mentioned below.

(IV) Captain Hezekiah Stone, son of Nathaniel Stone (3), was born in Framingham, Massachusetts, March 5, 1710-11. He was a captain of the Framingham military company.

He received from his father the homestead "Bridgefield" and his interest in Baiting Brook Meadow. He lived near Major J. Stone's, a cellar hole there marking the location. He held the office of selectman and other places of trust. He removed to Oxford, Massachusetts, where he died July 18, 1771. He married Ruth Howe, of Sudbury. She married, second, Deacon Bancroft, of Ward (now Auburn). Children: 1. Eliphalet, born December 5, 1735, mentioned below. 2. Jesse, September 28, 1737. 3. Hepsibah, July 8, 1741, married Jeremiah Belknap. 4. Ruth, February 10, 1743, married John Eames. 5. Sarah, February 24, 1746, married ——— Davis, of Oxford. 6. Lois, August 3, 1749, married Uriah Stone, of Oxford. 7. Israel, January 2, 1752, died in Ward. 8. Hezekiah, May 27, 1755.

(V) Eliphalet Stone, son of Hezekiah Stone (4), was born in Framingham, Massachusetts, December 5, 1735. Married Lydia Goddard, born September 4, 1737, daughter of William and Keziah (Cloyes) Goddard, of Berlin, Massachusetts. They removed to Marlborough, New Hampshire, in 1771, and he became a leading citizen; deacon of the church and town officer. He purchased of his brother-in-law, Moses Goddard, a lot of land near Stone Pond, now comprising the farm owned by Clark. Hill and the one adjoining, lately owned by Curtis F. Hunt. He was a soldier in the revolution in Captain James Lewis's company of Marlborough; Colonel E. Hale's regiment to reinforce the northern army. He died February 9, 1817; his wife March 18, 1821. Children: 1. Calvin, born in Framingham, January 11, 1761. 2. Beulah, born in Framingham, married Jonathan Frost, of Marlborough. 3. John, mentioned below. 4. Shubael, born December 14, 1765. 5. Cynthia, born 1768, married, March 29, 1796, John Farrar, of Marlborough. 6. Ruth, born in 1770, married, March 15, 1796, Silas Raymond, of Rindge, New Hampshire. 7. Abigail, born in 1772, married Phinehas Farrar. 8. Luther, born November 17, 1775, died in New Orleans in 1806, unmarried. 9. Patty, born January 13, 1777, drowned in Stone Pond, July 25, 1784. 10. Asa, born December 1, 1779, died April 14, 1785.

(VI) Captain John Stone, son of Eliphalet Stone (5), was born in Framingham, Massachusetts, in 1764, removed with the family when a young boy to Marlborough, New Hampshire. His farm was north of Stone Pond, the line between Dublin and Marlborough running through the center of his house. He was captain of the militia company and a citizen of prominence. He married first, Elizabeth Stanley, who died November 4, 1813; he married, second, Mrs. Rebecca (Coolidge) Ward, who died October 24, 1856. He died April 18, 1849. Children of Captain John and Elizabeth Stone: 1. John, born May 20, 1788, died November 29, 1804. 2. Polly, November 22, 1789, married Seth Fisher and removed to Francestown. 3. Betsey, October 2, 1791, married Jesse Worsley; died 1833. 4. Abigail, November 15, 1793, married, January 15, 1815, Robert Hardy; removed to Rutland. 5. Andrew, October 11, 1796, married Hannah Shirtleff, of Watertown, New York; died 1833. 6. Martha, January 19, 1798, married Socrates Fay; removed to Framingham. 7. Silas, January 12, 1800. 8. Aaron, February 28, 1802, mentioned below. 9. Mahala, February 20, 1804, died October, 1804. 10. Mahala, August 8, 1806, married, June, 1831, Francis Coolidge; removed to Framingham. 11. Lydia, June 4, 1808, married, April 13, 1830, Benjamin Alcott, of Keene. 12. Emeline, May 8, 1810, married, June, 1831, Peter Lawson; removed to Lowell, Massachusetts. 13. Louisa, January 14, 1812, died January 14, 1867. Children of Captain John and Rebecca Stone: 14. John C., August 22, 1819. 15. Caroline E., August 28, 1821, married, February 15, 1849, William J. Logan, of Bellows Falls, Vermont. 16. Ruth Helen, February 24, 1824, married Fred Rogers, of Bellows Falls. 17. George H., December 21, 1825, married Mrs. Starkweather, of Walpole, New Hampshire; removed to Bellows Falls.

(VII) Aaron Stone, son of Captain John Stone (6), was born in Marlborough, New Hampshire, February 28, 1802, married, June 12, 1828, Mary Ward, daughter of Reuben and Rebecca (Coolidge) Ward. The latter married his father, as his second wife. Children, born in Marlborough: 1. Ellen R., December 16, 1830. 2. Eliza Ann, January 4, 1833. 3. Mary Jane, December 7, 1836. 4. Andrew C., mentioned below.

(VIII) Andrew Coolidge Stone, son of Aaron Stone (7), was born in Marlborough, New Hampshire, March 16, 1839. He was educated in the public schools of his native town and attended sundry terms in the academies of Meriden and Ipswich, New Hampshire, Westminster, Vermont, graduating at Phillips Academy, Exeter, New Hampshire. Then for a short season he engaged in teaching school in Walpole, New Ipswich, Keene and Peterborough, New Hampshire, but having chosen the law as his profession commenced to study in the office of Hon. Daniel Saunders, of Lawrence, in 1861. Upon the breaking out of the civil war he postponed his legal studies for the duty of the hour and enlisted in Company A, Thirty-third regiment, Massachusetts Volunteers, served with credit to the close of the war. Then he resumed his study of law in the office of Hon. L. Sherwin at Ashtabula, Ohio, and was admitted to the bar in 1867. Immediately afterward he established himself in the practice of his profession at Lawrence, Massachusetts, and speedily won and held an honorable position as a lawyer. Mr. Stone's ambition has not led him much into political life and therefore he has never sought public employment. The first public office that he held was that of member of the common council of Lawrence, of which body he was president. He is a Republican and for a number of years was an active and influential member of the Republican state central committee of Massachusetts. He was chairman of the Republican city committee in 1884 and delegate to the Republican National convention at Chicago in 1884. He holds the judicial commission of master in chancery. He was elected state senator from his district for 1880 and 1882 and served with credit on the judiciary and railroad committees. In 1885 he was appointed city solicitor and in 1887 received the appointment to his present position as justice of the police court of Lawrence. He is prominent in the Masonic Order, being past master of Phenician Lodge of Lawrence; member of Mount Sinai Royal Arch Chapter; member of Bethany Commandery, Knights Templar; past senior grand warden and permanent member of the Grand Lodge of Massachusetts. In the Grand Army he was commander of Post 39, at Lawrence, in 1881, and judge advocate on the staff of the commander of the Department of Massachusetts for 1888. He is a member of the Home Club of Lawrence and has been its president. He married at Ashtabula, Ohio, January 19, 1869, Mary F. Hulbert, daughter of Joseph D. and Lucinda (Hall) Hulbert of that place. They have no children.

PINNOCK Thomas Pinnock (I) was a wool sorter in Durssey, Gloucestershire, England, and was born there, in that ancient shire from which came the first colony of adventurers who in 1623 planted a settlement on Cape Ann, within the limits of the present city of Gloucester in Massachusetts. Thomas Pinnock came to America in 1827, settled first in Lowell, and about two years later removed to North Billerica, where he died at the age of about forty years. He was industrious and hardworking, and was much respected in the town in which he lived. He married Sarah Lewith, also a native of Dursey, and who lived to attain the remarkable age of ninety-six years. She bore her husband two children. The elder child, Sarah, was born in 1814, and was thirteen years old when she came with her parents to America. She married first a Mr. Collins, by whom she had a large family of children, six of whom grew to maturity. Her second husband was a Mr. Culinana, by whom she had two children. She died in 1906, aged ninety years.

(II) Thomas Pinnock, son of Thomas and Sarah (Lewith) Pinnock, was born in old Gloucestershire, England, in 1817 and died in Salem, Massachusetts, October 22, 1877. He was a boy of ten years when he came to America, and when old enough was apprenticed to the trade of slate roofing. Afterward he worked as a journeyman roofer until 1857, when he went to Salem and set up in business for himself. He continued as sole proprietor until 1872, when his son Thomas became partner in the business and the firm name became Thomas Pinnock & Son. Mr. Pinnock died October 22, 1877, having been in active business in Salem for a period of twenty years. He was the pioneer in his line of trade in the city, and under the proprietorship of his father and son in succession the business has been carried on for more than a half century without interruption and with gratifying success. Mr. Pinnock was a man of quiet habits, a Republican in politics, but not active in that field. He was brought up under the influence of the Church of England, but in Salem he attended services at the Tabernacle Church (Congregational). He presented the Essex Institute with the oldest edition (St. James) of the Bible on exhibition there. He married Ann Lewis, born in Hyde, Lancashire, England, April 18, 1827, daughter of Widow Mary Lewis, who came to this country about 1835, her children following soon afterward. Mr. and Mrs. Pinnock had two children, Elizabeth and Thomas Goodwin. Elizabeth was born February, 1849, and lives with her brother. She never married.

(III) Thomas Goodwin Pinnock, only son of Thomas and Ann (Lewis) Pinnock, was born in Lowell, Massachusetts, November 1, 1851, and was a boy of six years when his father removed to Salem. He attended the public schools and afterward was a pupil in the Salem grammar school, but left early to learn the trade of slate roofing with his father. On reaching his majority his father took him as partner in the firm of Thomas Pinnock & Son, and five years later, upon the death of the senior partner, he became sole proprietor. Thus it is by the succession of the son to the interest of his father that Mayor Pinnock is proprietor of the oldest business concern of its kind in Salem, and both father and son were self-made men in every respect. The mayor himself never owned a dollar that he didn't earn, and about the first money he did earn was thirty-five cents paid him for picking up onions when he was a little boy. It may be said without any enlargement of fact that former Mayor Pinnock is probably one of the most widely acquainted men in Salem, and if it were permissible to pay him a compliment here, it might be said with equal truth that he probably is one of the most popular men in Salem today, and that notwithstanding the fact that he has been more or less active in city politics for the last ten or fifteen years. Mayor Pinnock did not enter Salem municipal politics because of any desire for public office, nor even for the emolument thereof, for during the years he was in the mayor's chair his expenditures were considerable in excess of his salary. He was member of the board of aldermen in 1899 and 1900, was elected mayor in the fall of 1905, re-elected in 1906, but declined to stand as a candidate for a third term. At the time of his first candidacy he consented to take the nomination only after much urging on the part of prominent business men who knew him to be well fitted for the office, and the same considerations again were presented a year later; and during both terms he acquitted himself well and to the entire satisfaction of the best element of the taxpaying population of Salem. He is a mason of high degree and member of many other fraternal, benevolent and philanthropic bodies of the city. In 1879 he was made a member of Essex Lodge, F. and A. M., and has been at the head of that and all other of the subordinate bodies of the craft; he is possessor of an interesting collection of past officers' jewels. Besides the lodge he is a member of Washington Chapter, R. A. M., Salem Council, R. and S. M., and Aleppo Temple, A. A. O. N. M. S.; member of Essex Lodge, I. O. O. F.; Naumkeag Encampment, P. M.; member and past chancellor of North Star Lodge, K. P.; past president and present treasurer of the Salem Mechanics Charitable Association; member of Salem Lodge, B. P. O. E., the Essex Institute and of the Salem Board of Trade.

On January 18, 1878, Mr. Pinnock married Emma Augusta, daughter of Thomas Littlefield, of Kennebunkport, Maine. Of this marriage four children have been born: 1. Harold, died when only a few days old. 2. A son, died in extreme infancy. 3. Thomas Wellington, born Salem, April 18, 1891, student at Salem high school. 4. Lorna, born Salem, January 18, 1894. Thomas Wellington and Lorna Pinnock, son and daughter of Thomas Goodwin and Emma Augusta (Littlefield) Pinnock, are descendants of the sixth generation of William Pinnock, of London, England, once a famous scholar and writer of school and other books. He was a great-uncle of Thomas Pinnock, the wool sorter, who came to this country in 1827.

FOLLANSBEE As might be expected from present variations in spelling of the surname Follansbee, or Follansby, the early records furnish an unusual variety of spellings. Falambee, Falansby, Folansbe, Folensbie, Folansby, Folinsbe, Follansbe, Follensbee, Follensbury, Follensby, Follingbe, Follingbee, Follingsby, Follinsbee, Follisbee, Follinsby, Follnsbe, Fallonsbee and Folnsby; while in England the spelling showed as many variations, but for the past century has been spelled Foliambe and Foljambe. The "s" sound seems to have been added in America. It is doubtless a norman family, dating back in England to the Conquest in 1066. When the mania for discovering great estates in England for American heirs became a profitable enterprise, a Follansbee estate was conjured up, an association formed, and an agent set at work in England. Judging from the report there was not even a family of importance using the spelling in vogue in America. A few wills were presented and one parish or village named Follansbee was discovered in Durham.

The coat-of-arms of the Follambe family of Croxdon, county Stafford, England: Sable a bend between six escallops or with a bordure engr. gu. Crest: A leg couped at the thigh quarterly or and sa., spurred of the first on the thigh a fesse indented gules, the arms and crest charged with a crescent for difference. This family is a branch of the following, and as there is but one coat-of-arms the American family seems entitled to use it. The family in Walton, Linacre Hall, Derbyshire, and Aldwark, county York, spells the name with a "j". The progenitor was Sir Thomas Fuljambe, of Oberton, bailiff of High Pearth, Derbyshire, in 1272, soon after the beginning of the use of surnames in England. The original arms he bore were: Sable a bend between six escallops or. Another branch of the family in Yorkshire uses, according to Burke, the same device.

(I) Thomas Follansbee, immigrant ancestor, born in England, about 1640, came to America when a young man and settled at Newbury, Massachusetts, and Portsmouth, New Hampshire. He married first, before 1672, Mary ———, and second, Sarah ———, who died probably November 4, 1683, at Newbury, and he married third, April 4, 1713, at Newbury, Jane Mossman, of Boston. He was of Portsmouth in 1665 and 1671; of Newbury in 1677 and later. He was the ancestor of all of this name in America, so far as discovered. He was living as late as 1713 and probably in 1721. Children: 1. Rebecca, born about 1660; married November 22, 1677, Thomas Chase (2). 2. Anne, married, November 10, 1684, Moses Chase; she died before 1713. 3. Mary, born about 1667; married December 1, 1686, Robert Pike; second, about 1691, William Hooke. 4. Thomas, born about 1671; mentioned below. 5. Francis, born October 22, 1677. 6. Hannah, born April 10, 1680.

(II) Thomas Follansbee Jr., son of Thomas Fallansbee (1), was born in Newbury, about 1671. He was an innholder and a housewright. He married first, June 19, 1694, Abigail Rolfe; second, after 1724, Mary ———. His will was dated July 30, 1753, and proved June 23, 1755. Children, born at Newbury: 1. Mary, April 24, 1695; married, April 17, 1712, Philip Chase. 2. Thomas, March 26, 1697; married January 5, 1715-6, at Newbury, Hannah March. 3. Francis, mentioned below. 4. William, March 14, 1701, married 1722, Mary Robinson, of Exeter, New Hampshire.

(III) Francis Follansbee, son of Thomas Follansbee (2), was born in Newbury, June 13, 1699; married there, December 15, 1719, Judith, daughter of Thomas Moody (3). His will was dated January 23, 1747-8, and proved February 15 following. Children, born in Newbury: 1. Judith, November 2, 1720; married ——— Spofford. 2. Anne, November 6, 1722; married ——— Noyes. 3. Francis, November 10, 1724. 4. Abigail, February 28, 1726. 5. Moody, November 6, 1729; soldier in revolution. 6. Hannah, born after 1730. 7. John, mentioned below. 8. Sarah.

(IV) John Follansbee, son of Francis Follansbee (3), was born in Newbury about 1732.

(V) Benjamin Follansbee, son or nephew of John Follansbee (4), was born in Newbury about 1760, removed to Salisbury, and thence to Pittston, Maine. He was a prominent ship-builder in his day. He was a soldier in the revolution, a private in Captain Henry Morrill's company, Colonel Caleb Cushing's regiment, on the Lexington alarm. He was a taxpayer in Pittston in 1803. Children: 1. Child, born 1788, died at Salisbury, March 26, 1797, aged eight and a half, drowned. 2. Benjamin, mentioned below. 3. John. 4. Samuel. 5. Daniel. The last three paid poll taxes in Pittston, Maine, in 1803.

(VI) Benjamin Follansbee, son of Benjamin Follansbee (5), was born in Newbury or Salisbury, Massachusetts, about 1780. He was a minute-man in the war of 1812. He followed in his father's footsteps as a ship-builder. He was but eleven years of age when the family located in Pittston, and he spent his active life in that town. He married Elizabeth, daughter of Thomas and Hannah Kenney, a native of Maine. He was a devout and prominent member of the Congregational church, and for many years was a deacon. Children, born at Pittston: 1. Alonzo, married Mary McIntosh. 2. Benjamin A., mentioned below. 3. Elizabeth. 4. James Crowell. 5. George, died young. 6. Emeline, married Eliphalet Lapham. 7. George, settled in California.

(VII) Benjamin A. Follansbee, son of Benjamin Follansbee (6), was born in Pittston, Maine, in 1816, and was educated in the schools of that state. When a young man he shipped before the mast and for many years he followed the sea, rising to the rank of master mariner. He sailed for the most part from New York City to Calcutta, China, Japan and the east. He was lost at sea in 1872, aged fifty-six. He married Apphia A. R. Tyler, born at Georgetown, D. C., daughter of William and Elizabeth (Pillsbury) Tyler. She is a Congregationalist in religion. Mrs. Follansbee survives at an advanced age, residing with her daughter in Amesbury, Massachusetts. Children: 1. William T., married Annette Pettingill. Their only child was: Ellen W. 2. Alice C., mentioned below.

(VIII) Alice C. Follansbee, daughter of Captain Benjamin A. Follansbee (7) was born Amesbury, Massachusetts. She was educated in private schools at Amesbury and at Bradford (Massachusetts) Academy, where she was graduated in 1873. She has lived in the old home at Amesbury with her mother, who is now eighty-six years old (1907). Miss Follansbee is librarian of the Amesbury Public Library. Her assistants in the management of this institution at present are Miss Alice D. Brown and Miss Ruth E. Osborne. The library is well equipped and conducted along modern lines. Miss Follansbee is a member of the Congregational Church of Amesbury.

CHILD This name dates back to the beginning of the use of surnames. It was spelled in many ways—Childe, Chyld, Chylde, etc.,—but seldom with an "s" added. Some branches of the Child family in America use the following coat-of-arms. Gules, a chevron engrailed ermine, between three eagles close argent. Crest, an eagle wings expanded enveloped with a snake proper. Motto, "Imitare quam invidere".

(I) William Child, one of the early emigrants to the Massachusetts colony, appears to have been the brother of Ephraim Child, who settled in Watertown, and to have come with his brother or shortly before him. He was made a freeman in 1634, and was a man of some landed estate. He married probably in England, and his eldest son was probably born there. His widow is mentioned in the will of Mrs. Elizabeth (Palmer) Child, wife of Ephraim, who left to her some of her wardrobe. William's sons were also mentioned in the will of Ephraim Child. Children: 1. Joseph, born about 1629; married 1654, Sarah Platt. 2. Richard, born in Watertown, Massachusetts, 1631; married first, March 30, 1662, Mehitable Dimick; second, January 16, 1678, Hannah Traine. 3. John, mentioned below.

(II) John Child, son of William Child (1), was born in Watertown, in 1636. He was a prominent man in the colonies, and was representative to the general court. By a nuncupative will witnessed by his brother Richard and two others he left to his eldest son John his "dwelling house with its lot of twelve acres, also some meadow land, and the reversion of all lands upon the little plains" His youngest son Daniel received the farm lands. He died October 15, 1676, aged forty. He married first, Mary ———; second, May 29, 1668, Mary Warren, born November 29, 1651, granddaughter of John Warren, who came to America in the "Arabella" with Governor Winthrop in 1630. She married again, and died May 12, 1734, aged eighty-three. Children: 1. Mary, born January 8, 1663. 2. John, born April 25, 1669; married, October 5, 1693, Hannah French. 3. Eliza, born July 24, 1670. 4. Daniel, mentioned below.

(III) Daniel Child, son of John Child (2), was born June 5, 1677, and died in 1724. He married January 29, 1702, Beriah Bemis. She married second, August 12, 1736, Joseph Pierce, and died aged eighty-eight. Children: 1. Sarah, born September 14, 1702; married, June 13, 1734, John Fisk. 2. Susanna, born March 6, 1705. 3. Elizabeth, born February 18, 1707; married, July 21, 1725, Deacon Isaac Stearns, of Waltham, Massachusetts. 4. Daniel, born April 9, 1709; mentioned below. 5. David, born December 27, 1711, married first, October 23, 1737, Grace Brown; second, Mehitable Richardson. 6. John, born December 2, 1713; married August 15, 1758, Ruhanna Pierce. 7. Joshua, born March 2, 1717; married April 30, 1741, Grace Bemis. 8. Samuel, born February 7, 1719; married first, October 19, 1745, Mary Ball; married second, Esther ———; married third, April 8, 1799, Mrs. Elizabeth Stimpson. 9. Elisha, born February 16, 1721; married first, Mary ———; second, Mehitable Garfield. 10. Mary, born June 10, 1722; married March 11, 1743, Joseph Whitney of Weston.

(IV) Daniel Child, son of Daniel Child (3), was born in Watertown, April 9, 1709. He married January 13, 1729, Mary, daughter of Nathaniel Bright. He was a selectman of Waltham, where he settled. Children, born in Waltham: 1. Anna, July 6, 1730. 2. Daniel, April 26, 1732; died May, 1733. 3. Abijah, January 12, 1734; mentioned below. 4. Daniel, February 21, 1736. 5. Lydia, February 25, 1738; married October 26, 1758, William Flagg. 6. Sarah, August 11, 1740; married January 2, 1760, William Benjamin. 7. Jonas, September 30, 1743; married January 11, 1770, Hannah Sanderson. 8. Mary, October 14, 1745; married October 6, 1763, William Hagar of Waltham. 9. Bettie, March 9, 1748; died September 24, 1751. 10. Josiah, June 17, 1750; died September 24, 1757. 11. Ephraim, baptized June 30, 1754.

(V) Abijah Child, son of Daniel Child (4),

was born in Waltham, January 12, 1734. He was captain in the Twenty-Fifth regiment, Continental army, in the revolution, in 1775. He was selectman of Waltham in 1774-5 and 1787. He married first, December 15, 1759, Beulah Harrington; second, December 2, 1790, Ann Bemis. Children, born in Waltham, all by first wife: 1. Ephraim, July 26, 1760; married November 6, 1784, Lydia Livermore. 2. Abijah (twin), January 14, 1762; died young. 3. Beulah (twin), January 14, 1762; married February 16, 1786, William Benjamin. 4. Sarah, June 2, 1764; died July 14, 1769. 5. Daniel, July 3, 1766; married January 7, 1787, Phebe Parks. 6. William, May 14, 1768; mentioned below. 7. Phebe, November 4, 1769. 8. Edward, January 12, 1772. 9. Elizabeth, December 8, 1773; married November 23, 1802, Antepas Maynard. 10. Anna, November 8, 1775; married April 1, 1791, Nathaniel Carter. 11. Abijah, January 25, 1779; married 1807, Polly Sanderson.

(VI) William Child, son of Abijah Child (5), was born May 14, 1768, and died about 1820. He removed to Maine with the family of David Marshall, and settled in what was then called Sudbury, Canada, now Bethel, Maine. Attacked by the Indians, the inhabitants were compelled to flee, and this family located in Minot, Maine. Here he married, about 1790, Anna Washburn, and removed to Livermore, Maine, where he settled upon a farm. He was a man of liberal religion. Children: 1. Lewis Washburn, born 1793; shipped in Decatur's fleet in 1815, sailed to the Mediterranean, and was never afterwards heard from. 2. Joseph, born January 5, 1795; married first, 1816, Olive Woodsum; second, 1841, Dorcas Andrews. 3. William, born April, 1797; married 1816, Lucinda Woodsum. 4. Anna, born 1799; married John Perham. 5. True Woodman, born 1802; married ——— Smith. 6. Elisha, born 1804; drowned when about twenty years of age. 7. Granville, born 1806; married Esther Godding. 8. Marshall, born 1808; mentioned below. 9. Aurelia, born 1810; married Elijah Parrington. 10. Eliza, born 1813; married Sulivan Andrews. 11. Adelphia, born 1816; married first, William Bradford; second, John Gordon.

(VII) Marshall Child, son of William Child (6), was born in Livermore, Maine, January 25, 1808. He received a common school education, and when a young man settled in Livermore, Maine, where he took up some land and built a small house. Here he remained until 1860, when he moved to Peru, Oxford county, Maine. In 1867 he returned to Livermore and died in the winter of 1889-90. He was a Universalist in religion and a Republican in politics, being a worker for his party, though he would never accept office. He was a Mason. He married first, in 1830, Olive Stetson of Hartford, Maine; second, Sarah Haskell. Children of first wife, born in Livermore, Maine: 1. Martha, January 2, 1834; died March 24, 1864. 2. Hiram, August 18, 1835. 3. Asa, born August 14, 1837; a soldier in the Union service. 4. Homer, September 2, 1839. 5. Martha F., April 21, 1841. 6. Harriet E., May 26, 1844. 7. Emerson (twin), May 11, 1846; died in United States service. 8. Elihu (twin), May 11, 1846; died in United States service. 9. Albert, February 17, 1849; died April 20, 1864. 10. Elmer P., December 12, 1850; died December 19, 1865. 11. Francis O., March 13, 1854; died July 23, 1855. Child of second wife: 12. Albert M., mentioned below.

(VIII) Albert M. Child, son of Marshall Child (7), was born in Peru, Maine, January 2, 1867. He received his early education in the public schools of Livermore, Maine, graduating from the high school in 1885. He taught school for a time and then worked at the trade of shoemaker in factories in Mansfield, Salem and Haverhill, Massachusetts, for a period of sixteen years. He has resided in Haverhill since 1890, and May 1, 1904, was elected secretary of the Haverhill Board of Trade, a position he has since filled with conspicuous credit. He is a Republican, and has been active in the management of the party and in the support of its candidates. In 1902 he was elected to the common council from Ward Two, and re-elected the following year and chosen president of the council for 1903. He was the candidate at the Republican caucus for mayor of the city in 1904, and made a good run. He was elected overseer of the poor January 1, 1904, and continues to hold this office. He is a member of the Lincoln Club of Haverhill. Mr. Child has demonstrated unusual executive ability, and possesses those qualities of mind and character that attract the confidence and friendship of men. Few men in the city are better known or more popular with all classes of people. He married, February 18, 1892, Celia G., born Naples. Maine, daughter of George P. and Abbie (Lord) Gammon. Children, born in Haverhill: 1. Frank M., December 10, 1892. 2. Roscoe, February 22, 1894.

TOBIN According to the authorities on surnames, Tobin is an Irish surname modified from the ancient English St. Aubyn to St. Tobyn, to Tobyn and Tobin. The family has been prominent in Ireland since the reign of Edward III, especially in county Tipperary. A writer in the *Quarterly Review* in 1860 cited as instances of names hibernicized, Fitz Urses, which became MacMahon, and St. Aubyn, which became Dobbin or Tobyn. O'Hart, in the "Irish Pedigrees," gives the following account of the family: "Geoffrey, one of the princes of Scotland, siding with the Irish monarch, Brian Boru, fought at the battle of Clontarf in 1014, and his descendants settled in Ireland. The family of Betagh, Beattie, Beatty or Beytagh, is directly descended from this Geoffrey."

The lineage: 1. Geoffrey or Jaffrey. 2. Conhgall, one of whose sons, Malcolm, was ancestor of the Beatty family, the name being assumed by John of the sixteenth generation. 3. Constantine. 4. Philip. 5. Thomas. 6. James. 7. John. 8. David. 9. Robert. 10. Christopher. 11. John. 12. Jeoffrey. 13. James. 14. John. 15. John. 16. Pierce. 17. John Tobin, who assumed the surname and all after him continued it.

Another line of the family: 1. Walter Mor Tobin, of Kelaghy, county Tipperary. 2. Thomas. 3. Walter. 4. Edmund. 5. John. 6. Walter P. 7. Edmund, of Kilvegsgonah, county Tipperary, married Margery, daughter of Edmund Tobin, of Kelaghy; died August 8, 1638. 8. Thomas Tobin, married Joanna, daughter of William Butler, of Polichiny, county Tipperary; children: John, Richard, Joar, Elin, Mary and Anastasia.

Tady Tobin, of this Irish family, was born in the year 1830. He was a nail maker by trade. He married Margaret McCarthy, who was born in Kinsale, county Cork, Ireland, about 1830, and died in Methuen, Massachusetts, in 1882. Mrs. Tobin had five brothers, four of whom served in the British army. Her uncle, Michael McCarthy, sent money for her brothers to come to America, but they being in the army, the money was transferred to her. She came with her infant son, and soon afterward her husband started also to make his home in this country, but the vessel on which he sailed was wrecked off the coast of Nova Scotia, in June, 1853, and all were lost. He was but twenty-three years old at the time of his death. Their only child was John, mentioned below.

John Tobin, son of Tady Tobin (1), was born in the city of Cork, County Cork, Ireland, March 10, 1853. He was but three months old when his mother brought him to the United States. She lived first in Lowell, Massachusetts, but after a few years went to live with relatives in Tewksbury. In 1860 the family removed to Lawrence, and John attended school there until he was ten years old, when he began to earn his own living in the Pacific Mills. His following occupation was in a hat factory in Ballardvale, but in 1865 he returned to Lawrence. For some years he worked out for W. E. Stevens, A. H. Harris and S. W. Williams, farmers of Methuen, attending the district school during the winter terms. In 1869 he clerked for A. A. Lamprey and James R. Simpson in the grocery business in Methuen, and later worked in the Everett Mill of Lawrence. In 1871 he started to learn the trade of plasterer in the employ of Rufus Page, of Methuen, completing his time in the employ of D. M. Prescott & Company of Lowell, Massachusetts. He worked at his trade in various places, but returned to Lawrence and in 1876 started his present business in a store on Common street, dealing in paints, oils, wall paper, etc. His business constantly increased, and after a few years he was compelled to seek more commodious quarters, removing to his present location. He is the largest contractor in his line in the city, employing from ten to thirty men as plasterers and decorators. Mr. Tobin is a prominent Democrat, and is at present alderman of the city of Lawrence. He is a member of Lawrence Lodge of Elks, No. 65; local Aerie of Eagles, No. 216, of which he has been treasurer since its organization; Knights of Columbus; Lawrence Board of Trade; Real Estate Owners' Association; St. Mary's Holy Name Society and of the Roman Catholic Church; he is a resident and generous supporter of St. Mary's parish, Lawrence.

Mr. Tobin married, August, 1871, at Lowell, Ann Maria Bush, born November 29, 1850, daughter of Francis Joseph and Ellen (McCarthy) Bush. Francis Joseph Bush was born in Baltimore, Maryland, and died in Lowell, Massachusetts, 1873; he removed to Salem; followed the life of a sailor, serving in that capacity during the civil war, and was a gunner in Admiral Farragut's fleet. Children of John and Ann Maria (Bush) Tobin: 1. Joseph F., born in Lowell, 1872; member of the Lawrence police force; married Ellen McGuire, of Lowell; children: Walter J. and Marion J. 2. John, born March, 1873, at Low-

John Tobin

ell, died aged five months. 3. Frank J., born August, 1875, died aged four years. 4. Margaret, born at Lawrence, died aged two years and a half. 5. Charles, born at Lawrence, died aged five months. 6. John, born at Lawrence, died aged four months. 7. Mary Ellen, born at Lawrence, died aged five years. 8. Albert H., born January 3, 1884, served five years in the American navy, and is now working for his father; married Lillie Fraze. 9. Gertrude Frances, died in infancy. 10. Gertrude Frances, born 1890, student in the public schools.

LLOYD Lloyd is a well-known Welsh personal name — sometimes corrupted to Floyd and Flood. As an hereditary surname it does not date beyond the sixteenth century, yet many of the families bearing it are of great antiquity as, for example,—Lloyd of Bronwydd is twenty-third lord of the Barony of Kemes, County Pembroke, in hereditary descent from Martin de Tours, a companion of William the Conqueror. Lloyd of Plymog claims descent from Marchudd ap Cynan, who flourished in the ninth century and founded the eighth noble tribe of North Wales, and Powys; King Henry VII sprang from this family. Lloyd of Ashton springs from the royal house of Powys. Lloyd of Dan-yr-allt descends from Cadivor ap Dyfnwall, Lord of Castle Howell, time of Henry II and Lineally sprung from Rhodri Mawr, King of Wales. Lloyd of Coedmore claims descent from an ancient prince of Ferlys. Lloyd of Clockfaen springs from the great Tudor Revor in the tenth century. Lloyd of Pale from Held Molwyrogg, a chieftain of Denbighland founder of the ninth noble tribe of North Wales and Powys. In proof of the prominence and number of the Lloyd families in the Gentry, it may be noted that more than thirty different coats-of-arms are ascribed to this name. A branch of the family in Maryland from Wales bears: Azure a lion rampant guardant or. Crest: A demi-lion rampant guardant or supporting in his paws an arrow in pale argent.

Burke in his General Armory says: "Plymog, County Denbigh; Gwerclas and Kymmeryn; Edeirnion, County Merionett, and Bashall Hall, county York. This very ancient family, is one of the most distinguished in the principality, derives in common with the royal house of Tudor the Bulkeley-Williams, baronets, Lord Mostyn and other eminent Welsh houses from Marchudd, Lord of Abergellen and Brynffenige in Carnarvon, Founder of the Eighth Noble Tribe of North Wales and Powys, living in the middle of the ninth century. The immediate ancestor of the Lloyds was Kenrig, Lord of Creuthyn-yn-Yale in Denbighland, third son of Ednyfed Vychan, Lord of Brynffenigl, chief counselor, chief justice and general of Iorwerth, King of North Wales, tenth in descent from Marchudd. The Lloyds were seated at Plymog for many centuries." The coat-of-arms of Ednyfed Vychan: i. Gules a chevron ermine between three Englishmen's heads in profile proper quartering the bearings of Iwfa ap Kendrig, Lord of Christianydvl; ii. Rhys ap Griffith derived from Ynyr, Lord of Yale; iii. Davies of Denbigh, derived from Ednor Wan Bendew, Lord of Tegaingle, founder of the Eighth Noble Tribe of North Wales; iv. Hughes of Gwerclas, barons of Kymmer-yn-Eideirnon; v. Walmsley of Cold Coates Hall, County Lancaster, and Bashall Hall. Motto: "Heb Dduw heb ddym Dduwadygan."

(I) The progenitor of the American family of this sketch lived in Birmingham, England, and among his children were: 1. Noah, died in Birmingham; married a woman of wealth and position. 2. John, mentioned below. 3. Thomas. 4. Edward; his son Edward was a music-publisher of London.

(II) John Lloyd, son of ——— Lloyd, was born at Birmingham, England, and died at East Cambridge, Massachusetts. His schooling was brief and elementary and most of his education he gained by reading and through contact with the world. His early years were spent in Birmingham Heath, a suburb of the city. He learned the trade of glass-maker in the glassworks in Birmingham and followed his trade there until about 1827, when he came with his brother, Thomas Lloyd, and other glass-makers to work for the New England Glass Company at East Cambridge, Massachusetts, being induced by the company's agent who was sent to Birmingham to secure skilled workmen. After his first year in this country, he sent for his family, who came in the sailing vessel, "Rodney of Ellsworth", the voyage lasting three months. He was an expert glass-worker and he continued in the employ of the same house the remainder of his life. The work in a glass factory is continuous and in those days the men worked six hours off and six hours on. The heat and the physical strain tested the endurance of the strongest. Mr. Lloyd was not only a clever glass-worker, but he was gifted with mechanical skill and gave evidence of it in many directions. He was confirmed in the Church of England, but after he came to America attended the Methodist Episcopal church at East Cambridge. He was a model of piety and religious zeal, strong in his faith, vigorous in supporting his beliefs, and inclined to austerity, always upright and honest in word and deed. He married, in England, Ann Bridgins, born in England and died at East Cambridge. She inherited a considerable estate, but was defrauded of it by a near relative, after she came to America. Children: 1. Jane, died at East Cambridge; married, November 8, 1842, Charles Benjamin Stevens, of Boston; children: i. Mary, unmarried; ii. Charles Stevens, born 1846; iii. Henry Stevens, born October 24, 1848; iv. Frances Stevens. 2. Matilda, died at East Cambridge, unmarried. 3. Emma, died at East Cambridge, unmarried. 4. Alfred, died at East Cambridge. 5. Henry, died at Brighton; married Mary Thwing, of Brighton (now Boston), Massachusetts, daughter of Reuben Thwing; children: i. Reuben; ii. Walter; iii. Grace, married George Simpson. 6. William, mentioned below.

(III) William Lloyd, son of John Lloyd, was born at Birmingham, England, July 30, 1821. He was seven years old when he came with his mother to East Cambridge. Here he attended the public schools until he was fifteen years old, working from time to time, when not in school, for the New England Glass Company, where later he learned the trade of glass-making. He also learned the trade of carpenter in his youth, serving an apprenticeship of four years and he worked at this trade for a number of years in the vicinity of Boston. Altogether, however, he spent ten years in the glass-making trade, six years in the New England Glass Company's works and four at the works of the South Boston Glass Company. He was employed for many years in the car-shops of the Boston & Albany railroad, Albany street, Boston, and he became superintendent of the planing mill there. He gave up work in the carshops on account of the failure of his health. Early in the seventies he retired, however, and since then has lived with his son, William E. Lloyd, at Arlington Heights. Mr. Lloyd inherited a talent for music and for some years played the clarionet in the best bands in Boston. He is a loyal and earnest member of the Park Avenue Congregational Church, of which he is a deacon, and he has served on various committees and as teacher in the Sunday school. In politics he is a Republican. He married Alice Maria Mooney, of Pittston, Maine, born September 22, 1827, died of endocarditis at Arlington, February 4, 1884, daughter of Patrick and Nancy Mooney, of Boston and Pittston. Her father was a farmer. Children: 1. William Edwin, born March 2, 1847, mentioned below. 2. Alfred, born June 8, 1849, died September 26, 1851. 3. Charles Augustus, born September 25, 1851, died at Cambridge, August 14, 1876; employed in the Boston Five Cents Savings Bank. 4. George Alvin, born January 11, 1854, married, February 2, 1883, Jennie Anderson, of Cambridge, Massachusetts; children: i. Constance; ii. Mabel Alice, married Ray Van Norman. 5. Mary Alice, born April 10, 1856, married, September 6, 1877, Joseph Crowell Holmes, treasurer of the Boston Five Cents Savings Bank, born September 16, 1851, son of William and Susan (Farris) Holmes, of Marshfield, Massachusetts; children: i. Charles Lloyd Holmes, born September 3, 1878, clerk in the Boston Five Cents Savings Bank, married, September 6, 1904, Edith Thayer Capen, of Dorchester, and had Virginia Capen Holmes, born June 16, 1905, Alice Holmes, born October, 1906, and Charles Lloyd Holmes, Jr., born February 15, 1908; ii. Joseph Edwin Holmes, born February 11, 1880, unmarried. 6. Gilbert, born June 25, 1858, died November 24, 1862.

(IV) Captain William Edwin Lloyd, son of William Lloyd, was born in Boston, March 2, 1847. He received his education in the Boston public schools, graduating from the Quincy grammar school at the age of fourteen. Early in life he acquired habits of industry. He was taught at home that an early start in the world of business was a great advantage, and when he left school he began at once to work in the office of the Old Colony railroad on Beach street, Boston. After three years there, he was employed one year in the ticket office of the Boston & Albany railroad. He then took a trip through the west to see the country. Upon his return, he became a clerk in the indexing department of the registry of deeds of Middlesex county, at East Cambridge, in 1866. He took the contract later for indexing the oldest records of the city of Cambridge. In 1880 he accepted the position of teller in the Cambridge National Bank, and for the next eight years discharged the duties of that responsible office with credit. He was elected treasurer of the East Cambridge Savings

Bank in 1889, a position he has efficiently filled to the present time. He is also a trustee of this bank. He resides at 154 Park avenue, Arlington Heights, a place he purchased in October, 1874. In politics he is independent, though formerly an active Republican, serving that party as delegate to county and other nominating conventions. He is a prominent member of the Union Church (Unitarian) of Arlington Heights and has been the treasurer and collector of the society. He enlisted in Company B, Fourth Battalion, which became a part of the First Regiment, Massachusetts Volunteer Militia, and rose through the various ranks to that of captain. He resigned in 1883. Captain Lloyd is treasurer of the Willard Hospital of Bedford, Massachusetts, and is interested in various other charities. He is a member of the Savings Bank Treasurers' Club of Massachusetts, and of the Ancient Order of United Workmen. He is much interested in music and is now the president of the "Singers Club" of Arlington Heights.

He married, January 1, 1879, Mary Elizabeth Haggens, born at South Berwick, Maine, January 13, 1843, daughter of Major Edmund and Mary Ann (Hamilton) Haggens, of South Berwick. Her father was a merchant in Charleston, South Carolina. Children: 1. George Hamilton, born June 3, 1880, of the Cambridge Trust Company, Cambridge; married, April 26, 1906, Dora Abbott Parsons, of Arlington Heights; child, Charlotte, born September 2, 1907. 2. William Millett, born October 4, 1882, now with W. O. Gay, broker, 24 Congress street, Boston; married, April 22, 1907, Amy Gorham, of Arlington. 3. Edward Haggens, born March 4, 1886.

ARCHAMBAULT The surname Archambault is of very ancient origin, and many of the family have been distinguished in civil, ecclesiastical and military life. The Paris family has this coat-of-arms: D'argent au saut d'azure ch. de cinq étoiles d'or; á la bord denchée de gules. The Archambaults of Orleans: D'azure á trois lions de'or sur le tout d'argent au pal de gules ch. de trois flanchis d'or.

(I) Jacques Archambault, the immigrant to America, was born in France. He settled in the Province of Quebec, probably, though the records give little about him and he may have remained in France. We know that he had a son born in France in 1634, mentioned below.

(II) Laurent Archambault, son of Jacques Archambault, was born in France in 1634, and was the progenitor of the family in Canada where he died February 15, 1688. He came to Quebec when a young man and married, at Montreal, January 7, 1660, Catharine Marchand, born 1634, died February 25, 1713, at Pointe aux Trembles. Children, born in Quebec: 1. Laurent, born 1668, died March 31, 1749; married, October 21, 1686, Anne Courtemanche. 2. Pierre, born March 24, 1669, married, November 21, 1701, Marie Lacombe, born 1681. 3. Jacques, born March 27, 1671, married, February 15, 1694, Francoise Aubuchon; he died October 9, 1725, at Longue Pointe. 4. Francoise, born August 29, 1681, married, November 20, 1697, Toussaint Baudry. 5. Jean, born October 6, 1683, mentioned below. 6. Marie Madeleine, born September 2, 1685, married Gilles Galipeau.

(III) Jean Archambault, son of Laurent Archambault, was born in Montreal, October 6, 1683, died before 1748. He married, June 4, 1708, Cecile Lefebvre, born 1688, daughter of Jean Baptiste Lefebvre. (See sketch of Lefebvre). Children, born at or near Montreal: 1. Jean Baptiste, born December 31, 1711, at Pointe aux Trembles, married, January 12, 1733, Denisse Labelle at St. Francois, I. J. 2. Louis, born June 20, 1714, married Marie Charlotte Froget; he died November 24, 1766, at Repentiguay. 3. André Jacques, born October 21, 171—, married Angelique Lorion. 4. Gervais, born January 8, 1718, mentioned below. 5. Jean Baptiste, born June 12, 1720. 6. Marie Anne, born April 18, 1722, died July 26, 1724. 7. Pierre, born June 8, 1724, married, November 7, 1746, Marie Labelle at St. Vincent de Paul. 8. Joseph, married, January 29, 1748, Agathe Baudry. 9. Cecile Annable, born 1730, married, October 16, 1752, Joseph Galipeau. 10. Charles, married, February 15, 1751, Marie Charlotte Limoges at Terrebonne.

(IV) Gervais Archambault, son of Jean Archambault, was born at Montreal, January 8, 1718, died July 9, 1787, at Repentiguy. He married Marie Charlotte Touin, born 1721, died June 4, 1781. Children: 1. Marie Therese, born about 1743, married, October 10, 1768, Joseph Gabriel Picard. 2. Marie Charlotte, born 1745, married, November 11, 1771, Michael Chaput. 3. Marie Joseph, married, October 5, 1772, Antoine Archambault. 4. Gervais, mentioned below. 5. Jean Baptiste, married, in 1774, Angelique Lebeau; children: i. Jean Baptiste, born May 20, 1775, at Repentiguy; ii. Antoine, born November

11, 1786, died August 17, 1789; iii. Marie Elizabeth, born October 10, 1790; iv. Marie Charlotte, born October 10, 1790, died March 30, 1791; v. Marie Joseph, born January 30, 1791. 6. Louis, married, January 31, 1780, Marie Agathe De Sautels; children: i. Marie, born and died September 13, 1781; ii. Marie Agathe, born January 3, 1786; iii. Jean Baptiste, born January 7, died July 25, 1787; iv. Marie Catherine, born August 12, 1789; v. Jean Baptiste, born July 23, died August 19, 1791. vi. Angelique, born October 5, 1792; vii. Alexis, born June 18, died August 9, 1794; viii. Louis, born October 22, 1795.

(V) Gervais Archambault, son of Gervais Archambault, was born at Longue Pointe, Quebec, Canada. He married, February 22, 1775, Marie Judith de Sautels, daughter of Nicolas de Sautels. (See sketch of De Sautels family herewith). Children: Gervais, mentioned below, Francois, Narcisse, Joseph, Elise, Annable.

(VI) Gervais Archambault, son of Gervais Archambault, was born in the Province of Quebec, Canada, died about 1878 in Michigan, whither he removed and engaged in the lumber business. He lived at St. Alexis, Quebec, Canada, before coming to the United States. He married Julie Martin de Bernabé, who was born about 1820 in the Province of Quebec, and died about 1874 in Michigan. Children: 1. Julienne, married John Moore. 2. Clement. 3. Joseph; mentioned below. 4. Celestine, married Joseph Gravelle. 5. Valerie, deceased. 6. Honorine, unmarried.

(VII) Joseph Archambault, son of Gervais Archambault, was born at St. Alexis, Province of Quebec, Canada, July 16, 1847. He attended the local schools. About 1865 he came to Massachusetts and found employment in a saw mill at Lowell. There he learned the trade of carpenter. From Lowell he went to Fitchburg, and thence to Framingham, Massachusetts, locating finally in Waltham, where he engaged in business as contractor and builder. He was a skillful craftsman himself and demonstrated exceptional business ability. His affairs prospered and he built many of the fine residences of the city of Waltham. His standing among business men was always of the highest. He retired from active business in 1906 and now devotes his time to the care of his real estate in which he has invested extensively in Waltham.

Mr. Archambault married, at Saxonville, Massachusetts, May 6, 1880, Nellie Rock, born November 27, 1853, at Saxonville, daughter of William and Anne (Kane) Rock. Child: Laura L., born October 11, 1884; the mother, Nellie (Rock) Archambault, died July 24, 1897. Mr. Archambault married second, July 11, 1906, Jennie (Greenlaw) Crafts, widow, born June 1, 1866, at Briston, Maine, daughter of Nathaniel and Susan (Poole) Greenlaw.

LEFEBVRE Jean Baptiste Lefebvre (1), immigrant ancestor, was born in 1651 and died April 27, 1715. He married, January 14, 1676, at Montreal, Cunigarde Gervaise, born 1651, died February 16, 1724. Children: 1. Jean Baptiste, born October 26, 1676, died July 18, 1703. 2. Geoffry, born December 27, 1677, married, June 30, 1704, Marie Madeleine Michaud. 3. Louis, born February 26, 1679, died November 14, 1707. 4. Marie Anne, born July 22, 1681, married, October 28, 1697, Jacques Picard; she died May 10, 1717. 5. Nicolas, born August 12, 1686, married, February 9, 1711, Marie Ann Ducharme. 6. Cecile, born September 9, 1688, married Jean Archambault. (See sketch of the Archambault family herewith). 7. Urbain, born July 19, 1691, married, May 17, 1716, Louise Catherine Rivard at Batiscan; died March 9, 1729, at Repentiguy. 8. Charles, born August 20, 1692, married, February 8, 1717, Francoise Gaudry. 9. Cunigarde, born December 2, 1694, married, April 6, 1717, Joseph Descarry. 10. Jean Baptiste, born February 2, 1697, married, September 19, 1723, Agnes Lafond; died January 5, 1752. 11. Jacques, born February 6, 1698, married, 1737, Jeanne Suzanne Picard. 12. Jeanne, born October 13, 1700, married, November 4, 1721, Jean Baptiste Descarry; married, second, April 19, 1728, Paul Tessier.

DE SAUTELS Pierre de Sautels (1), immigrant ancestor, was born in France in 1631, died in Canada, November 19, 1708. He married first, January 11, 1666, Marie Remy, born 1646, died November 11, 167—. He married, second, November 23, 1676, Catherine Lorion, born 1636, daughter of Mathurin Lorion and widow of Nicholas Millet. She died April 20, 1720. Children, born at Montreal: 1. Pierre, born September 13, 1677, mentioned below. 2. Gilbert, born December 17, 1679, married, January 30, 1708, Charlotte Etienne at Pointe des Trembles.

(II) Pierre de Sautels, son of Pierre de Sautels, was born in Montreal, September 13,

1677, died August 1, 1753, at Longue Pointe. He married, January 12, 1699, at Montreal, Therese Angelique Thuillier, daughter of Jacques Thuillier (1). She was born in 1683, died January 20, 1765. Children: 1. Angelique, born December 25, 1699, married, January 8, 1720, Simon Sicard. 2. Louis, born August 3, 1703, married first, February 15, 1734, Agathe Bandreau; second, April 20, 1739, Marie Anne L'archeveque, who died April 5, 1782. 3. Marie Francoise, born July 15, 1705, married, February 2, 1729, Joseph Patenote. 4. Jean Baptiste, born March 14, 1707, married, February 17, 1738, Marie Francoise Lefebvre. 5. Marie Joseph, born October 14, 1709, married, November 4, 1732, Nicolas Patenote. 6. Francois, born March 11, 1712, married first, February 6, 1747, Marie Marguerite Vinet; second, January 15, 1753, Marie Ann Bazinet. 7. Joseph, born April 10, 1714, died January 12, 1729. 8. Laurent, born February 16, 1716, died December 30 following. 9. Nicolas, born March 5, 1718, mentioned below. 10. Jacques, born November 22, 1720. 11. Anthoine, born May 6, 1722. 12. Charles Basile, born March 30, 1724. 13. Marie Anne, born 1726, died March 27, 1730. 14. Catherine, married, 1748, Jean Baptiste Chatel.

(III) Nicolas de Sautels, son of Pierre de Sautels, was born March 5, 1718, died February 17, 1783. He married, February 6, 1741, Marie Catherine Dufresne, daughter of Jean Baptiste Dufresne. Children: 1. Marie Angelique, born November 20, 1741, died April 15, 1742. 2. Marie Catherine, married, January 30, 1764, Joseph Picard. 3. Marie Marguerite, born March 23, 1743, married, February 11, 1771, Joseph Brunel. 4. Jean Baptiste, born August 17, 1744. 5. Marie Louise, born January 10, died August 3, 1746. 6. Marie Marguerite, born May 11, 1747. 7. Marie Judith, born January 4, died May 26, 1749. 8. Marguerite, born May 13, died July 25, 1750. 9. Marie Judith, born November 11, 1751, married, February 22, 1775, Gervais Archambault. (See sketch of Archambault family). 10. Amable, born March 29, 1753, married, September 30, 1782, Catherine Valiquet, at Terrebonne. 11. Nicolas, born December 9, 1754. 12. Joseph Marie, died November 6, 1769. 13. Marie Monique, born July 11, 1758, married, July 18, 1785, Pierre Descaris. 14. Marie Agathe, born November 28, 1760, married, January 31, 1780, Louis Archambault, brother of Gervais. 15. Antoine, born June 2, 1762. 16. Marie Madeleine, born July 23, 1766.

BITZER

Frederick Bitzer, the earliest ancestor of the Bitzer family of whom there is definite information, was born at Durrwangen, Wurtemburg, Germany, 1778, died there 1855. He was brought up on his father's farm, acquiring the usual education of a farmer's son at that period. He became proficient in his studies, and when a young man was the schoolmaster of the district for a number of years. Subsequently he purchased a hostelry which he conducted a number of years. He became later a trader of horses. On account of his wife's health he gave up the hotel, and entering the trading market was successful in that line of business. He was also the owner of a farm, which he conducted in a successful manner, raising products for his own consumption. He was of medium height, broad and powerful, and very industrious. He was the father of fifteen children, among them a son John, who was the father of Jacob Bitzer.

John Bitzer, son of Frederick and Regina Bitzer, was born at Durrwangen, Wurtemburg, Germany, September 7, 1818, died at Arlington, Massachusetts, August 9, 1879. He received his education in his native town, attending until fourteen years of age, when he was confirmed in the Lutheran church, this being the custom at that time after that period of school. He was brought up on his father's farm, continuing until he was apprenticed to the trade of millwright, serving until he attained his majority, under Herr Murlbach. At the age of twenty-one he was drafted for the army, in which he served eighteen months in the infantry, at the expiration of which time he was discharged but not allowed to marry until twenty-seven years of age, being held in reserve for the army until that age. He continued at the trade of millwright until 1845, when he was married and then became a millwright in his own behalf, contracting and making gear wheels for overshot water wheels and machine work. He continued at his trade up to 1854 when, owing to a depression in business, he decided to seek his fortune in the United States. After arriving at Boston he secured employment in the Ellis furniture factory at Cambridgeport, and was one of the workmen employed on the furnishing and chairs for the then new Boston Theatre. After eighteen months in the above named factory he entered the employ of Everett & Company at South Dedham, furniture makers, where he had charge of the moulding machine until 1860, in the spring of which year he returned to the Fatherland, and again took up his trade of wheelwright, remaining there eight years. He returned to Boston in May, 1868, and entered the employ of Charles Schwamb, a maker of picture mouldings, running a moulding machine until 1875, when he retired from active business. He resided at No. 49 Forest street up to the time of his death, August 9, 1879. In 1874 he built the homestead. In 1868 he purchased a tract of land on Forest street, which he divided into thirds, selling one lot to his son, John F.; one to his son-in-law, Gottlieb Rau, and retaining the other, on which he built in 1874. He was a man of very retired nature, very domestic, greatly endeared to his family, a man of strictly upright and honest principles, of a sunny disposition, very well read and well informed. He was a member of the Lutheran church, and a Republican in politics. He married, 1845, Dorothea Beck, born August 26, 1822, died at Arlington, April 26, 1906, daughter of Andrew and Elizabeth (Jetter) Beck, of Zillhausen, Wurtemburg, Germany. Andrew Beck was a horseman and trader. Children: 1. Elizabeth D., born May 2, 1846, married, September 14, 1868, Gottlieb Rau, of Zillhausen, Germany. Children: Annie E., Frederick, Christina Dorothea Elizabeth, William, Emily and Gottlieb. 2. John Frederick; see forward. 3. Christina, born July 29, 1853, died November 24, 1906; married, 1872, Jacob Dornbach, of Roxbury, Massachusetts; children: Emma, Bertha, Charles, Frederick. 4. Dorothea, born April 6, 1861, died February 8, 1907. 5. Jacob, see forward.

John Frederick Bitzer, oldest son of John and Dorothea (Beck) Bitzer, was born at Durrwangen, Wurtemburg, Bolingen county, Germany, February 19, 1850. He was educated in his native town in the common schools, attending until fourteen years of age, when he was confirmed in the Lutheran church. He then went to Balingen, a nearby town, where he learned draughting and designing. He later was apprenticed to his father for three years at his trade of millwright, and worked at his trade until he came to the United States, leaving his native land March 23, 1867, arriving at New York, May 2, 1867. He then came to Arlington, Massachusetts, entering the employ of Charles Schwamb in his picture frame factory, serving an apprenticeship of two years duration. He remained in the employ of Mr. Schwamb for thirty-six years, having charge of the manufacturing department of the business for a number of years. In 1903 he severed his connection with the business of Mr. Schwamb, entering the employ of the Theodore Schwamb Company, having charge of the moulder, which position he now holds. Mr. Bitzer and family attend the Unitarian church at Arlington. He is a Republican in politics. He was formerly a member of Arlington Fire Department, 1874-75-76, and is a member of Bethel Lodge, No. 12, I. O. O. F., at Arlington, and served that body as noble grand in 1890; was also treasurer and chaplain for four or five years. Mr. Bitzer married, March 19, 1870, Louisa Emily Bassing, of Arlington, Massachusetts, born in Newton, Massachusetts, February 23, 1853, daughter of Jacob and Gertrude (Wagner) Bassing, of Newton. Jacob Bassing was a farmer and casemaker. Children: 1. John Frederick, Jr., born January 3, 1871, married, September 19, 1906, Caroline Winterhalder, of Shelburn Falls, Massachusetts. Children: i. John Frederick (3), born January 6, 1907; ii. Helen Louise, March 14, 1908. 2. Gertrude D., born June 12, 1873, died September 25, 1873. 3. Henrich, born July 23, 1874, died September 6, 1874. 4. Charlotte Elizabeth, born July 18, 1875. 5. Robert, born March 29, 1878, married, November 24, 1906, Elizabeth Tucker, of Somerville, Massachusetts. 6. Dorothea Louise, born April 5, 1884. 7. Gertrude, born February 28, 1886. 8. Oscar, born July 31, 1888, married, September 25, 1906, Ethel Hawthorn Moore, of Dorchester, Massachusetts. 9. Bertha, born May 26, 1890. 10. Eliza Houstetter, born December 24, 1892. 11. Infant, born and died March 14, 1895.

Jacob Bitzer, youngest son of John and Dorothea (Beck) Bitzer, was born at Durrwangen, Balingen county, Wurtemburg, Germany, January 16, 1865. He remained in his native town until eight years of age, attending the common schools two years, and then came to the United States with his mother and sister Dorothea to join the father and other members of the family who had settled at Arlington, Massachusetts. Here Jacob attended the Cutter school, graduating in 1879. He then entered the employ of Welch & Griffiths, saw works in Arlington, serving a six years apprenticeship, at the expiration of which time the concern failed. Mr. Bitzer then entered the employ of Theodore Schwamb. a manufacturer of piano cases, starting as a mill hand on irregular moulding machine. Mr. Bitzer served in the various branches of the business of piano case working and mill work, and when the present business (1897) of Theodore Schwamb Company was incorporated Mr. Bitzer became a stockholder and clerk of the corporation, a position he now holds. He is also assistant superintendent of the business, having charge of the mill department. The Theodore Schwamb Company was originally started by Jacob Schwamb, a cabinet maker, who came to Boston in 1838 and established himself in business. Charles Schwamb came to West Cambridge in 1848 and apprenticed himself to Paul F. Dodge to learn the trade, at what is now 1171 Massachusetts avenue, later going into business with Mr. Dodge. Peter Schwamb came to West Cambridge in 1850 and learned the trade at their shop, and in 1853 Theodore and the younger Jacob came also. The two elder brothers entered into partnership, and at this time Theodore started in his apprenticeship. They made pianos and did turning and sawing. Theodore served his time and then was journeyman for two years, when he and his brother Peter were admitted into the firm under the firm name of Charles Schwamb & Brothers. They occupied the old Dodge mill site and continued in business until 1862 when the firm dissolved. Charles and Frederick continued the business and Jacob established himself in Boston. Theodore then began the manufacture of piano cases back in the old Hobbs milldam where 1093 Massachusetts avenue now is, and continued at this location until 1872 with great success. In 1871 he purchased the Stephen Cutter mill property, and the following year removed his business there. It was the original site of the Schwamb Brothers mill, and water power was available there. In 1881 steam power was installed, and in 1886 extensive additions were made to the buildings and plant, then employing twenty men. The corporation of Theodore Schwamb Company was formed in 1897 with Theodore Schwamb as president, Peter Schwamb as secretary and treasurer, and Philip Eberhardt and Jacob Bitzer as directors. Both Mr. Eberhardt and Mr. Bitzer had been actively engaged in the business for a number of years; the former was appointed superintendent in the factory, and the latter assistant superintendent, having charge of the mill department. The business increasing, in 1901 other additions were made, nearly doubling the former floor space, and in 1905, owing to the crowded condition of the plant, still further additions were made; desirable land was purchased in the rear of the buildings, giving access to the railroad and permitting the construction of a spur track for the conveniences of the delivery of lumber. A lumber storehouse and brick factory sixty by eighty feet were built in 1905, and in 1906 drying houses and a new boiler plant were added. About sixty-five men were employed, and the finest case work is manufactured at the plant. Many of the oldest piano makers in the country are customers of the company.

Mr. Bitzer purchased his father's old homestead at 49 Forest street of the heirs, where he resided, and in November, 1906, purchased the Charles Schwamb estate at 1130 Massachusetts avenue, where he now resides, it being one of the most valuable properties in that section. Mr. Bitzer is an attendant of the Unitarian church, and Republican in politics. He served on the committee of twenty-one on town appropriations; member of Republican town committee since 1890, serving for two years as secretary and chairman of same; and served his party as delegate to National convention at Chicago, 1904. He is a member of Bethel Lodge, No. 12, I. O. O. F., joining in 1888, and served that body as noble grand in 1892. He is a member of Arlington Veteran Firemen's Association. Mr. Bitzer is unmarried.

WOODS John Woods was born in Ireland and died in Newburyport, Massachusetts, in 1882, aged seventy-five. He came to America in 1862. He married, in Ireland, Esther Byrnes. Children: 1. Ellen, deceased; married William Walsh, of New York City. 2. Mary, deceased; married Thomas Lynch; child, Mary J. 3. William, born August 15, 1838, mentioned below. 4. John, married Ann Kelley; children; William S., Esther E., Elizabeth A., Theresa M., John J., Mary and Jennie. 5. Theresa married Bernard Doran. 6. Jane, married John Kelley; children: John and Esther.

William Woods, son of John Woods, born August 15, 1838, in the county of Dublin, Ireland, died at Newburyport, Massachusetts, September 17, 1904. He was educated in the old country. At the age of eighteen he came to America, landing in New York City and finding employment in a comb factory in Newark, New Jersey. After working there for several years and becoming a skillful craftsman in this trade, he removed to Newburyport where he worked for the Carr Brown Company, comb manufacturers. Several years later he left this concern to engage in business with his brother John as retail dealers in groceries, etc., with their store in Newburyport. The firm was very successful and the brothers continued in business there for the remarkably long period of thirty-two years. William Woods then retired from active business and devoted himself to the care of his property. He had invested extensively in real estate, and at the time of his death was the owner of ten tenement houses. He held to the religious faith of his fathers and was a devoted Catholic. In politics he was a Democrat. He was a member of the Father Lennon Benevolent Society of Newburyport. A man of upright character, one of best known and most popular citizens of Newburyport, his death was sincerely mourned.

William Woods married, May 1, 1873, Mary Ann Henry, born November 4, 1854, at Newburyport, daughter of Patrick Henry, born in Ireland, 1821, died August 22, 1873, and Anastatia (Grangel) Henry, born 1834, at Newfoundland, died June, 1906, at Newburyport. Children of Patrick Henry and wife: i. Thomas F. Henry, married Ann Bonner; children: Alice, married a Mr. Howard; Charles and Harold. ii. Mary Ann Henry, mentioned above; iii. Catherine Elizabeth Henry; iv. Margaret E. Henry, died aged twenty-one years; v. John J. Henry, a comb manufacturer by trade; married Annie L. Doyle; three children: Eugene, John and Edna; vi. Agnes Henry, married Frank J. Leonard, captain of the Lynn (1908) baseball club; children: Lucy, James, Ruth and Philip; vii. Lucy Henry; viii. Lizzie Henry, married John Bryan, of Newburyport. Children of William Woods and wife: 1. Esther E., unmarried. 2. William H., married Sarah A. Savery; children: Sarah A. and William S. 3. Edward P., a plumber, unmarried.

HOLLAND The Holland family has an ancient and honorable history in Ireland where the surname originated. Flanchadh (Flancha), brother of Cobthach of the ancient O'Madden family (No. 100 of the Connaught pedigree as given in O'Hart's Irish Pedigrees), was the ancestor of the Holland family. The Irish spelling O'h Uallachan has been modified after this family was dispossessed of their lands in Hy-Maine in Connaught, settling in Dublin, Galway, Kildare, Kilkenny, King's County, Mayo, Meath and Westmeath, into the following rather bewildering variety of surnames: Colaghan, Coolacan, Coolaghan, Halahan, Halegan, Halligan, Holahan, Holhane, Holhgane, Holighan, Holland, Hollighan, Hoolighan, Hoolaghan, Hoolaghane, Hoolahan, Houlaghan, Houlaghane, Houlahan, Howlegan, Hulegan, Huolaghane, Olehan, Oulahan, Oulaghan, Oullahan, Woolahan, and Merrie, Merry, FitzMerry, MacMerry, Nolan of Connaught, Noland in England, Proud, Proude, Soople, Suple, Supple, Vain, Vane, Whelton and Wilton. Uallachan is derived from uallach, Irish, meaning proud, haughty, merry, supple, vain. This lineage is traced from the earliest Irish kings to the present time in the Kildare branch, which spells the name Holahan.

(I) Jeremiah Holland, the first of the name of whom we have definite information, married Johannah Daley, and their children were: 1. Philip, born Ireland, died in New York. 2. Timothy, born Ireland, lived in Australia. 3. John, born Ireland, mentioned below. 4. Kate, the superior of the St. Joseph Convent of the Notre Dame order in England. 5. Margaret, married William Connell; she never came to this country. 6. Norah, married John Cocklin; six children. 7. Minnie, married (first) William Ragan; (second) a Mr. Burke; she was the mother of seven children. 8. Hannah, married ———, resided in Jersey City.

(II) John Holland, son of Jeremiah and Johannah (Daley) Holland, was born and died in Lisballard, county Cork, Ireland. He was a farmer. He married Ellen Collins, a native of the same place, whose death also occurred there. Their children, all natives of Lisballard, were: 1. Jeremiah. 2. Philip J., mentioned below. 3 Mary, married Joseph Kean. 4. Timothy. 5. Michael, died in Boston. 6. Hannah, unmarried. 7. Dennis, died Boston. 8. Norah, lived in Boston. 9. John, lived in Lawrence. 10. Patrick, lived in Lawrence. 11. Kate, lived in Ireland. 12. Margaret, lived in Ireland.

(III) Philip Joseph Holland, son of John and Ellen (Collins) Holland, was born February 21, 1868, in county Cork, Ireland. He was educated in the parish schools of his native place. When he was twenty years old he left his home and came to Lawrence, Massachusetts, where he was first employed at St. Mary's Church. He learned the trade of tool sharpener and followed his trade for a number of years. With his savings he started in business as a teamster and general contractor, excavating, making stone work of various kinds a specialty. He has built up an extensive and flourishing business, and is counted among the most substantial and reliable men in his line of business. Although a Democrat in politics, he has not been active in public af-

James Phelan

fairs and has held no offices. He is a member of the Knights of Columbus and of Lodge No. 65, Order of Elks. He married, October 18, 1895, Julia Frances McAuliffe, born December 28, 1836, daughter of John and Ann (Scollard) McAuliffe, both natives of Ireland. Children born in Lawrence: Mary J., John Joseph, Philip A., Ann Catherine, Frank and Augusta.

PHELAN James Phelan, long an honored citizen of Lynn, Massachusetts, and numbered among its most active and enterprising manufacturers and men of affairs, was a native of Ireland, born November 9, 1833, son of Edmond Phelan, who was a farmer, and lived and died in Ireland.

James Phelan attended school at his native home, and assisted in farm work until he was about sixteen years of age, when he came to the United States, first landing in Boston. Shortly after his arrival here he went to Yarmouth, Maine, where for about a year he lived with Professor Wood, principal of an academy, for whom he served as chore boy, and in return received such instruction as gave him a fair educational equipment. Young Phelan then returned to Boston, and thence to Appington, where he began to learn the shoe trade. After he had made considerable progress, he went to Lynn, where he completed his trade, working for several years in various leading factories. Owing to declining health he was obliged to lay aside his work, and he made a voyage to Australia and an extended tour through that country. Returning invigorated and with freshened ambition, he again went to Lynn, resuming work in the shoe factories. In 1861 he made his modest beginning on his own account, in a small upstairs room in a building on Monroe street. Success attended his effort, and he soon found his accommodations inadequate for his increasing trade, and removed to a larger building in the rear of the old Lynn railway station. His business continuing to expand, he was again obliged to seek larger quarters, and removed to Central Square, where he occupied more than one-half of a large factory on the site of what is now the Powers furniture store, and here carried on business with gratifying success until the building was destroyed by fire. This calamity drove Mr. Phelan to seek a new location, and he purchased a factory building on Monroe street. After several years, during which his business continued to expand, he built a factory of his own on Sea street, and which bears his name at the present time. Soon after entering upon the occupancy of this edifice, Mr. Phelan took his sons into partnership, they having thoroughly learned the trade and business under the masterly direction of the father. After a time Mr. Phelan practically retired from the business, yet still making almost daily visits to the establishment, advising and counselling with his sons as occasion arose, and affording them the advantage of his intimate acquaintance with every detail of the business, both mechanical and managerial. It was on the occasion of such a visit, on February 7, 1906, that he was taken suddenly ill, and died before aid could reach him.

While most widely known as the founder and manager of an extensive manufacturing establishment, Mr. Phelan was ever active in other enterprises, and ever gave his aid to all movements for the advancement of the city. He was independent in spirit and action, using his vote and influence in behalf of men of ability and energy, with little if any regard to their political creed or standing. Without ambition for distinction, he gave to the people service as a member of the common council during the administration of Mayor Bubier, and so efficiently that he was elected alderman in the following year. He was a director in the Five Cents Savings Bank, and had occupied a like position in the Lynn Safe Deposit and Security Bank from the day of its organization. He was a communicant of the Roman Catholic church, and a liberal contributor to its support and its various charities. He was a member of no secret orders, but was connected with the Park Club and the Oxford Club. In all relations with his fellows he was regarded with esteem and confidence.

Mr. Phelan married, in Lynn, November 1, 1861, Rebecca Griffin, a native of Ireland, who came to America with her parents when she was about four years old. Her father, John Griffin, was born in Ireland, and after finishing his schooling learned shoemaking. He came to the United States with his family about 1848, settling in Lynn, where he conducted business until retirement, and where he died about 1877. He was a Roman Catholic in religion, and a Democrat in politics. His wife, who was Mary Ann McCarty, also born in Ireland, is still living in Lynn, at the advanced age of eighty-five years. The children of Mr. and Mrs. Griffin were: Mary Ann; Rebecca, who became the wife of Mr.

James Phelan; Michael; Hannah; Katherine Frances; Michael; Gerald; Theresa; Elizabeth; James, and John. Mrs. Griffin has thirty-five grandchildren and eight great-grandchildren. Children of Mr. and Mrs. James Phelan, all born in Lynn, were: 1. Edmond Joseph, married May Chisolm, of Gloucester, Massachusetts; children: Priscilla and James. 2. John Andrew, died 1905. 3. Mary Ann, died 1898. 4. James Peter, married Helen Dempsey, of Lowell. 5. Katherine Frances, died 1891. 6. Michael Francis, married May Van Depoele (see sketch elsewhere), of Chicago, Illinois; child, Louis. 7. Joseph Charles, married Adeline Van Depoele; one child, John J. 8. William Henry, at home. Of the above children Joseph C. and James P. conduct the former business of their father, now one of the largest of its kind in the city. Michael F. is an attorney in Lynn.

(For ancestry see Jeremiah Belcher I.)

BELCHER (VIII) Henry M. Belcher, youngest child of Thomas Jefferson and Hannah (Tewksbury) Belcher, was born in Winthrop, Massachusetts, March 23, 1860, and for more than a quarter century has been closely identified with the business life of the town, and by his own native industry and enterprise has contributed his full share to the growth and prosperity of that municipality. After completing his education in the public schools he served an apprentice's term to the carpenter trade, and became a great master builder, taking contracts on his own account and increasing his operations as his means would permit until he became one of the most extensive building contractors in the town; and not only that, by reason of a certain quality and reputation he possessed for being a business man of the highest integrity, he exacted honest and faithful service from his own employees, with result that his contracts were always carried out according to the spirit as well as the letter, hence his finished work always was of the best character, and the ultimate result of his years of business endeavor is a competency fairly earned and richly deserved. During his active career Mr. Belcher was builder of several of the most substantial structures in Winthrop and among them may be mentioned the fire department building, the Winthrop Yacht Club house, Constitution hall and the Lewis block, although our list might be continued almost indefinitely. And in connection with a large general contract work during the period referred to, Mr. Belcher acquired considerable tracts of land, improved them by the erection of attractive residences and then sold them to purchasers who sought comfortable homes in the pleasant suburban town of Winthrop. In this manner he has been a considerable dealer in real estate in the town and is still possessed of much valuable property in lands and buildings.

While he has not at any time regarded himself as being a public man in Winthrop, Mr. Belcher has generally been found identified in some prominent manner with the several movements for promoting the public welfare. He is a Republican, but not a rabid partisan in political preference, and the several offices he has filled he has been induced to take more because the electors and taxpayers of Winthrop wanted him rather than because he wanted office. For the last six years he has been one of the town assessors, and is a trustee of the Winthrop Co-operative Bank and chairman of its investment committee; member of Winthrop Lodge, F and A. M.; Crystal Bay Lodge No. 133, I. O. O. F., and of Winthrop Lodge No. 153, D. R., of which latter order his wife also is an active and useful member.

On December 2, 1885, Mr. Belcher married, in Winthrop, Amelia J. Cobb, who was born in Charlotte Town, Prince Edward Island, October 20, 1863, and came to live in Winthrop in 1881. Her father, Samuel Cobb, was born in England and came with his father's family to America and settled on Prince Edward Island when Samuel was a child. The elder Cobb was a hard working farmer, an honest, thorough-going man and was much respected in the locality in which he lived. Samuel Cobb married Mary Brakey, who was born in the north of Ireland and came of a long line of Scotch ancestors. Samuel and Mary (Brakey) Cobb had six children: 1. Amelia J. (twin with Annie Elizabeth), born October 21, 1863; wife of Henry M. Belcher. 2. Annie Elizabeth (twin with Amelia J.), married Ellsworth Burr; live in Winthrop, and have daughter, Laura M. Burr. 3. Andrew, who met death by accident. 4. M. Leah, wife of Dr. H. J. Soule, of Winthrop; two children, Horatio and Nadene Soule. 5. Robert B., builder and contractor in Winthrop; married Alma Floyd, and had Edgar, Lewis and Edson Cobb. 6. Maud, living in Winthrop. Mary Brakey, wife of Samuel Cobb, is a daughter of the late Andrew and Mary (McKern) Brakey, who came to this country soon after marriage and settled on Prince Edward Island. They spent their lives on a farm near Charlotte Town, where both attained the age of more than four score years. They had nine children: 1. Robert, now dead; was a successful farmer and business man and accumulated a comfortable fortune. 2. James, married Betsey Curry and is a farmer on Prince Edward Island. 3. Jane, died in Winthrop at the home of her niece, Mrs. Belcher; never married. 4. Sarah, married and removed to Iowa. 5. Elizabeth, married Alexander McKenzie and went west. 6. Mary, married Samuel Cobb; is now a widow living in Winthrop. 7. Martha, married James Houston and lives at Charlotte Town, Prince Edward Island. Two others, names not known.

Henry M. and Amelia J. (Cobb) Belcher had three children, born in Winthrop: Harrison Otis, July 10, 1893; Mildred, died in infancy, and Ellsworth, died aged about six years.

NEWSHOLME Robert Newsholme, father of Alfred Newsholme, was born and died in Yorkshire, England. He belonged to the yeoman class, and the family trace their ancestry to The Conquest. Robert Newsholme (father) was a stone merchant during his active life. He married Phoebe Binns, who was born in England, and died there November 30, 1904. Their children were: Alfred, see forward; Robert, George H., Arthur and Mary. Alfred and George H. were the only members of the family who came to the United States.

Alfred Newsholme, son of Robert and Phoebe (Binns) Newsholme, was born in Haworth, England, June 23, 1849. He received his education in England under the instruction of his uncle William Binns, who was a college professor and who taught high school at Derby, England. He served an apprenticeship to the wool trade, and was afterwards a wool dealer in Bradford ten years. In 1881 he came to this country and entered the employ of the United States Bunting Company of Lowell, Massachusetts, as wool sorter, from which position he rose to that of wool buyer, which position he held up to his death. In 1895 he moved to Methuen, where he was instrumental in establishing the Arlington Heights district of that town. He bought up much of the land, and later sold it at very reasonable rates that a new settlement might be made. This section is now one of the most thickly populated districts in the town. Land upon which the church in this district stands was generously given by Mr. Newsholme. He was elected selectman in 1900, and two years later was elected to a three years' term as water commissioner. He was a member of John Hancock Lodge of Free Masons; Sons of St. George, of Lowell; Methuen Grange, P. of H.; and the Congregational church. He was honest and faithful in the discharge of his duties, and respected by all who knew him.

Mr. Newsholme was twice married, his first wife being Sarah Agnes Pratt, who was born and died in Bradford, England. Their children were: 1. Agnes Maud, born in Bradford, England, in 1879, died in 1890. 2. Robert H., born in 1880, a contractor and builder in Methuen. He married second, Emma Craven, born near Bradford, England, February 20, 1855, daughter of Jonathan and Elizabeth (Wood) Craven. Her father was born in Yorkshire, England, January 18, 1823. Children of Alfred and Emma Newsholme: 3. Arthur H., born in 1883, educated in the public schools of Methuen, a wool sorter by trade. 4. George H., born in 1885, died in 1890. 5. Mary E., born in 1887, educated in the high school of Methuen, and the Lowell State Normal School. 6. Charles E., born in 1890, attended the high school of Methuen. 7. Henry G., born in 1892. Mr. Newsholme died at his home in Methuen, November 14, 1905.

BEIRNE (The ancestry of the Irish Kings given under the Hart pedigree and elsewhere in this work brings the ancestry of the O'Beirne family down to Milsius of Spain (36) and his son Heremon, to whom most of the leading families of Ireland trace their ancestry.)

(I) Patrick Beirne, a descendant, as are all of this name, of Beirin (103), was born in county Cork, Ireland, and married Nancy Smith, of the same county, parish of Rathweny. Among their children were: 1. Patrick, mentioned below. 2. Mary. There were seven in all.

(II) Patrick Beirne, son of Patrick Beirne, was born in Corcrea, Ireland, married Anna Callahan, of Stickellen, county Meath, Ireland. Children, born in Corcrea, Ireland, 1. Michael, mentioned below. 2. Ann, married Peter Murray, a native of Ireland, at Stoneham, Massachusetts. 3. Matthew, married Mary McGough, at Ireland; children: Michael, Thomas, Peter, Mary, Rose, Bernard. 4. Mary, married Peter Mullen, of

Stoneham, Massachusetts; children, born in Woburn: Mary, Margaret, Thomas, Katharine, Anna, and Peter. 5. Peter, died at Stoneham, aged thirty-four years. 6. John, died in Cork. 7. Patrick, married ——— Donohue, of Donegal, county Galway, reside at Chelsea, Massachusetts. Patrick Beirne was educated in his native town and in his youth worked on the farm of his uncle. He learned the carpenter's trade in Dublin, serving his apprenticeship under a builder named Clarkane. He became a skillful craftsman and a trusted employee. Before his death Mr. Clarkane provided for Beirne by procuring for him a position with the McKeel firm of builders. But the young man decided to try his fortunes in the United States. He found employment with F. L. Whitcomb, a carpenter and builder, Somerville, Massachusetts, and after a few years engaged in business there on his own account. He was very successful in business and became one of the leading builders of Somerville.

(III) Michael Beirne, son of Patrick Beirne was born in Corcrea, Ireland, February 21, 1844, and came with his parents to America when a child. He was educated in the Somerville schools. While a young man, he learned the carpenter's trade of his father, at which he worked as a journeyman for a time and later took up contracting and building which he followed many years, building many fine homes in Backbay, Boston, Somerville, Woburn, and surrounding towns, employing at times as many as forty men. Mr. Beirne was an architect as well as a builder, and furnished his own plans for many of his buildings. He was a man highly respected by his friends and neighbors, a man of sterling character and integrity, his word was his bond, and though a selfmade man in every respect, commencing life a poor boy, with little or no financial aid from others he accumulated a fine property owning several buildings in Somerville and Woburn. In politics he was a Democrat, and in religion, a Roman Catholic, a member of the parish of St. Joseph. He died June 4, 1904, and he leaves a widow and three children to mourn his loss; they reside at 154 Linnwood street, Somerville. He married in Boston, November 11, 1872, Marion Kuirk, born at Rathweny, Ireland. His children: Patrick Henry, (see forward); Katharine, born in Somerville, December 10, 1880, graduated from high school, Somerville; Mary Elizabeth, born 1883, graduated from high school, Somerville.

(IV) Patrick Henry Beirne, son of Michael Beirne, was born in South Boston, July 21, 1876. He was educated in Somerville, graduated from the grammar school, and later attended Comer's Business College of Boston.

When fifteen he entered the shop of Blake, Bell & Co., to learn the trade of brass-finisher and tool-maker, where he served an apprenticeship of four years. In 1896 he entered the United States postal service, where he is still employed. In religion he is a Roman Catholic. Though a young man, he is well known and respected, and since his father's death has been a great help to his mother and sisters in looking after his father's property.

VAN DEPOELE It has been said that genius rarely finds full appreciation and frequently receives little reward; and again, that reward of true genius is fame, wealth and due appreciation. The man who conceives and develops new ideas, and brings them into practical use, generally lives in advance of his time, frequently meets with discouraging obstacles, and sometimes finds himself so beset with opposition and ridicule that his greatest aims never attain full fruition; but when genius in man is accompanied with the proper spirit of determination, fortitude sufficient to oppose adversity, courage enough to brave the clamor of opposition, and power of mind to defend a sound and rational principle in science, success and ultimate reward are almost sure to come.

These principles are illustrated most clearly in the life and achievements of one who laid no claim to a long and entirely respectable American pedigree, one who was his own ancestor in this country, and whose span of life measured less than a half century of years; but notwithstanding the fact that he was of foreign birth and ancestry, and was hedged about with many embarassments, lacked money for the early development of the scientific principles which originated in his mind, Charles J. Van Depoele at length provided the means with which to carry out his purposes and attain the full fruition of his hopes and receive the ample reward of his genius, fame and appreciation. The story of his life is his best eulogy.

Charles J. Van Depoele was born in Lichtervelde, Belgium, April 27, 1846, died March 18, 1892. His father was chief engineer on a railway, and it was there that young Van Depoele gained his first mechanical ideas and later learned his first lesson in the science of electricity. When only a child he began experimenting by using ink wells obtained at school for batteries, and later, when still only a boy, having become greatly interested in the elementary principles of electricity and steam valves, he earned sufficient money to purchase a couple of battery cells. From that time he was constantly engaged in experimental work, using for that purpose all the money he could earn. When about sixteen years old, he began to learn the trade of fancy wood carving in Paris, at the same time continuing his experiments evenings and frequently far into the night before laying aside his study and toil. At eighteen he began contracting the making of church altars and employing workmen to assist him, taking the contracts from large concerns to finish their work, making among others an altar for a cathedral in the Chinese Empire. In 1868 he came to the United States and located in Detroit, Michigan, where he started a shop for the making of church furniture, and continued this successfully for twelve years, employing finally upwards of two hundred skilled mechanics. During this time he was devoting every moment he could spare to the perfection of his various electrical devices. Among these was an electric light; first in a primative way with only two candle power lights with which he lighted Forepaugh's Circus; that was the result of his first attempt, and his next was the lighting of the Detroit Opera House.

His plans and undertakings were opposed by his father and friends to such an extent that they called a meeting with the intention of inducing him to abandon them, but he was determined, and instead of doing as they requested he placed his father at the head of his business, and erected a building for the especial purpose of producing his commodities and continuing his experimental work. In 1880 he moved to Chicago, Illinois, where he organized the Van Depoele Electric Light Company, and during the following summer, to demonstrate their idea, lighted some of the streets of that city without charge to the municipality. This experiment was of course expensive, but it resulted in several large contracts to the company which yielded a good profit. To this was later added the manufacture of electrical appliances for various structures, electric lights and general electrical appliances. This still continues as one of the largest of its kind in the country. Soon afterward, in the face of opposition, including that of Mr. Stiles, president of the company, Mr. Van Depoele suggested the idea of operating street railways with electric motive power, and in 1883 he built a short experimental line of road running out of Chicago for the purpose of demonstrating his principle. As a result of this Mr. Stiles was convinced of the practical value of Mr. Van Depoele's suggestion and offered no further opposition to his plans.

In 1884 he constructed a conduit road at the Toronto, Ontario, exposition, and followed it in 1885 with an overhead trolley system in the same city. During the following three years he was engaged in developing and improving upon his former work, taking out patents, and in building electric railways in Toronto, Canada; South Bend, Indiana; Minneapolis, Minnesota; and other large cities. In 1888 the Thompson-Houston Company of Lynn, Massachusetts, secured by purchase all of the Van Depoele railway patents, and from that time until his death Mr. Van Depoele was identified with the extensive operations of that company in the capacity of electrician and inventor. Mr. Van Depoele also perfected the electric percussion drill, having begun his experiments in 1882. Believing that electric power could be used in the operation of mines, he consulted with Mr. Stiles in regard to the subject, and was immediately offered money sufficient to perfect a drill for that especial purpose. On being tested it was found to be powerful enough to crush large stones to pieces. Mr. Van Depoele continued to improve these machines, and the results of his work can now be seen in the output of the Thompson-Van Depoele Electric Mining Company, which was recently purchased by the Thompson-Houston Electric Company. At the time of his death this became the General Electric Company which, while it has enormous works in Lynn, Massachusetts, has in addition branches in all the large cities of the United States, being the largest concern in the world. Though much interested in all branches of electrical mechanism, Mr. Van Depoele's most profitable inventions are the electric railway and electric reciprocating devices, both the result of his intelligent application of the principles of electrical science. At the time of his death he was developing and improving his earlier inventions, and had he lived he would have carried them to a point of perfection far in advance of any thing now known. Mr. Van Depoele was well known in scientific and electrical circles in Detroit,

Chicago, Boston, New York, Lynn and other large commercial centres, and his fame as an inventor was world-wide. His life was devoted to hard work. As a student and inventor he displayed wonderful ability and unflagging zeal, and had few equals in his special field of endeavor, and in his death the electrical and scientific world lost one of its most capable and useful men. The papers said his greatest fault was his generosity.

Mr. Van Depoele married, November 22, 1870, Ada Mina Van Hoogstraten, born in South Holland, at the village of Achthuizen, daughter of Cornelius Van Hoogstraten, born in North Brabond, died December 3, 1906, aged ninety years. He was a cabinet maker by trade; he came to the United States in 1866, and spent the remainder of his days in Detroit, Michigan. He married Cornelia Wevers, who bore him four children, two of whom died young, and the remaining two were: Cornelia A., married Peter Dingman, of Detroit, a well known sash and door manufacturer, and Ada Mina, wife of Mr. Van Depoele. The mother of these children died in 1884, aged seventy-two years. Mr. and Mrs. Van Depoele were the parents of nine children, the following living at the present time (1908): 1. Matilda, married John Griffin, of Lynn; two children: Charles Van Depoele and Helen Theresa Griffin. 2. Maria F., married Michael Phelan; one child, Lewis H. Phelan. 3. Adeline, married Joseph Phelan, one child, John Joseph Phelan. 4. Prudence, resides at home. 5. Henry M., now in Biltmore, North Carolina, at the school of forestry.

BUTTERWORTH James William Butterworth, sexton of the Episcopal church in Lawrence, Massachusetts, is a descendant of an honored family of England. His father was John Butterworth, and his grandfather William Butterworth.

James William Butterworth was born in Roachdale, England, June 10, 1859, and was educated in his native country. He came to the United States with his parents who settled in North Andover, Massachusetts. He served as an apprentice at Ballard Vale, Massachusetts, where he learned his trade of wool sorter; for a time worked in the Pacific Mills, and later worked in the Arlington. At present and for a number of years he has been a dealer in real estate, and he made a success of this line of business. He is a stanch upholder of the principles of the Republican party, but has neither sought nor held public office. He was one of the officers of the Episcopal church. He is a member of the Royal Arcanum. He married Martha Kay, born in England, June 2, 1852, who came to this country with her mother and four sisters, the husband and father having preceded them by a number of years and worked in the shoddy mills of Lawrence in order to prepare a home for their reception. Mr. and Mrs. Butterworth have had children: 1. Ellen, born July 4, 1882. 2. Carrie, October 20, 1884. 3. John Alfred, May 24, 1886. 4. Philip Kay, May 29, 1890.

COTTER Among the principal families of county Cork for many centuries we find the Cotters, though the family is found in many other counties of Ireland at the present time and also in various parts of America. It is supposed that this family is allied to the English Cotter or Cutter family. One Robert Cotta settled in Salem, Massachusetts, before 1636, coming from England.

In Gibson's History of Cork the Cotter family is stated to be of Danish origin. The name Cotter, also spelled Kotter, is common through Denmark and northern Europe; and so far as this family was concerned, was in Ireland anciently written Mac Cottyr, MacCotter and McCottin. Sometimes the name was written in Irish McCoithir, as well as MacCothir. The head of the family in the Commonwealth period was William Cotter, son of Edmond, of Coppingerstown Castle near Middleton, in County Cork. William forfeited his estates under attainder, consequent on his taking part in the Irish war of 1641. It would appear that for the same cause William Catter of Gearigh, in the barony of Imokilly, county Cork, then also forfeited his estates; which inclines us to believe that the two William Cotters were identical; as there is no other William Cotter or Catter mentioned in the list of the "Forfeiting Proprietors in Ireland under the Cromwellian Settlement." Edmond Cotter, (son of Garrett Cottir of Innismore; son of William Cottyr of Innismore; son of William Cottyr of the reign of Edward IV), the kinsman and contemporary of William Cotter of Coppingerstown Castle was the ancestor of the Cotters of Rockforest, Mallow, county Cork. That Edmond Cotter held considerable property, chiefly Anngrove, which was his principal residence, and situated near Carrigtwohill; he also had property in Innismore, where he held a great part of the site of the Queenstown (or "The Cove of Cork"), and land in other sections. (For his descendants see p. 613 in Irish Landed Gentry When Cromwell came to Ireland. O'Hart). James Cotter, of Ann-grove, son of Sir James Cotter, born August 4 1689, was for his devotion to the Stuarts executed May 7, 1720. The family has had many distinguished men in the church and in public life.

(I) Thomas Cotter, a native of county Cork, Ireland, was one of four brothers, the names of the others having been John, Edward and James; John died while on his way to this country, and his two children—John and Mary—who had preceded him, settled his estate; the son John fought in the civil war. Edward and James, the other two brothers, remained in their native land. Thomas Cotter was a farmer, devoting his time and attention exclusively to that occupation. He married Mary A'Hern, and they were the parents of the following named children: 1. Bridget, married Patrick Ormond, of county Cork, Ireland, parish Youghal; they came to this country accompanied by their three children in the year 1878. 2. Thomas, deceased. 3. Patrick, married Elizabeth Murphy, no children; he came to North Andover, Massachusetts, 1850, and was a railroad man and foreman. 4. Mary, married Dennis O'Brian, of Lowell, Massachusetts. 5. John, died in Wales. 6. William, see forward. 7. Thomas, went to Minnesota and there died; he left two children. 8. Margaret, married Thomas O'Brien, of Lawrence, Massachusetts; they settled in North Andover, Massachusetts. 9. ———, married Maurice Murphy; settled in North Andover.

(II) William Cotter, son of Thomas and Mary (A'Hern) Cotter, born in Fennoy, county Cork, Ireland, 1820, died 1885. He was educated in the common schools, and being a great reader he acquired considerable knowledge along various lines, collecting and forming a good library which is in the possession of the family at the present time. He was engaged for some time in the iron works of South Wales, and in 1853 emigrated to the United States, landing in New York. In the same year he went to Boston, Massachusetts, where he took out his naturalization papers, and from there went to Lawrence and was employed for some time in the Lawrence Machine (Iron) Shops. The following year he returned to Boston and for seven years was employed as foreman in the Smith & Felton Iron Works. He then took up his residence in North Andover, secured employment with the firm of Davis & Ferber, and remained until the fall of 1863, when he went to Missouri, where he remained a few months. He then returned to Lawrence, Massachusetts, securing employment as a blacksmith with the Everett Company, with whom he remained until 1877, in which year he retired from business. He purchased a home in Lawrence in which he resided until his death, June 24, 1885. He was a devout member of St. Mary's Church, Lawrence, to which he contributed generously of his means, and was a firm adherent of the principals of Democracy, casting his vote for the candidates of that party. He married, in St. Mary's Church, Lawrence, 1854, Bridget O'Callaghan, a native of the same parish and county in Ireland as her husband; her death occurred April 30, 1890; she was a daughter of Timothy and Mary (O'Keefe) O'Callaghan, who were the parents of eight children as follows: Elizabeth, Johanna, Ellen, Bridget, mentioned above; Catherine, twin of Bridget; Mary F., Margaret and Daniel; four of these children came to the United States, namely: Bridget, Mary F., Catherine and Daniel. Children of Mr. and Mrs. Cotter: 1. Mary A., born 1855, unmarried, resides in Lawrence. 2. Thomas, born 1856, died in Boston, March, 1860. 3. Margaret, died in childhood. 4. Catharine, born 1859, Boston, died there the following year. 5. Thomas Francis, see forward. 6. William Joseph, born November 20, 1863, resides with his sister Mary A.; he is unmarried; employed as blacksmith with D. J. Furber; he is the owner of a large three-story tenement house and a camp at Chrystal Lake· a Democrat in politics, and a member of the Foresters of America. 7. Catherine, born July, 1865, in North Andover, died 1874 in Lawrence. 8. John, born 1865, is a government printer in Washington, D .C.

(III) Thomas Francis Cotter, son of William and Bridget (O'Callaghan) Cotter, was born in North Andover, Massachusetts, May 29, 1861. He was educated in St. Mary's parochial school in Lawrence, and later learned the trade of iron moulder. After serving six years at his trade, he embarked in business as proprietor of a retail shoe store in Lawrence, which business he continued with much profit and success for a period of twenty years, investing his surplus in real estate. Becoming convinced that the real estate business demanded all his time, he accordingly disposed of his shoe business in February, 1905, and since then has given his entire attention to real estate ventures and the development and care of his property. Mr. Cotter is one of the most substantial and highly respected citizens of Lawrence, in the interests of which he is an active factor. He is an active member and liberal supporter of St. Mary's Roman Catholic Church of Lawrence, and in politics adheres to the principles laid down by the Democratic party.

Mr. Cotter married, October 7, 1891, Mary Elizabeth Shea, born May 12, 1869, daughter of John and Mary (Hopkins) Shea. John Shea was born in county Cork, Ireland, 1840, learned the trades of tailor and cutter in London, England, from whence he came to the United States in early manhood, landing in New York city. The greater part of his life was spent in the city of Boston; he died in Lawrence, Massachusetts, 1900; his wife was born in county Cork, Ireland, 1844. They were the parents of three children, all of whom were born in New Bedford, Massachusetts: Margaret, married Timothy McCarthy, of Haverhill, Massachusetts. Samuel, married Mary Mullins; one child, Samuel E. Mary Elizabeth, aforementioned as the wife of Mr. Cotter. Children of Mr. and Mrs. Cotter, born in Lawrence: William H., September 6, 1892. Samuel E., April 5, 1896. Thomas F., December 8, 1900. Augustine H., June 4, 1903.

DURANT Abel Durant of Dorchester, England, was born of English parents, a descendant of ancestors who lived in that kingdom for many generations one after another, and with the exception of a single intermarriage with a French family the Durants of the line here treated were of pure English blood. Abel Durant was a mason, plasterer, a workman who is said to have been skilled in his trade, which he learned by a regular apprenticeship covering several years. Having reached middle age he removed with his family to the Isle of Jersey, and both he and his wife lived there from 1853 to the time of their deaths, both well on in years, devout Methodists and much respected persons in the community in which their lives were spent. His wife's name was Jemima Strickland.

Job S. Durant, son of Abel and Jemima (Strickland) Durant was born in Dorchester, England, December 16, 1851, and learned the trade of his father as soon as he was old enough to work. In 1869, being then not quite eighteen years old the young man came to America, landed at Boston and soon afterward took up his residence in Malden. He not only was able to and willing to work, but he was a superior workman, hence had little difficulty in finding employment; and what was of equal importance, he was a young man of good character, frugal in his habits and had the good sense to save his wages for future use. In the course of a few years he was employed to do some work at his trade in Winthrop, and while there determined to make an investment in real estate in that growing town. In 1877 he bought a lot of land on Revere street and afterward erected a large combined business and apartment building. He then moved to Winthrop and later on gave up his former trade and became a painter, and dealer in paints and painters' supplies. From the beginning his business was successful and he continued it until his death, June 13, 1905.

Mr. Durant is remembered as a capable and reliable business man and one who deserved all of the success which was the reward of his industry. He was a Master Mason, a member of the Methodist Episcopal church, and in politics a Republican. He married February 10, 1890, at Margaretville, Annapolis county, Nova Scotia, Addie Fales, who was born in Margaretville, April 1, 1863, daughter of Hiram and Hepzibah (Downie) Fales, both parents being native Nova Scotians, both devout members of the Baptist church, and highly respected persons in the town in which they live. Mrs. Durant is their only child, and with her adopted daughter, Addie Beatrice, born January 2, 1891, divides her time between her own home in Winthrop and the home of her aged parents in Nova Scotia.

MILLER The surname Muller in Germany, an ancient and honorable family name, is the equivalent of the English surname Miller, having the same origin and meaning.

Gottfried Muller was born in Saxony, Germany, July 22, 1823. He was educated in the common schools, and followed the occupation of farming in his native place until he came to the United States, in 1870. The following year he settled in Methuen, Massachusetts, and purchased a farm. But his life in Amer-

J. S. Durant

ica was short. He died March 19, 1875, at his home in Methuen. He was a Lutheran in religion, a man of sturdy character devoted to his family, industrious, frugal and upright in all his dealings. His wife, Mary, born in Germany, November, 1824, died at Methuen, April, 1896. Children, born in Germany: 1. Emeline, October 31, 1850, died December 1, 1907; married Herman Kress, of Lawrence, Massachusetts. 2. Herman, January 22, 1852; farmer and coal dealer. 3. Emma, April 11, 1854; married William Kress, of Lawrence. 4. Frederick, August 4, 1856; mentioned below. 5. Augusta, November 24, 1858, (twin); died, aged twenty-eight years. 6. Minnie, twin with Augusta; died at age of twenty-eight years, within ten months of the date of death of her twin sister.

Frederick Miller, son of Gottfried Miller (as he spelled his name after coming to this country) was born in Saxony, Germany, and educated in the common schools of his native town. He was fifteen years old when he came with his parents to Lawrence, Massachusetts, and for the first eight months worked in a mill in that city. When his father bought the farm in Methuen he went to work with him and continued until he was twenty-one. He bought a small place in Methuen after he came of age and built a house and barn. He sold it in 1900 and bought a farm of seventy acres on Pleasant street, in Methuen, bulding a new barn and later a new house, and establishing a large milk route in Lawrence and vicinity and maintaining a large dairy for the production of milk for his customers. The milk route he has turned over lately to his son Frederick William Miller. The farm supports thirty-five head of cattle. He devotes his attention mainly at present to general farming. About 1892 he started in the wood business in Lawrence and continued successfully for ten years, selling out to advantage at the end of that period. His place of business was at the corner of Vine and Prospect streets. He has invested in real estate in the suburbs of Lawrence and has built and sold no less than seventy-five dwelling houses. He has amassed a competence and is still pursuing his varied lines of business activity with great success. His natural ability and energy have won him a position of prominence in business and public life. He has been appointed assistant street commissioner of the town of Methuen and is held in high esteem by his townsmen. In politics he is a Republican. He married, January 3, 1884, in Methuen, Emma Lena Muller, born March, 1864, in Saxony, Germany, daughter of Moritz Muller not related to his family. Children, born in Methuen: 1. Frederick William, October 16, 1884; educated in the schools of his native town, now manager of the milk route and living with his parents, Methuen. 2. Arthur, June, 1886, educated in Methuen, assisting his father on the homestead. 3. Eddie, January 13, 1888; died February 10, 1888. 4. Emma H., born August 24, 1891, student. 5. Walter Herbert, March 29, 1899.

EVANS The earliest known member of the family of which William F. Evans, of Bradford, is a representative, was John Evans, a native of Rathcarberry, in the north of Ireland, where he died in 1843, aged about seventy years. He was a large land owner, and was considered a very wealthy man for those days. He and his wife were members of the Congregational church, in the affairs of which they took an active interest. He married Martha Weir, who was of Welch descent; children: Margaret, Mary, Sally, Jane, David W., John, Robert.

David Weir Evans, eldest son of John and Martha (Weir) Evans, was born in the north of Ireland, December, 1801, died November 4, 1879. He was a linen manufacturer, the greater part of his goods being hand-made. He was also the owner of many horses and fox hounds, deriving great enjoyment from that sport. In 1848, accompanied by his wife, Agnes (Ferguson) Evans, who was born at or near Warren Point, Ireland, died January 21, 1898, and eight children, he emigrated to the United States, the voyage being made on the sailing vessel "Constitution," landing in New York. Their children were: 1. Sarah, born April 19, 1830. 2. Eliza, April 13, 1833, deceased. 3. Martha, April 25, 1835. 4. Robert, February 25, 1837, died August 25, 1863. 5. John W., June 19, 1839. 6. Mary J., December 23, 1841, died April 15, 1863. 7. Margaret, August 28, 1844, died in 1900. 8. William F., August 30, 1846, see forward. 9. Agnes, August 1, 1849. 10. Viola, July 2, 1852, died April 10, 1863. 11. David H., September 5, 1855, died January 29, 1879.

William Ferguson Evans, third son of David W. and Agnes (Ferguson) Evans, was born in Belfast, Ireland, August 30, 1846. He received a common school education in his youth, and in early life came to Haverhill, Massachusetts, where he became a shoemaker, later a manufacturer of shoes, remaining as such for a period of thirty years, from 1872 to 1902, retiring after the death of his wife, and since then has conducted a retail shoe store in Haverhill. He has invested extensively in real estate in Haverhill and in the stock of its various banks. He is a member of the Baptist church of Haverhill, and of the Saggahew Lodge of Free Masons of Haverhill. In politics he is a Republican. He married Emma Frances Robinson, born in Augusta, Maine, daughter of Captain William Robinson, of Augusta. Children: 1. Hattie V., unmarried. 2. William R., married Bessie Durgin, of Haverhill, Massachusetts. 3. Alfred W., married Mary Brooks. 4. Mildred, unmarried, resides at home.

CAMPBELL Among the residents of Lynn may be mentioned Thomas Campbell, a native of Ireland, born in county Fermanagh, October 22, 1841, son of William and Jane (McCoy) Campbell, of county Fermanagh, Ireland, and grandson of James Campbell, a native of the same place. William Campbell (father) followed farming in Ireland; he came to the United States in 1873, locating in Lynn, Massachusetts, where he died in 1874, aged seventy-three years. His wife died aged sixty-four years. William and Jane (McCoy) Campbell reared a family of nine children, seven of whom are still living, namely: James, now deceased; Thomas, see forward; Alexander, a resident of England; Margaret and William, residents of Australia; Annie Eliza, died in 1905; Phoebe, a resident of Northampton, New Hampshire; married Charles Orrin Stevens; Mary Jane, married Alexander Patterson; resides in Lynn; Francis, a resident of Texas.

Thomas Campbell acquired a practical education in the schools of his native land, and in 1866, at the age of twenty-five, emigrated to the United States, settling in Philadelphia, Pennsylvania. He followed the trade of carpenter in that city, having learned the same in Ireland prior to his emigration. In March, 1867, after a short residence in the "City of Brotherly Love," he removed to Lynn, Massachusetts, and there followed his trade for about eighteen months, after which he engaged in the building business in a small way, gradually increasing until at one time he employed over sixty men, being among the largest builders in the city, and erecting a large number of the finest and largest buildings, including shoe factories, churches and dwelling houses; among the latter may be mentioned the residences of Mr. C. A. Coffin, B. F. Spinney, Dr. C. A. Lovejoy, Dr. J. G. Pinkham and Waldo Pevear; also the Oxford Club house and the Episcopal church. He continued this line of work with marked success until his retirement in 1906, being then one of the oldest builders in the city, when he was succeeded by his sons—William A., Robert S. and Frederick J.—under the firm name of Campbell Brothers, contractors and builders. Their shop is located at Nos. 34 and 38 Suffolk street, and their offices at Nos. 99 and 101 Sagamore street, Lynn, and by their honorable business principles and straightforward methods of conducting affairs have maintained the reputation established by their father.

Thomas Campbell was prominent in the ranks of the Republican party, having been elected to the offices of city councilman, 1884-85-92, and member of the board of aldermen, 1895-96, in which capacities he served faithfully both the people and his constituents. He is also president of the Lynn water board, being elected in 1908 to serve five years, and is discharging his duties in that office at the present time. He is a member of Bay State Lodge, Independent Order of Odd Fellows; he is also a member of the Order of Free and Accepted Masons, affiliating with Golden Fleece Blue Lodge, William Sutton Chapter, Olivet Commandery, through the Scottish Rite bodies, including Aleppo Temple of the Mystic Shrine up to thirty-second degree, and of the Massachusetts Consistory. He is vice-president of Commonwealth Savings Bank, in which he is serving as trustee, being appointed at its incorporation, and as a member of the investment committee. He is a member of the Episcopal church, Oxford Club and Cabin Club.

Thomas Campbell married, in 1862, Emily Crozier, a native of county Fermanagh, Ireland, daughter of Armstrong Crozier, a contractor and builder in county Fermanagh. Seven children, all of whom are now (1908) living and residing in Lynn, were born to Mr. and Mrs. Campbell, namely: 1. William A. 2. Thomas Henry, married Sophia Haines, two children: Helen Geneva and Alice Marion. 3. Lizzie Maria. 4. Robert Spence, married Edith E. Roberts, two children: Dorothy and Arline. 5. Laura Jane. 6. Emily Crozier. 7. Frederick James, married Harriet Cunningham, one child, Richard C. Campbell.

HERLIHY Thomas Herlihy, now living in retirement in Lawrence, Massachusetts, is a fine example of what can be accomplished by thrift, industry and perseverance, although they have not been backed by an extensive education. John Herlihy, father of Thomas Herlihy, was a native of Ireland, where he was employed as a tailor. He married Ellen Mead.

Thomas Herlihy was born in county Cork, Ireland, in 1837. He emigrated to the United States, landing at Boston, May 6, 1873. From thence he came to Lawrence as a laborer, entering the employ of the Lawrence Lumber Company, for whom he worked for the long period of twenty-three years. He was frugal and determined and in the course of years amassed a competence on the interest of which he is now living in comfort retired from active labors. He is the owner of a number of fine large tenement houses. He came to this country alone, but in the course of two years had saved a sufficient fund to enable him to have his wife and family follow him. He is a Democrat but has never taken an active part in political affairs. He is a member of the Catholic church. He married Ellen Sweeny, of county Cork, Ireland, and they have had children: 1. Ellen, married J. Kiley Lawrence. 2. Honora, deceased. 3. Mary, married, February 2, 1888, Dennis Shine; children: i. Julia, born November 20, 1888, graduated from St. Mary's Convent and a commercial college, resides with parents; ii. Agnes, born March 10, 1892, now attending school; iii. Helen, born January 1, 1894, died September 29, 1894, aged nine months; iv. Timothy, born October 15, 1896; the family reside in Lawrence. 4. Bridget, twin of Mary, married Matthew Reynolds. 5. Anna. 6. Margaret, a nun; she was about eighteen when she entered the Notre Dame Convent in 1887, and at present (1908) is in East Boston. 7. John, died in early life.

LEONARD John Leonard was born in Ireland, 1835. He spent his early youth in his native land and acquired the rudiments of an education there. When he was fourteen he followed the exodus from his native land to America. He began to work in the mills at Lawrence, Massachusetts, and after six months was apprenticed to a marble cutter. He worked in Lawrence as marble cutter and maker of monuments and all kinds of cut stone work, continuing until 1900 when he retired from business on account of failing health. He was very successful in a financial way and had a reputation second to none for excellent and artistic work. He himself was an expert craftsman and his work was always in great demand. Upright, honorable, fair-dealing, Mr. Leonard has the respect and confidence of all with whom he has done business and with all his townsmen, and has been free to help others in need. In his active years he was one of the most industrious and hard-working men in business in the city. To the regret of many friends he has for many months been confined to his room by illness. In his family the father has the right to take great satisfaction. All his children have been given liberal educations and all have evinced unusual ability. Three are priests, one a physician and one a musician of note.

Mr. Leonard married Ellen Walsh, born in Forest Hill, Massachusetts. Children, born in Lawrence: 1. William, died in 1890; was a noted musician and composer. 2. Rev. Daniel, educated in St. Mary's Roman Catholic school at Lawrence and at St. Thomas College, Villinova, Pennsylvania; is a priest of the St. Augustinian Order. 3. Rev. Augustine, educated in the same school and college as his brother, but died on the threshold of his career as a priest in 1894; was ordained in Rome. 4. Thomas F., educated in St. Mary's school, Lawrence high school, St. Thomas College and New England Conservatory, took musical instruction under private teachers; is now a teacher of music with an office on Essex street, Lawrence, and organist of St. Mary's Roman Catholic Church. 5. Rev. John B., a graduate of Lawrence high school, was a student at St. Mary's school and St. Thomas College; is a priest of the St. Augustinian Order and a curate of St. Mary's Roman Catholic Church of Lawrence. 6. Dr. Andrew, a graduate of public school of Lawrence, St. Mary's school, Holy Cross College and Baltimore Medical College. 7. Loyola, whose only daughter graduated at the convent of St. Mary's and joined the order of Notre Dame nuns.

HAYES John Hayes was a shoemaker at Alton Bay, New Hampshire, and from that town removed to Georgetown, Massachusetts, where he died August 23, 1896. He was a native of Ireland and a descendant of sturdy Irish ancestors. He was a young man when he came to this country, and two of his brothers also came over and went to Wisconsin, then a new and comparatively wilderness region. They were railroad men, Thomas having charge of construction work on the line of road which was built through the present city of Janesville. The other brother was James, and both are now dead. John Hayes went to live in Georgetown that he might improve his condition in domestic life, educate his children and give them a start in useful vocations. All of them except one were graduated from the Georgetown high school. He was an industrious, honest man and was much respected in the town in which he lived. He married Catherine Mahoney, who died in August, 1903, having borne her husband six sons and one daughter. Their children: 1. James A., a railroad man in the employ of the Boston & Northern Railroad Company. 2. Francis E., died in Washington, D. C., in November, 1895; never married. 3. George H. W., lawyer of Ipswich, Massachusetts. 4. Joseph A., lives in Boston and is manager of the National Produce Company; married, but has no children. 5. David B., an employee and assistant manager of Danvers Electric Lighting Company. 6. Bernard, died when two years old. 7. Catharine, married; her husband an employee of the E. E. Gray department store, Boston.

(II) George H. W. Hayes, son of John and Catherine (Mahoney) Hayes, is a native of Georgetown, Massachusetts, born March 16, 1871, and received his literary education in the Georgetown grammar and high schools, graduating from the latter. After leaving school he took up the study of law, later matriculated at Boston University School of Law, completed the course there and graduated LL.B. in 1895. Having been admitted to practice in the courts of this state, Mr. Hayes began his professional career in Ipswich in February, 1896, and for more than twelve years has been numbered with the capable and rising members of the Essex bar. In legal circles he is looked upon as a good trial lawyer and an excellent advocate at the bar of the court and before the jury. His methods are careful but not laborious, and he never goes half prepared into the trial of a case. He takes a commendable interest in public affairs and the institutions of Ipswich, and during his residence in the town has been chosen in various official capacities. In 1904-05 he was a member of the school committee and since 1904 has served as member of the water and electric lighting boards. He is a member of Carrolton Council, No. 498, Knights of Columbus, recording and financial secretary of Agawan Aerie, No. 1588, Fraternal Order of Eagles, and member and keeper of the records of Chebacco Tribe, No. 93, Improved Order of Red Men.

Mr. Hayes married, April 30, 1901, Helen O'Brien, daughter of William F. and Sarah (Dunn) O'Brien, and by whom he has four children: 1. Althea V., born June 13, 1902. 2. William F., February 15, 1904. 3. Zelda M., May 26, 1905. 4. George M., July 23, 1907.

DICK The surname Dick is merely the diminutive form of the personal name Richard, and was undoubtedly commonly used as a personal name before becoming a family name. The family of Dick was located in Edinburghshire, Peebleshire, Orkneys and other parts of Scotland before A. D., 1300, and the family is reputed to be of Danish origin, dating back to the invasion of the British Isles by the Danes. A branch of the Scotch family of Dick is located in Ulster province, Ireland, chiefly in county Antrim.

(I) David Dick, of this ancient Scotch family, was born in Perthshire, Scotland, where he was educated in the common schools, and lived all his days. He learned the trade of mason, which he followed during his active life. He died at the age of sixty-three. He was an enthusiastic and active Free Mason. He belonged to the established church of Scotland. He married Margaret Wilson, born in Scotland, died aged seventy-six years. Children, born in Perthshire: 1. John, resided at Providence, Rhode Island, where he died. 2. George M. 3. Robert, resides at Sandiego, southern California. 4. David. 5. Alexander Wilson, mentioned below. 6. Peter. 7. Mary. 8. Euphemia. 9. Margaret.

(II) Alexander Wilson Dick, son of David and Margaret (Wilson) Dick, was born in Perthshire, Scotland, May 5, 1852. He received his education in his native land. When he came of age he decided to leave home and try his fortune in America. At the age of twenty-one he sailed in the ship "Columbia." He settled first in Springfield, Massachusetts, where he found employment as clerk in the dry goods house of Forbes & Smith. After working there two years he went to Boston as clerk in the store of Churchill, Gilchrist, Smith & Company, dealers in dry goods, at the time that Mr. Smith left the firm of Forbes

& Smith to become a partner in the Boston firm, and Mr. Dick came with him. In 1880 Mr. Dick established himself in the dry goods business at Lynn, Massachusetts, in a store in Market Square. A year later he formed a partnership with Mr. Dawson under the firm name of Dick, Dawson & Company and continued in the dry goods business on Market street. Mr. Dick bought out his partner two years later and became sole proprietor. In 1884 he sold his Lynn business and purchased the business of the firm of Zean, Leach & Company at Plymouth, Massachusetts, in the dry goods trade. He conducted it two years, and the following two years was engaged in the same line of business at Westfield, Massachusetts, buying out the firm of Towell & Buckton. In 1888 Mr. Dick returned to Lynn and started another dry goods and millinery store in one end of what was called the Boscabel Block. His business prospered, and at the end of ten years he purchased one-half of this block and occupied it with his business which grew rapidly. At one time he had three stores, one on Market street, one on Federal square and one on Market square. He continued with the utmost success in the dry goods business in Lynn until 1904, when he retired, and since then has been occupied in the care of his real estate in Lynn and other investments. Mr. Dick is a Republican in politics. He is a member of the lodge and Fraternity Encampment of the Independent Order of Odd Fellows, of Lynn, and of the Scots Charitable Society, established in Boston in 1654, the oldest Scotch organization in America, and of Clan McLan, of Boston, the Highland Dress Association, Burns Memorial Association and the Lynn Caledonian Club. He is a member of the Presbyterian church at the corner of Columbus avenue and Berkley street, Boston.

Mr. Dick married, in Lynn, June, 1879, Maria Lawson, born in Sherbrooke, Canada, daughter of William and Lucy (Carver) Lawson, both of Sherbrooke, later of Lynn. William Lawson was born in Sanguher, Scotland, was a shoemaker by trade, which line of work he followed until late in life, when he was employed by the Boston & Maine Railroad Company in Lynn. Mr. Lawson settled for a time in Montreal, Canada, removed to Sherbrooke, Canada, and finally to Lynn, Massachusetts, where he spent his last years, and where both he and his wife died; they were buried in Pine Grove cemetery. Their children were: Mary, Susan, Maria, Rebecca, William, Nancy, Lucy and James Lawson. Mr. and Mrs. Dick are the parents of one child, Margaret May, born in Lynn, June 17, 1881, resides at home with her parents.

HOGAN The Hogan family of Ireland is traced to one Ogan (meaning in Irish, a youth), son of Aitheir, and gradson of Cosgrach, brother of Cineidh, of the O'Brien family, Kings of Thomond. (See O'Brien family in this work). O'Hogan is the anglicized spelling of the name. Later generations in Ireland and America have preferred the spelling Hogan. The family is now well scattered through the counties of Ireland.

(I) Patrick Hogan lived in county Queens, Ireland. He married and among his children was George, mentioned below.

(II) George Hogan, son of Patrick Hogan (1), was born January 14, 1797, in King Tallamore county, Ireland. He received a common school education, and learned his trade, serving an apprenticeship of seven years at Kilmunum, in the woolen mills. In 1826 he came to America, and in 1837 settled at North Andover, Massachusetts, where he worked in the Stevens Mills. He died November 8, 1870, at Lawrence. He married, at Leeds, Ann O'Rielley, born April 7, 1805, died September 12, 1888, at Lawrence. Children: 1. Thomas A., born February 17, 1835. 2. James, born May 25, 1837, died July 10, 1864. 3. Elizabeth, born June 30, 1839, married William H. Harrison. 4. John Francis, born September 19, 1841, mentioned below. 5. Annie M., born July 22, 1843, unmarried. 6. George E., born February 28, 1846, mentioned below. 7. Joseph A., born August 8, 1848, died 1851. In politics he was a Democrat. He was a member of Division 1, Ancient Order of Hibernians, and of the St. Vincent de Paul Society. Children, Minnie, Nellie, Dr. Joseph A., George.

(III) John Francis Hogan, son of George Hogan (2), was born in North Andover, Massachusetts, September 19, 1841. He was educated in the public schools of his native town. He began to work in the mill of Moses T. Stevens, at North Andover, when he was only ten years old. He enlisted in the Union army in 1861, but after three months of drilling, his company disbanded without entering the service. He re-enlisted in the Sixth Massachusetts Regiment in 1862 and served nine months in Virginia. When he returned he went to work in the woolen mill of Hodge

Brothers, Lawrence, as overseer of the spinning room and continued for three years. Then he engaged in business on his own account in partnership with two others operating a woolen mill in New Hampshire under the firm name of Henry H. Wyman & Company. They invested sixteen thousand dollars in the plant and prospered for four years, when they lost their plant by fire with inadequate insurance and were unable to resume business afterward. In 1870 he went into partnership with his brother George E. in the milk business in Lawrence, and in 1872 established a retail grocery business. It proved successful, and in 1875 he admitted his brother George E. to partnership and they were in business together for a period of fourteen years when he retired, selling his interests to his partner. Since then he has invested freely in real estate in Lawrence, has built many houses and bought and sold much real estate. He has demonstrated expert knowledge of the value of property in Lawrence and has profited largely by his deals and investments. In politics Mr. Hogan is a Democrat; member of common council 1876-77, and has been on the board of overseers of the poor from ward three. He is treasurer of St. Patrick's Aid Society; of the Holy Name Society and of the funds of the Post, Grand Army of the Republic. He is vice-president of the Real Estate Association of Lawrence.

He married (first) Mary Remwich, born January 7, 1842, died June, 1873. He married (second) Hannah Callahan, daughter of Thomas Callahan, a mason and contractor of Lawrence. He married (third), May 26, 1891, Josephine McCarthy, born January 10, 1864, daughter of Joseph J. McCarthy. Children of John F. and Mary Hogan: 1. Mary Frances, born March 17, 1868, died March 9, 1886. 2. George F., born April 23, 1870, died June 12, 1873. 3. John, born April 12, 1872, died April 14, 1872. Children of John F. and Hannah Hogan: 4. Thomas, born February 4, 1880, died June 8, 1884. 5. Francis Xavier, born November 8, 1886, graduated from the Lawrence high school at the age of fifteen; he then took a special course at Harvard; now teaching in the Lawrence high school. Memorial Day, May 30, 1908, he delivered the oratorical address in the City Hall, Lawrence, which was very good and highly appreciated by all. Children of John F. and Josephine Hogan: 6. Agnes R., born March 14, 1892. 7. John J., born December 7, 1893. 8. Mary P., born March 17, 1895. 9. George, born July 5, 1899. 10. Margaret, born April 15, 1906.

(III) George E. Hogan, son of George Hogan (2), born February 28, 1846, died October 14, 1907, at Lawrence. He removed to Lawrence when eighteen years old and followed the trade of iron molder, later having a retail milk business and finally engaging in the grocery business on Common street. His business increased and he removed his grocery to the corner of Broadway and Haverhill street. Subsequently he engaged in the liquor business at 501 Broadway, continuing until a year before his death, when on account of failing health he sold out. He served as overseer of the poor for the city of Lawrence for a period of three years. In politics he was a Democrat. He was a member of Division 1, Ancient Order of Hibernians, and of the St. Vincent de Paul Society. He married, in May, 1869, in Lawrence, Sarah Claffay, born in Lowell, Massachusetts, in August, 1842, youngest daughter of Thomas and ——— Claffay, who reared seven daughters. Mrs. Hogan died in Lawrence, August, 1890, at the age of thirty-eight years. She left four children: Mary, a bookkeeper at the Arlington mills. Dr. Joseph A., a practicing physician of Lawrence, office corner of Franklin and Essex streets. Nellie, a resident of Lawrence. George E., Jr., a drummer for the Essex Brewing Company of Bradford, and a resident of Amesbury.

McLAIN It is impossible to distinguish between the surnames MacLain and MacClain. The variations of spelling of the two clans are infinite. The prefix Mac or Mc (meaning son of) is often dropped and many of the Lane families are of these Scotch clans, especially those of the state of Maine. The MacClean family was in Ayrshire, Moray and Mull county, Scotland, from time immemorial, and the McLean or McLane in Argyle and Mull before the year 1300. One branch of the McLane or McClain family is found in Francestown, New Hampshire, descendants of Malcolm McLane, who came there in 1784. He was born in Lear Castle, county of Argyle, Scotland; landed in Boston in the fall of 1773, and resided at Londonderry and New Boston, New Hampshire. His mother was Molly Beaton, his father Daniel McLane, who was in the army of Charles the Pretender at the battle of Culloden, April 16, 1746, and claimed descent from a younger branch of the family, as son

Charles O. McLain

of Sir John McLane. The clan McLane was located on Loch Buoy. Malcolm married Isabelle Livingston, born in Scotland, daughter of John and Jenny (Carmichael) Livingston. Malcolm's parents both died in Scotland, but a brother Hugh, who died unmarried came with him. Malcolm died January 19, 1831; his wife November, 1809; Hugh in 1859 at the age of ninety-six. Captain Obadiah McLane, of Goffstown, New Hampshire, was a clansman but not a near relative; he was a prominent officer in the revolution.

(I) Alexander McLain comes of one of the McLain pioneers who came about the time of the revolution. Malcolm McLane mentioned above had a grandson Alexander who removed to Vermont and the general similarity of names suggests relationship. But this Alexander lived at Appleton, Maine, where his father is said to have been a pioneer. He was a farmer in that town, but died when still young, leaving a widow and young children. He married Mary Barker. They were members of the Universalist church. Their children: 1. Henry. 2. Oscar. 3. Charles O., born August 12, 1840, mentioned below. 4. Fergus, deceased. 5. Fergus, deceased. 6. Furgus. 7. Nancy. 8. Elizabeth.

(II) Charles O. McLain, son of Alexander McLain (1), was born in Appleton, Maine, August 12, 1840. He was educated in the public schools of his native town, and worked at farming during his youth. When he was seventeen years old he came to Haverhill and worked at the trade of shoemaking for several years. At length he established his own business as a manufacturer of boots and shoes and gradually increased the volume of his production until he had one of the most extensive factories in the city and employed several hundred hands. He retired from business in 1889, after a long and honorable as well as an exceptionally successful career. His health failed at that time and he died May 24, 1899. He was a member of Saggahew Lodge of Free Masons. In politics he was a Republican and served one term in the common council of Haverhill. He was a man of public spirit and alive to the interests of the city in which his business was located. He invested of his savings in real estate and did much to upbuild and develop Haverhill. He built for investment ten dwelling houses, still owned by his widow. He was an active member of the Universalist church. He was a veteran of the civil war. He enlisted in Company G, Thirty-fifth Massachusetts Regiment of Volunteers, and was wounded in the battle of Antietam. He was a member of Major Howe Post, Grand Army, Haverhill. He was of sterling character and large influence in business and society, having the friendship of many men and the esteem of everybody who knew him.

He married, October 13, 1866, Martha A. Brown, born March 10, 1846, daughter of Henry and Ann (Simmons) Brown. Henry Brown, her father, was born in Bremen, Maine, and followed the sea for a livelihood; was a Methodist in religion. Her mother married, first, Samuel Jones, by whom she had two children, Ann and Samuel Jones. Children of Henry and Ann Brown: Martha A., mentioned above; Susan, Henrietta, George Brown. Children of Charles O. and Martha A. McLain: 1. Frank I., born June 24, 1868, resides at home; unmarried; a shoe cutter by trade. 2. Henry G., born August 12, 1870, died July 20, 1898. 3. Jesse, born January 1, 1872, married Clarence Dean. 4. Tafton, born April 29, 1877. 5. George T., born January 21, 1879, died August 5, 1879.

DALEY John Daley, prominent in the business world of Lawrence, Massachusetts, for many years, traces his descent to an old and honored family of Ireland.

(I) Timothy Daley was born in county Cork, Ireland, and spent his life in that country.

(II) John Daley, son of Timothy Daley, was born in Ireland, and died in this country, April 15, 1875. He emigrated to the United States with other members of the family in 1848. He married Ellen O'Neil, born 1797, died January 5, 1899.

(III) John Daley, son of John and Ellen (O'Neil) Daley, was born in Ireland and came to the United States with his family in 1848. He was the father of six children: Mary, Kate, Ellen, William, John and Timothy.

(IV) John Daley, son of John Daley, was born in Glandore, county Cork, Ireland, July 18, 1840. He was eight years of age when he came to this country with his parents, and his school education was acquired in Lawrence. He was ambitious and persevering, and his earnest efforts enabled him to rise to an enviable position in the business world. He worked for a time in a mill, then in the leather business, and is now the owner of a grocery and meat market. He has amassed a considerable fortune and owns a large block in South Lawrence. He married, January 1, 1867, Margaret Barry, died September 27, 1906, daughter of Andrew Barry. Children: 1. James, died September 9, 1869. 2. William H., died April 12, 1873. 3. Mary. 4. Timothy J. 5. Thomas, died at age of ten years. 6. Elizabeth, married George Kerrigan, of Haverhill, Massachusetts 7. Catherine, married Benjamin Devine, of Salem, Massachusetts. 8. Ella. 9. Margaret. 10. John. 11. Anna. 12. Josephine.

HOLT John Holt, born January 14, 1841, in Lancashire, England, is son of James and Sara (Cropper) Holt, and grandson of Richard Holt, who lived and died in England. James Holt (father) and his wife were natives of Rochdale, Lancastershire, England; they were the parents of seven children: Sarah, born 1839, married James Jepbron; John, see forward; Harriet, died young; Robert, unmarried; Thomas, living; William, deceased; Jane, married Thomas Giendrod.

John Holt was educated at a mill school, beginning to work in the woolen mill at the age of nine, and learning the trade of spinner. He worked for a time as fireman and stationary engineer. In 1869 he came to the United States and made his home in Lawrence, Massachusetts. He lived with Mr. J. Barnes. He worked at his trade in the Sutton Mills, Marland Mills and North Andover Mills. He was one of the first traveling men on the road for the Peter McGovern operating jack, setting them up and operating them. After two years he gave up his position. Later he was first overseer of the spinning room of the Sawyers new mill, at Dover, New Hampshire, a position he held for a year and a half, and he held a similar position for eight years in the Pemberton Mills, Lawrence, Massachusetts. When he left the spinning room he purchased two boarding houses and conducted them eight years, under the Pemberton Company. He then accepted a position as overseer in the woolen mills at North Andover and held it for nine years and a half. He went to the Marland Mill, where he held a similar position for eleven years and six weeks. He is now living in Lawrence, and is engaged in the Stanley Manufacturing Company of that city. He is a member of Blue Lodge of Free Masons, one of the oldest Free Masons in Lawrence. In politics he is a Republican.

Mr. Holt married (first), in England, Maria Fielding, born 1841, died July 11, 1864, in England. He married (second), in 1865, in England, Alice Stuart, born October 26, 1840, died 1902. Child of first wife: Robert, born March 26, 1864, died aged one and one half years. Child of second wife: Alice Maria, born 1873, married Moses Marshall, of Lawrence, register of deeds of that city; children: John Stuart and Alice Catherine Marshall.

KEATING Thomas Keating, son of Thomas and Bridget (Brophy) Keating, born in town of Old Beg, parish of Borris, Edron East, Carlo county, Ireland, 1836, died at Melrose, Massachusetts, January 4, 1894, aged fifty-nine years. He received his education in the common schools of his native parish. He left home at the age of thirteen, 1849, coming with the great movement of population from Ireland to America. He obtained employment as a gardener in Melrose, Massachusetts, and passed the remainder of his life in that town. He invested his savings in the livery stable business, during his early manhood, and built up a flourishing establishment from a humble beginning. His stable was located near the Wyoming station, and he became known as an expert judge of horses, being a careful buyer and trader. Mr. Keating was a Democrat in national affairs, independent in municipal affairs, and never sought or held political office.

Thomas Keating married (first), 1858, at Sacred Immaculate Conception Church, Malden, Massachusetts, Rose Powder, and their children were: 1. Thomas H., born May 10, 1860, at Melrose; piano maker; Emerson Piano Company of Boston; married, October 25, 1881, Rosalie M. Beh, of Boston; reared a large family; resides at Roslindale, Massachusetts. 2. James P., born March 14, 1864, at Melrose, afterwards resided in New York City. Thomas Keating married (second), 1868 at "Tommy's Rock" St. Joseph's Church, Boston, Ann Fleming, born in Borradagh, parish of Ballinoe, Cork county, Ireland, daughter of Thomas and Mary (McEnery) Fleming, the latter being a native of Ballylusky, parish of Ballinoe, Cork county, Ireland. Children: 3. William E., born September 24, 1869, at Melrose, married, June 29, 1898, Jennie D. Prior, of Randolph, Massachusetts; four children: Joseph, Mary, Marguerite and Josephine; William E. is an electrical superintendent of Boston & Northern Railroad. 4. John J., born April 2, 1871, in Melrose, mentioned below. 5. Philip S., born

November 26, 1874, at Melrose, married. July 21, 1903, Agnes McSweeney, of Revere, Massachusetts; has one son, Paul Sylvester, born December 31, 1907; Philip S. is engaged in the livery business.

(II) John Joseph Keating, son of Thomas and Ann (Fleming) Keating, was born in Melrose, Massachusetts, April 2, 1871. He was educated in the public schools of Melrose, graduating from the high school. He started upon a mercantile career as clerk in the store of Hawley, Folsom & Martin, of Boston, wholesale dealers in men's furnishing goods, and continued with the concern for four years. The following seven years he served as clerk for the firm of Farrar & Selee in the same line of business at Melrose. In 1898 he embarked in business in clothing and furnishing goods for men in a store in the Post Office block. He was successful from the first and his store prospered. In 1900 he had outgrown the original store and concluded to take larger quarters; accordingly he removed to his present location at Nos. 510-512 Main street. He carries a large stock of men's furnishing goods and clothing. He is independent in politics. He is a member of the Young Men's Catholic Lyceum and was its first president, serving three years, and was formerly a director of the Melrose Cycle Club in its palmy days. He is a charter fourth degree member of Melrose Council, Knights of Columbus, and has held in succession all the offices in that body, including that of grand knight. He is a member of Melrose Lodge, Benevolent and Protective Order of Elks, and a life member of the Melrose Athletic Club. He is a charter member and vice-president of the Melrose Board of Trade, was formerly its secretary for five years and active in the work of the board. Mr. Keating has devoted much time and energy to the matter of encouraging home industries as much as possible. He is fond of outdoor sports and a leader in athletics in Melrose, having served as chairman of Old Home Week and July 4th athletic committees many times. He is one of the most popular and best known of the younger business men of the city.

He married, at Melrose, February 24, 1908. Adah Marie, daughter of Mrs. Helen A. Nelson, of New Haven, Connecticut.

BEEDE The first of this name that we have any definite information of was Charles Beede, whose birth occured in or near Rumney, New Hampshire, and who faithfully performed the duties of citizenship. He married twice, one wife having been Sarah Flanders, who was probably a native of Boston, Massachusetts.

William Dustin Beede, son of Charles Beede, was born in Rumney, New Hampshire, June 24, 1859. After acquiring a practical education in the schools of his native town, he went to Waltham, Massachusetts, working for a time in the Waltham watch works. Later he changed his place of residence to Manchester, New Hampshire, and worked in the shoe factories there, after which he went to Lynn, Massachusetts. Shortly afterward, when the great fire swept the city, he removed to Newburyport, Massachusetts, but in the course of a few months returned to Lynn and engaged at his trade as a shoe laster, which he followed to the time of his death which occurred in August, 1893. He was a man of excellent character and strict integrity, and won and retained the esteem of all with whom he was brought in contact. He attended the Methodist church. In politics he cast his vote for the candidate who in his opinion was best qualified for office, and although no office seeker or office holder took an active interest in the affairs of his adopted city. He married Emma F. Wood, born in Lynn, February, 1857, daughter of Louis D. and Mary F. (Dickerson) Wood. There were no children of this marriage.

Louis D. Wood, father of Mrs. Beede, was born in Canada, November 20, 1830. He came to Lynn, Massachusetts, at an early age, and shortly afterward turned his attention to the trade of shoemaker. He had a small shop in the rear of his home on Franklin street and there manufactured shoes for many years previous to the introduction of shoe machinery to any extent in Lynn. In his later years he engaged as a shoe cutter, and worked at that trade until his retirement from active pursuits, since which he has enjoyed a life of ease, the fruit of many years of ceaseless activity. He is an adherent of the principles of the Republican party, but has always declined to take any active part in political affairs. He has always been an attendant of the First Methodist Church in Lynn, to the support of which he has been a willing contributor. In 1862 he enlisted as a private in the civil war, serving for a period of nine months; he is now a member of the Grand Army of the Republic Post in Lynn. He married, in Lynn, June 6, 1852, Mary F. Dickerson, born in Lynn, June 20, 1832, daughter of Edward A. Dickerson, born probably in Boston. In 1902 Mr. and Mrs. Wood celebrated the fiftieth anniversary of their marriage, at which time they received the congratulations and good wishes of their children and friends. At the present time (1908) they are both enjoying good health and take an active interest in all matters. Children of Louis D. and Mary F. (Dickerson) Wood: 1. William L., born in Lynn, April 6, 1853, died August 1, 1857. 2. Henry Eugene, born Lynn, September 20, 1855, died March 19, 1856. 3. Emma Frances, born Lynn, February 27, 1857, widow of William D. Beede, mentioned above. 4. Cora A., Born Lynn, October 2, 1860, married first, January 17, 1883, Charles Bancroft; second, George Bailey, of Maine, who left his home and went to Lynn when a young man, remaining there a number of years. About 1900 he removed to Beverly, where he was engaged as foreman in Woodbury's shoe factory. He later opened a restaurant in Beverly and has successfully conducted the same to the present time. 5. William L., born Lynn, April 1, 1866, received his education in the schools at Lynn, and was first employed as clerk in a shoe store. When about twenty years of age he removed to Pittsfield, Massachusetts, conducted a shoe store one year, when he reto South Berwick, where he had interests in a livery stable, and during his stay there he was also employed in the stitching room in one of the shoe factories. Some time later he returned to Beverly, opening a business of his own for stitching shoes and continued in same for a number of years. Subsequently he purchased a shoe business in Lynn, which he removed to Beverly and afterward sold. About 1897-98 he became interested in the insurance and real estate business, continuing to the present time, having his office in Beverly. Mr. Wood married first, Ida Whittier, of Danvers; second, Ruth Allen, born in Everett, who bore him three children: Rowland Louis and Robert Many, twins, born December 19, 1900, and Philip Allen, born March 8, 1903. 6. Frank, born August 26, 1868, resides in Lynn.

DEMPSEY Patrick Charles Dempsey, one of the large real estate holders of Lawrence, Massachusetts, is descended from Irish ancestry. His parents were John and Susan (Seaton) Dempsey, natives of Ireland, the former of whom was a successful farmer in Ireland. Their children were: 1. Patrick Charles, born 1842, mentioned below. 2. John, was a contractor and plasterer; retired; owner of real estate in Boston; resides on Washington street; married ———; children: William, Annie, Fred, Walter, Maggie, Harold. 3. Daniel, died in Haverhill; unmarried. 4. Timothy, died in Boston; unmarried. 5. Mary, deceased, married John Fallow, of Clinton. 6. Josephine, died in Clinton; unmarried.

Patrick Charles Dempsey was born in Cork, Ireland, 1842, and was educated in the district schools. He emigrated to the United States, coming to Pepperell, Massachusetts, June 20, 1850. From there he located in Shirley, Massachusetts; from there removed to Clinton, Massachusetts; from there to Lawrence, Massachusetts, February 11, 1865, and worked in the Pacific Mills for three months. He left the Pacific Mills for a period, but finally returned and secured employment again in Pacific Mills; he left again in 1870, going to Palmer, Massachusetts, and upon his return to Lawrence secured employment in the Pacific Mills where he remained until 1881, when he accepted a position as second hand in the Arlington Mills, cotton department, which position he holds at the present time. He married, in 1884, Mary E. Shortwell, born in Exeter, New Hampshire, 1850, died January 22, 1885. He remained single six years and then married (second), 1891, Nellie Kennedy, born in Killarney, county Kerry, Ireland, April 10, 1870. Two children born, one lived to be sixteen months old and the other died at time of birth.

LYLE In New England colonial history the surname Lyle was known as early as the first half of the eighteenth century, when Daniel Lyle came from the south and settled at Augusta, Maine, in 1737. This Daniel Lyle, according to well authenticated family tradition, was one of four brothers—Daniel, James, John and Matthew—who came from the north of Ireland about or soon after the year 1700 and settled in Rockbridge county, Virginia.

It may be said, however, that none of these Lyles were of Irish stock or blood, although all of the four brothers may have been born in that country, a region which for many years and perhaps for several generations was the safe temporary refuge sought out by thousands of English and Scotch families that they might be free from the persecutions to which they had been subjected on account of their religious convictions. The ancestors of these Lyles had once lived in Scotland, long seated there, but because they were Scotch Presbyterians and refused to yield to the domination of the ruling church they were driven out of the country by the Earl of Montrose and sought safety in the north of Ireland. Such is the accepted tradition, so well grounded in the established events of history during the period of religious persecution that it has come to be recognized as absolute truth. But far back of that period the patronymic Lyle was known in English history at the time of the conquest, and it is claimed with much reason to have been of Norman extraction from an ancient French root.

The original seat of the Lyle families on this side of the Atlantic ocean was in that part of Timberridge valley which was known as New Virginia, and there they dwelt for some time, although in later years they became scattered, some going farther south, others to new settlements in Virginia and still others coming to the New England provinces. Daniel Lyle found his way into Maine, and was progenitor of a considerable branch of the family there. One chronicler says that he settled there as early as the year 1737.

James Lyle came north sometime previous to the revolution, and from a New England port sailed to Nova Scotia, accompanied by a number of slaves. In Virginia he had been a planter, a man of means and much influence. In Nova Scotia he fixed his abode in the Straits of Canso, now Middle Milford, Guysborough county. There he married a Miss Martin, and by her had two sons, James and David, and one daughter, Nancy Lyle.

James Lyle was a son of James and —— (Martin) Lyle, born at Middle Milford, Nova Scotia, and spent his life in that region, where he was a farmer and owner of large tracts of land. He married Lydia Carter, who bore him fourteen children: David, James, Jeremiah Wood, John, Joseph, Bruce, Elizabeth, Caroline, Maria, Rhoda, Susanna, Nancy, Margaret and Lydia Lyle. Something like a half a century ago the families of David, Jeremiah and John Lyle came to live in New England, David taking up his residence on Cape Ann.

David Lyle, born March 22, 1819, at Middle Milford, Nova Scotia, died in Gloucester, Massachusetts, in 1886. He settled in that town in 1867, and was a cooper by trade, but his sons, with the exception of one or two, were engaged in the fisheries. He married, December 3, 1844, Susan A. Procter, born May 17, 1826, daughter of James Procter and Harriet Jane Grant. When Sir John and Sir Edward Hamilton left Halifax, Nova Scotia, to return to England, they left all of their property to John Procter, and Procter Square in that city is named in allusion to him in memory of the good he wrought for the inhabitants of that municipality. John Procter married Nellie Derby, and their children were Robert, John, James, Michael, Alexander, Nancy, Mary, Betsey and Susan. Of these, James Procter married Harriet Jane, daughter of Lewis Francis Grant and his wife, whose name before marriage was Susan Grant. The children of James Procter and Harriet Jane Grant were Susan, died young; Ann, James, Susan, John, Eliza, William, Alexander, Robert and Francis Procter.

Lewis Francis Grant and his wife Susan Grant were both descendants of Matthew Grant, who came with his wife to America in 1630 in the ship "Mary and John," and settled first at Dorchester, Massachusetts. He was made freeman there in 1631, and in 1635 was one of the colony of Dorchester settlers who founded a new plantation at Windsor, Connecticut. He was a land surveyor there, town clerk and also kept the records of the church. President Ulysses Simpson Grant was a descendant of the eighth generation of Matthew Grant of Dorchester and Windsor.

David Lyle and Susan A. Procter had children: 1. Harriet W., born September 17, 1845; married September 3, 1872, Isaac Patch of Gloucester, Massachusetts. 2. Joseph B., born May 24, 1847, died October 10, 1850. 3. James Jeremiah, born October 9, 1850; married Mary Macfarlane; children, James Macfarlane and Alexander Gordon Lyle. 4. David W., born September 10, 1852; married Laura Jane Witham; two children, Emeline B. and Harriett C. 5. Alexander A. G., born August 12, 1854; drowned at sea. 6. Alma Swan, born April 25, 1856; married David Frederick Scranton; lives in Cambridgeport, Massachusetts. 7. Joseph A. C., born January 10, 1858; married Hannah Nagle, lives in Gloucester. 8. Elizabeth F. N., born December 25, 1860; married Frederick Boyer. 9. Simpson W. A., born June 28, 1861 (see post). 10. Margaret J. M., born January 30, 1866; married Charles S. Miller; now a widow living in Gloucester.

Simpson W. A. Lyle, son of David and Susan A. (Procter) Lyle, was born at Steep Creek, Middle Milford, Guysborough county, Nova Scotia, June 28, 1861, and was a boy of five years when his father removed with his family to Gloucester. He was brought up to farm work on the old Patch farm, now the property of his sister and her children, while his own home and summer hotel, the Delphine, stand on a part of the original farm tract. In 1894 Mr. Lyle became proprietor of the Delphine, succeeding its former owner. It is one of the most comfortable and pleasantly situated summer hotels on Eastern Point, a locality noted for its many attractions and the number of its summer resorts and cottages. It has a capacity for one hundred guests. Mr. Lyle is a capable business and hotel man, a member of the various subordinate masonic bodies of Gloucester and frequently an officer of some of them, and with his family occupies a prominent position in the social life of the city of Gloucester. January 5, 1887, he married Edith Witham; children: Susan Lyle, born in Gloucester, August 11, 1889; Harris K. Lyle, born in Gloucester, May 27, 1895.

SMITH John Smith, a native of St. John, New Brunswick, came to the United States, and for a number of years was a resident of Lawrence, Massachusetts. He married Julia O'Leary, of that city, who was born in Cork, Ireland, February 1, 1837. She came to this country when a young woman and located in Lawrence, and by her exertions accumulated sufficient capital to purchase two large properties in that city, from which she derived a goodly income. Being a woman of great business ability, energy and perseverance, when left with the care of four small children, she turned her attention to the management of a corporation boarding house, which she conducted for a number of years successfully, and in this manner provided a comfortable home for her children and was enabled to give them excellent educational advantages. In addition to her many excellent traits, Mrs. Smith was exceedingly charitable, giving liberally of her means to alleviate the sufferings of others, and in addition to the care of her own children she adopted a child, to whom she gave a mother's loving care. Mrs. Smith had a wide circle of friends, who admired her for her many womanly qualities, and her death which occured in Lawrence, December 13, 1904, at the age of sixty-seven years, was sincerely mourned not only by her family but by all who had the honor of her acquaintance. Two of her children—Julia and Elizabeth—died in early life. The surviving members of the family are: James Robert, unmarried, at the present time (1908) employed in the real estate office of A. E. Mac, of Lawrence; he is a resident of Lawrence. Annie Maria, unmarried, also a resident of Lawrence.

DOWBRIDGE John Dowbridge (I), lived and died in Trieste, province of Kustenland, Austria, although doubtless he was of English birth and ancestry, and went over to the continent to take part in the wars and married there and ever afterward made his home in that country.

(II) Andrew Dowbridge, son of John Dowbridge, was born in Trieste, Austria, but spent little even of his younger life in that city. At the age of ten years he ran away from home and shipped as a cabin boy on board one of the numerous vessels that sailed from important seaports on the Adriatic sea. In the course of his life on the high seas the cabin boy became a sailorman, and it so happened that the ship in which he sailed made port at Salem, Massachusetts. From that time to the end of his days Andrew Dowbridge followed the sea, and he died in Salem, February 8, 1885. He married Mary, widow of John Martin, and whose family name was Gardner. She bore him four children: Andrew, who settled in Maine and died there; Lucy, who married Charles Briggs and died in Salem; Henry F., now dead; Mary, who became wife of Hugh Munsey and lives in North Beverly.

(III) Henry Francis Dowbridge, son of Andrew and Mary (Gardner-Martin) Dowbridge, was born in Salem and died there July 20, 1899, after an honorable and highly successful business career. As a boy he was sent to the public schools, but his opportunities of acquiring an education were quite limited. When old enough to work he learned the mason's trade, and from a journeyman he developed into a contracting and building mason, for besides being a competent workman he possessed native business qualities which served him well and yielded him a comfortable fortune. For many years Mr. Dowbridge was a well known figure in business circles in Salem, and always was recognized as a man of high character and strict integrity. Among the many large structures erected by him there may be mentioned the mills of the Naumkeag Steam Cotton Company, the Salem Fire Department building and scores of others were it necessary to enumerate all of them. In 1891 he was elected a

Henry J Dowbridge

member of the board of directors of the Salem Mutual Fire Insurance Company. He was a member of old Essex Lodge, Free and Accepted Masons and the Essex Institute. In politics a Republican and in religion preference was a Universalist. On November 1, 1855, Mr. Dowbridge married Joanna Frances Adams, born in Salem, May 23, 1836, daughter of Charles Hodgdon and Elizabeth (French) Adams (see Adams family). One daughter was born of this marriage, Clara Louise Dowbridge, born in Salem, June 21, 1856. She married (first) Archibald Nettles, and by him had one son; married (second) Stephen W. Abbott, of Beverly. Henry D. Nettles, son of Archibald and Clara L. (Dowbridge) Nettles, was born April 8, 1882, married Rita Viola Derby, of Beverly, and had three children: Clara D. Nettles, born October 8, 1900; Gladys D. Nettles, born November, 1901; Lucille Dorothy Nettles, born September 5, 1907.

ADAMS (I) Henry Adams, of Braintree, was one of the earliest planters in the locality known in colonial days as Mt. Wollaston and which in 1640 was incorporated as Braintree. He was born in England and came to New England about 1632-33, with his wife, eight sons and one daughter, and in 1640 had a grant of forty acres of land at "the mount," which seems to have been the allotment for his family of ten members. The name of his wife does not appear, nor the date of her death, but Henry died in Braintree in 1646. He was a malster and yeoman. Of his sons several bore military titles won in early colonial wars, and one of them fulfilled the office of deacon of the church. They were Lieutenant Thomas, Captain Samuel, Deacon Jonathan, Peter, John, Joseph and Ensign Edward.

(II) Joseph Adams, son of Henry Adams, immigrant, was born in England in 1626, and was a malster and yeoman; was made freeman in 1653, served as selectman in 1673, and died in 1694. He married, November 26, 1650, Abigail, daughter of Gregory and Margaret (Paddy) Baxter, of Boston. She died in 1692, having borne her husband twelve children: Hannah, Joseph, John (died young), Abigail, Captain John, Bethea, Mary (died young), Samuel, Mary, Captain Peter, Jonathan and Mehitable.

(III) Joseph Adams, son of Joseph and Abigail (Baxter) Adams, born in Braintree, December 24, 1654, died there February 12, 1737. He was a soldier of King Philip's war, 1676, and selectman of Braintree three years. He married (first), February 20, 1682, Mary Chapin, born August 27, 1662, died June 14, 1687; married (second) Hannah Bass, born June 22, 1667, died October, 1705, daughter of John and Ruth (Alden) Bass; married (third) Elizabeth, daughter of Caleb Hobart, of Braintree. She died February 13, 1739. By his first wife Joseph Adams had two children, Mary and Abigail; by his second wife he had Rev. Joseph, Deacon John, Samuel, Josiah, Hannah, Ruth, Bethia and Captain Ebenezer; and by his third wife he had son Caleb.

(IV) Rev. Joseph Adams, son of Joseph and Hannah (Bass) Adams, and uncle of the second president of the United States, was born in Braintree, January 4, 1688, and died in Newington, New Hampshire, May 21, 1783. He graduated from Harvard College in 1710, was ordained and settled at Newington, November 16, 1715, and was pastor there for the next sixty-six years. He married (first), October 13, 1720, Mrs. Elizabeth Janverin, daughter of John and Elizabeth (Knight) Janverin of Newington. She died February 10, 1757, and he married (second), January 3, 1760, Elizabeth Brackett, of Greenland, New Hampshire. Rev. Joseph Adams had children, all born of his first marriage: Elizabeth, Dr. Joseph, Deacon Benjamin, and a daughter.

(V) Dr. Joseph Adams, son of Rev. Joseph and Elizabeth (Janverin) Adams, born in Newington, New Hampshire, January 17, 1723, died in Barnstead, New Hampshire, March 22, 1801. He graduated from Harvard College in 1745, and entered the profession of medicine against the expressed wishes of his father. He settled first in Newington and in 1792 removed to Barnstead, where the last nine years of his life was spent. His wife was Joanna Gilman, daughter of Major Ezekiel Gilman, of Exeter, who commanded the New Hampshire forces at the capture of Louisburg in 1745. Dr. Joseph and Joanna (Gilman) Adams had twelve children: Ezekiel Gilman, Captain Joseph, Ebenezer, Dudley, Gilman, William, John, Elizabeth, Abigail, Benjamin, Nathaniel and Polly.

(VI) Nathaniel Adams, son of Dr. Joseph and Joanna (Gilman) Adams, was baptized in Barnstead, New Hampshire, March 31, 1770, and died there in 1853. He was familiarly known as "Uncle Nat." He married Olive, daughter of Honorable Charles Hodgdon, and had five children, all born in Barnstead: 1. Abigail, August, 1798, died September 4, 1874; married (first) David Chase, (second) Samuel Chase. 2. Charles Hodgdon, 1803. 3. Joanna, about 1805-06, married (first) Coffin Colcord, (second) Elbridge Earl; lived in Salem and died there in 1876. 4. Frances D., January 16, 1808, died in Portsmouth, New Hampshire, June 8, 1890; married Josiah, son of Nathan Webb and Elizabeth (Cole) Adams. 5. Mary Ann, April 26, 1812, died in Charlestown, Massachusetts, January 7, 1887; married, December 22, 1830, Isaac Harlow, of Beverly, Massachusetts, who died August 10, 1858.

(VII) Charles Hodgdon Adams, son of Nathaniel and Olive (Hodgdon) Adams, born in Barnstead, New Hampshire, 1803, died in Salem, Massachusetts, March 4, 1869. He married Elizabeth French, of Salem, Massachusetts, and had nine children, five born in Barnstead and four in Salem: 1. Joseph P., April 2, 1827, died May 10, 1827. 2. Elizabeth H., July 25, 1828, died September 10, 1828. 3. Elizabeth Ann, November 6, 1829, married William B. Wyman, of Marblehead. 4. Mary Jane, December 6, 1831, died unmarried December 11, 1855. 5. Charles Henry, March 11, 1833, died March 19, 1835. 6. Caroline F., November 2, 1834, died about 1875; married B. Frank Bartlett. 7. Joanna Frances, May 23, 1836, married, November 1, 1855, Henry F. Dowbridge (see Dowbridge family). 8. Clara Louisa, July 25, 1837, died November 11, 1855. 9. Charles H., born July 27, 1840, married, March 5, Isabelle Kelley, born November 1, 1842.

MICKEL The surname Mickel is of Dutch origin. The pioneer of this family came from Holland and settled at an early date in Nova Scotia.

(I) John Mickel, a descendant of the Nova Scotia immigrant, lived and died in Seneca county, New York. His father lived at Saratoga Springs and near Albany, New York. John Mickel married and was the father of five daughters and three sons, of whom Benjamin M. is mentioned below. The mother of William Moore, of Interlaken, Seneca county, New York, was another of the children.

(II) Benjamin M. Mickel, son of John Mickel, born near Mecklenburg, New York, August 11, 1835, died May 31, 1872. He married Hannah E. Wolcott, born November 7, 1836, died April 18, 1890. Among their children, born at Sand Lake, New York was: Orin Elijah, mentioned below.

(III) Dr. Orin Elijah Mickel, son of Benjamin M. Mickel, born in Sand Lake, New York, August 11, 1859, died at Haverhill, January 12, 1902. He was educated in the public schools, and began at an early age to study dentistry in Troy, New York, in the office of Dr. Charles Gabeler. From 1887 until the time of his death in 1902 he practiced his profession in Haverhill, Massachusetts, with marked success, having previously had offices for a short time at Pittsfield and Northampton, Massachusetts. He was a member of Pythian Castle, Knights of Pythias; Council, Royal Arcanum; and of Mutual Relief Lodge of Odd Fellows. He was a Republican in politics and took a keen interest in public affairs. He served the city of Haverhill in the common council In religion he was a Congregationalist. He married, October 8, 1886, Emma Brunell, born 1860, daughter of Louis and Phillis (Carpenter) Brunell, of Troy, New York. She was a native of Three Rivers, Canada, in the Province of Quebec. Her great-grandfather, Balfour by name, changed his name at the time of his marriage, to that of his wife, Brunell. Dr. and Mrs. Mickel had one child, Orene Jennie, born January 22, 1890, now living with her widowed mother in the home, 26 Park street, Bradford, Massachusetts.

TAYLOR William James Taylor, a respected citizen of Lynn, Massachusetts, for nearly fifty years, was born in Bladen county, North Carolina, 1840, son of William Taylor, who was born and reared in Bladen county, where he afterward remained a number of years, removing in later years to Samson county and making his home there until shortly after the close of the civil war, when he returned to his native part of the state and there spent the remainder of his life. His wife was Jane Taylor, of Bladen county, both dying there; and they were the parents of seven children: Thomas, Sarah, Mary Jane, Julia, William James, Eliza and Lucy. His wife Jane after his decease married James McCoy and they had children: James and two that were twins, the only surviving ones of the family being William James and Lucy, who reside in Lynn. William Taylor was oldest son of Thomas McKitcham Taylor, who was also a native of Bladen county where he lived during his life, he and his wife dying in Bladen county having reared children: William, Arthur, Gabriel, Hagar, Eva, Penny and Matilda.

William James Taylor remained in his native state and town until he was about twenty-two years of age, when he left the south and went from there to Philadelphia, Pennsylvania, and soon after went to Boston, Massachusetts, but after remaining in Boston a few months, he removed to Lynn in the year 1862. After settling in Lynn he found employment, working at odd jobs, and about a year after his arrival entered the lumber mill of James Buffum, where he remained nearly seven years, when he met with an accident and was completed to give up work for several months. The year following he was interested in the sale of fresh pork, buying and raising his stock. Mr. Taylor built the next year a small building where he conducted a small variety and grocery business. His trade, however, soon demanded larger quarters and he erected another building, removing into same where he carried on the grocery business about twenty-five years. He converted his former place of business into a dwelling house and at that time became interested in real estate, and in the following years, by constant purchase of land and buildings, his success in real estate warranted his resigning from the grocery business about 1893, that his entire interests might be devoted to the care of his property which he had accumulated, and it may be said that he has since continued as dealer in real estate successfully.

Mr. Taylor married in 1864, Harriet Robinson, of Boston, Massachusetts, daughter of Henry and Mary Ann Robinson, of Boston. Their children were: 1. Louis E., employed in General Electric Company, Lynn, married Charlotte Jacobs, daughter of Michael and Katherine Jacobs, and have two children, Issoline and Jesline; residing in Lynn. 2. Viola Jane, died at age of five years in Lynn.

McMANUS

The McManus or MacManus family is of very ancient Irish origin. O'Hart in his Irish Pedigrees states that Manus, brother of Giollaiosa, of the ancient Maguire family, was the ancestor of MacManus. Manus was son of Dun Mor Maguire. MacManus was a numerous clan in Fermanagh (chiefly in Tirkennedy) who had the control of the shipping on Lough Erne, and held the office of hereditary chief manager of the fisheries under Maguire. The surname Manus is derived from the Irish word mainis (lance or spear) (main: Irish, "the hand"; Latin manus) and O'Hart translates the name McManus as "the son of the man who could wield a spear."

(I) Dennis McManus was born in Ireland. He married Mary McMurray, also a native of Ireland. He came to America a few years after his marriage, landing in New York city at old Castle Garden, March 5, 1860, after a voyage lasting nine weeks, five days, bringing with him his son Timothy and two daughters. His wife followed a few years later. The family settled in Lowell, Massachusetts.

(II) Timothy McManus, son of Dennis McManus (1), was born in Ireland, November 22, 1846. He was fourteen years old when he came to America with his father and two sisters. The father started in the new world without capital, and the son began to work at gardening at twelve dollars a month. Soon afterward he began to work in the Fitchburg paper mill, at the rate of eighty cents per day, later at the Lawrence paper mills, operated by William A. Russell, and continued in various positions for the period of twenty-six years, when he retired to devote his time to the care of his real estate in which he had invested his savings. He now owns several large tenement houses and is possessed of a competence. He is independent in politics. He is a devout member and liberal supporter of the Roman Catholic parish in which he resides. He married (first) 1867, Rose Riley, born January 12, 1845. He married (second), July 4, 1877, Annie Gouldon, born 1848, in Ireland, daughter of Daniel Gouldon. His only child died soon after birth in 1868.

BAKE

Frank Bake, son of Frank and Grace (Butler) Bake, was born in England, December 15, 1842, and died in Lawrence, Massachusetts, February 11, 1907. His father was born February 20, 1808, and his mother July 24, 1806. He received his early education in the common schools in his native town. He learned a trade and worked in the mills in England until he came to America. He came to Lawrence, Massachusetts, and found employment in the mills there. He followed his trade and had the fullest confidence of the employers and employees. He retired in 1903 for a well earned rest and leisure. He was a quiet unobtrusive man, prudent, careful and upright. By his habits of industry and thrift and careful investment of his savings he acquired a competence. He was not interested in politics, preferring his home life to any other. He was a member of the Odd Fellows in England, and was transferred to the Manchester Unity Lodge of Lawrence after he came to this country.

He married December 10, 1864, first, Sarah Ann Butler, born October 1, 1843. Children: 1. Francis, born February 16, 1866, died March 6, 1866. 2. Emily, born July 4, 1867. 3. Annie E., March 17, 1869. 4. Herbert, February 29, 1872. 5. Frank, March 7, 1879. He married second, October 5, 1893, Mrs. Mary Barlow, born May 30, 1850, daughter of Samuel and Susan Lord. She had married first, Thomas F. Barlow, September 23, 1870, and the fololwing children were born to them: 1. Rhoda B., June 30, 1874. 2. Susie, October 22, 1875. 3. John E., June 12, 1878. 4. Wilfred, August 10, 1882.

HAYES John William Alton Hayes was born at Ipswich, Massachusetts, May 21, 1866, son of John W. Hayes and Bessie Alton, his first wife. John Hayes, Sr., was a native of England, born in Derby, in 1834, son of John Hayes. He came from England in 1866, and settled in Ipswich, Massachusetts, where he found employment in the Ipswich mills, becoming manager of the finishing department. Later on he was superintendent of a hosiery mill in Ipswich and still later became proprietor of a restaurant. He died in 1892. He was a member of Syracuse Lodge, Knights of Pythias. He married first, Bessie Alton, by whom he had children: Thomas, Eliza, Ellen, Annie, Arthur, John William Alton, Elizabeth and Frank. His wife died in 1875, and he married second, Ann Daly, by whom he had two children: 1. Annie became the wife of Dr. Ames, of Ipswich. 2. Arthur, died young.

John William Alton Hayes received his education in the public and high schools of his native place, Ipswich, and was there engaged in business until he retired from active pursuits in 1903. For eighteen years he was in the hotel business and became well known as a host in that long period. He is a member of Chebacco Tribe of Red Men, Lodge No. 93, and of Syracuse Lodge No. 30, Knights of Pythias. Mr. Hayes married March 1, 1892, Mary C. Ryan, daughter of William Ryan, of Norwich, Connecticut, and has one child, Mary Madeline Carrol Hayes, born December 23, 1892.

CATE The Cates are an old, numerous and highly respectable family in New Hampshire, where various of its representatives have lived through several generations from the time of the ancestor. In town and church records the name is written both Cate and Cates. Of the particular branch of the family here treated the earliest one of whom we have any reliable account is Alpheus D. Cate (1), grandfather of Edgar Alpheus Cate.

(I) Alpheus D. Cate was born in Tamworth, New Hampshire, April 19, 1810, spent his young years in that town and in the course of a few years after his marriage removed with his wife to Portsmouth, New Hampshire, where he died August 29, 1872. He married Margaret Shannon, of the old New England family of that surname which has been made the subject of an exhaustive genealogical record.

(II) John Shannon Cate, son of Alpheus D. and Margaret (Shannon) Cate, was born in Tamworth, New Hampshire, March 25, 1839, and went when a child with his parents to Portsmouth, where he was educated in the public schools, later attending the academy at Hampton, New Hampshire. After leaving school he worked for a time with his father, and on leaving home went to Chelsea, Massachusetts, and found employment with the firm of Chapman & Soden, Boston, manufacturers of and dealers in roofing material and supplies. He proved to be a competent employee and the interest he showed in the business of the firm was rewarded with his advancement to more responsible positions, first to that of superintendent of the manufacturing department and afterward to that of general manager of the extensive business operations of the firm. Mr. Cate retired from active business pursuits in 1889, but afterward took, as he had done before, a commendable interest in public affairs in the town and subsequently city of Everett, where he lived from 1877 until the time of his death, October 11, 1906. During the almost thirty years of his residence in Everett he was counted among the foremost men of that municipality, and having acquired considerable real estate there he naturally took much interest in its growth and welfare. He was an earnest Republican in his political preference, and as the candidate of his party was elected representative from Everett to the general court of Massachusetts in 1890. He was for two years a member of the board of selectmen of

Everett before the incorporation of the town as a city, and he was mayor of the city in 1895 and 1897. In 1893 and 1894 he was a member of the board of aldermen of the city. Mr. Cate was a member of the Methodist Episcopal church, a member of Palestine Lodge, Free and Accepted Masons of Everett, Chelsea Chapter, Royal Arch Masons, and of Palestine Commandery, Knights Templar, of Chelsea. He also held membership in the Ancient Order of United Workmen, the United Order of Pilgrim Fathers and the Knights of Honor. On November 2, 1862, Mr. Cate married Lydia B. Witham, born in York, Maine, December 3, 1840, daughter of Thomas Witham, a farmer of York, and Catherine (Moulton) Witham, his wife. Of this marriage two children were born: 1. Lucy Jane, born September 23, 1863, in Portsmouth, New Hampshire, died in infancy. 2. Edgar Alpheus Cate, born September 8, 1875.

(III) Edgar Alpheus Cate, son and only surviving child of John Shannon and Lydia B. (Witham) Cate, was born in Chelsea, Massachusetts, September 8, 1875. He was about two years old when his father removed with his family to Everett. He was educated in the public schools of that city and in Bryant and Stratton's Business College in Boston, and since 1897 has been clerk in the office of the water commissioners of Everett. He married, October 16, 1901, in Everett, Mertie L. White, born in Oldtown, Maine, November 6, 1876, daughter of Avery White, a native of Oldtown, and his wife, Almeda (Ellis) White, born in Belfast, Maine. Two children have been born of the marriage: 1. Marjorie Shannon, born Everett, September 1, 1903. 2. Irene Frances, born Everett, January 2, 1906.

PERONT The Peront family settled early in Canada. Daniel Perron, son of Francois and Marie Perron, came from La Rochelle, France, in 1664. The name is variously spelled in the early records.

(I) Cyriacque Peront was born at St. Hyacinthe, province of Quebec, 1805, died January 7, 1885. He always lived there. He was a farmer and drummer for wagons and plows. He married Morion Julie, born 1808, died August 3, 1867. They were the parents of twelve children, eight of whom are living in St. Hyacinthe, Canada.

(II) Clement Peront, son of Cyriacque Peront, was born at St. Hyacinthe, province of Quebec, February 24, 1841. He was educated in the schools of his native parish, and worked during his youth on his father's farm. He then learned the trade of mason. He came to Lawrence, Massachusetts, in 1865, and since then has made his home in that city. He has followed his trade as journeyman and contractor to the present time. He has been employed on many of the houses and buildings erected in Lawrence during the past forty years. He has invested his savings in Lawrence real estate, and is at present the owner of six large double tenement houses. In politics Mr. Peront is a Republican. He is a Roman Catholic and a generous contributor to the parish in which he lives. He is a member of a number of Catholic organizations and fraternal societies.

He married, February 12, 1866, Delima Lestage, born August 12, 1845. Children: 1. Eliza, born St. Hyacinthe, province of Quebec, February 5, 1867, married, July 26, 1886, ——, who was a wool sorter in Pacific Mills; two children: Clement and Edward. 2. Emelia, born September 10, 1868, died March 6, 1873. 3. Joseph E., born July 31, 1870. 4. Anna, born May 15, 1872; she is a nun, entered March 27, 1894. 5. Joseph H., born April 23, 1874, married, August 15, 1899, ——. 6. Emma, born October 6, 1876, married, November 20, 1901, Henry Burke. 7. Mary, born March 25, 1878, married, February 4, 1902, a Mr. Perre. 8. Arthur, born July 2, 1880, married, September 15, 1903, Victoria Guenette; children: Arthur and Leonne. 9. Clement, born July 4, 1882, married, June 8, 1903, Mary Johnes; child, Clement. 10. Helen, born November 8, 1883, died April 29, 1885. 11. Bertha, born June 2, 1885, died December 9, 1885. 12. Armond, born June 3, 1886, died March 10, 1888. 13. Delima, born June 24, 1888, died August 18, 1888.

WESSEL Julius Wessel, prominently identified with the financial, commercial and social interests of Lawrence, Massachusetts, traces his ancestry to that land of thrift and industry, Germany.

(I) Henry Dietrich Wessel, father of Julius Wessel, was a native of Germany, where he was occupied as a tailor. He married, and was the father of thirteen children. One of his sons, Fritz, emigrated to America in 1868 or 1869.

(II) Julius Wessel was born in Germany, January 17, 1857, and acquired his education in the district schools of his native land. He came to the United States in 1873, and settled in Worcester, Massachusetts, where he became an apprentice in a sausage shop. From there he went to the Iver Johnson Firearms Company, with whom he was employed from 1874 until 1877. His next venture was in the west, where he found employment in St. Louis, Missouri, from which city he went to Harrisburg and Philadelphia, and finally to the New Hartford Arms Company of New Haven, Connecticut. His next position was with the Smith and Wesson Firearms Company, returning to Worcester in 1882, and accepting a position with the American Arms Company, remaining with them until 1886. He then established the Tonic Bottling Shop in East Boston, a business he conducted until he sold it in 1892. While residing in Worcester he was a member for three years of Battery B. He was then engaged in the hotel business for some time in Lawrence, giving this up in favor of the Cold Spring Brewing Company, in which he was employed in the bottling department until the present time as manager. For the past eight years he has been a director and stockholder in this company, and at the same time conducts a restaurant in Park street. He is a stanch upholder of the principles of the Democratic party, and a member of the Free and Accepted Masons and the Order of Haruigari. He married, March 25, 1885, Matthes Augusta, daughter of Fritz Augusta, who came to Lawrence in 1854 and worked in the old Bay State mill as a wool sorter. Mr. and Mrs. Julius Wessel have had the following named children: Julius, Albert, Carl, Augusta, Catherine, Henry, Lena, Bertha, Ella, Minnie, and two who died in infancy. Of these, Henry, Lena, Bertha and Ella are now living.

ROBINSON David Robinson (1), farmer, a native of Ireland, who lived and died in county Downs, town of Scarvia, was a descendant of those English Protestants who followed in the wake of the English army and settled in the north of Ireland after the conquest of the country by the British forces. In his religious faith he was a Presbyterian.

(II) David Robinson, son of David Robinson, was born in the town of Scarvia, Ireland, 1821. At the age of twenty-three years he set forth from his native country with two of his brothers, William and John, to seek his fortune in America. He landed at the port of Boston in 1844, and having knowledge and previous experience in the culture of the soil, he turned his attention to landscape gardening, working throughout the region of Boston in eastern Massachusetts. He had success in that line and in the year 1876 established himself in Chelsea, Massachusetts, as landscape gardener, which business he conducted prosperously until the time of his death, which occurred October 29, 1902. Of the two brothers who accompanied him to America, William went west and became a prosperous ranchman in Nevada. He was killed by Indians. He had twelve thousand sheep on the prairies, which the Indians were stealing; he threatened them, they heard of his threat and swooped down upon him in his tent and riddled him with bullets, going so far as to shoot off every finger, eyes and mouth; that was in Montana; his descendants are living in California. John Robinson remained in Massachusetts and settled in Charlestown, where for forty-two years he had charge of the grounds of Bunker Hill monument, being familiarly known as "Monument John".

David Robinson married Mary McCarley, of Boston, daughter of John and Rosie (Moore) McCarley, who were the parents of eleven children, as follows: James and Ann, twins, died in infancy; David, Thomas, William John, Robert, Jane, Alexander, Martha, Mary, wife of David Robinson, and Rosie. Children of Mr. and Mrs. Robinson: 1. John, born in Charlestown, died young. 2. David Alexander, born July 11, 1865, see forward. 3. John, born in Chelsea, January 19, 1868; member of Robert Lash Lodge, Free and Accepted Masons; married Frances White; no children. 4. Francis H., born in Chelsea, August, 1870; member of Robert Lash Lodge, Free and Accepted Masons; married Gladys White; one child, Francis H., Jr. 5. William Moore, born in Chelsea, July 21, 1875, attended the public schools, including the high, and the Worcester Academy; was an athlete of American reputation by running hundred yard dash, ten seconds, at three hundred yards, indoor meet at Mechanics Building; held record four years; then won inter-scholastic meet at Madison Square Garden, New York City, fifty yards; was star football player Chelsea high school and Worcester Academy; he is connected with the Boston mercantile house of MacArthur & Company; was member of board of aldermen four years, and member of house of representatives two years; member of Robert Lash Lodge, Free and Accepted Masons, of Chelsea; married Florence Margeson;

one child, Marion Margeson Robinson. 6. Charles S., born in Chelsea, November 16, 1879, was known as a record bicycle rider, winning local road and track races, and receiving many prizes; he is a physician, a graduate of Bellevue Hospital; served one year on the training ship "Enterprise"; member of Robert Lash Lodge, Free and Accepted Masons; married Catherine Hogan; resides in Chelsea. All of the brothers are of an athletic build.

(III) David Alexander Robinson, second son and eldest surviving child of David and Mary (McCarley) Robinson, was born in Charlestown, Massachusetts, July 11, 1865. He was brought up in the vicinity of Boston and attended Carter school at Chelsea, Massachusetts. He was taken into the business established by his father, which has become widely and honorably known throughout Boston and outlying towns. He is a Mason, member of Robert Lash Lodge, and an Odd Fellow; politically a Republican, but takes no especial personal interest in public affairs. In his religious faith he is a Congregationalist. He married, July 25, 1902, Emmaline Tilden, born in Chelsea, Massachusetts, May 21, 1868, daughter of Coleman and Eliza (Howard) Tilden, the latter a daughter of Charles Howard, and a descendant of Dr. Coleman Tilden of the prominent family of that surname. Four children have been born of this marriage: 1. Helen Tilden, born April 29, 1903. 2. Elizabeth, died in infancy. 3. Dorothy, died in infancy. 4. Alice Moore, born December 4, 1906.

DRISCOLL The origin of the ancient Irish surname Driscoll seems to be a mystery. It may have been a local name, originally, perhaps of French origin. The family of Driscoll was numerous in Ireland as early as the sixteenth century.

(I) John Driscoll was born in county Cork, Ireland, about 1768, and died in Lawrence, Massachusetts, where his son had located, at the phenomenal age of one hundred and five years. He married in Ireland, Honora Harrington. Children, born in Ireland: 1. Patrick, came to America, and had a son John killed in the civil war. 2. Jeremiah, mentioned below. 3. John.

(II) Jeremiah Driscoll, son of John Driscoll (1), was born in county Cork, Ireland, in 1814, and died in March, 1906, at Lawrence, at the advanced age of ninety-two. He came to America in 1849 with the great tide of Irishmen seeking a better opportunity in the world. He worked in Lawrence at various occupations. During the later years of his life he was employed on the Lawrence dam, of the Essex Company. He was prudent and saving. He finally bought a house and some land in North Andover and worked on his place to the time of his death. He married in Lawrence, Mary Driscoll, daughter of Patrick Driscoll, of Ireland. Children: 1. John A., mentioned below. 2. Patrick, born 1856; a mason and brick layer; resides at the homestead in Lawrence; has a daughter Mary. 3. Ellen, born 1858; married ——— Harrington. 4. Catherine, died young. 5. Michael, resides in Lawrence.

(III) John Ambrose Driscoll, son of Jeremiah Driscoll (2), was born in Lawrence, May 8, 1855. He was educated in the public schools of his native town, and went to Boston in 1870 to begin to learn his trade as bricklayer and mason. He served his apprenticeship of four years and returned to Lawrence, working as journeyman under Captain Chatburn on the Arlington mills and other contracts. In 1884 he established himself in business. He was in partnership one year with Mr. Collins, and since then has been a member of the firm of Driscoll & O'Brien. This firm has been very successful, handling many of the largest masonry contracts in the city of Lawrence and vicinity. In many cases the firm takes the contract for the entire work on buildings and sub-lets the carpentering, plumbing, etc. They have the contract for the Chelsea high school, and erected most of the large brick or stone buildings of recent years in this section—the Rowling high school, Prospect Hill, Lawrence; the Lawrence high school; Plummer Block, of Lawrence; Halligan Block, Lawrence; Ancient Order of Hibernians Building; the Kidd Block; the John Breen Block, etc. Mr. Driscoll is a member of the Benevolent and Protective Order of Elks. Like his father and grandfather, he was a faithful Catholic, a generous supporter and constant attendant of the church in St. Augustine parish, North Andover. He married, November, 1877, Ellen Crowley, born in Lawrence, daughter of Michael and Ann (Coughlin) Crowley. Children: 1. Jeremiah, married ——— McGee; children: John and Ellen. 2. Ann, a school teacher. 3. Mary, lives at home with parents. 4. John, works for his father. 5. Catherine. 6. Daniel.

DAWSON Seth Frank Dawson, a well-known and influential citizen of Lawrence, Massachusetts, residing at No. 8 Jackson Terrace, traces his ancestry to an old family of England. His father, William Dawson, was a native of England, where he was a worker in one of the large mills. He married ———, and had children: William Henry, Jennie, Sirth, Anna and Seth Frank.

Seth Frank Dawson was born in Huddersfield, England, July 19, 1847. He was but an infant when he came to America with his father and the others of the family, and they settled in Lawrence, Massachusetts, where young Seth Frank was educated. The first step in his business career was in the meat and grocery line, but eighteen years ago he established himself in the leather board business, in which he has successfully been engaged since that time. He is also an extensive dealer in real estate and has done much to improve and increase the real values of the township. He has taken an active part in the councils of the Republican party, has served as councillor two terms and as president of the school board two terms. He is a member of the Independent Order of Odd Fellows and Pilgrim Fathers, and trustee and superintendent of the Methodist Sunday school. He married, October 26, 1876, Lizzie Abigail, daughter of Daniel Darius and Harriet Spears (Standridge) Cutting, who were the parents of three daughters and two sons. Daniel D. Cutting was a farmer in Standridge, Canada, and came to the United States in 1854. He settled in Vermont where he had purchased a farm and cultivated the same ten years. He then removed to the state of New York. Seth Frank and Lizzie A. (Cutting) Dawson had children: 1. Rose Edith, born November 3, 1877; married Arthur Barker; has three children. 2. Seth Frank, Jr., born June 17, 1879. 3. Florence Cutting, November 20, 1887.

MURPHY Bartholomew Murphy (I) was born in Ireland. He came to America when a young man and settled in Newburyport, Massachusetts, later removing to Merrimack, Massachusetts. He was employed there in a wheel factory connected with the carriage manufacturing industry of that city. He married Catherine Cleary. They were members of the Catholic church at Merrimack. Children, born in Ireland and Merrimack: 1. Patrick. 2. Frances, married Cornelius O'Shea. 3. Michael, 4. James, born in 1839, mentioned below. 5. John J. 6. Elizabeth, married Frank Lefevor, of Merrimack.

(II) James Murphy, son of Bartholomew Murphy (1), was born in Dungarven, county Waterford, Ireland, 1839. He came to America when a mere child with his parents and their children, and he received his education in the public schools of West Amesbury, where he lived the remainder of his life. He took up the trade of body maker in the carriage factories of Amesbury. When quite a young lad he ran away from home and enlisted in the United States navy on the ship "Niagara" under the assumed name of James Kimball, and served three years, the period of his enlistment. In 1861 he enlisted under his own name and served two years and a half in Company D, Seventeenth Regiment of Massachusetts Volunteers. He was discharged on account of disability from a wound received in battle, from which he finally died December 16, 1875. While in civil war he participated in the battle of Kingston, While Hall, Goldsboro, Blount Mills and Winton, North Carolina, and at the latter place is where he received the wound that was the principal cause of his death. He was fearless in the discharge of his duty, impulsive and generous, would dare the displeasure of his superior officers when prompted by principles of humanity. The wound was a gun shot, passing entirely through the body.

He married Bridget McCarron, born in Ireland, but came to America when two years old with her family. Children: 1. William Andrew, born February 15, 1868, mentioned below. 2. Charles B., died in childhood. 3. Annie E., born 1870. 4. Charles B., born 1872, resides in Petersburg, Michigan. 5. Mary Olive, born 1874, educated in the public schools, bookkeeper for Chase & Parker, Boston.

(III) William Andrew Murphy, son of James Murphy, was born February 15, 1868, in Merrimack, then South Amesbury, Massachusetts, a village near Amesbury, and was educated there in the public and high schools. After leaving school he worked two years as clerk in the grocery store of Senator James D. Pike, of Merrimack. He was then with John S. Payen & Company for ten years in the sale of carriage findings, and for about ten years with the firm of A. N. Perry & Company of Amesbury. After a year with the firm of Gray & Davis he was appointed postmaster of Amesbury by President Roosevelt for a term of four years. He is a member of Bethany Lodge of Free Masons of Merrimack; of Wonnesquam Club and of the Powow Canoe Club and Sons of Veterans. In politics he is a Republican. He is interested in public affairs; and as postmaster is perhaps the best known citizen of the younger generation. He has given eminent satisfaction to the people in this position and commands the confidence and esteem of his townsmen, regardless of partisan or other lines. He married Helen Erskine F. Drummond, daughter of Robert and Jennet (Plenderleith) Drummond. They have no children.

BARRY Richard Paul Barry, of Lynn, Massachusetts, who enjoys the high distinction of having been the first Roman Catholic layman ever elected a member of the school committee of that city, serving for a period of six years, and who also enjoys a wide acquaintance throughout the commonwealth of Massachusetts by reason of his prominent connection with the state board of conciliation and arbitration, and his efficient service as a member of that body during the last more than twenty years, is a native of Ireland, grandson of Edmund Barry (I), a man of character and ability, who was a land steward in Ireland. By his wife, Ellen (Ahearn) Barry, also a native of Ireland, Edmund Barry had sixteen children, among them a son Matthew.

(II) Matthew Barry, son of Edmund and Ellen (Ahearn) Barry, was born in Ireland, and was also a land steward for Sir William Richard Beecher. Sir William fell in love with and married Miss O'Neil, a celebrated actress, known as the Mary Anderson of the London stage, and one of the most famous actresses of that period, winning great renown not only for her histrionic ability but for her lofty standards of morality. As Lady Beecher she became mistress of Crea House, the summer home of Sir William—a great mansion located at Crea, in the western part of county Cork, looking toward Cape Clear, and it was over this vast estate that Matthew Barry had supervision, collecting rents, etc., and the mansion itself was supervised by his wife, she having charge of the numerous retinue of servants. It was in this mansion that Richard P. Barry was born, and shortly after that event Matthew Barry gave up his stewardship and located in the town of Fermoy, county Cork, where he engaged in general business, including exportation of products to English markets. Later he came with his family to the United States, settling in Alabama, where he resided seven years, coming thence to Lynn, Massachusetts, where he passed the remainder of his life with his son, Richard P. Barry, and dying there at the age of seventy years. He married Catherine, daughter of William Boylson, of Tipperary, Ireland, and among their children were: Edmund Boylson, who settled in Lynn, 1850, and married Mary Bowman, an Irish girl; Richard Paul, of whom further; and Elizabeth T. and William E., both of whom died young.

(III) Richard Paul Barry, son of Matthew and Catherine (Boylson) Barry, was born January 6, 1834, at Crea House, and spent his boyhood days in the town of Fermoy, county Cork, on the Black Water, frequently called the "Iris Rhine," a notable stream. He was educated in private and public schools. His intention was to prepare for the Catholic priesthood, but circumstances forbade. Having completed a course in English and mathematical studies, at the age of twelve and a half years he took up languages and classics, to which he devoted about five years. At the age of nineteen, in 1853, he came to the United States, joining his brothers and sisters, who had preceded him, and locating in Lynn, Massachusetts, which has since been his home. Mr. Barry worked many years in different local shoe factories. In 1877 he was elected a member of the school board, and served two terms of three years each. It was during this period and by his persistent effort that, against tremendous opposition and considerable prejudice, the first Irish Catholic school teacher was appointed, and she is yet serving in that capacity.

As a workman, Mr. Barry proved himself faithful and competent, and by reason of his intellectual attainments and just appreciation of the rights and mutual obligations of employer and employee soon gained an extended acquaintance and healthful influence in the councils of his fellow-workmen, and when in pursuance of an act of the legislature the state board of conciliation and arbitration was established, he was, entirely without solicitation on his own part, appointed by Governor Robinson, in 1886, an original member of that body, and has served to the present time, being the only one of the original members now serving. In this capacity he has been called upon frequently to adjust differences between employers and their workmen, settle strikes, and repress excited action on the part of workmen who felt themselves aggrieved at the hands of corporate and individual proprietors, and nowhere in all the varied experiences of his official position was his wise influence and sound judgment more clearly shown than in the settlement of the disturbances which arose in labor circles when international trouble was threatened on the occasion of the so-called Venezuela controversy during President Cleveland's administration. In that case Mr. Barry and one other member had sole charge of the settlement of the strike by the ship-building workmen, and made such satisfactory adjustment of existing differences that the progress of the work of construction on ship No. II (the "Marblehead") and some smaller craft, suffered very little delay. This was only one of a large number of important cases which have occupied the attention of this board, during the nearly quarter of a century of its existence. Scores of disputes between employers and employees have been satisfactorily settled, and thousands of men have resumed work. Although Mr. Barry has passed the allotted age of three score years and ten, he is still in possession of all of his faculties, and is acknowledged to be the most active member of the board.

Mr. Barry married, in St. Mary's Church, Lynn, on May 28, 1868, Mary Ann Griffin, who was born in Dripsy, near historic Blarney Castle, on the river Lee, county cork, Ireland, and came to this country in childhood. Children: 1. Mary Elizabeth, married James Clarence Mangan, of Lynn; children: Mary Regina, Charles James Mangan. 2. William J., in general real estate and insurance business, Lynn; married Jennie Baxter; child: William Paul Barry. 3. John M., graduate of Lynn high school, Bryant & Stratton's Business College, and Boston University Law School; is a lawyer in active general practice, in Lynn; served two terms of three years each on school committee, and as chairman the last years. 4. Richard Paul, Jr., received early education in Lynn public schools, graduating from high school; took up study of music and follows that profession as teacher, and organist of St. Mary's Church. 5. Joseph Lewis, attended public schools of Lynn, including high school, Lynn Business College, and Boston Law School; now a practicing lawyer in Lynn. 6. Edmund Augustine, attended public schools of Lynn, graduating from high school, and from Harvard University; holds clerical position in First National Bank of Lynn.

For many years Mr. Barry and his family have taken a prominent part in all matters connected with the Catholic church. It was through his efforts that the first Catholic Sunday school was started in Lynn, in a small frame building in West Lynn, where the Catholics of Lynn, Swampscott, Saugus and Nahant worshipped. This was known as St. Mary's Church, and, owing to Mr. Barry's change of residence and the burning of the church edifice, he with a number of others formed the society which later erected the magnificent St. Joseph's Church on Union street, in which Mr. Barry and his family have taken a prominent part for many years. Mr. Barry was for many years superintendent of its Sunday school, and president of its Holy Name Society. In addition, Mr. Barry has been connected with many charitable and benevolent organizations, including the Hibernian Benevolent Association, Land League, Home Rule Association, and the Citizens' Association, the latter being formed for the purpose of securing representation for Irish Catholics in the city councils. Mr. Barry has been president or treasurer of all these bodies.

BOEHM

Adolph G. Boehm was born in Germany, December 19, 1852, and was educated in the public schools of the fatherland. At the age of seventeen he sought his fortune in America. His first employment was in a textile mill at Manchester, New Hampshire. A few years later he removed to Lawrence, Massachusetts, where he lived the rest of his life. He worked for several years there in the mills. In 1885 he established the business in which he achieved great success and acquired a competence. He had a thorough knowledge of the restaurant business, and his ability to please his customers came largely from his ingenuity in devising unique and unusual bills-of-fare, etc. He had one of the best equipped restaurants in New England, and the service was unexcelled. Of late years his restaurant was a favorite stopping place in Lawrence for automobile tourists. Mr. Boehm knew how to please his customers with both meat and drink. Personally he could not help being popular. He was ideal as "Mine Host"—jovial, cheerful, witty and kindly to all. He had a host of friends in Lawrence, and many throughout New England. Mr. Boehm was for a time manager of the Cold Spring Brewery of Lawrence. In politics he was a Republican. He was very prominent and popular in the Lawrence Lodge, Benevolent and Protective Order

Adolph G. Boehm

of Elks, which had charge of his funeral. He was a member of the Ancient and Honorable Artillery Company of Boston; of the Haruiguri Society, the German Central Hall Association, the Bavarian Club, the Turn Verein, the Lyra Singing Society, the Arion Singing Society, and various Masonic bodies—Germania Lodge, of Boston, Chapter, Council, and the Commandery to the thirty-second degree, and was a noble of the Mystic Shrine.

Owing to ill health he undertook a trip to Germany in company with Daniel F. Conlon, of Lawrence. He had a hemorrhage while at Hamburg, Germany, and died suddenly, September 19, 1907. The body was brought home on the steamer "Blucher." The funeral was held October 9, 1907, at Lyra Hall, Lawrence, and was one of the largest ever held in the city. Deputations and friends came from Boston, New York, Manchester, Haverhill, Methuen, Andover, North Andover and elsewhere. The body lay in state in the hall from eleven until two, and thousands paid a visit of respect and farewell. The bearers were: Edward I. Koffman, Gustav Weigel, Reinhardt G. Knuepfer, G. P. Thumm, Daniel F. Conlon, Anton Weidner, Charles H. Rowe, of West Kennebunk, Me., and William Stoehrer, of Haverhill. The hall was draped in mourning, and flags were at halfmast on the various lodge buildings. The service of the Elks was conducted by Exalted Ruler Henry J. Koellen. A brief eulogy was delivered by August Sontag. Masonic services were held at Bellevue Cemetery. The floral offerings were extremely elaborate and numerous, a substantial evidence of the great affection in which he was held by men and women in all walks of life.

Mr. Boehm married Elizabeth Scheer, daughter of Gottlob. She died, and he married Anna C. Wagner, daughter of August F Wagner. His wife survives him. Child born of the first union, Gertrude, married Louis Matthes, of Lawrence and has one child, Adolph Louis, child born of the second union, Oswald Adolph, born July 26, 1888.

O'BRIEN The O'Briens were for many centuries the royal family of Ireland. Cormac Cas, brother of Owen Mor, of the McCarthy Mor family, was the ancestor of O'Briain, anglicized O'Brien, Bernard, Bryan and Bryant. The place of inauguration of the O'Briens as Kings and Princes of Thomond, was at Magh Adhair, a plain in the barony of Tullagh, County of Clare; and their battle cry was Lamhlaidir *An Uachdar,* which means The Strong Hand Uppermost. On their armorial ensigns were three lions rampant which were also on the standards of Brian Boru, borne by the Dalcassians at the battle of Clontarf. In modern times the O'Briens were marquises of Thomond, Earls of Inchiquin and barons of Borren, in the county of Clare; and many of them were distinguished commanders in the Irish Brigades in the service of France under the titles of earls of Clare and counts of Thomond. Brian Boroimhe (Boru) the 175th Monarch of Ireland, younger son of Cineadh, born 926; slain on the battlefield of Clontarf on Good Friday, April 23, 1014, was the ancestor of O'Briain of Thomond, anglicized O'Brien. The name means in Irish very great strength. Brian is represented by the old Irish annalists as a man of fine figure, large stature, of great strength of body and undaunted valor; and has been always justly celebrated as one of the greatest of the Irish monarchs, equally conspicuous for his mental endowments and physical energies; a man of great intellectual powers, sagacity and bravery; a warrior and legislator; and, at the same time, distinguished for his munificence, piety and patronage of learned men thus combining all the elements of a great character, and equally eminent in the arts of war and peace; a hero and patriot, whose memory will always remain famous as one of the foremost of the Irish kings, in wisdom and valor. Brian lived at his palace of Cean Cora (Kincora) in a style of regal splendor and magnificence unequalled by any of the Irish kings since the days of Cormac MacArt, the celebrated Monarch of Ireland in the third century. The more prominent branches of the O'Brien family trace their ancestry for more than a hundred generations through the royal family, as given by the ancient Irish annalists. (See Irish Pedigrees by John O'Hart. Dublin, 1881).

(I) Thomas O'Brien was born in Ireland, a descendant of the ancient O'Brien family mentioned above, and was a farmer. He married in Ireland, Hellen Burns, and in 1853 came to America with his wife and eldest children. The family settled in Lawrence. Children: Maurice, Honora, Margaret, Thomas, Michael, Catherine.

(II) Michael O'Brien, son of Thomas O'Brien (1), was born in Ireland in 1852. When he was about a year old his parents brought him to America and settled in Lawrence, Massachusetts, where he was educated in the public schools. He entered the employ of William E. Heald, and continued with him until he sold out his business in 1877 to Kurn and Joyce. Since then he has continued with the firm, and is one of the best known and most popular men in his line of business in this section.

In politics Mr. O'Brien is a Democrat, but has never been active in public or political affairs. He is a devout Catholic, and a liberal contributor to the benevolences of his church. He is a member of no clubs or societies, being devoted to his home life. He married, June, 1875, at Andover, Massachusetts, Elizabeth Ohearn, born January 5, 1854, daughter of Eugene and Mary (Ohearn) Ohearn. Children, born in Lawrence: 1. Mary A., May 11, 1878. 2. Charles A., October 13, 1879; died November 23, 1906. 3. Helen R., born April 30, 1884. 4. Eugene W., born September 26, 1887. 5. Thomas F., twin with Eugene W. 6. Joseph F., born September 28, 1890. 7. Elizabeth, twin with Joseph F.

BROWN Stephen Brown, of old Quaker stock, was born on Turkey Hill, West Newbury, Massachusetts, and was a farmer.

(II) John Brown, son of Stephen Brown (1), was born on Turkey Hill, West Newbury, January 14, 1784, and died September 12, 1855. He was educated in the common schools, and was a farmer in his native place during all his active life. He married first, Ruth Green, born 1782, died August, 1817; second, Mary Pillsbury, born January 20, 1795, died August 21, 1872. Children by first marriage: 1. Mary, born August 18, 1810, died October 10, 1887. 2. James N., born October, 1813, died December 21, 1816. 3. James, May 8, 1814. By second marriage: 4. Joseph P., born September 21, 1819, died October 12, 1820. 5. George F., born March 31, 1821, died July 10, 1898. 6-7. Susan M. and Susan L., twins, born July 27, 1823; Susan L. died August 29, 1823. 8. Marian M., born May 15, 1825. 9. William P., January 28, 1827. 10. Elizabeth C., March 19, 1829. 11. Sarah A., November 16, 1836. Those whose deaths are not noted, are living.

(III) James Brown, son of John and Ruth (Green) Brown, was born in West Newbury, May 8, 1814. He had a common school education, and during his youth worked on his father's farm at West Newbury. He himself became a farmer in West Newbury, and like most of his neighbors learned the trade of shoemaking and made shoes during the winter when work was slack on the farm. In later years he removed to Lynn, where he died June 14, 1906. In early life he was of the Society of Friends, like his ancestors for many generations, but in later years he attended the Congregational Church. In politics he was a Republican. He married Hannah Morse. Children: Mary Jane, Charles Warren, mentioned below, Ella, Allen, Arthur, all are deceased. All were born and died in West Newbury except Charles Warren.

(IV) Charles Warren Brown, son of James Brown (3), was born in West Newbury, April 28, 1847. He attended the public schools of his native town and also of Lynn, whither the family moved when he was a young man, in 1868. He learned the trade of shoemaker, and worked for various employers at this trade in Lynn until 1873, when he removed with his family to Hampstead, New Hampshire, and bought a farm. After nineteen years of farming he left Hampstead to return to Lynn, where for a few years he resumed his former trade of shoemaking. In 1898 he entered the employ of General Electric Company at Lynn and rose to the position of foreman of one of the departments, a position he held until his death. He was in the electric business for eight years. Mr. Brown was a capable mechanic and a resourceful man in any situation. He had the force of character and integrity of a race of Quakers and commanded the respect and esteem of all who knew him. He served the town of Hampstead on the school committees and various other offices of trust and responsibility. He was a loyal Republican in politics. He served in the army during the latter part of the civil war. He was a member of Bay State Lodge of Odd Fellows. In religion he was a Congregationalist. He married, in Lynn, October 1868, Anna Ruddock, born in West Newbury, daughter of Charles and Lottie (Brock) Ruddock, all of English birth. Her father came to America when a young man and followed his trade of shoemaker until his death, in the prime of life, aged thirty-eight years. Children of Charles and Lottie (Brock) Ruddock: i. Anna Ruddock; ii. Mercy Ruddock; married Frank Balch, of Groveland, Massachusetts; iii. Lovina, married John Melzard, of Swampscott (deceased); iv. Clara Ruddock married George Pettengill, of Lynn (she is deceased); v. Addie, died in infancy; vi. Etta Ruddock, married Charles Willey, of the General Electric Company.

Children of Charles Warren and Anna (Ruddock) Brown: 1. Arthur Allen, born in Lynn, December 12, 1869; at present purchasing agent for the General Electric Company. 2. Walter Scott, born in Lynn, August 5, 1871; died in Salem, New Hampshire, February 13, 1905; married Ella Grover, born in Sandown, New Hampshire; children: i. Hazel Eva, born April 7, 1901; ii. Ethel Grover, born August 29, 1902. 3. Herbert Austin, born in Hampstead, May 12, 1876; resides in Lynn, and is connected with the General Electric Company.

THOMAS The surname Thomas is said by genealogists and antiquarians to be of ancient Welsh origin, and while many bearers of the name came to this country from various parts of Wales, the Thomases have been seated in England for centuries and thus have come to be regarded as an English family. The particular family here under consideration is doubtless of Welch ancestry, as were very nearly all of the Thomases who settled in the Virginias, Maryland and Pennsylvania during the eighteenth and nineteenth centuries.

David Thomas, with whom this narrative begins, was born in Ohio, about 1826, and for many years previous to his retirement from active pursuits was proprietor of a pottery at Roseville, Ohio, near Zanesville, where he now lives. In his younger life he himself was a practical potter and stood many years at the wheel in turning earthenware. Later on he set up in business for himself, and having a thorough knowledge of the trade and possessing, moreover, an excellent business capacity his later endeavors were rewarded with gratifying success, hence he retired in 1886 and has since lived in comfort, enjoying the fruits of years of honest effort and earnest endeavor. He married Mary Bagley, who was born in Ohio, and died there September 15, 1907, aged seventy-two years. Both her husband and herself were devoted member of the Baptist church, and took an earnest interest in advancing its growth and influence. Her husband, surviving her, is yet a zealous church worker and has done much both in precept and example for the welfare of the community in which his life has been spent. Children: 1. William, deceased. 2. Charles Benjamin, deceased. 3. Emma, unmarried. 4. Herbert, married. 5. Florence, unmarried.

Charles Benjamin Thomas, second son and child of David and Mary (Bagley) Thomas, was born in Zanesville, Ohio, January 11, 1851, and died there suddenly, June 14, 1907, while on a visit to his old home and the scenes of his boyhood life. He was educated there and after his school days were over he was employed in and about his father's factory and thus became well acquainted with the business generally. Having attained his majority and possessing energy, capacity and a good character, he soon found a desirable position as traveling salesman for S. A. Weller, an extensive manufacturer of earthenware and crockery, and for the next more than twenty years represented that concern in the New England states. In his capacity of sole representative in this region Mr. Thomas found it desirable to take up his residence in this state and establish his house near Boston, living in the suburban town of Winthrop. As managing salesman for an entirely reliable and reputable manufacturer, Mr. Thomas gained an extensive acquaintance with trade throughout New England greatly to the profit of his principals and much to his own advantage, for his success commanded for him a high salary, and at the same time placed him among the most substantial business men of the region. More than that, he was a man of the highest character and strictest integrity, straightforward in every business transaction, taking no unfair advantage, and always the same candid, genial and companionable man, whether in affairs of business or social life. His unexpected taking off in the very prime of manhood was felt in his home town, and it seemed as if the entire community there had met with an unfortunate loss.

In Zanesville, Ohio, June 6, 1895, Mr. Thomas married Ana M. Reed, born in Princeton, New Jersey, July 17, 1866, daughter of James and Clara (Dillintash) Reed, and who lived in Princeton until about two years before her marriage. Her father, James Reed, was born in New Jersey, and died in 1866, about two months before the birth of Mrs. Thomas, who was his only child. Her mother afterward married Charles Hulmes, whom she survived, and still lives in Princeton. Mrs. Thomas is a communicant of the Protestant Episcopal church in Winthrop, taking an earnest interest in parish work. Having no children, she is sole possessor of one of the most comfortable houses with which that town abounds, and among its interior decorations are many much prized vases, jardinieres, and other similar treasures, all of which suggest pleasant memories of her husband's business life.

FRANCE John France, son of Mathew and Ann (Delmar) France, one of the prominent residents of Lawrence, Massachusetts, was born in Ashton, England, November 9, 1830. His father, was a tailor. When John France was a young led there were no laws regulating the employment of child labor, and he commenced active work as a wage earner at the early age of nine years. He attended school at the same time as was the custom of the day. He emigrated to the United States about 1854, settling in the state of New York, where he lived for one year, then went to Lawrence, Massachusetts, where he has since made his home. He engaged in the work of a spinner, and in the course of years rose to the rank of boss and was very successful. He has taken an active part in the political affairs of his city, having served two terms in the council and one term as alderman. He is one of the oldest members of the Episcopal church, and is affiliated with a number of organizations, among them being the Free and Accepted Masons, Independent Order of Odd Fellows, Veteran Massachusetts Firemen, of which latter he is president.

He married, first, Ellen Ward, native of Ireland, by whom he had two children: Edward William, born August 6, 1859, and an infant; mother died at same time as infant. He married, second, Harriet Maria Goodwin, native of Maine, and had children: Edwin N., deceased. John Westley, born August 26, 1867. Harriet, born March 5, 1869, married John Denniston, of Lawrence. He married, third, Mrs. Alice Marcroft, whose maiden name was Squibbs, native of England.

CROSS John Cross (I) was born in Cheshire, England, in 1804, and died in Liverpool, England, in 1883. On his father's side he came of a long line of English ancestors, his surname being distinctively English and one of great antiquity, according to the deductions of students of our English patronymics; on the maternal side his ancestors were of Welch stock. On both sides the families were noted for longevity, his father having attained the remarkable age of within three months of one hundred years, his mother less than four months of a century, while he himself lived to the age of almost eighty years.

As a young man John Cross early became connected in a clerical capacity with a railroad and canal company, and after several years of faithful service he was given the more responsible office of general manager of the Shropshire Union Railroad & Chester Canal Company, which duties he performed with satisfaction to his employers and much credit to himself. While serving as the company's manager he made his house in Ellsmereport, but afterward removed to Liverpool, where the latter part of his life was spent. He married in Cheshire, Elizabeth Shone, born in Arding, Wales, but whose life was chiefly spent in Cheshire, where her father was a smith and farrier, a superior workman at his trade as also was her brother Edward, who for many years was smith and farrier of the famous Royal Guards in his majesty's service. John and Elizabeth (Shone) Cross had children, nine of whom grew to maturity and five of whom are still living: John, William, Robert, George, Thomas H., Clement (died young), Clement Rider, Christopher Clement, Susanna, Clementine, Wilhelmina, Henrietta, and one other who died in infancy.

(II) Thomas H. Cross, son of John and Elizabeth (Shone) Cross, was born in Ellsmereport(Creshire, England, April 10, 1840, and was sent to a private guild school preparatory to more thorough education in marine engineering. After that he served an apprenticeship with Faucett, Preston & Co., and became a practical marine engineer. From that time he was in the service of John Ladd & Company until 1862, and in that year became engineer in the service of the Cunard Steamship Company, and is still in the employ of that great trans-Atlantic company, although not now in the capacity of engineer, for he proved himself worthy of a higher position and was advanced according to his merit. In 1871, after nine years of service as engineer, Mr. Cross was promoted in the company's service to the position of superintendent of engineers at the Cunard line docks in East Boston, and the duties of that position he has filled for more than thirty-seven years. Few men have a more extended acquaintance than he in maritime circles in this country, and few indeed are they who are so well known for rugged honesty and unquestionable integrity as Thomas H. Cross. The duties of his position have frequently called him into business transactions which require something beyond mere practical knowledge of marine engineering, matters of great importance to the

John France

company which have called for the exercise of sound business judgment, a knowledge of men as well as of affairs, but in whatever capacity he has been called upon to act he has acquitted himself well. In 1893 Mr. Cross took up his residence in the town of Winthrop, where he has acquired valuable property interests, and where he is looked upon as one of the substantial men of the town. His interest in local affairs is earnest and unselfish; and while frequently importuned he has consistently declined service in public office, although his counsel has been given freely in municipal affairs and the engineering corps of Winthrop has received substantial assistance at his hands. He is a Master and Royal Arch Mason, and a charter member of Crystal Bay Lodge, I. O. O. F., of Winthrop.

Mr. Cross married first, in Liverpool, England, July 16, 1867, Jane Robinson, born May 23, 1842, died in Winthrop, July 9, 1897. He married second, in Ashtabula, Ohio, in 1900, Mrs. Margaret Hill Crain, whose family name was Hill. She was born in Nashua, New Hampshire, and afterward removed to Burlington, Vermont, where she married William H. Crain, who died at St. Albans, Vermont, in 1896, from the effects of wounds received in battle during the civil war. Mrs. Cross had two children by her first husband: Henry C. Crain, now in the service of the N. Y. N. H. & H. R. R. Co., and living in Boston, and Daisy Crain, wife of Rev. William Babbitt, a clergyman of the Protestant Episcopal church, now living in the state of New York. Rev. William and Daisy (Crain) Babbitt have four children: William, Edward, Margaret and one other who died in extreme infancy. Mr. Cross has no children.

ERRATA AND ADDENDA.

The following errata and addenda were received after the narrative pages had gone to press:

Pope, p. 109, generation III, second line; for Fogler read Folger. In this and preceding paragraph, for Bethseda read Bethesda.

Bacon, p. 202, 2d col., ninth line from bottom of sketch; for Georgette read Georgietta.

Horsford, p. 261, 2d col., 16th line; for Katherine read Katharine.

Rand. p. 642, 2d col., last line; birth date of Vernon Waterman Rand should read October 1, 1852.

Brooks, p. 653, 2d col.; in connection with marriage of Reuben Brooks (5), see Cleaveland Family.

Shepard. p. 702, 2d col.; Rev. John William Shepard is of generation VI, instead of IV. Edward Olcott Shepard is of generation VII, instead of V.

Joint, p. 724, 2d col., five lines from bottom; for James C. Crutcheon read Cutcheon.

Morse, p. 778, last paragraph of sketch; Nathan Tingley Morse is of generation VIII, not IX.

Pattillo, p. 820, 2d col., 6th line; children of Alexander Manton Pattillo: Carlton Perkins, born January 15, 1886, died January 4, 1888; Alice Manton, born March 13, 1889; Gilbert Sayward, born September 26, 1890; George A., born October 17, 1894, died July 10, 1905.

Hills, p. 908; in connection with military service of Albert Smith Hills and Albert Perkins Hills: Total number men enrolled in 23d Massachusetts Regiment, 1380; killed in battle, 49; died of wounds, 28; died of disease, 79; died in rebel prisons, 39; died otherwise, 7; prisoners, 253; wounded, 200.

Bancroft, p. 923, 2d col.; marriage date of Thomas Bancroft (VII) should be June 1, 1815. His only living child is Caroline A. Bancroft.

Berry, p. 945. 2d col., 1st line, 2d parag.; Mr. Berry married Lorana Milton Ferrin.

Belcher, p. 1084, 2d col., 1st parag.; a daughter was born to Alphonso W. Belcher, November 7, 1908.

Palmer, p. 1451, cols. 1 and 2, for William Henry Palmer (VI) read William Hardy Palmer. Wililam H. H. Palmer (VII) fought in the civil war, in Company A, 50th Massachusetts Regiment; he was enrolled September 4, 1862, and was discharged August 24, 1863, by reason of expiration of term of service; he served in siege of Port Hudson from the beginning to the end.

Ingraham, p. 1525, 1st col., 2d parag.; George Henry Ingraham, who married Helen Maria Ballard, was born in Saxonville, Massachusetts, November 12, 1848, son of Augustus and Harriet A. (Atwood) Ingraham; he is a druggist in West Newton; all his children were educated in the public schools except Grace, who attended Allen's private school, West Newton.

Whiting, p. 1665, 2d col., 2d parag.; William H. H. Whiting was selectman one year and park commissioner four years, in town of Revere; his wife's father, A. J. Wilkinson, was a cotton manufacturer, a descendant of the Wilkinsons of the earlier days of cotton manufacturing in Rhode Island. His children were: 1-2. Died at birth. 3. Mary Tower, born March 4, 1879, died December 9, 1887. 4. George Walcott, born December 20, 1881, died December 23, 1887.

Moses B. Paige, p. 2001, last parag.: Robert Henry Wilkinson, born January 14, 1855, died September 22, 1884; married, April 18, 1883, Eliza Harris Poor, daughter of Nathan H. Poor; a son, Edward Poor Wilkinson, born August 5, 1884, died October 10, 1884.

Anderson, p. 2055, 1st col., 5th line from top; for John Anderson read John Mitchell Anderson.

INDEX.

ND - #0078 - 080424 - C0 - 229/152/38 - PB - 9781332310647 - Gloss Lamination